About the Authors

Francis Soen currently is working as an independent AutoCAD consultant in Pittsburgh, Pennsylvania. He has worked with AutoCAD for more than 10 years as a CAD administrator at a large AEC company, as the manager of support services for an AutoCAD dealer, as an instructor at the local authorized training center, and as a shareware developer. With civil engineering degrees from Lehigh University and the University of California at Berkeley, he has a particularly strong understanding of how to use AutoCAD in engineering applications.

David Pitzer is an AutoCAD instructor and consultant. He currently is a member of the adjunct faculty at Santa Rosa Junior College in northern California. Mr. Pitzer is a frequent contributor to *CADENCE* magazine, for which he serves as a contributing columnist. He also has published several articles in *CADalyst* magazine. He was a lecturer at the first Autodesk University in 1993. He first started using AutoCAD in 1986, and for five years was CAD Coordinator for an engineering/manufacturing firm near San Francisco.

Howard M. Fulmer is the president of HMF Consulting, based in Norristown, Pennsylvania. His firm is a full-service computer consulting enterprise, specializing in all aspects of hardware and software installation, training, customization, and support. He regularly conducts seminars and lectures at Fortune 500 companies as well as local high schools, sharing his 20-plus years of comput[illegible] to mainframe[illegible] faculty me[illegible] engineering [illegible] at Villanova U[illegible] Univer-sity, and Montg[illegible]y Community College. He was [illegible] Beta Kappa at Temple University and also has studied at the University of Minnesota.

He is one of the founders and long-standing members of the Philadelphia AutoCAD Users Group, having served as PAUG President, Vice-President, Program Chairman, and on executive steering committees. He has intensively utilized and customized AutoCAD since v1.4 (1984), and is an ATC trainer.

Thanks are extended to his wife, Joan, and father, Aaron, for their ongoing support during the writing of this book.

Jim Boyce has been a computer user and system administrator since the late 1970s. He worked for Marathon LeTourneau, a world leader in the design of offshore drilling platforms, as a production planner, designer, CAD system administrator, and programmer. Mr. Boyce also was a member of the faculty of Texas State Technical College for six years, where he taught courses in using, customizing, and programming AutoCAD and HP's ME-10 and ME-30 mechanical engineering software. Mr. Boyce also taught UNIX, DOS, and DOS applications. He is the author of *Maximizing Windows*, co-author of

AutoCAD for Beginners, and contributing author to numerous books from New Riders Publishing.

Kevin McWhirter is the training director for Diversified Graphics, in Indianapolis, Indiana. He graduated from Indiana University with a degree in education. Mr. McWhirter has seven years of experience with AutoCAD as an operator and a project manager. He currently is doing training and technical support for Diversified Graphics. Mr. McWhirter worked as a technical editor on *AutoCAD: The Professional Reference,* published by New Riders Publishing, and was a 1992 national winner for curriculum development from Autodesk's Learning Systems Group.

Michael Todd Peterson is a lecturer at the University of Tennessee College of Architecture and a computer consultant for architects and engineers for AutoCAD and 3D Studio. He graduated from the University of Tennessee College of Architecture in 1992.

Rusty Gesner was born and raised in Indianapolis and educated at Antioch College and the College of Design, Art, and Architecture at the University of Cincinnati before migrating to Oregon. He is a registered architect, formerly practicing in Oregon and Washington before buying a copy of the original PC release of AutoCAD in early 1983. Prior to joining New Riders in 1986, he was founder and president of CAD Northwest, Inc., one of the first AutoCAD dealerships. Rusty is co-author or developer of various editions of many New Riders books, including *Maximizing AutoCAD, Maximizing AutoLISP,* and *Inside AutoCAD.* He now resides in Boring, Oregon, with his wife, Kathy, their two children, and seven pets (cats, dogs, and horses). In his meager spare time, Rusty skis (volunteering with the Mt. Hood Ski Patrol), bicycles, and rides his tractor in circles.

Jeff Beck graduated from Pulaski Area Vocational-Technical School as a drafter/detailer. He graduated from Columbia State Community College as an engineering technician. Mr. Beck worked at General Electric of Columbia, Tennessee, as a drafter for four years, taught AutoCAD classes for Columbia State Community College for six months, and taught AutoCAD, drafting, physics, algebra, and trigonometry for ITT Technical Institute for four years. He currently works as CAD Manager/Systems Administrator for ENSAFE, Inc., of Nashville, and does private CAD and computer graphics consulting and drafting with his wife, Lisa Beck. Mr. Beck's previous publishing works include *Hands On AutoCAD Release 12* by New Riders Publishing.

Kevin Coleman is a Product Development Specialist at New Riders Publishing. He has been with New Riders Publishing since 1989. Kevin has been using AutoCAD and other computer graphics applications since 1985. He attended the University of Oregon where he studied telecommunications and film.

Andrew Morris is a freelance engineer in the broadcast, cable, and telecommunications industries. Employed for more than 20 years by television and radio networks in New York City, he often has used

AutoCAD for the design and documentation of audio, video, and RF systems.

Tom Boersma is a Certified Manufacturing Engineer, an instructor at Grand Rapids Community College, and a training consultant for West Michigan manufacturing companies. His training specialties are CAD/CAM/CNC, manufacturing processes, and shop floor continuous improvement processes. He is a co-author of *Inside AutoCAD for Windows, Inside AutoCAD Release 12 for Windows, Inside AutoCAD Release 12, Learn CAD with AutoSketch,* and *Inside AutoCAD LT for Windows,* all from New Riders Publishing.

Jim Fitzgerald is a CAD Product Development Specialist for New Riders Publishing in Gresham, Oregon. Prior to joining New Riders he was the Director of Training for a CAD training and consulting organization in Philadelphia. He has been working with AutoCAD since 1988. He studied mathematics and education at Linfield College in McMinnville, Oregon.

Cathleen Jones was born in San Francisco, studied Animal Science at the University of California at Davis, and somehow found herself addicted to computers. She worked 13 years in production-related CAD drafting and design before moving into technical support for Autodesk. During almost five of those design years, Cathleen found time to teach CAD at a local vocational school and junior college in the Denver Metro Area, Colorado. When she's not on the support phones, you can find Cathleen on CompuServe in the AutoCAD forum where she is a designated "Threadmaster."

Trademark Acknowledgments

Contents at a Glance

Table of Contents

Introduction

AutoCAD is a software phenomenon; its users far outnumber those of any other CAD system. Since its introduction, AutoCAD has grown from a micro-curiosity to a full-fledged CAD system by any set of standards. AutoCAD also has grown from a relatively simple program to a large and complex one, but do not be intimidated by its size and complexity. More than a million designers and drafters have learned to use AutoCAD with the help of Inside AutoCAD, *the best-selling AutoCAD book for more than ten years.*

Inside AutoCAD Release 13c4 *is your guide to a significant step in the evolution of AutoCAD: AutoCAD Release 13. Because AutoCAD Release 13c4 for Windows, Windows 95, and Windows NT utilizes the flexibility of Windows, it offers you a far more productive design environment and interface than AutoCAD under DOS, and includes several advanced features not available in the DOS version.*

Inside AutoCAD Release 13c4 is organized to be of primary benefit to professional AutoCAD users: those who use AutoCAD on a regular basis in the course of their work. It assumes some basic understanding of the AutoCAD and Windows user interfaces, and aims at sharpening the skills you need to use AutoCAD effectively and efficiently.

This book is written specifically for the Release 13c4 version of AutoCAD. If you are upgrading from AutoCAD Release 11 or 12, AutoCAD Release 13c4 offers many new features, which are comprehensively covered in this book. In addition, Release 13c4 is a significant upgrade from previous versions. Features which are new to the 13c4 version are highlighted in the text.

Even if you are experienced with previous releases of AutoCAD, Release 13 has enough new features to make this book valuable to you. There are new ways of working with text, linetypes, hatching, and dimensions; new construction line objects; mathematically true ellipses; additional object snap options; and a flexible, powerful new capability to group objects. This book not only shows you how these new features work, but it goes on to suggest ways you can apply them to help you be more productive.

How This Book Is Organized

Inside AutoCAD Release 13c4 is designed to help you master AutoCAD and sharpen the professional skills you need to use AutoCAD effectively and efficiently, beyond simply understanding the basics of the program. To accomplish this goal, the book is organized into parts, each of which covers a specific group of concepts and operations. Each part is a collection of related chapters, presented more-or-less in order of increasing complexity.

Part One: The Working Environment

Part One covers the wide range of issues involved in planning for, setting up, and managing AutoCAD's working environment. The key to working quickly and easily in AutoCAD is to take control of the workspace—setting system variables, organizing layers, taking full advantage of AutoCAD's accuracy, controlling your display, working in both Model and Paper space, and getting the plotted output you need.When you complete Part One, you will have your AutoCAD system tuned to your design and drafting needs, so that you can begin drawing more productively.

Part Two: Object Creation Tools

Part Two covers basic 2D construction tools, from drawing simple lines and circles, through creating and manipulating polylines, to assembling complex blocks, and taking advantage of XREFs. Obviously, it is essential that you understand the use of these tools. These chapters take you beyond the basics, showing you when to use which tool and how to quickly achieve exactly the results you need. When you finish Part Two, you will be able to quickly construct virtually any 2D design, making your drafting much more efficient.

Part Three: Object Editing Tools

Part Three covers editing commands and techniques, including editing with grips; selecting, grouping, and modifying objects; and querying your drawings. The capability to copy, modify, and reuse objects and even entire drawings, is one of the greatest benefits AutoCAD brings to the design process. These chapters take you from basic object editing commands through *constructive editing*, which combines the power of editing and construction.When you complete Part Three, you will have mastered the skills you need to quickly and accurately create and manipulate your designs.

Part Four: Text, Graphic, and Dimensioning Tools

Finally, Part Four covers the range of commands and techniques required to complete your drawings with annotation, graphic linetypes, hatching, and dimensioning. Many of the most useful improvements in Release 13 were made to these functions, and they are thoroughly covered here—multiline text, associative hatching, and an extensively revised and enhanced set of dimensioning tools. When you complete Part Four, you will have learned how to efficiently create professional quality, complex 2D drawings.

Part Five: The Appendixes

Inside AutoCAD Release 13c4 also has several useful appendixes.

Appendix A covers installation and configuration issues.

Appendix B covers optimizing the AutoCAD Release 13 tools and interface.

Appendix C lists all AutoCAD commands, and the tools, menu items, and aliases that issue them.

Appendix D provides useful tables of AutoCAD's system and dimensioning variables.

You'll also find a handy reference glossary of all the commands covered in the book. This glossary, found at the back of the book, also provides page references for each command so you know where to read for more information on how to use the command.

How to Use the Tutorials

Each chapter is divided into a series of exercises, each of which teaches one or more AutoCAD commands. Explanatory text accompanies each exercise, puts commands and techniques into context, explains how commands behave, and shows you how to use different options. If you just read the text and exercises and look at the illustrations, you will learn a great deal about the program. But if you want to gain a greater mastery of AutoCAD Release 13, you need to sit down at a computer equipped with AutoCAD Release 13 and work through the exercises.

A sample exercise follows. You do not need to work through it or understand the content, but you should look over the format so that you will know how the book's exercises are presented. Most exercises are accompanied by one or more illustrations, most of which were captured from the screen during an actual exercise. Exercises are arranged in two columns, with direct instructions on the left and explanatory notes on the right. Lengthy instructions or explanations sometimes extend across both columns.

TRYING A SAMPLE EXERCISE

Continue in the SAMPLE drawing from the preceding exercise.

`Command:` *Double-click on the* SNAP *button*	Turns on snap mode and highlights the button
`Command:` *Choose Line (Draw, Line)*	Issues the LINE command
`_line From point:` **1,1** ↵	Starts a line at ① (see fig. I.1)

To point: *Pick* ②	Draws the line
To point: ↵	Ends the LINE command
Command: *Choose Arc Start Center Angle*	Issues the ARC command with Center and *(Draw, Arc)* Angle options
_arc Center/<Start point>: **@** ↵	Starts at last point, ②
Center/End/<Second point>: _c	The tool issues the Center option
Center: *Pick* ①	
Angle/Length of chord/<End point>: _a	The tool issues the Angle option
Included angle: **-90** ↵	Draws the door arc to ③
Command: *Choose* File, Save	Issues QSAVE command and saves the drawing

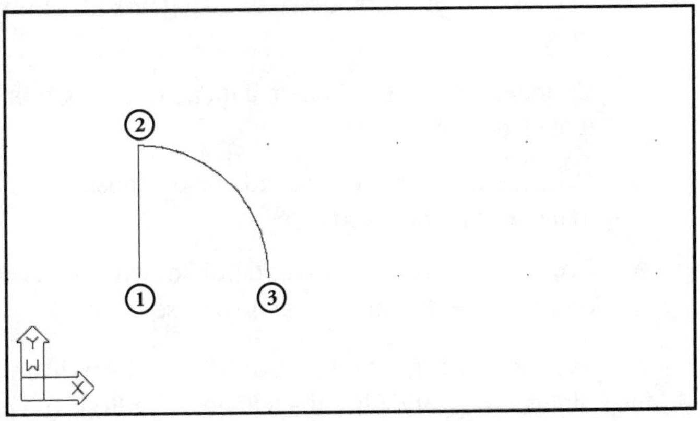

Figure I.1

A sample exercise illustration.

Because AutoCAD Release 13c4 for Windows is a Windows application, its interface uses many standard Windows elements. The toolbars provide tools for most commonly used commands. The Special Object Properties toolbar above the drawing area and the status bar below the drawing area also provide information on the current drawing settings. The menu bar always appears above the top toolbar.

You will be using your mouse for much of your input in AutoCAD. You should become familiar with the following terms, which are used to describe mouse actions:

- **Click.** To press and release the pick button.
- **Click on, click in.** To position the cursor on the appropriate user interface object (icon, input box, menu item, and so on) and click the pick button.
- **Double-click.** To press and release the pick button twice, in rapid succession.
- **Pick.** To position the cursor on the appropriate object or point and click the pick button.
- **Select.** To highlight an object in the AutoCAD drawing area by picking it or by using other object selection methods. Also, to highlight an item, word, or character in a drop-down or dialog box list or text input field by clicking on it.
- **Choose.** To select an item in a menu or dialog box by either clicking on it or typing its hot-key letter.
- **Drag.** To move the mouse and cursor, causing lines or objects on the screen to move with the cursor.
- **Press and drag.** To press and hold down a mouse button, drag something on screen, and then release the mouse button.

When you see an instruction such as "Choose Item" in an exercise, it means to move the pointer to Item and click the left mouse button. The instructions usually specify the location from which you are to initiate a command. Exercise steps that use the toolbars instruct you to choose the tool, such as "*Choose Line (Draw, Line)*." Exercise steps that use the pull-down menus instruct you to choose the menu, then the item, as in "*Choose* File, Save." You also can use a hot key—a key combination consisting of the Alt key and the letter underlined in the menu—to display the File menu; for example, you would press Alt+F.

If a pull-down menu or dialog box is currently displayed, "choose" refers to an item on it. If no specific direction is given for the source of the command, feel free to use whatever serves you best. As you progress through the book, you will learn a variety of ways to issue a command. See Chapters 2 and 3 for more information on using the AutoCAD interface.

Your computer may have a key labeled Enter, or one labeled Return, or one with an arrow symbol. In any case, *Press Enter* or the symbol ↵ means to press the key that enters a return.

You often enter commands from the keyboard. Similarly, point coordinates, distances, and option keywords must be typed. The exercise text generally indicates when typed input is required by showing it in bold text following a prompt, such as `Command:` **`UNITS`** or `To point:` **`3,5`**. You should type the input as it appears, and then press Enter.

You should save your drawings when instructed, to help you build a habit of saving drawings at regular intervals. If you want to proceed at a leisurely pace, you can save and close your drawing whenever you see the save instruction and reload your drawing later.

Notes, Tips, and Warnings

Inside AutoCAD Release 13c4 features many special sidebars, which are set apart from the normal text as follows. The book includes three distinct types of sidebars: Notes, Tips, and Warnings. These passages have been given special treatment so that you can instantly recognize their significance and easily find them for future reference.

NOTE

A Note includes extra information you should find useful. A Note might describe special situations that can arise when you use AutoCAD under certain circumstances, and might tell you what steps to take when such situations arise.

TIP

A Tip provides quick instructions for getting the most from your AutoCAD system. A Tip might show you how to speed up a procedure, or how to perform one of many time-saving and system-enhancing techniques.

WARNING

A Warning tells you when a procedure can be dangerous—that is, when you run the risk of a serious problem or error, even losing data or crashing your system. Warnings generally tell you how to avoid such problems or describe the steps you can take to remedy them.

New Riders Publishing

The staff of New Riders Publishing is committed to bringing you the very best in computer reference material. Each New Riders book is the result of months of work by authors and staff who research and refine the information contained within its covers.

As part of this commitment to you, the NRP reader, New Riders invites your input. Please let us know if you enjoy this book, if you have trouble with the information and examples presented, or if you have a suggestion for the next edition.

Please note, though: New Riders staff cannot serve as a technical resource for AutoCAD or for questions about software- or hardware-related problems. Please refer to the documentation that accompanies AutoCAD Release 13c4 or to the applications' Help systems.

Make sure to visit the New Riders web site at `www.mcp.com\newriders` for updates and corrections to this book. You can also post corrections to the book through the Web site.

If you have a question or comment about any New Riders book, there are several ways to contact New Riders Publishing. We will respond to as many readers as we can. Your name, address, or phone number will never become part of a mailing list or be used for any purpose other than to help us continue to bring you the best books possible. You can write us at the following address:

New Riders Publishing
Attn: Publisher
201 W. 103rd Street
Indianapolis, IN 46290

If you prefer, you can fax New Riders Publishing at (317) 581-4670.

You can also send electronic mail to New Riders at the following Internet address:

`abuckley@newriders.mcp.com`

NRP is an imprint of Macmillan Computer Publishing. To obtain a catalog or information, or to purchase any Macmillan Computer Publishing book, call (800) 428-5331.

Thank you for selecting Inside AutoCAD Release 13c4 for Windows 95, Windows NT, and Windows 3.1!

part

The Working Environment

chapter 1

Drawing Setup and File Management

In many ways, setting up a CAD drawing is like preparing to draw on a drafting board. From the information you know about the drawing you want to make, you determine the size of the paper sheet you will need and the tools you will use. In AutoCAD, you determine such things as the units you will use, the size of the drawing area, and what scale factor you need to apply to text and symbols. Unlike working on the board, you also need to manage your drawings as electronic files, instead of sheets of paper. This chapter discusses these issues and shows you some ways to take advantage of the way AutoCAD handles them. Topics covered include the following:

- *Understanding full-scale electronic drawing*
- *Determining scale factors for symbols and text*
- *Setting a drawing's working units and sizing its limits*
- *Opening existing drawings and creating new ones*
- *Using prototype drawings to save and reuse setups*
- *Saving your work*

Setting up your drawing is a key step. By understanding and using the electronic tools available in AutoCAD, you can draw more efficiently and accurately. If you plan ahead and anticipate your requirements, you can devote more time to the drawing itself and less time to the details of organizational concerns and how they affect the drawing outcome.

Organizing Your Drawing

This chapter is about setting up and managing your AutoCAD drawings. Before you start to draw, you can take certain steps that will save you time and make your drawing proceed much more efficiently. In this respect, drawing with AutoCAD is not that different from manual drafting, where you gather the tools you need and prepare the work area before you even put pencil to paper. When doing manual drafting, for example, one of the first questions that must be answered is at what scale the drawing will be carried out. Unless the drawing will fit comfortably on the drawing sheet at full scale, some reduction or enlargement must be applied. Although CAD drawings work somewhat differently in this respect, consideration for the form, scale, and size of the final output also must be given as you organize the electronic workspace. Other important aspects, such as the drawing units to be used and the settings that affect the way AutoCAD works, should be determined as you set up and organize your drawing.

Perhaps the most important of all these considerations is understanding how working with AutoCAD differs from conventional manual drafting with respect to the concept of scale. Once the concept of CAD scale is understood, you can better understand the other steps you take to organize your drawings.

Drawing in Real-World Units

AutoCAD drawing elements are stored in real-world units. Therefore, when using AutoCAD, you always draw in real-world units; that is, you always draw full scale. AutoCAD stores dimensional data—the length of a line, the radius of a circle—in real units of inches, feet, meters, millimeters, or just about any unit of measurement you need to use.

When you draw on a drafting board, you usually create the drawing to fit on a certain sheet size. If the objects your drawing represents are larger than the drawing sheet, you must scale them down as you draw. Conversely, if you are representing relatively small objects on a large sheet, you scale up the dimensions by some factor, again, as you draw. In effect, you draw and plot simultaneously. As a consequence, the text, symbols and line widths remain about the same size from drawing to drawing.

In AutoCAD, this process is reversed. You always draw objects at actual size (full scale) in real-world units. You do not need to worry about applying a scale factor as you actually draw. In fact, if your drawing is never plotted onto paper or some other physical medium, you need never worry about scale at all.

Most drawings, however, do get plotted onto some form of "hard" output; therefore, size and scale factor become a consideration at this stage. At plot time, AutoCAD enables you to scale the full-sized electronic drawing up or down to fit the plot sheet. In other words, you must apply some overall scale factor to the full-scale drawing as it is plotted. This scale factor affects everything in the drawing equally. You must, therefore, plan ahead for scaling a full-sized AutoCAD drawing and make the settings that adjust the scale of the text, symbols, and line widths as they are added to the drawing, so that they appear at an appropriate size on the scaled plot. The first step in this process is determining how much your full-scale drawing must be scaled up or down to fit the actual plot sheet. This determination yields the scale factor.

Determining a Scale Factor and Drawing Limits

Consider, first, an architectural drawing of a floor plan that has an overall dimension of 24 feet by 13 feet. Assume that you want to plot the drawing at a scale of 1/4" = 1' (12"). What is your scale factor, and what size electronic sheet are you going to use? You set the size of the electronic sheet by choosing the drawing's limits. AutoCAD's LIMITS command sets the X and Y values of the lower right and upper left corners of your electronic sheet. But what values will you use?

If you convert your intended drawing scale to a ratio of 1:*n*, then *n* is your scale factor. If you already have selected a drawing scale, you easily can determine the scale factor. In the case of your floor plan, you want a final plotted scale of 1/4" = 1'-0" so the scale factor is 48. The conversion can be thought of in this way:

1/4" = 1' (or 12") converts to 1" = 48" or a ratio of 1:48

Therefore, your scale factor is 48. If you select a scale of 3/8" = 1'-0", the scale factor is 32. The following is the conversion:

3/8" = 1' (or 12") converts to 3" = 96" or 1" = 32" or 1:32

Calculating Sheet Size for a Known Scale and Object Size

Now you can use the scale factor to determine the limits for your electronic drawing sheet by performing some test calculations for common plotting sheet sizes. The following is a sample set of calculations:

Size of floor plan: 24'×13'

Scale: 1/4" = 12"

Scale factor: 48

Now test for a 17-by-11-inch B-sheet:

17"×48 = 816" or 68'

11"×48 = 528" or 44'

A 17-by-11-inch sheet equals 68'×44' at a scale of 1/4" = 12".

The B-sheet is certainly large enough; the 24-by-13-foot floor plan would easily fit. In fact, at this plotted scale, the floor plan would perhaps appear too small. Try the next smaller standard sheet, an 11-by-8.5-inch A-sheet:

11"×48 = 528" or 44'

8.5"×48 = 408" or 34'

An 11-by-8.5-inch sheet equals 44'×34' at a scale of 1/4" = 12". This size offers a better fit with adequate room for dimensions, notes, and a border, and perhaps a title block.

In this example, you determined your limits by the number of units that fit across a standard A-sheet (44' across 11" at 1/4" = 12"). Sometimes you need to fit the full-scale drawing to a predetermined sheet size. In these instances, use the sheet size and the size of what you are drawing to calculate the plot scale. The following calculation applies to an 11-by-8.5-inch sheet and a 24-by-13-foot object:

24' = (24'×12" per foot) = 288"

11": 288" (ratio of sheet size to object size)

11:288 equals a ratio of 1:26 (approximately)

The next highest scale is 1:32, or .375:12, or 3/8" = 1' scale.

Setting the Drawing Units and Limits

Now that you have determined the scale factor for a particular drawing and a final plotting scale, the next step in setting up your electronic drawing's environment is setting the units for the drawing and then setting the limits. It is easier to figure and set the limits if you first set the units using AutoCAD's Units Control dialog box.

Setting Units

AutoCAD offers drawing units that are suitable for drawings in virtually any profession or discipline. If you normally use architectural units, for example, use AutoCAD's architectural units. Technical researchers might use decimal or scientific units; a mechanical designer would use metric units or inches; and a surveyor might choose decimal feet or miles. A wide range of precision settings also is available. Setting units accomplishes two things in the drawing setup process. First, it determines the input format you use for entering distances and angles from the keyboard. Second, it sets up the output format that AutoCAD uses when displaying the dimensioning distances and angles.

To get started with your drawing setup for the 24-by-13-foot architectural floor plan, perform the steps in the following exercise to create a new drawing and set the units and precision you want to use.

Using the UNITS Command

`Command:` *Choose* File, New	Opens the Create New Drawing dialog box
Type **ARCH** *in the* New Drawing Name *box, then choose* OK	Creates a new drawing named ARCH in the current directory
`Command:` *Choose* Data, Units	Issues the DDUNITS command and displays the Units Control dialog box (see fig. 1.1)
Choose the Architectural *radio button*	Selects architectural units
Click in the Precision *list box in the* Units *area, then select* 0'-0 1/64"	Opens drop-down list and changes precision from 1/16" to 1/64"
Verify that the Decimal Degrees *radio button is selected in the* Angles *area*	Specifies the default, decimal degrees angles

Figure 1.1

The Units Control dialog box.

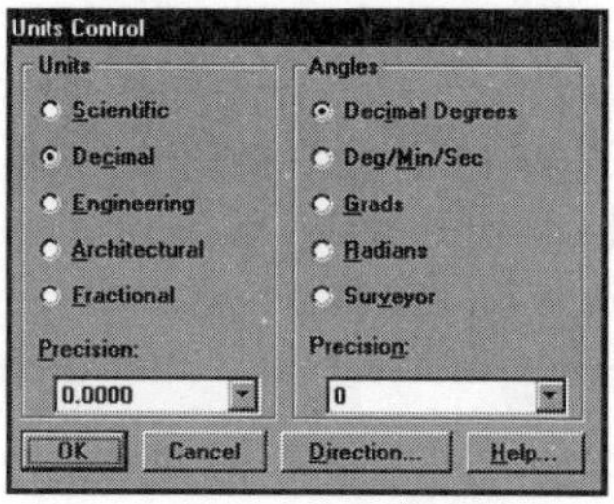

Click in the Precision *list box in the* Angles *area, then select* 0.00	Changes the angular measurement precision from zero to two decimal places
Choose Direction	Opens the Direction Control dialog box (see fig. 1.2)

Figure 1.2

The Direction Control dialog box.

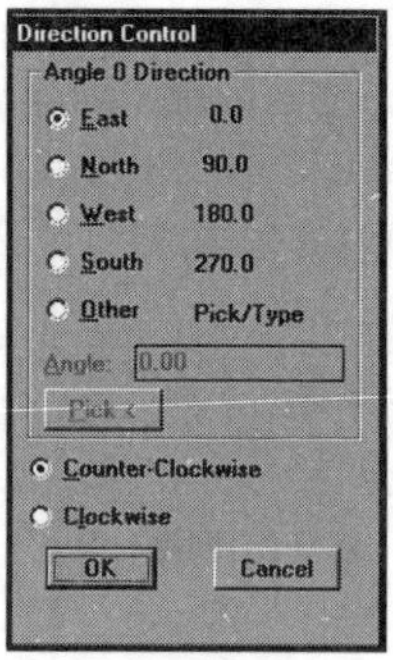

Verify that the East *radio button in the* Angle 0 Direction *area is selected*	Specifies the default, East (right of screen) as the direction for angle 0
Verify that the Counter-Clockwise *radio button is selected*	Specifies angles to be measured counter-clockwise (the default) from 0
Choose OK, *then* OK *again*	Closes both dialog boxes and saves settings
`Command:` *Move the cursor in the drawing and note the coordinate display in the status bar*	The coordinates display as feet and inches and are rounded to the nearest 1/64 inch.
`Command:` *Choose* File, Save	Saves your changes to ARCH.DWG

The coordinate display now shows Architectural units: feet, inches, and fractions. If the format of the current coordinate is too long to fit in the coordinate display area, it appears in scientific units, such as 1.704450E+03,95'–9 5 1/64".

TIP

If the status bar coordinate display is turned off, you can press F6 or Ctrl+D to turn it on. You also can double-click in the coordinate display area.

DDUNITS Command Options

The Units Control dialog box, displayed by the DDUNITS command, provides the following areas and options:

- **Units area.** Displays and sets the current format for units of linear measure. The Precision list box sets and displays the precision for the current units format.
- **Angles area.** Displays and sets the current angle format. The Precision list box sets and displays the precision for the current angle format.
- **Direction button.** Displays the Direction Control dialog box, which is used to control the direction of angles.

You also can use the UNITS command to set linear and angular units and precision; however, the DDUNITS command and its Units Control and Direction Control dialog boxes are quicker and easier to use. The UNITS command simply steps you through the linear and angular settings as prompts on the command line, gathering the same information you supply with the DDUNITS dialog box.

NOTE

Duplicate dialog box and command-line commands, such as DDUNITS and UNITS, might appear to be needless redundancy. Often the command-line version is a holdover from earlier versions of AutoCAD that did not support a dialog box user interface. These command-line commands have been retained, however, to provide a programming interface for AutoCAD scripts, menu macros, and user-defined AutoLISP functions. From a user's point of view, it is almost always preferable to use the dialog box version of these commands.

In the previous exercise, you set the precision to 1/64". Even though you might not need fractions finer than 1/2", consider setting the precision to a much higher value (such as 1/32" or 1/64"). Doing so will help ensure precision in your drawing. For example, say you are attempting to draw a line 1/2" long and have the precision set to 1/2". If you accidentally draw a line 5/16" long, AutoCAD will round off the distance and display the length as 1/2" even though the line is actually 5/16" long! If, however, you have the precision set to 1/64", AutoCAD will display the correct length and you can then detect and correct the error. Setting a higher precision makes drawing errors more likely to show up.

Entering and Displaying Values in Various Units

No matter which units you are using, you can enter values in integer, decimal, scientific, or fractional formats. When you are using architectural or engineering units, you can enter values as feet, inches, or both. AutoCAD assumes that the value is in inches unless you use a foot mark (') to indicate feet. You can omit the inches mark ("), and if the inches value is zero, you do not need to type anything. The values 2'0", 2'0, 2', and 24" all are equivalent in engineering units. Thus, to signify one foot, three inches, you can enter 1'3" or 1'3.

AutoCAD displays values in a manner different from the way you input them. If, for example, you input a value of 1'3-1/2", AutoCAD displays it as 1'-3 1/2". You can force feet and inches, angles, and fractions to appear in the same form as their entries by setting the UNITMODE system variable to 1. Enter UNITMODE at the `Command:` prompt and then enter the value 1.

WARNING

AutoCAD interprets the press of the spacebar as a press of the Enter key. Do not use the spacebar in an attempt to separate elements of a linear distance input. No space is required between feet and whole inches; use a hyphen between whole and fractional inches, as in 1'3-1/2" or, more simply, 1'3-1/2.

AutoCAD's scientific, decimal, and fractional units have no associated dimension, such as feet or inches. You can use them to represent any units. You can use AutoCAD's dimension text suffix feature to add an appropriate symbol. To represent millimeters, for example, use decimal units and then add mm as a suffix. See Chapters 19, "Introduction to Dimensioning," and 20, "Styling and Editing Dimensions," for details.

Setting Limits and Drawing Aids

After you establish your drawing's units, set up your electronic drawing sheet using the LIMITS command. The drawing limits define the area you want to draw in and are useful for viewing and plotting your drawing. You also can set up various other drawing aids such as a cursor snap increment and a visual reference grid of dots. You set these to functions or multiples of the units you have specified. You can type `LIMITS` at the `Command:` prompt or use the Drawing Limits item on the Data pull-down menu.

NOTE

AutoCAD has two drawing environments: model space and paper space, each having its own separate drawing limits. For more on model space and paper space, see Chapter 5, "Working with Model and Paper Space Viewports."

LIMITS Command Options

The LIMITS command issues the following command-line options:

- **ON.** Turns on limits checking to prevent points from being specified outside the limits.
- **OFF.** Turns off limits checking (the default) to enable you to specify points outside the limits.
- **Lower left corner.** This prompt sets the coordinates for the lower left corner of the limits (the default is 0,0).
- **Upper right corner.** This prompt sets the coordinates for the upper right corner of the limits (the default is 12,9).

You previously determined that your 24-by-13-foot architectural floor plan would plot adequately on an 11-by-8-1/2-inch A-sheet at a scale of 1/4" = 1'-0", yielding a full-scale "sheet size" of 528×408 inches or 44×34 feet. Therefore, you now can apply this full-scale "sheet size" to the LIMITS command.

SETTING THE LIMITS FOR AN ARCHITECTURAL DRAWING

Continue from the previous exercise, in the ARCH drawing.

`Command:` *Choose* Data, Drawing Limits — Issues the LIMITS command

`'_LIMITS`

`Reset Model space limits:`

`ON/OFF/<Lower left corner>`
`<0'-0",0'-0">:` ↵ — Retains the default 0,0 lower left corner

`Upper right corner`
`<1'-0",0'-9">:` **44',34'** ↵ — Sets the value for the upper right limit

The value in the preceding step is the sheet size value in drawing units, which you calculated earlier. Note that you could have entered the value in inches.

`Command:` *Choose Zoom All (Standard Toolbar, Zoom) (refer to Appendix C if needed)* — Issues the ZOOM command with the All option and zooms to area bounded by current limits and regenerates the drawing

`Zoom All/Center/Dynamic/Extents/`
`Left/Previous/Vmax/Window/`
`<Scale(X/XP)>:` **_a**

`Regenerating drawing.`

Move the cursor around the drawing area and notice the coordinate display on the status bar. Near the upper right corner of the drawing area, note that the display indicates approximately 57', 32'. You will see the upper left extent of the limits more clearly and precisely in the next section, when you turn on the grid and snap.

`Command:` *Choose Save (Standard Toolbar)* — Issues the QSAVE command and saves the drawing

In the preceding exercise you set the limits of the ARCH drawing to the dimensions of an 11-by-8-1/2-inch physical sheet scaled *up* by an amount equal to the scale factor. This, in effect, defines an electronic drawing area within which you can create your 24-by-13-foot floor plan at full scale. When you actually plot the drawing, you scale the drawing *down* by the reciprocal of the scale factor (1/48 in this case) so that the objects in the drawing are physically plotted at a ratio of 48:1; or 48 real-world inches equals one plotted inch; or 12 real-world inches equals 1/4 plotted inches. Stated another way, 1/4" = 1'-0".

Setting the Snap and Grid

Now that you have set the limits of your electronic sheet, it would be useful to have some means of visualizing the limits. Unlike manual drafting whereby the physical sheet on the drawing board clearly defines your boundary, AutoCAD's electronic screen has no physical bounds. You can use AutoCAD's Drawing Aids dialog box or the GRID command to establish a drawing grid that automatically extends to the current drawing limits. The grid also is useful in visualizing and estimating coordinate values and distances. You also can set a snap increment in the Drawing Aids dialog box that causes the crosshairs to move in accurate increments. Appropriate snap and grid values, and the coordinates display, enable you to visually pick points accurately.

In the following exercise you establish a drawing grid and snap increment and further investigate the function of the drawing limits.

SETTING A GRID TO DISPLAY THE DRAWING'S LIMITS

Continue from the previous exercise, in the ARCH drawing.

`Command:` *Choose* Options, Drawing Aids	Issues the DDRMODES command and displays the Drawing Aids dialog box (see fig. 1.3)
Put a check in the Grid On *check box*	Turns on the grid
In the Grid *area, double-click in the* X Spacing *edit box, and then enter* **12**	Sets the X spacing to 12 and changes the Y spacing to 1'0" when you press Enter
Put a check in the Snap On *check box*	Turns on snap
In the Snap *area, enter* **3** *in the* X Spacing *box*	Sets X and Y spacing to 3"
Choose OK	Closes the dialog box and displays the grid—an array of dots
`Command:` **Z** ↵	Issues the ZOOM command
`All/Center/Dynamic/Extents/ Left/Previous/Vmax/Window/ <Scale(X/XP)>:` **.75** ↵	Zooms so that limits and grid cover 75 percent of the graphics window (see fig. 1.4)

Move the cursor around the drawing area and notice the coordinate display on the status bar. Near the upper right corner of the drawing area, note that the display indicates precisely 44'0", 34'0" at the upper right grid dot.

`Command:` *Choose Save (Standard Toolbar)*	Saves the drawing

Figure 1.3

The Drawing Aids dialog box.

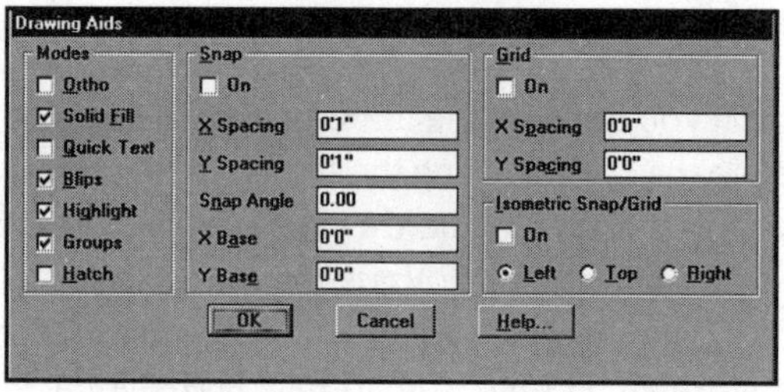

Figure 1.4

Drawing limits shown by a grid.

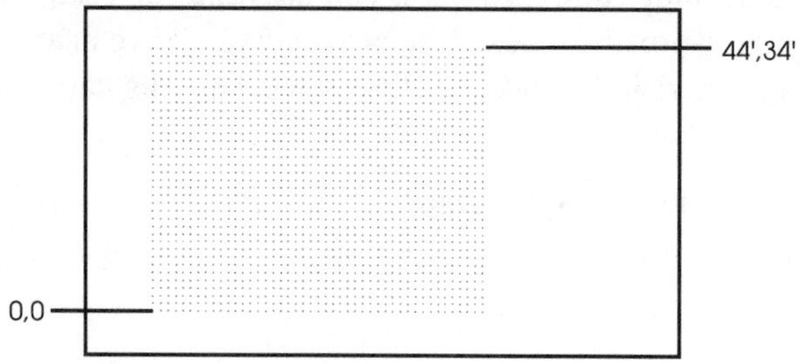

As shown in figure 1.4, the grid provides both a functional and visual boundary for your drawing. The area covered by the grid is the defined limits, representing an 11-by-8$^1/_2$-inch sheet scaled up by a scale factor of 48, or 44'×34' (528"×408"). For clarity, the upper right limits of the drawing are identified in figure 1.4.

This time, as you move the cursor to the upper right, the coordinates display showed X,Y values in increments of three inches. This increment is the snap increment. The grid and snap are aids for accurately picking points. The grid and snap settings are fully discussed in Chapter 3, "Drawing Accurately," which you develop methods to increase the accuracy of your drawings.

Turning On the Limits Checking

You can use AutoCAD's grid to visually identify the drawing's limits. The LIMITS command can actually prevent you from drawing outside of these limits. This feature is called *limits checking*, and it is off by default. The ON/OFF options in the LIMITS command prompt signify limits checking. When limits checking is on, AutoCAD checks each point you specify to determine whether the point is within the drawing's current limits. If the point is outside the limits, AutoCAD prevents you from using the point.

Setting Limits Automatically with MVSETUP

After you have determined either the size of the plotted sheet or the final plotted scale for your drawing, you can determine the all-important scale factor that you use during plotting. As you saw in the previous exercises, setting the drawing's limits is then largely a matter of simple arithmetic. You can use AutoCAD's MVSETUP command to perform most of these calculations for you. MVSETUP prompts for the drawing units, the drawing scale factor, and the intended sheet dimensions, and then calculates the drawing's limits. MVSETUP also draws a border representing the limits of the drawing.

MVSETUP Prompts

For use in non-paper-space applications, MVSETUP has the following prompts:

- Enable paper space? (No/<Yes>). You must enter **N** or **n** to use the non-paper-space functions of this command.
- Units type (Scientific/Decimal/Engineering/Architectural/Metric). Entering one of these options (initial letter acceptable) displays a list of appropriate scales and associated scale factors.
- Enter the scale factor. Enter a value.
- Enter the paper width. Enter a value in actual sheet-size units.
- Enter the paper height. Enter a value in actual sheet-size units.

The following exercise uses MVSETUP to determine the limits for a civil engineering drawing. For the purpose of this exercise, assume that the drawing is to be plotted at a scale of 1" = 20' and the plotted sheet is to be 17"×11".

Using the MVSETUP Command To Determine Limits

`Command:` *Choose New (Standard Toolbar)*	Issues the NEW command and opens the Create New Drawing dialog box
Type **ENG** *in the drawing name box, and then choose* OK	Begins a new drawing titled ENG using the default ACAD prototype drawing
`Command:` **MVSETUP** ↵	Starts the MVSETUP command
`Initializing...`	Indicates loading the command—it might take several seconds

`Enable paper space? (No/<Yes>):` **N** ↵	Forces the non-paper-space prompts
`Units type (Scientific/Decimal /Engineering/Architectural/Metric):` **E** ↵	Specifies engineering units and prompts for engineering scale

AutoCAD switches to the text window and displays the following common engineering scales and their associated scale factors:

Engineering Scales
==================
(120) 1"=10'
(240) 1"=20'
(360) 1"=30'
(480) 1"=40'
(600) 1"=50'
(720) 1"=60'
(960) 1"=80'
(1200) 1"=100'

`Enter the scale factor:` **240** ↵	Specifies 1" = 20' scale
`Enter the paper width:` **17** ↵	Specifies sheet width
`Enter the paper height:` **11** ↵	Specifies sheet height

MVSETUP calculates the drawing's limits, sets units, and draws a border defined by the calculated limits, and then zooms to the limits. Next, you zoom out a little farther.

`Command:` **Z** ↵	Issues the ZOOM command
All/Center/Dynamic/Extents/Left/ Previous/Vmax/Window/<Scale(X/XP)>: **.75** ↵	Zooms limits to cover 75 percent of drawing window
`Command:` *Choose* Options, Drawing Aids	Displays the Drawing Aids dialog box
Put a check in the On *check box in the* Snap *area*	Turns on snap
Double-click in the X Spacing *edit box in the* Snap *area, and then enter* **10'**	Sets both the X and Y snap interval to 10' when you press Enter
Put a check in the On *check box in the* Grid *area*	Turns on the grid
Choose OK	Closes the dialog box and displays the grid (see fig. 1.5)

Move the cursor around the drawing and note that it moves in 10-foot increments coincident with the displayed grid. In the upper right corner, note that the coordinate display reads 340'-0.000", 220'-0.000".

Save the drawing.

NOTE

The MVSETUP command is also used to set up multiple viewports in AutoCAD drawings using paper space. For this use, MVSETUP is available from the View menu. For non-paper-space use, the command must be entered at the `Command:` prompt. See Chapter 6, "Plotting and Sheet Composition," for details of MVSETUP use.

Figure 1.5 shows the ENG drawing after you have configured it for a 1"=20' scale. The border drawn by the MVSETUP command surrounds an area 340'×220' within which you create your drawing at full scale. In the exercise, you turned on AutoCAD's snap feature and set the interval to a distance of 10'. Then you turned the grid feature on but left the grid spacing at the default of 0. The grid automatically displays at the snap interval when the grid spacing is set to 0. The snap feature restricts cursor movement to specified intervals. As you move the cursor around, it snaps to 10' intervals.

At plot time you instruct AutoCAD to plot ENG drawing at a scale of 1 plotted inch equals 240 drawing units (20'). The border also will be scaled down to 17"×11". This border makes the edge of the sheet—you need to draw or insert a standard title block and border.

Whether you set the limits for your drawing automatically with MVSETUP or manually with the LIMITS command, defining limits is an important step in preparing your drawings for final output. The drawing limits define a work area that is useful in both plotting and viewing your drawing, and limits checking provides extra protection against erroneous drawing objects.

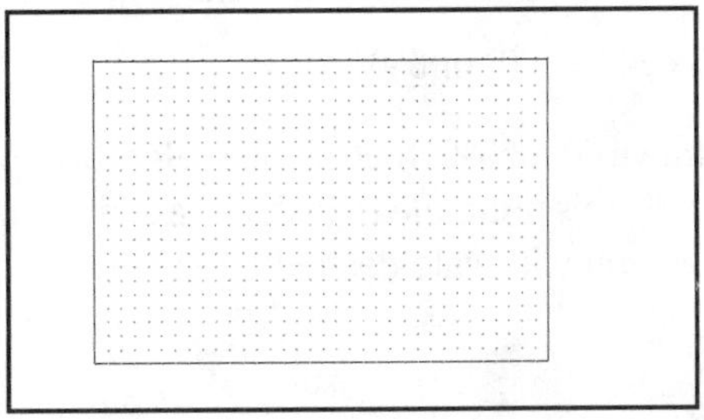

Figure 1.5

The drawing set up with MVSETUP.

Applying Scale Factors to Text and Symbols

As noted previously, when drawing using conventional manual drafting techniques, you add such features as text, standard symbols (such as mapping symbols, schematic electrical or piping symbols) linetypes, and line widths uniformly from drawing to drawing, in accordance with your own drawing standards and conventions. When using AutoCAD and drawing in real-world units and then plotting at a scale, however, you need to apply a different technique. For example, if you want certain text elements in your plotted drawing to be 1/8" in height and you are plotting at a scale of 1/4 plotted inch equals 12 drawing inches, what height must the text be in real-world units as you add it to your drawing? How wide do you make a line in your full-scale drawing if you want it to be 1/16" wide when reduced to fit the plotted sheet at any given scale?

You easily can answer these and similar questions if you know the scale factor for your particular drawing size and plotted scale. Simply determine the size you want your symbols, text, and other elements to be in the final plot and then multiply that size by the scale factor. This is actually an extension of the principle involved in the scaling of all CAD drawings discussed earlier in this chapter. You can use the following general formula:

Plotted Size × Scale Factor = Electronic Size

Applying this formula, 1/8" plotted text in a 1/4" = 1'-0" architectural drawing would be drawn at a height of 1/8" × 48, or 6". In a similar manner, a symbol you want plotted at a standard 3/4" height in an engineering drawing with a scale factor of 24 (1" = 2') would be drawn at a real-world size of 3/4" × 24 = 18" (for more on scaling and creating symbols, see Chapter 10, "Basic Building Blocks for Repetitive Drawing").

Use this formula with your ENG drawing (scale factor 240) and add some text as a title. Suppose, for example, that you want to add the title *I-24/SR-12 Interchange* in the lower left corner. Assume that you want the text to appear at a height of 1/4" on the plotted sheet. You use the following calculation:

1/4" × 240 = 60" or 5'-0"

Text drawn 60" or 5'-0" high at full scale will appear 1/4" in height on the plotted sheet. You apply this principle to text and a symbol in the following exercise. Later in this chapter, you will scale dashed linetypes.

SETTING TEXT HEIGHT

Continue from the previous exercise, in the ENG drawing.

Command: **DTEXT** ↵	Starts the DTEXT command
Justify/Style/<Start point>: *Pick at point* 10',10'	Specifies the text insertion point for the text
Height <0'-0.2000">: **60** ↵	Specifies a height of 60"
Rotation angle <0>: ↵	Accepts the default 0 degrees

In the following step, enter the text from the keyboard:

Text: **I-24/SR-12 Interchange** ↵	Draws the text (see fig. 1.6)
Text: ↵	Ends the DTEXT command

Save the drawing.

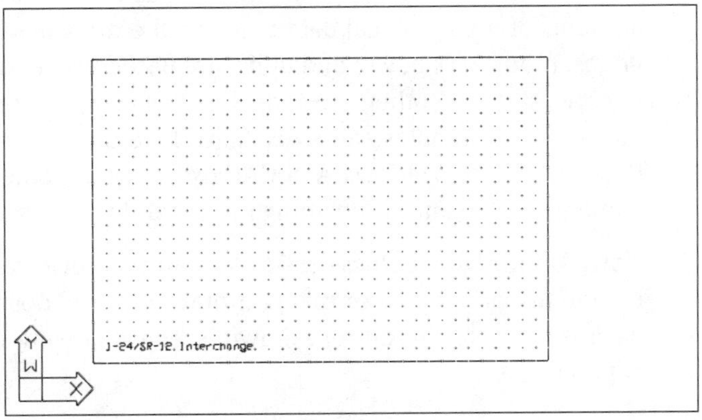

Figure 1.6

Text added to the drawing.

In this section you have learned about several tools you can use to set up your working environment. AutoCAD stores these settings, along with your work, as electronic files. You can take advantage of this fact to minimize the work required when you start a new drawing or project by saving "prototype" drawings within which you have made these settings. You learn how to do so in the next section, which describes AutoCAD's file commands.

Opening and Creating Drawings

The first section of this chapter covered several general settings you can employ to create an environment suited to the type of drawing you are creating. Often these settings are common to much of the work you do routinely. If you are preparing architectural drawings, for instance, you will probably work in one of a set of standard drawing scales, use architectural units, and perhaps use a standard sheet size for plotting.

One powerful and flexible aspect of using AutoCAD is the capability to easily make use of any existing work when starting a new drawing. This capability is especially useful in preparing "prototype" drawings in which you can store many of the settings described in the preceding section. This provides you with a ready-made working environment when you need to create many similar drawings. This section starts by describing the commands you use to open existing drawings and how to create new drawings using "prototype" drawings.

Previewing and Opening Existing Drawings

AutoCAD is a graphics application. Although AutoCAD is capable of linking large amounts of nongraphical data between the drawings it creates and external programs, AutoCAD's power and utility are based upon visual data. File management interfaces, on the other hand, deal exclusively with textual/numerical data—file names, creation dates and sizes, hard drive directories, and subdirectories. With Release 13c4 for Windows, AutoCAD extends its graphical functionality into the file-management realm by including the capability to visually preview its .DWG files.

Now, AutoCAD's graphics-based files can be previewed prior to performing such operations as opening or saving a drawing, or choosing another drawing file to be inserted into the current drawing. The following exercise demonstrates this capability.

PREVIEWING AUTOCAD DRAWINGS

Continue from the previous exercise, in the ENG drawing.

Command: *Choose Open (Standard Toolbar)*	Issues the OPEN command and opens the Select file dialog box
Click on any file name	Displays a preview of the drawing in the Preview box (see fig. 1.7)

You can preview drawing files one at a time by clicking once on the file name. To view all the drawings in an entire directory, perform the following steps:

Choose the Find File *button*	Displays the Browse page of the Browse/Search dialog box (see fig. 1.8)

All the drawing files in the currently selected directory are displayed. If there are more files than can fit in the preview box, use the scroll bars to move within the display. The drawing's name appears below the image.

Click on the Size *list box and select* Medium, *then repeat and select* Large	Displays the drawing previews at medium and large size
Choose the Exit *button*	Closes the Browse/Search dialog box
Click on the Cancel *button in the* Select File *dialog box*	Closes the Select File dialog box and cancels the OPEN command

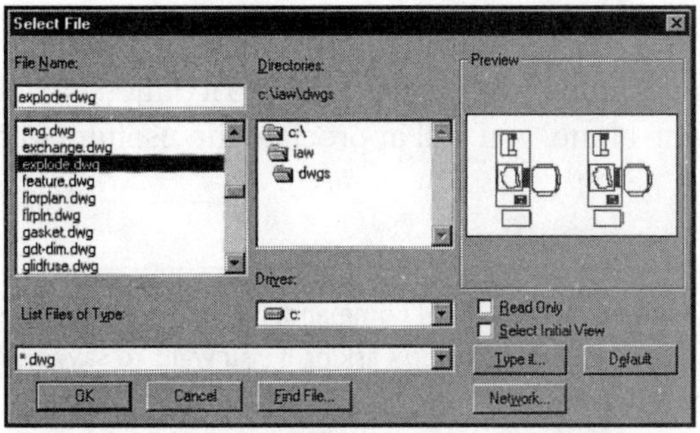

Figure 1.7

Previewing a single drawing.

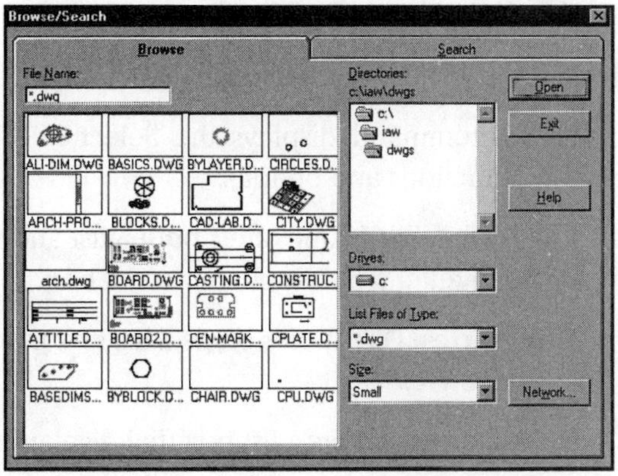

Figure 1.8

Viewing multiple drawings.

When drawing preview images are displayed in the Browse/Search dialog box, you can open a drawing by double-clicking on its image or by selecting the image (with a single click) and then choosing the Open button. If you find the drawing you want to open in the Select File dialog box, you can open it by double-clicking on the file name or by choosing OK (see fig. 1.9).

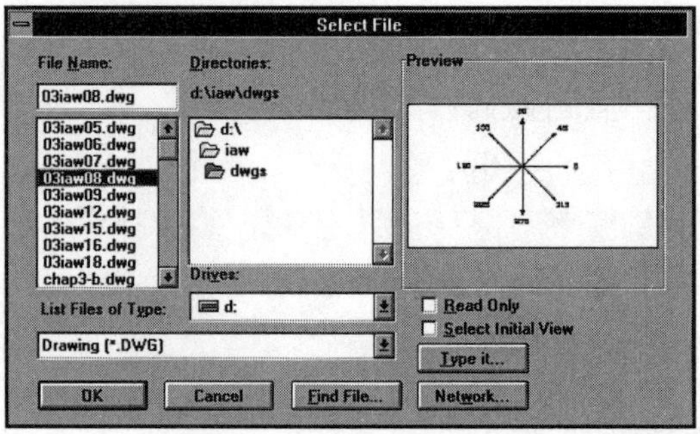

Figure 1.9

The Select File dialog box.

Drawing files—especially files stored in the same directory—often have similar file names, and if you have ever found it difficult to locate a particular drawing by its file name alone, you will appreciate the usefulness of this AutoCAD feature.

NOTE

When issuing the OPEN command, if the current drawing has not been saved, AutoCAD displays an alert dialog box asking if you want to save the current drawing before opening a new drawing.

Select File Dialog Box Options

The OPEN command displays the Select File dialog box, which provides the following functions and options:

- **File Name.** File Name offers both a list and text box. You can select a file name or enter a file name in the text box.
- **Directories.** Directories offers a list box that displays the directories on the current drive.
- **Drives.** Drives offers a list box that displays the names of all available drives.
- **Preview.** Preview is an area that displays a bitmap of the selected file.
- **List Files of Type.** List Files of Type offers a list box that displays files by extension.

- **Read-Only Mode.** The Read-Only Mode check box opens a drawing in Read-Only Mode. You can edit a drawing and save it to another file name.
- **Type it.** The Type it button prompts for the drawing file name to be entered at the `Command:` prompt.
- **Find File.** The Find File button enables you to search for files using standard search criteria such as wild cards. It displays the Find File dialog box.
- **Network.** The Network button enables you to connect to network drives.

Creating New Drawings

The command to start a new drawing is NEW. As with many of the commands in AutoCAD, there are several ways to issue the NEW command. From the command line, you can type NEW. You also can use the NEW tool from the standard toolbar or the New item on the File pull-down menu. All these methods display the Create New Drawing dialog box.

Understanding the NEW Command Options

The NEW command provides the following options in the Create New Drawing dialog box:

- **Prototype.** This option enables you to specify the prototype drawing you want to use.
- **No Prototype.** This option enables you to bypass a prototype drawing and use AutoCAD's default settings for all parameters.
- **Retain as Default.** This option enables you to set No Prototype as the default or set the specified drawing as the default prototype drawing.
- **New Drawing Name.** You enter the name of the new drawing in this box. Choosing the New Drawing Name button displays a file dialog box that enables you to view and select the names of existing drawings.

WARNING

Until you save a new drawing using any of AutoCAD's save commands, the work you perform in a new drawing is stored only in the computer's temporary memory. It is vulnerable and can be completely lost due to accidents such as power failure or equipment malfunctions. Save your drawings often! Refer to the section "Saving Your Work" later in this chapter for more information.

Using Prototype Drawings

Anytime you open a new drawing, AutoCAD refers to a *prototype drawing* to obtain the many settings needed to begin the drawing. If you do not specify a specific prototype drawing, AutoCAD uses it own prototype, named *ACAD.DWG*. AutoCAD reads the settings from ACAD.DWG and uses them to get started. ACAD.DWG contains only the bare necessities you need to start drawing any objects. It has one layer, layer 0; one linetype, CONTINUOUS; and a few other basic settings. Defining your own prototype drawings will save you innumerable hours of drawing setup time and also provide a consistency to your work.

After you set up units, limits, and scale factor and other settings, it is likely you will want to make many drawings with most, if not all, of the same settings. In an architectural setting, for example, you might need to make hundreds of drawings plotted at a scale of 1/8"=1'-0". If you use AutoCAD for a civil engineering application, you might need many drawings plotted at 1"=20'. The layers you use in one typical drawing might be the same layers you use in many others. You can make a single drawing in which the settings that you use regularly can be stored and used again and again. Such prototype drawings can be used as the basis for new drawings. You can have many prototype drawings, each serving as the basis for new drawings of a specific type.

The Create New Drawing dialog box has a section for specifying a prototype drawing name to be used as the starting point for a new drawing. Choosing the Prototype button opens the Prototype Drawing File dialog box. The Prototype Drawing File dialog box contains the following elements:

- **File Name.** You enter a file name in the File Name edit box. If the cursor is not already in this box, a single click places it there; a double-click highlights the text for replacement.

- **Drives.** The Drives drop-down list box enables you to select a different disk. A single click selects a drive and changes the list in the Directories box to the drive's current path setting.
- **Directories.** The Directories box lists the current drive and directory along with any subdirectories. A double-click selects a directory and lists the files that match the type specified in the List Files of Type box.
- **List Files of Type.** The List Files of Type drop-down list sets the file extension for the files listed in the File Name edit box. The default is Drawing (*.DWG).

Prototype drawings are used throughout this book as the basis for new drawings. Follow in the next exercise as one of the book's prototype drawings, IAW-MECH, is used as the prototype for a new drawing named CHAP01B drawing.

USING AN EXISTING DRAWING AS A PROTOTYPE

Command: *Choose* File, New	Issues the NEW command and opens the Create New Drawing dialog box
Choose the Prototype *button*	Opens the Prototype Drawing File dialog box (see fig. 1.10)
In the File Name *list box, choose the* IAW-MECH *drawing file (scroll the list if required)*	Selects the IAW-MECH file as the prototype drawing file and the Preview box

The Preview box displays a blank drawing.

Choose OK	Closes the Prototype Drawing File dialog box
In the New Drawing Name *edit box, type* **CHAP01** *and choose* OK	Closes the Create New Drawing dialog box and starts a new drawing named CHAP01

In the next step, take a look at the layer setup for the new CHAP01 drawing.

Command: *Choose Layers (Standard Toolbar)*	Issues the DDLMODES command and opens the Layer Control dialog box

Note the 13 layers and their colors and linetypes.

Choose Cancel	Closes the Layer Control dialog box

You do not need to save this drawing.

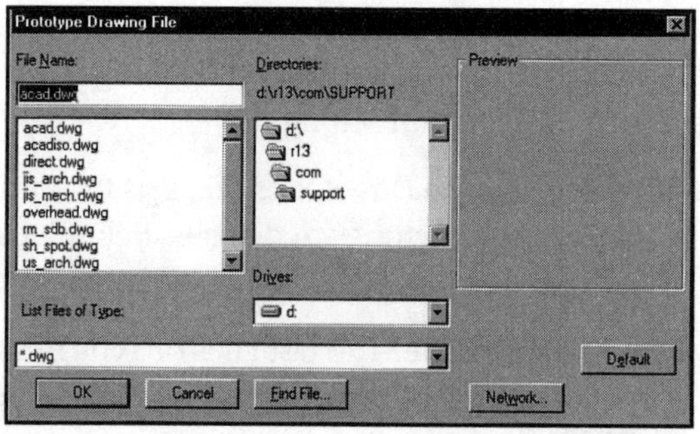

Figure 1.10

The Prototype Drawing File dialog box.

The CHAP01 drawing is an exact copy of the prototype IAW-MECH drawing with all its settings, loaded linetypes, and layer configuration. After you expend the time and effort to set up the prototype, you can make an unlimited number of prototype clones. By their very nature, prototype drawings attempt to anticipate all layers, linetypes, and other named items and settings that might be needed in the clone drawing. Therefore, they can contain layers and linetypes that you do not need in a specific drawing. You can easily use the AutoCAD commands to fine-tune the new drawing to your needs.

TIP

You have an alternative to using the Prototype Drawing File dialog box for specifying a prototype drawing; you can enter the file name (and path) directly in the input box next to the Prototype button.

Prototype drawings help avoid repetitious setup procedures, and using prototypes provides an excellent means to establish standards. Keep in mind also that any drawing can serve as a prototype. Because the prototype procedure essentially copies, renames, and opens a drawing in one step, existing drawings can serve as a starting point for new drawings. After the new drawing has been opened, erase the unneeded portion of the old drawing and keep the remaining portion as the basis for the new drawing.

Prototype drawings are a powerful tool that you can use in setting up many of your drawings. Three prototype drawings are included on the CD-ROM that comes with this book and are installed in the book's \DWGS directory. IAW-ARCH provides settings and layers appropriate for many architectural drawings. IAW-MECH is a prototype drawing suitable for many mechanical applications. IAW-MTRC provides similar settings with metric units and ISO standards. In addition, AutoCAD ships with its own set of standard prototype drawings that includes ACADISO, US_ARCH, and US_MECH, among others. These can be found in the R13\COM\SUPPORT directory of your AutoCAD installation. Prototypes are used extensively in the remainder of this book and you can use them in your work with AutoCAD to save drawing setup time and establish and maintain drawing standards.

In this section, you have learned how to start a new drawing using a prototype drawing to replicate settings you previously made. To create a new prototype drawing, you need to start a new drawing, make any changes you need to the environment, and then use one of AutoCAD's commands for saving the file to disk. The next section describes these commands.

Saving Your Work

AutoCAD provides several commands that save the drawing by writing the drawing's database as a file on a permanent storage device such as a hard drive. The drawing is saved with a .DWG file-name extension. Three commands save drawings to a permanent file: SAVE, QSAVE, and SAVEAS. AutoCAD's terminology and menu structure are confusing here because the command labeled Save: on the screen menu, the Save item on the File pull-down menu, and the Save tool on the standard toolbar actually issue the QSAVE command. The SAVE command is available only at the command line. The various commands used to save drawings to files are described in the following section.

The QSAVE command is a quick and easy way to ensure that changes made to the drawing are stored on a permanent storage medium—typically a hard drive. In addition, AutoCAD automatically makes a backup copy of the drawing each time you issue the QSAVE command. The current drawing file becomes the most recent backup copy at the completion of the next QSAVE. This backup procedure ensures that you have a copy of the current drawing that is no older than the elapsed time since your previous QSAVE. Using the QSAVE command frequently and habitually is a small investment of time that pays large dividends should you need to recover a drawing due to equipment failure.

TIP

AutoCAD provides a keyboard shortcut, Ctrl+S, that issues the QSAVE command.

The SAVE command, available only at the command line, works similarly to the QSAVE command, but prompts for the name of the file to which to save the drawing. The default file name is the current one, but you may supply any valid file name. The drawing is saved as a file with the name you supply. Note that the current drawing name does not change even if you supply a different name to the SAVE command. AutoCAD provides a different command with which to accomplish this task.

Saving a Drawing Under a Different Name

If you attempt to save an unnamed drawing, AutoCAD displays the Save Drawing As dialog box, which enables you to assign a name prior to saving the drawing. The SAVEAS command also displays the Save Drawing As dialog box, enabling you to save an unnamed drawing to a file name you specify. The SAVEAS command also enables you to simultaneously save and rename the current drawing.

As you saw in the definition of the SAVEAS command, you can save the current drawing to a different name. In the following exercise, you save the current CHAP01 drawing using the SAVEAS command and rename it to CHAP01B.

SAVING A DRAWING TO A DIFFERENT NAME

Choose File, Save As	Issues the SAVEAS command and displays the Save Drawing As dialog box (see fig. 1.11)
Type **CHAP01B** *in the* File Name: *input box, then choose* OK	Saves the drawing to a new file and closes the dialog box

```
_saveas
Current drawing name set to
C:\IAW\DWGS\CHAP01B.
```

`Command:` *Choose* File, New, *then choose* OK	Clears the drawing database without assigning a drawing name
`Command:` *Choose* File, Open	Displays the Select File dialog box

The drawing you saved with the SAVEAS command, CHAP01B, appears in the File Name: list box.

Select CHAP01B	Highlights drawing name and displays a preview of the drawing in the Preview box (see fig. 1.12)
Choose OK	Loads the drawing into the graphics window

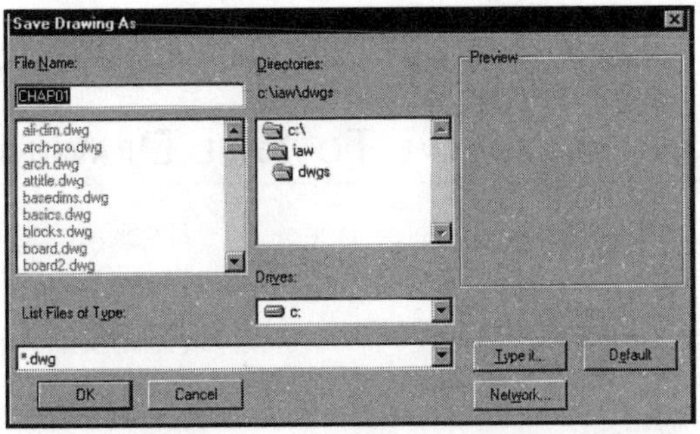

Figure 1.11

The Save Drawing As dialog box.

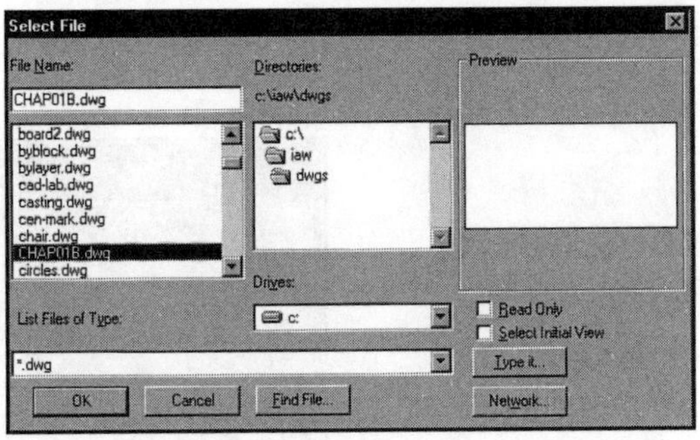

Figure 1.12

The Select File dialog box.

If you want to exit AutoCAD at this point, you can choose File, Exit, which issues the QUIT command. You can return to this drawing later by using the OPEN command as described in this exercise.

TIP

If you have made changes to your drawing since it was last saved, these changes will be discarded if you answer No to the prompts in the Drawing Modification dialog box. Many AutoCAD users, however, use the QSAVE command immediately before issuing the QUIT command. This precludes accidentally discarding changes to the drawing.

Saving Your Drawing Automatically

AutoCAD has an automatic drawing file-saving feature often referred to as autosave. You can set a timer to automatically save the current drawing at intervals of from 1 minute to 2 hours (the default interval). You also can disable the autosave feature. In the following exercise you set the autosave interval to 15 minutes using the Preferences dialog box.

USING AUTOSAVE TO SAVE DRAWINGS AUTOMATICALLY

`Command:` *Choose* Options, Preferences	Displays the Preferences dialog box (see fig. 1.13)
Double-click in the input box in the Automatic Save section of the System *page*	Highlights the current text
Type **15**	Places the number 15 in the input box
Choose OK	Closes the Preferences dialog box

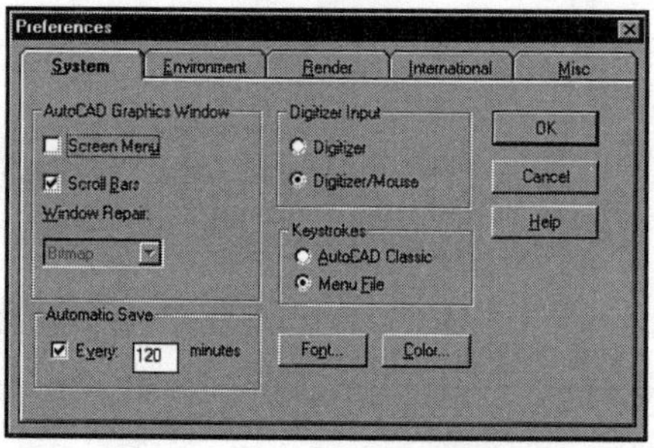

Figure 1.13

The System page of Preferences dialog box.

As a result of the preceding exercise, you have reconfigured AutoCAD so that any drawing you are working in will be saved automatically every 15 minutes. Removing the check from the Every box in the Automatic Save section of the Preferences dialog box disables the autosave feature and grays out the current interval time in the minutes input box.

NOTE

You also can set the autosave time interval using the Auto save time item on the Options pull-down menu.

Automatic saves are made to a special file, AUTO1.SV$, in the current directory. Should you need to use this file (due to a problem with the parent drawing), rename AUTO1.SV$ to a name with a .DWG extension and open it as a drawing.

Using Release 13 File Options

AutoCAD R13 introduced several new aspects to the issue of saving drawing files. These issues are the following:

- Compatibility with Release 12 format
- Using Windows 95 and NT long-file-name format
- Speeding up the file save process

First, because the file format used in Release 13 is different from the file format of Release 12, AutoCAD provides a way to save files that is *backward compatible*. The SAVEASR12 command enables you to save the current drawing in Release 12 format.

When a Release 12 drawing is opened in Release 13, the drawing is automatically converted to the current file format. If it is saved using the QSAVE or SAVE commands, it is saved in Release 13 format, and anyone who is using Release 12 will no longer be able to open it. If you are saving drawings that will be worked on in the future with Release 12, you should use the SAVEASR12 command to maintain this compatibility.

WARNING

If your drawing contains objects or accesses features which are new to Release 13, they will be lost when the drawing is saved using SAVEASR12. Examples of this include multi-line text and ellipse objects, hatch associativity, and object groups.

Second, AutoCAD Release 13c4 for Windows is fully compatible with Windows 95 and Windows NT, including support for long file names. If your system is set up to save files using this format, you can save your AutoCAD drawings using descriptive names up to 255 characters long. Long file names also can contain several additional special characters (including spaces) that are not acceptable within the DOS or Windows 3.x file-naming scheme.

TIP

Conscientious use of the long file-name feature can make it far easier to recognize drawings, especially if you have multiple versions. The downside of this feature is that its indiscriminate use could just as easily create a new level of confusion. As with many aspects of using AutoCAD, this feature will provide the greatest benefit only with thoughtful and consistent application.

You can learn more about the details of working with long file names in the Windows 95 documentation. New Riders also publishes several informative books on the subject of optimizing your use of Windows 95 features.

Third, AutoCAD's new drawing file format introduced in Release 13 results in file sizes that can be considerably larger than the equivalent files saved in earlier versions. One side effect of this increase in file size is that files can take significantly longer to be written to disk. In response to users' complaints about this side effect, Releases 13c3 and later provide a feature known as *incremental saves*. With this feature enabled, when you issue a SAVE or QSAVE command, AutoCAD appends only the drawing objects that have changed to the previously saved file. This has the effect of reducing the time it takes to write the file, at the expense of increasing the file's size in the interim.

Two system variables control the action of the incremental save feature:

- **ISAVEPERCENT** is an integer value between 0 and 100, which specifies the amount of "estimated waste space" within the file. Waste space results from objects being deleted or modified—the previous definition is retained in the file, while the new definition is added to the end. The default setting of ISAVEPERCENT is 50, which permits up to half of the original file's size to be accumulated as waste space before a "full" save is performed. You can disable the incremental save feature by setting this variable to 0.

- **ISAVEBAK** specifies whether AutoCAD creates a duplicate .BAK file for each incremental save. Its value is either 1 (enabled—the default) or 0 (disabled). Copying the entire file to create the backup each time accounts for a substantial portion of the time required for the save operation, so disabling this function can speed things up, at the expense of some file security.

WARNING

In the event of a system crash, an ISAVEBAK setting of 0 can result in a loss of data.

If you often work with very large drawings and find that routine saves take an inordinate amount of time, examine the setting of ISAVEPERCENT. You might want to experiment to find an optimum setting.

In this chapter you have seen how proper drawing setup is one of the keys to putting AutoCAD to work for you. Understanding and applying the concepts of drawing units, limits, and scale factors make working in real-world units intuitive and natural. You also learned how you can leverage these basic settings by creating and using prototype drawings to apply them to any similar drawings you need to create in the future. In the next chapter, you learn how (like making basic environment settings) preparing a set of appropriate layers with their associated colors and linetypes can make your drawings both efficient and easy to work with. Keep the concept of prototype drawings in mind as you read it.

chapter

2

Organizing Drawings with Layers

Layers are one of the most effective tools you can use to help organize your AutoCAD drawings. Almost everything you design or draw can be thought of as being separated into layers. Buildings are layered by floors; individual floors can be divided into electrical, plumbing, and structural elements. Even the simplest schematic drawing might have a layer devoted to annotation and another devoted to the schematic elements. AutoCAD offers a virtually unlimited number of electronic layers giving you a high degree of flexibility and control in organizing your drawing. Layers also are used in CAD to separate different types of objects so that they easily can be assigned different linetypes and plotted with different line weights.

In manual drafting, physical layers made from clear plastic sheets often are used to separate groups of related drawing elements. Think of AutoCAD's layers as similar transparent electronic sheets that are laid over one another. A typical AutoCAD 2D drawing looks like a stack of these transparent sheets (see fig. 2.1). You can see your entire drawing as it is being built from the superimposed sheets. You can "remove" sheets from the stack so that they do not interfere with the view of the other sheets, and you can add new sheets as the need arises. Each layer can have any of AutoCAD's colors and linetypes associated with it.

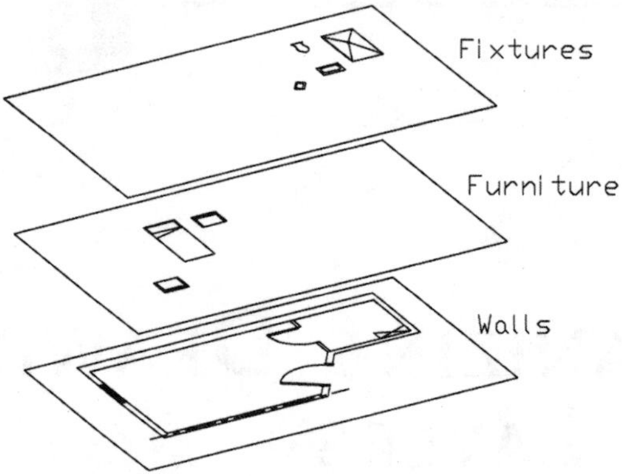

Figure 2.1

Using layers in AutoCAD.

In this chapter you learn about object properties, such as color and linetype, how to create new layers, set their properties, and use these properties to select groups of layers. You also learn the benefit of developing and using a system of layers to organize your work. Some of the topics covered in this chapter include the following:

- Working with layers in your drawings
- Creating and naming new layers
- Assigning properties to layers
- Changing layer visibility and accessibility
- Renaming layers and other named objects
- Removing unneeded layers
- Assigning properties to individaul objects

When you use any of AutoCAD's drawing tools to draw on one of the electronic layers, you create a *drawing object.* Lines, circles, and text are examples of AutoCAD objects. In addition to its geometric position, each object has an associated layer, color, and linetype. AutoCAD calls these associations *object properties*. Normally, the color and linetype are inherited from the layer on which the object is drawn, although this association can be overridden.

NOTE

The color of an object can have special significance, because most plotting and printing devices used with AutoCAD assign line weight or other visual properties according to color. This and other plotting topics are discussed in Chapter 6, "Plotting and Sheet Composition."

With this amount of flexibility, one of the most important steps in organizing your drawing is devising the layering scheme you use: which parts of the drawing you place on which layers, and the names, colors, and linetypes of each layer. You can make as many or as few layers as you need. There are many schemes for creating layers. Different professions have established standards and conventions that you can adopt, or you can devise your own.

Working with Layers

As a reflection of their importance, AutoCAD provides several ways of working with layers:

- Opening the Layer Control dialog box by either choosing the Layers tool on the Object Properties toolbar (see fig. 2.2), choosing Data, Layers from the pull-down menu, or entering the DDLMODES command at the `Command:` prompt
- Entering the LAYER command, then entering options and layer names on the command line
- Clicking on the icons in the Layer Control drop-down list on the Object Properties toolbar (see fig. 2.2)

Figure 2.2

The Object Properties toolbar's layer facilities.

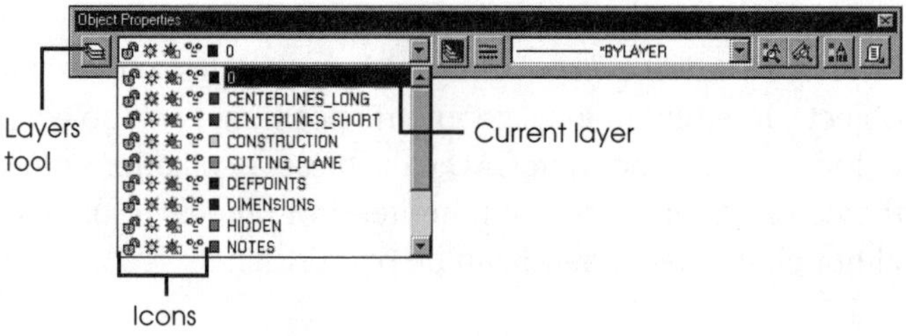

In the preceding list, the first two methods afford complete layer control. Because of its advanced interface, you probably will use the Layer Control dialog box most often when creating layers and performing operations on groups of layers. The Layer Control dialog box is shown in figure 2.3.

Figure 2.3

The Layer Control dialog box.

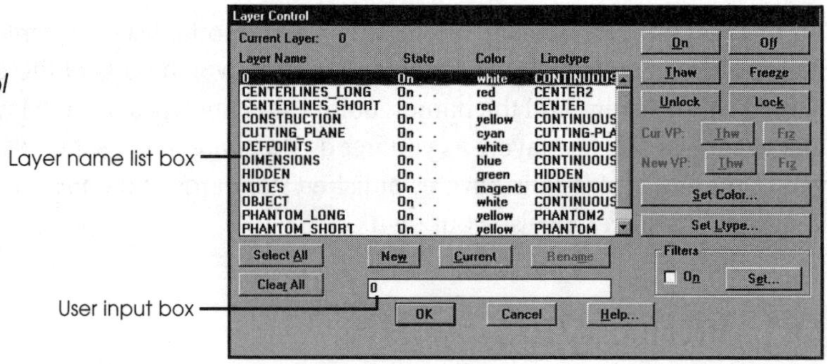

The Layer Control dialog box provides the easiest way to create layers, to change their colors and linetypes, and to manipulate groups of layers. The Layer Control drop-down list provides the easiest way to control layer visibility and set the current layer for drawing.

Using the Layer Control Dialog Box

The Layer Control dialog box is composed of a layer name list box, a user input box, and several buttons. The Layer Name list box displays a list of all the layers defined in the drawing along with their assigned color, linetype, and current state (to be discussed later). The Layer Name list box always contains a layer named 0. Layer 0 is AutoCAD's default layer and it is assigned the default layer properties: color white and linetype continuous. Layer 0 has some special properties that are explained later. The input box enables you to enter layer names. The various buttons are explained later. The Layer Control dialog box is opened by the DDLMODES command.

Creating New Layers

Although you always have layer 0 available, you need to begin setting up a layer system by making some new layers. In the following exercise you begin a new drawing named LAYERS and begin using the Layer Control dialog box.

Creating New Layers

Use the NEW command to begin a new drawing named LAYERS using the default ACAD.DWG prototype drawing.

`Command:` *Choose* Options, UCS, Icon	Turns off the UCSICON

The UCSICON is covered in Chapter 3. It is turned off here for visual clarity.

`Command:` *Choose Layers (Object Properties)*	Issues the DDLMODES command and displays the Layer Control dialog box
Type **OBJECT** *in the name input box and choose* New	Creates a new layer named OBJECT and adds it to the Layer Name list box (see fig. 2.4)
Select OBJECT *in the* Layer Name *list box*	Selects OBJECT layer for a subsequent operation
Choose Current	Makes OBJECT the current layer
Choose OK	Closes the Layer Control dialog box and saves the changes

Note that OBJECT now shows as the current layer in the Layer Control drop-down list box of the Object Properties toolbar.

Use the LINE command and enter the coordinates shown in figure 2.5 to draw the "Upper Shim" widget.

Save the drawing.

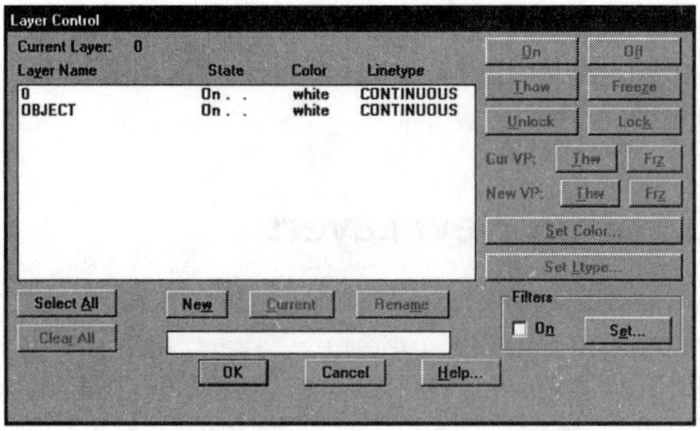

Figure 2.4

Creating the OBJECT layer in the Layer Control dialog box.

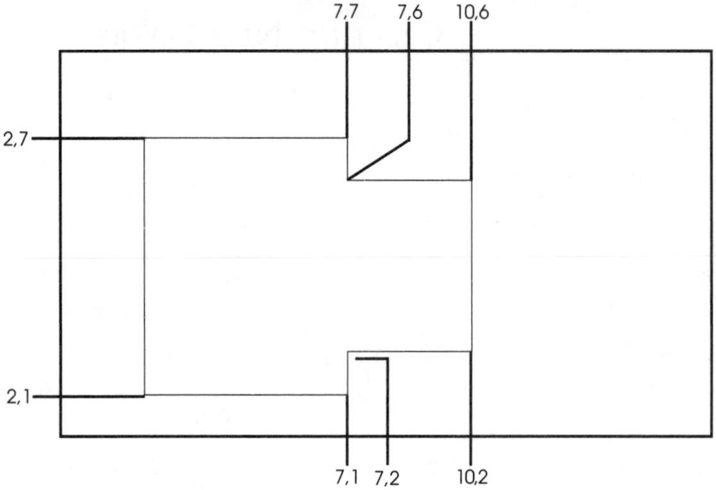

Figure 2.5

An Upper Shim widget drawn on the OBJECT layer.

After you created the new layer OBJECT, you made it the current layer, then drew the shim. Any objects you draw automatically are assigned to the current layer. The shim, therefore, appears on the OBJECT layer and has the associated properties of that layer. All new layers, by default, have a color of white and a linetype of continuous associated with them unless and until you change that association. You learn how to change the default color and linetype of layers later in this chapter.

NOTE

If you are using a white graphics background, AutoCAD's color 7 (white) appears black. Although it appears black, AutoCAD always calls it white. Certain light colors, such as yellow, can be difficult to see on a light background. You can use the Color button on the System page of the Preferences dialog box to change the graphics window background color. The Preferences dialog box can be opened by choosing Options, Preferences on the pull-down menu.

Knowing which layer is the current layer is important, and AutoCAD displays the name of the current layer in the layer control section of the Object Properties toolbar (refer to figure 2.2).

NOTE

You can use the keyboard and the hot keys in the Layer Control dialog box to select layer names in the Layer Name list box. Press Alt+Y, use the up- and down-arrow keys to move the dotted box to the desired layer name, and then press the spacebar to select or de-select it.

Layer Control Dialog Box Options

The Layer Control dialog box displayed by the DDLMODES command contains numerous options and features that provide complete information about and control of AutoCAD layers (refer to figure 2.3).

- **Current Layer.** The Current Layer area displays the name of the current layer.
- **Layer Name.** The Layer Name list displays the name, visibility state, color, and linetype of each layer in the drawing. To modify layer settings, select a layer name (or names) from the list and then choose an option. The layer names listed can be controlled through the use of filters. When only one layer is chosen, its name appears in the input box.
- **Select All.** The Select All button selects and highlights all the layers currently displayed in the Layer Name list box.
- **Clear All.** The Clear All button deselects and dehighlights all selected and highlighted layers.
- **New.** The New button creates new layers with the name or names in the input box.
- **Current.** The Current button sets a selected layer current.
- **Rename.** The Rename button renames the selected layer to match the name in the input box.
- **Input box.** If only a single layer is selected, the input box displays the name of the selected layer. If multiple layers are selected, the input box is blank. Or, you can enter one or more layer names as input for the New or Rename buttons. A layer name can be up to 31 characters long. The input box holds up to 255 characters for multiple entries.

- **On/Off.** The On/Off buttons control the On/Off states of selected layers. Layers that are on are visible; layers that are off are invisible, but are still regenerated. If you turn the current layer off, any new objects you draw will not be visible until you turn the layer on. The word ON in the State column of the Layer Name list box indicates which layers are on.
- **Thaw/Freeze.** The Thaw/Freeze buttons control whether the selected layers are frozen or thawed. A frozen layer is neither displayed nor regenerated. An F in the State column of the Layer Name list box indicates a frozen layer.
- **Unlock/Lock.** The Unlock/Lock buttons control the Unlock/Lock state of selected layers. *Locking* a layer prevents you from editing objects on that layer. Locked layers are displayed and their objects can be used for object snaps. An L in the State column of the Layer Name list box indicates a locked layer.
- **Cur VP Thaw/Frz.** The Cur VP Thaw/Frz buttons control the Thaw/Freeze status of layers within individual floating viewports in paper space. See Chapter 5, "Working with Model and Paper Space Viewports," and Chapter 6, "Plotting and Sheet Composition," for more on paper space.
- **New VP Thaw/Frz.** The New VP Thaw/Frz buttons control the default layer Thaw/Freeze status in subsequently created floating viewports (see Chapter Chapter 6, "Plotting and Sheet Composition").
- **Set Color.** The Set Color button opens the Select Color dialog box, which assigns a color to the selected layer(s).
- **Set Ltype.** The Set Ltype button opens the Select Linetype dialog box, which assigns a linetype to the selected layer(s).
- **Filters Set.** The Filters Set button opens the Set Layer Filters dialog box, which enables you to choose the criteria by which layer names are displayed in the Layer Name list box. You can filter layers based on their state, name, color, or linetype. You also can filter layers based on whether they are frozen in the current viewport or in new viewports. Filters can use wild cards, which are explained later in this chapter.
- **Filters On.** The Filters On check box filters the names displayed in the Layer Name list box based on the criteria defined in the Set Layer Filters dialog box. When checked (on), only layer names matching the currently defined filter are displayed.

- **OK.** The OK button closes the Layer Control dialog box and saves the current settings.
- **Cancel.** The Cancel button closes the Layer Control dialog box and discards any changes.
- **Help.** The Help button activates AutoCAD Help for the Layer Control dialog box features.

Creating Multiple Layers

Unlike mechanical drafting and design, where using a large number of overlays can become unwieldy and self-defeating, you easily can add as many layers to an AutoCAD drawing as necessary—there is no limit. Large drawings often contain hundreds of layers. On the other hand, needless or superfluous layers can be eliminated or combined more meaningfully with other layers. Again, some thought to a layering scheme while you are setting up your drawing will save time and increase efficiency.

You easily can create multiple layers at one time with the Layer Control dialog box. Simply enter several layer names, separated by commas (without spaces), into the input box and then choose New.

In the next exercise you create three additional layers in your LAYERS drawing and then place objects on two of them.

Creating Multiple Layers and Setting the Current Layer

Continue from the preceding exercise, in the LAYERS drawing.

`Command:` *Choose* Data, Layers	Issues the DDLMODES command and displays the Layer Control dialog box
Type **CENTER, TEXT, DIMS** *in the input box and choose* New	Creates three new layers—CENTER, TEXT, and DIMS—and lists them in the Layer Name list box
Select the CENTER *layer name in the* Layer Name *list box*	Selects and highlights the CENTER layer
Choose Current	Sets the selected layer—CENTER—current and displays its name as the current layer

Choose OK	Chooses the dialog box

Draw a line from point 1,4 to point 11,4 through the center of the shim as shown in figure 2.6.

`Command:` *Click in the Layer Control drop-down list box on the Object Properties toolbar*	Displays the Layer Control drop-down list (see fig. 2.7)
Select the TEXT *layer (click on it)*	Sets the TEXT layer current and displays the TEXT layer status in the Layer Control drop-down list box
`Command:` **DTEXT** ↵	Starts the DTEXT command
`Justify/Style/<Start point>:` **2,7.25** ↵	Sets insertion point for text shown above shim in figure 2.6
`Height <0.2000>:` **0.25** ↵	
`Rotation angle <0>:` ↵	
`Text:` **Upper Shim** ↵	Draws text (see fig. 2.6)
`Text:` ↵	Ends DTEXT command

Save the drawing

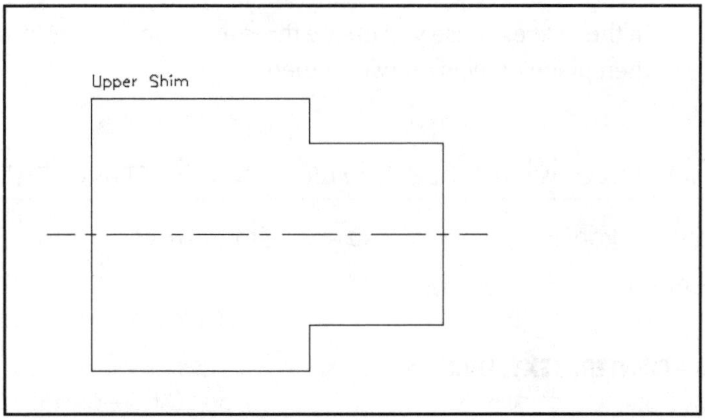

Figure 2.6

Creating objects on various layers.

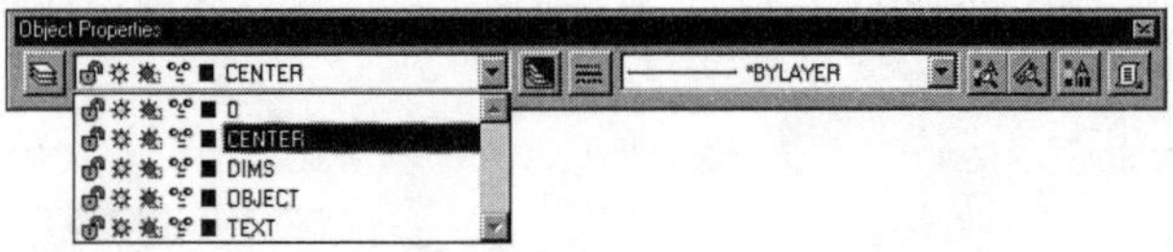

Figure 2.7

The layer names drop-down list.

Assigning Layer Properties

Currently all your layers have the same default properties: color white, linetype CONTINUOUS. Distinguishing between your layers will be difficult because everything looks the same. You need to take full advantage of the power of layers by assigning different colors and linetypes to some layers. AutoCAD supports 255 colors and well over 20 predefined linetypes. These colors and linetypes enable you to differentiate your layers.

Using Colors and Linetypes

Not only do various colors and linetypes make it easier to distinguish objects on the screen while you are drawing, they convey other important information. Some objects, for example, might require different line weights (widths) either to make them stand out or to convey functional meanings. Colors are assigned to layers (or to objects—see Chapter 15, "Object and Drawing Modification and Inquiry Tools,") and then to different plotting pens.

Various design and drafting practices and standards require that certain linetypes be used to convey established meanings; examples of this include the use of the standard center linetype to denote the center of circles and other objects such as the shim in your LAYERS drawing. In mapping applications, certain standard linetypes denote various types of borders and other lines of demarcation. AutoCAD also offers a few complex linetypes with embedded text and symbols, and you can create custom linetypes—see Chapter 18, "Linetypes and Hatching," for more on creating and using linetypes.

Before assigning linetypes (other than CONTINUOUS) to any of your layers, you must first load the linetypes you need into your drawing as shown in the next exercise.

Loading Linetypes

Linetype definitions are stored in specialized text files that AutoCAD uses to describe how a linetype appears. Standard linetypes are kept in a file called ACAD.LIN. Other special linetypes are stored in similar files. (See Chapter 18.) Before you can assign linetypes to layers with the Layer Control dialog box, you must first load them. AutoCAD provides several ways of loading linetypes. In this chapter you use the linetype features of the Layer Control dialog box—see Chapter 18, "Linetypes and Hatching," for use of the DDLTYPE command and for other methods. Before you can access the linetype features of the Layer Control dialog box, you must select one or more layers. The following exercise explains how to load all the linetypes available in the ACAD.LIN file.

Loading Linetypes

Continue from the previous exercise, in the LAYERS drawing.

`Command`: *Choose Layers (Object Properties)*	Opens the Layer Control dialog box
Select CENTER *in the* Layer Name *list box*	Selects and highlights the layer
Choose Set Ltype	Opens the Select Linetype dialog box (see fig. 2.8)
Choose Load	Opens the Load or Reload Linetypes dialog box (see fig. 2.9)
Choose Select All	Selects and highlights all available linetypes from the ACAD.LIN file
Choose OK	Closes the Load or Reload Linetypes dialog box, loads all selected linetypes into the drawing, and displays them in the Loaded Linetypes list box

All the linetypes in the ACAD.LIN file are now loaded in the LAYERS drawing and are available to be assigned to layers.

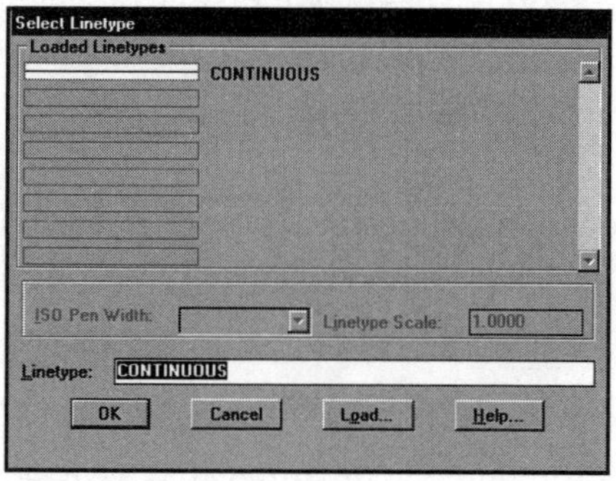

Figure 2.8

The Select Linetype dialog box.

Figure 2.9

The Load or Reload Linetypes dialog box.

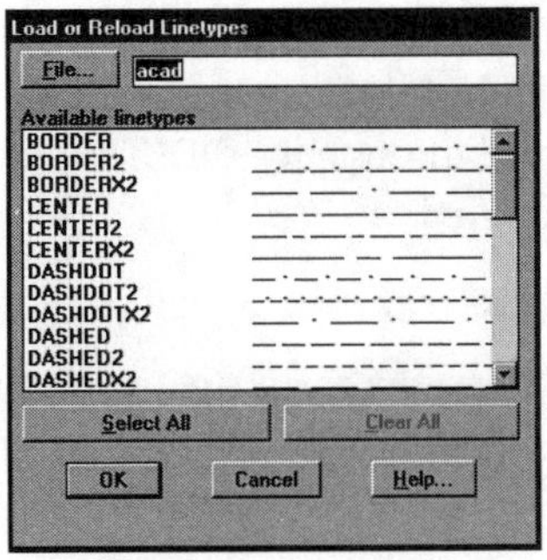

Normally a single drawing does not use all the available linetypes. The Load or Reload dialog box provides the capability to select individual linetypes so that you can load a few or as many as you require. Selectively loading linetypes reduces the overall storage size of your drawing; alternatively, you might find it more convenient to load all linetypes and then later use the PURGE command to remove unneeded ones.

You can select one or more linetypes in the Load or Reload linetypes dialog box by clicking on the linetype names of interest. Clicking on a selected linetype deselects it.

TIP

You can remove linetype definitions that are not used in your drawing with the PURGE command. The PURGE command is covered later in this chapter.

DDLTYPE Command Options

The DDLTYPE command opens the Select Linetype dialog box (refer to figure 2.8), which contains the following elements:

- **Loaded Linetypes list box.** Displays the names and diagrams of available (loaded) linetypes. Clicking on the diagram selects the linetype and places its name in the Linetype text box.
- **ISO Pen Width list box.** Specifies pen width (in millimeters) for International Standards Organization (ISO) linetypes. This is available only for linetypes assigned directly to objects, not those assigned by layer, so it is grayed out when accessed through the Layer Control dialog box. See Chapter 18, "Linetypes and Hatching," for information about ISO linetypes.

- **Linetype Scale.** Displays the current linetype scale factor. This cannot be modified when accessed through the Layer Control dialog box. When accessed through the DDLTYPE command (see Chapter 18 for details), it can be modified.
- **Linetype text box.** Specifies the name of the current linetype.
- **Load button.** Opens the Load or Reload linetypes dialog box (see Chapter 18 for details). This dialog box loads linetypes from a linetype definition file.

NOTE

The 'LINETYPE command, available only at the command line, offers many of the capabilities available with the Select Linetype dialog box and the additional capability to create linetypes on the fly. The 'LINETYPE command is covered in Chapter 18.

Assigning Colors and Linetypes

Now that you have loaded a series of linetypes to your LAYERS drawing, you can assign linetypes to individual layers. In the following exercise you assign nondefault colors and linetypes to some of your layers.

ASSIGNING PROPERTIES TO LAYERS

Continue from the preceding exercise, with layer CENTER selected, all linetypes loaded, and the Select Linetype dialog box open (see fig. 2.10).

Click on the linetype pattern next to CENTER	Specifies and highlights the CENTER linetype; CENTER appears in the Linetype input box

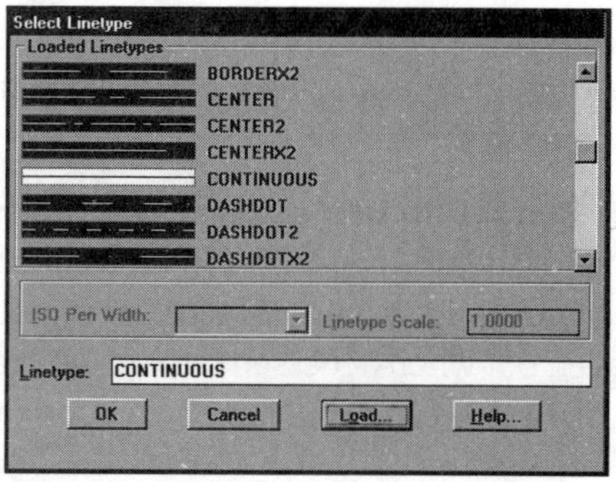

Figure 2.10

The Select Linetype dialog box.

Choose OK	Closes the Select Linetype dialog box

Note that the linetype name CENTER appears in the Linetype column of the selected layer, CENTER, in the Layer Name list box.

Choose Set Color	Opens the Select Color dialog box (see fig. 2.11)

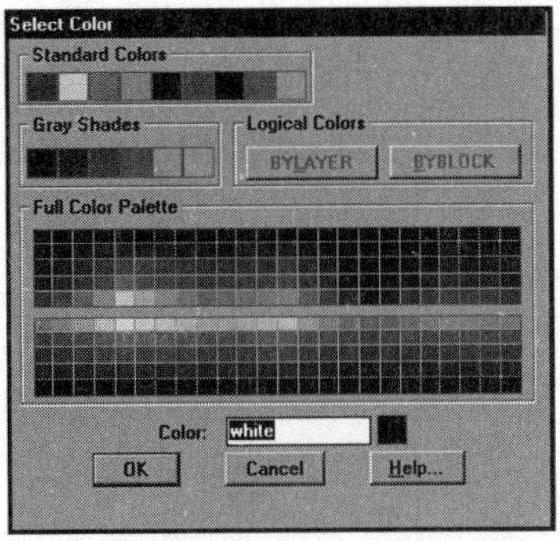

Figure 2.11

Selecting a color in the Select Color dialog box.

Click on the green box in the Standard Colors *area*	Specifies the color for the selected layer; green appears in the Color input box
Choose OK	Closes the Select Color dialog box and lists green in the color column of the CENTER linetype
Choose OK	Closes the Layer Control dialog box and saves the settings

The drawing regenerates and displays the center line with the CENTER linetype and color green properties. The green center line might be difficult to see if you have a white graphics background.

`Command:` ↵	Repeats the DDLMODES command
Click on the TEXT *layer in the* Layer Name *list box*	Selects the layer TEXT
Choose Set Color, select blue, then choose OK	Assigns blue to the TEXT layer
Click on the OBJECT *layer in the* Layer Name *list box*	Selects the layer OBJECT, the TEXT layer remains selected
Click on the TEXT *layer in the* Layer Name *list box*	Deselects the layer TEXT

Choose Set Color, select red, then choose OK	Assigns red to the OBJECT layer
Choose OK	Closes the Layer Control dialog box with the new settings

The drawing will regenerate to show the new setting (see fig. 2.12). Notice that the center line is green with the CENTER linetype, the lines on the OBJECT layer are now red, and the text drawn on the TEXT layer is now blue.

Choose Save (Standard Toolbar)	Saves the changes to the drawing

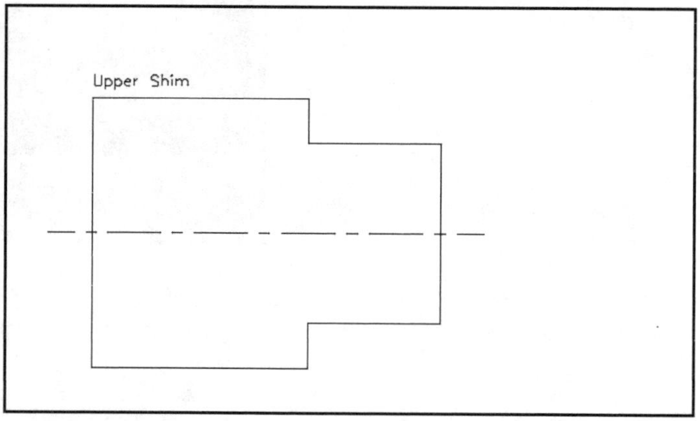

Figure 2.12

The center line displayed with the CENTER linetype on the CENTER layer.

Understanding Linetype Scales

AutoCAD's standard linetypes are composed of repeating patterns of dashes, spaces, and, optionally, dots. The number of defining patterns drawn per unit length is controlled by the linetype definition itself and AutoCAD's system variable LTSCALE.

System variables are the settings and values used by AutoCAD to store its operating environment and many of its commands. The name of the current drawing, for example, is stored in a system variable. You learn more about system variables in Chapter 3, "Drawing Accurately."

The LTSCALE system variable acts as a multiplier, directly affecting the number of linetype repetitions per unit distance. LTSCALE acts globally on all noncontinuous linetypes in the drawing. The lower the value of LTSCALE, the smaller the size of the dashes and spaces, and therefore, the greater number of repetitions per unit distance, as shown in figure 5.24. With a default value of 1.0, for example, setting LTSCALE to 0.5 doubles the number of repetitions in a given distance.

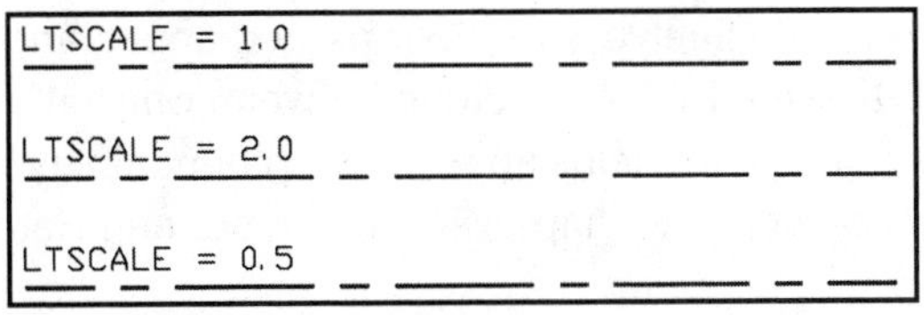

Figure 2.13

The effect of LTSCALE on a linetype.

In the LAYERS drawing, the CENTER linetype assigned to your CENTER layer has the default LTSCALE value of 1.0 applied to it. You might want linetypes to appear at a smaller scale to meet a specific drafting standard or convention. In the following exercise you change the LTSCALE.

CHANGING THE APPEARANCE OF LINETYPES WITH LTSCALE

Continue from the preceding exercise.

`Command:` **LTSCALE** ↵	Accesses the LTSCALE system variable
`New scale factor <1.0000>:` **.5**	Sets the drawing's LTSCALE to 0.5 and regenerates the drawing to apply the new scale (see fig. 2.14)
`Regenerating drawing`	

Save the drawing.

In this drawing, an LTSCALE factor of 0.5 yields an appropriate center line.

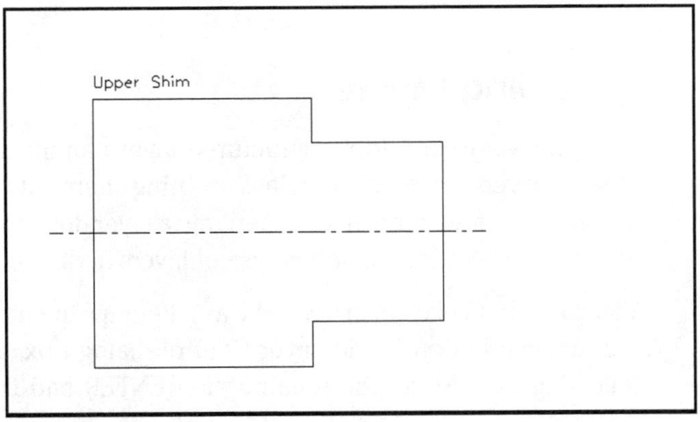

Figure 2.14

The center line with an LTSCALE of 0.5.

You scale linetypes for their plotted appearance, not their displayed appearance. Setting the LTSCALE setting between one-half and one-fourth the drawing's scale factor usually yields appropriate plotted linetypes. You can also set linetype scale per object (see Chapter 18, "Linetypes and Hatching").

WARNING

Assigning too small or too large a value to LTSCALE can result in all linetypes appearing continuous on the screen.

Understanding AutoCAD's Colors

A palette of 255 colors is available in AutoCAD, even if your graphics display supports fewer. The first seven colors are standard and have both names and numbers: 1 = red, 2 = yellow, 3 = green, 4 = cyan, 5 = blue, 6 = magenta, and 7 = white. You can enter the color by name or number in the Color input box in the Select Color dialog box. Other colors are designated by numbers. You also can enter a color from the Select Color dialog box by clicking on the color patch. If your display supports fewer than 255 colors, the unsupported colors appear gray in the dialog box. You still can choose these unsupported colors; however, they will appear in shades of gray on-screen. Assigning unsupported colors to layers in this manner still enables plotter pens to be assigned to these colors. Plotter pens also can be used to designate textures or other special effects when AutoCAD drawings are exported to other graphics programs.

Renaming Layers

As you develop or adopt a structured layer naming scheme, you might want to rename layers on older drawings to bring them into agreement with your new scheme. You also might need to rename a layer due to a misspelling, or to make the name more descriptive, or because of layers in drawings received from others.

You can rename layers in several ways. Perhaps the most convenient method uses the Rename button in the Layer Control dialog box. You use this method in the following exercise as you rename the CENTER and DIMS layers in your LAYERS drawing.

Renaming Layers Using the Layer Control Dialog Box

Continue from the previous exercise, in the LAYERS drawing.

`Command`: *Choose* Layers *(Object Properties)*	Opens the Layer Control dialog box
Select CENTER *in the* Layer Name *list box*	Selects the layer to rename and displays CENTER in the input box
Click to the right of the word CENTER *in the input box and type* **LINE**	Changes CENTER to CENTERLINE in the input box
Choose Rename	Renames the layer in the Layer Name list
Click on DIMS *in the* Layer Name *list box*	Selects DIMS, but grays out the Rename button because two layers are selected
Click on CENTERLINE *in the* Layer Name *list box*	Deselects CENTERLINE and displays DIMS in the input box
Double-click on DIMS *in the input box and type* **DIMENSIONS**	Replaces DIMS with DIMENSIONS in the input box
Choose Rename	Renames the layer in the Layer Name list
Choose OK	Closes the Layer Control dialog box and saves the new names

Save the drawing

You also can rename layers by using the Rename item on the Data pull-down menu. This issues the DDRENAME command and displays the Rename dialog box. You also can use the RENAME command at the `Command:` prompt to rename named items. Both of these commands are discussed later in this chapter.

Controlling Layer Status

Although assigning an adequate number of layers to your drawing is an effective way to help organize your work, having a large number of layers visible at one time can lead to confusion and actually decrease your efficiency. This is particularly true if you have created a large number of layers and your drawing is complex. AutoCAD provides a number of ways to control the visibility and behavior of layers. A layer can be characterized by six states, or conditions, that affect layer visibility and behavior: on or off, frozen or thawed, and locked or unlocked. These states affect layers in the following combinations:

- **On, thawed, and unlocked.** Objects are visible, selectable, and require regeneration time.
- **Off and thawed.** Objects are invisible, not selectable, and require regeneration time.
- **Frozen.** Objects are invisible, not selectable, and do not require regeneration time.
- **Locked, on, and thawed.** Objects are visible, not selectable, require regeneration time, and can still be snapped to with object snap (see Chapter 3).

Several circumstances cause AutoCAD to regenerate a drawing. These include certain viewing operations (see Chapters 4 and 5), text style and block redefinitions (see Chapters 17 and 10), and changing linetype scale. When you altered the LTSCALE for your LAYERS drawing earlier in this chapter, for example, AutoCAD automatically regenerated the drawing to affect the change. AutoCAD automatically regenerates a drawing under many other circumstances.

Regeneration might take a noticeable amount of time—especially with large drawings. Freezing layers can speed up regeneration because when a layer is frozen, AutoCAD ignores the objects on that layer during regeneration. Freezing a layer also renders the objects on the layer invisible.

Turn layers off to suppress display of their objects in a crowded area of the drawing you are editing. Freeze layers when you want their objects to be invisible and not participate in regenerations. Lock layers when you want their objects to be visible for reference but do not want their objects to be selectable.

Even though the objects on a locked layer are not selectable for editing, you can use these objects as a reference and as object snap points. You learn about object snaps in Chapter 3, "Drawing Accurately."

Using the Layer Control Box Drop-Down List

The Layer Control drop-down list on the Object Properties toolbar provides a convenient way to quickly set the current layer or change the On/Off, Freeze/Thaw, and Lock/Unlock states of layers. The Layer Control box is shown both closed and open in figure 2.15.

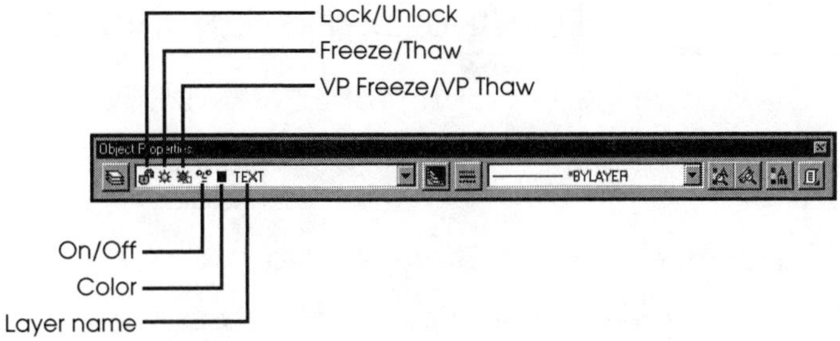

Figure 2.15

The Layer Control box on the Object Properties toolbar.

When closed, only the current layer, its assigned color, and its states are displayed in the Layer Control box, as shown in figure 2.15. By clicking in the layer name area or on the down-arrow button, a drop-down list box appears displaying the same information for all the drawing's layers, as shown in figure 2.15.

By clicking on the various icons associated with each layer name, you can change the condition of the layer state associated with the icon. The icons also change to indicate the current status; for example, clicking on an On icon—a face with open eyes—closes the eyes and turns the layer off. The icons are identified in figure 2.15. You also can change the current layer by clicking on the layer to set it current. That layer's data then appears at the top of the layers list and in the closed Layer Control box on the Object Properties toolbar. You cannot set a frozen layer current.

The Layer Control box offers an efficient way to view and change layer states and to set the current layer without having to use the Layer Control dialog box. When using the Layer Control box, however, you cannot create new layers, rename layers, or use the filters and multiple selection methods available in the Layer Control dialog box.

Turning Layers Off and On

Turning a layer off or on controls the visibility of the objects on that layer. You might want to turn layers off that contain objects that are not relevant to your current work. You also might want to turn certain layers off for plotting purposes. A layer containing annotations or material schedules, for example, might not be needed or wanted on some plots.

In the following exercise, you use both the Layer Control dialog box and the Layer Control drop-down list controls to control whether a layer is on or off.

Turning Layers On and Off

Continue from the previous exercise, in the LAYERS drawing.

`Command:` *Click in the Layer Control drop-down list*	Displays the drop-down list of layers and layer states

Note that the current layer, TEXT, is highlighted.

Click on the open eyes icon for the TEXT *layer*	Changes the icon to closed eyes and sets the layer TEXT to off
Click on the CENTERLINE *layer name*	Sets CENTERLINE current and closes the drop-down list

Note that the text Upper Shim is not visible. The TEXT layer has been turned off. Also note that CENTERLINE is now the current layer.

`Command:` *Choose Layers (Object Properties)*	Opens the Layer Control dialog box

Note that the TEXT layer shows a dot instead of On in the State column because you turned it off in the preceding step.

Select CENTERLINE *in the Layer Name list box*	Selects and highlights the layer name
Choose the Off *button*	Removes On from the State column

Notice the Warning in the lower left corner of the dialog box: **`Current layer is off.`** (see fig. 2.16).

Choose OK	Closes the dialog box and saves the change

AutoCAD displays another warning box. Choose OK. CENTERLINE still is the current layer but is set to off.

`Command:` **L** ↵	Issues the LINE command
`From point:` **3,2** ↵	Specifies the beginning point for the line
`To point:` **5,2** ↵	Specifies the next point for the line
`To point:` ↵	Ends the LINE command

Notice that the line you just drew is not visible. The current layer is turned off.

Click in the Layer Control drop-down list box	Displays the layer drop-down list

Note that the icons for both TEXT and CENTERLINE indicate that these layers are turned off and that CENTERLINE is current and highlighted.

Click on the closed eyes (off) icons for the CENTERLINE *and* TEXT *layers*	Changes the icons to open eyes (on)
Click on the OBJECT *layer name*	Closes the drop-down list and sets OBJECT layer current

The line you drew is now visible because the CENTERLINE layer is now on (see fig. 2.17). Note also that OBJECT, the new current layer, appears in the Layer Control drop-down box.

`Command:` *Pick the line you drew and choose Erase (Modify)*	Selects the line, issues the ERASE command, and erases the line

Save the drawing.

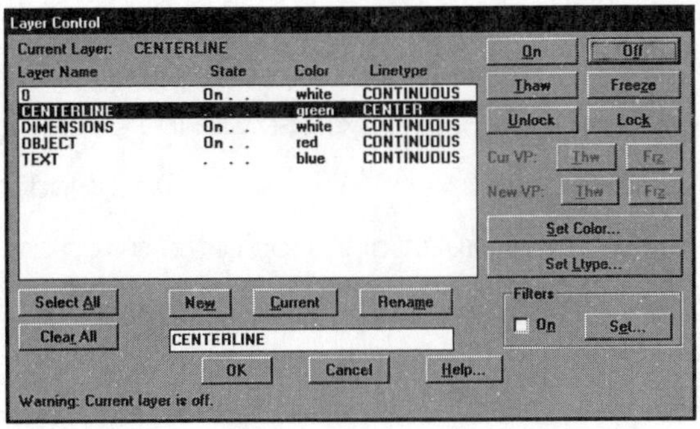

Figure 2.16

The Layer Control dialog box with the `Current Layer is Off` *message.*

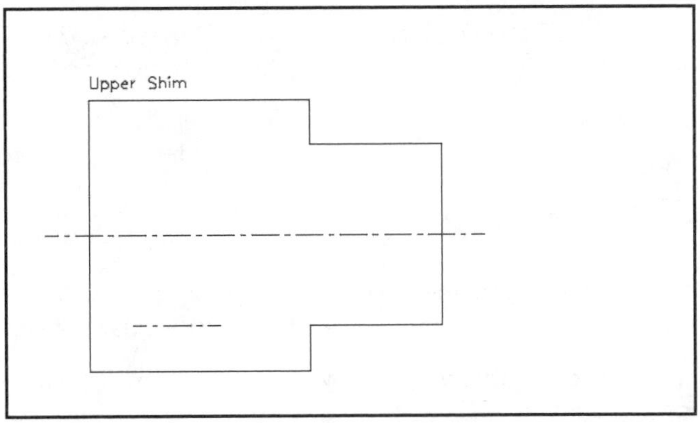

Figure 2.17

The LAYER drawing with a second CENTERLINE line.

To close the Layer Control drop-down list without changing the current layer setting, you can click either on the current layer name or anywhere in the drawing window.

Freezing and Thawing Layers

Freezing a layer makes objects on the layer invisible and exempt from screen regenerations. By freezing layers that you do not need to refer to, you can continue your work for an extended period of time.

When a frozen layer is thawed, AutoCAD performs a regeneration to update the objects on the formerly frozen layer. The current layer cannot be frozen.

In the following exercise, you attempt to freeze the current layer and then freeze and thaw the TEXT layer.

FREEZING AND THAWING LAYERS

Continue from the preceding exercise with the OBJECT layer current.

`Command:` *Choose* Data, Layers	Opens the Layer Control dialog box

Notice `Current Layer: OBJECT` at the top of the dialog box.

Select OBJECT *in the* Layer Name *list box*	Selects the layer to modify
Choose Freeze	Displays `Cannot freeze the current layer.` at the bottom of the dialog box
Click on OBJECT *then* TEXT *in the* Layer Name *list box*	Deselects OBJECT and selects TEXT as the layer to modify
Choose Freeze	Sets the State to frozen and displays an F in the State column (see fig. 2.18)
Choose OK	Closes the Layer Control dialog box and saves the setting

Notice that the text on the TEXT layer, Upper Shim, is not visible. Next, thaw the TEXT layer using the Layer Control box on the Object Properties toolbar.

Click on the down arrow of the Layer Control drop-down list	Displays the layer drop-down list

Notice that the Freeze/Thaw icon for the TEXT layer shows frozen and that the TEXT name is grayed-out and unavailable for setting as the current layer (see fig. 2.19).

Click on the freeze/thaw icon for the TEXT *layer*	Changes the icon to indicate thawed and ungrays the layer
Click in the drawing window	Closes the Layer Control drop-down list, retains OBJECT as the current layer, regenerates the drawing, and displays the TEXT layer

Save the drawing.

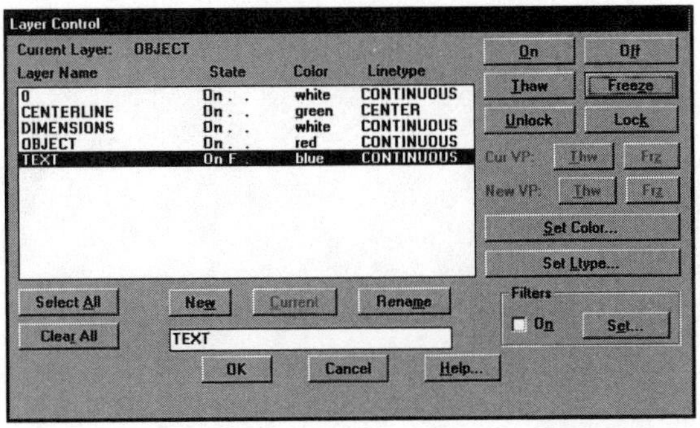

Figure 2.18

Freezing the TEXT layer.

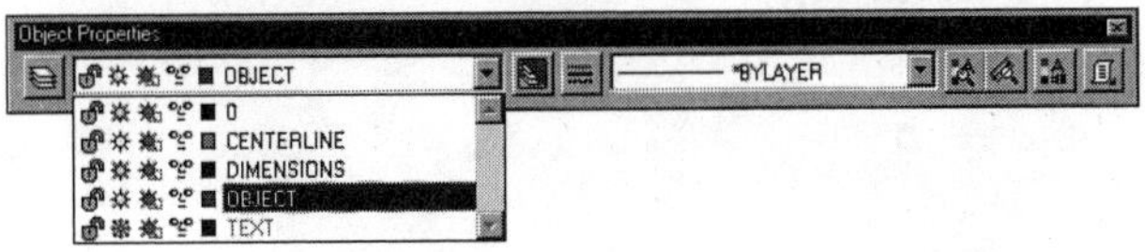

Figure 2.19

The frozen TEXT layer in the Layer Control drop-down list box.

Locking Layers

Locking a layer prevents you from editing any of the objects on the locked layer, but keeps the objects visible for reference. You also can make a locked layer current and add objects to it, and you can apply object snap modes to objects on a locked layer.

In the following exercise you add objects to the Upper Shim in your LAYERS drawing while you investigate how locked layers work. The Lock/Unlock icon is the padlock symbol in the Layer Control drop-down list.

Locking and Unlocking Layers

Continue from the preceding exercise.

First, using any of the methods you have used so far in this chapter, make certain that all layers are on, thawed, and unlocked, and that the OBJECT layer is current.

`Command:` *Click in the Layer Control drop-down list box*	Displays the layer drop-down list
Click on the lock/unlock icon for the OBJECT *layer*	Closes the padlock and locks the layer (see fig. 2.20)
Click in the drawing area	Closes the drop-down list; all layers are displayed
Choose Erase (Modify)	Issues the ERASE command
`Command: _erase`	
`Select objects:` **ALL** ↵	Specifies the ALL option to select all objects in the drawing
`10 found`	
`8 were on a locked layer.`	Reports objects on locked layer; these will be ignored by the ERASE command
`Select objects:` ↵	Erases the two objects not on a locked layer
`Command:` **OOPS** ↵	Restores the objects deleted by the ERASE command

The objects on the locked layer were ignored by the ERASE command.

Use the following steps to unlock the layer.

`Command:` *Choose* Data, Layers	Issues the DDLMODES command and opens the Layer Control dialog box

Notice that an L appears in the State column for the OBJECT layer in the Layer Name list box (see fig. 2.21).

Select OBJECT *in the* Layer Name *list box, then choose* Unlock	Unlocks the layer and removes the L from the State column
Choose OK	Closes the Layer Control dialog box and saves the change

Save the drawing.

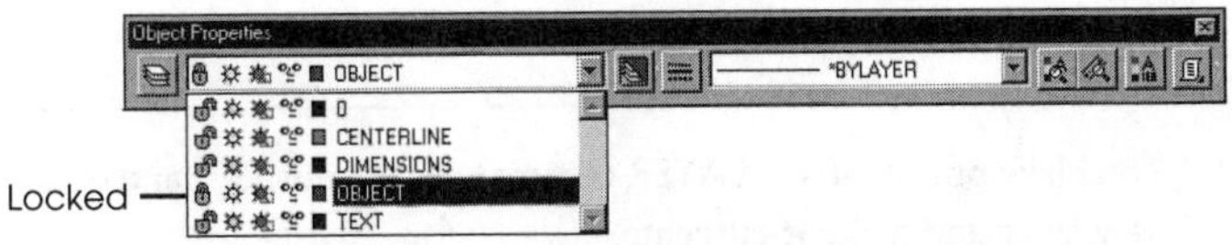

Figure 2.20

Locking the OBJECT layer in the Layer Control box

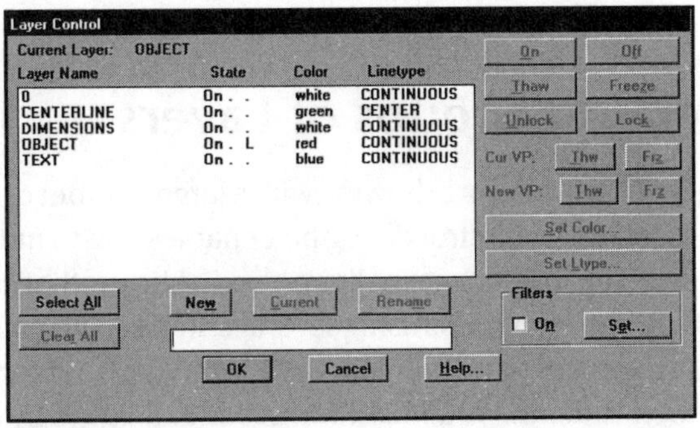

Figure 2.21

Unlocking a layer in the Layer Control dialog box

Using the 'LAYER Command

Although the Layer Control dialog box and the Layer Control list box on the Object Properties toolbar provide complete control of AutoCAD's layers and usually are easier to use, you also can use the LAYER command available from the command line.

The 'LAYER command displays the following prompt:

```
?/Make/Set/New/ON/OFF/Color/Ltype/Freeze/Thaw/LOck/Unlock
```

The `?` option displays a list of all current layers, their current state, and their color and linetype. You can filter this listing with the ? and * wild cards. The `Make` option creates a new layer and sets it current. The `Set` (current), `New`, `ON`, `OFF`, `Color`, `Ltype`, `Freeze`, `Thaw`, `LOck`, and `Unlock` options behave as they do in the Layer Control dialog box displayed by the DDLMODES command. These functions are described earlier in this chapter in the section "Using the Layer Control Dialog Box."

NOTE

> The 'LAYER command offers no control over the freezing of layers in specific mview viewports in paper space. See Chapter 5, "Working with Model and Paper Space Viewports," for details about paper space viewports and layers.

TIP

The Make option of the 'LAYER command is the quickest and easiest way to create a single new layer and make it current.

Selecting Groups of Layers

When working in a drawing with a large number of layers, the Filters facility available in the Layer Control dialog box enables you to narrow the list of displayed layers by selectively filtering smaller groups of layers that share a common trait or property. You can filter layers using several criteria. You might, for example, want to have only layers sharing a common state, such as all locked layers, listed to globally change their state. Or, you might want to list all layers by a common characteristic of their name, such as all layers beginning with the characters "TXT-". Other filtering criteria are available and you can combine these criteria to narrow the layer listing even further. By combining a well-thought-out layer naming scheme with AutoCAD's layer filter feature, you can perform operations on groups of layers easily and quickly.

Filtering Layers by State

In working with layers you often want to group layers by their state. That is, you might want to thaw some or all frozen layers; you might want to list all of the layers that are currently turned off; or you might want to group all the currently locked layers together before unlocking any. Filtering layer names by their state is an effective way to manage a large number of layers in a drawing in which you are changing layer states frequently.

In the following exercise you will use the accompanying CD drawing SITE.DWG. This drawing represents a site plan for an imaginary office complex. Even though this drawing is not complete, it already has some 22 layers. By using your knowledge of the operation of the Layer Control dialog box and applying layer filters, you continue to learn how to make your work with layers more efficient. To open the drawing, use the prototype drawing option of the Create Drawing File dialog box that you learned earlier in the chapter.

Filtering Layers

Begin a new drawing named CHAP02A, using the SITE drawing from the accompanying CD-ROM as a prototype drawing. (The fonts are located on the R13\COM\FONTS directory by default.)

`Command`: *Choose Layers (Object Properties)*	Opens the Layer Control dialog box

Using the scroll bar, scroll through the Layer Name list box to familiarize yourself with the layer names and their states, colors, and linetypes. Note that some layers are frozen. You will make a filter to list only these layers.

Choose Set *in the* Filters *section*	Opens the Set Layer Filters dialog box (see fig. 2.22)

Notice that all of the visibility settings input boxes read "Both." This means that both of the two options will be shown in the list box. For example, by choosing Both for On/Off filter, AutoCAD will display layers that are both On and Off.

Click on Both *next to* Freeze/Thaw	Opens the Freeze/Thaw drop-down list
Select Frozen	Specifies that frozen layer names will be displayed
Choose OK	Closes the Set Layer Filters dialog box and checks the On box in the Filters section

As shown in figure 2.23, only the layers that are frozen now appear in the Layer Name list box.

Click on the On *check box in the* Filters *section to remove the* ✓	Removes the layer name filter and displays all layers in the Layer Name list
Click on the On *check box to restore the filter*	Reinstates the filter and displays the previously defined filtered list again

Stay in the Layer Control dialog box for the next exercise.

Figure 2.22

The Set Layer Filters dialog box.

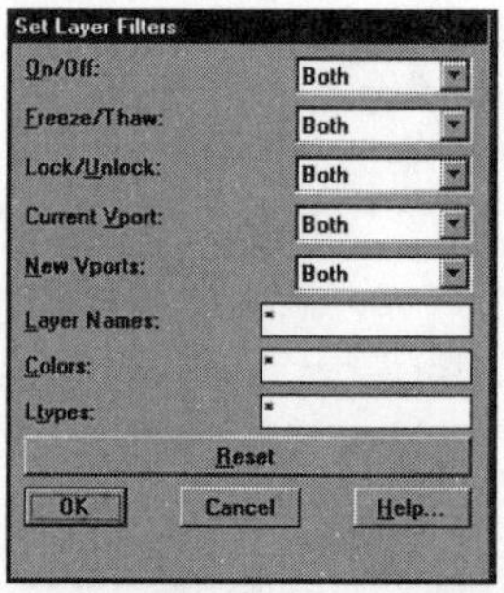

Figure 2.23

Filtering Layer names by state.

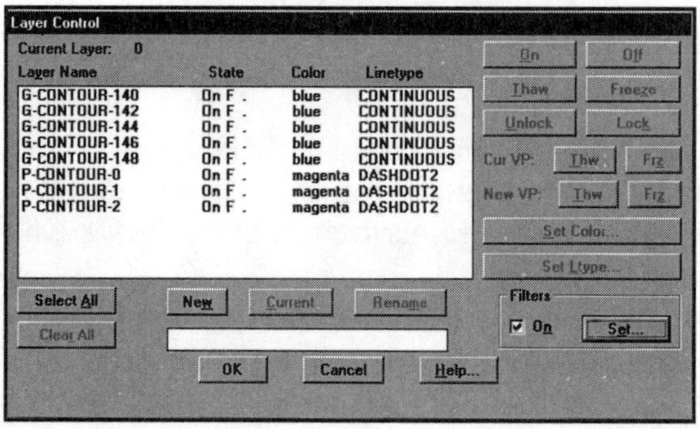

Filtering Layers by Layer Name

In addition to filtering layer names by state, you also can limit the number of layers displayed in the Layer Name list box by displaying only layers that have a common characteristic in their names. At this point, having a structured layer naming scheme makes it easy to take advantage of this feature.

In the following exercise, continuing from the preceding exercise, you further filter the layer list that you isolated by layer state by applying an additional filter based on layer name. In the filtered list you defined in the preceding exercise, all of the layer names begin with the letter *P* or *G*. In the following exercise you define a filter to thaw all the layers beginning with *G* and leave the *P* layers frozen.

Filtering Layers by Layer Name

Continue from the preceding exercise, with the Layer Control dialog box open and your filtered layer name list displayed (refer to figure 2.23).

Choose Set *in the* Filter *section*	Opens the Set Layer Filters dialog box

Double-click in the Layer Names *input box and type* **G***	Defines a filter that matches all layer names beginning with G followed by any other characters
Choose OK	Closes the Set Layer Filters dialog box and displays a new filter layer name list (see fig. 2.24).

Your filter is further refined by filtering only frozen layers beginning with the letter "G." In the following steps you select these layers and thaw them.

Choose Select All	Selects and highlights all displayed layers in the Layer Name list box
Choose Thaw	Thaws selected layers and displays the message `No layers match filter criteria.` in the lower left corner of the dialog box

Note that when you thawed all the filtered layer names, no names met the filter criteria any longer, so the Layer Name list box is empty.

Choose On *in the Filters section to remove the* ✓ *from the check box*	Deactivates the filter and displays all layers in the Layer Name list box

Notice that the F is removed from the State column of the G* layers.

Choose OK	Closes the Layer Control dialog box and regenerates the drawing with the filtered layers now thawed

Save the drawing.

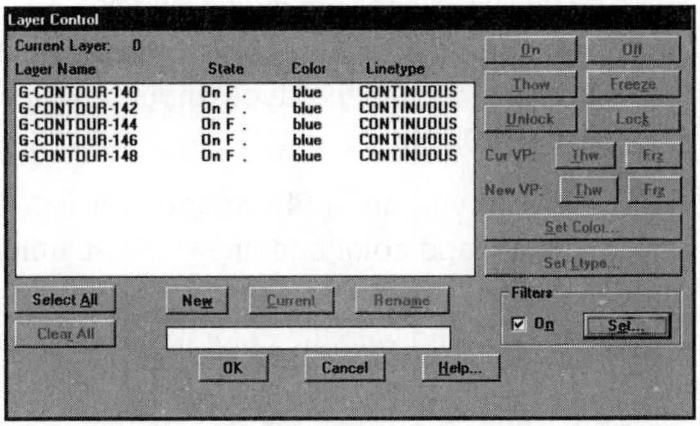

Figure 2.24

Filtering layers by name.

The thawed layers depict topographical contour lines that are now visible (see fig. 2.25).

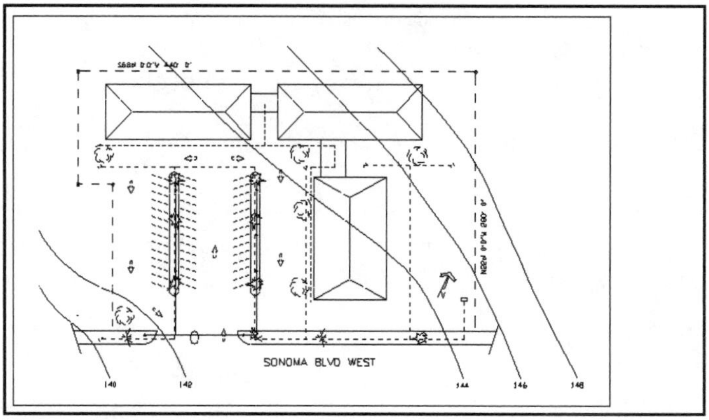

Figure 2.25

The CHAP02A drawing with filtered layers thawed.

WARNING

If the Filters On box is checked in the Layer Control dialog box, any filter you have previously defined is applied to the Layer Control box in the Object Properties toolbar as well. You should either deactivate your filter by clearing the Filter On check box or reset the filter to its default of no filter using the Reset button in the Set Layer Filters dialog box when the filter is no longer needed.

Filtering Layers by Color and Linetype

You can filter layer names based on their assigned color or linetype in a manner similar to that used in the preceding exercise. To display all layers assigned the color blue, for example, enter blue in the Colors input box of the Set Layer Filters dialog box. Entering hidden in the Ltypes input box filters all layers except those assigned the linetype HIDDEN.

Again, filter criteria are additive and you can filter for layer states, layer name characteristics, and color and linetype assignments simultaneously. For example, you can define a filter that would display only frozen layers beginning with the characters "1F-" and with the color red and the linetype DASHED assigned.

TIP

When defining filter criteria for layer names, linetypes, or colors, you can specify multiple criteria by separating them with a comma. For example, specifying a layer filter of G* and a color filter of RED,BLUE results in a list of layers whose names start with G and have either red or blue color assignments.

NOTE

Even though the Layer Control and the Set Layer Filters dialog boxes display layers names in uppercase letters, filter input data is not case-sensitive; you can enter filter criteria in either upper- or lowercase.

Filter Wild Cards

To increase the functionality of layer filters even further, you can use a number of wild-card characters in addition to the standard ? and *. These wild cards also can be used in many other places where AutoCAD accepts text string input, such as with many commands that list items. The following wild cards are available:

Table 2.1

Available Wild Cards

Wild Card	*Meaning*
@	Matches any alphanumeric character.
#	Matches any number.
*	Matches any character or characters including an empty character string. You can use the asterisk anywhere in the string.
. (period)	Matches any nonalphanumeric character.
?	Matches any single character.
~ (tilde)	Matches any character except the one that follows the tilde.
[ ]	Matches any single instance of any characters enclosed between the brackets.
[~]	Matches anything except the enclosed characters.
- (hyphen)	Matches a range of characters when used within brackets, such as [5-9] to match 5, 6, 7, 8, or 9.
‘	Matches the special character that follows; for example, ‘? matches a ? instead of using the ? as a wild card.
, (comma)	Separates wild cards, such as red,blue.

With such flexibility in filtering layer names and a structured layer naming scheme, you can filter practically any set of layers using a wide variety of criteria. If you are devising a standard layer naming format that you plan to utilize frequently, it might be worth the initial time and effort to consider groups of layers that you want to isolate using these wild cards and establish your layer names accordingly. Do not be overwhelmed by the possibilities these wild cards afford. You probably can utilize a few of them to accomplish your filtering needs.

Renaming Layers with the DDRENAME Command

There are other instances in AutoCAD where wild cards can be used to edit named objects. The DDRENAME command is used to rename objects in AutoCAD that are referred to by name, such as layers. The DDRENAME command also is used to rename blocks, dimension styles, linetypes, text styles, views, and user coordinate systems.

Rename Dialog Box Features

The DDRENAME command opens the Rename dialog box, which has the following features:

- **Named Objects list box.** Displays the types of objects you can rename.
- **Items list.** Displays the named objects, if any, that correspond to the category selected in the Named Objects list.
- **Old Name text box.** Specifies the object(s) to be renamed. Select a name from the Items list or enter a name in the Old Name text box. Wild cards can be used in the Old Name text box.
- **Rename To button.** Specifies the new name for the object. Type the new name in the Rename To input box, then choose the Rename To button. Wild cards can be used in the Rename To input box.

In the following exercise you rename some layers in the CHAP02A drawing using the DDRENAME command. The * wild card is used to rename all layers beginning with the character *G* that you filtered in the preceding exercise. Assume that you want to rename these layers so that they conform to a different layering convention by replacing the *G* with *TOPO*. Using the DDRENAME command and a wild card enables these five layers to be renamed in a single operation. You also rename another layer so that its name is more descriptive.

USING DDRENAME TO RENAME LAYERS

Continue from the preceding exercise, or begin a new drawing named CHAP02B, using the SITE drawing from the accompanying CD as a prototype.

`Command`: *Choose* Data, Rename	Issues the DDRENAME command, and opens the Rename dialog box (see fig. 2.26)
If not already highlighted, select Layer *in the* Named Objects *list box*	Lists named objects, if any, of the selected category in the Items list box
Use the Items *list box scroll bars to display all five* G-CONTOUR-14X *layers*	
Choose the Old Name *input box, type* **G***, *and press Enter*	Highlights and selects all layers beginning with G followed by any other characters (see fig. 2.27)

Notice in the Items list box that only layers meeting the criteria of the G* filter are highlighted for renaming.

Click in the Rename To *input box and type* **TOPO***	Defines the new layer name prefix
Choose the Rename To *button*	Renames the selected layers in accordance with the wild-card specification

The renamed layers are moved to their alphabetical position at the bottom of the Items list.

Scroll to the bottom of the Items list to verify the name change. In the next step you rename the layer PROP to the more descriptive name PROPLINE.

Find and choose the layer PROP *in the* Items *list*	Highlights the PROP layer name and copies it to the Old Name input box
Double-click in the Rename To *input box and type* **PROPLINE**	Specifies the new layer name
Choose the Rename To *button*	Renames the layer
Choose OK	Closes the dialog box and saves changes

Save the drawing.

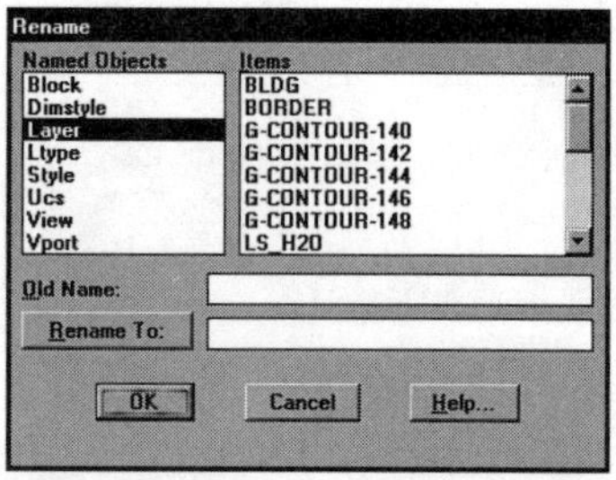

Figure 2.26

The Rename dialog box.

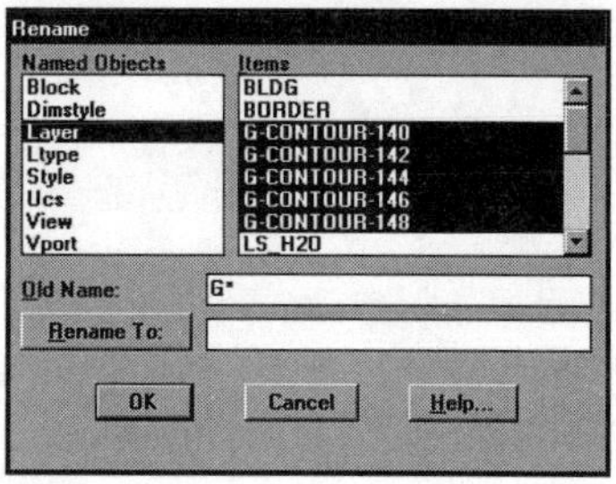

Figure 2.27

Applying filters with the DDRENAME command.

TIP

You can copy an old (current) name to the new name box and edit it. To copy the old name, double-click on the Old Name box, press Ctrl+Ins, then click or double-click in the Rename To edit box and press Shift+Ins. You then can edit the name.

The RENAME Command

The RENAME command is available at the `Command:` prompt only. Unlike the DDRENAME command and the Rename dialog box, the RENAME command does not display a listing of current objects, nor does it enable you to rename groups of objects with the use of wild cards. The RENAME command displays the following prompt:

```
Block/Dimstyle/LAyer/LType/Style/Ucs/VIew/VPort:
```

Enter the option for the category of the named object you want to rename (displayed uppercase letters for each option accepted). Enter the current name for the object, press Enter, then enter the new name.

Deleting Named Items with the PURGE Command

Earlier, when setting up the LAYERS drawing, you loaded all the linetype definitions available in the ACAD.LIN file at once using the Select Linetype dialog box. Although you can load specific linetypes with this dialog box, placing all the linetype definitions into your drawing is often the easiest and fastest way to make a wide variety of linetypes available. This can be especially true when you are first setting up a drawing and you don't know all the linetypes you might need. The disadvantage to this method is that storing unneeded linetype definitions in your drawing increases the size of the drawing, requiring more disk storage space. You might also find your drawing populated with unused layer definitions, especially if the drawing was created from a prototype drawing containing a large number of layers. In cases such as this, you can use the PURGE command to delete named items such as unused blocks, dimension and text styles, layers, linetypes, and shapes.

In the following exercise you delete an unused layer. Although several loaded linetypes will not be used in the drawing, the drawing is not yet completed. Therefore you should defer deleting linetypes until later.

Purging Unused Layers

Continue from the preceding exercise.

`Command:` *Choose* Data, Purge, Layers — Issues the PURGE command, Layers option

```
Command: _PURGE
Purge unused
Blocks/Dimstyles/LAyers/LTypes/
SHapes/STyles/APpids/
Mlinestyles/All: _la
```

Notice in the above prompt that the menu issues the la (LAyers) option. In the next step, all unused layers (only one in this case) are offered as candidates for purging from the drawing database.

`Purge layer LY_CITY? <N>` **Y** ↵ — Deletes the LY_CITY layer

Verify that the LY_CITY layer has been removed from the database by displaying Layer Control drop-down list.

You cannot purge an item that is referenced in any object or by any other item. If the LY_CITY layer contained a text object using the ROMANS text style, for example, neither the LY_CITY layer not the ROMANS text style could be purged. You can view items eligible for purging from several categories of named items by repeating the PURGE command and specifying different options each time. Alternatively, you can specify the All option to examine all categories in turn.

The PURGE command also is available from the command line. The prompts and mode of operation are the same as when issued from the pull-down menu; the pull-down menu adds the convenience of specifying an option as the command is issued.

NOTE

Many of the categories of named items subject to the PURGE command have not been covered in this book yet. The PURGE command acts on all categories in the manner shown here.

The PURGE command is useful as a tool in setting up your AutoCAD drawing because it can be used to delete layers and other named items that might be included in prototype drawings. Prototype drawings are discussed earlier in this chapter.

Developing a Layering Scheme

The subject of this chapter has been setting up a CAD drawing and it is no mistake that a large amount of attention has been given to AutoCAD's layering capabilities and the various ways in which layers can be manipulated and controlled, renamed, and even deleted.

You have seen the importance and advantages of having layer names that conform to an overall pattern or scheme. This extends to the use of layer colors, which often control plotted line weight, as well as the assignment of layer linetypes. The ability to perform operations on groups of layers, such as freezing a number of layers that you do not need at the moment or isolating all layers of a specific linetype, is a very powerful tool that you can use to speed up your editing tasks as well as help you organize your drawing into functional "layer units" that can be viewed, edited, or plotted separately. By intelligently using AutoCAD's layer building and modification tools, one drawing can be made to do the work of several. In an architectural floor plan, for example, the layers containing specific data, schedules, and annotations might be of little interest to the client, whereas this same information is essential to the contractor. From the same base drawing you can selectively plot or display on-screen the layers you choose.

You might already have developed a layer naming procedure that serves you well in the particular type of work you perform. Based on what you learn in this chapter, there might be ways to alter or customize your present procedure with AutoCAD's electronic layer capabilities in mind. On the other hand, if you are developing the ways and means to handle one of AutoCAD's most powerful drafting tools, knowing how layers can be used and manipulated will be helpful as you develop a system to meet your needs as well as the needs of others with whom you exchange drawings.

Assigning Object Properties

So far, you have been using layer definitions to control the color and linetype of objects in a drawing. When you draw an object, it takes on the color and the linetype of the current layer. If you change either the color or the linetype of a layer, all of the objects on that layer update to match the new layer definition. It is, however, possible to override the layer definition and explicitly assign a color and linetype to drawing objects.

The Bylayer Color and Linetype

When you draw an object, AutoCAD stores a description of the object in the drawing file. This description includes information such as what type of object it is (line, arc, circle, and so on), where it is located in the drawing (coordinates), as well as its layer, color, and linetype. By default, AutoCAD assigns each object a linetype and a color called *bylayer.*

The bylayer color is known as a *logical color.* This means that instead of explicitly giving the object a color, AutoCAD displays the object according to its assigned layer definition. The bylayer linetype works the same way, instead of explicitly assigning a linetype, AutoCAD looks to the object's layer definition to see how to display it. When the layer definition changes, AutoCAD redisplays the objects.

NOTE

Whereas AutoCAD uses colors 1–255 to explicitly define a color, the bylayer color is actually color number 256. One other color (color 0) exists, and is called byblock. (There is also a byblock linetype.) For more information on using the byblock color and linetype, see Chapter 11, "Block Structure, Editing, Organization, and Management."

Assigning Object Colors and Linetypes

AutoCAD uses the bylayer colors and linetypes by default, but it is possible to override the default color and linetype using the 'DDEMODES command.

The 'DDEMODES Command

The 'DDEMODES command displays the Object Creation Modes dialog box (see fig. 2.28), which enables you to set a number of drawing modes, including the default color and linetype.

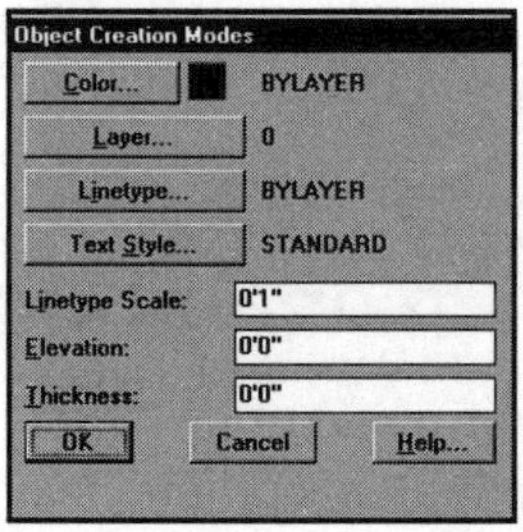

Figure 2.28

The Object Creation Modes dialog box.

The Object Creation Modes dialog box has the following options:

- **Color.** The Color button displays the Select Color dialog box (refer to figure 2.11), which enables you to set the current color. Any new objects are assigned the current color.
- **Layer.** The Layer button displays the Layer Control dialog box (refer to figure 2.3), which enables you to set the current layer as well as define and edit layer definitions.
- **Linetype.** The Linetype button displays the Select Linetype dialog box (refer to figure 2.8), which enables you to load linetypes into the current drawing as well as set the current linetype. Any new objects are assigned the current linetype.

- **Text Style.** The Text Style button displays the Select Text Style dialog box, which enables you to view and set the current text style. For more information on creating text and text styles, see Chapter 17, "Annotation with Text."
- **Linetype Scale.** This option enables you to set the current linetype scale. The current linetype scale is stored in the system variable LTSCALE.
- **Elevation.** This option enables you to set the default Z coordinate for drawing 3D objects.
- **Thickness.** This option enables you to set the default extrusion thickness for drawing 3D objects.

In the following exercise, you will assign a new default color and linetype and create some new lines.

CHANGING THE DEFAULT COLOR AND LINETYPE

Continue from the previous exercise. Using the Layer Control drop-down list, set layer PROPLINE current.

`Command:` *Choose Object Creation (Object Properties)*	Issues the DDEMODES command and opens the Object Creation Modes dialog box
Choose the Color *button, choose the Magenta color from the* Standard Colors *area, then choose* OK	Sets the default color to Magenta (6)
Choose the Linetype *button, choose* DIVIDE *from the* Loaded Linetypes *list, then choose* OK *twice*	Sets the default linetype to DIVIDE and closes the dialog box
`Command:` *Choose Line (Draw, Line)*	Issues the LINE command
`From point:` **200',400'** ↵	Places the first point of the line
`To point:` **400',400'** ↵	Places the second point of the line
`To point:` ↵	Ends the LINE command

Notice that the new line is magenta and has a linetype of DIVIDE, even though the current layer is red and has a linetype of DASHDOT. The line is still on layer PROPLINE but has an explicit color and linetype.

The 'DDLTYPE and 'LINETYPE Commands

There are other ways to set the current color and linetype as well. The 'DDLTYPE and 'LINETYPE commands both enable you to set the current linetype. An easier way is to use the Linetype Control drop-down list in the Object Properties toolbar. This drop-down list presents you with a list of currently loaded linetypes. Simply select the linetype you want to be current. The current linetype can also be changed with the CELTYPE system variable.

The 'DDCOLOR and 'COLOR Commands

The 'DDCOLOR command displays the Select Color dialog box, which enables you to set the current color. This dialog box is opened by issuing both the DDLMODES and DDEMODES commands.

The 'COLOR command also enables you to change the current color from the `Command:` prompt.

In addition to the 'DDCOLOR and 'COLOR commands, the current color can also be set with the CECOLOR system variable.

Although there might be instances in which you want to explicitly assign a color or linetype to an object, the BYLAYER color and linetype should be used routinely. In fact, assigning a color or linetype other than BYLAYER can lead to confusion. As we saw in the previous exercises, drawing objects are typically organized by their layer, and thus are identified by their layer properties. For example, if you define your PROPLINE layer as red with a DASHDOT linetype, when you see a red object with a DASHDOT linetype, it will most likely be a property line. If, however, you assign a color and linetype other than BYLAYER, you cannot visually tell what layer the object was drawn on. Using the BYLAYER color and linetype also gives you the ability to globally update the appearance of objects by simply changing the layer definition.

chapter

3

Drawing Accurately

Many of the tasks required to create a CAD drawing are, of course, the same tasks you encounter in traditional manual drafting. The solutions in CAD, however, are often quite different and almost always are achieved more quickly. One major contributor to this speed and power is the accuracy built into the tool. Instead of using your hands and eyes to carefully position a straight-edge or compass, and align a pencil with marks on paper, AutoCAD provides tools to effortlessly align drawing objects with incredible accuracy.

In this chapter, you begin by exploring the coordinate system that provides the foundation for this accuracy. You also look at the way AutoCAD handles typed coordinate input and how you can use either absolute or relative coordinates to specify the position of objects in your drawings. Then you learn about the drawing aids AutoCAD provides that enable you to use the pointing device to accurately locate points in your drawing. The topics covered in this chapter include the following:

- Understanding AutoCAD's coordinate system
- Using a reference grid to locate points
- Using snap to control points
- Using ortho mode to control angles
- Adjusting the UCS coordinate system in 2D
- Using object snap to snap points to existing objects
- Using direct distance input
- Using point filters to align points
- Using construction lines to place objects
- Using the tablet to digitize points

Exploring AutoCAD's Coordinate Systems

AutoCAD's default coordinate system is called the *World Coordinate System* (often referred to as the WCS throughout this book). One of the reasons many new users find AutoCAD easy to use right away is that the WCS is based on a standard Cartesian (or rectangular) coordinate system. This system is known to anyone who has experience with standard manual drafting, and is easy to understand and apply to CAD drafting methods. Although AutoCAD supports other coordinate systems, such as spherical coordinates for 3D work, most of the points you need to specify are based upon the standard Cartesian coordinate system.

The World Coordinate System

When you begin a new drawing, AutoCAD places you in the WCS. You can think of AutoCAD's opening graphics window as a sheet of drafting paper with the WCS extending across the entire sheet. The WCS's coordinates consist of left-right horizontal, or X axis, displacements and up-down vertical, or Y axis, displacements. (There also is a Z axis displacement above and below the plane of the paper that is used in 3D work.) Displacements are from an assumed zero point that is initially located at the bottom left corner of the sheet. Displacements to the right along the X axis and upward along the Y axis are considered positive.

Any point on the sheet can be described by specifying the distance, or displacement, from the zero point. By convention, points are described by specifying the X distance first followed by the Y distance with a comma separating the two. The zero point is called the origin and has a coordinate designation of 0,0. Figure 3.1 shows two points along with their coordinates. The point labeled 3,2, for example, is located three units to the right and two units up from 0,0. The X and Y axes in figure 3.1 are represented by two lines originating at 0,0. The tick marks along each axis represent one unit. Notice that as you pass through the 0,0 point, or origin, the numbers become negative. The point −2,−1 in figure 3.1 is located two units to the left and one unit below point 0,0.

Figure 3.1

Measuring in coordinates in AutoCAD.

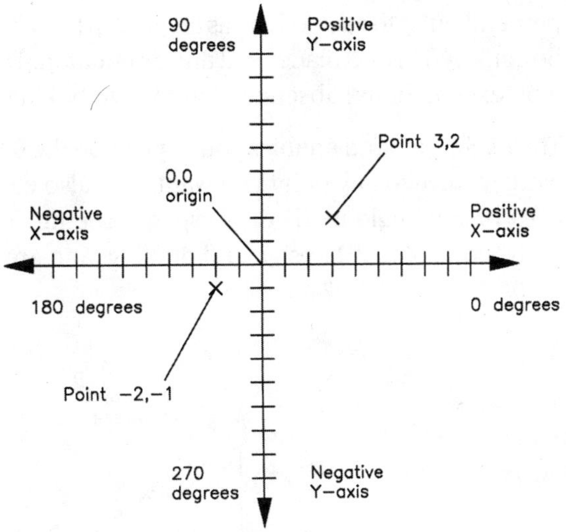

To assist you in visualizing this system of coordinates, AutoCAD superimposes the WCS icon near the lower left corner of the drawing window or at the 0,0 point. The WCS icon is shown in figure 3.2, along with two points labeled with their respective coordinates.

Figure 3.2

The World Coordinate System.

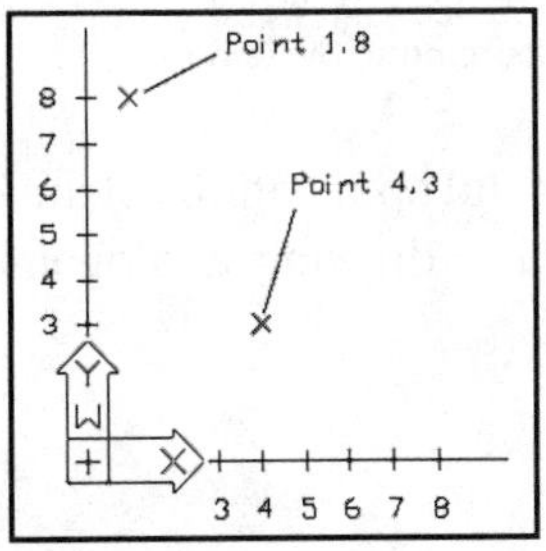

The X arrow points to the right, or positive, direction on the X axis and the Y arrow points upward in the positive Y axis direction. The *W* on the Y arrow indicates that you are in the default World Coordinate System.

Creating Your Own Coordinate System

Although the World Coordinate System is the default, you can create your own coordinate systems called *User Coordinate Systems* or *UCSs*. As its name suggests, a UCS is controllable by you, the user. In a UCS, the origin, as well as the directions of the X, Y, and Z axes, can be moved and rotated and even made to align with particular objects in the drawing. Even though the three axes of any UCS are mutually perpendicular to each other (as they are in the WCS), a great degree of flexibility can be achieved in UCS placement and orientation. The UCS icon is identical to the WCS icon except for the absence of the *W* symbol in the UCS icon.

The UCS command enables you to position the 0,0 origin anywhere so that you can work relative to any point you want. You also can rotate the X and Y (and even Z) axes to any angle in 2D or 3D space (see fig. 3.3). User Coordinate Systems are indispensable in 3D design and drafting, and are also of value in 2D applications.

Figure 3.3

The World Coordinate System and a User Coordinate System.

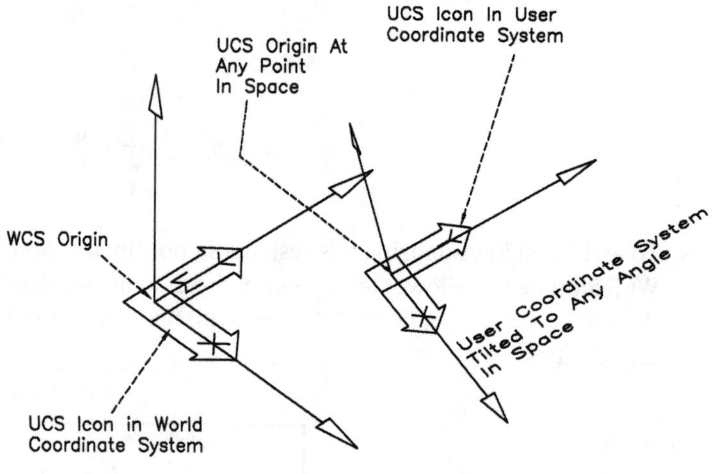

One of the most useful applications of the UCS in 2D drafting is aligning a UCS with a feature or object in a drawing, analogous to rotating the drafting machine used in manual drafting.

The following exercise demonstrates how to align the UCS with any two 2D points. To rotate the UCS in 2D, you rotate it about the Z axis. The exercise uses the CENter object snap. Object snaps are covered in detail later in this chapter.

ALIGNING THE UCS WITH AN OBJECT

Start a new drawing named CHAP03, using the CIRCLES drawing from the accompanying CD as a prototype. The OBJECT_LINES layer should be current. CHAP03 drawing should resemble figure 3.4. Note that the W in the UCS icon indicates the default World Coordinate System is current.

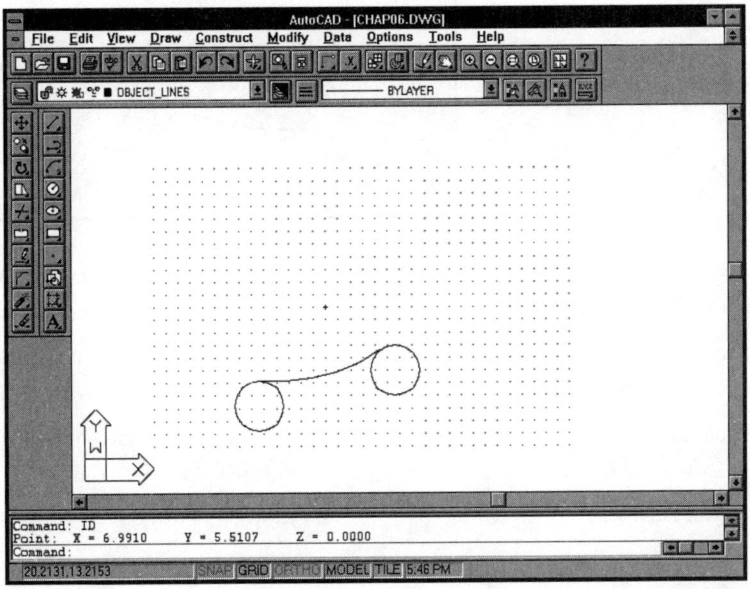

Figure 3.4

Adding a grid to the CHAP03 drawing.

`Command:` *Choose* View, Set UCS, Z Axis Rotate	Issues the UCS command and the Z option
`_ucs`	
`Origin/ZAxis/3point/OBject /View/X/Y/Z/Prev/Restore/ Save/Del/?/<World>: _Z`	
`Rotation angle about Z axis <0>:` **CEN** ↵	Specifies CENter object snap
`of` *Pick the left circle*	Snaps the angle's start point to the circle's center

`Second point:` **CEN** ↵	Specifies CENter object snap
`of` *Pick the right circle*	Snaps the angle to the circle's center and aligns the UCS icon with the circle's

Note that the W is not displayed in the UCS icon, because the UCS is no longer the World Coordinate System (see fig. 3.5).

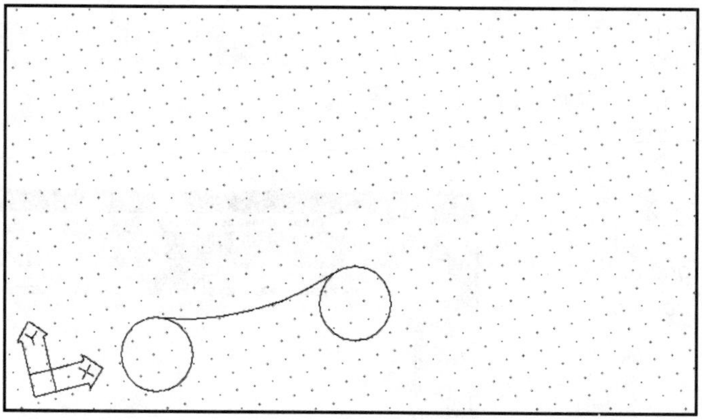

Figure 3.5

The User Coordinate System aligned to angle between circles.

In the next steps, you make a copy of the two circles and the arc four units above the current objects.

`Command:` *Pick each of the two circles and the arc*	Selects and highlights the three objects
`Command:` *Choose Copy Object (Modify, Copy)*	Issues the COPY command and prompts for objects
`_copy 3 found`	
`<Base point or displacement>/Multiple:` *Pick any point*	Sets a base point
`Second point of displacement:` *Pick point at* 4.0000<90 *on coordinate display*	Specifies a displacement of 4 units at 90 degrees in the current UCS and copies the objects

Save the drawing.

The objects are copied 4 units along the Y axis of the UCS, as shown in figure 3.6.

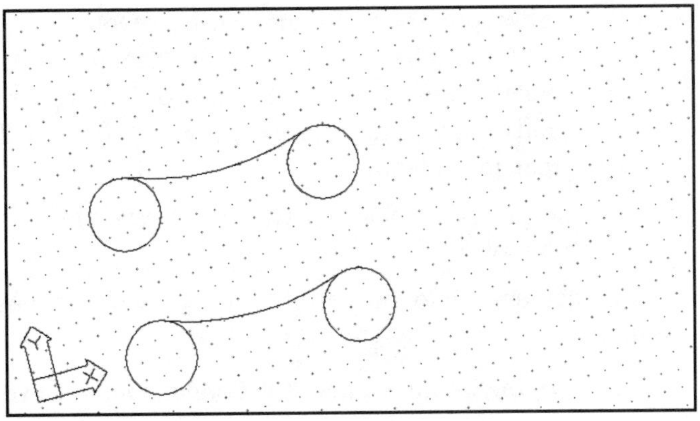

Figure 3.6

Objects in new User Coordinate System.

In a short editing operation, such as copying a few objects as you did in the previous exercise, you might not have to align newly defined UCSs with the graphics window. However, for more extended editing operations, you probably would want to do so for visual orientation or convenience.

In the preceding exercises, the UCS commands that you used were found as items on the Options and View pull-down menus. Figure 3.7 shows the UCS toolbar.

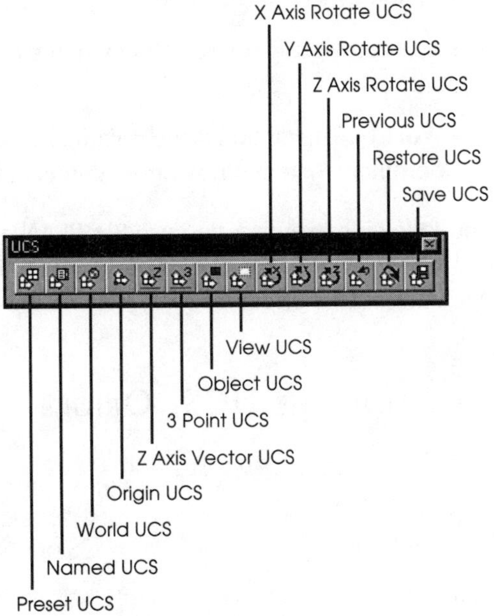

Figure 3.7

Tools of the UCS toolbar.

With the exception of the Follow item in the Options, UCS menu, these items actually issue the UCS or UCSICON commands with appropriate preset options. The UCSICON command is covered in the next section of this chapter. Both the UCS and UCSICON commands also are available at the `Command:` prompt. If you use the UCS command rather than the pull-down menu items, you see the following prompt:

```
Origin/ZAxis/3point/OBject/View/X/Y/Z/Prev/Restore/Save/Del/?/
➥World>:
```

You can use the following subset of options with most two-dimensional applications:

- **Origin.** Specifies a new X,Y,Z origin point relative to the current origin.
- **OBject.** Defines a new coordinate system based upon a selected object.
- **Z.** Rotates the X,Y axes around the Z axis.
- **Prev.** Steps back to the previous UCS. You can back up through as many as 10 previously used UCSs.
- **Restore.** Sets the UCS to a previously saved UCS.
- **Save.** Enables you to store the current UCS under a name, which you specify.
- **Del.** Removes a saved UCS.
- **?.** Lists previously saved UCSs by name to display point of origin and orientation.
- **<World>.** This option is the default. It sets the current UCS to the World Coordinate System. Press Enter to accept this option.

In the following exercise, you use the PLAN and UCSICON commands to change your UCS view to a plan view and verify the origin of the UCS by moving the UCS icon to the current UCS origin.

CONTROLLING THE UCS, ORIGIN, ICON, AND PLAN VIEW

Continue from the preceding exercise.

`Command:` *Choose* View, 3D Viewpoint Presets, Plan View, Current	Issues the PLAN command with the Current UCS option

`Command: _plan`
`<Current UCS>/Ucs/World:`
`Regenerating drawing.`
	Changes to plan view; regenerates the drawing

Use the UCSICON command to set the UCS icon at the origin of the current UCS.

`Command:` *Choose* Options, UCS, Icon Origin	Issues UCSICON command with ORigin option
`_UCSicon`	Sets the UCS icon at the current origin
`ON/OFF/All/Noorigin/ORigin<on>: _OR`	

You see no effect; the UCS is rotated, but still at the WCS 0,0 origin. If there isn't room for the entire UCS icon at the origin, AutoCAD ignores the UCSICON origin setting. Try relocating the UCS to the lower left circle's center to see the UCS icon indicate the origin.

`Command:` *Choose* View, Set UCS, Origin	Issues UCS command with Origin option
`_ucs`	
`Origin/ZAxis/3point/OBject/View/X/Y/Z/`	
`Prev/Restore/Save/Del/?/<World>: _o`	
`Origin point <0,0,0>:` **CEN**↵	
`of` *Pick the left circle*	Sets the 0,0 origin and UCS Icon at the circle's center (see fig. 3.8)
`Command:` *Choose* View, 3D Viewpoint Presets, Plan View, World	Returns to plan view in the WCS orientation
`Command:` *Choose* View, Set UCS, World	Returns UCS to WCS origin and alignment

Save the drawing.

Figure 3.8

The UCS icon placed at the current UCS origin.

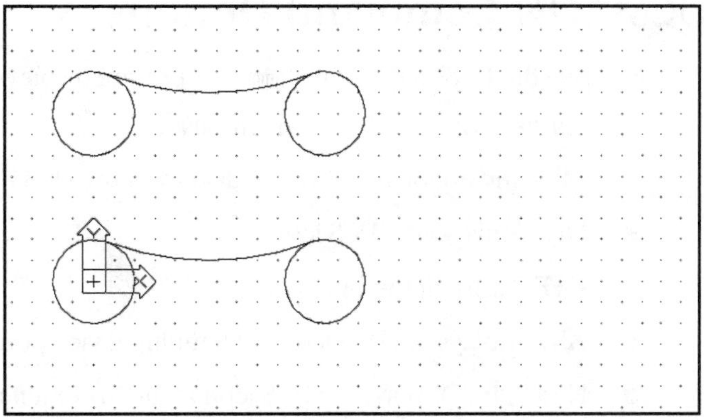

Notice that the UCS icon no longer fits at the origin.

WARNING

> The PLAN command provides a quick way to orient the drawing view to a UCS. Be careful; if you set the view "plan" to something other than the WCS, you may not later realize you are not working in the default World Coordinate System.

You might want to offset the origin of the UCS in 2D drawings to facilitate some aspect of editing or to carry out certain dimensioning tasks. Figure 3.9, for example, shows a part with holes dimensioned from the lower left corner of the bar. Adding these features is quick and accurate if you first define a UCS that has its origin at this corner.

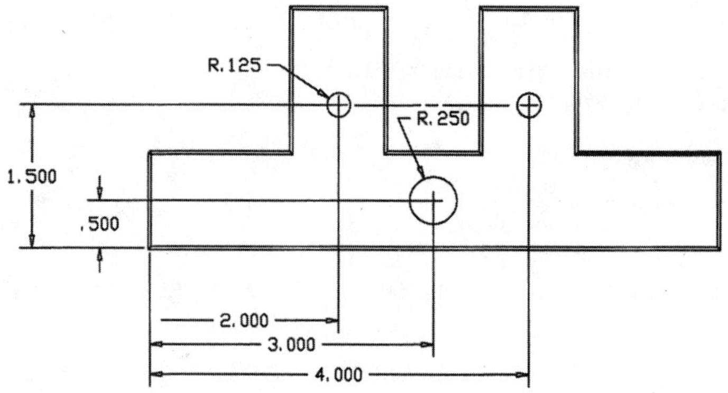

Figure 3.9

The guide bar with holes added.

UCSICON Command Options

Entering the UCSICON at the `Command:` prompt displays the following prompt:

```
ON/OFF/All/Noorigin/ORigin <ON>:
```

The following options control the display of the UCS icon.

- **ON.** Turns on the UCS icon.
- **OFF.** Turns off the UCS icon.
- **All.** Displays the UCS icon in all multiple viewports.
- **Noorigin.** Displays the UCS icon at the lower left corner of the viewports.
- **ORigin.** Displays the UCS icon at the 0,0 origin of the current UCS, unless the origin is out of the drawing area or too close to the edge for the icon to fit. The icon then appears at the lower left corner.

Figure 3.10 shows the UCS icon. The X arrow points along the positive X axis, and the Y arrow points along the positive Y axis. The *W* on the Y arrow indicates that the current UCS is the default World Coordinate System (WCS). The + on the UCS icon indicates that the icon is placed at the origin of the current UCS.

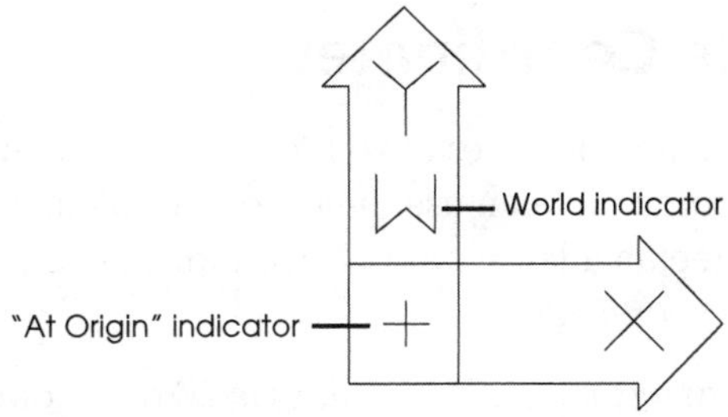

Figure 3.10

The UCS icon at the WCS origin.

The following is a list of the Options, UCS pull-down menu options (see fig. 3.11):

- **Icon.** Uses the UCSICON command to turn the UCS Icon on or off. A check mark appears before the option if the UCS Icon is on.
- **Icon Origin.** Uses the UCSICON command to turn on or off the Origin option. A check mark appears before the option if the Origin option is on.
- **Follow.** When on, this option automatically changes the view to the plan view of the current UCS; it sets the UCSFOLLOW system variable to 1. If UCSFOLLOW is on, a check mark precedes the option.

Figure 3.11

The Options, UCS pull-down menu options.

The power and flexibility that the User Coordinate System gives you is essential when you work in 3D drawings. The preceding few exercises in this chapter, however, show that being able to manipulate the orientation and origin of UCSs that you define enables you to work much more efficiently in many 2D drawings as well.

Entering Points

Many of the drawings you create in AutoCAD—from the very simple to the very complex—are composed of a relatively few basic AutoCAD objects: lines, arcs and circles, and text elements. All these require you to enter points that specify their location, size, and direction. The center of a circle, the beginning of a line, and the end of an arc all are defined by points. Coordinate points are as basic to CAD as words are to word processing. There are several ways to enter coordinates in AutoCAD.

Using Absolute Coordinates

If you know the exact coordinates of your points, or their angle and distance from the drawing's 0,0 point, you can use the keyboard to enter coordinates in several formats including rectangular, spherical, cylindrical, and polar. These formats are known as *absolute coordinates.*

Absolute Cartesian or *rectangular coordinates* in 2D treat coordinate entries as X and Y displacements from the 0,0 origin of the current UCS. The absolute Cartesian coordinates 6,5, for example, define a point that is 6 units in the positive X direction and 5 units in the positive Y direction. This point is shown in figure 3.12. The UCS icon is also shown in figure 3.12. By default, the initial 0,0 point of your drawing is located at the lower left of the graphics window.

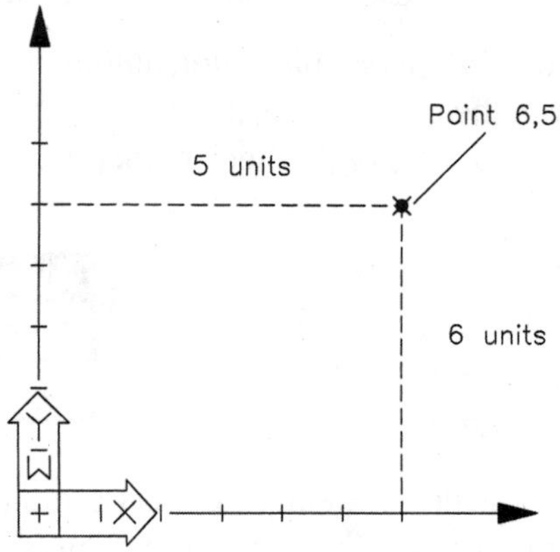

Figure 3.12

Locating a point with absolute Cartesian coordinates.

If your displacement is positive, you do not need to use a plus (+) sign; it is assumed. Negative displacements are to the left of and down from point 0,0. You precede a negative displacement coordinate with a minus (–) sign; for example, –3.5,2.5 specifies a point 3.5 units below and 2.5 units to the right of the 0,0 point.

Absolute Polar coordinates also treat 2D coordinate entry as a displacement from 0,0, but you specify the displacement as distance and angle. The distance and angle values are separated by a left-angle bracket (<). Positive angles are measured clockwise relative to an assumed 0 degrees that lies, by default, along the positive X axis. In this system, then, 90 degrees lies in the direction of the positive Y direction, 180 degrees in the direction of the negative X axis, and 270 degrees in the negative Y direction, all radiating from the drawing's 0,0 point. The default angle directions are shown in figure 3.13.

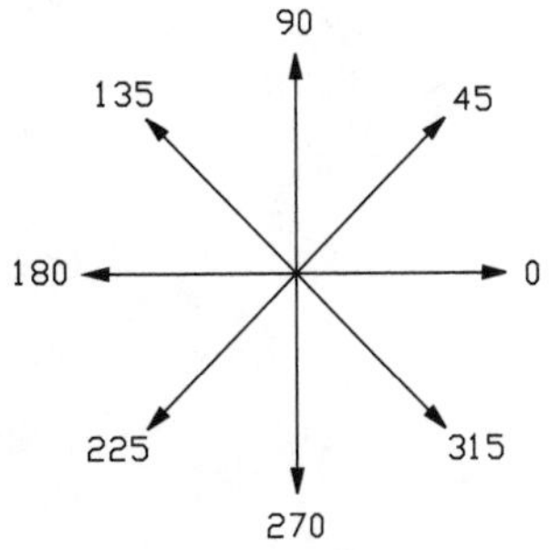

Figure 3.13

Default angle directions.

In figure 3.14, the 2D point is defined using a distance of *D* and an angle of *a*. At the keyboard, this is entered as *D<a*. A specific polar coordinate, 2<60 for example, defines a point 2 units from 0,0 at an angle of 60 degrees from the X axis.

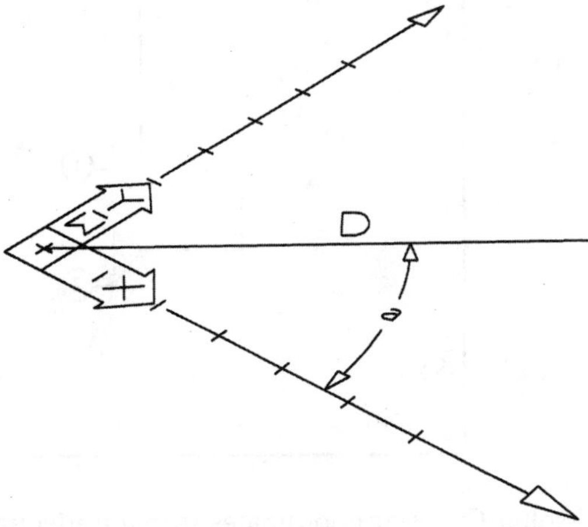

Figure 3.14

Locating a point using absolute polar coordinates.

In the following exercise, you use both absolute Cartesian and absolute polar coordinates to draw a fastener outline.

SPECIFYING POINTS WITH ABSOLUTE COORDINATES

Continue working in CHAP03 drawing.

`Command:` *Choose Line (Draw, Line)*	Issues the LINE command
`Command: _line From point:` **4.5,4**↵	Specifies an absolute Cartesian point
`To point:` **4.5,5**↵	Specifies an absolute Cartesian point
`To point:` **6.5,5**↵	Specifies an absolute Cartesian point
`To point:` **9<38.34**↵	Specifies an absolute polar point
`To point:` **7.8<25.36**↵	Specifies an absolute polar point
`To point:` **6.5,4**↵	Specifies an absolute Cartesian point
`To point:` **C**↵	Specifies the Close option; completes the outline

Your drawing should now look like figure 3.15.

In the preceding exercise the limitations of absolute coordinates are apparent.

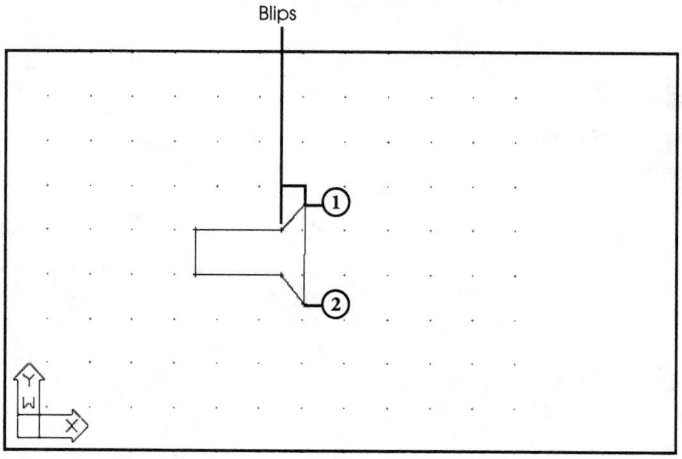

Figure 3.15

Fastener outline drawn with absolute coordinates.

While absolute Cartesian coordinates are often adequate to specify the starting point of a line, subsequent points measured from the drawing's 0,0 point are cumbersome and invite mistakes when constructing an object consisting of "connected" line segments. When the lines of the object (such as the fastener in the preceding exercise) are not orthogonal, both absolute Cartesian and absolute polar coordinates are inadequate if any degree of accuracy is desired.

In the following exercise you measure the endpoints of the vertical line of the fastener in the preceding exercise.

Measuring a Line's Endpoints

Continue from the preceding exercise. In the first step refer to the map of tools and toolbars in the back of the book if necessary.

`Command:` *Choose Locate Point (Object Properties, Inquiry)*	Issues the ID command
`Command: id`	
`Point:` **ENDP**↵	Specifies the ENDPoint object snap
`of` Pick the upper end of the line at ① (refer to figure 3.15)	

The ID command displays the coordinates of the upper endpoint of the line.

```
X = 7.0591  Y = 5.5829  Z = 0.0000
```

`Command:` ↵	Reissues the ID command
`ID Point:` **ENDP**↵	Specifies the ENDPoint object snap
`of` *Pick the lower end of the line at* ②	

The ID command displays the coordinates of the lower endpoint of the line.

```
X = 7.0483      Y = 3.3408      Z = 0.0000
```

In the preceding exercise, notice that the X coordinates for the opposite ends of the line are not the same. Although in this instance the difference is small (0.0108 units), this is unacceptable for most CAD work, in which this small amount of inaccuracy can become significant—especially if it is magnified by a cumulative error effect. This inherent inaccuracy is a major disadvantage of absolute polar coordinate entry.

Viewing the Coordinate Display

The coordinate display area on the application window's status bar is a useful aid when entering coordinates from the keyboard or picking points with the pointing device. The display has three modes of operation and, depending on the mode selected and the command in progress, is capable of showing either absolute or relative coordinates. You can cycle through the three modes at any time by pressing F6, by pressing Ctrl+D, or by double-clicking in the coordinate display area itself.

The three modes of coordinate display are as follows:

- **Mode 0.** Mode 0 displays the absolute coordinates of the last picked point. The display is updated only when a new point is picked. Entering a point from the keyboard does not affect this mode of display. The coordinate display is considered off in this mode.
- **Mode 1.** Mode 1 displays the absolute coordinates of the cursor. The display is continuously updated. The coordinate display is considered on in this mode. This is the default mode.
- **Mode 2.** When Mode 2 is selected, the distance and angle relative to the last point are displayed whenever a prompt requesting a distance or angle is active. This mode displays a relative polar coordinate.

When mode 0 is selected, the coordinate display appears grayed-out, indicating that the coordinate display is off. The coordinates of the last picked point are still readable, however. At an "empty" `Command:` prompt or at a prompt that does not accept a distance or angle as input, you can only switch between mode 0 and mode 1. At a prompt that does accept a distance or angle as input, you can switch among all three modes. The following exercise demonstrates the three coordinate display modes. Pay particular attention to the coordinate display on the status bar during this exercise.

SWITCHING COORDINATE DISPLAY MODES

Continue from the preceding exercise. First, ensure that the display mode is set to mode 0 by pressing F6 until the coordinate display appears grayed-out.

`Command:` *Move the cursor within the drawing window*

Note that the coordinate display remains static, displaying the last point picked.

`Command:` *Double-click in the coordinate display area* — Changes display to non-grayed-out state

Note that when you move the cursor now the coordinate display is continuously updated as it tracks the cursor movement. Coordinate display is now in mode 2.

`Command:` *Choose Line (Draw, Line)* — Issues the LINE command

Move the cursor within the drawing window

Note that the display continuously updates. The `From point:` prompt does not accept a distance-angle input; the display remains in absolute coordinate format.

`From point:` **8,4** ↵ — Specifies the start point for the line; line rubber-bands from start point

Notice that once a point has been specified, the coordinate display changes to relative polar (distance-angle) format as you move the cursor.

`To point:` **8,5** ↵ — Specifies an absolute Cartesian point; line rubber-bands from newest point

Press Ctrl+D — Changes coordinate display to mode 1

`To point:<Coords on>` — Indicates that you changed modes

Note that in mode 1 the display is once again in absolute Cartesian format.

Press F6 — Changes coordinate display to mode 0

`To point: <Coords off>`

Note that in mode 0 the display is grayed-out and static as you move the cursor.

`To point:` **10,5** ↵ — Specifies endpoint for line in absolute Cartesian format

In the following step you use the U option of the LINE command.

`To point:` **U** ↵ — Undoes the last line segment; prompts for new point

`To point:` *Double-click in the coordinate display area* — Changes coordinate display to mode 2

`To point: <Coords on>`

Note that the display is once again in relative polar format.

`Command:` **U** ↵ — Undoes the previous line segment; prompts for a new point

`Command:` *Press Esc* — Cancels the LINE command

Note that the coordinate display reverts to absolute Cartesian mode because no prompt accepting distance-angle input is active.

In the preceding exercise you utilized all three methods of switching among the three coordinate display modes. Although absolute coordinates are limited in their usefulness in many situations, they frequently are used to locate and specify the first point of an object or to specify a set of known points in surveying applications, for example.

Using Relative Coordinates

The utility of absolute coordinates is limited, and if all points had to be entered in absolute coordinates, drawing in AutoCAD would be awkward indeed. You more often know the X,Y displacement or the distance and angle of points relative to previous points you have specified. Coordinates entered in this manner are called *relative coordinates*. In 2D work, both Cartesian and polar coordinates can be specified as relative coordinates. In relative coordinates, the last point entered is treated as the drawing's new 0,0 point. Otherwise, the positive direction of the X and Y axes and the method of measuring angles is the same as in describing absolute coordinates.

To distinguish between absolute and relative point entry, precede *all* relative coordinates with an at symbol (@). If during the LINE command, for example, you want to add a line segment that is 2 units in the X direction and 1 unit in the Y direction from the last point you entered, type @2,1 at the `To point:` prompt. A relative polar coordinate would be entered as @2<33, defining a point 2 units at an angle of 33 degrees from your last specified point.

In the following exercise, both relative Cartesian and relative polar coordinates are used to draw a second fastener outline.

DRAWING WITH RELATIVE COORDINATES

Continue in CHAP03 drawing.

`Command:` *Choose Line (Draw, Line)*	Issues the line command
`_line From point:` **8,4** ↵	Specifies the first point with an absolute Cartesian coordinate
`To point:` **@0,1** ↵	Specifies a relative Cartesian coordinate
`To point:` **@2<0** ↵	Specifies a relative polar coordinate

Recall that positive angles are measured counterclockwise from zero degrees.

`To point:` **@8<45** ↵	Specifies a relative polar coordinate
`To point:` **@2.1314<270** ↵	Specifies a relative polar coordinate
`To point:` **@.8<135** ↵	Specifies a relative polar coordinate

Recall that X axis directions "to the left" are negative.

`To point:` **@-2,0** ↵	Specifies a relative Cartesian coordinate
`To point:` *Press Esc*	Ends the LINE command

Your CHAP03 drawing should now resemble fig. 3.16.

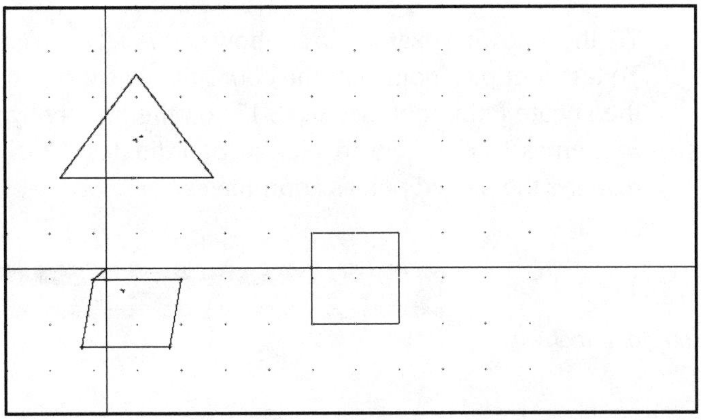

Figure 3.16

Second fastener drawn with relative coordinates.

In some instances, it is easier to specify points using relative polar coordinates; in others, relative Cartesian coordinates seem more appropriate. The angles involved or the distance information available often determines which system to use. Keep in mind that coordinate input is useful when you already have the distance or angle information of drawing elements.

Understanding Drawing Accuracy

The first step of creating an accurate drawing is to locate your drawing points. One way to do this is to enter coordinates from the keyboard. You can be as precise as you need to be with this method. However, although you might know some of the coordinate values to start a drawing, you rarely know all of them as you begin a drawing. Besides, entering coordinates at the keyboard is grueling, tedious work and leaves you vulnerable to typing errors.

By contrast, using your pointing device to pick locations in your drawing is comparatively easy, and doesn't require that you know any of the actual coordinates. But how accurate is it?

How Accurate Are Pick Points?

Picking a point accurately with your cursor is difficult. As you move the cursor, the digital readout of your coordinates should display the crosshair cursor's current X,Y position. If the coordinates are not active, you can turn on your coordinate display by double-clicking on the coordinate display in the status bar, pressing Ctrl+D, or pressing F6.

Try the following exercise to see how accurately you can pick your drawing points. To test your pick point, use the coordinate display and the ID command issued by the Locate Point tool (see fig. 3.17) on the Inquiry flyout, which is on the Object Properties toolbar. Try to pick at coordinates 3.25,5. The ID command simply displays the picked point's coordinates.

Figure 3.17

The Locate Point tool.

USING ID COMMAND TO TEST PICK POINTS

Continue from the preceding exercise and make sure that your coordinate display is turned on by pressing Ctrl+D, if necessary.

`Command:` *Choose Locate Point (Object Properties, Inquiry)*	Issues the ID command
`Command: '_id Point:` Try to pick the point 3.2500,5.0000, using the coordinate display to guide the crosshairs	
`X = 3.2456   Y = 4.9710   Z = 0.0000`	Your point might differ, but you can't pick it exactly

The ID command shows the X,Y,Z position of your pick point. Try the same thing with a few more points. As you can see, it is nearly impossible to accurately pick the point you want. AutoCAD's precision is actually working against you here.

AutoCAD stores numbers to at least 14 significant digits. If you pick your drawing points without some form of control, however, AutoCAD must translate the cursor's pixel position into the current drawing units. That is, AutoCAD must approximate the coordinates you actually want. If you try to pick the point 2.375,4.625, for example, you might get such numbers as 2.3754132183649,4.6248359103856. Even if you use the grid or other objects to visually align the crosshairs, you seldom locate the point you want with complete accuracy.

WARNING

If you set the coordinate display to show only three decimal places, these numbers appear to be rounded accurately, but AutoCAD stores them internally with their true precision—with several more decimal places of "inaccuracy."

AutoCAD provides several methods for controlling the movement of your cursor so that you can accurately select pick points. One method involves using the grid and snap functions; another involves using object snap. Still other methods involve using ortho mode, XYZ point filters, *direct distance entry*, and two types of construction lines. All of these tools, used separately or in combination, enable you to take advantage of AutoCAD's capability to store data in a highly accurate drawing database.

Using Drawing Aids

As a first step to achieve some degree of drawing accuracy, you can use AutoCAD's *grid* or snap to control your pick points. The grid serves as a visible template that shows the location of a set of points. It is a visual aid. Although it does help you see the location of points, it does not round the input points to accurate locations. *Snap,* on the other hand, is an invisible grid template that does control the points that you use your cursor to select. If you set snap to 0.5, you can select only points that fall exactly on 0.5-unit increments.

Grid and snap work well together and you can easily control many pick points by coordinating AutoCAD's grid and snap capabilities. If you set them equally, you can select only the visual grid points. If you set the snap increments to half the grid increments, you can select only the grid points or points that lie halfway between the grid points. Snap enables you to control the accuracy of your point selection; grid enables you to keep track visually of the points to which you snap.

A special form of snap, called *object snap,* enables you to accurately locate geometric points on objects or in relation to objects. Object snaps are among the most powerful tools available in AutoCAD for accurately defining relationships in your drawing. Object snaps are discussed in detail in the section "Snapping to Objects with Object Snaps" later in this chapter.

The simplest way to control drawing accuracy is with the GRID, SNAP, and ORTHO commands and by using the Drawing Aids dialog box (see fig. 3.18). You access this dialog box by choosing the Drawing Aids item in the Options pull-down menu. You also can turn grid, snap, and ortho on and off by double-clicking the SNAP, GRID, and ORTHO buttons on the status bar. When the text in the box is highlighted, the corresponding mode is on.

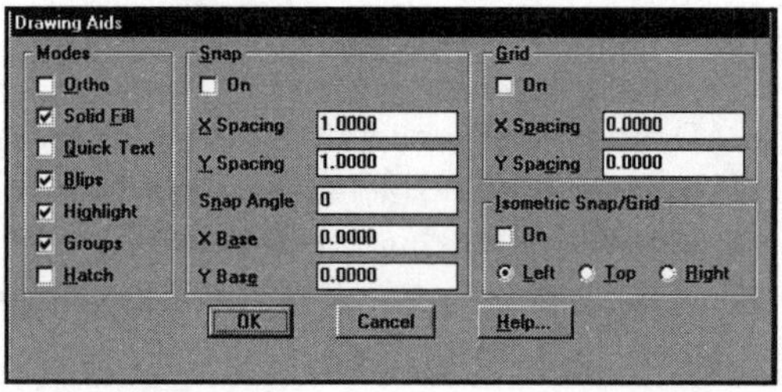

Figure 3.18

The Drawing Aids dialog box.

The Drawing Aids dialog box provides the following settings and controls:

- **Ortho.** Turns ortho mode on or off (same as using the F8 key).
- **Solid Fill.** Notifies AutoCAD whether to show solids and thickened polylines or to show only their edges. This box is checked by default.
- **Quick Text.** Notifies AutoCAD to display text normally or with a boundary box that shows the limits of the text. If you do not activate the box, AutoCAD displays text normally.

TIP

Text, solids, and wide polylines add to drawing regeneration time on very large drawings. If your editing does not currently involve these items, turn off Solid Fill and turn on Quick Text to dramatically decrease regeneration time.

- **Blips.** Notifies AutoCAD to place blips at every point you have picked in the drawing editor.
- **Highlight.** Notifies AutoCAD to display selected objects with a temporary dashed linetype. This is on by default.
- **Groups.** Enables you to select objects by groups. For example, if you select an object within a group, you select the entire group. This is on by default.
- **Snap.** You use options in the Snap area to turn snap mode on or off (same as pressing F9) and to change the snap X and Y spacing (the default is 1), the snap angle (default 0), and the snap base (default 0,0).
- **Grid.** You use the options in the Grid area to turn the drawing grid on or off (same as pressing F7) and change the grid X and Y spacing (the default is 0).
- **Isometric Snap/Grid.** You use the options in the Isometric Snap/Grid area to turn isometric drawing mode on or off and determine which isometric plane is currently in use (same as cycling F5). The default value is off.

NOTE

You also can use keyboard function keys to turn grid, ortho, and snap on and off. Use the F7 key for grid, F8 for ortho, and F9 for snap. In addition, the key combinations of Ctrl+B and Ctrl+G turn snap and grid on and off, respectively. No Ctrl+key combination turns ortho mode on and off in the Windows platform.

Using the Grid Display

To get accurate points, you first set up a grid template that helps you see points on the screen. A grid serves the same purpose as the lines or dots on a sheet of graph paper—it provides a frame of reference as you draw. AutoCAD's grid consists of an array of points that appear on-screen but are not part of the drawing file.

You set up a grid by using the GRID command or the Drawing Aids dialog box. In the next exercise, you set up a one-half-inch grid. When you try to pick a grid point, you see that grid points do not actually control input points.

USING GRID TO SET UP A GRID

Continue from the previous exercise.

`Command:` *Choose* Options, Drawing Aids	Displays the Drawing Aids dialog box (see fig. 3.18)
In the Grid area, put a check in the On *box*	Turns on the grid
Double-click in the X Spacing edit box, enter **0.5**, *then choose* OK	Sets X to 0.5 units and, when you press Enter, defaults Y to equal X, then displays the 0.5 grid (see fig. 3.19) and turns on the GRID button on the status bar

Now use the ID command as before to try to pick a point that lies exactly on one of the grid marks.

`Command:` **ID** ↵

`Point:` *Try to pick the point* 7.00,5.50	Displays the point you picked
`X = 7.0170    Y = 5.5547    Z = 0.0000`	Your point might differ, but you still can't pick it exactly

Save the drawing.

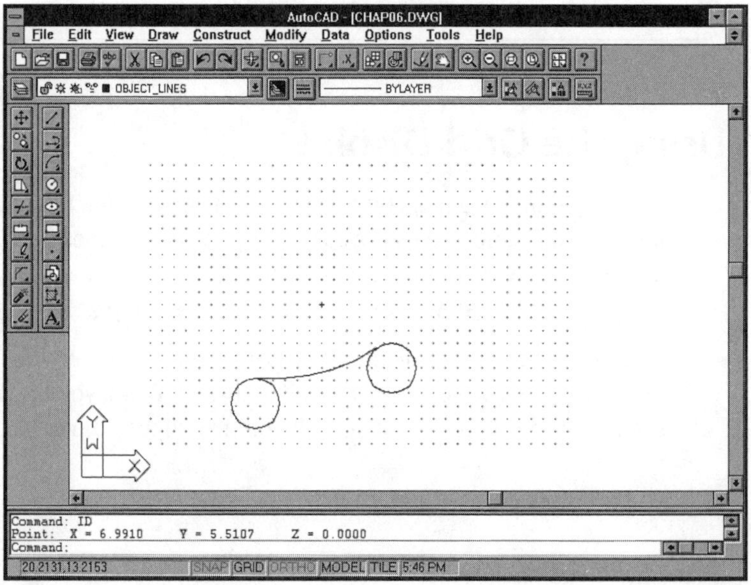

Figure 3.19

Adding a grid to CHAP03 drawing.

This exercise shows that points you pick are not necessarily precisely located on the grid. Using the grid, however, can give you a "target" and a better sense of the distances represented by the graphics window display. In addition, the grid gives you a visual indication of the drawing's limits because the extent of the grid is defined by the current limits when the UCS is set to the default.

Tip

> When you set the grid spacing, avoid setting a grid that is too dense (one whose points are too close together). A too-dense grid obscures the drawing and causes slow screen redrawing.

You have several options when you set up a grid, and you are not limited to a square grid. Sometimes a grid that has an aspect ratio other than 1:1 might be useful. Figure 3.20, for example, shows a grid aspects ratio of 2X:1Y (the actual settings for the grid shown are X = 1.0, Y = 0.5).

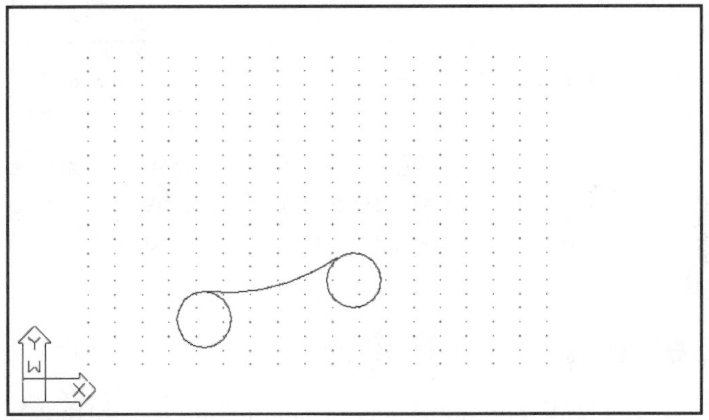

Figure 3.20

A grid that has a 2X:1Y aspect ratio.

You can set the grid by using the Drawing Aids dialog box, as you did in the previous exercise, or with the GRID command. The GRID command prompt appears with the following options:

```
Grid spacing(X) or ON/OFF/Snap/Aspect <0.0000>:
```

Grid Command Options

The GRID command options perform the following functions:

- **Grid spacing(X).** Sets the X,Y grid increment and activates it. If you enter **0**, AutoCAD makes the grid equal to the snap spacing, automatically adjusting when snap changes. If you enter a number followed by an X, AutoCAD sets the grid to the current snap increment multiplied by the specified number.
- **ON.** Makes the grid visible.
- **OFF.** Makes the grid invisible.
- **Snap.** Sets the grid increment so that it is equal to the current snap increment (when you enter **0** or **1X** for the grid spacing, for example), except that it does not automatically change the grid as snap changes.
- **Aspect.** Enables you to set different increments for grid's horizontal and vertical dots.

TIP

You also can press Ctrl+G or F7 to turn the grid on and off.

Although the grid helps indicate how much you are zoomed into or out of the drawing and, along with the coordinate display, it helps you find points, it provides no direct capability to pick points accurately. For that you need snap.

Setting Snap Points

The SNAP command sets the smallest increment that AutoCAD can recognize when you move the cursor. If you turn snap on and set a spacing value, your cursor moves with a incremental motion; it jumps from snap point to snap point instead of tracking smoothly. When you set snap spacing values, all drawing pick points are forced to multiples of your snap values.

A good practice is to set your snap to some fraction of your grid spacing. AutoCAD normally aligns snap points with the grid. As you draw, you can easily eyeball points that are one-quarter to one-fifth of the distance between grid points. In the following exercise, you set the snap increment to 0.25 units, or one-half of your grid spacing.

USING SNAP TO SET SNAP POINTS

Continue from the preceding exercise with the grid on.

`Command:` *Choose* Options, Drawing Aids	Displays the Drawing Aids dialog box
In the Snap area, *choose the* On *check box*	Turns on snap
Double-click in the X Spacing *box, enter* **.25**, *and choose* OK	Sets the X spacing and defaults the Y spacing to equal the X spacing
Try to move the cursor around	The crosshairs now jump to the snap increments

Save the drawing.

The SNAP box on the status bar is now highlighted, indicating that snap mode is on, and the coordinates display accurately in 0.25-unit increments. Think of snap as an invisible grid that constrains the points you can pick with the pointing device. Snap adds some real control to picking points. Combined with the grid and coordinate display, snap permits you to achieve a degree of accuracy comparable to that offered by manually typing coordinates.

NOTE

You can turn snap on and off by double-clicking on the SNAP button on the status bar, pressing Ctrl+B, or pressing F9. Turning snap off is necessary if you want to pick a point that is not on the snap grid.

Using Snap Points To Draw Objects

After you set a snap value, you can draw accurately in the CHAP03 drawing, as long as the points you need to pick are on snap points. The coordinate display shows the correct crosshairs position as it rounds the X,Y values to 0.25 units in your CHAP03 drawing.

Figure 3.21 shows a dimensioned drawing of a guide bar. Note that at this stage of its design, all the points that you need to draw its outline fall upon convenient snap points. In the following exercise, you use the dimensions from figure 3.21 to duplicate the guide bar, aided by the current snap and grid settings.

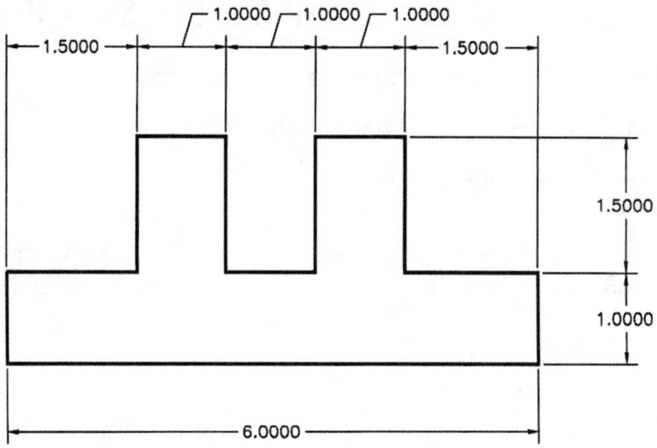

Figure 3.21

The dimensional guidebar needed.

Use the grid and coordinate display to help you pick the points in the following exercise. As you pick the points, notice that the cursor snaps to the snap increments.

USING SNAP TO DRAW A GUIDE BAR

Continue in CHAP03 drawing. Use the Layer Control drop-down list to set the layer CONSTRUCT current, then set the layer OBJECT_LINES to off.

`Command:` *Choose Zoom All (Standard, Zoom)*	Issues the ZOOM command and the All option and zooms drawing to limits
`Command:` *Choose Line (Draw, Line)*	Issues the LINE command
`_line From point:` *Using the grid and coordinate display, pick point* 3.0000,3.0000	Starts the outline at 3,3, which is the guide's lower left corner

As you move the cursor, the coordinate's display now should display distance and angle from the last picked point. If necessary, double-click one or more times in the coordinate display box to cycle the display to this mode.

`To point:` *Drag the line to* 6.0000<0, *as indicated by the coordinate display, and pick*	Draws the base line of the figure and prompts for the next point
`To point:` *Pick at coordinates* 1.0000<90	Draws the right end line

Use the dimensions from figure 3.21 and the coordinate display, and proceed counter-clockwise to each point, defining the outline of the guide. Enter **C** instead of picking the last point. C draws the closing line segment and ends the LINE command.

Save the drawing.

After you finish, your figure should look like the guide bar outline in figure 3.21.

As you work with grid and snap, you might need to adjust the grid and snap settings as you zoom so that you can work in greater detail. If you start with a snap at 1 unit and a grid at 5 units on a whole drawing, you might want to reset your snap to quarter-units and your grid to 1 unit when you zoom in to work on a portion of the drawing. To be useful as a visual aid, you need to be able to see the grid in a context appropriate to the distances with which you work.

You can coordinate your snap and grid spacing to suit your needs. Make it a practice to set your grid and snap, and then leave them on most of the time. If you do not pick your drawing points with snap (or object snap) turned on, your drawings are not accurate.

TIP

In most real drawings, points are often not so conveniently coincide with small increments, so you usually draw with the other accuracy methods covered in this chapter. However, it is usually a good idea to keep snap on for consistent placements, annotation, and dimensions.

SNAP Command Options

The SNAP command offers the following options:

```
Snap spacing or ON/OFF/Aspect/Rotate/Style <current>:
```

- **Snap spacing.** Prompts you for a value to set the snap increment and to turn on snap.
- **ON.** Turns on snap.
- **OFF.** Turns off snap. This is the initial default setting.
- **Aspect.** Prompts for different horizontal (X) and vertical (Y) snap increments (except in isometric mode; see the description of the Style option).
- **Rotate.** Prompts you to specify an angle and a base point, around which you can rotate the snap grid (and crosshairs).
- **Style.** Prompts for Standard or Isometric style. Standard sets the normal (default) snap style.

NOTE

The UCS command provides a better way to rotate snap, the grid, and the entire coordinate system. Rotating the snap grid does not affect the orientation of the drawing's X and Y axes. You use the User Coordinate System (UCS) to control axis orientation, discussed later in the "Creating Your Own Coordinate System" section.

Using Ortho Mode as a Special Snap

If you draw horizontal and vertical lines, you can constrain your cursor movements by turning on ortho mode. Ortho stands for *orthogonal* and limits cursor movement to right angles from the last point. When ortho is on, any lines you enter with the cursor are aligned with the snap axes. In effect, you can draw only at right angles. To turn on ortho mode, double-click on the ORTHO button on the status bar. You also can use the Drawing Aids dialog box, the ORTHO command, or F8.

Ortho is easy to use and helpful any time you draw sets of horizontal and vertical lines. When you turn on ortho mode, `<Ortho on>` appears at the `Command:` prompt and the ORTHO button on the status bar is highlighted. The rubber-band cursor that normally trails from the last point to the intersection of the crosshairs now goes from the last point to the nearest perpendicular point on the X or Y crosshairs.

Many drawings—or portions of drawings—can be quickly laid out using Ortho mode. Creating geometry that is parallel to the axes with ortho is simple, fast, and accurate if you also use snap.

Snapping to Objects with Object Snaps

Snap is useful if you want to draw an element that fits the snap increments exactly—such as the guide bar you drew earlier in this chapter. If you need to align new points, lines, and other objects with geometric points on objects you already have drawn, however, you need an easier, more accurate method.

Understanding Object Snap

As your drawing becomes more complex, points on circles, arcs, and intersections of angled lines no longer fall directly on snap points. AutoCAD offers a set of tools called *object snaps* to help you accurately pick such points. To understand object snaps, remember that objects such as lines have middle points and endpoints, and circles have center, quadrant, and tangent points. When you draw, you often need to attach lines to these points.

AutoCAD's *object snaps* are geometric filters that enable you to select your drawing-attachment points. If, for example, you want to draw to an intersection of two lines, you can set the object snap to filter for intersections, and then pick a point close to the intersection. The point snaps to the precise intersection of the lines. Although it takes a little time to get used to setting object snaps, it is the best way to maintain geometrically accurate drawings.

AutoCAD's OSNAP command and Running Object Snap dialog box (DDOSNAP command) set running object snap modes that calculate the attachment points you need to make accurate drawings. You can also enter object snap modes directly at any prompt that accepts point input. You tell AutoCAD which object snap attachment mode(s) to use—such as INT for INTersection or TAN for TANgent. After you pick a point or enter coordinates near the geometric point you want, AutoCAD snaps to the precise attachment point. Figure 3.22 shows all the filter modes you can use for picking attachment points on objects or for picking points in relation to objects. The OSNAP and DDOSNAP commands are discussed in the "Using Overrides versus Running Modes" section of this chapter.

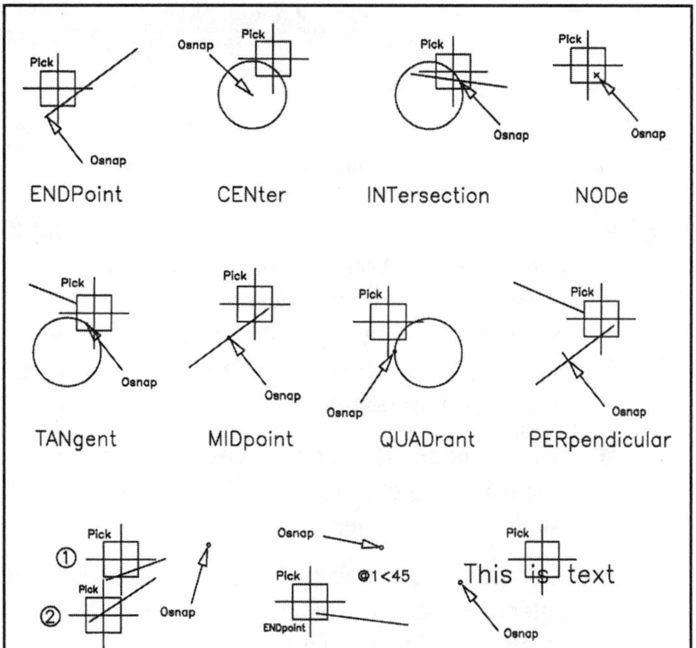

Figure 3.22

Object targets and the points they pick.

Using Overrides versus Running Modes

You can use object snaps as single-pick override filters at point-input prompts, or you can set a running object snap mode that is active until you turn it off. The OSNAP command sets running object snaps and is described later in this chapter.

You can select object snaps as overrides (which interrupt any current running object snap) using several methods, as follows:

- **Object Snap toolbar.** The object snap flyout toolbar (see fig. 3.23) is located on the Standard toolbar. The object snap toolbar can also be shown and docked in the graphics window or floated anywhere in the application window.

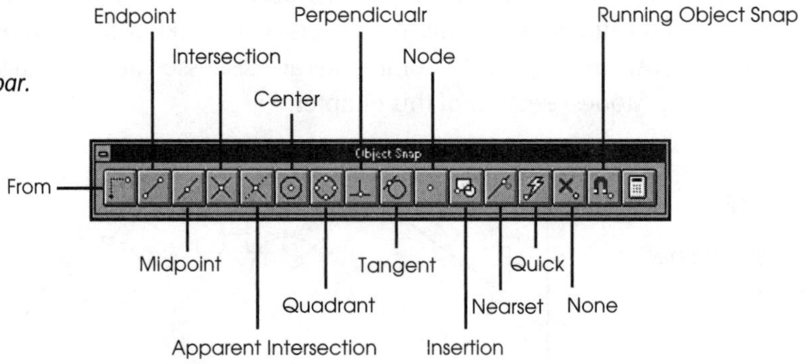

Figure 3.23

The Object Snap toolbar.

- **Pop-up menu.** The cursor pop-up menu (see fig. 3.24) appears at the current cursor position. You can display it by clicking the middle (pop-up) button on three-button pointing devices, or by pressing Shift while clicking the Enter button on two-button pointing devices. On other multibutton devices, use the button following the Enter button. (See the construction methods section of this chapter for point filter.)

- **Screen menu.** The screen menu provides access to both the OSNAP command and object snap overrides. Click on the **** line beneath the standard AutoCAD screen menu's title.

- **Keyboard.** Each object snap mode has a unique abbreviation that you can enter on the command line. This abbreviation is indicated by uppercase letters in the following list.

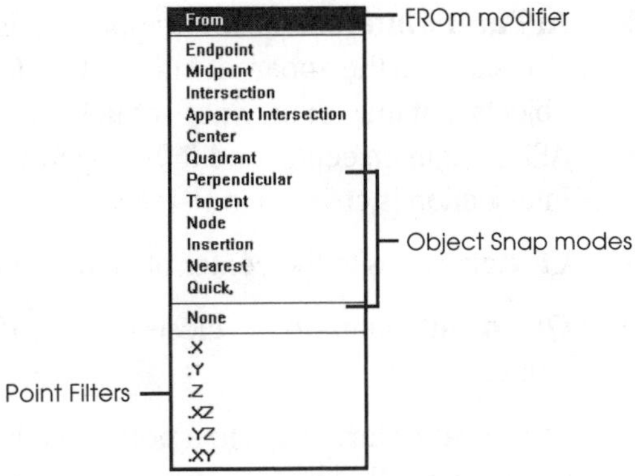

Figure 3.24

The cursor or pop-up menu with object snap modes.

Note

When chosen at the `Command:` prompt, the object snap tools issue the OSNAP command and the selected mode to set a running object snap. When chosen during a command, the object snap tools issue only the selected mode as an object snap override. This feature, however, is incompatible with AutoLISP- or ADS-define commands, such as those in third-party applications, or the AutoCAD RECTANG command. When chosen during AutoLISP or ADS-defined commands, the object snap tools cause an error.

Whether invoked in the running or override mode, AutoCAD has 13 object snap modes. The following list gives a description of each.

Note

In the following list, "line" includes polyline and spline segments and floating viewports borders.

- **ENDPoint.** Snaps to the nearest endpoint of a line or arc.
- **MIDpoint.** When you use the MIDpoint option, AutoCAD snaps to the midpoint of a line or arc.
- **INTersection.** Snaps to the nearest intersection of any combination of two lines, arcs, or circles. If only one object is selected with the first pick, AutoCAD prompts for a second object and the snap is to the real or projected intersection of the two objects.

- **APParent Intersection.** This option is identical to INTersection, except it also snaps to the apparent intersection from the current viewpoint of two objects that may or may not actually intersect in 3D space. In 2D, the APParent Intersection and INTersection modes are equivalent. APParent Intersection is covered in Part Five.
- **CENter.** Snaps to the center of an arc or circle.
- **QUAdrant.** Snaps to the closest 0-, 90-, 180-, or 270-degree point on an arc or circle.
- **PERpendicular.** Snaps to a point on a line, arc, or circle that, for the object you pick, would form a perpendicular (normal) line from the last point to the object you pick. The resulting point need not even be on the object.
- **TANgent.** Snaps to a point on an arc, spline, or circle that forms a tangent to the picked arc, spline, or circle from the last point.
- **NODe.** Snaps to a point object.
- **INSertion.** Snaps to the origin of text, attributes, and symbols (block or shape) that have been inserted into the drawing file. (You learn more about blocks, shapes, and attributes in Chapter 11, "Block Structure, Editing, Organization, and Management.")
- **NEArest.** Snaps to the nearest point on an object; generally an endpoint, normal, or perpendicular point.
- **QUIck.** Forces all other object snap options to find the first potential target quickly. The point QUIck chooses is not necessarily the closest target. QUIck finds the potential point that is on the most recently qualified object in the target box.
- **NONe.** Removes or overrides any running object snap.

WARNING

Although you can activate the ENDPoint object snap mode by entering END, use the four-letter abbreviation ENDP to help avoid accidentally issuing the END command and thereby ending your AutoCAD session.

Although it is technically not an object snap mode, the FROm modifier is often used in conjunction with object snaps and is included on the object snap menus and toolbar, but not the OSNAP command or Running Object Snap dialog box. The

FROm modifier prompts for a base point to use when specifying for the next supplied point with relative coordinates. It establishes a temporary reference point similar to the last point used by the @ prefix for input. Dragging is disabled while you use FROm.

You can use running object snaps or overrides. You use object snaps as overrides that apply to the next pick only. Running object snaps are described later in this chapter.

Using Object Snaps as Single-Pick Filters

To learn how overrides work, you will draw the dimensioned transfer arm shown in figure 3.25. Refer to this illustration to obtain distances and other dimension data as you duplicate the part in the following exercise.

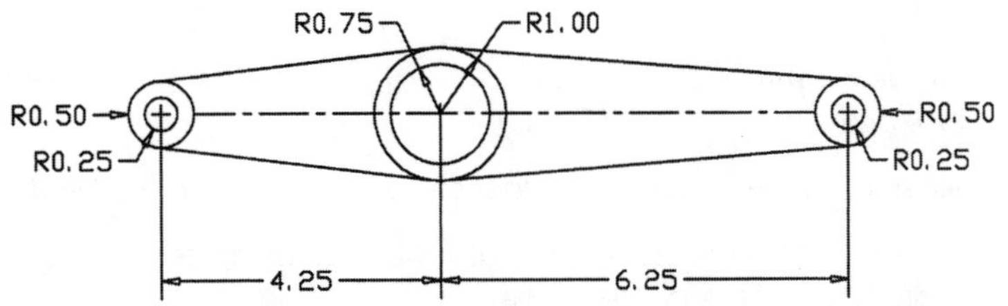

Figure 3.25

A dimensional transfer arm.

As you might in conventional drafting, begin with the large circle in the center of the arm and work from there. Follow the steps of the exercise as you use object snaps and the FROm modifier to accurately create and place objects. In this exercise you issue object snaps using the tools on the Object Snap toolbar (refer to figure 3.23).

USING OBJECT SNAP OVERRIDES

Begin a new drawing named CHAP03A using the OBJECTS drawing from the IAW Disk as a prototype. The grid is set to .25, and snap is off. The X in the middle of the drawing is a point object.

`Command:` *Choose Circle Center Radius (Draw, Circle)*	Issues the CIRCLE command
`Command: _circle 3P/2P/TTR/ <Center point>:` *Choose Snap to Node (Standard, Object snap)*	Specifies the NODe object snap override

`_nod of` *Pick the point object at* ① *(see fig. 3.26)*	Snaps to the point object
`Diameter/<Radius>:` **1** ↵	Draws a circle with 1-inch radius
`Command:` ↵	Repeats the CIRCLE command
`CIRCLE 3P/2P/TTR/<Center point>:` *Choose Snap to Center (Standard, Object snap)*	Specifies the CENter object snap override
`_cen of` *Pick anywhere on the circle*	Snaps to the center of the circle
`Diameter/<Radius> <1.00>:` **.75** ↵	Draws a second circle concentric with the first (see fig. 3.26)
`Command:` ↵	Repeats the CIRCLE command
`CIRCLE 3P/2P/TTR/<Center point>:` *Choose Snap From (Standard, Object Snap)*	Specifies the FROm modifier
`_from Base point:` *Choose Snap to Center (Standard, Object Snap)*	Specifies the CENter object snap
`_center of` *Pick anywhere on either circle*	Establishes the FROm base reference point

Next, you supply the distance, as a relative coordinate, from the center of the concentric circles to set the center of the left circles.

`<Offset>:` **@4.25<180** ↵	
`Diameter/<Radius> <0.75>:` **.5** ↵	Draws the circle
`Command:` ↵	Repeats the CIRCLE command
`Command: _circle 3P/2P/TTR/ <Center point>:` *Choose Snap to Center (Standard, Object Snap)*	
`_center of` *Pick on the left circle at* ②	
`Diameter/<Radius> <0.50>:` **.25** ↵	Draws the smaller concentric circle

Repeat the steps used to draw the two left circles to draw two right circles. Use a relative coordinate of @6.25<0 to draw the first circle. Your drawing now should resemble figure 3.27.

Save the drawing.

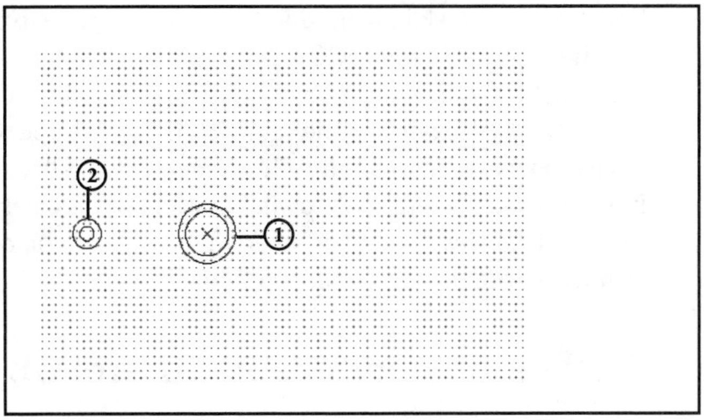

Figure 3.26

Placing the circles for the transfer arm.

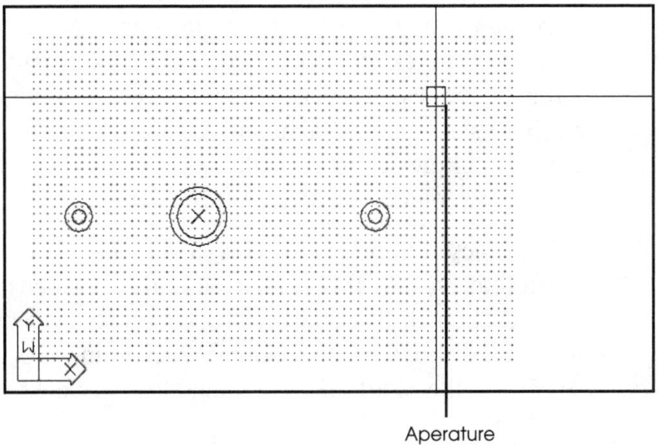

Figure 3.27

The Object Snap aperture.

NOTE

If an object snap override pick fails to find an object to which to snap, AutoCAD warns you and reprompts for the point, discarding the object snap setting.

To begin this drawing, you used the NODe object snap to place the center of the first circle. Point objects are covered later in the construction methods section of this chapter. The NODe object snap finds the location of point objects exclusively. You can take advantage of the unique nature of point objects and the NODe object snap by placing points in drawings that are, or will become, crowded with other objects. Then later, you can use the NODe object snap to snap to the point when other objects present too many potential candidates for other snap modes.

You next used the FROm modifier to set a base point to place accurately two circles at either end of the arm. FROm is actually not an object snap but usually is used in combination with an object snap specification followed by a relative coordinate, as in the previous exercise. The relative coordinate specifies an offset distance and angle from the point set by the FROm modifier and its associated object snap mode. In the previous exercise, knowing that the circles were inline and knowing their relative distances from each other enabled you to place the end circles at relative distances from the center of the middle circles.

Setting the Aperture To Control Object Finding

A dense drawing can have several attachment points close to your pick point. If you want to snap to an intersection, AutoCAD might find one, but it might not find the intersection you want. Object snap uses an *aperture box* to identify the points it considers to be candidates for the snap attachment (refer to figure 3.27). The aperture serves as an electronic bull's-eye that homes in on object snap points. AutoCAD uses the object snap only for objects that fall in the aperture. You should size your aperture according to the objects you select, the drawing's zoom settings, the display resolution, and the drawing density.

You can adjust the aperture by using a slider bar in the Running Object Snap dialog box. The other features of this dialog box are discussed in the "Using Running Object Snaps" section of this chapter. To access this dialog box, use the DDOSNAP command or choose Running Object Snap from the Options pull-down menu. You also can use the APERTURE command to adjust the size of the aperture.

TIP

A smaller aperture size enables you to pick better specific objects to snap to, but requires a slow steady hand. A larger aperture makes it harder to select specific objects but requires less coordination. The APERTURE and DDOSNAP commands can be issued transparently, so you can adjust the aperture size while being prompted for an object snap pick point. To avoid confusion with the pickbox, you should usually make the aperture a couple of pixels larger than the pickbox.

In the following exercise, you continue with the transfer arm drawing as you learn about some other object snap modes.

Continuing with Object Snap Modes

Continue from the previous exercise in CHAP03A drawing. Turn off grid mode to provide a clearer working screen. In this exercise, you issue object snaps using the pop-up menu.

`Command:` *Choose Line (Draw, Line)*	Issues the LINE command
`_line From point:` *Click the middle button on your pointing device*	Opens the pop-up menu
Choose Tangent	Specifies the TANgent object snap
`_tan to` *Pick near* ① *in figure 3.28*	Selects the circle but doesn't display rubber-band line yet
`To point:` *Choose* Tangent *from the pop-up menu*	Specifies TANgent object snap
`_tan to` *Pick near* ②	Draws a line tangent to the two circles
`To point:` *Press Enter twice*	Ends, then reissues the LINE command
`_line From point:` *Choose* Tangent *from the pop-up menu*	Specifies the TANgent object snap
`_tan to` *Pick near* ②	Select the circle but doesn't display rubber-band line yet
`To point:` *Choose* Tangent *from the pop-up menu*	Specifies TANgent object snap
`_tan to` *Pick near* ③	Draws a line tangent to the two circles
`To point:` *Press Enter twice*	Ends, then reissues the LINE command

Continue as in the previous steps, drawing lines tangent to the bottom of the circles, picking near points ④, ⑤, and ⑥. Your drawing should resemble figure 3.28 after you finish.

Save the drawing.

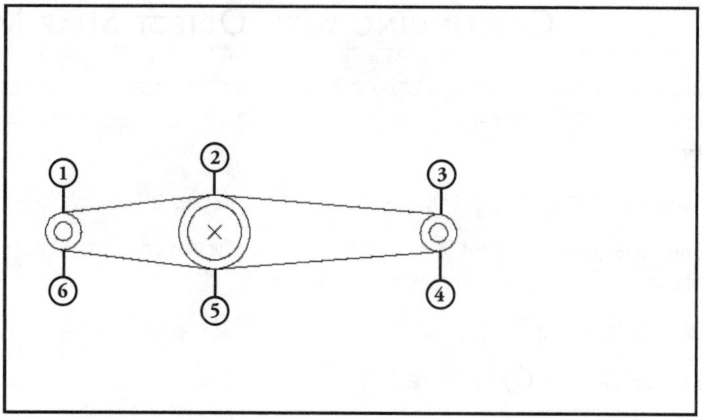

Figure 3.28

The completed transfer arm outline.

TIP

If you accidentally specify the wrong object snap override mode, pick a point in a clear area. AutoCAD issues an error message and reissues the prompt for a point. You then can specify the correct mode.

When you use the TANgent object snap, the first end, the second end, or both ends of a line can snap to a tangent point. When you issue the TANgent object snap at the LINE command's `From point:` prompt, no rubber-band line appears until you pick the next point, at the `To point:` prompt. This same behavior is exhibited by the PERpendicular object snap. Circles and arcs often have more than one point that qualifies for a TANgent or PERpendicular snap. In such cases, AutoCAD uses the point on the side closest to the pick point.

As you continue in the following exercise, you learn about the INSertion and NEArest object snap modes. In this exercise, you issue the object snap modes from the keyboard. You need enter only the uppercase letters (the first three) from the keyboard.

THE INSERTION AND NEAREST OBJECT SNAP MODES

Continue from the preceding exercise and turn on layer TEXT.

`Command:` *Choose Line (Draw, Line)*	Issues the LINE command
`_line From point:` **INS**	Specifies the INSertion object snap
`_ins of` *Pick anywhere on the text object* Centered	Snaps to insertion point of the center-justified text object

`To point:` **INS**	Specifies the INSertion object snap
`_ins of` *Pick anywhere on the text object* Left	Snaps to the insertion point of the left-justified text object
`Command:` ↵	Ends the LINE command
`Command:` **U** ↵	Issues the U command and deletes the line LINE GROUP
`Command:` *Choose Move (Modify)*	Issues the MOVE command
`_move`	
`Select objects:` *Pick anywhere on the arrow*	
`1 found`	
`Select objects:` ↵	Ends the Select objects prompts
`Base point or displacement:` **INS**	Specifies the INSertion object snap
`_ins of` *Pick anywhere on the arrow*	Snaps to insertion point of block object
`Second point of displacement:` **NEA**	Specifies the NEArest object snap
`_nea to` *Pick at* ① (see fig. 3.29)	Snaps to nearest object

Your drawing should resemble figure 3.29.

Save your work.

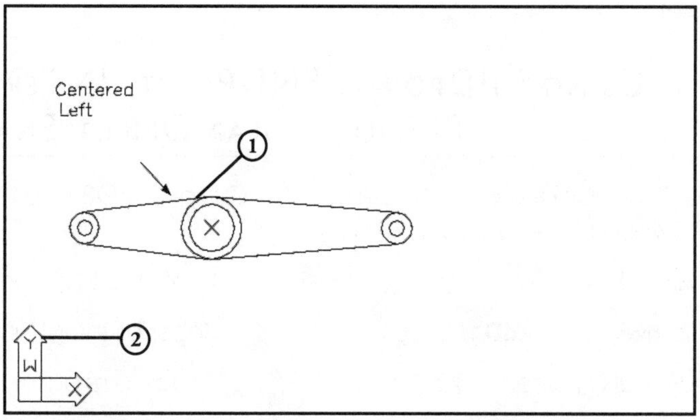

Figure 3.29

Working with the NEArest and INSertion object snaps.

The INSertion object snap snaps to the insertion point of block objects and text objects. The insertion point for text objects is determined according to the type of justification you specify when you create the text. Blocks have their insertion points defined when they are created. Neither of these object types have natural geometric snap points other than their insertion points. You can, however, snap to the objects within blocks. Being able to use the INSertion object snap to snap to the insertion point of text objects is valuable if you must move the text or align it with other text or drawing geometry.

The NEArest object snap simply finds a point on an object closest to the point you specify—that is, closest to the center of the aperture box. NEArest object snap, although unable to snap to specific geometry, such as an endpoint or tangent point, has many uses. It is frequently used with measurements in conjunction with such commands as DIST. You use the NEArest object snap again in an exercise later in this chapter.

The next exercise looks at the ENDPoint, INTersection, MIDpoint, and PERpendicular object snaps. The ENDPoint and INTersection object snaps are two of the most frequently used object snaps in mechanical drafting and design, and the PERpendicular and MIDpoint object snaps are essential in most geometric construction. In the following exercise, object snaps again are specified by their typed abbreviations. Now that you have used all three methods of issuing object snap overrides in the preceding exercises (toolbar, pop-up menu, and typed abbreviation), feel free to use the method(s) you prefer. The exercise consists of completing a not-to-scale diagram of a simple roof truss.

USING MIDPOINT, ENDPOINT, INTERSECTION, AND PERPENDICULAR OBJECT SNAPS

Continue from the previous exercise. Turn off layers TEXT and OBJECT, then turn on layer TRUSS and make it current.

`Command:` **L** ↵	Issues the LINE command
`LINE from point:` **MID** ↵	Specifies the MIDpoint object snap
`of` *Pick at* ① *(see fig. 3.30)*	Snaps to midpoint of line
`To point:` **ENDP** ↵	Specifies the ENDPoint object snap
`of` *Pick at* ②	Snaps to nearest ENDPoint
`To point:` *Press Enter twice*	Ends and reissues LINE command

`LINE from point:` **INT** ↵	
`of` *Pick at the intersection of the base and the line just drawn* ③	Snaps to intersection of lines
`To point:` **MID** ↵	Specifies the MIDpoint object snap
`of` *Pick at* ④	Snaps to MIDpoint of line
`To point:` **PER** ↵	Specifies the PERpendicular object snap
`to` *Pick at* ⑤	Snaps to PERpendicular point (see fig. 3.30)

Complete the right side of the truss by performing the following steps.

`Command:` *Press Enter twice*	Ends and reissues LINE command
`LINE from point:` **ENDP** ↵	Specifies the ENDPoint object snap
`of` *Pick at* ① *(see fig.3.31)*	Snaps to nearest ENDPoint
`To point:` **MID** ↵	Specifies the MIDpoint object snap
`of` *Pick at* ②	Snaps to MIDpoint
`To point:` **PER** ↵	Specifies the PERpendicular object snap
`to` *Pick anywhere on base line*	
`To point:` ↵	Ends LINE command

The truss diagram is complete and your drawing should look like figure 3.31.

Save your work.

Figure 3.30

The truss figure, half completed.

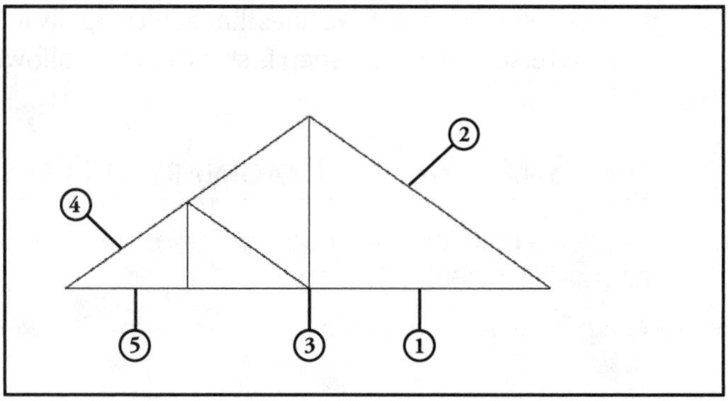

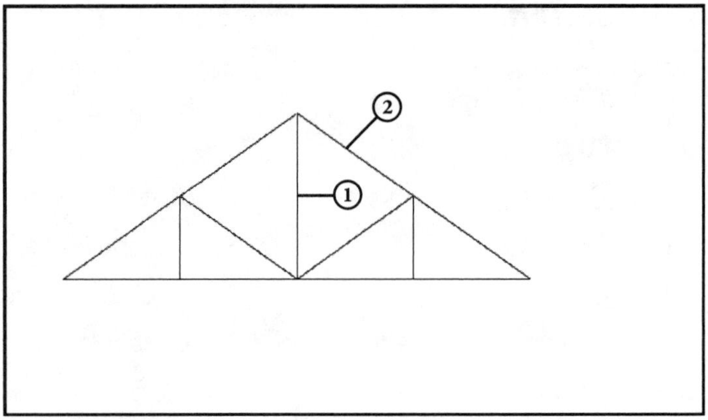

Figure 3.31

The completed truss outline.

You can be fairly indiscriminate when you pick ENDPoint, MIDpoint, and PERpendicular object snaps. Picking anywhere past the midpoint on a line with ENDpoint, for example, results in a snap to the nearest endpoint. Likewise, picking anywhere on a line or arc suffices when you snap to the MIDpoint. This can be beneficial in dense drawings when the geometric point to which you want to snap is crowded in with other objects or even out of view. INTersection object snaps must be precise or you'll be prompted to pick the second object. Often, snapping to an ENDPoint rather than an INTersection is easier if you know that the ENDPoint of a line or arc coincides exactly with the INTersection. In dense drawings, changing the size of the aperture and zooming the view are beneficial.

The INTersection object snap has the added flexibility of being able to find the projected intersection of two lines that don't actually intersect. This added flexibility of the INTersection object snap is shown in the following exercise.

SNAPPING TO IMAGINARY INTERSECTIONS

Continue from the preceding exercise. First, turn off layer TRUSS, then turn on layer VALVE and make it current.

`Command:` *Choose Circle Center Radius (Draw, Circle)*	Issues the CIRCLE command
`_circle 3P/2P/TTR/<Center point>:` **INT ↵**	Specifies the INTersection object snap
`of` *Pick at ① (see fig. 3.32)*	Selects one object

and *Pick at* ② — Selects another object and snaps to the imaginary extended INTersection of the two objects

`Diameter/<Radius> <0.25>:` **ENDP** ↵

`of` *Pick at* ② — Draws the circle (see fig. 3.32)

Save your work.

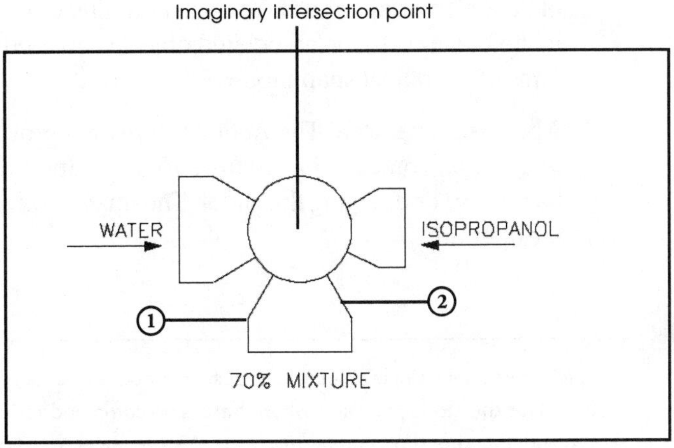

Figure 3.32

Snapping to an imaginary intersection.

Using QUIck To Optimize Object Snap

When you use an object snap, AutoCAD must search every object in the drawing window to find all the objects that cross the aperture box. AutoCAD then calculates potential points for all qualified objects to find the best (closest) fit for the object snap you issue. This process can take some time if the drawing contains many objects.

You can shorten the object snap search process by reducing the size of the aperture to keep extraneous objects out of the target. You also can use the QUIck object snap option, which enables AutoCAD to take the most recently created object that meets your object snap criteria, instead of doing an exhaustive search and comparison to find the closest object. You invoke QUIck by using it as a prefix for other object snap option(s), such as QUI,INT for a quick intersection.

When you invoke QUIck, AutoCAD occasionally finds a different fit from the one you want. If this happens, simply cancel the current command and initiate the object snap process again without the QUIck modifier.

Using Running Object Snaps

An object snap condition that is set to be in effect until you change it is called a *running object snap mode*. You use the DDOSNAP command to open the Running Object Snap dialog box, or the OSNAP command to set running object snap modes.

The Running Object Snap dialog box provides the following functions:

- **Select Settings area.** The Select Settings area provides check boxes for each of the object snap modes. You set a running object snap by placing a check in the box next to the associated object snap mode. The Clear All button turns off all object snap modes.

- **Aperture Size area.** The Aperture Size area provides a slider bar and an image box. You can change the size of the aperture by clicking on the slider bar arrows or dragging the slider. The image box shows the current size of the aperture.

TIP

A quick way to set a single running object snap mode is to click on the tool (in the standard toolbar) for the mode you want when there is no command active. This issues the OSNAP command and sets the running mode to the one selected. You cannot use this to set multiple (combined) object snap modes. The cursor pop-up menu does not support this mechanism.

Running object snap modes remain in effect until you replace them with another running mode setting. If a pick fails to find an object to snap to when a running mode is set, AutoCAD finds the point it would have found if no object snap mode were set. Unlike SNAP, GRID, and ORTHO, the OSNAP command is not transparent; fortunately, overrides are transparent. Use the NONe override or any other override you need to suppress a running mode temporarily.

In the following exercise, you set a running QUAdrant object snap and place a square inside a circle on the transfer arm drawing you completed in a previous exercise.

USING A RUNNING OBJECT SNAP

Continue from the previous exercise. Turn off the layer VALVE, turn on the layer OBJECT, and set OBJECT current.

`Command:` *Choose* Options, Running Object Snap	Displays the Running Object Snap dialog box (see fig. 3.33)

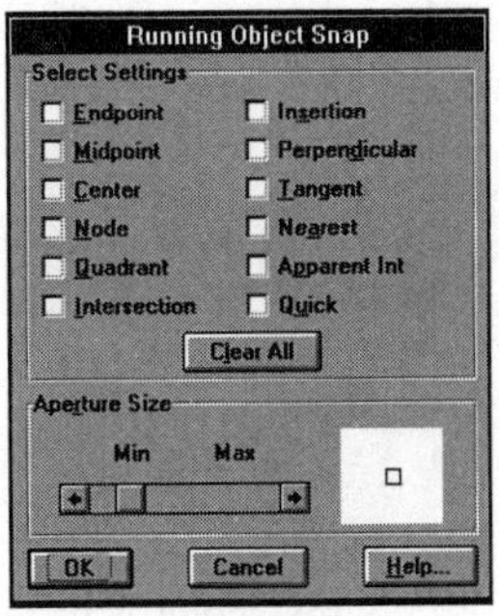

Figure 3.33

The Running Object Snap dialog box.

`Command:` *Put a check in the Quadrant check box, then choose* OK	Sets QUAdrant as the running object snap mode
`Command:` *Choose Line (Draw, Line)*	Issues the LINE command and displays the object snap aperture box
`_line From point:` *Pick a point near* ① *in fig. 3.34*	Snaps to the nearest quadrant of the circle
`To point:` *Pick a point near* ②	Snaps to the quadrant
`To point:` *Pick a point near* ③	Snaps to the quadrant
`To point:` *Pick a point near* ④	Snaps to the quadrant
`To point:` **C**↵	Closes the square (see fig. 3.34)

Set the running object snap to NONE and save the drawing.

You can specify two or more running or override modes at once; AutoCAD finds the calculated point of the mode that is closest to the crosshairs. Specify multiple modes by checking multiple check boxes in the Running Object Snap dialog box. If you use the OSNAP command at the `Command:` prompt, include multiple object snap modes at the `Object snap modes:` prompt and separate them with commas, as in END,MID,CEN. Depending on the type of drawing or editing tasks at hand, a running object snap combination of ENDP,INT,MID should cover the majority of your object snap requirements.

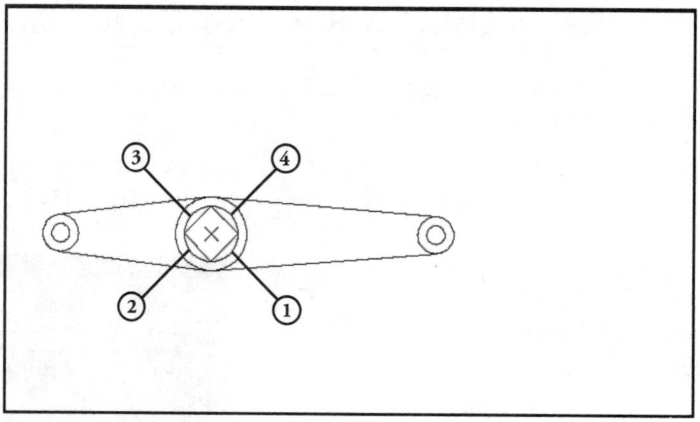

Figure 3.34

The completed transfer arm.

TIP

CENter, INTersection, ENDPoint is probably the most useful combination for running object snaps. It will find most of the points you want and can be overridden in the few cases when you need another mode or no object snapping.

Some object snap mode combinations are tricky. For example, when you use the ENDpoint mode with the MIDpoint mode, AutoCAD finds the endpoint or midpoint nearest to the point you specify; the point you pick must be less than halfway to the endpoint or the midpoint depending on which point you want AutoCAD to find. When you combine the PERpendicular and the TANgent modes, proximity distance determines which mode you want applied to an arc or a circle.

Some object snap mode combinations just don't work. The NEArest mode does not combine well with anything because the nearest point is usually the first point found.

The CENter and QUAdrant object snap modes do not combine well either. If the radius of a circle or arc is larger than the aperture, it is impossible to snap to its center because the distance from the pick point to the center is always greater than the distance to a quadrant point. However, you can still snap to the center of small circles and arcs by placing the crosshairs as close as possible to the center point while the aperture touches the circle or arc. When in doubt, just override the running mode combination with a mode that you know will work.

Use the override modes whenever the need arises; they override running modes. Set up a running object snap whenever you repeatedly use the same object snap mode(s). The Running Object Snap dialog box provides a fast and efficient way to set running object snaps.

NOTE

When you use AutoCAD's grips autoediting feature, you can snap to various object-specific positions, such as an endpoint, without using object snaps. As you move the cursor over a grip, it snaps to the grip. Grips are discussed in Chapter 13, "Autoediting with Grips."

Using Construction Methods

In manual drafting, you often draw light guidelines or temporary lines as construction lines to help you align or place objects accurately. The AutoCAD grid sometimes takes the place of guidelines, but you sometimes need to use construction line methods in CAD drafting. AutoCAD offers two types of construction lines: infinitely long lines called *xlines*, and rays. AutoCAD also provides two alternative construction methods: *point filters*, and *direct distance entry*.

Specifying Points with Direct Distance Entry

Starting with Release 13c4, AutoCAD includes a method of specifying point locations that has been popular with users of AutoSketch and AutoCAD LT—*direct distance entry*. Direct distance entry is not a command, rather it is an option you can use any time AutoCAD presents a rubberband cursor from a previous point and is prompting for another. In this situation you can enter a distance value with the keyboard to specify a point at the given distance, in the direction indicated by the cursor.

Direct distance entry works like specifying relative polar coordinates, except that you rely on the direction the cursor is pointing for the angle input. Therefore, direct distance entry works best with ortho on, or when you can use snap to align the cursor at the angle you need.

In the following exercise you use direct distance entry, combined with ortho, to draw a simple rectangle.

Using Direct Distance Entry to Draw a Rectangle

Continue in CHAP03A drawing. Turn off all layers, then turn layer FILTERS on and make it current. Make sure that grid and ortho are on and snap is off.

`Command:` *Choose Zoom All (Standard, Zoom)*	Issues the ZOOM command with the All option
`_ZOOM`	

`All/Center/Dynamic/Extents/Left/`
`Previous/Vmax/Window/`
`<Scale(X/XP)>: _all`
	Zooms to the drawings limits and regenerates drawing

`Command:` *Choose Polyline (Draw, Polyline)*	Issues the PLINE command
`_pline`	
`From point: 3,3`	Specifies start point

`Current line-width is 0.00`
`Arc/Close/Halfwidth/Length/Undo/Width/`
`<Endpoint of line>:`	

Move your pointing device to the right so the cursor extends horizontally.

`Arc/Close/Halfwidth/Length/Undo/Width/` `<Endpoint of line>:` **4.125** ↵	Specifies a point 4-1/8 units to the right

Now move your pointing device so the cursor extends vertically.

`Arc/Close/Halfwidth/Length/Undo/Width/` `<Endpoint of line>:` **6.125** ↵	Specifies a point 6-1/8 units up

Repeat the 4.125 distance entry, but with the cursor dragged to the left, then enter C to close the rectangle. Your drawing should look like figure 3.35

Save the drawing.

Direct distance entry makes drawing orthogonal figures easy if you use ortho. It also works with many of AutoCAD's editing commands, such as MOVE, COPY, and STRETCH. It even works with most of the grips autoediting modes. Think of it as a point input shortcut, and look for opportunities to use it.

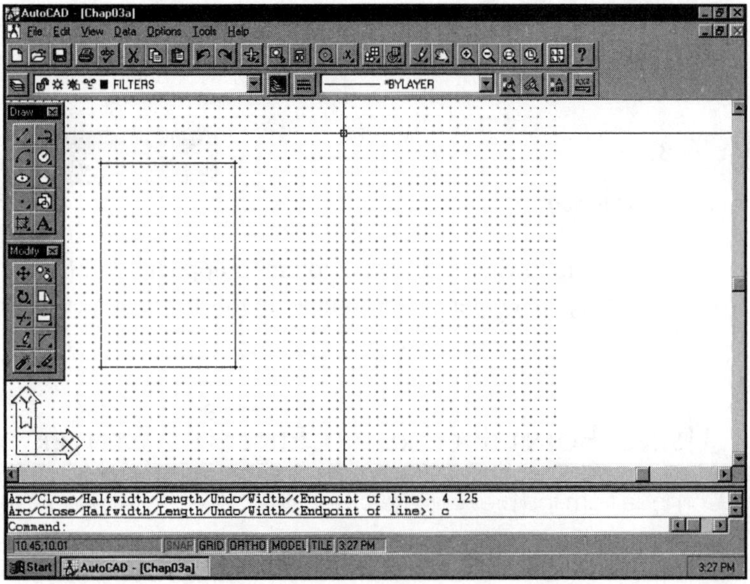

Figure 3.35

Drawing with direct distance entry.

Using Point Filters

Point filters enable you to specify coordinates by choosing one value at a time, such as only the X value, and then combining values to form a complete 2D or 3D point. When you choose values, you can use object snaps to extract X, Y, or Z values from existing geometry to locate another point. Using point filters you could, for example, extract the X coordinate of the center point of an arc and combine that value with the Y coordinate of the midpoint of a line to yield an X,Y coordinate to serve as the center for a circle.

When AutoCAD requests a point, you can respond with a point filter of the general form *coordinate*, where *coordinate* is one or more of the letters X, Y, and Z. For instance, .X and .XY are valid filters. When you specify such a filter, AutoCAD responds with `(of)` and then extracts only those coordinates specified by the filter from the next point you designate. Point filters are used with object snaps to pick the filtered points. If a full point has not been formed, a prompt such as `(need YZ)` appears to tell you what is needed before a full point is complete. In 2D usage, the Z coordinate is the current elevation.

In addition to being able to enter point filters from the keyboard, you also can select them from the Point Filters flyout (see fig. 3.36) from the Standard toolbar as well as from the pop-up menu displayed by clicking the middle button (or Shift+clicking the

Enter button) of the pointing device (refer to figure 3.36). In the following exercises using point filters, keyboard entry is indicated—but use the method you prefer.

Figure 3.36

The Point Filters toolbar.

In the following exercise, a common application of point filters is demonstrated: finding the center of a rectangle. In this exercise you begin a drawing of a simple flange.

Using Point Filters To Find the Center of a Rectangle

Continue from the previous exercise, in the CHAP03A drawing.

You draw a 1-unit radius circle centered in the rectangle.

`Command:` *Choose Circle Center Radius (Draw, Circle)*	Issues the CIRCLE command
`Command: _circle 3P/2P/TTR/ <Center point>:` **X**↵	Specifies X coordinate filter
`of` **MID**↵	Specifies the MIDpoint object snap
`of` *Pick either the top or bottom line*	Filters the X coordinate of the midpoint of the line and prompts you for the Y and Z coordinates
`(need YZ):` **MID**↵	Specifies the MIDpoint object snap
`of` *Pick either the left or right line*	Filters the Y and Z coordinates of the midpoint of the line and combines them with X coordinate; uses the result

Note that after a valid X,Y,Z coordinate forms from the filters, the original prompt for a center point is answered.

`Diameter/<Radius> <1.49>:` **1**↵	Draws the circle (see fig. 3.37)

Save your work.

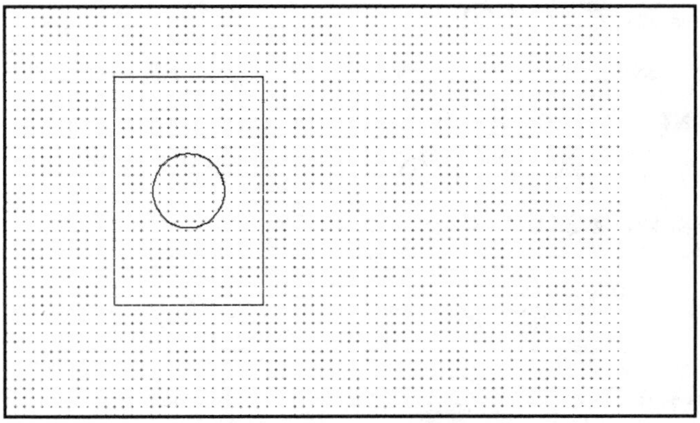

Figure 3.37

Using point filters to find the center of a rectangle.

In the preceding exercise, after you issued the prompt for the center of the circle, you isolated the X coordinate of the midpoint of either of the horizontal lines (the X coordinate of the midpoint of both lines are the same). Then, using the MIDpoint object snap, you ensured that the exact midpoint was chosen. Next, AutoCAD prompted for the Y,Z components, which you supplied by snapping to the midpoint of either vertical line, yielding a complete X,Y,Z coordinate for the circle's center. You can also type enter coordinates at the filter prompt.

In the following exercise, you begin a section view of the flange, using point filters to form points from existing drawing objects. Remember, you cannot use the object snap toolbar during the RECTANG command, so use the pop-up menu or just type the object snap modes.

USING POINT FILTERS TO MAKE A NEW VIEW

Continue from the preceding exercise. Turn on ortho (double-click on the ORTHO button).

`Command:` *Choose Rectangle (Draw, Polygon)*	Issues the RECTANG command and prompts for first corner
`Command: rectang`	
`First corner:` *Choose .Y (Standard, Point Filters)*	Specifies a Y point filter
`of` **INT** ↵	Specifies the INTersection object snap
`_int of` *Pick the intersection at ① in figure 3.38*	Obtains Y coordinate of intersection

`(need XZ):` *Pick near* ②	Obtains X,Z coordinate; places first corner
`Other corner:` **.Y** ↵	Specifies a Y point filter
`of` **INT** ↵	Specifies the INTersection object snap
`of` *Pick the intersection at* ③	Obtains Y coordinate of intersection
`(need XZ):` **@.25,0** ↵	Supplies X,Z coordinate and draws the rectangle

Next, you draw the cross-section of the hole on a hidden-line layer. Set the layer HIDDEN on and current.

`Command:` *Choose Line (Draw, Line)*	Issues the LINE command
`_line From point:` **.Y** ↵	Specifies a Y point filter
`.Y of` **QUA** ↵	Specifies the QUAdrant object snap
`of` *Pick the top of the circle at* ④	Obtains the Y coordinate of the quadrant point
`(need XZ):` **NEA** ↵	Specifies the NEArest object snap
`to` *Pick anywhere on line at* ⑤	Obtains the X,Z coordinate of the line; establishes beginning of line
`To point:` **PER** ↵	Specifies the PERpendicular object snap
`to` *Pick anywhere on second line*	Draws the line
`to point:` ↵	Ends the LINE command

Draw the bottom cross-section line using the same steps as for the top line, but obtain the Y coordinate from the bottom quadrant of the circle.

Set layer CENTER on and current and draw the center line. Use a Y point filter and CEN object snap to locate its Y position, then pick with snap on to set its X position at 6 and second end at 7—ortho keeps it horizontal.

Next, you add some text centered below the front view of the flange. The DTEXT command is covered in Chapter 17, "Annotation with Text."

Set the layer FILTERS current.

`Command:` **DTEXT** ↵	Begins the DTEXT command
`Justify/Style/<Start point>:` **C** ↵	Specifies the Center justification option
`Center point:` **.X** ↵	Specifies an X point filter
`of` **MID** ↵	Specifies the MIDpoint object snap

`of` *Pick bottom line of flange, front view*	Obtains the X coordinate of the midpoint of the line
`(need YZ):` *Pick at* ⑧	Obtains the Y,Z coordinate of the text start point
`Height <0.20>:` **.25** ↵	Sets text height
`Rotation angle <0>:` ↵	Accepts the default angle of 0 degrees
`Text:` **0.25 Flange** ↵	Draws the text and starts a new line
`Text:` ↵	Ends the DTEXT command

Turn off the grid, and your flange drawing should resemble figure 3.38.

Save your work.

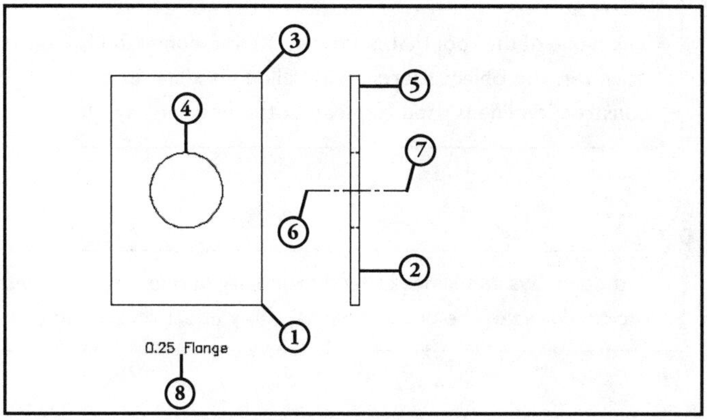

Figure 3.38

Two views of the flange.

In effect, specifying a new point with the X value taken from one existing point and the Y value from another existing point finds the intersection of imaginary orthogonal construction lines projecting from each of the two points. Combining the accuracy of object snaps with point filters provides a powerful tool.

Using Xlines and Rays as Construction Lines

AutoCAD provides two methods of creating construction lines for use as reference objects in drawings. One method is the RAY command and the other is the XLINE command. AutoCAD's construction lines offer unique characteristics and methods of placement that you do not find in conventional line objects.

These special construction line objects extend to infinity in one or both directions, and are known as *rays* and *xlines*, respectively. Rays have finite starting points and extend from that point to infinity. Xlines have no starting point and extend to infinity in both directions.

Rays are created with the Ray (Draw, Line) tool and xlines are created with the Construction Line (Draw, Line) tool (see fig. 3.39).

Figure 3.39

The Line toolbar.

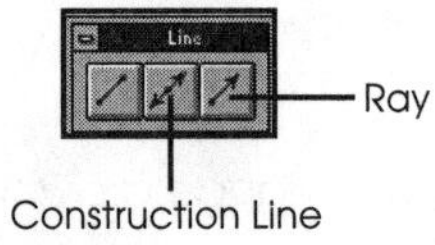

NOTE

The name of the tool that issues the XLINE command is Construction Line (Draw, Line); however, the object it creates is called an xline. In discussing xlines and rays, the term construction line is used to mean both xline and ray objects.

NOTE

Although rays and xlines extend to infinity in one or both directions, they do not change the total area of the drawing or have any effect on zooming or viewpoints.

XLINE Command Options

The XLINE command provides the following six versatile options:

- **From point.** The From point option is the default option. It specifies both the location of the infinite line and the point through which it passes. After you specify the first point, AutoCAD prompts you for the through point. Specify the point through which you want the infinite line to pass. The first point you chose becomes the conceptual "midpoint" of the line. You can specify successive lines through this midpoint until you press Enter to end the command.
- **Hor.** The Hor (Horizontal) option creates an infinite line that passes through the point you specify. The line is parallel to the X axis of the current UCS.

- **Ver.** The Ver (Vertical) option creates an infinite line that passes through the point you specify. The line is parallel to the Y axis of the current UCS.
- **Ang.** The Ang (Angle) option creates an infinite line at a specified angle. After you specify the angle for the line, AutoCAD asks for the point through which the line, at the specified angle, is to pass. Enter **R** at the initial prompt if you want to specify a reference line, then an angle. The angle is measured counterclockwise from the reference line. You then specify the point through which the line at the specified angle is to pass.
- **Bisect.** The Bisect (Bisector) option creates an infinite line that passes through an angle vertex you select and bisects the angle formed between two points you specify. You can specify successive bisectors until you end the command by pressing Enter.
- **Offset.** The Offset option creates an infinite line parallel to another line object. You can specify the offset distance and direction or you can specify a point through which the line is to pass.

RAY Command Options

The RAY command displays the following prompts:

- **From point:.** At the `From point:` prompt, you specify the point from which you want the line to start.
- **Through point:.** At the `Through point:` prompt, you specify the point through which you want the ray to pass. You are prompted for successive through points until you end the command by pressing Enter.

Other than their length and methods of placement, AutoCAD's construction lines behave similarly to a conventional line object; for example, you can copy, rotate, move, break, and trim them. Certain editing operations, such as lengthening, do not apply to infinite lines, although you can extend a ray object. You might want to create construction lines on a separate layer so that you can freeze or turn them off before you plot.

In the following exercise, you use the XLINE and RAY commands to create construction lines. For a point of departure, you use a rectangle identical to the one you used to begin the flange drawing in the previous exercise.

WORKING WITH INFINITE CONSTRUCTION LINES

Continue in the CHAP03A drawing or begin a new drawing named CHAP03B, using the OBJECTS drawing from the IAW Disk as a prototype.

Turn all layers off, then turn layer CONSTRUCTION on and set it current. Turn grid, snap, and ortho off. Set a running INTersection object snap.

The following steps draw construction lines through the opposite corners of the rectangle.

`Command:` *Choose Ray (Draw, Line)*	Issues the RAY command
`_ray From point:` *Pick the intersection at ① (see fig. 3.40)*	Snaps to the intersection
`Through point:` *Pick the intersection at ②*	Snaps to the intersection and draws the ray
`Through point:` *Press Enter twice*	Ends and repeats the RAY command
`ray From point:` *Pick the intersection at ③*	Snaps to the intersection
`Through point:` *Pick the intersection at ②*	Snaps to the intersection and draws the ray
`Through point:` ↵	Ends the command (see fig. 3.40)

Save the drawing.

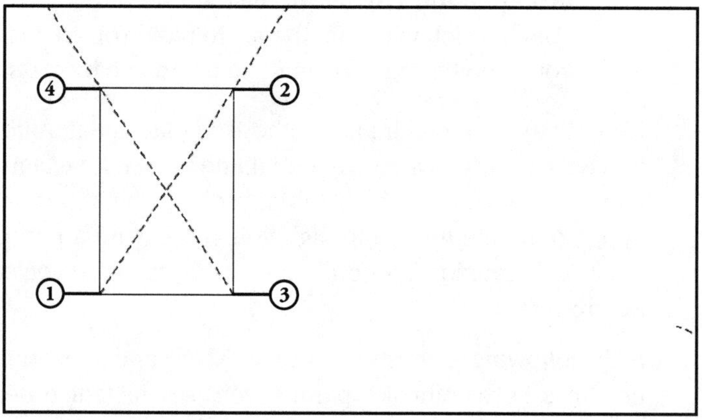

Figure 3.40

Finding the center of a rectangle with rays.

After you draw the construction lines, you can change layers and use their intersection (with an INTersection object snap) to accurately place a circle as you did in the earlier exercise in which you used point filters to find the center of the rectangle.

In the following exercise, you use the XLINE command to place construction lines to use in drawing a side view of the flange.

USING THE XLINE COMMAND TO DRAW CONSTRUCTION LINES

Continue from the previous exercise.

`Command:` *Choose Construction Line (Draw, Line)*	Issues the XLINE command
`_xline Hor/Ver/Ang/Bisect/Offset/ <From point>:` *Pick intersection at ① (see fig. 3.41)*	Snaps to the INTersection object snap
`Through point:` *Pick at ②*	Snaps to the intersection and draws the construction line

Note that another `Through point:` prompt appears. As you move the cursor, a potential second line appears with the same "anchor" point.

`Through point:` *Press Enter twice*	Ends, then reissues the XLINE command

To draw the next construction line, you use the horizontal option.

`XLINE Hor/Ver/Ang/Bisect/Offset/ <From point>:` **H** ↵	Specifies the horizontal option
`Through point:` **NEA** ↵	Specifies the NEArest object snap
`_nea to` *Pick anywhere along the top line of the rectangle*	Draws a horizontal construction line and prompts for another point

Note that as you move the cursor, a potential second horizontal line appears at the cursor.

`Through point:` *Press Enter twice*	Ends and reissues the XLINE command

Next, you create the vertical construction lines using the Offset option. Recall that the thickness of the flange is 0.25 units.

`xline Hor/Ver/Ang/Bisect/Offset/ <From point>:` **O** ↵	Specifies the Offset option
`Offset distance or Through <Through>:` **4** ↵	Specifies the offset distance for the side view

`Select a line object:` *Pick the rectangle at* ③	Selects and highlights the rectangle
`Side to offset?` *Move the cursor any distance to the right and pick*	Specifies the offset direction and draws the line
`Select a line object:` *Press Enter twice*	Ends then reissues the XLINE command
`XLINE Hor/Ver/Ang/Bisect/Offset/ <From point>:` **O** ↵	Specifies the Offset option
`Offset distance or Through <4.00>:` **.25** ↵	Specifies the offset distance
`Select a line object:` *Pick the xline you just created*	Selects and highlights the xline
`Side to offset?` *Move the cursor any distance to the right and pick*	Specifies the offset direction and draws the line (see fig. 3.41)
`Select a line object:` ↵	Ends the command

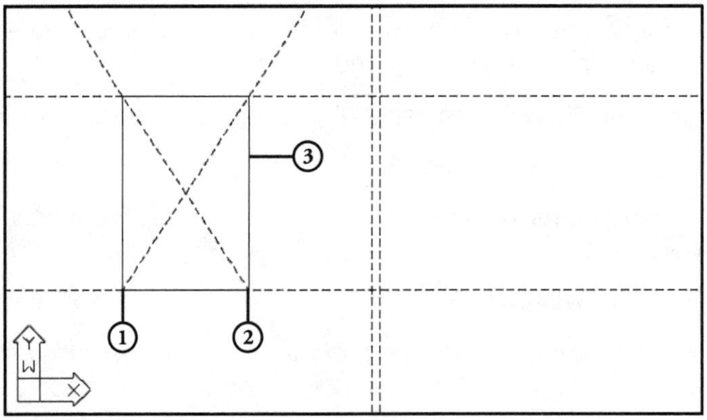

Figure 3.41

Completed construction lines.

In the preceding exercise, you used several of the options available to you for creating construction lines. All the constructions you drew were placed on the layer CONSTRUCT. CONSTRUCT has the color red and a linetype of HIDDEN assigned to it. Using a separate layer devoted to construction lines enables you to display these lines in a specific color and linetype to enhance their visibility. In the preceding exercise, you could use the geometry created by the construction lines (for example, intersections) to accurately place new objects (on another layer) by using point filters and object snaps. You could then freeze the layer that contains the construction lines, or erase the lines. Alternately, you could leave the construction lines in place, then edit and transfer them to another layer. You learn about transferring objects to different layers in Chapter 15, "Object and Drawing Modification and Inquiry Tools."

TIP

If you want automatically to have construction lines visible while drawing but not have them plot, place them on the DEFpoints layer. The DEFpoints layer is never plotted—it is used by AutoCAD's associative dimensions.

The construction lines you drew in the previous exercise (see fig 3.41) can be turned into lines forming the plate profile by using the FILLET or TRIM command.

Transferring coordinate or geometric data from one location in the drawing to another is a basic technique used to build and develop your drawings. Using object snaps, point filters, and construction lines enables you to apply this technique to your CAD drawings with ease and accuracy.

Using the Tablet To Digitize Points

If you have a digitizer, you can use it to trace and digitize drawings into AutoCAD. AutoCAD has two modes for using digitizers: the screen pointing mode you usually use and a calibrated digitizing mode. You use the calibrated digitizing mode to establish a relationship between points on a drawing taped to the tablet and points in your AutoCAD drawing. After that relationship is calibrated, you can pick points in the AutoCAD drawing fairly accurately by digitizing the corresponding points on the paper drawing. Although this is not as accurate as creating a new drawing entirely from accurate coordinate and measurement data, it often is the only efficient way to import existing drawing data.

Digitizing is well suited to tracing contours, which do not demand absolute precision, with sketched lines. Digitizing, however, is not limited to sketching. You can use the full range of drawing commands and controls, even inserting blocks at datum points picked on the tablet.

To digitize, first use the CALibrate option of the TABLET command. It prompts you for two known points on the paper drawing and for the drawing coordinates to which to assign them. After calibration, the relationship between the drawing and tablet is maintained, even if you pan and zoom. The X and Y axes are calibrated with equal scales. If the tablet drawing is distorted (as are many paper drawings), you can compensate after you trace by blocking the results and inserting them with differing X and Y scales. If your paper drawing does not fit on the tablet menu's screen pointing area, you can reconfigure the tablet to use its full area for digitizing. To exit the calibrated tablet mode, use the TABLET command's OFF option; to reenter tablet mode, use ON. You also can switch between tablet mode and screen pointing mode by pressing Ctrl+T. For more information about tablet calibration and configuration, see Appendix A, "Installation and Configuration."

TABLET Command Options

The TABLET command provides the following options:

- **ON.** Turns on tablet mode, as does setting the system variable TABMODE to 1.
- **OFF.** Turns off tablet mode, as does setting the system variable TABMODE to 0.
- **CAL.** Calibrates your digitizer to an outside coordinate system, such as a paper drawing or map, that is attached to the tablet, enabling you to digitize points on the drawing or map and transform them to coordinates in AutoCAD.
- **CFG.** Enables you to specify areas on the tablet for screen pointing and for menus to use.

The TABLET command offers extensive capabilities for transferring data from outside sources such as maps, drawings, and photographs.

This chapter provided several methods for ensuring accuracy in your drawings. Use the GRID command for a frame of reference; use the SNAP command to limit crosshairs and picks to preset increments. If you need to draw at 90-degree increments, activate the ORTHO command. If you need to align your coordinate system with your drawing, you can change the UCS.

To construct geometrically accurate objects, use coordinate entry and object snap to snap to objects. You can invoke the object snap options temporarily to override any command that requests a point. A running object snap mode sets up a full-time mode and aperture that you still can override. Try to find a good aperture setting to control the reliability and speed of your object snap searches. The toolbars provide easy access to commands you use often.

Throughout the rest of this book, you often see coordinates given in response to prompts with the exercises. You can type them and press Enter, or you can use your pointing device to pick the coordinates if you are sure the pick is accurate. Remember that the crosshairs position is only accurate with snap on or with object snap. Use object snap whenever you can—your drawing productivity will improve, and you can be confident that your work is accurate.

chapter

4

Controlling the Display

Whether you use AutoCAD to draw a tiny machine screw or the side of a barn, you instruct the system to use real-world coordinates. Then, the AutoCAD drawing database maintains accurate sizes of objects. However, this can create a dilemma—for example, how do you represent the side of a barn at full scale on a screen that measures, say, 20 inches maximum?

To create drawings, you need to move around the drawing, locating and magnifying the work areas. This chapter includes the following tools and techniques that you can use to control the view of the graphics screen:

- *Using the ZOOM and PAN commands to magnify and reposition areas*
- *Using the VIEW or DDVIEW commands to manipulate named areas*
- *Using the Aerial View to zoom and pan the display*
- *Using the scroll bars to pan the display*
- *Controlling the display size and resolution*
- *Understanding the virtual screen and regenerations*

Chapter 5, "Working with Model and Paper Space Viewports," discusses controlling the display by using viewports.

What you see in the AutoCAD graphics window is actually a viewport into your drawing, enabling you to zoom in and out (like using a magnifying glass) and pan around (like using a pair of binoculars).

How far can you zoom in? Figure 4.1 shows the solar system, drawn at full scale (about 7 million miles across). If you include enough detail, you can position your view to the edge of the galaxy, and then zoom in (see fig. 4.2) to read the plaque attached to the leg of the lunar lander! AutoCAD is capable of such magnification levels because it is precise within at least 14 significant digits.

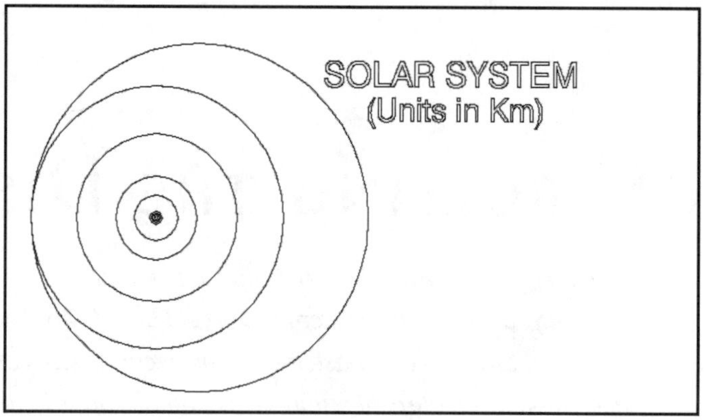

Figure 4.1

The solar system, drawn at full scale.

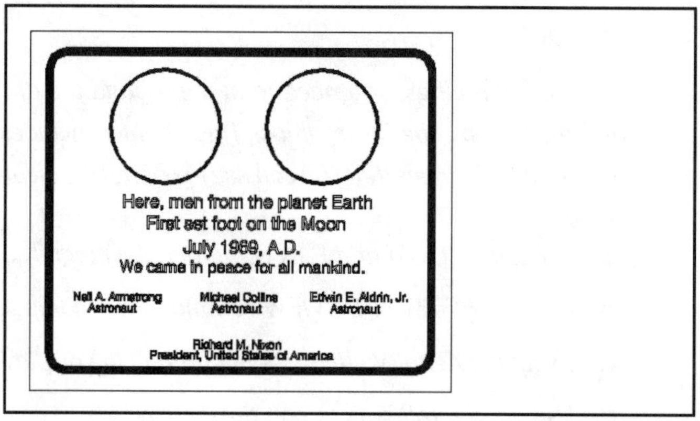

Figure 4.2

View of the lander plaque.

AutoCAD's display controls make drawing easier. Basic display-control commands, such as ZOOM and PAN, function in AutoCAD just like their photographic counterparts. You use the ZOOM command to magnify the drawing for detailed work, and you use the PAN command to shift the drawing view at the current magnification. Panning enables you to work on large objects without having to return to a full-drawing view to determine your drawing location. Use the VIEW and DDVIEW commands to save and restore views by names you supply. Simple controls, such as REDRAW and REGEN, enable you to clean up your drawing or display its most current view.

AutoCAD's display controls are the Aerial View, the scroll bars, the commands issued by the View pull-down menu, and several tools and a flyout on the Standard toolbar (see fig. 4.3).

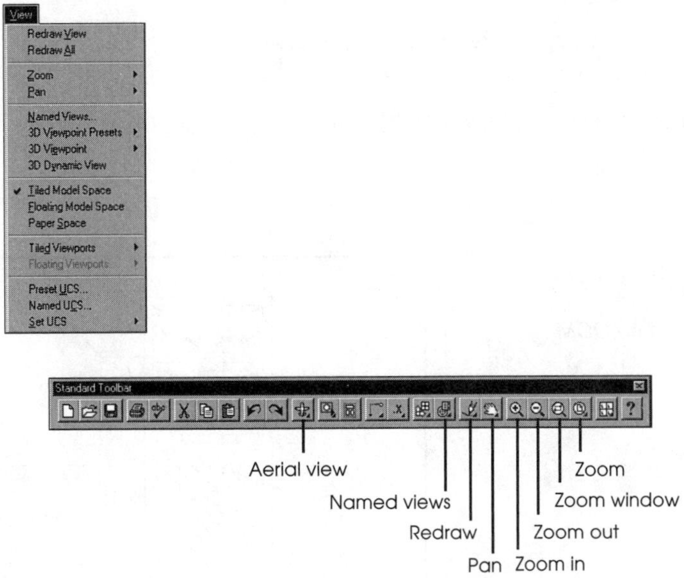

Figure 4.3

The View pull-down menu and related tools.

Controlling the Drawing Display

Whenever you reopen a drawing, AutoCAD displays the last view that was on-screen at the time of the last save (not unlike an electronic bookmark). To look more closely at the current display, you might need to zoom in on the drawing. The most common way to tell AutoCAD what part of the current drawing you want to enlarge is to use the ZOOM command to pick diagonal corners of a box, or *window*, around the area of interest.

Using ZOOM Window

Do the following exercise to become more familiar with the ZOOM Window option. You do not need to pick exact coordinates; just indicate roughly the area you want to see in more detail.

USING ZOOM WINDOW

Begin a new drawing called CHAP04A, using the TOWER486 drawing from the accompanying CD as the prototype.

`Command:` *Choose Zoom Window (Standard)*	Issues the ZOOM command with the Window option
`Command:_zoom`	
`All/Center/Dynamic/Extents/Left/Previous/` `Vmax/Window/<Scale(X/XP)>:_w`	
`First corner:` *Pick ① (see fig. 4.4)*	Sets the window's lower left corner
`Other corner:` *Pick ②*	Sets the window's upper right corner and zooms to the view in figure 4.4

Figure 4.4

Creating a ZOOM Window

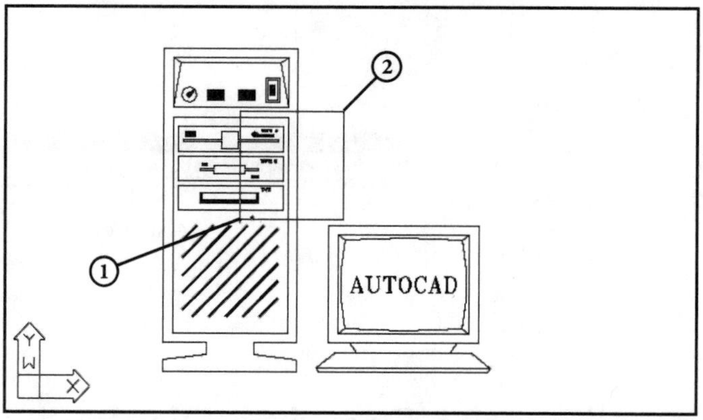

Notice that after you pick the first corner, your cursor changes to a rubber-band box rather than the normal crosshairs. As soon as you pick the second corner, AutoCAD displays the area of the drawing that you enclosed in the window, as shown in figure 4.5. The corners that you pick guide AutoCAD in determining the new area to display.

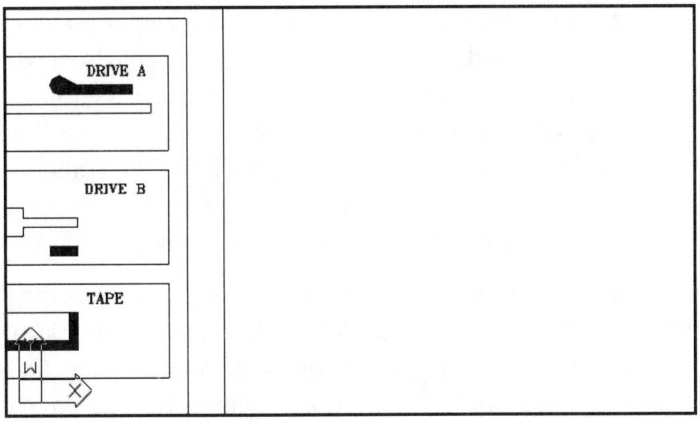

Figure 4.5

The view of the drawing after ZOOM Window.

Note

Zooming a very tall, narrow window or a very long, thin window results in negligible magnification. AutoCAD makes up the difference between the shape of the zoom window you point to and the actual aspect ratio of the drawing window by including more of the drawing either up or to the right. Therefore, you can use this feature to simulate a pan operation.

You do not have to issue the Window option to perform a ZOOM Window. The default ZOOM command accepts two corner points and zooms to the window that they define. In fact, you do not even have to enter ZOOM, because AutoCAD defines Z as an alias that issues the ZOOM command. Just enter Z and then pick two points to perform a ZOOM Window.

Examining ZOOM's Other Options

The Window option enables you to move in closer to your drawing. The ZOOM command includes other options for display management, as described in the following list:

- **All.** This option displays the entire drawing, defined by the larger of the drawing's limits or extents. In a 3D view, All is the same as Extents. All always causes a regeneration.

- **Center.** This option prompts for a center point, and then a magnification (denoted by appending an X) or height (in drawing units). AutoCAD then zooms to the center point and displays the drawing at the specified magnification or height. Pick a new center and press Enter to pan (move the display at the current zoom magnification). The center point you pick becomes the viewport's center. To retain the center point and modify only the magnification or height, press Enter at the new center point prompt.
- **Dynamic.** This option graphically combines the PAN command with the ZOOM command's All and Window options. Dynamic displays an image of the entire generated portion of your drawing, and you use the cursor to tell AutoCAD where to zoom. Dynamic can zoom in or out, or it can pan the current viewport.
- **Extents.** This option displays the entire drawing as large as possible in the current viewport. Extents always causes a regeneration.
- **Left.** This option prompts for a lower left corner point, and then a magnification (denoted by appending an X) or height (in drawing units). AutoCAD then zooms to the lower left corner point and displays the drawing at the specified magnification or height. Pick a new lower left corner and press Enter to pan (move the display at the current zoom magnification). The lower left corner point you pick becomes the viewport's lower left corner. To retain the lower left corner point and modify only the magnification or height, press Enter at the new lower left corner point prompt.
- **Previous.** This option restores a previous display for the current viewport, whether it was generated by the ZOOM, PAN, VIEW, or DVIEW commands. AutoCAD stores up to ten previous views for each viewport; you can step back through them by using the Previous option repeatedly.
- **Vmax.** This option zooms to the currently generated virtual screen to display the maximum possible drawing area without a regeneration.
- **Window.** This option zooms to the rectangular area you specify by picking two diagonally opposite corner points. When you issue the ZOOM command, you can automatically begin a window by picking a point on the screen. Unless the X,Y proportions of the window you specify exactly match the proportions of the viewport, a little extra image width or height shows.

- **Scale(X/XP).** This option uses the current view center as the center point, and zooms by an entered relative factor. The input must be one of three types: a number by itself zooms the image relative to the drawing limits; a number followed by an X displays the image enlarged or reduced relative to the current view; or a number followed by XP zooms the current viewport relative to paper space.

NOTE

Zooms occasionally require a drawing regeneration. The ZOOM command's All and Extents options always cause at least one drawing regeneration. Such regens are not time-consuming in small or simple drawings, but large or complex drawings can take a long time to regenerate. If you use the ZOOM command's Previous or Vmax options, you often can avoid forcing AutoCAD to regenerate your drawing. There is more advice on avoiding regens in the section "Tips for Avoiding Regenerations," later in this chapter.

Keeping Track of Zoom Displays

Every time you zoom in or out, AutoCAD keeps track of the previous display, up to 10 zooms. In the following exercise, you learn how to use the ZOOM command's Previous, Center, Scale, Left, and Extents options.

USING ZOOM PREVIOUS, CENTER, SCALE, LEFT, AND EXTENTS

Continue in the CHAP04A drawing.

If the SNAP button is on, turn it off.

`Command:` *Choose Undo (Standard)*	Undoes the last zoom
`Command:` *Choose View, Zoom, Left*	Issues ZOOM with the Left option
`Command: '_ZOOM All/Center/Dynamic/Extents/Left/ Previous/Vmax/Window/<Scale(X/XP)>: _L`	Sets the lower left corner
`Lower left corner point:` *Use* **INT** *object snap and pick the bottom left of the tape drive (see fig. 4.6) at* ①	Sets the lower left corner

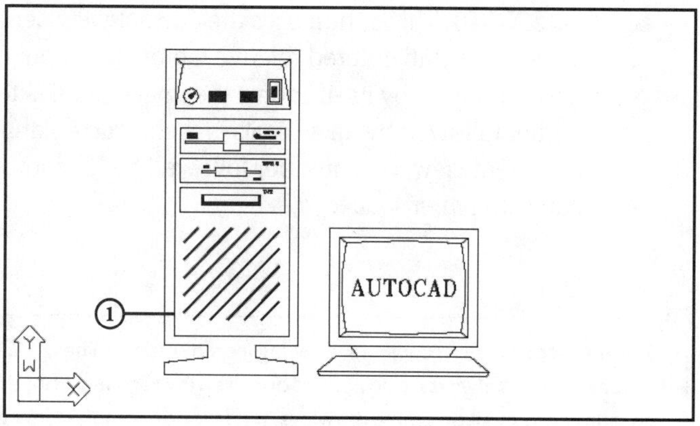

Figure 4.6

The drawing before using ZOOM Left.

`Magnification or Height <26.946>:` **10** ↵	Specifies the window's height and zooms (see fig. 4.7)

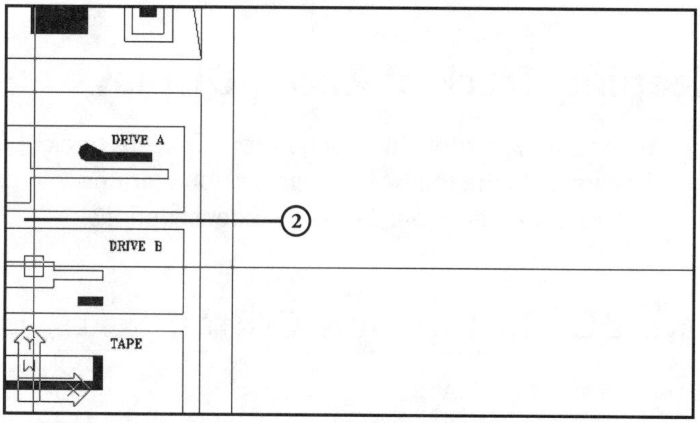

Figure 4.7

After ZOOM Left and before ZOOM Center.

`Command:` *Choose Zoom Center (Standard, Zoom)*	Issues ZOOM with the Center option
`Command: '_zoom` `All/Center/Dynamic/Extents/Left/` `Previous/Vmax/Window/<Scale(X/XP)>:_c`	
`Center point:` *Use* MIDpoint *object snap and pick* ② *(see fig. 4.7) at the top of drive B*	Sets the window's center point
`Magnification or Height <10.000>:` **15** ↵	Specifies the window's height and zooms (see fig. 4.8)

Figure 4.8

After ZOOM Center and before ZOOM 0.25X.

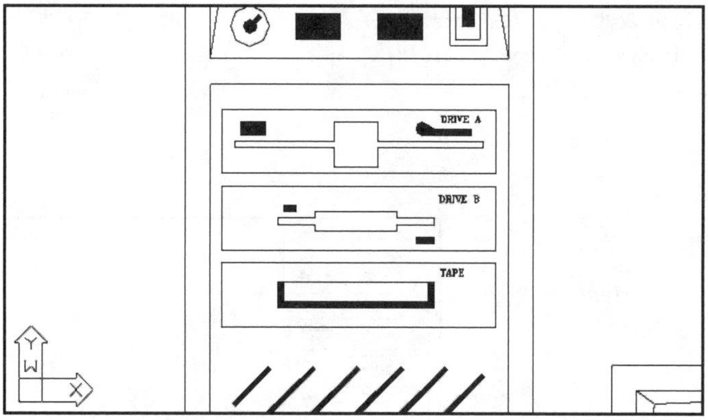

`Command:` ↵ — Repeats the ZOOM command

`'ZOOM`

`All/Center/Dynamic/Extents/Left/Previous/Vmax/Window/<Scale(X/XP)>:` **0.25X** ↵ — Zooms to one-fourth of the current scale (see fig. 4.9)

Figure 4.9

After the ZOOM Scale 0.25X.

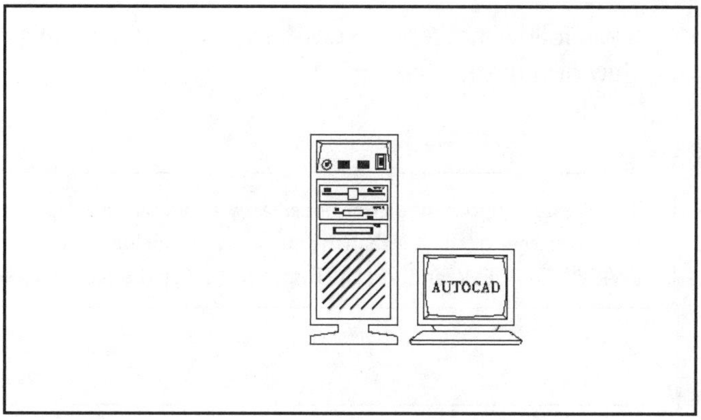

`Command:` ↵ — Repeats the ZOOM command

`'ZOOM`

`All/Center/Dynamic/Extents/Left/Previous/Vmax/Window/<Scale(X/XP)>:` **P** ↵ — Zooms to the previous view

`Command:` ↵ — Repeats the ZOOM command

`'ZOOM`

```
All/Center/Dynamic/Extents/Left/
Previous/Vmax/Window/<Scale(X/XP)>:
E↵
```

Zooms to the drawing extents (see fig. 4.10)

```
Regenerating drawing.
```

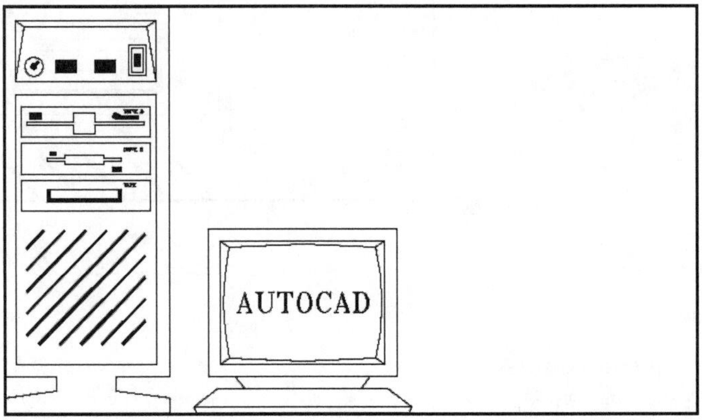

Figure 4.10

After ZOOM Extents

Save your work.

If you follow the steps successfully, the window's height should be filled with a full view of your drawing.

NOTE

The Previous option does not necessarily zoom out. It simply returns to a previous view, whether larger or smaller than the current view, including views created by the PAN, VIEW, DVIEW, DDVIEW, and VPOINT commands, or the Aerial View.

TIP

Use the ZOOM Extents option just before you end your drawing session as a quick check to visually verify whether you drew outside your limits. Another advantage to using ZOOM Extents just before leaving a drawing is that the next person to open that drawing is oriented within the file immediately. You can terminate the zoom to save time while the screen is updating by pressing Esc.

You might have noticed a speed difference between zooms that regenerate the drawing and those that do not. In a complex drawing, this time difference can be considerable. To control drawing regenerations, you need to understand how ZOOM works. The following section explains AutoCAD's virtual screen.

Understanding AutoCAD's Virtual Screen

During a zoom operation, AutoCAD might redisplay the screen at a quick, redraw speed or at a slower, regen speed. When you load a new drawing or use the REGEN command, AutoCAD recalculates the current view to its full 14 places of precision. The program treats the display as a 32,000-by-32,000-pixel screen area, referred to as the *virtual screen*. The virtual screen contains the last regeneration, or recalculation, of the graphic database. AutoCAD translates this calculated image to your actual display area and redraws the current viewport. AutoCAD performs a redraw much quicker than a regeneration. This translation is what occurs when you use the REDRAW command, turn on the grid, turn on layers, or change other settings that cause a redraw.

Many kinds of zooms require only a redraw, not a regeneration. The drawing does not regenerate as long as you do not use certain ZOOM options, zoom outside of the current virtual screen, or zoom so far into tiny detail that AutoCAD cannot translate accurately from the virtual screen. When a zoom occurs without a regeneration, it occurs at redraw speed.

Procedures available for minimizing the frequency of regens are listed at the end of this chapter.

NOTE

Resizing the AutoCAD graphics window also causes a regeneration. If the window is not maximized, you can resize it by moving the cursor to any edge or corner where the cursor changes to a double arrow. Then, press the pick button, drag the corner or edge, and release the button. (If the window is maximized, first click on the maximize button at the upper right corner of the window.)

You not only can alter the current magnification, but you also can slide your current view from side to side (called *panning*). The next section explains how to use the PAN command to position the view to your specifications.

Using PAN To Slide a View

The PAN command enables you to view other areas of the drawing by relocating the drawing across the current viewport. If you are zoomed in and need to draw outside the current viewport, use the PAN command to shift the drawing to display the area of interest. Like a camera pan, the PAN command enables you to move around the drawing at your current magnification.

The Pan Point tool issues the plain PAN command. The Pan submenu on the View pull-down menu and the Pan flyout on the Standard toolbar also include eight Pan tools with predefined displacements. These work the opposite of the way in which many people expect because they are named for the movement of the viewport (like an imaginary camera) as it pans across the drawing. For example, the Pan Left tool pans the viewport to the left, resulting in the drawing image being displaced to the right.

To use the PAN command, you supply AutoCAD with a displacement. A *displacement* is defined by two points, which determine the pan distance and direction. When you specify two points to identify a displacement, you specify a point at which AutoCAD picks up the drawing (the first displacement point) and then specify another point at which to place the drawing (the second displacement point). AutoCAD stretches a rubber-band line between the two displacement points.

In the following exercise, continue to use the CHAP04A drawing. Use the PAN command to shift the display to another area of the drawing.

USING PAN TO SHIFT THE DISPLAY

Continue in the CHAP04A drawing.

If the ORTHO button is on, turn it off.

`Command:` *Choose View, Pan, Point*	Issues the PAN command
`Command: _'pan Displacement:` *Use* INT *object snap and pick the lower right corner of the main tower at* ① (see fig 4.11)	Specifies the first displacement point
`Second point:` *Pick the upper right corner of the monitor at* ②	Specifies the second point and pans

Save the drawing for a later exercise.

Figure 4.11

Using the PAN command to show displacement.

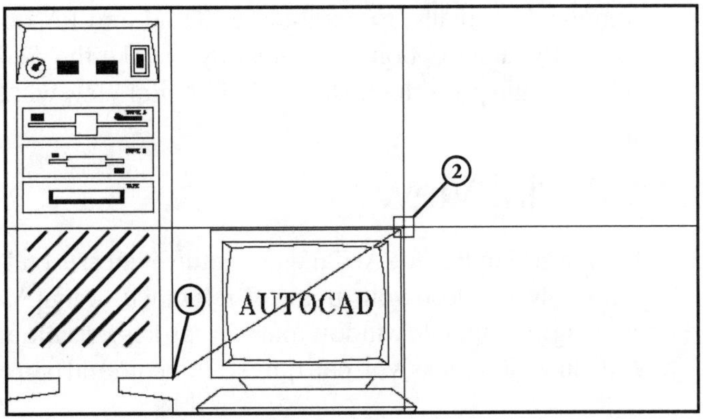

Your screen should appear as shown in figure 4.12.

Figure 4.12

The view after the PAN command.

NOTE

You also can pan left, right, up, down, and in various combinations of directions by selecting from the Pan pull-down menu or its tool flyout. These methods shift the view approximately half the window in the indicated direction. In addition, you can use the Aerial View and the ZOOM Center and Left options to perform similar pan operations.

You've explored some of the more common options of the ZOOM and PAN commands, and might be wondering if zooming and panning can be combined without further menu selections. Is there a ZOON command? Perhaps a PAM command? Actually, to combine a ZOOM and PAN operation, you can use the ZOOM Dynamic option, or preferably, invoke the Aerial View. The next section illustrates the powerful features of the Aerial View window.

Using Aerial View

As its name implies, the Aerial View feature is most useful in a large drawing, in which you easily can lose your point of reference. Aerial View can display the entire drawing in a separate window that you can keep visible and immediately accessible. With only a few picks, you can quickly indicate and pan or zoom to any desired area.

Using the Aerial View and Scroll Bars To Zoom and Pan

AutoCAD Release 13 for Windows includes two viewing features not available in the DOS version (and most other versions) of AutoCAD: Aerial View and graphics window scroll bars. You can use one or both of these features, depending on your configured display driver. If you have configured AutoCAD with either the "WHIP" driver, or the Windows accelerated display-list driver (with the Display-list option on), then you can use the Aerial View, a separate window in which you can specify zooms and pans, as well as the graphics window scroll bars to pan the drawing. If you have configured AutoCAD with the nondisplay-list Windows driver by Autodesk, then you can cannot use the Aerial View, only the scroll bars.

Activating the Aerial View

The 'DSVIEWER command displays the current extents or virtual screen (whichever is less—usually the entire drawing) in the Aerial View window. Depending on the Aerial View option settings, you might need to redisplay Aerial View and/or click in the Aerial View to use it.

TIP

When the Aerial View is open, choosing the Aerial View tool both closes it and returns to the AutoCAD window.

The Aerial View window (see fig. 4.13) contains the pull-down menus View, Mode, and Options, and also contains a toolbar.

Figure 4.13

The Aerial View window activated.

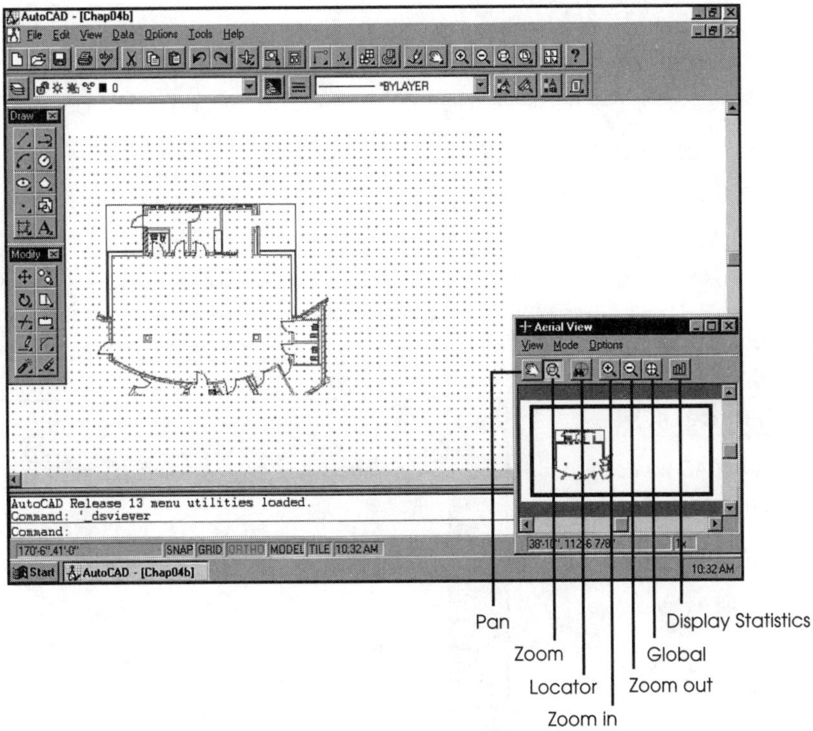

The Zoom mode (on the Mode pull-down menu) is selected and active by default. You simply pick two points in the Aerial View window to zoom the AutoCAD graphics window, as shown in the following exercise. To fully appreciate the productivity boost compared to using ZOOM D or multiple zooms, use a moderately complex drawing for this exercise. If you did not install the AutoCAD sample drawings, use any other moderately complex drawing.

Activating Aerial View and Using it To Zoom

This exercise assumes that AutoCAD is configured for the default accelerated display-list driver. See Appendix A, "Installation and Configuration," for details on video display configuration.

Begin a new drawing named CHAP04B, using the ROOMPLAN drawing from the accompanying CD as a prototype.

Notice how long the drawing takes to regen, and compare it to how quickly it zooms later in this exercise.

`Command:` *Choose Aerial View (Standard, Tool Windows)*	Issues the DSVIEWER command
`_DSVIEWER`	Displays the Aerial View window
Click on the Aerial View title bar	Highlights title bar and activates window

Press and drag on the title bar to position the Aerial View window, as shown in figure 4.13.

The Aerial View window is now active, with its default Zoom tool highlighted and active.

Pick a point in the middle of the building, then a second point beyond the upper right corner	Defines a zoom window and zooms the AutoCAD graphics window to its upper right corner (see fig. 4.14)

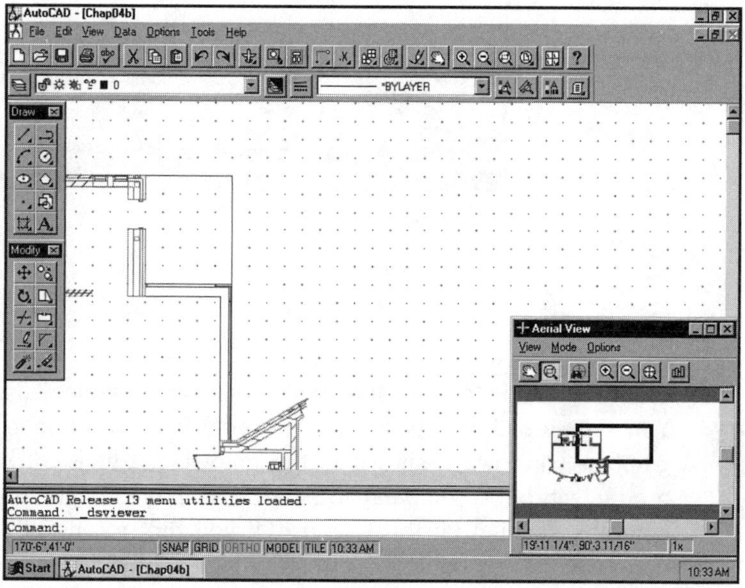

Figure 4.14

AutoCAD window zoomed by Aerial View.

Click in the AutoCAD window	Returns to AutoCAD

Save your work.

Notice that in the Aerial View window a heavy rectangular line now indicates the zoomed area of the drawing.

Note

The current Aerial View configuration is saved in the ACAD.INI file when you exit AutoCAD.

Note

Like most forms of ZOOM, you can use Aerial View transparently within most AutoCAD commands in model space (in tiled or floating viewports); however, it is disabled in paper space and viewports displaying perspective views.

Aerial View accomplishes its action in the AutoCAD window by issuing the ZOOM command, so you can use ZOOM Previous to return the AutoCAD window to previous views.

Note

The U and UNDO commands also can return the AutoCAD window to previous views. In some cases, however, AutoCAD also can undo previous commands.

Examining the Aerial View Tools and Menu

Although Zoom is the Aerial View default, the Aerial View menu bar offers several menus and tools. The aerial view menus are described in the following list.

- **View.** Offers the choice of Zoom In, Zoom Out, and Global. Zoom In magnifies the image in the Aerial View window 2x to display less of the drawing, Zoom Out shrinks the image .5x to display more of the drawing, and Global zooms to display the entire drawing. None of the options affects the AutoCAD window.
- **Mode.** Offers the choice of Zoom and Pan. Zoom magnifies the drawing in the AutoCAD window to the area defined by the two corner points you pick in the Aerial View window. Pan shifts the drawing in the AutoCAD window to the view you pick in the Aerial View window (does not change the zoom magnification). The Aerial View window displays a dashed box sized to the current view to aid your view selection.

- **Options.** Offers the choice of Auto Viewport, Dynamic Update, Locator Magnification, and Display Statistics. When Auto Viewport is checked, AutoCAD displays the model space view of the active viewport automatically; otherwise, AutoCAD updates the view only when you click on the title bar of the Aerial View window. When Dynamic Update is checked, AutoCAD updates the view while you edit the drawing. Locator Magnification is used with the Locator tool, described in the following list. It enables you to adjust the magnification under the cursor, up to 32 times. Display Statistics presents a dialog box of display driver information.

The Aerial View toolbar contains tools for the following functions:

- **Pan.** The crosshairs change to a dashed-line box the same size as the current view box. You specify the next view for the AutoCAD window by dragging the box to a new position and picking in the Aerial View window.
- **Zoom.** Operates similarly to AutoCAD's ZOOM window. Pick two points, or press and drag to create a rectangle in the Aerial View window. When you pick, or release the button at the second point, the AutoCAD window zooms to the new view. To zoom out, make the view box larger; to zoom in, make it smaller. Zoom is the default tool.
- **Locator.** Displays a magnified view (up to 32 times) directly under the cursor. When you press on the tool and drag the cursor, a zoom window box drags with it and the image in the Aerial View window moves in real time. You can drag the cursor anywhere on the entire Windows screen—it behaves as if the drawing covers the entire screen regardless of the size of the AutoCAD window. When the desired view is shown, release the button and AutoCAD zooms to display the view that was in the cursor's zoom window. This option enables you to discover a small detail in a cluttered drawing.
- **Zoom In.** Magnifies the Aerial View image 2x. Does not affect AutoCAD window.
- **Zoom Out.** Shrinks the Aerial View image .5x. Does not affect AutoCAD window.
- **Global.** Shows the entire drawing in the Aerial View image. Does not affect AutoCAD window.
- **Display Statistics.** Shows display driver information.

TIP

> Backing out of an active Aerial View function can be tricky. To cancel a zoom, press the Enter button on the pointing device, or click on the Zoom tool. To cancel a pan, click on the Zoom tool. To cancel a locator function, keep a portion of the active locator box within the Aerial View window, then release the pick button.

In addition to these items, you also can use the Aerial View window's scroll bars to pan the view in the Aerial View window. The scroll bars are at the right side and bottom of the Aerial View window. You can click on the arrow buttons at the top/bottom or left/right of the scroll bars, or drag the slider box (the box in the center of the scroll bar) up/down or left/right to pan the view in the Aerial View window. The scroll bars do not affect the AutoCAD window.

NOTE

> When instructed to activate Aerial View in the following exercises, click on the DSVIEWER icon on the toolbar and/or click in the Aerial View as needed to display the Aerial View window and highlight its title bar. Aerial View then is ready to pan or zoom your drawing. To return to the AutoCAD window when the Aerial View title bar is highlighted, simply click in the AutoCAD window.

Try several of the Aerial View commands and options in the following exercise.

Using Aerial View Commands and Options

Continue in the CHAP04B drawing from the preceding exercise.

Activate the Aerial View *window and choose* Mode, Pan	Displays cursor as a dashed box

Notice that the Pan tool and Pan on the Mode pull-down menu are now the defaults.

Drag the box to the lower left corner of the building and click	Zooms AutoCAD window to match area in box
In Aerial View, choose the Zoom Out tool	Displays more of the drawing in the Aerial View window (see fig. 4.15)

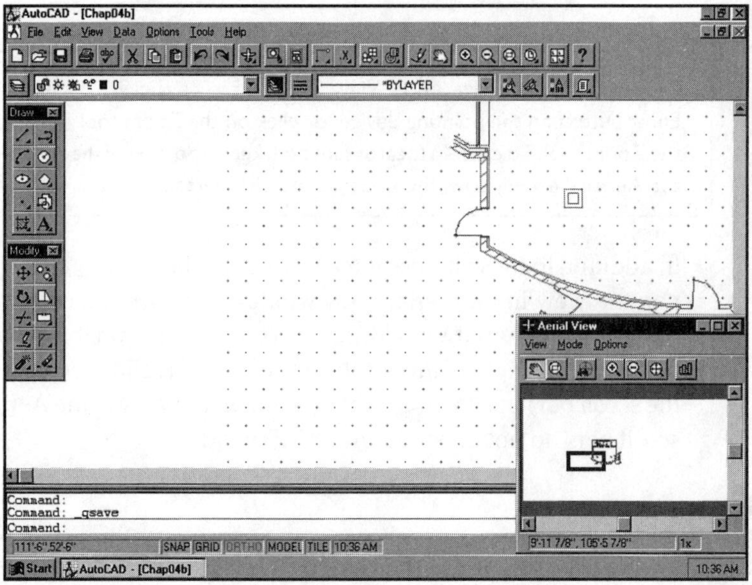

Figure 4.15

Aerial View window zoomed out, with Pan active.

In the Aerial View window, choose the Global tool	Displays full image (entire drawing) in the Aerial View
Choose the Zoom Out tool three times	Magnifies view area three times

Notice that these last three steps left the AutoCAD window unchanged. Next you use the Locator tool.

Choose Options, Locator Magnification	Displays the Magnification dialog box
Enter **4** *in the Magnification input box that appears and choose OK*	Sets Aerial View to magnify area under Locator box 4x
Press on the Locator tool and drag the Locator box that appears around until the left building support column appears in the Aerial View, then release (see fig. 4.16)	Zooms Aerial View window to match Locator box until you release, then Zooms AutoCAD window to match Aerial View, then restores prior Aerial View

Figure 4.16

Using the Aerial View locator function.

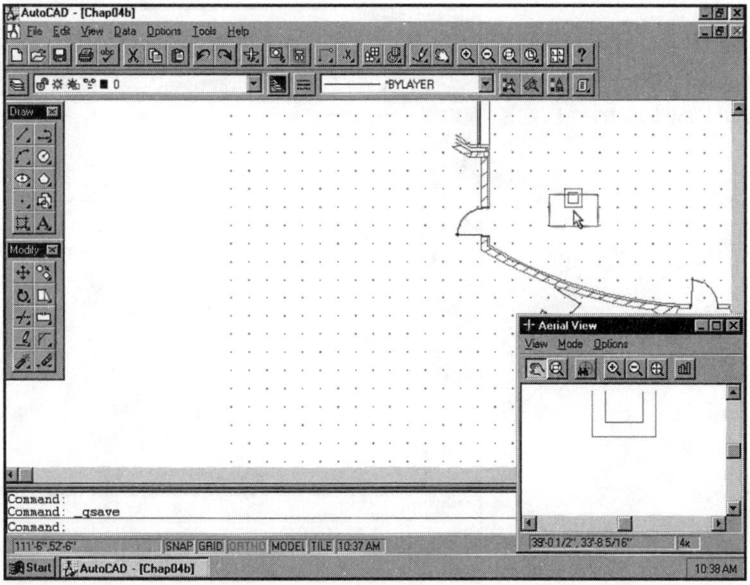

Choose Options, Locator Magnification, *then choose* - *three times, then choose* OK	Sets Locator box Magnification back to 1x
Press on the Locator tool and drag locator box to the left building support column, shown in figure 4.17, then release	Zooms Aerial View, then when you release, zooms AutoCAD window to match and restores Aerial View

Aerial View now returns to its previous view (see fig. 4.17).

In Aerial View, choose Global, then Zoom Out, then Zoom and specify a window to match the view in figure 4.15. Then choose Zoom In. Next you use the scroll bars to position the view in Aerial View.

In the Aerial View window, press and drag the right-side slider box down, and the bottom-side slider box to the left	Pans the Aerial View to approximately match the AutoCAD window's view
Click on the scroll bar's arrow buttons	Fine-adjusts the Aerial View to match the AutoCAD window's view

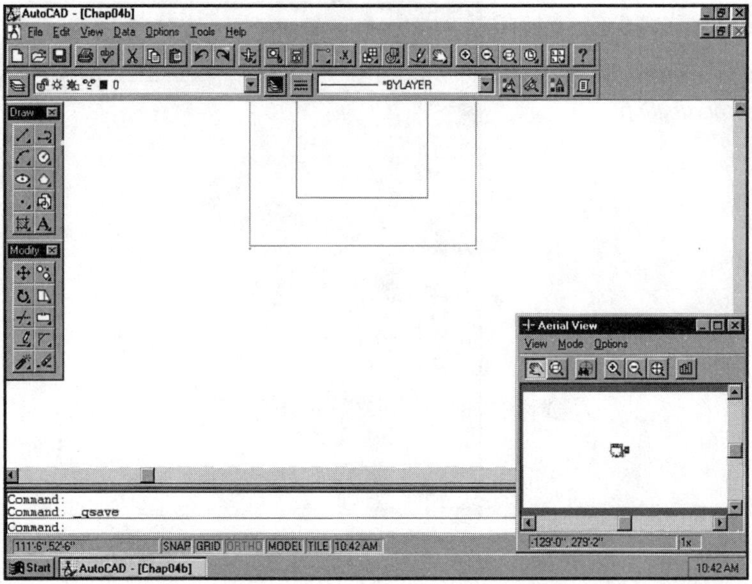

Figure 4.17

AutoCAD window after Aerial View Locate.

Click in the AutoCAD window, select several objects, and enter **E**	Erases the objects and updates Aerial View
`Command:` **U** ↵	Unerases the erasure in AutoCAD and updates Aerial View
Activate the Aerial View window, then choose Options, Dynamic Update	Turns off updating during editing
In the AutoCAD window, select several objects and enter **E**	Erases the objects but does not update Aerial View
Activate the Aerial View window	Updates Aerial View
Choose Global, then specify a zoom window enclosing the entire building	Restores original views
Choose Options, Dynamic Update	Turns updating back on

Save your changes.

TIP

You might want to turn off Dynamic Update to speed up complex operations.

If you configure AutoCAD with the Windows driver by Autodesk instead of the accelerated display-list driver, you cannot use the Aerial View. You can, however, use the scroll bars in the AutoCAD graphics window to pan the drawing.

TIP

There is no reason that the Aerial View needs to be small—you can resize it like any other window. You can see more detail and pan and zoom more accurately with a large Aerial View.

Saving and Restoring Working Views by Name

As you develop a drawing, you might find that your zooms and pans frequently return to the same area. You can expedite the development process by naming a selected window of the current display. You can use either the VIEW command or the View Control dialog box (DDVIEW command).

The VIEW command has the following five options:

- **?.** This option displays a list of all saved viewport configurations when you enter an asterisk (*). The ? option lists a specific set of views when you enter names using wild cards. The list includes an M or P with the view's name to indicate whether the view is defined in model space (M) or paper space (P). See Chapter 5, "Working with Model and Paper Space Viewports," for a discussion of model space and paper space.
- **Delete.** This option prompts you to enter the name of a view to delete. You can use wild cards to delete a group of similarly named views.
- **Restore.** This option prompts you for the name of a saved view to display in the current viewport.
- **Save.** This option saves the current viewport's view.
- **Window.** This option enables you to define a window to save as a view by specifying its corners. You are prompted to enter a name for the view.

NOTE

You can rename an existing view by using the RENAME command or the Rename dialog box (the DDRENAME command). The RENAME command is described in Chapter 2, "Organizing Drawings with Layers."

The following exercise shows you how to use AutoCAD's VIEW command to save and restore named views.

Using VIEW To Save and Restore a View

Reopen the CHAP04A drawing from an earlier exercise, then zoom to the view shown in figure 4.18.

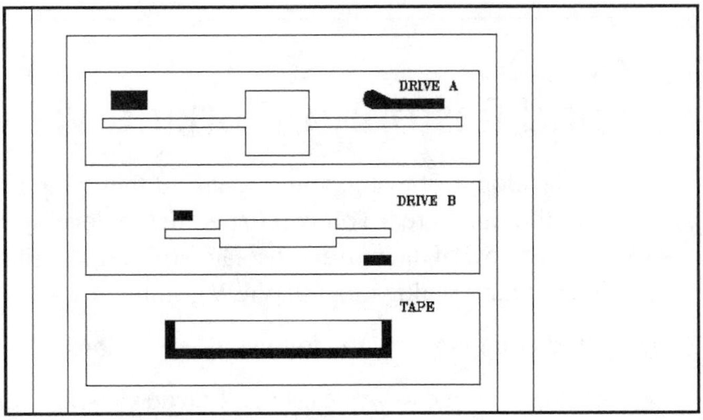

Figure 4.18

The saved and restored view named DRIVES.

`Command:` **VIEW** ↵	
`?/Delete/Restore/Save/Window:` **S** ↵	Issues the Save option
`View name to save:` **DRIVES** ↵	Saves the current view under the name DRIVES
`Command:` *Choose Zoom Extents (Standard, Zoom)*	Zooms to display the entire drawing as large as possible (see fig. 4.19)

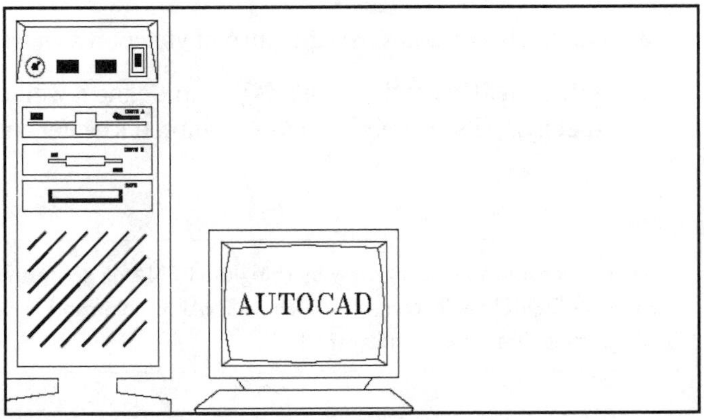

Figure 4.19

The view after ZOOM Extents.

Command: **VIEW** ↵

?/Delete/Restore/Save/Window: **R** ↵ — Issues the Restore option

View name to restore: **DRIVES** ↵ — Restores the saved view named DRIVES, as shown in figure 4.18

Save the drawing.

TIP

Two useful named views are L for Limits or A for All. Both are easy to type and can be used rather than the ZOOM command's All option to avoid regenerations. Use the view names LL, LR, UL, and UR to easily restore a drawing's four quadrants. Similarly, use a standard named view called PLOT for consistency in plotting.

The View Control dialog box (see fig. 4.20) is a useful tool when saving and restoring multiple view names. Enter DDVIEW or choose View, Named View to display this dialog box. The Views list box shows all defined view names. Use the buttons at the bottom of the dialog box to restore a named view, create a new view, delete an existing view, or see a description of a view's general parameters. The edit box enables you to type or change view names. As is the case with most dialog boxes, you can choose OK to accept the most recent changes in the dialog box; click on Cancel to disregard the changes.

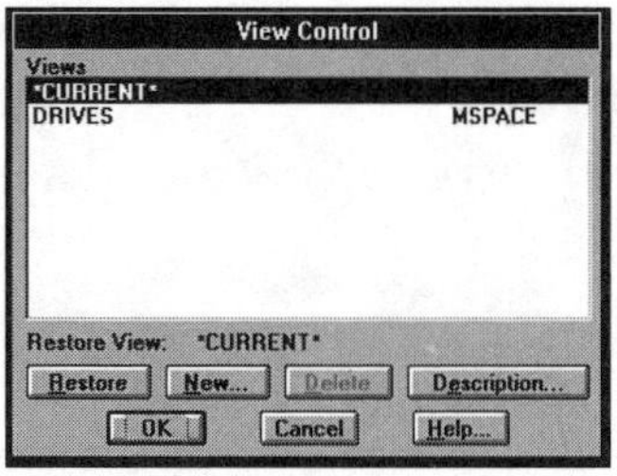

Figure 4.20

The View Control dialog box.

In the following exercise, you use the View Control dialog box to restore and save named views of the drawing.

Using DDVIEW To Work with Views

Continue from the preceding exercise.

`Command:` *Choose Zoom All (Standard, Zoom)*	Returns to the full view
`Regenerating drawing.`	Notice that it regenerates
`Command:` *Choose* View, Named Views	Issues the DDVIEW command and displays the View Control dialog box
Select DRIVES *in the Views list box, then choose* Restore, *then* OK	Restores the view named DRIVES and closes the dialog box
`Command:` *Choose Zoom Previous (Standard, Zoom)*	Issues ZOOM with Previous option and restores previous view
`Command:` *Choose* View, Named Views	Issues the DDVIEW command and displays the View Control dialog box
Choose New	Opens the Define New View dialog box
Choose the Define Window *radio button*	Enables (ungrays) the Window button and corner coordinates
Choose Window	Closes dialog boxes and prompts for window corner points
`First Corner:` *Pick the lower left corner of the monitor*	
`Other Corner:` *Pick the upper right corner of the monitor*	Specifies window to save and reopens dialog boxes
Type MONITOR, *then choose Save View*	Names the windowed view MONITOR and closes the Define New View dialog box
Choose OK	Closes the View Control dialog box and saves the view
`Command:` ↵	Repeats DDVIEW and displays the view names DRIVES and MONITOR in the View Control dialog box
Select MONITOR, *then choose* Restore, *then* OK	Closes the dialog box and restores the MONITOR view

Controlling Display Size and Resolution

Adding more detail to a drawing increases its file size. AutoCAD uses the virtual screen to keep only a portion of the drawing generated at all times. With a small, uncomplicated drawing, the time difference between a redraw and a regen is negligible. But as your drawing file gets larger, the calculations necessary to regenerate the virtual screen take longer.

Usually, you use a PAN or ZOOM command at redraw (fast) speed to move between views in the generated portion of the drawing. At times, however, AutoCAD requires a regen (slow) to recalculate a different set of data that lies outside the virtual screen. The next section discusses a method of balancing display speed against drawing accuracy.

Using VIEWRES To Control Smooth Curve Regeneration

The AutoCAD VIEWRES (VIEW RESolution) command controls the speed of your zooms and regenerations in two ways. First, it turns fast zoom on and off. *Fast zoom* means that AutoCAD maintains a large virtual screen so that it can do most pans and zooms at redraw speed. If fast zoom is off, all pans and zooms cause a regeneration. Second, VIEWRES determines how finely the curves should be displayed. When circles or arcs are tiny, AutoCAD need display only a few straight lines to fool your eye into seeing smooth curves. When arcs are larger, AutoCAD needs more segments (or vectors) to make an arc appear smoother. The VIEWRES circle zoom percent tells AutoCAD how smooth you want your curves, and AutoCAD then determines the number of segments necessary for the display contents.

NOTE

Views defined in model space (either tiled or floating model space viewports) are restored in model space, and views defined in paper space are restored in paper space. See Chapter 5, "Working with Model and Paper Space Viewports," for details on paper space.

Figures 4.21 and 4.22 demonstrate the effect of VIEWRES on circles.

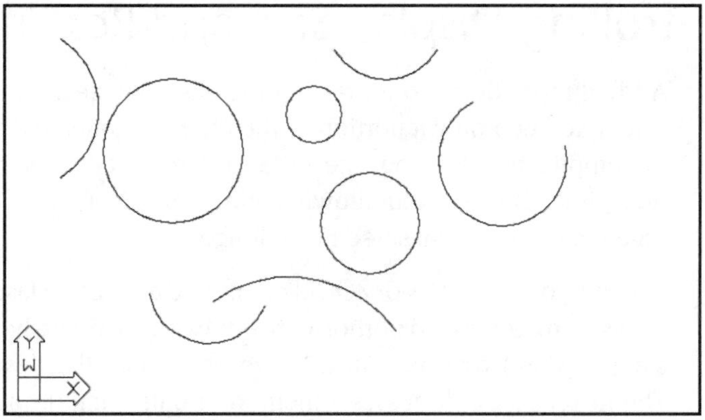

Figure 4.21

Smooth curves with a normal VIEWRES setting of 100.

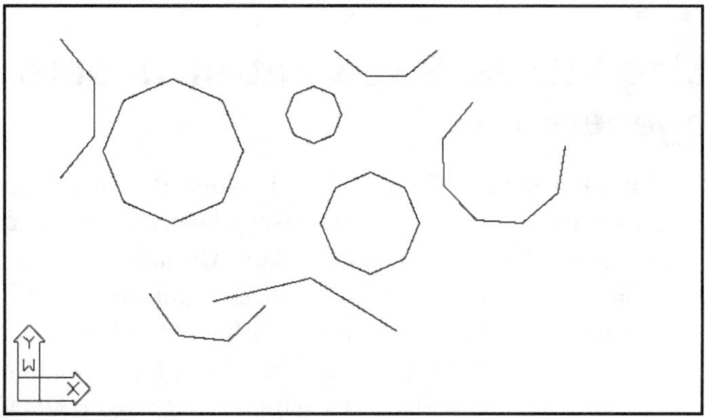

Figure 4.22

Curves after the VIEWRES command.

Fast zooms must be turned on to enable AutoCAD's large virtual screen, which effectively decreases the frequency of regens. When fast zoom is off, PAN and ZOOM operations always regenerate the drawing. So then, why not always keep fast zooms on? The minor disadvantage of fast zoom is that when a regeneration is required, AutoCAD takes longer than if fast zoom is off, because AutoCAD must then recalculate a larger area.

NOTE

When fast zoom is off, pans and zooms always cause a drawing regeneration. Although you probably never should turn off fast zoom, you might find that AutoCAD is more efficient when zooming large text-filled drawings or doing work that often causes regenerations, even if fast zoom is on. In addition, setting the VIEWRES circle zoom percent too large can cause slow regenerations.

NOTE

VIEWRES has no effect on the plotted smoothness of circles and arcs—only the way circles and arcs appear on the screen.

TIP

The default VIEWRES setting of 100 can yield some confusing results. Some unfortunate side effects include door swings that look like stop signs and lines trimmed against an arc appearing too short. On today's more powerful PCs, try setting VIEWRES to a much higher value in the prototype drawing, such as 5000. This enables you to zoom in much further without curves becoming faceted.

Understanding REDRAW and REGEN

You can use two commands—REDRAW and REGEN—to refresh the graphics window to provide a clearer look at your drawing. Using REDRAW simply removes extraneous blips and pixels left over from prior editing operations. However, issuing the REGEN command recalculates the drawing database and updates the virtual screen—a more CPU-intensive task. Therefore, for larger drawings, regenerations take time. Experienced AutoCAD users know that a desirable objective of drawing development is to avoid using REGEN. The next section lists some tips, tricks, and techniques to avoid, limit, or speed up the redraws and regenerations required.

Tips for Avoiding Regenerations

Although it is impossible to develop an entire drawing without a single redraw or regeneration, you can employ methods that greatly reduce the need to redraw or regen. As the situation arises, use any or all of the following suggestions:

- **Set BLIPMODE OFF.** Avoid placing blips in your drawing with each pick to minimize the frequency of redraws.
- **Set FILLMODE OFF.** Replace wide, filled-in object regions (polylines, solids, and traces) with their boundaries only. On some slower displays and plotters, this setting could enhance the regeneration speed or plotting time.
- **Set QTEXT ON.** Replace lines of text with approximate rectangular boundaries to speed the time required to regenerate more elaborate fonts. See Chapter 17, "Annotation with Text," for a discussion of QTEXT.

- **Use ZOOM Vmax.** Choose this option to zoom out as much as possible in the current viewport without forcing a regeneration.
- **Use ZOOM Dynamic.** Choose this option (with fast zoom on) to enable both panning and zooming without forcing a regeneration.
- **Avoid frequent ZOOM All or Extents.** These options always cause a regen.
- **Use LAYER Freeze.** Frozen layers are not subject to regeneration; therefore, any required regens are speeded up. Make sure you freeze any layers that are not involved in your current editing processes.
- **Use REGENAUTO OFF.** With this setting, whenever AutoCAD requires a regen, you are prompted to proceed. Then, you can decline the regen and try another strategy. If you perform many linetype or text style changes, for example, turn off REGENAUTO until all the changes are made. AutoCAD then queues the regen until appropriate.
- **Adjust VIEWRES.** Keep fast zooms on. Then, maintain a circle zoom percentage large enough to discern true circles from polygons, but still within an acceptable regeneration time. This value depends on the CPU speed, so experiment!
- **Use VIEWs.** Define view names in prototype drawings to make them automatically available in generated drawings. Saving and restoring views minimizes the number of regens.
- **Limit active VIEWPORTs.** Turn off any viewports that you don't need, although viewports with zoomed drawing portions can save time. See Chapter 5, "Working with Model and Paper Space Viewports," for a discussion on viewports.
- **Use DSVIEWER.** The Aerial View enables you to maintain the big picture on-screen at all times, without sacrificing a regen.
- **Check your LIMITS.** Make sure that the LIMITS match the area within which you actually draw. For example, keeping the default LIMITS of 0,0 to 12,9 while drawing out to 50000,50000 usually increases the likelihood of regeneration when zooming in and out. If your drawing needs these new limits, zoom to this new size and set LIMITS to the sheet size or to a zoom factor slightly larger than the extents.

- **Use the Zoom Limits tool.** This tool appears on the ZOOM flyout of the Standard toolbar. To avoid regens when zooming back to the full drawing view, make sure the drawing extents do not exceed your defined limits.

AutoCAD offers many ways to get around the graphics window, including zooming, panning, Aerial View, scroll bars, and using view names. The ZOOM command adjusts the display magnification and the PAN command shifts the display at the current zoom level. The DSVIEWER command (Aerial View) creates another drawing window for intuitive zooms and pans. Scroll bars, a Microsoft Windows feature, provide another panning method. Finally, the VIEW command saves and restores selected drawing areas for convenient redisplay.

chapter

5

Working with Model and Paper Space Viewports

In Chapter 4, you learned to adjust the displayed view with the ZOOM and PAN commands which enable you to determine exactly what portion of your model is to be displayed. But there are times when you want to have multiple views of your model displayed in the drawing window, such as is shown in figure 5.1.

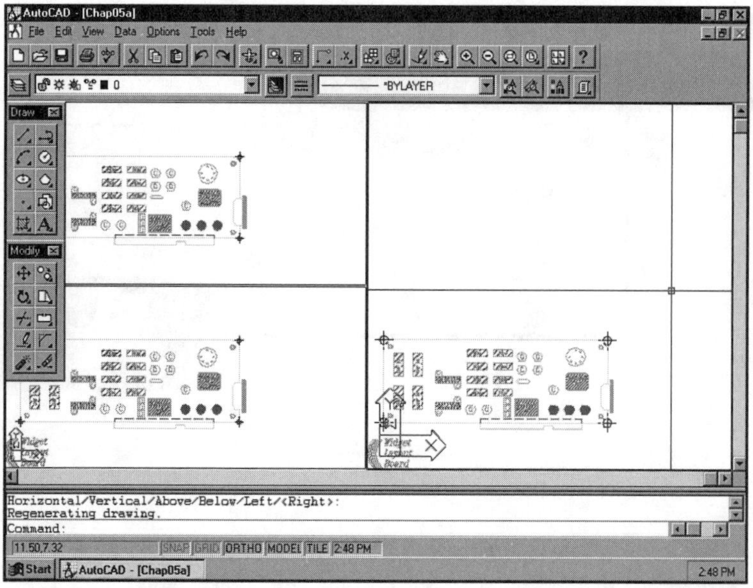

Figure 5.1

A drawing window with multiple viewports.

In this chapter you learn how to display and control several views on your monitor using multiple viewports. You can subdivide the drawing window into two or more viewports and view different parts of your drawing in different viewports. You might want to have multiple viewports for a variety of reasons. For example, you might want multiple views of your model to facilitate a side-by-side comparison of different areas of the model. Multiple views also enable you to display a magnified view of the area you want to edit while simultaneously having an overall view of the model for reference (similar to the effect you get with the aerial viewer). You can eliminate switching back and forth between different views of the model by displaying the needed views simultaneously in the drawing window.

When you subdivide the drawing window, you create *tiled viewports*—so called because the viewports must fill the drawing window like tiles. Creating tiled viewports and controlling what is displayed in each viewport is relatively easy. In the first part of this chapter, you will learn to how to create and manipulate multiple tiled viewports.

There are certain restrictions that govern the creation of additional tiled viewports:

- The additional tiled viewports are created by subdividing the current viewport. This means that the additional viewports get smaller and smaller in size as more are created.

- Additional viewports can only be created in preset arrangements.
- Although there are certain settings that can be made individually for each viewport, layer visibility is not one of them. You cannot have a layer turned off in one viewport and have that same layer displayed in another viewport.

If you find these restrictions limiting, you can use *floating viewports*, which overcome these restrictions. With floating viewports, you are free to determine the size of each viewport, the arrangement of the viewports, and the layer visibility settings for each viewport. Whereas tiled viewports exist in the drawing environment called *tiled viewport mode* or *model space* (the environment you have used so far), floating viewports exist in the environment called *paper space*. Just as a piece of paper has two sides, these two environments are like the two sides of an AutoCAD drawing. In this chapter, you learn how to switch between the two environments and how to use paper space as a drawing and editing tool. Paper space is a vital tool for composing a drawing with multiple views at multiple scales. The use of paper space as a composition tool is not covered in this chapter but is covered in detail in Chapter 6, "Plotting and Sheet Composition."

Working with Tiled Viewports

AutoCAD has two distinct drawing environments: paper space with floating viewports and tiled viewport mode with tiled viewports. You use the system variable TILEMODE to switch between these environments. TILEMODE is set to 1 (by default), which is tiled viewport mode (also referred to as model space). To switch to the paper space environment, set TILEMODE to 0. The menu item Paper Space in the View pull-down menu sets TILEMODE to 0 (off) and issues the PSPACE command to make sure you are in paper space itself, not a floating model space viewport within paper space. Choosing View, Tiled Model Space sets TILEMODE to 1 (on). More on paper space and floating viewports later; for this portion of the chapter on tiled viewports, you need to continue to work exclusively in model space only. So, be sure that there is a check mark next to the menu item Tiled Model Space.

To display multiple views, you must use multiple viewports. A *viewport* is a rectangular area in which a single view of your model appears. In previous chapters, you have used only a single tiled viewport that has automatically been made equal in size to your drawing window. In effect, your drawing window has been your single viewport.

To display and control multiple tiled viewports, use the VPORTS command.

The VPORTS command provides the following options:

- **Save.** Enables you to save and name the current viewport configuration.
- **Restore.** Enables you to restore a saved viewport configuration.
- **Delete.** Enables you to delete a saved viewport configuration.
- **Join.** Enables you to merge the current viewport with another viewport. The resulting viewport also must be rectangular in shape.
- **SIngle.** Enables you to restore the drawing window to a single viewport. The current viewport configuration is lost unless previously saved.
- **?.** Enables you to list any or all saved viewport configurations. You then can enter * for all viewports, or any combination of names or wild cards.
- **2.** Enables you to divide the current viewport into two viewports.
- **3.** Enables you to divide the current viewport into three viewports (the default).
- **4.** Enables you to divide the current viewport into four viewports.

To access the VPORTS command using the pull-down menus, choose View, Tiled Viewports (see fig. 5.2). Each menu item in the Tiled Viewports submenu triggers the VPORTS command and then the appropriate option.

Figure 5.2

The Tiled Viewports submenu.

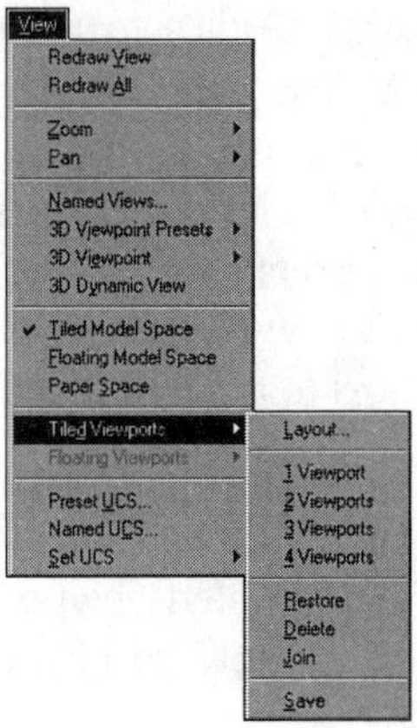

In the sections that follow, you learn how to create and use tiled viewports.

Opening Tiled Viewports

Each tiled viewport displays a single view of the drawing. To display multiple views in your drawing window, you create additional viewports. You divide the current viewport into as many as four viewports. In the Tiled Viewports submenu, the following options create the additional viewports:

- **Layout.** Displays an icon menu with various tiled viewport arrangements that you can choose from. Whereas the other menu items that create viewports create the additional viewports from the current viewport, the Layout menu item does not. If you already have multiple viewports opened, the current viewport is expanded to a single viewport and then subdivided into the arrangement of viewports selected by you.
- **2 Viewports.** Divides the current viewport into two viewports. You can divide the current viewport vertically (the default) or horizontally (see fig. 5.3).
- **3 Viewports.** Divides the current viewport into three viewports. You can divide the current viewport vertically or horizontally, placing the major viewport above, below, left, or right, which is the default (see fig. 5.3).
- **4 Viewports.** Divides the current viewport into four equal viewports (see fig. 5.3).

The initial view in each of the new tiled viewports is the same as in the previous current viewport. You learn to change the individual views in the next section.

TIP

If you can choose to divide the current viewport vertically or horizontally, which should you choose? Choose the option that gives you viewports that best fit the area(s) of your model that you need to see. If the area's extents is greater in the X than in the Y direction, divide horizontally. If the area's extents is greater in the Y than in the X direction, divide vertically.

Figure 5.3

The various arrangements of viewports you can choose from.

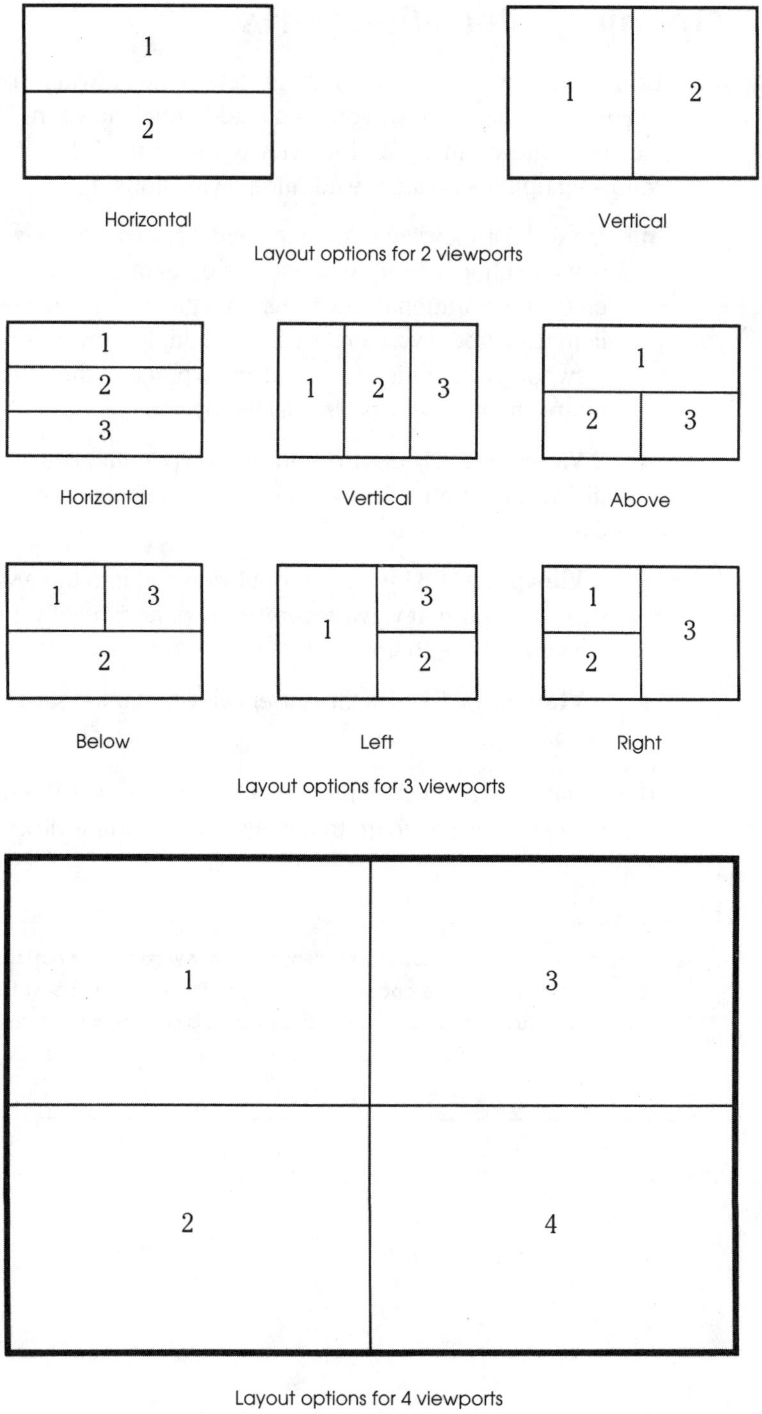

In the following exercise, you display three views of a model simultaneously.

CREATING TILED VIEWPORTS

Begin a new drawing named CHAP05A using the accompanying CD drawing BOARD as the prototype.

`Command:` *Choose* View, Tiled Viewports, 3 Viewports	Issues the VPORTS command using the 3 Viewport option
`Save/Restore/Delete/Join/SIngle/?/2/<3>/4:` **3**	
`Horizontal/Vertical/Above/Below/Left/<Right>:` ↵	Specifies the largest viewport to be on the right side

Save your drawing.

The board is now displayed in all three viewports, as shown in figure 5.4.

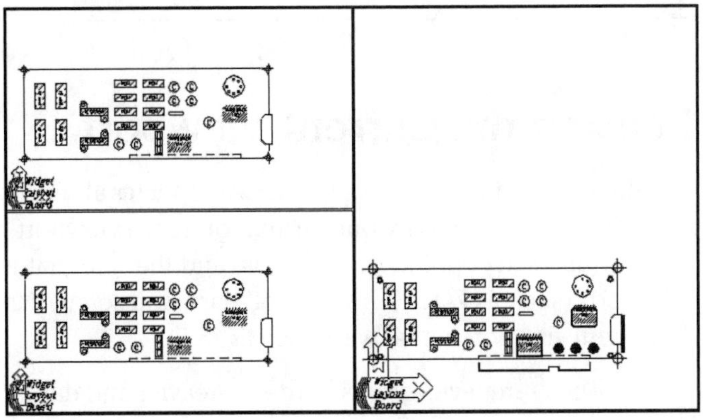

Figure 5.4

The CHAP05A drawing with three properties.

Opening More Tiled Viewports

You can have more than 4 viewports open simultaneously by taking the current viewport and dividing it into multiple viewports. You can do this to each viewport, but the succeeding viewports get smaller and smaller. In practical terms, the maximum number of viewports you can work with depends on the type of drawing and the size and resolution of your monitor. If you have a 14-inch monitor, two viewports probably is the practical limit; if you have a 19-inch monitor, four viewports is quite usable. AutoCAD will refuse to create more than 96 simultaneous viewports, and will refuse to subdivide a viewport that it deems too small, but both of these limits are well beyond the number of viewports you would realistically use.

TIP

AutoCAD does have to do more work with multiple viewports. If you notice a performance degradation when you use multiple viewports with large drawings, cut back on the number of viewports. Alternatively, you might want to freeze unneeded layers rather than turn them off. Remember that when you freeze a layer, AutoCAD ignores all the objects residing on the layer.

Choosing the Current Viewport

When you change the model, AutoCAD updates all viewports to reflect any changes. There is, however, only one current or active viewport, the one in which you can draw and select points and objects, and the one that is affected by display commands (such as ZOOM, PAN, scroll bars, and so on). You can visually identify the current viewport in two ways (see fig. 5.5):

- The current viewport's border is heavier and darker than the other viewports' borders.
- The current viewport is the only viewport in which you can see the crosshairs. All other viewports display the pointer.

To set another viewport as the current viewport, just move the system pointer to that viewport and click the pick button once. Immediately, the crosshairs will appear in the selected viewport and the viewport's border becomes thicker and darker.

Alternatively, you can press Ctrl+R to switch to the next viewport in a counterclockwise direction.

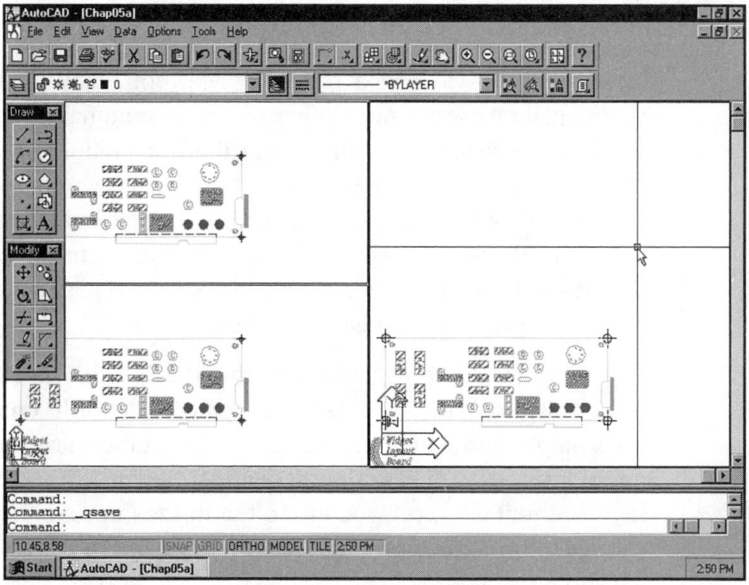

Figure 5.5

The current viewport has crosshairs and a heavier border.

In the next exercise, you practice setting the current viewport.

SETTING THE CURRENT VIEWPORT

Continue in the drawing CHAP05A.

Notice that the right viewport has a heavier border than the other two. The right viewport is the current viewport.

Move the cursor from one viewport to the next. Notice that the crosshairs appear in only the current viewport and that the system pointer appears in the other viewports.

`Command:` *Click in the upper left viewport*	Sets the upper left viewport current and displays a heavier border and crosshairs
`Command:` *Move the pointer to the lower left viewport*	Displays the pointer
`Command:` *Click the pick button*	Sets the lower left viewport current and displays a heavier border and crosshairs
`Command:` *Press* Ctrl+R *several times*	Sets viewports current

Getting the View You Want

To change the view in a particular viewport, make that viewport the current viewport, then use the Aerial View or display commands (such as ZOOM and PAN) to adjust the view. If you wish, you can think of multiple viewports as a bank of video monitors with each monitor hooked up to its own camera. The display in each viewport is the view as seen through the lens of the viewport's camera and you can determine the view by setting the position and zoom factor of the camera with the ZOOM and PAN commands. Since each viewport has its own camera, the view can be set independently for each viewport.

You can have different settings for the SNAP, GRID, and UCSICON commands in each viewport. You can have one spacing for the GRID command in one viewport, for example, and a different grid spacing in another viewport. You cannot, however, adjust the display of layers per individual viewport. If you turn off or freeze a layer in the current viewport, you turn off or freeze that layer in all the viewports. If you change the color of a layer in the current viewport, you change the color in all the viewports.

The REDRAW and REGEN commands affect only the current viewport. If you want to affect all viewports, you must use the equivalent commands REDRAWALL and REGENALL. You can activate REDRAWALL by choosing View, Redraw All or the Redraw All tool on the Redraw flyout of the Standard toolbar. You must, however, type the REGENALL command, because it does not appear in a menu.

If you use the Aerial View window (DSVIEWER), the view in the Aerial View window is automatically that of the current viewport. As you change current viewports, the view in the Aerial View Window changes accordingly. You can disable this action by disabling the Auto Viewport option in the Options pull-down menu of the Aerial View window. When Auto Viewport is disabled, you must click on the title bar of the Aerial View window if you want to update the displayed view to that of the current viewport.

In the next exercise, you change the views in the viewports you created in the previous exercise.

CHANGING THE VIEWPORT VIEWS

Continue using the drawing CHAP05A.

`Command:` *Click in the upper left viewport*	Sets the current viewport
`Command:` *Choose Zoom Extents (Standard, Zoom)*	Zooms the view in the current viewport to the model's extents
`Command:` *Turn on the* SNAP *button*	Turns on snap in the current viewport
`Command:` *Set the lower left viewport current*	
`Command:` *Turn on the* GRID *button*	Turns on grid in the current viewport
`Command:` *Choose Zoom Window (Standard)*	
`First corner:` **6,3** ↵	
`Other corner:` **7.5,4.5** ↵	Changes the view in the current viewport

Set the right side viewport current, then zoom its view with a window from 4.5,3 to 7,6.

`Command:` *Choose Aerial View (NRP)*	Displays Aerial View window

In turn, make each of the viewports current; the view in the Aerial View window changes to reflect the current viewport as long as the Auto Viewport option in the options pull-down menu of the Aerial window is enabled.

`Command:` *Close the Aerial View window*	
`Command:` *Click on the* Layer Control *drop-down list and turn off the layer HATCHING, then close the drop-down list.*	Selects the change in all viewports—the ROMs are no longer hatched

Click on the Layer Control *drop-down list and turn on the layer* HATCHING, *then close the drop-down list*

`Command:` *Choose* View, Redraw All	Issues the REDRAWALL command and redraws all viewports

Save your drawing.

Editing in Tiled Viewports

You always draw and edit in the current viewport, and you do all your object selection and point picking in the current viewport. Any changes you make to the model automatically appear in all viewports, assuming that the viewports show portions of the model to which you made the changes.

You can change your current viewport while executing a command. You can start to draw a line in one viewport, for example, and change the current viewport before you pick the next point for the line. In general, the only commands during which you cannot change the current viewport are the display commands, such as ZOOM, PAN, and VIEW.

You even can change the current viewport during object selection. Only the objects selected in a viewport are highlighted in that viewport, but after you select all objects, all selected objects are dragged in the current viewport (if applicable) for the duration of the command.

In the next exercise, you edit the drawing VIEWS using multiple viewports.

EDITING WITH VIEWPORTS

Continue in the CHAP05A drawing.

Set the lower left viewport current.

`Command:` *Choose Copy Object (Modify, Copy)*	Issues the COPY command
`Select objects:` *Select a crossing window from ① to ② (see fig. 5.6)*	Selects the circle and letter C
Select objects: ↵	Ends selection
`<Base point or displacement>/ Multiple:` *Using CEN object snap, pick the circle at ③*	Sets the center of the circle as the base point
`Second point of displacement:` *Click in the right viewport, then turn on the* SNAP *and* ORTHO *buttons*	Changes the current viewport and settings during the COPY command

Figure 5.6

Copying and erasing with multiple viewports.

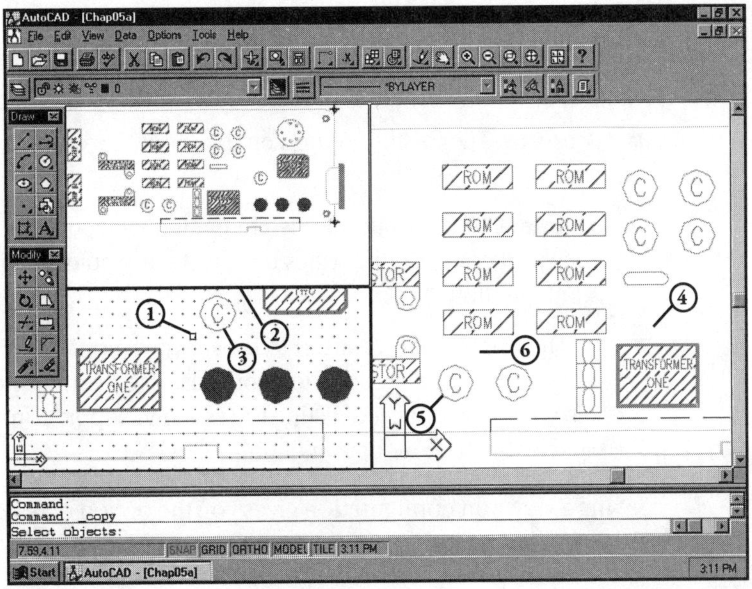

`Second point of displacement:` *Pick point* ④ *at coordinates* 6.80,4.30	Specifies the point in the right viewport to copy to
`Command:` *Choose Erase (Modify)*	Issues the ERASE command
`Select objects:` *Select a crossing window from* ⑤ *to* ⑥	
`Select objects:` ↵	

Save your drawing.

In the preceding exercise, you discovered that you can use any viewport to edit the drawing and even change viewports while in the middle of a command (the COPY command in the exercise). The ability to change viewports while executing a command enables you to switch to whichever viewport clearly shows the objects or points you want to pick even when that viewport is not the one you started with.

Saving and Restoring Viewport Configurations

Just as you can save, restore, delete, and list named views (DDVIEW command), you can save, restore, delete, and list tiled viewport arrangements (also referred to as viewport configurations) using the following options of the VPORTS command:

- **Save.** This option enables you to assign a name to the current arrangement of tiled viewports. The snap, grid, and ucsicon settings and the view in each viewport is recorded and can be restored with the Restore option.
- **Restore.** The Restore option enables you to restore a saved viewport configuration.
- **Delete.** Use this option to delete named viewport configurations. Deleting a viewport configuration does not delete any objects, only the named viewport configuration.
- **?.** The listing option is used to list viewport configurations specified by you. If you wish to list all saved viewports, use the * name specification. You will also have the option of listing the saved viewport configurations when you specify the Restore option.

Saving a viewport configuration gives you the option of restoring the saved group of views at a later date.

TIP

If you use the same viewport configurations repeatedly, consider defining the viewport configurations in your prototype drawing so that every new drawing will have the viewport configurations already defined and ready for you to use.

In the exercise found in the next section, you will practice saving and restoring a viewport configuration.

Closing Tiled Viewports

To close unneeded viewports, use either the Join or SIngle options of the VPORTS command:

- **SIngle.** Choosing this option expands the current viewport to fill the entire drawing window and closes all other viewports.
- **Join.** This option enables you to merge two adjacent viewports into a single viewport. You select the two viewports to be merged. The view in the first viewport (also referred to as the *dominant* viewport) will be the view that is displayed in the final viewport. By default, the first viewport is the current viewport. The outline of the two viewports you select to join must combine to form a rectangle. In figure 5.7, for example, you could join viewports 1 and 2, but not 1 and 3, nor 2 and 3.

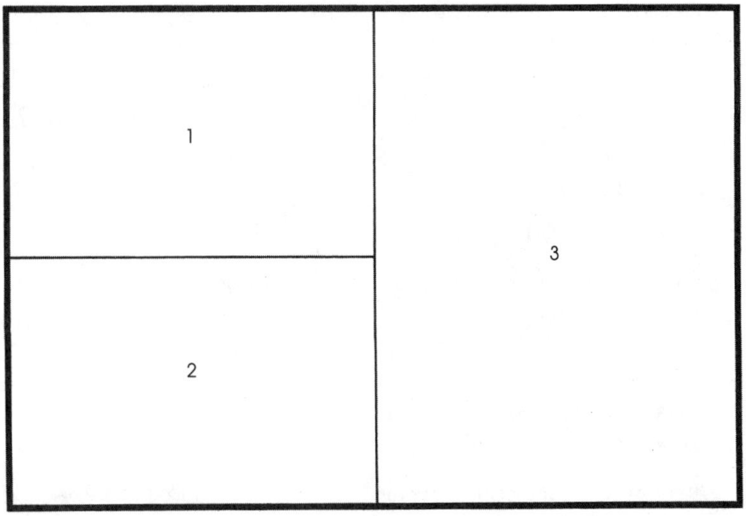

Figure 5.7

Joining viewports.

In the following exercise, you use the Save, Restore, Join, and SIngle options to manipulate the current viewport configuration.

Changing and Restoring the Viewport Configuration

Continue in the drawing CHAP05A.

`Command:` *Choose* View, Tiled Viewports, Save	Issues the VPORTS command with the Save option specified

`_vports`
`Save/Restore/Delete/Join/`
`SIngle/?/2/<3>/4: _s`	

`?/Name for new viewport configuration:` **3PORTS** ↵	Saves the current viewport arrangement with the name 3PORTS
`Command:` *Choose* View, Tiled Viewports, Join	Issues the VPORTS command with the Join option specified
`Select dominant viewport <current>:` *Click in the upper left viewport*	Makes the upper left viewport the dominant viewport
`Select viewport to join:` *Click in the lower left viewport*	Merges the lower left viewport with the dominant viewport

`Command:` *Choose* View, Tiled Viewports, 1 Viewport — Issues the VPORTS command with the SIngle option specified and makes the current (left) viewport a single viewport

```
_vports
Save/Restore/Delete/Join/
SIngle/?/2/<3>/4: _si
```

Perform a ZOOM Extents

`Command:` *Choose* View, Tiled Viewports, Restore — Issues the VPORTS command with the Restore option

```
Command: _vports
Save/Restore/Delete/Join/
SIngle/?/2/<3>/4: _r
```

`?/Name of viewport configuration to restore:` **?** ↵ — Specifies the listing option of the Restore option

`Viewport configuration(s) to list <*>:` ↵ — Accepts the default of listing all saved viewport configurations which, displays the following information for the configuration TRIVIEW

```
Current configuration:
id# 3
corners: 0.0000,0.0000 1.0000,1.0000
Configuration 3PORTS:
0.5000,0.0000 1.0000,1.0000
```

The information displayed simply lists the identification numbers and screen positions of the active and saved viewports. The id# 3 title represents the single current viewport. The Configuration 3PORTS: title refers to the viewport configuration you just saved. The coordinates represent the screen position of the viewport that was active when you saved the 3PORTS configuration. The coordinates displayed are not the standard XY coordinates of the drawing; 0,0 is the lower left corner of the screen while 1,1 is the upper right corner of the screen.

`?/Name of viewport configuration to restore:` **3PORTS** ↵ — Restores the viewport arrangement 3PORTS

Save your drawing.

Working with Paper Space Viewports

Paper space originally was conceived as a tool to help you compose the layout of a drawing before you plotted it, hence the term *paper space*. Paper space also can be a useful environment from which to edit the model, and its usage as such is discussed in the remainder of this chapter.

In the sections that follow, you learn how to enter the paper space environment, switch between paper and model space, and how to create and use floating viewports for drawing and editing the model.

Entering the Paper Space Environment

You switch between the tiled viewport and paper space environments by changing the setting of the system variable TILEMODE. When TILEMODE is set to 1 (on), you are in the tiled viewport environment (also referred to as model space). When TILEMODE is set to 0 (off), you are in the paper space environment. Within the paper space environment, you can either be in model space within a floating viewport, or in paper space itself. Paper space is a special drawing space intended for title blocks, borders, and similar features, and for the placement of floating viewports. Paper space is supposed to represent an actual piece of paper. You use the MVIEW command to place floating viewports in paper space, then you can enter model space and draw in the viewports. More on MVIEW and floating viewports later—first you need to know how to enable the paper space environment. You can type TILEMODE at the `Command:` prompt or you can use the View pull-down menu to set TILEMODE off. The Paper Space menu item not only turns off TILEMODE but also issues the PSPACE command, which ensures you enter paper space itself and not model space within a floating viewport. When you are in paper space, a check mark appears by this menu item.

You also can turn TILEMODE on or off by double-clicking on the TILE button on the status bar. When the TILE button appears bold, TILEMODE is on and double-clicking on it turns it off. When the TILE button appears grayed, TILEMODE is off and double-clicking on it turns it on.

After you turn off TILEMODE, you are in the paper space environment, as corroborated by the following indicators:

- The TILE button on the status bar appears grayed.
- The MODEL button on the status bar is now the PAPER button (the function of this button is discussed shortly).
- The paper space UCS icon appears, as shown in figure 5.8, instead of the normal model space UCS icon.

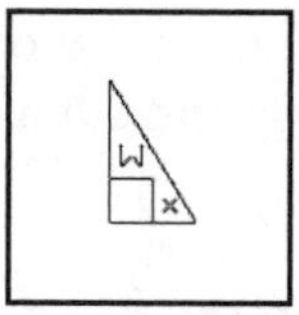

Figure 5.8

The UCS icon in paper space.

If, when TILEMODE is turned off, you are in model space within a floating viewport in the paper space environment, you will see the following indicators:

- The TILE button appears grayed.
- The MODEL button appears on the status bar.
- The normal model space UCS icon appears in each viewport.

The model space that exists in tiled viewports is the same model space that exists in floating viewports; however, paper space itself and model space are two separate areas of the same drawing file, and have a dividing wall between them. In the next exercise, you use various methods to move between tiled model and paper space.

Changing TILEMODE

Continue in the CHAP05A drawing.

`Command:` *Make the upper left viewport the current viewport if it is not already*

`Command:` *Choose* View, Paper Space — Changes to paper space

Notice the paper UCS icon and the TILE and PAPER buttons on the status bar, and that you cannot see your model yet.

`Command:` *Choose* View, Tiled Model Space — Changes back to tiled model space

Notice the normal UCS icon and the TILE and MODEL buttons on the status bar.

`Command:` *Turn off the TILE button on the status bar*	Changes to paper space
`Command:` *Turn on the TILE button on the status bar*	Changes back to tiled model space
`Command:` *Double-click on the* MODEL *button on the status bar*	Sets TILEMODE to 0 but does not change anything because you have no floating viewports in paper space

When you are in tiled model space, the dividing wall between the two spaces prevents you from seeing what is on the paper space side. When you are in paper space, you can see what is on the model space side only by opening some windows (viewports) in the wall. The viewports in model space are referred to as *tiled viewports,* but the viewports in paper space are referred to as *floating viewports*. In the following sections, you learn how to create and use floating viewports.

Opening Floating Viewports

When you opened tiled viewports in model space, you divided the current viewport into smaller multiple viewports. You had limited control over the size and positioning of the viewports. In contrast, when you create viewports in paper space, you specify the size and location of the viewports. The viewports can be positioned anywhere in paper space, hence the term *floating viewports* (in contrast to having fixed positions as in tiled viewport mode).

To work with the model in paper space, you use MVIEW to create floating viewports.

With MVIEW, you have the following options:

```
ON/OFF/Hideplot/Fit/2/3/4/Restore/<First Point>:
```

- **ON.** Turns on a floating viewport.
- **OFF.** Turns off a floating viewport. Turning off a viewport instructs AutoCAD to not display the model in the viewport.
- **Hideplot.** Tags a floating viewport to have its hidden lines removed during plotting.
- **Fit.** Creates a single viewport to fit the drawing window.
- **2.** Divides a user-specified rectangular area into two viewports (refer to figure 5.3). It prompts you to specify the orientation (Horizontal or Vertical) and the location by specifying Fit or picking two points.

- **3.** Divides a user-specified rectangular area into three viewports (refer to figure 5.3). It prompts you to specify the orientation (Horizontal or Vertical) and the location by specifying Fit or picking two points.
- **4.** Divides a user-specified rectangular area into four viewports (refer to figure 5.3). It prompts you to specify the orientation (Horizontal or Vertical) and the location by specifying Fit or picking two points.
- **Restore.** Creates the equivalent of a tiled viewport configuration (saved using the VPORTS command) in paper space, using floating viewports.
- **First point.** The default option enables you to create a new floating viewport by picking two points that define its size and location.

To access the MVIEW command by using the pull-down menus, choose View, Floating Viewports (see fig. 5.9). Each menu item in the Floating Viewports submenu triggers the MVIEW command and then the appropriate option. The Floating Viewports submenu is active only in paper space.

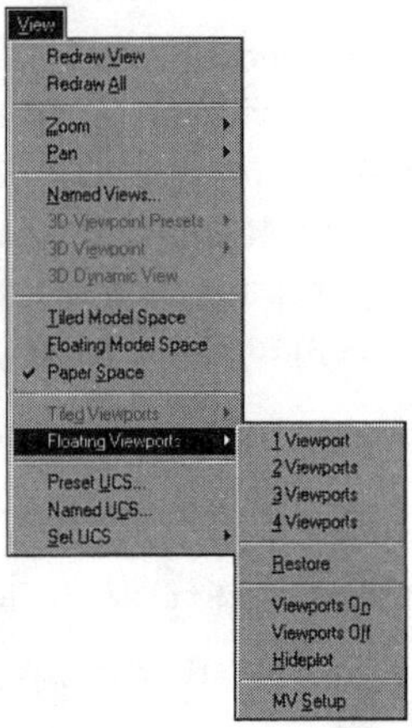

Figure 5.9

The Floating Viewports submenu.

The default option of the MVIEW command enables you to define the size and location of the floating viewport by defining an area with two points or entering F to fill the paper space view. If you use the 2 or 3 options, you will be prompted for orientation. You may specify horizontal or vertical orientation, or with the 3 option, you may instead specify whether the major (larger) viewport is created above, below, left, or right of the others. If you are creating more than one viewport, you will see the following prompt:

```
Fit/<First Point>:
```

At this prompt, you can define the area by defining the area with a window (the default First Point option) or by specifying the area as the entire area visible in paper space (the Fit option).

The MVIEW options for creating floating viewports are very similar to the VPORTS options for creating tiled viewports, except that you get to choose the location and size of the floating viewports.

The menu items on the Floating Viewports submenu of the View menu (except MV Setup) all issue the MVIEW command. The 1 Viewport item issues MVIEW without options, and the rest of the menu items issue MVIEW with the options indicated in their menu labels.

In the following exercise, you use MVIEW to create several floating viewports.

Creating Floating Viewports

Continue in the CHAP05A drawing, in paper space.

`Command:` *Choose Layers (Object Properties) create a new layer named FVPORTS, assign the color green, set it current, and choose* OK

`Command:` *Choose* View, Floating Viewports, 3 Viewports	Issues the MVIEW command with the 3 option
`ON/OFF/Hideplot/Fit/2/3/4 /Restore/<First Point>:` **_3**	
`Horizontal/Vertical/Above/ Below/Left/<Right>:` ↵	Accepts the default arrangement, major viewport on the right
`Fit/<First Point>:` **2,0.5** ↵	Specifies lower left corner of the viewports
`Second point:` **12,8** ↵	Specifies upper right corner of the area and creates the three viewports (see fig. 5.10)

Save your drawing.

Figure 5.10

The VIEWS drawing in paper space.

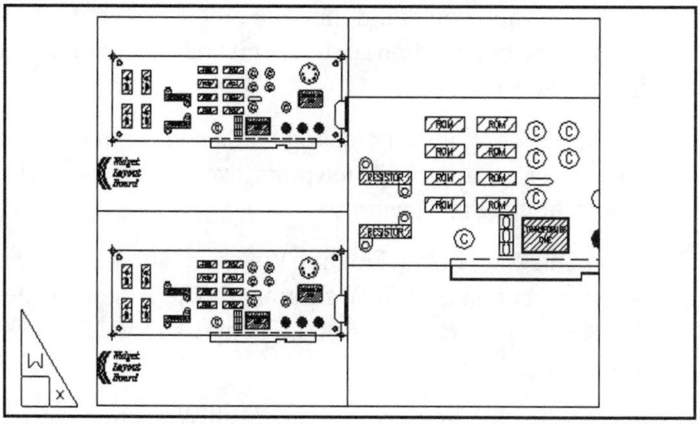

If you have several multiple floating viewports open, you might notice a degradation in your system's performance. Such a degradation is understandable when you consider that AutoCAD must do much more work to update multiple viewports. If the degradation becomes serious, you might want to turn off any unnecessary viewports temporarily. AutoCAD will not update the display in any viewports that are turned off. You can use the MVIEW command to turn viewports on and off.

NOTE

You can create as many viewports as you want. AutoCAD, however, by default updates the views in only 16 of them. The limit of 16 is set in the MAXACTVP (MAXimum ACTive ViewPorts) system variable. You can raise or lower it. The maximum number of active viewports that you can have is dependent on the display driver you are using. The standard drivers provided with AutoCAD will only support a maximum of 16 active viewports (the default value of MAXACTVP). If you create a new viewport that causes you to exceed the limit set in MAXACTVP, AutoCAD automatically turns off one of the older viewports. At no time does AutoCAD maintain (update) more floating viewports than is set in MAXACTVP.

To adjust the view in a floating viewport or to edit the model, you have to access the model space within the viewport. Right now, you are in paper space and are not able to access the model space in any of the floating viewports. To access the model space within a particular viewport, you have to make that viewport current and how to do that is the topic of the next section.

Choosing the Current Viewport and Entering Model Space

To make the default floating viewport current and enter model space within that viewport, you use the MSPACE command.

When you access model space through a floating viewport, the model space is called *floating model space*. However, be aware that there is only one model space. Floating model space simply refers to the fact that you are accessing model space through a floating viewport. The View, Floating Model Space menu item actually is a macro that checks whether you are in model space (TILEMODE=1). If you are, it first sets TILEMODE to 0 to move you into paper space. If you already have floating viewports established, the menu macro then issues the MSPACE command. If you do not have any floating viewports, the MVIEW command is then triggered so that you can create one or more floating viewports before the macro issues MSPACE.

The views in the floating viewports are always current unless you have a particular viewport turned off or have exceeded the maximum number of active viewports (MAXACTVP). All viewports are normally active, so when you make changes to the model, AutoCAD updates all viewports to reflect the changes. There is, however, only one current viewport. The current viewport is the viewport in which you pick points and select objects, and that is affected by your display commands, such as ZOOM, PAN, scroll bars, and so on. When you are in floating model space you can identify that fact and the current viewport based on the following indicators (see fig. 5.11):

- The model space UCS icon appears in each floating viewport (if you have not turned off the UCS icon for that viewport).
- The PAPER button on the status bar is replaced with a MODEL button.
- The current viewport has a heavier, darker border than the others.
- The crosshairs no longer cross the entire drawing window. The crosshairs appear only in the current viewport and only when the cursor is over that viewport. In the rest of the drawing window, the system pointer appears in place of the crosshairs.

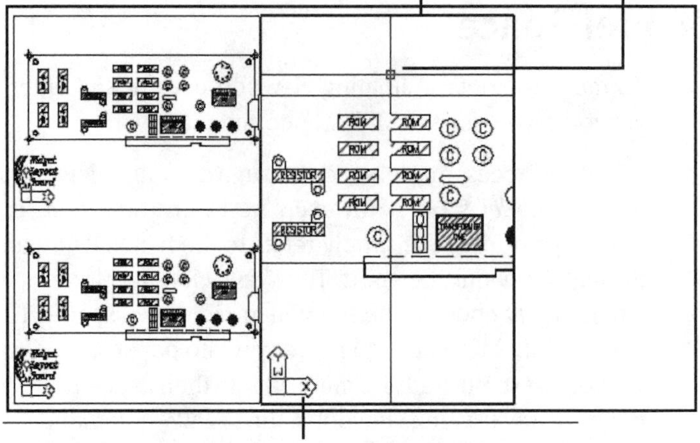

Figure 5.11

Indicators pointing to the current viewport.

NOTE

If you are in model space when you issue the MVIEW command, it temporarily changes to paper space until the command is complete.

When you are in model space, to set another viewport current, move the pointer to the viewport you want to make current and click the pick button once. That viewport immediately becomes the current viewport. Alternatively, you can press Ctrl+R to sequentially select the next viewport in a counterclockwise direction. After you make a viewport current, you can draw, edit, and adjust the view in that viewport.

In the following exercise, you set various floating viewports current.

Entering Model Space and Setting the Current Viewport

Continue in the CHAP05A drawing, with three floating viewpoints visible.

`Command:` *Double-click on the* PAPER *button on the status bar*	It changes to read MODEL; you now are in floating model space

Now, look at the viewports. Notice that the right viewport has a heavier border than the other two. The right viewport is the current viewport.

`Command:` *Move the cursor from one viewport to the next.*

Notice how the crosshairs appear only in the current viewport (see fig. 10.14). In all other viewports, you see the system pointer. Notice that the model space UCS icon now appears in each viewport.

`Command:` *Click in the upper left viewport*	Sets the upper left viewport current, displaying heavier border and crosshairs
`Command:` *Click in the lower left viewport*	Sets the lower left viewport current, displaying heavier border and crosshairs
`Command:` *Press* Ctrl+R *several times*	Changes current viewport in a counterclockwise direction

Save your drawing.

Changing the View

When you open up a new floating viewport, the view displayed in the viewport will correspond to the view in the current tiled model space viewport (TILEMODE=1). Just as with tiled viewports, you can adjust the view in each floating viewport to show a different portion of the drawing. After you make the floating viewport you want to affect the current viewport (see the previous section), you can use the display commands (such as ZOOM and PAN) to adjust the displayed view. If you wish, you can think of multiple viewports as a bank of video monitors with each monitor hooked up to its own camera. The display in each viewport is the view as seen through the lens of the viewport's camera and you can determine the view by setting the position and zoom factor of the camera with the ZOOM and PAN commands. Since each viewport has its own camera, the view can be set independently for each viewport. The view in one viewport could be a view of the overall model while the other viewports could be displaying selected close-ups of the model.

Each viewport may also have individual settings for layer visibility and for the SNAP, GRID, and UCSICON states. You can, for example, have one spacing for the GRID command in one viewport and a different grid spacing in another viewport.

REDRAW and REGEN affect only the current viewport. If you want to affect all viewports, you must use the equivalent commands REDRAWALL and REGENALL. You can activate REDRAWALL by choosing View, Redraw All. You must enter REGENALL at the `Command:` prompt because it is not on a menu.

If you use the Aerial View window (DSVIEWER command), the view in the Aerial View window is by default the same as the view of the current floating viewport. As you change current viewports, the view in the Aerial View window changes accordingly. You can disable this action by removing the check mark from the Auto Viewport option in the Options pull-down menu of the Aerial View window. If Auto Viewport is disabled, you must click on the title bar of the Aerial View window to update the displayed view to that of the current viewport. Aerial View is not available while in paper space; you must be in floating model space.

In the following exercise, you adjust the views and snap and grid settings in the floating viewports you created.

Adjusting the Viewport Views

Continue in the CHAP05A drawing, in model space, with three floating viewports visible.

Set the upper left viewport current.

`Command:` *Choose* View, Zoom, Extents — Zooms the current viewport to the model's extents

`Command:` *Turn off the* SNAP *button* — Turns off SNAP in the current viewport *only*

Set the lower left viewport current.

`Command:` *Turn on the* GRID *button* — Turns on GRID in the current viewport

`Command:` *Choose Zoom Window (Standard) and zoom to a window from* 6,3 *to* 7.5,4.5 — Changes the view in the current viewport

Set the right side viewport current.

`Command:` ↵ — Repeats the ZOOM command

`Zoom`

`All/Center/Dynamic/Extents/Left/Previous/`
`Vmax/Window/<Scale (X/XP)>:` **4.5,3** ↵

`Other corner:` **7,6** ↵ — Zooms to the specified window

`Command:` *Choose Aerial View (NRP)* — Displays the Aerial View window

Make each of the viewports current in turn and watch how the view in the Aerial View window changes to reflect the current viewport.

Close the Aerial View window.

`Command:` *Choose* View, Redraw All — Issues the REDRAWALL command

Save your drawing.

Editing the Viewports

Each floating viewport is itself an object—a VIEWPORT object. As an object, it resides on the layer on which it was drawn and has the current color and linetype. You even can edit it just as you would with other objects.

To adjust the location of the viewport, use the MOVE command to move it. To change the size of the viewport, use STRETCH or SCALE to change its size. You even can use GRIPS on a viewport object.

To edit the viewports themselves, you need to be in paper space, not in floating model space. If you are in floating model space, you can use the PSPACE command to get back to paper space.

If you are in floating model space, you will find a button on the status bar labeled MODEL. If you double-click on that button, you issue the PSPACE command. The MODEL button is then replaced with one labeled PAPER.

In the following exercise, you edit the viewport objects.

Adjusting Floating Viewports

Continue in the CHAP05A drawing.

`Command:` *Double-click on the* MODEL *button*	Changes to paper space and displays the PAPER button.
`Command:` *Choose Move (Modify)*	Issues the MOVE command
`Select objects:` *Pick viewport border at ① (see fig. 5.12)*	Selects the upper left viewport object to be moved
`Select objects:` ↵	
`Base point or displacement:` **0,1** ↵	Specifies displacement
`Second point of displacement:` ↵	Moves viewport by specified displacements

Repeat the MOVE command and move the right viewport object one unit to the right. The three viewports should now be separated.

`Command:` *Choose Stretch (Modify, Resize)*	Issues the STRETCH command

`Select objects to stretch by crossing window or polygon...`

`Select objects:` *Select a crossing window from 14,9 to 7.5,6.5* — Selects the right viewport as the object to be stretched

`Select objects:` ↵

`Base point or displacement:` **0,1** ↵ — Specifies displacement

`Second point of displacement:` _ — Stretches viewport by specified displacement (see fig. 5.13)

`Command:` *Choose* View, Floating Viewports, Viewports Off — Issues MVIEW with the OFF option

`Command: _mview`
`ON/OFF/Hideplot/Fit/2/3/4/Restore/`
`<First Point>:` **_OFF**

`Select objects:` *Select the rightmost viewport and press Enter* — *Turns off the rightmost viewport*

It is almost like turning off a TV monitor. To get back the picture, you need to turn the viewport back on.

`Command:` *Choose* View, Floating Viewports, Viewports On — Issues MVIEW with ON option

`Command: _mview`
`ON/OFF/Hideplot/Fit/2/3/4/Restore/`
`<First Point>:` **_ON**

`Select objects:` *Select the rightmost viewport and press Enter* — *Turns back on the right viewport*

`Select objects:` ↵

Save the drawing.

Figure 5.12

Selecting viewport to move.

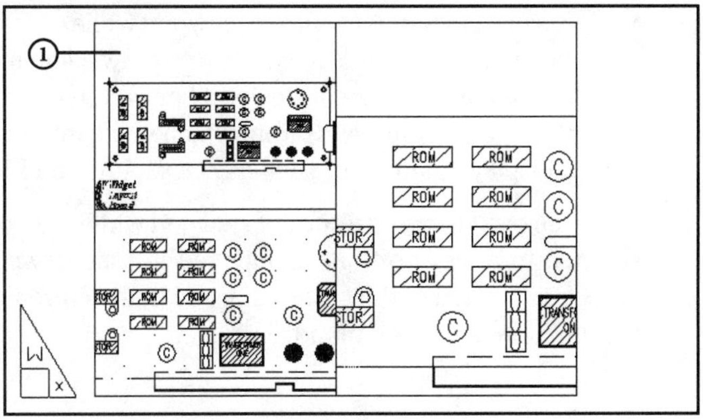

Figure 5.13

Results of moving and stretching the viewports.

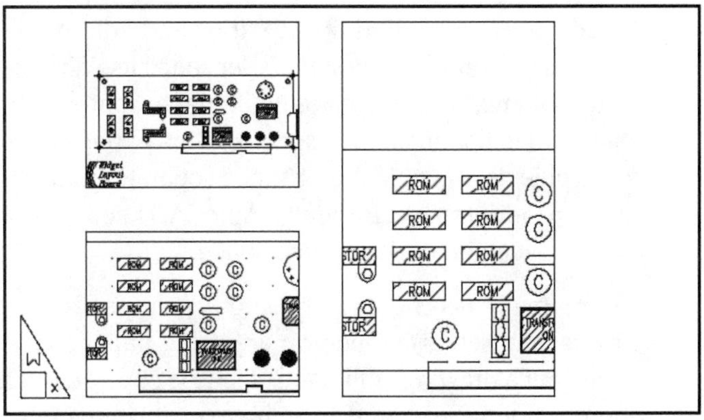

Editing in Model Space in Floating Viewports

After you make one of the floating viewports current, you also can edit the model in floating model space. (See Chapter 19, "Introduction to Dimensioning," for dimensioning in viewports.) Editing objects in model space using floating viewports (TILEMODE=0) is no different from editing the drawing in tiled model space (TILEMODE=1). You draw and edit in the current viewport. You do all your object selection and point picking in the current viewport. Any changes you make to the model automatically appear in all active viewports, assuming that they show portions of the model to which you made the changes and the appropriate layers are thawed.

You even can change your current viewport while executing a command, just as you can with tiled viewports. You can start to draw a line in one viewport, for example, and then change the current viewport before you pick the next point for the line. In general, the only commands from which you cannot change the current viewport are the display commands, such as ZOOM, PAN, and VIEW.

You even can change the current viewport while selecting objects. Only the objects selected in a viewport are highlighted in that viewport, but after you select all objects, all selected objects are dragged in the current viewport (if applicable) for the duration of the command.

Editing in Paper Space

So far, you have learned how to draw and edit in floating model space. You also know how to draw and edit in paper space itself. (See Chapter 19, "Introduction to Dimensioning," for dimensioning in paper space.) All the layers created in model space and in floating model space exist in paper space as well. AutoCAD, however, keeps objects drawn in paper space separate from the objects drawn on the same layers in model space. Basically, AutoCAD keeps two versions of the layers, one for model space and one for paper space.

You normally need only draw and edit in paper space (other than the viewport objects themselves) when you are using paper space to compose your drawing. Laying out a drawing with paper space is covered in Chapter 6, "Plotting and Sheet Composition." For now, do not draw or edit in paper space. Always be sure to draw and edit in floating model space, with TILEMODE set to 0 (off).

For now, restrict the editing you do in paper space to editing the viewport objects themselves. Remember that you do not have the option of changing the size and location of the viewports in tiled model space (TILEMODE=1), whereas you do have those options when dealing with paper space viewports. Furthermore, because you are not restricted in the layout of paper space viewports, you can actually layout several arrangements of viewports to accommodate different purposes. For example, you could open up a cluster of floating viewports to show a group of related details and then open up another cluster of viewports to show a different group of related details. In the next section, you will learn of another advantage that paper space viewports have over model space viewports, and that is layer visibility.

Setting Layer Visibility in Viewports

You can control the display of layers globally (in all viewports) or individually for each viewport. In contrast, you can affect layers in tiled viewports only globally. The only layer operations that you can set for an individual viewport are freezing and thawing. Setting a layer's color and linetype or turning a layer on or off affects the views in all floating viewports. If you decide to freeze a layer, you can do it globally or for the current viewport only. In the Layer Control dialog box, if you choose the Freeze button, you freeze the layer globally. To freeze the layer for the current viewport only, choose the Frz button next to the label Cur VP. The letter C appears in the state column to indicate that the layer is frozen in the current viewport (see fig. 5.14).

Figure 5.14

The Layer Control dialog box.

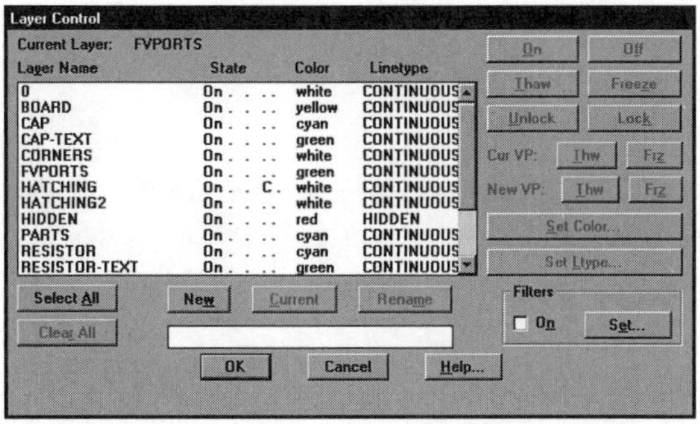

To thaw a layer that is frozen for the current viewport, choose the Thw button next to the Cur VP label. If you choose the regular Thaw button, you affect only the viewports that do not have the selected layers frozen for these viewports.

You also can use the VPLAYER command to set the freeze/thaw status. VPLAYER is discussed in greater detail after the following exercise in which you freeze a layer in the current viewport. To begin, continue from the previous exercise.

CONTROLLING VIEWPORT LAYER VISIBILITY

`Command:` *Choose Layers (Object Properties)*	Opens the Layer Control dialog box
`Command:` *Select layer* HATCHING, *then choose* Freeze (*not the* Frz *button*), *then* OK	Freezes layer HATCHING in all viewports (the ROMs are no longer hatched)
`Command:` ↵	Reopens the Layer Control dialog box

Select layer HATCHING, *then choose* Thaw *(not the* Thw *button), then* OK	Thaws layer HATCHING in all viewports
Turn off the PAPER *button*	Changes to model space

Set the lower left viewport current

`Command:` *Choose Layers (Object Properties)*	Reopens the Layer Control dialog box
Select layer HATCHING, *then choose* Frz *(button next to Cur VP, not the* Freeze *button)*	Freezes layer only in the current viewport and displays the letter C in the state column for HATCHING

The "C" indicates that the layer is frozen for the current viewport.

`Command:` *Choose* OK	Freezes the layer HATCHING only in the current viewport; the hatching on the ROMs remains visible in the others

Set the right viewport current.

`Command:` ↵	Reopens the Layer Control dialog box

Notice that the HATCHING does not have a letter C now. This is because for this viewport, HATCHING is not frozen. Exit the Layer Control dialog box.

`Command:` *Click in the* Layer Control *drop-down list box (Object Properties)*	Opens drop-down list (see fig. 5.15); the layer HATCHING's sun/viewport icon is bright, indicating HATCHING is thawed in the current viewport
Click in the lower left viewport	Closes drop-down list and sets lower left viewport current
`Command:` *Click in the Layer Control drop-down list box*	Opens drop-down list; the layer HATCHING's sun/viewport icon is dark, indicating HATCHING is frozen in the current viewport

TIP

You also can click on the sun or sun/viewport icons in the Layer Control drop-down list to quickly freeze or thaw layers for all viewports (the sun icon) or only the current viewport (the sun/viewport icon).

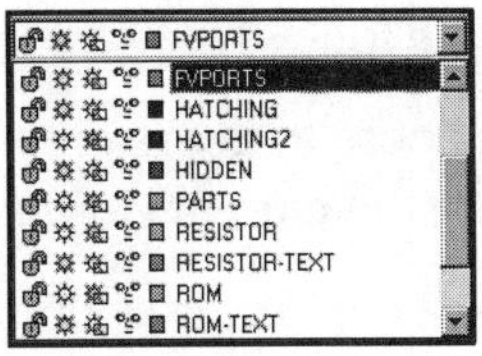

Figure 5.15

Checking the Freeze/Thaw status with the drop-down list.

There also is a pair of buttons labeled Frz and Thw next to the label New VP. If you choose the Frz button, all selected layers automatically are frozen in any new floating viewports you create. The letter *N* appears in the State column to indicate that the layer will be frozen in new viewports. To remove the *N* state from a layer, choose the Thw button next to the label New VP.

Another command you can use to manipulate layer visibility in lieu of DDLMODES on the layer drop down list is VPLAYER.

With VPLAYER, you have the following options:

```
?/Freeze/Thaw/Reset/Newfrz/Vpvisdflt:
```

- **?.** Lists all frozen layers in a selected viewport.
- **Freeze.** Enables you to freeze specified layers in a selected viewport.
- **Thaw.** Enables you to thaw specified layers in a selected viewport.
- **Reset.** Resets layers in a selected viewport to the default settings.
- **Newfrz.** Creates a new layer that is frozen in all current floating viewports and new viewports. The letters *C* and *N* appear in the State column to indicate that the layer is frozen in the current viewport and will be frozen in new viewports.
- **Vpvisdflt.** Enables you to set the default visibility of existing layers to be used when you create new viewports. When you choose the Freeze option, the letter *N* appears in the State column.

If you specify the Freeze, Thaw, or Reset options, you see the following prompt:

```
All/Select/<Current>:
```

This prompt enables you to choose whether you want to apply the action to the current viewport (the default option), to all viewports, or to viewports that you select. If you choose the Select option while in floating model space, you will be switched back to paper space so that you can select the viewport objects you want to affect.

VPLAYER has the following two advantages over DDLMODES:

- You can choose to freeze or thaw selected layers for several viewports rather than just for the current viewport.
- You can use the Newfrz option to create a new layer that is frozen in all viewports and then thaw it for the current viewport, which is very handy when you want to create a layer to be visible in only a single viewport.

WARNING

Unlike a frozen layer in tiled model space (TILEMODE=1), a layer that is frozen for the current floating viewport (TILEMODE=0) can be the current layer. You receive a warning, but the action is carried out. If a layer is frozen globally, you cannot make it the current layer, nor can you freeze the current layer globally (using the FREEZE button).

In the following exercise, you edit the model in floating model space, with the help of VPLAYER.

EDITING IN FLOATING MODEL SPACE

Continue in the CHAP05A drawing.

`Command:` *Choose* Data, Viewport Layer Controls, Freeze	Issues VPLAYER with the Freeze option specified
`Command: _vplayer ?/Freeze/Thaw/Reset/Newfrz/Vpvisdflt: _f`	
`Layer(s) to Freeze:` **HATCHING2** ↵	Specifies layer to be frozen
`All/Select/<Current>:` **S** ↵	Specifies the Select option
`Switching to Paper space.`	Message indicating the user is being switched back to paper space (PSPACE command)
`Select objects:` *Select the upper left viewport*	Selects the upper left viewport as one to be frozen
`Select objects:` *Select the lower left viewport*	Selects the lower left viewport as one to be frozen
`Select objects:` ↵	
`Switching to Model space.`	Message indicating the user is being switched back to model space (MSPACE command)

`Command: _vplayer ?/Freeze/Thaw/Reset/ Newfrz/Vpvisdflt:` ↵	Ends the VPLAYER command
`Command:` *Choose* Data, Viewport Layer Controls, New Freeze	Issues VPLAYER with the New option specified
`?/Freeze/Thaw/Reset/Newfrz/ Vpvisdflt:` **_n** ↵	
`New Viewport frozen layer names:` **TITLE** ↵_	Creates a new layer named TITLE that is made frozen for all current viewports and new viewports
`?/Freeze/Thaw/Reset/Newfrz/ Vpvisdflt:` **T** ↵	Specifies the Thaw option
`Layer(s) to Thaw:` **TITLE** ↵	Specifies TITLE as the layer to be thawed
`All/Select/<Current>:` **S** ↵	Specifies the Select option
`Switching to Paper space.`	Message indicating the user is being switched back to paper space (PSPACE command)
`Select objects:` *Select the upper left viewport*	Selects viewport in which layer TITLE is to be thawed
`Select objects:` ↵	
`Switching to Model space.`	Message indicating the user is being switched back to model space (MSPACE command)
`?/Freeze/Thaw/Reset/Newfrz/ Vpvisdflt:` ↵	

Make the upper left viewport current and the layer TITLE the current layer.

`Command:` *Choose Dtext (Draw, Text)*	Issues DTEXT
`Justify/Style/<Start point>:` **4.5,6** _ ↵	Specifies left justification point for text
`Rotation angle <0.00>:` ↵	Specifies rotation angle

`Text:` **Model 100X I/O Board** *Press Enter twice*

Examine the right viewport. Notice that the text you just drew does not appear in the right viewport, because the layer TITLE was created as a frozen layer in all viewports except the viewport in which you thawed it (the upper left viewport).

Closing Floating Viewports, and Opening More

Unlike tiled viewports, MVIEW does not have options you can use to merge or close multiple floating viewports. Instead, all you have to do to close a viewport is erase the viewport object. Deleting a viewport object does not delete the objects displayed in it.

When you fill up your drawing window with floating viewports, you might find that you want to open up some more. You can make room for additional viewports by shrinking (scaling down) some of the existing viewports, or you can use ZOOM to zoom out to see more paper space in the drawing window. If you choose to zoom out, make sure that you are in paper space; otherwise, you change the view in the current viewport.

TIP

If you want to blow up the view in a particular viewport before you work on the model, switch to paper space and zoom in on the viewport. If you issue ZOOM while in floating model space, only the view within the viewport confines is affected; before you can zoom in on or pan the viewports, you must be in paper space.

In this chapter you have learned to create multiple views of your model in both tiled model space and in paper space and how to switch between the two environments (TILEMODE). You can edit the model using viewports in either environment but there are crucial differences between tiled and floating viewports. With floating viewports, you have more flexibility to size and locate them and also more control over the visibility of layers within each viewport.

chapter

6

Plotting and Sheet Composition

Most of the skills you need to develop to become proficient with AutoCAD center on configuring your electronic workspace, and creating a model of your design within it. For some purposes, the resulting virtual drawing might suffice, but most design work eventually needs to be presented as hard copy—a printed or plotted image. In this chapter, you learn how to control the output of your model and transfer it to a piece of paper, vellum, or other media—in a word, plotting. This chapter covers the following:

- *Configuring and selecting a plot device*
- *Using the PLOT command*
- *Plotting specific areas of a drawing*
- *Composing a plot in paper space*
- *Using the MVSETUP command*

You also learn how to compose the layout of your plotted output in both model and paper space. When you sit at a drafting board deciding what views to draw and where to place them on the sheet of paper, you are composing the layout of the drawing. This chapter describes the equivalent process for an AutoCAD drawing.

You begin by learning about the details of the plotting process.

Plotting

Despite incessant talk of a "paperless" office, the reality is that producing plots is still a big part of CAD work. You create plots for checking (sometimes called *check plots*), and of course, you create plots as the finished product. The primary command for producing hard copy output is the PLOT command.

Issuing the PLOT command opens the Plot Configuration dialog box (see fig. 6.1), which provides the range of options required to control the output process. These options are described in detail in the sections that follow.

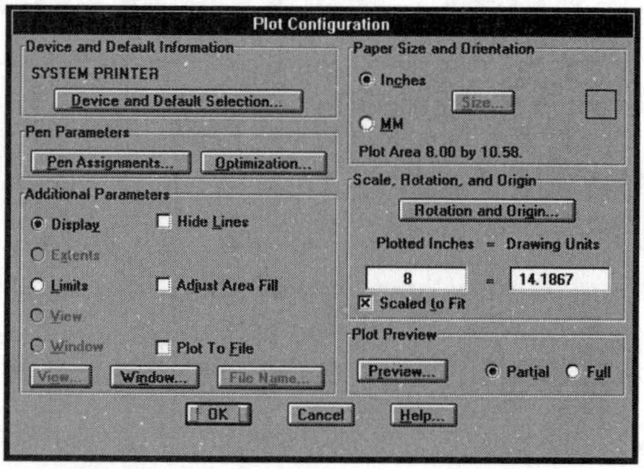

Figure 6.1

The Plot Configuration dialog box.

The basic procedure for producing a plot is as follows:

1. Make sure that your plotter is ready to plot.
2. Issue the PLOT command.
3. Select the plotter you want to use.
4. Set the pen assignments.
5. Specify the area of the drawing to plot.
6. Select a sheet size.

7. Set a plot scale.
8. Preview the output and, if you are satisfied, start the plot.

Checking Your Plotter Configuration

You can configure AutoCAD to use a particular output device during the initial installation of AutoCAD or any time thereafter (using CONFIG). The exact options available in the Plot Configuration dialog box vary from one plotter model to another. To ensure that you can carry out the exercises, you configure an HP 600 Design Jet plotter as your output device for this chapter.

NOTE

Even if you do not have an HP 600 plotter, you can configure for it and follow the exercise. You then can use the Preview Full feature in the Plot Configuration dialog box to simulate the plot, then use Cancel rather than OK to exit the dialog box.

To find out whether you even have a plotter currently configured, simply issue the PLOT command. If AutoCAD has not yet been configured to use an output device, an error message box appears (see fig. 6.2).

Figure 6.2

The error message box that appears if no plotter is configured.

If you are configured for an output device, the Plot Configuration dialog box appears, as shown in figure 6.1.

This chapter does not intend to teach you how to configure AutoCAD for your specific plotter. If you need to do so, consult the *AutoCAD Installation Guide* and the plotter manufacturer's installation guide.

In the following exercise, you go through the configuration process for an HP 600 Design Jet plotter. If you do not have the plotter that is specified in the following instructions, do not be alarmed. You do not actually plot to the specified plotter.

Configuring a Plotter

Begin a new drawing named CHAP06A, using the accompanying CD drawing BOARD as the prototype.

`Command:` *Choose* Options, Configure	Issues the CONFIG command and displays your current configuration settings
↵	

The main configuration menu appears.

```
Configuration menu
 0. Exit to drawing editor
 1. Show current configuration
 2. Allow detailed configuration
 3. Configure video display
 4. Configure digitizer
 5. Configure plotter
 6. Configure system console
 7. Configure operating parameters
```

`Enter selection <0>:` **5** ↵	Specifies the plotter configuration option

Next, you see the plotter configuration menu, which has options that you can use to add, delete, or modify plotter configurations.

```
Plotter Configuration Menu
 0. Exit to configuration menu
 1. Add a plotter configuration
 2. Delete a plotter configuration
 3. Change a plotter configuration
 4. Rename a plotter configuration
```

`Enter selection, 0 to 4 <0>:` **1** ↵	Specifies the Add plotter option

```
Available plotter:
  1. None
  2. AutoCAD file output formats (pre 4.1) - by Autodesk, Inc
  3. CalComp ColorMaster Plotters ADI 4.2 V2.8 - by Autodesk, Inc
  4. CalComp DrawingMaster Plotters ADI 4.2 V2.8 - by Autodesk, Inc
  5. CalComp Electrostatic Plotters ADI 4.2 V2.8 - by Autodesk, Inc
  6. CalComp Pen Plotters ADI 4.2 V2.8 - by Autodesk, Inc
  7. Canon Laser Printer ADI 4.2 - by Autodesk, Inc
  8. Hewlett-Packard (HP-GL) ADI 4.2 - by Autodesk, Inc
```

9. Hewlett-Packard (PCL) LaserJet ADI 4.2 - by Autodesk, Inc
10. Hewlett-Packard (PCL) PaintJet/DeskJet ADI 4.2 - by Autodesk, Inc
11. Hewlett-Packard HP-GL/2 devices, ADI 4.2 - for Autodesk by HP
12. Houston Instrument ADI 4.2 - by Autodesk, Inc
13. PostScript device ADI 4.2 - by Autodesk, Inc
14. Raster file export ADI 4.2 - by Autodesk, Inc
15. System Printer ADI 4.2 - by Autodesk, Inc

Select device number or ? to repeat list <1>: **11** ↵ — Specifies the HP-GL/2 driver

The list of plotters might vary from version to version, so make sure that the number 11 still corresponds to HP-GL/2 devices before you enter 11.

Supported models:

1. HP DesignJet 650C
2. HP DesignJet 600
3. HP DesignJet 200
4. HP DraftMaster with Roll Feed
5. HP DraftMaster Plus Sheet Feed
6. HP DraftMaster SX/RX/MX Sheet Fd
7. HP PaintJet XL300
8. HP DraftPro Plus
9. HP 7600 Color (obsolete)
10. HP 7600 Monochrome (obsolete)
11. HP LaserJet III
12. HP LaserJet 4

Enter selection, 1 to 12 <1>: **2** ↵ — Specifies the HP DesignJet 600 plotter

The list of HP models might vary from version to version, so make sure that the number 2 still corresponds to the DesignJet 600 before you enter 2.

You then get some device-specific instructions, after which you see the following prompt.

Press a key to continue ↵ — Continues the configuration process

Is your plotter connected to a <S>erial, or <P>arallel port? <P> ↵

Enter parallel port name for plotter or . for none <LPT1>: ↵

Accepting the defaults of the previous two prompts configures AutoCAD to plot on parallel port LPT1.

Plot will NOT be written to a selected file Sizes are in Inches and the style is landscape Plot origin is at (0.00,0.00) Plotting area is 43.00 wide by 33.00 high (E size) Plot is NOT rotated Hidden lines will NOT be removed Plot will be scaled to fit available area	
Do you want to change anything? (No/Yes/File) <N>: ↵	Accepts the listed defaults
Enter a description for this plotter: **IAW PLOTTER** ↵	Assigns the name IAW PLOTTER to the new plotter configuration and returns you to the plotter configuration menu
Plotter Configuration Menu 0. Exit to configuration menu 1. Add a plotter configuration 2. Delete a plotter configuration 3. Change a plotter configuration 4. Rename a plotter configuration	
Enter selection, 0 to 4 <0>: ↵	Exits plotter configuration menu and returns you to the configuration menu
Configuration menu 0. Exit to drawing editor 1. Show current configuration 2. Allow detailed configuration 3. Configure video display 4. Configure digitizer 5. Configure plotter 6. Configure system console 7. Configure operating parameters	
Enter selection <0>: ↵	Exits configuration menu
If you answer N to the following question, all configuration changes you have just made will be discarded.	
Keep configuration changes? <Y> ↵	Saves configuration and returns you to the drawing editor

You use the IAW PLOTTER configuration in the following exercises.

Previewing Your Plot

As you decide upon the exact settings for the plot, you can preview the expected results at any time by using the Plot Preview options, shown in figure 6.3.

Figure 6.3

The Preview options from the Plot Configuration dialog box.

You can perform a Partial (default setting) or a Full preview. If you select a Partial preview, you see a dialog box similar to the one in figure 6.4.

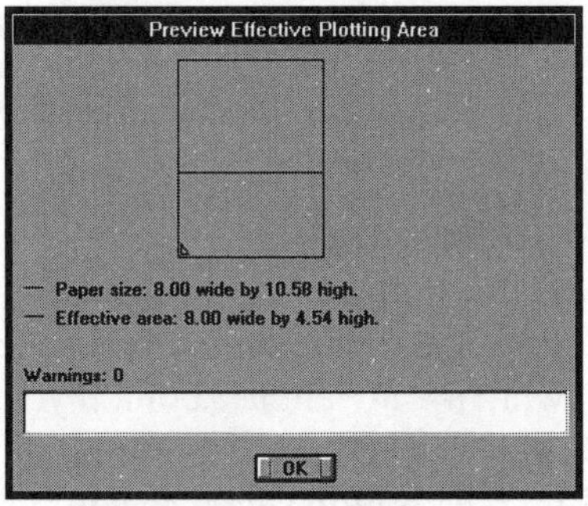

Figure 6.4

A partial preview.

The larger rectangle (red color) usually represents the specified plot area (paper size) and the smaller rectangle (blue color) usually represents the area that the plot actually uses. You are given the actual dimensions below the rectangles. The preview function warns you if it detects any possible errors, such as specifying a scale that requires more plot area than you indicate is available.

If you opt for a full preview, you see an image of the actual plot itself, similar to figure 6.5.

Figure 6.5

A full preview.

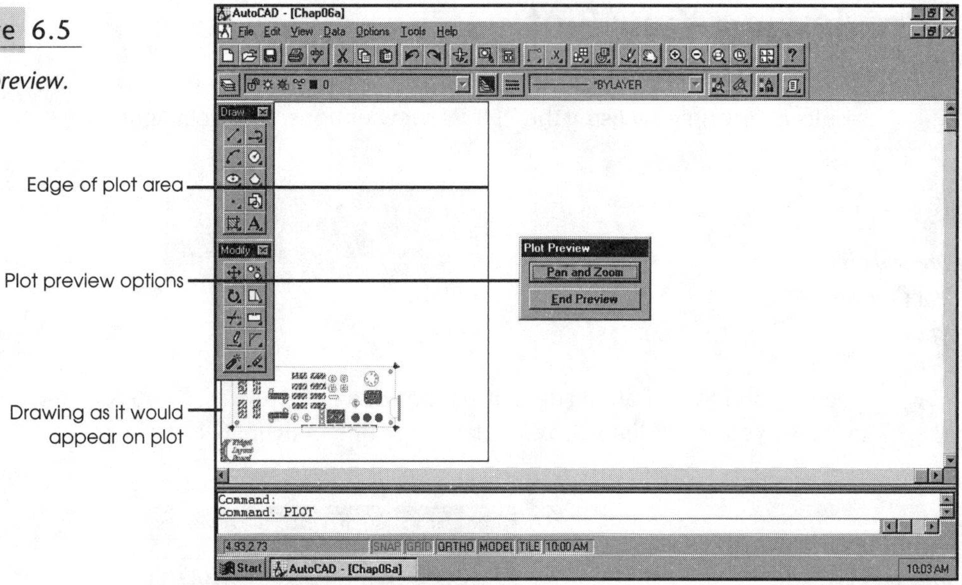

You can zoom into an area by using the Pan and Zoom button. If you choose Pan and Zoom, a rectangle replaces your normal cursor. You position the rectangle in the area into which you want to zoom. If you click the pick button, you can size the rectangle. If you click the pick button again, you can position the resized rectangle. Clicking the pick button switches you between resizing and positioning the rectangle. Dynamic zoom works in a similar manner. After you are satisfied with the size and location of the rectangle, press Enter or the spacebar, and the specified area appears. You then see the following options, as shown in figure 6.6.

Figure 6.6

Plot Preview options.

If you want to zoom into another area, choose the Zoom Previous button. The previous view appears and you can zoom and pan to another area. After you are satisfied, you can end the preview by choosing End Preview. Naturally, it takes longer to generate a full preview than a partial preview.

If you do not like what you see in the preview, go back and change your settings. After you decide that everything looks satisfactory, choose OK in the Plot Configuration dialog box to proceed with the actual plot.

Note

Zooming and panning in preview mode do not actually change the view that is plotted. They simply enable you to see the details of the plot that might be too small to read.

In the exercises that follow, you use the preview function to view the effects of changing the various Plot Configuration settings.

Selecting the Plotter

You can configure AutoCAD to work with multiple output devices. If you have only one plotter configured, PLOT automatically uses it. If, however, you have several plotters configured, you need to select the plotter you want to use by choosing the Device and Default Selection button in the Device and Default Information group of the Plot Configuration dialog box (refer to figure 6.1). Choosing the Device and Default Selection button displays the Device and Default Selection dialog box, as shown in figure 6.7.

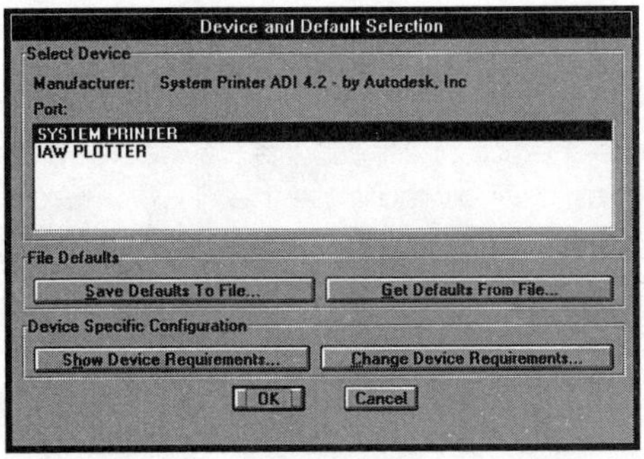

Figure 6.7

The Device and Default Selection box.

To select a particular plotter configuration, simply select it from the list that appears in the Select Device list box in the Device and Default Selection dialog box. At times, you can set some device-specific options. To see if the selected plotter has any options, choose the Show Device Requirements button. If you want to set device-specific options, choose the Change Device Requirements button. The device-specific options, of course, vary from device to device, and are nonexistent for some devices.

TIP

The plotter configuration names that appear in the list are the names you specify during the configuration process. Use descriptive names that will be meaningful even to a novice user.

In the following exercise, you issue the PLOT command and select the plotter you configured in the previous exercise.

SELECTING A PLOTTER CONFIGURATION

Continue using the drawing CHAP06A from the previous exercise.

`Command:` *Choose Print (Standard Toolbar)*	Issues the PLOT command and opens the Plot Configuration dialog box
`Command:` *Choose the* Device and Default Selection *button*	Displays the Device and Default Selection dialog box

If you have multiple plotter configurations, you select the plotter configuration you want to use in the Device and Default Selection dialog box.

Select IAW PLOTTER *from the device list*

`Command:` *Choose the* Change Device Requirements *button*	Displays the Change Device Requirements dialog box

You set device-specific options in the Device Requirements dialog box. The HP DesignJet displays settings, but you must use the HPCONFIG command (supplied with the plotter driver) to change them.

`Command:` *Choose* OK	Exits the Device Requirements dialog box
`Command:` *Choose* OK *again dialog box*	Exits the Device and Default Selection
Choose the Full *button*	Specifies the Plot Preview Full option
Click on the Preview *button*	Displays the full plot preview

The full preview accurately simulates plotting the drawing. The simulated plot is scaled to fit in the drawing area. You need to consider several other options before actually creating a finished plot.

Click on the End Preview *button*	Returns to the Plot Configuration dialog box

Remain in the PLOT command for the next exercise. If you cancel, your settings are lost.

Setting Pen Parameters

After you select the device to use, you want to set up the pen assignments for the plot. Correctly setting the pen assignments ensures that AutoCAD knows the plotter's pen characteristics so that it can create accurate plots. You access the pen assignments through the Pen Assignments dialog box (see fig. 6.8), which you bring up by choosing the Pen Assignments button in the Pen Parameters group of the Plot Configuration dialog box (refer to figure 6.1).

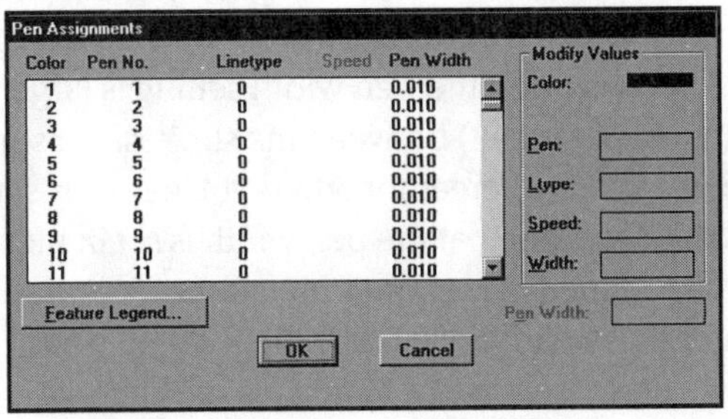

Figure 6.8

The Pen Assignments dialog box.

The Pen Assignments dialog box enables you to assign a pen, speed, linetype, and line weight to a particular drawing color. AutoCAD uses the analogy of *pens* (even though many plotters today use inkjet, electrostatic, or laser technology), based on the historical use of multiple-pen plotters, where pens of different widths (or colors) are identified by their numbered positions within the plotter's carousel.

In AutoCAD, pens are associated with drawing objects based on the object's color. By setting the pen table, you can instruct PLOT to use pen #2 for all objects drawn in red or pen #1 for all objects drawn in green. Using a multiple-pen plotter, if you insert pens with color ink into the carousel, you end up with a color plot, or if you put pens of different widths into the carousel, then you can create a plot that has multiple line weights.

Non-pen or *raster* plotters extend this analogy, so you can instruct an inkjet or laser plotter to draw lines of various widths or colors by assigning *logical pen* numbers to the range of drawing object colors.

The linetype and speed parameters are similar holdovers from the older plotting technology. Even with a pen plotter, you can generally leave the linetype setting at the default value of 0 (for continuous) and use AutoCAD's linetypes when you want to draw objects that have noncontinuous linetypes.

Using a pen plotter, depending on the media on which you plotted and the type of pen you used, you might need to adjust the speed at which the pens travel so that the ink will flow properly. With most raster plotters the pen speed setting is not relevant and you can leave it at the default. Some devices use the pen speed setting to control some other parameters, such as the darkness of lines for a laser printer.

The pen width setting enables you to set the pen width of a particular pen. AutoCAD uses this information when it draws solid filled areas and for the Adjust Area Fill option of the Plot Configuration dialog box. To fill in a solid area, AutoCAD draws one stroke and then moves the pen over one pen width to draw the next stroke. If the pen width setting is smaller then the actual pen width, you get redundant overlapping of strokes. If the pen width setting is larger than the actual pen width, you get gaps (blank space) between the strokes. For some plotters, you can set a pen width for each pen, whereas for others you can only set a global pen width for all pens. You must remember that the pen width is set in inches, not in millimeters, if your paper size is defined in inches (which is the default setting). So, if you use a 0.35-mm pen, enter a pen width of 0.014 inches. Usually leaving this setting at its default value of 0.01 (equivalent to 0.254 mm) is satisfactory.

TIP

If you are used to working with line weights defined in millimeters, set the paper size units to mm, then assign the pen widths. After you assign the pen widths, you can change the paper size units back to inches.

To set the values for a particular pen, just select the pen you want to set. AutoCAD then places the pen's current values into the edit boxes on the right side of the Pen Assignments dialog box, where you can change them. To set several pens simultaneously, first select several pens and then change the values in the edit boxes.

NOTE

The ISO Pen Width setting the Select Linetype dialog box only controls the linetype scale of ISO linetypes. You control the plotted width of an ISO linetype as you would any other linetype—by specifying an appropriate pen width for the object's color.

In the following exercise, you change the default pen table.

CHANGING THE PEN ASSIGNMENTS

Continue to use the drawing CHAP06A. If you canceled the PLOT command in the previous exercise, reissue it and make sure that the IAW PLOTTER is still the selected configuration.

In the following steps, you use the Pen Assignment button located in the upper left portion of the Plot Configuration dialog box.

`Command:` *Choose the* Pen Assignments *button* — Displays the Pen Assignments dialog box

`Command:` *Select colors* 1, 2, 3, *and* 4

To assign pen # 1 to colors 1, 2, 3, and 4, replace the value in the Pen edit box with the value 1 and press Enter. Even if the Pen edit box already shows 1, press Enter to assign 1 to all four selected colors.

`Command:` *Deselect colors* 1, 2, 3, *and* 4

`Command:` *Select colors* 5, 6, *and* 7

To assign pen # 2 to colors 5, 6, and 7, replace the value in the Pen edit box with the value 2 and press Enter.

`Command:` *Choose* OK — Exits the Pen Assignments dialog box

Remain in the Plot Configuration dialog box for the next exercise.

NOTE

If you need to exit, choose OK so that your settings are saved, then quickly choose Cancel when the small `Printing CHAP06A` message box or AutoCAD Alert box appears. If you choose Cancel in the Plot Configuration dialog box, your settings are not saved.

Defining the Area To Be Plotted

You specify the portion of the drawing you want to plot in the Additional Parameters section of the Plot Configuration dialog box (see fig. 6.9).

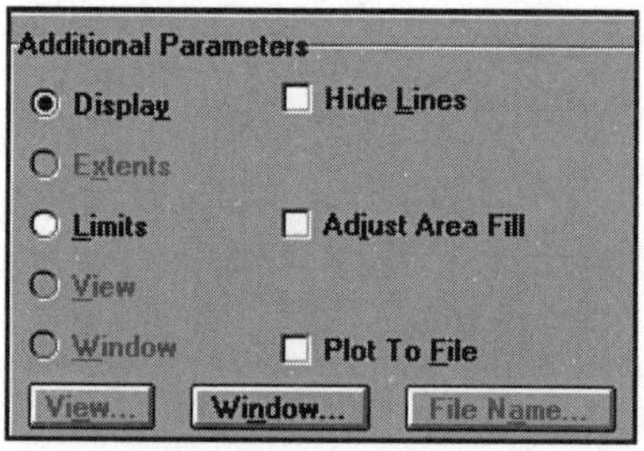

Figure 6.9

The Additional Parameters section from the Plot Configuration dialog box.

You have the following choices in the Additional Parameters section:

- **Display.** Choose this radio button to plot the portion of the drawing in the current viewport. If you are in paper space itself or in the default single tiled viewport, Display plots the portion of the drawing displayed in the drawing window. If you are in a model space tiled or floating viewport, then the portion of the drawing visible in that viewport is plotted.
- **Extents.** Choose this radio button to process the rectangular portion of your drawing that actually has objects drawn in it.
- **Limits.** Choose this radio button to process the area defined by the drawing limits (as set by using the LIMITS command).
- **View.** This radio button initially is grayed and disabled. Choose this button to plot previously saved views with DDVIEW or VIEW. If you opt to plot a view, choosing the View button at the bottom of the Additional Parameters area opens the View Name dialog box, in which you can select from a list of defined views. Then the View radio button becomes enabled and ungrayed so that you can choose it. If the drawing has no defined views the View button is grayed.
- **Window.** This radio button initially is disabled. To window a rectangular area to be plotted, first you define the area by choosing the Window button at the bottom of the Additional Parameters area. The Window Selection dialog box appears (see fig. 6.10) which displays the points defining the current window. If you want to define another window area, choose the Pick button. When you choose OK to close the Window Selection dialog box, the Window radio button is ungrayed and enabled.

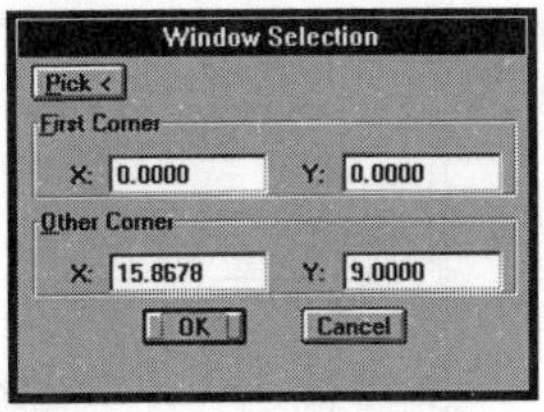

Figure 6.10

The Window Selection dialog box.

Warning

If you recently changed the extents you might need to perform a ZOOM All or ZOOM Extents before plotting. You can change extents accidentally, for example, if you mistakenly move or copy an object to somewhere "out in space." Even if you use Undo to reverse the mistake, the extents will be oversized. If you find your plot is scaled small and placed in a corner of the plotted area, this probably is the cause. Use ZOOM Extents to correct this problem.

In the following exercise, you use the various options for defining the area to plot. You also use the preview buttons located in the lower right corner of the Plot Configuration dialog box to simulate the plot.

Defining the Area to Plot

Continue to use the drawing CHAP06A. If you canceled the PLOT command in the previous exercise, reissue it and make sure that the IAW PLOTTER is still the selected configuration and that the previous pen assignments are intact.

Choose Extents	Specifies the Extents option
`Command:` *Choose* Preview	Displays a partial preview (default setting) of the plot using the current settings
`Command:` *Choose* OK	Ends the partial preview
`Command:` *Choose* Full	Enables a full preview for the next preview operation
`Command:` *Choose* Preview	Displays a full preview of the plot using the current settings and displays the Plot Preview dialog box (see fig. 6.11)

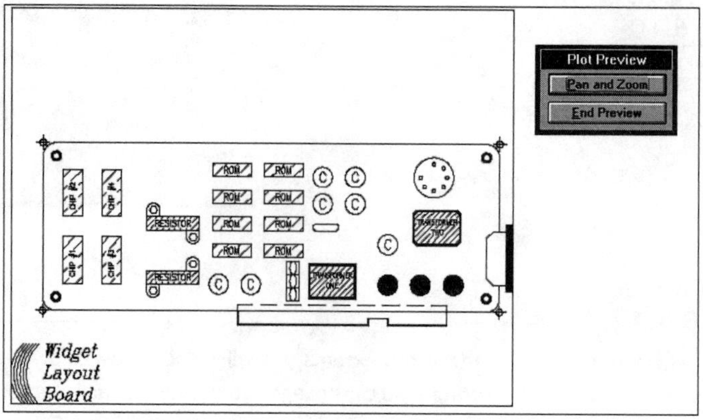

Figure 6.11

Full plot preview of the drawing.

`Command:` *Choose* Pan and Zoom	Enters the Pan and Zoom mode

Your cursor is replaced with a box that represents the area you are panning or zooming. Position the box anywhere on the screen. Click the pick button once and you can size the box. If you want, click the pick button once again and you can reposition the box. After you are satisfied with the size and location of the box, press Enter to redisplay the Plot Preview dialog box.

`Command:` *Choose* End Preview	Ends the preview function and reopens the Plot Configuration dialog box

In the following steps, you work with the options for defining the area to be plotted. These options are on the left side of the Plot Configuration dialog box in the Additional Parameters section.

`Command:` *Choose the* Window *button at the bottom*	Displays the Window Selection dialog box with the coordinates of the current window
`Command:` *Choose* Pick	Closes dialog boxes and prompts for a new windowed area
`First corner:` *Pick* ① *(see fig. 6.12)*	
`Other corner:` *Pick* ②	Defines new windowed area and reopens the Window Selection dialog box
`Command:` *Choose* OK	Accepts the new windowed area and automatically selects the Window radio button
`Command:` *Choose* Preview	

You should see the area you windowed as the area on the plot preview (see fig. 6.13).

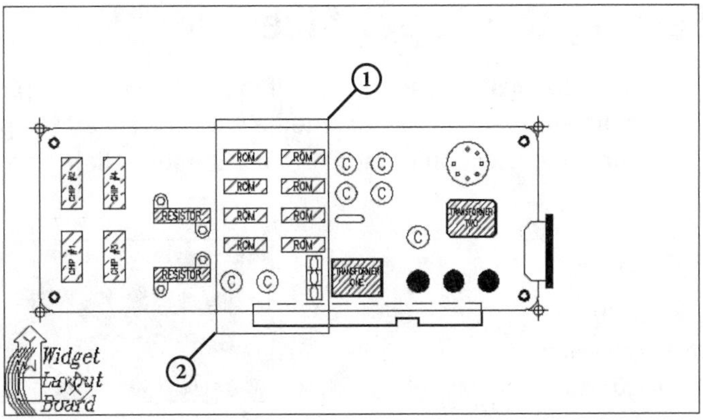

Figure 6.12

The windowed area to be plotted.

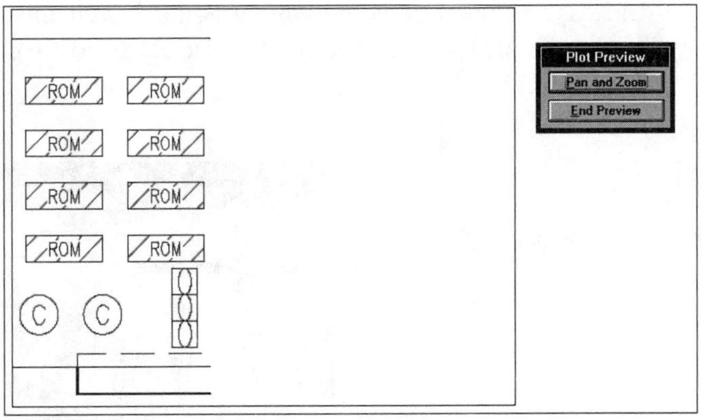

Figure 6.13

Preview of window area plot.

`Command:` *Choose* End Preview

Remain in the Plot Configuration dialog box for the next exercise.

TIP

Standardizing on the name PLOT for a single plot view, or PLOT1, PLOT2, and so on. for multiple plot views, can help you avoid confusion about what view to plot.

Setting the Paper Size

You also must decide the size of media on which to plot and the units—inches or millimeters—to define that media size. You set these options in the Paper Size and Orientation section of the Plot Configuration dialog box, as shown in figure 6.14.

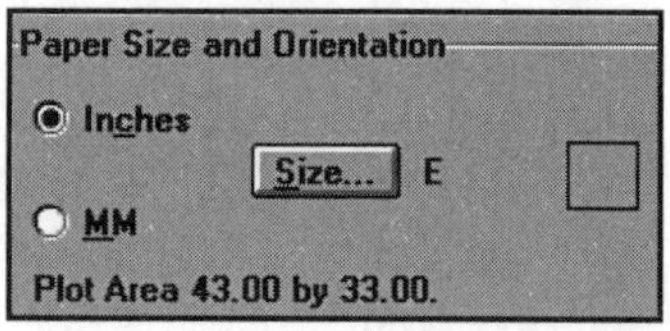

Figure 6.14

The Paper Size and Orientation section from the Plot Configuration dialog box.

Unless you work with metric standards, the default units of inches is appropriate. To set the actual paper size, click on the Size button to display the Paper Size dialog box (see fig. 6.15).

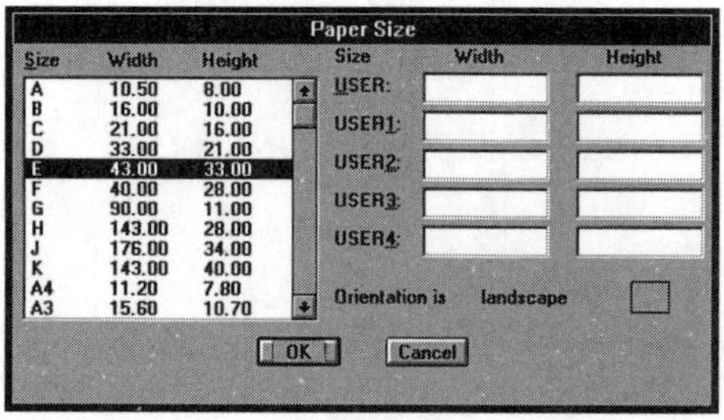

Figure 6.15

The Paper Size dialog box.

The term *paper size* is misleading because what you really define is the area on which you plot (also referred to as the *plot area*). The difference is that a plotter cannot plot right up to the edges of a sheet of paper. There always is a margin around the edges that the plotter cannot access, as shown in figure 6.16.

The actual margin varies from plotter to plotter, so you need to look up that information in the plotter manuals. When you subtract the margins from the sheet size, you obtain the maximum available plot area, which is what you usually want to enter in the Paper Size dialog box. Suppose that the instruction manual of your plotter states that the plotter leaves a half-inch margin all the way around the edge of the paper. Then on a 24-by-36-inch piece of paper, the maximum usable area (or plot area) is going to be 23 inches by 35 inches.

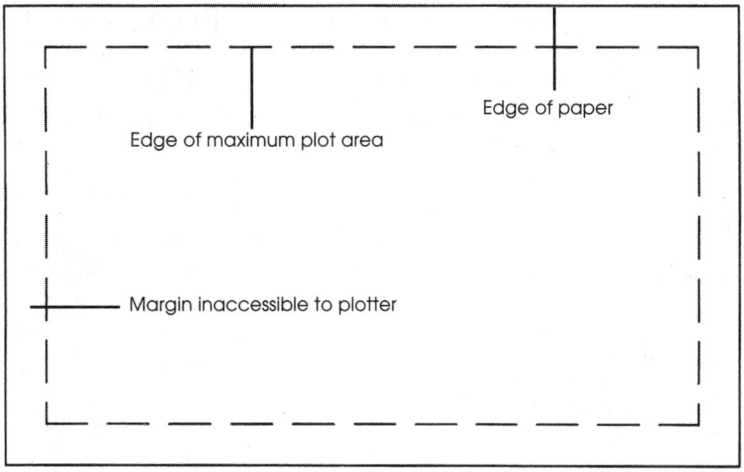

Figure 6.16

Physical area versus maximum available plot area.

On the left of the Paper Size dialog box is a list of standard sheet sizes and their associated plot areas. You can select a plot area from the list or you can enter custom dimensions by using the edit boxes on the right labeled USER, USER1, and so on. A sheet size defined using these edit boxes is referred to as a *user defined sheet*. After you define a sheet size, the associated label (USER, USER1, and so on) appears in the list of available sheet sizes.

TIP

The list of predefined plot areas usually is not optimized for the specific plotter you are using. You usually can get more plot area for a specific sheet size than what is stated on the list. If this is true for your plotter, use the edit boxes to define your own user-defined sheet size. You can test the maximum available plot area by selecting the MAX size and separately plotting two xline objects (one horizontal and one vertical), then measuring the results of each plot. Use a tall, skinny window for the vertical xline plot and a short, wide window for the horizontal one.

In the bottom right corner of the Paper Size dialog box is a message that indicates the orientation of the paper. This is the assumed orientation of the loaded media. It is just a message, not a choice. The message varies for different plotters. For some, it indicates landscape; for others, it indicates portrait.

In the following exercise, you select the paper size for the plot.

SETTING THE PLOT AREA

Continue to use the drawing CHAP06A. If you canceled the PLOT command in the previous exercise, reissue it and make sure IAW PLOTTER is still the selected configuration.

In this exercise, you work with the paper size options located in the upper right portion of the Plot Configuration dialog box.

`Command:` *Choose the* Extents *radio button*	Sets the drawing extents as the area to be plotted
`Command:` *Choose* Size	Displays the Paper Size dialog box
`Command:` *Select the A-size sheet from the list*	Sets the current plot area to that of an A-size sheet
`Command:` *Choose* OK	Closes the Paper Size dialog box

Remain in the Plot Configuration dialog box for the next exercise.

Setting the Rotation and Origin

Choosing the Rotation and Origin button in the Plot Configuration dialog box opens the Plot Rotation and Origin dialog box (see fig. 6.17).

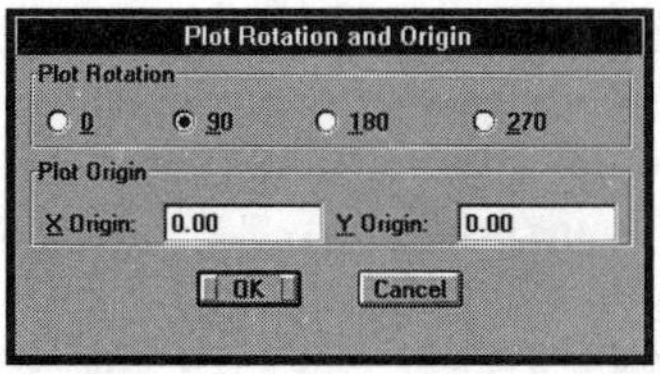

Figure 6.17

The Plot Rotation and Origin dialog box.

A plotter has its own X,Y axes and origin point. A rotation angle setting of 0 and an origin setting of 0,0 ensures that the area to be plotted (whether it be limits, extents, or whatever) is oriented on the paper so that the model's X axis is parallel to the plotter's X axis and that the lower left corner of the area to be plotted coincides with the plotter's origin point.

You might want to change the orientation so that the area to be plotted can be better accommodated on the paper. Typically, the paper is loaded in a plotter so that the plotter's X axis runs along the longer length of the sheet. If your model's extents is greater in the Y direction than in the X direction, you might need to rotate the plot to get the largest possible plot onto the paper.

WARNING

Be careful when you change the rotation angle. The settings rotate the plot in a clockwise direction and you can rotate the plot off the physical paper area. If this occurs, no plot is produced, and you have to adjust the origin point to accommodate the rotation angle.

Some plotters have a smaller margin on one side of the paper than the other. In such cases, your plot might appear off balance with more blank space on one side than the other. To even the margins out, you can adjust the origin to center the plot.

You also can use the origin option to fit several small plots onto a single large sheet of paper. After you generate the first plot, you would set the origin so that the next plot does not overlap the area occupied by the first plot. Not all plotters enable you to use this technique because it requires that you reuse the same sheet of paper for several plots. This technique is most commonly used with pen plotters. Composing your plot in paper space, as discussed later in this chapter, is probably easier than offsetting multiple plots.

In the following exercise, you set the rotation and origin of the plot.

SETTING THE ROTATION AND ORIGIN

Continue to use the drawing CHAP06A. If you canceled the PLOT command in the previous exercise, reissue it and make sure that the IAW PLOTTER is still the selected configuration.

In this exercise, you set the origin and rotation of the plot (using the right side of the Plot Configuration dialog box).

`Command:` *Choose* Rotation and Origin	Displays the Plot Rotation and Origin dialog box
`Command:` *Type* **2.0** *in the* Y Origin *edit box*	Offsets the origin of the plot 2 inches along the plotter's Y axis
`Command:` *Choose* OK	Returns you to the Plot Configuration dialog box
`Command:` *Choose* Full, *then* Preview	Offsets the plot in the vertical (Y axis) direction *(see fig. 6.18)*

Figure 6.18

Plot preview with the plot origin moved.

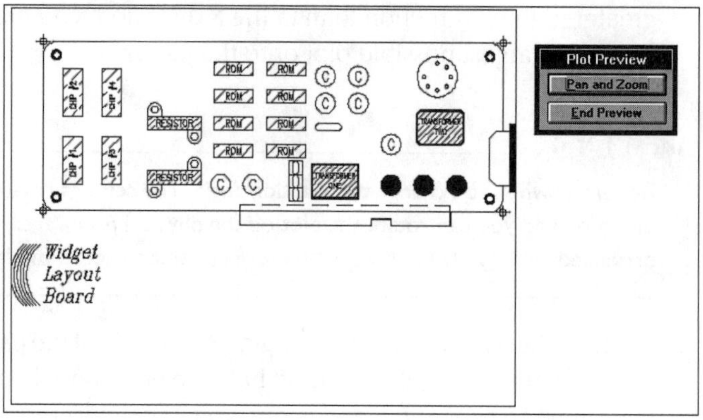

`Command:` *Choose* End Preview	
`Command:` *Choose* Rotation and Origin	
`Command:` *Choose the* 90 Plot Rotation *radio button*	Rotates the plot 90 degrees clockwise
`Command:` *Type* **0.0** in *the* Y Origin *edit box*	Resets the plot origin back to 0,0
`Command:` *Choose* OK	
`Command:` *Choose* Preview	Previews the plot, rotated clockwise 90 degrees (see fig. 6.19)

Figure 6.19

Plot preview of rotated plot.

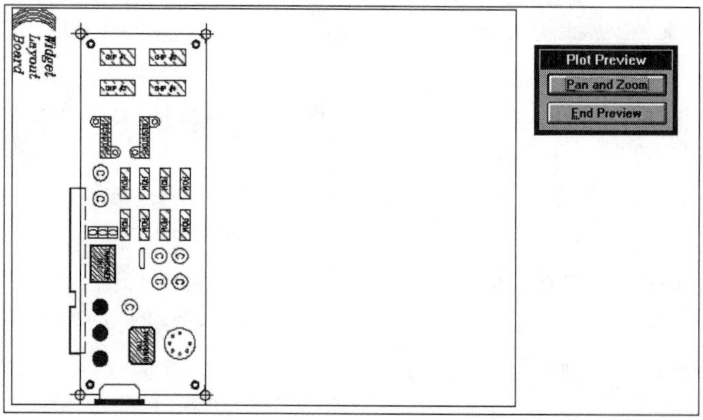

`Command:` *Choose* End Preview

Remain in the Plot Configuration dialog box for the next exercise.

Setting the Plot Scale

The *plot scale* is the relationship you set between a distance on your final plot (inches or millimeters) to the equivalent distance in your drawing (drawing units). A common scale is 1/8 plotted inch to 1' in the actual drawing. You set the plot scale in the Scale, Rotation, and Origin section of the Plot Configuration dialog box (see fig. 6.20).

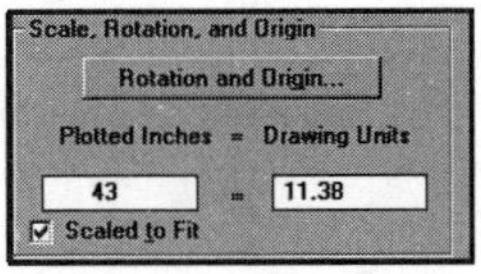

Figure 6.20

The Scale, Rotation, and Origin section of the Plot Configuration dialog box.

If you have your units set for architectural or engineering units, you can include the foot and inch marks in your scale specification. Regardless of the units you have set, you always can set the scale in decimal units. For example, if you are working on a drawing that you have set up in architectural units and intend to plot at a 1/8"=1' scale, you can enter any of the following values for the scale:

1" = 8'

1/8" = 1'

1 = 96"

1 = 96

At times, you might want to generate a plot that has no particular scale. In such situations, use the Scaled to Fit option. Turning on Scaled to Fit instructs AutoCAD to calculate and use the largest scale possible to fit the area to be plotted onto the specified plot area (Paper Size section). The drawback to using Scaled to Fit is that you cannot scale anything off the drawing because a nonstandard scale was used for the plot.

In the following exercise, you set the plot scale for the plot.

SETTING THE PLOT SCALE

Continue to use the drawing CHAP06A. If you canceled the PLOT command in the previous exercise, reissue it and make sure the IAW PLOTTER is still the selected configuration.

Choose Rotation and Origin, *set plot rotation to* 0 *and then choose* OK.

`Command:` *Choose* Size	Displays the Paper Size dialog box
`Command:` *Select* B *size from the list*	Sets the paper size to the B size
`Command:` *Choose* OK	
`Command:` *Clear the* Scaled to Fit *check box*	

Disabling the Scaled to Fit option enables you to set a specific scale. The default is a 1:1 scale. Make sure that the values in the scale edit boxes read 1 = 1.00", meaning that 1 inch on the plot is equal to 1 inch in the model.

`Command:` *Choose* Preview

Notice how the plot no longer fills the sheet (see fig. 6.21). End the preview after you finish examining it.

Figure 6.21

Preview plot at 1:1 scale.

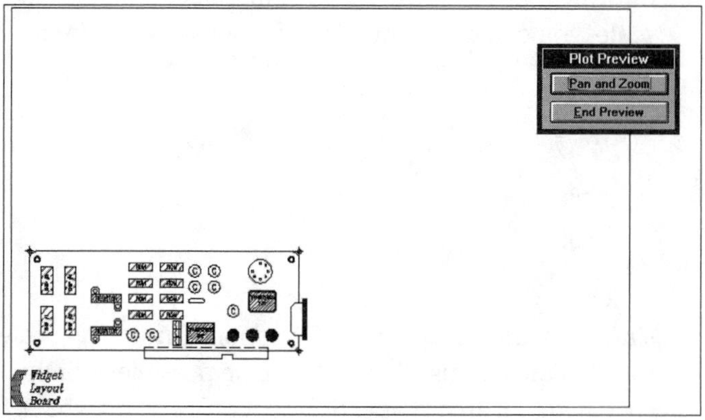

Change the values in the scale edit boxes to read 1=2.00". This scale shrinks the plot because 1 inch on the plot is equal to 2 inches in the model.

`Command:` *Choose* Preview	Decreases the plot size

End the preview after you examine it.

Change the values in the scale edit boxes to read 1=0.25". This scale enlarges the plot because 1 inch on the plot is equal to 0.25 inches in the model.

Command: *Choose* Preview

Notice that the plot is larger but not complete because only a portion of the model fits on the specified paper size (see fig. 6.22). End the preview after you examine it.

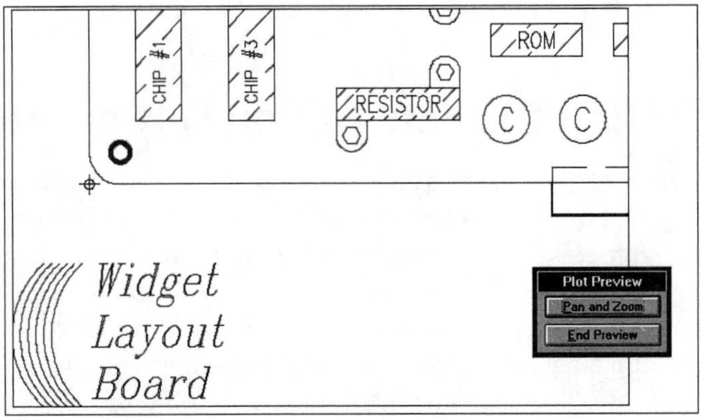

Figure 6.22

Preview of plot 4:1 scale.

Remain in the Plot Configuration dialog box for the next exercise.

Where Does the Plot Information Go

After you choose the OK button in the Plot Configuration dialog box, where does the plot information go? By default, the data is sent to the parallel or serial port that you specified by your plotter configuration. You can, however, send the plot data to a file by enabling the Plot To File option. You then can specify a file name by choosing the File Name button. If you do not specify a file name, a default file name is used that is the same as the drawing file name but with a PLT extension. The plot file is written in the current working directory (IAW\DWGS).

Plotting to a file is often used to send a drawing out to a plotting service that may not have AutoCAD. The service bureau can simply transfer the plot data directly to the plotting device. Plot files are also useful for importing drawings into illustration packages or word processors for creating documentation.

If you specify the file name as LPT1, LPT2, LPT3, COM1, COM2, COM3, or COM4, the file is sent directly to the associated parallel or serial port.

To enable AutoCAD's plot spooler, you use the file name AUTOSPOOL. For details on how to configure a spooling program to work with AutoCAD, see the *AutoCAD Installation Guide*.

If your plotter is connected to a network, you should consult your network administrator concerning how you should send the plot information.

Setting the Pen Motion Optimization

When you process the drawing data for plotting, you can instruct AutoCAD to try to optimize the order in which the information is sent to the plotter. The goal of the process is to minimize wasted motion (such as moving pens or changing pens) that the plotter physically must undertake to plot. For example, it is more efficient for a pen plotter to draw all the lines that require a particular pen before it draws the lines that require another pen, instead of jumping around and switching pens all through the plot. If you turn on *pen sorting,* AutoCAD processes the entire drawing and sends out all plotting instructions for pen one first, then repeats the process for the next pen, and so on.

There are other pen motions that can be optimized. To set the level of pen motion optimization, choose the Optimization button in the Pen Parameters section of the Plot Configuration dialog box. The Optimization button displays the Optimizing Pen Motion dialog box (see fig. 6.23).

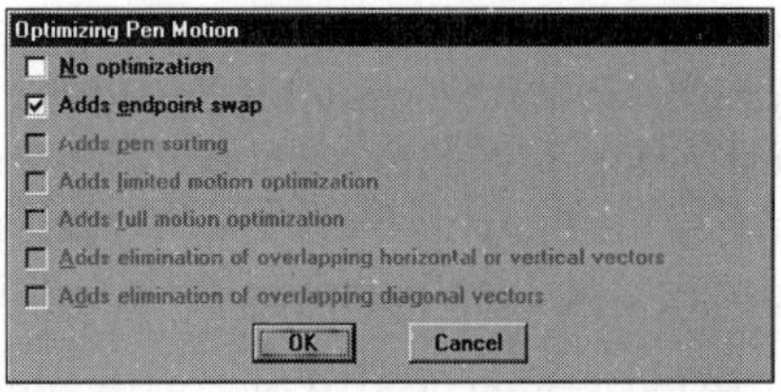

Figure 6.23

The Optimizing Pen Motion dialog box.

You can set various levels of optimization within the Optimizing Pen Motion dialog box. The levels are arranged in order of complexity and are cumulative. If you select the 3rd level of optimization, the 1st and 2nd levels are selected automatically. The greater the optimization, the more time AutoCAD requires to generate plot data, but it usually enables pen plotters to plot more quickly. Normally, the configuration process includes the automatic setting of the optimization level. For raster image devices (laser jets, inkjets, and so on), optimizing the data is a waste of time because physical pen movements are not involved. If you use such a device, you want to choose the No optimization level.

TIP

Plot optimization can improve the consistency of plotted lines drawn by pen plotters, particularly by eliminating overlapping vectors.

In the following exercise, you set the level of pen optimization.

SETTING THE PEN OPTIMIZATION LEVEL

Continue to use the drawing CHAP06A. If you canceled the Plot Configuration dialog box in the previous exercise, reissue it and make sure that the IAW PLOTTER is still the selected configuration.

`Command:` *Choose* Optimization	Displays the Optimizing Pen Motion dialog box
`Command:` *Put a* ✓ *in the* No Optimization *box*	Disables all optimization

For raster devices such as the Design Jet, this setting is optimal.

`Command:` *Choose* OK

Remain in the Plot Configuration dialog box for the next exercise.

NOTE

Some plotters have their own built-in plot and pen optimization that might be more efficient than AutoCAD's.

Hiding Lines for 3D Drawings

If you plot a 3D drawing, choosing the Hide Lines check box (in the Plot Configuration dialog box) results in *hidden lines*—lines that lie behind an opaque surface—being removed from the plotFor 2D plots, enabling this option is unnecessary.

Enabling the Adjust Area Fill Option

If you turn on the Adjust Area Fill check box, plotting adjusts for the pen width when you draw solid filled areas. This adjusts the location of the plotter pen inward by half its pen width when you draw the edges of a filled area.

If Adjust Area Fill is enabled, the edges of filled areas better match the coordinates of the filled area boundaries as measured in the drawing. Objects that are affected by this setting include traces, solids, and polylines that have width.

Unless you require an extreme degree of accuracy in the placement of lines on your plots (such as for printed circuit board artwork), it is not necessary to enable the Adjust Area Fill option.

Saving Your Plot Parameters

The current plot parameters are stored in the ACAD.CFG file when you exit the Plot Configuration dialog box. Sometimes, however, you need multiple sets of plot parameters.

In the Device and Default Selection dialog box (refer to figure 6.7), you can choose the Save Defaults To File button to save the current plot parameters to a file. You supply the filename and a file is created that has a filename extension of PCP (Plot Configuration Parameters). Choose the Get Defaults From File button from the same dialog box to restore a saved set of plot settings. The Get Defaults From File option is especially handy for saving and restoring pen settings when you switch from one set of pen settings to another.

TIP

> You can store the name of the PCP file to use with a drawing in an invisible attribute of an inserted block, such as the title block. Then, in a couple of years when you replot the drawing, you can check the name and quickly access the PCP file.

In the next exercise, you save the current plot settings to a file.

SAVING THE PLOT SETTINGS

Continue to use the drawing CHAP06A. If you canceled the Plot Configuration dialog box in the previous exercise, reissue it and make sure the IAW PLOTTER is still the selected configuration.

`Command:` *Choose* Device and Default Selection	Opens the Device and Default Selection dialog box
`Command:` *Choose* Save Defaults to File	Displays the Save to File dialog box
`Command:` *Type* **PLTSET1** *in the* File Name *box*	Specifies saving the plot parameters as PLTSET1.PCP
`Command:` *Choose* OK	Initiates the save operation
`Command:` *Choose* Get Defaults From File	Displays the Obtain from File dialog box, listing pltset1.plt in the file list
`Command:` *Click on* Cancel	Closes the Obtain from File dialog box
`Command:` *Choose* OK	Closes the Device and Default Selection dialog box

You now can cancel the PLOT command. If you choose OK, AutoCAD will attempt to generate a plot.

Plotting Hints and Tips

Inevitably, you run into problems plotting at one time or another. To minimize the chances of problems, check on the following items before you trigger the PLOT command:

- Make sure that the plotter is turned on and is online.
- Make sure that the necessary paper and pens are loaded. If you use a raster device, make sure that the ink cartridges have sufficient ink, especially if you plan multiple plots.
- Make sure that you know the scale you should use.
- Decide what area (extents, window, and so on) of the drawing you want to plot.
- Make sure that the appropriate layers are turned on or off.

Some other steps you can take to ensure fewer problems when plotting are as follows:

- Read the instructions that came with the plotter and the driver you use. Different models of plotters have different capabilities. You must read the instructions to get the most out of your plotter. In some cases, AutoCAD might come with a driver for your device, but a more up-to-date driver might be supplied by the plotter manufacturer. The instructions would indicate if such a device driver is supplied.
- Create standards for your pen settings. If you have standard pen settings for your plots, you can save them in PCP files and restore them when necessary.
- Create standards for your drawing creation. Everyone in your organization should set up the drawing the same way. A standard setup makes it easier to standardize the settings used for plotting.
- Always check out drawings from other sources. If you get drawings from a client or a subcontractor, do not assume that the drawings are set up the same way as your drawings. Check the units and colors. Ask whoever supplied the drawings how the drawings were set up.
- Use a monochrome driver for black-and-white plots with color plotters. Colored objects might plot as shades of grey or not plot at all on some color plotting devices if monochrome plots are plotted with color drivers. Create an alternate plotter configuration that uses a monochrome driver for creating monochrome plots. If your plotter does not have a monochrome driver, substitute a driver for a similar device that only supports black line plots.
- Clean the print head of inkjet plotters that create streaked plots. Use a soft cloth moistened with rubbing alcohol. Print heads can clog if unused for a long period of time.

Some of the more common problems encountered when you plot are as follows:

- Part of the plot gets chopped off. Be sure to specify the right scale and sheet size. You might accidentally specify a scale that requires more paper than you have. Alternatively, you might specify a plot area smaller than what is really available. PLOT does not plot beyond the plot area you specify, even if plenty of space is available.
- Solid filled areas are not getting filled. Do you have FILL turned off? Also, check on the pen widths. If the pen width is too large, PLOT might move the pen over too far to overlap the previous pen stroke. A common mistake is to specify the pen widths in millimeters when the units are still set for inches.

- Text characters are being connected together or are missing parts. Again, check your pen widths. When the width is too large, text characters are chopped off or connected together.
- The plot comes out the size of a postage stamp. Check the scale. If you specify a Fit scale with the plot area set to Extents, check the drawing extents. Sometimes the drawing extents are not reset correctly prior to plotting, so PLOT thinks the drawing occupies more room than it actually does. The easiest way to check the extents is to issue the ZOOM command using the Extents option.
- The PLOT command completes, but the plotter does not respond. This problem is most commonly encountered on networks. Usually, the problem is that the plot data gets sent to the wrong device. Make sure that the correct LPT ports are being captured correctly by the network.
- The PLOT command says the plotter is not responding. Check to see if the plotter is online. Make sure that the cable is correctly connected and that the plotter configuration is set to the right parallel or serial port.
- The pen seems to be skipping on the plot. The pen is moving too fast. Lower the pen's speed. Also, check the type of pens you are using. The types of pens that work best with different types of media vary.

Composing Plots in Tiled Model Space and Paper Space

In this section, you learn how to compose the layout of your plot. You can compose the layout in tiled model space or paper space. You first learn how to compose a layout in tiled model space. Then, you learn how to compose a layout with floating viewports in paper space and why paper space is preferable to model space for complicated layouts. See Chapter 5, "Working with Model and Paper Space Viewports," for more information about paper space, viewports, and model space.

The MVSETUP command is a helpful tool for plot composition. MVSETUP actually is two routines in one: one routine is for model space and one routine is for paper space. The details of using MVSETUP are covered in the following sections.

Sheet Composition in Tiled Model Space

The drawings you produce can have one of two types of layouts: layouts with scale and layouts without scale. These layouts can be created in model space or paper space. We do not recommend sheet composition in model space. Sheet composition in model space requires repetition of information and is inflexible when changes to the model occur. For this reason, creating plot layouts is only briefly described.

Layouts with Scale

In general, you are encouraged to draw your model full size—that is, as the model would appear in the real world. This approach eliminates scaling errors and enables you to use your model as a design tool for making accurate measurements. Of course, you have to take into account the scale you eventually use to plot the model, in drawing elements such as text and symbols (border, bubbles, north arrows, and so on). This approach works well if you produce a drawing that has a single view or multiple views at the same scale. But what if you want to create a plot with multiple views at varying scales? Suppose, for example, you want to produce the drawing in figure 6.24.

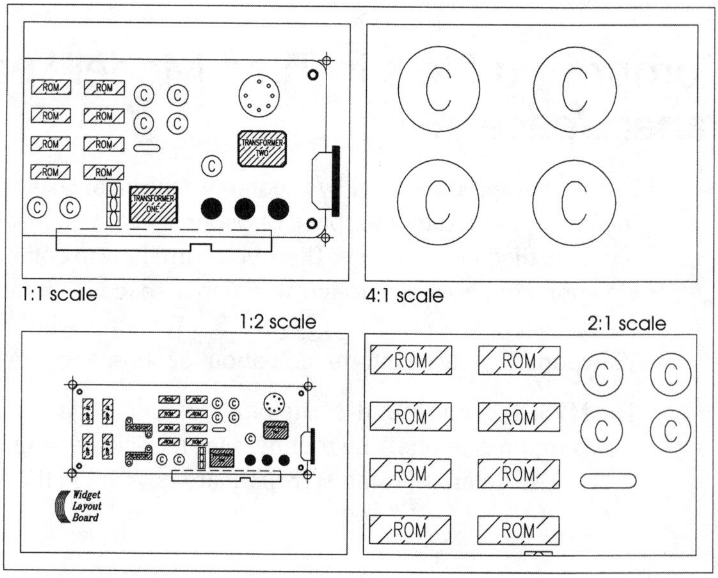

Figure 6.24

A layout that has multiple scales.

The best approach is to use paper space to depict the various views. If for some reason you choose not to utilize paper space, you can use the following approach to compose the layout in model space. In effect, you use model space as a substitute for paper space. If you use the preceding figure as an example, you could do the following:

1. Create a new drawing with limits set to the actual size of your plot sheet and insert or draw your title block and border to fit the sheet. Use a prototype drawing to automate this process.
2. Insert the drawing that contains your model (drawn at full scale) at an appropriate scale factor for the view you want to show. For the drawing shown in figure 6.24, the 1:2 view was inserted at .5 scale, the 1:1 view at 1, the 4:1 at 4, and the 2:1 at 2.
3. Draw a border for the view you want to show. The border does not have to be a rectangle.
4. Use TRIM, BREAK, and ERASE to remove all objects that extend beyond the view border.

If all this seems like too much work, it is. Using paper space to compose a plot is much easier.

Layouts without Scale

Some types of drawings are not scaled, such as schematics and sketches. The best way to deal with these types of drawings is to treat the model space like the final plot sheet. Treat each drawing unit as equal to 1 inch on the final plot. Then, size everything you draw just as you would on a piece of paper. If you want a 23"-by-35" border, you draw a 23-by-35-unit border. If you want 1/8" high text, draw 1/8" high text. You then use a 1=1 scale to plot the drawing.

Using MVSETUP in Model Space

You can find the MVSETUP command in the Floating Viewports submenu of the View pull-down menu. The Floating Viewports submenu is inactive when you are in tiled model space, so you have to enter MVSETUP at the `Command:` prompt. After you start MVSETUP, you see the following prompts:

```
Enable paper space? (No/<Yes>):
```

Answer No to this prompt if you want to use MVSETUP for model space.

```
Units type (Scientific/Decimal/Engineering/Architectural/Metric):
```

Specify the length of units you want to use in the drawing.

```
Enter the scale factor:
```

A list of commonly used scale factors appropriate to the units chosen appears. If you specify architectural units, for example, you see the following list of scales:

```
Architectural Scales=====================
(480) 1/40"=1'
(240) 1/20"=1'
(192) 1/16"=1'
(96) 1/8"=1'
(48) 1/4"=1'
(24) 1/2"=1'
(16) 3/4"=1'
(12) 1"=1'
(4)  3"=1'
(2)  6"=1'
(1)  FULL
```

Respond with the decimal scale factor in parentheses or enter your own scale factor.

```
Enter the paper width:
```

Specify the width of the border to be created.

```
Enter the paper height:
```

Specify the height of the border to be created.

MVSETUP then sets the length in units, sets the limits, and draws a rectangle to represent the border. The limits and rectangle size are adjusted for the specified scale.

Sheet Composition in Paper Space

When you compose the layout of a drawing that has multiple views at varying scales, you should use paper space. Paper space provides a method for sheet composition that is flexible and automatically reflects updates to the model. In paper space, you compose and scale the viewports, then plot at 1:1 from paper space. The views themselves might be completely different from each other (for example, a plan view versus an elevation view) or they might be different views of a common model.

Either way, the general approach is the same. In Chapter 5, "Working with Model and Paper Space Viewports," you learned how to switch to paper space using TILEMODE, create the needed floating viewports, and use the viewports to edit the model. Now, you learn how to use paper space to compose a layout for your plot. The procedure itself is quite simple and is broken down in the sections that follow. To help with the explanation, assume that you are composing the layout shown earlier in figure 6.24.

Using MVSETUP

Although you do not need to use MVSETUP to perform the procedure described in the sections that follow, using MVSETUP speeds things up quite a bit. When you start MVSETUP in paper space, you are prompted with the following options:

```
Align/Create/Scale viewports/Options/Title block/Undo:
```

The following sections explain these options.

Align

If you use the Align option, you can align and rotate views. Your alignment options are as follows:

```
Angled/Horizontal/Vertical alignment/Rotate view/Undo:
```

- **Angled.** You pick a base point in the first viewport and then a point in the second viewport. Then you specify a distance and angle from the basepoint. MVSETUP then pans the view in the second viewport so that the two points align at the specified angle (see fig. 6.25). The distance specified is in model space units. The purpose of the angled alignment is to align views of inclined surfaces.

NOTE

The Angled option only works properly if the view in the base point's viewport is perpendicular to the WCS.

- **Horizontal.** You pick a base point in the first viewport and then a point in the second viewport. MVSETUP then pans the view in the second viewport so that two points line up horizontally (see fig. 6.26).

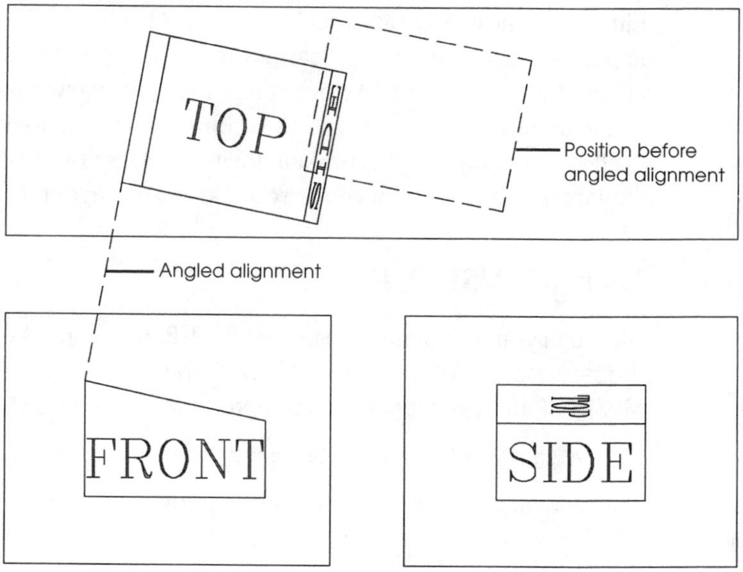

Figure 6.25

Angled alignment.

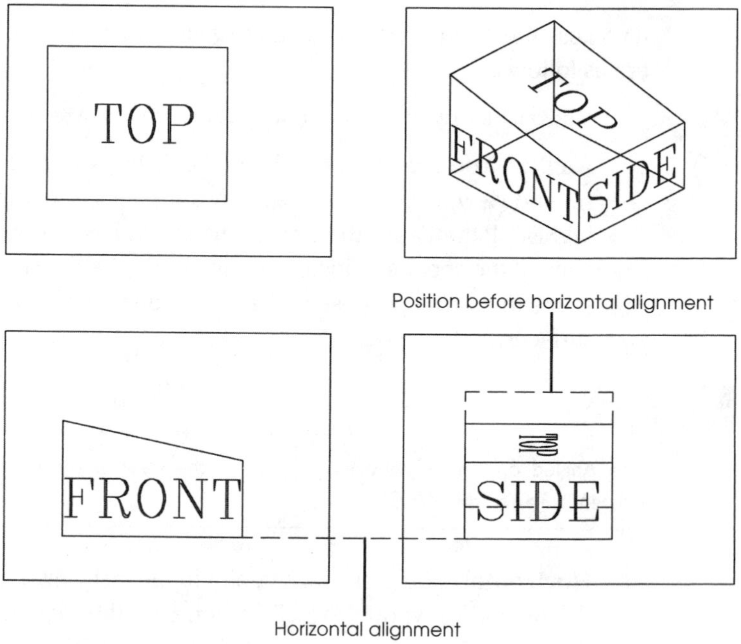

Figure 6.26

Horizontal alignment.

- **Vertical alignment.** You pick a base point in the first viewport and then a point in a second viewport. MVSETUP then pans the view in the second viewport so that the two points line up vertically (see fig. 6.27).

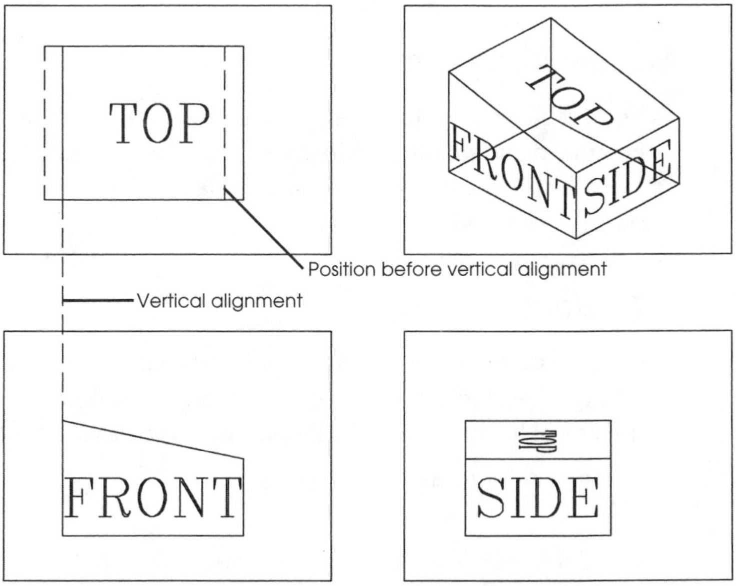

Figure 6.27

Vertical alignment.

- **Rotate view.** You also can rotate the view in a viewport. Bear in mind that the model itself is not rotated, just the view. The rotation angle is relative to the WCS.

Create

You use the Create option to create viewports. You have the following choices:

- **0: None.** Skips viewport creation.
- **1: Single.** If you choose to create a single viewport, then you are prompted to locate and size the viewport by windowing an area. This option is identical to the MVIEW command's default option of creating a single viewport.
- **2: Std. Engineering**. If you choose to create a standard engineering arrangement of viewports, you are asked to window an area that is divided into four viewports. This option is similar to the MVIEW command's 4 viewport option, except that you also can specify a vertical (X) and horizontal (Y) separation distance between the viewports.

- **3: Array of Viewports.** If you choose to create an array of viewports, then you are asked to window an area that is then divided into *m* rows and *n* columns of viewports. You get to specify the *m* and *n* values and the vertical (X) and horizontal (Y) separation distance between the viewports.

Scale Viewports

You use this option to scale the view in a viewport. This option issues the ZOOM command and supplies it with an XP scale factor. You select the viewports to scale. The viewports can be scaled individually or a scale can be applied across all selected viewports.

Options

Options enables you to change several default settings. Because these default settings affect the defaults of other options, you should select this option before you use any of the other MVSETUP options. You can set the following settings:

```
Set Layer/LImits/Units/Xref
```

- **Set Layer.** This option enables you to specify the layer on which to draw the title block. The specified layer can be an existing or new layer. If it is new, MVSETUP creates it for you.
- **LImits.** This option determines whether the drawing limits are reset to the extents of the title block.
- **Units.** This option enables you to determine whether to interpret paper space units as inches, feet, meters, or millimeters.
- **Xref.** This option enables you to determine whether the title block is inserted as a block or attached as an xref.

Title Block

Selecting this option brings up another list of options, as follows:

```
Delete objects/Origin/Undo/<Insert title block>:
```

- **Delete objects.** This option enables you to delete selected objects.
- **Origin.** This option enables you to determine a new insertion point for the title block. The default origin point is 0,0.

- **Undo.** Undoes the last option.
- **Insert title block.** If you select the default option of inserting a title block, you see a list of available title blocks:

```
0:      None
1:      ISO A4 Size(mm)
2:      ISO A3 Size(mm)
3:      ISO A2 Size(mm)
4:      ISO A1 Size(mm)
5:      ISO A0 Size(mm)
6:      ANSI-V Size(in)
7:      ANSI-A Size(in)
8:      ANSI-B Size(in)
9:      ANSI-C Size(in)
10:     ANSI-D Size(in)
11:     ANSI-E Size(in)
12:     Arch/Engineering (24 x 36in)
13:     Generic D size Sheet (24 x 36in)
```

If a drawing that has the name of the selected size is found in the directory that the ACADPREFIX system variable specifies, that drawing is inserted as the title block. This mechanism enables you to use your own title block drawings with MVSETUP. The name of the drawing should be of the form ANSI-? (where ? is V, A, B, C, D, or E) or ISO_?? (where ?? is A0, A1, A2, A3, or A4) if you want MVSETUP to recognize and use it as a title block drawing. If a drawing that has the name of the selected size is not found, MVSETUP creates one and you then have the option of writing out (WBLOCK) to a drawing file. The directories listed in the ACADPREFIX system variable are determined by the ACAD system variable or the support field in the environment section of the PREFERENCES command.

NOTE

The title block normally is inserted at 0,0 unless you specify a different origin by using the Options option.

The Initial Steps

Begin by drawing all the views in the model space of a single drawing file. In the case of the example problem, create views A, B, C, and D in the model space of a single drawing. If the views are different views of a single model, just draw the one model. Draw the views at full size, not scaled down.

Next, switch over to paper space by turning off TILEMODE.

Now, draw the border in paper space. Treat paper space like your sheet of paper. To end up with a 23-inch-by-35-inch border on the plot, draw a 23-inch-by-35-inch border in paper space. Eventually, you plot the entire paper space layout at a 1=1 scale.

To view the model, use MVIEW to create the necessary floating viewports. If you do not want to have the viewport borders on the final plot, be sure to draw the viewports on a separate layer. Before you plot, you can turn off the layer that contains the viewport objects, which makes the viewport borders invisible but still leaves the views in them visible.

TIP

Draw the viewports on the defpoints layer. If you do so, the viewports will not plot even if the defpoints layer is on.

When you use noncontinuous linetypes that are visible in multiple viewports at varying scales, you want the various linetypes to have the same appearance in all viewports. It is poor practice to have the dashed linetype in one viewport appear different from the dashed linetype in another viewport or from that drawn in paper space. To prevent this from occurring, you need to turn on the PSLTSCALE system variable. When PLTSCALE is on and CELTSCALE is 1, all linetypes in all viewports are drawn at a 1 to 1 scale factor, as if they were drawn in paper space. If CELTSCALE is set to a value other than 1, the linetypes are proportionately affected. To see the effect on existing linetypes, you must issue a REGENALL.

TIP

If you use a limited number of layouts, consider creating the layouts in your prototype drawings. That way, every new drawing has the paper space already prepared for usage.

In the following exercise, you compose an initial layout in paper space using the MVSETUP command.

CREATING FLOATING VIEWPORTS WITH MVSETUP

Begin a new drawing named CHAP06B using the accompanying CD drawing BOARD as the prototype.

`Command:` *Choose* View, Paper Space	Switches to paper space
`Command:` *Choose* View, Floating Viewports, MV Setup	Issues the MSVSETUP command

`Initializing...`
`Align/Create/Scaleviewports/`
`Options/Title block/Undo:` **O** ↵
	Specifies the Options option

`Set Layer/LImits/Units/Xref:` **L** ↵	Specifies the Layer option
`Layer name for title block or . for current layer:` **TITLE_BLOCK** ↵	Sets the layer TITLE_BLOCK as the layer on which the title block is to be drawn
`Set Layer/LImits/Units/Xref:` ↵	Returns you to the main MVSETUP options list
`Align/Create/Scale viewports/` `Options/Title block/Undo:` **T** ↵	Specifies the Title block option
`Delete objects/Origin/Undo/<Insert title block>:` ↵	Accepts the default of inserting a new title block

```
Available title block options:
 0:  None
 1:  ISO A4 Size(mm)
 2:  ISO A3 Size(mm)
 3:  ISO A2 Size(mm)
 4:  ISO A1 Size(mm)
 5:  ISO A0 Size(mm)
 6:  ANSI-V Size(in)
 7:  ANSI-A Size(in)
 8:  ANSI-B Size(in)
 9:  ANSI-C Size(in)
 10:  ANSI-D Size(in)
 11:  ANSI-E Size(in)
 12:  Arch/Engineering (24 x 36in)
 13:  Generic D size Sheet (24 x 36in)
```

`Add/Delete/Redisplay/<Number of entry to load>:` **8** ↵	Specifies ANSI-B as the title block to be inserted
`Create a drawing named ansi-b.dwg? <Y>:` **N** ↵	Declines the option of writing the newly created title block out to a file (WBLOCK)
`Align/Create/Scale viewports/ Options/Title block/Undo:` ↵	Ends MVSETUP

Make a new layer named VPORTS and set it current.

`Command:` *Choose* View, Floating Viewports, MV Setup	Issues the MVSETUP command
`Align/Create/Scale viewports/ Options/Title block/Undo:` **C** ↵	Specifies the Create option
`Delete objects/Undo/ <Create viewports>:` ↵	Accepts the default option of creating viewports

```
Available Mview viewport layout options:
 0:  None
 1:  Single
 2:  Std. Engineering
 3:  Array of Viewports
```

`Redisplay/<Number of entry to load>:` **3** ↵	Specifies the Array layout
`Bounding area for viewports. Default/<First point >:` *Pick* ① *(see fig. 6.28)*	Sets the right corner

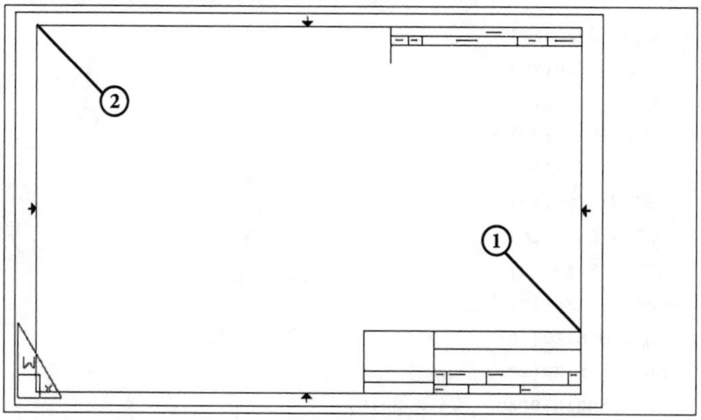

Figure 6.28

Specifying the area for viewports.

`Other point:` *Pick* ②	Finishes specifying the area that will be divided into viewports
`Number of viewports in X. <1>:` ↵	Accepts the default of 1 column of viewports
`Number of viewports in Y. <1>:` **2** ↵	Defines 2 rows of viewports to be created
`Distance between viewports in Y. <0.0>:` **.25** ↵	Specifies a separation of 0.25 inches in the Y direction
`Align/Create/Scale viewports/ Options/Title block/Undo:` ↵	Ends MVSETUP

Save your work.

Adjusting the Views

To adjust the view in the viewports, you must enter model space (MSPACE) and, in turn, make each viewport current (refer to figure 6.28). To scale each view correctly, you use the XP option of the ZOOM command. XP stands for "relative to paper." The number you enter should be the scale of the view. For example, for the 1:2 view in Figure 6.28, after you trigger the ZOOM command, enter .5XP (1 plotted inch equals 2 drawing units). For the 4:1 view, use a zoom factor of 4XP. These are the same scale factors you would use if plotting each viewport separately; instead, you scale the viewports and plot at 1:1 from paper space. The MVSETUP command is a convenient tool for setting the scale of floating viewports.

TIP

Because there is no way to "lock in" a view, you might want to draw some reference points or lines after you set your views. These objects can act as registration points to help you realign the views, should it ever be necessary. For example, you might draw several points in paper space that coincide with the ends of several lines that appear in a view.

After a view is scaled correctly, you use PAN to center the view in the viewport. You even can enlarge or shrink the viewport itself to better accommodate the view.

TIP

> Using the LIST command on a viewport will tell you the zoom scale.

In the following exercise, you adjust the views in the viewports and resize the viewports.

Adjusting the Views

Continue to use the drawing CHAP06B.

`Command:` *Choose* View, Floating Model Space	Issues the MSPACE command, making one of the viewports current
`Command:` *Pick in the top viewport*	Makes the top viewport current
`Command:` **Z** ↵	Starts the ZOOM command
`All/Center/Dynamic/Extents/Left/ Previous/Vmax/Window/<Scale(X/XP)>:` **1XP** ↵	Zooms the view in the current viewport to a scale relative to paper space of 1=1 (1 paper space inch = 1 model space draw ing unit)
Use PAN *to center the view in the viewport if necessary*	
Make the lower viewport current	
`Command:` **Z** ↵	
`All/Center/Dynamic/Extents/Left/ Previous/Vmax/Window/<Scale(X/XP>:` **2XP** ↵	Zooms the view in the current viewport to a scale relative to paper space of 2=1 (2 paper space inches = 1 model space drawing unit)

Pan the view in the viewport until you can see the left upper area of the board.

Next you align the views in the viewports using two objects, one in each viewport.

`Command:` *Choose* View, Floating Viewports, MV Setup	Issues MVSETUP
`Align/Create/Scale viewports /Options/Title block/Undo:` **A** ↵	Specifies Align option
Angled/Horizontal/Vertical alignment/Rotate view/Undo: **V** ↵	Specifies Vertical alignment option

`Base point:` *Set the upper viewport current, then use ENDpoint object snap to pick ① (see fig. 6.29)*	Sets the point that the second view will be aligned with

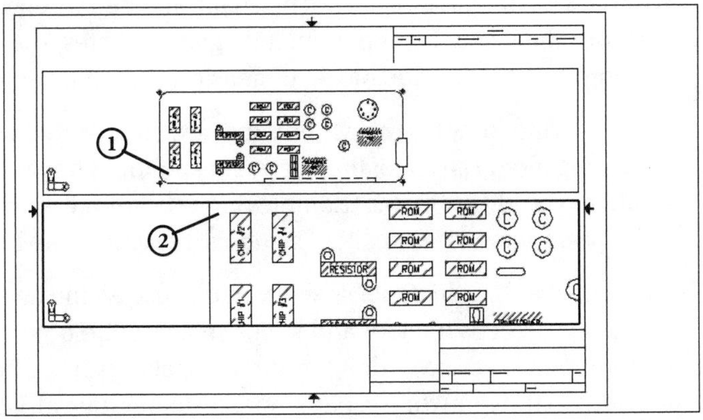

Figure 6.29

Aligning the views vertically.

`Other point:` *Set the lower viewport current, then use ENDpoint object snap to pick ②*	Sets the point that will be aligned with the base point and pans the view
`Angled/Horizontal/Vertical alignment/Rotate view/Undo:` ↵	Returns you to the main MVSETUP options list
`Align/Create/Scale viewports/ Options/Title block/Undo:` ↵	Ends MVSETUP

Switch to paper space and then edit (use STRETCH or grips) the lower viewport object itself to isolate the four chips on the left. The process is just like stretching a rectangular polyline object. You should end up with something similar to figure 6.30.

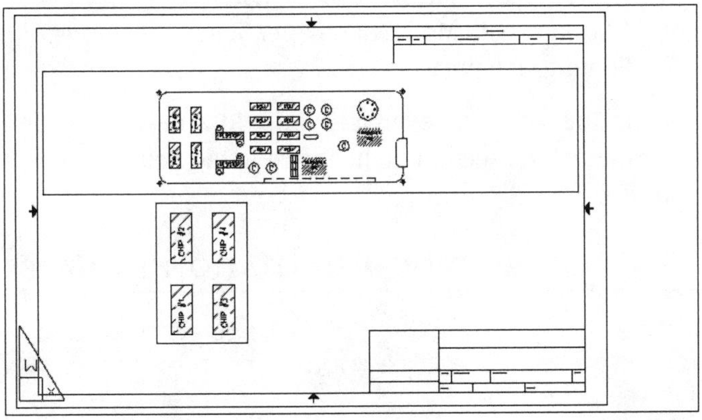

Figure 6.30

The views aligned with MVSETUP.

Save your work.

Annotating the Paper Space Layout

You also must annotate the drawing with necessary symbols or text. You should draw text or symbols that are not directly related to the views in paper space. These should be objects that are not normally affected when you edit (stretch, move, and so on) the views. Examples include general notes, scale bars, labels for the views, information in the title block, dimensions that span across viewports, and so forth.

You should draw text or symbols that are directly related to a particular view in the floating model space of that view. These should be objects that should be affected when you edit the views. Examples include normal dimensions, section lines, labels for parts of the views, callout symbols, revision symbols, and so forth.

When you draw in paper space, you can use all the layers created in model space. AutoCAD keeps track of and keeps separate the objects you draw in paper space from the objects you draw in model space. If need be, you can create and use additional layers while in paper space. Remember, all objects drawn in paper space are not visible when you switch back to tiled model space (TILEMODE=1).

Remember that although you can pick points and use object snap to snap to objects in floating model space when you are in paper space you cannot select those objects. While you are in paper space, you can select and edit only objects that reside in paper space. While in floating model space, you can select and edit only objects that reside in model space.

With floating viewports, you can freeze a layer in specific viewports and leave it on in the remaining viewports. When you deal with multiple views of the same model, you can use this feature to draw text and other objects so that they appear only in specific viewports. You begin by drawing the objects specific to the current view, on a separate layer. Then use DDLMODES or VPLAYER to freeze that layer in the other viewports so that the layer is visible only in selected viewports. See Chapter 5, "Working with Model and Paper Space Viewports," for more information on using floating viewports.

In the following exercise, you add a dashed border and lines in paperspace to denote the section of the board in the detail veiw.

Adding Annotation in Paper Space

Continue in the drawing CHAP06B. Make sure that you are in paper space before proceeding with the exercise. If you are not sure, choose View, Paper Space.

Make a new layer named DASHED, assign the linetype DASHED, and set it current.

`Command:` *Choose Rectangle* (Draw, Polygon)	Issues RECTANG
`First corner:` *Pick* ① (see fig. 6.31)	

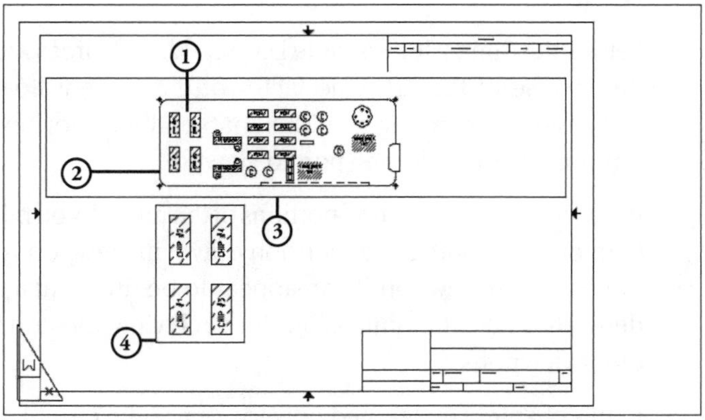

Figure 6.31

Points for rectangles.

`Other corner:` *Pick* ②	
`Command:` ↵	Repeats RECTANG
`First corner:` *Pick* ③	
`Other corner:` *Pick* ④	
`Command:` *Turn off layer* VPORTS	Makes the outlines of the viewports invisible

Draw lines to connect the rectangles as shown in figure 6.32.

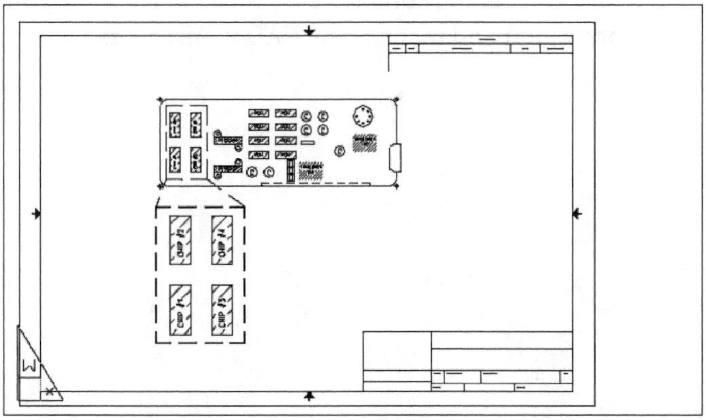

Figure 6.32

The completed detail view.

Dimensioning the Views

If a view requires dimensions, draw them in floating model space so that the measured distances are the correct real-world dimensions. Drawing the dimensions in model space also enables you to edit (move, stretch, and so on) them while you edit the model.

Setting the dimension variable DIMSCALE to 0 forces AutoCAD to automatically use the inverse of the XP scale factor of the current floating viewport as you draw dimensions in model space. This enables dimension text and arrowheads to appear uniform in size from viewport to viewport.

If the views show common portions of the model, you might see a dimension in more than one viewport. If a dimension drawn in viewport A is visible in viewport B, the dimension in viewport B can appear to be drawn at a different size. To avoid this, dedicate a layer for dimensions for each viewport and then freeze that layer for all other viewports.

In this chapter you learned how to control the output of your drawing to a plotting device. You looked at the options provided by the PLOT command, to adjust the appearance of your hard copy image.

You also learned how to compose a plot sheet, and how the MVSETUP command can help automate the process. You saw how composing the plot sheet in paper space is more flexible than using model space, and how to avoid pitfalls such as drawing dimensions in paper space, which, while convenient to draw, are not associated to model space objects and are not updated if the model changes.

Extending your control of the CAD environment to the hard-copy output process complements and completes the range of skills that you need to master to effectively work within and manage the CAD workspace.

part

II

Object Creation Tools

chapter

7

Drawing Basic Objects

No matter how complicated the drawing, no matter how many layers and linetypes, almost all AutoCAD drawings are comprised of relatively few basic shapes and forms. Circles and circular arcs, lines, rectangles, regular polygons, and ellipses are the elements from which both simple and complicated drawings are built. This chapter shows you the tools with which you need to be familiar before you can draw these simple objects. In this chapter you learn to draw the following objects:

- *Lines*
- *Circles*
- *Circular arcs*
- *Points*
- *Donuts*
- *Regular polygons*
- *Rectangles*
- *Ellipses and elliptical arcs*

The tools to draw these objects are found in flyouts located on the Draw toolbar, identified in figure 7.1.

Figure 7.1

The Draw toolbar and its flyouts.

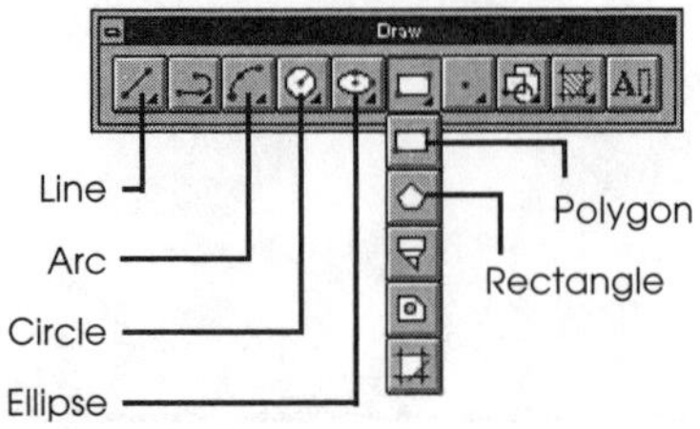

The logical place to begin is with the simplest of AuotCAD's basic drawing objects—lines.

Using the LINE Command

The LINE command is one of AutoCAD's basic commands; you use it in most drawings. The LINE command draws line segments. You specify the beginning and endpoints in answer to the LINE command's prompts. After a segment is created, AutoCAD assumes that you want to continue drawing lines. As you continue to pick points, AutoCAD draws additional segments, with the endpoint of one segment coinciding with the starting point of the next, until you end the command by pressing Enter on the keyboard or the Enter button of your pointing device.

There are several ways to issue the LINE command, with the Line tool on the Draw toolbar being, perhaps, the most readily available. The Line tool is shown in figure 7.2.

Figure 7.2

The Line toolbar.

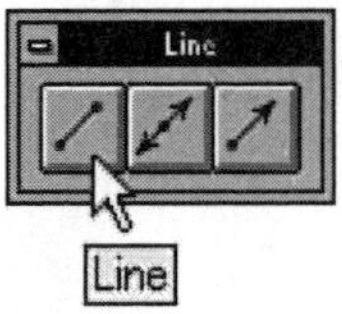

The LINE command has three useful options: continue, Close, and Undo. These options extend the functionality of the LINE command and are summarized here and demonstrated in exercises throughout the remainder of this book.

Line Command Options

The LINE command has five prompts and options:

- **From point.** At the `From point:` prompt you specify the point for the beginning of the first (and perhaps only) segment.
- **Enter.** Pressing Enter at the `From point:` prompt causes the line to begin from the end of the most recently drawn line or arc. If you drew an arc most recently, the line is drawn tangent to the endpoint of the arc, and you are prompted for the length of the segment.
- **To point.** At the `To point:` prompt you specify the point to which a line is drawn from the previous point.
- **Undo.** At the `To point:` prompt you enter Undo (or simply U) to erase the last line segment, stepping back to the previous point.
- **Close.** At the `To point:` prompt you enter Close (or simply C) to close a series of two or more line segments.

NOTE

After you complete the LINE command, AutoCAD's U command will undo all the segments you just drew (within a single command), not just the last one, as the LINE command's internal Undo option does.

Creating Circles

You find circles in most drawings, representing various objects such as holes, wheels, trees, instruments, and numerous other real and symbolic objects. In mechanical drafting, as in AutoCAD, isolated circles and circles that stand alone are not particularly difficult to produce; you need only know the center point location and the radius or the diameter. Circles tangent to other objects—such as other circles, arcs, or lines—are somewhat more difficult if you use traditional means. AutoCAD, however, gives you the capability to draw tangent circles with an ease and precision impossible if you use only a compass, ruler, and straightedge.

AutoCAD offers five ways to construct a circle. The method you choose depends on the information you have about the geometry of the circle. Often, you know the center point and radius or diameter. At other times, you might know only where you want points on the circumference to lie, or the radius and tangent points. The CIRCLE command offers options to cover all these possibilities, as well as other situations. The various methods are illustrated in figure 7.3.

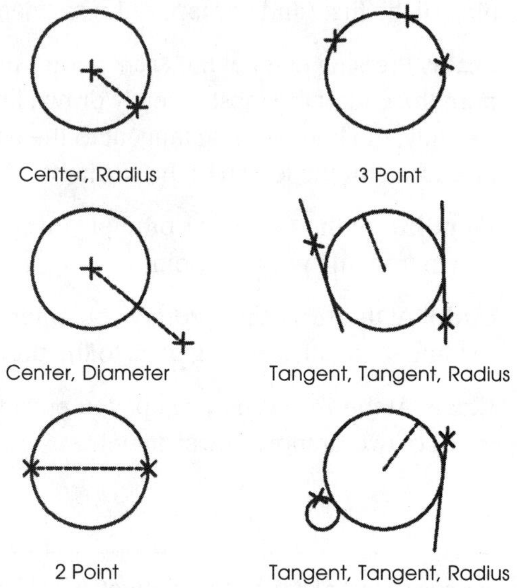

Figure 7.3

Methods of drawing circles.

NOTE

Notice the difference between Center point/Diameter and 2P. Both options enable you to specify a diameter, but if you pick the second point with Center point/Diameter, it merely indicates the diameter's distance, and the circle does not draw through the point. If you pick two points with 2P, you see a circle appear between those two points, and the distance is the diameter. The 2P option enables you to draw a diameter circle the way most people intuitively think about diameter.

CIRCLE Command Options

The CIRCLE command offers the following options:

```
3P/2P/TTR/<Center point>:
```

- **Center point.** Type or pick the center point and the CIRCLE command then prompts for a radius or diameter. This is the default option.

- **Radius.** If you choose `Center point:`, you then use the Radius option to enter a distance or pick two points to show a distance for the radius.
- **Diameter.** If you choose `Center point:`, use the Diameter option to specify a radius. You can either enter a distance or pick two points to show a radius.
- **3P (3 Point).** Use this option to specify the circumference by entering or picking three points.
- **2P (2 Point).** Use this option to specify two diameter points on the circumference.
- **TTR (Tangent-Tangent, Radius).** Use this option to select two lines, arcs, or circles (any combination) that form tangents to the circle. Then specify the circle's radius.

These options also are provided by the Circle toolbar, as shown in figure 7.4.

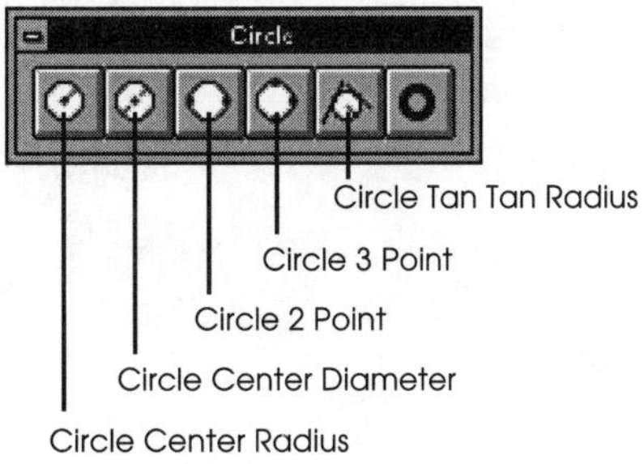

Figure 7.4

The Circle toolbar.

Using the CIRCLE Command

In the following exercise, you use the CIRCLE command as you begin to draw the components of a typical circuit board. Use the CIRCUIT-BOARD layer of the BASICS drawing. The outline of the circuit board and text already have been drawn on this layer. You now draw the outlines of two capacitors. You can use the coordinates display and the 0.25 snap to pick the points shown.

USING THE CIRCLE COMMAND

Begin a new drawing named CHAP07, using the BASICS drawing from the accompanying CD as a prototype. Use the Layer Control drop-down list to turn on the CIRCUIT-BOARD layer and set it to current, and turn all other layers off.

`Command:` *Choose Circle Center Radius (Draw, Circle)*	Issues the default CIRCLE command
`_circle 3P/2P/TTR/<Center point>:` **3,8** ↵	Specifies the center at ① (see fig. 7.5)
`Diameter/<Radius> <1.25>:` **1** ↵	Draws the circle with a 1-unit radius

In the next step, you specify a circle with the `Center point: Diameter` option.

`Command:` *Choose Circle Center Diameter (Draw, Circle)*	Issues the CIRCLE command and the Diameter option
`_circle 3P/2P/TTR/<Center point>:` **6,8** ↵	Specifies the center at ②
`Diameter/<Radius> <1.00>:d`	The tool issues the Diameter option
`Diameter <2.00>:` **2.2** ↵	Draws the circle with a 2.2-unit diameter

Note that in the previous step, the default diameter value (2.00) is based on the most recent radius used (1.00).

Save the drawing.

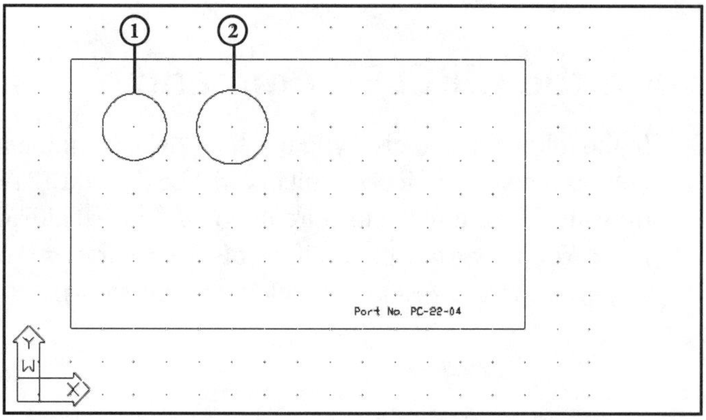

Figure 7.5

Drawing circles with a known radius or diameter.

Drawing circles with the `Center point:` option and then specifying a radius or a diameter is easy. You can drag the circle to the size you want or enter a value from the keyboard. You also can use object snap to place the circumference in relation to other geometry. The tools from the Circle toolbar issue the appropriate option, such as Diameter, depending on which tool you choose. If you issue the CIRCLE command from the `Command:` prompt, you can accept the default options by pressing Enter, or you can override the defaults by typing the command or option. Entering a D, for example, selects the diameter option at the `Diameter/<Radius>:` prompt.

In the following two exercises, you use the 2P, 3P, and TTR options to construct circles that are related to other drawing geometry. The 2P and 3P options, by definition, do not require radius or diameter input; AutoCAD calculates that information from the points you specify. You used the TTR option in the opening exercise; in this exercise you learn more about its capabilities. You also use the object snap and point filter features here, you can type them as shown or choose them from the toolbars or pop-up menu.

USING THE 2P OPTION

Continue from the preceding exercise. Turn the CIRCUIT-BOARD layer off, then turn on the CIRCLE layer and set it current. Your drawing should look like figure 7.6, except the circles are not yet drawn.

`Command:` **C** ↵	Issues the CIRCLE command
`CIRCLE 3P/2P/TTR/<Center point>:` **2P** ↵	Issues the 2 Point option
`First point on diameter:` **ENDP** ↵ `of` *Pick* ① (see fig. 7.6)	Specifies the ENDPoint object snap Establishes the first point on diameter

Notice that as you move the cursor, the circle drags.

`Second point on diameter:` **ENDP** ↵ `of` *Pick* ②	Specifies the ENDPoint object snap; draws the circle

Next, you use a point filter to help define the radius of a TTR circle.

`Command:` *Choose Circle 2 Point (Draw, Circle)*	Issues the CIRCLE command with the 2 Point option
`_circle 3P/2P/TTR/<Center point>: _2P` `First point on diameter:` **ENDP** ↵	Specifies the ENDPoint object snap

`of` *Pick the line at* ③	Specifies first point
`Second point on diameter:` **ENDP** ↵	Specifies the ENDPoint object snap
`of` *Pick the line at* ④	Specifies second point and draws the circle

Save your drawing.

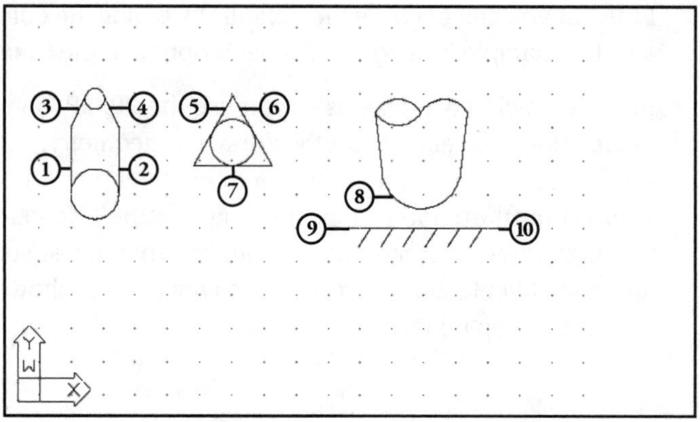

Figure 7.6

Drawing circles with the 2P, 3P, and TTR options.

The 2P option of the CIRCLE command along with object snap is often useful. In the preceding exercise, it enables you to specify a diameter equal to the distance between the ends of the lines without having any information about that distance.

TIP

You can always use the CAL command to specify a point halfway between two other points, regardless of whether adjacent geometry is available.

In the following exercise, you draw a circle using the 3P option and again use the TTR option.

THE 3P OPTION AND MORE ABOUT THE TTR OPTION

Continue from the preceding exercise.

`Command:` *Choose Circle 3 Point (Draw, Circle)*	Issues the CIRCLE command and the 3P option
`_circle 3P/2P/TTR/<Center point>:`	Specifies the MIDpoint object snap

`_3p First point:` **MID** ↵	
`_mid of Pick point` ⑤ *(refer to figure 7.6)*	Specifies first point on circumference
`Second point:` **MID** ↵	Specifies the MIDpoint object snap
`_mid of Pick point` ⑥	Specifies second point on circumference
`Third point:` **MID** ↵	
`_mid of Pick a point at` ⑦	Specifies third point on circumference and draws the circle
`Command:` *Choose Circle Tan Tan Radius (Draw, Circle)*	Issues the CIRCLE command and the TTR option
`_circle 3P/2P/TTR/<Center point>: _ttr`	
`Enter Tangent spec:` *Pick the arc at* ⑧	Selects the first tangent object
`Enter second Tangent spec:` *Pick the line at* ⑨	Selects the second tangent object
`Radius <0.70>:` **.4** ↵	Specifies the radius and draws the circle (see fig. 7.7)
`Command:` ↵	Reissues the CIRCLE command
`3P/2P/TTR/<Center point>:` **T** ↵	Specifies the TTR option
`Enter Tangent spec:` *Pick the arc at* ⑧	Selects the first tangent object
`Enter second Tangent spec:` *Pick the line at* ⑩	Selects the second tangent object
`Radius <0.40>:` ↵	Accepts the default radius and draws a second circle (see fig. 7.7)

Save your drawing.

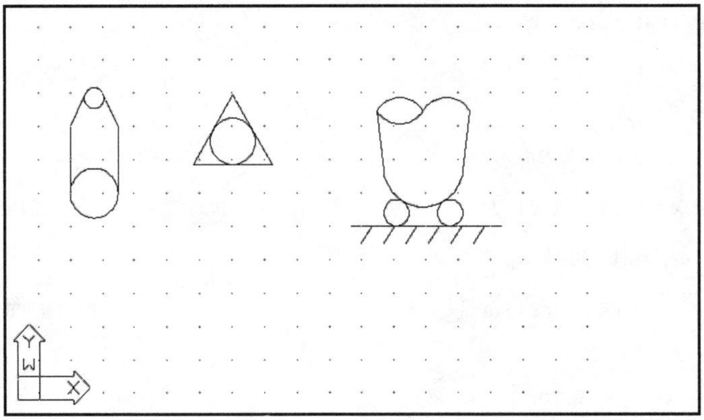

Figure 7.7

The completed CIRCLE command exercise.

The 3P (3 Point) option of the CIRCLE command enables you to construct circles, even when you have neither center point nor radius values. In the preceding exercise, for example, drawing the circle inside the triangle without center point or radius values would have been difficult. Neither value would be easy to obtain from the information in the drawing. Because it was an equilateral triangle, the 3P option and the MIDpoint object snap made the task easy.

TIP

> To draw a circle tangent to any three lines (or arcs or curves), use the 3 Point option and then use the TAN object snap to pick each of the three lines.

When you use the TTR (Tangent, Tangent, Radius) option, some situations occur in which more than one circle matches the criteria specified by the command. In the preceding exercise, for example, two possible circles could be drawn to satisfy the radius and tangent specifications—one on either side of the arc's quadrant. In such situations, AutoCAD draws the circle whose tangent points are closest to the selected points. In the exercise, you forced both possible circles by picking near the opposite ends of the line.

Depending on the information you have about the circle, the five options of AutoCAD's CIRCLE command enable you to accurately draw and place virtually any circle. Combined with object snaps and point filters, you need never calculate or guess the information you need to draw circles correctly.

Creating Arcs

Unlike circles, which have only a center point and radius, arcs are more difficult to draw. In addition to center points and radii, arcs require that you begin and end angles to fully define them. Arcs, therefore, also have either a clockwise or counter-clockwise nature to their creation, and are a little more difficult to draw than circles. AutoCAD offers 11 different methods for constructing arcs. Although this many choices might seem intimidating, you must understand only a few principals before you can use all the various methods. As with the five options of drawing circles, the information you have about the arc largely determines the method you choose. Often, more than one method can yield the arc you want with a given set of parameters. In the exercises in this section, you practice applying the most commonly used methods of constructing arcs in AutoCAD.

ARC Command Options

Figure 7.8 shows the various arc construction methods. The labels for the construction methods shown in figure 7.8 correspond to their ToolTip labels on the Arc toolbar.

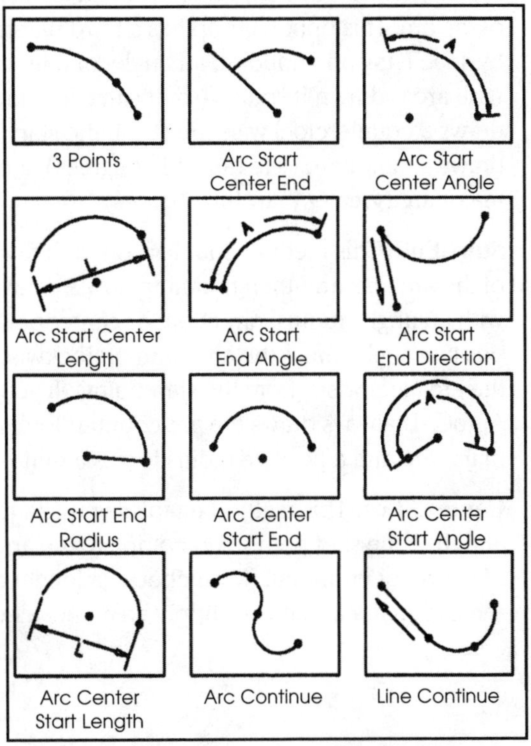

Figure 7.8

Methods of constructing arcs.

When you enter ARC at the `Command:` prompt, the following prompt appears:

```
Center/<Start point>:
```

If you pick a start point, your construction methods narrow to those that begin with Start (including 3 Points); if you begin with the C, AutoCAD restricts your options to those that accept the center point first. If, for example, you begin the arc with a center point, followed by a start point, the following prompt appears:

```
Angle/Length of chord/<End point>:
```

In this way, you are presented with possible remaining options as you supply each successive arc parameter. In most methods, when adequate information is supplied, AutoCAD drags the arc on-screen, and then when you supply the third necessary parameter, draws the arc. Varying the order of the options enables you to choose the easiest order of input. An example of input order is center-start-end versus start-center-end. The following list explains some combinations of the arc options.

- **3-Point.** This method creates an arc that passes through three specified points. The first point is the start point, the third point is the endpoint, and the second point is any other point on the arc. This is the default construction method.

- **Start,Center.** This method requires an arc starting point and the center point of the arc. This option group has a third parameter, which completes the arc by specifying an endpoint, an angle, or a length of chord. A counterclockwise arc is drawn if you give a positive included angle; a negative angle draws a counterclockwise arc (from the start point). A positive chord length draws a minor arc (less than 180 degrees); a negative chord length draws a major arc (greater than 180 degrees).

- **Start,End.** This method enables you to define the starting and ending points of the arc first, and then to define how to draw the arc. You define the arc with an angle, radius, direction, or center point. If you supply an angle, a positive angle draws the arc counterclockwise and a negative angle draws the arc clockwise (from the start point). If you choose the radius option, AutoCAD always draws the arc counterclockwise. A negative radius forces a major arc and a positive radius forces a minor arc.

- **Center,Start.** This method enables you first to identify the center of the arc, and then the start point. You complete the arc by supplying an angle, length of chord, or endpoint. If you choose a length of chord, a negative length forces a major arc. If you supply an angle, a negative angle draws a clockwise arc.

- **Continue.** This method is a further default—invoked by pressing Enter at the first arc prompt—that begins a new arc tangent to the last line or arc drawn. Similarly, pressing Enter at the first prompt of the LINE command starts a new line at the end of the last arc.

You can have additional control over the way AutoCAD draws the arc in several options by supplying negative values. A negative radius, for example, forces a major arc using the start, end, radius method; and if you specify negative included angles, AutoCAD constructs arcs in a clockwise direction. The 11 methods of arc construction are available on the Arc toolbar (see fig. 7.9). Choosing a tool from the toolbar automatically issues the appropriate prompts as the command progresses.

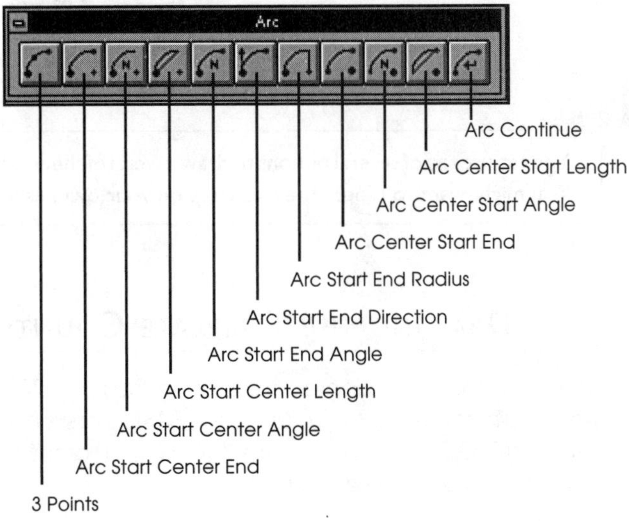

Figure 7.9

The Arc toolbar.

Using ARC Command Options

You gain an understanding of several of the frequently used arc construction methods in the next two exercises. First, you use several options of the ARC command to draw the template shown in figure 7.10, beginning at the lower left corner and proceeding counterclockwise. Then, in the second exercise, you use other arc options to draw the same part in a clockwise direction. As you proceed through these exercises, refer to the ARC command's options list and figure 7.8, if necessary, to make sure that you understand why you use specific options.

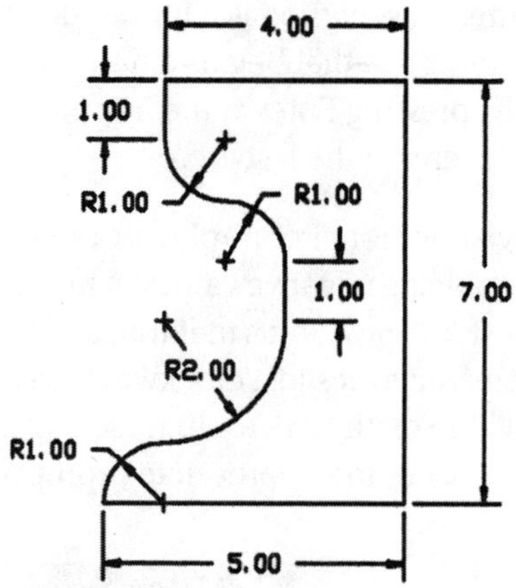

Figure 7.10

The dimensional template.

NOTE

You can use any of several options to draw several of the arcs in the following two exercises. You might want to repeat the exercises on your own, using other methods.

DRAWING THE TEMPLATE COUNTERCLOCKWISE

Continue from the preceding exercise, using the CHAP07 drawing, or begin a new drawing again named CHAP07, using the BASICS drawing as a prototype. First, turn on the layer TEMPLATE and set it to current. Turn off all other layers. See figure 7.10 for dimensions. Turn on snap and ortho.

`Command:` *Choose Line (Draw, Line)* — Issues the LINE command

In the following six steps, you can type the relative coordinates or use ortho and snap along with the coordinate display to draw the lines from ① to ②.

`_line From point:` **1,2** ↵ — Starts the lines at ① (see fig. 7.11)

`To point:` **@5<0** ↵

`To point:` **@7<90** ↵

`To point:` **@4<180** ↵

`To point:` **@1<270** ↵

`To point:` ↵ — Ends the LINE command at ②

Next, you use the continue method to begin the first arc at ② where the last line segment ends. First turn off ortho.

`Command:` *Choose Arc Continue (Draw, Arc)*	Issues the ARC command and an Enter for the Continue option; displays a rubber-band arc
`_arc Center/<Start point>:` **@1,-1** `End point:` **@1,-1** ↵	Draws the arc from ② to ③

You must draw the next arc clockwise. Although you could use the continue method, use the start, center, angle method instead and specify a —90 degree angle.

`Command:` *Choose Arc Start Center Angle (Draw, Arc)*	Issues the ARC command and the Center option
`_arc Center/<Start point>:` **@** ↵	Specifies the last point—the end of the previous arc at ③
`Center/End/<Second point>:` **_c**	The tool issues the Center option
`Center:` **@1<270** ↵	Sets the center point; the arc rubber-bands as you move the cursor
`Angle/Length of chord/<End point>:` `_a Included angle:` **-90** ↵	Draws the 90° arc in a clockwise direction

Next you draw a 1-unit straight-line segment beginning from the end of the last arc, using the Continue option of the LINE command.

`Command:` *Choose Line (Draw, Line)*	Issues the LINE command
`_line From point:` ↵	Specifies the Continue option; starts the line tangent to the end of the last arc
`Length of line:` **1** ↵	Draws the line to ④
`To point:` ↵	Ends the LINE command

You must draw the next arc clockwise (beginning at ④). Use the start, end, angle method with a negative angle. The radius of the arc is 2 units.

`Command:` *Choose Arc Start End Angle (Draw, Arc)*	Issues the ARC command with the End and Angle options
`_arc Center/<Start point>: @` ↵	Starts the arc at the last point ④
`Center/End/<Second point>: _e`	The tool issues the End option
`End point:` **@-2,-2** ↵	Rubber-bands an arc in counterclockwise direction

`Angle/Direction/Radius/<Center point>:` **_a**	The tool issues the Angle option
`Included angle:` **-90** ↵	Draws the arc in clockwise direction

Next, draw the last arc. Several methods work. Use start, center, end.

`Command:` *Choose Arc Start Center End (Draw, Arc)*	Issues the ARC command and the Center option
`_arc Center/<Start point>:` **ENDP** ↵	Specifies the ENDPoint object snap
`_endp of` *Pick the end of the arc at* ⑤	Specifies the arc start point
`Center/End/<Second point>:` **_c**	The tool issues the Center option
`Center:` **PER** ↵	Specifies the PERpendicular object snap
`to` *Pick the line at* ⑥	
`Angle/Length of chord/<End point>:` **ENDP** ↵	Specifies the ENDPoint object snap
`_endp of` *Pick at* ①↵	Draws the arc and completes the template

Save your drawing.

In figures 7.11 and 7.12, the template is shown in dashed lines as it is being drawn.

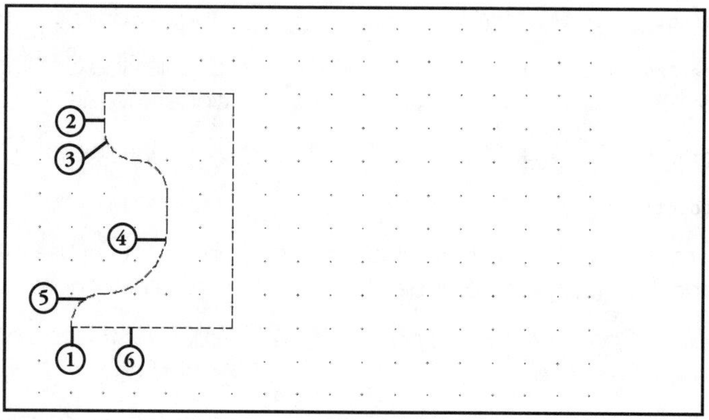

Figure 7.11

Drawing the template counterclockwise.

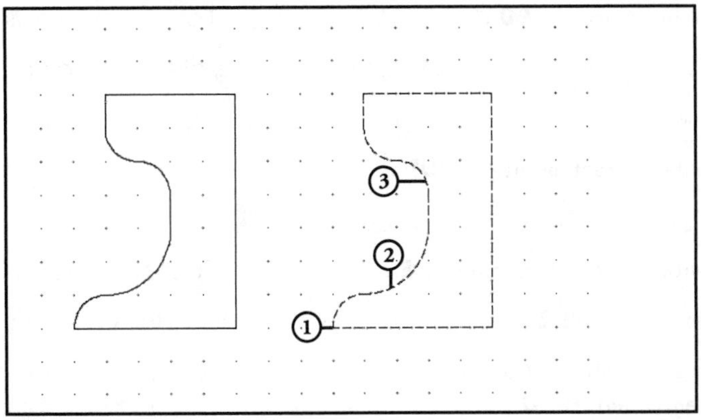

Figure 7.12

Drawing the template clockwise.

By using object snaps, relative coordinates, last point references, and four of the arc construction methods, you drew the template outline quickly and accurately. When you encounter a clockwise arc construction, choose an option that forces arcs in that direction, if possible.

Now, you use some of the same and some other arc construction methods to draw the template in a clockwise direction. Now that you have experience with arcs from the preceding exercise, the steps in the following exercise are somewhat abbreviated. Again, refer to figure 7.10 for dimensions.

DRAWING THE TEMPLATE CLOCKWISE

Continue from the preceding exercise. Begin in the lower left corner and proceed clockwise; the first arc you draw is the last arc from the preceding exercise.

`Command:` **A** ↵	Issues the ARC command
`ARC Center/<Start point>:` **9,2** ↵	Specifies the arc start point (refer to ① in figure 7.12)
`Center/End/<Second point>:` **C** ↵	Specifies the Center option
`Center:` **@1<0** ↵	Sets the center; drags a rubber-band arc as you move the cursor
`Angle/Length of chord/<End point>:` **A** ↵	Specifies the Angle option; arc drags in counterclockwise direction

Notice that the rubber-band angle drags from 0° (to the right of the center point), not from the start point.

`Included angle:` **-90** ↵	Forces and draws a clockwise arc

Now draw the next arc, using the start, end, direction method.

`Command:` ↵	Issues the ARC command
`Center/<Start point>:` **ENDP** ↵	
`of` *Pick the end of the arc at* ②	
`Center/End/<Second point>:` **E** ↵	Specifies the End option
`End point:` **@2,2** ↵	Sets the end point
`Angle/Direction/Radius/` `<Center point>:` **D** ↵	Specifies the direction option; move the cursor and watch the arc drag with direction
`Direction from start point:` **0** ↵	Draws the arc

Note that in the last step, direction is reckoned in degrees from the start point. Now draw the line segment using the Continue option of the LINE command.

`Command:` **L** ↵	Issues the LINE command
`From point:` ↵	Specifies the continue option; drags a line
`Length of line:` **1** ↵	Draws the line
`To point:` ↵	Ends the LINE command

Use the center, start, angle method to draw the next arc.

`Command:` **A**	Issues the ARC command
`Center/<Start point>:` **C** ↵	Specifies the Center option

Next, use the @ (lastpoint) to specify the arc's center. Recall that the current lastpoint is the end of the line from the preceding step.

`Center:` **@1<180** ↵	
`Start point:` **ENDP**↵	Specifies the ENDPoint object snap
`of` *Pick at* ③	
`Angle/Length of chord/<End point>:` **A** ↵	Specifies the Angle option; drags a counterclockwise arc
`Included angle:` **90** ↵	Draws the arc

For the last arc, use the Continue option of the ARC command.

`Command:` *Press Enter twice*	Reissues the ARC command and specifies the Continue option
`End point:` **@-1,1** ↵	Draws the arc
`Command:` **L** ↵	Issues the LINE command
`From point:` ↵	Specifies the Continue option
`Length of line:` **1**	Draws the line
`To point:` ↵	Ends the LINE command; you need not draw the remainder of the outline

The TEMPLATE layer of your CHAP07 drawing should now resemble figure 7.13.

Save your drawing.

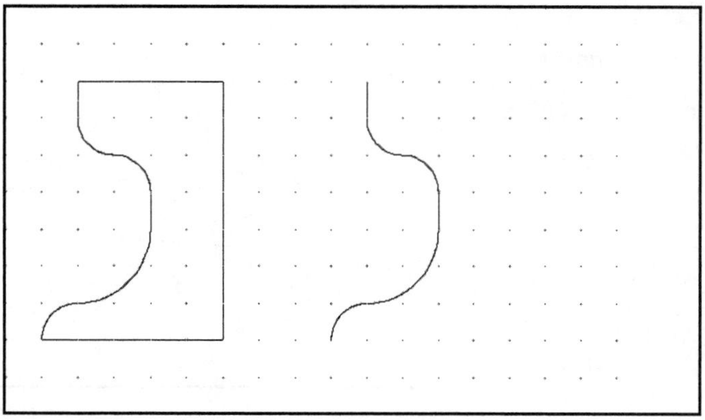

Figure 7.13

The completed templates.

In the two preceding exercises, you gained experience with seven of the arc construction methods. Again, more than one method often would work to construct the arc you need. In the template figure you used in those exercises, you had the opportunity to use the Continue options of both the ARC and LINE commands. In drawings that consist largely of orthogonal lines and arcs, these options often are available. In any situation, however, knowing the various options available with the ARC command enables you to construct just the arc you need. You use few other AutoCAD commands in which thinking and planning ahead a step or two is as beneficial as when you use the ARC command.

Drawing Points

The POINT command is the simplest of AutoCAD's drawing commands. It creates a point object. When you use the Point tool to issue the POINT command it repeats until canceled. This is useful when you need to locate a number of points in sequence. You terminate the command by pressing Esc. If you issue the POINT command by typing it at the `Command:` prompt, AutoCAD requests only one point location, then the command terminates.

The X in the center of the transfer arm (see fig. 7.14) is a point object. Point objects can be displayed in 20 different styles, as shown in figure 7.15. If you use style 0, you must perform a display redraw after you create the point to see the actual point object.

Figure 7.14

The completed transfer arm.

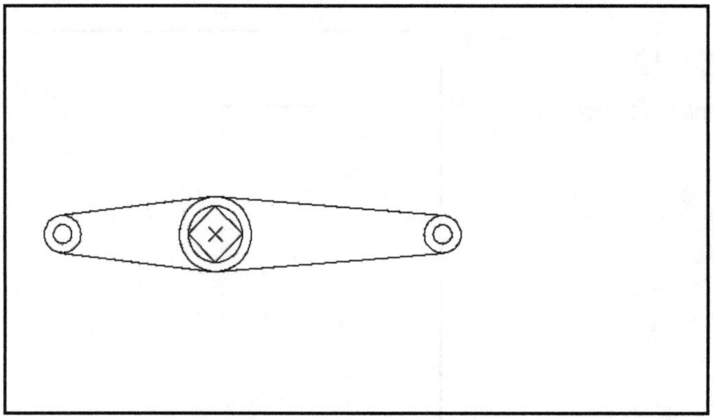

NOTE

Point objects are most useful in designating reference locations, such as pivot points in mechanical designs, or survey points in civil work. You can control their appearance so that they either stand out or remain invisible. They can be located with the NODE object snap, which enables you to snap to them even within otherwise crowded areas of a drawing, where other object snap modes might produce ambiguous results.

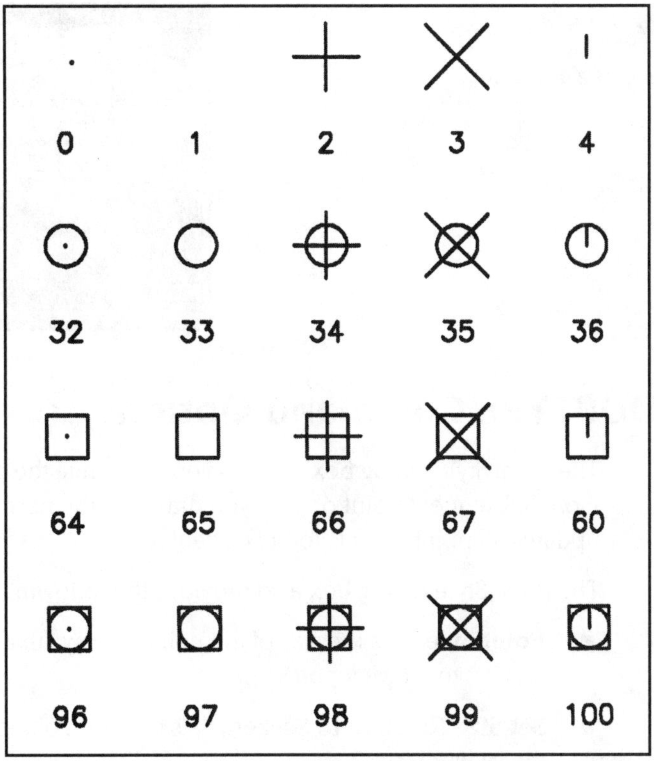

Figure 7.15

The 20 available point styles and their PMODE numbers.

Twenty different "styles" of point objects are available (shown in figure 7.15 along with their corresponding number designation). You can use the corresponding style number to set the style after you enter the PDMODE system variable at the command prompt. The system variable PDSIZE controls the display size of the point object. A positive PDSIZE value specifies an absolute size in drawing units for the point object; a negative value specifies a point object size that is a percentage of the viewport size. Entering a size of 0 creates a point object that is 5 percent of the drawing window height.

Using the Point Style dialog box (refer to figure 7.16), which you access from the DDPTYPE command, is a much easier way to control point object style and size.

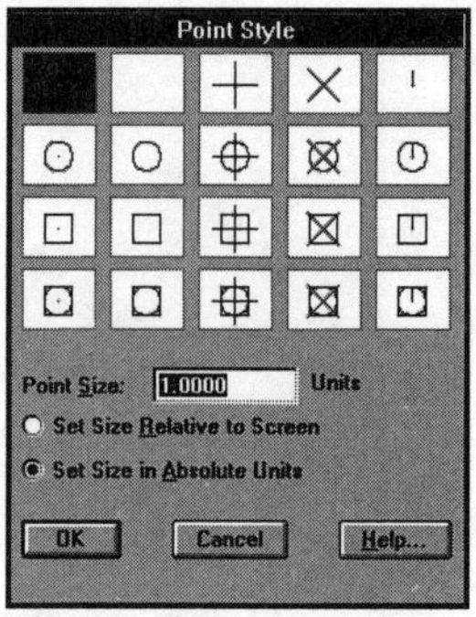

Figure 7.16

The Point Style dialog box.

DDPTYPE Command Options

The Point Style dialog box enables you to change the point display by selecting an icon. Subsequent point objects you draw use the new style. The next regeneration updates all point objects to the current style.

The Point Style dialog box also provides the following controls:

- **Point Size.** Sets the size of the point display (in absolute drawing units or relative to the viewport).
- **Set Size Relative to Screen.** Sets the point object size as a percentage of the viewport size.
- **Set Size in Absolute Units.** Sets the point object size in actual units.

TIP

Use an easily noticeable point style when drawing, but remember to set it to the default dot (PDMODE 0) before plotting. Or, if you don't want points to plot, set them to the blank point style (PDMODE 1). You can also place construction points on their own layer and turn off or freeze the layer before plotting.

Creating Donuts, Polygons, and Rectangles

Donuts, Polygons, and Rectangles are three AutoCAD objects that are useful in many drawings. Each is comprised of a special type of line called a *polyline*. Polylines differ from the individual line segments you create with the LINE command. Although line segments can appear to be connected, they are actually separate objects which share common endpoints. A multi-segment polyline, on the other hand, is created and treated as a single object. A pentagon created using the POLYGON command, for example, behaves as a single object, not as five individual line segments. This special quality of polylines aids in the creation and editing of donuts, rectangles, and polygons.

NOTE

Polylines also differ from independent line segments in their capability to have width properties. Polylines also can have arc segments (as in donuts) and can be edited in several ways. All of the special qualities of polylines are covered in Chapter 8, "Drawing and Editing Polylines and Splines."

Creating Donuts

As you might imagine, the DONUT command enables you to create an object that looks like a doughnut. Donuts can have any inside and outside diameter. In fact, as figure 7.17 demonstrates, donuts that have an inside diameter of 0 appear as a filled-in circle. Donuts can serve many useful functions in a drawing, such as mounting holes, lugs, grounds, dots, and so forth.

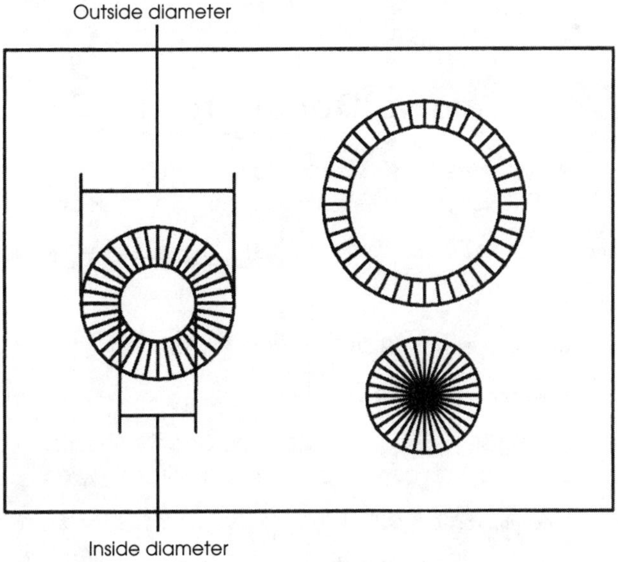

Figure 7.17

Some examples of donuts.

As shown in figure 7.18, you can find the Donut tool on the Circle toolbar.

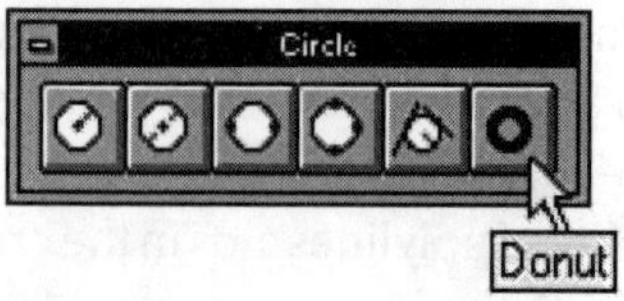

Figure 7.18

The Donut tool on the Circle toolbar.

DONUT Command Options

The DONUT command has the following options.

- **Inside diameter <current>.** At the `Inside diameter` prompt, you specify the inside diameter or press Enter to accept the default value. A diameter of 0 is acceptable; it causes DONUT to draw solid filled dots.
- **Outside diameter <current>.** At the `Outside diameter` prompt, you specify the outside diameter or press Enter to accept the default value.
- **Center of doughnut.** At the `Center of doughnut` prompt, you specify a point for the center of the donut.

You can edit donuts with the PEDIT command; see Chapter 8, "Drawing and Editing Polylines and Splines."

In the following exercise, return to the CIRCUIT-BOARD layer of the CHAP07 drawing and use the DONUT command to add mounting grommets and a grounding lug to the circuit board.

ADDING DONUTS TO THE CIRCUIT BOARD

Continue to use the CHAP07 drawing from the earlier circuit board exercise. Turn on the CIRCUIT-BOARD layer and set it to current. Turn off all other layers. Turn on snap mode.

`Command:` *Choose Donut (Draw, Circle)*	Issues the DONUT command
`_donut`	
`Inside diameter <0.50>:` **.2** ↵	Specifies the inside diameter
`Outside diameter <1.00>:` **.4** ↵	Specifies the outside diameter

In the following steps, you can use snap and the coordinate display to locate the donut centers, or you can type the coordinates shown.

`Center of doughnut:` **1.5,9.5** ↵	Draws the donut
`Center of doughnut:` **14.25,9.5** ↵	Draws the donut

`Center of doughnut:` **14.25,2.5** ↵	Draws the donut
`Center of doughnut:` **1.5,2.5** ↵	Draws the donut
`Center of doughnut:` ↵	Ends the command

In the following steps, you place a grounding lug on the board.

`Command:` ↵	Repeats the command
`Inside diameter <0.20>:` **0** ↵	Specifies the inside diameter
`Outside diameter <0.40>:` **.5** ↵	Specifies the outside diameter
`Center of doughnut:` **14,5** ↵	Draws the donut
`Center of doughnut:` ↵	Ends the DONUT command

Save your drawing.

Your circuit board drawing should now resemble figure 7.19.

Figure 7.19

Circuit board with donuts added.

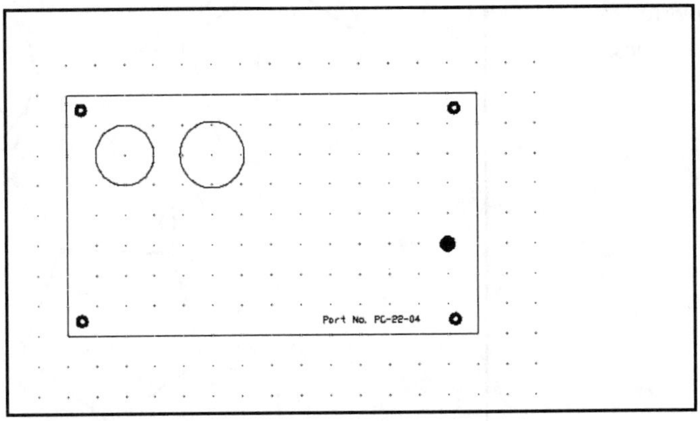

Notice that the DONUT command continues to prompt for donut center points until you end the command by pressing Enter.

TIP

You can type DONUT or DOUGHNUT; AutoCAD recognizes either spelling.

Drawing Regular Polygons

Another composite polyline AutoCAD object is the polygon, which you create using the POLYGON command. The POLYGON command enables you to draw regular (equilateral) polygons with from 3 to 1,024 sides. POLYGON gives you two ways to define the size of your figure (see fig. 7.20). You can show the length of one of the edges or you can define it relative to a circle. You then can inscribe the polygon in the circle or circumscribe it about the circle.

Polygon Command Options

The POLYGON command offers the following options.

Figure 7.20

Three ways to draw regular polygons.

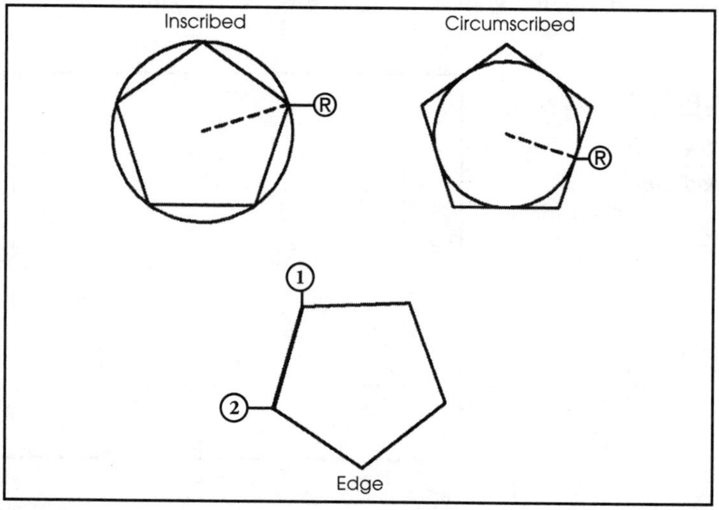

- **Number of sides <current>.** At the `Number of sides` prompt, you enter the number of sides between 3 and 1,024 or press Enter to accept the default.
- **Edge/<Center of polygon>.** At this prompt, you choose whether you want to define the polygon by specifying its center or the endpoints of an edge.

- **Inscribe in circle/Circumscribe about circle (I/C)<I>.** If you specify the center of the polygon, this prompt appears. If you choose `inscribe in circle`, all vertices of the polygon fall on the circle; if you choose `circumscribe about circle`, the radius equals the distance from the center of the polygon to the midpoints of the edges. If you use the pointing device to specify the radius, you dynamically determine the rotation and size of the polygon. If you specify the radius of the circle by typing a specific entry, the angle at the bottom edge of the polygon equals the current snap rotation angle.
- **First endpoint of edge, Second endpoint of edge.** If you place the polygon by specifying its edge, these prompts enable you to specify the endpoints of an edge (refer to figure 7.20).

The POLYGON command is available on the Polygon toolbar, as shown in figure 7.21. Regular polygons are easy to draw in AutoCAD. In the following exercise, you add two hexagonal inductance coils to the circuit board. You use the Edge option to place the first hexagon and you use the Center option to place the second hexagon.

Figure 7.21

The Polygon tool on the Polygon toolbar.

DRAWING REGULAR POLYGONS

Continue from the preceding exercise. Make sure that snap is on.

`Command:` *Choose Polygon (Draw, Polygon)*	Issues the POLYGON command
`_polygon Number of sides <4>:` **6** ↵	Specifies a hexagon
`Edge/<Center of polygon>:` **E** ↵	Specifies the edge option
`First endpoint of edge:` *Pick point* 9,7 (①) (see fig. 7.22)	Drags the polygon
`Second endpoint of edge:` *Pick point* 10,7 (②)	Draws the polygon
`Command:` ↵	Repeats the POLYGON command
POLYGON `Number of sides <6>:` ↵	Accepts the default hexagon

`Edge/<Center of polygon>:` *Pick point* 12,8 (③)	Defaults to set the center point
`Inscribed in circle/ Circumscribed about circle (I/C) <I>:` ↵	Accepts the default inscribed option

In the following step, you type the radius value to force the bottom edge of the hexagon to be parallel to the current snap angle (0 degrees).

`Radius of circle:` **1** ↵	Draws the polygon (see fig. 7.22)

Save your drawing.

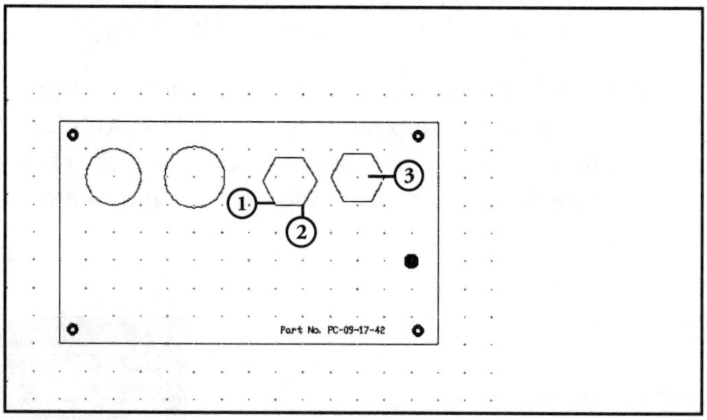

Figure 7.22

Adding a polygon to the circuit board.

After you draw a polygon object, you can use the PEDIT and EXPLODE commands to edit it. See Chapter 8, "Drawing and Editing Polylines and Splines," for information about editing polylines.

When you draw polygons, if you know the intended center point, the inscribed or circumscribed methods are the obvious choice. The edge method, on the other hand, enables you to align the polygon with other objects. The edge method generates a polygon figure that continues counterclockwise from the two edge endpoints you specify.

Drawing Rectangles

Perhaps the simplest of the composite polyline objects is the rectangle drawn by the RECTANG command. The command requests the opposite corners of the rectangle, then draws the rectangle.

The RECTANG command is available on the Polygon toolbar, as shown in figure 7.23.

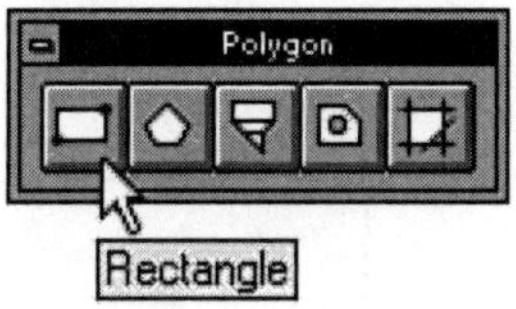

Figure 7.23

The Rectangle tool on the Polygon toolbar.

RECTANG Command Prompts

Whether you issue the RECTANG command by using the Rectangle tool or entering the command at the keyboard, RECTANG presents the following prompts:

- **First corner.** At this prompt, you specify a point to represent one corner of the rectangle. A rectangle drags on-screen as you move the cursor.
- **Other corner.** At this prompt, you specify a point to represent the opposite corner of the rectangle.

In the following two exercises, you draw several rectangles to represent additional elements on the circuit board: a transformer, three resistors, and a trimming capacitor. Use snap, the coordinate display, and figure 7.24 to help you find the points.

Adding a Rectangle to the Circuit Board

Continue from the previous exercise, with snap on.

`Command:` *Choose Rectangle (Draw, Polygon)* — Issues the RECTANG command

`_rectang`

`First corner:` *Pick point* 2,6

Note that as you move the cursor after you specify the first corner, a rectangle drags on-screen.

`Other corner:` *Pick point* 7.0,3.0 — Draws the rectangle

Draw another rectangle inside the first.

`Command:` ↵ — Repeats the command

`First corner:` *Pick point* 2.5,5.5

`Other corner:` *Pick point* 6.5,3.5 Draws the second rectangle

Repeat the command to create the other rectangles shown in figure 7.24.

Save your drawing.

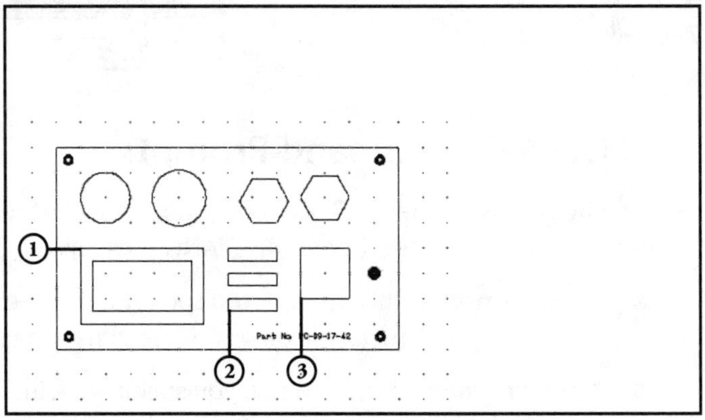

Figure 7.24

Circuit board with rectangles added.

Creating Ellipses and Elliptical Arcs

In AutoCAD you can create full ellipses, as well as elliptical arcs. Both use true mathematical representations of ellipses. Ellipses created in this manner have both center and quadrant object snap points; elliptical arcs have center object snap points and may have quadrant object snap points.

NOTE

In previous releases of AutoCAD, ellipses were created using polyline approximations. True ellipses and elliptical arcs were not possible. The same ellipse approximations are supported in Release 13 although true ellipses and elliptical arcs are more accurate. The system variable PELLIPSE controls which type of ellipse is drawn. If PELLIPSE is set to 0 (the default), true ellipses are drawn.

When older drawings are opened in Release 13, the older ellipse approximations are not converted to the newer, true ellipses.

The default method of creating an ellipse is to specify the endpoints of one axis and the distance from the center of the other axis. You can also draw an ellipse by specifying the center, one axis endpoint, and the other axis distance. The second axis can also be specified by a rotation which defines the major to minor axis ratio (see fig. 7.25).

Figure 7.25

Methods of drawing an ellipse.

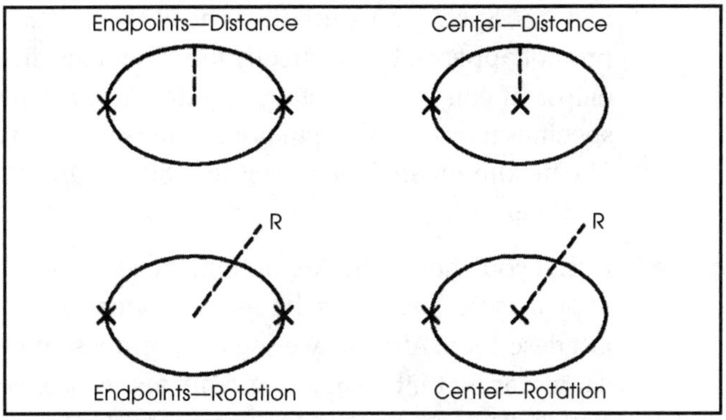

The Ellipse toolbar is shown in figure 7.26. If the system variable PELLIPSE is set to 1, the last tool, Ellipse Arc, is not functional.

Figure 7.26

The Ellipse toolbar.

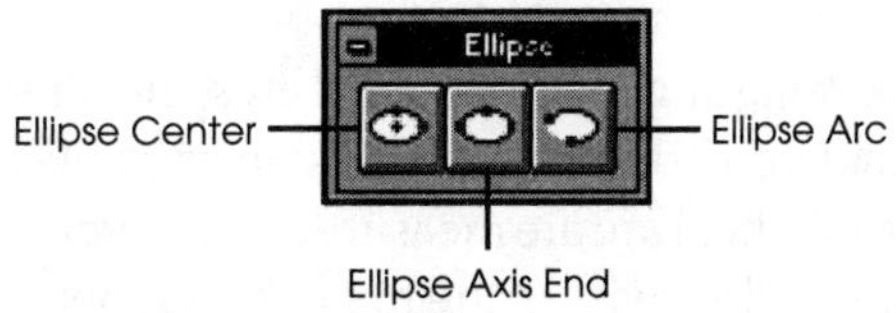

ELLIPSE Command Options

When you issue the ELLIPSE command from the `Command:` prompt, AutoCAD issues the following initial prompt:

```
Arc/Center/<Axis endpoint 1>:
```

- **Axis endpoint 1.** You specify an axis (major or minor) endpoint. The `Axis endpoint 2` prompt appears, at which you specify the second axis endpoint. The `<Other axis distance>/Rotation` prompt appears. If you specify the other axis distance, AutoCAD draws the ellipse. If you specify Rotation, AutoCAD prompts for an angle. The angle specifies the ratio of the major to minor axis. An angle of 0 defines a circle. The maximum angle acceptable is 89.4 degrees which yields a "flat" ellipse.

- **Center.** If you choose the Center option, the `Center of ellipse` prompt appears, at which you specify a center point. The `Axis endpoint` prompt appears. Specify an endpoint. The `<Other axis distance>/Rotation` prompt appears. If you specify the other axis distance, AutoCAD draws the ellipse. If you specify Rotation, AutoCAD prompts for an angle. The angle specifies the ratio of the major to minor axis. An angle of 0 defines a circle. The maximum angle acceptable is 89.4 degrees, which yields an essentially "flat" ellipse.

- **Arc.** If you choose the Arc option, the `<Axis endpoint 1>/Center:` prompt appears, which requests the same information as the prompt for a full ellipse just described. After answering the prompt sequence for the full ellipse, the `Parameter/<start angle>:` prompt appears. Specifying a point defines the start angle of the arc and the `Parameter/Included/<end angle>:` prompt appears. Specifying an end angle draws the arc. Specifying I, for Included, allows you to specify an included angle for the arc, beginning with the start angle. The Parameter option in the arc prompts is covered later in this chapter.

In reckoning angles for elliptical arcs, the direction of the first point of the major axis is considered 0 degrees. If the system variable ANGDIR is set to 0 (the default), angles for the elliptical arc are measured counterclockwise. If ANGDIR is set to 1, angles are measured clockwise. If the minor axis is defined first, the major axis zero point is 90 degrees in a counterclockwise direction. If you choose the Included angle option, this angle is measured from the start point, not the 0 degree point.

TIP

When specifying elliptical arc angles, it is helpful to refer to the coordinate display area of the status bar. Make sure the system variable COORDS is set to 2 to obtain a polar coordinate display.

Using either ellipse tool from the ellipse toolbar automatically issues responses to some of the options of the ELLIPSE command.

In the following exercise, you add an ellipse to the trimming capacitor on your circuit board. You use the Center option with both the second axis distance and rotation options.

Adding an Ellipse to the Circuit Board

Continue from the preceding exercise.

`Command:` *Choose Ellipse Center (Draw, Ellipse)*	Issues the ELLIPSE command and the Center option
`_ellipse` `<Axis endpoint 1>/Center:` **_c**	
`Center of ellipse:` Pick point 12,5 at ① (see fig. 7.27)	
`Axis endpoint:` **@.75<0** ↵	Specifies the axis endpoint with a relative coordinate and drags an ellipse
`<Other axis distance>` `/Rotation:` **@.5<90**	Specifies the second axis distance from center with a relative coordinate and draws the ellipse
`Command:` **U** ↵	Deletes the ellipse
`Command:` *Choose Ellipse Center (Draw, Ellipse)*	Issues the ELLIPSE command and Center option
`_ellipse` `<Axis endpoint 1>/Center: _c`	
`Center of ellipse:` *Pick point 12,5 at* ①	
`Axis endpoint:` **@.75<0** ↵	Specifies the axis endpoint with a relative coordinate; drags an ellipse
`<Other axis distance>` `/Rotation:` **R**	Specifies the rotation option

Next, move the cursor about the ellipse center point so that you can see what happens when you increase the angle from 0 degrees (to the right) to 90 degrees.

`Rotation around major axis:` **45** ↵	Draws the ellipse

Your circuit board is now complete and should resemble figure 7.27.

Save your drawing.

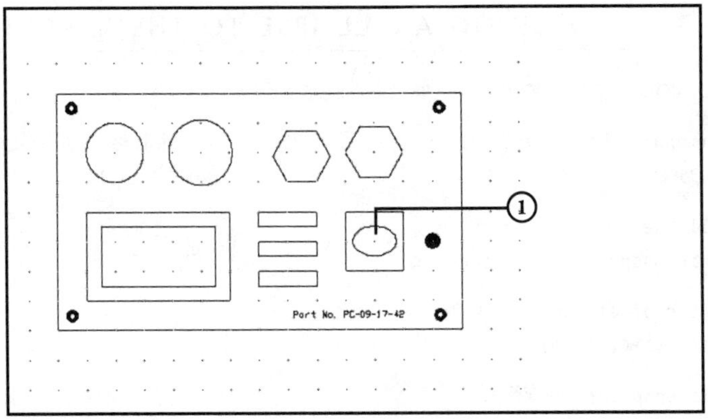

Figure 7.27

The completed circuit board.

Drawing Elliptical Arcs

Elliptical arcs are easy to draw in AutoCAD Release 13. The first stage involves constructing the parent ellipse. The same options and prompts required to construct a full ellipse appear first. Then prompts requesting the starting and ending arc angles allow you to define the arc. You can also specify a starting angle and an included angle. When specifying elliptical arc angles, you can use keyboard entry or pick points in the drawing window. When picking points, you can employ object snap points.

In the following two exercises you draw a rocker arm assembly. The drawing requires four elliptical arcs, and you use several of the options available for constructing these arcs. Pay particular attention to the scheme of measuring the arc angles once the parent ellipse has been drawn.

DRAWING ELLIPTICAL ARCS

Begin a new drawing, CHAP07B, using the IAW-MECH drawing on the accompanying CD as a prototype. First, make the OBJECT layer current and draw the three pairs of concentric circles at the coordinates shown in figure 7.28. Draw the construction line on layer CONSTRUCTION, then ensure that layer OBJECT is again current.

`Command:` *Choose Ellipse Arc (Draw, Ellipse)*	Issues the ELLIPSE command and the Arc option
`Arc/Center/<Axis endpoint 1>: _a`	Selects Arc option automatically
`<Axis endpoint 1>/Center:` **QUA** ↵	Specifies the QUAdrant osnap

`_qua of` *Pick a point near* ① *(see fig. 7.29)*

`Axis endpoint 2:` — Drags the ellipse in the drawing window

`qua of` *Pick a point near* ②

`<Other axis distance>/Rotation:` **@.25<0** ↵ — Specifies the minor axis distance from the the ellipse center point; draws ellipse

As you move the cursor around the ellipse, note the polar coordinate display on the status bar. Because the axis points defined the major axis, the first axis endpoint is the 0 degree point for measuring the arc.

`Parameter/<start angle>:` **0** ↵ — Specifies the start angle for the arc

`Parameter/Included/<end angle>:` **180** ↵ — Specifies the end angle for the arc; draws the arc

Depending upon your display hardware, portions of the entire arc might still be visible. In the remainder of this exercise and the next, issue the REDRAW command, as required, to clean up the screen display.

`Command:` *Choose Ellipse Arc (Draw, Ellipse)* — Issues the ELLIPSE command and the Arc option

`Arc/Center/<Axis endpoint 1>:` **_a**

`<Axis endpoint 1>/Center:` **_C** ↵ — Specifies the Center option

`Center of ellipse:` **QUA** ↵

`qua of` *Pick a point near* ① — Specifies the arc's center point

`Axis endpoint:` **QUA** ↵

`_qua of` *Pick a point near* ③

`<Other axis distance>/Rotation:` **@1.375<0** ↵ — Specifies the arc's minor axis

As you move the cursor around the ellipse, note that the point defining the major axis, ③, establishes the 0 degree point for arc angle. Note also the 270 degree point is measured counterclockwise from the 0 degree point.

`Parameter/<start angle>:` **270** — Specifies the start angle for the arc

`Parameter/Included/<end angle>:` **I** ↵ — Specifies the Included angle option

`Included angle <180.00>:` **90** ↵ — Draws a 90 degree arc

Your drawing should now resemble fig. 7.29.

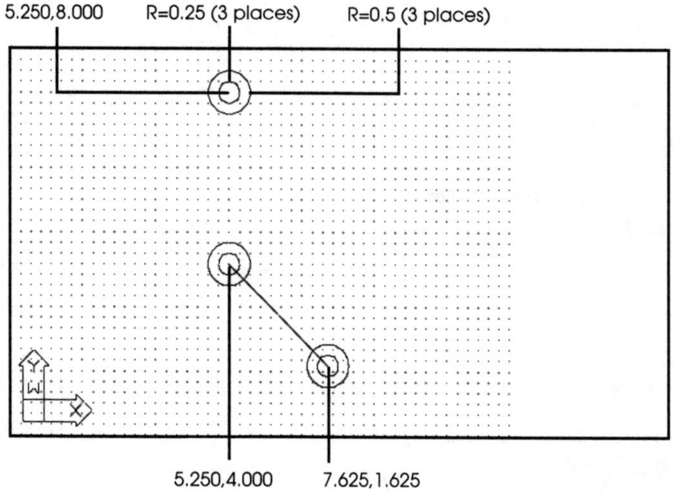

Figure 7.28

Setting up for elliptical arcs.

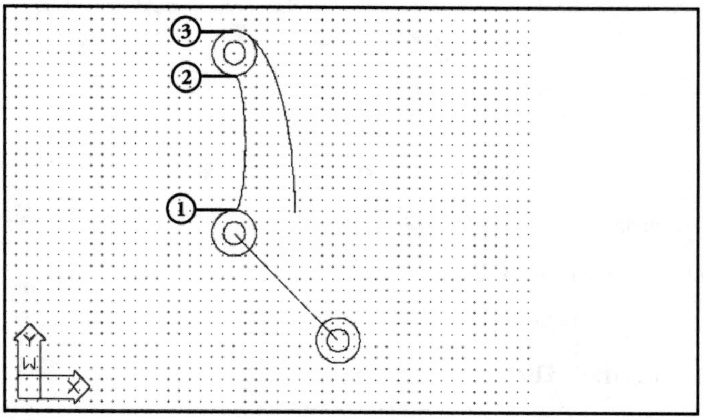

Figure 7.29

The first two arcs for the rocker arm.

Notice in the preceding exercise that once the parameters for the parent ellipse have been defined, the polar coordinate display on the status bar is based upon the direction of the ellipse's major axis, not the conventional drawing window directions. This will become more apparent in the following exercise as you draw elliptical arcs whose axes are not orthogonal to the drawing window's 0 degree direction.

CONTINUING WITH ELLIPTICAL ARCS

Continue from the preceding exercise.

`Command:` *Choose Ellipse Arc (Draw, Ellipse)*	Issues the ELLIPSE command and Arc option
`Arc/Center/<Axis endpoint 1>:` **_a**	
`<Axis endpoint 1>/Center:` **INT** ↵	Specifies the INTersection osnap
`int of` *Pick the intersection at* ① *(see fig. 7.30)*	Specifies axis endpoint 1
`Axis endpoint 2:` **INT** ↵	
`int of` *Pick the intersection at* ②	Draws the ellipse
`<Other axis distance>/Rotation:` **@.325<45** ↵	Specifies minor axis distance and direction

Note that the 0 degree point is the first point of the major axis at a.

`Parameter/<start angle>:` **180**	
`Parameter/Included/<end angle>:` **INT** ↵	
`int of` *Pick the intersection at* ①	Draws the arc
`Command:` *Choose Ellipse Arc (Draw, Ellipse)*	Issues the ELLIPSE command and Arc option
`Arc/Center/<Axis endpoint 1>:` **_a**	
`<Axis endpoint 1>/Center:` **_C** ↵	
`Center of ellipse:` **INT** ↵	Specifies the INTersection object snap
`int of` Pick near the end of the construction line at ③	
`and` *Pick anywhere on the larger middle circle*	Specifies the center of the ellipse
`Axis endpoint:` **INT** ↵	
`int of` *Pick near the end of the construction line at* ④	
`and` *Pick anywhere on the larger lower circle*	Specifies an axis endpoint; draws the ellipse

`<Other axis distance>/Rotation:` **@1.45<45 ↵**	Specifies the minor axis
`Parameter/<start angle>:` **0 ↵**	

In the next step, drag the arc through and past the second arc you drew in the preceding exercise.

`Parameter/Included/<end angle>:` *Pick a point near* ⑤	Draws the arc
`Command:` **TRIM ↵**	Issues the TRIM command
`Select cutting edges:` (Projmode = UCS, Edgemode = No extend)	
`Select objects: 1 found` *Pick the arc at* ⑥	Selects and highlights the arc
`Select objects: 1 found` *Pick the arc at* ⑦	Selects and highlights the arc
`Select objects:` ↵	
`<Select object to trim>/Project/Edge/Undo:` *Pick the end of the arc at* ⑤	Trims the arc
`<Select object to trim>/Project/Edge/Undo:` *Pick the end of the arc at* ⑧	Trims the other arc
`<Select object to trim>/Project/Edge/Undo:` ↵	Ends the TRIM command
`Command:` *Choose Erase (Modify)*	Issues the ERASE command
`Command: _erase`	
`Select objects:` *Pick the construction line*	
`1 found`	Selects and highlights the line
`Select objects:` ↵	Erases the line

Save your drawing.

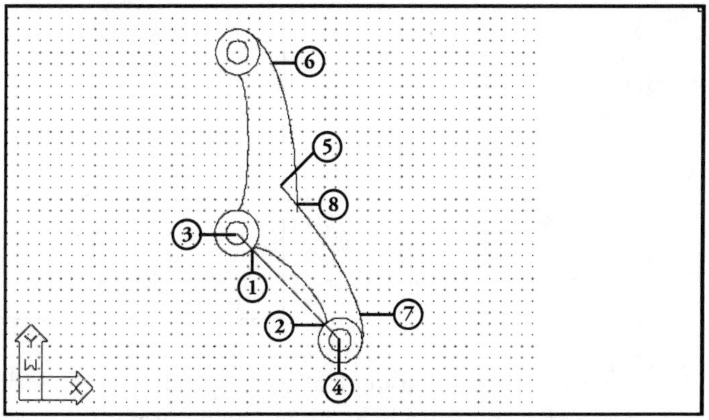

Figure 7.30

The second two arcs for the rocker arm.

Using the Elliptical Arc Parameter Option

When drawing elliptical arcs, a Parameter mode is offered in prompts requesting starting, ending, or included angles. If the Parameter mode option is chosen, by entering P, AutoCAD uses the following parametric equation to calculate the arc:

p(u) = (Cx + a*cos (u))*i + (Cy + a*sin(u))*j

Cx is the x value of the ellipse center
Cy is the y value of the ellipse center
a is -(1/2 of the major axis length)
b is -(1/2 of the minor axis length)
u is any angle between 0 and 360 degrees
i and j represent unit vectors in the x and y directions, respectively

Using the Parameter mode yields elliptical arcs that are proportional to the area of the parent ellipse. For example, specifying an arc with a starting angle of 45 degrees and an ending angle of 135 degrees parametrically draws an arc which subtends an angle, not of 90 degrees, but of approximately 127 degrees. This is shown in figure 7.31 where the elliptical sector on the left was derived from an arc drawn parametrically. The parametric specification for this arc is 30 degrees to 120 degrees—90 degrees. The resulting elliptical sector has an area of one quarter of that of the parent ellipse. The elliptical sector shown at the right of figure 7.31 was derived from an arc using the Angle mode. The area enclosed by this figure bears no proportional relationship to the area of the parent ellipse.

Figure 7.31

Elliptical arcs drawn in Parameter and Angle mode.

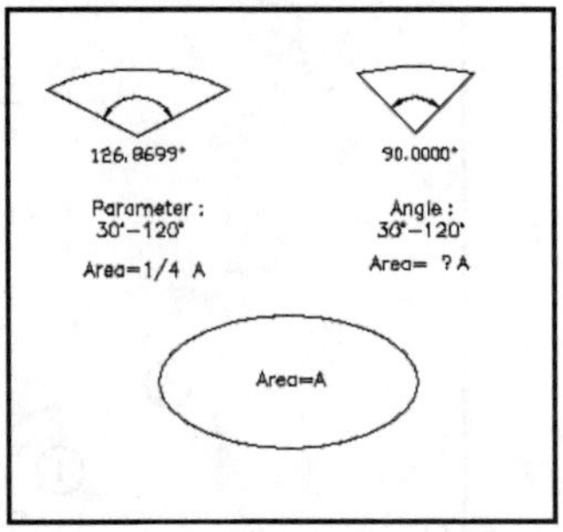

If you specify the Parameter mode option you can switch between the Parameter mode and Angle mode at the following prompt requesting angle input. The mode you are in when you specify an angle determines how AutoCAD calculates the ellipse.

In the following exercise, you draw an elliptical arc parametrically, specifying angles in both the Arc mode and Parameter mode.

DRAWING PARAMETRIC ARCS

Continue in your CHAP07B drawing. First turn off layer OBJECT and set layer CONSTRUCTION current.

`Command:` *Choose Ellipse Arc (Draw, Ellipse)*	Issues the ELLIPSE command and the Arc option
`Arc/Center/<Axis endpoint 1>:` **_a**	
`<Axis endpoint 1>/Center:` *Pick point 6.75,5.75*	Specifies axis endpoint 1
`Axis endpoint 2:` *Pick point 2.50,5.75*	Specifies axis endpoint 2
`<Other axis distance>/Rotation:` *Pick point 4.625,6.75*	Specifies minor axis; shows the ellipse

Note that since axis endpoint 1 defines the start point of the major axis, arc angles are measured from this point in a counterclockwise direction.

`Parameter/<start angle>:` **45** ↵	Specifies the starting angle in Angle mode
`Parameter/Included/<end angle>:` **P**↵	Changes to Parameter mode
`Angle/Included/<end parameter>:` **I** ↵	Specifies that next angle input is an included angle
`Included parameter <90.00>:` **36** ↵	Specifies the included angle; draws the arc parametrically

`Command:` *Choose Erase (Modify)*	Issues the ERASE command
`Command:` **_erase**	
`Select objects:` *Pick the elliptical arc*	
`1 found`	
`Select objects:` ↵	Ends the ERASE command; erases the arc

Turn layer OBJECT on and set it current. Save your drawing. You are now finished with CHAP07B drawing. You might want to use it to practice drawing the AutoCAD objects you learned about in this chapter.

In the preceding exercise, you specified an angle of 36 degrees. Because you drew this arc while in the Parameter mode, it subtends an angle which would yield an elliptical sector whose area would equal one-tenth the area of the parent ellipse.

The use of the parametric, or proportional, mode of specifying elliptical arc angles makes tasks such as projecting an arc onto a nonparallel plane simple and accurate. The choice between the Angle and Parametric mode depends upon the desired end result.

In this chapter, you have used the commands AutoCAD provides for drawing basic objects, from simple lines and points, to parametrically specified elliptical arcs. Mastering their use forms the basis of the range of skills required to use AutoCAD most effectively.

Although the LINE command involves few options, used in combination with the other basic objects and construction aids such as ORTHO and object snaps, it is a fundamental component of many AutoCAD drawings.

When drawing circles and arcs, as with many other AutoCAD commands, several methods are available. The method you select depends on the information you have. You can often use more than one method to accomplish the task. Understanding how and when to use each method enables you to quickly construct complex designs.

The polyline objects—donuts, polygons, and rectangles—are common objects found in many drawings. Knowing how to draw them quickly and accurately increases your efficiency.

True mathematical ellipses and elliptical arcs are possible for the first time in AutoCAD Release 13. Ellipses have true center and quadrant object snap points. Elliptical arcs can be specified with absolute angles or drawn parametrically in proportion to the area of the parent ellipse.

chapter

8

Drawing and Editing Polylines and Splines

When you use line and arc objects to draw straight lines and curves, each line and arc segment is a separate object, even when connected from end to end. If, for example, you use four lines to draw a box, you have to select all the lines to move the box. Polylines are multisegmented objects; they can contain multiple straight and curved segments. If you want to move a box drawn with a polyline, you only need to select any one segment to select the entire box.

In most CAD drawings, you use traditional drawing elements: lines, circles, ellipses, arcs, and so on. Sometimes, however, you need to draw smooth, irregular curves. You use splines to draw free-form, irregular curves. Splines are useful when you draw map contours, roads, walkways, and other smooth, flowing curves.

In this chapter, you learn how to do the following:

- Draw and edit multisegmented and multiwidth polylines
- Create a polyline from nonpolyline objects
- Fillet polylines and other objects
- Sketch freehand polylines
- Spline-fit a polyline
- Draw and edit splines

Although the PLINE, PEDIT, SPLINE, and SPLINEDIT commands consist of more options and suboptions than any other command in AutoCAD, you mostly use them with their defaults. As you become familiar with polylines in this chapter, you gain an understanding of when to use polylines to your advantage.

Creating Polylines

You use the PLINE command to create polylines. Instead of using a wide plotter pen or creating multiple lines to get a thick line, or creating independent arcs and then connecting them to lines, you can create a polyline. A polyline does the work of separate objects. Some samples of polylines are shown in figure 8.1.

Figure 8.1

Several kinds of polylines.

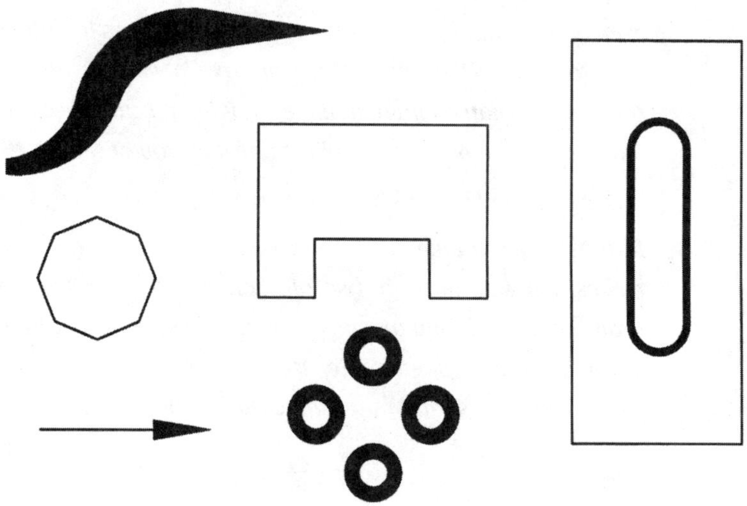

Polylines versus Lines

Polylines are different from independent line objects that you create by using the LINE command, which only appear to be joined. AutoCAD treats a multisegment polyline as a single object. Polylines can include both line and arc segments connected at vertices (endpoints). AutoCAD stores information, such as tangent direction and line width, at each vertex.

Polylines offer two advantages over lines. First, versatility: they can be straight or curved, thin or wide, one width or tapered. You can, for example, draw a curved leader with an arrowhead as a single polyline.

Second, editing operations are easier and you make fewer errors when you use crosshatching or work in 3D, because a polyline is a single object. You can edit a polyline by selecting any segment, because all of a polyline's segments are connected. If you crosshatch or create 3D objects from 2D lines, you must have edges that connect. Objects drawn with lines and arcs can have tiny gaps that cause hatch or 3D errors. Use polylines to draw any closed or connected object or polygon, particularly if you anticipate hatching it or working with your drawing in 3D.

TIP

If you plan to import your AutoCAD drawing into 3D Studio, polylines are indispensable. Use polylines to create all outlines, contours, and perimeters that you plan to loft in 3D Studio. Convert lines that make up walls in plan view drawings to polylines.

The PLINE Command

The PLINE command enables you to draw two basic kinds of segments, straight lines and curves, so some PLINE prompts are similar to the LINE and ARC prompts. If you draw straight polyline segments, options such as Endpoint, Close, and Undo appear. Check out the possibilities on the PLINE prompt line. The default set of options applies to line mode, as described in the following list:

- **Arc.** Switches from drawing polylines to drawing polyarcs and issues the polyarc options prompt.
- **Close.** Closes the polyline by drawing a segment from the last endpoint to the initial start point, and then exits from the PLINE command.

- **Halfwidth.** Prompts you for the distance from the center to the polyline's edges (half the actual width). See the Width option that follows for details.
- **Length.** Prompts you to enter the length of a new polyline segment. AutoCAD then draws the new segment at the same angle as the last line segment or tangent to the last arc segment. AutoCAD stores this angle in the LASTANGLE system variable. The last line or arc segment can be that of a previous polyline, line, or arc object.
- **Undo.** Undoes the last drawn segment. It also undoes any arc or line option that immediately preceded drawing the segment, but will not undo width options.
- **Width.** Prompts you to enter a width (default 0) for the next segment to create polylines. To taper a segment, define different starting and ending widths. After drawing the tapered segment, AutoCAD draws the next segment with the ending width of the tapered segment. Unless you cancel the PLINE command before drawing a segment, the ending width is stored as the new default width.
- **Endpoint of line.** Prompts you to specify the endpoint of the current line segment. This option is the default.

The Arc option presents a set of arc mode options, including some familiar arc prompts, such as Angle/CEnter/Radius, Second pt, and Endpoint of arc.

The PLINE Arc options include the following:

- **Angle.** Prompts you to enter the included angle (a negative angle draws the arc clockwise).
- **CEnter.** Prompts you to specify the arc's center.
- **Close.** Closes the polyline by using an arc segment to connect the initial start point to the last endpoint, and then it exits the PLINE command.
- **Direction.** Prompts you to specify a tangent direction for the segment.
- **Halfwidth.** Prompts you to specify a halfwidth, the same as for the Line option.
- **Line.** Switches back to line mode.
- **Radius.** Prompts you to specify the arc's radius.
- **Second pt.** Selects the second point of a three-point arc.

- **Undo.** Undoes the last drawn segment.
- **Width.** Prompts you to enter a width, the same way as in line mode.
- **Endpoint of arc.** Prompts you to specify the endpoint of the current arc segment. This option is the default.

NOTE

When a polyline has width, you can control the line fill by turning FILL on or off.

Although using PLINE to draw lines and arcs is similar to using LINE and ARC to draw equivalent elements, you should be aware of several important differences.

- You get all the line or arc mode prompts every time you enter a new polyline vertex.
- Additional prompts, such as for Halfwidth and Width, control the width of the segment.
- You can switch back and forth from straight segments to curved segments and add additional segments to your growing polyline.
- Linetypes can be applied continuously across vertices.
- The MEASURE and DIVIDE commands can be applied to complex polyline paths.
- The AREA command can be used to find lengths and areas of polylines.
- The OFFSET command can be used to great advantage to create new complex features, such as offsetting a foundation perimeter outline to create a footing.

Using PLINE To Draw Multisegment and Wide Lines

In the following exercises, you use polylines to draw a diagram of a street intersection as you use the PLINE command to create the most common types of objects: multisegmented lines and lines of varying widths.

You use normal zero-width polylines to draw the edge of the road where it meets the curb in the first exercise. You use the Arc, Line, and Length options. Use the 5' grid and 6" snap to pick points.

DRAWING BASIC POLYLINES

Start a new drawing named CHAP08A, using INTERSEC.DWG as a prototype.

`Command:` *Choose Polyline (Draw, Polyline)*	Issues the PLINE command
`From point:` *Pick point at* ① *(see fig. 8.2)*	Specifies the starting point of the polyline
`Current line-width is 0'-0.0000"`	Tells you the current line width
`Arc/Close/Halfwidth/Length/Undo/Width/` `<Endpoint of line>:` *Pick point at* ②	Specifies vertex of line segment
`Arc/Close/Halfwidth/Length/Undo/Width/` `<Endpoint of line>:` **A** ↵	Changes to polyline arc mode
`Angle/CEnter/CLose/Direction/Halfwidth/` `Line/Radius/Second pt/Undo/Width/` `<Endpoint of arc>:` *Pick point at* ③	Specifies vertex of arc segment
`Angle/CEnter/CLose/Direction/Halfwidth/` `Line/Radius/Second pt/Undo/Width/` `<Endpoint of arc>:` **L** ↵	Changes to polyline line mode
`Arc/Close/Halfwidth/Length/Undo/Width/` `<Endpoint of line>:` *Pick point at* ④	Specifies vertex of line segment
`Arc/Close/Halfwidth/Length/Undo/Width/` `<Endpoint of line>:` **A** ↵	Changes to polyline arc mode
`Angle/CEnter/CLose/Direction/Halfwidth/` `Line/Radius/Second pt/Undo/Width/` `<Endpoint of arc>:` *Pick point at* ⑤	Specifies vertex of arc segment
`Angle/CEnter/CLose/Direction/Halfwidth/` `Line/Radius/Second pt/Undo/Width/` `<Endpoint of arc>:` **L** ↵	Changes to polyline line mode
`Arc/Close/Halfwidth/Length/Undo/Width/` `<Endpoint of line>:` **L** ↵	Specifies Length option
`Length of line:` **21'6** ↵	Draws segment to ⑥
`Arc/Close/Halfwidth/Length/Undo/Width/` `<Endpoint of line>:` **A** ↵	Changes to polyline arc mode
`Angle/CEnter/CLose/Direction/Halfwidth/` `Line/Radius/Second pt/Undo/Width/` `<Endpoint of arc>:` *Pick point at* ⑦	Specifies vertex of arc segment

`Angle/CEnter/CLose/Direction/Halfwidth/ Line/Radius/Second pt/Undo/Width/ <Endpoint of arc>:` **L** ↵	Changes to polyline line mode
`Arc/Close/Halfwidth/Length/Undo/Width/ <Endpoint of line>:` *Pick point at* ⑧	Specifies vertex of line segment
`Arc/Close/Halfwidth/Length/Undo/Width/ <Endpoint of line>:` *Press Enter twice*	Ends and repeats the PLINE command
`PLINE` `From Point:` *Pick at* ⑨ *and use the* Arc *and* Line *options to draw segments to* ⑩, ⑪, *and* ⑫	Completes the curbs as shown in figure 8.2

Next, you move the right road edge to widen the lanes.

`Command:` *Select the right polyline and choose Move (Modify)*	Issues the MOVE command with polyline selected
`Base point or displacement:` *Pick any point*	
`Second point of displacement:` **@9'6<0**	Moves the polyline (see fig. 8.3)

Next, you draw two polylines for the center lane stripes. You edit them into wide polylines in a later exercise.

`Command:` *Choose Polyline (Draw, Polyline) and draw a line from* ① *to* ②

`Command:` *Choose Polyline (Draw, Polyline) and draw a line from* ③ *to* ④

Save the drawing.

Figure 8.2

Polyline boundaries.

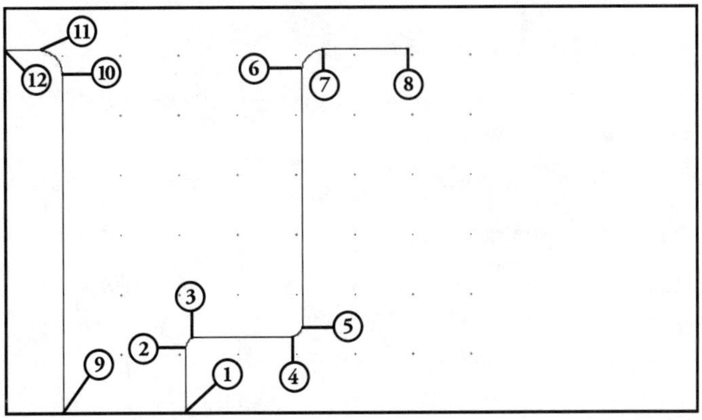

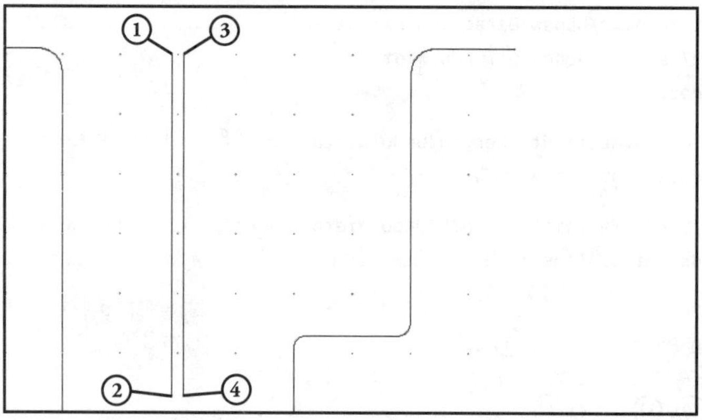

Figure 8.3

Polyline moved as one object.

The drawing of the intersection looks anemic for now, but you add some wide polylines in the next exercise to fill in the drawing. Later in this chapter, you edit the zero-width polylines into wide polylines.

A common use for wide and multiwidth polylines is for symbols and markings. Next, you add a stop line and some lane markers with wide polylines, and a fancy multiwidth polyline for the right-turn arrow. You use the Width and Halfwidth options.

Drawing Wide Polylines

Continue to work in the CHAP08A drawing from the previous exercise.

`Command:` *Choose Polyline (Draw, Polyline)*	Issues the PLINE command
`From point:` *Pick point at* ① *(see fig. 8.4)*	Specifies the starting point of the polyline
`Current line-width is 0'-0.0000"`	Tells you the current line width
`Arc/Close/Halfwidth/Length/Undo/Width/ <Endpoint of line>:` **W** ↵	Specifies the Width option
`Starting width <0'-0.0000">:` **10**	Specifies a starting width of 10 inches
`Ending width <0'-10.0000">:` ↵	Accepts starting width as ending width
`Arc/Close/Halfwidth/Length/Undo/Width/ <Endpoint of line>:` *Pick point at* ②	Specifies the endpoint of the polyline

`Arc/Close/Halfwidth/Length/Undo/Width/` `<Endpoint of line>:` *Press Enter twice*	Ends and repeats the PLINE command
`PLINE` `From point:` *Pick point at* ③	Specifies the starting point of the polyline
`Current line-width is 0'-10.0000"`	Tells you the current line width (AutoCAD remembers!)
`Arc/Close/Halfwidth/Length/Undo/Width/` `<Endpoint of line>:` *Pick point at* ④	Specifies the endpoint of the polyline
`Arc/Close/Halfwidth/Length/Undo/Width/` `<Endpoint of line>:` *Press Enter twice*	
`PLINE` `From point:` *Pick point* **28'-6",22'**	
`Current line-width is 0'-10.0000"`	Tells you the current line width
`Arc/Close/Halfwidth/Length/Undo/Width/` `<Endpoint of line>:` *Pick point* **28'-6",23'**	
`Arc/Close/Halfwidth/Length/Undo/Width/` `<Endpoint of line>:` **H** ↵	Specifies the Halfwidth option and prompts with the current half-width
`Starting half-width <0'-5.0000">:` ↵	Accepts the default
`Ending half-width <0'-5.0000">:` **15** ↵	Specifies an ending width of 15 inches
`Arc/Close/Halfwidth/Length/Undo/Width/` `<Endpoint of line>:` **A** ↵	Changes to arc mode

Drag the cursor around and observe the tapered outline of the polyline arc.

`Angle/CEnter/CLose/Direction/Halfwidth/`
`Line/Radius/Second pt/Undo/Width/`
`<Endpoint of arc>:` *Pick point* **30'-6",25'**
	Specifies the endpoint of the wide tapered polyline arc

`Angle/CEnter/CLose/Direction/Halfwidth/`
`Line/Radius/Second pt/Undo/Width/`
`<Endpoint of arc>:` **L** ↵
	Changes to line mode

`Arc/Close/Halfwidth/Length/Undo/Width/` `<Endpoint of line>:` **W** ↵	Specifies the Width option
`Starting width <2'-6.0000">:` **60** ↵	Specifies a starting width of 60 inches

`Ending width <5'-0.0000">:` **0** ↵	Specifies an ending width of 0
`Arc/Close/Halfwidth/Length/Undo/Width/ <Endpoint of line>:` *Pick point* **32'-6",25'**	Specifies endpoint of tapered polyline segment
`Arc/Close/Halfwidth/Length/Undo/Width/ <Endpoint of line>:` ↵	

Save the drawing.

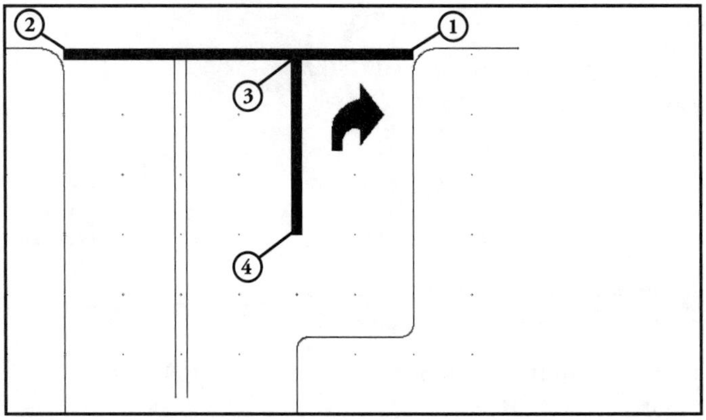

Figure 8.4

Enhanced drawing with wide polylines.

The preceding exercise emphasizes the versatility of polylines. Not only can polylines have varying width, but each segment can have different starting and ending widths. You also might have noticed that AutoCAD remembers the polyline width setting. Polyline width is stored in the PLINEWID system variable.

Controlling Polyline Appearance with FILL

A drawing that consists of many wide polylines can severely increase the amount of time AutoCAD expends to redraw the screen or plot a drawing. AutoCAD provides the FILL command to enable you to control the visibility of the filled portion of wide polylines, multilines, traces, and solids. When you turn FILL off, AutoCAD displays or plots only the outline of the filled object. You must regenerate the drawing before you can see the effect of the FILL command.

There is a pull-down menu item that controls FILL, but it directly controls the FILLMODE variable and does not use the FILL command. If you choose Options, Display, you see the Solid Fill item on the Display menu. If a check is made by this item, FILL is on (the default). If no check is made, FILL is off. The setting is stored with the drawing.

Creating Polylines with SKETCH

You use the SKETCH command as a freehand drawing tool or use a drawing tablet as an input device to trace curves on a paper drawing. (See Appendix A, "Installation and Configuration," for information on tablet calibration.) SKETCH creates a contiguous series of lines or polyline segments as you move the cursor. It draws wherever you move your cursor, as you move it. Because AutoCAD does not know where your sketching might lead, you and the program must take precautions to keep the amount of sketch information from getting out of hand. Just a few quick motions of the cursor while using the SKETCH command can create a huge number of short segments in the drawing file.

The Sketch screen menu also contains the SkpolOn: and SkpolOff: items, which turn SKPOLY on and off.

Setting SKETCH Parameters

To help AutoCAD keep sketch information under control, you specify the length of segment to use for storing your sketch data. This is known as the *record increment*. AutoCAD creates a new segment every time your pointer moves a distance away from the last segment endpoint that amounts to more than the record increment. If you want to minimize the number of lines, try to keep the record increment as large as possible.

The record increment is in current drawing units, but the effect on your input coordination also depends on the area your mouse or digitizer cursor must move in your currently zoomed view. For example, if the width of your screen represents 300 feet (3,600 inches), and the screen pointing area on your digitizer is 6 inches wide, a 60-inch increment means your sketch segments are 5 feet and that AutoCAD records a new segment every time you move your pointing device about one-tenth of an inch (6 inches × 60 inches, divided by 3,600 inches). The record increment is stored in the SKETCHINC system variable.

NOTE

Some mouse drivers are speed sensitive; the faster you move the mouse, the faster the cursor moves across the screen. These drivers enable you to have fine positioning control while you move the mouse slowly for detail work, yet cover large distances on-screen for accessing menus and tools when you move the mouse quickly. When you use the SKETCH command with speed-sensitive mouse drivers, move them at a slow, steady speed for best results.

You also must inform AutoCAD when it needs to consider the sketching pointer up (off the paper) or down (sketching). AutoCAD keeps all sketch input in a temporary buffer until you press R to record it into the drawing file database. SKETCH input appears in green until you record the input. You can press E to erase sketched lines before you record them. If you record sketched lines, AutoCAD turns them into regular line (or polyline) entities.

To achieve smooth contour curves, you need to sketch with polylines rather than with lines (the default).

NOTE

You easily can sketch and edit polylines, but the biggest advantage of using polylines is that you can curve fit them and end up with a smooth curve. When you set SKPOLY to sketch polylines, set your record increment higher than when you sketch with lines. Use an increment one-half the smallest radius or turn that you sketch. This might seem too large—until you apply a curve fit to it.

When you use the SKETCH command, AutoCAD ignores all other input, other than the sketch mode controls (and toggles such as F8 for ortho mode and F9 for snap mode). To control SKETCH, using the following options, press the first character of the option without pressing Enter.

- **Pen.** This option tells AutoCAD to pick up or put down the tracing pen. Just type P, without pressing Enter, to change the mode. You also can click the pick button to raise or lower the pen.
- **eXit.** This option records the sketch segments you have been creating in the drawing file and returns you to the `Command:` prompt. You also can exit by pressing the spacebar or Enter.
- **Quit.** This option leaves SKETCH without storing the segments you have been creating. Pressing Esc does the same thing.
- **Record.** This option keeps you in SKETCH, but stores the segments you have been creating in the drawing file. This function is just like a save, but after you record, stored segments are not available for Erase from SKETCH.
- **Erase.** This option erases any unrecorded segment from a point you pick to the last segment drawn.
- **Connect.** This option connects the pen to the end of the last endpoint of an active sketch chain. You also can use normal AutoCAD editing techniques to connect finished sketch lines to other elements after you finish the sketch.

In the following exercise, you use the SKETCH command to make some contour lines, a common and extremely useful application of SKETCH. Getting the hang of sketching takes a little time, so don't hesitate to undo or erase and try again. First, you set up SKETCH to draw using polylines and then you sketch the contours.

Sketching Polylines

Continue to work in the CHAP08A drawing from the previous exercise.

`Command:` **SKPOLY** ↵	Accesses the SKPOLY system variable
`New value for SKPOLY <0>:` **1** ↵	Causes SKETCH to draw polylines
Turn off snap	
`Command:` *Choose* Tools, Toolbars, Miscellaneous	Opens Miscellaneous toolbar
`Command:` *Choose Sketch (Miscellaneous)*	Issues the SKETCH command
`_sketch Record increment <0'-0.1000">:` **1'** ↵	Specifies record increment
`Sketch.  Pen eXit Quit Record Erase Connect.`	
Move the cursor to the start of a contour and press **P** *(see fig. 8.5)*	Puts pen down and begins sketching
`<Pen down>`	
Move the cursor along the contour	Draws sketch segments
Press **P** *again*	Raises the pen and stops sketching
`<Pen up>`	
Draw the other three contour lines	
After you finish drawing the contour lines, press **R**	Records the sketch data
`4 polylines with 76 edges recorded.`	Tells you how many polylines and how many segments were drawn by SKETCH (your number will vary)
Press **X**	Exits the SKETCH command
`Nothing recorded`	

Save the drawing and close the Miscellaneous menu.

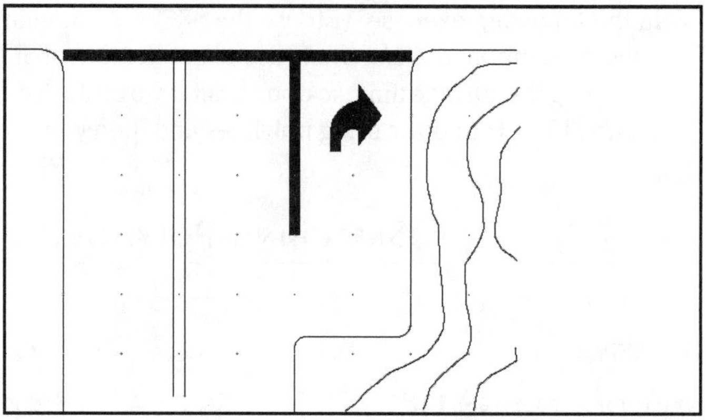

Figure 8.5

Contour lines created with the SKETCH command.

Do not be concerned if your sketched contours look too uneven; you smooth them with PEDIT in the next section.

TIP

Set the linetype to CONTINUOUS when you use the SKETCH command to create line objects. Noncontinuous linetypes do not work well for short line segments, such as those that SKETCH creates.

Next, you learn how to use the PEDIT command to change the characteristics of existing polylines.

Editing Polylines

Polylines can contain a complex continuous series of line and arc segments, so AutoCAD provides the PEDIT command, which you use only to edit polylines. PEDIT also contains a large list of subcommands for polyline properties. To manage this list, AutoCAD divides PEDIT into two groups of editing functions. The primary group of functions works on the entire polyline that you edit, and the second group works on the vertices that connect segments within the polyline.

When PEDIT prompts `Select polyline:`, you can pick a polyline line, arc, or polyline object. The PEDIT command operates on only one polyline at a time. PEDIT does not support noun/verb object selection. Before you can select a wide polyline for editing you must pick it at a vertex or an edge. This is true for any editing command—not just PEDIT. You can use a Window or Crossing selection, but to do so you must first enter W or C—PEDIT disables the implied windowing selection feature. You also can use the Last, Box, All, Fence, WPolygon, and CPolygon selection options. Selection ends as soon as PEDIT finds a line, arc, or polyline. If you select more than one, PEDIT finds only one, generally the most recently created one. If the first object you select is not a polyline, AutoCAD asks you if you want to turn it into one.

Although in this chapter you concentrate on editing two-dimensional polylines, you also can use PEDIT to modify three-dimensional polylines and meshes. The PEDIT command has fewer options and more restrictions when you edit three-dimensional polylines, as noted in the following list.

The primary PEDIT options are as follows:

- **Close/Open.** Adds a segment (if needed) and joins the first and last vertices to create a continuous polyline. When the polyline is open, the prompt shows Close; when closed, the prompt shows Open. A polyline can be open, even if the first and last points coincide and it appears to be closed. A polyline is open unless you use the Close option when you draw it, or later use the PEDIT Close option.
- **Join.** (2D only) Enables you to add selected arcs, lines, and other polylines to an existing polyline. Endpoints must coincide exactly to be joined.
- **Width.** (2D only) Prompts you to specify a single width for all segments of a polyline. The new width overrides any individual segment widths already stored. You also can edit the width of individual segments by using a suboption of the Edit vertex option.
- **Edit vertex.** Presents a prompt for a set of options that enable you to edit vertices and their adjoining segments. See the section "Editing Polyline Vertices with PEDIT" later in this chapter.
- **Fit.** (2D only) Creates a smooth curve through the polyline vertices.
- **Spline curve.** Creates a curve controlled by, but not usually passing through, a framework of polyline vertices. The type of spline and its resolution are controlled by system variables.
- **Decurve.** Undoes a Fit or Spline curve back to its original definition.
- **Ltype gen.** (2D only) Controls whether linetypes are generated between vertices (Ltype gen OFF) or between the polylines' endpoints (Ltype gen ON), spanning vertices. This is ignored for polylines with tapered segments.
- **Undo.** Undoes the most recent editing function.
- **eXit.** This option is the default <X> and exits PEDIT to return you to the `Command:` prompt.

Using PEDIT Width and Undo to Modify Polylines

In the following exercise, you use the Width option of the PEDIT command to modify the width of the center lane markings and the road boundaries. You also use the Undo option. These objects were created with zero-width polylines and need to have some width to fit into the diagram.

Changing the Width of Polylines

Continue to work in the CHAP08A drawing from the previous exercise.

`Command:` *Choose Edit Polyline (Modify, Special Edit)*	Issues the PEDIT command
`Select polyline:` *Pick left road edge at ① (see fig. 8.6)*	Selects the polyline for editing
`Close/Join/Width/Edit vertex/Fit/Spline/ Decurve/Ltype gen/Undo/eXit <X>:` **W** ↵	Specifies the PEDIT Width option
`Enter new width for all segments:` **6** ↵	Specifies new width and redraws entire polyline
`Close/Join/Width/Edit vertex/Fit/Spline/ Decurve/Ltype gen/Undo/eXit <X>:` ↵	Exits the PEDIT command

Press Enter to repeat the PEDIT command and use the above steps to change the right road edge at ② to 6" width.

Repeat the PEDIT command two more times, changing both center lane markers to 4" width.

Next, you try out the PEDIT Width option on a polyline that has multiple widths.

`Command:` ↵	Repeats PEDIT command
`PEDIT`	
`Select polyline:` *Pick the right-turn arrow at ③*	Selects the arrow for editing
`Close/Join/Width/Edit vertex/Fit/Spline/ Decurve/Ltype gen/Undo/eXit <X>:` **W** ↵	Specifies the PEDIT Width option
`Enter new width for all segments:` **10** ↵	Changes the width of all the segments in the polyline

`Close/Join/Width/Edit vertex/Fit/Spline/ Decurve/Ltype gen/Undo/eXit <X>:` **U** ↵	Restores the polyline to its original form
`Command has been completely undone.`	Tells you that all of the modifications to the polyline have been undone
`Close/Join/Width/Edit vertex/Fit/ Spline/Decurve/Ltype gen/Undo/eXit <X>:` ↵	Exits the PEDIT command

Save the drawing.

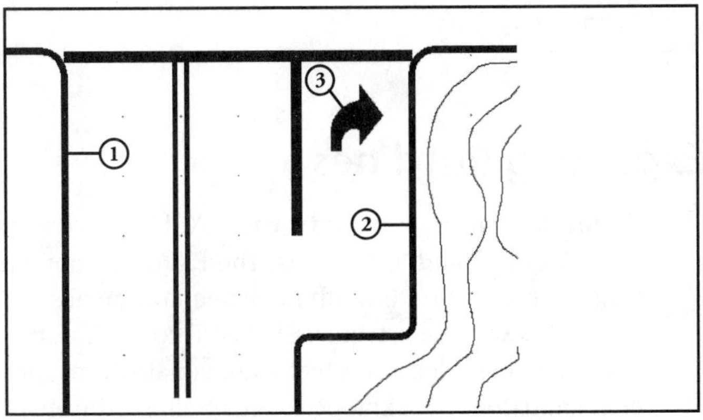

Figure 8.6

The INTERSEC drawing with modified polylines.

In the preceding exercise, you used the PEDIT Width option to change the width of all the polyline segments to the same value. The effect was particularly evident when you changed the width of the right-turn arrow. All the options at the main PEDIT prompt operate at the polyline level. The width of individual polyline segments is controlled at the vertex level. You use the PEDIT Edit vertex option and its suboptions to change information at the vertex level. The Edit vertex option is explained in more detail later in the section "Editing Polyline Vertices with PEDIT."

The ends of wide polylines are always square. When wide polylines are trimmed or extended, they still have square ends, regardless of the angle of the object to which they are being trimmed or extended. If you trim a wide polyline to a nonperpendicular line, for example, AutoCAD does not miter the end of the wide polyline segment to the angle of the intersecting line. AutoCAD trims polylines so that the midpoint of the end segment exactly meets the trim boundary. This can cause half of the width to go beyond the trim boundary and the other half to fall short of the boundary. The more acute the angle of the two objects, the more pronounced this effect becomes.

TIP

> You can create a wide polyline with a seemingly mitered end by using a trick when drawing the polyline. After specifying the last vertex endpoint, set the width to taper from the full width to zero width. Then draw another extremely short segment using typed relative polar input. The end of the polyline will appear to be mitered perpendicular to the angle you enter. Calculate the angle relative to the current UCS, not the angle of the polyline.
>
> For example, enter @0.00000001<45 to miter the top of a vertical polyline with width to an angle of 135 degrees (45 plus 90). The end of the last segment is actually pointed, but the 0.00000001 segment is short enough to have the effect of ending the previous segment with a miter.

Exploding Polylines

In the following exercise you use the EXPLODE command to change a polyline into individual line and arc objects. The EXPLODE command removes all width and tangent information from the polyline and breaks each segment into line or arc objects between each vertex. EXPLODE converts curve-fit and spline-fit polylines to many arc or line segments that approximate the shape of the spline. The EXPLODE command does not explode spline or ellipse objects.

The EXPLODE command also reduces other complex objects, such as blocks, dimensions, groups, multilines, 3D meshes, 3D solids, bodies, polyface meshes, polygon meshes, and regions, into their component parts. See Chapter 10 for more information on using the EXPLODE command with blocks, and Chapters 19 and 20 for information on dimensions. There also is a related XPLODE command, which is covered in Chapter 11.

Try out the EXPLODE command in the following exercise.

EXPLODING POLYLINES

Continue to work in the CHAP08A drawing from the previous exercise.

`Command:` *Choose Explode (Modify, Explode)*	Issues the EXPLODE command
`Select objects:` *Pick the right road boundary*	Selects an object to explode
`1 found`	
`Select objects:` ↵	Explodes all selected objects

`Exploding this polyline has lost width information. The UNDO command will restore it.`	Warns you about explode and tells you how to fix an accidental explode
`Command:` *Pick line at* ① *(see fig. 8.7)*	Selects one of the exploded polyline line segments and shows its grips

The polyline is exploded into its component parts; each polyline segment is now a separate object.

Save the drawing.

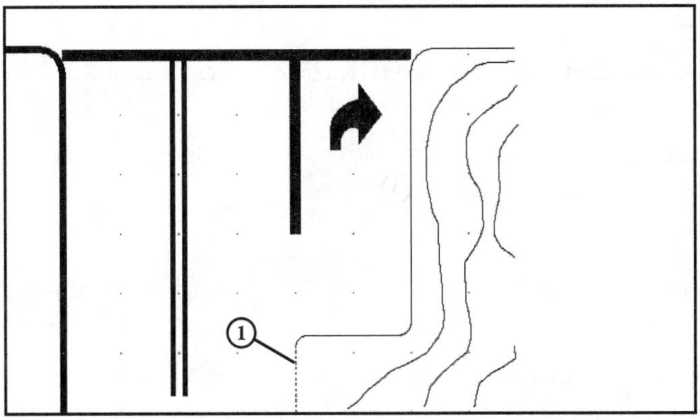

Figure 8.7

Wide polyline after EXPLODE.

Joining Polylines with PEDIT

The PEDIT Join option enables you to add additional objects to a polyline to create a single larger polyline. You can add polylines, lines, or arcs—they must be contiguous and the endpoints must coincide exactly. The Join option tells you the number of segments you add to the polyline.

You can use the PEDIT command to turn a line or arc object into a polyline. If you select a line or arc at the PEDIT `Select object:` prompt, AutoCAD asks you if you want to turn it into a polyline:

```
Object selected is not a polyline
Do you want to turn it into one? <Y>
```

Now that the right road boundary is exploded into lines and arcs, you use the PEDIT command to turn a line into a polyline and then join the rest of the lines and arcs back together to again form a polyline in the following exercise.

ADDING SEGMENTS TO A POLYLINE

Continue to work in the CHAP08A drawing from the previous exercise.

`Command:` *Choose Edit Polyline (Modify, Special Edit)*	Issues the PEDIT command
`Select polyline:` *Pick line at* ① *(see fig. 8.8)*	Selects an object for editing

`Object selected is not a polyline`
`Do you want to turn it into one?`
`<Y>` ↵
	Turns the line object into a polyline

`Close/Join/Width/Edit vertex/Fit/Spline/` `Decurve/Ltype gen/Undo/eXit <X>:` **J** ↵	Specifies the PEDIT Join option
`Select objects:` *Select objects with a crossing window from* ② *to* ③	Selects objects to add to polyline
`14 found`	
`Select objects:` ↵	Ends the selection process and adds segments to the polyline
`6 segments added to polyline`	Tells you the number of segments added
`Close/Join/Width/Edit vertex/Fit/Spline/` `Decurve/Ltype gen/Undo/eXit <X>:` ↵	Exits the PEDIT command
`Command:` *Pick line at* ①	Selects entire polyline and shows its grips

The lines and arcs are now joined back into a single polyline object.

Save the drawing.

The PEDIT Join option starts with the initially selected (or converted) polyline and sequentially joins each of the objects selected at the Join `Select objects:` prompt. It ignores all but line, arc, and polyline objects, and only joins an object if its endpoint exactly coincides with that of the previously joined segment. If more than one joinable object coincides, the results can be unpredictable. You can use object snaps and editing commands to fix the endpoints of objects that don't perfectly coincide before using PEDIT to join them.

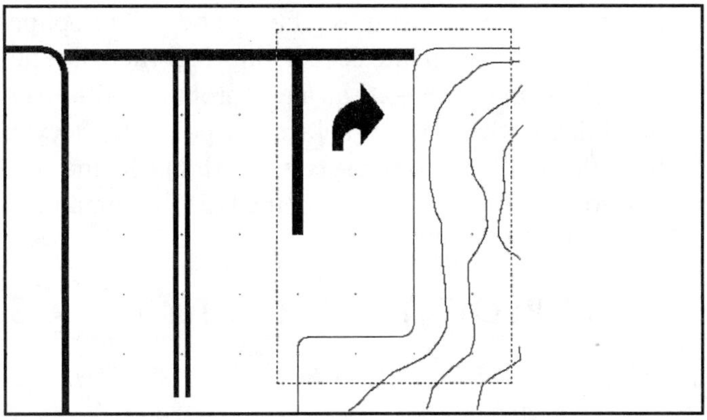

Figure 8.8

Adding segments to a polyline.

Using the PEDIT Fit and Spline Options

The PEDIT command provides two options for making polyline curves that pass through control points: a fit curve and a spline curve. A *fit curve* passes through vertex control points and consists of two arc segments between each pair of vertices (see fig. 8.9). A *spline curve* interpolates between control points but does not usually pass through the vertices (see fig. 8.10). The framework of vertices is called the *spline frame*.

PEDIT spline curves create arcs or short-line segments that approximate the curve of the arc. To help you visualize a spline curve, AutoCAD provides a system variable called SPLFRAME. You can set SPLFRAME to 1 to show you the reference frame and vertex points for a spline curve. If you choose Options, Display, you see a Spline Frame menu item that turns SPLFRAME on and off. If there is a check mark next to this item, SPLFRAME currently is on.

You use the SPLINESEGS system variable to control the fineness of the approximation and type of segment. The numeric value controls the number of segments. A positive value generates line segments; a negative value creates arc segments. Arcs are more precise, but slower.

You can generate two kinds of polyline spline curves: a quadratic b-spline (type 5) or a cubic b-spline (the default, type 6). You use the SPLINETYPE system variable to control both types of spline curves. The PolyVars: item on the Pedit screen menu (choose MODIFY, Pedit:) opens the Set Spline Fit Variables dialog box. The Quadratic and Cubic selections control SPLINETYPE. All the Spline settings are stored with the drawing.

In the next exercise, you use the Fit and Spline options to smooth the sketched contour lines in your intersection drawing. Then, in a new drawing, you try both fit and spline curves to create an airfoil profile for a radio-controlled glider. The rough profile is already created using a closed polyline. After you generate the spline curve, turn SPLFRAME on to see the reference frame for the curve. The exercise shows you how to draw the polyline within the PEDIT command to make the frame visible.

USING PEDIT TO MAKE A FIT AND A SPLINE CURVE

Begin a new drawing named CHAP08B using GLIDFUSE.DWG as a prototype, and zoom to the view that is similar to figure 8.9.

`Command:` *Choose Edit Polyline (Modify, Special Edit)*	Issues the PEDIT command
`Select polyline:` *Pick the rough airfoil profile*	
`Open/Join/Width/Edit vertex/Fit/ Spline/Decurve/Ltype gen/Undo/eXit <X>:` **F** ↵	Specifies the Fit option and curve fits as shown in figure 8.9

The PEDIT Fit option does not work well in this situation.

`Open/Join/Width/Edit vertex/Fit/ Spline/Decurve/Ltype gen/Undo/eXit <X>:` **S** ↵	Specifies the Spline option and spline fits as shown in figure 8.10

The PEDIT Spline option produces a better profile, but not a perfect one.

Choose Options, Display, Spline Frame	Turns on the spline frame (but you cannot see it yet)
`Open/Join/Width/Edit vertex/Fit/ Spline/Decurve/Ltype gen/Undo/eXit <X>:` **S** ↵	Specifies the Spline option and redraws the polyline, making the frame visible—you can see the vertices
`Open/Join/Width/Edit vertex/Fit/Spline/ Decurve/Ltype gen/Undo/eXit <X>:` ↵	Ends the PEDIT command

Save the drawing.

Open the CHAP08A drawing from the previous exercise and use both PEDIT Fit, then Spline to smooth the most jagged contour line. Fit smooths it, but Spline smooths it even more. Continue using PEDIT to smooth the rest of the contour lines, then save the drawing.

Figure 8.9

Airfoil using the Fit curve option.

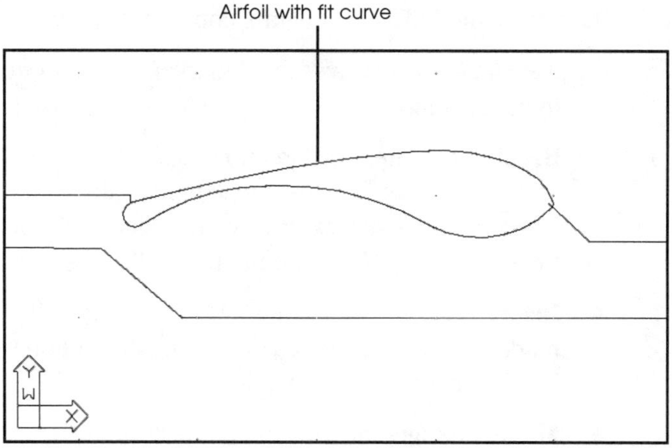

Figure 8.10

Airfoil using the Spline curve option.

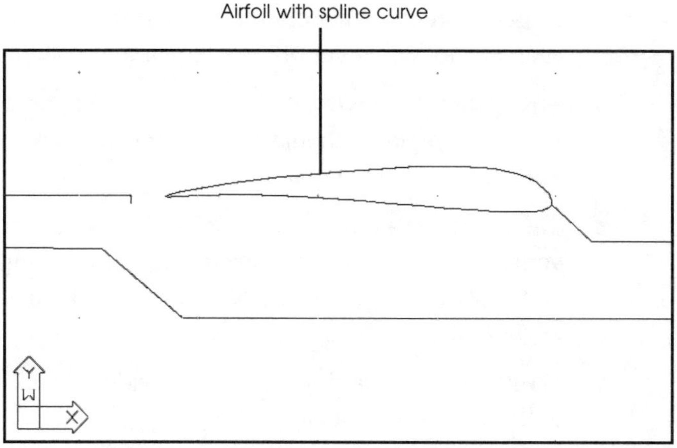

Neither curve option creates a satisfactory airfoil profile with a closed polyline. The next section shows you how to open a polyline and insert a vertex.

Editing Polyline Vertices with PEDIT

Each polyline segment belongs to, and is controlled by, the preceding vertex. The PEDIT Edit vertex option provides another prompt with a separate set of Edit vertex suboptions. When you use these options, the current vertex of the polyline is marked with an X, which shows you the vertex you are editing. Move the X until you mark the vertex you want to edit.

Options for the PEDIT Edit vertex command are as follows:

- **Next/Previous.** Moves the X marker to a new current vertex. Next is the initial default.
- **Break.** Splits the polyline into two, or removes segments of a polyline at existing vertices. The first break point is the vertex on which you invoke the Break option. Use Next/Previous to access another vertex for the second break point. The Go option performs the break.
- **Insert.** Adds a vertex at a point you specify, following the vertex currently marked with an X. You can combine this option with the Break option to break between existing vertices.
- **Move.** Changes the location of the current (X-marked) vertex to a point you specify.
- **Regen.** Forces a regeneration of the polyline so that you can see the effects, such as width changes or the spline frame visibility, of your polyline editing.
- **Straighten.** Removes all intervening vertices from between the two you select and replaces them with one straight segment. It also uses the Next/Previous and Go options.
- **Tangent.** Sets a tangent to the direction you specify at the currently marked vertex to control curve fitting. You can see the angle of the tangent at the vertex with an arrow, and you can drag it with the cursor or enter it at the keyboard.
- **Width.** Sets the starting and ending width of an individual polyline segment to the values you specify.
- **eXit.** Exits vertex editing and returns to the main PEDIT command.

TIP

Often the easiest way to edit the position of polyline vertices is to use grips rather than the PEDIT Edit vertex Move option, especially if you want to edit splined polylines.

The airfoil profile needs a sharp trailing edge, but the closed polyline causes the splined polyline to use the common start/end vertex to influence the curve of the spline. If a splined polyline is open, the polyline starts and ends exactly on the first and last vertex. The PEDIT Edit vertex Break option cannot break a closed polyline at the first or last vertex. To get around this problem, you must first open the polyline, then add a new ending vertex.

The PEDIT Open option appears only when you edit closed polylines; otherwise, the Close option appears. The Open option deletes the closing segment of a polyline and, if the polyline is splined, updates the spline information. If the polyline's start and end points coincided when the polyline was closed, the Open option simply changes the definition of the polyline and doesn't remove anything. In this case, the only visible effect is to polylines that have been spline-fit, as described.

NOTE

Choosing Undo at the main PEDIT prompt undoes an entire vertex editing session.

In the following exercise, you use the PEDIT Edit vertex Insert option to open the splined polyline of the airfoil profile and insert a new ending vertex. The open polyline produces a nice, sharp edge for the airfoil trailing edge.

OPENING A POLYLINE AND INSERTING A VERTEX

Open the CHAP08B drawing from the previous exercise.

`Command:` *Choose Edit Polyline (Modify, Special Edit)*	Issues the PEDIT command
`Select polyline:` *Pick the airfoil profile*	
`Open/Join/Width/Edit vertex/Fit/Spline/ Decurve/Ltype gen/Undo/eXit <X>:` **O** ↵	Specifies the Open option and opens the polyline by deleting the last segment (notice the difference in the spline format)

AutoCAD updates the polyline spline information when you open the polyline. The polyline now starts at the first vertex.

`Close/Join/Width/Edit vertex/Fit/Spline/ Decurve/Ltype gen/Undo/eXit <X>:` **E** ↵	Specifies the Edit vertex option and displays the Edit vertex prompt
`Next/Previous/Break/Insert/Move/Regen/ Straighten/Tangent/Width/eXit <N>:` *Press Enter six times*	Moves the X to the last vertex
`Next/Previous/Break/Insert/Move/Regen/ Straighten/Tangent/Width/eXit <N>:` **I** ↵	Specifies the Insert suboption and displays a rubber band from the last vertex to the cursor
`Enter location of new vertex:` *Choose Snap to Endpoint (Object Snap) and pick point ① (see fig. 8.11)*	Snaps the location for the new vertex to the line's endpoint

Choose Options, Display, Spline Frame	Turns off SPLFRAME
`Next/Previous/Break/Insert/Move/Regen/ Straighten/Tangent/Width/eXit <N>:` **R** ↵	Regenerates the polyline and hides the frame
`Next/Previous/Break/Insert/Move/Regen/ Straighten/Tangent/Width/eXit <N>:` **X** ↵	Exits vertex editing
`Close/Join/Width/Edit vertex/Fit/Spline/ Decurve/Ltype gen/Undo/eXit <X>:` ↵	Exits PEDIT

Save the drawing.

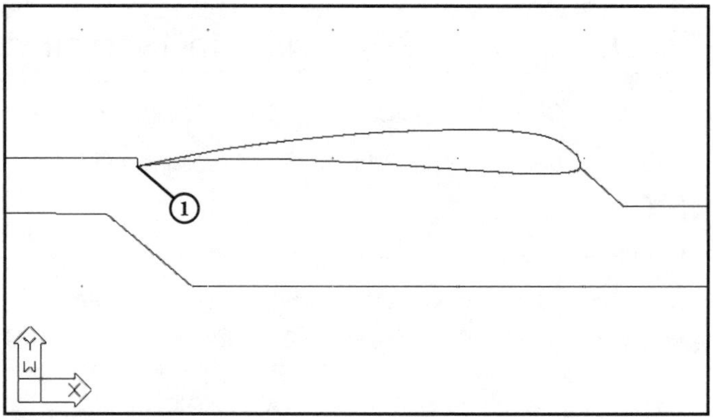

Figure 8.11

The completed airfoil profile.

The airfoil looks much better. In the following section, you are introduced to the FILLET command and you fillet all vertices of the polyline fuselage at once.

Rounding Edges with the FILLET Command

A *fillet* is a tangent arc swung between any two lines, circles, or other arcs to create a round corner. In traditional drafting terms, a fillet is a rounded interior corner, and a *round* is a rounded exterior corner. AutoCAD uses the FILLET command to create both.

You can specify the radius of the arc to create the fillet corner. The default radius is 0. The fillet radius you set becomes the new default. The fillet radius must be less than the maximum distance between two line or polyline objects. You can use the Polyline option to fillet all of a polyline's segments at once. If the fillet radius is 0, the fillet command trims or extends two lines or polylines so that the endpoints meet exactly.

FILLET works on any combination of two arcs, circles, or lines; or on a single polyline. The FILLET command is fully covered in Chapter 16, "Constructive Editing;" here we are interested in applying it to polylines. The Polyline option enables you to fillet an entire polyline at once. You can fillet only 2D polylines. AutoCAD ignores segments of a polyline that are shorter than the fillet radius. AutoCAD reports the number of lines filleted and the number ignored. If you fillet a polyline with a radius of 0, AutoCAD removes all arcs and replaces them with a single vertex.

In the next exercise, you use the fillet command to fillet an entire polyline at once, rounding the edges of the glider fuselage to make it more aerodynamic. You will work in a paper space viewport, which is already in the drawing.

FILLETING POLYLINES

Continue to use the CHAP08B drawing from the previous exercise.

Turn off the TILE *button*	Turns off TILEMODE and changes to a floating viewport in paper space, displaying three viewports (see fig. 8.12)
`Command:` *Choose Fillet (Modify, Feature)*	Issues the FILLET command
`_fillet` `(TRIM mode) Current fillet radius = 0.1250`	
`Polyline/Radius/Trim/ <Select first object>:` **R** ↵	Specifies the Radius option
`Enter fillet radius <0.0000>:` **1.25** ↵	Specifies a new fillet radius distance
`Command:` ↵	Repeats the FILLET command
`FILLET` `(TRIM mode) Current fillet radius = 1.2500`	
`Polyline/Radius/Trim/ <Select first object>:` **P** ↵	Specifies the Polyline option

`Select 2D polyline:` *Pick fuselage polyline at* ①	Fillets all corners that are equal to or greater than the fillet radius
`4 lines were filleted` `2 were too short`	Tells you the number of lines filleted, the number not filleted, and why
Turn on the TILE *button*	Turns on TILEMODE and changes back to tiled model space

Save the drawing.

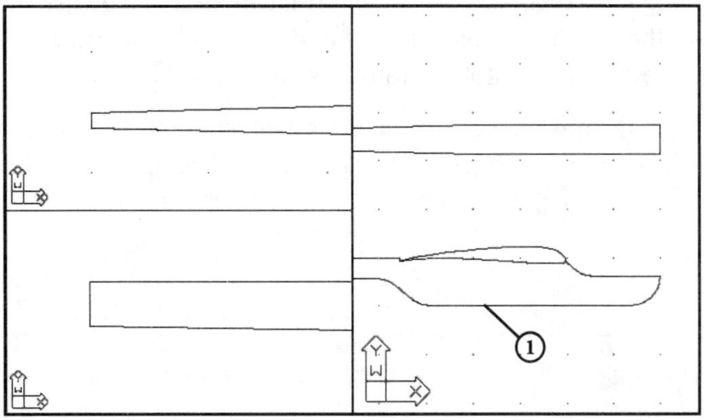

Figure 8.12

The filleted fuselage.

You might wonder why the bottom corner of the fuselage nose was filleted rather than the top corner. The FILLET command progresses around the polyline from the start to the end when making fillet arcs. When the bottom corner was filleted, no segment was left to fillet at the top corner of the nose. The tail, in the lower left viewport, was not filleted because the vertices were too close together. When you fillet polylines, you must consider the direction of the polyline and distances between vertices.

In the next section, you learn about the BOUNDARY command and use it to create a profile of the glider fuselage.

Creating Polyline Boundaries

The BOUNDARY command creates a polyline boundary from contiguous or overlapping objects. The edges of the overlapping objects must form a completely enclosed area; if the perimeter has a gap, the command is doomed to fail. The BOUNDARY command also enables you to create a region object. BOUNDARY works like the

BHATCH command, except it creates regions or polylines instead of hatches. See Chapter 9, "Drawing with Complex Objects," for more information on regions, and Chapter 18, "Linetypes and Hatching," for more on hatches.

The BOUNDARY command has the following options:

- **Object type.** You use the Object type option to specify whether to create a polyline boundary object or a region boundary object. The default setting is Polyline.
- **From Everything on Screen.** This option uses all objects to determine the boundary. This option is on by default.
- **From Existing Boundary Set.** This option uses specific objects you select to create the boundary. Use this option if you want to avoid using certain objects for boundary determination or if you want to reduce the number of objects AutoCAD considers for the boundary perimeter. This option is available only after you use the Make New Boundary Set option and select objects.
- **Ray Casting.** The Ray Casting option controls the way AutoCAD looks for boundary objects. This option is enabled only if the Island Detection option is disabled. The default setting, Nearest, creates a correct boundary in most situations. If the boundary set contains objects that produce a narrow passage or slot, however, you might need to change the direction of the ray casting to parallel the slot. Chapter 18, "Linetypes and Hatching," discusses the BHATCH command and ray casting in more detail.
- **Island Detection.** When activated, the Island detection option causes polylines or regions to be created for each object wholly contained within the boundary. BOUNDARY ignores islands when this option is off. Island Detection is on by default.
- **Pick Points.** The Pick Points option prompts you to pick point(s) inside the perimeter of the boundary(ies). After you specify the point(s), the command creates the polyline or region boundary(ies). If you fail to define a valid perimeter, the `Nothing was found to make a boundary out of` error message appears and AutoCAD reprompts you to specify a point. If you pick more than one valid point, a boundary is created for each. The Pick Points option is the default.

In the following exercise, you use the BOUNDARY command, set to its defaults, to create a polyline boundary of the fuselage and airfoil profile.

CREATING A POLYLINE BOUNDARY

Continue to use the CHAP08B drawing from the previous exercise and restore the BOUNDARY view shown in figure 8.13. The boundary you will create is the lowest of the three objects in the figure.

`Command:` *Choose Boundary (Draw, Polygon)*	Issues the BOUNDARY command and displays the Boundary Creation dialog box
Choose the Pick Points *button*	Prompts you to pick an internal point for the boundary calculation
`Select internal point:` *Pick point at* ①	Specifies what area to include inside the boundary

`Selecting everything...`
`Selecting everything visible...`
`Analyzing the selected data...`
`Analyzing internal islands...`
	Tells you the status of the boundary calculation and highlights the selected boundary elements

`Select internal point:` ↵	Ends the BOUNDARY command
`BOUNDARY created 1 polyline`	Draws the polyline
`Command:` *Choose Move (Modify)*	Issues the MOVE command
`Select objects:` **L** ↵	Selects the last object, the boundary
`1 found`	
`Select objects:` ↵	Ends selection
`Base point or displacement:` **0,-5.25** ↵	Specifies displacement
`Second point of displacement:` ↵	Accepts displacement and moves boundary
`Command:` **R** ↵	Issues REDRAW

REDRAW

Save the drawing. It should now look like figure 8.13.

The boundary you created follows perfectly the curve of the fuselage and the airfoil profile. Although the airfoil and fuselage consisted of three objects, the boundary was created as a single polyline.

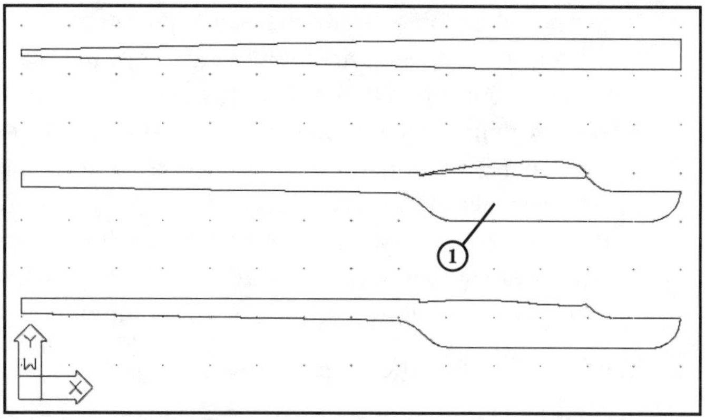

Figure 8.13

The polyline boundary created using the BOUNDARY command.

TIP

To create the boundary of the outside of a collection of objects, simply draw a polyline enclosing but not touching all the objects, then use BOUNDARY, picking a point within the enclosing polyline but outside the collection of objects. BOUNDARY will create two polylines, one duplicating the enclosing polyline you drew, and one that is the outside boundary of the collection of objects. If you enclose more than one collection of objects, you get an additional boundary polyline for each additional collection. This is useful for finding the area or perimeter of a building plan or any other object, as AutoCAD's AREA and LIST commands can easily extract the area and perimeter of polyline objects.

In the next section, you learn about spline objects and how to create them. Spline objects are not the same as a splined polyline; they are a separate object type.

Creating Splines

You use the SPLINE command to draw smooth, curved lines. Splines can be 2D or 3D objects. You draw the curve by specifying fit-data points (vertices) through which the curve passes. The fit-data points determine the location of the spline object's control points. The control points contain the curve information for the spline. Spline objects are true splines—unlike the spline approximation of spline-fit polylines. AutoCAD draws nonuniform rational B-splines (or NURBS) with the SPLINE command.

You use spline objects for the same purposes as you use spline-fit polylines. However, spline objects are far more accurate and can pass through their defining data points. Although they are more accurate, NURBS take less memory and disk resources than their polyline cousins; AutoCAD uses mathematical equations, rather than many short line or arc segments, to draw spline objects. You can use the SPLINE command to convert 2D and 3D spline-fit polylines to spline objects. If a portion of a boundary set is defined by a spline, the BOUNDARY command can create only region boundaries. The SPLINETYPE system variable does not affect the type of spline you draw using the SPLINE command.

The SPLINE command options are:

- **Object/<Enter first point>.** The default option of the main prompt specifies the starting point of the spline. After you specify a starting point, AutoCAD prompts you to specify a second point. Spline objects must consist of a minimum of three points.
- **Object.** The Object option enables you to convert existing spline-fit polylines to spline objects. After you specify this option, AutoCAD prompts you to select a splined polyline.
- **Close/Fit Tolerance/<Enter point>.** After you specify a second point for the spline, AutoCAD displays this prompt. The default option is to continue to specify additional data points for the spline you are drawing. If you press Enter here, AutoCAD prompts you to specify the tangent information for the start and endpoints of the spline, then ends the command. Entering U at this prompt undoes the last pick point.
- **Close.** The Close option operates identically to the SPLINE command's close option. This option causes the start and end of the spline to coincide and share a common vertex and tangent information. When you close a spline, AutoCAD prompts you only once to specify the tangent information.
- **Fit Tolerance.** The Fit Tolerance option controls how closely the spline curve follows the data points. The distance of the Fit Tolerance is in current drawing units. The smaller the tolerance, the closer the spline fits the data points. A value of 0 causes the spline to follow the data points exactly.
- **Undo.** Although this option does not appear in the prompt, you can enter U after any point to undo the last segment.

In the following exercise, you use the SPLINE command. The fuselage of the glider is still a bit clunky, and a spline should give it a nice aerodynamic and sleek look.

In the exercise, you first explode the existing fuselage polyline and erase the bottom section. Then, you use the SPLINE command to draw a new profile. It takes some practice to get the feel for drawing with the SPLINE command. If you don't like the profile you draw, feel free to use the Undo option to back up, or even cancel and start over.

Drawing a Spline

Continue to use the CHAP08B drawing from the previous exercise.

`Command:` *Choose Explode (Modify, Explode)*	Issues the EXPLODE command
`Select objects:` *Pick the lower polyline of the middle fuselage profile and press Enter*	Explodes the polyline
`Command:` *Select all the lines and arcs of the bottom of the fuselage profile from ① to ③, then choose Erase (Modify)*	Issues the ERASE command and erases the selected objects
`Command:` *Choose Spline (Draw, Polyline)*	Issues the SPLINE command
`Object/<Enter first point>:` *Use ENDPoint object snap to pick the line at ① (see fig. 8.14)*	Specifies the start of the spline
`Enter point:` *Pick another point near ②*	
`Close/Fit Tolerance/<Enter point>:`	

Continue to pick points until you are ready to end the spline. You do not need many points to define the curve. Four points and a start and end vertex is enough. If you don't like the way the curve looks, don't worry—you edit it in the next exercise.

`Close/Fit Tolerance/<Enter point>:` *Use ENDPoint object snap to pick point ③*	
`Close/Fit Tolerance/<Enter point>:` ↵	Ends the vertex input process
`Enter start tangent:` *Pick a point to the left of the first pick point ①*	Specifies the starting tangent
`Enter end tangent:` *Pick a point at 90 degrees to the spline endpoint at ③*	Specifies the ending tangent—this makes the nose bulbous, but you edit it in the next exercise

Save the drawing.

Figure 8.14

The spline fuselage bottom.

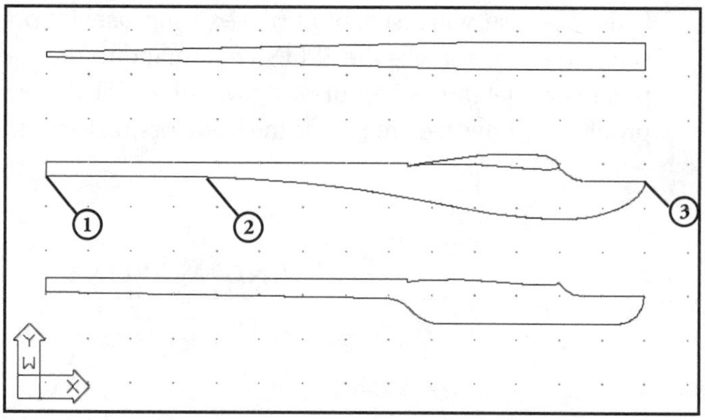

Spline objects are special objects that have their own editing command—similar to the relationship between PLINE and PEDIT. In the next section, you learn about the SPLINEDIT command and use it to change spline objects.

Controlling Splines Using SPLINEDIT

The SPLINEDIT command enables you to edit control points of all spline objects and for spline objects that have them, fit-data points. When you draw a spline, you pick fit-data points. The fit-data points are used to calculate the location of the spline's control points. You can add additional control or fit-data points or move them. You can change the weight of control points and the tolerance of the spline. You also can close or open a spline and adjust the tangent information of the start and endpoints.

Control points usually are not located on the spline curve (except for the start and endpoints), but they control the shape of the spline. AutoCAD uses the fit-data points to calculate the position of the control points. However, after AutoCAD determines the control points, it no longer needs the fit-data points to draw the spline. If the fit data is removed from a spline, you cannot use any of the fit data editing options of the SPLINEDIT command to edit the shape of the spline.

When you select a spline for editing, AutoCAD displays its control points as if you had selected the spline for grip editing (see fig. 8.15). However, you cannot perform grip editing on the spline with the SPLINEDIT command. The SPLINEDIT command works on only one spline object at a time. Also, you cannot use noun/verb selection with SPLINEDIT.

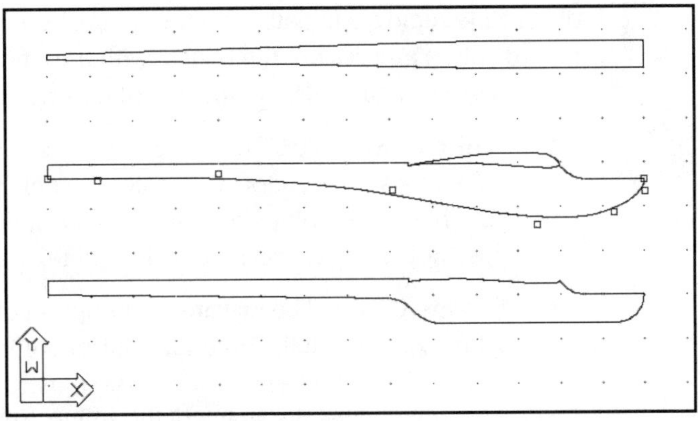

Figure 8.15

Control points of the fuselage spline.

The SPLINEDIT command has the following options:

- **Fit Data.** Enables you to edit the fit-data points for spline objects that have them. AutoCAD displays another prompt of Fit Data options when you choose this option. AutoCAD does not present this as an option if the spline does not have any fit data information. The Fit Data suboptions are listed following this option list.
- **Close.** Closes an open spline. This option adds a curve that is tangent between the start and end vertices for splines that do not have the same start and endpoints. If the spline does have the same start and endpoints, the Close option makes the tangent information for each point continuous. If the spline is already closed, the Close option is replaced by the Open option.
- **Open.** Opens a closed spline. If the spline did not have the same start and endpoints before you closed it, this option removes the tangent curve and removes tangent information from the start and endpoints. If the spline shares the same start and endpoint before you close it, the option removes the tangent information from the points, but they continue to share the same point.
- **Move Vertex.** Enables you to move control point vertices of a spline. You specify a vertex to edit by moving the current vertex to the next or previous vertex. Often, using the grip editing features of AutoCAD to edit the control point vertices is easier. See Chapter 13, "Autoediting with Grips," for information on grip editing.
- **Refine.** Displays suboptions that enable you to add control points and adjust the weight of control points. You can add individual control points in areas where you want finer control of the curve. Performing any refine operation

on a spline removes fit data from the spline. You can reverse the effect of the Refine option and restore the fit data with the Undo option before ending the SPLINEDIT command. The following list describes the Refine suboptions:

- **Add control point.** This option enables you to add a single control point to a spline. AutoCAD locates the new control point as close as possible to the point you specify on the spline. Adding a control point does not change the shape of the spline.
- **Elevate Order.** The Elevate Order option elevates the order of the spline's polynomial. This adds control points evenly over the spline, thus, giving you finer control of the spline. The Elevate order option does not change the shape of the spline. You cannot decrease the order of the polynomial after you increase it.
- **Weight.** Controls the amount of tension that pulls a spline towards a control point.
- **eXit.** Returns to the main SPLINEDIT prompt.
- **rEverse.** Changes the direction of the spline; the start becomes the end and the end becomes the start.
- **Undo.** Undoes the most recently performed SPLINEDIT option.
- **eXit.** Ends the SPLINEDIT command.

The following are the suboptions of the Fit Data option, for editing spline object fit-data. When you choose the Fit Data option, the grip-like boxes change to highlight the fit-data points.

- **Add.** Adds additional fit-data points to the curve. Adding fit-data points changes the shape of the spline curve. Added fit-data points obey the current tolerance of the spline.
- **Close.** Performs the same function as the control point Close option, but using fit-data points.
- **Open.** Performs the same function as the control point Open option, except that it uses fit-data points. The Open option replaces the Close option if the spline is already closed.
- **Delete.** Removes fit-data points and redraws the spline to fit the fit-data points that remain.

- **Move.** Enables you to move fit-data point vertices of a spline. You specify a vertex to edit by moving the current vertex to the next or previous vertex. Fit-data information cannot be edited with AutoCAD's grip editing feature.
- **Purge.** Removes all fit data from the spline.
- **Tangents.** Enables you to change the tangent information of the start and endpoints of a spline.
- **toLerance.** Changes the tolerance of the spline's fit-data points and redraws the spline. A spline loses its fit data if you change the tolerance and move a control point or open or close the spline.
- **eXit.** Returns to the control point editing prompt.

In the following exercise, you edit the spline of the bottom of the fuselage. First, you reduce the number of fit-data points, then you add additional control points to the spline.

EDITING SPLINES

Continue to use the CHAP08B drawing from the previous exercise.

`Command:` *Choose Edit Spline (Modify, Special Edit)*	Issues the SPLINEDIT command
`Select spline:` *Pick the fuselage spline (see fig. 8.16)*	Specifies the spline to edit
`Fit Data/Close/Move Vertex/Refine/ rEverse/Undo/eXit <X>:` **F** ↵	Specifies the Fit Data option
`Add/Close/Delete/Move/Purge/Tangents/ toLerance/eXit <X>:` **D** ↵	Specifies the Delete option
`Select point:` *Pick a few control points*	Deletes the points you pick
`Select point:` ↵	Exits the delete points mode
`Add/Close/Delete/Move/Purge/Tangents/ toLerance/eXit <X>:` **T** ↵	Specifies the Tangents option
`System Default/ <Enter start tangent>:` ↵	Keeps current start tangent

`System Default/<Enter end tangent>:` *Pick a tangent point at about 60° from the endpoint*	Specifies new end tangent information to make a more aerodynamic profile (see fig. 8.17)
`Add/Close/Delete/Move/Purge/Tangents/ toLerance/eXit <X>:` ↵	Exits to the main control point prompt
`Fit Data/Close/Move Vertex/Refine/ rEverse/Undo/eXit <X>:` **R** ↵	Specifies the Refine option
`Add control point/Elevate Order/ Weight/eXit <X>:` **E** ↵	Specifies the Elevate Ordeeditingr option
`Enter new order <4>:` **6** ↵_	Elevates order of spline polynomial and adds intermediate control points
`Add control point/Elevate Order/ Weight/eXit <X>:` ↵	Returns to the main prompt
`Close/Move Vertex/Refine/rEverse/ Undo/eXit <X>:` ↵	Exits the SPLINEDIT command

Save the drawing. This completes the fuselage for this chapter.

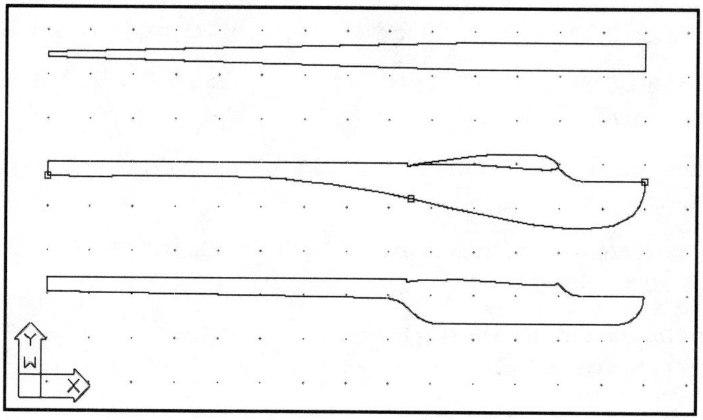

Figure 8.16

Fuselage spline with fit-data points deleted.

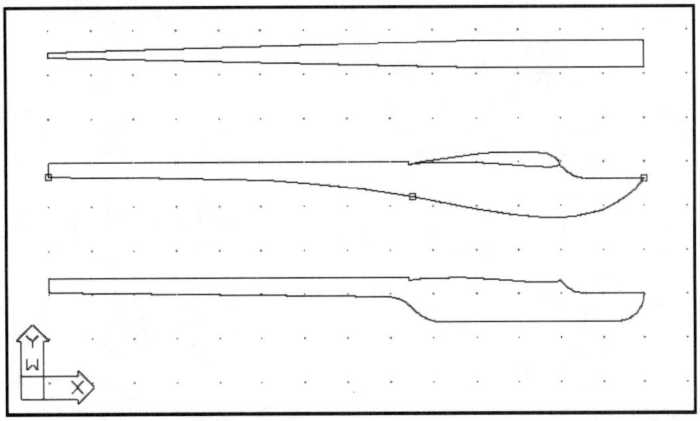

Figure 8.17

Fuselage with adjusted ending tangent.

In this chapter, you explored the extremely versatile polyline. Using polylines can simplify drawing and editing by replacing separate line and arc segments with one continuous object. Polylines can be used to create graphic features, such as wide lines and spline curves, that would be difficult or impossible otherwise. You can use the AREA command to derive perimeter and area information about polylines, and closed polylines make excellent hatch boundaries. Look for opportunities to apply the benefits of polylines in your drawings.

chapter

9

Drawing with Complex Objects

In Chapter 8, "Drawing and Editing Polylines and Splines," you learned about two of AutoCAD's more complex objects, polylines and splines. In addition, AutoCAD offers a number of other complex objects that you can use to increase your drawing productivity. You learn about two of them in this chapter.

This chapter covers the following topics:

- *Region modeling*
- *Boolean operations*
- *Creating multiple-line objects*
- *Creating custom multiline styles*

Creating Regions

A *region* is a 2D solid object formed from a closed area. You can think of a region as a flat surface. Although many commands in AutoCAD enable you to create closed shapes, regions are unique in the information they contain and in the way they can be modified.

Understanding Wire Models versus Solid Models

The CIRCLE command creates closed areas. The PLINE, SPLINE, and LINE commands all have a Close option. The BOUNDARY command will create closed polylines from any group of objects that overlap to form a closed area. All of these commands create what are known as wireframe models. A *wireframe model* consists only of the edges of an object. It is similar to taking a piece of wire and bending it into the shape of your model. The edges of the model are defined but the model has no surfaces.

Regions are solid 2D surfaces. A solid contains not only the edge information, but also information about what is between the edges, such as holes, slots, and so on. AutoCAD can use this information to calculate engineering properties such as surface area, centroids, and moments of inertia.

The REGION Command

The REGION command prompts you to select objects that you want to convert to regions. Valid selections are closed lines, polylines, splines, circles, or any group of objects whose endpoints connect to form a closed loop. Self-intersecting objects or objects whose endpoints do not connect do not qualify. Figure 9.1 shows some examples of valid and invalid selections for the REGION command. The REGION command converts the valid selections to regions.

TIP

By default, the REGION command replaces the selected objects with regions and deletes the original objects. If you want to keep the original objects, set the AutoCAD system variable DELOBJ to 0 (off). AutoCAD then keeps the original objects.

Figure 9.1

Examples of valid and invalid region selections.

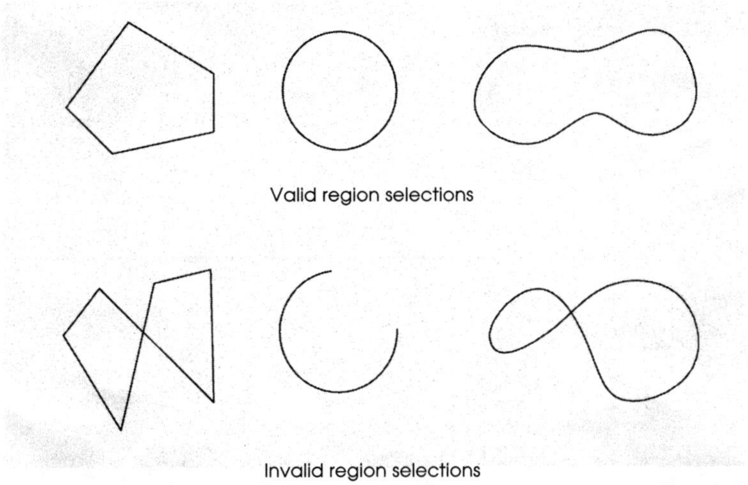

In the following exercise, you use regions to create the front elevation of a small house.

CREATING REGIONS

Create a new drawing named CHAP09A using the accompanying CD drawing PLANELEV.DWG as a prototype. The layer ELEV should be current.

`Command:` *Choose Rectangle (Draw, Polygon) and draw a rectangle from* 60',30' *to* 82',38'	Issues the RECTANG command and draws the rectangle (see fig. 12.5)
`Command:` *Choose Polyline (Draw, Polyline)*	Issues the PLINE command
`From point:` *Using the* ENDPoint object snap, pick ① *(see fig. 9.2)*	Places the first point of the polyline
`Arc/Close/Halfwidth/Length/Undo/Width /<Endpoint of line>:` **@11',14'** ↵	Places the second point of the polyline
`Arc/Close/Halfwidth/Length/Undo/Width /<Endpoint of line>:` *Using the ENDPoint object snap, pick* ②	Places the third point of the polyline
`Arc/Close/Halfwidth/Length/Undo/Width /<Endpoint of line>:` **C** ↵	Closes the polyline
`Command:` *Choose Region (Draw, Polygon)*	Issues the REGION command

`Select objects:` **ALL** ↵ Selects the polylines

`Select objects:` ↵ Creates two regions from the polylines

Save your drawing.

The regions you created don't look any different from the polylines. But later in the chapter, you see how differently they act.

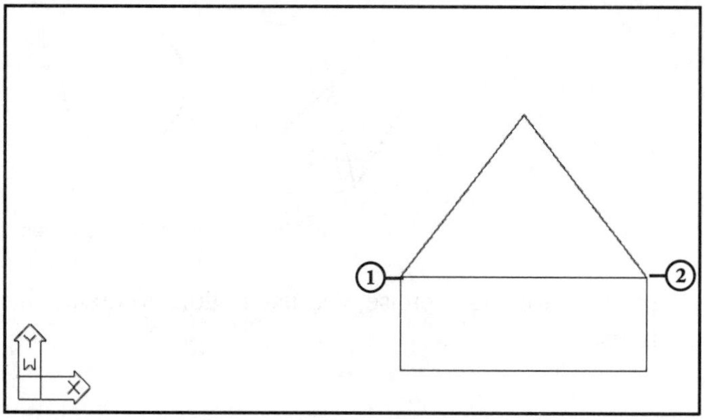

Figure 9.2

Creating regions from polylines.

Creating Regions with BOUNDARY

You can create regions in one other way. Chapter 8, "Drawing and Editing with Polylines and Splines," introduced the BOUNDARY command, which enables you to create closed polylines by selecting a point within an enclosed area. You also can use the BOUNDARY command to create regions by setting the Object Type to Region in the Boundary Creation dialog box (see fig. 9.3).

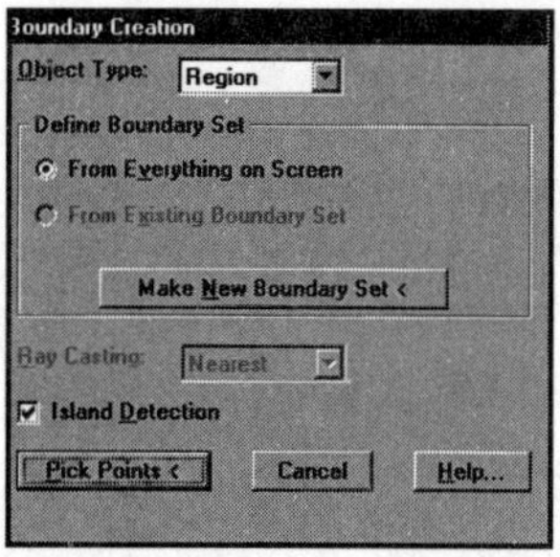

Figure 9.3

The Boundary Creation dialog box.

Note

Unlike the REGION command, BOUNDARY creates new regions but leaves the original objects in place regardless of the setting of the DELOBJ system variable.

In the following exercise, you create some windows using the Region option of the BOUNDARY command.

Creating Regions with BOUNDARY

Continue from the previous exercise. Thaw the layers CONST, ELEV_WINDOWS, and ELEV_DOORS. The layer ELEV should remain current.

`Command:` *Choose Boundary (Draw, Polygon)*	Issues the BOUNDARY command and opens the Boundary dialog box
In the Object Type *drop-down list, select Region*	Selects the Region option
Choose Pick Points *and pick* ①, ②, ③, ④, ⑤, *and* ⑥ *(see fig. 9.4) and press Enter*	Determines the boundary areas and creates six regions

Freeze layers CONST, ELEV_WINDOWS, and ELEV_DOORS to see the six regions created by the BOUNDARY command. Your drawing should now resemble figure 9.5.

Save your drawing.

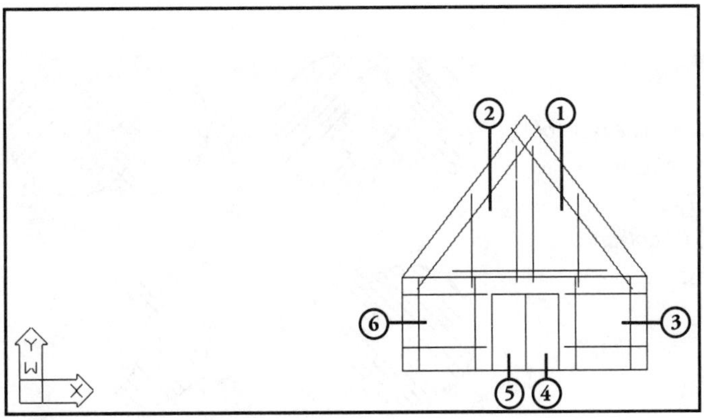

Figure 9.4

Creating boundary regions.

Figure 9.5

The new boundary regions.

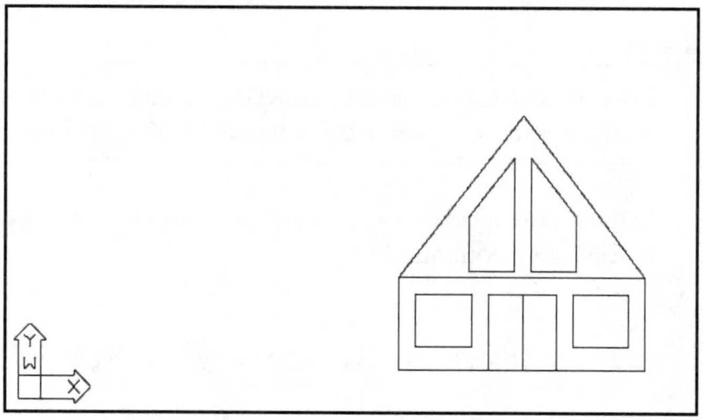

Understanding Boolean Operations

Because regions are solid objects, you act on them in the same manner as you would if you were to use real-world solid objects. If you had a flat piece of material, you might drill some holes in it, attach other pieces of material to it, or trim off excess material. You can act on AutoCAD regions in a similar fashion by using three commands known collectively as *Boolean operations*. The three Boolean operations are the UNION, SUBTRACT, and INTERSECT commands.

The UNION command enables you to join two or more regions into a single region of their combined areas. The regions do not have to touch before you can join them. You can see the effect of the UNION command in figure 9.6.

Figure 9.6

Examples of the effects of using the UNION, SUBTRACT, and INTERSECT Boolean operations.

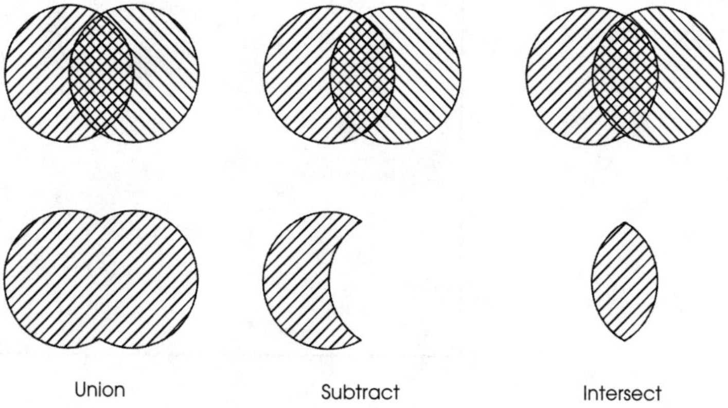

The SUBTRACT command enables you to cut holes in regions. These holes and cutouts become a part of the region. If you move the region, the holes move as well. You can see the effect of using the SUBTRACT command in figure 9.6. AutoCAD prompts you for the region you want to keep, then prompts you to select the regions you want to subtract.

The INTERSECT command creates a region from the area common to two or more overlapping regions. You can see the effect of the INTERSECT command in figure 9.6.

WARNING

Using INTERSECT on regions that do not overlap creates a region that has no area (a null region). AutoCAD deletes all the regions you selected. If this occurs, you can use an UNDO to restore the regions.

In the following exercise, you create some window and door openings in the elevation view.

Boolean Operations

Continue from the previous exercise. The layer ELEV should remain current.

`Command:` *Choose Union (Modify, Explode)*	Issues the UNION command
`Select objects:` *Select the objects at ① and ② (see fig. 9.7) and press Enter*	Selects the two regions and joins them into a single region
`Command:` *Choose Subtract (Modify, Explode)*	Issues the SUBTRACT command
`Select solids and regions to subtract from...`	
`Select objects:` *Pick ① (see fig. 9.7) and press Enter*	Selects the building elevation
`Select solids and regions to subtract...`	

`Select objects:` *Pick the point* ③ *and drag to* ④	Selects the door and window regions
`Select objects:` ↵	Ends the UNION command and subtracts the door and window regions from the elevation

Notice that the door sections have been subtracted from the shape.

Save your drawing.

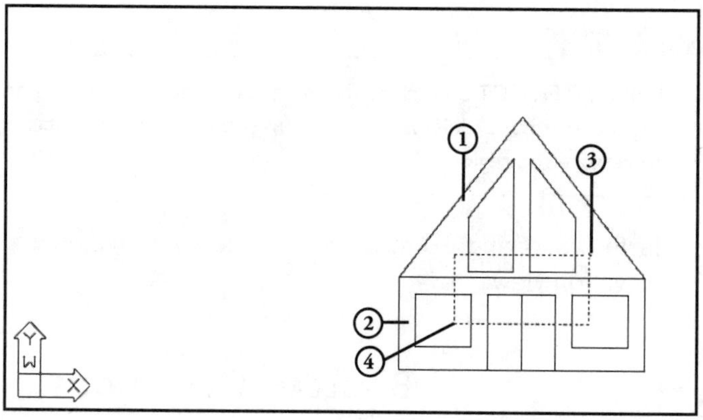

Figure 9.7

Adding and subtracting regions.

NOTE

Because regions are solid models, you can change their shape only by using Boolean operations. If you want to convert regions back into lines and arcs, you must use the EXPLODE command.

Extracting Data from a Region Model

Because regions are solid objects, they contain a great deal more information than their wireframe counterparts. The MASSPROP command enables you to display engineering information about solid models.

The MASSPROP command prompts you to select a region or regions. After you select the region(s), AutoCAD displays a list of engineering properties. The following is an example of the engineering data AutoCAD calculates.

```
---------  REGIONS  ---------

Area:                       12165.1412
Perimeter:                  935.1617
Bounding box:             X: 34.0000  —  381.3532
Y: 21.0000  —  111.0000
Centroid:                 X: 232.1490
Y: 66.0000
Moments of inertia:       X: 56095150.3085
Y: 774080785.1308
Product of inertia:      XY: 186392266.8312
Radii of gyration:        X: 67.9054
Y: 252.2520
Principal moments and X-Y directions about centroid:
I: 3103795.1893 along [1.0000 0.0000]
J: 118462957.3496 along [0.0000 1.0000]
```

After you display the information, you can save the information to an ASCII text file.

Chapter 15, "Object and Drawing Modification and Inquiry Tools," offers more information on using AutoCAD's inquiry commands to obtain information from 2D wireframe objects.

Creating Multiple Lines

Multilines (mlines) are new in Release 13. *Multilines* are objects that contain multiple parallel lines called *elements*. Each element is defined by its distance or *offset* from the center. The center is *zero offset*. Figure 9.8 shows the parts of a typical mline object.

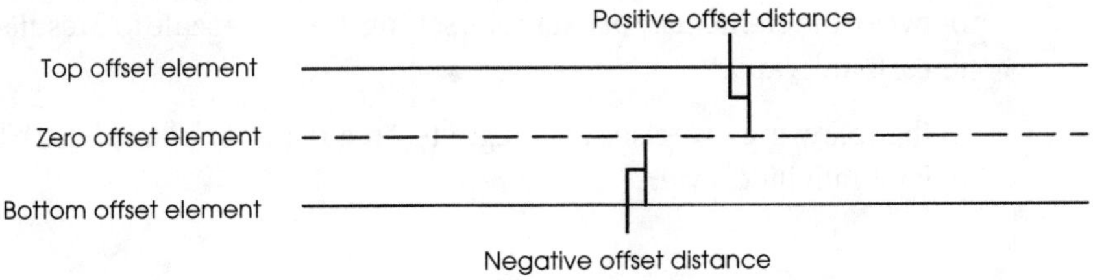

Figure 9.8

Multiline elements.

Drawing with the MLINE Command

Multilines are created with the MLINE command, which has the following prompts:

```
Justification/Scale/STyle/<From point>:
```

- **Justification.** The Justification option enables you to control whether AutoCAD draws the mline from the top offset, the zero offset, or the bottom offset.
- **Scale.** This option enables you to control the scale at which AutoCAD draws the mline. AutoCAD multiplies the offset distances by this scale factor.
- **STyle.** The STyle option enables you to set the current mline style. You use the MLSTYLE command to define mline styles. Entering **?** at this prompt displays a list of currently defined mline styles.
- **From point.** This is the default option, which prompts you for the starting point of the mline. After you pick a starting point, AutoCAD prompts you for the To point. You also can use an Undo option to undo the last drawn segment. After you pick two points, you can use a Close option to close the mline and clean up the last corner.

NOTE

The MLINE command creates only straight line objects. Curved multiline objects are not supported in R13.

By default, AutoCAD draws multilines with two elements, one having an offset of 0.5 and the other having an offset of –0.5, which results in an mline that consists of two elements, 1 unit apart. By adjusting the mline scale, you can control the distance between the elements. For example, setting the mline scale to 6 results in two parallel lines, 6 units apart.

In the following exercise, you begin to create a floor plan of the house, using the default multiline style.

CREATING MULTILINES

Continue from the previous exercise. Set the layer PLAN current.

`Command:` *Choose Multiline (Draw, Polyline)*	Issues the MLINE command
`Justification/Scale/STyle/` `<From point>:` **S** ↵	Specifies the Scale option
`Set Mline scale <1.00>:` **6** ↵	Sets the multiline scale factor
`Justification/Scale/STyle/` `<From point>:` **30',30'** ↵	Places the starting point
`<To point>:` **@22'<0** ↵	Draws an mline segment
`Undo/<To point>:` **@26'<90** ↵	Draws another segment
`Close/Undo/<To point>:` **@22'<180** ↵	
`Close/Undo/<To point>:` **C** ↵	Closes the multiline

Save your work.

Your drawing should now resemble figure 9.9.

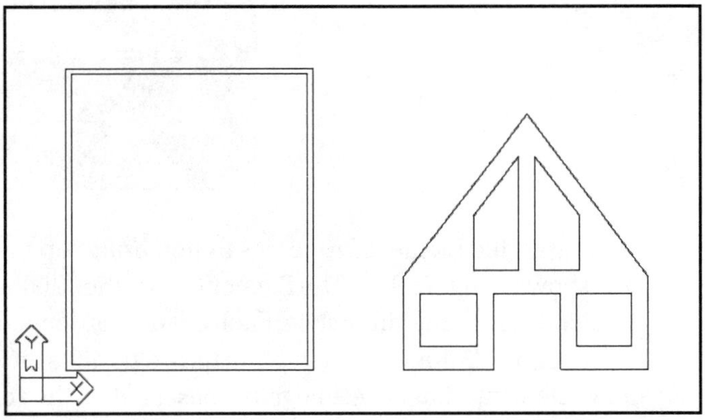

Figure 9.9

Floor plan outline with mlines.

Defining Mline Styles with MLSTYLE

The default multiline style consists of two lines, each .5 units from the zero offset. This is known as the *Standard mline style*. By adjusting the scale and justification, the Standard mline style can serve many purposes, but is limited to only two lines. The MLSTLYE command enables you to create much more complex multiline styles.

Issuing the MLSTYLE command opens the Multiline Styles dialog box, shown in figure 9.10. The Multiline Style area of the dialog box gives you information about the multiline styles available in the drawing and gives you options for loading, saving, adding, and renaming multiline style definitions. Unless you save them to a file, multiline styles exist only in the current drawing. To share multiline styles between drawings, you must save the multiline style definitions to a file. Multiline styles are stored in MLN files. The Standard multiline style is stored in ACAD.MLN, in the \ACADR13\COMMON\SUPPORT directory.

Figure 9.10

The Multiline Styles dialog box.

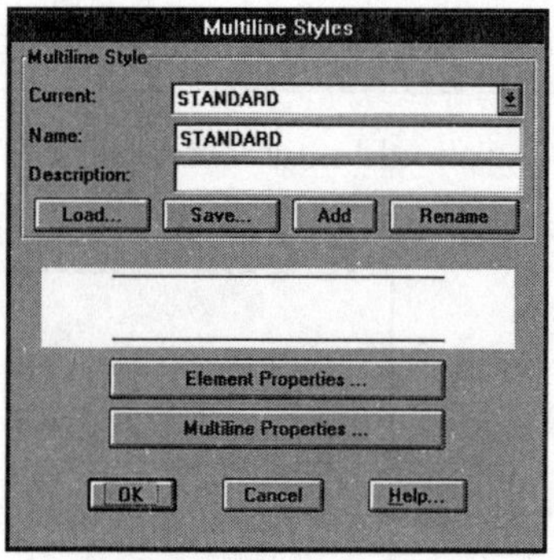

Clicking on the Element Properties button brings up the Element Properties dialog box, shown in figure 9.11. The Element Properties dialog box enables you to define the elements of a multiline style. Each element is defined as a distance from the zero offset. AutoCAD draws elements that have a positive offset above the zero offset and draws elements that have a negative offset below the zero offset. The elements that have the greatest positive and negative offsets become the top and bottom justification elements.

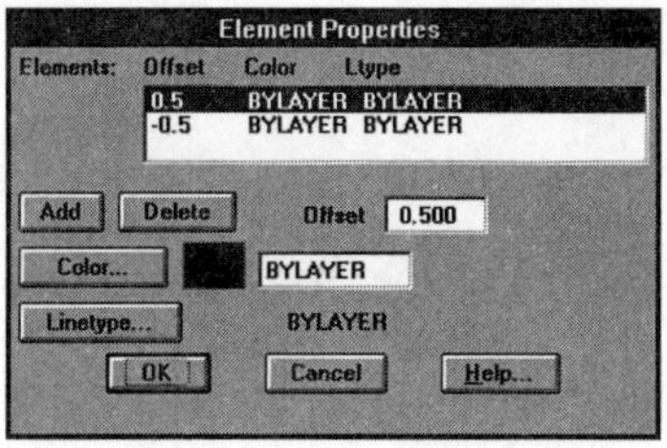

Figure 9.11

The Element Properties dialog box.

You can define as many as 16 elements in a multiline style. In addition to an offset distance, you assign each element a linetype and color, which enables you to create very complex multiline styles. For more on assigning linetypes and colors, see Chapter 2, "Organizing Drawings with Layers." See Chapter 18, "Linetypes and Hatching," for more on creating custom linetypes.

NOTE

Although you can assign a separate linetype and color to each multiline element, the multiline itself resides on a single layer. If you freeze a layer that contains a multiline, you freeze the entire multiline.

Clicking on the Multiline Properties button opens the Multiline Properties dialog box (see fig. 9.12). The Multiline Properties dialog box presents you with some options for the display and generation of the multilines. The Display joints check box provides you with the means to control the display of corner joints (see fig. 9.13).

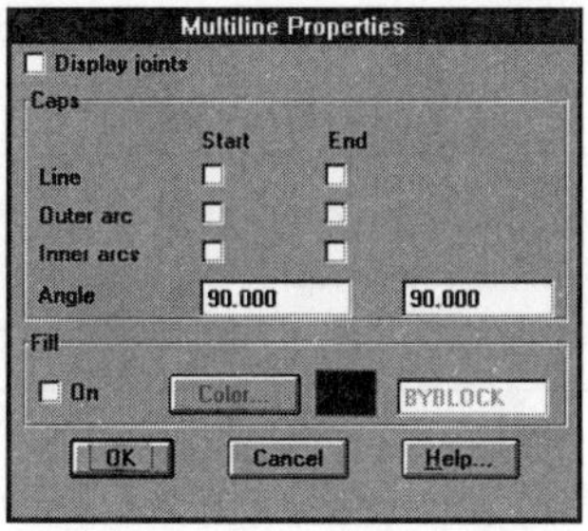

Figure 9.12

The Multiline Properties dialog box.

Figure 9.13

Multilines with and without joint display.

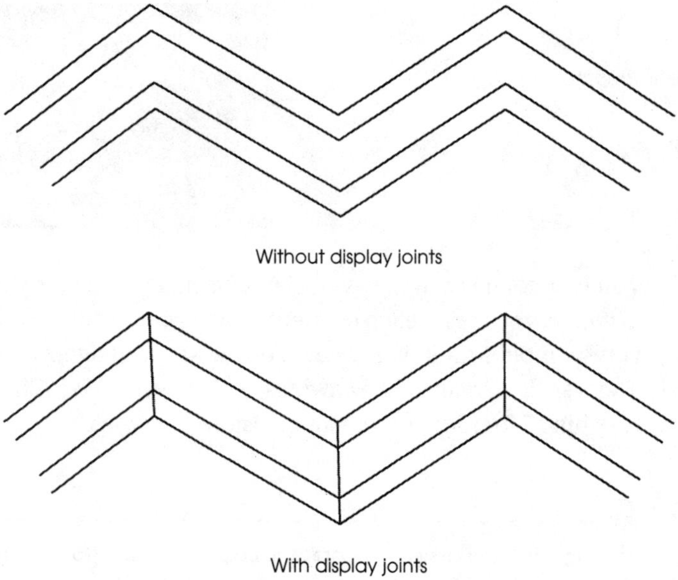

The Caps area of the dialog box enables you to control the creation of the start and end of the multilines. The Angle option enables you to control the miter angle of the end cap. The various capping effects are shown in figure 9.14.

The options in the Fill area of the Multiline Properties dialog box enable you to fill in the multiline with a solid color. If you set the Fill option to on (mark the On check box), AutoCAD fills in the area between the outermost offset elements with the color you define in the multiline style.

NOTE

> You use the [']FILL command or the FILLMODE system variable to control the global display of solid fill. See Chapter 8, "Drawing and Editing Polylines and Splines," for more information regarding the [']FILL command and the FILLMODE system variable.

In the following exercise, you create two new multiline styles for the interior walls and closet shelves.

Figure 9.14

Multiline end cap options.

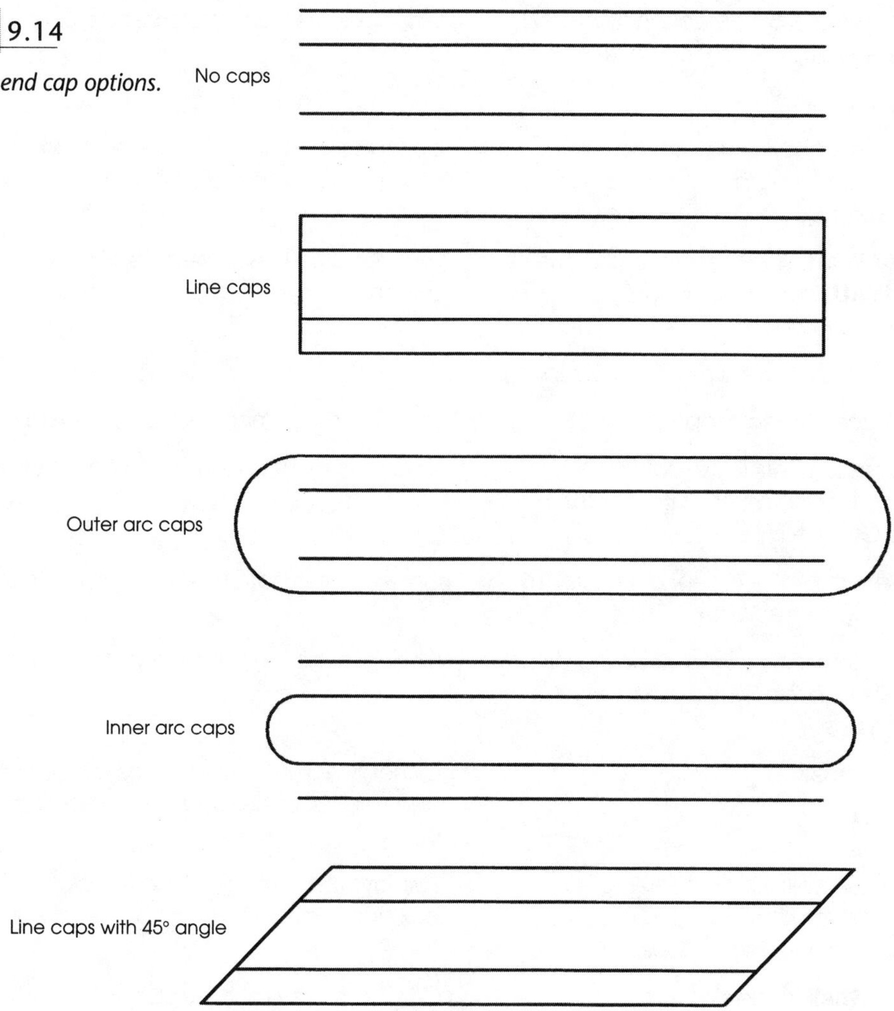

Creating Multiline Styles

Continue from the preceding exercise. Make the layer PLAN current.

`Command:` *Choose Multiline Style (Object Properties)*	Issues the MLSTYLE command and displays the Multiline Style dialog box
Choose the Element Properties *button*	Displays the Element Properties dialog box
In the Elements *list, select the* 0.5 *element and enter a value of* **2** *in the* Offset *edit box*	Changes the top element to an offset of 2

Select the -0.5 element and enter a value **-2** *in the* Offset *edit box*	Changes the bottom element to an offset of –2
Choose OK	Exits the Element Properties dialog box
Choose the Multiline Properties *button, place an* X *in the* Start *and* End Line *boxes, then choose* OK	Displays the Multiline Properties dialog box and turns on the start and end caps
Type **WALL_4** *in the* Name *box, type* **4" WALL** *in the* Description *box, and choose* Add	Creates a new multiline style with the current setting.

Next, you create a multiline style for a closet shelf

Choose Element Properties	Displays the Element Properties dialog box
In the Elements *list, select the 2.0 element and enter a value of* **20** *in the* Offset *edit box*	Changes the top element to an offset of 20
Select the -2.0 element and enter **16** *in the* Offset *edit box*	Changes the bottom element to an offset of 16
Choose Linetype *and double-click on* Dashed *in the list of available linetypes*	Changes the element linetype to Dashed
Choose OK	Closes the Element Properties dialog box and returns to the Multiline Style dialog box
Choose Multiline Properties, *clear the X's from the* Start *and* End Line *check boxes, then choose* OK	*Displays the Multiline Properties dialog* box and turns off the start and end caps
Type **Shelf** *in the* Name *box, type* **20" Closet Shelf** *in the* Description *box, and choose* Add	Creates a new multiline style with the the current setting
Choose OK	Closes the Multiline Styles dialog box

Save your drawing.

In addition to the Standard multiline style, you now have two additional multiline styles. In the following exercise, you use these multiline styles to create the interior walls of your house.

USING MULTILINE STYLES

Continue from the previous exercise. Before you begin, turn on ortho.

`Command:` *Choose Multiline (Draw, Polyline)*	Issues the MLINE command
`Justification/Scale/STyle/ <From point>:` **S** ↵	Specifies the Scale option
`Set Mline scale <6.00>:` **1** ↵	Sets the multiline scale to 1
`Justification/Scale/STyle/ <From point>:` **ST** ↵	Specifies the STyle option
`Mstyle name (or ?):` **WALL_4** ↵	Sets the multiline style to WALL_4
`Justification/Scale/STyle/ <From point>:` *Using FROM and the ENDPoint object snap, pick* ① *(see fig. 9.15)*	Picks a reference point at the end of the wall

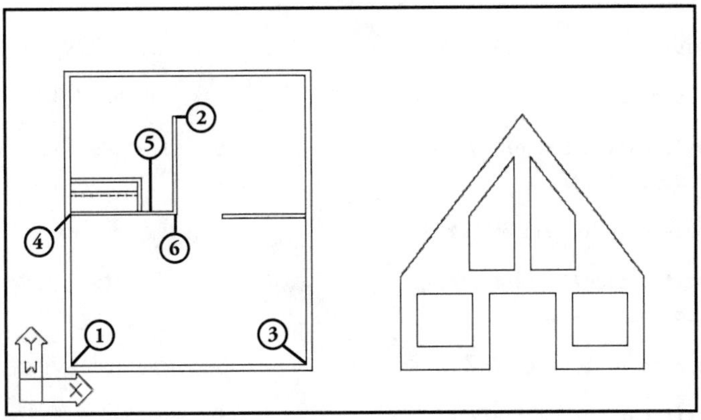

Figure 9.15

Floor plan with interior walls and a shelf.

`<Offset>:` **@13'<90** ↵	Places the first point of the mline
`<To point>:` **@9'6<0** ↵	Places the second point of the mline and draws a segment
`Undo/<To point>:` *Pick* ②	Draws another segment

Note that this line is too short, but you clean this up later.

`Close/Undo/<To point>:` ↵	Ends the MLINE command
`Command:` ↵	Repeats the previous command

`Justification/Scale/STyle/` `<From point>:` *Using the FROM and ENDPoint object snap, pick* ③	Places a reference point at the end of the wall
`<Offset>:` **@13'<90** ↵	Places the first point of the mline
`<To point>:` **@7'6<180** ↵	Draws a segment
`Undo/<To point>:` ↵	Ends the MLINE command
Notice the end cap on the wall.	
`Command:` ↵	Repeats the MLINE command
`Justification/Scale/STyle/` `<From point>:` *Using FROM the and ENDPoint object snap, pick* ④	Picks a reference point at the end of the interior wall
`<Offset>:` **@30<90** ↵	Places the first point of the mline
`<To point>:` **@6'<0** ↵	Places the second point of the mline
`Undo/<To point>:` *Using the PERPendicular object snap, pick* ⑤	Places the last point of the mline
`Close/Undo/<To point>:` ↵	Ends the MLINE command
`Command:` ↵	Repeats the MLINE command
`Justification/Scale/STyle/` `<From point>:` **ST** ↵	Specifies the STyle option
`Mstyle name (or ?):` **SHELF** ↵	Sets the multiline style to SHELF
`Justification/Scale/STyle/` `<From point>:` **J** ↵	Specifies the Justify option
`Top/Zero/Bottom <top>:` **Z** ↵	Sets the justification to 0
`Justification/Scale/STyle/` `<From point>:` *Using the ENDPoint object snap, pick* ⑤	Places the first point of the mline
`Undo/<To point>:` *Using the ENDpoint object snap, pick* ⑥	Draws the closet shelf
`Undo/<To point>:` ↵	Ends the MLINE command

Save your drawing.

Note

There currently is no way to redefine or reload a multiline style once it has been created. To make changes to a multiline style you must either EXPLODE or ERASE all multilines having that style, PURGE the multiline style from the drawing, re-create the mutliline, and re-create any multilines that use the new style.

If you have saved the multiline to an MLN file, you can redefine the style by changing the DXF codes listed in the MLN file. However, the changes will only affect new multilines. Existing multilines will not change. See The AutoCAD Customization Guide for more on DXF codes.

Editing Multilines with MLEDIT

Multilines are rather unique objects in AutoCAD R13. Being unique, they have a unique set of editing tools. The MLEDIT command gives you a set of tools for cleaning up and editing multilines.

MLEDIT doesn't actually cut or break the multilines, but simply supresses the display of the various multiline cut segments. This is done so that you may later redisplay (or heal) the cut segments. So, what appears to be many multiline segments, might in fact be a single multiline, and vice versa.

Tip

To tell if a multiline has cut segments in it, simply pick on any portion of the multiline. The entire multiline segment will highlight, and grips will appear at each multiline vertex.

When you issue the MLEDIT command, you open the Multiline Edit Tools dialog box (see fig. 9.16), which provides 12 tools for editing multilines. You can divide the MLEDIT tools into four categories: crosses, tees, corners, and cuts.

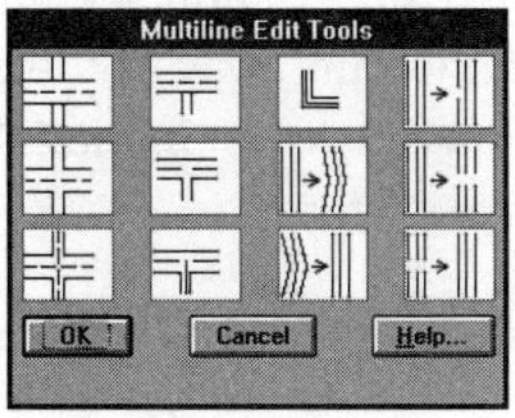

Figure 9.16

The Multiline Edit Tools dialog box.

Crosses

The MLEDIT command's three cross tools (Closed Cross, Open Cross, and Merged Cross) enable you to clean up various crossing intersections. You can see the various effects of these tools in figure 9.17.

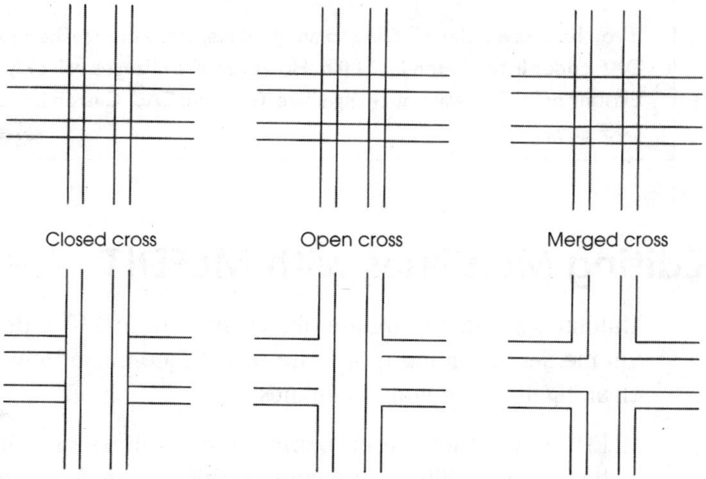

Figure 9.17

Closed, open, and merged crosses.

When you choose one of the cross tools, AutoCAD prompts you to select two mlines. AutoCAD always cuts the first mline you choose. AutoCAD cuts the second mline you choose according to the tool you use.

For merged crosses, AutoCAD creates a corner out of matching pairs of mline elements. In other words, the outermost elements of the first mline create a corner with the outermost elements of the second mline, the second pair of elements in the first mline creates a corner with the second pair of elements in the second mline, and so on. If an unmatched element is left in one of the mlines, it is left uncut.

Tees

You use the next three multiline editing tools to clean up tee intersections. The tools behave much the same way as the crossing tools. Figure 9.18 shows the effects of using the various tee tools on multilines.

Figure 9.18

Closed, open, and merged tees.

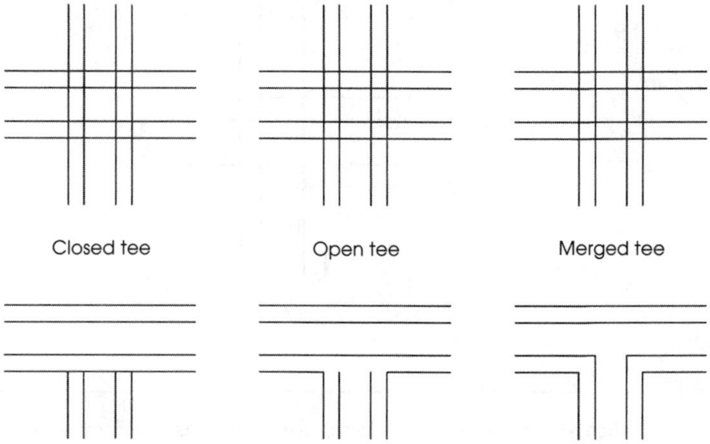

As with the cross tools, AutoCAD prompts you to select two mlines. AutoCAD cuts the first mline to make the base of the tee and cuts the second mline according to the tool you use.

Warning

In early versions of Release 13, a certain bug causes a Fatal Error when you use any of the tee tools on mlines created with a zero justification. This bug causes an AutoCAD Fatal Error and terminates your AutoCAD session!

Corners

The MLEDIT command's corner tools enable you to clean up corner intersections between two multilines, as well as give you the capability to add and remove vertices from multilines. The corner joint tool creates a clean corner joint from two multilines. You can see the effect of the corner joint in figure 9.19.

When you select the corner joint tool, AutoCAD prompts you to select two mlines. Pick points on the portions of the mlines you want to keep. AutoCAD trims or extends the mlines to their respective intersection points.

Figure 9.19

A corner joint.

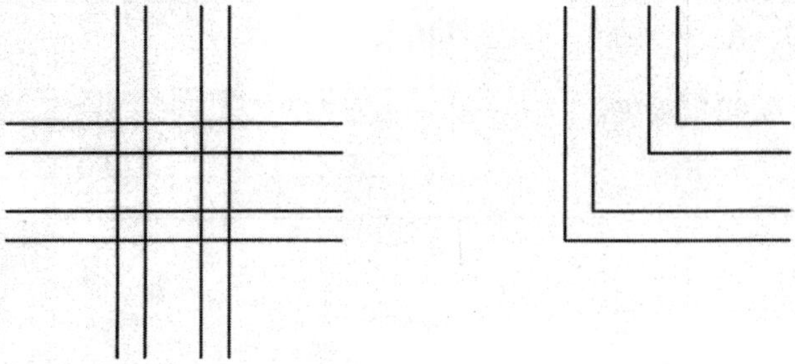

TIP

When you make a corner joint, make sure that each mline has the same number of elements. This helps ensure that the corners miter properly. Making a corner joint out of mlines that have a different number of elements can lead to unexpected results.

When you create a multiline, AutoCAD places a vertex at each of the points you pick. The Add Vertex and Delete Vertex tools enable you to create and remove vertices from a multiline. Figure 9.20 shows the effect of adding a vertex. The top multiline is the original mline with a vertex at each endpoint. The middle multiline shows the effect of adding a new vertex, and the bottom shows the mline after you use grips to stretch the mline.

Figure 9.20

Adding a vertex to a multiline.

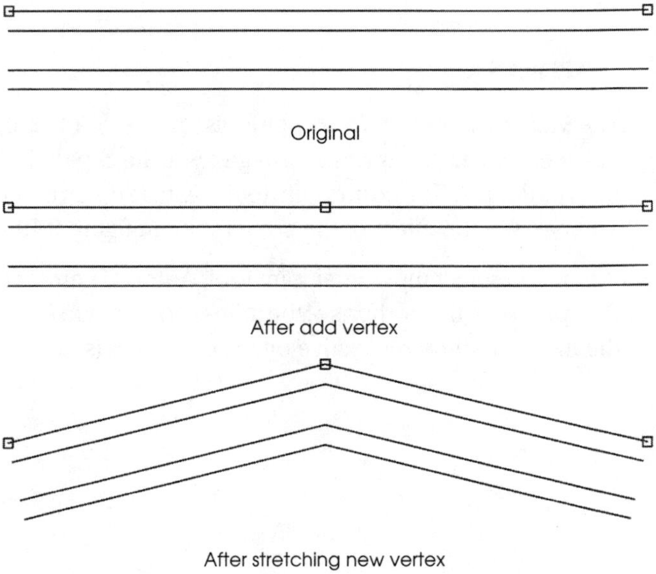

You can use the Delete Vertex tool to remove a vertex from multilines that have three or more vertices. If you select an mline that has only two vertices, AutoCAD simply ignores the pick and allows you to try again.

Cuts

The cut tools enable you to break sections out of the individual elements of a multiline. You can use the Cut Single tool to break a section out of a single element of a multiline. You simply pick two points on the element and AutoCAD cuts the portion of the element between the two points. The Cut All tool works similarly, but cuts all of the elements. Figure 9.21 shows the effects of using the Cut Element and Cut All tools.

Figure 9.21

The multiline cut tools.

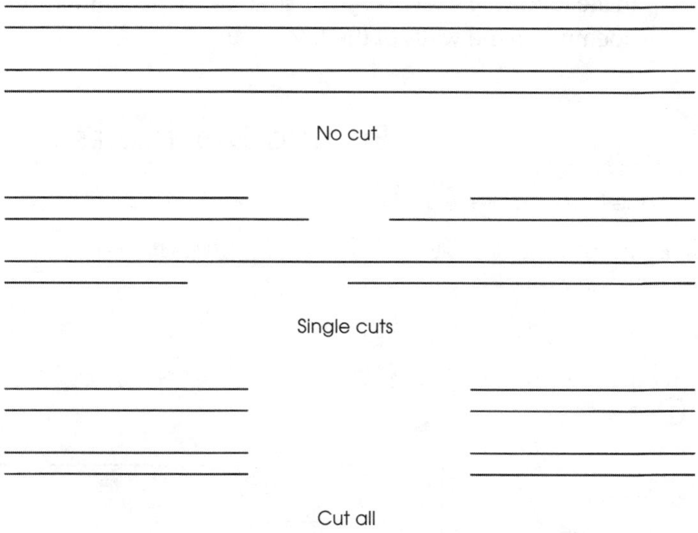

AutoCAD doesn't actually cut the multiline itself—it simply suppresses display of those sections. The multiline is still a single object. The Weld All tool prompts you to pick two points on a multiline. AutoCAD redisplays any cut sections between the two points you pick. The fact that AutoCAD doesn't actually break the multiline enables you to reverse the effects of the cut tools, using the Weld All tool. You can see the effect of the Weld All tool in figure 9.22.

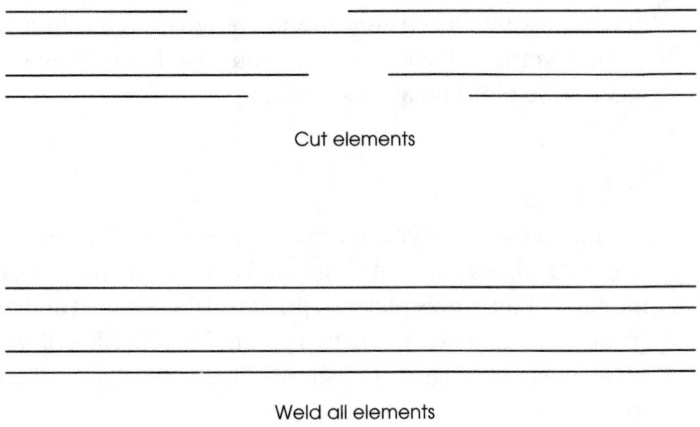

Figure 9.22

Welding a cut mline.

In the following exercise, you use some of the multiline editing tools to create door openings in the walls of the floor plan.

EDITING MULTILINES

Continue from the preceding exercise. Make the PLAN layer current.

`Command:` *Choose Edit Multiline (Modify, Special Edit)*	Issues the MLEDIT command
Double-click on the Closed Tee icon	Activates the Closed Tee tool
`Select first mline:` *Pick the mline at ① (see fig. 9.23)*	Selects the base of the tee intersection

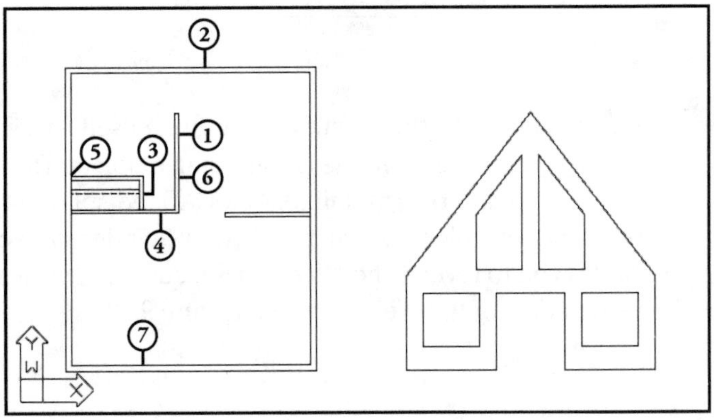

Figure 9.23

Editing with MLEDIT.

`Select second mline:` *Pick the mline at* ②	Creates a closed tee intersection
`Select first mline(or Undo):` ↵	Ends the MLEDIT command
`Command:` ↵	Repeats the MLEDIT command
Double-click on the Merged Tee *icon*	Activates the Merged Tee tool
`Select first mline:` *Pick the mline at* ③	Selects the base of the tee intersection
`Select second mline:` *Pick the mline at* ④	Creates a merged tee intersection
`Select first mline(or Undo):` ↵	Ends the MLEDIT command

Next, you use the Cut All tool to create some door openings.

`Command:` ↵	Repeats the MLEDIT command
Double-click on the Cut All *icon*	Activates the Cut All tool
`Select mline:` *Using the From and ENDPoint object snaps, pick* ⑤	Sets a reference point at the end of the closet wall
`<Offset>:` **@6<0**	Places the first point of the cut
`Select second point:` **@4'8<0**	Cuts a door opening in the wall

Notice that the cut ends are not automatically capped. Later, you cap these lines manually.

`Select mline(or Undo):` *Using the FROM and ENDPoint object snaps, pick* ⑥	Sets a reference point at the inside corner of the wall
`<Offset>:` **@6<90**	Places the first point of the cut
`Select second point:` **@30<90**	Creates a 30" door opening
`Select mline(or Undo):` *Using the FROM and MIDpoint object snaps, pick* ⑦	Sets a reference point at the midpoint of the wall
`<Offset>:` **@3'<180**	Places the first point of the cut
`Select second point:` **@6'<0**	Creates a 6' door opening
`Select mline(or Undo):` ↵	

Next, you use the LINE command and a running ENDPoint object snap to clean up the cut openings.

`Command:` *Choose Snap to Endpoint (Standard, Object Snap)*	Sets a running ENDPoint object snap
`Command:` *Choose Line (/Draw, Line)*	Issues the LINE command
`From point:` *Pick ① (see fig. 9.24)*	Places the start point of the line

Figure 9.24

Capped door openings.

`To point:` *Pick ②*	Draws the cap line
`To point:` ↵	Ends the LINE command

Use the LINE command to continue to connect the endpoints of the door openings. After you finish, your drawing should resemble figure 9.24. Leave the running ENDpoint object snap turned on—you use it in the next exercise.

Save your drawing.

The complex objects you have learned about in this chapter extend your AutoCAD drawing capabilities by enhancing the effect of a single command.

By combining several simple objects into a region using Boolean operations, you can quickly create complex geometry that would be difficult or impossible to produce using any other method. You can then query AutoCAD to provide additional information about the resulting objects.

The MLINE command, by contrast, enables you to create complex objects, with a single command, which would require multiple commands to replicate, and the MLEDIT command provides editing tools for the mlines objects that you could not otherwise accomplish.

chapter

10

Basic Building Blocks for Repetitive Drawing

In this chapter you explore how to create and use blocks. Blocks are drawing elements grouped together so that you can place them easily throughout a drawing or use them in many different drawings. The use of blocks is similar to the use of templates in board drafting, but if you use blocks you control the scale and proportions of the symbols you draw. Just as when you use templates, using blocks eliminates repetitive drawing tasks and ensures standard symbols. You also are shown in this chapter how to attach text information to a block. Text information can be constant or can be defined each time you place the block.

In this chapter you learn how to do the following:

- *Create a block of drawing objects*
- *Place blocks in your drawing*
- *Use blocks to increase drawing speed and accuracy and decrease file size*
- *Attach text attributes to a block*
- *Use attributes for data storage and extraction*

Using blocks enables you to increase the speed, uniformity, and efficiency of your work with AutoCAD. You increase drawing speed by eliminating the time you spend re-creating common elements, such as title blocks and drawing symbols. Uniformity of symbols within a drawing or from one drawing to the next also increases, because the same block is being used to define each occurrence of the symbol. The drawing file size decreases when blocks are used for repetitive features, because the block's geometry needs only to be defined once in the drawing file.

When to use blocks is as important to know as how to use them. Figure 10.1 shows some typical uses of blocks for common drawing symbols and parts. Using blocks as the CAD version of a template is the most obvious use. Other uses of blocks, however, go well beyond the capabilities of templates. For instance, if you create a standard title block with *attributes* (text attached to a block), you can automate the repetitive process of filling in the title block information for each drawing. Also, if you insert blocks that have different X and Y scale factors, you can use the same block for many applications, as shown in figure 10.2.

Figure 10.1

Blocks used as drawing symbols.

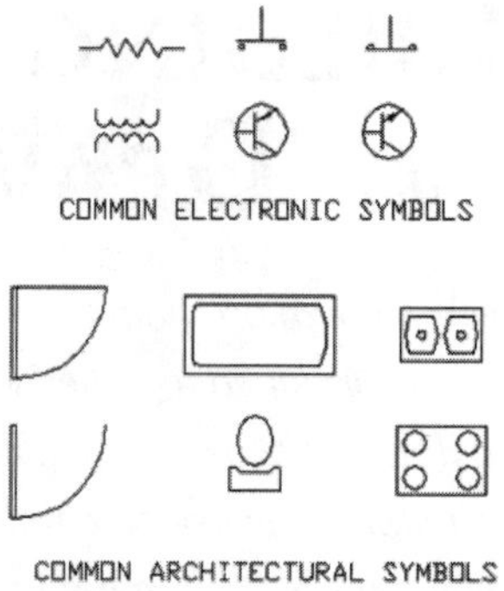

Figure 10.2

Scaling a block's proportions.

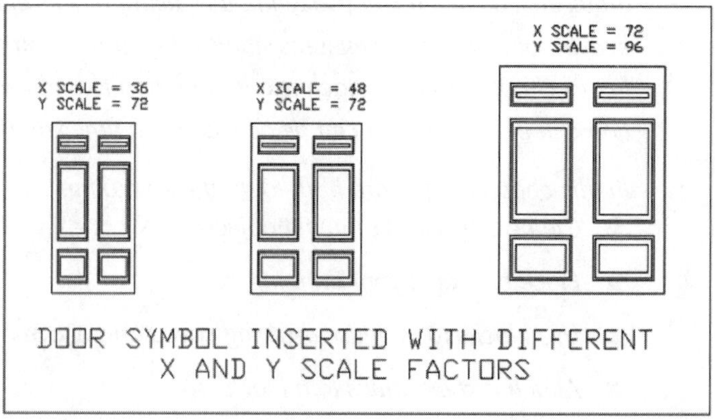

Blocks also can offer editing advantages. To move or copy symbol objects as individual drawing objects, you collect the individual objects into a selection set. As drawings become crowded, however, selecting the objects you want becomes more difficult. You can make selection much easier if you group the objects together as a block. AutoCAD blocks enable you to operate on the group as a whole. Objects in blocks stick together; if you move one part of the block, the whole block moves.

You save a block with a name and reuse it any number of times later in the same drawing or in other drawings. If you need to edit the individual elements of a block, you can explode the block.

The following exercise introduces you to some of the capabilities of blocks. In the exercise, you open a drawing of a simple office floor plan, insert a block of a title block, supply title information, and insert a full-scale block of a workstation. Next, you insert a block of a chair twice—once at full scale and again at a 3:1 scale to create a couch.

You use the Insert Block tool to place blocks into your drawing. Figure 10.3 shows you where you can find this tool.

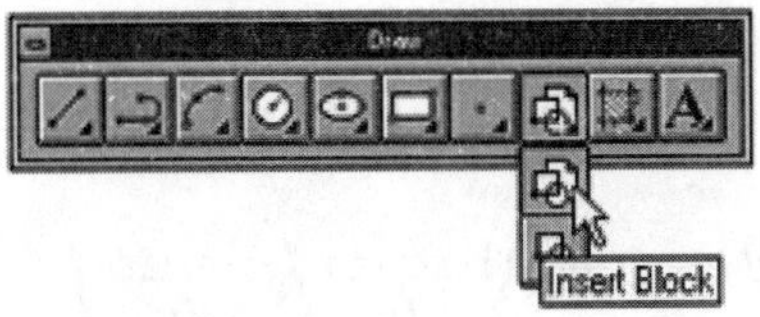

Figure 10.3

The Insert Block tool on the Block flyout.

Blocks and Drawing File Size

Using blocks helps minimize a drawing's file size. If you draw 100 lines, for example, you add 100 objects to your drawing. If you make a block that contains 100 lines, AutoCAD creates a block definition that contains 100 objects, which then is stored as one object in the drawing file. When you insert a block in your drawing, you add only one new object—a reference to the block definition.

If you insert the block only once, you save nothing because the definition containing 100 lines is also stored in the drawing. However, if you insert a block that contains 100 lines into your drawing in 12 places, AutoCAD must store only 112 objects. These 112 objects include 100 lines in the block definition and 12 block references (properly called *insert objects*) for the visible references. If you draw and copy 12 groups of 100 lines, but do not use blocks, you add 1,200 objects to your drawing file.

You can see, then, how using blocks can save huge amounts of disk and memory space. Using blocks to reduce the size of the drawing file also lowers the time required to load the file and leaves more memory free for other uses.

Understanding Types and Uses of Blocks

Drafting uses many symbols (such as thread symbols and surface finish symbols in mechanical drafting, window and door symbols in architectural drafting, fittings and equipment in pipe drafting, and so on) and common drawing elements (such as title blocks, standard details, and company logos). The varied use of symbols calls for various types of blocks.

You generally can divide types of drafting symbols into three categories. Certain common elements are not related to a specific type of drawing, such as the symbols illustrated in figure 10.4. Some common elements might pertain only to a specific drawing, such as the pump arrangements illustrated in figure 10.5. Also, you would use some symbols only on specific types of drawings, such as those illustrated in figure 10.6. Although these three categories certainly don't cover every application of blocks for symbols, they do represent the largest use of blocks.

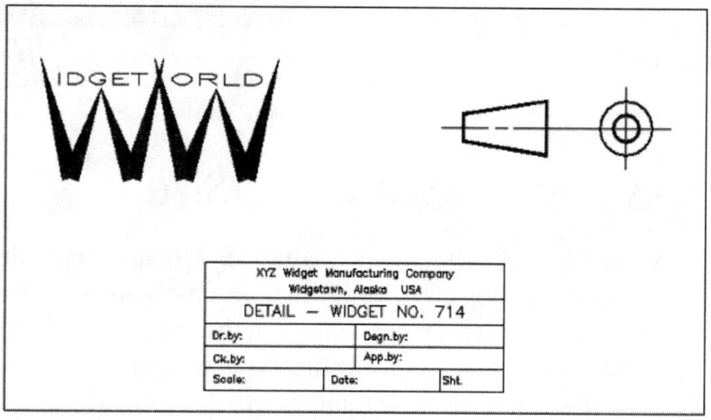

Figure 10.4

Common elements used in a variety of drawings.

Figure 10.5

Common elements within a specific drawing.

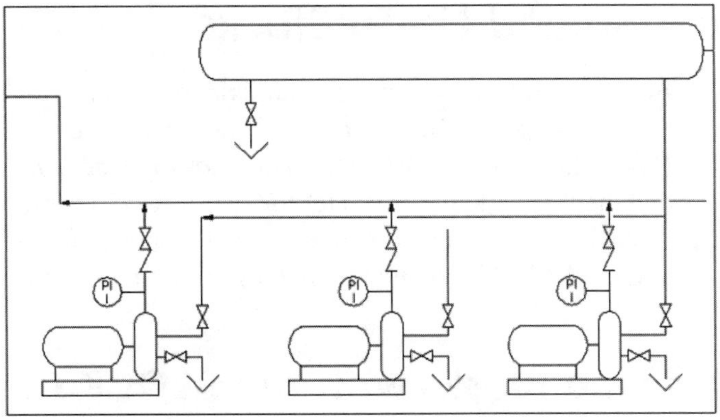

Figure 10.6

Symbols used within a specific type of drawing.

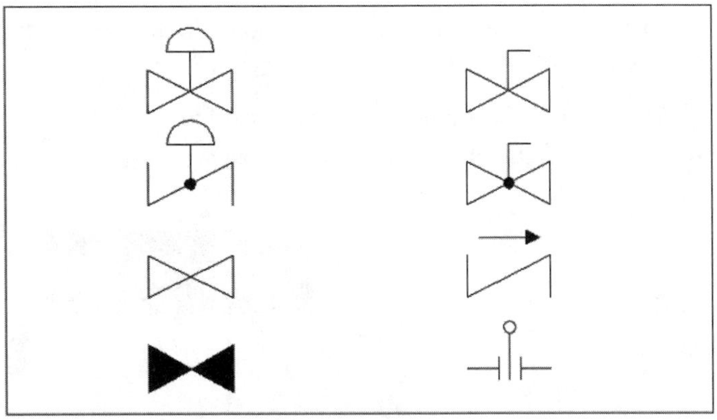

In addition to their use as symbols, blocks often are used for real-world parts, such as toilets, light fixtures, fittings, or furniture. Blocks used as real-world parts usually are defined at full scale and inserted at 1:1 scale.

To accommodate these applications, you use different methods of creating blocks. The WBLOCK command usually is suited best for common elements used in many drawings, such as a title block. The BLOCK command usually is suited best for common elements within a drawing. Finally, for symbols related only to specific types of drawings, creating a symbol library of blocks is likely to be the most efficient method. This chapter introduces you to the BLOCK and WBLOCK commands. Chapter 11, "Block Structure, Editing, Organization, and Management," deals with symbol libraries.

Creating and Using Blocks

AutoCAD provides several commands for grouping objects into blocks and inserting them. You use the BLOCK command to create a block definition, the DDINSERT (Insert dialog box) or INSERT commands to place a block reference in a drawing, and the WBLOCK command to store a block's objects as a separate drawing file on disk. The BASE command enables you to reposition a block's insertion base point, and the MINSERT command enables you to insert blocks in a rectangular array.

Defining Blocks with the BLOCK Command

The BLOCK command is used to create a block definition. You must specify a name for the block, what objects make up the block, and a point to use as an insertion point when placing the block.

The BLOCK command can be accessed from the Block tool on the Draw toolbar, as shown in figure 10.7.

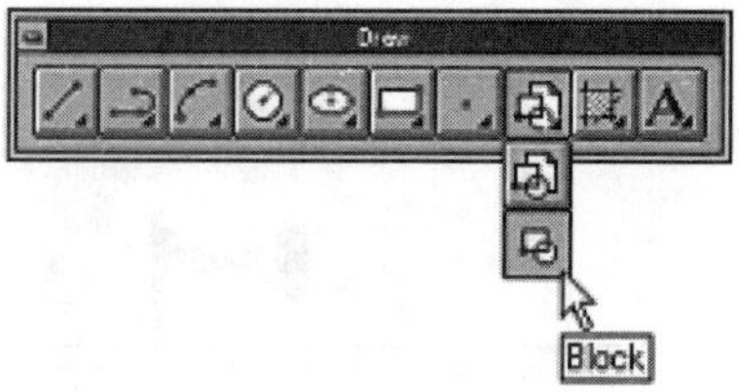

Figure 10.7

The Block tool on the Block flyout.

When you use the BLOCK command, AutoCAD prompts you for a block name. The block name can consist of any combination of letters and numbers up to a maximum length of 31 characters. In addition to letters and numbers, you can use the following characters: $, -, and _. At the `Block name (or ?):` prompt, AutoCAD also gives you an opportunity to see a list of named blocks in the drawing if you type **?**. AutoCAD lists the names of all blocks, and shows the number and types of blocks. The four types of blocks are described in the following list:

- **User blocks.** Blocks you use the BLOCK command to create.
- **External reference blocks.** Reference drawings attached to the drawing. (See Chapter 12, "Using Xrefs for Efficiency and Sharing Data," for more about reference drawings.)

- **Dependent blocks.** Blocks that belong to reference drawings.
- **Unnamed blocks.** Blocks that AutoCAD creates to perform hatching, associative dimensioning, PostScript importing, and solid modeling functions.

Next, AutoCAD prompts you for an insertion base point. You can enter the insertion base point as a coordinate or you can select it on-screen. The insertion base point becomes the point from which a block is justified when you place it in your drawing. Usually, you want to use an object snap mode to select the block insertion base point. Before you pick a practical insertion base point, you must consider the placement of the block when you use it. The insertion base point can be thought of as a "handle" by which the block will be positioned in your drawing. Figure 10.8 shows some typical block insertion base points.

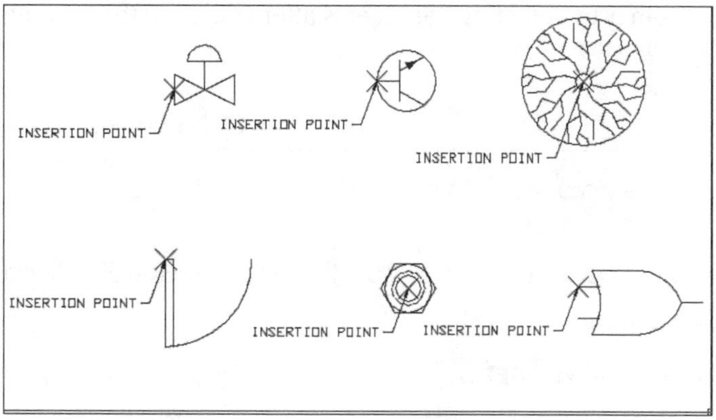

Figure 10.8

Typical block insertion base points.

NOTE

Consider the orientation of the objects in the block, and how the block is used. Symbols that point in a specific direction, such as North Arrows, should be defined pointing toward angle 0. This way, the rotation angle for the block will coincide with AutoCAD's standard method of specifying direction (90° points the arrow straight up).

Finally, AutoCAD prompts you to select the objects of which the block is to consist. You can use any of the object selection methods described in Chapter 14, "The Ins and Outs of Editing." After you select the objects, press Enter to create the block. At this time, all the objects that comprise the block are removed from the screen.

TIP

If you want to restore the objects used to define a block to the drawing, use the OOPS command. Using UNDO or U restores the objects, but also removes the block definition.

You also can select the objects that make up a block from the `Command:` prompt before you issue the BLOCK command. If you do so, AutoCAD bypasses the `Select objects:` prompt and creates the block as soon as you specify a name and an insertion base point.

After you create a block, AutoCAD stores the information that defines the block in the drawing file so that the next time you open this drawing file, you still have access to the block.

In the following exercise, you create blocks of a tree and a group of shrubs. You create one by selecting the objects before you issue the BLOCK command and the other by selecting the objects after you issue the command.

CREATING BLOCKS

Begin a new drawing named CHAP10A, using the file BLOCKS from the accompanying CD as a prototype.

`Command:` *Choose Block (Draw, Block)*	Issues the BLOCK command
`Command: _block`	
`Block name (or ?):` **TREE** ↵	Defines the block's name
`Insertion base point:` *Use CENter object snap to pick center of circle at ① (see fig. 10.9)*	Specifies base point
`Select objects: _` *Select a window from ② to ③*	Selects the objects for the block TREE
`4 found`	
`Select objects:` ↵	Ends object selection

Now the objects that make up the TREE block are erased from the screen and are stored in the drawing's block definition table. To return the original objects to the screen, you can use the OOPS command.

`Command:` **OOPS** ↵	Starts the OOPS command

Next, use the noun-verb method of object selection.

Select a window from ④ *to* ⑤	Selects the objects that will make up the block named SHRUBS
`Command:` *Choose Block (Draw, Block)*	Issues the BLOCK command with the selected objects

Note that the Select objects: prompt is not issued when using the noun-verb method.

`Command: _block` `Block name (or ?):` **SHRUBS** ↵	Specifies the block's name
`Insertion base point:` *Pick* ⑥	Creates the block and deletes selection
`16 found`	
`Command:` **OOPS** ↵	Returns the original objects

AutoCAD has defined the two blocks. Use the ? option of the BLOCK command to list all blocks in the drawing's block table.

`Command:` Choose Block (Draw, Block)

`Command: _block` `Block name (or ?):` **?**	Specifies the list blocks option
`Block(s) to list <*>:` ↵	Accepts the default to list all blocks

```
Defined blocks.
  SHRUBS
  TREE
User      External      Dependent    Unnamed
Blocks    References    Blocks       Blocks
    2          0             0            0
```

Hide the AutoCAD text window and save your drawing.

Figure 10.9

Tree and shrubs symbols, showing pick points for "Creating Blocks" exercise.

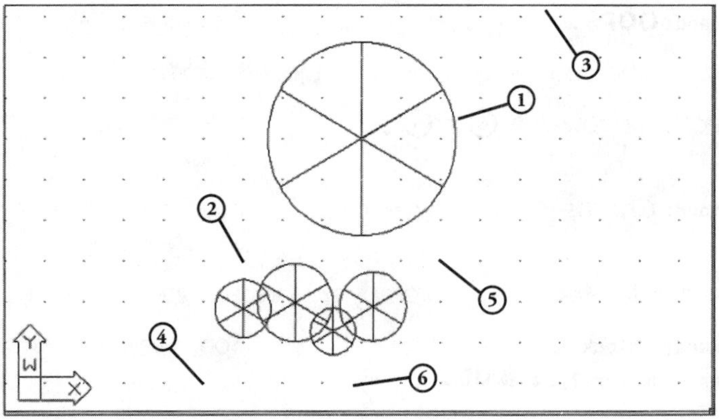

Placing Blocks into Drawings

Obviously, creating a block would be a pointless exercise without some means of placing it in your drawing. Consequently, AutoCAD provides a number of methods for inserting blocks, including the DDINSERT, INSERT, and MINSERT commands.

Remember that after you place a block in your drawing, AutoCAD considers the block to be one object, regardless of the level of complexity of the block. If you want to edit individual parts of a block, you must first explode the block, which you have the option of doing when you use the INSERT or DDINSERT commands to place the block. You also can use the EXPLODE or XPLODE command later to explode a block; these commands are covered in the next chapter.

Using the DDINSERT Command

Once you have created a block with the BLOCK command, the DDINSERT command allows you to place it in your drawing. When placing the block with DDINSERT, you can specify the block's location, scale factors, and rotation angle. DDINSERT may also be used to place a separate drawing file into your drawing; this is described in this chapter in the section "Using DDINSERT To Place a File into a Drawing."

The Insert dialog box has two sections: Block and Options (see fig. 10.10).

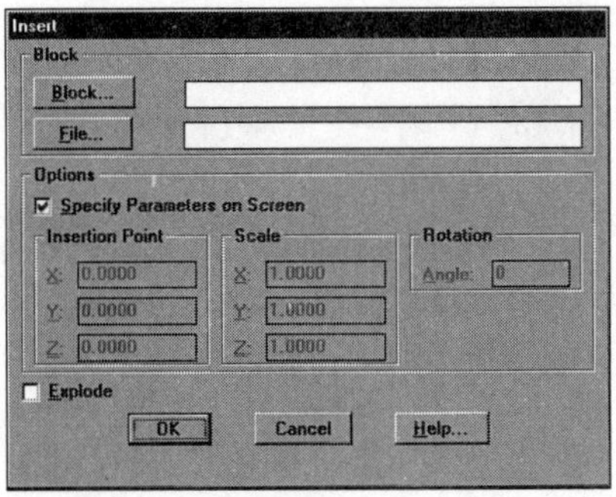

Figure 10.10

The Insert dialog box.

In the Block section of the Insert dialog box, you must choose either the Block button or the File button. Because you want to insert a block you created by using the BLOCK command, you would choose the Block button. The File button is explained later in this chapter, in the section "Using DDINSERT To Place a File into a Drawing." After you choose the Block button, AutoCAD displays a list of all user blocks in the drawing. Simply select the block you want to insert from this list.

The Options section of the Insert dialog box is divided into three sections. These sections normally are grayed out because the Specify Parameters on Screen check box is selected. Normally, you specify a block's insertion point, scale, and rotation angle on-screen. To access the options, you must deselect this check box. The first section, Insertion Point, enables you to supply an insertion point for the block using absolute coordinates. The second section, Scale, enables you to specify a scale for the X, Y, and Z axes of the block to create scaled blocks. The third section, Rotation, enables you to specify a rotation angle for the inserted block.

Also note the Explode check box at the bottom of the dialog box. If you mark this check box, AutoCAD inserts the block as individual objects rather than as one object. This is discussed in detail in Chapter 11, "Block Structure, Editing, Organization, and Management."

In the following exercise, you use the DDINSERT command to insert blocks identical to those you created in the previous exercise. You will insert them in a landscape drawing of a small park. The drawing contains the TREE and SHRUBS blocks, as well as several other blocks to be used in other exercises in this chapter.

USING DDINSERT TO INSERT BLOCKS INTO A DRAWING

Create a new drawing named CHAP10B, using the drawing PARK from the accompanying CD as a prototype.

`Command:` *Choose Zoom Window (Standard, Zoom Window) and zoom to a window from* 20',195' *to* 170',350'	Zooms in to get a closer look at the park entrance (see fig. 10.11)

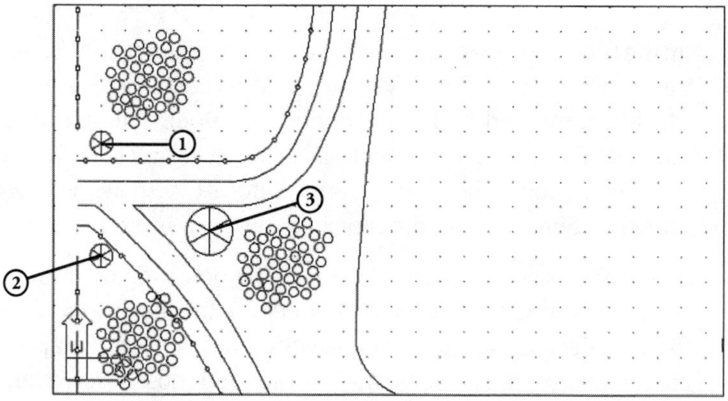

Figure 10.11

Zoomed view of park entrance.

Next, place a few trees around the entrance.

`Command:` *Choose Insert Block (Draw, Block)*	Issues the DDINSERT command and opens the Insert dialog box
`Command: _ddinsert`	
`Initializing...  DDINSERT loaded.`	
Choose the Block *button*	Opens the Defined Blocks dialog box with a list of block names
Select the block TREE *from the list, then choose* OK	Returns to the Insert dialog box
Check the Specify Parameters on Screen *check box, then choose* OK	Closes Insert dialog box
`Insertion point:` *Pick* ① *(refer to figure 10.11)*	
`X scale factor <1> / Corner / XYZ:` ↵	Accepts the default X scale

`Y scale factor (default=X):` ↵	Accepts the default Y scale
`Rotation angle <0>:` ↵	Accepts the default rotation
`Command:` ↵	Repeats the DDINSERT command and opens the Insert dialog box
Choose OK	Defaults to the block TREE, the last one you selected
`Insertion point:` *Pick* ②	
`X scale factor <1> / Corner / XYZ:` ↵	Accepts the default X scale
`Y scale factor (default=X):` ↵	Accepts the default Y scale
`Rotation angle <0>:` ↵	Accepts the default rotation

The trees that you have been inserting have a foliage diameter of about 8'. Next, place a 16'-diameter tree where the walking path divides.

`Command:` ↵	Repeats the DDINSERT command
Choose OK	Defaults to place another tree
`Insertion point:` *Pick* ③	
`X scale factor <1> / Corner / XYZ: 2` ↵	Specifies an X scale factor of 2
`Y scale factor (default=X):` ↵	Y scale defaults to 2 because X scale was entered as 2
`Rotation angle <0>:` ↵	Accepts the default rotation

Note that the scale factor of 2 doubles the size of the tree.

Next, you insert a tree by specifying its insertion point and scale factor in the Insert dialog box. First, zoom out to the view shown in figure 10.12.

`Command:` *Choose Zoom Out (Standard, Zoom Out)*	Issues ZOOM command with .5x scale preset
`Command: '_zoom All/Center/Dynamic/Extents/Left/Previous/ Vmax/Window/<Scale(X/XP)>: .5x`	Zooms out
`Command:` *Choose Insert Block (Draw, Block)*	Issues DDINSERT command and opens the Insert dialog box

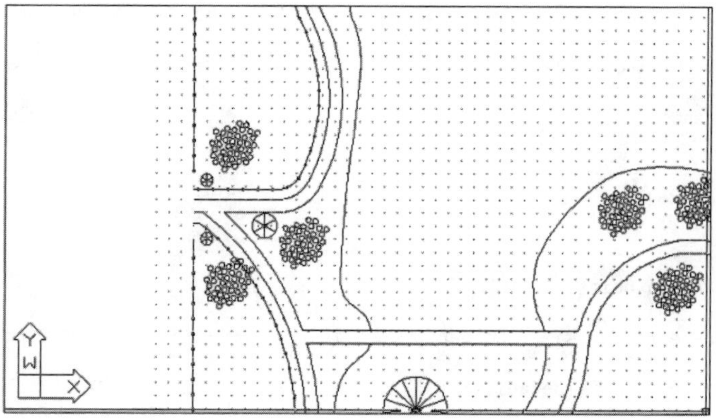

Figure 10.12

Zoomed out view of park entrance.

Select the TREE block you want to insert, then clear the Specify Parameters on Screen check box. Type **120'** in the X edit box of the Insertion Point section. Type **190'** in the Y edit box of the Insertion Point section. Type **2** in the X edit box of the Scale section. Clicking in the Y edit box of the Scale section causes the Y default to change to 2, because you set the X scale to 2. Figure 10.13 shows the dialog box with the proper settings.

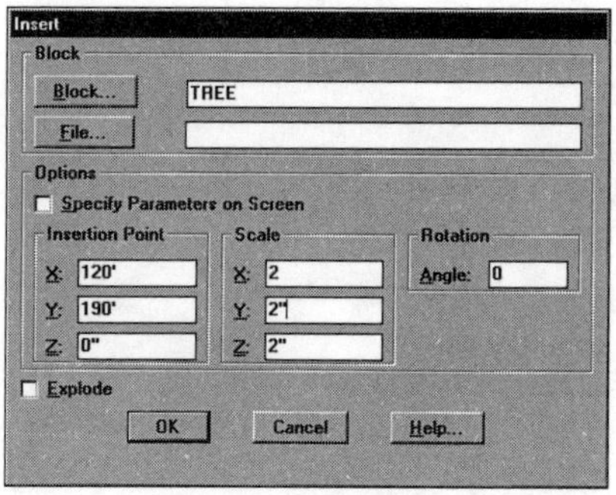

Figure 10.13

The Insert dialog box with insertion point and scale settings.

Choose OK	Inserts the tree without further prompts

Save the drawing.

Using the INSERT Command

The INSERT command provides another method for placing a block in your drawing. This command places the block without the use of a dialog box.

TIP

> The INSERT command is useful for placing blocks from a custom menu macro or a LISP routine, because you do not need to select the block name from a list.

When you insert a block without the dialog box, you must type the INSERT command from the `Command:` prompt or choose it from the screen menu. AutoCAD then asks you to supply a block name. You type the name of the block (or file) you want to insert, or type **?** if you want AutoCAD to list the names of all defined blocks in the current drawing. To insert a block as individual objects (exploded), you enter the block's name preceded by an asterisk (*). After you supply a block name, AutoCAD prompts for an insertion point, which you can supply by entering the coordinates or, more commonly, by picking it on-screen.

To insert a block reference, you can enter different values for the block's scale and rotation. To scale, you can enter X and Y scale factors. The default scale prompt for the Y factor uses the X factor you enter by default, which simplifies the process of scaling your drawing symbol at a 1:1 ratio. You can use different X and Y scales by entering different responses (the XYZ option is for 3D control). You also can supply an angle of rotation by entering an angle or by dragging the rotation and picking a point.

In the following exercise, you use the INSERT command to place the blocks you made previously. You also use the autoedit move copy mode to copy a block.

USING INSERT TO INSERT BLOCKS INTO A DRAWING

Continue in the CHAP10B drawing from the preceding exercise, or create a new drawing again named CHAP10B using the drawing PARK from the accompanying CD as a prototype, and thaw layer EXER_2 and set layer SHRUBS current.

`Command:` *Choose Zoom Window (Standard, Zoom Window) and zoom to a window from* 100',140' *to* 360',220'

`Command:` **INSERT** ↵	Starts the INSERT command
`Block name (or ?) <TREE>:` **SHRUBS** ↵	Specifies the block to insert
`Insertion point:` **155',185'** ↵	Specifies insertion point by coordinates
`X scale factor <1> / Corner / XYZ:` ↵	Accepts the default X scale

`Y scale factor (default=X):` ↵	Accepts the default Y scale
`Rotation angle <0>:` ↵	Accepts the default rotation
`Command:` *Pick at* ① *(see fig. 10.14)*	Selects the block
Select its grip	Makes it a "hot" grip, and enters autoedit mode

`** STRETCH **`
`<Stretch to point>/Base point/Copy/`
`Undo/eXit:` ↵
	Cycles to MOVE mode

`** MOVE **`
`<Move to point>/Base point/Copy/`
`Undo/eXit:` **C** ↵
	Specifies the Copy option

`** MOVE (multiple) **`
`<Move to point>/Base point/Copy/`
`Undo/eXit:` *Pick at each of the shrub locations shown in figure 10.14*
	Copies the inserted shrubs to several places

Save the drawing.

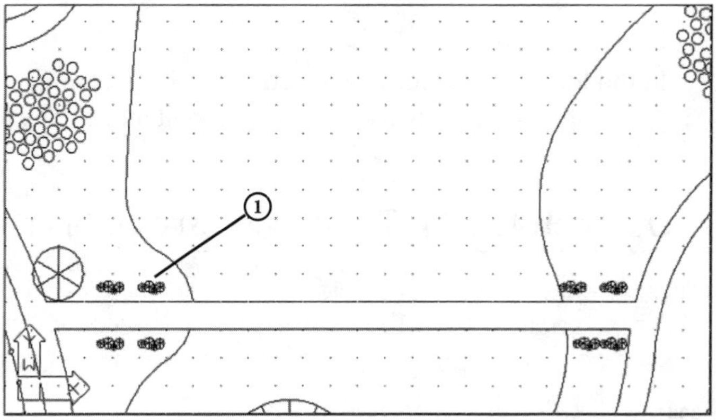

Figure 10.14

Location to copy shrubs.

TIP

If you need to move a block by one of its component object's grips, choose Grips, then turn on the Enable Grips Within Blocks check box.

When you accepted the default INSERT scale values in the preceding exercise, you might have noticed a second option, called Corner. When you use the Corner option to enter the scale values, you can scale the block by indicating the X and Y size of a rectangle. The insertion point is the first corner of the rectangle. Drag and pick the other corner to determine scale. AutoCAD uses the width as the X scale and the height as the Y scale, in current drawing units.

You do not need to enter C to use corner point scaling. If you move the pointer at the X scale prompt, you see the block being dynamically scaled. The Corner option is used in menus because it limits scale input to corner point picking and issues an `Other corner:` prompt.

TIP

Whether you use keyboard scale entry or the Corner option, you can specify negative scale factors to mirror the block's insertion, turn it upside-down, or both.

Be careful when you use corner point scaling. When you use a corner scale input, use snap or object snap to control accuracy. The dragged scale is relative to one drawing unit square, and it works well if your block definition is about one unit in size. (See the section "Using Versatile Unit Size Blocks" later in this chapter.) If your block definition is many drawing units in size, however, even a small rectangle yields a large size.

Using Preset Scales and Rotation Angle with INSERT

You have inserted blocks by specifying an insertion point, a scale, and an angle. You can preset the scale factor and rotation angle before you select the insertion point. When you preset the block's scale and angle, AutoCAD suspends insertion point dragging until you finish setting those options. You then see the block's scale and angle as you drag it to pick the insertion point.

Preset Scale and Rotation Options

Several options are available for presetting values, but they are not shown as prompts during the INSERT command. The following list shows every option.

- **Scale and PScale.** These options prompt for scale factor preset to X, Y, and Z axes.

- **Xscale and PXscale.** These options preset only the X-scale factor.
- **Yscale and PYscale.** These options preset only the Y-scale factor.
- **Zscale and PZscale.** These options preset only the Z-scale factor.
- **Rotate and PRotate.** These options preset the rotation angle. Enter this value from the keyboard or pick two points.

Type the first one or two characters of the preset option to tell AutoCAD what you want to preset.

The letter *P* stands for preliminary, not preset. Options prefixed with a *P* establish a preliminary scale and rotation value to visually aid in insertion. After you select the insertion point, you see the normal insert prompts and defaults.

Preset scale factors have limitations. You cannot mix fixed presets (such as Xscale) with preliminary presets (such as PYscale). If you try to mix them, the preliminary presets become fixed, and AutoCAD does not prompt you again for their values.

In the following exercise, you use preset values to insert a couple of blocks.

Using INSERT with Preset Scales

Continue from the previous exercise, or create a new drawing again named CHAP10B using the drawing PARK from the accompanying CD as a prototype, and thaw layers EXER_2 and EXER_3. Zoom a close-up view of the park entrance as shown in figure 10.15.

Use the Layer Control drop-down list to set layer BENCHES current.

`Command:` **INSERT** ↵	Starts the INSERT command
`Block name (or ?) <SHRUBS>:` **BENCH** ↵	Specifies a block to insert
`Insertion point:` **X** ↵	Requests a preset X scale prompt
`X scale factor:` **2** ↵	Presets the X axis scale factor
`Insertion point:` **Y** ↵	Requests a preset Y scale prompt
`Y scale factor:` **1** ↵	Presets the Y axis scale factor
`Insertion point:` **R** ↵	Requests a preset rotation angle prompt
`Rotation angle:` **270** ↵	Presets the block rotation angle
`Insertion point:` **25',300'** ↵	Specifies the block insertion point at ① (see fig. 10.15)

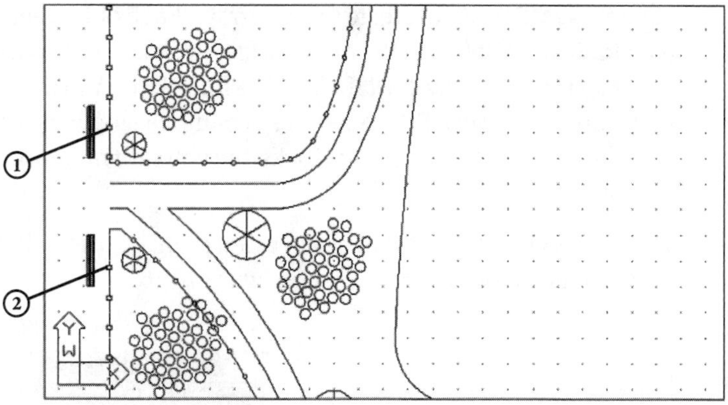

Figure 10.15

View of the park entrance.

The block you just inserted, BENCH, is a 3' by 10' park bench symbol. However, by inserting it with an X axis scale factor of 2 and a Y axis scale factor of 1, you have created a 3' by 20' bench.

Now repeat the procedure to place another bench with the same scale at 25',250' on the other side of the entrance at ②.

Save the drawing.

NOTE

Preset options are most valuable when you use them in custom menu macros. Macros can apply preset options transparently, which simplifies the task of placing the block by enabling dragging with predetermined scale and rotations during an insertion.

Using the MINSERT Command

A block is more than a block if you use the MINSERT command to insert it. Suppose you want to put many blocks in your drawing in a rectangular pattern, such as placing columns or beams in a structural drawing or an array of tables and chairs in a school cafeteria. You could insert one copy of the block and then use the ARRAY command to make several columns and rows of copies, but each of these copies duplicates much of the insert object.

The MINSERT command provides another method. Think of MINSERT (Multiple INSERTion) as a single command that combines inserts and rectangular arrays. (You cannot use MINSERT to create a polar array.) Each object generated by using ARRAY is an individual object in the drawing file—you can edit, delete, copy, or even array the object individually. MINSERT differs from ARRAY in that each block component in the array that MINSERT generates is part of a single inserted object. You cannot edit the individual component blocks, but you save memory by not storing repetitive information.

The MINSERT command can be accessed from the Insert Multiple Blocks tool on the Miscellaneous toolbar, as shown in figure 10.16.

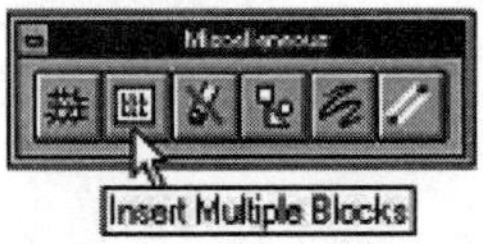

Figure 10.16

The Insert Multiple Blocks (MINSERT) Tool on the Miscellaneous Toolbar.

In the following exercise, you use MINSERT to placesprinklers in the park.

Using MINSERT To Insert an Array of Blocks

Continue from the preceding exercise, or create a new drawing again named CHAP10B using the drawing PARK from the accompanying CD as a prototype, and thaw layers EXER_2, EXER_3, and EXER_4.

Use the Layer Control drop-down list to set layer IRRIGATION current.

`Command:` *Choose Zoom Window (Standard, Zoom Window) and zoom a window from* 400',240' *to* 700',480'	Zooms to view shown in figure 10.17
`Command:` *Choose* Tools, Toolbars, Miscellaneous	Displays the Miscellaneous toolbar
`Command:` *Choose Insert Multiple Blocks (Miscellaneous, Insert Multiple Blocks)*	Issues the MINSERT command
`Command: _minsert Block name (or ?) :` **SPRINKLER** ↵	Specifies the block to insert
`Insertion point:` **450',260'** ↵	Specifies insertion point
`X scale factor <1> / Corner / XYZ:` ↵	Accepts default X scale factor
`Y scale factor (default=X):` ↵	Accepts default Y scale factor

`Rotation angle <0>:` ↵	Accepts default rotation
`Number of rows (—) <1>:` **7** ↵	Specifies 7 vertical rows of blocks
`Number of columns (¦¦¦) <1>:` **8** ↵	Specifies 8 horizontal columns of blocks
`Unit cell or distance between rows (—):` **30'** ↵	Specifies row spacing
`Distance between columns (¦¦¦):` **30'** ↵	Specifies column spacing and draws the sprinkler array (see fig. 10.17)

Save the drawing.

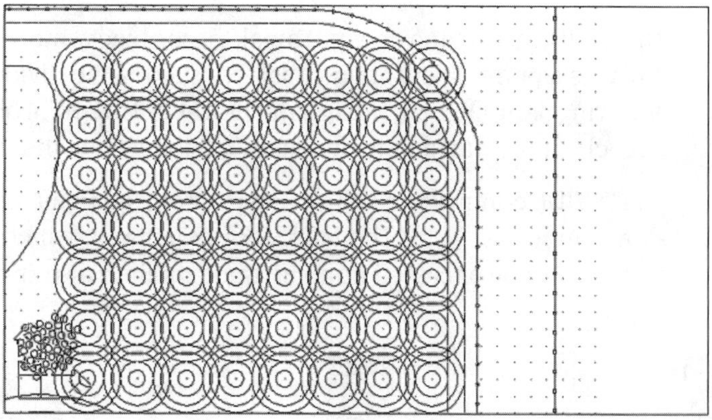

Figure 10.17

Sprinklers inserted with the MINSERT command.

NOTE

When you specify a rotation in MINSERT, AutoCAD rotates the array, and the individual blocks maintain their position in the array.

MINSERT is an efficient way to place multiple copies of a block in a drawing file. In an array, every object occurrence takes up disk space. If you use MINSERT to insert, the block reference occurs once and includes information about the number of rows, columns, and spacing of elements.

NOTE

Individual objects of MINSERT cannot be edited with ERASE or otherwise edited, and objects inserted with MINSERT cannot be exploded.

AutoCAD provides two additional commands, DIVIDE and MEASURE, that you can use to insert multiple copies of a block along a path.

Using the DIVIDE Command

Sometimes you need to divide an object into an equal number of segments while laying out a drawing. For instance, a mechanical design might call for equally spaced holes along a part, or a landscape designer might want to plant shrubs at equal intervals along a pathway. The DIVIDE command provides a method by which you can do this automatically. You can accurately divide lines, circles, arcs, ellipses, polylines, donuts, polygons, and rectangles into equal intervals.

The DIVIDE command does not break these objects into separate segments. Instead, it places a point object at equal intervals along the divided object (see Chapter 7, "Drawing Basic Objects," for information about the point object). Or, you can specify a block rather than a point for AutoCAD to insert at these intervals.

The DIVIDE command can be accessed from the Point tool on the Draw toolbar, as shown in figure 10.18. The MEASURE command, which is explained in the next section, can be accessed from the same toolbar, also shown in figure 10.18.

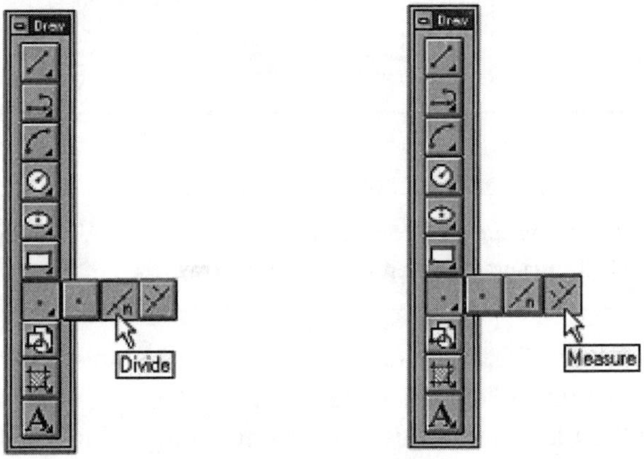

Figure 10.18

The Divide and Measure tools on the Point flyout.

All you have to do after you issue the DIVIDE command is pick the object you want to divide, then specify the number of divisions. AutoCAD calculates the interval distance and places a point at each interval. If you want to place a block rather than a point, choose the Block option of DIVIDE before you specify the number of divisions.

TIP

Remember, you can use the NODE object snap to snap to a point object.

In the following exercise, you practice using the DIVIDE command to place the shrub block at equal intervals along the property line of the park. Then you place some benches along the park pathway, using the DIVIDE command to align the benches with the pathway.

USING DIVIDE TO INSERT BLOCKS

Continue from the preceding exercise, or create a new drawing again named CHAP10B using the drawing PARK from the accompanying CD as a prototype, and thaw layers EXER_2, EXER_3, EXER_4, and EXER_5.

Set layer SHRUBS current and zoom to the view shown in figure 10.19.

`Command:` *Choose Divide (Draw, Point)*	Issues the DIVIDE command
`Command: _divide`	
`Select object to divide:` *Pick* ① *(see fig. 10.19)*	Selects the perimeter fence
`<Number of segments>/Block:` **B** ↵	Specifies placing blocks rather than points
`Block name to insert:` **SHRUBS** ↵	Specifies the block
`Align block with object? <Y>` ↵	Accepts defaults to align blocks
`Number of segments:` **200** ↵	Inserts Shrub blocks along fence

Dividing the object 200 times inserts 199 blocks (one at each division).

`Command:` ↵	Repeats the DIVIDE command
`Select object to divide:` *Pick* ②	Selects edge of pathway
`<Number of segments>/Block:` **B** ↵	
`Block name to insert:` **BENCH** ↵	Specifies block to place
`Align block with object? <Y>` ↵	
`Number of segments:` **20** ↵	Inserts blocks along pathway

Save the drawing.

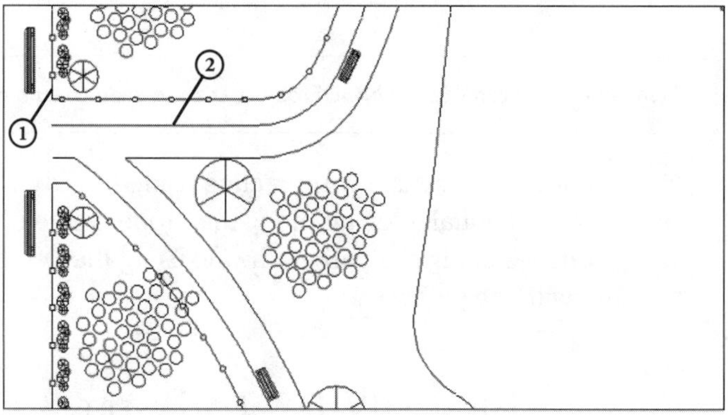

Figure 10.19

Zoomed view of park entrance, showing pick points for the "Using DIVIDE to Insert Blocks" exercise.

When you use DIVIDE to insert blocks (or points), AutoCAD saves the objects as a Previous selection set. To edit the group you can use the Previous selection set option to select it again. If, for example, you want to change the layer of the benches in the previous exercise, to select all of them, you would use the Previous selection set option.

TIP

You can use groups (see Chapter 14, "The Ins and Outs of Editing") to save the selection for later access.

DIVIDE does not enable you to scale a block (nor does MEASURE). If you want to insert the original one-unit size trees at a different scale, for example, you need to create a larger block and insert it, or rescale each block after you insert it. You also might need to adjust a block's insertion base point, original rotation angle, or both to use it with DIVIDE and MEASURE.

Using the MEASURE Command

Placing objects at a set distance apart is another common necessity in drafting—placing a 2-by-6 stud every 24 inches along a wall in an architectural floor plan, for instance, or threads spaced 18 per inch in a mechanical drawing. AutoCAD enables you to do this automatically with the MEASURE command.

The MEASURE command works like DIVIDE, but, instead of dividing an object into equal parts, MEASURE enables you to specify the segment length. After you select the object to measure along, you can specify a block name to insert. Next, you specify a segment length (by entering a value or by picking two points), and

AutoCAD inserts a point or the specified block at the segment-length intervals. As with DIVIDE, MEASURE works with blocks or points, and it forms a Previous selection set that you can use for subsequent editing.

In the following exercise, you use MEASURE to place some lightpoles along the pathway opposite the benches you placed earlier, using MEASURE to align the lights.

USING MEASURE TO INSERT BLOCKS

Continue from the preceding exercise and set layer LIGHTING current.

`Command:` *Choose Measure (Draw, Point)*	Issues the MEASURE command
`Command: _measure`	
`Select object to measure:` *Pick* ② *(refer to figure 10.19)*	Selects edge of pathway
`<Segment length>/Block:` **B** ↵	Specifies placing blocks instead of points
`Block name to insert:` **LIGHTPOLE** ↵	Specifies block to insert
`Align block with object? <Y>` ↵	Accepts the default
`Segment length:` **100'** ↵	Places a lightpole every 100' around the pathway

Zoom out to see the shrubs, benches, and lights along the complete fence and path (see fig. 10.20).

Save the drawing and hide the Miscellaneous toolbar

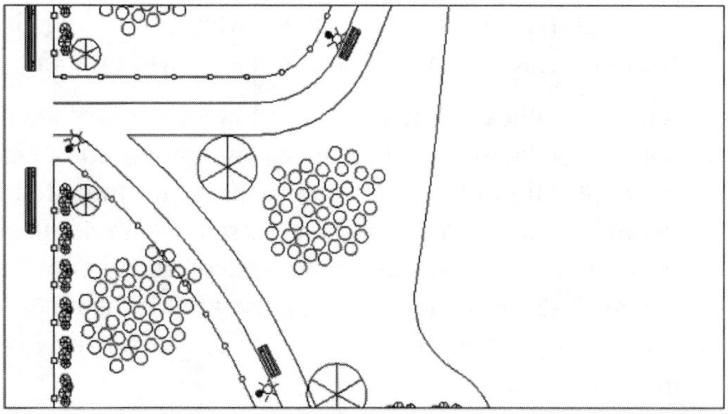

Figure 10.20

Shrubs, benches, and lights along the fence and path.

Using Blocks as Symbols

You use many common symbols that never vary in shape or size in drafting. In board drafting, you have many templates to create these symbols. In AutoCAD, you can use blocks for the same purpose. Blocks are much more versatile because you can scale the symbol, and because the amount of detail you can place in a block far exceeds what is possible when you use a template.

You might need to access these types of blocks from many different drawings. You can use two methods to make this possible—the WBLOCK command, discussed later in this chapter, and symbol libraries, discussed in Chapter 11, "Block Structure, Editing, Organization, and Management."

Using Versatile Unit Size Blocks

A very important and versatile type of block is the unit size block, which you use for symbols that always have the same geometry, but vary in size and proportion. The unit size block is more versatile than the use of drafting templates, because one block can be used to represent many symbols or parts. If the only differences between many symbols are their sizes or proportions, one unit size block is all that is needed.

The applications of unit size blocks are not as obvious as the applications of blocks you use as symbols. Many situations occur in drafting in which symbols vary only in size and proportion. For instance, in structural drafting the basic geometry for most steel shapes is similar from one size to another—in mechanical drafting the geometry for fastener symbols is also consistent from one size to another. In architectural details, a 1×1 unit box with an X through it can be inserted at various scales to represent any piece of dimensioned lumber.

A unit size block is drawn to a 1 unit by 1 unit size, then inserted with appropriate X and Y scale factors to adjust its size and proportions. Figures 10.21 and 10.22 show the application of two unit size symbols for threaded holes. In figure 10.21, the symbols are drawn at a 1 unit by 1 unit scale—the circular view uses a major diameter of 1 unit, and the side view uses a major diameter of 1 unit and a depth of 1 unit. Figure 10.22 shows how you can insert this same block to create various threaded hole symbols simply by using the hole dimensions as X and Y scale factors when you insert the block.

Figure 10.21

Threaded hole symbols drawn at a 1 × 1 scale.

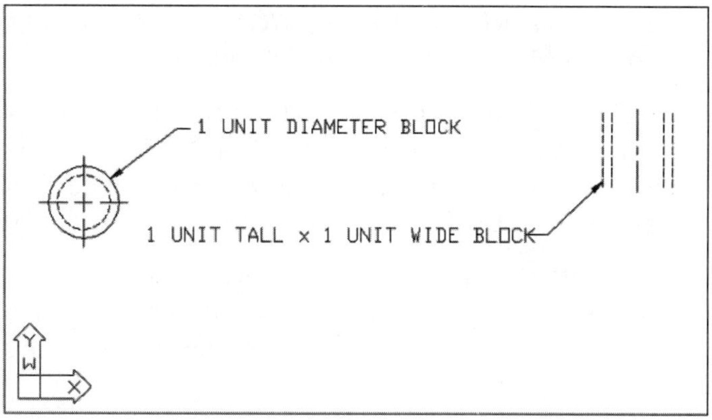

Figure 10.22

Threaded hole symbols inserted with various X and Y values.

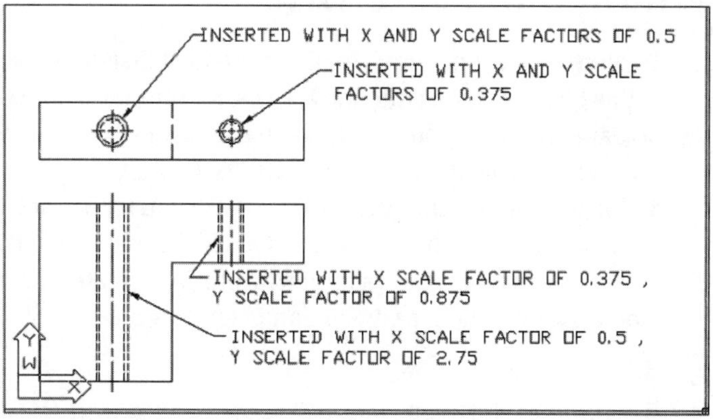

Storing Blocks with the WBLOCK Command

You have seen the way the BLOCK command enables you to make and use symbols repeatedly in a drawing. If this were the extent of its capabilities, the only advantage it would have over the COPY command would be a reduced file size. The main purpose of the WBLOCK command is to enable you to reuse the same block from one drawing to another.

When you create a block, AutoCAD adds information that describes that block to a portion of the drawing file known as the *block table*. Because AutoCAD stores this information in the drawing file, you can access it only from within the drawing in which the information is stored. You use the WBLOCK command to write a separate drawing file (a file that has the DWG extension) that contains the block information to disk, which enables access of the block information from any drawing.

When using the Insert dialog box to place a file created with WBLOCK into a drawing, you use the File button instead of the Block button. This opens the Select Drawing File dialog box, where you specify the directory and file name to insert. Or, if the file is on the search path, you simply can enter its name in the box next to the File button.

The WBLOCK command has more uses than writing a block to disk. You also can create the disk file by using a selection set to define the objects that make up the WBLOCK, instead of supplying an existing block name to send to disk.

Writing a Block to Disk

To write an existing block to disk, you must first define a block as described earlier in this chapter, then issue the WBLOCK command. The Create Drawing File dialog box appears, and you supply the name with which you want to store the drawing. After you supply the name, choose OK in the Create Drawing File dialog box. The dialog box closes, and AutoCAD prompts you for a block name. You can specify the name of a block you have defined, or you can type = if the block name is the same as the drawing name you supplied. AutoCAD creates a drawing file that contains the block you specified, and you can insert this file as a block in any other drawing.

NOTE

When you write a block to disk, the block's insertion point becomes the origin of the drawing file created.

Suppose you have decided to use the SHRUBS block and the EVERGREEN block in another drawing. In the following exercise, you write the blocks to disk files using the WBLOCK command and the EXPORT command. After writing the blocks, you start a new drawing and use the DDINSERT command to insert the files.

WRITING A BLOCK TO DISK

Continue from the preceding exercise, or create a new drawing again named CHAP10B using the drawing PARK from the accompanying CD as a prototype, and thaw layers EXER_2, EXER_3, EXER_4, EXER_5, EXER_6, and EXER_7.

Zoom to the view shown in figure 10.23.

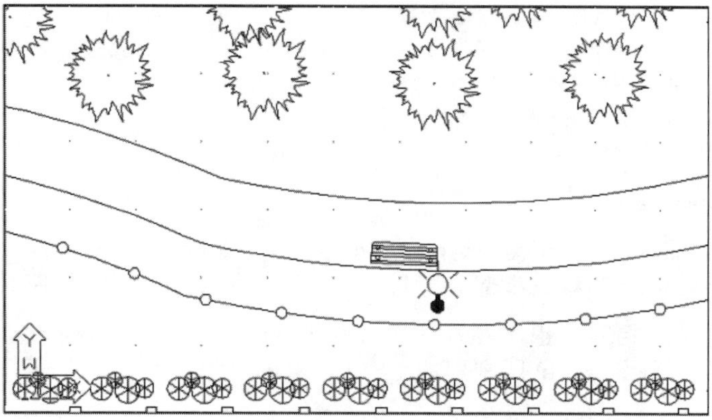

Figure 10.23

A zoomed view showing EVERGREEN and SHRUBS blocks.

`Command:` **WBLOCK** ↵	Starts the WBLOCK command and opens the Create Drawing File dialog box
Select IAW\DWGS *in the* Directories *list box*	Specifies the directory in which to store the SHRUBS file
In the File Name *edit box, type* **SHRUBS**, *then choose* OK	Specifies the file name to create
`Block name: =` ↵	Specifies that the block name is the same as the file name and writes the file

Next, to create a file of the EVERGREEN block, you use the File menu's Export option. Because a DOS file name can consist of no more than eight characters, you must give the file a shorter name than the block.

`Command:` *Choose* File, Export	Issues the EXPORT command and opens the Export Data dialog box (see fig. 10.24)

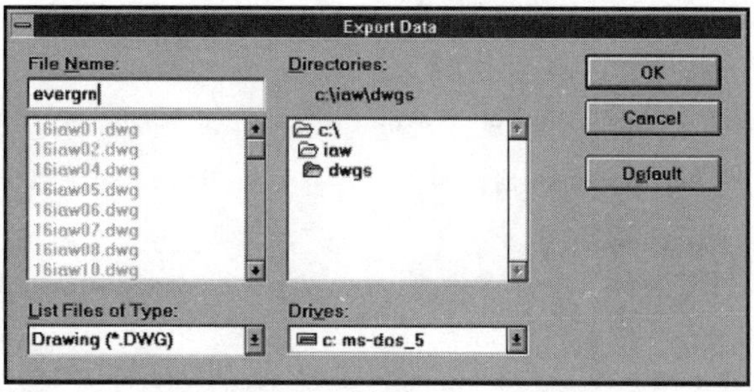

Figure 10.24

The Export dialog box.

Select \IAW\DWGS *in the* Directories *list box, select* Drawing(*.DWG) *in the* List Files of Type *list box, type* **EVERGRN** *in the* File Name *edit box, then choose* OK	Specifies the path, file type, and name, and closes the dialog box
`Command: export`	
`File name: C:\IAW\DWGS\EVERGRN.DWG` `Block name:` **EVERGREEN** ↵	Specifies an existing block name and writes the EVERGRN.DWG file to disk

The files have been created. You do not need to save your changes; this will not delete the SHRUBS and EVERGRN files you just created.

Begin a new drawing named CHAP10C, using PROTOC as a prototype drawing from the IAW Disk.

`Command:` *Choose Insert Block (Draw, Block)*	Issues the DDINSERT command and opens the Insert dialog box
Type **EVERGRN** *in the box next to the* File *button, then choose* OK	Specifies file name and exits dialog box
`Insertion point:` *Drag the block and pick at* 35',25'	Specifies location
`X scale factor <1> / Corner / XYZ:` ↵	Accepts the default X scale factor
`Y scale factor (default=X):` ↵	Accepts the default Y scale factor
`Rotation angle <0>:` ↵	Accepts the default rotation angle
`Command:` ↵	Repeats the DDINSERT command
Type **SHRUBS** *in the* File *input box, then choose* OK	
`Insertion point:` *Drag the block and pick at* 35',20'	
`X scale factor <1> / Corner / XYZ:`	Accepts the default X scale factor
`Y scale factor (default=X):` ↵	Accepts the default Y scale factor
`Rotation angle <0>:` ↵	Accepts the default rotation angle and inserts the block

Repeat the DDINSERT command and choose the Block button of the Insert dialog box. You can see the block SHRUB and EVERGRN added to the current drawing, and you can now place it anywhere in the drawing without having to reload the files. Their block definitions now are a part of the drawing CHAP10C. Cancel the Insert dialog box. You do not need to save this drawing.

Writing a Selection Set to Disk

If you have drawn a symbol that you know you will need to write to disk using WBLOCK, you do not need to use the BLOCK command to define the block first. Instead, when the WBLOCK command prompts for a block name, press Enter. When no block name is supplied, AutoCAD enables you to define the block within the WBLOCK command. AutoCAD first prompts for an insertion point, then asks you to select the objects that comprise the block—exactly the same prompts AutoCAD issues when you use the BLOCK command.

As when you use the BLOCK command, when you use WBLOCK in this way, the objects you select are erased from the display. You can use OOPS or U (UNDO 1) to restore these objects to the screen. Using U deletes a block definition created using the BLOCK command, but does not affect a drawing file created using the WBLOCK command.

Writing an Entire File with WBLOCK* to Disk

Often as you create a drawing, you create many named items. Named items include blocks, dimension styles, layers, linetypes, and text styles. You can end up with many more named items than you need, depending on how you create the drawing. You might, for instance, use a prototype drawing with preset layers, linetypes, dimension styles, and text styles. If you complete the drawing and fail to use any one or more of these named items, they are saved along with the drawing file anyway. You can use the PURGE command to selectively delete the definitions of unused blocks and other named items. A simple way to remove *all* unused named items, thus decreasing the file size, is to issue the WBLOCK command and use the asterisk (*) as a block name.

If you respond to the WBLOCK `Block name:` prompt with an asterisk, it writes most of the entire current drawing to a disk file. AutoCAD does not write any unreferenced table definitions, such as unused blocks, text styles, layers, or linetypes. AutoCAD does write drawing-environment settings for UCSs, views, and viewport configurations, however.

TIP

Like the PURGE command, WBLOCK* often is used to remove unused blocks, layers, linetypes, and text styles. If you use WBLOCK* with the same file name as the current drawing, AutoCAD asks you if you want to replace it. If you answer Yes, AutoCAD saves the current drawing without any unused blocks, layers, and so on. Then simply quit the current drawing. This trick is commonly called a wblock star. Use it with care—unlike PURGE, it does not prompt before deleting definitions.

Placing a Drawing File into a Drawing

Beyond placing blocks into a drawing, occasions arise in which you might want to place an entire drawing into another drawing. You might have a standard detail, such as a wall section, for example, that applies to many drawings. AutoCAD provides several ways in which you can perform such an action.

NOTE

AutoCAD provides a command that enables you to visually attach one drawing file to another without merging their data. This is the XREF command, discussed in Chapter 12, "Using Xrefs for Efficiency and Sharing Data." However, this command differs from the methods shown in this chapter, as the attached xref does not save the inserted objects as part of the current drawing file.

Using DDINSERT To Place a File into a Drawing

In an earlier exercise, you used the Insert dialog box DDINSERT command to place a file into a drawing. In that exercise, the file used had been created using the WBLOCK command. However, you can place any drawing file on disk into your drawing using the same method. Simply choose the File button in the Insert dialog box, then select the path and drawing file name. When inserting a drawing file into a drawing as a block, the origin point of the file (0,0) is used as an insertion base point of the block.

TIP

If the file is on the AutoCAD support file search path, you need only enter the file name in the input box next to the File button in the Insert dialog box and AutoCAD will find the file. You also can enter a path and file name in the File input box if you want.

Using INSERT To Place a File into a Drawing

The INSERT command provides another way to insert a drawing file into the current drawing. You can specify the file name to insert at the command's `Block name (or ?):` prompt, or select the file from the Select Drawing File dialog box.

When you use the INSERT command, AutoCAD first prompts you for a block name to insert. When you supply a block name to the INSERT command, AutoCAD first searches the current drawing's block table for the name you specify. If AutoCAD does not find the block there, it then searches the current directory. If it still doesn't find a match, AutoCAD finally searches through the path defined by the Preferences dialog box and stored in your ACAD.INI file. You also can enter a drawing file name with its path, such as "\drawings\details\wallsect", in response to the block name prompt.

An alternative to typing the name of the file to insert is to enter the tilde character (~) at the block name prompt, which causes AutoCAD to display the Select Drawing File dialog box, in which you can select the directory and drawing file name from lists.

In the following exercise, you use the DDINSERT command and the INSERT command to place a drawing file into a drawing.

USING DDINSERT AND INSERT TO PLACE A DRAWING FILE INTO THE CURRENT DRAWING

Begin a new drawing named CHAP10D using the PROTOD file from the accompanying CD as a prototype drawing.

`Command:` *Choose Insert Block (Draw, Block)*	Issues the DDINSERT command and opens the Insert dialog box
`Command: _ddinsert` Initializing... DDINSERT loaded	
Choose the File *button*	Opens the Select Drawing File dialog box
Set the Directories *list to* IAW\DWGS, *select* KEYBOARD *from the* File Name *list, then choose* OK	Specifies the file and closes the Select Drawing File dialog box
Choose OK	Closes Insert dialog box and prompts for insertion
`Insertion point:` **1,1** ↵	Specifies insertion point ① in figure 10.25

`X scale factor <1> / Corner / XYZ:` ↵	Accepts the default X scale factor
`Y scale factor (default=X):` ↵	Accepts the default Y scale factor
`Rotation angle <0>:` ↵	Accepts the default rotation angle

Next, you use the INSERT command and the tilde (~) option to insert another file.

`Command:` **INSERT** ↵	Starts the INSERT command
`Block name (or ?) <KEYBOARD>: ~` ↵	Opens the Select Drawing File dialog box
Select the PHONE *file in the* IAW\DWGS *directory, then choose* OK	Specifies the file to insert, then closes the dialog box
`Insertion point:` **1,1** ↵	Specifies insertion point
`X scale factor <1> / Corner / XYZ:` ↵	Accepts the default X scale factor
`Y scale factor (default=X):` ↵	Accepts the default Y scale factor
`Rotation angle <0>:` ↵	Accepts the default rotation angle

To demonstrate that the drawing files are inserted as blocks, perform a simple edit operation on the phone.

`Command:` *Select the phone, then choose Move (Modify, Move)*	Issues the MOVE command with the phone selected
`1 found`	
`Base point or displacement:` **-5,-1** ↵	Specifies displacement
`Second point of displacement:` ↵	Accepts displacement and moves phone block

The completed drawing should look like figure 10.25.

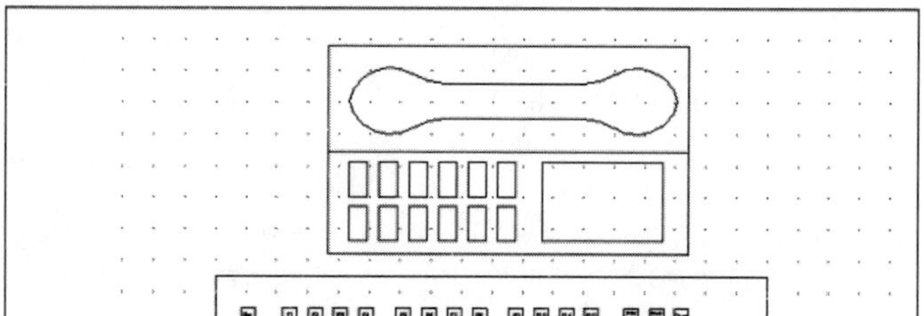

Figure 10.25

The completed drawing CHAP10D.

The KEYBOARD and PHONE blocks were inserted with their insertion base points set by the 0,0 origin in their DWG files. As you saw in the exercise, these insertion base points were not well coordinated and required moving the PHONE after insertion. A good common practice is to define the insertion base point at the lower left corner of an object, or at a center line or center point. Another common practice for aligning multiple blocks is to coordinate their insertion base points so that the blocks properly align when all are inserted at the same point.

Using Windows Drag-and-Drop to Place a File into a Drawing

Another method for inserting one drawing file in another is to use the Windows drag-and-drop feature. You can use the Windows File Manager or Explorer to get parts from another directory to insert into your drawing. You can also use these applications to help find a lost file, and then drag it into your current drawing.

From the AutoCAD `Command:` prompt, you activate the Windows File Manager and size it so that AutoCAD is still partially visible. Use the File Manager to select the drive and directory that holds the drawing file you want. You can use the By File Type feature in the View menu to limit the file display to DWG files. Click on the file name you want to insert and drag the file icon out of the File Manager window and into the AutoCAD window. AutoCAD issues the INSERT command, using the file name you have selected, and then issues the INSERT command's normal prompts and options.

Using the BASE Command

When you create Idrawing files that you might use later as blocks, you need an easy way to control their insertion-base points. The BASE command sets the INSBASE system variable, which establishes the insertion-base point for a drawing file. (Setting INSBASE directly has the same effect as using BASE.)

The *base point* is an insertion handle, like the insertion-base point on a regular block. (It is not an object or visible point.) If you make a drawing, store it on disk, and later insert it in another drawing, the insertion-base point (INSBASE) defaults to 0,0,0 unless you specify a base point with the BASE command. If you use WBLOCK to create a drawing the insertion-base point you specify becomes the INSBASE value for the resulting drawing file.

The BASE command has only one prompt: `Base point:`. You may specify the new insertion base point for a drawing by absolute coordinate entry or by picking a point on the drawing.

Automating Annotation with Attributes

Many types of information besides the graphical objects themselves are associated with a drawing. When you place symbols on a drawing, you often need to use textual information to provide specific information about that symbol. A window or door symbol on a floor plan contains a callout that refers it to a schedule in which more detailed information is provided. An electronic component on a schematic also would contain a reference designator to key it to a parts list.

In AutoCAD, you can assign attributes to any block to provide extra information about that item. Attributes are like paper tags attached to merchandise with a string. They can contain all kinds of information about the item to which they are tied: the item's manufacturer, model number, materials, price, stock number, and so on. The information stored in the attribute is the attribute's *value*. Usually, you attach attributes to a symbol by selecting the attributes along with the objects that make up the symbol when you use the BLOCK command. You also can make a block that contains nothing but attributes.

Attributes originally were designed as a means of assigning information to blocks and exporting that information to generate reports. Attributes also are extremely useful as a means of automating and controlling text that appears in a drawing in the title blocks, schedules, and other items, even if you never need to export the text as data. Attributes can be used to predefine the text location, style, or even its content. They can be used to prompt the drafter for the text and can offer defaults.

The remainder of this chapter deals with methods you can use to create and insert attribute information. The process of editing attributes is covered in Chapter 11.

Creating Block Attributes

You can use the ATTDEF or DDATTDEF commands to create block attributes. In this chapter, you use the DDATTDEF command to create some simple attributes.

The DDATTDEF command can be accessed from the Define Attribute tool on the Attribute toolbar, as shown in figure 10.26.

Figure 10.26

The Define Attribute tool on the Attribute flyout.

Issuing the DDATTDEF command, opens the Attribute Definition dialog box (see fig. 10.27). This dialog box has several sections: Mode, Attribute, Insertion Point, and Text Options.

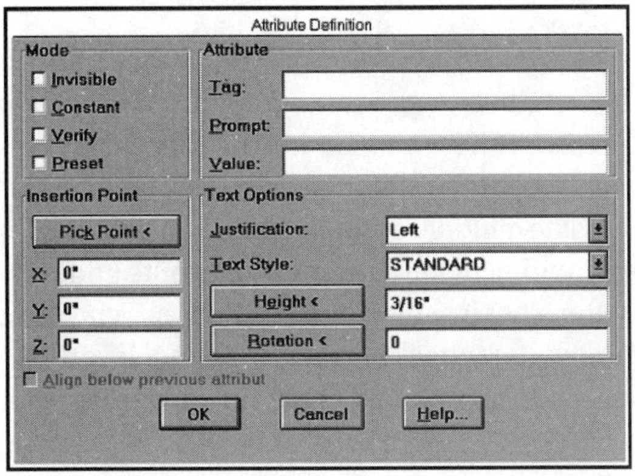

Figure 10.27

The Attribute Definition dialog box.

The Mode section of the dialog box enables you to create invisible attributes (the Invisible check box). Remember that attributes are text attached to a symbol—so why would you want invisible text? You can attach much information to a block that does not belong on the drawing, such as cost, catalog number, supplier, and so on. By attaching this information to the block, you can later extract the invisible (and visible) attributes to generate reports.

In the Attribute area, you define a name for the attribute (the Tag edit box), enter the prompt AutoCAD displays when inserting the attribute (the Prompt edit box), and optionally create default attribute text (the Value edit box). The following list describes each setting.

- **Tag.** Tag is a descriptive name for the attribute. It does not appear on the drawing after you insert the attribute, but it is needed for attribute data extraction. The tag name cannot have spaces; you need to use a hyphen or an underscore if you want to use a space, such as ITEM_COST. All attributes must have a tag.

- **Prompt.** When you insert a block that has an attribute attached, AutoCAD prompts you for the information. You define the prompt you receive, such as ENTER COST OF ITEM, here. You can have spaces in the attribute prompt. If you do not define a prompt, AutoCAD uses the attribute tag as a prompt.
- **Value.** The attribute's value generally is supplied when you insert the block that contains the attribute. However, if the value is often the same, such as 1/4"=1' for a title block scale attribute, you can specify for AutoCAD to use this as a default to save the time it takes to type the attribute's value. Supplying a default value is optional.

The Insertion Point section of the dialog box enables you to define an insertion point for the attribute text, just as you must define an insertion point when you use the TEXT or DTEXT command. You can supply absolute coordinate values, or, by clicking on the Pick Point button, you can select the insertion point on-screen. When you create multiple attributes, you can use the Align below previous attribute check box to automatically line up one attribute under another. When you select this check box, the other Insertion Point options are grayed out. If you have not yet created any attributes, this check box is grayed out. If you do not specify the insertion point for an attribute, it is placed at the drawing origin.

WARNING

Although you can create an attribute tag and an attribute prompt of up to 256 characters each, the Enter Attributes dialog box (described later in this chapter) can only display tags and prompts of 24 characters or less, so you should try to keep tags and prompts within this range.

When you use the TEXT or DTEXT commands to place text on a drawing, you specify the text style, height, rotation angle, and justification. The Text Options section of the Attribute Definition dialog box enables you to make the same settings for the attributes you create. If you select a text style that has a predefined height or rotation angle, these buttons are grayed out.

In the following exercise, you use DDATTDEF to create some attributes for a title block. First you define an attribute for the drafter's name in the title block.

USING DDATTDEF TO CREATE ATTRIBUTES

Begin a new drawing named CHAP10E, using the drawing ATTITLE from the accompanying CD as a prototype.

`Command:` *Choose* Tools, Toolbars, Attribute	Displays the Attribute toolbar
`Command:` *Choose Define Attribute (Attribute, Define Attribute)*	Issues DDATTDEF command and opens the Define Attribute dialog box
`Command: _ddattdef`	
`Initializing...  DDATTDEF loaded.`	
Enter **DRAFTER** *in the* Tag *edit box, enter* **Drawn By** *in the* Prompt *edit box, and enter your name in the* Value *edit box*	Specifies the tag, prompt, and default (value) text
Choose the Height *button in the Text Options section of the dialog box*	Returns to the drawing for height specifications
`Height:` **.125** ↵	Specifies the text height and returns to the dialog box
In the Insertion Point *section, choose the* Pick Point *button*	Returns to drawing for point
`Start point:` *Pick* ① (see fig. 10.28)	Specifies start point of text and returns to dialog box

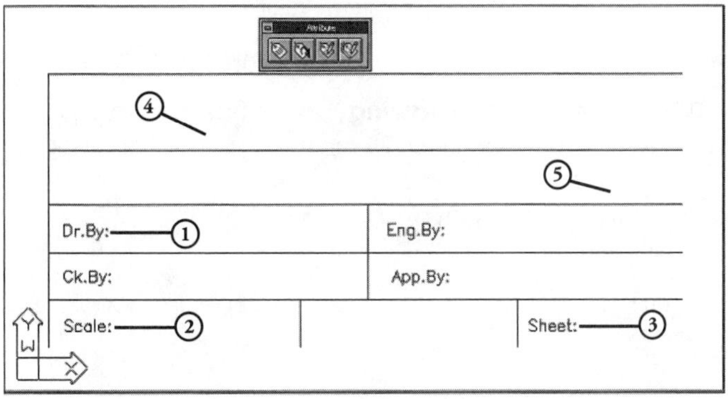

Figure 10.28

View of title block drawing, showing pick points for the "Using DDATTDEF To Create Attributes" exercises.

Choose OK	Closes dialog box and inserts the attribute's tag at the start point

Next, create an attribute for the drawing scale. Note that no prompt or default value need be defined.

`Command:` ↵	Repeats the DDATTDEF command and opens the Attribute Definition dialog box
Type **SCALE** *in the* Tag box, *then choose* Pick Point	Specifies tag and prompts for location
`Start point:` *Pick* ②	Specifies location and returns to dialog box
Choose OK	Closes dialog box and inserts tag at start point
`Command:` ↵	Repeats the last command

`_DDATTDEF`

Next, create an attribute for the drawing sheet number.

`Command:` ↵	Repeats the DDATTDEF command
Type **SHEET** *in the* Tag box *and* **Sheet Number** *in the* Prompt box, *then choose* Pick Point	Specifies the tag and prompt, then prompts for location
`Start point:` *Pick* ③	Specifies location and returns to dialog box
Choose OK	Closes dialog box and inserts tag at start point

Next, create an attribute for the drawing title.

`Command:` ↵	Repeats the DDATTDEF command
Type **TITLE** *in the* Tag box, **Drawing Name** *in the* Prompt box, *and* **.25** *in the* Height box, *then select* Fit *text from the* Justification *list box and choose* Pick Point	Specifies tag, prompt, height, and text justification, then prompts for location
`Start point:` *Pick* ④	Specifies location and returns to dialog box
Choose OK	Closes dialog box
`First text line point:` *Pick* ④	Closes dialog box and prompts for justification points
`Second text line point:` *Pick* ⑤	Specifies Fit width and inserts tag

Command: **BASE** ↵	Starts the BASE command
Base point <0.0000,0.0000,0.0000>: *Pick ① (see fig. 10.29)*	Specifies insertion base point

Save the drawing.

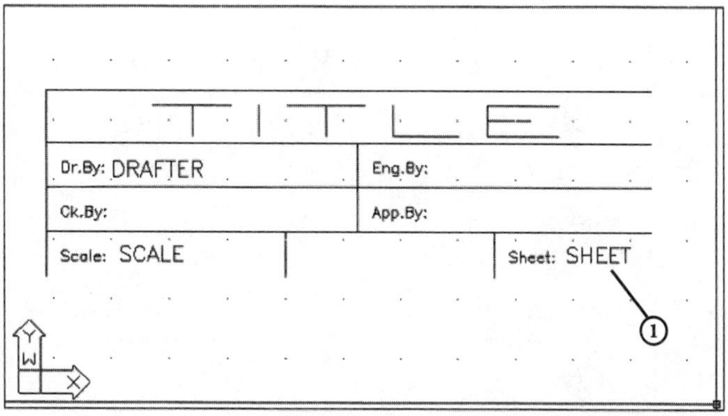

Figure 10.29

Title block with attribute tags, showing pick point for the "Using DDATTDEF to Create Attributes" exercises.

You do not need to use either the BLOCK or WBLOCK command to be able to use the title block with attributes in other drawings. You can set the insertion base point with the BASE command, then save the drawing and later insert it in any drawing.

Inserting Blocks with Attributes

After you attach an attribute to a block or define one in a drawing, you simply insert the block or drawing in any of the methods described earlier in this chapter. When you insert a block or drawing that contains (or consists entirely of) attributes, AutoCAD prompts you for the information for the attribute. Then you define the attribute's value. You can supply the necessary information in a dialog box or at the `Command:` prompt.

You use the system variable ATTDIA to control whether AutoCAD displays the attribute prompts from the command line or in a dialog box. ATTDIA is set to 0 by default, which specifies for AutoCAD to prompt from the command line. Type **ATTDIA** and set its value to 1 to tell AutoCAD to issue the attribute prompts in a dialog box. Remember, you used DDATTDEF to assign the attribute prompt when you created the attribute.

In the following exercise, you use DDINSERT to insert the file you created in the previous exercise. You insert the file twice: once with ATTDIA at its default setting of 0, and once after you set ATTDIA to 1. Before you insert the title block, create a border on which to place it by drawing a 16-by-10-inch border with the RECTANG command, in which to place it.

Inserting a Block with Attributes

Begin a new drawing named CHAP10F, using the file IAW-MECH from the accompanying CD as a prototype, and set the layer TITLE current.

`Command:` *Choose* Data, Drawing Limits *and enter limits of* **0,0** *to* **17,11**	Issues LIMITS command and specifies new limits for a B-size sheet
`Command:` *Choose Rectangle (Draw, Rectangle) and draw a rectangle from* .5,.5 *to* 16.5,10.5	Issues the RECTANG command and draws rectangular border
`Command:` *Choose Zoom All (Standard, Zoom All)*	Zooms to new limits
`Command:` *Choose Insert (Draw, Insert)*	Issues the DDINSERT command and opens the Insert dialog box
Choose the File *button, then select the file CHAP10E*	Specifies a file from the Insert dialog box to insert as a block
Choose OK *twice*	Closes both dialog boxes and prompts for location
`Insertion point:` *Pick* ① *(see fig. 10.30)*	Specifies insertion point of block
`X scale factor <1> / Corner / XYZ:` ↵	Accepts the default X scale factor

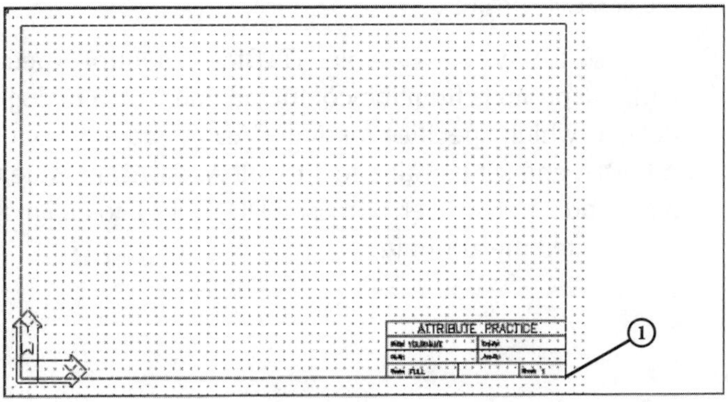

Figure 10.30

Inserted title block and attribute values, showing pick point for "Inserting a Block with Attribute" exercises.

`Y scale factor (default=X):` ↵	Accepts the default Y scale factor
`Rotation angle <0>:` ↵	Accepts the default rotation angle
`Enter attribute values`	
`Drawn By <Your name here>:` **YOURNAME** ↵	Specifies value for the DRAFTER attribute
`SCALE:` **FULL** ↵	Specifies value for the SCALE attribute
`Sheet number:` **1** ↵	Specifies value for the SHEET attribute
`Drawing name:` **ATTRIBUTE PRACTICE** ↵	Specifies value for the TITLE attribute

After you enter the last attribute value, the block is inserted with the attribute values in place of the attribute tags.

Next, erase the block you just inserted and place it again by using the Enter Attributes dialog box (ATTDIA set to 1).

`Command:` *Select the title block, then choose Erase (Modify, Erase)*	Erases the title block
`Command:` **ATTDIA** ↵	Accesses the ATTDIA system variable
`New value for ATTDIA <0>:` **1** ↵	Changes the system variable setting
`Command:` *Choose Insert (Draw, Insert)*	Issues the DDINSERT command and opens Insert dialog box
Choose OK	Closes dialog box and prompts for location (it defaults to insert the last block, TTLBLOCK)
`Insertion point:` *Pick* ① (refer to figure 10.30)	Specifies insertion point of block
`X scale factor <1> / Corner / XYZ:` ↵	Accepts the default X scale factor
`Y scale factor (default=X):` ↵	Accepts the default Y scale factor
`Rotation angle <0>:` ↵	Accepts the default rotation angle and opens the Enter Attributes dialog box
Fill in the attribute value edit boxes as shown in figure 10.31, then choose OK	Specifies attribute values and inserts title block

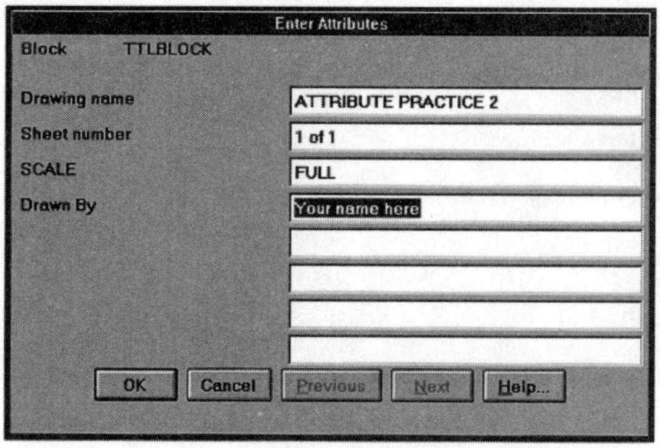

Figure 10.31

The values for the Enter Attributes dialog box.

Save the drawing.

NOTE

The order of attributes in the prompts or dialog box depends on the order of creation or selection. If you want the attributes in a specific order, select them in that particular order when creating the block definition. Selection by window makes the order unpredictable. If you create attribute definitions in a drawing which you later insert as a block, the order in which you are prompted for them is the order in which they were selected.

Using Attributes for Data Storage and Extraction

Attributes are great for automating and controlling text, and for minor data applications. They also can be used for applications that require significant data storage and extraction, but we recommend that you use AutoCAD's SQL (Structured Query Language) features (see the AutoCAD User's Guide) for those applications.

You can print extracted attribute data as lists or use the data in other programs, such as database, spreadsheet, and word processing programs. You also can put the data into a table and bring it back into your drawing as an mtext object.

Planning and Inserting Attribute Data

When you plan for attributes, lay out the data in a simple table. For example, the drawing shown in figure 10.32 lists the name, type of phone, and extension number for each employee. Similar kinds of tables form the basis for bills of materials (BOM) lists, schedules, and specifications that regularly accompany professional drawings.

After planning the data, you define attributes and create a block or place the attributes in a drawing file for insertion in other drawings, using the techniques covered in the previous exercises. The accompanying CD drawing named PHN-BLK contains attribute definitions for employee name, type of phone, and extension number. In the following exercise, you insert this block and enter attribute data.

Inserting Blocks with Attribute Data

Begin a new drawing named CHAP10G, using the OFFICE drawing from the accompanying CD as a prototype. Zoom to the view shown in figure 10.32, then copy and mirror the furniture in the lower left cubicle to match the figure. Create a new layer named PHONES and set it current.

`Command:` *Choose Insert Block (Draw, Block), enter* **PHN-BLK** *in the* File *edit box, then choose* OK	Opens the Insert dialog box, specifies the block, and closes the dialog box
`Insertion point:` *Pick ① (refer to fig. 10.32), then press Enter three times to accept default scale and rotation*	Inserts phone and opens Enter Attribute dialog box (because ATTDIA was on in *rom* OFFICE prototype drawing)

Enter **Sam Smith** for the name, **Reception** for the type, and **586** for the extension, then choose OK to complete the DDINSERT command and attribute entry.

Repeat for name **Tonya White**, type **Desk**, and extension **486**.

Repeat for name **Susan Driscoll**, type **Desk**, and extension **386**.

Repeat for name **Harriet Sands**, type **Desk**, and extension **286**.

Save the drawing.

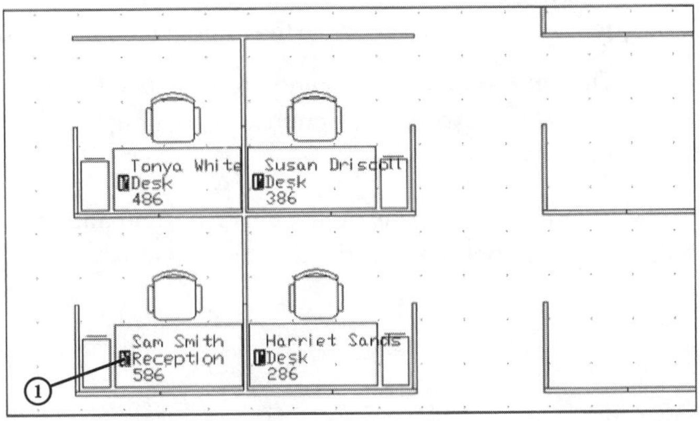

Figure 10.32

Office with attribute data phone books inserted.

Using ATTEXT and DDATTEXT Commands To Extract Data

Although the ATTEXT command sounds like a text operation, it stands for ATTribute EXTraction. ATTEXT provides a way to extract attribute information from the drawing file and use that information in a text report.

The ATTEXT command is provided for compatibility with previous versions of AutoCAD and for programming access to attribute extraction. It has no advantage over the DDATTEXT command, which is easier to use. DDATTEXT performs the same function with the Attribute Extraction dialog box. DDATTEXT is used in this chapter.

ATTEXT and DDATTEXT (Attribute Extraction Dialog Box) Options

The functions and options of the DDATTEXT (Attribute Extraction dialog box) commands are described in the following list.

- **Comma Delimited File (CDF).** Specifies the format for the extracted data file.
- **Space Delimited File (SDF).** Specifies the format for the extracted data file.
- **Drawing Interchange File (DXF).** Specifies the format for the extracted data file.
- **Select Objects.** This button closes the dialog box, prompts for object selection to extract data from specific blocks, and reopens the dialog box upon completion of object selection.
- **Template File.** This button and text box specifies the name and path of the template file. If you choose the button, it opens the Template File dialog box.
- **Output File.** This button and text box specifies the name and path of the data file to create. If you choose the button, it opens the Output File dialog box.

The prompts and options of the ATTEXT command are similar to the DDATTEXT functions and options described in the previous list.

WARNING

The output file overwrites existing files of the same name without warning you.

Examining ATTEXT Formats

AutoCAD provides three ways to extract attribute values from a drawing file and format them in a disk file. The following attribute extraction formats are templates that define the way the data is formatted in the extracted text file:

- **CDF (Comma Delimited Format).** CDF is easy to use with BASIC programs or with dBASE's "APPEND FROM . . . DELIMITED" operation.
- **SDF (Standard Data Format).** SDF is for FORTRAN and other programs that read a dBASE "COPY . . . SDF" file, or a dBASE "APPEND FROM . . . SDF" operation.
- **DXF (Drawing Interchange Format).** DXF is a subset of AutoCAD's full DXF file format that is used by many third-party programs.

You can extract data in any format suitable for your application. Many users (and vendors of third-party software) now have applications built around AutoCAD by using one or more of these data extraction interfaces.

Extracting Attribute Data Using CDF or SDF

CDF creates a file that has commas separating the data fields in the attribute extraction. The following is a simple example of a CDF format:

```
'Name1','Type1','Extension1'
'Name2','Type2','Extension2'
...
...
...
'Name9','Type9','Extension9'
'Name10','Type10','Extension10'
```

To format extract files, you need to place alphanumeric characters, commas, and spaces. In the CDF format, each data field is separated by a comma. The spacing of the data field is dependent on the data width in the field. `Name10` in the preceding example takes up more room than `Name9`.

The SDF format creates a file similar to CDF, but without commas and with a standard field length and spacing, as shown in the following list:

```
Name1     Type1     Extension1
Name2     Type2     Extension2
...  ...  ...
...  ...  ...
Name9     Type9     Extension9
Name10    Type10    Extension10
```

In SDF format, the data field length is standardized and preformatted to a standard value, regardless of the data value length. If the data exceeds the length, the data is truncated.

Creating an Attribute Report Template File

Before you can extract attributes AutoCAD needs a template file to create the SDF or CDF file. The *template file* is a format instruction list that tells AutoCAD what to put where in the extract data file. The accompanying CD contains a template file called PHONE.TXT. This file provides an SDF template for the telephone data that you added to the office plan in the previous exercise. You use this file to create a report file.

The PHONE.TXT file was created as an ASCII text file. You can create similar files by using the Windows Notepad utility. Use spaces, not tabs. Make sure you end the last line of your file with a return character (↵). Also, make sure you do not have any extra spaces at the end of lines, or extra returns after the last line of text.

Table 10.1 shows the PHONE.TXT template file for your sample telephone data. The template outputs NAME first, TYPE second, and EXTENSION third.

Table 10.1
Viewing an SDF Template File

Data Code	*Format Code*
BL:NAME	C011000
BL:X	N006002
DUMMY1	C002000
BL:Y	N006002

Data Code	*Format Code*
DUMMY2	C002000
NAME	C015000
TYPE	C010000
EXTENSION	N005000

If you look at the right column, you can easily decipher the formatting information. The first C or N says this is a character or a number. The next three digits (`011` in the `BL:NAME` line) tell the number of spaces to leave for the data. The final three digits specify the number of decimal places for floating point (decimal) numeric data. Integer data have 000 in the last three columns.

The `BL:X` and `BL:Y` are not blocks or attributes. They extract the X,Y coordinate values for the block.

`DUMMY1` and `DUMMY2` are not blocks or attributes; they are "dummy" codes used to provide space in the report. These dummy lines force a two-space blank between the X,Y coordinates (BL:X,BL:Y) and a two-space blank between the Y coordinate and the NAME, making the output easier to read.

NOTE

If you get a `** Field overflow in record nn` message from the ATTEXT or DDATTEXT commands, it means that the data for one of the fields in line nn of the output file contains too many characters.

Table 10.2 shows the complete list of the kinds of data that ATTEXT or DDATTEXT can extract.

Table 10.2

ATTEXT Template Fields

Field Data Type	*Data Type*	*Description*	*Field*
BL:LEVEL decimal	integer	Block nesting level	BL:XSCALE

continues

Table 10.2, ***CONTINUED***

ATTEXT Template Fields

Field Data Type	*Data Type*	*Description*	*Field*
BL:NAME decimal	character	Block name	BL:YSCALE
BL:X decimal	decimal	X insert coord	BL:ZSCALE
BL:Y decimal	decimal	Y insert coord	BL:XEXTRUDE
BL:Z decimal	decimal	Z insert coord	BL:YEXTRUDE
BL:NUMBER decimal	integer	Block counter	BL:ZEXTRUDE
BL:HANDLE integer	character	Object handle	*attribute*
BL:LAYER character	character	Insertion layer	*attribute*
BL:ORIENT	decimal	Rotation angle	

Integer fields are formatted Nwww000, floating point (decimal) fields are Nwwwddd, and character fields are Cwww000, in which www is overall width (such as 012 for 12 characters wide and 000 is 0) and ddd is the width to the right of the decimal point.

Extracting the Data File

After you have the template file, you can extract data for all or some of the attributes. If you have the PHONE.TXT file, switch to AutoCAD. Extract the attribute data into a file called PHN-DATA.

USING DDATTEXT TO CREATE AN SDF DATA FILE

`Command:` **DDATTEXT** ↵	Opens the Attribute Extraction dialog box
`Initializing... DDATTEXT loaded.`	
Choose Space Delimited File (SDF)	Specifies a space-delimited format
In the Template File *edit box, enter* **PHONE**	Specifies the template to use

Leave the default, the drawing name, and TXT extension, in the Output File edit box.

Choose OK	Closes the dialog box and creates the file on disk
`4 records in extract file.`	

If you choose Select Objects, AutoCAD closes the dialog box, prompts for object selection to extract data from specific blocks, and reopens the dialog box upon completion of object selection.

NOTE

Do not use the same name for your template file as that of your extract file, or the extract file overwrites the template.

The extracted SDF report file in the IAW\DWGS directory, CHAP10F.TXT, is shown in the following list. You can examine the file by using the Windows Notepad. Take a look at your data text file.

SDF Report Example

```
PHN-BLK    646.00  384.00  Tonya White    Desk        486
PHN-BLK    646.00  288.00  Sam Smith      Reception   586
PHN-BLK    722.00  384.00  Susan Driscoll Desk        386
PHN-BLK    722.00  288.00  Harriet Sands  Desk        286
```

Notice that the extracted data gives useful spatial information about this drawing as well as the attribute data. The X and Y data fields give the X and Y insertion points of each PHONE block. Your X,Y fields can vary from the ones shown here, depending on where you insert the blocks. The PHONE column is set up to print the name of the block that acts as the attribute data source. The PHONE column has character data (see the C in the template) and an 11-character print width.

The next two columns give the X and Y locations of the block insertion point in numeric form (see N in the template). (Your data can vary from the example.) The X and Y data have two decimal places and the decimal point in a six-character print width. The X and Y fields and the employee name would all run together if the two-character dummy fields were not included. The other extracted attribute fields (a character field and a numeric field) are in the last two columns. If an employee's name is unusually long, you can see that the name would be truncated by the print width.

This chapter has dealt with various methods of creating and using blocks and attributes. You've seen the advantages of using blocks for standard parts and symbols, and probably can identify several applications for blocks and attributes in your particular field. Before creating blocks for your application, however, there are several aspects of block storage and block properties that need to be addressed.

The following chapter describes the block considerations you need to know before creating blocks for your application. The relationship of blocks to layer, linetype, and color properties is thoroughly explored. Different approaches to block storage are compared and contrasted, and strategies for managing your blocks are suggested. Advanced techniques for editing block references in your drawing are also covered. These techniques can be used to make your work with blocks much more flexible and efficient.

chapter

11

Block Structure, Editing, Organization, and Management

Chapter 10 illustrated several advantages of using blocks for recurring elements in your drawing, such as improved speed and uniformity of drawing symbols. Along with these advantages, blocks can represent a large reduction in drawing file size, which frees valuable disk space and leaves more memory free for AutoCAD to load its program modules. In this chapter, you explore specifically how AutoCAD stores this block information.

This chapter identifies the powerful methods AutoCAD provides for editing block references in your drawing, as well as the limitations imposed. This includes editing individual elements of a single block reference as well as simultaneously changing all occurrences of a block reference in your drawing.

A large number of standard symbols are used in many drafting disciplines, thus you might need to create a large number of blocks. You learn some specific methods for storing and organizing your blocks, either as individual drawing files or in a special drawing file called a block library.

You learn about some special considerations when creating and editing block references; for instance, how blocks and layers relate to each other, the uses of and differences between EXPLODE and XPLODE, and the use of nested blocks.

Understanding Block Storage and Structure

You learned in Chapter 10 that using blocks can significantly reduce file size, which uses less disk space and less of AutoCAD's memory when loading the file. This section describes just how using blocks reduces file size. This section also describes a technique known as nesting blocks, which is very efficient if a block contains redundant features within itself. Nested blocks also can be useful for certain editing operations.

One of the biggest problems AutoCAD users encounter when working with blocks is the way blocks and layers interact. A thorough understanding of the relationships between blocks and layers can save you quite a bit of frustration and expand the usefulness of your blocks.

Block Storage

The AutoCAD drawing file contains a section known as the block table. In the block table, AutoCAD stores the information it needs to display the objects that comprise each unique block reference in your drawing, which is why the objects disappear when you create a block—the information needed to display the objects has been moved to the block table. When you insert a file into your drawing, the block table again is used to store all the object information for the file.

Because this information is stored, all AutoCAD needs to store in the drawing file when you insert a block reference is the block's name, insertion point, scale factors, and rotation angle. This tells AutoCAD where and how to display that particular block reference.

Because the information describing a block's objects is stored in the block table, you can insert the block more than once in the drawing, and the information needed to display the objects doesn't need to be duplicated in the drawing file; this can represent a significant reduction in file size, especially if you have a complex block with multiple occurrences in the drawing. The only thing you actually are adding to the drawing is the insertion information. Copying a block reference has the same effect as multiple insertions—all you actually are copying is the insertion information.

TIP

If you are going to reuse a group of objects a number of times in a drawing, it might be more efficient to make a block of them rather than copying them as a group.

Nested Blocks

A block can be made up of other blocks, a technique called *nesting*. You can place a block inside a block inside a block. AutoCAD does not place a limit on the number of block-nesting levels, although editing nested blocks can be confusing if you go more than a few levels deep.

When using the BLOCK command, you are prompted to select the objects that make up the block. If any of the objects you select are blocks themselves, you create a nested block. You can use standard editing commands with nested blocks, such as ARRAY, COPY, and MOVE, just as you use them with normal block references.

Nested blocks further increase the efficiency and control of blocks. In figure 11.1, the chair is a nested block, and the outer TABLE block needs to contain the table itself and six block references, rather than all the objects that make up each chair. Another advantage to nesting the TABLE block is that the CHAIR block can be redefined (changed) easily and independently of the TABLE block definition. Redefining blocks is covered later in this chapter in the section "Redefining a Block."

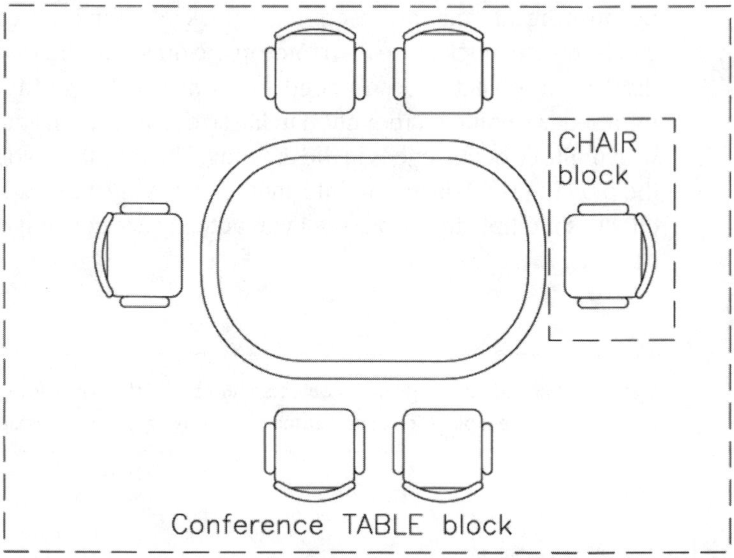

Figure 11.1

An example of a nested block.

WORKING WITH NESTED BLOCKS

Begin a new drawing named CHAP11A, using the file NESTED from the accompanying CD as a prototype.

`Command:` *Choose Block (Draw, Block)*	Issues the BLOCK command
`Block name (or ?):` **WORKSTATION** ↵	Names the block
`Insertion base point:` *Pick ① (see fig 11.1)*	Defines the block's insertion point

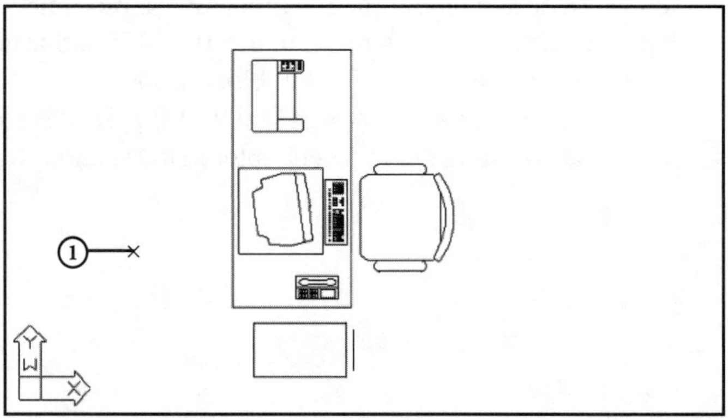

Figure 11.2

The workstation, showing the pick point.

`Select objects:` **ALL** ↵	Selects all objects in the drawing
`8 found`	
`Select objects:` ↵	Ends object selection
`Command:` *Choose Insert Block (Draw, Block)*	
Choose Block *and select* WORKSTATION *from the list of blocks, then choose* OK *twice*	Selects the block and starts the insertion process
`Insertion point:` *Pick some point near the middle of the drawing window*	Specifies insertion point
`X scale factor <1> / Corner / XYZ:` ↵	Accepts the default X scale factor
`Y scale factor (default=X):` ↵	Accepts the default Y scale factor
`Rotation angle <0>:` ↵	Accepts the default rotation angle

Now reposition the block reference with the MOVE command to see how AutoCAD performs editing commands on block references.

`Command: Choose Move (Modify, Move)`	Issues the MOVE command
`Command: _move`	
`Select objects:` **L** ↵	Selects the last object drawn
`1 found`	
`Select objects:` ↵	Ends object selection
`Base point of displacement:` **2'<30** ↵	Specifies displacement
`Second point of displacement:` ↵	Specifies distance to move with relative coordinates

That's all there is to creating a nested block: simply select block references as the objects that make up a block. Any combination of objects and block references can be used for block creation.

Save this drawing for use in an exercise later in this chapter.

Blocks, Layers, and Linetypes

AutoCAD keeps track of much more than the geometry of an object drawn on-screen. As you know, each object has certain properties, such as color, linetype, and layer, which provide very useful and even necessary features, but if unconsidered when creating blocks, they can provide unexpected results.

When a block is created, the objects' properties of color, linetype, and layer are stored with the objects' data in the block definition. If the block is inserted in another drawing, these properties go along with it.

For example, take a block created from objects drawn on layer PART and with color and linetype set to BYLAYER (the default setting for these properties). If layer PART was defined as having blue phantom lines, the block table not only defines the objects, but also specifies these objects are drawn with blue phantom lines on a layer named PART. If you insert this block in a drawing that does not have this layer, AutoCAD automatically creates the layer for the block reference objects to reside on.

Taking the example one step further, what if you inserted the block in a drawing that *does* have a layer named PART, but the layer has different properties—such as yellow continuous lines? In this case, the block would not create a new layer, and the drawing's layer settings would override the block's settings. In other words, your block reference would end up with yellow continuous lines.

As you can see, the inner workings of blocks and their properties can become rather confusing. To understand these issues more clearly, look at the three methods of defining an object's linetype and color, and see how they relate to block insertions. These three methods are BYLAYER, BYBLOCK, and explicit settings given with the LINETYPE and COLOR commands. Another method of controlling a block's color and linetype is called the LAYER 0 block. Layer 0 blocks are covered in the section "Special Properties of Layer 0 Blocks."

Using BYLAYER with Blocks

The default setting for color and linetypes properties is BYLAYER, which simply means the color and linetype of any object drawn is defined by the settings of the layer on which it resides. If you create a block of objects drawn on a specific layer, the color and linetype of that layer stay with the block, regardless of the layer on which it is inserted. This often is the desired effect. If you create a block of a tree using green continuous lines, you probably don't want to insert the tree and have it turn red with phantom lines.

For example, you could create a block of objects whose properties are set to BYLAYER, and the objects reside on layer RED, which is defined as having a linetype setting of continuous lines and a color setting of red. Regardless of the settings of the layer on which this block is inserted, it keeps red continuous lines. If it is inserted in a drawing that does not have a congruous layer named RED, AutoCAD creates one and assigns the continuous linetype and red color to it.

One result of inserting blocks with BYLAYER properties can be rather confusing. If you insert the block on a layer named BLUE with a color setting of BLUE and a linetype setting of HIDDEN, the block reference still appears red and has continuous lines, but if you select it with the DDCHPROP command, AutoCAD reports that the block reference is blue and has a hidden linetype! What's more, if you turn off the layer BLUE, the block reference is still displayed, even though it was inserted on layer BLUE.

The block reference is still displayed because AutoCAD places the insertion point of the block reference on the layer BLUE, but the actual objects are still on whatever layer they were on when you created the block. The seemingly erroneous report from the DDCHPROP command is reporting the layer, color, and linetype of the block reference, not the block objects. For the objects not to be displayed, you would have to turn off the layer RED. Freezing the layer BLUE also causes the objects not to be displayed.

NOTE

A block created from objects residing on layer 0 with the BYLAYER property settings does not behave as described in this section. The special case of layer 0 blocks is discussed later in this chapter.

See a later section of this chapter, "Using the EXPLODE Command," for special considerations when exploding blocks with BYLAYER properties.

If all this seems confusing, then you're on the right track. The following exercise helps clear things up by demonstrating the principles of blocks with BYLAYER properties.

BLOCKS WITH BYLAYER PROPERTIES

Begin a new drawing named CHAP11B, using the drawing BYLAYER from the accompanying CD as a prototype.

This drawing contains a symbol for an evergreen tree, drawn with a polyline. The polyline was drawn on the layer EVERGREEN, with its color and linetype properties set to BYLAYER, as shown in figure 11.3. You can verify this with the DDCHPROP command.

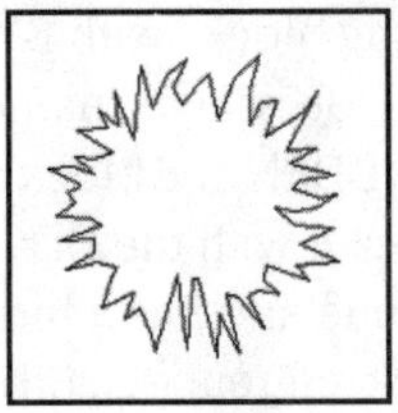

Figure 11.3

The symbol for an evergreen tree.

`Command:` *Choose Properties (Object Properties)*	Beginsobjectselection
`Select Objects:` **L** ↵	Selects the last object in the drawing
`Select Objects:` ↵	Ends object selection and issues the DDMODIFY command

You can see in the Change Properties dialog box that the color and linetype for the evergreen symbol are set to BYLAYER. Choose OK to exit the dialog box.

`Command:` *Choose Block (Draw, Block)*	Issues the BLOCK command
`Block name (or ?):` **EVERGREEN** ↵	Defines the block name
`Insertion base point:` *Pick a point near the middle of the evergreen symbol*	Sets the insertion point of the block
`Select objects:` **P** ↵	Reselects the previous selection set
`Select objects:` ↵	Ends object selection, erases the object, and creates the new block definition

Click on the Layer Control drop-down list and set layer EVERBLUE current. Verify the color and linetype settings for this layer with the 'DDLMODES command.

`Command:` *Choose Layers (Object Properties)*	Issues the 'DDLMODES command

You can see in the Layer Control dialog box that the current layer (EVERBLUE) has its color property set to blue and its linetype property set to hidden. Now see what happens when you place the EVERGREEN block on this layer.

`Command:` *Choose* OK	Ends 'DDLMODES
`Command:` *Choose Insert Block (Draw, Block)*	
`Command: ddinsert` *Choose* Block *and select* EVERGREEN *from the list of blocks, then choose OK twice*	Selects the block and starts the insertion process

`Insertion point:` *Pick a point near the middle of the drawing window*	Specifies the block insertion point
`X scale factor <1> / Corner / XYZ:` ↵	Accepts the default X scale factor
`Y scale factor (default=X):` ↵	Accepts the default Y scale factor
`Rotation angle <0>:` ↵	Accepts the default rotation angle

You can see that even though you inserted the block reference on a layer with blue hidden lines, it has retained its original green continuous lines. Now see what information AutoCAD gives you about this block reference with the DDMODIFY command.

`Command:` *Choose Properties (Object Properties)*	Begins object selection
`Select Objects:` **L** ↵	Selects the last object in the drawing
`Select Objects:` ↵	Ends object selection and issues the DDMODIFY command

Note that AutoCAD says the block reference for EVERGREEN is blue and resides on the layer EVERBLUE. Sure looks green to me! Remember, AutoCAD is showing you the properties of the block reference, not its objects. The objects actually are on layer EVERGREEN, where they resided when you created them.

`Command:` *Choose* OK	Ends DDMODIFY

Now, look at how layer settings will affect this block. From the Layer Control drop-down list, turn off layer EVERBLUE and set layer 0 current. Note that even though the layer the block reference resides on is turned off, the objects that make up the block are still displayed.

Now turn off the layer EVERGREEN from the Layer Control drop-down list. The objects that make up the block disappear. Turn back on all the layers to redisplay the block.

Next, from the Layer Control drop-down list, freeze layer EVERBLUE. Again, the block disappears. Finally, thaw layer EVERBLUE and freeze layer EVERGREEN. The block is still frozen.

To summarize, if you want to suppress the display of a block reference with BYLAYER properties, you can either freeze or turn off the layer(s) on which the objects were created or freeze the layer they were inserted on.

From the Layer Control drop-down list turn on and thaw all layers, then save this drawing.

Using BYBLOCK with Blocks

You can also create blocks from objects with color and linetype properties defined as BYBLOCK. These blocks' properties behave quite differently than blocks with BYLAYER properties. You will be glad to know their behavior is much simpler.

WARNING

Remember that the default settings for object color and linetype properties is BYLAYER. If you want to create a block with BYBLOCK properties, you must define the objects' properties as BYBLOCK before creating the block. This can be done with the DDCHPROP, DDMODIFY, CHPROP, or CHANGE commands if the objects have already been drawn, or by setting the color and linetype to BYBLOCK with the COLOR and LINETYPE commands before drawing the objects.

If a block is created from objects whose color and linetype properties are set to BYBLOCK, the objects have no established color or linetype until they are inserted. They are displayed white with a continuous linetype. Upon insertion, they assume the color and linetype current in the host drawing, making these blocks act as sort of chameleon blocks, assuming whatever color and linetype is set for the environment in which they are placed, whether these properties were set by layer settings or explicitly with the COLOR and LINETYPE commands. The layer on which the objects were drawn still stays with the block reference, just as it did for the BYLAYER blocks.

See the section of this chapter titled "Using the EXPLODE Command" for special considerations when exploding block references with BYBLOCK properties.

In the following exercise, you will explore the methods of creating blocks with BYBLOCK properties.

BLOCKS WITH BYBLOCK PROPERTIES

Begin a new drawing named CHAP11C, using the :drawing BYBLOCK from the accompanying CD as a prototype.

Figure 11.4 shows a hexhead bolt symbol as it was drawn on the OBJECT layer with its linetype property set to BYLAYER.

Before making a block of the bolt head, change its color and linetype setting to BYBLOCK.

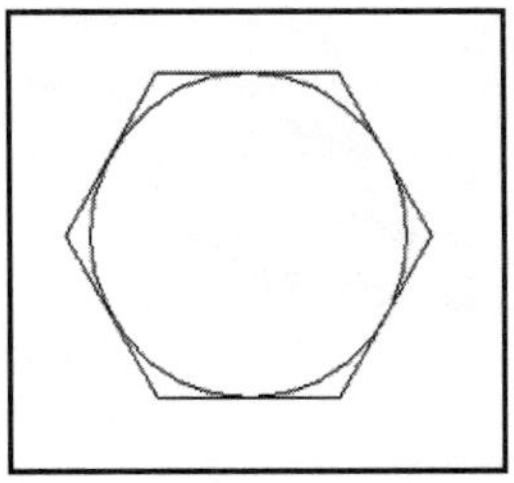

Figure 11.4

The symbol for a hexhead bolt.

`Command:` *Choose Properties (Object Properties)*	Begins object selection
`Select objects:` **All** ↵	
`Select objects:` ↵	Ends object selection and issues 'DDCHPROP

In the Change Properties dialog box, choose the Color button. In the Select Color dialog box, choose BYBLOCK. Choose OK to exit the Select Color dialog box. Now from the Change Properties dialog box, choose the Linetype button and select BYBLOCK from the list box in the Select Linetype dialog box. Choose OK to exit the Select Linetype dialog box and choose OK again to exit the Change Properties dialog box.

`Command:` *Choose Block (Draw, Block)*	Issues the BLOCK command
`Block name (or ?):` **HEXBOLT** ↵	Names the block
`Insertion base point:` *Using the CENter object snap, select the circle*	Selects the insertion point of the block
`Select objects:` **P** ↵	Reselects the previous selection set
`Select objects:` ↵	Ends object selection and creates the block
`Command:` *From the Layer Control drop-down list, choose* HIDDEN	Sets layer HIDDEN current
`Command:` *Choose Insert Block (Draw, Block)*	Issues the DDINSERT command
`Command:` *Choose* Block *and select* HEXBOLT *from the list of blocks, then choose* OK *twice*	Selects the block and starts the insertion process
`Insertion point:` *Pick a point near the center of the drawing window*	Sets the insertion point of the block
`X scale factor <1> / Corner / XYZ:` ↵	Accepts the default X scale factor

`Y scale factor (default=X):` ↵	Accepts the default Y scale factor
`Rotation angle <0>:` ↵	Accepts the default rotation angle

As you see, the block reference takes on the color and linetype of the layer on which it was inserted. Now see what properties AutoCAD reports for the block reference with the DDMODIFY command.

`Command:` *Choose Properties (Object Properties)*	Begins object selection
`Select Objects:` **L** ↵	Selects the last object in the drawing
`Select Objects:` ↵	Ends object selection and issues the DDMODIFY command

The block reference's color and linetype properties have been changed to BYLAYER because that was the color and linetype setting when the block was inserted.

Choose Cancel	Closes dialog box

Next you can see what happens when you insert a block with BYBLOCK properties when the color and linetype have been set explicitly.

`Command:` *Choose Color Control (Object Properties)*	Issues the DDCOLOR command
`Command:` *Choose the color red from the Standard Colors area and choose* OK	Sets the current object color to red (1)
`Command:` *Choose Linetype Control (Object Properties) and select the Center linetype*	Sets the current object linetype to center
`Command:` *Choose Insert Block (Draw, block)*	Issues the DDINSERT command
`Command:` *Choose* Block *and select* HEXBOLT *from the list of blocks, then choose* OK *twice*	Selects the block and starts the insertion process
`Insertion point:` *Pick a point to the right of the last block reference you placed*	Sets the insertion point of the block
`X scale factor <1> / Corner / XYZ:` ↵	Accepts the default X scale factor
`Y scale factor (default=X):` ↵	Accepts the default Y scale factor
`Rotation angle <0>:` ↵	Accepts the default rotation angle

This time the block reference was inserted to the current specifications of color red and linetype center, even though it is still on the layer HIDDEN. See what AutoCAD reports for this block reference's properties.

`Command:` *Choose Properties (Object Properties)*	Begins object selection
`Select Objects:` **L** ↵	Selects the last object in the drawing
`Select Objects:` ↵	Ends object selection and issues the DDMODIFY command

The block reference's color and linetype properties have been changed to RED and CENTER because these were the color and linetype settings when the block was inserted. Figure 11.5 shows the two inserted block references of the block created with BYBLOCK properties.

`Command:` *Choose* OK	Ends DDMODIFY

Save your drawing.

Figure 11.5

Inserts of block created with BYBLOCK properties.

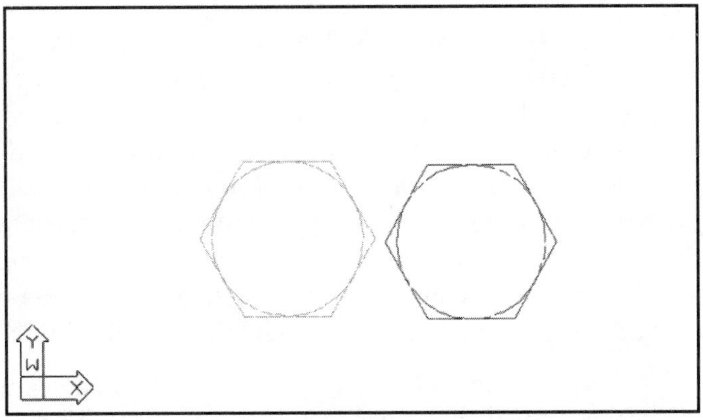

Using COLOR and LINETYPE with Blocks

You can create a block that always has the same color and linetype properties, regardless of the property settings in effect when the block is inserted. To do this, explicitly assign these properties to the objects before making a block of them.

Assignment is easily done by one of two methods. You can use the COLOR and LINETYPE commands to set explicit properties before drawing the objects, or you can use DDCHPROP, DDMODIFY, CHPROP, or CHANGE commands to reset these properties if the objects are already drawn.

Special Properties of Layer 0 Blocks

For general-purpose symbols, you might find that creating and blocking all objects on Layer 0 is the most efficient and least confusing method. Block objects created this way "float" to the layer current at the time of their insertion, meaning that the block reference's objects and its insertion point will always reside on the same layer. If you work with different layer schemes from one drawing to another, this can simplify block standardization.

Layer 0 blocks with properties set to either BYLAYER or BYBLOCK assume the color and linetype of whatever layer they are inserted on. If the objects in a Layer 0 block were created with an explicit color or linetype setting, these settings are preserved.

See a later section of this chapter, "Using the EXPLODE Command," for special considerations when exploding block references with Layer 0 objects.

Editing Blocks

In the first exercise of this chapter, you moved a chair block reference and saw that it moved as a single object. Block references perform similarly when controlled by several editing commands, including COPY, MIRROR, and ROTATE. There are, however, certain editing functions that cannot be performed on block references because of the nature of blocks. If you try to TRIM or EXTEND a block reference, for example, AutoCAD has no way of describing this action in the block table, so it cannot enable you to use these commands on a block reference. Other editing functions that cannot be performed on block references include the OFFSET, STRETCH, BREAK, CHAMFER, FILLET, and LENGTHEN commands.

To edit individual objects within a block reference, the EXPLODE and XPLODE commands enable you to turn a block reference back into the original objects used to create it. After a block reference has been exploded, it is stored as individual objects in the drawing file and no longer can be edited as a unit without first using the BLOCK command to redefine it as a block. Block attributes also can be edited in many ways, using the DDEDIT, ATTEDIT, and DDATTE commands.

By far the most powerful aspects of block editing are the block substitution and block redefinition features. With these techniques, you automatically can change all occurrences of a block reference within a drawing simultaneously. These techniques have many applications that increase your productivity.

Editing a Block's Component Objects

When a block is placed in a drawing, AutoCAD treats it as a single object. If you try to select any part of the block reference for an edit command, such as ERASE or COPY, the entire block reference is selected. This can be very handy if you want to edit the entire block reference. If you want to edit any of the block reference's individual components, however, you must return the block reference to the original objects used to create it. This can be done with either the EXPLODE or the XPLODE commands.

If you know you will need to edit a block reference's individual components, you can insert the block as component objects, using either the Explode check box in the Insert dialog box or using a feature known as INSERT*.

Using the EXPLODE Command

The EXPLODE command is a simple command to use—it has no options; you are simply prompted to select the objects to explode. Exploding a block reference returns the block reference back into its original objects.

When exploded, blocked objects created from BYLAYER objects return to their original layer and its property settings. Block objects created from BYBLOCK objects return to their original layer and retain their BYBLOCK color and linetype settings, but they are displayed as white objects of continuous linetype because they have no block to define these settings. Layer 0 blocks return to layer 0 with their original color and linetype settings.

When a nested block is exploded, it is broken down to the component blocks used to create it, not to its original objects. These component blocks then can be exploded to their original objects, providing they are not also nested blocks.

WARNING

If you explode a block with attributes, any assigned attribute values are lost. The attribute definition is retained and the attribute tag is displayed.

When all block references are exploded, they are stored as separate objects and are defined in the block table. The PURGE command, covered later in this chapter, should be used to remove these unneeded block definitions.

Using the XPLODE Command

When a block reference is exploded with the EXPLODE command, its component objects revert to their original property settings. If this is not what you want them to do, you might want to use XPLODE instead. The XPLODE command enables you to explode the block and to specify what layer, color, and linetype you want the component objects to be given.

The XPLODE command provides more control over exploding block references than EXPLODE does, letting you specify in many ways how the component objects shall be displayed once exploded. To provide this kind of control, XPLODE has a number of options that overcome the limitations of EXPLODE but add a lot of complexity to the task of exploding a block reference.

If you select more than one block reference at the XPLODE command's `Select objects:` prompt, you will be asked if you want to explode the objects individually or globally. If you explode individually, you can define different properties for each block reference selected. AutoCAD highlights the block reference currently being exploded while it prompts you for the object properties of its components. If you choose to explode globally, the properties you specify are applied to all block references selected. If you only select one block reference to explode, this prompt does not appear.

After specifying whether to explode selected objects individually or globally, you are prompted for layer, color, and linetype information. The following list describes these prompts and their effects:

- **All.** Tells AutoCAD you want to change the layer, color, and linetype for the selected block reference. You will receive all the prompts described for the next three options in this list.
- **Color.** You can enter for this option the first letter of colors 1 through 7 or the number of any color. You can enter BYLayer or BYBlock.
- **LAyer.** You can type the name of any existing layer for the component objects to reside on.
- **LType.** You may set the linetype of the component objects to BYLAYER, BYBLOCK, CONTINUOUS, or to any linetype that has already been loaded.

- **Inherit from parent block.** If you have blocks that were created on layer 0 and have their color and linetype set to BYBLOCK, this option will change the layer, color, and linetype of these objects to match the properties of their block reference. This enables you to explode blocks with BYBLOCK objects and have them retain their appearance after being exploded.
- **Explode.** This option causes AutoCAD to explode the block in the same manner as it would with the EXPLODE command.

NOTE

In early releases of R13, the Inherit from parent block option of XPLODE does not work properly. The blocks are simply exploded without changing the layer, color, and linetype properties.

WARNING

The XPLODE command does not explode block references placed with the MINSERT command. It also cannot explode block references whose X, Y, and Z scale factors have unequal absolute values.

In the following exercise, you try both the EXPLODE and XPLODE commands.

USING EXPLODE AND XPLODE

Begin a new drawing named CHAP11D using the drawing EXPLODE from the accompanying CD as a prototype. This drawing has two blocks, each containing a number of nested blocks created from objects on layer 0, having BYLAYER linetype and color. The blocks were inserted on layer WORK-STATION.

First, you will explode the left workstation using the EXPLODE command.

`Command:` *Choose Explode (Modify, Explode)*	Issues the EXPLODE command
`Select Objects:` *Select the block at ① (see fig. 11.6) and press Enter*	Explodes the block

Figure 11.6

Workstation blocks to be exploded.

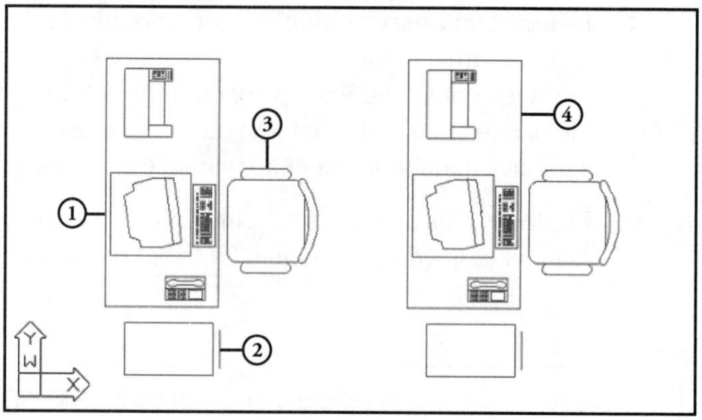

Notice that the objects that made up the block return to the layer, color, and linetype on which they were created. Verify this by looking at the object properties.

`Command:` *Choose Properties (Object Properties)*	Begins object selection
`Select Objects:` *Select the blocks at ② and ③ and press Enter*	Selects the objects and issues the DDCHPROP command

You can see how the objects that made up the block return to their original state. This may not always be desirable. In the next steps, you will use XPLODE to change the layer and color of block components.

`Command:` *Choose OK*	Ends the DDCHPROP command
`Command:` **XPLODE** ↵	Starts the XPLODE command
`Select objects to XPlode.` *Select the block at ④ and press Enter*	Selects the second block to explode
`All/Color/LAyer/LType/Inherit from parent block/<Explode>:` **A** ↵	States the All option
`New color for exploded objects. Red/Yellow/Green/Cyan/Blue/Magenta/ White/BYLayer/BYBlock <BYLAYER>:` ↵	Accepts the default color for the component objects
`Enter new linetype name. <BYLAYER> :` ↵	Accepts the default linetype for the component objects
`XPlode onto what layer? <CENTERLINES_SHORT>:` **WORKSTATION** ↵	Specifies the layer for the component objects

```
Object exploded with color of Bylayer
linetype of BYLAYER, and layer
WORKSTATION.
```

Notice that this block exploded onto the current layer instead of onto the layer in which it was created. Also notice that you were able to separately set the color of the new objects. You can verify this by checking the properties of the new objects with DDCHPROP.

Save your drawing

Inserting Blocks as Component Objects

If you have foreseen that a block reference will need editing after its insertion, you can insert it as an exploded block reference. If a block is inserted as an exploded block reference, AutoCAD disables dragging, which means the block is invisible to you as you place it. AutoCAD also does not enable the insertion of an exploded block reference with different X, Y, and Z scale factors. The property settings of a block reference inserted this way are the same as they would be if you inserted and then used the EXPLODE command on a block reference.

There are two methods of inserting blocks as component objects. You can use the DDINSERT command and choose the Explode check box of the Insert dialog box. Alternatively, you can use the INSERT command and simply type an asterisk (*) in front of the block name. The following exercise demonstrates both of these options.

INSERTING BLOCKS AS COMPONENT OBJECTS

Begin a new drawing named CHAP11E using the drawing SLOTS from the accompanying CD as a prototype.

`Command:` *Choose Insert (Draw, Block)* Issues the DDINSERT command

Select the block SLOT to be inserted. Place an X in the Explode check box and remove the X from the Specify Parameters on Screen check box. Set the X insertion point to 7.125 and the Y insertion point to 3.625. Set the X scale to .5. (Note the Y and Z scales are grayed out.) Set the Rotation Angle to 90. The Insert dialog box should appear like the one in figure 11.7. Choose OK to complete the insertion process.

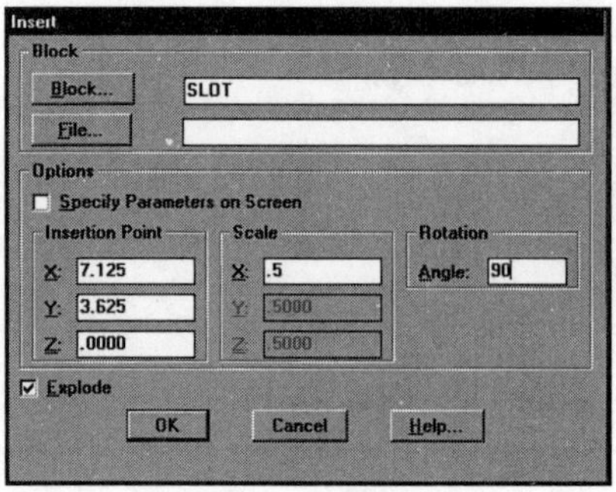

Figure 11.7

Settings for the Insert dialog box.

`Command:` **INSERT** ↵	Starts the INSERT command
`Block name (or ?) <SLOT>:` ***SLOT** ↵	Specifies the block to insert
`Insertion point:` **2.875,3.625** ↵	Specifies insertion point by coordinates
`Scale factor <1>:` **.5** ↵	Scales the insertion to half scale
`Rotation angle <0>:` ↵	Accepts the default rotation angle

The slots should be inserted and appear as they do in figure 11.8. Next, you see why you inserted them as component objects.

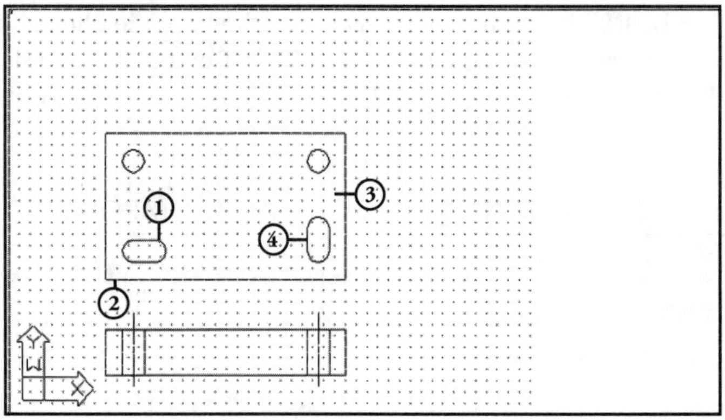

Figure 11.8

Pick points for STRETCH command.

`Command:` *Choose Stretch (Modify, Stretch)*	Issues the STRETCH command
`Select objects:` *Pick* ① *(refer to fig. 11.8)*	Selects right end of slot with a crossing box
`Other corner:` *Pick* ②	Selects the other corner of the crossing box

`Select objects:` ↵	
`Base point or displacement:` **.5<0** ↵	Sets the displacement for the stretch
`Second point of displacement:` *Press Enter*	Stretches the slot
`Command:` ↵	Repeats the last command
`Select objects:` *Pick* ③	Selects top of slot with a crossing box
`Other corner:` *Pick* ④	Selects the other corner of the crossing
`Select objects:` ↵	Ends object selection
`Base point or displacement:` **.5<90** ↵	Sets the displacement for the stretch
`Second point of displacement:` ↵	Completes the stretch

The slot you inserted was a 1-by-1 unit block—it was created with a 1-unit diameter and a center-to-center distance of 1 unit. By placing it as components with a .5 scale factor, you get a .5-wide slot that you can STRETCH to any desired length.

Editing Attribute Information

Rather than editing the component objects of block references, you might need to edit their attributes, which could be the result of design changes, insertion errors, or to position the attributes more appropriately for cosmetic reasons. In cases such as these, do not explode the block reference. Remember, exploding a block reference causes it to lose any attribute values you assigned when inserting the block.

There are only three commands with which to edit attributes, covered in the following section. The DDEDIT command can be used to edit text or attribute definitions. Note that it does not enable you to edit an attribute value, only its definition. It is useful only when creating attributes or after exploding a block reference with attributes.

The DDATTE command enables you to change an attribute value. After you select a block for attribute editing with this command, the Enter Attributes dialog box appears with the current values listed in the appropriate edit box. You simply make any changes needed in the edit box, then choose OK.

The ATTEDIT command gives you the most control over attributes, and has many options. Not only can you change an attribute's value, but you can change its position, text height, angle, text style, layer, and color.

Using DDEDIT To Change an Attribute Definition

If you make a mistake or change your mind about an attribute definition before you create a block of an attribute, it easily can be modified with the DDEDIT command, which also can be used to change the attribute definition of a block reference after it has been exploded.

All you need to do is select the attribute definition you want to change, and you are presented with a dialog box to make your changes. The following exercise demonstrates the use of DDEDIT.

MODIFYING AN ATTRIBUTE DEFINITION

Begin a new drawing named CHAP11F using the drawing TRANSIST from the accompanying CD as a prototype.

First, you will create a couple of attributes with the DDATTDEF command.

From the Tools menu, choose Toolbars, Attribute to display the Attribute toolbar in the drawing window.

`Command:` *Choose Define Attribute (Attribute, Define Attribute)* — Issues the DDATTDEF command

Type **Transistor_Number** *in the* Tag *box and* **Enter Transistor Number** *in the* Prompt *box; in the* Value *box, enter* **01**, *then select* Bottom Center *from the* Justification *drop-down list and choose* Pick Point — Specifies the tag, prompt, and justification, then prompts for the insertion point of the attribute

`Start point:` *Pick* ① (see fig. 11.9) — Selects insertion point for attribute text

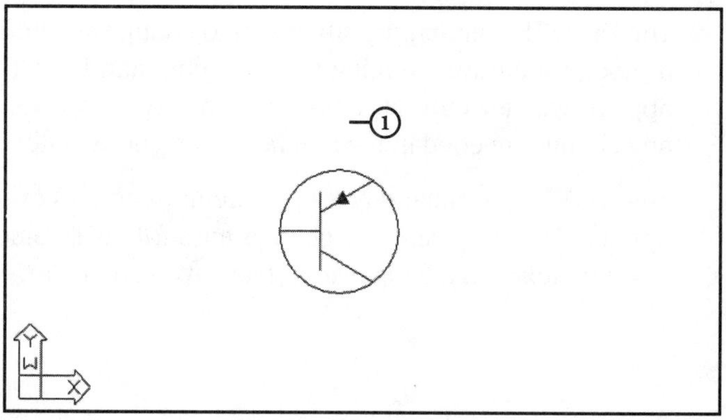

Figure 11.9

Pick point for DDEDIT exercise.

Choose OK

`Command:` ↵	Repeats the last command
Type **Part_Number** *in the* Tag *box and* **Enter Transistor Part Number** *in the* Prompt *box, then place a checkmark in the* `Align below previous attribute` *check box and press* OK	Specifies the tag, prompt, and placement of the attribute and inserts the attribute

Your drawing now should look like the one in figure 11.10.

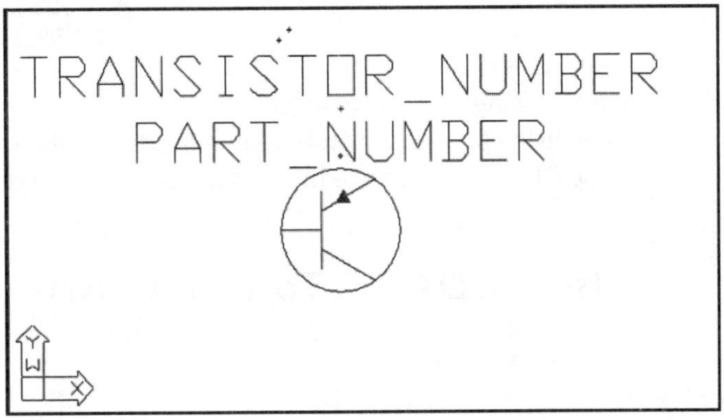

Figure 11.10

The transistor with attributes in place.

Suppose you decide on a better prompt for the TRANSISTOR_NUMBER attribute.

`Command:` *Choose Edit Text (Modify, Special Edit)*	Issues the DDEDIT command
`Command: _ddedit` `<Select a TEXT or ATTDEF object>/Undo:` *Select the TRANSISTOR_NUMBER attribute*	Specifies attribute definition to edit and displays the Edit Attribute Definition dialog box
Type **Enter Reference Designation** *in the Prompt box and choose* OK	Changes the attribute prompt
<Select a TEXT or ATTDEF object>/ Undo: ↵	Ends editing selection

Save this drawing for use in the next exercise.

Using DDATTE To Change an Attribute Value

The DDATTE command is used to change an attribute's value after the attribute has been placed. It cannot be used to change attribute values defined as constant. Upon selecting a block with attributes, the Edit Attribute dialog box is displayed to make changes. The Edit Attribute tool is shown in figure 11.11.

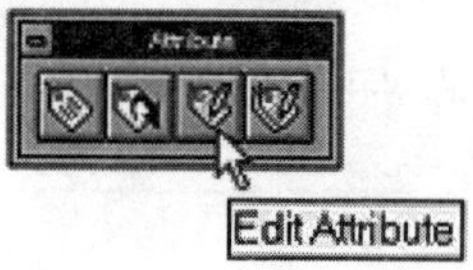

Figure 11.11

The Edit Attribute tool.

In the following exercise, you will create a block of the transistor and its attributes defined in the previous exercise. After inserting a block reference of this block, you will use DDATTE to change one of the values supplied on insertion.

USING DDATTE TO EDIT AN ATTRIBUTE VALUE AFTER INSERTION

Continue with the previous exercise.

To begin with, you must create a block containing the symbol and both of its attributes.

`Command:` *Choose Block (Draw, Block)*	Issues the BLOCK command
`Block name (or ?):` **TRANSISTOR** ↵	Names the block
`Insertion base point: _int of` *Use INTersection object snap to pick* ① (see fig. 11.12)	

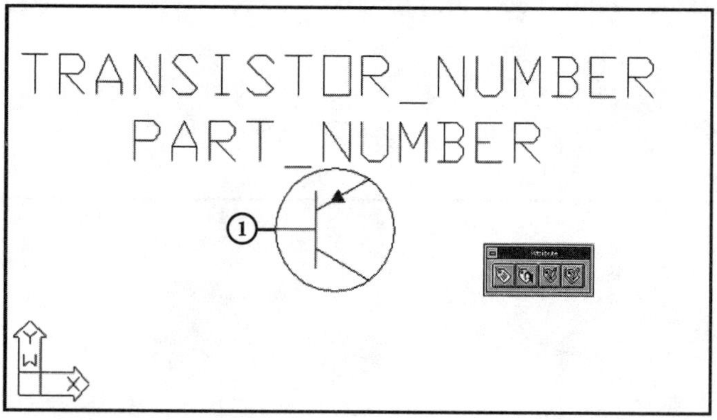

Figure 11.12

Pick points for the BLOCK command.

`Select objects:` ALL ↵	Selects all nonfrozen objects
`Select objects:` ↵	Ends object selection, erases objects, and creates new block definition
`Command:` *Choose Zoom All (Standard, Zoom All)*	Issues the ZOOM ALL command
`Command:` *From the Control Layer drop-down list, thaw layer* SIGNAL_PATH	Thaws the layer SIGNAL_PATH
`Command:` *Choose Insert Block (Draw, Block)*	Issues the DDINSERT command
Choose Block *and select* TRANSISTOR *from the list of blocks, then choose* OK *twice*	Selects the block and starts the insertion process
`Insertion point: _endp of` *Use ENDpoint object snap to pick* ① (see fig. 11.13)	Sets the insertion point for the block

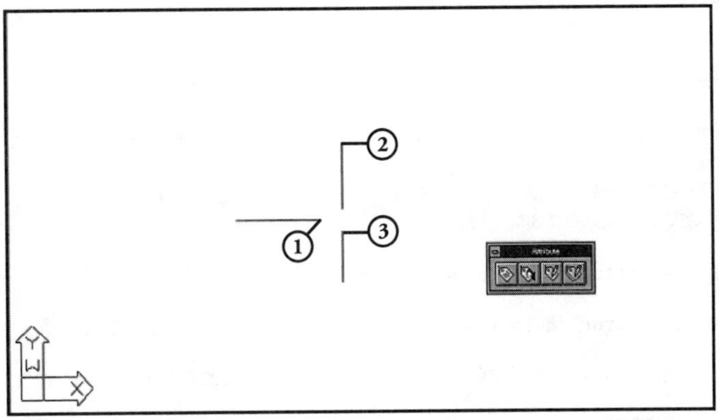

Figure 11.13

Pick points for the DDINSERT command.

`X scale factor <1> / Corner / XYZ:` ↵	Accepts default X scale factor
`Y scale factor (default=X):` ↵	Accepts default Y scale factor
`Rotation angle <0>:` ↵	Accepts default rotation angle
Enter attribute values	
`Enter Transistor Part Number:` **2N6114** ↵	Enters attribute value
`Enter reference designation <Q1>:` ↵	Accepts default value

If you prefer entering values from a dialog box, remember that the ATTDIA system variable controls how AutoCAD will prompt for attribute values.

`Command:` **ATTDIA** ↵	Accesses the ATTDIA system variable
`New value for ATTDIA <0>:` **1** ↵	Turns on dialog box entry
`Command:` *Choose Insert Block (Draw, Insert)*	Issues the DDINSERT command
Choose OK	Inserts the TRANSISTOR block
`Insertion point: _endp of` *Use ENDpoint object snap to pick* ②	
`X scale factor <1> / Corner / XYZ:` ↵	Accepts default X scale factor
`Y scale factor (default=X):` ↵	Accepts default Y scale factor
`Rotation angle <0>:` **90** ↵	Specifies a rotation angle
Enter **2NB601** *in the* Enter Transistor Part Number *box and* **Q2** *in the* Enter reference *designation box and choose* OK	Specifies the attribute information and inserts the block
`Command:` ↵	Repeats the last command
Choose OK	Inserts the TRANSISTOR block
`Insertion point: _endp of` *Use ENDpoint object snap to pick* ③	
`X scale factor <1> / Corner / XYZ:` ↵	Accepts default X scale factor
`Y scale factor (default=X):` ↵	Accepts default Y scale factor
`Rotation angle <0>:` **270** ↵	Specifies a rotation angle
Enter **2B8088** *in the* Enter Transistor Part Number *box and* **Q3** *in the* Enter reference designation *box and choose* OK	Specifies the attribute information and inserts the block

Suppose you made a typo—you specified the third transistor's PART_NUMBER as 2B8088 when you meant to type 2N8080. This easily will be corrected using the DDATTE command.

`Command:` *Choose Edit Attribute (Attribute, Edit Attribute)*	*Issues the DDATE command*

`Select block:` **`L`** ↵	Selects the last block and displays the Edit Attribute dialog box

Make the necessary change in the Edit Attribute dialog box, then choose OK. Figure 11.14 shows the final drawing. The attribute text is not very well placed; this can be fixed with the next command covered, the ATTEDIT command. Save this drawing for use in the next exercise.

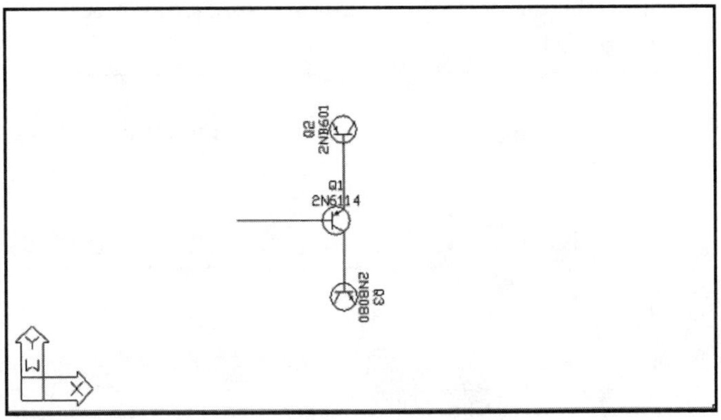

Figure 11.14

The current drawing with block references and attributes in place.

Using ATTEDIT To Change Attribute Values Globally or Change the Way an Attribute is Displayed

The ATTEDIT command is used to change more than just attribute values; it is used to change the way the information is presented. With ATTEDIT, you can change the position, height, angle, style, layer, and color of attribute text. Figure 11.15 shows the Edit Attribute Globally tool.

Figure 11.15

The ATTEDIT tool.

The first thing ATTEDIT asks is whether you want to edit attributes one at a time. If you want to change the way an attribute is displayed, you must answer yes (the default). If you answer no, you perform a global attribute edit. Global attribute editing enables you to change only attribute values, but it changes the value for all attributes selected at once. If you wanted to change the *Q* to a *V* in the transistor symbols in the previous exercise, for instance, you could change them all with one global edit.

If you answer yes to edit the attributes one at a time, you are allowed to select as many attributes as you want, then prompted to make changes to each attribute.

TIP

> When selecting attributes to edit, AutoCAD does not allow all normal object selection procedures. If you want to select more than one attribute, you must type W to select attributes with a window or C to use a crossing. Any objects selected that are not attributes are ignored.

The following exercise takes you through the ATTEDIT options.

Using ATTEDIT for Global Editing Attributes

Continue with previous exercise.

To begin with, you will perform a global edit as described earlier—changing the Q designator for all transistors to a V.

`Command:` *Choose Edit Attribute Globally (Attribute)*	Issues the ATTEDIT command
`Edit attributes one at a time? <Y>` **N** ↵	Specifies global editing of attribute values
`Global edit of attribute values.` `Edit only attributes visible on screen? <Y>` ↵	Accepts the default to edit only visible attributes
`Block name specification <*>:` **TRANSISTOR** ↵	Specifies which block's attributes to edit

You also could accept the default <*>, because TRANSISTOR is the only block reference in the drawing.

`Attribute tag specification <*>:` ↵	Accepts the default to edit all attributes
`Attribute value specification <*>:` ↵	Accepts the default to edit all attributes regardless of the present value

This option would be useful if you needed to change only a particular value. For instance, change all PART_NUMBER attributes set to 2N6017 to a new value of 2N8017.

`Select Attributes:` **W** ↵	Specifies window selection
`First corner:` *Pick* ① (see fig. 11.16)	

Figure 11.16

Pick points for Global Attribute Edit.

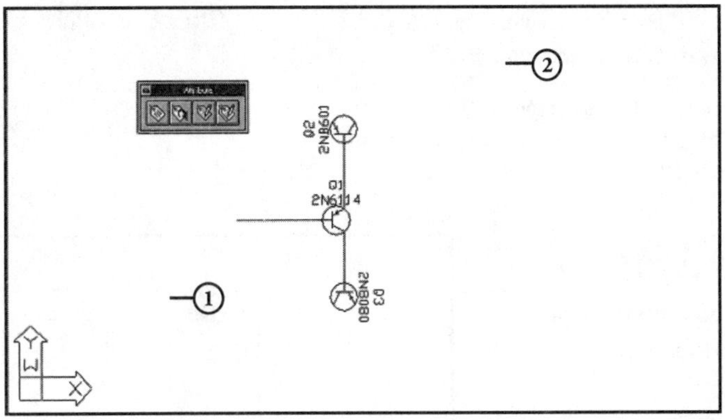

`Other corner:` *Pick* ②	
`String to change:` **Q** ↵	Specifies text to change
`New string:` **V** ↵	Specifies text to replace it with

A text string can be any number of letters to change. To change the text string BATTER to BOATER, for example, the string to change would be AT, and the new string would be OA.

You should now see all the transistors labeled Vn instead of Qn. Now you can edit attributes one at a time to clean up the drawing a bit.

`Command:` *Choose Edit Attribute Globally (Attribute)*	Issues the ATTEDIT command
`Edit attributes one at a time? <Y>` ↵	Accepts the default
`Block name specification <*>:` ↵	Accepts default
`Attribute tag specification <*>:` ↵	Accepts default
`Attribute value specification <*>:` ↵	Accepts default
`Select Attributes:` **W** ↵	Specifies window selection
`First corner:` *Pick* ① (see fig. 11.16)	Specifies first corner
`Other corner:` *Pick* ②	Specifies second corner, highlights first attribute, and marks it with a large X
`Value/Position/Height/Angle/Style /Layer/Color/Next <N>:` **A** ↵	Specifies the angle option
`New rotation angle <90>:` **0** ↵	Sets angle for attribute text to 0

`Value/Position/Height/Angle/Style /Layer/Color/Next <N>:` **P** ↵	Changes attribute's position
`Enter text insertion point:` *Move attribute text to position shown in figure 11.17*	

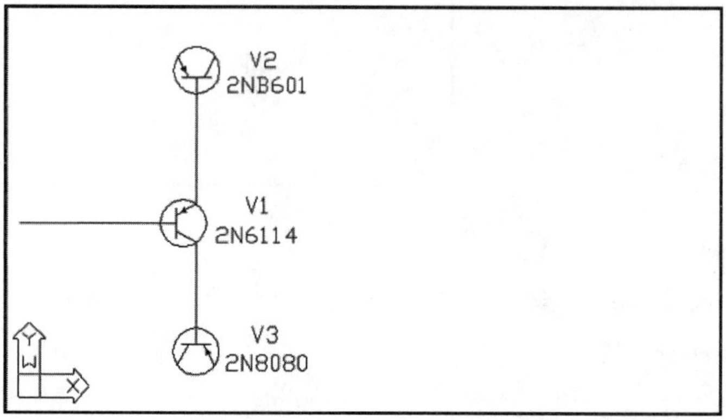

Figure 11.17

Final positions and angles for all attributes.

`Value/Position/Height/Angle/ Style/Layer/Color/Next <N>:` ↵	Goes to next attribute to edit
`Value/Position/Height/Angle/Style /Layer/Color/Next <N>:` **A** ↵	Changes the attribute's angle
`New rotation angle <90>:` **0** ↵	Sets angle for attribute text to 0
`Value/Position/Height/Angle/Style /Layer/Color/Next <N>:` **P** ↵	Changes attribute's position
`Enter text insertion point`: *Move attribute text to position shown in figure 11.17*	
Value/Position/Height/Angle/ Style/Layer/Color/Next <N>:	

Continue to arrange the attributes so they appear as shown in figure 11.17.

TIP

Grips are great for repositioning attributes, but not rotating them.

Redefining a Block

You have seen how to edit individual block references, but what if you need to edit all occurrences of a block reference throughout a drawing? What if your client's standard for a resistor symbol differs from your company's standard symbol? If you have placed quite a few resistors in your drawing, editing them individually would be very time-consuming.

AutoCAD enables you to change all occurrences of a symbol in your drawing simultaneously through a technique called *block redefinition,* with which you begin to see how the power to edit block references can be a real time-saver.

Block redefinition typically is accomplished with the BLOCK command, after placing the block reference with the BLOCK command, then using the EXPLODE command before making required changes. There are no new commands to learn, only a new application of these basic commands.

Figure 11.18 shows an office layout with 16 computer workstations. Each of these workstations is a nested block, as you might remember from a previous exercise—each workstation contains eight component blocks, one of which is a printer. Say you install a network so that these computers can share a printer, and at the same time add a mouse to each workstation. Without block redefinition, this would mean exploding each workstation block reference, erasing each printer block reference, and adding a mouse to each workstation. With block redefinition, the task is greatly simplified; simply explode one workstation, make the necessary changes, and redefine the workstation block. All workstation block references are automatically updated.

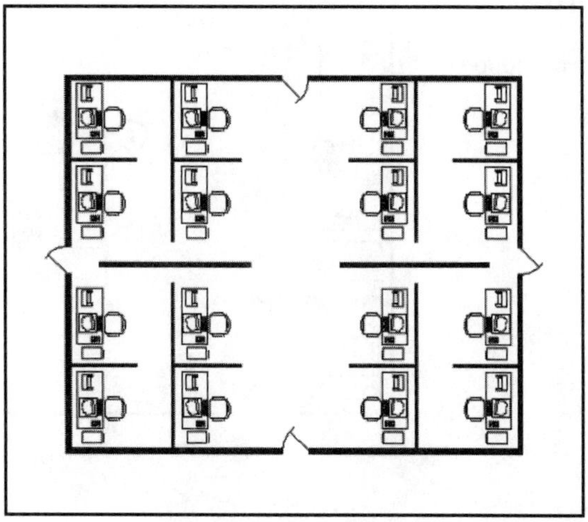

Figure 11.18

An office layout with 16 workstation block references.

The following exercise helps to illustrate the concept of block redefinition. You will make the changes to the office layout previously described.

REDEFINING BLOCK REFERENCES

Begin a new drawing named CHAP11G using the file REDEFINE, from the IAW disk, as a prototype. First, you will insert an exploded copy of the WORKSTATION block to edit.

`Command:` *Choose Insert Block (Draw, Block)*	Issues the DDINSERT command
Choose the Block *button and double-click on* WORKSTATION, *then place an X in the* Explode *box and choose* OK	Specifies the block to be inserted and starts the insertion process
`Insertion point:` *Pick a point in the middle of the building*	Places the block insertion point
`Scale factor <1>:` ↵	Accepts the default scale factor
`Rotation angle <0>:`	Accepts the default rotation angle

Next, you will edit the block by erasing the printer and replacing it with a mouse. First, zoom in on the workstation as shown in figure 11.19

`Command:` *Choose Erase (Modify)*	Issues the ERASE command
`Select objects:` Pick ① (see fig. 11.19)	Selects the PRINTER block reference

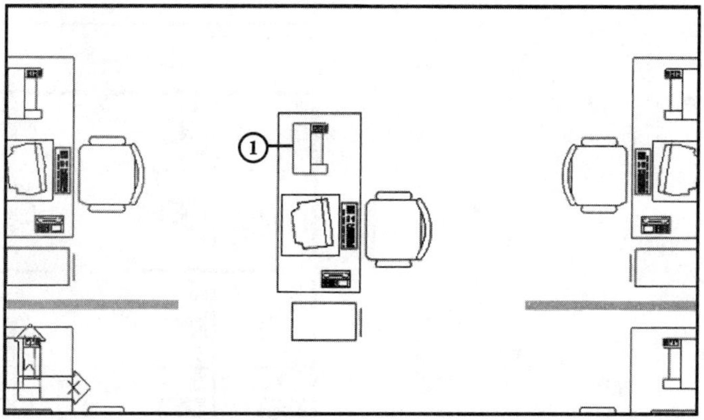

Figure 11.19

The exploded workstation.

`Select objects:` ↵	Ends object selection

A block for the mouse and mousepad has already been created, so you can insert the mouse block at the workstation.

`Command:` *Choose Insert Block (Draw, Block)*	Issues the DDINSERT command
`Command:` *Choose* Block *and select* MOUSE *from the list of blocks, then choose* OK *twice*	Selects the block and starts the insertion process
`Insertion point:` *Pick a point on the desk to the right of the keyboard.*	Places the insertion point of the block
`X scale factor <1> / Corner / XYZ:` ↵	Accepts default X scale factor
`Y scale factor (default=X):` ↵	Accepts default Y scale factor
`Rotation angle <0>:` ↵	Accepts default rotation angle

Now that the block reference has been exploded and modified, use the BLOCK command to redefine it.

`Command:` *Choose Block (Draw, Block)*	Issues the BLOCK command
`Block name (or ?):` **WORKSTATION** ↵	Gives the new block the same name as the original block
`Block WORKSTATION already exists.` `Redefine it? <N>` **Y** ↵	Redefines the block
`Insertion base point:` *Using the MIDpoint object snap, pick point* a *(see fig. 11.20)*	Specifies the midpoint of the back of the desk

Figure 11.20

Modified WORKSTATION and PRINTER erased and MOUSE added.

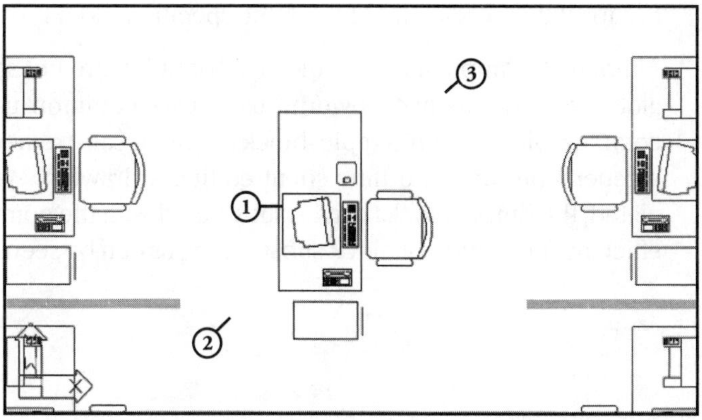

`Select objects:` *Select a window from ② to ③ and press Enter*	Selects the objects and redefines the WORKSTATION block

To see that the redefinition changed all occurrences of the block reference WORKSTATION, zoom out to view the entire drawing.

`Command:` *Choose Zoom All (Standard Toolbar, Zoom)*	Issues the ZOOM command with the All option

Save this drawing for use in the next exercise.

TIP

Before using EXPLODE on a block reference you want to redefine, note the location of the current block insertion point, which enables you to choose the same insertion point when creating the new block. This prevents other references to the redefined block from shifting their positions.

Block Substitution

As you have seen, block redefinition is a method of globally editing block references—changing all occurrences of a particular block reference in a drawing simultaneously. Another method of globally editing block references is the block substitution method.

Block substitution is simply the replacement of all occurrences of a block reference with a separate file, using the INSERT command. When supplying a block name for the INSERT command, you can set an existing block equal to a file, causing AutoCAD to substitute the specified file for the specified block.

Although the applications of block substitution are not so obvious, this method of global editing has two powerful uses. One common use is the replacement of complex blocks with simple blocks, which can tremendously reduce drawing regeneration time and time spent editing a drawing. When the drawing is completed, the simple blocks can be substituted with the complex blocks. This is a very efficient application of block substitution, as can be seen in the following exercise.

Using Block Substitution for Efficient Drawing

Continue from the previous exercise. Zoom in on the upper left desk, as shown in figure 11.21, and turn on ortho mode.

First, you will draw an outline around the workstation to show its overall dimensions.

`Command:` *Choose Pline (Draw, Pline)* — Issues the PLINE command

`From point:` *Pick* ① (see fig. 11.21) — Specifies start point for polyline

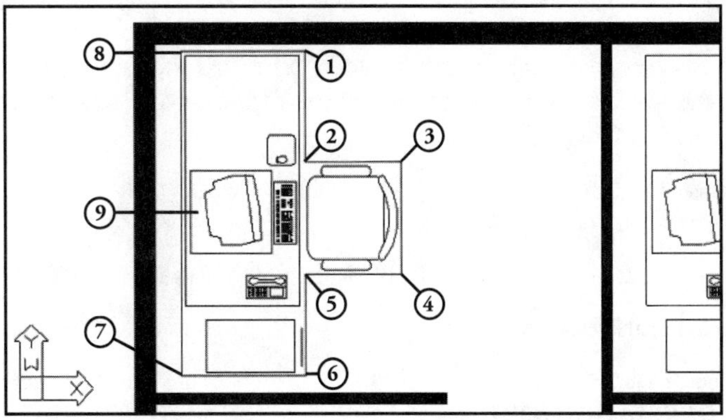

Figure 11.21

Envelope outline of the workstation.

`Arc/Close/Halfwidth/Length/Undo/Width/ <Endpoint of line>: <Ortho on>` *Pick* ②, ③, ④, ⑤, ⑥, ⑦, and ⑧ — Specifies next point on polyline

`Arc/Close/Halfwidth/Length/Undo/Width/ <Endpoint of line>:` **C** ↵ — Closes the polyline

Now you need to create a drawing file from the outline of the workstation.

`Command:` **WBLOCK** ↵ — Starts the WBLOCK command

In the Create Drawing File *dialog box, specify the file name* OUTLINE, *then choose* OK — Specifies the name OUTLINE as the new drawing name

`Block name:` ↵ — Specifies that no block is being used to create file

`Insertion base point:` *Using the INSertion object snap, pick* ⑨ — Snaps to the insertion point of the block

`Select objects:` **L** ↵ — Selects the last object drawn to create the WBLOCK file

`Select objects:` ↵ — Ends object selection

`Command:` ↵ — Repeats the last command

In the Create Drawing File *dialog box, specify the file name* WORKSTAT, *then choose* OK — Specifies the name WORKSTAT as the new drawing name

`Block name:` **WORKSTATION** ↵ — Specifies the block to write to disk

To get an idea of how much time you will save substituting the simple outline for the workstation, note how long the drawing takes to regenerate when you select Zoom All. The time will vary depending on your hardware and configuration, but as an example, the author's 486DX66 machine took about 20 seconds to regenerate this drawing. Later in this exercise, you can compare this regeneration speed to the regeneration time using the simple outline block.

`Command:` *Choose Zoom All (Standard, Zoom All)* — Zooms to the drawing limits

Next you will substitute the OUTLINE block for the WORKSTATION block.

`Command:` **INSERT** ↵ — Starts the INSERT command

`Block name (or ?) <MOUSE>:` **WORKSTATION=OUTLINE** ↵ — Substitutes all block references to the block WORKSTATION with references to the block OUTLINE

At this time, the OUTLINE block should replace the WORKSTATION block, as shown in figure 11.22. Because you do not need to create any new references to the block, you should abort the command when you are prompted for an insertion point.

Figure 11.22

The WORKSTATION block replaced with the OUTLINE block.

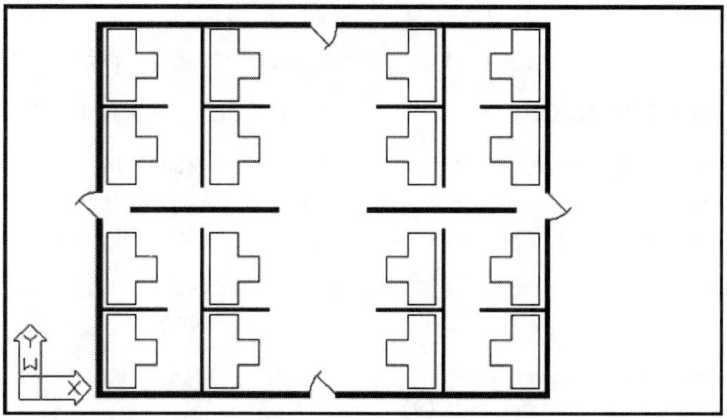

`Insertion point:` *Press Esc* — Cancels the INSERT command

Use the REGEN command to get an idea of regeneration time differences.

`Command:` *Choose Regen (NRP)* — Issues the REGEN command

`Regenerating drawing.`

The author's computer, which took approximately 20 seconds to regenerate the drawing with the complex WORKSTATION blocks, regenerated the drawing with the substituted OUTLINE blocks in less than 1 second!

Save your drawing for the next exercise.

This exercise demonstrated the timesaving capabilities of block substitution, but there is another powerful application of block substitution.

Suppose the office layout from the previous exercise is not the only option you want to show your client. Perhaps you want to provide the client with several other workstation design choices; for example, have one optional layout with smaller desks and another that eliminates the file cabinets. These changes do not require several layout drawings, only several files that can substitute the WORKSTATION block. These substitutions can be performed and the resulting layout plotted, or they can be incorporated into a presentation during which the client can watch as the layout transformations take place in seconds with the use of one command, INSERT. This use of block substitution is demonstrated in the following exercise.

Using Block Substitution for Multiple Designs

Continue from the previous exercise.

`Command:` **INSERT ↵** — Starts the INSERT command

`Block name (or ?) <MOUSE>:` **WORKSTATION=WORKSTA2 ↵** — Substitutes all block references to the block WORKSTATION with references to the block WORKSTA2

As the block is substituted, you may see some messages about duplicate block definitions. That's okay; remember this is a nested block, and AutoCAD is telling you that its component blocks are already defined in this drawing.

`Insertion point:` *Press ESC* — Cancels the INSERT command

You should now see the new workstation layout as shown in figure 11.23.

Save your drawing for the next exercise.

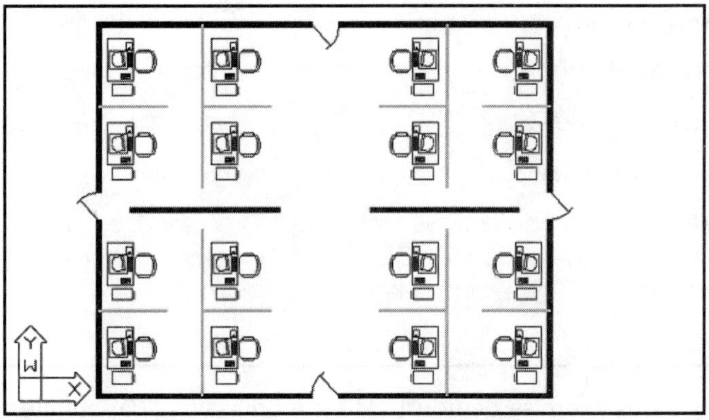

Figure 11.23

Office Layout Alternative 2—desks shortened from 6′ to 4.5′.

There is one more concept to illustrate involving block substitution. If you want to substitute a block reference with a file having the same name as the block, just type **BLOCKNAME=** when the INSERT command prompts for a block name, where *BLOCKNAME* is the name of the block being substituted.

For example, in the office layout of the previous exercises, suppose you also want to show your client a layout using tower PC cases rather than desktop cases. Because the case is the part of the nested block WORKSTATION defined by a block named CPU, you can substitute a file named CPU for the block named CPU. All occurrences of the block are automatically updated, even though it is nested in the WORKSTATION block. The following short exercise illustrates this point.

Using Block Substitution With BLOCKNAME=

Continue from the previous exercise.

`Command:` **INSERT** ↵	Starts the INSERT command
`Block name (or ?): CPU=` ↵	Substitutes all block references to the block CPU with references to the file named CPU
`Insertion point:` *Press ESC*	Cancels the INSERT command

You should now see the CPU block redefined in all of the WORKSTATION blocks.

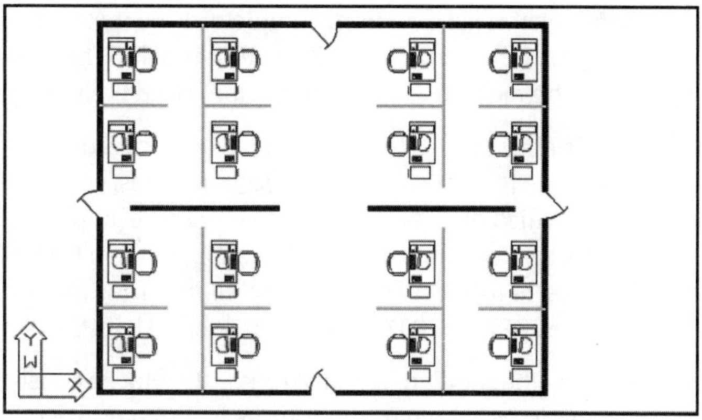

Figure 11.24

Office Layout Alternative 4—desktop CPUs replaced with tower CPUs.

Managing and Organizing Blocks

It should be obvious by now that an efficient CAD department makes extensive use of blocks. The amount and types of blocks you use depends on the types of drawings you produce, but any CAD discipline will find the use of blocks very advantageous.

When using large numbers of blocks, management and organization of your blocks greatly affects their efficiency. Block management encompasses the method used to organize your blocks, but also includes planning how your blocks should be created and used, as well as the setting of standards to ensure consistency in your block schemes.

Planning your block scheme involves deciding, before creating blocks, how they are to be used. Some of the questions you might ask at the planning stage are as follows:

- What is the most practical insertion point for each block?
- How will the block be placed (picked from a menu, inserted with an AutoLISP routine, with INSERT, with DDINSERT, as an XREF, and so forth)?
- Can several blocks be derived from one unit size block?
- Can several blocks be derived from one exploded block?
- Is the block complex enough to warrant the use of a simplified block and block substitution?
- How do the layer, linetype, and color properties of blocks relate to this block?
- At what scale should the block be drawn?

Although this list is far from complete, these questions are fairly generic and would apply to almost any extensive use of blocks. The answers to these questions will affect the methods used to create and store the blocks.

Consistency in your block scheme would include how your blocks will be named. If you are storing your blocks as separate files, you are limited to an eight-character name, which often isn't enough to be very descriptive. The use of mnemonic names or abbreviated names is a good solution, but don't get so elaborate with this that they become hard to interpret. An example of an abbreviated mnemonic file name would be 25SHCS20.DWG for a 1/4" Socket Head Cap Screw with 20 threads per inch.

Keeping the standards used to create the blocks consistent with the standards used to create the drawings themselves is another aspect of block consistency. Layer names, linetypes, colors, and text style of attributes or blocked text are some of the things to consider in this area.

There are two basic approaches to block organization: blocks can be stored as individual files in an intuitive directory structure, or they can be grouped into symbol libraries. A *symbol library* is a file made of a group of blocks, usually blocks that fall into some category, such as electronic control symbols, floor plan symbols, and so on. You often will find that a combination of these two approaches best suits your needs. The remainder of this chapter deals with the two approaches to block organization.

Symbol Directories

Storing symbols as individual files makes editing and retrieving them easy. The most common method of creating these files is to create a block of the symbol with the BLOCK command, then write the block to disk with the WBLOCK command. This enables you to create symbols on-the-fly; you simply draw the symbol the first time you need it, then use WBLOCK to store it as a file.

Another method of creating these files is to draw the symbol as a separate drawing and save it. If you create symbols this way, the origin point (0,0,0) is the insertion point of the symbol, unless you use the BASE command to specify the insertion point. Storing a block as an individual file works best if you have a symbol that doesn't fall into a category of symbols. For instance, symbols for mechanical fasteners probably would be better stored in a symbol library, whereas symbols for your company's logo or a title block are good candidates for storage as individual drawing files.

As a rule of thumb, symbols that need to be accessed from a variety of drawings rather than from a particular type of drawing probably should be stored as individual drawing files. Also, symbols that are to be inserted from a menu selection or an AutoLISP routine usually should be stored as individual files.

If you decide to store symbols as individual files, you can save yourself a lot of time by creating a meaningful directory structure in which to store the files. A good directory structure makes selecting the files with the DDINSERT command much easier than if the files are all stored in one directory. The Select Drawing File dialog box only lists 10 files at a time. If there are more than 10 files in a directory, you must scroll to the file you need. The more files you have in the directory, the more you must scroll to get to the file you need. Figure 11.25 shows an example of a directory structure that would make symbols files easy to locate and would keep the directories from becoming too cluttered. In figure 11.25, the directory named SYMBOLS has two subdirectories: ARCHITEC and ELECTRIC. Both of these subdirectories have their own subdirectories to organize the symbols in specific groups.

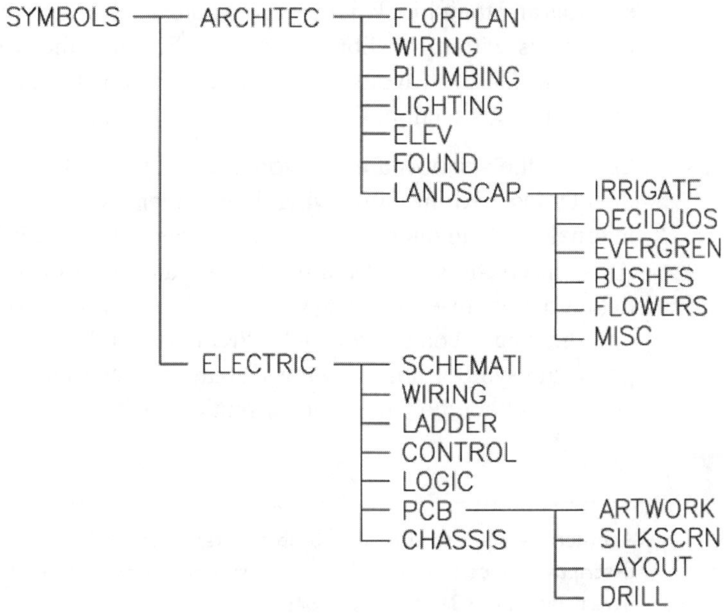

Figure 11.25

A sample directory structure.

There are disadvantages to storing symbols as separate files. Your computer's hard disk can quickly become cluttered with files stored this way, bogging down the hard disk and causing a decrease in your overall system performance.

Another less obvious disadvantage has to do with the way files are stored on a hard disk. File size limitations exist on your disk and operating system, and the end result is that a simple symbol can take more bytes of disk space than are needed to describe the symbol. Disk space for files is allocated in blocks of memory, so virtually every symbol stored as a separate file is eating up more disk space than it requires. There also is a lot of information stored in a drawing file that might not be needed to describe the symbol, eating up even more bytes unnecessarily. These factors can account for several thousand bytes of disk space. Multiply that by several hundred symbol files and you can see this can be a real problem.

Symbol Libraries

Storing symbols in symbol libraries can overcome most of the disadvantages mentioned about storing symbols as separate files, but libraries have their own limitations.

You create a symbol library by creating a drawing that contains nothing but the symbols and their block definitions. You use the BLOCK command to create block definitions within the library drawing. Because the symbols are not saved as individual files, you avoid the hard disk clutter and hard disk space losses described in the previous section.

Because the symbols are not stored as individual files, however, they cannot be directly inserted into a drawing. Remember, the BLOCK command creates only internal block definitions—these blocks are defined only in the symbol library file. If you insert the symbol library file into another drawing, however, all its block definitions are inserted along with it, and these blocks are then accessible from the new drawing. If you cancel the INSERT command when it prompts for an insertion point, the symbol library is not displayed in the current drawing, but its block definitions become part of the current drawing's block table.

TIP

Another advantage to using symbol library files is the capability to give your symbols more descriptive names. Not limited to 8-character names, symbols defined within a drawing can have names up to 31 characters long.

You also can place the blocks' names adjacent to the symbols, then plot the library drawing and use it as a reference for the symbols.

Symbol libraries have two disadvantages. First, an extra step is added to the process of inserting a block. Before the symbol can be inserted into a drawing, the symbol library must first be inserted. This makes it necessary to add extra lines of code to insert the symbol library first when inserting the symbol from a menu selection or an AutoLISP program.

Another disadvantage is the fact that all the block definitions from the symbol library are stored in the current drawing's block table—even if you need to load only one block definition. You can overcome this with the use of the PURGE command, which is described at the end of this chapter, or with the WBLOCK* technique, described in Chapter 10, "Basic Building Blocks for Repetitive Drawing."

Figure 11.26 shows a typical symbol library drawing. The symbols are generally associated in some way. In this example, they all are logic diagram symbols. The Xs represent the block insertion points. The labels and Xs have been added so that the drawing can be plotted and used as a reference. They are not part of the symbols.

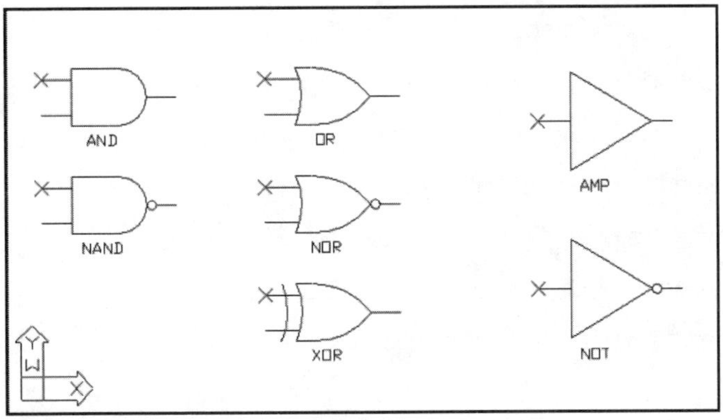

Figure 11.26

A symbol library for logic symbols.

Inserting Symbols from a Library File

Using a symbol library file is a simple procedure. Before you can access the block definitions in the library file, you must insert the library file itself. It is helpful to think of the library file as a nested block. When you insert a nested block, AutoCAD stores a block definition for all nested blocks in the current drawings block table.

In the following exercise, you use the symbol library created in the preceding exercise to complete a logic diagram.

USING BLOCKS FROM A SYMBOL LIBRARY FILE

Begin a new drawing named CHAP11H using the default ACAD.DWG prototype drawing. Set the SNAP spacing to .25 and the GRID spacing to 1. Turn both GRID and SNAP ON.

`Command:` *Choose Insert Block (Draw, Block)*	Issues the DDINSERT command
Choose the File *button and select* LOGIC.DWG *from the file list, then choose OK twice*	Inserts the file LOGIC.DWG into the current drawing
`Insertion point:` *Press Esc*	Cancels the INSERT command
`Command:` *Choose* Block *and select* AND *from the list of blocks and choose* OK, *remove the X from the* Specify Parameters on Screen *box, enter* **2** *in the* X Insertion Point *box, enter* **8** *in the* Y Insertion Point *box, and choose* OK	Inserts the block AND at the coordinate 2,8

Insert the block AND at the coordinate 2,6.

Insert the block OR at the coordinate 2,4.

Insert the block XOR at the coordinate 2,2.

Insert the block OR at the coordinate 6,7.

Insert the block AND at the coordinate 6,3.

Insert the block NOR at the coordinate 10,5.

You should have all the symbols in place now, completing the diagram is just a matter of adding a few lines to connect the symbols. Figure 11.27 shows the completed logic diagram.

After adding the connecting lines, save your drawing for the next exercise.

Figure 11.27

The completed logic diagram.

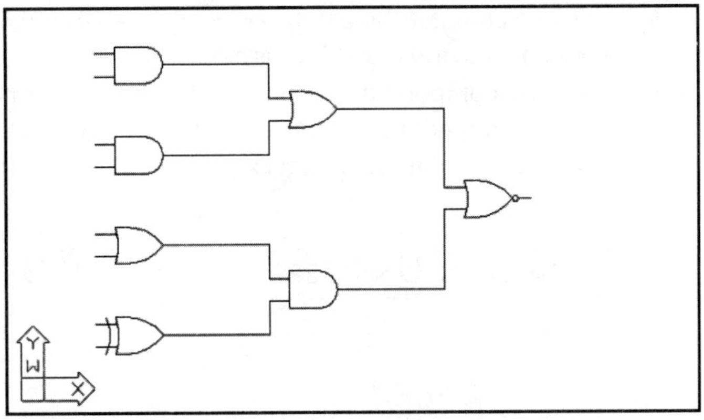

Purging an Unused Block from the Block Table

In the preceding exercise, you inserted into a drawing a symbol library file containing seven block definitions, which added eight block definitions to the block table of your drawing—seven definitions for the nested blocks in the symbol library file and one for the symbol library file itself. To create the drawing, however, you needed only four block definitions. The NAND, AMP, and NOT blocks and the file LOGIC.DWG were not used. Now that the drawing is complete, you should PURGE the unused blocks from your drawing.

The PURGE command enables you to purge unreferenced block definitions from your drawing. *Unreferenced* block definitions are block definitions that have no block references inserted in the drawing, or whose block reference(s) has been exploded. These block definitions are just taking up space; they increase the size of your drawing file and are not needed.

As the size of your symbols libraries and the complexity of your block definitions increase, the need to purge a drawing after inserting the symbol library becomes more and more important.

An alternative to using the PURGE command to remove unreferenced block definitions is the WBLOCK* procedure, which is discussed in Chapter 10.

In the following exercise, you use the PURGE command to remove the unreferenced block definitions from the logic diagram completed in the previous exercise.

The PURGE command acts only on the top level of nested blocks, not the component blocks. After the top level block is purged, you can reissue the PURGE command to remove the component blocks. If any of the component blocks are also nested blocks, this procedure must be repeated as many times as is necessary to purge the lowest level of component blocks.

Purging Unreferenced Block Definitions

Continue from the previous exercise.

`Command:` Choose Data, Purge, Blocks	Issues the PURGE command with the Blocks option
`Purge block LOGIC? <N>` **Y** ↵	Purges the definition from the block table

Now that the highest level block (the drawing file) has been purged, you can purge the remaining unused blocks.

`Command:` ↵	Repeats the purge command
`Purge unused Blocks/Dimstyles/LAyers/ LTypes/SHapes/STyles/APpids/ Mlinestyles/All:` **B** ↵	Specifies the Block option
`Purge block NAND? <N>` **Y** ↵	Purges the definition from the block table
`Purge block AMP? <N>` **Y** ↵	Purges the definition from the block table
`Purge block NOT? <N>` **Y** ↵	Purges the definition from the block table

In this chapter, you have explored the intricacies of block storage and structure. You looked at the way AutoCAD stores block data and insertion information in the block table, and learned about the relationships of blocks to color, layer, and linetype object properties. You also worked with methods of editing blocks, including exploding a block to edit its individual components, and substituting and redefining blocks. You learned commands that AutoCAD provides to edit block attributes. These techniques make your use of blocks more flexible, as well as more efficient. Finally, you looked at different strategies for organizing and managing a library of blocks. This and the previous chapter have shown that you can greatly increase your efficiency with AutoCAD by making extensive and appropriate use of blocks.

chapter

12

Using Xrefs for Efficiency and Sharing Data

This chapter explains the xref, or external reference, an AutoCAD object that in many ways is similar to a block. An xref is a reference in a drawing to another drawing. All objects in an externally referenced drawing, including named items such as layers, linetypes, and blocks, are part of the xref in the active drawing.

This chapter covers the following topics:

- *Explanation of xrefs*
- *When to use an xref*
- *How to use an xref*
- *New xref capabilities in Release 13*
- *Working in a multiple-user environment*

Xrefs have two primary purposes. First, xrefs are an efficient way to import standard elements that you need not modify, such as title blocks, into a current drawing. Second, they provide a means by which you can use identical drawing data in multiple drawings. AutoCAD automatically updates any changes in an externally referenced drawing in all drawings that have xrefs to that drawing.

Through the use of xrefs, several people can work on a project in a coordinated manner, using the same data. For example, a building design team can simultaneously work on the building's structural plan, floor plan, electrical plan, and plumbing plan. All members of the team can use the same base plan by attaching or overlaying it as an xref. If anyone makes a change to the base plan, AutoCAD automatically updates it in the drawings to which it is attached or overlaid.

Understanding Xrefs

An xref is similar to a block in that it is a single object that can contain multiple objects. Like a block, an xref appears as an image of the referenced objects. The difference between an xref and a block is that whereas a block's data is stored in the current drawing, xref data is stored in an external drawing. When you use an xref, only an image of the data is placed in the current drawing session—the xref data remains defined in the external drawing. You can create an xref as an attachment or as an overlay, and you can scale and rotate an xref when it is attached or overlaid.

WARNING

AutoCAD ignores block attributes contained in an xref.

The XREF command has the following options:

- **Attach.** This is the default option.
- **?.** This option lists the name, path, and type of each external reference in the drawing. The ? option does not indicate if an external reference was loaded or not.
- **Bind.** The bind option converts an xref to a block. In addition, all dependent symbols, such as layers and linetypes, are renamed and placed into the current drawing.
- **Detach.** The Detach option removes xref objects from the current drawing. You can specify xref objects to delete using AutoCAD's standard wild-card options.

- **Path.** The Path option is used to update the path of an xref object's associated drawing file.
- **Reload.** This option is used to force a reload of an attached drawing without having to reopen the current drawing. This option is used in a networked workgroup environment.
- **Overlay.** This option is similar to attach; however, nested, overlaid external references are not loaded. Nested, attached external references are loaded as usual.

Advantages of Using Xrefs

There are several advantages to using xrefs over blocks or copied objects. First, an xref reduces the amount of disk space consumed by a drawing by storing data in an external drawing file. The external drawing can be referenced by several other drawings. Each time the external drawing is referenced, it saves the duplication of its contents in other drawings. The external data does not exist in each referencing file, only in the externally referenced drawing.

An xref also enables you to update drawing data easily. Each time a drawing that contains an xref is opened, the referenced drawing is loaded, and any changes in the referenced drawing are automatically reflected in the drawing that contains the xref. You also can force a reload of the referenced drawing in the current drawing session by using the XREF command's Reload option.

WARNING

In a team situation, the person who makes a change to a referenced drawing is responsible for notifying the others; the XREF command does not provide automatic notification or identification of changes.

Working with Xrefs

You can attach or overlay any drawing file as an xref. Although xrefs take up less space in a drawing file than blocks, you cannot edit them from within the drawing to which they are attached or overlaid. To edit the contents of an xref, you must edit the original external drawing file. You can not use the EXPLODE command on xrefs to edit them in the current drawing as you can with blocks. Editing an external drawing affects all drawings that have a reference to that drawing.

After an xref is attached or overlaid in a drawing, you can update the xref image, update the path to the external file, and remove them from the drawing with the XREF command. You also can list the xrefs in a drawing.

Attaching Xrefs

You use attached xrefs whenever you need to nest more than one level of xref. For example, attached xrefs are used when a master plan drawing references a new-construction drawing which, in turn, references an old-construction drawing. In this arrangement, the master drawing depends on information in the new-construction drawing, and the new-construction drawing depends on information in the old-construction drawing.

Attached xrefs cannot be circular. In other words, if drawing A references B, and drawing B references C, drawing C cannot reference drawing A.

The following exercise demonstrates how to attach nested xrefs. In the exercise you place an xref to a plan drawing in a furniture layout drawing, and then place an xref to the furniture drawing in a master drawing. If the plan drawing changes, the changes will be visible in the furniture layout drawing and the master drawing. Figure 12.1 shows the visual result of nesting attached xrefs.

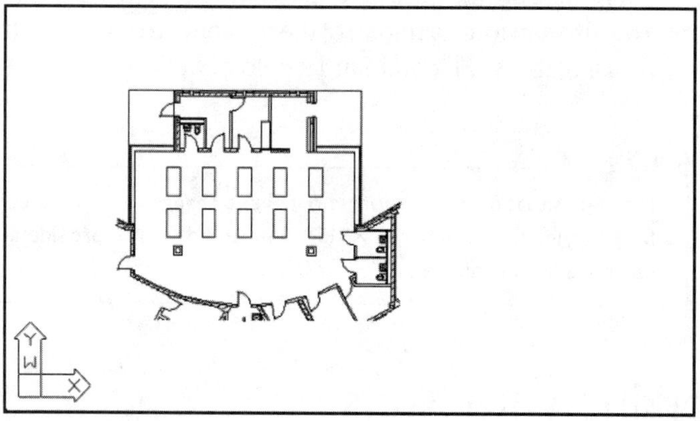

Figure 12.1

Xref ATCHROOM with nested xref ROOMPLAN in current drawing.

ATTACHING NESTED XREFS

Start a new drawing named ATCHROOM.DWG using DESKS.DWG as a prototype.

`Command:` *Choose Tools, Toolbars, External Reference*	Displays External Reference toolbar
`Command:` *Choose Attach (External Reference)*	Issues the XREF command with the Attach option

The Attach option displays the Select file to attach dialog box to enable you to specify a file name for the xref. When the dialog box appears, choose Type it.

`Select file to attach:` **PLAN=ROOMPLAN** ↵	Specifies the drawing to attach and an alternate xref name
`Insertion point:` **0,0** ↵	Specifies insertion point
`X scale factor <1> / Corner / XYZ:` ↵	Accepts default X scale factor
`Y scale factor (default=X):` ↵	Accepts default Y scale factor
`Rotation angle <0>:` ↵	Accepts default rotation angle
`Command:` *Save the drawing*	

Start a new drawing named CHAP12A using XREFPROT as a prototype.

`Command:` *Choose Attach (External Reference)*	Issues the XREF command with the Attach option

Select the drawing ATCHROOM to attach to CHAP12A.

`Insertion point:` **0,0** ↵	Specifies insertion point
`X scale factor <1> / Corner / XYZ:` ↵	Accepts default X scale factor
`Y scale factor(default=X):` ↵	Accepts default Y scale factor
`Rotation angle<0>:` ↵	Accepts default rotation angle
`Command:` *Choose List (External Reference)*	Issues XREF command with the List option

```
Xref(s) to list <*>: ↵
```
Lists all names and paths in the AutoCAD Text Window

```
  Xref name          Path              Xref type
  ---------          -------           -----
  ATCHROOM           ATCHROOM.DWG      Attach
  PLAN               ROOMPLAN          Attach

Total Xref(s): 2
```

`Command:` *Save the drawing*

In the previous exercise, you placed an xref to ROOMPLAN.DWG in ATCHROOM.DWG and then placed an xref to ATCHROOM.DWG in CHAP12A.DWG. Now, whenever CHAP12A is opened, it loads ATCHROOM which, in turn, loads ROOMPLAN.

External references are named according to the referenced drawing file name by default. However, in the previous exercise, the xref to ROOMPLAN.DWG was named PLAN. You can use this technique to name xrefs to specify longer or more meaningful xref names than eight-character file names allow. Also, this technique enables you to keep the names of dependent symbols the same if the xref file name changes.

NOTE

Although you cannot select individual objects in an xref, you can use object snap modes to snap to them.

Overlaying Xrefs

The capability to overlay an xref is a new feature in Release 13. Overlaid xrefs are more flexible than attached xrefs. However, overlaid xrefs do not display nested, overlaid xrefs; an overlaid xref is not visible in a drawing if it is more than one attached or overlaid xref level deep. Overlaid xrefs can have circular references because nested overlaid xrefs are ignored when loaded.

You use overlaid xrefs to see the way your current drawing relates to drawings of others in a concurrent-design workgroup. Overlaid xrefs enable each designer in the workgroup to see any other designer's drawings without worrying about creating circular xrefs or inflexible drawing interdependencies.

For example, what if the electrical designer attaches HVAC and plumbing information to his drawing at the same time as the HVAC designer needs electrical information? If the HVAC designer attaches the electrical drawing, a circular reference to the HVAC drawing occurs and the extra plumbing information is also loaded. With overlaid xrefs the electrical designer can see both HVAC and plumbing information in his drawing and the HVAC designer doesn't have to worry about getting plumbing information and referencing his own HVAC drawings.

TIP

If you use xrefs to share data in a concurrent design environment, use overlaid xrefs rather than attached xrefs to prevent circular xrefs and rigid, complex dependencies.

In the next exercise, you use the Overlay option of the XREF command to create a more flexible design drawing.

OVERLAYING XREFS

Start a new drawing named OVLYROOM.DWG using DESKS.DWG as a prototype.

`Command:` *Choose Overlay (External Reference)*	Issues the XREF command with the Overlay option

The Overlay option displays the Select file to overlay dialog box to enable you to specify a file name for the xref. When the dialog box appears, choose Type it.

`Select file to overlay:` **PLAN=ROOMPLAN** ↵	Specifies the drawing to overlay and an alternate xref name
`Insertion point:` **0,0** ↵	Specifies insertion point
`X scale factor <1> / Corner / XYZ:` ↵	Accepts default X scale factor
`Y scale factor (default=X):` ↵	Accepts default Y scale factor
`Rotation angle <0>:` ↵	Accepts default rotation angle
`Command:` *Save the drawing*	

Start a new drawing named CHAP12B using XREFPROT as a prototype.

`Command:` *Choose Overlay (External Reference)*	Issues the XREF command with the Overlay option

Select the drawing OVLYROOM to overlay on CHAP12B.

`Insertion point:` **0,0** ↵	Specifies insertion point
`X scale factor <1> / Corner / XYZ:` ↵	Accepts default X scale factor
`Y scale factor(default=X):` ↵	Accepts default Y scale factor
`Rotation angle<0>:` ↵	Accepts default rotation angle
`Command:` *Choose List (External Reference)*	Issues XREF command with the List option
`Xref(s) to list <*>:` ↵	Lists all names and paths in the AutoCAD Text Window

```
Xref name        Path           Xref type
---------        ------         -----
OVLYROOM         OVLYROOM.DWG   Overlay

Total Xref(s): 1
```

ROOMPLAN isn't displayed because overlaid xrefs are displayed only one level deep (see fig. 12.2). If you want both the desks and the plan to show, you must overlay both xrefs (see fig. 12.3).

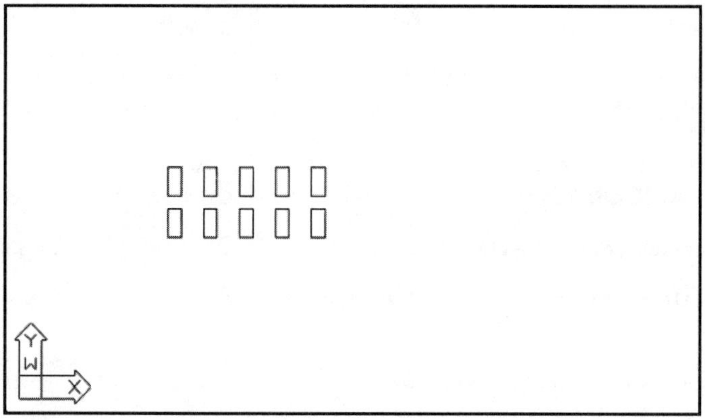

Figure 12.2

Xref OVLYROOM overlaid in current drawing.

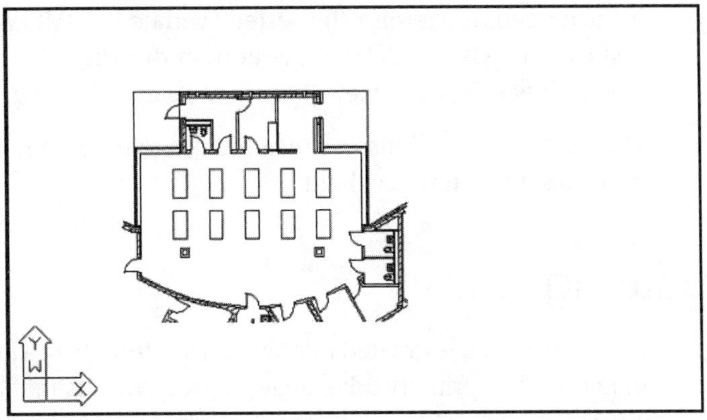

Figure 12.3

Xref OVLYROOM and ROOMPLAN overlaid separately in current drawing.

`Command:` *Choose Overlay (External Reference)*	Issues the XREF command with the Overlay option

When the Select file to overlay dialog box appears, choose Type it.

`Select file to overlay:` **PLAN=ROOMPLAN** ↵	Specifies the drawing to overlay and an alternate xref name
`Insertion point:` **0,0** ↵	Specifies insertion point
`X scale factor <1> / Corner / XYZ:` ↵	Accepts default X scale factor
`Y scale factor (default=X):` ↵	Accepts default Y scale factor
`Rotation angle <0>:` ↵	Accepts default rotation angle
`Command:` *Choose List (External Reference)*	Issues XREF command with the List option
`Xref(s) to list <*>:` ↵	Lists all names and paths in the AutoCAD Text Window

```
Xref name        Path            Xref type
---------        -------         -----
OVLYROOM         OVLYROOM.DWG    Overlay
PLAN             ROOMPLAN        Overlay

Total Xref(s): 2
```

`Command:` *Save the drawing*

In the preceding exercise, the nested overlaid ROOMPLAN xref did not appear when you overlaid OVLYROOM in the current drawing. You overlaid the desks and the plan independently to view them in the same drawing.

The next section discusses how changes to externally referenced drawings affect drawings that reference them.

Updating Xrefs

Now that you have created references to external drawing files, it's time to see them in action. The primary advantage to using xrefs is that AutoCAD always loads the current version of the externally referenced drawing each time the referencing drawing is opened. This enables externally referenced design elements to change independently and ensures the referenced drawing is up-to-date at the moment the referencing drawing is opened.

If an externally referenced drawing in your current open drawing changes, you can force a reload of the xref with the XREF command's Reload option. The Reload option is covered later in this chapter.

In the following exercise, you open and edit the ROOMPLAN drawing, the source of the PLAN xref. The demand for AutoCAD classes is so great that space for more desks is needed in the lecture room. Later you reopen CHAP12A to see the effects.

MODIFYING THE EXTERNALLY REFERENCED DRAWING

Continue from the preceding exercise. Create a backup copy of ROOMPLAN.DWG named ROOMPLAN.SAV using the Windows File Manager or AutoCAD's file utilities. After you have created the backup, open the ROOMPLAN drawing.

`Command:` *Choose Stretch (Modify, Resize)* Issues the STRETCH command

`Select objects:` Specify a *crossing window from* ① *to* ② *(see fig. 12.4)*

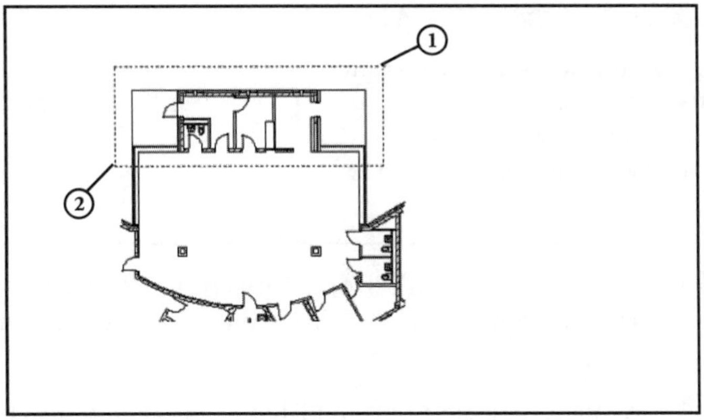

Figure 12.4

The drawing ROOMPLAN during STRETCH

```
Select objects: ↵
Base point or displacement: 0,8' ↵
Second point of displacement: ↵
Command: Save the drawing
```

You have now edited the xref object's source drawing, the externally referenced file, just as any drawing might be edited. Next, you open the CHAP19A drawing, which contains the xref to ATCHROOM which contains the xref to ROOMPLAN, to see the effect of this modification (see fig. 12.5).

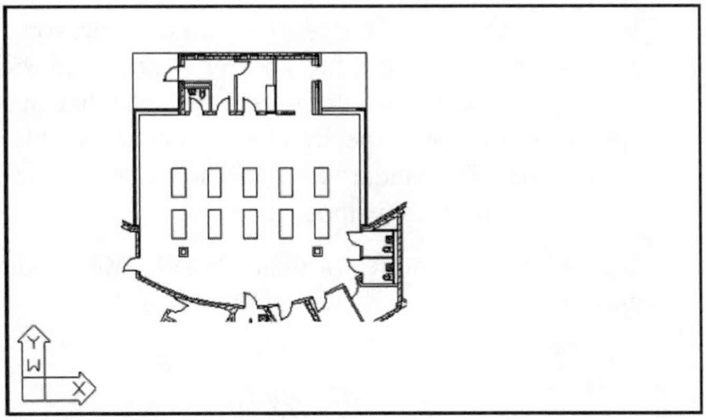

Figure 12.5

The CHAP19A drawing with the ROOMPLAN xref automatically updated.

`Command:` *Open the CHAP12A drawing*

`Resolve Xref ATCHROOM: ATCHROOM.DWG`	Loads each external reference drawing
`ATCHROOM loaded.`	and reports the status
`Resolve Xref PLAN: ROOMPLAN`	
`PLAN loaded. Regenerating drawing.`	
`Command:`	

If you open the CHAP12B drawing with the overlaid xrefs it would appear visually the same as CHAP12A. However, the drawing database contains two separate overlaid xrefs.

As AutoCAD loads a drawing, it finds and loads any external references. If an external drawing itself contains any attached xrefs, those drawings also are loaded. If drawings are found and loaded without any problem, AutoCAD reports them as loaded.

If AutoCAD has difficulty when it tries to load any of the externally referenced drawings, a message dialog box appears. The dialog box reports where AutoCAD looked for the external reference files. Make sure that all external reference files are in a directory in the AutoCAD search path. You can use XREF's Path option to respecify the drawing name and path for any unresolved xrefs.

Removing Xrefs

To remove an external reference from a drawing, you use the Detach option of the XREF command. Detaching an xref removes an xref object from the current drawing's database. You can detach both attached and overlaid xrefs. The Detach option prompts you to specify the name or names of the xrefs to detach. You can use any of AutoCAD's standard wild cards to specify xref names, or you can separate the names with commas (without spaces).

In the following exercise, you detach the ROOMPLAN drawing from the ATCHROOM drawing.

DETACHING XREFS

Continue from the previous drawing and open the ATCHROOM drawing.

`Command:` *Choose Detach (External Reference)*	Specifies the XREF command's Detach option
`Xref(s) to detach:` **ROOMPLAN** ↵	Specifies the XREF name to detach
`Scanning...`	

`No matching Xref names found.`

The xref name was not found because ROOMPLAN.DWG was attached with the PLAN xref name.

`Command:` *Choose Detach (External Reference)*	Specifies the XREF command's Detach option
`Xref(s) to detach:` **PLAN** ↵	Specifies the XREF name to detach
`Scanning...`	Scans the drawing database and removes the xref
`Command:` *Save the drawing*	
`Command:` Open CHAP12A	

When CHAP12A was reopened in the preceding exercise, only the ATCHROOM xref is loaded because the PLAN xref was detached (see fig. 12.6).

Figure 12.6

ATHCROOM drawing without PLAN xref.

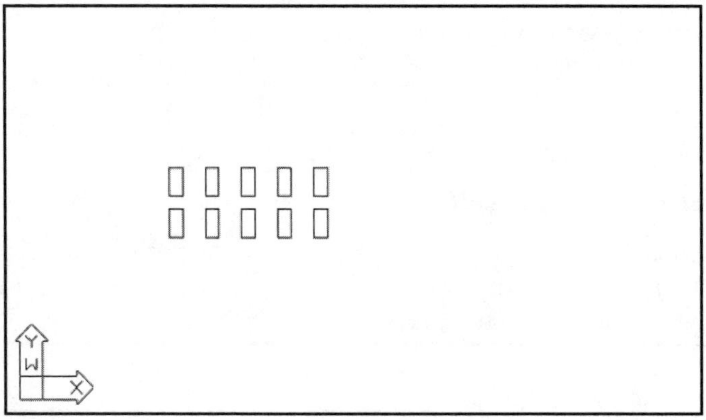

Reloading Xrefs

Should another colleague in your workgroup update a drawing referenced by your current drawing, you can use the XREF command's Reload option to update your xref. The Reload option enables you to reload a specific xref or group of xrefs. Reloading specific xrefs saves time over reopening your current drawing; you don't have to save changes to your drawing, open the drawing, and then wait while every xref loads again.

The Reload option prompts you to specify the name or names of the xrefs to reload. You can use any of AutoCAD's standard wild cards to specify xref names, or you can separate the names with commas (without spaces).

The XREF command's Reload option usually is used in a networked, team design situation because AutoCAD Release 13 for Windows can edit only one drawing at a time. In a non-networked environment, the Reload option can be used to reload updated drawings copied from floppy disk or other storage device.

In the next exercise you open the CHAP12B drawing, which loads the OVLYROOM and PLAN xrefs. After the drawing is opened you copy the backup ROOMPLAN drawing over the ROOMPLAN drawing referenced by PLAN and then reload the PLAN xref. Figure 12.7 shows the reloaded xref.

Reloading an Xref

Continue from the preceding exercise and open the CHAP12B drawing. Using the Windows File Manager or AutoCAD's file utilities, copy the ROOMPLAN.SAV backup file to ROOMPLAN.DWG.

`Command:` *Choose Reload (External Reference)*	Specifies the XREF command's Reload option
`Xref(s) to reload:` **PLAN** ↵	Specifies the XREF name to reload

`Scanning...`
`Reload Xref PLAN: ROOMPLAN`
`PLAN loaded. Regenerating drawing.`
	Scans the drawing database for the specified XREF and reloads the external file

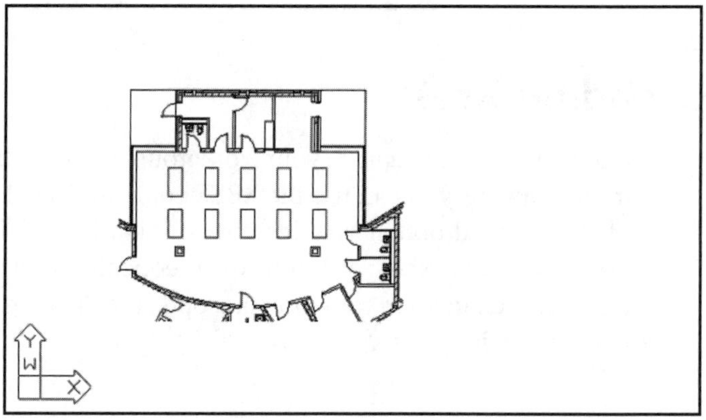

Figure 12.7

Updated ROOMPLAN reloaded.

Your drawing should now use the original unstretched version of ROOMPLAN. Because AutoCAD does not update the image of an xref in the current drawing when changes are made to the source file, it is necessary to force a reload.

In the preceding exercise you were aware that the ROOMPLAN drawing was updated. In a networked environment, it is likely that you will not be aware of changes as they occur. Take steps to make sure you're working with the latest drawing version as suggested in the following tip.

Tip

AutoCAD does not notify you when an externally referenced drawing has been updated. In a networked environment, it is important, therefore, to reload xrefs periodically or adopt a departmental policy requiring all workgroup members to notify each other of significant changes as they occur. A network workgroup broadcast message is an easy way to handle notification.

Changing Xref Paths

The path to each external file is stored as data in an xref object. If the structure of your project changes and referenced files are moved to another subdirectory, hard drive, or file server, you must also update the path information in the xref object. The XREF command Path option enables you to respecify a path to an external file.

The XREF command's Path option also enables you to specify a different file name for the xref. This is useful for using simplified stand-in drawings in place of large complex drawings for positioning or rough-in purposes. When the detail of the complex drawing is needed, you can substitute the file name of the alternate drawing in the xref.

In the following exercise, you move a referenced drawing to another subdirectory and use the XREF command's Path option to update the xref path.

Changing the Path of an External File

Using the Windows File Manager (or any other method you prefer), create a \IAW\TEMP subdirectory and move the ROOMPLAN drawing to the new subdirectory. After the file is moved, start AutoCAD and open the CHAP12B drawing.

When you open the drawing, a message box appears warning you that ROOMPLAN.DWG could not be found (see fig. 12.8). Choose OK.

`Command:` *Choose Path (External Reference)*	Specifies the XREF command's Path option
`Edit path for which xref(s):` **PLAN** ↵	Specifies the xref name to change
`Scanning...`	Searches the drawing database for the xref
`Xref name: PLAN` `Old path: ROOMPLAN`	Informs you of the old path and specifies
`New path:` **C:\IAW\TEMP\ROOMPLAN.DWG** ↵	Specifies the new path and file name
`Regenerating drawing.`	

`Reload Xref PLAN:`
`C:\IAW\TEMP\ROOMPLAN.DWG`
`PLAN loaded. Regenerating drawing.`
	Reloads the xref

`Command:` *Save the drawing*	

Use the Windows File Manager (or any other method you prefer) to copy ROOMPLAN back the original directory so it can be used by the remainder of the exercises in this chapter.

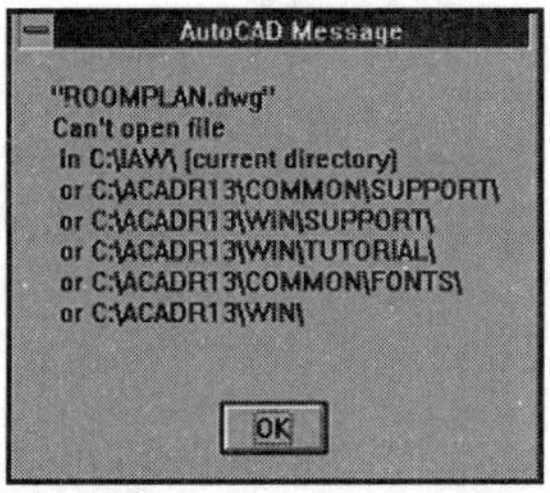

Figure 12.8

AutoCAD Message indicating it cannot locate externally referenced files.

Archiving Xrefs

When a project is finished it is a common practice to archive it to make space for new projects. It often is easier to archive a single project drawing rather than a master drawing and its many individual external drawings. The XREF command's Bind option makes an xref a permanent part of a drawing. Binding xrefs to the master drawing is safer than trying to remember to store a master drawing with its xrefs.

The Bind option prompts you to specify the name or names of the xrefs to bind to the current drawing. You can use any of AutoCAD's standard wild cards to specify xref names, or you can separate the names with commas (without spaces).

WARNING

The All (External Reference, Bind) tool automatically binds every xref in the drawing! You can reverse the operation with the UNDO command.

Binding an xref to a drawing converts the xref to a block, making it a permanent part of the drawing and no longer an externally referenced file. You can bind the entire drawing's database by using the XREF Bind option, or you can use the XBIND command to individually bind the named items (referred to as *dependent symbols*) in the current drawing. The XBIND command is discussed later in this chapter.

The following exercise uses the All (External Reference, Bind) tool to bind all the xrefs in CHAP12B into a single drawing.

ARCHIVING AN XREF

Continue in the CHAP12B drawing from the previous exercise.

`Command:` *Choose All (External Reference, Bind)*	Issues XREF command with Bind option

```
Xref(s) to bind: *
Scanning...

Regenerating drawing.
```

`Command:` *Choose List (External Reference)*

```
?/Bind/Detach/Path/Reload/Overlay/
<Attach>: ?↵
Xref(s) to list <*>: ↵

  Xref name          Path        Xref type
  ------------       -------     -----

  Total Xref(s): 0
```

`Command:` *Save the drawing*

When you opened the CHAP12B drawing in the preceding exercise again, AutoCAD did not load the xrefs; they no longer exist in the drawing. Visually, no changes occur when you bind an xref. However, when bound, the entire external file, including its dependent symbols, is incorporated into the referencing drawing. The dependent symbols are renamed so you easily can differentiate them from dependent symbols of xrefs.

Clipping Xrefs

New in Release 13 is the XREFCLIP command. This command enables you to create a specific view of an xref at a specific scale. XREFCLIP is useful for creating scaled detail views of a drawing in a plot drawing. XREFCLIP also is useful for importing standard details.

The XREFCLIP command attaches an xref on a layer you specify; displays the entire xref and prompts you to specify the area to display, the scale, and insertion point; and then creates a floating viewport based on your input. If TILEMODE is on, XREFCLIP prompts you to enable paper space. If you answer no to the prompt, the command fails; XREFCLIP requires paper space to be enabled. The layer you specify for the xref must not exist in the current drawing.

WARNING

The XREFCLIP command does not function properly if the xref you want to clip is already attached to the drawing. Use the XREF command's Detach option to remove the XREF before using the XREFCLIP command.

In the following exercise you use XREFCLIP to create a detailed view of a bathroom in ROOMPLAN and a full view of ROOMPLAN.

USING XREFCLIP

Start a new drawing named CHAP12C using XREFPROT as a prototype.

`Command:` *Choose Clip (External Reference)*	Issues the XREFCLIP command
`Initializing...`	
`Enable paper space? <Y>: ↵`	Enables paper space
`Regenerating drawing.`	
`Xref name:` **ROOMPLAN** ↵	Specifies drawing name for xref
`Clip onto what layer? DET-BATH-1 ↵`	Specifies the xref layer
`First corner of clip box:` *Pick* ① *(see fig. 12.9)*	Specifies first corner of clip box

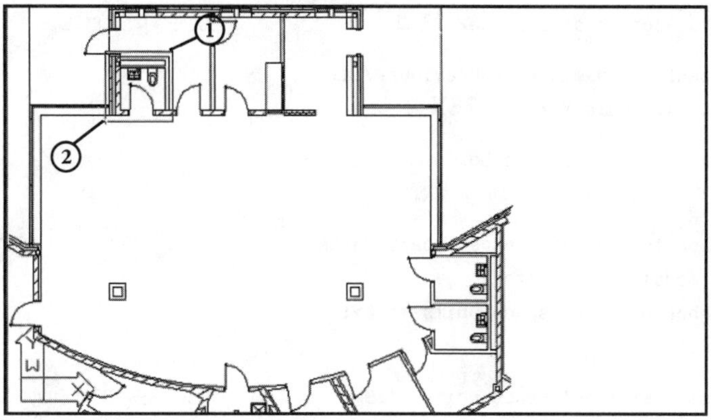

Figure 12.9

Specifying clip area for detail view of bathroom.

`Other corner:` *Pick* ②	Specifies second corner of clip box

`Enter the ratio of paper space units to model space units...`
`Number of paper space units <1.0>:`
12↵
	Specifies the number of paper space units

`Number of model space units <1.0>:` **1 ↵**	Specifies the number of model space units
`Insertion point for clip:` *Pick* ① *(see fig. 12.10)*	Specifies point for lower left corner of clip box

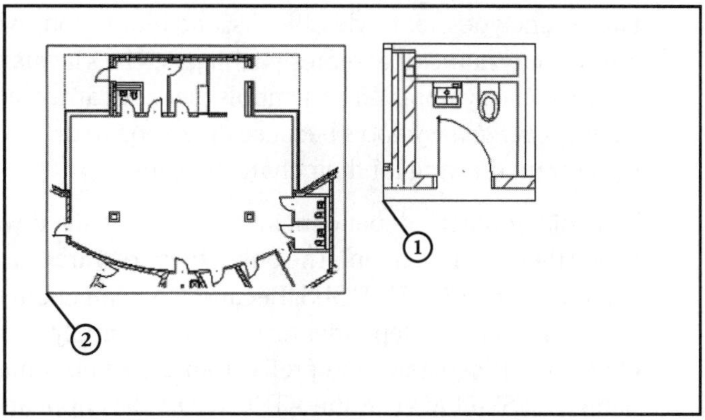

Figure 12.10

Two clipped xrefs created with XREFCLIP.

`Command:` *Choose Clip (External Reference)*	Issues the XREFCLIP command
`Xref name:` **ROOMPLAN ↵**	Specifies drawing name for xref
`Clip onto what layer?` **PLAN-1 ↵**	Specifies the xref layer

`First corner of clip box:` **'Z** ↵	Issues transparent zoom
`>>Center/Dynamic/Left/Previous/Vmax/ Window/<Scale(X/XP)>:` **.75X** ↵	Shrinks the view
`First corner of clip box:` *Enclose the entire xref with the clip window*	
`Enter the ratio of paper space units to model space units...`	Specifies the number of paper space units
`Number of paper space units <1.0>:` **48** ↵	
`Number of model space units <1.0>:` **1** ↵	Specifies the number of model space units
`Insertion point for clip:` *Pick* ②	Specifies point for lower left corner of clip box
`Command:` *Save the drawing*	

The next section explains what dependent symbols are and how they relate to xrefs. Up until this point dependent symbols have almost been ignored, but they are an important part of xrefs.

Understanding Xref Dependent Symbols

Layers, linetypes, text styles, blocks, and dimension styles are symbols; that is, they are arbitrary names that represent things such as layers or styles (not to be confused with graphic symbols). The symbols that are carried into a drawing by an xref are called *dependent symbols* because they depend on the external file, rather than on the current drawing for their characteristics.

To avoid conflicts, dependent symbols are prefixed with the name of the xref for which they are dependent. The only exceptions are unambiguous defaults like layer 0 and linetype CONTINUOUS. Because you can change text style STANDARD, it is prefixed. Prefixed dependent symbols also apply to nested xrefs. A vertical bar character (|) separates the prefix from the symbol name. For example, the layer named DESK-PLAN-1 in the ATCHROOM xref appears as the ATCHROOM|DESK-PLAN-1 dependent symbol.

To protect the integrity of an xref, AutoCAD limits the capability to change dependent symbols in your current drawing. You cannot make an xref's layer current and draw on it, for example, as you can with a standard drawing layer. You can modify an xref's appearance, however, by changing the color, linetype, and visibility of an xref's layers. Any changes you make are only temporary unless you set the VISRETAIN system variable to 1 (on). If you set VISRETAIN to 0 (off), AutoCAD restores all original dependencies when you reload the drawing or the xref.

NOTE

If you change the linetype of an xref-dependent layer to any linetype defined in the current drawing, you cannot reset it back to its original linetype without reloading the drawing or xref.

The names of other dependent symbols, such as blocks, dimension or text styles, are similarly displayed but cannot be modified unless you use the XREF BIND or XBIND commands.

As you learned earlier in this chapter, the XREF command's Bind option creates a block from an xref. The Bind option also renames the dependent symbols that belong to xrefs. It replaces the vertical bar (|) in the symbol name with $*n*$ (*n* is a number); for example, layer XSYMBOL|SYMLAYER changes to XSYMBOL0SYMLAYER. When AutoCAD renames binded symbols, it first uses 0 for the number. If a layer by that name already exists, AutoCAD increments the number by 1. AutoCAD continues trying higher numbers until it reaches a unique layer name. You can use the RENAME command to change these strange layer names to whatever layer name you like.

TIP

If you want to insert a drawing as a block into your current drawing (and there are conflicting layer names), attach the drawing as an xref first, then bind it as a block. This step preserves the incoming block's unique layers.

You can selectively import these dependent symbols into your current drawing with the XBIND command. You learn about the XBIND command later in this chapter.

TIP

You can use the Filters feature of the Layer Control dialog box to display a specific group of dependent layers.

Using XBIND To Import Part of an Xref

In an earlier exercise, you used the Bind option of XREF to convert an xref to a block. AutoCAD converted all the dependent symbols in the xref's file to make them part of the current drawing. The XBIND command binds only portions of an xref to the current drawing. Use XBIND if you only want to bring in a text style, block, or layer defined in the xref without binding the entire xref.

In addition to any symbols you explicitly bind by using XBIND, linetypes and other symbols that can be bound to one another are automatically bound to the current drawing. A linetype bound to a layer is one such example. The entities (lines and so on) contained in the xref are not bound to the drawing. If you bind a block, however, you can then use INSERT to insert it in the current drawing.

In the following exercise, you bind the DOORR block and its layers from ROOMPLAN. Then you set the bound layer current and insert a new door.

Binding Only Parts of an Xref by Using XBIND

Start a new drawing named CHAP12D using XREFPROT as a prototype, attach ROOMPLAN at 0,0 with default scale and rotation, then zoom to the view in figure 12.11.

`Command:` **LAYER ↵**	Issues the LAYER command
`?/Make/Set/New/ON/OFF/Color/Ltype/ Freeze/Thaw/LOck/Unlock:` **? ↵**	Specifies List option
`Layer name(s) to list <*>:` **ROOMPLAN* ↵**	Specifies layers to list

```
Layer name           State      Color        Linetype
----------           -----      -----        -------
ROOMPLAN¦A-DOOR       On        1 (red)      CONTINUOUS      Xdep: ROOMPLAN
ROOMPLAN¦A-FLOR-BATH  On        1 (red)      CONTINUOUS      Xdep: ROOMPLAN
ROOMPLAN¦A-FLOR-WALL  On        2 (yellow)   CONTINUOUS      Xdep: ROOMPLAN
ROOMPLAN¦A-IDEN-DIMS  Frozen    1 (red)      CONTINUOUS      Xdep: ROOMPLAN
ROOMPLAN¦A-OVHD-FLOR  On        1 (red)      ROOMPLAN¦SDASHED  Xdep: ROOMPLAN
ROOMPLAN¦A-WALL-FULL  On        3 (green)    CONTINUOUS      Xdep: ROOMPLAN
ROOMPLAN¦A-WALL-FURR  On        8            CONTINUOUS      Xdep: ROOMPLAN
ROOMPLAN¦A-WNDW-EXTR  On        1 (red)      CONTINUOUS      Xdep: ROOMPLAN
ROOMPLAN¦A-WNDW-INTR  On        1 (red)      CONTINUOUS      Xdep: ROOMPLAN
ROOMPLAN¦S-COLS       On        4 (cyan)     CONTINUOUS      Xdep: ROOMPLAN
```

`Current layer:` **ROOM-LAYOUT**	
`Command:` *Choose Layer (External Reference, Bind)*	Issues XBIND command with Layer option
`Block/Dimstyle/LAyer/LType/Style:` **_la**	
`Dependent Layer name(s):` **ROOMPLAN|A-DOOR** ↵	Specifies layer to bind
`Scanning...`	Scans the drawing database and binds layer
`1 Layer(s) bound.`	
`Command:` **BLOCK** ↵	Issues the block command
`Block name (or ?):` **?** ↵	Specifies the list option
`Block(s) to list <*>:` ***** ↵	Lists all blocks

```
Defined blocks.
  ROOMPLAN                          Xref: resolved
  ROOMPLAN¦COLCONC                  Xdep: ROOMPLAN
  ROOMPLAN¦DOORR                    Xdep: ROOMPLAN
  ROOMPLAN¦LAVFS                    Xdep: ROOMPLAN
  ROOMPLAN¦WCWALL                   Xdep: ROOMPLAN

User      External      Dependent    Unnamed
Blocks    References    Blocks       Blocks
   0          1            4            7
```

`Command:` *Choose Block (External Reference, Bind)*	Issues XBIND command with Block option
`Block/Dimstyle/LAyer/LType/Style: _b`	
`Dependent Block name(s):` **ROOMPLAN|DOORR** ↵	Specifies block to bind
`Scanning...`	Scans drawing database and binds block
`1 Block(s) bound. Regenerating drawing.`	
`Command:` *Make the ROOMPLAN0A-DOOR layer current*	
`Command:` *Choose Data, Rename*	Issues the DDRENAME command and displays the Rename dialog box

In the Rename *dialog box, select* Block *from the* Named Objects list *and* ROOMPLAN0DOORR *in the* Items *list, type* **DOORR** *in the* Rename to: *text box, click on the* Rename to: *button, then choose* OK	Renames the block
`1 Block renamed.`	
`Command:` **INSERT** ↵	Issues the INSERT command
`Block name (or ?):` **DOORR** ↵	Specifies block to insert
`Insertion point:` *Using endpoint object snap pick* ① *(see fig. 12.11)*	Specifies insertion point
`X scale factor <1> / Corner / XYZ:` **36** ↵	Specifies insertion scale Accepts default scale
`Rotation angle <0>:` ↵	Accepts default rotation angle
`Command:` *Save the drawing*	

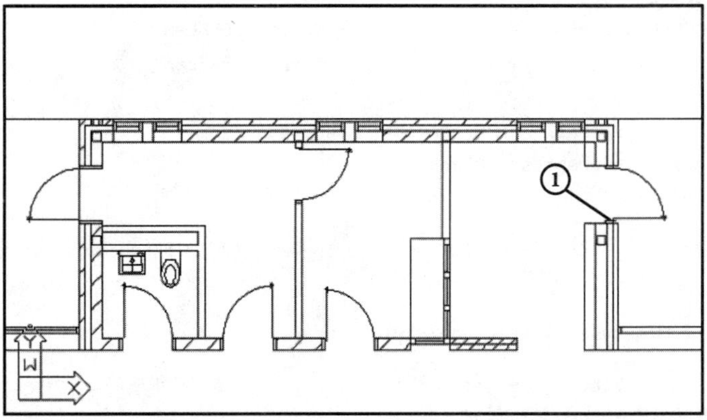

Figure 12.11

Bound DOORR block inserted on bound A-DOOR layer.

Use BIND if you want to bind the entire xref to make it a block. Use XBIND if you only want to bind layer, linetype, dimension styles, nested blocks, or text styles without binding any actual entities in the xref.

TIP

You can attach a library file that contains predefined named items, such as dimension styles or blocks. Use XBIND to import specific items, rename them to usable names, and then detach the xref.

Reading the XREF Log File

AutoCAD maintains a log file of all xref activity in ASCII-text format. The log file is stored in the same directory as your drawing, and it uses your drawing's name with an XLG extension. The log file continues to grow as the drawing is edited over many sessions. Occasionally, you may want to delete all or part of the log file to save disk space. AutoCAD maintains this log file if the XREFCTL system variable is set to 1 (on). The default setting is 0 (off).

The log file indicates nested xrefs, dependent symbols, and any errors that occur. AutoCAD displays many of these messages in the command line, as well as writing them to the XREF log file. This log file can be a useful troubleshooting tool when you manage xrefs in your drawings. It can also be used to double check when giving drawings containing xrefs to others.

Managing Xref Layers, Colors, and Linetypes

When you insert a block into a drawing, any layers in the block's definition are added to the drawing. If a layer in a block already exists in the drawing, and the object properties in the block are set to BYLAYER, the block's objects take on the characteristics of the existing drawing's layer.

Xrefs work a little differently than blocks. When you attach an xref that contains layers other than layer 0, AutoCAD modifies the xref layer names to avoid duplication. A vertical bar (|) prefixes the xref layer names to separate the prefix from the layer name. The renaming of the layers prevents the xref's entities from taking on the characteristics of existing layers in the drawing.

As usual, the exception is layer 0. Any objects that exist on layer 0 in the xref come in on layer 0 in the destination drawing. They then assume the characteristics of the destination drawing's current layer, as would a block insert. The following list describes how xref objects created on layer 0 behave when you attach them to a drawing, based on their color and linetype settings:

- **BYLAYER.** The objects assume the color and linetype characteristics of the destination drawing's current layer.
- **BYBLOCK.** The objects assume the color and linetype characteristics that are current at the time the xref is attached.
- **EXPLICIT.** The objects retain their original explicit color and linetype settings.

Because an xref's layers do not merge with the destination drawing's layers (except layer 0), you can simply create the xref's objects on any layer other than 0 to make layers, colors, and linetypes remain as they are in the original drawing.

If you want an xref to temporarily assume different characteristics in the destination drawing, you can change the settings of the xref's layers in the destination drawing. Unless the VISRETAIN system variable is set to 1 (on), however, the changes do not survive from one drawing session to another or if the xref is reloaded in the current drawing session.

Multiple Access Network Support Features

AutoCAD manages file locking in a networked workgroup environment. If simultaneous reads and writes were allowed, files would become corrupt and AutoCAD could crash.

There are two type of locks used by AutoCAD: write locks and read locks. A write lock is placed on a file when the file is opened for editing. Write locks prevent other users on the network from opening a drawing that is being edited. If you attempt to open a write-locked file, AutoCAD informs you that the file is write locked and reports who is using the file and when it was opened. A file remains write locked for the entire editing session.

A write locked file can be opened as read only or used as an external reference by another AutoCAD user. While the write locked file is being loaded by another AutoCAD drawing session, a read lock is placed on the file. A *read lock* prevents the user editing the drawing from saving or writing a block to the opened drawing while it is being read by another user. If the user editing a drawing attempts to write to a read-locked file, AutoCAD informs you that the file is read locked and reports who is reading the file and when the read lock was placed on the drawing. The read lock is removed after the file is finished being loaded.

If AutoCAD crashes during an editing session, or during a file read, read and write locks might not be removed. You can remove a lock using AutoCAD's file utilities. Be sure to only unlock files that are not in use by another AutoCAD user.

In this chapter, you learned how to use references to external drawings to improve drawing efficiency and enable concurrent design practices. Xrefs give the same benefits as blocks, but they work with multiple drawings. Xrefs are most useful for keeping file size to a minimum and for ensuring that a drawing has the most up-to-date revision of the parts it contains. Xrefs act like blocks, and you can consider them special types of blocks. If controlling the proliferation of common data, keeping drawing size down, and decreasing disk usage are critical problems, use xrefs.

The use of xrefs benefits from sound CAD management practices. Plan ahead when developing a project that will involve a set of interrelated drawings that you want to use as xrefs. For example:

- Use a common origin point for each reference drawing to simplify the process of assembling and coordinating them.
- Decide which elements are truly common to your various drawings that reference base drawings. Sometimes labels and annotations are best stored in separate drawings that can be referenced as required, thus reducing the clutter in drawings that do not need them.
- Set up an appropriate directory structure in which to store the project's drawings if you foresee the use of many external reference drawings. Although the XREF command's Path option enables you to update the path to referenced drawings, if you change the location of a large number of xref files in the middle of a project, it can be very time-consuming.

part III

Object Editing Tools

chapter

13

AUTOEDITING WITH GRIPS

As your skills with AutoCAD develop, you use more editing commands than drawing commands. You can, for example, use LINE and ARC (drawing commands) to represent a single chair in a room. You then would use COPY or ARRAY (editing commands) to generate the duplicates and fill up the room with chairs.

In addition to editing commands, such as MOVE, TRIM, and ARRAY, AutoCAD provides several quick, interactive, easy-to-use autoediting modes, such as Stretch, Move, and Rotate. To use autoediting modes, you select objects and then manipulate them by their geometric points, called grip points. This chapter focuses on using autoediting modes with grips. Chapter 14, "The Ins and Outs of Editing," continues the discussion of editing techniques and selection options in more depth.

To perform edit operations, AutoCAD must know which objects are selected. In this chapter, you learn the following:

- How to select objects at the `Command:` prompt
- How to use grips with the stretch, move, rotate, scale, and mirror autoediting methods
- How to use multiple hot grips to manipulate multiple points or objects
- How to control grip and selection behavior with DDGRIPS and DDSELECT settings

Picking an object at the `Command:` prompt causes grips to appear. A *grip* is a convenient location on the object to help control and manipulate that object, much like a modern suitcase with wheels has a couple of handles. Each AutoCAD object has several grip points, which can be chosen accurately (without specifying object snap modes) by picking with the point in the grip box. Figure 13.1 shows the grip locations of common objects.

Figure 13.1

Common object grip locations.

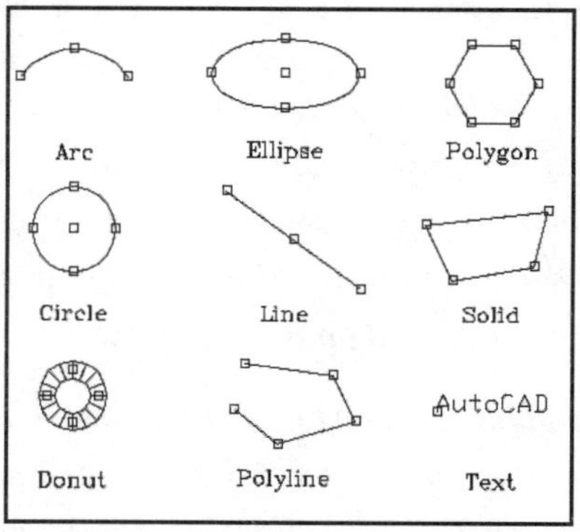

The grip points on a line, for example, are the endpoints and the midpoint. When grips are enabled (the default), the grips appear on an object when that object is selected at the `Command:` prompt.

When you click on a visible grip, it becomes "hot" (selected) and appears highlighted. A hot grip becomes a base point for one of the autoediting modes to manipulate the object.

The next section explains the important features of grips and shows how proper grip usage can make editing tasks less tedious. In this chapter, you will further develop the TOOLPLAT drawing from the IAW Disk. Figure 13.2 shows the initial view of the drawing.

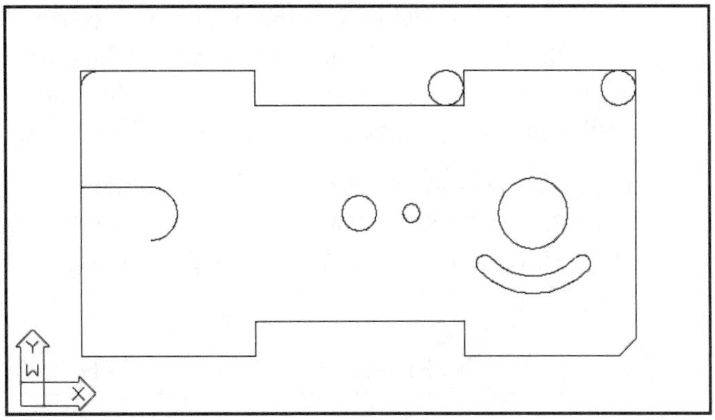

Figure 13.2

Selected objects with grip points.

Introducing Autoediting Modes

Autoediting modes are a special group of common editing methods that are available when a base grip is chosen. These modes are briefly explained in the following list.

- **Stretch.** This mode modifies objects by moving one or more grips to another location while leaving the other part of the object intact. This can easily change the size or shape of an object or a group of objects. In some cases, the stretch mode moves an object.
- **Move.** This mode relocates objects from a base point to another specified location. The size and orientation do not change.
- **Rotate.** This mode revolves objects around a base point. The angle can be entered, dragged, or shown using the Reference option.
- **Scale.** This mode resizes objects up or down by a given scale factor about a specified base point. Scale factors can be entered, dragged, or shown using the Reference option.
- **Mirror.** This mode reflects selected objects about a line described by the base point grip or specified point and another specified point.

All these autoediting modes have common properties. First, when objects are selected and a base grip is chosen to issue the command, you can choose the desired mode by entering the first two letters of the mode (SC for scale, for example) or by pressing Enter, the spacebar, or the pointing device Enter button. Pressing Enter repeatedly cycles through the autoediting modes in the order shown in the preceding list. Each mode displays a set of options, such as the Copy option. If you want to make a copy while executing any autoediting mode, use the Copy option or hold down the Shift key while making multiple second point picks. The Undo option undoes the last edit, and the eXit option exits the autoediting modes. These modes and their options are similar to the corresponding commands, such as STRETCH and MOVE, which are discussed in Chapter 14, "The Ins and Outs of Editing."

The following exercises introduce you to selecting and editing objects using grips to modify the TOOLPLAT drawing from the IAW Disk. You use grips to stretch the top and side lines to the ends of the arc to form a fillet for the upper left corner.

Stretching Lines with Grips

Begin a new drawing named CHAP13 using the TOOLPLAT drawing as a prototype. Zoom to the drawing area shown in figure 13.3.

`Command:` *Pick a point on the upper left arc*	Selects and highlights the arc and displays its grips
`Command:` *Pick line at* ① (see fig. 8.4)	Selects and highlights the top line and displays grips
`Command:` *Pick grip at* ②	Enters stretch autoediting mode

`** STRETCH **`
`<Stretch to point>/Base point/Copy/`
`Undo/eXit:` *Pick arc's grip at* ③
	Stretches the line to the arc endpoint

Choose View, Zoom, Previous	

Figure 13.3

Grip points and pick points.

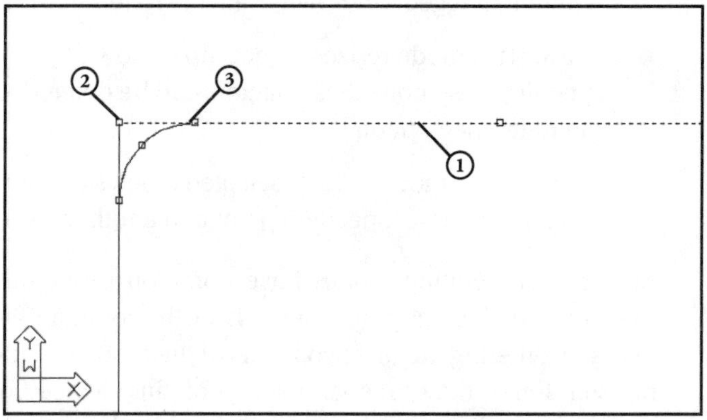

NOTE

> If you miss the object when picking, a rubber-band box (a window) appears from the pick point. Pick again at the same point, and then try again. Window selection is covered later in this chapter in the section "Controlling Press and Drag."

The preceding exercise could have used the endpoint object snap to lock the line onto the arc's endpoint. Because the cursor automatically snaps to grips, however, you generally do not need to use object snaps while grip editing.

TIP

> You can grip-edit objects with minimal use of object snaps. First, select object geometry and the objects to edit to snap to (displaying all grips). Then, click on the grips of the objects to edit (making those grips hot). Finally, snap to any of the displayed grips, eliminating the need for most (but not all) object snap modes. All grips remain displayed until you enter a command or press Esc at the `Command:` prompt.

To better control editing with grips, you must understand AutoCAD's grip and selection settings and methods. You can create a selection set of objects either before or after you choose the editing command. The next section explains how.

Understanding Object Selection Order

AutoCAD supports two methods of object editing—verb/noun selection and noun/verb selection. To illustrate the distinction grammatically, consider the active-voice sentence "John threw the ball." Here, the verb (throw, an action) precedes the noun (ball, an object). The passive-voice sentence "The ball was thrown by John." places the noun before the verb. Both sentence variations convey the same meaning.

As an AutoCAD user, however, you are not interested in throwing balls, but editing graphical objects! You can choose an edit operation first, then create the selection set (verb/noun), or you can pick objects first, then apply a modification (noun/verb). Which method to use is purely a personal preference. The result is the same—object editing occurs. The next section compares these two schemes.

Verb/Noun Selection

This selection method is analogous to a scientist verbally ordering a robot to perform some movement: "Push chair!" or "Drop package!" The robot applies the commands (verbs) to the appropriate set of objects (nouns). These directives are simple yet effective.

Historically, this command execution sequence was the sole means of editing AutoCAD objects since version 1.2, back in 1983. More recently, AutoCAD provided an alternate method of object editing called noun/verb selection, discussed next.

Noun/Verb Selection

In most Microsoft Windows applications, you can edit objects by creating a selection set (noun) first, then choosing the desired operation (verb). AutoCAD Release 13 for Windows is no different. In fact, as of Release 12, the AutoCAD developers included noun/verb selection as an editing method to answer the "wish list" request of the growing number of Windows users.

To use noun/verb selection, make sure the mode is checked in the Object Selection Settings dialog box (see fig. 13.5). You can display this dialog box by using the DDSELECT command or by choosing Options, Selection.

NOTE

For a more thorough discussion of object selection through verb/noun and noun/verb ordering, refer to Chapter 14.

Controlling GRIPS and Selection Parameters

Grips must be on for autoediting modes to function. You can display the Grips dialog box (see fig. 13.4) by using the DDGRIPS command or by choosing Options, Grips.

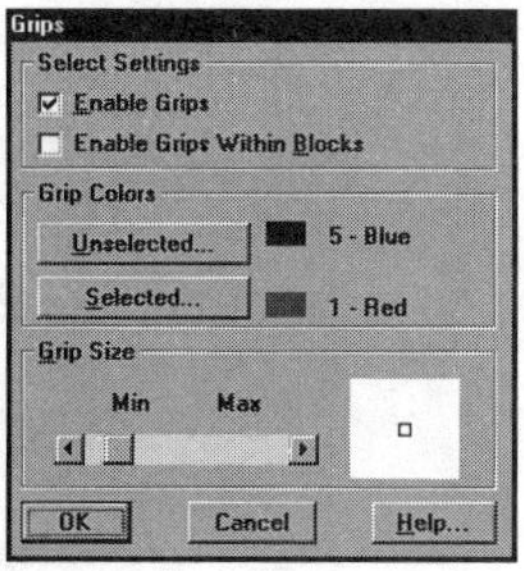

Figure 13.4

The Grips dialog box.

Putting a check mark in the Enable Grips check box turns on the GRIPS system variable; clearing the box turns it off. You can easily adjust the grip size, which works similarly to object snap aperture size, with the slider bar. You also can specify the color of both displayed and selected grips in this dialog box by choosing the Unselected and Selected buttons.

Tip

The GRIPS system variable stores the grips on/off setting. On is 1 and off is 0. To check all the AutoCAD system variables related to grips, enter SETVAR at the Command: prompt, then ?, then GRIP*. See Appendix F, "System and Dimension Variables Tables," or use online help for the details on the corresponding values.

Controlling Selection with DDSELECTA

Two other selection settings, Use Shift to Add and Press and Drag, improve the versatility and interaction of editing with grips. They are found in the Object Selection Settings dialog box (see fig. 13.5), which is accessed through the DDSELECT command or by choosing Options, Selection. The other settings in the Object Selection Settings dialog box are covered in Chapter 14, "The Ins and Outs of Editing."

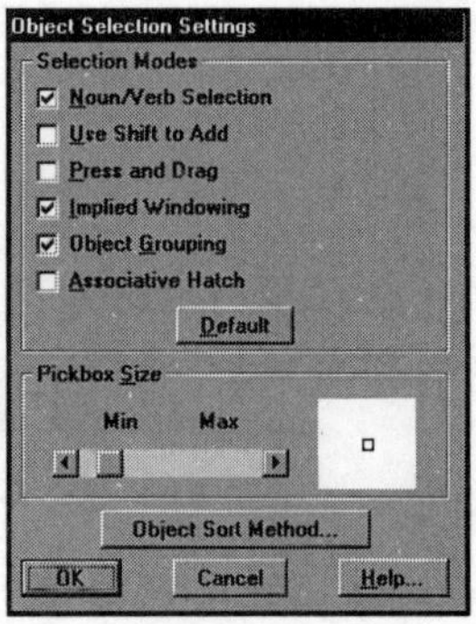

Figure 13.5

The Object Selection Settings dialog box.

AutoCAD editing modes and commands operate on a *selection set* of objects that you select. The current selection generally is indicated by highlighting the objects. The Use Shift to Add setting controls how objects are added to the selection set. When this setting is off (the default), objects are added to the selection set as they are selected. When this setting is on, newly selected objects replace the existing selection set unless you hold down Shift as you select them. Holding down Shift and selecting (Shift+pick) currently highlighted objects removes those objects from the selection set, independent of the Use Shift to Add setting. To add objects when Use Shift to Add is on, hold down Shift while selecting objects. After you remove a selected object from the selection set, its grips still appear until you clear them, as described later in this section. Experiment with Use Shift to Add in the following exercise.

CONTROLLING SELECTION

Continue in the CHAP13 drawing from the preceding exercise.

`Command:` *Choose* Options, Selection	Clears the selection set and displays the Object Selection Settings dialog box
Choose Default, then OK	Ensures default setting
`Command:` *Pick any object*	Highlights the object and starts a selection set
`Command:` *Pick two other objects*	Highlights the objects and adds them to the set
`Command:` *Shift+pick one of the highlighted objects*	Removes the object from the set, but leaves grips

Command: *Choose* Options, Selection	Clears the selection set and displays the Object Selection Settings dialog box
Put a check mark in the Use Shift to Add *check box, then choose* OK	Turns Use Shift to Add on and exits
Command: *Pick any object*	Starts a new selection set
Command: *Pick any other object*	Clears the selection set (leaving grips on) and starts a new set
Command: *Shift+pick two other objects*	Adds the objects to the existing set
Command: *Shift+pick a highlighted object*	Removes the object from the set

The current Use Shift to Add setting (off or on) is obvious as you select objects and is really a personal preference. Even if you are used to having it off, with practice you probably will find it more convenient to set it on. Just remember to use Shift to unselect objects or select additional objects.

The exercises throughout the rest of this book assume that Use Shift to Add is checked on.

NOTE

The Use Shift to Add setting is stored in the PICKADD system variable. Confusingly, Use Shift to Add on means PICKADD=0 (off) and Use Shift to Add off (the default) means PICKADD=1 (on).

As an alternative to pressing Esc to clear a selection set or to clear grips (press Esc twice to clear both), you also can select in a clear area to accomplish the same result. When you do so, you are actually selecting to clear the selection set. If Press and Drag is off (the default), you must pick twice. (Press and Drag is discussed in the next section.) If your first pick finds an object, it selects the object. If, however, the first pick misses, it sets the base corner of a rubber-banded window or crossing box. A second pick completes the window or crossing selection. A window selects all objects totally enclosed in its box; a crossing selects all objects in the box or that cross its box. You pick window points left-to-right, and the rubber-band box is shown solid; you pick crossing points right-to-left, and the rubber-band box is dashed. If the selection set is already empty, or if you just emptied it with a window or crossing selection of empty space, making another empty window or crossing selection removes all grips from the drawing window. You often need to clear grips to keep the drawing area from becoming too cluttered. Alternatively, you can press Esc twice to clear the grips and selection set.

Window and crossing selections, including clearing a selection set and grips using the preceding method, are easier if you change the way AutoCAD makes window and crossing selections. The next section explains how and why.

Controlling Press and Drag

In earlier releases, AutoCAD always required two picks to show a window. In most software with a graphical interface, you can make a window selection by pressing and holding the button at the first point, dragging to the second point, and then releasing the button. The Object Selection Settings dialog box now offers a choice in the way a window or crossing is specified. When the Press and Drag box is checked (the PICKDRAG system variable is on, set to 1), a window is created by pressing the pick button, moving to the other corner of the window, and releasing. Even if you are accustomed to the old two-pick method, once you get used to Press and Drag you will find it faster and more efficient.

TIP

Keeping Press and Drag on avoids the nuisance of starting a selection window by mistake. If you inadvertently pick a clear area of the drawing without moving the pointing device, no damage is done.

Press and Drag also behaves the same as other software you might use and enables you to clear selection sets or grips with a single pick.

WARNING

Throughout the rest of the book, Press and Drag (PICKDRAG on, 1) is the default window/ crossing selection mode. When exercises direct you to use a crossing or window selection, remember to use the Press and Drag technique to select as directed.

Controlling the Pick Box Sizes

The pick box is a small box that enables you to select objects. Unless both Noun/ Verb selection (see Chapter 14, "The Ins and Outs of Editing") in the Object Selection Settings dialog box and grips are disabled, the pick box appears on the crosshairs at the `Command:` prompt. The pick box also appears without the crosshairs at the `Select` `objects:` prompt during editing commands such as ERASE, MOVE, and COPY. The pick box size is controlled through a system variable. You can easily adjust the size by clicking and dragging a horizontal slider in the Object Selection Settings dialog box, accessed from the Options pull-down menu. The size units are pixels and the value usually ranges between 1 and 15, depending on your graphics resolution. Use whatever is comfortable for your display and pointing device, but be sure to set it to a different size than the aperture.

NOTE

A large pick box size can either increase the time required to select objects, or increase the likelihood of picking an object by mistake in a crowded area. Conversely, a small pick box can be difficult to manage. Experiment with pick box and aperture sizes to find a "happy medium."

To set the values transparently, enter either 'PICKBOX or 'APERTURE.

Editing with the Autoediting Modes

Now that you have an understanding of Use Shift to Add and Press and Drag, you can use the techniques to simplify editing tasks.

Object Snapping and Stretching with Grips

When snap is on, as you have seen, the cursor snaps to points on the snap grid. Similarly during a grip operation, the cursor snaps to grip points. When you move the cursor near a grip box, it snaps to the grip's center. This mechanism works in any grip mode and provides a geometric snap function similar to the object snap modes (see Chapter 3, "Drawing Accurately"). Because geometric points include center points, endpoints, and midpoints, snapping to grips enables you to precisely and easily stretch, move, and rotate existing geometry.

The following exercises continue the use of the stretch autoediting mode and show you how to snap to specific points by using only grips. Grip editing usually involves fewer steps than regular object snap editing; thus, it is a great time-saver.

OBJECT SNAPPING WITH GRIPS

Continue with the CHAP13 drawing from the preceding exercise and zoom to the view shown in figure 13.6.

`Command:` *Pick the arc at* ① (see fig. 13.6)	Selects the arc and displays its grips
`Command:` *Pick line at* ②	Clears the previous set, selects the vertical line, and shows grips
`Command:` *Pick grip at* ③	Grips the line and enters stretch mode
`** STRETCH **` `<Stretch to point>/Base point/Copy/` `Undo/eXit:` *Pick the lower left grip on the arc at* ④ *in figure 13.7*	Snaps the line to the arc endpoint

Figure 13.6

Grip and object selection points before stretching lines.

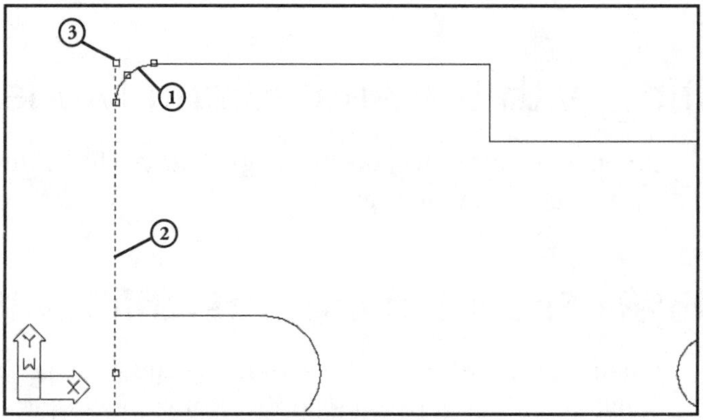

Figure 13.7

Tool plate after stretching lines.

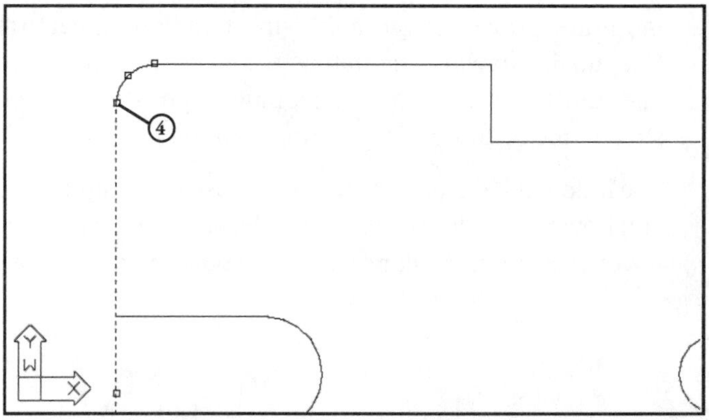

The stretch autoediting mode enables you to stretch various types of objects by moving selected grips to new locations. With a few exceptions, depending on which grip you pick, the stretch autoediting mode changes the shape of objects. In the next exercise, you change one of the arcs in the radial slot.

STRETCHING ARCS WITH AUTOEDIT

Continue with CHAP13 drawing from the previous exercise.

Zoom to the previous view.

`Command:` *Pick any arc*	Selects arc and displays grips
`Command:` *Pick the arc's midpoint grip*	Grips the midpoint and enters stretch mode

`** STRETCH **`
`<Stretch to point>/Base point/Copy/`
`Undo/eXit:` *Move and pick any other point*
	Changes the arc's shape

`Command:` *Pick an endpoint grip on the arc*	Grips the endpoint and enters stretch mode

`** STRETCH **`
`<Stretch to point>/Base point`
`/Copy/Undo/eXit:` *Pick any other point*
	Changes the arc's shape

`Command:` *Choose Undo (Standard)*	Undoes the last change
`Command:` *Choose Undo (Standard)*	Returns the arc to its original shape

Copying and Moving with Stretch Autoediting Mode

The stretch autoediting mode can move an object, change an endpoint, or resize an object, depending on the object type and selected grip. Some grips move the object rather than stretching it. For example, selecting a line's midpoint or circle's center grip moves the object, whereas picking the line's endpoint or circle's quadrant grip stretches it. You also can use the Copy option or hold the Shift key down while choosing the second point to create copies while stretching.

In this next exercise, you experiment with these methods and options, and use the Copy option of the stretch autoediting mode to complete the guide slot at the left of the tool plate.

Copying with Autoediting Modes

`Command:` *Pick the line at* ① *(see fig. 13.8)*	Selects the line and displays grips
`Command:` *Pick the mid grip on the line*	Grips line and enters stretch mode, moving line

`** STRETCH **`
`<Stretch to point>/Base point/Copy/`
`Undo/eXit:` *Pick a point above the tool plate*
	Moves the line

`Command:` *Choose Undo (Standard)*	Undoes the stretch move
`Command:` *Select the guide slot arc*	Selects and displays grips
`Command:` *Pick at* ①	Clears the arc from the set, selects the *line*, and displays its grips
`Command:` *Pick the line's midpoint grip*	Grips the line and enters stretch autoediting mode, moving the line

`** STRETCH **`
`<Stretch to point>/Base point/Copy/`
`Undo/eXit:` **B** ↵
	Specifies the Base point option

`Base point:` *Pick the right end grip of the line*	Changes the base (from) point for moving the line

`** STRETCH **`
`<Stretch to point>/Base point/Copy/`
`Undo/eXit:` **C** ↵
	Specifies the Copy (multiple stretch) option

`**STRETCH (multiple) **`
`<Stretch to point>/Base point/Copy/`
`Undo/eXit:` *Pick the bottom grip on the arc at* ②
	Copies the line

`<Stretch to point>/Base point/Copy/` `Undo/eXit:` *Pick another point below the base plate*	Copies the line again
`<Stretch to point>/Base point/Copy/` `Undo/eXit:` *Choose Undo (Standard)*	Undoes the last copy
`<Stretch to point>/Base point/Copy/` `Undo/eXit:` ↵	`Exits from autoediting mode`
`Command:` *Choose Save (Standard)*	Clears the selection sets and grips, and saves the drawing

Figure 13.8

Copying with stretch autoediting mode.

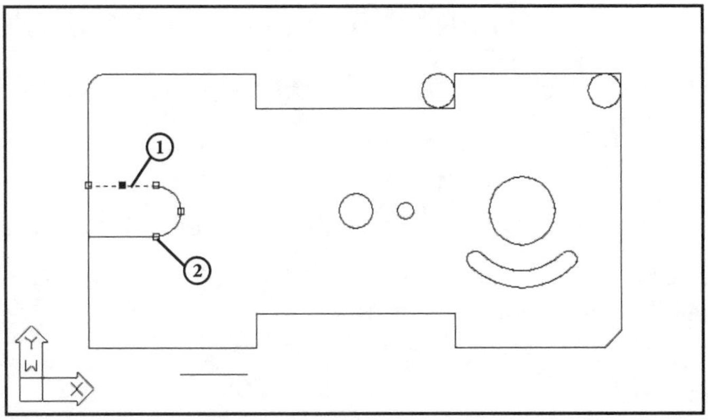

Note

You can exit from the multiple autoediting modes by pressing Enter, the spacebar, or Esc, or by entering an X. If you are not in multiple mode, you can exit from autoediting by pressing Esc or by entering an X.

Because it is so versatile—capable of stretching, moving, and copying objects—stretch is the default autoediting mode when grip editing. The move autoediting mode works similarly to stretch and is explained in the next section.

Using the Move Autoediting Mode

Instead of using the stretch autoediting mode to move an object, try using the move mode. To do so, enter MO at the autoedit prompt or press Enter or the spacebar once, and the move mode prompt appears. Specifying a point moves the selected object or objects the distance between the base point (selected grip) and the specified point. If you want a base point other than the selected hot grip, the Base point option enables you to respecify it, as in the preceding exercise. You can specify points by any combination of grips, object snaps, or coordinate entry.

Tip

When attempting to move or stretch a grip point a small distance, the destination point might be within the grip box of the gripped point, frustrating your efforts. In such cases, just move or stretch the grip to an out-of-the-way point, repick the grip, and then repick the destination point, which is now clear of the grip.

Try using the move autoediting mode in the next exercise.

USING MOVE AUTOEDITING MODE

Continue with the CHAP13 drawing from the previous exercise.

`Command:` *Pick, drag, and release to select from ① to ② (see fig. 13.9)*	Selects the radial slot and displays grips
`Command:` *Pick either large arc's mid grip*	Enters stretch mode

`** STRETCH **`
`<Stretch to point>/Base point/Copy/`
`Undo/eXit:` ↵
	Switches to move mode

`** MOVE **`
`<Move to point>/Base point/Copy/`
`Undo/eXit:`	

Move the cursor and note that the entire radial slot (the entire selection set) now moves with the cursor.

Pick any point below the tool plate	Relocates the slot
`Command:` *Choose Undo (Standard)*	Undoes the move and removes grips

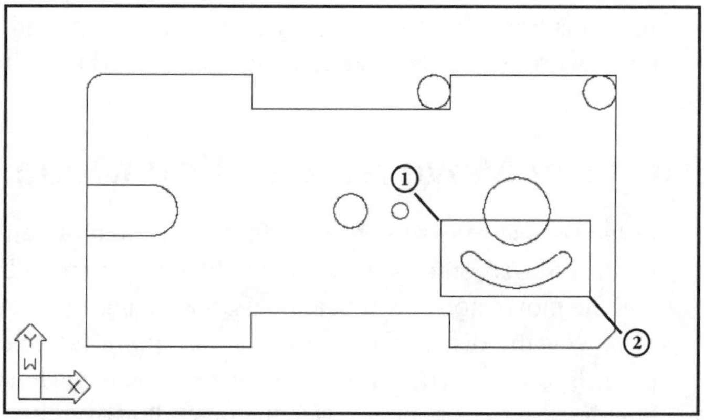

Figure 13.9

Window selection points for moving the slot.

As with stretch mode, you can make one or more copies from the original by using move mode. Use the Copy option or hold down the Shift key while picking the first destination point. The next exercise uses the Copy option with the move mode.

Copying with the Move Autoediting Mode

Continue with the CHAP13 drawing from the previous exercise.

`Command:` *Select a window from* ① *to* ② *(refer to figure 13.9)*	Selects the radial slot and displays grips
`Command:` *Pick any of the large arc's grips*	Enters stretch mode
`** STRETCH **` `<Stretch to point>/Base point/Copy/` `Undo/eXit:` *Press the spacebar*	Switches to move mode
`** MOVE **` `<Move to point>/Base point/Copy/` `Undo/eXit:` **C** ↵	Specifies the Copy (multiple) option
`** MOVE (multiple) **` `<Move to point>/Base point/Copy/` `Undo/eXit:` Pick two points below the tool plate (see fig. 13.10)	Copies two new slots to below the tool plate
`<Move to point>/Base point/Copy/` `Undo/eXit:` ↵	Exits from autoediting mode

Save the drawing.

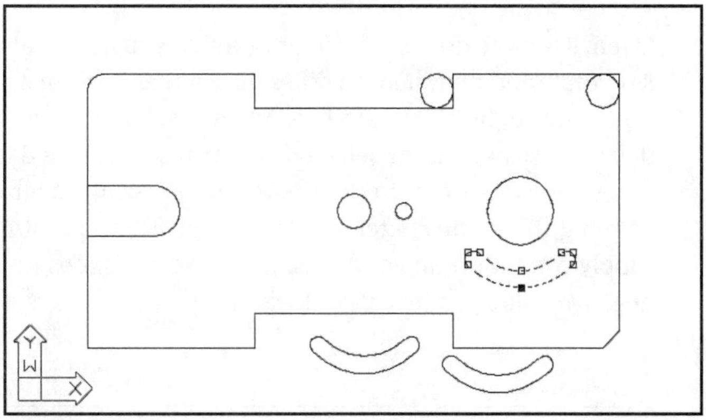

Figure 13.10

Two copies of the radial slot.

Placing Multiple Copies at Equally Spaced Intervals

Through autoediting, you can also generate several copies at regular intervals defined by an *offset snap*. This value is the distance between the original object and the first copy.

To create this grouping, first use the Copy option of the Move autoediting mode. After selecting the first copy offset, use Shift+pick to place additional copies.

WARNING

This offset snap technique is primarily used for orthogonally arranged copies; however, it may cause spurious or erratic behavior under other conditions. Use the ARRAY command (see Chapter 16, "Constructive Editing") for more predictable results.

The preceding exercise illustrated the move autoedit mode and how you can make multiple copies, if necessary. It is important to select all the objects to be included in the command, as well as to have any additional grips displayed that might be needed for point selection. Rotate mode is shown next.

Rotating with Autoediting Mode

Often, it is more convenient to draw a shape in a normal orientation and then rotate it or rotate and copy it into a different orientation than it is to draw it at an odd angle. You can use the rotate mode to revolve selected objects about a base point. The default base point is the selected grip; you can use the Base point option to respecify a new one. You enter rotate mode by pressing Enter or the spacebar twice, or entering RO at the stretch mode prompt. Then, point to a new rotation angle, or supply a rotation angle. A positive value produces counterclockwise rotation; a negative value produces clockwise rotation.

NOTE

The autoediting modes are stretch, move, rotate, scale, and mirror. Autoedit cycles through the modes, in this order, when you press Enter, the spacebar, or the pointing device Enter button. Pressing Enter when in mirror mode cycles back to stretch mode. You also can pick the modes and options from the screen menu.

Try using rotate mode in the following exercise.

Rotating and Moving Objects with Autoedit

Continue with the CHAP13 drawing from the preceding exercise.

`Command:` *Select a window from* ① *to* ② *(see fig. 13.11)*	Selects the radial slot and displays its grips
`Command:` *Pick either large arc's midpoint grip*	Highlights grip and enters stretch mode
`** STRETCH **` `<Stretch to point>/Base point/Copy/Undo/eXit:` *Press the spacebar twice*	Switches to rotate mode
`** ROTATE **` `<Rotation Angle>/Base point/Copy/Undo/Reference/eXit:`	

Move the cursor, and note that the slot rotates dynamically as you do so.

`<Rotation angle>/Base point/Copy/Undo/Reference/eXit:` *Turn on the Ortho button, then click at a 90° counterclockwise rotation. Then, turn off the Ortho button.*	Rotates the objects

Now, using figure 13.12 as a guide, move the slot into position near the guide slot at the left of the tool plate.

`Command:` *Pick either of the mid grips*	Enters stretch mode
`** STRETCH **` `<Stretch to point>/Base point/Copy/Undo/eXit:` *Press the spacebar once*	Switches to move mode
`** MOVE **` `<Move to point>/Base point/Copy/Undo/eXit:` **B** ↵	Prompts for a base point
`Base point:` *Click the pop-up menu button, choose* CENTER*, then pick either of the large arcs*	Sets the base point at the arc's center
`<Move to point>/Base point/Copy/Undo/eXit:` *Click the pop-up menu button, choose* CENTER*, and pick center of guide slot arc*	Moves the slot to a new location

Save the drawing.

Figure 13.11

Slot selection window and grips.

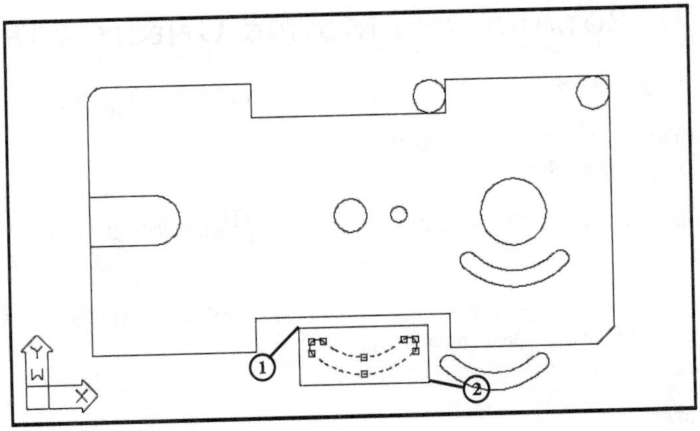

Figure 13.12

The rotated and relocated slot.

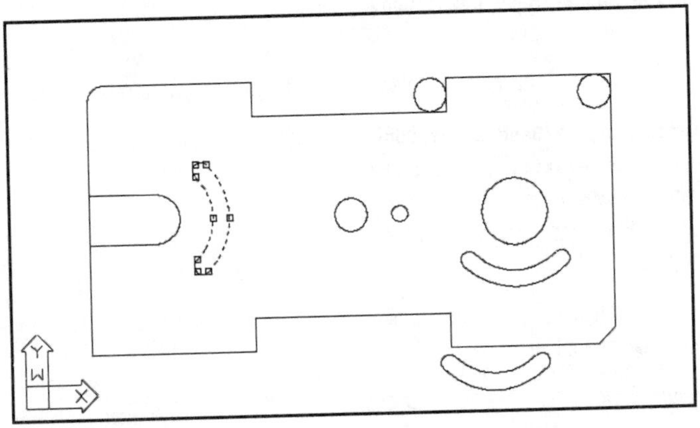

The autoedit rotate and move modes oriented the slot and moved it to the proper location. The exercises used object snaps instead of grips because arc centers do not have grips.

Next, use the Copy option of the rotate autoediting mode to complete the hole pattern at the center of the tool plate. You'll use the Shift+pick feature of Copy to snap copies to 45° increments.

ROTATING AND COPYING WITH AUTOEDIT

Continue in the CHAP13 drawing from the preceding exercise.

`Command:` *Pick the circle at* ① *(see fig. 13.13)*	Creates the set and displays grips
`Command:` *Pick the smaller circle at* ②	Clears the previous set, selects the circle, and displays grips

`Command:` *Pick the smaller circle's center grip*	Enters stretch mode

`** STRETCH **`
`<Stretch to point>/Base point/Copy/`
`Undo/eXit:` *Press Enter twice*
	Switches to rotate mode

`** ROTATE **`
`<Rotation angle>/Base point/Copy/`
`Undo/Reference/eXit:` **B** ↵
	Prompts for a base point

`Base point:` *Pick center grip of larger circle*	Sets the rotation base point
Turn on the Snap button	
`<Rotation angle>/Base point/Copy/` `Undo/Reference/eXit:` *Shift+pick cursor to 45° position at* ③	Makes the first copy at 45 degrees

`** ROTATE (multiple)`
`<Rotation angle>/Base point/Copy/`
`Undo/Reference/eXit:` *Shift+pick cursor to 90° position at* ④
	Makes the next copy at 90 degrees

`** ROTATE (multiple) **`
`<Rotation angle>/Base point/Copy/`
`Undo/Reference/eXit:` *Shift+pick cursor to 135° position at* ⑤
	Makes the next copy at 135 degrees

`** ROTATE (multiple) **`
`<Rotation angle>/Base point/Copy/`
`Undo/Reference/eXit:` *Shift+pick cursor to 180° position at* ⑥
	Makes the next copy at 180 degrees

`** ROTATE (multiple) **`
`<Rotation angle>/Base point/Copy/`
`Undo/Reference/eXit:` ↵
	Exits from autoediting mode

Turn off the Snap button	
`Command:` *Choose Save (Standard)*	Clears grips and the selection set, and saves the drawing

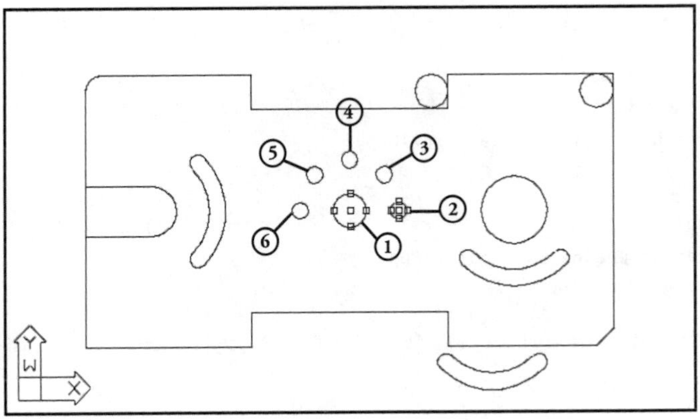

Figure 13.13

Circles copied with rotate autoediting mode.

The autoedit rotate mode conveniently changes the orientation of objects or creates circular patterns. Most of its options—Base point, Copy, Undo, and eXit—work the same as with the other autoediting modes. Use the Reference option to specify the current and new rotations. This latter method works well when you do not know the increment between the old and new rotations. See Chapter 14, "The Ins and Outs of Editing," for details.

In this drawing, some of the work that can be accomplished by rotating also can be done with mirroring, which is discussed next.

Mirroring Objects with Autoedit

The mirror mode creates a reflected image of the selected objects across an indicated mirror line. The mirror line is defined with endpoints of the base point and a specified second point. The base point is assumed to be the selected grip, unless overridden through the Base point option. If ortho mode is on, you easily can pick a second point for a horizontal or vertical mirror line. The Copy option creates a mirrored copy of the original objects; otherwise, the original objects are transformed. Enter MI at the autoedit prompt or cycle through the options by pressing Enter to access the mirror mode.

Try the mirror autoediting mode on the tool plate. Mirror the right radial slot to make a copy above the hole.

MIRRORING OBJECTS WITH AUTOEDITING MODE

Continue with the CHAP13 drawing from the previous exercise.

Command: *Select the circle at ① (see fig. 13.14)*	Creates the set and shows grips
Command: *Select a window from ② to ③*	Selects the radial slot and displays grips
Command: *Pick one of the grips on the slot*	Enters stretch mode
** STRETCH ** <Stretch to point>/Base point/Copy/Undo/eXit: *Press Enter four times*	Switches to mirror mode
** MIRROR ** <Second point>/Base point/Copy/Undo/eXit: **B** ↵	Prompts for a base point
Base point: *Pick center grip of the circle*	Specifies the new base point
<Second point>/Base point/Copy/Undo/eXit: *Pick the circle's right grip at ①*	Locates the second point directly to the right of the base point and mirrors the slot

Because you did not use the Copy option, the original slot was deleted.

Command: *Choose Undo (Standard)*	Undoes the edit
Command: *Select the circle at ① and a window from ② to ③ (see fig. 13.14)*	Selects the circle and radial slot and displays grips
Command: *Pick one of the grips on the slot and press the spacebar four times*	Enters stretch mode and switches to mirror mode
** STRETCH ** <Stretch to point>/Base point/Copy/Undo/eXit: *Press the spacebar four times*	
** MIRROR ** <Second point>/Base point/Copy/Undo/eXit: **B** ↵	
Base point: *Pick the center grip of circle*	
Second point>/Base point/Copy/Undo/eXit: **C** ↵	Specifies the Copy option

`** MIRROR (multiple) **`
`<Second point>/Base point/Copy/Undo/`
`eXit:` *Pick the circle's right grip at* ①
	Copies and mirrors in one operation

`** MIRROR **`
`<Second point>/Base point/Copy/Undo`
`/eXit:` ↵
	Exits from autoedit

Save the drawing.

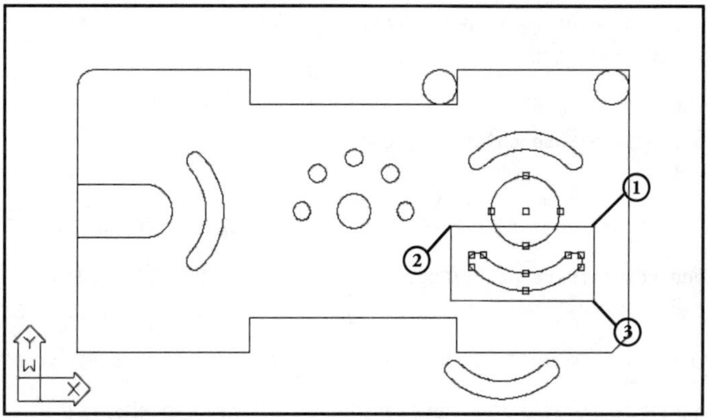

Figure 13.14

Upper slot created with mirror autoediting mode.

Next, use the mirror mode to complete the hole pattern at the center of the tool plate. This time, instead of using the Copy option, press Shift as you pick the second point. Using Shift is an alternative way to copy with autoedit.

Finishing the Hole Pattern by Mirroring

Continue with the CHAP13 drawing from the previous exercise.

`Command:` *Pick the circle in the center of the hole pattern*	Creates the set and displays grips
`Command:` *Select a crossing window from points* ① *to* ② *(see fig. 13.15)*	Selects three circles and displays grips
`Command:` *Pick any one of the grip points on the small holes*	Enters stretch mode

`** STRETCH **`
`<Stretch to point>/Base point/Copy/`
`Undo/eXit:` **MI** ↵
	Enters mirror mode

`** MIRROR **`
`<Second point>/Base point/Copy/Undo/`
`eXit:` **B** ↵	

`Base point:` *Pick the center hole's center grip*	Sets a new base point

`** MIRROR **`
`<Second point>/Base point/Copy/Undo/`
`eXit:` *Shift+pick the right grip of the center hole*
	Enters copy (multiple) mode to make copies while picking second point(s)

`** MIRROR (multiple) **`
`<Second point>/Base point/Copy/`
`Undo/eXit:` ↵
	Exits autoedit mode

Your drawing should look like figure 13.16.

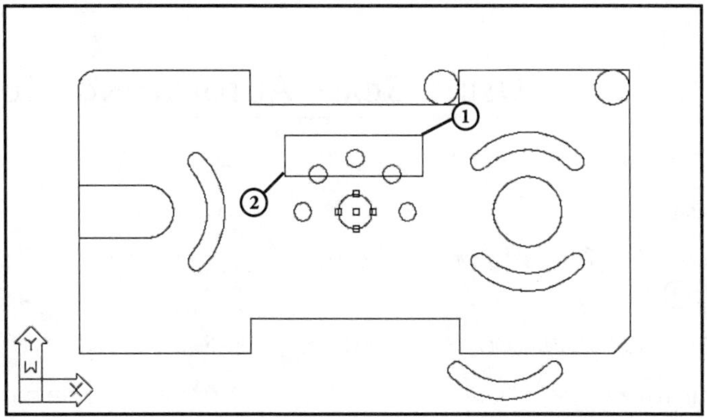

Figure 13.15

Crossing selection of holes to mirror.

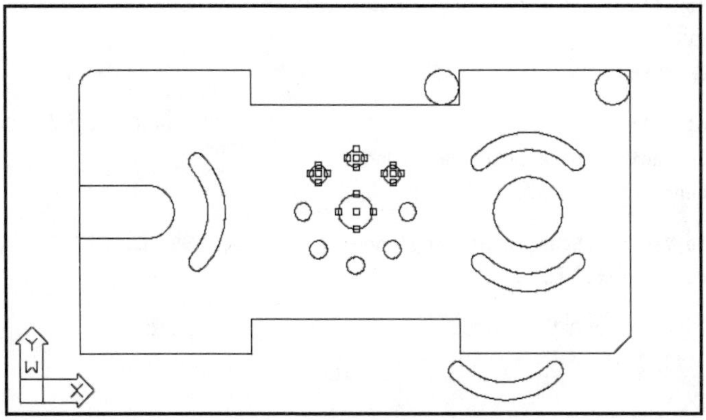

Figure 13.16

The completed hole pattern, with grips.

Look for opportunities to use mirror mode in your drawings to save time when creating objects. Remember to properly specify the two points that form the mirror line. Also, determine whether the Copy option is needed.

Scaling with Autoedit

Scaling is another editing feature that is a great time-saver. You might need to use this autoedit mode to create blown-up views, resize standard shapes, or change from English to metric units. As with the rotate mode, scaling is done from a base point. Unless otherwise specified, the base point is the selected grip point.

Continuing with the project, assume that an engineering change requires a size reduction of the hole and radial slots at the right side of the tool plate. The pattern is proportional to its original size—just smaller. Use the scale autoediting mode in the following exercise to shrink the slots to three-fourths of their original size.

USING SCALE AUTOEDITING MODE

Continue with the CHAP13 drawing from the previous exercise.

`Command:` *Double-click in empty space*	Clears the selection set and grips
`Command:` *Pick a crossing window from ① to ② (see fig. 13.17)*	Selects slots and circle
`Command:` *Pick center grip of center circle*	Enters stretch mode
`** STRETCH **` `<Stretch to point>/Base point/Copy/Undo/eXit:` *Press the pointing device Enter button three times*	Switches to scale mode
`** SCALE **` `<Scale factor>/Base point/Copy/Undo/Reference/eXit:` *Move the cursor*	Dynamically scales objects in proportion
`<Scale factor>/Base point/Copy/Undo/Reference/eXit:` **.75** ↵	Scales objects to 3/4 original size

Save the drawing. It should now look like figure 13.18.

Figure 13.17

Crossing selection of slots.

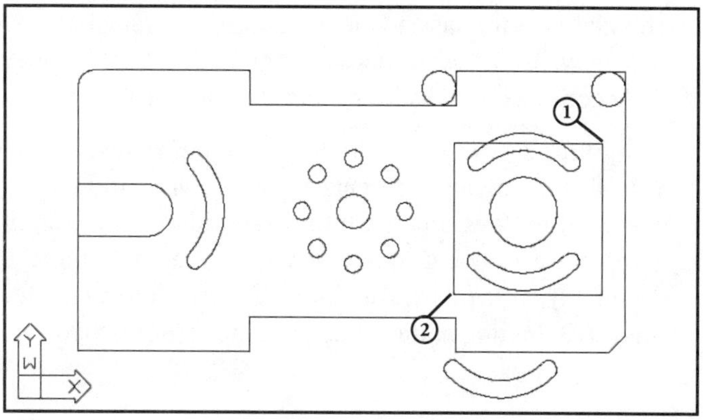

Figure 13.18

Scaled slots.

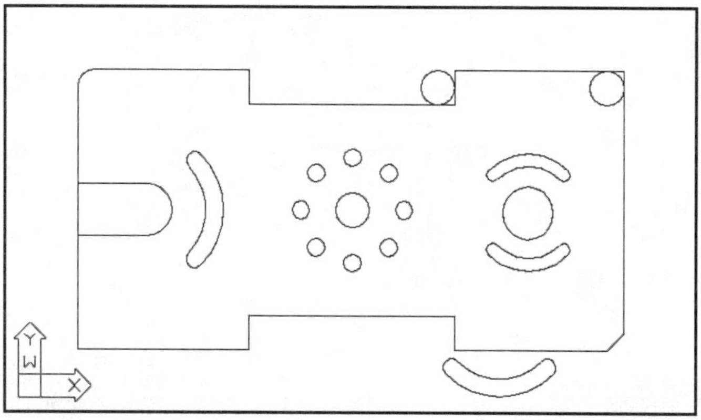

Because the proper scale—usually full—is so important in a CAD database, be sure to scale objects to their proper size. The scale mode is handy for adjusting items such as text, title blocks, and borders to complete a drawing. The autoediting modes have the same effect on text as on other graphics objects. You can scale, copy, move, and rotate text just like any other object.

TIP

The Reference option of Scale is very valuable. You can use it, for example, to scale one object to align with another. See Chapter 14, "The Ins and Outs of Editing," for examples of using the SCALE command.

This chapter emphasized the procedures to create and modify objects from existing geometry, using the techniques of grip editing. As you have seen, one can generate fairly complex models from simple prototypes!

Many more drawing and editing techniques are explained in the following chapters. Your first challenge is to master the drawing and editing commands themselves, then start to develop a style of CAD drafting that best fits your needs. When you complete a drawing, think of ways to draw it more efficiently the next time. Eventually, you refine your skills and tap into those techniques that make your AutoCAD drafting and design work more productive.

chapter

14

The Ins and Outs of Editing

The Greek philosopher Heraclitus is credited with the observation that "Change alone is unchanging." Although it is unlikely he was anticipating the use of AutoCAD, his statement is certainly true of engineering drawings—a change request invariably occurs even before the drawing is issued. To use AutoCAD successfully and professionally within such an environment, you must be adept at applying the program's editing functions. The benefits of electronic drawing editing are clear—as you master the commands and their options, you stay ahead of project changes without falling behind in your drawings.

In this chapter, you learn about the following:

- The various methods of selecting objects for editing
- The MOVE and COPY commands
- Using UNDO to recover from mistakes
- Rotating objects using ROTATE and ALIGN
- Editing objects using the TRIM, EXTEND, and LENGTHEN commands
- How to change the size and shape of objects using STRETCH and SCALE
- How to group objects together

Chapter 13, "Autoediting with Grips," explores several grip editing methods. AutoCAD includes many more powerful and versatile modification commands and options. Figures 14.1 and 14.2 identify commands used to develop and refine the main exercise drawing in this chapter.

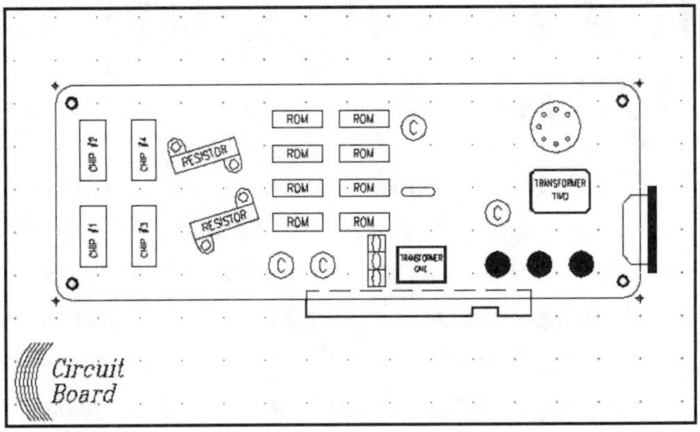

Figure 14.1

The CHAP14 drawing before editing.

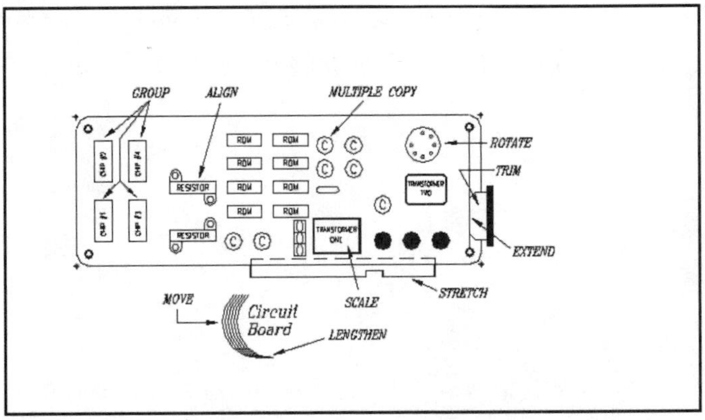

Figure 14.2

The CHAP14 drawing after editing.

You perform three basic kinds of edits to drawings: changing, copying, and erasing objects. You can change an existing object's location, layer, and visual properties, such as color and linetype. You also can *break* objects by deleting portions of line and arc segments. Breaking an object reduces its length or divides it into multiple objects. You can copy objects, singly or in a regular pattern. You also can erase objects to get rid of mistakes.

Most of AutoCAD's editing commands are gathered on the Modify toolbar, and the Select Objects flyout on the Standard toolbar contains tools for picking objects. In addition, the Options pull-down menu includes the Selection item, which opens the Object Selection Settings dialog box. This latter dialog box was introduced in Chapter 13 and is covered in greater detail later in this chapter. Figure 14.3 shows the important toolbars and flyouts for editing.

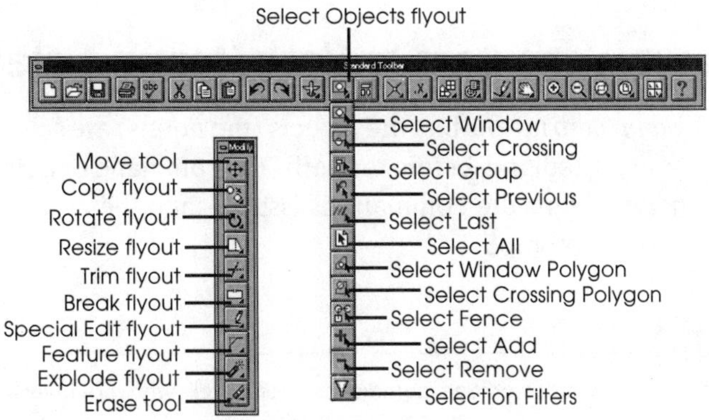

Figure 14.3

The Modify toolbar and the Select Objects flyout.

This chapter shows you how to change the spatial (location) properties of existing objects. Only a few basic editing commands are required to perform these simple functions. Chapter 15, "Object and Drawing Modification and Inquiry Tools," covers methods for changing the appearance (color and linetype) properties of existing objects.

TIP

If you want to practice individual editing commands as you work through the chapter, create a layer named SCRATCH. Create some objects on this layer, try out some editing variations, then freeze your SCRATCH layer and pick up again with the exercise sequences.

How Editing Selection Works

Most editing commands involve deciding what kind of edit you want to do, which objects you want to edit, and how you want to edit them. The steps are as follows:

- Issue the editing command
- Select the objects
- Enter the appropriate parameters and pick points
- The edit occurs

With most editing commands, the order of the first two steps depends on whether you prefer noun/verb editing or verb/noun editing.

Noun/Verb versus Verb/Noun Selection

Noun/verb means that the objects (the nouns) are selected at the `Command:` prompt, as in grip editing, before the verb (the command or autoedit mode) is issued. *Verb/noun* means the command is issued, then the objects are selected at the `Select objects:` prompt.

NOTE

Although most editing commands work well with noun/verb selection, some editing commands, such as FILLET and TRIM, ignore selections made prior to the command.

When you select objects at the `Command:` prompt, then issue most editing commands, such as MOVE, AutoCAD accepts the selected objects, skips the command's `Select objects:` prompt, and enters the command's editing mode. This is noun/verb editing.

When you issue most editing commands without objects selected, AutoCAD enters object selection mode, displaying the `Select objects:` prompt. At this prompt, you tell AutoCAD which objects you want to edit. When you complete object selection, AutoCAD enters the command's editing mode. This is verb/noun editing.

The following exercise demonstrates both the noun/verb and verb/noun selection methods with ERASE, AutoCAD's simplest editing command.

Noun/Verb and Verb/Noun Editing

Begin a new drawing named CHAP14A, using TOOLPLAT from the accompanying CD as a prototype.

`Command:` *Choose Erase (Modify)*	Issues the ERASE command and prompts for selection

`_erase`

`Select objects:` Pick the two circles at ① and ②, then select the radial slot using a window from ③ to ④ (see fig. 14.4). Hold down Shift while picking the second circle and slot to add them to the selections.

`Select objects:` ↵	Erases the objects
`Command:` **U** ↵	Restores the objects
`Command:` *Select the circles and the slot again, then choose Erase (Modify)*	Highlights selected objects and displays grips, then issues the ERASE command and erases the selections without additional input

`erase 6 found`

Figure 14.4

Selection points for editing.

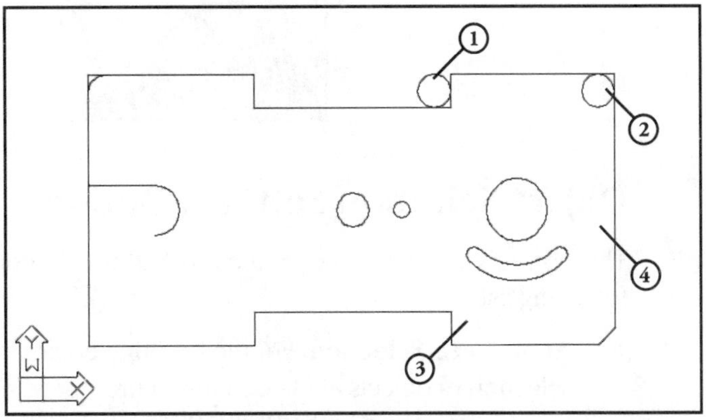

Verb/noun editing is always available. Noun/verb selection with editing commands is enabled by the Noun/Verb Selection setting in the Object Selection Settings dialog box, which is discussed in the next section. The default setting for Noun/Verb Selection is on. The availability of noun/verb editing with grips and autoediting modes is controlled by the Enable Grips setting in the Grips dialog box (see Chapter 13), regardless of the Noun/Verb Selection setting. The default setting for Enable Grips is on.

There are several other aspects of object selection behavior that you can control.

Setting Object Selection Behavior

Object selection behavior, including the availability of noun/verb editing for editing commands, is controlled by the Object Selection Settings dialog box (see fig. 14.5). You open the Object Selection Settings dialog box by issuing the DDSELECT command.

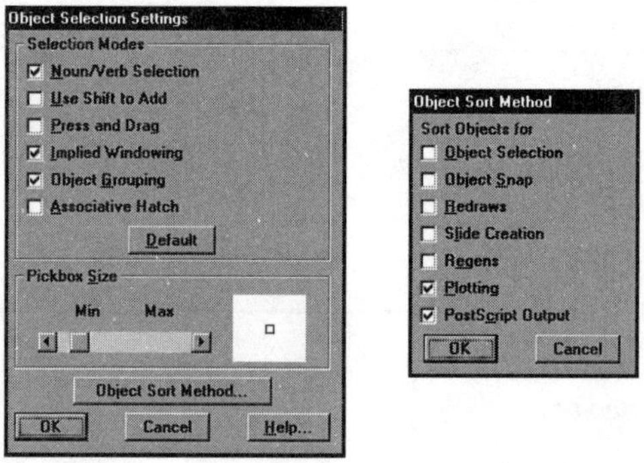

Figure 14.5

The Object Selection Settings and Object Sort Method dialog boxes.

Object Selection Settings Options

The controls in the Object Selection Settings dialog box are described in the following list:

- **Noun/Verb Selection.** For most editing commands, this setting enables selection of objects at the command prompt when turned on (the default). Its setting is stored in the PICKFIRST system variable (ON=1, OFF=0). Setting Noun/Verb Selection on adds versatility to editing by allowing both noun/verb and verb/noun object selection methods. The crosshair cursor includes a pickbox at the `Command:` prompt when either grips (see Chapter 13) or Noun/Verb Selection is turned on, but if Noun/Verb Selection is turned off, the only method available to editing commands is the verb/noun selection at the `Select objects:` prompt.

- **Use Shift to Add.** When Use Shift to Add is on, additional objects selected by picking or implied windowing replace the previous selection set and start a new one. When on, objects selected while holding down Shift and picking or using implied windowing adds them to the existing selection. To remove previously selected objects from the selection set, hold down Shift as you pick or use implied windowing to select them. If you use Shift and an implied window to select both unselected and previously selected objects, the unselected ones are added and none are removed.

  When Use Shift to Add is off, objects are automatically added to the selection set as they are chosen. To remove previously selected objects from the selection set, hold down Shift as you select them. If you use Shift as you pick or use implied windowing to select both unselected and previously selected objects, the unselected ones are ignored and the previously selected ones removed.

  This setting is stored in the PICKADD system variable, but Use Shift to Add *off* means PICKADD is *on* (1), and Use Shift to Add *on* means PICKADD is *off* (0). See the Adding and Removing objects section of this chapter for more details and examples.

- **Press and Drag.** To make a window or crossing selection, if Press and Drag is on, you press the pick button at the first corner point, move (drag) the cursor to the opposite corner point, then release. If it is off (the default), a separate pick is required for each corner point. Other window specifications, such as for ZOOM, always require two picks and are unaffected by this setting. This also affects clearing of a noun/verb selection and grips at the `Command:` prompt—if on, one pick clears grips and one pick clears a selection, but if off, two picks are required to clear grips and two more to clear a selection. The setting is stored in the PICKDRAG system variable (1=on, 0=off).

- **Implied Windowing.** If Implied Windowing is on (the default) a pick (or the press of a press and drag selection) at the `Select objects:` prompt selects an object, if any are in the pickbox. If no object is in the pickbox, the pick (or press) starts a selection window. If Implied Windowing is off, the pick (or press) either selects an object or returns a 0 found message. If off, you must use the Window or Crossing selection options to make window selections (see the Building the Selection Set section later in this chapter). This setting does not affect noun/verb selection at the `Command:` prompt, which always behaves as if Implied Windowing were on. This setting is stored in the PICKAUTO system variable (1=on, 0=off).

- **Object Grouping.** If Object Grouping is on, groups are selectable (selecting a member selects its group—see the Grouping Objects section at the end of this chapter). If off, groups are not selectable.
- **Associative Hatch.** If Associative Hatch is on, selecting an associative hatch entity also selects its boundary elements. If off, only the hatch entity will be selected.

  The setting for Object Grouping and Associative Hatch is stored in the PICKSTYLE system variable. If this system variable is set to 0, both Object Grouping and Associative Hatch are off. If set to 1, only Object Grouping is on. When set to 2, only Associative Hatch is on. When set to 3, both Object Grouping and Associative Hatch are on.
- **Default.** The Default button restores AutoCAD's initial default Selection Modes: all modes on except Use Shift to Add and Press and Drag.
- **Pickbox Size.** Drag the slider box or click on the slider bar or arrows to set pickbox size from 1 or 20 pixels. The current size is indicated to the right of the slider. The size is stored in the PICKBOX system variable, which can directly set the size from 0 to 32,767 pixels. The size is the pixel distance from the crosshairs to the pickbox.
- **Object Sort Method.** The Object Sort Method button opens the Object Sort Method dialog box (see the following "Controlling Object Sorting" section in this chapter).

Press and Drag and Implied Windowing work well together. Without Press and Drag on, Implied Windowing can be a nuisance, because an accidental pick always either selects an object or starts a selection window.

TIP

You can tailor object selection by varying the pickbox size. A large size makes selection quick and sloppy, and a small setting makes picking slower and more precise. You also can change the pickbox size transparently in the middle of a command by entering 'PICKBOX, and then entering a new value. If you use the system variable to set it, you can set a 0 size pickbox for pinpoint accuracy.

Controlling Object Sorting

AutoCAD provides options for processing objects in their creation order. You can use these sort options if your drawing or application depends on the order in which objects were created. For example, the controller for a CNC milling machine critically depends on the vertex order of generated polylines to cut or route the proper tool paths.

AutoCAD Release 12 and later uses an oct-tree (octal tree) method of sorting the data base. This sometimes affects object selection. The newer oct-tree method sorts, selects, displays, and outputs objects in a grid arrangement of rectangular areas, whereas the older sort method favored the most recently created objects to process. These areas are visually evident during a complex redraw or regen because AutoCAD redraws or regenerates each area in sequence. By localizing the processing, AutoCAD optimizes tasks such as object selection and object snapping.

TIP

To see the effect of an oct-tree sort, create a 50-row-by-60-column array of circles and perform a ZOOM All. (Refer to Chapter 16, "Constructive Editing," for details on the ARRAY command.)

Usually, the order of the objects is not important. However, you can use the Object Sort Method dialog box (see fig. 14.8) to override oct-tree sorting and consider the order of creation for specific operations.

To open the Object Sort Method dialog box, choose the Object Sort Method button from the Object Selection Settings dialog box (refer to figure 14.5). A checked box indicates object creation sorting; an unchecked box (the default) indicates oct-tree sorting. The operations affected by the sorting method are as follows:

- **Object Selection.** If several objects fall within the pickbox and oct-tree sorting is in effect, it is difficult to predict which object will be selected. Under object creation sorting, the most recent object will be found. When you are editing recently created objects, as is often the case, setting oct-tree off will help select them. When making a window or crossing selection with oct-tree on, objects will be selected in an unpredictable order. With oct-tree off, they will be selected in the reverse of the creation order.

- **Object Snap.** As with Object Selection, oct-tree affects locating objects when using object snap. Turn it off when you use the QUIck object snap option if you want to reliably find the most recently drawn objects.

- **Redraws.** If the order in which objects appear during a redraw matters to you, turn oct-tree off to make them redisplay in creation sequence. Because many zooms merely redraw rather than regenerate, this might be an advantage. If, for example, you first draw a basic part outline, framework, or building grid in your drawings, you can use it to locate your zooms. With oct-tree off, any initial outline, framework, or grid appears first. You can do a rough zoom, cut the zoom short with Esc, and then zoom more precisely, using the outline, framework, or grid. With oct-tree on, the order of appearance is less predictable.
- **Slide Creation.** As with redraws, oct-tree controls the order of appearance of objects in slides created by using MSLIDE. This order is often important in a complex slide; a presentation might look odd if all the windows of a building appear before the wall outlines.
- **Regens.** As with redraws, oct-tree controls the order of appearance of objects during regens. See the preceding Redraw discussion.
- **Plotting.** Because AutoCAD's plot routine, and many plotters, perform their own vector sorting, oct-tree is generally not important here. If you plot to an image file format, however, you might want to control the order of appearance, as discussed in the preceding Slide Creation option.
- **PostScript Output.** As with slides and image file plotting, set oct-tree off if you need to control the order of appearance in the PostScript file.

Setting oct-tree off for any option causes only that option's operations to use old-style sorting; other operations still use oct-tree sorting. The SORTENTS system variable stores the current oct-tree sort setting; see Appendix F for more information.

Building the Selection Set

AutoCAD offers more than a dozen ways to collect objects for editing. You can, for example, pick individual objects or enclose multiple objects within a window. As you select objects, AutoCAD sets up a temporary selection set and highlights the objects by temporarily changing their colors, making them blink, or giving them dotted lines. This highlighting confirms the objects that you have selected. You can enter any valid selection or selection option at the `Select objects:` prompt. If you enter invalid input, AutoCAD prompts you with all the available modes and reissues the `Select objects:` prompt, as follows:

```
Expects a point or
Window/Last/Crossing/BOX/ALL/Fence/WPolygon/CPolygon/Group/Add/
Remove/Multiple/Previous/Undo/AUto/SIngle
Select objects:
```

After you select all the objects you want, press Enter to end object selection and continue with the editing command.

Verb/noun editing is always available. Noun/verb selection with editing commands is enabled by the Noun/Verb Selection setting in the Object Selection Settings dialog box. The default is on. The availability of noun/verb editing with grips and autoediting modes is controlled by the Enable Grips setting in the Grips dialog box (see Chapter 13), regardless of the Noun/Verb Selection setting. The default for Enable Grips is on.

There are several other aspects of object selection behavior that you can control.

The Select Objects Options and Methods

AutoCAD provides many ways to add objects to a selection set, as follows:

- **Object pick.** Enables you to pick individual objects. This method is the default. As you pick, AutoCAD finds the most recently created object that falls within or crosses the pick box. If you use snap and object snap together, AutoCAD snaps first, then performs the object snaps from that snapped point.
- **Window.** Selects objects within a window you specify. AutoCAD selects only those objects that are enclosed entirely within the window. AutoCAD considers lines that the window edge overlaps to be within this window. Technically, window selection selects an object which partially extends outside the current viewport if its entire visible portion is within or overlapped by the window; however, it is difficult to specify such a window. If Implied Windowing is on in the Object Selection Settings dialog box, you can select a window without first specifying the Window option.
- **Last.** Selects the last object created that is visible in the drawing window.
- **Crossing.** Works the same as Window, except that Crossing also selects any objects that are partially within, crossing, or touching the window. If Implied Windowing is on, you can select a crossing window without specifying the Crossing option.

- **BOX.** Combines Window and Crossing into a single selection. Picking the points of your box from left to right produces a Window selection; picking from right to left produces a Crossing selection.
- **ALL.** Selects all objects in the drawing that are not on locked or frozen layer.
- **Fence.** Enables you to draw an open, multiple-point fence with which to select objects. All objects touched by the fence are selected.
- **WPolygon.** This method is similar to Window selection but enables you to draw an irregular closed polygon to select objects. All objects completely within the polygon are selected.
- **CPolygon.** This method is similar to the Crossing selection but enables you to draw an irregular closed polygon to select objects. All objects inside of or crossed by the polygon are selected.
- **Group.** Enables you to include a predefined group of objects by a specified name. (The GROUP command is covered later in this chapter.)
- **Remove.** Switches to Remove mode, so that you can remove selected objects from the selection set (not from the drawing). The Remove mode acts the same regardless of the setting of the Use Shift to Add setting in the Object Settings dialog box—picking a previously selected object removes it from the selection set. Picking unselected objects in the Remove mode has no effect. Previously selected objects, however, can be removed from the selection set without using the Remove option by simply holding the Shift key while picking them.
- **Add.** Switches from Remove mode back to normal, so that you again can add objects to the selection set, according to the setting of the PICKADD system variable.
- **Multiple.** Enables you to pick multiple objects in close proximity and speeds up selection by enabling you to make multiple selections without highlighting or prompting. Pressing Enter an extra time is required to complete the multiple selection and return to normal object selection.
- **Previous.** Selects the entire preceding selection set (from a previous command) as the current selection set. Previous does not recognize selections made at the `Command:` prompt for autoediting with grips.
- **Undo.** Undoes or reverses the last selection operation. Each U undoes one selection operation.

- **AUto.** Combines individual selection with the BOX selection. This selection performs the same as BOX, except that if the first pick point finds an object, that single object is selected and the BOX mode is aborted. This method is always available without entering AU if Implied Windowing is on in the Object Selection Setting dialog box.
- **SIngle.** Works in conjunction with the other selection options. If you precede a selection with SIngle, object selection automatically ends as soon as an object is detected; pressing Enter to confirm is not required.

When do you use which mode? The default option, picking objects, is fast and simple, even for picking three or four objects, and it requires no mode setting. Selecting by window and crossing window are also always available without having to enter a W or C if Implied Windowing is turned on in the Object Selection Settings dialog box. Last and Undo are obvious. Previous is great for repeated operations on the same set of objects, like a copy and rotate operation. The WPolygon, CPolygon, and Fence options are powerful tools for building complex selection sets, particularly when you must make the selections in a crowded area of the drawing. These selections take longer to specify than the Window and Crossing, but are more flexible and can save steps.

NOTE

The selection set options BOX, AUto, and SIngle are primarily for use in menus. They offer no real advantages over the other options discussed in the preceding list when specifying modes via the keyboard.

Sometimes objects are so close to each other that you cannot pick the one you want; additional picks simply locate the same object over and over again. In older versions of AutoCAD, you used Multiple and picked repeatedly to find multiple objects within the pickbox. However, because each additional pick added objects to the selection set, you then had to remove any undesired objects—a tedious process.

AutoCAD Release 13 now supports object selection cycling. To obtain a single object in a crowded area, press Ctrl while picking repeatedly. Objects within the pickbox then highlight one at a time with each pick. When AutoCAD selects the desired object, simply release Ctrl, then press Enter—you now have the object you want.

Note

Some editing commands, such as FILLET, TRIM, and EXTEND, require that you select a single object during the prompting sequence. In these cases, you must select by picking instead of using Crossing, Window, and so on.

You will use most of the preceding selection methods and options in the rest of this chapter and in subsequent chapters. First, you will take a better look at one of the most commonly used editing commands, MOVE, then use it as you further explore selection.

Exploring Selection and Editing with the MOVE command

Because the MOVE command is a fairly typical editing command, it is used in the following sections to explore further object selection and editing. The MOVE command is one of the simplest editing commands to use. To move an object, you select it and issue the MOVE command, or vice versa, then specify the object's new location. Although the options for specifying the new location are unique to this command, the way you go about selecting objects for the MOVE command is typical of the way commands that prompt you to `Select objects:` work.

Note

To specify a displacement, type 2,3 for an X,Y displacement or 2<30 for a polar displacement. Do not enter it with an @ sign, such as @2,3 or @2<30, or you will get unexpected results because you will have specified a point relative to the last point instead of a displacement value. You will also probably get unexpected results if you pick a point at the `Base point or displacement:` prompt, then press Enter at the second prompt. In both cases, the displacement will be the distance and angle from 0,0 to the point you specified and the results often move the object out of the visible drawing area. If this happens, Undo and try again.

In the following exercise, you use the MOVE command to relocate the logo in the circuit board drawing. You move the logo using a window selection. The destination point (second point of displacement) is near the bottom center of the board. You use verb/noun selection, and two points to indicate displacement, then noun/verb selection and a displacement value.

USING MOVE TO REPOSITION THE LOGO

Begin a new drawing named CHAP14B, using the BOARD2 drawing from the accompanying CD as a prototype.

`Command:` *Choose Move (Modify)*	Issues the MOVE command (verb)
`Select objects:` **?↵**	Specifies invalid selection option
`*Invalid selection*`	
`Expects a point or Window/Last/Crossing/BOX/ALL/Fence/ WPolygon/CPolygon/Group/Add/Remove/ Multiple/Previous/Undo/AUto/SIngle`	Displays list of valid options
`Select objects:` **W** ↵	Specifies Window option
`First corner:` *Pick at* ① *(see fig. 14.6)*	Starts a window
`Other corner:` *Drag to* ② *and release*	Completes window and selects objects (noun)
`8 found`	
`Select objects:` ↵	Ends selection and enters edit mode
`Base point or displacement:` *Pick at* ③ *point near the logo*	Specifies first point of displacement
`Second point of displacement:` *drag and pick at the crosshairs at* ④	Specifies second point of displacement and moves the object
`Command:` **U** ↵	Undoes the previous MOVE command
`Command:` *Select the logo with an implied window selection from* ① *to* ②	Selects the objects (noun)
`Command:` *Choose Move (Modify)*	Issues the MOVE command (verb) with the objects selected
`move 8 found`	
`Base point or displacement:` **3.1<0** ↵	Specifies a displacement
`Second point of displacement:` ↵	Accepts displacement and moves the logo

Save the drawing.

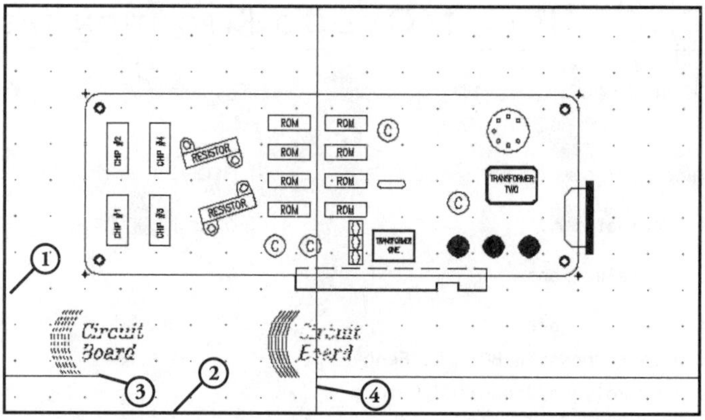

Figure 14.6

Moving the circuit board logo.

If you have set Implied Windowing on, you did not actually have to use the Window option to select a window. Sometimes, however, using the Window or Crossing option explicitly is essential. With Implied Windowing, picking selects an object (if any) within the pickbox. If such an object exists at the corner of the window selection area, it will be selected by the pickbox rather than the point starting a selection. To override this behavior, you must use the W or C options before you make your selection.

Object selection and moving is easy. After you select the logo with a window, the objects highlight. With verb/noun selection, you stop collecting objects by pressing Enter in response to the `Select objects:` prompt. With noun/verb selection, the command immediately enters editing mode. Then, pick your displacement points, and your logo moves.

AutoCAD offers several alternative methods to perform the same task. In the case of a move operation, you can choose between many ways to define the distance, or *displacement.* The next section further explains the various techniques.

Displacement and Drag

The use of the MOVE command involves specifying a displacement. If you know the absolute X,Y, or polar displacement, you can enter it at the `Base point or displacement:` prompt. Entering **3.2,0** or **3.1<0** (do not preface the displacement with an @), for example, duplicates the second move made in the previous exercise. Press Enter, instead of entering a value, at the `Second point:` prompt to tell AutoCAD to use the first value as an absolute offset.

Often, you want to show a displacement by entering two points. Think of the first point (base point) as a handle on the selection set. The second point, then, specifies the new location for this handle and the selection set relative to it. The *displacement* is an imaginary line from the base point to the second point. AutoCAD calculates the difference between the base and second points. The new location of the object(s) is determined by adding this displacement to its current location. For visual confirmation, AutoCAD shows a rubber-band line from the first point to the second, during the command.

TIP

When you set a base point, try to pick one that is easy to visualize (and remember). Use a corner point for rectangular objects, a center point for circular objects, and appropriate object snap points for all other types of geometry. Otherwise, you appear to be carrying the selection set around without touching it.

Adding and Removing Objects from the Selection Set

AutoCAD's selection options include Add and Remove modes. In Release 12 and later, however, you rarely need to use Add or Remove. You can control adding and removing objects in the selection set using only the Shift key and picking, or the implied windowing methods.

If you have the Use Shift to Add setting on in the Object Selection Settings dialog box anything you select by picking or an implied window or crossing box replaces the current selection set. To add objects to the selection set, press the Shift key while selecting them. To remove already selected objects from the selection set, just select them again by picking an implied window or crossing box while pressing the Shift key. If you press Shift and make a selection that includes both already selected and newly selected objects, the newly selected ones are added but the already selected ones are not removed.

If you have the Use Shift to Add setting off anything you select by any method without pressing Shift is added to the current selection set and anything you select by picking or an implied window or crossing box while pressing Shift is removed from the current selection set.

Although adding and removing objects from the selection set may seem simpler with the Use Shift to Add setting off, you will probably find that, with practice, Use Shift to Add setting on is more efficient.

To remove selections with options other than by picking or an implied window or crossing box, such as CPolygon, Previous, Last, of Fence, you do need to use the Remove option. To exit Remove mode and again add to the selection set, you need to use the Add option. Add mode is the default, indicated by the `Select objects:` prompt. To enter Remove mode, you enter an R (for Remove) at the `Select objects:` prompt. When the `Remove objects:` prompt appears, remove objects from the selection set by using any type of object selection. Enter an A to return to Add mode.

Adding and removing objects from the selection set is demonstrated in the next exercise, after you explore a few more options.

Using the Previous Selection Option

The Previous selection option is helpful when you cancel an editing command or use several commands on the same selection set. Previous object selection reselects the object(s) you selected in your most recent editing command.

Previous enables you to edit the preceding set without having to select its objects individually again. Note that Previous is different from Last, which selects the most recently created object visible in the drawing area.

TIP

The Previous option is useful for removing specific objects from a difficult selection—if you plan ahead. For example, you sometimes can turn off certain layers to simplify selection, use the SELECT command to create a selection set of objects you want to remove from a later selection set, then turn the layers back on, make the major selection, and finally use Remove mode and Previous to remove the previous selection from the current selection set.

Keeping Track of the Selection Set

Every time you select objects at the `Select objects:` prompt, AutoCAD shows the number of objects you selected and the number it actually finds. These numbers do not always match for two reasons. First, you can select objects that do not qualify for editing. For example, when you are in model space, ALL finds but then rejects paper space objects. In most cases, AutoCAD reports the number of objects rejected and the reason for their rejection. Second, you might already have selected an object. In the latter case, AutoCAD informs you that it found a duplicate. In all cases (except multiple mode selections), AutoCAD uses highlighting to show you what is currently in the selection set.

TIP

In a complex drawing, you might notice the time it takes AutoCAD to search through the drawing file for objects that qualify for the selection set. To expedite the selection of large selection sets, turn off the HIGHLIGHT system variable, enter HIGHLIGHT, and set it to 0 (off). If you operate in this mode, select carefully because you cannot tell which objects are selected. Highlight off is useful for selecting large, easily defined portions of the drawing. Also, consider using the DDSELECT dialog box to set Object Sort Method to fit your selection situation. (Object Sort is discussed later in this chapter.)

Using the COPY Command

The COPY command is similar to the MOVE command. The only differences between a copy and a move are that COPY leaves the original objects in place and provides a *multiple* option.

The Multiple option of the COPY command enables you to copy the contents of your selection set several times without having to respecify the selection set and base point. If you respond to the `Base point or displacement:` prompt by entering M, AutoCAD reprompts for base point, then repeatedly prompts you for multiple second point of displacement points. Press Enter or Esc to end the Multiple loop.

In the following exercise, you use a Fence selection with the COPY Multiple option to generate several copies of one of the circuit board's capacitors. The *capacitors* are the circles with Cs in them.

USING COPY TO DUPLICATE THE CAPACITORS

Continue in the CHAP14B drawing from either of the previous two exercises.

`Command:` *Choose Copy Object (Modify, Copy)*	Issues the COPY command
`_copy`	
`Select objects:` **F** ↵	Specifies Fence option

`First fence point:` *Pick* ① *(see fig. 14.7)*	Specifies first fence point
`Undo/<Endpoint of Line>:` *Pick* ②	Specifies next fence point
`Undo/<Endpoint of Line>:` ↵	Ends fence specifications
`2 found`	Selects objects touching fence
`Select objects:` ↵	Terminates object selection
`<Base point or displacement>/ Multiple:` **M** ↵	Specifies Multiple option
`Base point:` *Pick* ③	Specifies copy base point
`Second point of displacement:` **@0.5<0** ↵	Specifies offset to location of first copy
`Second point of displacement:` **@0.4<270** ↵	Specifies offset to location of third copy
`Second point of displacement:` **7.3,6.8** ↵	Specifies location for third copy
`Second point of displacement:` ↵	Ends COPY command

Save the drawing.

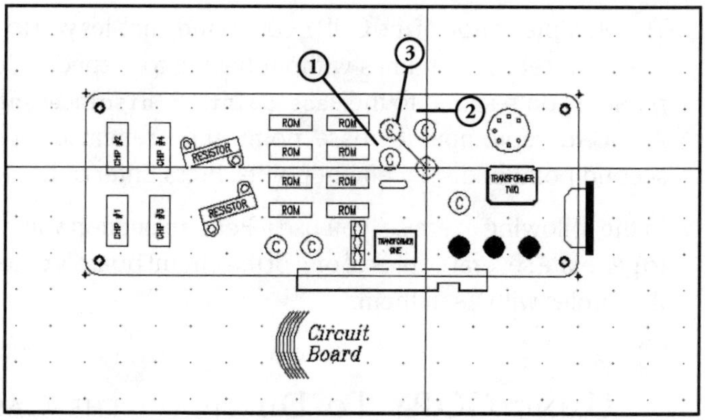

Figure 14.7

Copying multiple capacitors.

Using ROTATE To Turn Objects

The ROTATE command enables you to turn existing objects at precise angles. ROTATE, like MOVE, requires you to specify a rotation base point. After you specify the base point, you point to or enter a rotation angle. Negative angles produce clockwise rotation; positive angles produce counterclockwise rotation.

Another way to specify an angle is to use the reference method. You can specify a reference angle other than angle 0, then point to or enter a second angle relative to this reference angle. You need not know the actual angles—you can use pick points to instruct AutoCAD to calculate the angles. To align with existing objects, use object snaps when you pick the points of the angle(s).

In the following exercise, you use ROTATE to spin the contact plate so that the missing inner circle is in the upper-left corner. The contact plate is the circular object that encloses a radial arrangement of smaller circles. You use two rotation methods in the exercise; figure 14.8 shows the final results.

USING ROTATE TO SPIN THE CONTACT PLATE

Continue in the CHAP14B drawing from the previous exercise, and zoom to the view shown in figure 14.8.

`Command:` *Press and drag a window around the contact plate, then choose Rotate (Modify, Rotate)*	Issues the ROTATE command with the objects selected
`8 found`	
`Base point:` *Use CENter object snap to select the outer circle's center*	Specifies center of rotation
`<Rotation angle>/Reference:` *Drag the cursor around and the objects rotate, then pick point ① at 180 degrees*	Specifies the rotation angle relative to zero degrees and rotates the selected objects
`Command:` **R** ↵	Issues REDRAW command and redraws
`Command:` *Choose Rotate (Modify, Rotate)*	Issues the ROTATE command
`Select objects:` *Choose P (OPTIONS_I) then press Enter*	Specifies Previous selection set and ends object selection
`Base point:` *Use CENter object snap to select the outer circle's center*	Specifies center of rotation

`<Rotation angle>/Reference:` **R** ↵	Specifies the Reference option
`Reference angle <0.00>:` *Choose Last Point (OPTIONS_II)*	Specifies last point (circle's center) as base point of reference angle
`Second point:` *Pick ① again*	Specifies 180 degree reference angle, from circle's center to 1

Drag the cursor around and see that it now drags relative to 180 degrees.

`New angle:` **135** ↵	Rotates the selected objects to position shown in figure 14.8
`Command:` **R** ↵	Issues REDRAW command and redraws

Save the drawing.

Figure 14.8 shows the rotated contact plate.

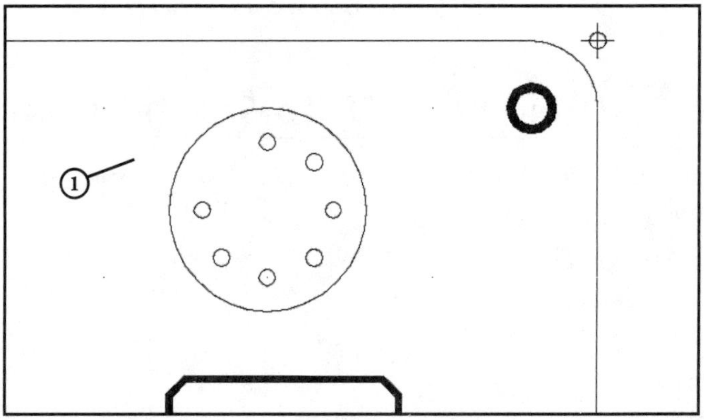

Figure 14.8

The contact plate after ROTATE.

The rotation base point does not need to be on the objects being rotated, although using an alternate point for rotation can be confusing if it is not logically placed relative to the objects being rotated.

Using the UNDO Command To Recover

You can use the ERASE command to delete objects from your drawing and OOPS to restore them. You also can use U to reverse the most recent procedure. But what if you want to undo several steps, to a much earlier drawing state—can it be done? Sure, just use the UNDO command, the U command's big brother.

The Undo tool on the Standard toolbar issues the U command, not the UNDO command. The UNDO command provides the following options:

- **Number.** You can enter a number to tell AutoCAD to undo the last *number* of commands issued.
- **Auto.** Causes UNDO to interpret menu picks as one command. After you select this option, the following prompt appears:

  `ON/OFF <default>:`

  When set to ON, UNDO reverses the effects of a menu selection, no matter how many steps it includes. For example, if a menu selection changes layers, inserts a block, and rotates it as needed, one execution of UNDO treats all these steps as one. If the Auto option is set to OFF, each step is removed individually. The *default* displays the current setting. If the Control option has been turned off or has limited the UNDO command in some way, the Auto option is not available.
- **Control.** Enables the normal UNDO, disables it, or limits it to one step or command. If you select this option, the following options appear:

  `ALL/None/One <ALL>:`

  - **All.** Enables the UNDO command to operate.
  - **None.** Disables completely the UNDO and U commands. If you select this option and then later enter the UNDO command, the `Control:` prompt immediately appears.
  - **One.** Restricts U and UNDO to a single step. You cannot perform multiple UNDO commands if you select this option. When this mode is active, UNDO displays the prompt `Control /<1>` rather than the standard UNDO prompt. Press Enter to UNDO a single action, or enter **C** to modify the settings.
- **BEgin.** The BEgin and End options work together to group a sequence of commands together into one Undo operation. This option treats a sequence of commands as one command. Precede the commands with **UNDO BEgin**, finish the set with **UNDO End**, then you can use a single U command to undo all the commands. Undo End is required to close a group. If a group is not properly Ended, the next BEgin option starts a new group, discarding the previous one. Also, issuing Undo will not back up past the Undo BEgin point. If an Undo Mark exists, it disappears inside the group.

- **Back.** Instructs AutoCAD to undo all commands until a mark is found. You can use the Mark option (explained later) to place multiple marks throughout the drawing. If no mark is in the drawing, AutoCAD displays the following prompt: `This will undo everything. OK? <Y>`.
- **End.** Closes a group of commands entered after the BEgin option was issued.
- **Mark.** Works in conjunction with the Back option. You can place marks periodically as you enter commands. Then you can use Undo Back to undo all the commands that have been executed since the last mark. Marks can be thought of as bookmarks—holding your place for a subsequent Undo operation.

The list of commands reported as undone includes any commands issued and canceled, so take that into account when you use UNDO *<number>*. Also, some menu items and tools cause their functions to be grouped as an UNDO Group, so they are undone as one operation and reported as GROUP. The operations of AutoLISP and ADS programs are also considered as single groups, even if they issue multiple commands.

WARNING

If you use transparent commands, such as 'ZOOM or make settings, such as snap, ortho, or grid during another command, then undo the command, the transparent commands and settings are also undone, without warning or notice.

WARNING

The UNDO Mark and Back options provide an excellent way to perform a "what if" scenario in your drawing. If you later determine the changes are not workable, simply undo back to the mark. UNDO resembles an "electronic bookmark" or even a "time machine" in your drawing.

Advanced Editing

You can use advanced editing commands, such as EXTEND, STRETCH, and TRIM, for more than copying and moving objects. These commands build on AutoCAD's capability to recognize drawing geometry. By combining these commands with construction techniques, you can make a rough draft of a drawing quickly, and then finish it perfectly.

The key to using the TRIM, EXTEND, ALIGN, SCALE, STRETCH, and LENGTHEN editing commands in the next few sections is to plan ahead. The operational details of the commands can involve several objects, so think about the ways you will use them.

The TRIM and EXTEND commands shorten and lengthen existing lines, arcs, circles, ellipses, polylines, rays, and splines to meet existing polylines, arcs, circles, ellipses, lines, floating viewport edges, rays, regions, splines, text, and xlines.

Trimming Objects

The TRIM command either shortens the object or removes a section, depending on the objects and points you specify.

Frequently, you need to trim existing lines in a drawing. If you work with a large number of objects, breaking individual objects is time-consuming. You can get the same results faster by using TRIM. The TRIM command uses boundary objects that include lines, arcs, circles, polylines, and, in paper space, viewports. The objects that you select as your boundary edge become your cutting edge(s). After you select your cutting edge, you individually pick or use Fence to select the objects you want to trim. You can trim lines, arcs, circles, and polylines. AutoCAD ignores other objects when you use the TRIM command; therefore, you can select extra objects that are in the area.

Extending Objects

The EXTEND command is analogous to the TRIM command. EXTEND uses boundary edges, whereas TRIM uses cutting edges and projects objects back to the cutting edges.

TRIM and EXTEND Prompts and Options

Because the commands act in a similar fashion, the TRIM and EXTEND commands share the same prompts. The only difference between the prompts is that the TRIM command prompts for cutting edges, while the EXTEND command prompts for boundary edges. When you start either command, you see one of the following prompts:

```
Select cutting (or boundary) edges: (Projmode = UCS, Edgemode = No
extend)
```

- **Select objects.** This prompt displays the current projection mode and Edge-mode for the TRIM and EXTEND commands. These can be changed at subsequent prompts. Select the objects that you want to use as the boundary or cutting edges for the command using any object selection method. If the view plan is not aligned with the current UCS, you see the warning, `View is not plan to UCS. Command results might not be obvious.` After you select the appropriate edges, you see one of the following prompts:

  ```
  <Select object to trim>/Project/Edge/Undo:
  ```

  ```
  <Select object to extend>/Project/Edge/Undo:
  ```

- **<Select object to trim>** or **<Select object to extend>.** Pick the object to trim or extend. Only one object can be picked at one time unless you use the Fence object selection method. The prompt repeats until you press Enter. If no intersection can be found between the object and the cutting edge, the message, `Object does not intersect an edge`, appears.

- **Project.** This option enables you to specify the mode of projection for subsequent options. The default mode is UCS. The Project option displays the following prompt:

  ```
  None/Ucs/View <Ucs>:
  ```

- **None.** This options specifies that no projection will be used for trimming or extending. This means that the objects must intersect with the edges in order to be edited.

- **UCS.** This default projection method means that AutoCAD will project the objects and the edges onto the current UCS X,Y plane. The objects projected do not have to intersect the cutting edges in 3D space to be trimmed.

- **View.** This projection method projects the objects onto the current viewing plane along the current view direction. The objects do not necessarily have to intersect the cutting edges in 3D space to be trimmed.

- **Edge.** The Edge option determines whether the objects are trimmed or extended to the implied edges or only to the edge it actually intersects in 3D space.

- **Extend.** This option extends the edges through 3D space for objects that may intersect it.

- **No Extend.** This default option ensures that the objects are trimmed or extended only if they intersect the actual edges selected.

- **Undo.** Use the Undo option to reverse the most recent trim or extend operation. You can Undo to the start of selecting objects to trim or extend.

You can use lines, polylines, arcs, circles, and viewport objects (when in paper space) as the boundary edge(s). Use normal object selection to select the boundary edge(s) to which you want to extend, then pick the objects that you want to extend. You must individually pick or use Fence to select each object to extend—you cannot use other modes to fill a selection set of objects to extend simultaneously. You cannot extend closed polylines or shorten objects (use the TRIM command to shorten lines).

TIP

If an object to be trimmed or extended passes through or extends to multiple cutting or boundary edges, you can pick it multiple times until it meets the desired edge—each pick trims or extends it to the next edge.

In the next exercise, use TRIM and EXTEND to modify the geometry near the port connector. The *port connector* is located at the lower right corner of the circuit board.

Using TRIM and EXTEND To Adjust the Port Connector

Continue with the CHAP14B drawing from the previous exercise and zoom to the view shown in figure 14.9.

`Command:` *Choose Trim (Modify)*	Issues the TRIM command

`_trim`
`Select cutting edges: (Projmode = UCS,`
`Edgemode = No extend)`	

`Select objects:` *Select a crossing window from ① (see fig. 14.9) to ②, then press Enter*	Selects several lines and ends cutting edge selection
`8 found 1 was not a valid edge.`	
`<Select object to trim>/Project/Edge/Undo:` *Pick line through port connector at ③*	Removes portion of the line between the nearest two selected cutting edges

`<Select object to trim>/Project/ Edge/Undo:` *Pick the same line again, near* ①	Trims it back to the next vertex, near ④, because it is a polyline and was selected as both a cutting edge and object to trim
`<Select object to trim>/Project/ Edge/Undo:` **U** ↵	Undoes the last trim
`<Select object to trim>/Project/ Edge/Undo:` ↵	Exits TRIM
`Command:` *Choose Extend (Modify, Trim)*	Issues the EXTEND command
`_extend` `Select boundary edges: (Projmode = UCS, Edgemode = No extend)`	Notice that the prompt displays the current Projmode and Edgemode status
`Undo/<Endpoint of Line>:` *Select a crossing window from ④ to ⑤, then press Enter*	Selects the donuts near ④ and ⑤, and several other lines, and ends boundary edge selection
`12 found 2 were not a valid edge.`	
`<Select object to extend>/Project/ Edge/Undo:` *Pick rear line of port at ⑥ and again at ⑦*	Extends each picked line to nearest boundary object beyond the picked end—to the donuts
`<Select object to extend>/Project/ Edge/Undo:` **E** ↵	Specifies Edgemode option
`Extend/No extend <No extend>:` **E** ↵	Specifies Extend mode
`<Select object to extend>/Project/ Edge/Undo:` *Turn off snap, and pick the left end of each diagonal line at ⑧ and ⑨*	Extends each line to meet the other
`<Select object to trim>/Project/ Edge/Undo:` *Enter* **U** *twice*	Undoes the last two extends
`<Select object to extend>/Project/ Edge/Undo:` ↵	Exits EXTEND

Save the drawing.

Figure 14.9 shows the results of trimming and extending the port connector.

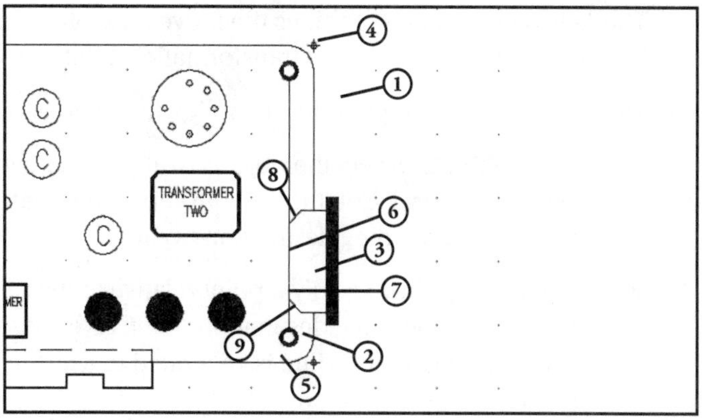

Figure 14.9

Detail of port connector after TRIM and EXTEND.

NOTE

Trimming a closed polyline creates two polylines unless the portion trimmed includes the starting or ending vertices.

You may have noticed in the previous exercise, the pick points used for selecting the edges were not very specific. In general, you don't have to be too careful in selecting cutting or boundary edges; a few extra objects in the selection set often do not interfere.

You might also have noticed that some of the objects used as edges were actually either trimmed or extended. The same object can act as both a cutting (or boundary) edge and an object to trim (or extend). After you trim (extend) it, it is no longer highlighted, but it still functions as an edge.

TIP

You can use the Fence selection option to select multiple objects to trim or extend. All eligible objects are simultaneously trimmed or extended when you end the fence specification. Ineligible objects are ignored.

Using ALIGN as a MOVE/ROTATE Alternative

Sometimes, you need to be able to move objects to another location and then rotate them in place. In prior versions of AutoCAD, you have to issue separate MOVE and ROTATE commands to perform the task.

The ALIGN command combines the move and rotate operations into a single task. It is primarily intended for 3D transformations, but is also useful in 2D.

The ALIGN command provides the following options:

- **Select objects.** Select the objects to align in a new location by any object selection method. You then are prompted alternatively for a source point and its corresponding destination point.
- **1st source point.** Specify a point relative to the selected objects to align with its corresponding destination point. As each source point is specified, a rubber-band reference line is generated to assist in the specification of the associated destination point.
- **1st destination point.** Specify the location corresponding to the 1st source point.
- **2nd source point.** If you press Enter at this point, the ALIGN command moves the selected objects relative to the points specified. To perform 2D transformations, select a second source point.
- **2nd destination point.** Specify the location corresponding to the 2nd source point.
- **3rd destination point.** If you press Enter at this point, you receive an additional prompt prior to performing a 2D alignment. To perform a 3D transformation, specify a third point outside the plane of the first two pairs of points.
- **3rd destination point.** Specify the location corresponding to the 3rd source point. The 3D transformation is then performed and the Align command is complete.
- **<2d> or 3d transformation.** This prompt is issued only when you press Enter at the 3rd source point prompt. If you specify a 2D transformation, any Z axis differences in the pairs of source-destination points is ignored. If you enter **3** to specify a 3D transformation, the Z components of the source-destination points you specified are included in moving and rotating the selected objects.

In the following exercise, you use ALIGN to relocate and rotate the resistors on the circuit board. The resistors are clearly labeled.

Using ALIGN To Adjust the Resistors

Continue to use the CHAP14B drawing and zoom to the view shown in figure 14.10

`Command:` *Choose Align (Modify, Rotate)*	Issues the ALIGN command
`_align`	
`Select objects:` *Press and drag a window around both resistors, then press Enter*	Selects objects to align, and ends object selection
`1st source point:` *Use* INT *object snap to pick* ①	Specifies base "move-from"
`1st destination point:` *Turn on snap and pick* ②	Specifies base "move-to"
`2nd source point:` *Use INT object snap to pick* ③	Specifies "rotate-from"
`2nd destination point:` *Pick* ④	Specifies "rotate-to"
`3rd source point:` ↵	Confirms object move and rotation
`<2d> or 3d transformation:` ↵	Accepts 2D default and moves and rotates the resistors
`Command:` **R** ↵	Issues the REDRAW command (see fig. 14.11)

Save the drawing.

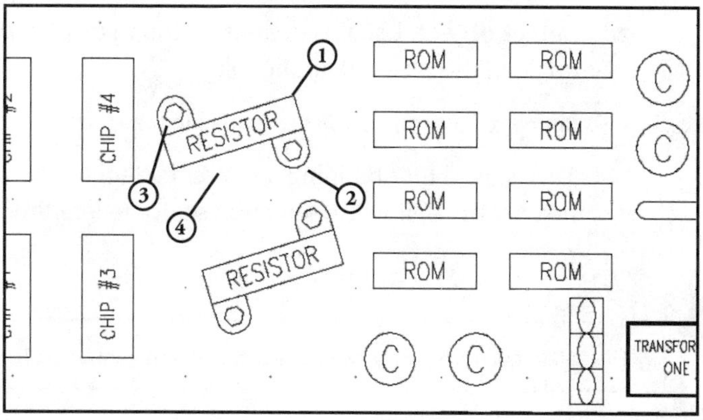

Figure 14.10

Detail of resistors before ALIGN.

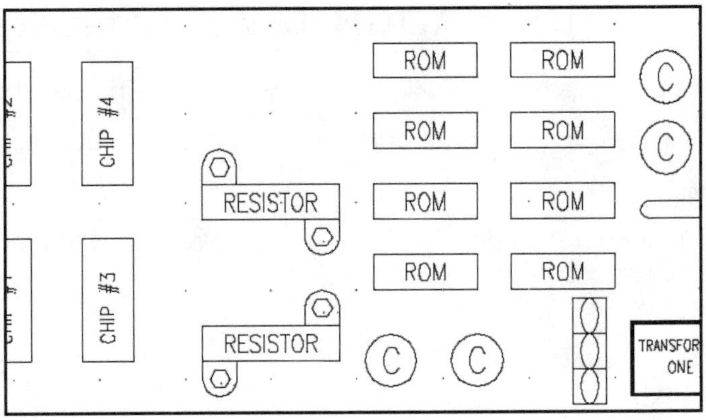

Figure 14.11

Detail of resistors after ALIGN.

Using LENGTHEN To Increase Sizes

Another editing task that you often are required to perform is to alter the length of a line or arc by a specific amount. In prior versions of AutoCAD, you must select a line, extend it to a boundary, offset that boundary, and finally, trim the line accordingly—quite a few steps. For arcs, the construction tasks are even more involved!

The Release 13 LENGTHEN command solves this problem with a minimum of fuss.

The LENGTHEN command presents the following options:

```
DElta/Percent/Total/Dynamic/<Select object>
```

- **Select object.** Use this default option to display the length and included angle of the object if applicable:

  ```
  Current Length: 3.5633, included angle: 205.6419
  ```

  This is used for obtaining a reference length and angle only and does not necessarily define the selection set to be lengthened.

NOTE

The spline object typically can be shortened, but cannot be lengthened.

- **DElta.** Use the DElta option to lengthen or shorten an object by a specified increment. Specify a non-negative value to lengthen an object or a negative value to shorten the object. You can specify a length or an angle. The object is lengthened or shortened by the specified amount from the endpoint closest to the pick point used to select the object. The DElta option issues the prompt `Angle/<Enter delta length (0.0000)>`.

- **Angle.** Use the Angle option to incrementally change the included angle of an arc. Enter a positive or negative angle value at the prompt `Enter delta angle <0.0000>`; and select an object to modify at the prompt `<Select object to change>/Undo`. The Undo option reverses the change made to the last object.

- **Enter delta length.** This is the default option for the DElta method. Enter a positive or negative value at this prompt and select the object to modify at the prompt `<Select object to change>/Undo`. The Undo option reverses the change made to the last object.

- **Percent.** Use the Percent option to specify a percentage change for the object. A 50-percent change, for example, results in the object being shortened by half. A 200-percent change doubles the length of the object. This option changes the included angle of an arc by the specified percentage. The percentage must be a positive value greater than zero.

  The Percent option issues the prompt `Enter percent length <0.0000>:`. Enter the percent change and select an object to modify at the prompt `<Select object to change>/Undo`. The Undo option reverses the change made to the last object.

- **Total.** Use the Total option to set an explicit length of an object from a fixed endpoint. For an arc, the Total option determines the total included angle of the arc. The Total option issues the prompt `Angle/<Enter total length (0.0000)>:`.

- **Angle.** The Angle option is used to specify the total included angle of an arc. Enter a value at the prompt `Enter total angle <0.0000>`; and select an object to modify at the prompt `<Select object to change>/Undo`. The Undo option reverses the change made to the last object.

- **Enter total length (0.0000).** At this prompt, enter the total length of the object and select an object to modify at the prompt `<Select object to change>/Undo`. The Undo option reverses the change made to the last object.

- **DYnamic.** Use this option to dynamically drag the length of the selected object. The endpoint closest to the pick point of the object is dragged to the desired length or included angle (for an arc), while the other endpoint remains fixed. The DYnamic option issues the prompt `<Select object to change>/Undo`. The Undo option reverses the change made to the last object. You cannot use the Dynamic option with Spline objects.

In the following exercise, you use LENGTHEN to increase all arc lengths within the circuit board logo to exactly 1.5".

USING LENGTHEN TO MODIFY THE LOGO

Continue in the CHAP14B drawing and zoom the view shown in figure 14.12.

`Command:` *Choose Lengthen (Modify, Resize)*	Issues the LENGTHEN command
`_Lengthen`	
`DElta/Percent/Total/` `DYnamic/<Select object>:` *Pick rightmost arc at* ①	Selects an arc to process
`Current Length: 1.01` `included angle: 95.85`	Reports arc data
`DElta/Percent/Total/` `DYnamic/<Select object>:` **T** ↵	Specifies Total option
`Angle/<Enter total length` `(1.00)>:` **1.5** ↵	Specifies new total length but does not lengthen it yet
`<Select object to change>/Undo:` *Pick all arcs in sequence, right to left, and press Enter after the last pick*	Lengthens each arc in order

Save the drawing.

Figure 14.12

Detail of logo after using LENGTHEN.

Using STRETCH for Versatile Changes

The STRETCH command enables you to move and stretch objects. You can lengthen objects, shorten them, and alter their shapes. The results of stretching depend on the object types you select and how you select them.

In a stretch operation, you normally use a crossing window to select your objects and then indicate a displacement from a base point. Everything you select inside the crossing window moves, and objects crossing the window are stretched. The phrase *inside the window* means all endpoints and vertices of an object are within the window. The phrase *crossing the window* means that endpoints and other object elements can lie both inside and outside the window.

The STRETCH command provides the following options:

- **Select objects to stretch by crossing-window or -polygon...Select objects:** At this prompt, you must use a crossing window or crossing polygon to select entities. AutoCAD accepts only one selection window. The STRETCH command ignores multiple selection sets, using the last one only. Use the BOX crossing option, Crossing window (C), or the Crossing Polygon (CP) object selection method to select the entities for stretching. You can use the Remove (R) option to remove objects from the selection set. You cannot use the Add (A) option, however, as AutoCAD ignores objects other than those originally selected using a crossing option. The prompt repeats until your selection set is complete. Press Enter to terminate object selection.
- **Base point or displacement.** Enter the base point of displacement or a coordinate amount of displacement.
- **Second point of displacement.** Enter the new point for the stretched entities.

In the following exercise, you use STRETCH to elongate the right side of the slot connector by 0.49". The *slot connector* runs along the bottom of the circuit board. This time, you use Noun/Verb selection.

Using STRETCH To Elongate the Slot Connector

Continue in the CHAP14B drawing from the previous exercise, and zoom to the view shown in figure 14.13.

`Command:` *Choose Stretch (Modify, Resize)* — Issues the STRETCH command

```
_stretch
Select objects to stretch by crossing-window
or -polygon...
```

`Select objects:` *Select a crossing window from ① to ②* — Selects objects and specifies window that determines what gets stretched

```
7 found
```

Notice which endpoints are within the window. The selection includes the polyline edge of the board, but no polyline endpoints are in the window. The selection also includes the objects at 3 and 4, which you next deselect.

`Select objects:` *Press Shift and pick the objects at ③ and at ④* — *Removes both objects from selection set*

```
1 found, 1 removed
1 found, 1 removed
```

`Select objects:` ↵ — Ends selection

`Base point or displacement:` **.49<0** ↵ — Specifies a polar displacement

`Second point of displacement:` ↵ — Accepts first point as displacement and stretches the objects

Notice that the endpoints within the window were moved, those outside the window were not, and the lines between those endpoints were stretched. The polyline edge of the board was unaffected.

`Command:` **R** ↵ — Cleans up the screen

Save the drawing.

In the previous exercise, you also selected the bottom edge of the circuit board with the crossing window. Because neither endpoint of this line fell within the crossing window, it was not stretched.

NOTE

The following explanation of the effect of STRETCH is not well known, or even correctly documented in Autodesk's own documentation.

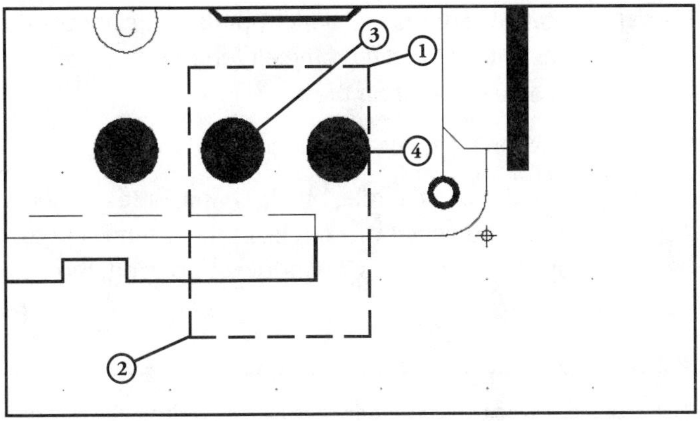

Figure 14.13

Detail of slot connector after STRETCH.

The results of STRETCH are controlled by the following three things:

- The selected objects. You can add or remove objects by any selection method.
- A window or polygon selection. Despite the command's prompt, it does not have to be a crossing selection. At least one window or polygon must be specified, although it does not have to select anything. You can use other methods to select the objects to be stretched or moved. It is only the relationship of each object's defining points to the last, and only the last, specified window or polygon that determines what gets stretched, moved, or ignored.
- The types of objects selected. Different types are affected differently.

TIP

In a crowded drawing, use the SELECT command before using STRETCH to select the objects you don't want to be affected. Then start the STRETCH command, use a crossing window to select the objects to be stretched (and possibly many others), and determine the control points. Then switch to Remove mode and enter P to remove the objects selected by SELECT.

The effects of object stretching depend on the type of object. Some significant points to remember when you use STRETCH are as follows:

- The defining endpoints or vertices of lines, arcs, polyline segments, viewports, traces, and solids determine what stretches or moves. Those within the window or polygon get moved, those outside it remain fixed, and the geometry in between gets stretched.

- AutoCAD adjusts the center points of arcs or polyline arcs to keep the sagitta constant. The *sagitta* is the altitude or distance from the chord midpoint to the nearest point on the arc.
- Viewport contents remain constant in scale.
- A point, object, circle, block, shape, or text object never stretch. If the point object, the center of a circle, or the insertion point of a block, shape, or text object is in the stretch window or polygon, the object gets moved.

TIP

Use the grip edit stretch mode to quickly stretch an object. You also can stretch a circle's radius with the grip edit stretch mode.

Using the SCALE Command

Occasionally, you use the wrong drawing symbol and text scale or need to change an object's size. The SCALE command enables you to shrink or enlarge existing objects. During a scaling operation, you use a scale factor or reference length to change the size of objects around a given base point. The base point remains constant; everything around it grows or shrinks by your scale factor. You can enter an explicit scale factor, pick two points to have AutoCAD compute the distance, or specify a reference length. To use the reference method, define a current length (generally on an object), then specify its new length.

The SCALE command prompt sequence is as follows:

- **Select objects.** Choose all the objects you want to enlarge or reduce by means of any of the object selection methods.
- **Base point.** Enter a base point in the current coordinate system around which to scale objects. When the scaling occurs, all points on selected objects move closer to the base point or farther away from the base point as their scale is reduced and enlarged.

TIP

Choose a base point that relates to the object or objects being scaled and positions them correctly after scaling. You generally pick a corner or the center of the object being scaled.

After selecting a base point, you see the following prompt:

```
<Scale factor>/Reference.
```

- **Scale factor.** Specify a scale factor by which to scale objects. A number greater than one enlarges the objects; a number between zero and one reduces the objects. You can enter a number or pick a point to show a distance. If you pick a point, a rubber-band line appears between the base point and the crosshairs. The objects to be scaled are highlighted and dragged as you move the crosshairs.
- **Reference.** Enter **R** for the Reference option if you want to define the scale factor in reference to a length, such as the size of an existing object.

NOTE

You cannot scale the X, Y, or Z values independently.

- **Reference length <1>.** If you specify the Reference option, the scale factor is defined by the ratio of the two lengths that you specify. You also can pick two points, usually on an existing object, to show the reference length.
- **New length.** Enter the new length to scale the reference length to. The selected objects are then scaled by the ratio between the reference length and the new length. You also can pick one point to show the new length as a distance from the base point. As you move the cursor to pick the new length, AutoCAD shows a rubber-band line from the base point.

In the following exercise, you use the SCALE Reference option to make transformer number one exactly 0.8" long. The transformer is clearly labeled. To describe the original reference length to AutoCAD, you pick two points.

USING SCALE TO ENLARGE THE TRANSFORMER

Continue to use the CHAP14B drawing and zoom to the view shown in figure 14.14.

`Command:` *Press and drag a crossing window around the transformer, from ① to ②, then Choose Scale (Modify, Resize)*	Issues SCALE with preselected objects
`_scale 3 found`	
`Base point:` Use INT object snap to pick ③ (see fig. 14.14)	

Drag the cursor around and watch the selection scale relative to a one-unit length.

`<Scale factor>/Reference:` **R** ↵	Specifies the Reference length method
`Reference Length <1>:` *Choose Last Point (OPTIONS_II)*	Issues @ to specify the last picked point at ③
`Second point:` *Use INT object snap to pick* ④	Specifies existing transformer length as reference length

Drag the cursor around and watch the selection scale relative to the reference length.

`New Length:` **0.8** ↵	Specifies the new transformer length and scales the text proportionally

Save the drawing.

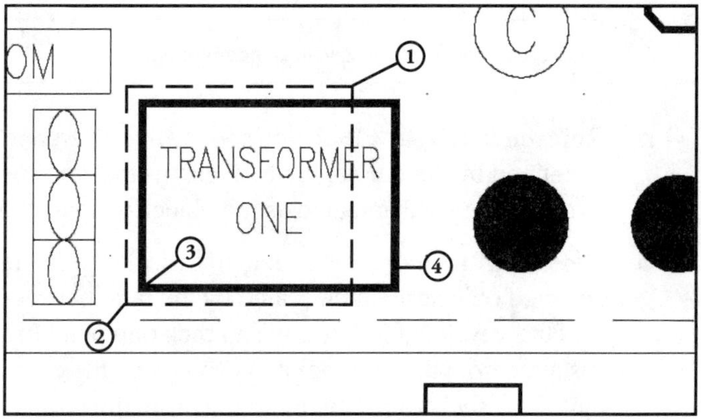

Figure 14.14

Detail of transformer number one after SCALE.

TIP

The scale base point is also the base point of the new length. You can pick points for the reference length on another object, but if you want to show the new length by picking points on another object, first use MOVE to move the selection to place the base point on the other object, then scale the selection, then use the MOVE command to move the selection back to its original location. Use Previous to reselect the objects and object snaps to specify the moves.

In the next section, you use selection *filters* to include and exclude specific objects, by object type and property, from your object selection sets.

Filtering the Selection Set

Despite the vast number of selection set options available, choosing the objects you want is still sometimes tricky in a complex drawing. Object-selection filters enable you to select only those objects that you specify in the filter description. Common filters can include object type, color, layer, or coordinate data. Although the concept of specifying filters is simple, the process can be confusing because AutoCAD provides so many filter specifications and options for using them.

To explore the filter options, choose Selection Filters from the Select Objects flyout on the Standard toolbar. AutoCAD then presents the Object Selection Filters dialog box (see fig. 14.15). You can enter 'FILTER to transparently open this dialog box at the `Select objects:` prompt.

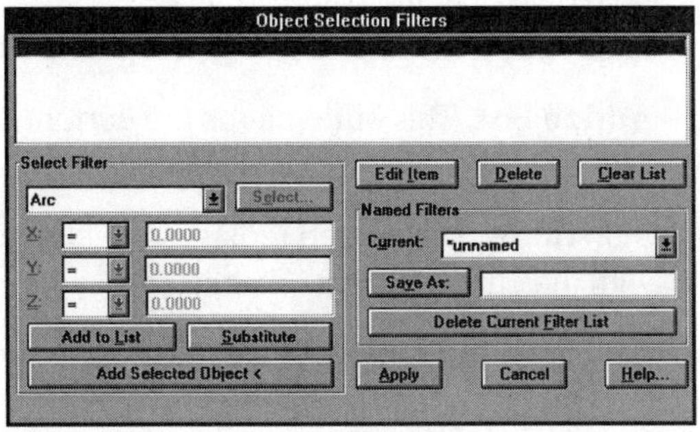

Figure 14.15

The Object Selection Filters dialog box.

NOTE

FILTER finds objects by color or linetype only when they have been directly assigned, rather than by layer.

You use the list box at the top of the Object Selection Filters dialog box to display and edit the filter criteria.

- **Select Filter.** This area of the dialog box contains features for specifying the filter criteria for object selection.
- **Select Filter drop-down list box.** This list displays all the filter types available. If you are editing an existing filter, this option shows the current filter's type.

- **Select.** This button displays a dialog box with all the available items of the filter type being edited. Valid types for the select are Xdata ID, Block Name, Color, Dimension Style, Layer, Linetype, or Text Style Name.
- **X.** This drop-down list box displays the relational operators from which you can choose. The relational operators are =, !=, <, <=, >, >=, *. X displays an X coordinate value in the edit box when working with coordinates, such as the starting point of a line. X displays the selected attribute when working with properties such as the color of a layer.
- **Y.** Y displays the relational operators from which you can choose. The relational operators are =, !=, <, <=, >, >=, *. This option displays a Y coordinate value in the edit box when working with coordinates.
- **Z.** Z displays the relational operators from which you can choose. The relational operators are =, !=, <, <=, >, >=, *. This option displays a Z coordinate value in the edit box when working with coordinates.
- **Add to List.** This button adds the current Select Filter settings to the Filters list box above the highlighted filter.
- **Substitute.** This button replaces the filter highlighted in the Filter list box with the current Select Filter settings.
- **Add Selected Object.** This button adds the properties of a selected object to the Filter list box. The dialog box is temporarily cleared from the screen while you select an object in your drawing.
- **Edit Item.** This option moves the filter highlighted in the Filters list box to the Select Filter group for editing.
- **Delete.** This option deletes the filter highlighted in the Filters list box.
- **Clear List.** This option deletes all the filters in the Filters list box.

The Named Filters group contains the following options:

- **Current.** This drop-down list box displays a list of the available named filter.
- **Save As.** This button saves the current set of filters in the Filter list box to the name entered in the Save As edit box. This creates a named filter list. You can have up to 18 named filters, each up to 25 characters in length, stored in the FILTER.NFL file.

TIP

> If you have a complicated selection filter that you want to use in other drawings, type a name in the Save As edit box and click on the Save As button. Your filter will be stored in the FILTER.NFL file in your AutoCAD directory. Use the Current drop-down list box to choose your saved filter and apply it.

- **Delete Current Filter List.** This button deletes the current filter from the list of available named filters in the FILTER.NFL file.
- **Apply.** This button exits the Object Selection Filters dialog box and applies the defined filter to all the objects you select. You are prompted to `Select objects`.
- **Select Objects.** You select the objects to which you want to apply the filter. This prompt appears after you click on Apply in the Object Selection Filters dialog box. You can use any valid object selection method. Use ALL to apply the filter to all objects in the drawing. AutoCAD reports how many objects were found and how many were filtered out.

You can specify object-selection filters by choosing an item from the drop-down list under Select Filter, then clicking on the Add to List button. That filter then appears in the current filter list at the top of the dialog box. You can repeat this process to add more conditions to the filters. If you want to save the filter list to use at a later time, enter a name (up to 18 characters) in the edit box next to Save As and then choose the Save As button. You can find and retrieve all the defined filter names in the list box next to the Current button. Choosing the Apply button closes the dialog box and prompts you for object selection, using the current filter. Choose Cancel to leave the dialog box without applying the filter.

The PARTS layer of the board drawing contains several objects in the default BYLAYER (red) color: the circular contact plate at the upper right, the switchbank at the bottom center, and the four chips at the left side. The PARTS layer also contains several other objects, which are magenta, with their color set explicitly. In the following exercise, you use filtering to select only the objects on the PARTS layer in the default BYLAYER (red) color.

Using FILTERS To Qualify Objects

Continue in the CHAP14B drawing from the previous exercise and zoom to the extents.

`Command:` *Choose Selection Filters (Standard, Select Objects)*	Issues the Filter command and opens the Object Selection Filters dialog box
Click in the Select Filter *drop-down list box and select Layer*	Puts Layer in Select Filter list box
Choose the Select *button, then select* PARTS, *then choose OK*	Opens Select Layer dialog box, enters PARTS in box below the Select button
Choose Add to List	Enters Layer = PARTS in the filter list at the top of the dialog box
Choose Apply	Closes the dialog box and prompts for objects
`Applying filter to selection.` `Select objects:` **ALL** ↵	Selects all, but filters out objects that do not meet the filter criteria
`136 found, 97 were filtered out.`	Highlights all objects on PARTS layer
`Select objects:` ↵	Exits selection
`Exiting filtered selection`	

The filtered selection included the unwanted magenta objects. You need to refine the filter specification, as follows.

`Command:` ↵	Repeats FILTER command and reopens Object Selection Filters dialog box with Layer = PARTS in the filter list
Click below the Layer = PARTS line	Highlights the next blank line
In the Select Filter *drop-down list, select* ** Begin NOT *from the end of the list, then Choose* Add to List	Puts ** Begin NOT in Select Filter list box and in the filter list
In the Select Filter *drop-down list, select* Color, choose Select, *select the magenta color box, then choose* OK	Puts Color in Select Filter list box, opens Select Color dialog box, and returns to filters dialog box
Choose Add to List	Enters Color = 6-Magenta in filter list

In Select Filter *drop-down list, select* ** End NOT *from the end of the list, then Choose* Add to List	Puts ** End NOT in Select Filter list box and in the filter list
Choose Apply	Closes the dialog box and prompts for objects
`Applying filter to selection.` `Select objects:` **ALL** ↵	Selects all, but filters out all but the desired objects
`136 found, 106 were filtered out.`	Highlights all objects on PARTS layer except the magenta ones
`Select objects:` ↵	Exits selection
`Exiting filtered selection`	
`Command:` *Choose Erase (Modify)*	Issues the ERASE command
`Select objects:` *Choose P (OPTIONS_II)*	Specifies Previous selection
`_P 30 found`	Reselects the filter selection set
`Select objects:` ↵	Ends selection and erases objects
`Command:` *Choose Undo (Standard)*	Restore objects

When a filter is active, AutoCAD selects only those objects that conform to that filter; it ignores all other objects. In the preceding exercise, the command prompt displays the number of objects selected and the number filtered out. You can use the Previous selection option to recall those objects during a subsequent editing command.

In the Object Selection Filters dialog box, you can create a list of filters to apply. After you add a filter to the list, you can highlight it by clicking on it. You might need to follow this procedure before you click on the Delete, Edit Item, or Substitute button. You can define and then save filters with a name that you specify, so that you can later recall and use them.

Do not get discouraged the first time you explore object filtering; with a little practice, filters can increase your productivity. If your drawings are not very complex, however, you might find the use of locked layers (see Chapter 2, "Organizing Drawings with Layers") to be more intuitive—just keep an open mind and see what works for you.

Object Grouping

AutoCAD provides many ways to select objects. If you want to select several objects for subsequent reference, the Previous object selection option is somewhat limited, because it stores only the most recent set of edited objects.

One of the new Release 13 features is called *object grouping*, in which you can assign group names (saved with the drawing) to sets of selected objects. You can edit groups by referencing their names at any time during a drawing session; enter G at the `Select objects:` prompt to include a group of objects to process.

You use the Object Grouping dialog box (see fig. 14.16) to create groups.

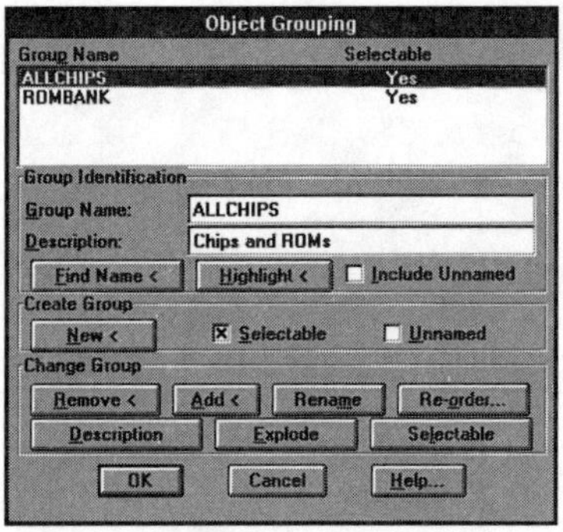

Figure 14.16

The Object Grouping dialog box.

The Object Grouping dialog box contains four basic areas: the Group Name list box, the Group Identification area, the Create Group area, and the Change Group area. The Group Name list box contains the names of all the groups defined within the drawing and whether they are selectable. *Selectable* means that if you select any one object within a group, the entire group is selected. Selectability is determined when you create a group and also can be changed at any time using the Selectable button.

The following sections discuss the other basic areas of the Object Grouping dialog box.

Group Identification

The Group Name edit box is used for entering the name of a new group to create or showing the name of the highlighted group in the Group Name list box. Group names can be up to 31 characters in length, but cannot contain any spaces. AutoCAD converts the names to uppercase.

Use the Description edit box to type an optional description of the group. Descriptions can be up to 64 characters in length and can contain spaces.

Choose the Find Name button to list the groups that any one selected object belongs to. The Find Name button prompts you to pick a member of a group. If the object you select is not a member of a group, AutoCAD prompts you as such. If you select an object that belongs to a group, the Group Member List dialog box appears, listing all the groups that include the selected object.

The Highlight button is used to highlight all the objects in a drawing that belong to the selected group. First select the desired group in the Group Name list box, and then choose the Highlight button.

Use the Include Unnamed check box to cause AutoCAD to display all group names, regardless of whether they are assigned an explicit name. All group names assigned by AutoCAD begin with *A*n* where *n* is a sequential number. (See the following Unnamed check box.)

TIP

When you copy a group, the copy is defined as an unnamed group. Use the Include Unnamed option to list such groups and then use the Change Group options to rename them, explode them, change their selection status, and so on.

Choose the New button to define a selection set for a new group. You must have a valid name entered in the Group Name edit box unless the Unnamed check box is checked. Selecting the objects for the group is the last step in defining a group. Be sure you have entered the name and description for the group before choosing New.

The Selectable check box affects only newly created groups and determines whether the new group will be selectable. Selectability means that the entire group is selected if any one object within a group is selected.

Use the Unnamed check box to specify whether you can create unnamed groups.

Change Group

Choose the Remove button to remove items from a group. You are prompted to `Select objects to remove`. If an object belongs to more than one group, it is removed only from the current group.

Choose the Add button to add items to the current group. You are prompted to `Select objects to add`. If an object already belongs to other groups and any of those groups are selectable, the entire group is added to the current group.

Choose the Rename button to rename a group. Highlight the group you want to rename in the Group Name list box. Type over the name in the Group Name edit box and choose the Rename button.

Objects are added to groups in the order you select them. If it is important to have them in a specific order, use the Re-order button. When you choose this button, an Order Group dialog box is displayed. This dialog box provides functions for changing the position of objects within a group.

The Order Group dialog box contains the following options:

- **Group Name.** This list box displays the names of the groups defined in the drawing.
- **Description.** This text area list the description, if any, of a selected group.
- **Remove from position (0 - nnn).** Object numbering with a group begins with 0. This edit box label shows the number of items within the selected group, starting at 0. In this edit box, enter the number of the item you want to move within the group.
- **Replace at position (0 - nnn).** Use this edit box to determine to what position within the group the item in the Remove from position edit box gets moved.
- **Number of objects (1 - xxx).** Use this edit box to enter a value or range of values to specify how many objects within the group will be moved to the new position.

The Re-order button performs the reordering of the objects within the group as specified earlier.

Choose the Highlight button to selectively highlight individual objects within a group. When you select this button, the Object Grouping Highlight dialog box appears. This dialog box contains a Next and Previous button as well as a text label showing the current position of the highlighted object within the group. Use the buttons to work forward or backward through a group as AutoCAD highlights the object occupying that position within the group.

Choose the Reverse Order button to totally reverse the positions of objects within a group. In other words, the last becomes first and the first becomes last.

The Description button in the Object Grouping dialog box is used to change a group description for an existing selected group. Type the new description in the Description edit box and choose the Description button to effect the change.

Choose the Explode button to destroy a group, removing the objects from the group. The objects are not erased—they simply have their individual identity restored. The group name is deleted from the drawing.

The Selectable button turns the selectability of the highlighted group on or off.

The command-line equivalent of the GROUP command (-GROUP) has options that correlate closely with the dialog items discussed previously.

In the following exercise you define two groups: one of all ROMs, and the other of all ROMs and chips, which includes the first group. You then experiment with group selectability.

USING GROUPS TO CLASSIFY OBJECTS

Continue in the CHAP14B drawing from either of the two previous exercises and zoom to the extents.

`Command:` *Choose Object Group (Standard)*	Issues the GROUP command and opens the Object Grouping dialog box
In the Group Identification *area, click in the* Group Name *edit box and enter* **ROMBANK**	Names group
Press Tab (or choose Description*) and enter* **Bank of eight ROM chips**	Describes group
Choose New	Closes dialog box and prompts for selection
`Select objects for grouping:` `Select objects:` *Select the eight ROMs with a window, then press Enter*	Selects ROMs (each is a polyline and text label), ends selection, reopens dialog box, and enters the name in Group Name list at the top of the dialog box
Enter another Group Name **ALLCHIPS**, *and* Description **Chips and ROMs**, *then choose* New	Names and describes group, closes dialog box, and prompts for selection

`Select objects for grouping:`	Selects CHIPs
`Select objects:` *Select the four CHIPs at the lift with a window*	
`Select objects:` *Press Shift and pick one of the ROMs*	Selects all eight ROMs as a group
`16 found, 1 group`	
`Select objects:` ↵	Reopens dialog box, and enters the name in the Group Name list
`Choose` OK	Closes dialog box
`Command:` *Pick any ROM or CHIP*	Selects all objects in both groups
`Command:` *Choose Object Group (Standard)*	Opens Object Grouping dialog box
Select ALLCHIPS *in the* Group Name *list, and choose* Selectable, *then* OK	Changes the group's selectability from Yes to No, and closes dialog box
`Command:` *Pick any ROM*	Selects all ROMs
`Command:` *Pick any CHIP*	Selects only one object—the group's selectability is turned off

TIP

You can control group selectability globally with the Object Grouping check box in the Object Selection Settings dialog box.

After you finish the preceding exercise, the group name ROMBANK is now stored in the drawing. You can enter G and then the group name at any `Select objects:` prompt to edit a named group. Applications of group names are limited only by your imagination.

The advantages of groups over blocks includes the following:

- You can use the Selectable option to control access to the individual members of a group.
- You can edit members of groups without affecting other members or removing them from the group.
- Blocks are more efficient for multiple occurrences, but groups avoid increasing drawing size for single occurrences.
- Any AutoCAD drawing object could be assigned membership in one or more groups, just as you can be a member of several groups.

Tip

When you use EXPLODE, AutoCAD replaces the selected object with component objects. When you use DIVIDE or MEASURE (see Chapter 10), AutoCAD creates points along the selected object. Use Previous to select the objects created (the points or exploded objects), and GROUP to name them. You can later select the objects by specifying the corresponding group name.

Final Editing Tips

From this chapter, you have seen the importance of editing during drawing development. Your job is to produce high-quality drawings in an efficient manner, so learning valuable techniques and adopting good work habits are key steps toward achieving your goal.

The following list outlines some procedures to help you edit your drawings in a professional style:

- Consider any repetitive or symmetric features. A good phrase to remember is "draw once, edit many."
- Familiarize yourself with all of the editing commands.
- Use snap, ortho, and object snaps to set up your MOVE and COPY displacements. If you find yourself in a tight space, try object selection cycling.
- Learn all of the object-selection options, including the Remove and Shift key usage. All selection-set options have their merits. Last and Previous are frequently used. The object-picking method is best for detail work, especially with object snap. If you want to edit most of the objects at once, use the All option, then remove the objects you did not want to include.
- Window is powerful, but it is not all inclusive. Remember, what you see in the window is what goes into the selection set. You can use Crossing as a knife to slice out a selection set. The WPolygon window is nice when a rectangular window can not enclose the objects. Previous saves time in repetitive editing. And lest you forget, a U undoes the last object selection operation.
- Explore the new Release 13 GROUP command, in combination with object filtering, to provide great flexibility with named selection sets.

When you work with all of the editing commands and investigate their capabilities, you expand your drawing knowledge and become a more valuable asset to your organization. In the next chapter, you will learn about direct modification of objects and their properties.

chapter

15

Object and Drawing Modification and Inquiry Tools

As you develop a drawing, you often need to check your work for accuracy. Did you place the center of the circle at coordinates 3,5 or 4,5? Is that line 6" or 6.5" long? Did you draw that object on the right layer? Based on the answers you get, you may have to change one or more properties of the object or even the object itself.

You can use AutoCAD drawings, drawn to full size, to make critical measurements. For example, with a floor plan of a building, you can measure areas and lengths very accurately and base design/construction decisions on those measurements.

AutoCAD has several commands that enable you to make such measurements and to query the drawing database. Together, these are referred to as *inquiry* commands. The inquiry commands enable you to find out specific information about an object or about an aspect of the drawing. Other commands enable you to change the properties of an object and are referred to as *object property* commands. The object property commands enable you to edit the object and geometric properties of objects. Geometric properties define an object's size and location. Endpoints are a line's geometric properties, for example, while the center point and radius are a circle's geometric properties. Object properties are an object's color, linetype, layer, linetype scale, and thickness.

Quite a number of commands are covered, so the new commands are presented as four groups, as follows:

- Commands that give you general information about the drawing, such as the drawing extents and limits.
- Commands that give you specific information about selected objects or points, such as the coordinates of the endpoints of a line.
- Commands that enable you to view and change specific properties of selected objects, such as changing an object's layer or color.
- The CAL command, which invokes the powerful, built-in calculator.

Getting General Drawing Data

STATUS and TIME are two commands that display information about the general state of your drawing. Additionally, several commands have a listing option you can use to get information about a specific aspect of your drawing, such as a listing of all layers and their states. All of these commands are covered in this section.

The STATUS Command

The STATUS command generates a report in the text window that describes the overall status of your drawing. STATUS has no options, and using it has no affect on the drawing.

Figure 15.1 shows a typical report that STATUS generates. You can see in the figure that the report contains much information. At the top of the report you see the total number of objects in the drawing and name of the drawing.

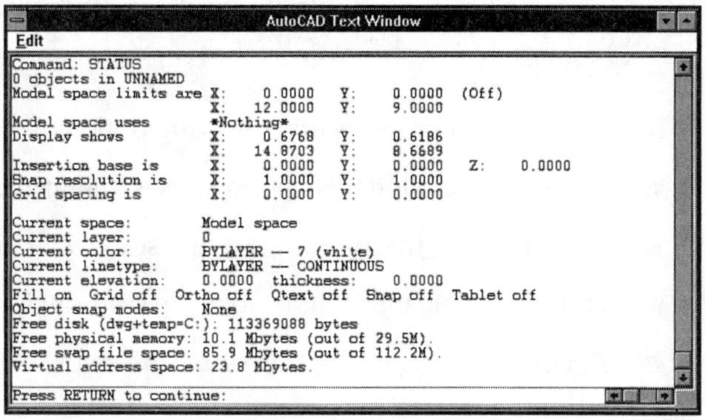

Figure 15.1

A typical report generated by STATUS.

Next, the coordinates of the lower left and upper right corners of the drawing limits (set using the LIMITS command) are shown. This is followed by the coordinates of the lower left and upper right corners of the drawing extents, and the lower left and upper right corners of the area that you see in the current viewport.

After those, you see the current settings for the drawing insertion base point (set using the BASE command) and the spacing settings for the SNAP and GRID commands. You also are told whether you currently are in model or paper space.

The values for the current layer, color, linetype, elevation, and thickness settings also are displayed. You use the DDLMODES and DDEMODES commands to set these settings.

Next, the on/off status of various commands, such as SNAP and GRID, is listed. The last item of the report is the amount of free space on the hard drive, RAM memory, and swap space (see Appendix B, "Optimizing AutoCAD for Windows," for further explanation).

The TIME command

The TIME command enables you to keep track of time from within the drawing editor. Figure 15.2 shows the typical output generated by TIME.

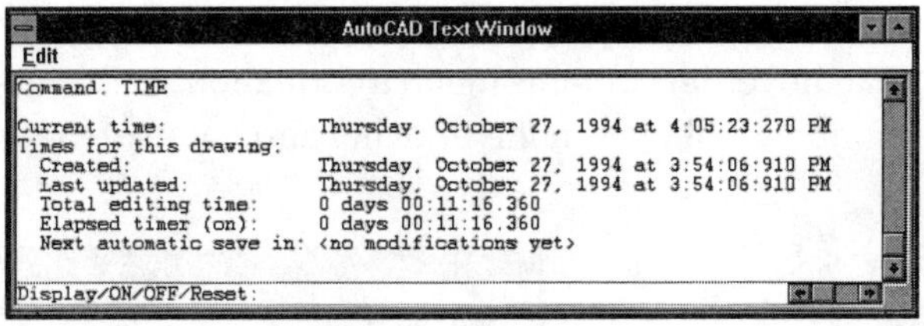

Figure 15.2

The typical output generated by TIME.

The TIME prompt presents the following options:

- **Display.** Choosing this option causes TIME to redisplay the time information.
- **ON.** Choosing this option starts the stopwatch function.
- **OFF.** Choosing this option stops the stopwatch function.
- **Reset.** Choosing this option resets the stopwatch function.

You can start TIME transparently, and its usage does not affect the drawing.

WARNING

You might be tempted to use total editing time to track time for accounting purposes, but be careful. If an operator opens a drawing and then heads out for an hour lunch, AutoCAD includes that hour in the cumulative time if the operator subsequently updates the drawing file using the END command or the SAVE command.

In the following exercise, you use the TIME command to get some times relevant to the drawing file.

Checking on Some Times

Begin a new drawing again named CHAP15 using the CPLATE drawing from the IAW Disk as the prototype.

`Command:` *Choose* Data, Time	Issues the TIME command

The current date and time, date and time of drawing creation, date and time of last update, elapsed time since opening the drawing, and time to next autosave are displayed. The stopwatch function is automatically turned on when you open a drawing.

`Display/ON/OFF/Reset:` **OFF** ↵	Turns off the stopwatch function
`Display/ON/OFF/Reset:` **R** ↵	Resets the stopwatch function to zero
`Display/ON/OFF/Reset:` **D** ↵	Displays the current time information

Notice that the elapsed timer is now off and the time is 0.

`Display/ON/OFF/Reset:` **ON** ↵	Turns on the stopwatch function

Wait for several seconds before proceeding to the next step. The wait gives the stopwatch function some elapsed time to record.

`Display/ON/OFF/Reset:` **D** ↵	Displays all time values

Notice that the elapsed timer is now on and the time has changed.

`Display/ON/OFF/Reset:` **OFF** ↵	Turns off the stopwatch function
`Display/ON/OFF/Reset:` ↵	Terminates TIME

Using the stopwatch options does not affect the drawing in any way.

Other Listing Commands

A number of commands include a listing option, represented by the symbol ? in the command's options list. The following is a list of those commands:

Command	*Listing Option*
BLOCK	? displays a list of currently defined block definitions.
DIMSTYLE	? displays a list of currently defined dimension styles.
HATCH	? displays a list of all hatch patterns that reside in the ACAD.PAT file.
INSERT	? displays a list of all currently defined block definitions (similar to the ? option of HATCH).
LAYER	? displays a list of all layers and their states.
LINETYPE	? displays a list of all currently loaded linetypes.
MLINE	If you select the Style option and then enter ?, you get a list of all currently defined mline styles.
SHAPE	? displays a list of currently loaded shapes.
STYLE	? displays a list of all currently defined text styles and their settings.
TEXT	If you select the Style option and then enter ?, you get a list of all currently defined text styles and their settings.
UCS	? displays a list of all saved UCSs.

continues

Command	*Listing Option*
VIEW	? displays a list of saved views.
VPORTS	? displays a list of all saved viewport configurations.
XREF	? displays a list of all currently attached XREFS.

NOTE

Of the preceding listed commands, you can use only LAYER, SETVAR, and VIEW transparently.

After you specify the ? option of one of the preceding commands, you usually see another prompt that asks you for the name of the item you want to list. The ? option of the LAYER command, for example, prompts you as follows:

```
Layer name(s) to list <*>:
```

The default value is the asterisk wild-card character, which specifies to list all layer names. If you want a specific layer or group of layers, type that layer or a layer name pattern (defining patterns is covered in Chapter 2, "Organizing Drawings with Layers").

Some of the commands in the preceding list have been superseded by dialog box equivalents. The newer dialog box versions of the commands usually have the information that was produced by the ? option incorporated directly into the dialog box format. The LAYER command, for example, has been superseded by the DDLMODES command, and the DDLMODES dialog box shows a list of all layers and their states.

One advantage the older commands have over their newer, dialog box—based successors is that the listing appears in the text window, which enables you to use Windows' Copy and Paste functions to copy the listing into another application or to print the listing.

WARNING

Unlike STATUS or TIME, commands like BLOCK and LAYER can affect your drawing. The ? option itself is harmless, but you can use the other options of these commands to save, delete, or change definitions and settings in your drawing.

In the following exercise, you get listings of various aspects of a drawing file.

Displaying Some Lists

Continue using the drawing CHAP15.

`Command:` **LAYER** ↵	Starts the LAYER command
`?/Make/Set/New/ON/OFF/Color/Ltype/ Freeze/Thaw/Lock/Unlock:` **?** ↵	Specifies the listing option
`Layer name(s) to list <*>:` ↵	Instructs LAYER to list all layers

There should be four layers in the list.

`?/Make/Set/New/ON/OFF/Color/Ltype Freeze/Thaw/LOck/Unlock:` ↵	Ends the LAYER command

Next, you get a listing of all currently defined text styles and their settings.

`Command:` *Choose* Data, Text Style ↵	Issues the STYLE command
`Text style name (or ?) <STANDARD>:` **?** ↵	Specifies the listing option
Text style(s) to list <*>: ↵	Instructs STYLE to list all text styles

There should be two styles in the list.

The SETVAR Command

Many drawing, editing, and dialog-box commands affect or are affected by settings. AutoCAD maintains these settings as system variables. SETVAR provides a means to access these settings.

System variables perform several functions. Certain variables control various aspects of the drawing editor. FILEDIA, for example, controls whether a file dialog box appears anytime you are prompted for a file name.

Other variables hold the results of various commands, such as AREA, which holds the last area recorded by the AREA command. Some variables even contain some environment settings. The variable DWGNAME, for example, contains the name of the current drawing file. DWGNAME also is an example of a read-only variable. *Read-only* means that the variable is maintained by AutoCAD and although you can view its value, you cannot change it directly.

Yet other variables hold the results of and control the actions of a number of AutoCAD commands. When you turn SNAP on or off, for example, the action is stored in the variable SNAPMODE as a 0 (for off) or 1 (for on). On the other hand, if you set the value of SNAPMODE directly, you can turn SNAP on or off.

SETVAR was once the only means of accessing system variables. As AutoCAD underwent revisions and improvements, you were given the ability to access system variables like commands, by typing them at the `Command:` prompt. As AutoCAD was improved, access to a number of the system variables (not all) was integrated into the menu and command system. For example, many of the settings that you enable/disable in dialog boxes are directly linked to various system variables. A prime example is the DDIM dialogue box which you use to set the parameters that govern dimensioning; all the dimension settings are stored in system variables. Another example is the TILEMODE variable which controls paper and model space. TILEMODE can be accessed via the TILE button in the status bar or through the View pull-down menu. On the other hand, some system variables are still not integrated into the menu or dialog boxes. A prime example is FILEDIA which controls the usage of the file dialog box. To set FILEDIA, you must use SETVAR or enter it at the `Command:` prompt.

TIP

As a general rule, you can execute system variables transparently. If you are in the middle of the LINE command, for example, you can still execute the variable SNAPUNIT (which controls the snap spacing) and resume the LINE command.

System variables are stored in either the AutoCAD configuration file or the Drawing file, or not at all. As a general rule, any variables that are related to the drawing environment or editor (such as FILEDIA) are saved in the configuration file. All other variables are saved with the drawing file or are not saved at all. If a particular variable is saved in the configuration file, then its setting carries over from one drawing session to another. If a variable is saved with the drawing, then its current value depends on the current drawing.

Quite a number of system variables exist in AutoCAD. This chapter does not focus on system variables; to learn more about specific system variables, see Appendix A, "Installation and Configuration," of this book, or Appendix A of the *AutoCAD Command Reference.*

Although dated, SETVAR still has its uses. For one, the system variable AREA conflicts with the command AREA. If you enter the command AREA, you execute the command AREA; the only way to view the system variable AREA is to use SETVAR. More importantly, SETVAR is the only command you can use to list all or a group of system variables. You can use any of the wild cards listed earlier in this chapter to list specific sets of system variables.

In the following exercise, you use SETVAR to list and set some system variables.

EXAMINING THE SYSTEM VARIABLES

Continue using the drawing CHAP15.

`Command:` *Choose* Options, System Variables, List	Issues the SETVAR command and specifies the ? option and * wild card automatically

At various points in the listing, you are prompted to press Return to continue; press Enter to see the next portion of the listing.

Also, note that some variables are accompanied by the notation "(read only)." This notation indicates that you can view, but not change, the system variable's value.

Continue to press Enter until the `Command:` prompt returns.

`Command:` *Choose* Options, System Variables, Set	Issues SETVAR and gives you the option of specifying a system variable name or the ? option
`Variable name or ?:` **?** ↵	
`Variable(s) to list <*>:` **A*** ↵	Instructs SETVAR to list all system variables that begin with the letter A
`Command:` Choose Options, System, Variables, Set	
`Variable name or ?:` **SAVETIME** ↵	Specifies the system variable SAVETIME
`New value for SAVETIME <120>:` **20** ↵	Sets a new value for SAVETIME of 20 minutes

SAVETIME is the system variable that determines the time interval (in minutes) at which the autosave function is carried out.

System variables are a handy feature. They enable you to set various settings directly and often are quicker to use than the commands that would normally set them. SETVAR is especially useful if you customize AutoCAD with custom menus and AutoLISP or ADS routines.

TIP

The AutoCAD documentation still makes a distinction between a command and a system variable, even though system variables behave like commands. If you look up a command in the AutoCAD Command Reference and cannot find it, check in Appendix A of the *AutoCAD Command Reference* because it might be listed as a system variable.

Getting Object-Specific Data

General information on the state of the drawing is handy, but you also need the capability to get object-specific information. In this section, you learn commands that enable you to inquire about specific objects.

The DDMODIFY Command

You can use DDMODIFY to view geometric and property information on any drawing object. As its name implies, you can also use DDMODIFY to make changes to objects, and it is described in greater detail later in this chapter.

In figures 15.3 and 15.4, you can see the typical DDMODIFY dialog boxes for a line and a circle. Note that although both dialog boxes are produced by DDMODIFY, the dialog box title and format is adjusted to suit the selected object. The adjustments make it easier to read the object and geometric properties of the selected object.

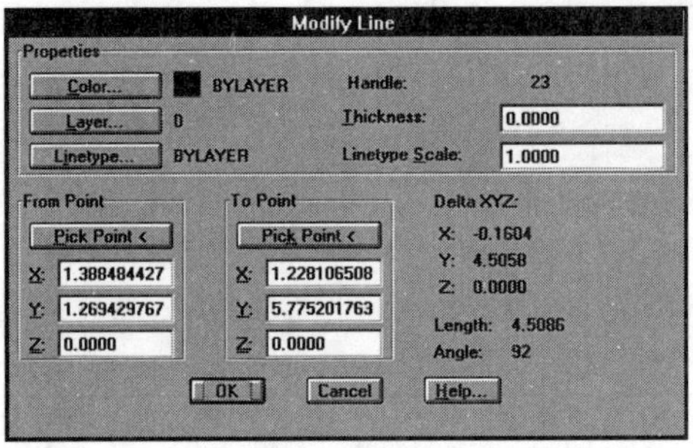

Figure 15.3

DDMODIFY dialog box for a line.

Figure 15.4

DDMODIFY dialog box for a circle.

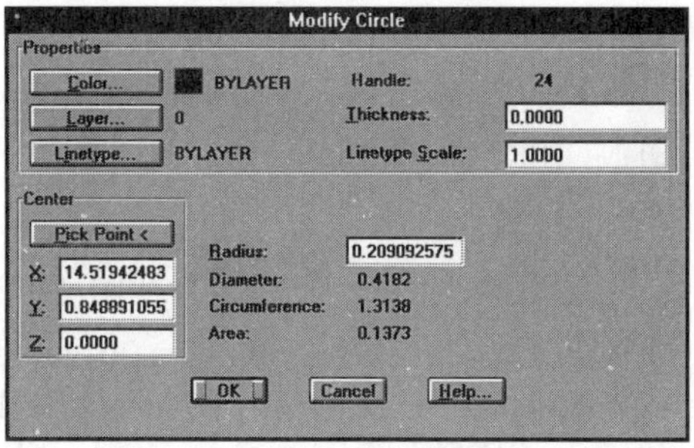

WARNING

DDMODIFY actually enables you to modify some of the object's properties and geometry, so use it as an inquiry tool with care. The properties that you can change (such as the layer) appear next to buttons or in edit boxes. To prevent unintended changes to an object's properties, press Esc or choose the Cancel button to exit the dialog box rather than choose the OK button.

The LIST Command

You can use the LIST command to list the object and geometric properties of an object, or several objects simultaneously.

Unlike the DDMODIFY command, LIST displays the information in the text window. The typical output of the LIST command is shown in figure 15.5.

Figure 15.5

The typical output of LIST for an arc.

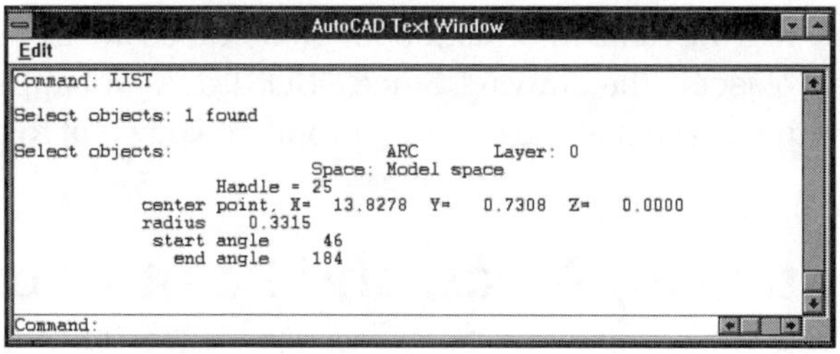

LIST and DDMODIFY display similar information; however, they differ on the following points:

- DDMODIFY uses a dialog box to show the information, whereas LIST uses the text window.
- You cannot use LIST to change selected objects, unlike DDMODIFY.
- DDMODIFY and LIST sometimes display different calculated values for the same object. For example, LIST displays the area and perimeter of a polyline, whereas DDMODIFY does not. DDMODIFY displays the length of an arc, but LIST does not.
- If LIST displays an area, it updates the value of the AREA system variable with the area of the selected object. DDMODIFY does not affect AREA.
- LIST enables you to select more than one object. You can use this characteristic to display the information of several objects on one text window, for easier comparison.
- LIST does not have to be initialized. If you have a slow machine, you might find that LIST responds significantly faster than does DDMODIFY.

TIP

Because LIST uses the text window, you can use the text window's scroll bars to view previous displays of the LIST command, which facilitates the comparison of multiple objects. Furthermore, you can use Windows' copy and paste functions to copy the information from the text window to another application.

There is also the DBLIST command which is a cousin of the LIST command. DBLIST lists the same information for an object as the LIST command but does so for every object in the drawing. Since DBLIST does not appear anywhere in the menus, you must type it at the `Command:` prompt if you want to use it.

Distances, Areas, and Point Coordinates

Measuring distances, areas and identifying points are tasks that you will find yourself doing quite often. The DIST, AREA, and ID commands are the inquiry commands that enable you to perform the aforementioned tasks and are the focus of this section.

The DIST Command

You use the DIST command to measure distances. It prompts you to select the two points you wish to measure the distance between. You may select any two points you wish but if you are picking points on objects, be sure to use object snaps to pick the points exactly, otherwise, the measurement will not be accurate. DIST not only displays the distance between the points but also the angle from the 1st point to the 2nd point, and even the coordinates of the points. Keep in mind that some distances are automatically measured and displayed for you by the LIST and DDMODIFY commands. For example, the length of a selected line is given by both LIST and DDMODIFY. The DIST command may be used transparently.

TIP

AutoCAD records the distance value returned by the DIST command in the DISTANCE system variable.

The AREA Command

Measuring areas is another common task. You can use the AREA command to do so.

Issuing the AREA command displays the following prompt:

```
<First point>/Object/Add/Subtract:
```

- **First point.** The default option enables you to pick points to define the area to be measured. After picking the first point, the displayed prompt changes to `Next point:`. Continue to pick the points necessary to define the area. When you are done picking points, press the Enter key and the area and perimeter are calculated.
- **Object.** To measure the area of a closed object such as a circle or closed polyline, specify this option and select the object. If you select an open polyline, AREA assumes that a closing segment connects the first and last points of the polyline and calculates the corresponding area. The calculated perimeter of an open polyline is its actual length.
- **Add.** The Add option enables you to measure the area and perimeter of an area and add the area to a running count of the net area. Once you specify the Add option, the prompt changes to:

```
<First point>/Object/Subtract:
```

You can measure an area by using either the First point or Object options. Alternatively, you may switch to subtract mode or end the AREA command by pressing the Enter key.

- **Subtract.** The subtract option enables you to measure the area and perimeter of an area and subtract the area from a running count of the net area. Once you specify the Subtract option, the prompt changes to:

  `<First point>/Object/Add:`

  You can measure an area by using either the First point or Object options. Alternatively, you may switch to add mode or end the AREA command by pressing the Enter key.

By using the Add and Subtract options, you can measure the net area of a section with cutouts.

In the following exercise, you measure several areas.

Measuring Areas

Continue using the drawing CHAP15.

`Command:` *Choose* Area (*Object Properties, Inquiry*)	Issues AREA
`<First point>/Object/Add/Subtract:` **A** ↵	Chooses the Add mode of AREA

AREA now adds the areas measured to the total area it keeps track of. When AREA is started, the total (net) area value is initially set to zero.

`<First point>/Object/Subtract:` **O** ↵	Signals AREA that you will be selecting objects
`(ADD mode) Select objects:` *Pick* ⑤ (see fig. 15.6)	

`Area = 27.7854, Perimeter = 21.1416`

`Total area = 27.7854`

Area measures the area and perimeter of the polyline and adds the area to the value of the running total area (27.7854) which initially was 0.

`(ADD mode) Select objects:` ↵	Ends the Add mode of AREA

`<First point>/Object/Subtract:` **S** ↵ — Chooses the Subtract mode of AREA; AREA now subtracts the areas measured from the total area it is keeping track of

`<First point>/Object/Add:` **O** ↵

`(SUBTRACT mode) Select objects:`
Pick ①

`Area = 0.0491, Circumference = 0.7854`

`Total area = 27.7363`

AREA displays the area and circumference of the circle and then subtracts the circle's area from the running total area. Continue to pick points at 2, 3 and 4 (refer to figure 15.6).

`(SUBTRACT mode) Select objects:` ↵ — Ends the Subtract mode of AREA; the last area is the area of the polyline minus the total areas of the circles

`<First point>/Object/Add:` ↵ — Ends the AREA command

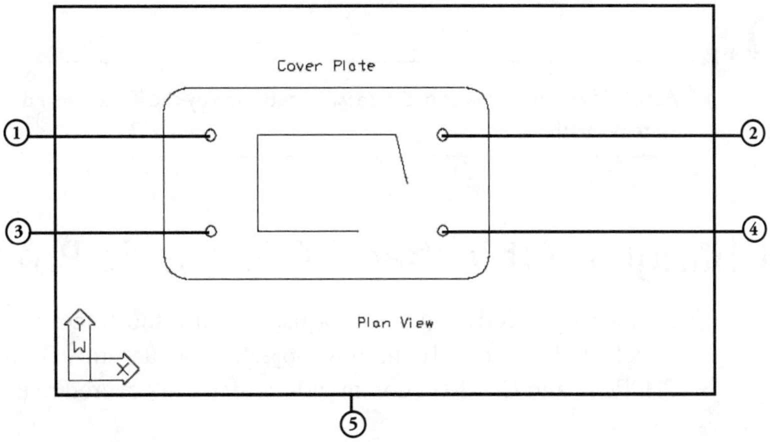

Figure 15.6

Measuring areas of objects.

TIP

AutoCAD records the last area measured in the system variable AREA. Because the variable name is identical to the command name AREA, you must use the SETVAR command to retrieve the value of the AREA system variable. The AREA system variable is a handy way to retrieve the results of the last AREA command.

Similarly, AutoCAD records the perimeter value calculated by the most recent AREA command, in the PERIMETER system variable.

The LIST command also calculates and displays the area and perimeter of circles and polylines. So, you could use BOUNDARY to outline the overall area with a polyline, then simply list the polyline for its area and perimeter. If you don't want to bother with the vertex data, just use AREA with the generated polyline. If islands are in the overall area, BOUNDARY can create polylines to delineate the islands, and you still can use AREA (using its Add and Subtract options) to get a net area.

The ID command

Identifying the coordinates of a point is another type of inquiry you need to do. You can use the ID command to do so.

If you are identifying a point on an object, it is important to pick the exact point, so use the appropriate object snap mode. Prior to Release 13, ID was the best way to reset the last point recorded by AutoCAD, so that you could use relative coordinates from the identified point. The FROM object snap mode replaces ID as the preferred means to reset the base point for relative coordinates. FROM object snap enables you to pick a base point from which you specify relative coordinates to the point you actually want to pick.

TIP

AutoCAD records the coordinate value returned by the ID command, in the LASTPOINT system variable.

Changing Object and Geometric Properties

At times, you need to change, not just examine, the object and geometric properties of selected objects. To modify objects, you use the DDMODIFY, DDCHPROP, CHPROP, and CHANGE commands, which are covered in this section.

The DDMODIFY Command

DDMODIFY not only displays information about a selected object, but it can also be used to change various object and geometric properties of the object. The appearance of the DDMODIFY dialog box is adjusted to suit the selected object. Refer to figures 15.3 and 15.4 for examples of DDMODIFY dialog boxes for a line and a circle. As a general rule, any piece of information that appears next to a button or is in an edit field, may be changed.

For all types of objects, you can use DDMODIFY to change:

- Layer
- Assigned color
- Assigned linetype
- Linetype scale
- Thickness

The geometric properties of the object (a circle's center point and radius) are also displayed. For some objects, additional geometric information is also calculated and displayed; for example, a circle's circumference and area. The geometric properties that define the object appear in text edit boxes, enabling you to modify their values. Values that are calculated may not be modified, but are maintained and updated automatically by DDMODIFY. For example, if you change a circle's radius, the area and circumference values in the dialog box are updated.

DDMODIFY allows you to select only a single object at a time. If you need to modify several objects at a time, use DDCHPROP, CHPROP, or CHANGE, all of which are covered in the next section.

TIP

DDMODIFY handles text, mtext, and dimension objects especially well. For example, using DDMODIFY, you can alter a text object's oblique angle and width factor, and you can determine whether the text is generated upside down or backward. No other editing command enables you to change all these aspects of a text or mtext object.

In the following exercise, you use DDMODIFY to edit selected objects.

MODIFYING OBJECTS

Continue using the drawing CHAP15, or create a new drawing named CHAP15 using the CPLATE drawing as a prototype.

`Command:` *Choose* Edit, Properties	Prompts for selection
`Select objects:` *Pick* ① *(see fig. 15.7) and press Enter*	Selects the circle, issues DDMODIFY, and opens the Modify Circle dialog box
Click in the Radius *edit box and change the radius to* 0.25, *then choose* **OK**	Redraws circle with 0.25 radius

`Command:` Select the circle at ②, *then choose* Edit, Properties — Preselects object and issues DDMODIFY

In the Radius edit box, change the radius to 0.25, then choose OK

`Command:` *Choose Properties (Object Properties)*

Repeat DDMODIFY, choosing Edit, Properties or the Properties (Object Properties) tool and change each of the circles at ③ and ④ to a 0.25 radius. Do not select both circles at once, or the DDCHPROP command (Change Properties dialog box) will open rather than DDMODIFY.

`Command:` **DDMODIFY** ↵ — Starts DDMODIFY

Notice that the Properties menu item and tool, from which you can issue DDMODIFY or DDCHPROP, prompts for multiple object selection, but when you enter DDMODIFY directly, it prompts for a single object.

`Select object to modify:` *Select the text string* Cover Plate

In the Obliquing box, change the angle to 10. In the Height box, change the text height to 0.4. From the Style drop-down list, select HEADING. Choose OK after you make the changes.

Your drawing should look like figure 15.8.

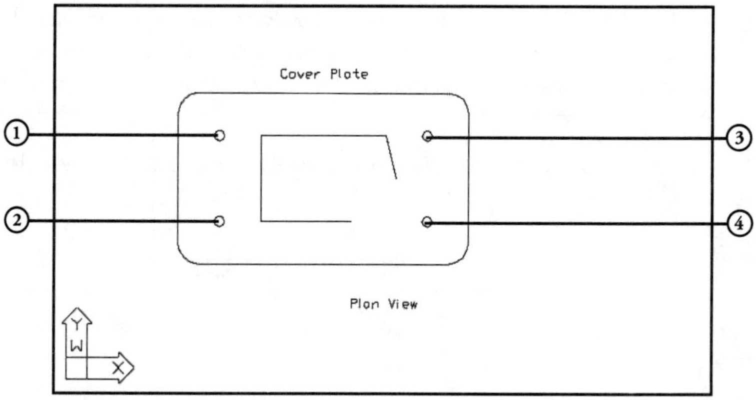

Figure 15.7

Changing the circles with DDMODIFY.

DDMODIFY gives you the most control over an object's properties, but unfortunately it works on only one object at a time.

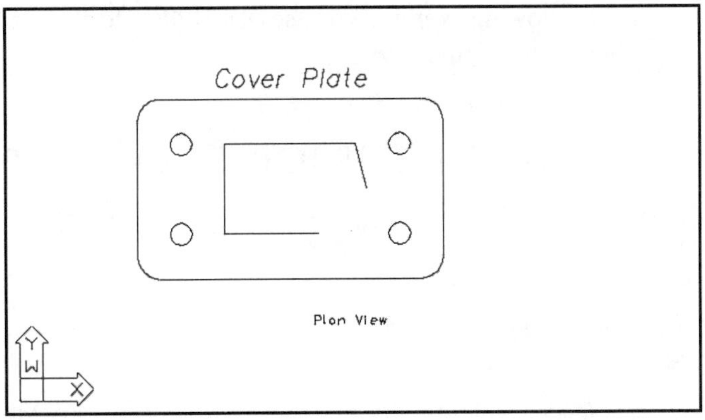

Figure 15.8

The modified cover plate.

The DDCHPROP Command

The DDCHPROP command does not enable you to change as many aspects of an object as does DDMODIFY, but it does allow you to edit multiple objects at one time.

Issuing the DDCHROP command opens the Change Properties dialog box, as shown in figure 15.9.

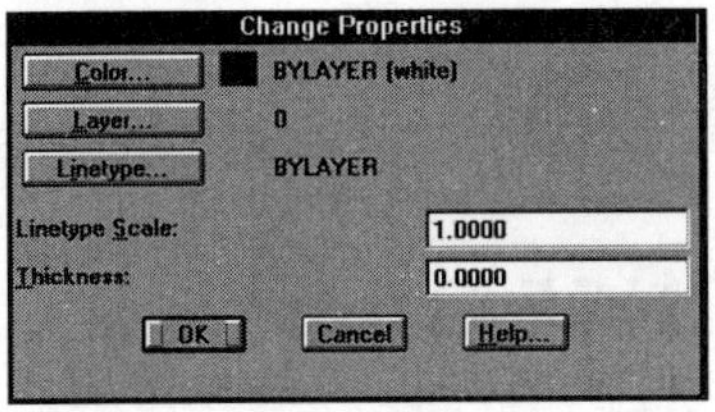

Figure 15.9

The Change Properties dialog box.

Using DDCHPROP, you can change any of the following object properties:

- Layer
- Color assignment
- Linetype assignment
- Linetype scale
- Thickness

DDCHROP cannot be used to change geometric properties. If a particular property is not identical for all the selected objects, the dialog box will display the word "varies" for the property value.

In the following exercise, you use DDCHPROP to change the layer property of several objects simultaneously.

Using DDCHPROP To Change Properties

Continue using the drawing CHAP15.

`Command:` *Choose* Edit, Properties	Prompts for selection
`Select objects:` *Select the four circles and press Enter*	Opens Change Properties dialog box with the circles selected

Because you selected more than one object, the same menu item that you earlier used to start DDMODIFY now starts DDCHPROP. Notice that the dialog box shows color BYLAYER (white) and layer 0.

Choose Layer	Opens the Select Layer dialog box
Select layer SCREW_HOLES, *then choose* OK	Sets layer and returns to the Change Properties dialog box

Notice that the color shows BYLAYER (red) and the layer shows SCREW_HOLES.

Choose OK	Closes dialog box and redraws circles on layer SCREW_HOLES in red

You have just changed the four circles from layer 0 to layer SCREW_HOLES.

The CHANGE Command

The CHANGE command is the grandfather of all the commands covered in this section. CHPROP, DDCHPROP, and DDMODIFY evolved from CHANGE. Despite its age, CHANGE still has its uses.

You can use CHANGE to change an object's geometry, including its elevation (Z coordinate), by specifying a *change point*. A change point is a point you pick that is used to change the geometry of the selected objects. The CHANGE command has the following two options:

- **Properties.** If you specify the Properties option, you are presented with six properties that you can modify: Color, Elev, Layer, Ltype, ltScale, and Thickness.

- **Change point.** The default option is to specify a point to use to change the selected objects. You are prompted as follows:

  ```
  Properties/<Change point>:
  ```

  You can pick the change point, or press Enter (or the spacebar) to accept the default option.

You pick the change point, and it is used to modify the object itself. The effect of the change point depends on the type of object:

- **Attribute Definition.** The attribute definition moves to the change point. If you press Enter instead of picking a change point, you are prompted for the new text insertion point. In either case, you also are prompted for the attribute definition's style, height, rotation angle, tag, prompt, and default value.
- **Block.** The inserted block moves to the change point. If you press Enter instead of picking a change point, you are prompted for a new insertion point. In either case, you also are prompted for a new rotation angle.
- **Circle.** The circle's radius adjusts so that the circle passes through the change point. If you press Enter instead of picking a change point, you are prompted for a new radius for the circle. Figure 15.10 illustrates the effect of picking a change point from a circle.

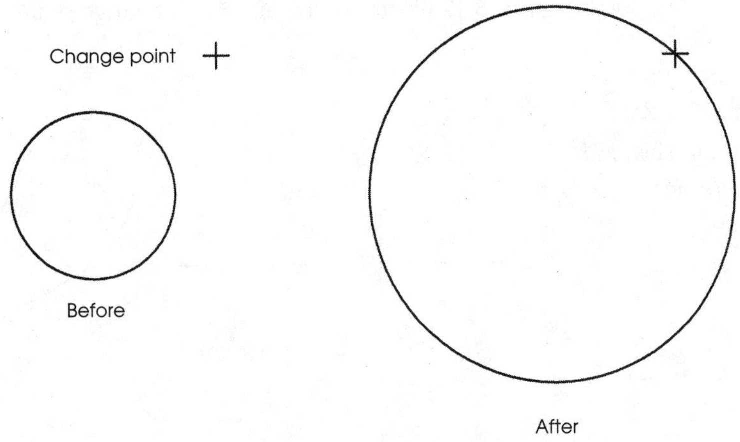

Figure 15.10

A change point with a circle.

- **Line.** The nearest endpoint of the line moves to the change point. If you press Enter, you are not prompted again for a change point. Figure 15.11 illustrates the effect of a change point for a line.

Figure 15.11

A change point with a line.

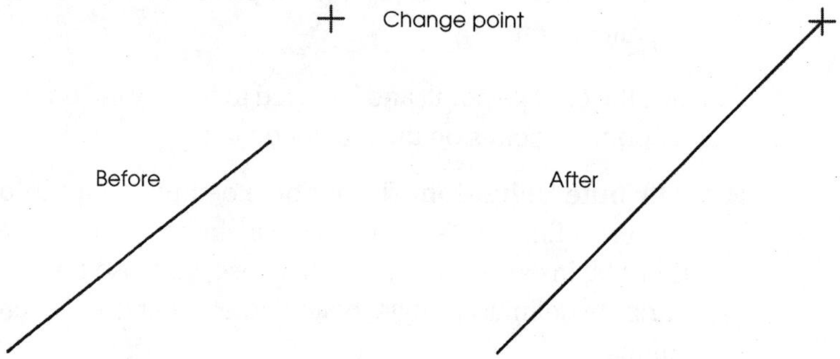

- **Text.** The text moves to the change point. If you press Enter instead of picking a change point, you are prompted for a new text insertion point. In either case, you are prompted for the text's style, height, rotation angle, and value.

If you select multiple objects and pick a change point, CHANGE cycles through the selection set one object at a time, enabling you to pick a different change point for each object. One exception exists to this rule: if multiple lines are selected, all the lines are modified so that the nearest endpoint of each line moves to the change point. Figure 15.12 illustrates the effect of a change point for multiple lines.

Figure 15.12

A change point with multiple lines.

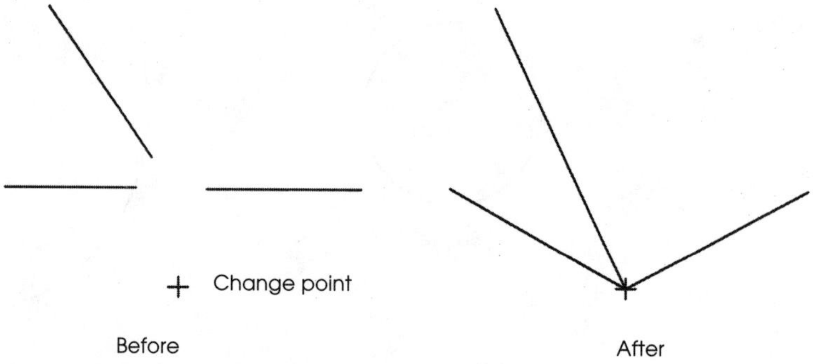

In the following exercise, you use CHANGE to alter the location and appearance of text and line objects.

Changing Some Objects

Continue using the CHAP15 drawing.

`Command:` **CHANGE** ↵	Starts the CHANGE command
`Select objects:` *Select the text* Plan View *and press Enter*	
`Properties/<Change point>:` **6.5,2** ↵	Moves the insertion point of the text object to the point 6.5,2
`Text style:` **STANDARD**	
`New style or RETURN for no change:` **HEADING** ↵	Changes the text style to HEADING
`New height <0.2000>:` **0.3** ↵	Changes the text size to 0.3 units
`New rotation angle <0>:` ↵	Accepts the current setting
`New text <Plan View>:` **Plan View (nts)** ↵	Changes the text string

Next, you modify the two lines shown in figure 15.13 so that they meet at the point 8,4.

`Command:` ↵	Repeats the last command
`CHANGE` `Select objects:` *Select the lines* ① *and* ② *and press Enter (see fig. 15.13)*	Selects the lines
`Properties/<Change point>:` **8,4** ↵	Stretches the lines to the change point 8,4

Because only lines were selected, the lines were simultaneously changed so that the endpoint of each line nearest to the change point was moved to the change point. Your drawing should now look like figure 15.14.

Figure 15.13

Modifying the text with CHANGE.

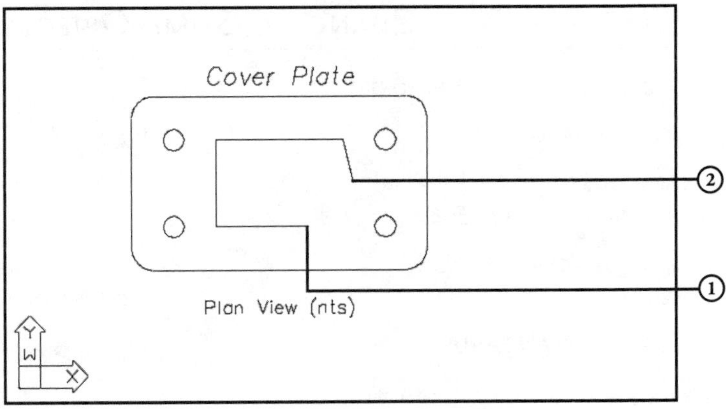

Figure 15.14

Changed text and points.

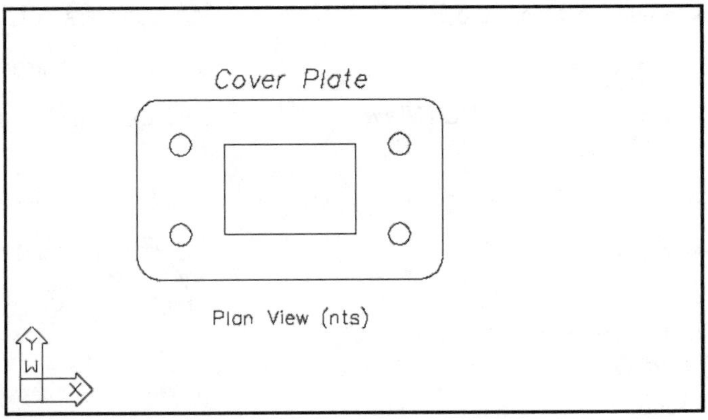

Using the Calculator

CAL is a powerful built-in calculator that you can use to perform numeric calculations, calculations involving point coordinates, and even calculations involving distances and angles. It is tightly integrated into the drawing editor, which gives you capabilities you do not have with an ordinary desktop calculator.

You can execute CAL transparently. If you are prompted for the radius while using the CIRCLE command, for example, you can call CAL to help you calculate the radius without interrupting the CIRCLE command.

CAL is such a powerful tool with so many capabilities that it is best to approach it in stages, as is done in the following sections. First, you learn how to use CAL as an ordinary desktop calculator. Then you learn how to use it to calculate points, distances, and angles of objects in your drawing.

CAL as a Desktop Calculator

You can use CAL to evaluate any mathematical expression that involves addition, subtraction, multiplication, division, or any of a range of scientific functions. In the following exercise, you perform several such calculations.

If you execute CAL at the command prompt, the result of your expression echoes to the screen. If you execute CAL transparently from within an AutoCAD command, the calculated value is interpreted as an input value by the AutoCAD command.

CAL supports most of standard mathematical functions found on a scientific/ engineering calculator, including the following:

sin(angle)	Returns the sine of the angle
cos(angle)	Returns the cosine of the angle
tang(angle)	Returns the tangent of the angle
asin(real)	Returns the arc sine of the number
acos(real)	Returns the arc cosine of the number
atan(real)	Returns the arc tangent of the number
ln(real)	Returns the natural log of the number
log(real)	Returns the base 10 log of the number
exp(real)	Returns the natural exponent of the number
exp10(real)	Returns the base 10 exponent of the number
sqr(real)	Returns the square of the number
sqrt(real)	Returns the square root of the number
abs(real)	Returns the absolute value of the number
round(real)	Returns the number rounded to the nearest integer
trunc(real)	Returns the integer portion of the number
r2d(angle)	Converts an angular value from radians to degrees
d2r(angle)	Converts an angular value from degrees to radians
pi	The constant pi

Unlike AutoLISP functions, CAL expects you to enter angles in decimal degrees and returns angular values in decimal degrees. You enter complicated expressions just as you would write them, using parentheses as required. CAL evaluates expressions using AOS (Algebraic Operating System) rules.

Suppose you need to calculate the cost of moving dirt on your construction site. The calculation involves taking the volume in cubic feet, which you convert to cubic yards (27 cubic feet per cubic yard) and then multiply by a cost per cubic yard of $1.27. You then multiply the calculated dollar amount by a factor of 1.5 to get the amount you bill the client. To calculate the billable cost of moving 15,000 cubic feet, and round it to the nearest dollar, you would enter the following expression:

```
round((15000/27)*1.27*1.5)
```

Note that you do not enter commas as part of a number (such as 15,000). Integer values that you enter must be in the range of -32768 and 32767.

Variables

Just like a desktop calculator, you can store the results of CAL in memory locations (variables) and then recall those values as the need arises. You can name the memory locations anything by using a combination of digits, letters, and other characters, except ( ) . ' " ; and spaces.

TIP

Keep variable names short but meaningful. The variable name SUM, for example, communicates its purpose better than the name S.

You create the named memory location and store a value in it, when you enter the expression at the CAL prompt by typing the variable name, followed by an equal sign and then the expression to be evaluated. For example, to store the results of dividing 5 by 32 in the variable FRACTION, at the CAL command prompt, you would enter:

```
FRACTION=9/32
```

To use the value stored in a variable in a CAL expression, simply reference the variable name in the expression. For example, if you wanted to take the value of FRACTION and divide it by 2, at the CAL command prompt, you would enter:

```
FRACTION/2
```

If you want to reference the value stored in a variable at the AutoCAD command prompt or at the prompt of an AutoCAD command, you simply type the variable name with an exclamation mark prefix. For example, if you want to use the value stored in FRACTION as the radius of a new circle, then at the radius prompt of the CIRCLE command, you would enter:

```
Diameter/<Radius>: !FRACTION ↵
```

NOTE

> If you are familiar with AutoLISP, then you may have guessed by now that when you store a value in a variable, you are actually creating a global variable.

You can even use the value stored in a variable to calculate a new value to replace the current value in the same variable. For example, if you want to take the value stored in FRACTION, divide the value by two and store the result back in FRACTION, at the CAL command prompt, you would enter:

```
FRACTION=FRACTION/2
```

Any references to a variable occurring on the right side of the equal sign reference the current value stored in the variable. Writing expressions this way is standard practice for programmers and allows the programmer to recycle variables and to use a variable as a running counter.

Variables only exist for the duration of the drawing session they are created in. As soon as you open another drawing, the variable and the value stored in it cease to exist.

CAL as a Point Calculator

You also can use CAL to evaluate expressions that involve point coordinates. You can specify a point in any of the standard AutoCAD formats, but the most commonly used ones are Cartesian and polar coordinates.

Cartesian	[X,Y,Z]
Polar	[dist<angle]
Relative	Use @ prefix, for example, [@dist<angle]

In CAL, you must enclose the coordinates in brackets [].

CAL can perform standard +—/* operations with points in the following manner:

multiplication	number * point or point*point
division	point/number or point/point
addition	point + point
subtraction	point — point

Expressions that involve point coordinates are also referred to as *vector expressions*. Suppose you want to find the coordinates of the point midway between the points 2,3 and 3,4. You can calculate the midpoint by averaging the X and Y values of the two points, as follows:

```
Command: CAL
>> Expression: ([2,3]+[3,4])/2
 (2.5 3.5 0.0)
```

Performing operations with specific point coordinates in isolation probably does not excite you. But what if you could evaluate expressions using points that you select using any of the standard methods allowed by AutoCAD, like picking, typing coordinates, and object snap? The function CUR instructs CAL to let the user pick a point. The preceding example can be generalized as the following:

```
Command: CAL
>> Expression: (cur+cur)/2
```

Furthermore, you can incorporate object snap into your expressions by entering one of the following CAL functions rather than CUR:

CAL Function	*Equivalent Object Snap Mode*
end	endpoint
ins	insert
int	intersection
mid	midpoint
cen	center
nea	nearest
nod	node
qua	quadrant
per	perpendicular
tan	tangent

To take the preceding example a little further, you can calculate the point midway between an endpoint of a line and the center of a circle (see fig. 15.15). The command sequence might go as follows:

```
Command: CAL
>> Expression: (end+cen)/2
```

Figure 15.15

Finding a point midway between two other points.

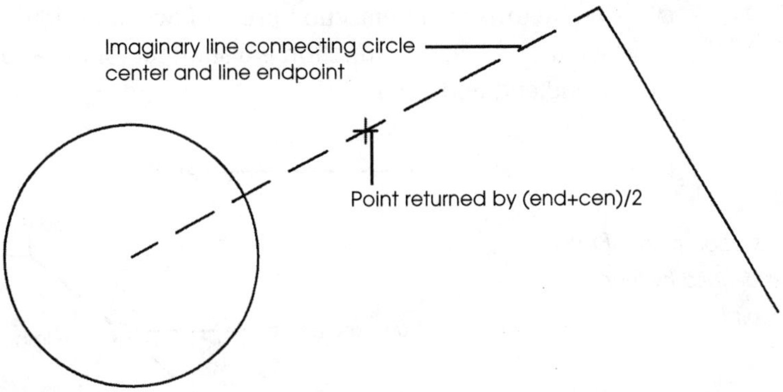

CAL also provides a set of functions to calculate points for certain specific scenarios:

- **ill(P1,P2,P3,P4).** Returns the intersection point of lines (P1,P2) and (P3,P4) (see fig. 15.16).

Figure 15.16

Intersection point of lines (P1, P2) and (P3, P4).

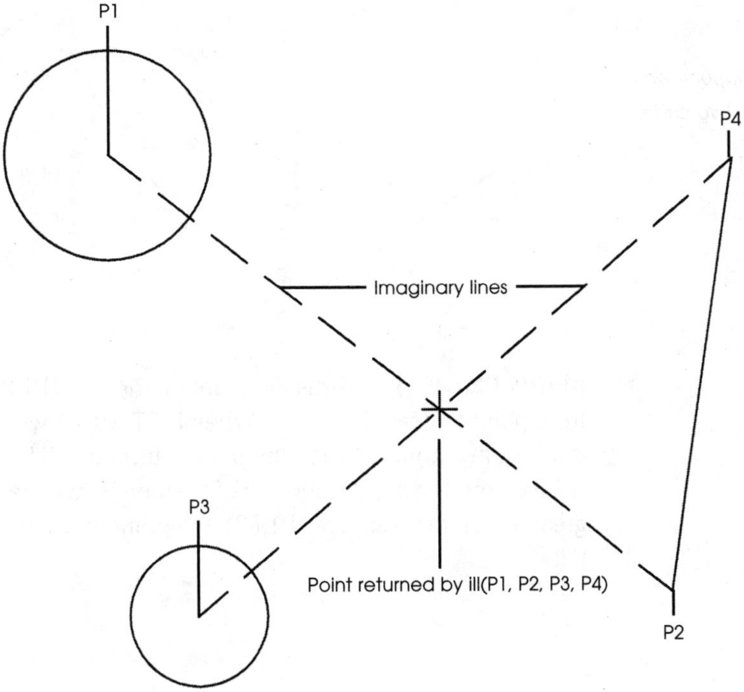

- **ille.** Returns the intersection point of two lines defined by four endpoints (see fig. 15.17). This function is a shortcut for the expression ill(end,end,end,end).

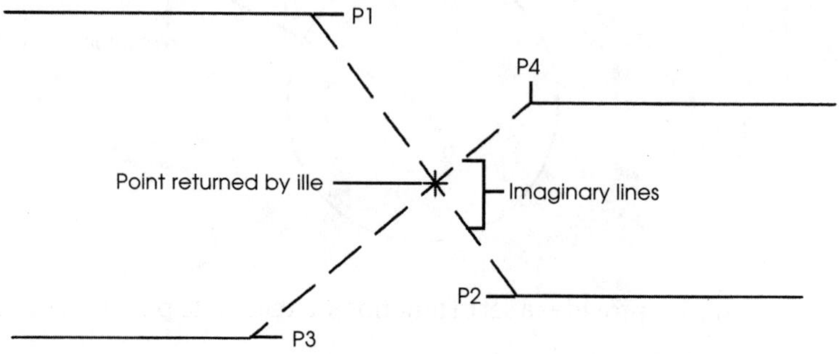

Figure 15.17

Intersection point of two lines defined by four endpoints.

- **mee.** Returns the midpoint between two endpoints (see fig. 15.18).

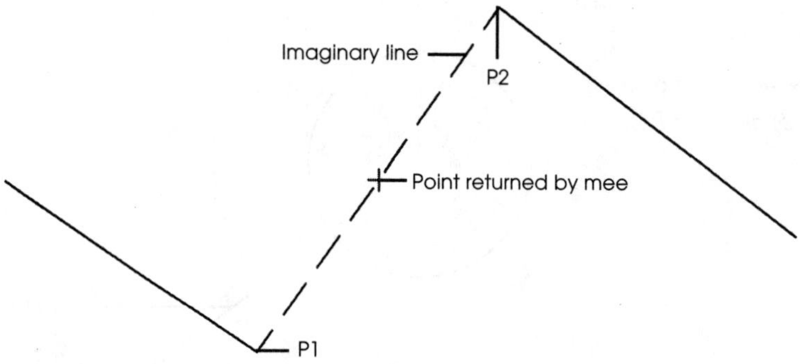

Figure 15.18

Midpoint on line defined by two endpoints.

- **pld(P1,P2,DIST).** Returns the point on the line (P1,P2) which is *dist* units from point P1 (see fig. 15.19). When DIST = 0, P1 will be returned. When DIST is a negative number, then the point returned will be positioned before P1. If DIST is equal to the distance (P1,P2), then P2 will be returned. If DIST is greater than the distance (P1,P2), the point returned will be positioned after P2.

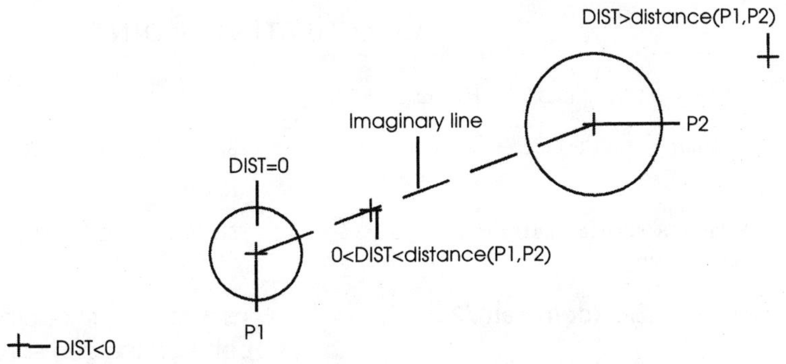

Figure 15.19

Illustration of pld(CEN,CEN,DIST).

- **plt(P1,P2,T).** Returns the point on the line(P1,P2) a T of the distance from P1, where T is the ratio of the distance from P1 to the desired point, to the distance from P1 to P2 (see fig. 15.20). When T = 0, P1 will be returned. When T = 1, then P2 will be returned. If T is negative, then the point returned will be positioned before P1. If T is greater than 1, the point returned will be positioned after P2.

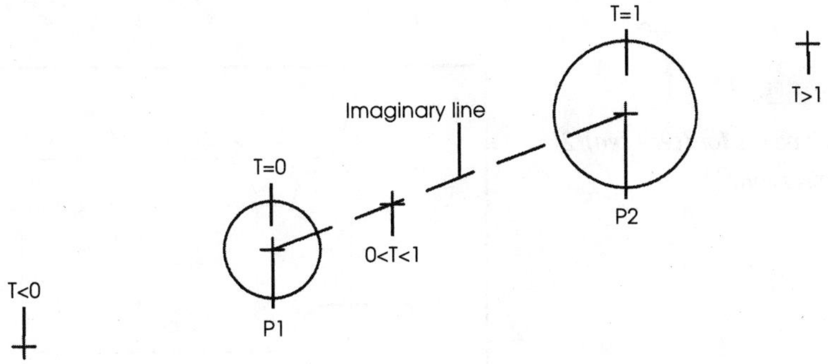

Figure 15.20

Illustration of plt (CEN, CEN, T).

TIP

> By invoking CAL from within AutoCAD commands, you can calculate point coordinates anytime the need arises, which enables you to use CAL not only as an inquiry tool, but as a powerful construction tool.

In the following exercise, you use CAL to draw a new circle.

Calculating Points

Continue using the CHAP15 drawing.

`Command:` *Choose Circle Center, Radius (Draw, Circle)*	Issues the CIRCLE command
`3P/2P/TTR/<Center point>:` *Choose* Tools, Calculator	Issues CAL transparently
`>>Expression:` **(cen+cen)/2** ↵	Instructs CAL to return the point midway between the centers of two circles that you select next
`>>Select entity for CEN snap:` Pick 1(see fig. 15.21)	
`<ET>>>Select entity for CEN snap:`	Sets center of circle Pick 2
`Diameter/<Radius>:` **0.5** ↵	Finishes the CIRCLE command by specifying a radius of 0.5 units

Your drawing should look like figure 15.22.

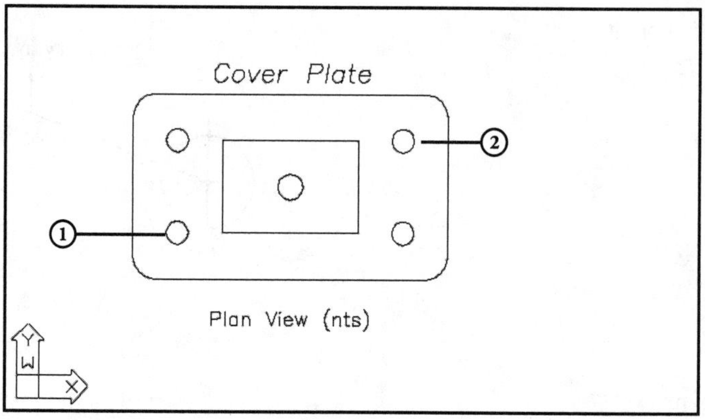

Figure 15.21

Pick points for (cen+cen)/2 expression.

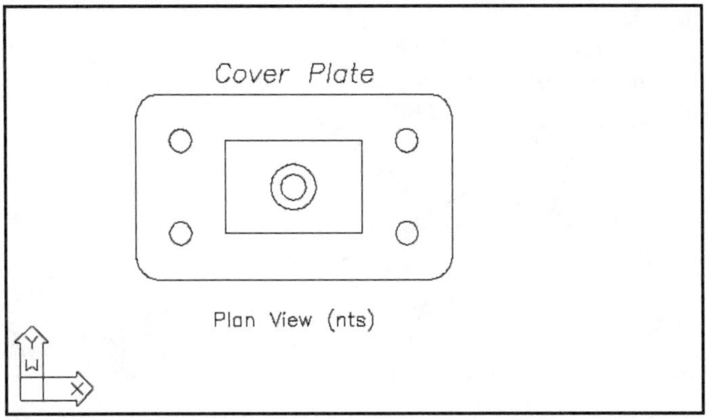

Figure 15.22

The circle is drawn at the calculated midpoint.

As you see in the exercise, using CAL can eliminate the need to draw intermediate construction lines.

CAL as a Distance Calculator

CAL also has the following functions for calculating distances:

- **dist(P1,P2).** Measures the distance between P1 and P2 (see fig. 15.23).

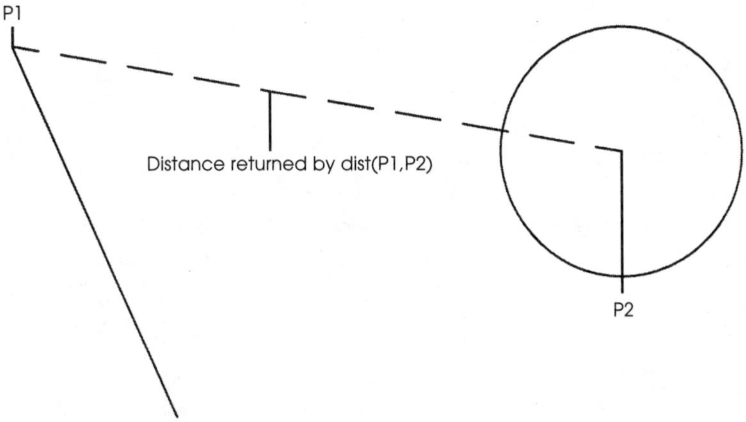

Figure 15.23

Illustration of dist(END+CEN).

- **dee.** Measures the distance between two endpoints; short for dist(end,end) (see fig. 15.24).

Figure 15.24

Illustration of dee with the two endpoints P1 and P2.

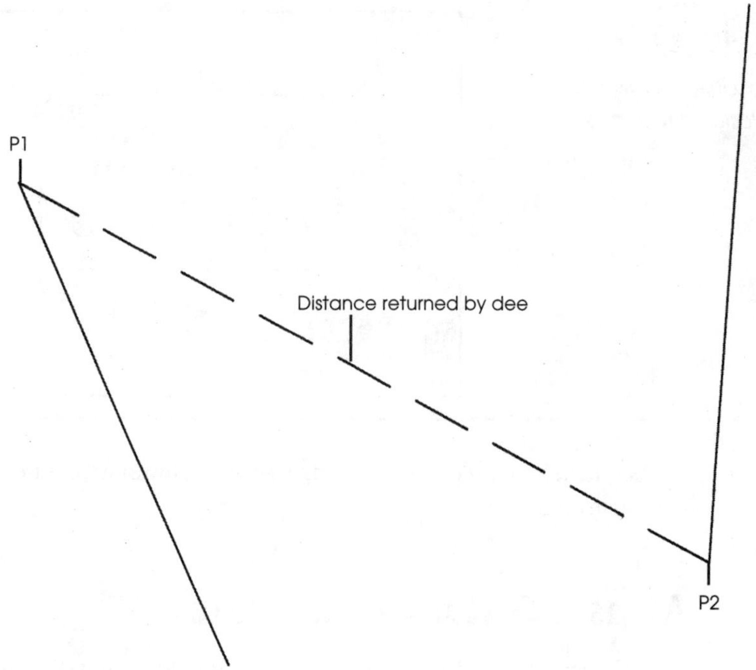

- **dpl(P,P1,P2).** Measures the distance between the point P and the line (P1,P2) (see fig. 15.25).

Figure 15.25

Illustration of dpl(CUR,END,CEN).

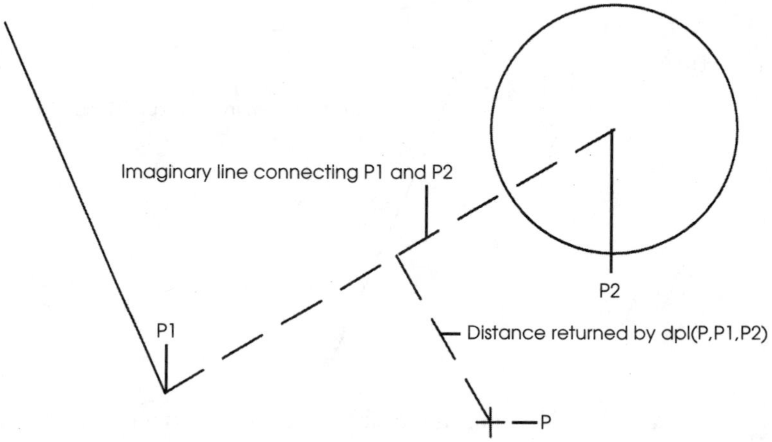

- **rad.** Measures the radius of the selected object.

You can, of course, use DIST to measure distances, but with the preceding function, you can integrate distance measurements into your CAL expressions.

Angle Measurements with CAL

Although you can use DIST to measure distances and AREA to measure areas, you do not have an equivalent command for measuring angles CAL has two functions that enable you to make angular measurements:

- **ang(P1,P2).** Measures the angle between the X axis and the line(P1,P2) (see fig. 15.26).

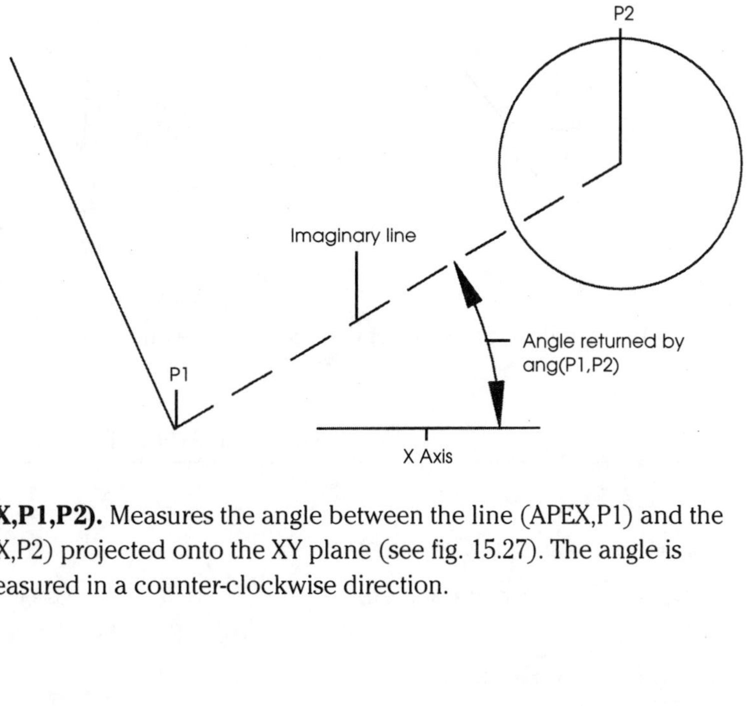

Figure 15.26

Measuring the angle of the line (P1,P2) with ang(END,CEN).

- **ang(APEX,P1,P2).** Measures the angle between the line (APEX,P1) and the line (APEX,P2) projected onto the XY plane (see fig. 15.27). The angle is always measured in a counter-clockwise direction.

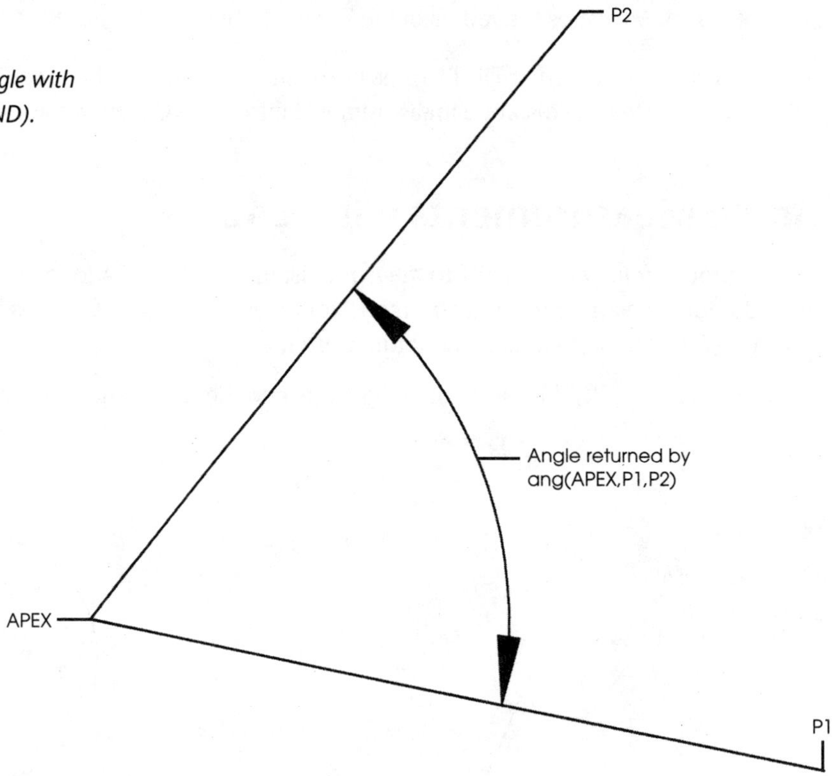

Figure 15.27

Measuring the angle with ang(APEX,END,END).

In the following exercise, you measure the angle between two lines.

Measuring Angles

Continue using the CHAP15 drawing.

`Command:` *Choose* Tools, Calculator

`>> Expression:` **ang(cen,cen,cen)** ↵	Instructs CAL to use the ang function with three center points you supply
`>> Select entity for CEN snap:` *Pick* ① *(see fig. 15.28)*	Selects the apex for the measurement
`>> Select entity for CEN snap:` *Pick* ②	Selects the end of the line from which the measurement begins
`>> Select entity for CEN snap:` *Pick* ③	Selects the end of the line at which the measurement ends

`21.8014`

`Command:` *Choose* Tools, Calculator	
`>> Expression:` **ang(cen,cen,cen)** ↵	Instructs CAL to use the ang function with three center points you supply
`<ET>>> Select entity for CEN snap:` *Pick* ①	Selects the apex for the measurement
`>> Select entity for CEN snap:` *Pick* ③	Selects the end of the line from which the measurement begins
`>> Select entity for CEN snap:` *Pick* ②	Select the end of the line at which the measurement ends
`338.199`	

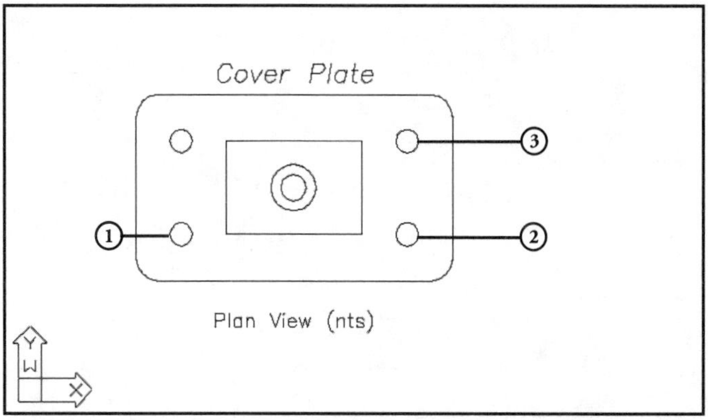

Figure 15.28

Measuring angles with ang(CEN,CEN,CEN).

The angle measured the second time differed from the first angle because the angle is measured counterclockwise from the line (APEX, P1) to the line (APEX, P2). The order in which the points are selected is very important.

Other Uses for CAL

CAL has many other functions that enable you to calculate vectors, unit vectors, normal vectors, to filter point coordinates, and to convert points between the UCS and the WCS. To learn more about CAL, you can find a complete listing of CAL functions in the *AutoCAD Command Reference*, under CAL.

This chapter has explored the range of commands available to you for verifying and/or improving the accuracy of your drawings, retrieving valuable information from them, and even combining these functions to construct new geometry based on relationships between existing objects. Using commands such as DDMODIFY and ID, you can find the object and geometric properties of objects and, if necessary, modify the objects with commands such as DDMODIFY and DDCHPROP. You can use commands such as DIST and CAL to determine angular and spatial relationships between objects and points. You can apply the CAL command to directly incorporate information about such relationships into other editing and drawing commands.

The wealth of information associated with each object in an AutoCAD drawing is what elevates working in AutoCAD beyond anything possible in the traditional drafting realm. When you recognize your CAD drawings as graphical databases of information, and learn to apply the inquiry commands to access and manipulate that information, you extend your design skills to a new level.

chapter

16

CONSTRUCTIVE EDITING

Previous chapters introduced the concepts of drawing and editing. Many of AutoCAD's editing commands enable you to modify existing objects. This chapter merges the topics of drawing and editing to explain commands that you can use to edit existing geometry to create new geometry, a process known as constructive editing. This chapter covers the following constructive editing topics:

- *Creating offset geometry using the OFFSET command*
- *Applying fillets and chamfers with the FILLET and CHAMFER commands*
- *Measuring and dividing objects with the MEASURE and DIVIDE commands*
- *Creating rectangular and polar arrays with the ARRAY command*
- *Breaking objects with the BREAK command*
- *Mirroring objects with the MIRROR command*

Chapter 14, "The Ins and Outs of Editing," introduced the concept of editing, which in AutoCAD generally means modifying existing objects in some way. Typical editing includes erasing, copying, and moving objects. Many of AutoCAD's editing commands modify existing objects without changing the appearance of the original objects. When you copy or move a selection set, for example, the objects in their new location appear identical to the original objects.

Many of AutoCAD's editing commands, however, are *constructive editing commands*, the tools that enable you to refine a sketchy design into a finished drawing. Like other editing commands, constructive editing commands modify existing objects, but they also create new objects, which enables you to construct a drawing quickly.

A good example of this type of command is the ARRAY command, which enables you to copy an existing object in a rectangular or circular (polar) array. Figure 16.1 shows a drawing before and after an array.

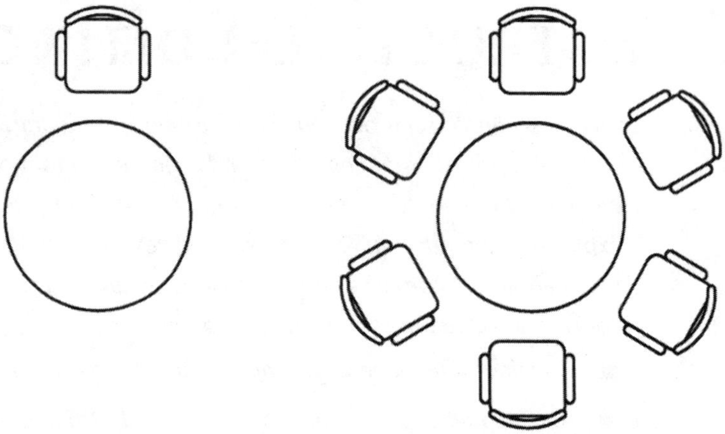

Figure 16.1

A drawing before and after an array.

By enabling you to use existing geometry, AutoCAD's constructive editing commands significantly speed up the drawing process. With the ARRAY command, for example, you can quickly create numerous copies of an object rather than individually draw or copy and rotate each new object.

AutoCAD's constructive editing commands enable you to modify existing objects quickly to add new features to the drawing. These commands make it possible for you to turn roughed-in construction objects into finished drawing geometry, modify existing parts and symbols to create new ones, and otherwise complete a drawing in as little time as possible. As you become proficient using AutoCAD, you will find that you use constructive editing commands even more than the primary drawing commands to complete a drawing. For this reason, applying constructive editing is one of the most important skills you can learn.

Applying Fillets and Chamfers

A *fillet* is an arc that is applied to the intersection of two objects—two lines, a line and an arc, two polyline segments, and so on. A *chamfer* is a line segment that is applied to the intersection of two objects or two polyline segments. Figure 16.2 shows two lines before and after a chamfer.

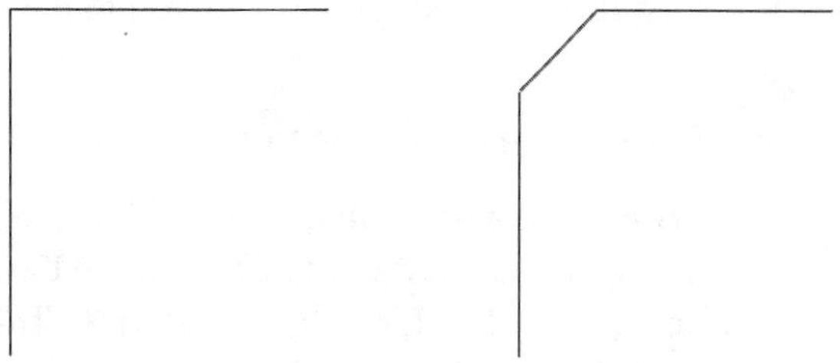

Figure 16.2

Two lines before and after a chamfer.

AutoCAD simplifies the process of applying fillets and chamfers by completely automating the process. Rather than draw the fillet or chamfer manually, you simply specify a fillet radius or chamfer distances or angle and select the objects to which you want to apply the fillet or chamfer. AutoCAD modifies the objects automatically.

Understanding the FILLET Command

The FILLET command enables you to apply a fillet to various types of objects, which include the following:

- Lines
- Polyline vertices or entire polylines
- Arcs
- Circles

The most common use for the FILLET command is to apply an arc to the intersection of two objects, but other uses for the FILLET command also exist. Because the two objects to which you're applying the fillet do not have to meet at an intersection, for example, you can use the FILLET command to join two objects. You also can specify a radius of zero for the fillet, which enables you to "un-fillet" two objects and extend them to an intersection. In all cases, applying a fillet is as simple as specifying a radius and then picking two objects.

FILLET Command Options

The FILLET command provides three options that enable you to control the way in which the fillet is applied:

- **Polyline.** This option enables you to fillet all vertices of a polyline in a single operation.
- **Radius.** Use this option to specify the radius of the fillet arc.
- **Trim.** This option can be set to Trim (the default) or No Trim. If set to Trim, this option causes AutoCAD to trim to the arc tangent points the objects being filleted. If this option is set to No Trim, AutoCAD applies the fillet arc but does not trim the objects in any way.

NOTE

If you select two parallel lines, they will be filleted with a 180-degree arc, regardless of the fillet radius setting.

Applying Fillets

You used the FILLET command in the first exercise in this chapter to apply a fillet to the intersection of two construction lines. You also can apply a fillet to two objects that do not intersect. If the Trim option is set to Trim, AutoCAD automatically trims or extends the objects as necessary to move their endpoints to the tangent points of the fillet arc.

Using the Trim Option

Although you probably will most often want the objects to which you're applying a fillet to be trimmed to the tangent points of the fillet arc, you occasionally might want the objects to remain as they are. For example, you might want to draw a tangent arc at the intersection of two lines, but don't want the lines to be trimmed. With the FILLET command's Trim option, you can control whether AutoCAD trims the objects.

The Trim option can be set either to Trim or to No Trim. If this option is set to Trim, AutoCAD trims the objects when it applies the fillet arc. If you set the Trim option to No Trim, AutoCAD does not trim the object, but instead leaves them as they are.

Tip

The points at which you select the objects to be filleted determines the location of the fillet and which part of the object it trimmed. The portion of the object on the same side of the intersection as the selection point is retained and the rest of the object is trimmed. Figure 16.3 illustrates the importance of the selection point location.

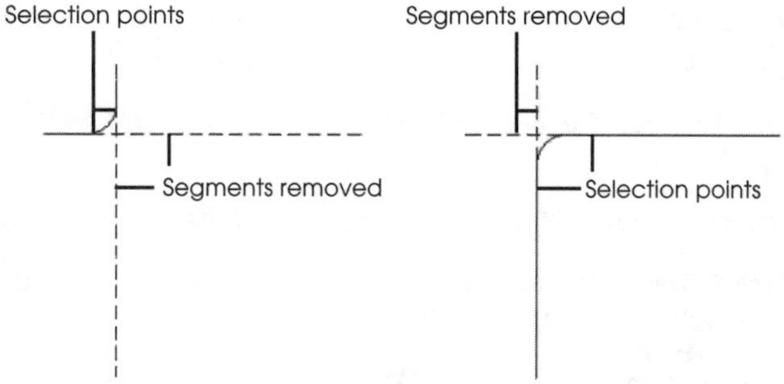

Figure 16.3

The selection point affects how objects are trimmed.

Experiment with the Trim option in the following exercise. Add a fillet to the upper right corner of the scraper blade with the Trim option set to No Trim. Figure 16.4 shows the selection points for the exercise.

Figure 16.4

A scraper blade before applying fillets.

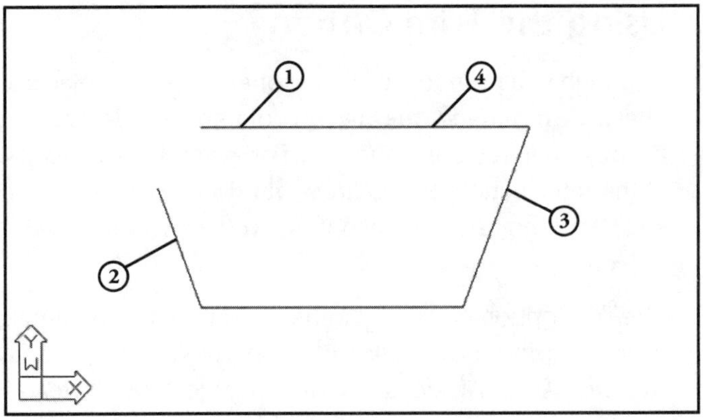

USING THE TRIM OPTION

Begin a new drawing named CHAP16A using FEATURE as a prototype.

`Command:` *Choose Fillet (Modify, Feature)*	Issues the FILLET command
`_fillet` `(TRIM mode) Current fillet radius = 0.5000`	Notice that the prompt indicates TRIM mode and the default radius
`Polyline/Radius/Trim/<Select first object>:` **T** ↵	Specifies the Trim option
`Trim/No trim <Trim>:` **N** ↵	Sets the Trim option to No Trim
`Polyline/Radius/Trim/<Select first object>:` *Pick line ① (see fig. 16.4)*	Specifies first line to fillet
`Select second object:` *Pick line ②*	Specifies second line and creates fillet
`Command:` ↵	Repeats the FILLET command
`FILLET` `(NOTRIM mode) Current fillet radius = 0.5000`	Notice that the prompt indicates NOTRIM mode
`Polyline/Radius/Trim/<Select first object>:` *Pick line ③*	Specifies first line to fillet
`Select second object:` *Pick line ④*	Specifies second line and creates fillet

Save your drawing, which should look like figure 16.5.

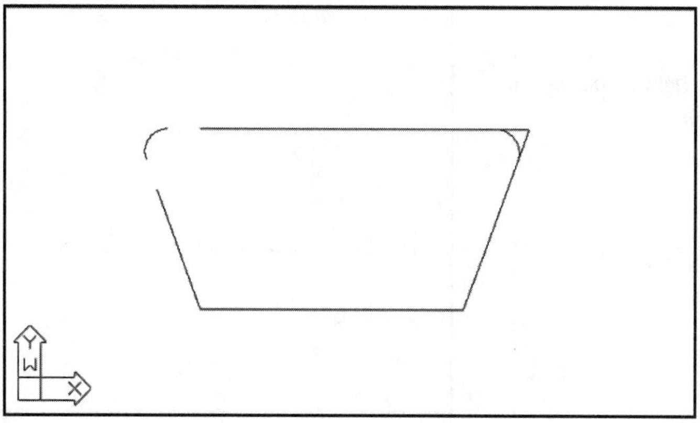

Figure 16.5

Fillets created with No Trim.

You can see from the exercise that AutoCAD does not alter the existing objects in any way when you apply a fillet with No Trim mode set.

Trimming and Extending with a Zero-Radius Fillet

Although you can undo a fillet just like you can undo nearly any AutoCAD command, it sometimes is impractical to do so. For example, you might apply a fillet, then realize an hour later—after a considerable amount of other editing—that you did not want the objects to be trimmed. Fortunately, you don't have to erase the objects and redraw them. Instead, you can use the FILLET command to extend the objects to an intersection again.

If you specify a radius of zero for the fillet and TRIM mode is set, AutoCAD automatically extends the two objects to intersect. AutoCAD does not remove the fillet arc, if any, however.

TIP

You can use the zero-radius feature of FILLET to extend or trim lines and arcs. This enables you to roughly draw objects, and then later clean up intersections and adjust endpoints with FILLET, as shown in figure 16.6.

Figure 16.6

A corner before and after a zero-radius fillet.

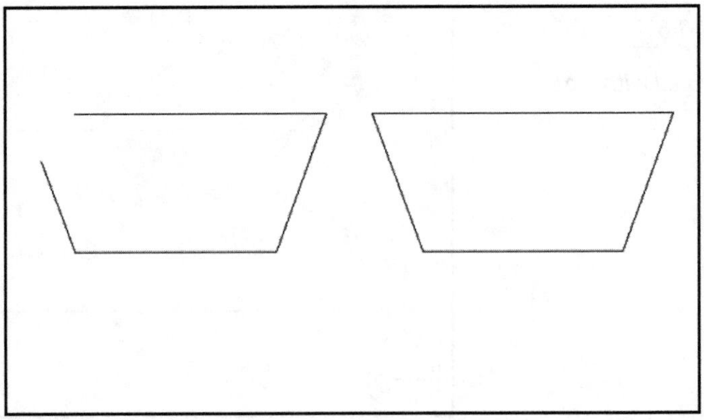

In the following exercise, remove a fillet you applied in the previous exercise. Use the FILLET command with a radius value of zero to extend the lines to their original intersection point.

Filleting with a Zero Radius

Continue with your drawing from the previous exercise.

`Command:` *Choose Fillet (Modify, Feature)*	Issues the FILLET command
`_fillet` `(NOTRIM mode) Current fillet radius = 0.5000`	
`Polyline/Radius/Trim/<Select first object>:` **T** ↵	Specifies the Trim option
`Trim/No trim <No trim>:` **T** ↵	Turns on Trim
`Polyline/Radius/Trim/<Select first object>:` **R** ↵	Specifies the Radius option
`Enter fillet radius <0.0000>:` **0** ↵	Sets the radius to zero
`Command:` ↵	Repeats the FILLET command
`FILLET` `(TRIM mode) Current fillet radius = 0.0000`	

`Polyline/Radius/Trim/<Select first object>:` *Pick line ① (see fig. 16.7)*	Specifies first line to fillet
`Select second object:` *Pick line ②*	Specifies second line and extends lines to their intersection

Save your drawing.

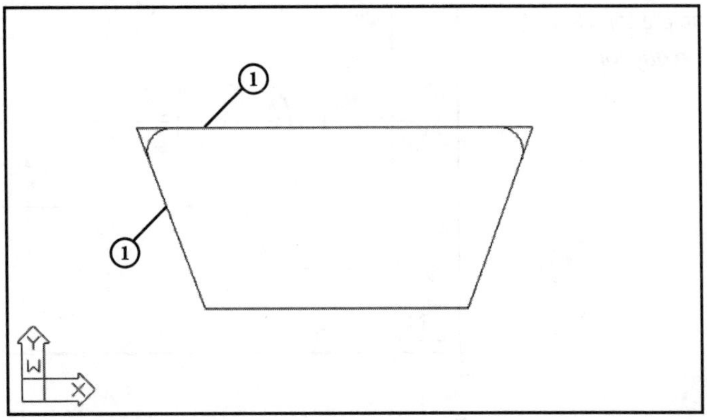

Figure 16.7

A zero-radius fillet.

TIP

You also can extend the objects to an intersection after applying a fillet by using the EXTEND command. Set the EXTEND command's Edge option to Extend to cause AutoCAD to extend the lines to their projected intersection.

When you use FILLET with a zero radius, AutoCAD does not remove the previous fillet arc if one exists. You must manually remove the fillet arc using the ERASE command.

Filleting Arcs and Circles

In previous exercises, you filleted line segments. You also can fillet arcs and even circles. Applying a fillet to a line and arc, or to two arcs, creates a tangent arc between the two objects. If the Trim option is set to Trim, AutoCAD trims the two objects to the tangent points of the fillet arc. If Trim is set to No Trim, AutoCAD only draws the tangent arc and does not trim the objects.

Circles behave differently with fillets, however. AutoCAD does not trim a circle in any way when you apply a fillet to it, regardless of the Trim setting.

In the following exercise, you set the fillet radius to 20 and fillet lines, arcs, and circles, using figure 16.8 as a reference.

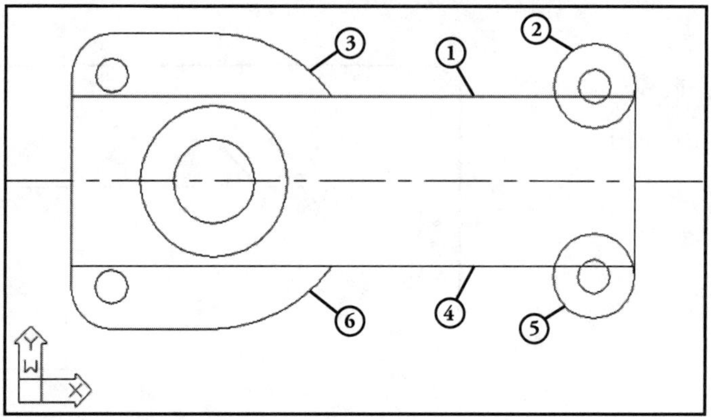

Figure 16.8

An incomplete top view of a casting ready for filleting.

FILLETING ARCS AND CIRCLES

Begin a new drawing named CHAP16B using CASTING as a prototype and zoom to the view shown in figure 16.8.

`Command:` *Choose Fillet (Modify, Feature) and set the fillet radius to 20*

`Command: ↵`	Repeats the FILLET command
`FILLET` `(TRIM mode) Current fillet radius = 20.0000`	
`Polyline/Radius/Trim/<Select first object>:` *Pick line* ① *(see fig. 16.8)*	Specifies the first object to fillet
`Select second object:` *Pick circle* ②	Specifies second object, trims line and arc, and creates fillet
`Command: ↵`	Repeats FILLET command
`FILLET` `(TRIM mode) Current fillet radius = 20.0000`	
`Polyline/Radius/Trim/<Select first object>:` *Pick line* ①	

`Select second object:` *Pick arc* ③	Creates fillet and trims the line but not the circle
`Command:` ↵	Repeats the FILLET command
`FILLET` `(TRIM mode) Current fillet radius = 20.0000`	
`Polyline/Radius/Trim/<Select first object>:` **T** ↵	Specifies the Trim option
`Trim/No trim <Trim>:` **N** ↵	Sets Trim to No Trim
`Polyline/Radius/Trim/<Select first object>:` *Pick line* ④	Specifies first object
`Select second object:` *Pick circle* ⑤	Creates fillet without trimming the line or circle
`Command:` ↵	Repeats the FILLET command
`FILLET` `(NOTRIM mode) Current fillet radius = 20.0000`	
`Polyline/Radius/Trim/<Select first object>:` *Pick line* ④	
`Select second object:` *Pick arc* ⑥	Creates fillet without trimming

Save your drawing, which should look like figure 16.9.

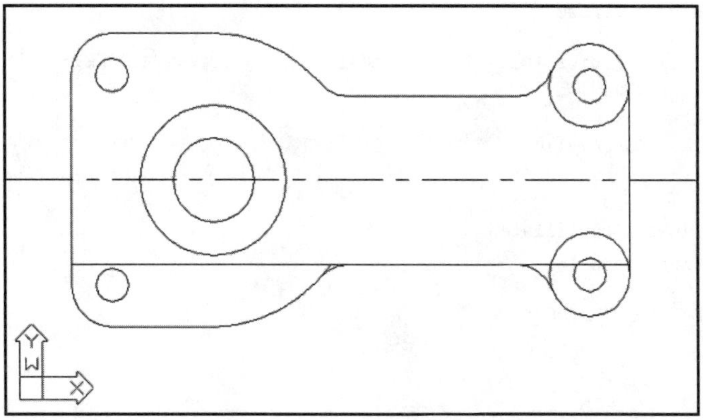

Figure 16.9

The casting after filleting arcs and circles.

You can see from this exercise that, regardless of the Trim setting, AutoCAD doesn't trim circles when you fillet them.

Filleting Polylines

You have applied fillets in the previous exercises primarily to noncomposite objects such as lines and arcs. The FILLET command also is useful for applying fillets to the vertices of polylines. You can apply a fillet to two polyline segments, just as you can to two line segments. The real advantage of using the FILLET command with a polyline is to apply fillets to all the vertices of a polyline. The Polyline option of the FILLET command applies fillets to all qualified vertices of the polyline in a single operation.

In the following exercise, try applying a common fillet radius to all the vertices of a polyline.

APPLYING FILLETS TO ALL VERTICES

Begin a new drawing named CHAP16C using GASKET as a prototype.

`Command:` *Choose Fillet (Modify, Feature) and set the fillet radius to .25*	
`Command:` ↵	Repeats the FILLET command
`fillet` `(TRIM mode) Current fillet radius = 0.2500`	
`Polyline/Radius/Trim/<Select first object>:` **P** ↵	Specifies the Polyline option
`Select 2D polyline:` *Pick any point on the polyline*	Selects the polyline to fillet and fillets the polyline (see fig. 16.10)
`4 lines were filleted` `10 were parallel`	

Save the drawing.

Figure 16.10

Fillets added to a polyline.

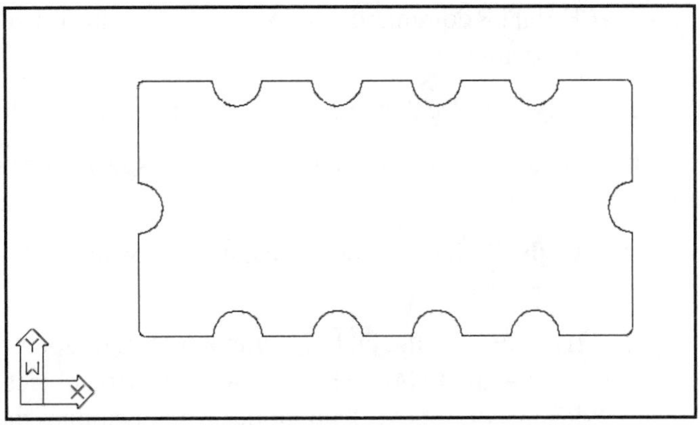

As you can see in figure 16.10, AutoCAD did not apply a fillet to each vertex. AutoCAD will not fillet polyline arc segments. Instead, AutoCAD filleted only the four corners of the object. In addition, AutoCAD ignores all vertices that result in the loss of a polyline segment (the length of a segment is less than the radius of the fillet). The FILLET command behaves in this way with polylines only if the Trim option is set to Trim. If Trim is set to No Trim, AutoCAD creates the fillet arcs even when the polyline segments are too short to meet them with tangency. When set to Trim, Fillet modifies the original polyline with the fillet arcs. When set to No Trim, individual arc objects are created and the polyline is unchanged.

NOTE

Applying a zero-radius fillet to a polyline when the trim is on removes existing polyarc segments, effectively undoing a previous fillet.

Understanding the CHAMFER Command

The CHAMFER command is similar to the FILLET command in the way it functions, but the results of the CHAMFER command are very different from those of the FILLET command. The CHAMFER command applies a chamfer to two objects; for example, you can quickly "trim" a corner where two line segments intersect, joining them with a third line at a specific angle. You can base the chamfer on distances along each segment, or a distance and angle from one segment.

The CHAMFER command options in the following list enable you to control how the chamfer is applied.

- **Polyline.** Use this option to apply a chamfer to all the vertices in a polyline.
- **Distance.** This option enables you to specify the chamfer distance along both objects.
- **Angle.** With this option you can specify the angle of the chamfer from the first object.
- **Trim.** As with the FILLET command, this option enables you to specify whether the CHAMFER command trims the objects (Trim mode—the default) or not (No Trim mode) when it applies the chamfer.
- **Method.** Use this option to choose between chamfering using two distances (the distance along each object) or chamfering using a distance and an angle.
- **Select first line.** This option, which is the default, enables you to pick the first object of the two to be chamfered.

Applying Chamfers

Two methods exist for applying chamfers with the CHAMFER command. In the first method, you specify two distances, one along each of the objects to be chamfered. AutoCAD then draws the chamfer based on those two distances.

In the following exercise, use distances to apply a chamfer to one corner of a guide block. Use figure 16.11 as a reference.

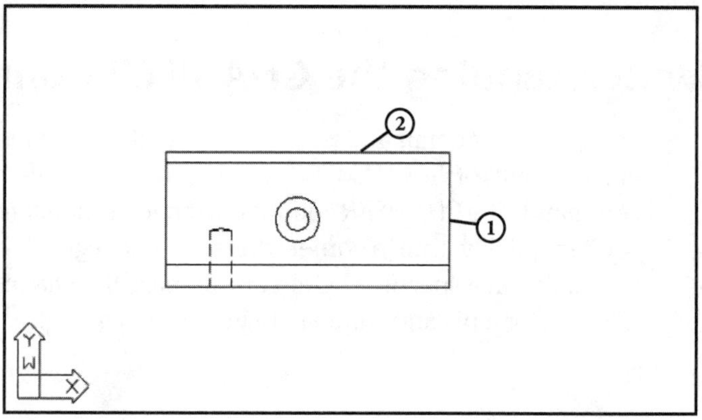

Figure 16.11

Guide block prior to chamfering corners.

Applying a Chamfer to a Corner

Begin a new drawing named CHAP16D using GUIDEBLK.DWG as a prototype.

`Command:` *Choose Chamfer (Modify, Feature)*	Issues the CHAMFER command

`_chamfer`
`(TRIM mode) Current chamfer`
`Dist1 = 0.0000, Dist2 = 0.0000`
	Notice that the prompt indicates TRIM mode and the default distances

`Polyline/Distance/Angle/Trim/Method/` `<Select first line>:` **D** ↵	Specifies the Distance option
`Enter first chamfer distance` `<0.0000>:` **1.25** ↵	Sets the distance for the chamfer along the first object
`Enter second chamfer distance` `<1.2500>:` **2.5** ↵	Sets the distance for the chamfer along the second object
`Command:` ↵	Repeats the CHAMFER command

`CHAMFER`
`(TRIM mode) Current chamfer`
`Dist1 = 1.2500, Dist2 = 2.5000`
	Notice the new default distances

`Polyline/Distance/Angle/Trim/Method/` `<Select first line>:` *Pick line* ① *(see fig. 16.11)*	Specifies to which object to apply the 1.25 distance
`Select second line:` *Pick line* ②	Specifies the object for the 2.5-unit distance and creates the chamfer

Use the TRIM command (see Chapter 14) to trim the line that represents the inner guide surface to the chamfered line at ① as shown in figure 16.12.

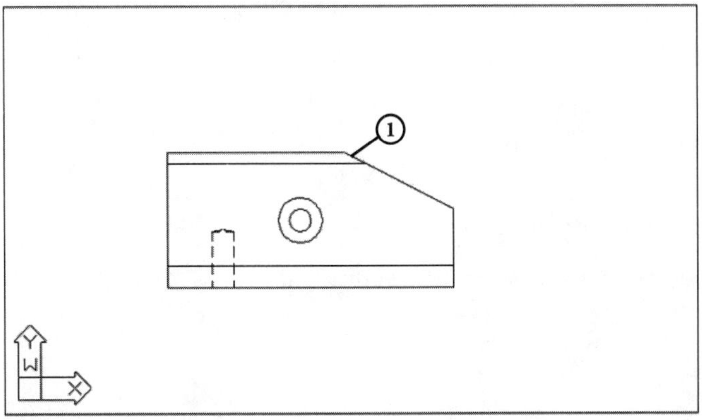

Figure 16.12

Guide block after chamfering and trimming

The order in which you pick the objects to be chamfered is significant when using the Distance option. The first distance is applied to the first object picked and the second distance is applied to the second object picked. The points at which you pick the lines also determine which portion of the line is chamfered. This is similar to the way in which the FILLET command works.

TIP

> You can create an equal-leg chamfer by specifying the same value for each of the two distances. To create an unequal-leg chamfer, specify different values for the two chamfer distances.

When you apply a chamfer, the two objects do not have to intersect. If the Trim option is set to Trim, AutoCAD automatically extends the objects to intersect the newly created chamfer line segment. If Trim is set to No Trim, AutoCAD draws the chamfer line but does not modify the existing segments.

In addition to creating chamfers based on two distances, you can specify a distance and an angle to create the chamfer. The distance you specify is the distance from the theoretical point of intersection of the two objects to the starting point of the chamfer on the first segment. You then specify the angle between the first segment and the chamfer line. AutoCAD creates the chamfer accordingly.

In the following exercise, apply a 1", 30° chamfer to the other corner of the guide block. Use figure 16.13 as a reference. Your drawing should look similar to figure 16.14 when you complete the exercise.

Creating a Chamfer at a Specific Angle

Continue with your drawing from the previous exercise.

`Command:` *Choose Chamfer (Modify, Feature)*	Issues the CHAMFER command
`_chamfer`	
`(TRIM mode) Current chamfer` `Dist1 = 1.2500, Dist2 = 2.5000`	
`Polyline/Distance/Angle/Trim/Method/` `<Select first line>:` **A** ↵	Specifies the Angle option

`Enter chamfer length on the first line <0.0000>:` **1.25** ↵	Specifies the distance along the first object at which to start the chamfer
`Enter chamfer angle from the first line <0.0000>:` **30** ↵	Specifies the chamfer angle based from the first object
`CHAMFER`	
`Length = 1.2500, Angle = 30.0000`	(Trim mode) Current chamfer

`Polyline/Distance/Angle/Trim/Method/`
`<Select first line>:` *Pick line* ① (See fig. 16.13)

`Select second line:` *Pick line* ②

On your own, try using FILLET with Trim mode on and a zero radius to trim the inside guide line to meet the newly created chamfer line at ③ (see fig. 16.13). Save the drawing.

Figure 16.13

Guide block after angle chamfer.

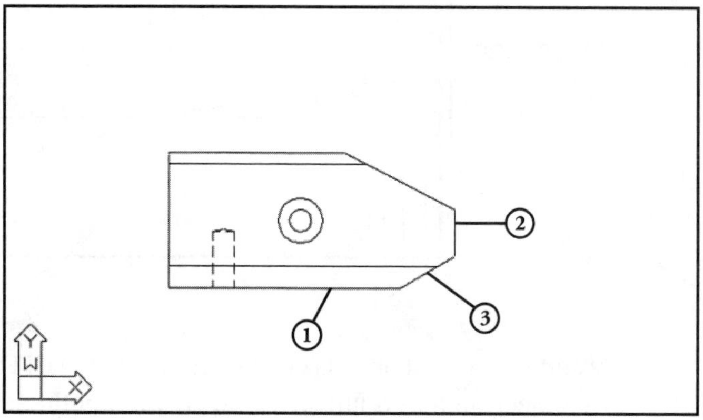

Applying Chamfers to Polylines

By using the Polyline option of the CHAMFER command, you can apply a chamfer to all of a polyline's vertices with a single operation. As with the FILLET command, the CHAMFER command ignores vertices whose segments are shorter than the resulting chamfer distance if the Trim option is set to Trim. If the Trim option is set to No Trim, CHAMFER creates the chamfer lines regardless of the length of the chamfer lines or their relationship to the original vertices.

Creating Offset Geometry

The OFFSET command enables you to offset certain types of objects through a point or at a specified distance from the original object. You can offset lines to represent the thickness of a wall, for example, or offset the outline of a gasket to create an interior cutout that is equidistant from the outer perimeter of the gasket. You can offset an object on one side of the object or offset the object on both sides. Figure 16.14 shows examples of offset geometry.

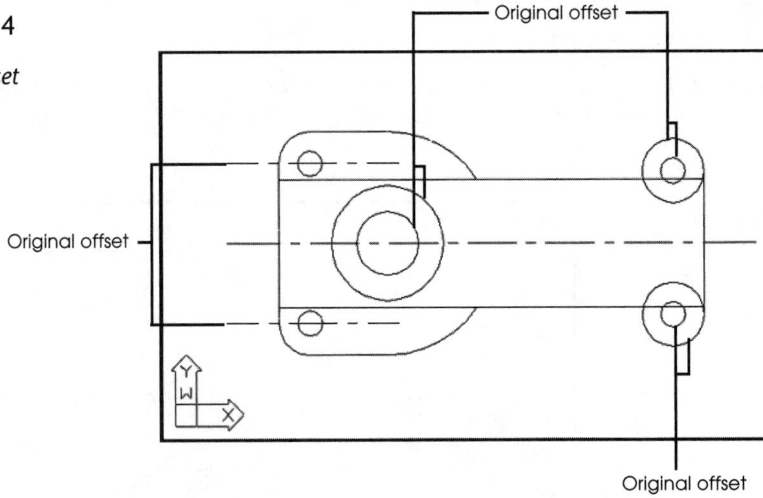

Figure 16.14

Examples of offset geometry.

Only certain types of objects can be offset with the OFFSET command. Offsetting a single object such as a line or circle creates another singular object. Offsetting a polyline creates a new polyline with the same general shape as the original, although with a different size.

OFFSET Command Options

The OFFSET command offers two options:

- **Offset distance.** This option specifies a distance from the original object to the new offset copy of the object.
- **Through.** This option enables you to specify a point through which the new offset object passes.

Creating Offsets at a Distance

The OFFSET command provides two methods for offsetting geometry. In the first method, you specify the offset distance between the original object and the new object. You can enter a value or pick two points to specify this distance. Then pick a point on either side of the object to specify the general location of the new object. AutoCAD then constructs the offset geometry on the selected side of the original object, but spaces it away from the original object by the distance you have specified.

NOTE

Offset distances cannot be negative values.

In the following exercise, create the inner boundary of a complex gasket by offsetting the gasket's outer perimeter. Your drawing should look similar to figure 16.15 when you have completed the exercise.

Creating an Offset Boundary with OFFSET

Open the drawing CHAP16C that you worked with earlier in this chapter.

`Command:` *Choose Offset (Modify, Copy)*	Issues the OFFSET command
`_offset`	
`Offset distance or Through <Through>:` **.5** ↵	Specifies the offset distance
`Select object to offset:` *Pick the polyline at any point*	Specifies which object to offset
`Side to offset?` *Pick a point inside the polyline*	Creates the offset and prompts for another object
`Select object to offset:` ↵	Ends OFFSET command

Save the Drawing.

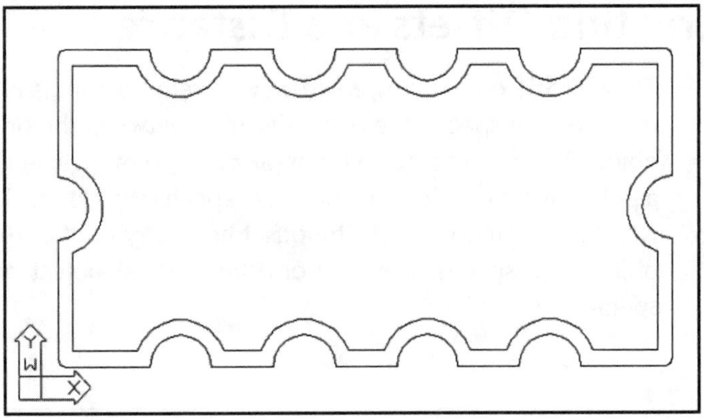

Figure 16.15

Inner perimeter of a gasket created with offset.

NOTE

If offsetting an arc will result in a radius of less than zero, AutoCAD doesn't create the arc. In figure 16.15, for example, you can see that the arcs at the four outer corners of the gasket were not duplicated in the interior perimeter of the gasket.

After you start the OFFSET command, you're not limited to creating a single offset. Instead, you can continue to specify offset distances and pick points to locate other offset copies of the original object. You can, for example, create an inner and outer offset of an object without exiting and reissuing the OFFSET command. Once an offset distance had been specified, the offset command no longer prompts for the distance, and all subsequent offsets are made at that distance. Any object can, however, be selected for offsetting, in the same command, including those just created by the command itself.

Creating Offsets Through a Point

The second way to offset objects is to pick the object you want to offset and then pick a point through which the object is to be offset. You can enter a coordinate or pick the point, and you can use any point specification method—including object snap modes and filters—to pick the point. If this point falls beyond the end of the new object, the offset is calculated as if the new object extended to the through point, but the object is drawn without that imaginary extension.

In the following exercise, assume you want to modify the CHAP16B drawing you worked with in a previous exercise. To add center lines to the two holes at the left side of the casting use the OFFSET command to offset the existing center line.

CREATING AN OFFSET THROUGH A POINT

Open the CHAP16B drawing you created in a previous exercise.

`Command:` *Choose Offset (Modify, Copy)*	Issues the OFFSET command
`_offset`	
`Offset distance or Through <Through>:` ↵	Specifies the through option
`Select object to offset:` *Pick line* ① *(see fig. 16.16)*	Specifies which object to offset
`Through point:` *From the pop-up menu, choose* Center	
`_center of` *Pick circle* ②	Creates the offset line
`Select object to offset:` *Pick the line at* ①	
`_Through point:` *From the pop-up menu, choose* Center	
`_center of` *Pick circle* ③	Creates offset line
`Select object to offset:` ↵	Ends OFFSET command

Save your drawing.

TIP

Sometimes you need to offset a perimeter made up of several objects. Use PEDIT to join objects and/or BOUNDARY to create a continuous object to offset.

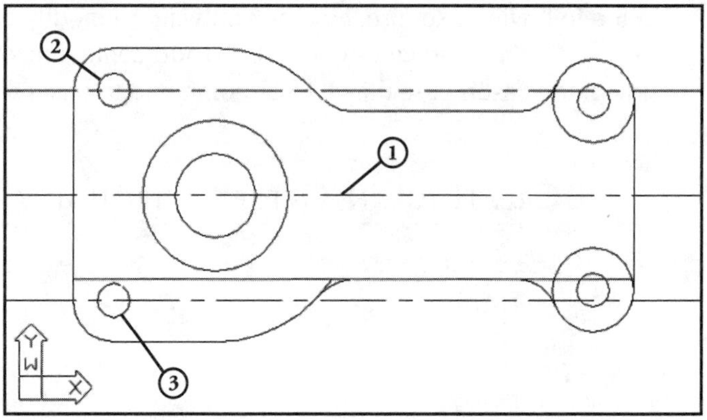

Figure 16.16

Offsets created through a point.

Also, you can use the OFFSET command to create concentric circles.

Objects that you can offset include lines, arcs, circles, splines, and 2D polylines. You also can offset objects that are created from polylines, which include donuts, ellipses, and polygons. Each offset creates a new object with the same linetype, color, and layer settings as the original object. Polylines also have the same width and curves as the original object, although the radius of curves and endpoints of objects change in order to allow a consistent offset distance between the original and the offset objects.

TIP

OFFSET forms a new object by drawing the object parallel to the original object. OFFSET cannot form a new object inside an arc or circle if the offset distance exceeds the original radius. (You cannot create a negative radius.) Donuts, polygons, and polyarcs or short segments in other polylines are treated similarly. OFFSET attempts to duplicate small zigzag segments and loops with polylines, but you might get confused results. Use TRIM, BREAK, and/or PEDIT to clean up offset polylines if you do not like the results.

Creating Arrays of Objects

One of AutoCAD's most useful commands is the ARRAY command. ARRAY enables you to create a rectangular or circular array by copying one or more existing objects. Figure 16.17 shows a rectangular and a polar array.

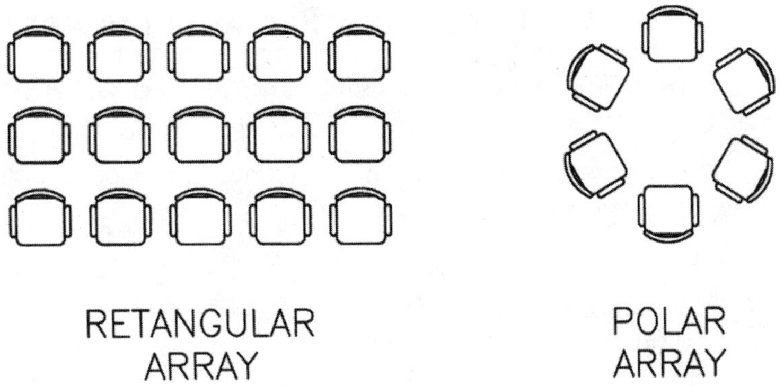

Figure 16.17

A rectangular and a polar array.

As with other commands that copy objects, new objects in an array have the same layer, color, and linetype settings as the original object. If necessary, however, you can change these object properties after creating the array.

Creating a Rectangular Array

A *rectangular array* is a group of objects arranged in rows and columns. To create a rectangular array, you first select the object(s) to be copied. Then you specify the number of rows and columns in the finished array and the distance between rows and columns. AutoCAD automatically copies the object(s) into an array.

In the following exercise, create an array of workstations in an office floor plan. Begin with a single four-cubicle group, then array more workstations to complete the layout. Use figure 16.18 as a reference. Your drawing should look similar to figure 16.19 when you complete the exercise.

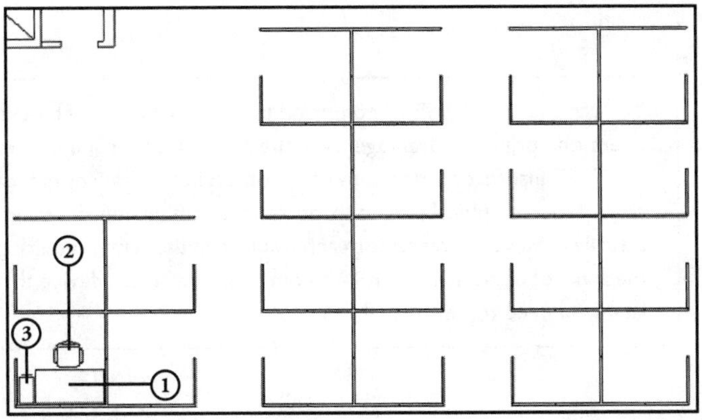

Figure 16.18

Workstation objects to array.

CREATING A RECTANGULAR ARRAY

Begin a new drawing named CHAP16E using OFFICE as a prototype, then zoom to the view shown in figure 16.18.

`Command:` *Choose Rectangular Array (Modify, Copy)*	Prompts for object selection
`_select`	
`Select objects:` *Select objects ①, ②, and ③ and press Enter*	Specifies the objects to be arrayed

`Command: _array`
`Select objects: _p`
`3 found`
`Select objects:`
`Rectangular or Polar array (R/P) <R>: _r`
	The tool issues the ARRAY command with the Rectangular option and selected objects

`Number of rows (—) <1>:` **2** ↵	Specifies number of rows horizontally in the array
`Number of columns (¦¦¦) <1>:` **2** ↵	Specifies number of columns vertically in the array
`Unit cell or distance between rows (—):` **8'1** ↵	Specifies the distance vertically between objects in the array
`Distance between columns (¦¦¦):` **7'11** ↵	Specifies the distance horizontally between objects and draws the array

You can see from the exercise that using the ARRAY command can be much faster than trying to copy or draw each workstation manually, particularly for large arrays.

TIP

> You can use the MINSERT command to create an array of blocks in a drawing. MINSERT offers one primary advantage over the ARRAY command in creating rectangular arrays. MINSERT inserts only one copy of the object in the drawing database, then represents that single block graphically in each of its locations in the drawing. The ARRAY command actually copies the objects for each instance in the array, requiring more memory to store the array of objects. The ARRAY command is a better device than MINSERT, however, if later you need to edit the objects.

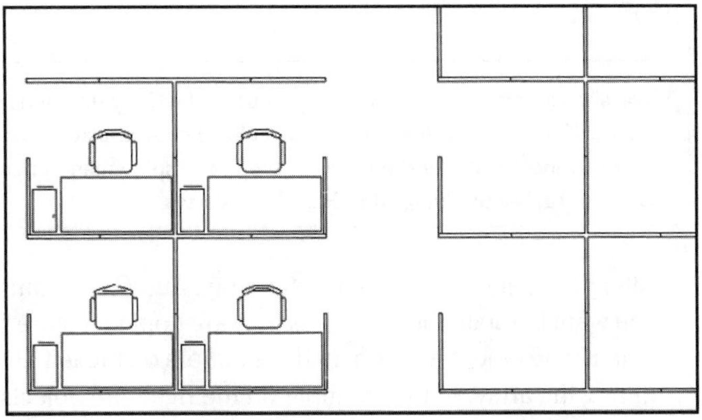

Figure 16.19

A two-by-two array of workstations.

You often need to create one-column or one-row arrays. A *one-row array* is a single horizontal row of objects, and a *one-column array* is a single column of objects. You can create one-row and one-column arrays easily with the ARRAY command. To create a one-row array consisting of 12 objects, for example, you specify a value of 1 for the number of rows and a value of 12 for the number of columns in the array. The result is a horizontal "line" of 12 objects.

A positive row spacing causes objects to be arranged to the right. Positive column spacing results in objects being arrayed up. A negative row spacing causes the object(s) to be arrayed to the left, rather than to the right. Using a negative column spacing causes the object(s) to be arrayed down, rather than up. You can use a combination of positive and negative row and column spacing values to control the directions in which objects are arrayed.

Creating a Polar Array

A *polar array* is an array of objects created around a center point. To create a polar array, pick the objects to be arrayed and choose a center point. AutoCAD then prompts you for the angle to fill. Accepting the default angle of 360° arrays the objects in a complete circle. Specifying an angle less than 360° arrays the objects in a partial circle. For example, specifying an angle of 180° creates a semicircle of objects. If you specify a positive angle, AutoCAD copies the objects counterclockwise. Specifying a negative angle causes AutoCAD to copy the objects in a clockwise rotation.

TIP

You also can copy objects in an array by using the Copy (multiple) option with autoediting modes. If you press Shift while picking multiple copy displacements (to points), the cursor jumps to increments of the offset of the first displacement, in an array-like fashion. See Chapter 13, "Autoediting with Grips," for details.

After you specify the angle for the array, AutoCAD prompts you to specify whether you want to rotate the objects as they are copied. Figure 16.20 shows two examples to illustrate object rotation. In the example on the left, the objects were not rotated during the array. In the example on the right, the objects were rotated.

Figure 16.20

The effects of object rotation on an array.

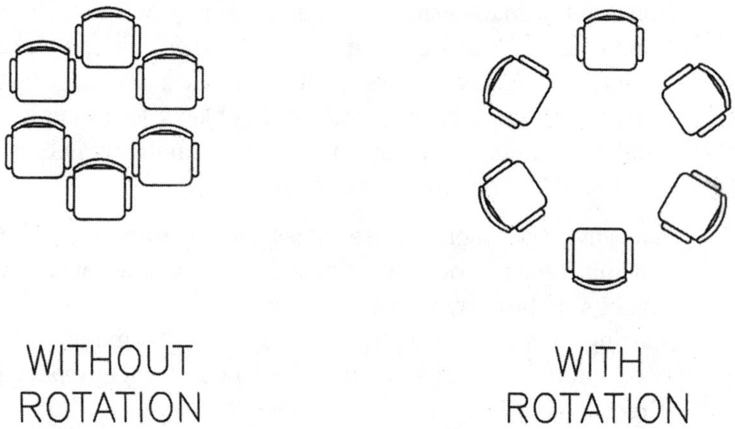

NOTE

In some situations, it doesn't matter if you rotate the objects during the array. Objects such as circles, for example, look the same whether or not you rotate them during the array.

In the following exercise, copy the chairs around a table using a polar array. Your drawing should look similar to figure 16.22 when you complete the exercise.

Creating a Polar Array

Continue with your CHAP16E (OFFICE) drawing from the previous exercise, and zoom to the view shown in figure 16.21.

`Command:` *Choose Polar Array (Modify, Copy)*	
`_select` `Select objects:` *Pick the chair at* ① *(see fig. 16.21) and press Enter*	Specifies an object to array

`Command: _array`
`Select objects: _p`
`1 found`
`Select objects:`
`Rectangular or Polar array (R/P) <R>: _p`
	The tool issues the ARRAY command with the Polar option and the selected object

`Center point of array:` *From the pop-up menu, choose* Center	Sets Center object snap
`_center of` *Pick circle* ②	Snaps the center of the array to the center of the circle
`Number of items:` **3** ↵	Specifies the total number of objects in the array
`Angle to fill (+=ccw, -=cw) <360>:` **180** ↵	Specifies the included angle of the array
`Rotate objects as they are copied? <Y>` ↵	Causes AutoCAD to rotate the chairs as it creates the array

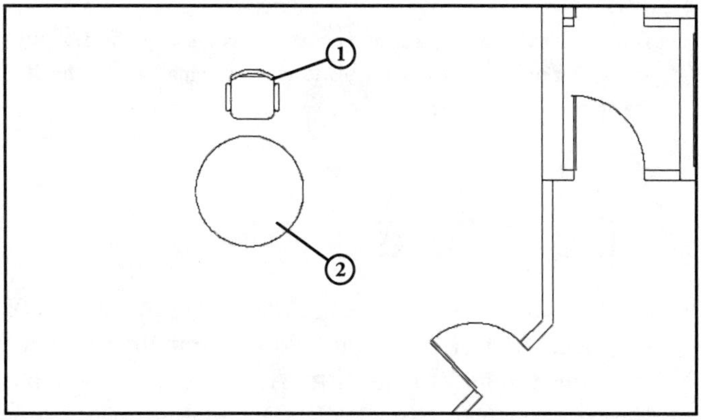

Figure 16.21

A table before a polar array.

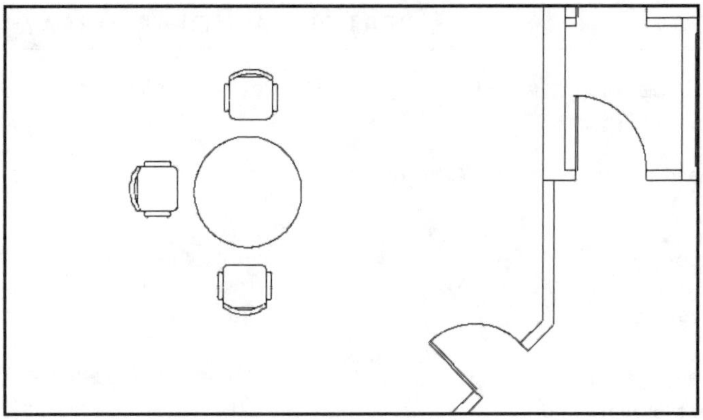

Figure 16.22

Chairs after completing the array.

You can use included angle and number of objects to determine the angle between each object. To determine a combination of included angle and number of copies that will result in a specific angle between objects, multiply the angle between objects by the number of new objects. You also can divide the included angle by the angle between all objects to determine the required number of objects in the array.

TIP

Pressing Enter when prompted for the number of objects simply proceeds to the `Angle to fill` prompt, then to an `Angle between items` prompt. Specifying a number of items, then giving a value of 0 (zero) for the `Angle to fill` prompt also issues the `Angle between objects` prompt.

NOTE

You can create rectangular and polar 3D arrays with the 3DARRAY command. In addition to copying objects in the same plane as the original object, the 3DARRAY command copies the array in the Z axis.

Mirroring Objects

Many designs contain symmetrical objects, and AutoCAD's MIRROR command simplifies the task of drawing these symmetrical objects. The MIRROR command functions similarly to the Mirror Autoedit mode, which is introduced in Chapter 13, "Autoediting with Grips." MIRROR enables you to create a mirror image of an existing object and gives you the option of retaining the original object (creating a mirrored copy) or deleting the original object.

After you start the MIRROR command, AutoCAD prompts you to select the objects to be mirrored. Then, AutoCAD prompts you to define a mirror line about which the selected objects will be mirrored. You can pick two points to specify the mirror line. AutoCAD then uses this imaginary line as the axis about which it mirrors the selected objects.

The only command option that the MIRROR command offers is a choice of whether AutoCAD should retain the original objects or delete them. Directing AutoCAD to delete the original objects is similar in concept to reversing (flipping) the selected objects. Directing AutoCAD to retain the original objects results in a mirror-image copy of the original.

Using the MIRROR Command

In the following exercise, use the MIRROR command to copy a fixture and stall between two rest rooms in the office layout you worked with in previous exercises. You will specify a mirror line that falls midway between the original object and its mirrored copy. In this example, this means that the mirror line runs through the middle of the wall separating the two rest rooms. Use figure 16.23 as a reference. Your drawing should look similar to figure 16.24 when you complete the exercise.

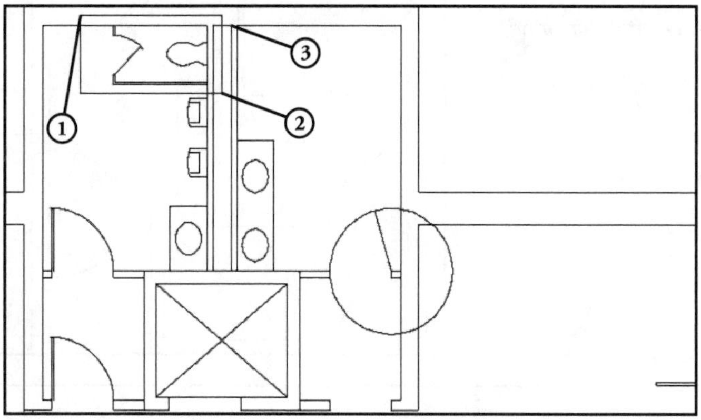

Figure 16.23

The rest room layout prior to mirroring.

Mirroring an Object

Continue with your CHAP16E (OFFICE) drawing from the previous exercise, and zoom to the view shown in figure 16.23.

`Command:` *Choose Mirror (Modify, Copy)*	Issues the MIRROR command
`_mirror` `Select objects:` *Pick points* ① *and* ② *(see fig. 16.23) and press Enter*	Selects objects with a window
`11 found`	
`First point of mirror line:` *From the pop-up menu, choose* Midpoint	Sets Midpoint object snap
`_mid of` *Pick line* ③	Specifies first point on mirror line
`Second point:` *Turn on Ortho and pick any point above or below the first point*	Defines the vertical mirror line
`Delete old objects? <N>` ↵	Creates a mirrored copy

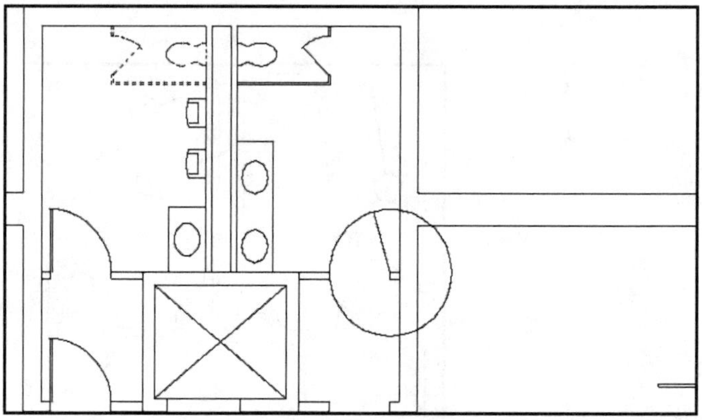

Figure 16.24

The fixture after mirroring.

To examine the effect of deleting the original object with the MIRROR command, mirror one of the towel holders from the left rest room to the right rest room. Because the towel holders are mounted on the wall, you can use the same points to define the mirror line that you used in the previous exercise.

DELETING THE ORIGINAL OBJECTS

Continue with your CHAP16E (OFFICE) drawing from the previous exercise, with Ortho on.

`Command:` *Choose Mirror (Modify, Copy)*	Issues the MIRROR command
`_mirror`	
`Select objects:` *Pick points* ① *and* ② *(see fig. 16.25) and press Enter*	Selects objects with a window
`7 found`	
`First point of mirror line:` *From the pop-up menu, choose* Midpoint	Sets Midpoint object snap
`_mid of` *Pick line* ③	Specifies first point of mirror line
`Second point:` *Pick any point above or below the first point*	Defines mirror line
`Delete old objects? <N>` **Y** ↵	Creates mirrored copy and deletes original objects

Save your drawing. It should look like figure 16.26

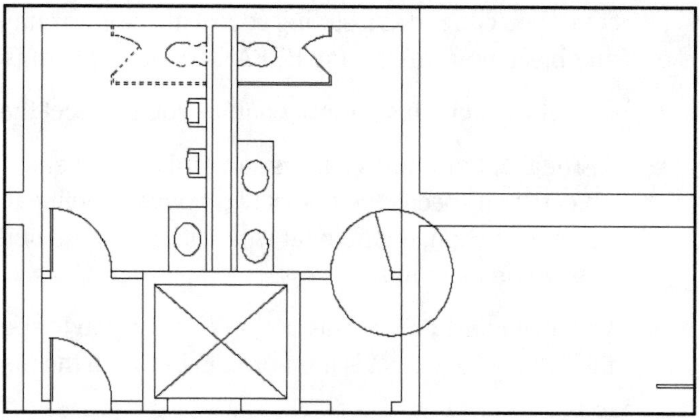

Figure 16.25

The towel fixture prior to mirroring.

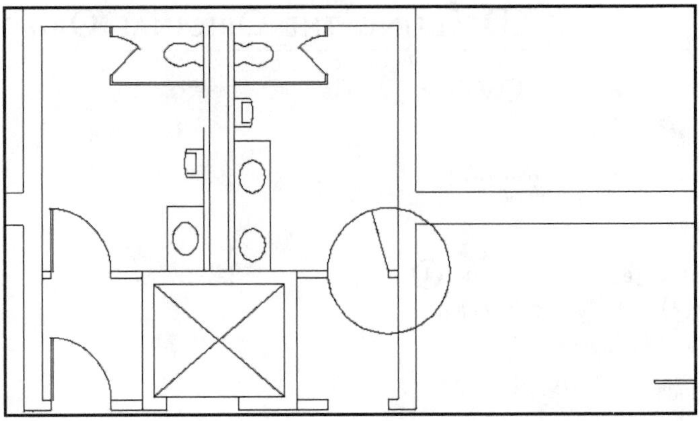

Figure 16.26

The towel fixture mirrored.

The MIRROR command is very similar in function to Mirror Autoedit mode. The MIRROR command is more useful than Mirror Autoedit mode when you need to work with a complex selection set, because the MIRROR command supports all of AutoCAD's object selection methods.

Breaking Objects with BREAK

You often will erase only a portion on an object. Although you can use the TRIM command in many situations, TRIM is not useful unless your drawing contains an object that you can use as a cutting edge. If there is no cutting edge that will properly trim an object, you can use the BREAK command to erase a part of the object.

- **Select Object.** This prompt enables you to select the object to be broken.
- **F.** The F option stands for First, and this option enables you to pick the object, then specify the first of two points to define the break. If you do not use the F option, the point at which you pick the object becomes the first of the two break points.
- **Enter Second Point.** This option enables you to specify the second point for the break. The object is then broken between the first and second points.

The BREAK command requires selection of two points to define the points between which the object will be broken.

The Break toolbar offers four predefined methods you can use to select the object to be broken and the points at which to break it. The following list defines these methods by their tool names:

- **1 point.** With this option you pick a point on the object and AutoCAD breaks the object at that point. If you pick a line, for example, AutoCAD breaks the line at the pick point and creates two separate lines that share an endpoint at the picked point.
- **1 point select.** AutoCAD prompts you to select the object to be broken, then prompts you for the first break point. AutoCAD automatically uses the same point for the second break point, breaking the object into two separate objects that share a common endpoint. This option is useful when you want to specify a break point other than the one by which you pick the object.
- **2 points.** AutoCAD prompts you to pick the object, then pick a point. The point at which you pick the object is used as the first break point. AutoCAD breaks the object between the two points, removing the portion of the object that falls between the two points.
- **2 points select.** AutoCAD prompts you to select the object, then pick two points. The point at which you pick the object is not used to determine the break points.

TIP

Circles are broken counterclockwise. Also, break points that you pick do not have to fall on an object. For example, ③ in figure 16.27 specifies the second point of the break, but does not fall on the circle being broken. AutoCAD calculates the apparent intersection between the point and the object based on the geometry of the object. If the second point is beyond the end of the object, the end is removed and no new object is created.

Depending on the type of object and the points specified, the BREAK command might both modify the existing object and create a new object, or simply modify the existing object.

In the following exercise, use the BREAK command to create a simplified door symbol. You will use the 2 points select method. Use figure 16.27 as a reference. Your drawing should look similar to figure 16.28 when you complete the exercise.

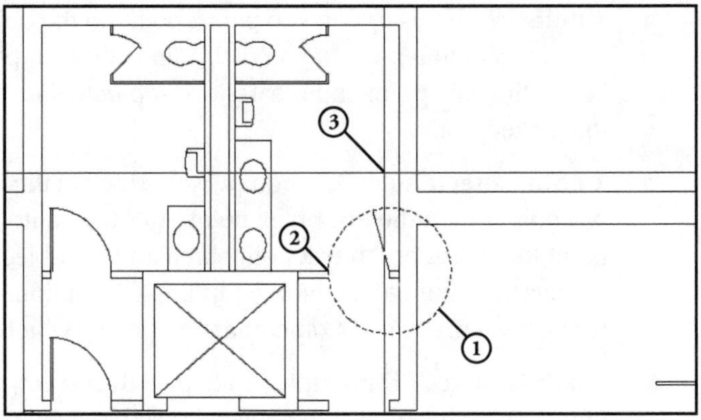

Figure 16.27

The door symbol prior to break.

Using the BREAK Command

Continue with your CHAP16E (OFFICE) drawing from the previous exercise.

`Command:` *Choose 2 points select (Modify, Break)*	Issues the BREAK command for the 2 points select method
`_break Select object:` *Pick circle* ① *(see fig. 16.27)*	Specifies object to break
`Enter second point (or F for first point): _f`	
`Enter first point:` *From the pop-up menu, choose* Endpoint	
`_endp of` *Pick point* ②	Specifies first point at which to break the object
Enter second point: *Pick point* ③	Specifies second point and breaks the circle

In some situations, it is easier to use TRIM to erase a portion of an object. In situations in which no trimming object exists, or in which drawing a trimming object is not feasible, the BREAK command is a good tool for erasing a portion of an object.

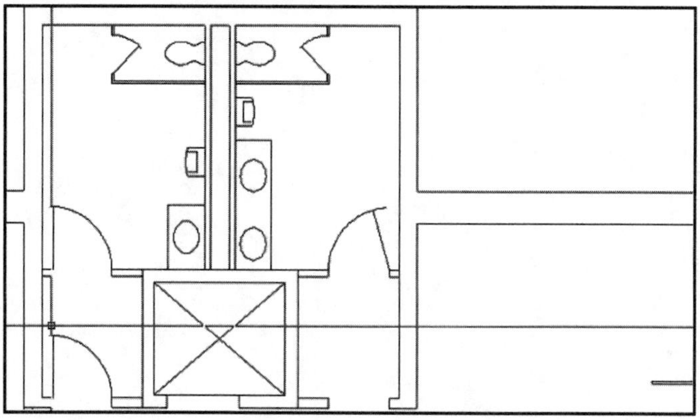

Figure 16.28

The door swing created using BREAK.

Mastering the techniques of constructive editing enables you to take advantage of the CAD concept of "draw it once." The FILLET and CHAMFER commands enable you to work in *sketch* mode; blocking out geometry with lines and arcs, then cleaning up the intersections. Using the MIRROR command, you can quickly complete symmetrical designs. The ARRAY command can multiply a carefully created detail part into a drawing full of replicas. Planning ahead to apply these techniques will leverage your AutoCAD drawing effort.

part

IV

Text, Graphic, and Dimensioning Tools

chapter

17

Annotation with Text

You often need to place lines of text in drawings to explain graphic objects. Although international logo symbols do support the philosophy that a picture is worth a thousand words (or at least a few words), accompanying text can specify, clarify, and simplify drawing details. Textual data can refer to notes, specifications, schedules, leader callouts, or anything "character-string" based.

Historically, hand lettering a drawing was time-consuming and error-prone. Correcting a misspelled or omitted word was difficult. Today, using AutoCAD Release 13's powerful, yet easy-to-use text entry and editing methods, the resultant lettering generates faster, is more accurate, and follows a more uniform style than manual techniques.

This chapter covers the following procedures related to drawing annotation:

- Using TEXT, DTEXT, and MTEXT to place single, multiple, and paragraph text objects
- Using text styles and fonts
- Basic line and paragraph text formatting
- Formatting special characters and strings
- Advanced paragraph text formatting
- Importing text
- Editing and spell-checking

Placing AutoCAD Text

AutoCAD provides the TEXT, DTEXT, and MTEXT commands to place text in your drawings. You use TEXT, the Single-Line Text tool, to create a single line of text. DTEXT, the Dtext tool, enables you to generate multiple lines of text *dynamically,* by displaying the characters as you type them. You use MTEXT, the Multi-line Text tool, to create paragraph-style text to fit within points you specify, which AutoCAD then treats as one object.

Plotted versus Drawn Text Height

In general because AutoCAD draws all objects at full size, you need to determine the corresponding text height so that geometry and text descriptions are properly proportioned. The question really becomes, What text height should I draw at, so that the plotted height meets acceptable industry standards?

Suppose you want to plot your drawing at a scale of 1/4"=1', and you want the text height to appear 1/8" high on the final plot. What should the drawn text height be? At this plot scale, every 1/4" *plotted* represents 1' *drawn*; therefore, a 1/8" plot height calculates to a 6" drawn height.

Refer to Chapter 6, "Plotting and Sheet Composition," for a table of common plot scales with their corresponding drawn text heights.

Using TEXT to Place Text

AutoCAD has always had a TEXT command since its initial release. However, no one really needs to use it, because the DTEXT and MTEXT commands are much more versatile. The TEXT command is retained solely for compatibility with older versions of the software.

In the following exercise, you place a single text label in the drawing at a specified location.

PLACING A SINGLE TEXT LABEL

Begin a new drawing again named CHAP17, using the HOSPROOM drawing from the IAW Disk as the prototype. Zoom to the view shown in figure 17.1, then set snap to 3" and grid to 6". Set the FURNITURE layer current.

`Command:` *Choose Single-Line Text (Draw, Text)*	Issues the TEXT command
`_text Justify/Style/<Start point>:` **12',11'6"** ↵	Specifies the start point 12',11'6"
`Height <0'-0 1/4">:` **6** ↵	Specifies 6" text height
`Rotation angle <0>:` ↵	Accepts default baseline rotation
`Text:` **CHAIR** ↵	Draws text as shown in figure 17.1

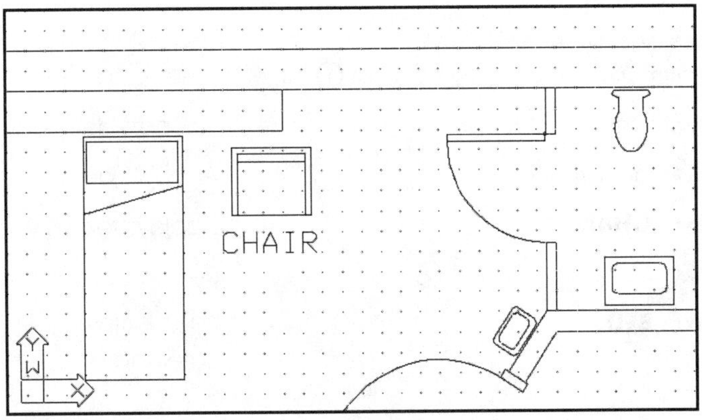

Figure 17.1

The chair annotated with TEXT.

Using DTEXT to Place Text

The DTEXT command provides more flexibility than TEXT. The D in DTEXT stands for dynamic. As you enter text using DTEXT, it appears in the drawing, so you can see how its size and position relate to the other drawing elements. When you press Enter, DTEXT starts a new line of text, aligned directly below the last, or you can reposition the box cursor on the drawing area at any time to create a new line anywhere you choose. This feature enables you to place text throughout your drawing with a single DTEXT command.

WARNING

Be sure to press Enter a second time at the end of a long sequence of DTEXT input. Although the text appears to be part of the drawing, clicking on another tool to issue a new command cancels the DTEXT command and deletes the text input.

In the next exercise, you use DTEXT to label the remaining pieces of furniture in the room.

PLACING MULTIPLE TEXT LABELS

Continue from the preceding exercise and zoom to view shown in figure 17.2. Label the remaining pieces of furniture in the hospital room. Turn on the snap and grid modes.

`Command:` *Choose Dtext (Draw, Text)*	Issues the DTEXT command
`Command:` _dtext Justify/Style/ `<Start point>:` *Pick point* 5',7" at ①	Specifies start point for chair text (see fig. 17.2)
`Height <0'-6">:` ↵	Accepts default 6" text height
`Rotation angle <0>:` ↵	Accepts default rotation
`Text:` **CHAIR** ↵	Displays text as you type
`Text:` *Pick point* 9',7'6 at ②	Relocates next insertion point
`Text:` **BED**	Displays text; notice that you didn't press Enter this time

`Text:` *Pick point* 12',6'6 at ③	Relocates next insertion point
`Text:` **SOFA** ↵	Displays text
`Text:` ↵	Completes the DTEXT command

Save the drawing.

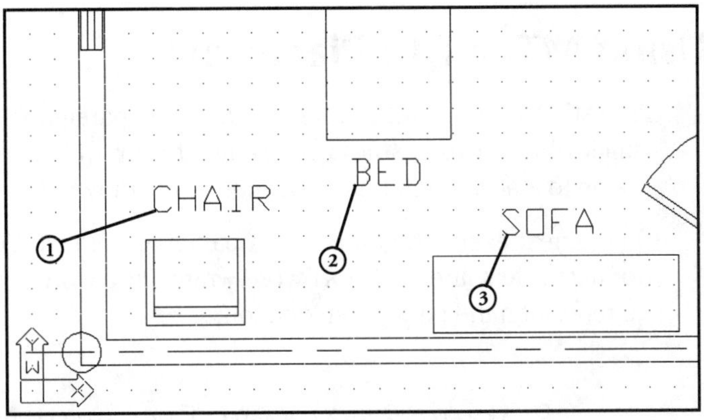

Figure 17.2

Bedroom furniture labeled with DTEXT.

In the preceding exercise, you picked alternate text insertion points by reading the coordinate display in the status line. A single DTEXT command enables you to enter all three text labels.

If you use a justification other than the default left (such as right or middle), input for DTEXT is still shown as left-justified during entry, but completing the command adjusts the alignment to the format you specify.

TIP

You also can use object snap modes to help place text. To add a line below existing text, use DTEXT with object snap mode INSert, pick the existing text, and enter only a space on the first line. Then press Enter to space down for the next line.

As shown in the preceding exercise, the DTEXT command enables you to place multiple lines of text at various locations in the drawing. Often, however, grouping several lines of text together to be treated as a single block becomes handy. Some examples are door schedules, design and build specifications, and mechanical tolerance notes. Instead of using the BLOCK command (see Chapter 10, "Basic Building Blocks for Repetitive Drawing"). to "glue" the text lines together, you can utilize a powerful, new Release 13 feature called MTEXT—text treated as paragraphs.

Using MTEXT to Place Text

The MTEXT command enables you to create paragraph-style text that is treated as a single object. This enables you to enter the text quickly and reposition its boundary frame to a new, uncluttered location in the drawing.

In the next exercise, you create a paragraph of text. You need not press Enter to format the text lines—MTEXT word-wraps like a word processor. Then, you see how to reposition the paragraph location.

PLACING PARAGRAPH TEXT WITH MTEXT

Continue in CHAP17 drawing from the previous exercise, and zoom to the view shown in figure 17.3.

`Command:` *Choose Text (Draw, Text)*	Issues the MTEXT command
`Attach/Rotation/Style/Height/Direction/ <Insertion point>:` *Pick point at* ① *(see fig. 17.3)*	Specifies upper left corner of paragraph
`Attach/Rotation/Style/Height/Direction/ Width/2Points/<Other corner>:` *Pick point at* ②	Specifies width of paragraph and opens Edit MText dialog box
Enter the text shown in the Edit MText dialog box (see fig. 17.4), then choose OK	
`Command:` *Pick the text*	Selects the text and displays grips at its corner points
Pick any grip, then press Enter	Makes grip hot, enters autoediting move mode, and drags text box with the cursor

Move the cursor around to see it drag, then press Esc three times to cancel

Save the drawing.

Figure 17.3 shows the results of this exercise.

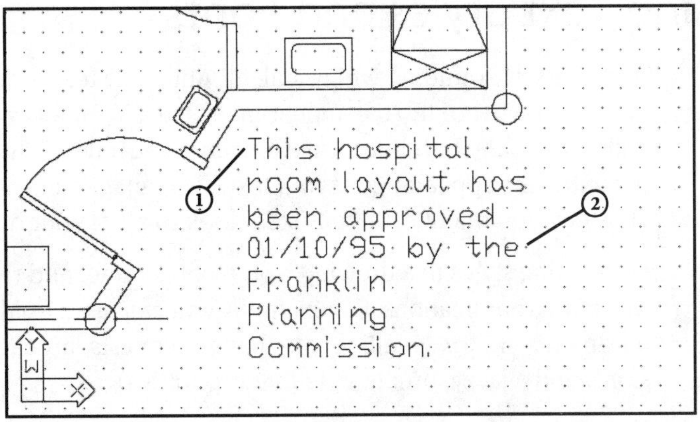

Figure 17.3

Completed approval note.

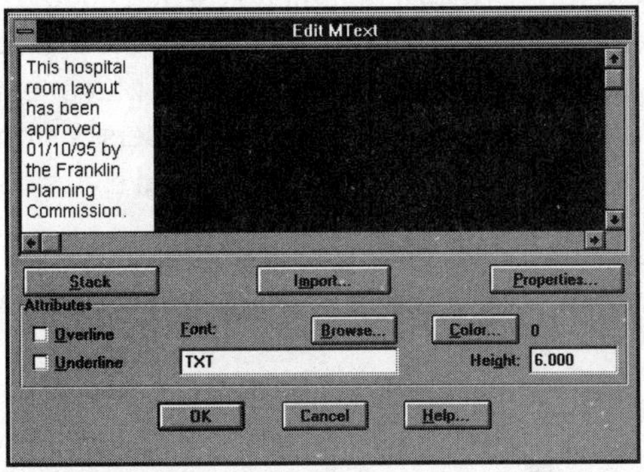

Figure 17.4

Approval note in Edit MText dialog box.

Although MTEXT word-wraps text as you type, it doesn't always format perfectly—the text lines might break differently on screen. If this happens, use DDEDIT to reedit the text in the Edit MText dialog box, and use the Enter key to force lines to break where you want. The better the MTEXT drawing font matches the MTEXT editing font, the better the word-wrapping will match. See the section "Font Mapping and Substitution" later in this chapter for more information.

NOTE

Entering -MTEXT at the Command: prompt displays all prompts at the command line instead of providing a dialog box.

Using Text Styles and Fonts

At the risk of sounding whimsical, all AutoCAD text is drawn with style! AutoCAD enables you to control the appearance of text in many ways, such as font, character width, slant, and baseline format. Because you have all these parameters with which to control the appearance of your text, file management can become a critical issue. How can you maintain a consistent look to all of your drawings?

By defining styles in a drawing, you create, name, and recall different text formats for various applications. For example, you can use a bold style for section markers, a slanted style for specification change requests, an easy-to-read style for dimensions, and a jazzy, ornate style for corporate logos.

You define a *text style* to alter the basic shape of a character set typeface, or *font*. AutoCAD provides a default text style called STANDARD, which uses a basic stick-lettering font called TXT. This is what the previous exercises used. Because at least one style must exist before you can place text, some users find the default style sufficient. However, the majority of users customize the STANDARD style by linking it to another font, or define additional styles.

13c4 Modifying Text Styles with DDSTYLE

AutoCAD Release 13c4 introduced a welcome replacement for the aging STYLE command—the Text Style dialog box, which you open with the DDSTYLE command. Using the Text Style dialog box you can select a new current text style from a list of previously defined styles, make changes to existing styles, or define new ones. It provides a graphical preview of selected characters with the current settings applied, and can show you the entire character set for a selected font.

To access the DDSTYLE command, choose Data, then Text style, or choose the Object Creation tool on the Object Properties toolbar, then choose Text Style.

In the following exercise, you use the Text Style dialog box to assign another font to the default STANDARD style, and make changes to two other settings, to enhance the appearance of text in the drawing.

Revising a Text Style

Continue to use the CHAP17 drawing from the previous exercise.

`Command:` *Choose* Data, Text Style	Issues the DDSTYLE command
`'_ddstyle`	Opens the Text Style dialog box (see fig. 17.5)

Click on the Browse button next to the Font File edit box, to open the Select Font File dialog box (see fig. 17.6). In the Files of Type list box, choose Shape Compiled. Use the Drives and Directories list boxes as required to locate the directory with the AutoCAD font files (typically C:\ACADR13\COMMON\FONTS), click on the file ROMANS.SHX, then choose Open. Notice that as soon as you return to the Text Style dialog box the text in the Character Preview window is changed to reflect the new font.

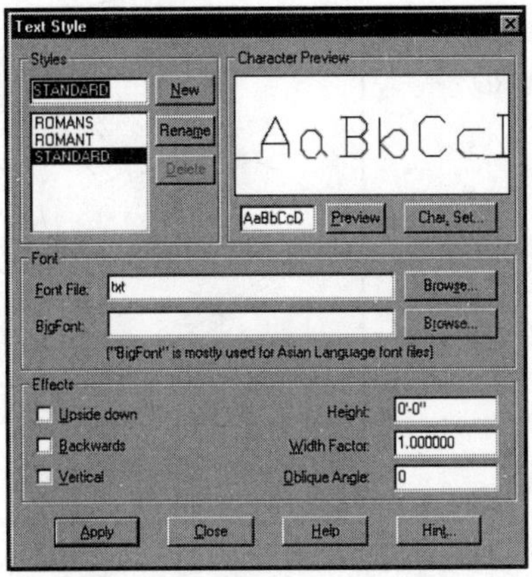

Figure 17.5

The Text Style dialog box.

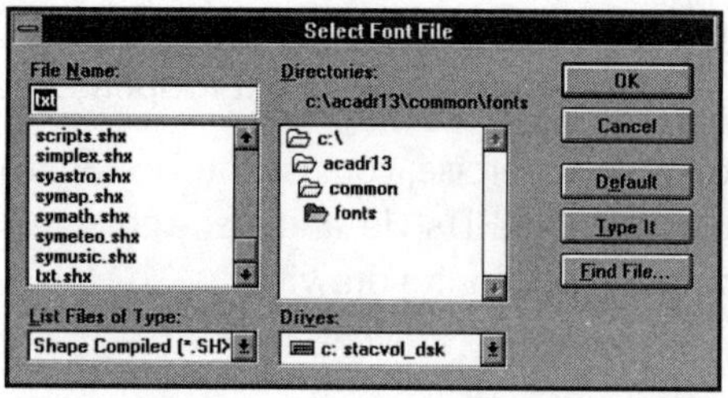

Figure 17.6

The Select Font dialog box.

Double-click in the Width Factor edit box and enter **0.8**, then double-click in the Oblique Angle edit box and enter **10**. Try clicking on some of the check-box items in the Effects section of the dialog box, and notice the changes to the Character Preview display.

Make sure none of the Effects check-box items are selected, click on Apply, then Close.

`Regenerating drawing.` Regenerates text with new style

After you complete the exercise, your STANDARD style uses the smoother ROMANS font and is slanted (italicized) and slightly narrower than normal, as shown in figure 17.7. If you zoom back to display the whole drawing, you will notice that the text objects created using the TEXT and DTEXT command have been updated to the new font, but did not acquire the new width or obliquing effects.

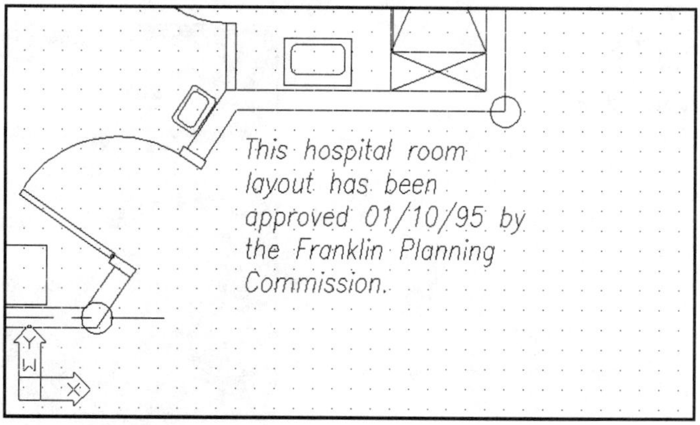

Figure 17.7

The modified STANDARD style.

WARNING

When you change the effects settings of an existing text style, the changes are not applied to existing text objects, and only the width and obliquing effects are applied to existing mtext objects. You can use the DDMODIFY command, select each object in turn, and reselect the style name in the list box, to update text effects.

Text Style Dialog Box Options

The Text Style dialog box comprises four sections—Styles, Character Preview, Font, and Effects. These sections interact to show you the currently defined text styles in your drawings, and enable you to make changes to a variety of settings.

The Styles section displays the current text style in an edit box, and the list of defined styles in a list box. You can make any style current by clicking on it in the list box. If this is all you want to do, simply choose the Close button, and the style you selected becomes the current text style. To make changes to the current style, use the options described below in the Font and Effects sections, and choose Apply, then Close.

You have several other options in the Styles section. If you enter a new style name, or edit the current name, you can choose New to create a new text style. You can also choose Rename to simply rename the current text style to the new or edited name. In either case, the new or renamed style retains all the properties currently set in the other sections of the dialog box.

TIP

Like blocks and layers, you can assign names to the text styles you create that help you remember their appropriate uses, like NOTES, DIMS, or TITLE. Another approach is to simply use the font name for the style name. If your standard text styles have fixed heights, you can combine the font name with a height designation, like ROMANS-125 for 1/8" text. However you do it, setting up meaningful text style names is an easy way to establish and maintain one aspect of your drawing standards.

As long as there are text or mtext objects in the drawing that reference the selected text style, the Delete button is grayed out. If this button is enabled, you can choose it to remove the selected text style definition, equivalent to using the PURGE command. The appearance of this button is a handy way to determine which of the defined text styles is actually used in the drawing.

The Character Preview section shows you a graphic representation of the selected text style. This representation is automatically updated to reflect any changes you make to the other settings in the dialog box, such as entering a different font file or changing the effects. You can specify the characters displayed in the graphic box, by entering them in the edit box below it and choosing Preview.

TIP

Most font files consist of alpha-numeric characters, so when you enter an A, for example, you get that font's version of the character A. However, some font files consist of symbols (for such things as maps, or musical notation), that are *mapped* to the standard alpha-numeric character set. In this case, the Preview option is a handy way to determine the symbols mapped to specific characters.

Choosing the Char. Set button opens the Text Style Symbol Set dialog box, which displays the entire symbol set for the selected text style. The symbols are displayed eight lines at a time, with 32 symbols per line. To move forward and backward through the symbol set, choose the Next or Previous buttons. When you are done viewing the symbol set, choose OK to return to the Text Styles dialog box.

The Font section enables you to specify the font file to associate with the selected text style. Figure 17.8 shows a selected sample of text fonts (in alphabetical order) included with AutoCAD.

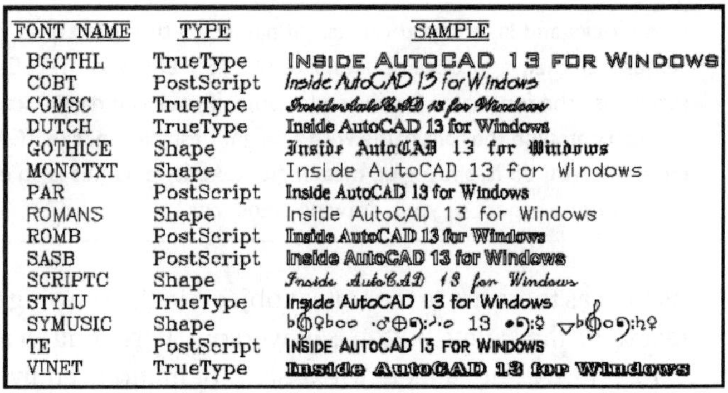

FONT NAME	TYPE	SAMPLE
BGOTHL	TrueType	INSIDE AUTOCAD 13 FOR WINDOWS
COBT	PostScript	Inside AutoCAD 13 for Windows
COMSC	TrueType	Inside AutoCAD 13 for Windows
DUTCH	TrueType	Inside AutoCAD 13 for Windows
GOTHICE	Shape	Inside AutoCAD 13 for Windows
MONOTXT	Shape	Inside AutoCAD 13 for Windows
PAR	PostScript	Inside AutoCAD 13 for Windows
ROMANS	Shape	Inside AutoCAD 13 for Windows
ROMB	PostScript	Inside AutoCAD 13 for Windows
SASB	PostScript	Inside AutoCAD 13 for Windows
SCRIPTC	Shape	Inside AutoCAD 13 for Windows
STYLU	TrueType	Inside AutoCAD 13 for Windows
SYMUSIC	Shape	[illegible]
TE	PostScript	INSIDE AUTOCAD 13 FOR WINDOWS
VINET	TrueType	Inside AutoCAD 13 for Windows

Figure 17.8

AutoCAD font sampler.

NOTE

The previous figure is by no means all-inclusive. AutoCAD ships with many more fonts, and also supports a variety of fonts from third-party vendors. Besides its native source (SHP) and compiled (SHX) shape file font formats, AutoCAD now handles Type I PostScript source (PFB) and compiled (PFA) fonts, as well as Windows TrueType (TTF) fonts. The AutoCAD User's Guide depicts the native AutoCAD fonts, as well as the PostScript fonts supplied, in its Standard Libraries appendix. A sample drawing called TRUETYPE.DWG shows an example of each of the included TrueType fonts.

To specify a font file, enter its name in the Font File edit box, adding the drive and path if it is not located on your AutoCAD search path. You also can choose the Browse button to open the Select Font File dialog box (refer to fig. 17.6). The Select Font File dialog box has a Files of Type list box, from which you can choose one of three file specifications corresponding to the file types AutoCAD recognizes as font files. The default filespec includes all three font file types. You can use the drives and directories list boxes to locate a font file, then choose OK. The selected file name with the full path is entered in the Font File edit box.

Warning

When you use the Select Font File dialog box to specify the font file, the full path is stored with the font file name for the style. This can cause problems if another user tries to open the drawing on a system that does not have the same path structure. In this case, AutoCAD uses the TXT font and/or displays an error message.

To prevent this error, if you use the Select Font File dialog box to load a font file which is on your path, highlight the drive and path in the edit box and delete it, leaving just the file name. This stores the font name without a path. If you encounter this error in an existing drawing, redefine the style, using the same process to remove the path string from the font file name.

The Font section also includes the Bigfont edit box, along with its corresponding Browse button. *Bigfonts* are font files which can include and access thousands of characters, beyond the range possible using the ASCII codes. They are most commonly used for Asian languages, fractions, or other extensive symbol collections. The use of bigfonts is not covered in this book.

Finally, the Effects section of the Text Style dialog box enables you to apply a variety of effects to modify the appearance of the selected font. You can combine all the available effects to create distinct text styles. The effects settings include:

- **Height.** If you enter a value other than zero in the height edit box, all text and mtext objects which reference this text style will be drawn with the specified height. This is referred to as *fixed height* text. A 0 in this edit box specifies *variable height* text. When you create text using a variable height style, you are prompted for the text's height. Negative values for height are not permitted.

- **Width Factor.** A width factor of 1.0 draws text using the character widths and spacing defined in the font file. Setting this value greater than 1.0 expands the text width; values less than 1.0 compress the text. Like height, negative width factors are not permitted.

- **Oblique Angle.** You can enter an angle value in the Oblique Angle edit box to specify a slant for the text. A 0 value draws text with no slant angle applied. Positive oblique angles slant the text to the right, giving an *italic* effect, negative values slant to the left.

- **Upside down.** If the Upside down check box is checked, text drawn with this style is mirrored vertically.

- **Backwards.** If the Backwards check box is checked, text drawn with this style is mirrored horizontally.

- **Vertical.** If you specify a native AutoCAD (SHX) font file which is defined with the vertical option, you can check the Vertical check box to cause text to be drawn vertically. PostScript and TrueType fonts do not support this option.

When you select a different font file, or make changes to the effects settings, the Character Preview graphic box is usually updated. If not, click on the Preview button. To apply the changes to the currently selected text style, choose Apply. If you have made changes to any of these settings and choose Close without first choosing Apply, AutoCAD displays an alert box asking if you want to apply the changes. Choosing No in this alert box discards any changes.

Using the STYLE Command

AutoCAD also includes the STYLE command, which is the command-line predecessor of the DDSTYLE command. The STYLE command enables you to create and modify text styles with all the same options as the Text Style dialog box, but without the preview feature. The STYLE command provides the following options:

- **Style name.** This option prompts you to name a new style to create or an existing style to edit. This style becomes the current default.

- **?.** This option lists named styles defined in the current drawing. You can enter an asterisk (the default) to list all named styles or use wild cards to list a specific set of styles.

- **Font file.** This option prompts you to specify a font file name for the style to reference. The default <TXT> references the TXT.SHX file.

- **Height.** This option prompts you to specify text height for a fixed height style, or enter **0** (the default) for a variable-height style. Text commands do not prompt for height unless you use a variable-height style.

- **Width factor.** This option prompts you for a width factor to expand or condense text (default 1 = normal).
- **Obliquing angle.** This option prompts you to specify a number to slant the text characters, italicizing them (default 0 = vertical). To slant toward the right, use a positive number; to slant toward the left, use a negative number.
- **Backwards.** This option mirrors text horizontally.
- **Upside-down.** This option mirrors text vertically.
- **Vertical.** This option stacks text vertically, each character below the preceding one.

Managing Text Style Features

Using text styles effectively enables you to produce drawings which are highly legible, make clear distinctions between different kinds of annotation, and look professional. Consider some of the following aspects of applying text styles in your drawings:

- Text styles offer an excellent opportunity to establish drawing standards. For example, creating a series of fixed height text styles, although somewhat inflexible, helps to ensure that drawings have a consistent appearance.
- Rather than define a standard set of styles each time you begin a new drawing, simply add your standard styles to your default prototype drawing. Or, save them as part of another drawing file and insert them as a block (this does not override any existing definitions in an existing drawing).
- Avoid using too many different fonts within a drawing. Consider using a simple font (like ROMANS) in several sizes. You can use different colors which plot with different line widths to differentiate between standard and bold text.
- Limit a text style's obliquing angle to within 20 degrees. A little slant goes a long way!

Font Mapping and Substitution

AutoCAD accesses a variety of support files when you open a drawing for its initial screen display. In particular, AutoCAD checks to ensure that all the font files exist because text styles are linked to separate font files. If a font file does not exist or is linked to an invalid directory path, AutoCAD will either use an alternate font or display an error message and prompt for an alternative font file.

These situations can arise if you fail to load all the fonts during AutoCAD installation (see Appendix A for details). Another problematic scenario that involves missing fonts can occur if you send a drawing on disk to another user at another site. The drawing can contain styles linked to third-party, separately purchased font files. If the font files are not included on the disk (which could be a license infringement), the second user cannot access and exactly match the corresponding styles.

WARNING

Text styles are stored in the DWG file, but the fonts they reference are not. The font file must be available when the drawing is loaded. If it is not, AutoCAD might use the TXT font and display error messages.

AutoCAD Release 13 provides a new mechanism, font mapping, to substitute and link text styles between otherwise incompatible systems. There are three components to AutoCAD's font mapping. First, the FONTALT system variable specifies a single alternate font for AutoCAD to use if it cannot find the requested font file. If an alternate font is specified for FONTALT, it is used during the drawing session, but the style is not redefined. The default for FONTALT is TXT. If FONTALT is not set, you will see an error message and a prompt or dialog box requesting a font selection. Selecting a font redefines the style, but if you close the drawing without making other changes, you are not prompted to save the change. Second, you can force multiple font translations, or *mappings*, on a one-to-one basis, by setting the FONTMAP system variable to the name and extension of a font mapping file. On each line of this file, specify a single font mapping by separating the original and substitute fonts with a semicolon, as in the following line:

```
complex;c:\windows\system\cour.ttf
```

When you specify the original font name, omit the directory name or path. After the semicolon, specify the substituted font name with the file-name extension. Unless it can be found on AutoCAD's support path, specify the file. The preceding example replaces Complex compiled shape font with the Courier TrueType font. Font mappings specified by FONTMAP override the fonts for the drawing session, but do not redefine the style or cause any change in the drawing file—they only change the displayed and plotted appearance.

The third type of font mapping controls the fonts used by Windows to display text in the Edit MText dialog box. It does not affect the fonts seen in the drawing, only those seen in the Edit MText dialog box while editing. MTEXT requires two font specifications: the font displayed in the drawing and the font displayed in the Edit MText dialog box while editing. Like all dialog boxes, it uses only standard Windows fonts for display while editing. AutoCAD drawing fonts are mapped to Windows fonts for display in the Edit MText dialog box by settings in the MTE Fonts section of the ACAD.INI file, formatted like the following:

```
 [MTE Fonts]
txt=Arial;400;0
...
romans=Times New Roman;400;0
C:\WINDOWS\SYSTEM\BGOTHL.TTF=BankGothic Lt BT;400;0
```

These specify mappings in the following format:

<name>=<face>;<weight>;<italic>

where:

name	AutoCAD font name
face	Windows typeface name
weight	1–1000, or 0 for default
italic	0 for normal or 1 for italic

If the mapped fonts don't closely match in character width, then the word-wrapping in the Edit MText dialog box might differ from that seen in the mtext paragraph in the drawing.

If MTEXT does not find a font mapping for the specified drawing font, even if it is also already loaded as a Windows font, it opens the Select Font dialog box for an editing font selection. Even if you select a standard Windows font and a drawing font, MTEXT prompts you to select it again for the display font while editing. The selections you make are then written to the ACAD.INI file as font mappings for future use.

You can add mappings directly to the ACAD.INI file by using the Windows Notepad text editor. Editing the INI file is the only way to change a mapping. If the AutoCAD font is not on the support path, you must specify a full path, as shown in the last line of the preceding example. You can select Windows fonts and drawing fonts, and can load AutoCAD's TTF and PostScript fonts as Windows fonts.

TIP

Loading AutoCAD TrueType and PostScript fonts into Windows enables you to select them as editing fonts in the Select Font dialog box, for a perfect match between drawing and editing fonts. To manipulate Windows fonts, open Control Panel and choose the Fonts icon to open the Fonts dialog box. The Fonts dialog box has a Help button that provides more information. Load the desired fonts from the \ACADR13\COMMON\FONTS directory.

You can also specify an MTE font-mapping file by choosing Options, Preferences, Misc in AutoCAD. Type the full path of the font mapping file, then choose OK. The format of the mapping file is the same as for the ACAD.INI MTE Fonts section.

The FONTMAP.PS and FONTMAP.BD files in the FONTS directory are not for the type of font mapping discussed here. They are used by AutoCAD's PostScript engine for PostScript font mapping.

The SAVEASR12 command redefines any text style that uses an R13-specific font to use the TXT font.

Formatting Text

When you use the TEXT or DTEXT command to place text in a drawing, AutoCAD needs to know the format. The following options are available during text placement. The following four options apply to the initial `Justify/Style/<start point>:` prompt:

- **Justify.** This option issues the prompt for text justification. You also can enter justification directly at the `Justify/Style/<start point>:` prompt, or let it default to left justification.
- **Style.** This option specifies a new text style default. The style must have already been created with the STYLE command.
- **Start point.** This default option specifies the bottom left justification point.
- **Press Enter.** This option highlights the last text entered and prompts for a new text string when you press Enter at the prompt. AutoCAD places the new

text directly below the highlighted text, using the same style, height, and rotation. When you use DTEXT, you also can specify a new pick point before you enter the text.

After you specify the above information, you are prompted for each of the following options:

- **Height.** This option specifies the text height (the default is 0.2). The height prompt is omitted if you use Align justification or any text style that has a predefined nonzero height.
- **Rotation angle.** This option specifies the baseline angle for text placement (the default is 0).
- **Text.** This option specifies the text string.

The default height shown in the TEXT command is rounded off to your units setting and might not accurately display its true value.

When you use AutoCAD text, you need to consider two angles. The *obliquing angle* is the slant of each character, and you use the DDSTYLE command to control it. The *rotation angle* is the slope of the text baseline, and you control it by using the TEXT, DTEXT, and MTEXT commands.

TIP

Whenever AutoCAD prompts for a text-related height or angle, it displays a rubber-band line from the start point to the cursor. To indicate the desired measurement, you can pick a point rather than type a value. When you do so, use snap for precision.

Text Justification

Justification (or alignment) specifies the positioning of the text, relative to the start and optional endpoint(s) you specify. The justification prompt shows all the options:

```
Align/Fit/Center/Middle/Right/TL/TC/TR/ML/MC/MR/BL/BC/BR:
```

The following list describes each option:

- **Align.** Specify the beginning and ending points of the text baseline. The text height is scaled so that the text between these points is not distorted.

- **Fit.** Specify the beginning and ending points of the text baseline. The text width is distorted to fit the text between these points without changing the height.
- **Center.** Specify a point for the horizontal center and the vertical baseline of the text string.
- **Middle.** Specify a point for the horizontal and vertical midpoint of the text string.
- **Right.** Specify a point for the right baseline of the text string.
- **TL.** Specify a point for the left of the text string, aligned with the top of the tallest character.
- **TC.** Specify a point for the center of the text string, aligned with the top of an uppercase character.
- **TR.** Specify a point for the right side of the text string, aligned with the top of an uppercase character.
- **ML.** Specify a point for the left side of the text string, aligned halfway between the top of an uppercase character and the text baseline.
- **MC.** Specify a point for the center of the text string, aligned halfway between an uppercase character and the bottom of the text baseline.
- **MR.** Specify a point for the right side, between the top of an uppercase character and the text baseline.
- **BL.** Specify a point for the left side of the text string, aligned at the bottom of a descender.
- **BC.** Specify a point for the center of the text string, aligned at the bottom of a descender.
- **BR.** Specify a point for the right side of the text string, aligned at the bottom of a descender.

Figure 17.9 presents a graphical depiction of each option. Once you have learned these options, you can enter them directly at the `Justify/Style/<start point>:` prompt, without first specifying the Justify option.

Figure 17.9

Text justification options.

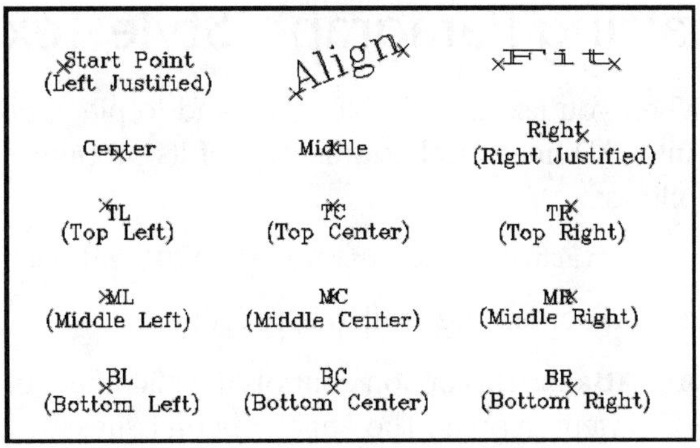

The TL, TC, TR, ML, MC, MR, BL, BC, and BR justifications are the nine possible combinations of the Top, Middle, and Bottom vertical alignments and the Left, Center, and Right horizontal alignments. The default Left and the simple Center and Right justifications all are baseline alignments, which could have fit into this same matrix if B was not already taken by Bottom. You cannot use Fit-, TL-, TC-, TR-, ML-, MC-, MR-, BL-, BC-, and BR-justified text with vertical text styles; the others work vertically or horizontally.

Middle-justified text (unlike ML, MC, and MR) floats vertically, depending on whether the particular text string includes uppercase characters or characters that have descenders. The other options have three vertical positions relative to a standard text cell height of a capital letter. The options TL, TC, TR, ML, MC, MR, BL, BC, and BR each maintain vertical text positioning, regardless of the string entered. Middle is designed to always be centered in both axes, for use in bubbles and similar applications. The other justifications are designed to give consistent results for most other applications.

TIP

If you respond to the DTEXT (or TEXT) start point prompt by pressing Enter, the new text starts one line below the last text you entered in the drawing. The new text assumes the height, style, and justification of the previous text, even if you have used intervening AutoCAD commands.

Formatting Paragraph-Style Text

When you use the MTEXT command to place paragraph-style text in a drawing, AutoCAD needs to know several of its properties. The initial prompt appears as follows:

```
Attach/Rotation/Style/Height/Direction/<Insertion point>:
```

Several options are available, as follows:

- **Attach.** This option controls the alignment of the text boundary to the insertion point. The Attach option issues the `TL/TC/TR/ML/MC/MR/BL/BC/BR:` attachment prompt, where T = top, M = middle, B = bottom, L = left, C = center, and R = right. TL (top left) is the default if you do not specify an attachment. You also can enter any of these attachment options directly at the `<insertion point>:` prompt without first using the Attach option. Attachment determines text justification and spill. Justification governs the text alignment to the left, center, or right of the text boundary, as in DTEXT. Spill manages the way excess text flows from the text boundary.
- **Rotation.** This option specifies the baseline angle of the text boundary.
- **Style.** This option specifies the default style used by the mtext paragraph. The style must already have been created with the STYLE command; its name, however, can later be changed within the Edit MText dialog box.
- **Height.** This option specifies the default height of uppercase text for the mtext paragraph. This value can be changed within the Edit MText dialog box.
- **Direction.** This option specifies the drawing direction (horizontal or vertical) of the paragraph text. In early versions of Release 13, vertical does not work correctly.
- **Insertion point.** This option (the default) specifies the text boundary corner at its insertion point. This is the upper left corner of the paragraph, unless you first specify a different attachment. The insertion point is a grip point and can be snapped with the INSertion object snap.

If you respond to the insertion point prompt, AutoCAD presents three additional options:

- **Width.** This option specifies the horizontal width of the text boundary. You can pick a point to indicate the width, or enter a width value.

- **2Points.** This option specifies the width of the text boundary, by specifying any two points.
- **Other corner.** This option (the default) specifies the diagonally opposite corner of the text boundary that the prompt implies. The point you specify does not define the extents, direction, justification, or spill of the mtext paragraph—only its width.

The default style and height properties used by the mtext paragraph are the current text settings stored in the TEXTSTYLE and TEXTSIZE system variables, which are set by the prototype drawing or the TEXT or DTEXT commands (the current style can also be set by the STYLE command). The default style and height properties can be changed by MTEXT command options or by the Text Style and Text Height settings in the MText Properties dialog box (choose Properties in the Edit MText dialog box). The settings set by MTEXT do not affect the TEXT or DTEXT commands or the TEXTSTYLE and TEXTSIZE system variables.

An important concept in understanding how MTEXT works is that the mtext object has default *properties* (including style and height) but each character within the mtext object can have character *attributes* (including font and height) assigned to it, much like assigning italic or bold in a word processor. The default properties are overridden by the character attribute settings in the Edit MText dialog box, as you see in the following exercise.

In this exercise, you use several options to place an MTEXT paragraph.

Using MTEXT Paragraph Insertion Options

Continue in the CHAP17 drawing from the preceding exercise. Zoom to the view shown in figure 17.12.

`Command:` *Choose Text (Draw, Text)*	Issues the MTEXT command
`_mtext`	
`Attach/Rotation/Style/Height/Direction/ <Insertion point>:` **A** ↵	Specifies the Attach option
`TL/TC/TR/ML/MC/MR/BL/BC/BR:` **BL** ↵	Specifies bottom left attachment
`Attach/Rotation/Style/Height/Direction/ <Insertion point>:` **H** ↵	Specifies the text Height option
`Height <0'-6">:` **4"** ↵	Changes text height to 4"

`Attach/Rotation/Style/Height/Direction/` `<Insertion point>:` *Pick* ① *(see fig. 17.12)*	Specifies the lower left corner
`Attach/Rotation/Style/Height/Direction/` `Width/2Points/<Other corner>:` *Pick* ②	Specifies width and displays Edit MText dialog box (see fig. 17.10)

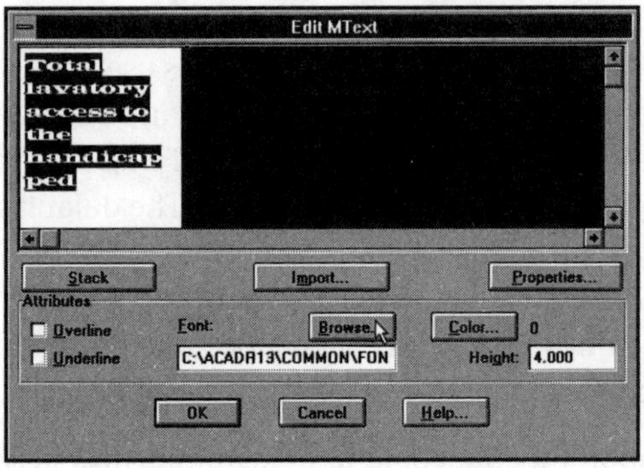

Figure 17.10

Completed paragraph text.

Notice that the default Font is shown as romans and Height as 4.000.

Enter **Revise to meet**	Displays text in Times New Roman typeface, as mapped in ACAD.INI file
Choose Browse	Opens the Change Font dialog box
Change Directories *to* C:\ACADR13\COMMON\FONTS, *select* *.pfb *from the* List of Files Type: *list box, then from the* File Name *list box,* cibt____.pfb, *then choose* OK	Specifies AutoCAD's City Blueprint PostScript font and opens the Select Font *dialog box*
Open the list box, select Arial, *then choose* Italic	Displays sample of editing typeface (see fig. 17.11)

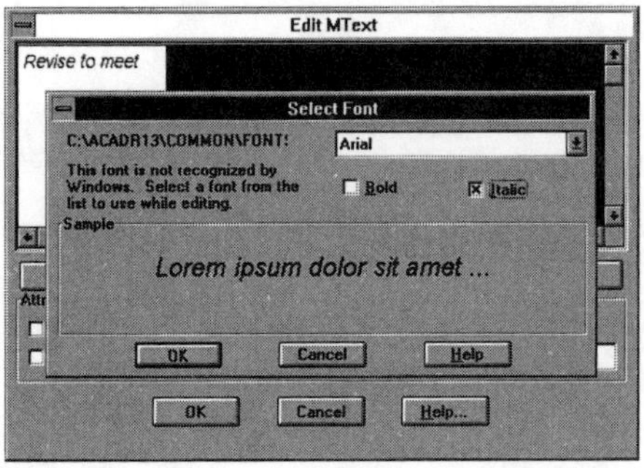

Figure 17.11

Sample typeface in the Select Font dialog box.

Choose OK	Closes the Select Font dialog box, writes new mapping to the ACAD.INI, and returns to the Edit MText dialog box

Watch the typeface closely as you enter the following text.

Enter **accessibility standards**	Displays text in Arial italic as you type

In early versions of R13, the text may revert to Times New Roman when it starts to word-wrap. If so, don't worry; the next step fixes it.

Press and drag from the first to the last character of the text, choose Browse, *select* File Name cibt.pfb, *then choose* OK	Selects all the text, opens Change Font dialog box, specifies font, and returns to the Edit MText dialog box

This time, the Select Font dialog box didn't appear because the City Blueprint to Arial italic mapping was already defined. All the display text is now shown in the Arial italic typeface.

Choose OK	Closes Edit MText dialog box and draws the text in the City Blueprint PostScript font, as shown in figure 17.12

Save the drawing.

Figure 17.12 shows the results of this exercise.

Figure 17.12

Inserted paragraph text.

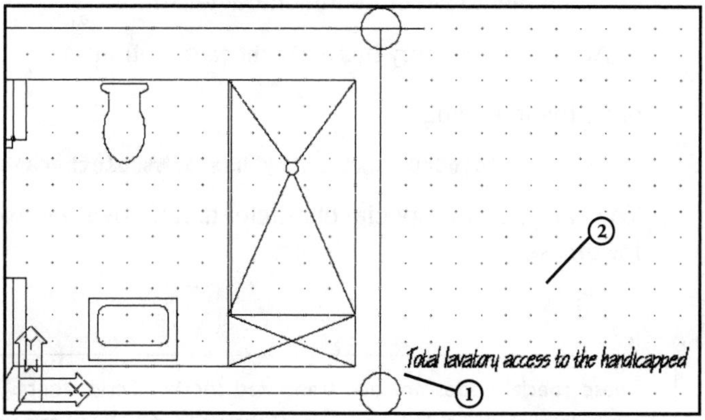

Using Special Characters with TEXT or DTEXT

Some symbols used in engineering drawings are not found on standard keyboards. These symbols include underscores, overscores, plus/minus, and so on. To generate these symbols, you type special code entries that AutoCAD will translate, as shown in table 17.1.

Table 17.1

Special Characters with TEXT, DTEXT, or MTEXT

Code Entry	*Unicode Entry*	*Symbol Translation*
%%O		Overscore
%%U		Underline
%%D	%\U+00B0	Degree
%%C	%\U+2205	Circle diameter
%%P	%\U+00B1	Plus/minus

The %%*x* codes are interchangeable with the TEXT, DTEXT, and MTEXT commands. Unicode codes provide better international compatibility.

For example, to generate the character string

AutoCAD text entry has a `plethora` of options.

enter the following:

```
Text: AutoCAD text entry has a %%uplethora%%u of options. ↵
```

You can enter the special character that follows the two percent signs in upper- or lowercase.

NOTE

These special codes are not translated for PostScript fonts. International and special symbols, such as %%213, are properly translated by PostScript output; however, they do not display translated in the drawing on screen.

In the following exercise, use DTEXT to dynamically enter multiple lines of text that include special symbols.

USING DTEXT SPECIAL CHARACTERS

Continue from the previous exercise, in the CHAP17 drawing, and zoom to the area shown in figure 17.14.

`Command:` *Choose Dtext (Draw, Text)*	Issues the DTEXT command
`_dtext Justify/Style/ <Start point>:` *Pick ① (see fig. 17.13)*	Specifies text insertion point
`Height <0'-6">:` **4"** ↵	Specifies text height
`Rotation angle <0>:` ↵	Specifies baseline rotation
`Text:` **Due to the nature of convalesince,** ↵	Misspells first text line (see fig 17.13) and spaces down to next line
`Text:` **do %%Unot%%u use 68%%D** ↵	Specifies second text line, displaying %% codes
`Text:` **thermostat setback.** ↵	Specifies third text line
`Text:` ↵	Completes DTEXT entry and redraws text with underline and degree symbol

Save the drawing.

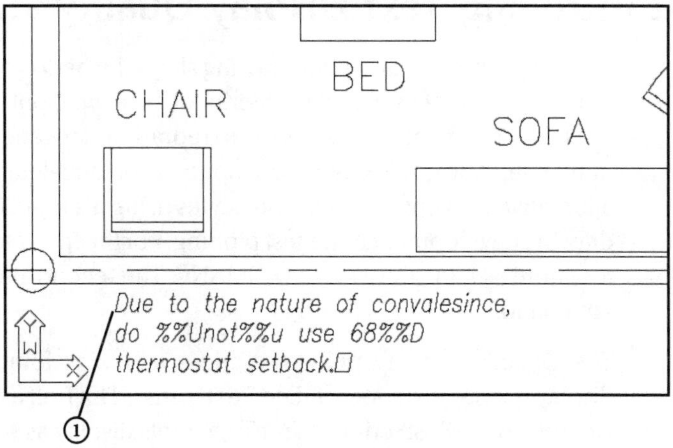

Figure 17.13

DTEXT during text entry with special characters code.

Figure 17.14

Completed DTEXT with formatted.

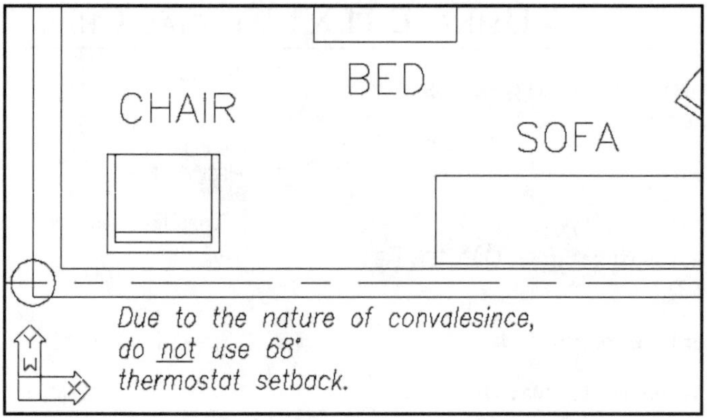

As you type DTEXT entries, AutoCAD displays the characters without modification or justification. When you type the final Enter on a separate line, AutoCAD translates any special character %% sequences and rejustifies the text as requested.

When you look at figures 17.13 and 17.14, you probably will notice a misspelled word. Don't worry—that was intentional! You use AutoCAD Release 13's new spelling checker to fix it later.

Controlling Text Display Quality and Speed

Adding many objects to your drawing slows the performance of subsequent zooms, redraws, and regens. Filled PostScript or TrueType fonts and multistroke fonts such as COMPLEX are particularly slow to redraw and regenerate. To decrease regeneration time, AutoCAD offers two options for accelerating text display. The first alternative is to enter all text with styles using a simple font, such as TXT, for initial drawing development or for test plotting. For the final plot, you can define the styles to a more elegant font, such as ROMANC. The second alternative is to use the QTEXT command.

The Options, Display pull-down menu contains four selections that affect text display quality and speed. Filled Text turns QTEXT off and sets the TEXTFILL system variable to 1—PostScript or TrueType fonts display as solid-filled. Outline Text also turns QTEXT off but sets TEXTFILL to 0—these font types then display in outline form. Text Frame Only turns QTEXT on. Finally, Text Quality sets the TEXTQLTY system variable to adjust the font display resolution. A higher value yields a smoother appearance.

As shown in figures 17.15 and 17.16, turning on quick text mode reduces the regeneration time for drawings that contain many text objects.

Figure 17.15

QTEXT turned on.

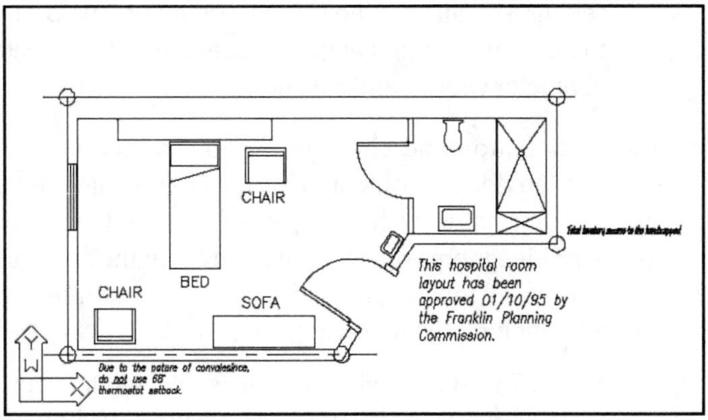

Figure 17.16

QTEXT turned off.

NOTE

The effect of turning QTEXT on or off is not seen until the next regeneration.

The next section illustrates character formatting for MTEXT paragraphs.

Using Special Characters and Formats with MTEXT

MTEXT provides greater flexibility with formatting options than TEXT or DTEXT. There are several formatting properties and character attributes you can apply to MTEXT paragraphs. As you read the following, remember that an mtext object has global default *properties* (including style and height), but each character within the mtext object can have overriding character *attributes* (including font and height) assigned to it.

With the MText Properties dialog box (choose Properties in the Edit MText dialog box), you can change the following overall default properties of the mtext object:

- **Content properties.** The options in the Content Properties section change the settings specified at the MTEXT command-line prompts and affect the default format of the entire mtext paragraph: Text Style, Text Height, and Direction. In some early versions of Release 13, the Direction setting is ignored.
- **Object properties.** The options in the Object Properties section change the settings specified at the MTEXT command-line prompts and affect the form of the entire mtext paragraph: Attachment, Width (of the paragraph, not character width), and Rotation.

The Stack button and character Attributes section of the Edit MText dialog box override the default content properties to change the appearance of the text you subsequently enter, or the text you select prior to specifying attributes. Text with a font override ignores subsequent changes in the Style property, but still is affected by changes in the Height and Direction properties. The Edit MText character overrides include the following:

- **Stack.** The Stack button reformats selected text containing a slash as numerator over denominator. For example, 3/16 or this/that would be reformatted as:

  $\frac{3}{16}$ $\frac{\text{this}}{\text{that}}$

- **Attributes.** The character attributes you specify affect the text you subsequently type, or the text you preselect before choosing attributes. The Attributes section contains the following options:
  - **Overline.** The Overline button applies overscore character formatting.
  - **Underline.** The Underline button applies underline character formatting.

- **Font and Browse.** The Font option enables you to specify a font file override by entering its name in the Font edit box. The Browse button opens the Change Font dialog box for font file override specification. If you specify a font that does not have a defined mapping, the Select Font dialog box is opened for selection of a Windows font for display in the Edit MText dialog box while editing.
- **Color.** The Color button opens the Select Color dialog box for color specification.
- **Height.** The Height edit box accepts a character height override.

The height attribute setting overrides the global height property setting. If you have text with the height property set to 0.2 and use the Height input box in the Attributes section of the main Edit MText dialog box to assign a height of 0.3 to selected characters, then you will have some text with a height of 0.2 and some with a height of 0.3. Then, if you use Properties to change the global height to 0.4, the change is applied globally in proportion: the 0.2 default-height text becomes 0.4 and the 0.3 overridden-height text becomes 0.6 high.

As you type text in the Edit MText dialog box, the input cursor assumes the character settings of the following character for new input. If nothing is selected when you make new settings, the text you enter uses those settings until you move the input cursor.

In the Edit MText dialog box, you can enter the following keys and special Unicode codes to create special formatting or characters for the degree symbol, plus/minus tolerance symbol, and the diameter symbol:

- **Press Enter.** Press Enter while typing text to force a new line.
- **%\U+00B0.** Enter %\U+00B0 (or %%D) to draw a degree symbol.
- **%\U+00B1.** Enter %\U+00B1 (or %%P) to draw a plus/minus tolerance symbol.
- **%\U+2205.** Enter %\U+2205 (or %%C) to draw a diameter symbol.

In the following exercise, you use MTEXT to enter a paragraph that includes text stacking and character changes.

USING MTEXT PARAGRAPH FORMATTING

Continue from the preceding exercise in the CHAP17 drawing, and zoom to the extents.

`Command:` *Choose Text (Draw, Text)*	Issues the MTEXT command
`_mtext`	
`Attach/Rotation/Style/Height/Direction/ <Insertion point>:` *Pick ① (see fig. 17.17)*	Specifies the upper left corner
`Attach/Rotation/Style/Height/Direction/ Width/2Points/<Other corner>:` **24',17'** ↵	Specifies the paragraph width and opens the Edit MText dialog box
Type **HOSPITAL ROOM LAYOUT by HIGH/LOW Associates**	Enters text in the Edit MText dialog box, using the default style
Press and drag from the first to the last character of the text, then enter DUTCH *in the* Font *edit box and press Enter*	Selects all of the text, finds DUTCH.TTF font in FONTS directory, then opens the Select Font dialog box
Open the drop-down list and select a font for display, then choose OK	Specifies display font for MText Edit dialog box, closes Select Font dialog box, and reformats text
Select text HIGH/LOW *and choose* Color	Opens Select Color dialog box
Click on the red box in Standard Colors, *then choose* OK	Sets color of HIGH/LOW to red (appears green while selected)
Enter **3** *in* Height *box and press Enter*	Changes height of HIGH/LOW
Choose Stack	Places HIGH over LOW (see fig. 17.18)
Choose OK	Draws the text in the drawing (see fig. 17.17)

Save the drawing.

Figure 17.17

Completed MTEXT paragraph formatting.

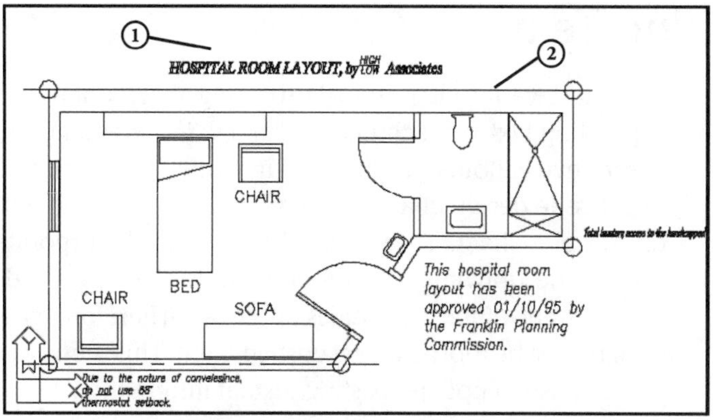

Figure 17.18

The Edit MText dialog box with text stacking.

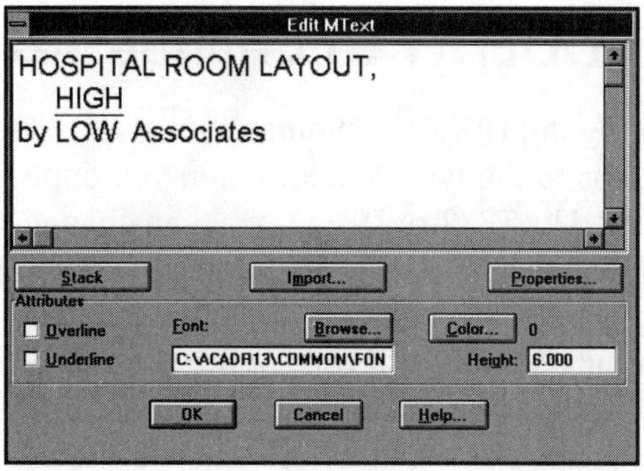

Figure 17.17 shows the results of this exercise. In early versions of Release 13, the color, height, or font of the stacked text might not correctly display.

Editing existing mtext paragraph text works exactly the same as creating it. See the "Editing Paragraph Text" exercise later in this chapter for more examples of applying attributes and properties in the Edit MText dialog box.

TIP

Use the LIST command to examine the properties and font codes of an MTEXT object.

Editing Text

You must verify an AutoCAD drawing that contains both graphic objects and supporting text for technical accuracy. If the geometry is not consistent with the descriptive callouts, you lose the integrity of the design. For example, an architect might issue design changes to an initial proposed layout and place revision marks on the plot sheet. Then, the CAD operator incorporates these modifications to update the drawing. The process could then proceed through several revision phases, until a final proposal is approved. Therefore, checking and rechecking the design must be thorough, yet cost-efficient. This section covers the various methods you can use to update existing textual information.

Using DDEDIT to Change Text

Issuing the DDEDIT command presents selected text in a dialog box that corresponds to the type of text. When you apply the DDEDIT command to an object created by TEXT or DTEXT, you can change the characters of a single line of text. Applied to an attdef (see Chapter 10, "Basic Building Blocks for Repetitive Drawing"), DDEDIT enables you to change the tag, prompt, and default values of the attribute definition. If you apply it to an object, DDEDIT opens the same Edit MText dialog box as does the MTEXT command. The only difference between accessing this dialog box with DDEDIT and with MTEXT is that DDEDIT presents the selected text. You can change any of the properties and attributes of the text in the Edit MText dialog box.

Selecting a text object opens the Edit Text dialog box. When the Edit Text dialog box appears, AutoCAD highlights the entire string for replacement. Clicking in the box positions the cursor. Any new text is inserted at the cursor's location and replaces all highlighted text. Choosing OK closes the dialog box and applies the changes. The command continues to prompt for another text string to edit until you press Enter at the next selection prompt or cancel the command. You also can enter U to undo the previous change.

Changing TEXT or DTEXT Objects

In the next exercise, you use DDEDIT to make a simple change to a line of text. You modify one of the furniture text labels.

Changing a Single Text Label

Continue the CHAP17 drawing from the preceding exercise. If you did not perform or save the results of the earlier DTEXT exercise, use DTEXT to label the chair, as shown in figure 17.20, then continue.

`Command:` *Choose Edit Text (Modify, Special Edit) (see fig. 17.19)*	Issues the DDEDIT command
`_ddedit`	
`<Select a TEXT or ATTDEF object>/Undo:` *Pick the text* CHAIR *next to the bed*	Opens the Edit Text dialog box with the with the existing text highlighted
Type **RECLINER** *(see fig. 17.20), then choose* OK	Closes dialog box, replaces text, and reprompts
`<Select a TEXT or ATTDEF object>/ Undo:` ↵	Exits the DDEDIT command

Save the drawing.

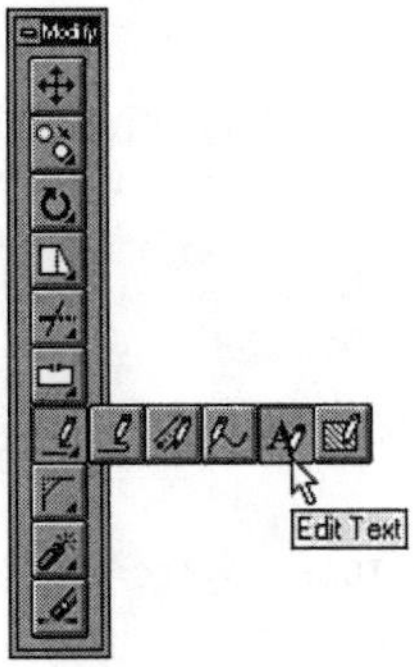

Figure 17.19

The Edit Text (DDEDIT) toolbar icon.

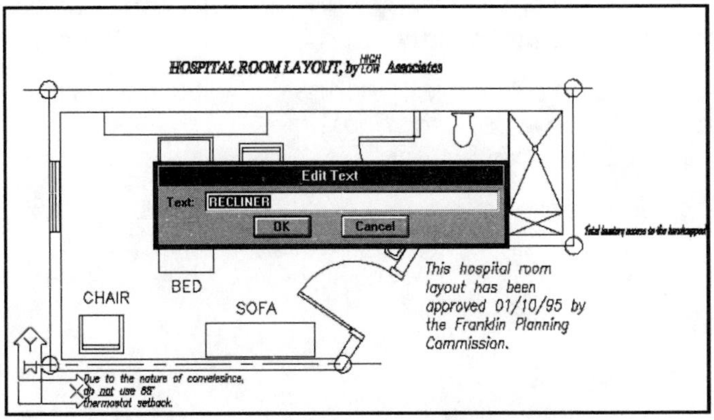

Figure 17.20

Modifying single-line text using the Edit Text dialog box.

TIP

The Windows cut-and-paste feature is a handy way to move text from one string to another. In the Edit Text dialog box, highlight the string you want and press Ctrl+Ins to store it (copy) or Shift+Del to store and delete it (cut). Then close the dialog box and select the second text string to receive the text. Position the cursor in the second text string in the Edit Text dialog box, and press Shift+Ins to insert it.

You also can use the cut-and-paste feature to import and export text and graphic objects between AutoCAD and another program by using the Windows Clipboard.

Changing MTEXT objects

In the next exercise, you use DDEDIT to change the content and format of a text paragraph. You change the phrase "hospital room" to "preliminary," underline the name "Franklin Planning Commission," then change the width of the entire paragraph.

EDITING PARAGRAPH TEXT

Continue from the previous exercise in the CHAP17 drawing

`Command:` *Choose Edit Text (Modify, Special Edit)*	Issues the DDEDIT command
`_ddedit`	
`<Select a TEXT or ATTDEF object>/ Undo:` *Pick the* Franklin Planning Commission *paragraph*	Opens the Edit MText dialog box with the selected text displayed
Press and drag over the text hospital room, *and type* **preliminary**	Highlights hospital room and replaces it with preliminary
Press and drag over the text Franklin Planning Commission, *and choose the* Underline *check box*	Underscores the selected text
Choose Properties	Opens the MText Properties dialog box (see fig. 17.21)

Change the Width *to* 70 *and choose* OK	Closes MText Properties dialog box and makes the editing area narrower
Choose OK	Closes Edit MText dialog box and redraws text with changes

Save the drawing.

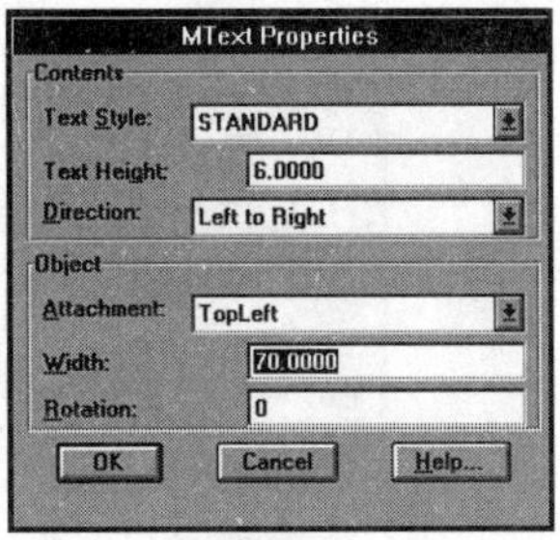

Figure 17.21

The Mtext Properties dialog box.

TIP

> In the preceding exercise, you used the Properties button in the Edit MText dialog box to open the MText Properties dialog box. Another way to change the properties of an existing mtext object is to enter **MTPROP** at the `Command:` prompt.

Importing Text

So far, you have explored various methods for placing and editing text in a drawing. However, all the methods share a common text source—the keyboard. Occasionally, you need the capability to import text from an external file. For example, an engineer or secretary could type job specifications into a word processing document, save it as a plain ASCII file, then hand you the disk or, in a networked environment, load the file into a shared directory.

In the Windows operating environment, you can open and run several applications at once. To bring a text file into a drawing, open the Windows File Manager so that you can drag icons into the AutoCAD graphics window. Then, press and drag the file icon from the directory tree to the AutoCAD drawing. The resulting text appears as an MTEXT object using the current default mtext properties. This import method is called *drag-and-drop*. Dragging and dropping a text file to create an mtext object uses the exact same process as dragging and dropping a drawing file to insert it as a block. This process is shown in an exercise in Chapter 10, "Basic Building Blocks for Repetitive Drawing."

Figure 17.22 shows a text file in File Manager being dragged into the AutoCAD graphics window. Releasing the pointing device in the AutoCAD window inserts the MTEXT object. Then, you can use AutoCAD editing techniques to modify the text.

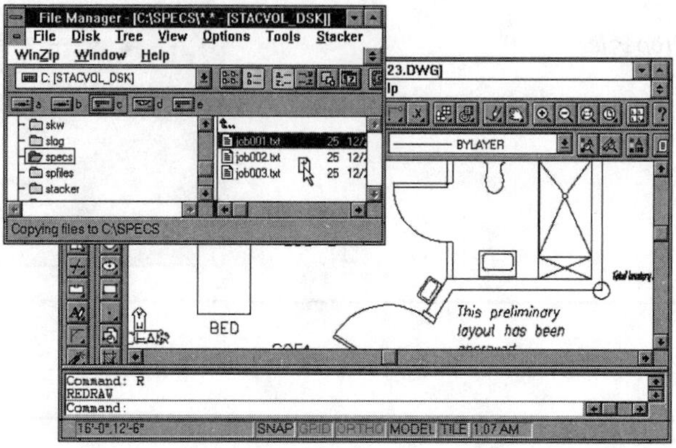

Figure 17.22

Using drag-and-drop to import text.

TIP

If you use the drag-and-drop feature, make sure that the imported text file has a TXT suffix.

In AutoCAD, you need to remember that the versatile Import option in the File pull-down menu works only with graphic formats, not text.

You also can use the Windows Clipboard to import text into AutoCAD, either directly into the drawing or into the Edit MText dialog box. In the Edit MText dialog box, and in most Windows text-based applications, pressing Ctrl+Ins copies selected text to the Windows Clipboard, pressing Ctrl+Del cuts (copies and deletes) it, and pressing Shift+Ins inserts the text from the Clipboard.

The Edit MText dialog box also contains a direct text file import feature. The Import button opens the Import Text File dialog box, which you use to select any ASCII text file. When you specify a file and choose OK, the contents of the file are inserted into the Edit MText dialog box, where you can format and edit the text.

Warning

When you use the Import button to open the MTEXT import feature to import an ASCII text file, the Release 13 for Windows MTEXT command does not translate any mtext formatting codes used in the file. Release 13 for DOS, however, requires these mtext formatting codes in text you import with the MTEXT command. This means that if you import standard text files into both Release 13 for Windows and Release 13 for DOS, you need two sets of files, one set with codes and one without. See New Riders Publishing's *Inside AutoCAD Release 13 for DOS* for these codes. You also can see the codes in Release 13 for Windows by using the LIST command to examine an mtext object.

After you place and edit your text, you are ready to print or plot your drawing. Oh, really? Have you checked your spelling?

For a long time, AutoCAD users bemoaned the lack of a built-in spelling checker. However, this latest release of AutoCAD makes this wish-list item a reality. The next section shows you how to use the AutoCAD Release 13 SPELL command.

Using the Spell Checker

The SPELL command enables you to verify the spelling of any selected text in your drawing. Sometimes AutoCAD flags a word that you know is spelled correctly. By creating and maintaining custom dictionaries, you can store words that AutoCAD never again flags as an error. For example, you can add employee names, product model names, or any industry-specific nomenclature to a custom dictionary.

In the following exercise, you verify the spelling of the text in the hospital room layout drawing.

Using the Spell Checker

Continue in the CHAP17 drawing.

`Command:` *Choose Spelling (Standard)*	Issues the SPELL command
`_spell`	
`Select objects:` **ALL** ↵	Selects all objects in drawing
`77 found`	

`Select objects: ↵`	Ends selection and opens the Check Spelling dialog box (see fig. 17.23)

AutoCAD displays %%unot%%u in the Current Word section—this code confuses the spell checker.

Choose Ignore	Skips to next word

AutoCAD displays the misspelled convalesince in the Current Word section, convalesce in the Suggestions box, and the correct convalescence in the Suggestions list box (see fig. 17.23).

Select convalescence, *then choose* Change	Corrects the spelling and displays box with "Spelling check complete." message
Choose OK	Closes message box and makes correction to drawing

Save the drawing.

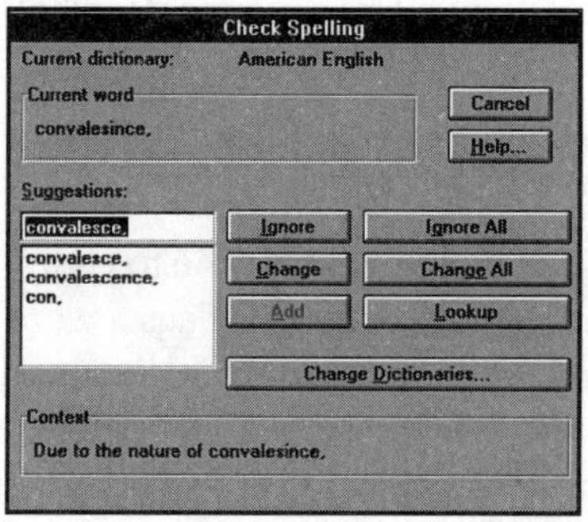

Figure 17.23

The Check Spelling dialog box.

As you saw in the exercise, the spell checker ignores all selected objects except text, mtext, and attdef objects.

In the preceding exercise, you selected all objects in the drawing by simply typing ALL when AutoCAD prompted you. Chapter 14, "The Ins and Outs of Editing," discusses the methods of selecting objects in more detail.

In this chapter, you learned that the TEXT, DTEXT, and MTEXT commands place lines or paragraphs of text into an AutoCAD drawing. Text also can be imported from external files. Using QTEXT optimizes the screen and plotted text display to roughly approximate the actual text characters.

The Text Style dialog box enables you to customize an existing font or create new ones for special purposes. The number and variety of styles are unlimited, truly to generate different strokes for different folks.

Formatting codes can be placed into text to generate special effects, either by character, line, or paragraph. The DDEDIT command is the primary method of editing text, whereas the MTPROP command alters the properties of paragraph-style text.

Finally, the new Release 13 SPELL feature is an extremely powerful tool to ensure that existing text is free of typographical errors.

chapter

18

Linetypes and Hatching

This chapter covers two major features of AutoCAD, linetypes and associative hatching. Linetypes are graphic properties which you can apply to most drawing objects. You use hatching to fill bounded areas with graphic patterns. Both enable you to highlight features in your drawings, add information, and make them clearer and easier to interpret.

This chapter covers the following topics:

- *What linetypes are available*
- *How to assign linetypes to layers and objects*
- *How to edit linetypes of existing objects*
- *How to control the scale of linetypes*
- *How to define your own linetypes*
- *What hatch patterns are available*
- *How to define the areas to be hatched*
- *How to obtain additional hatch patterns*

- The parameters that control the hatching, such as angle and scale factor
- How to edit existing hatched areas

Working with Linetypes

When you use multiple linetypes in your drawing, you have to decide which linetypes you want to use and how you want to assign linetypes to objects.

AutoCAD includes a library of linetypes ready for you to load and use, and enables you to create additional linetype definitions. Three basic categories of linetypes are available (see fig. 18.1):

- Lines that have a repeating pattern of dashes, spaces, or dots
- Lines that have a repeating pattern of text strings, dashes, spaces, or dots
- Lines that have a repeating pattern of shapes, dashes, spaces, or dots

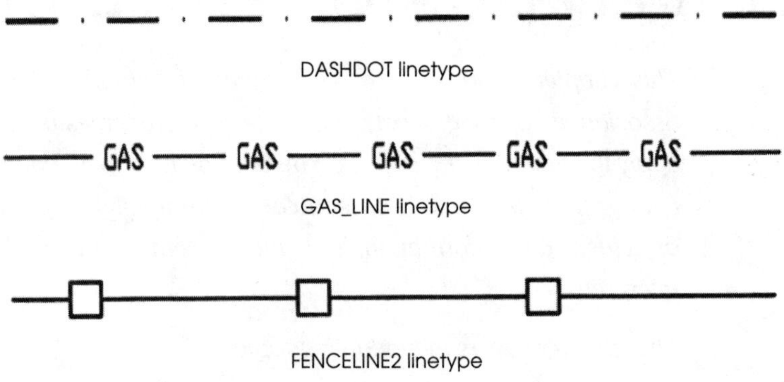

Figure 18.1

Sample linetypes.

Despite the differences in appearance, you define, apply, and edit all linetypes in the same manner.

There are three methods for applying linetypes to an object:

- You can assign linetypes to layers and then draw objects with a current linetype setting of BYLAYER. The BYLAYER setting draws objects using the linetype assigned to the layer they are drawn on.

- You can explicitly set the current linetype setting to the desired linetype. From that point on, all objects drawn will use the current linetype regardless of the layer the objects are drawn on.
- You can change the linetype of existing objects by assigning a linetype explicitly to the object or by moving the object to the layer that has the desired linetype assignment.

Loading Additional Linetypes

By default, new drawings use the continuous linetype. To use any other linetypes, you must first use the DDLTYPE command to open the Select Linetype dialog box. This enables you to load linetypes from the library file ACAD.LIN or the file LTYPESHP.LIN (both stored in the directory \R13\COM\SUPPORT), or other linetype definition files.

In the following exercise, you use the Select Linetype dialog box to load linetypes from the file ACAD.LIN.

Loading Linetypes

Begin a new drawing named CHAP18, using the drawing TOPO from the accompanying CD as the prototype (see fig. 18.2).

`Command:` *Choose Linetype (Object Properties)*	Issues DDLTYPE and opens the Select Linetype dialog box
Choose Load	Opens Load or Reload Linetypes dialog box
Select both DASHED *and* BORDER *from the list of available linetypes, then choose* OK	Selects linetypes to load
Choose OK *again*	Loads linetypes

Now that DASHED and BORDER are loaded in your drawing, you can assign them to objects or layers. Save the drawing.

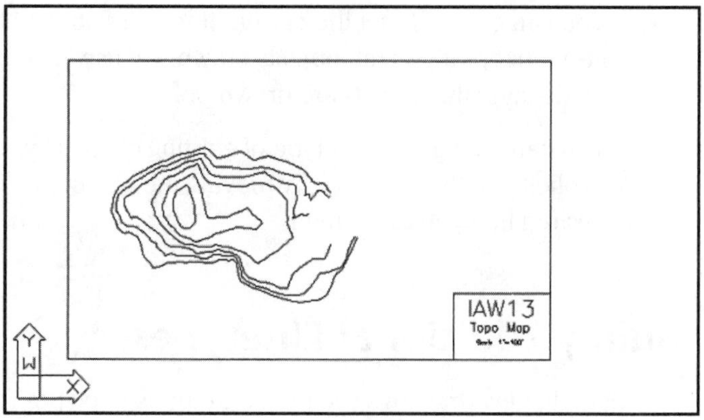

Figure 18.2

The TOPO drawing.

To load additional linetypes into a drawing, use the Load button to open the Load or Reload Linetypes dialog box (see fig. 18.3).

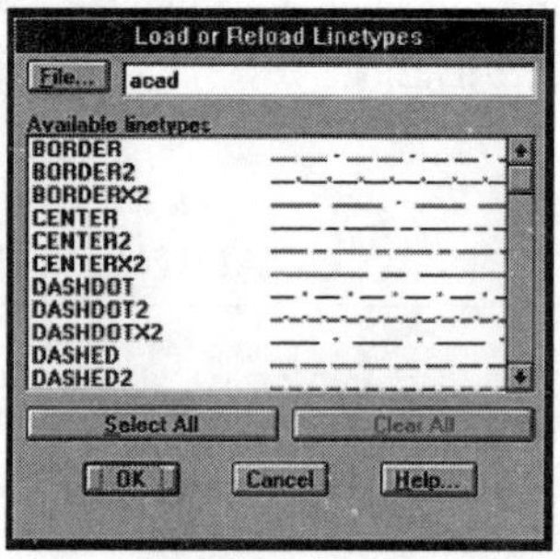

Figure 18.3

The Load or Reload Linetypes dialog box.

By default, the contents of the ACAD.LIN library are listed in the dialog box. ACAD.LIN contains quite an extensive set of linetypes (see fig. 18.4).

NOTE

Not all the linetypes stored in ACAD.LIN are shown in figure 18.4. For each linetype shown, there are two other linetype variations, with names that have the same prefix but end with 2 or X2. In addition to the linetype BORDER, for example, there are two linetypes in ACAD.LIN named BORDER2 and BORDERX2. Linetypes whose names end in 2 have dashes and spaces half as long as those used in the original linetypes. BORDER2, for example, is the same pattern as BORDER, but the lengths of the dashes and spaces are one-half of those used in BORDER. Linetypes whose names end in an X2 have dashes and spaces that are twice as long as those used in the original linetypes. BORDERX2, for example, is the same pattern as BORDER, but the lengths of the dashes and spaces are twice those used in BORDER.

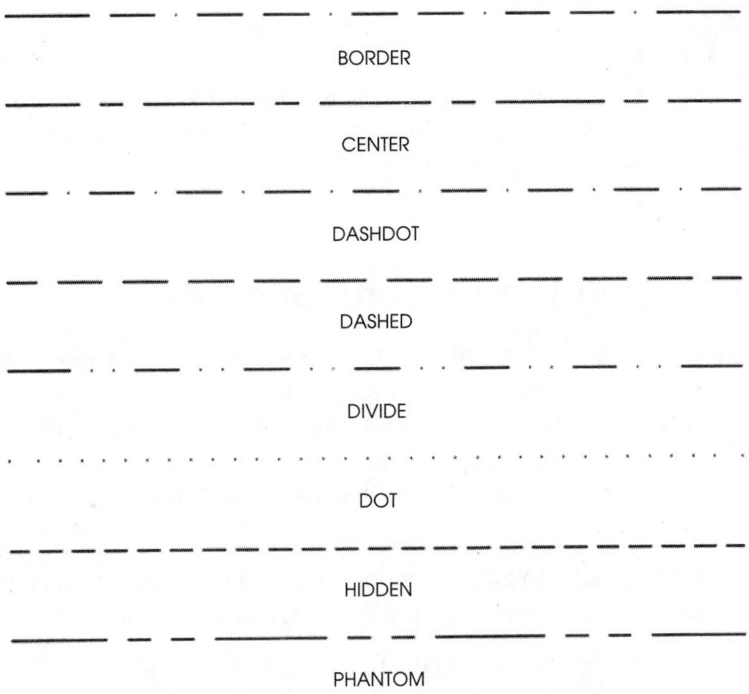

Figure 18.4

Linetypes that are stored in ACAD.LIN.

To load or reload a linetype, select the linetype from the list of available linetypes and choose OK. AutoCAD loads the linetype and returns you to the main Select Linetype dialog box. To browse through another linetype file, use the File button to specify the file name and location. For information about defining your own linetype definitions and storing them in your own files, see "Working with Linetype Files" and "Defining Complex Linetypes," later in this chapter.

TIP

> If you know you are going to use quite a few linetypes, you can save time by loading all the linetypes at one time and then purging the unused ones later. To load all linetypes, choose the Select All button in the Load or Reload Linetypes dialog box and then choose OK.
>
> To forego loading linetypes completely, load the linetypes you use into your prototype drawing(s). Then, when you begin a new drawing, the linetypes will be in the new drawing ready for you to use.

NOTE

If you assign a linetype to a layer by using the LAYER command, you do not need to load the linetype before you assign it; LAYER automatically looks in the ACAD.LIN file for the linetype and loads it if it finds it.

Setting the Current Linetype

Chapter 2, "Organizing Drawings with Layers," describes how all objects (other than points, mtext, text, trace, xlines, rays, viewports, and 3D objects) are drawn with the current linetype. You can set the current linetype by using the Select Linetype dialog box. Type the name of the linetype you want in the Linetype edit box, or select one from the list of available linetypes. The current object linetype is set to one of the following:

- **BYLAYER.** Draws objects with the linetype assigned to the layer the objects are drawn on. BYLAYER is the default setting.
- **Specific linetype.** Draws objects with the specified linetype, regardless of the linetype assigned to the layer the objects are drawn on.
- **BYBLOCK.** This special setting is used to create block definitions. See Chapter 11, "Block Structure, Editing, Organization, and Management," for a detailed discussion of this special linetype property.

The Object Properties toolbar has a linetype drop-down list, which lists the current linetype and all other loaded linetypes (see fig. 18.5). You can use this list to set the current linetype. The linetype displayed for the BYLAYER linetype reflects the linetype assigned to the current layer. For example, if the linetype assigned to the current layer is HIDDEN, the linetype displayed for the BYLAYER setting in the drop-down list is HIDDEN.

You also can set the current linetype with the Object Creation Modes dialog box (DDEMODES command). Choose the Linetype button in the Object Creation Modes dialog box to open the Select Linetype dialog box. See Chapter 2, "Organizing Drawings with Layers," for details.

Figure 18.5

The linetype drop-down list on the Object Properties toolbar.

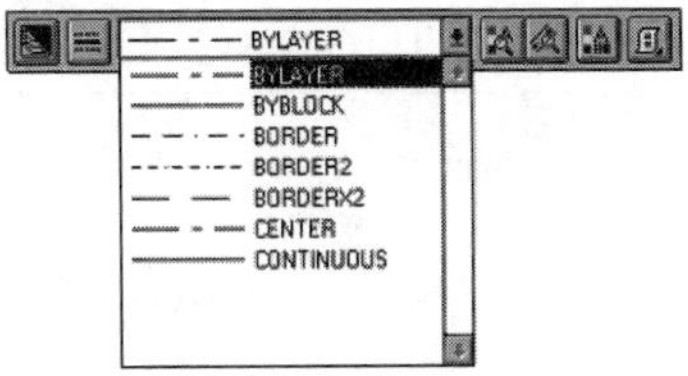

Using BYLAYER versus Specific Linetypes

Use the BYLAYER linetype setting when you want to be able to modify the linetypes of all objects on the same layer. You typically want that flexibility with objects that describe a common feature and reside on the same layer, such as the centerlines of an HVAC duct system. If objects have BYLAYER linetype assignments, all you have to do to change their linetypes is assign a new linetype (using DDLMODES) to the layer where the objects reside.

To draw using the current linetype setting of BYLAYER, load the desired linetypes with DDLTYPE. Then assign the linetypes to the appropriate layers using DDLMODES. As you draw objects, make current the layer to which the appropriate linetype is assigned. Don't forget that you can access the Select Linetypes dialog box through the Layer Control dialog box.

Sometimes, a particular feature in your drawing might require several linetypes. A common example is a company border sheet that utilizes several linetypes. If you want to draw the border and title block on one layer, you need to set the current linetype to the required linetypes as you draw your border sheet.

TIP

Use the BYLAYER setting when you need the capability to isolate a particular group of subelements, such as phantom lines for a border sheet, by turning layers on and off. Dedicate a layer for that group of objects, and draw those objects with a BYLAYER linetype and assign the linetype to the layer.

In the following exercise, you draw objects both ways: with the current linetype set to a specific linetype and then set to BYLAYER. The exercise uses the LTSCALE command, which is discussed later in this chapter.

SETTING THE CURRENT LINETYPE

Continue from the previous exercise, in the CHAP18 drawing.

`Command:` *Choose* Options, Linetypes, Global Linetype Scale	Issues LTSCALE system variable
`Command: _ltscale New scale factor <40.0000>:` **100** ↵	Sets LTSCALE to 100
`Command:` *Choose Object Creation (Object Properties)*	Issues DDEMODES, which opens the Object Creation Modes dialog box
`Command:` *Choose* Linetype	Opens the Select Linetype dialog box
`Command:` *Choose* Load	Opens the Load or Reload Linetypes dialog box
`Command:` *Select* DASHED *from the list of available linetypes and choose* OK	Loads DASHED into drawing
`Command:` *Select* DASHED *from the list of loaded linetypes and choose* OK	Sets the current linetype to DASHED

Set the layer TITLE_BLOCK current and draw a rectangle from 0,0 to 1700,1100. Because you set the current linetype to DASHED, the rectangle (polyline) is drawn with a DASHED linetype rather than the continuous linetype assigned to layer TITLE_BLOCK.

`Command:` *Select the* Linetype drop-down *list*	Displays the linetype drop-down list
`Command:` *Select the* BYLAYER *linetype*	Sets the current linetype setting back to BYLAYER; now all objects drawn will assume the linetype assigned to the layer the objects reside on
`Command:` *Choose Layers (Object Properties)*	Issues DDLMODES

Make a new layer named PROPERTY_LINES, change its color to magenta, and with only the PROPERTY_LINES layer selected, choose Set Ltype.

Choose Load, select PHANTOM2 from the list of available linetypes, and choose OK. Select PHANTOM2 from the list of loaded linetypes and choose OK.

Make PROPERTY_LINES the current layer and choose OK.

Use LINE to draw a line from point 310,620 to 740,620 to 840,550 to 820,350 to 550,430 to 340,425 and back to 310,620.

Draw another line from 550,620 to 550,431.

Draw another line from 550,550 to 840,550.

Draw another line from 690,550 to 820,350.

Your drawing should now look like figure 18.6. Save your drawing.

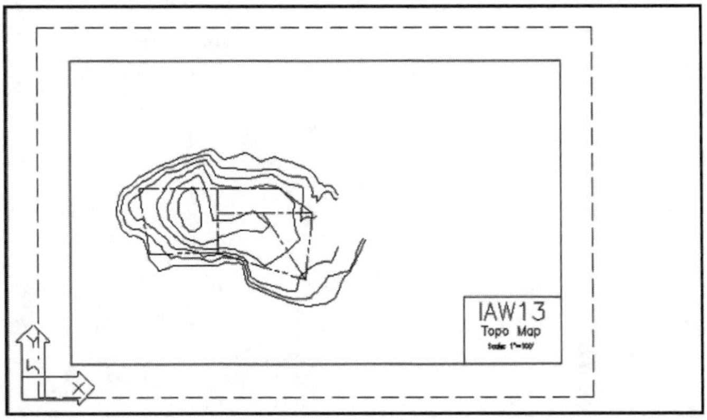

Figure 18.6

CHAP18.DWG with trimlines and property lines drawn.

Modifying Existing Linetypes

To change the linetype for all objects on a layer, use the Layer Control dialog box (DDLMODES) or the LAYER command to assign a different linetype to the layer. All objects on the selected layer drawn using the BYLAYER linetype setting take on the appearance of the newly assigned linetype. Objects on that layer drawn using a linetype other than BYLAYER are not affected by the change in linetype.

To change the linetype of a selected group of objects drawn using the BYLAYER linetype setting, use the DDMODIFY, DDCHPROP, CHPROP, or CHANGE commands to move them to a layer that has the linetype you want, thus preserving their BYLAYER linetype setting.

To change the linetype of a select group of objects without moving them to another layer or editing the layer settings, use DDMODIFY, DDCHPROP, CHPROP, or CHANGE to change the objects' assigned linetype. You can change an object's linetype from BYLAYER to a specific linetype (or vice versa) at any time.

In the following exercise, you edit the linetypes of existing objects.

EDITING THE LINETYPES OF OBJECTS

Continue from the previous exercise, in the CHAP18 drawing.

`Command:` *Choose* Properties *(Object Properties), select the dashed rectangle, and end the selection*	Issues DDMODIFY
Choose Linetype, *select* CONTINUOUS *from the list of linetypes and choose* OK*; choose OK again to exit* DDMODIFY	Changes the linetype of the polyline to CONTINUOUS and leaves the polyline on layer TITLE_BLOCK
`Command:` *Select the rectangle*	Selects rectangle you just edited
`Command:` *Choose* Properties *(Object Properties)*	Issues DDMODIFY with the rectangle you just selected
Choose Linetype, *then select* DASHED *from the list of linetypes and choose OK, then choose* OK *again*	Changes the linetype of the polyline to DASHED, but leaves the polyline on layer TITLE_BLOCK
`Command:` *Choose* Layers *(Object Properties)*	Issues DDLMODES
Select the PROPERTY_LINES *layer so that it is the only one selected; choose* Set Ltype*; select* CONTINUOUS *from the list of linetypes and choose* OK*; choose* OK *again to exit* DDLMODES	Assigns the CONTINUOUS linetype to layer, thereby affecting all objects on PROPERTY_LINES that were drawn with a BYLAYER linetype setting
Use DDLMODES *again, to reset the linetype assignment of* PROPERTY_LINES *to* PHANTOM2	Assigns the PHANTOM2 linetype to layer, thereby affecting all objects on PROPERTY_LINES that were drawn with a BYLAYER linetype setting

Controlling Linetype Scales

Every linetype has a linetype definition. A *linetype definition,* in its simplest form, consists of a series of numbers that tells AutoCAD how long to make the dashes and spaces. The definition of the DASHED linetype, for example, tells AutoCAD to draw dashes 0.5 units long and spaces 0.25 units long.

When you draw a DASHED line and you plot it at a 1=1 scale, the lengths of the dashes and spaces on the paper will be 0.50 inches and 0.25 inches, respectively. If you use a plot scale that reduces the drawing, the lengths of the dashes and spaces will be proportionately reduced; for example, a plot scale of 1=4 will result in a HIDDEN line with 0.125 inches (0.50/4) dashes and 0.0625 inches (0.25/4) spaces.

To adjust the lengths of the dashes and spaces of the linetypes to compensate for a plot scale, do one of the following:

- Change the global linetype scale factor, LTSCALE, which affects all existing objects and any objects drawn after the change.
- Set the current linetype scale factor, CELTSCALE, which affects all objects drawn after the change.
- Change the linetype scale of existing objects.

Setting the Global Linetype Scale

Each object capable of displaying a linetype is assigned its own individual linetype scale. In displaying the linetype for an object, AutoCAD takes the object's individual linetype scale and multiplies the scale by another linetype scale, the global linetype scale stored in the system variable LTSCALE (LineType SCALE):

Object's final linetype scale = Object's individual linetype scale × global linetype scale (LTSCALE)

By default, the object's individual linetype scale is set to 1 and is assigned to the object at the time the object is drawn. In the next section, you learn how to set and change an object's individual linetype scale. In this section, you learn how to control and set the global linetype scale, LTSCALE. Assuming the object's individual linetype scale is 1, the preceding equation becomes

Object's final linetype scale = global linetype scale (LTSCALE)

Just as you must consider the final plot scale when you draw text objects, you must take into account the final plot scale when you draw with noncontinuous linetypes such as DASHED or PHANTOM2. You can easily compensate for the plot scale by changing the global linetype scale factor stored in the system variable LTSCALE.

By default, LTSCALE is set to 1, which causes AutoCAD to draw a linetype with the length specifications in the linetype's definition. For example, when LTSCALE is set to 1, the DASHED linetype is drawn as a series of 0.5-unit dashes and 0.25-unit spaces. When LTSCALE is changed, the dashes and spaces in a linetype are affected proportionately. For example, when LTSCALE is set to 4, the DASHED linetype is drawn as a series of 2-unit (0.5 × 4) dashes and 1-unit (0.25 × 4) spaces. If you then apply a plot scale of 1=4 at plotting time, the DASHED linetype will appear on the final plot as a series of 0.5-inch dashes and 0.25-inch spaces. You use LTSCALE to adjust the linetypes in your drawing so that they appear correctly on your final plot. If you want the linetypes in a drawing to appear on the final plot with the dash and space lengths defined in the linetype definitions, then you set LTSCALE to the inverse of the plot scale. Here are some examples:

Plot scale	*LTSCALE Setting*
1/4"=1' (1=48)	48
1/8"=1' (1=96)	96
1/16"=1' (1=192)	192

You can change LTSCALE using one of the following three methods:

- Type LTSCALE at the command prompt. Remember that you use any system variable as a command just by typing it at the command prompt.
- Choose Options, Linetypes, Global Linetype Scale. This pull-down menu item issues LTSCALE.
- Change the Linetype Scale setting in the Select Linetype dialog box, which is opened by the DDLTYPE command. You can issue DDLTYPE by choosing the Linetype tool from the Object Properties toolbar or by choosing Linetype from the Data pull-down menu.

Changing LTSCALE affects both new objects and existing objects. It also causes an immediate regeneration of the drawing (unless REGENAUTO is off), so the linetypes of existing objects immediately reflect the current LTSCALE setting. If REGENAUTO is off, issue the REGEN command to see the effects on existing objects of a change in LTSCALE.

Setting New Objects' Linetype Scale

Setting LTSCALE is great when you want to adjust all linetypes in a drawing by the same proportion. Sometimes, however, you want to change the linetype scale of individual objects. Suppose, for example, that you want to draw two circles with the dashed linetype, but for one circle, you want the dashed pattern to be scaled down. Changing LTSCALE would affect both circles, but each circle can be assigned its own linetype scale.

The linetype scale factor assigned to each new object is stored in the system variable CELTSCALE (Current Entity LineType SCALE). By default, this setting is 1. You can change CELTSCALE one of two ways:

- Type CELTSCALE at the command prompt. Remember that you use almost any system variable as a command just by typing it at the command prompt.
- Change the Linetype Scale setting in the Object Creation Modes dialog box (DDEMODES command, see fig. 18.7). You can type DDEMODES, choose the Object Creation menu item from the Data pull-down menu, or choose the Object Creation tool from the Object Properties toolbar.

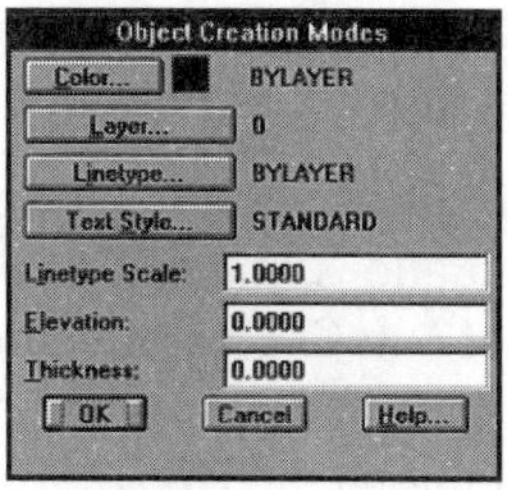

Figure 18.7

The Object Creation Modes dialog box.

NOTE

You can access the Select Linetype dialog box by choosing Linetype from the Object Creation Modes dialog box, as well as with the DDLTYPE command. The linetype scale setting in the Select Linetype dialog box, however, will be different in each case. The linetype scale setting displayed in the Select Linetype dialog box opened using the DDLTYPE command is the value of the global linetype scale factor LTSCALE. The linetype scale setting displayed in the Select Linetype dialog box opened from the Object Creation Modes dialog box is the value of CELTSCALE.

Unlike LTSCALE, which affects existing objects as well as new objects, CELTSCALE affects only new objects. This means that you have to set CELTSCALE before you draw the objects you want to affect.

TIP

Set LTSCALE to the general scale factor you want to use for all linetypes in the drawing. Set CELTSCALE to a value other than 1 for the objects that you want to deviate from the general scale factor. If you leave LTSCALE at 1 and use CELTSCALE as the primary mechanism for setting the linetype scaling for the drawing, you lose the flexibility of changing the scaling of linetypes in the drawing by simply changing LTSCALE.

When both CELTSCALE and LTSCALE are set to a value other than 1, the two factors interact with each other to determine the final scale of an object's linetype. If you draw an object after CELTSCALE has been set to 0.5 and LTSCALE has been set to 2, for example, the object will be displayed with a final linetype scale of 0.5×2, which results in a net linetype scale of 1.

Sometimes, all you want to do is scale the linetype of an object up or down by a factor of 2. In such situations, you might not need to change the CELTSCALE of the object. Remember that AutoCAD provides not one but three versions of the linetypes shown in figure 18.8. The three definitions are the original definition (such as DASHED), the half-scale definition (such as DASHED2), and the double-scale definition (such as DASHEDX2). Figure 18.8 shows the three versions of the DASHED linetype.

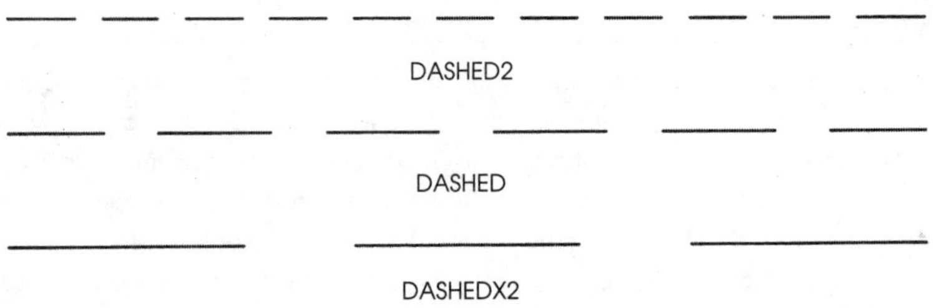

Figure 18.8

The DAHSED2, DASHED, and DASHEDX2 linetypes.

Changing Existing Objects' Linetype Scale

To change the linetype scale of an existing object, you change either the global linetype scale LTSCALE or the object's individual linetype scale. To modify the linetype scale of all linetypes in a drawing uniformly, change LTSCALE. To modify the linetype scale of a select group of objects, use DDMODIFY, CHANGE, CHPROP, or DDCHPROP to change the objects' individual linetype scales. Remember that the object's linetype scale interacts with the global linetype scale to produce the object's final linetype scale.

In the following exercise, you change LTSCALE and the linetype scale of existing objects in the drawing CHAP18.

DEALING WITH LINETYPE SCALES

Continue from the previous exercise, in the CHAP18 drawing.

`Command:` *Choose* Options, Linetypes, Global Linetype Scale	Issues the LTSCALE system variable
`Command: _ltscale New scale factor <100.0000>:` **50** ↵	Changes the global linetype scale factor from 100 to 50 and regenerates drawing to display the change
`Command:` *Choose Object Creation (Object Properties)*	Issues DDEMODES, which displays CELTSCALE (still 1), not LTSCALE, in the Select Linetype dialog box
Click on the Cancel *button*	Exits from the Object Creation Mode dialog box
`Command:` *Choose Properties (Object Properties)*	
`Select Objects:` *Select the dashed rectangle you drew and end the selection*	Issues the DDMODIFY command
Change the Linetype Scale *value from* 1.0 *to* 2.0 *and choose* OK	

The linetype of the rectangle should change, but none of the other objects should change.

The linetype scale that appears in DDMODDIFY, DDCHPROP, CHPROP, and CHANGE is that of the object, not the global linetype scaling factor LTSCALE.

Applying Linetypes to Polylines and Splines

When you apply a linetype pattern to an object, AutoCAD begins the pattern generation from the object's start point and continues to the object's next vertex point or endpoint. If there is not enough space between the start and endpoint of an object to allow one instance of the pattern to be drawn, AutoCAD draws the linetype pattern as a continuous line. Suppose, for example, that you tried to draw a 0.25-inch long line with a dashed linetype using LTSCALE and CELTSCALE settings of 1. There is not enough space between the start and endpoints of the line to accommodate a pattern of 0.5-inch dashes and 0.25-inch spaces, so AutoCAD draws the 0.25-inch line as a continuous line but records the linetype as DASHED.

If conditions ever change to allow the linetype to be generated, AutoCAD automatically regenerates the object with the assigned linetype. What type of changes could cause a regeneration? If you set the object's linetype scale factor to a smaller value, the pattern could be reduced enough to fit between the existing endpoints of the object. Or you could increase the distance between the object's endpoints (that is, you lengthen the line) to allow the linetype pattern to be generated.

A polyline has a start point and an endpoint and, usually, numerous intermediate vertex points. A good example of such a polyline is one drawn to represent a contour line on a topographic drawing. Unlike other objects that have a start and endpoint (such as lines and arcs), AutoCAD considers the space between each pair of vertex points to see whether the linetype pattern can be generated along that portion of the polyline. So no matter how long a polyline might be, it still might not have enough space for the linetype pattern because of closely spaced vertex points. Another polyline might have enough space between adjacent vertices along only certain portions of its length to accommodate the linetype pattern (see fig. 18.9).

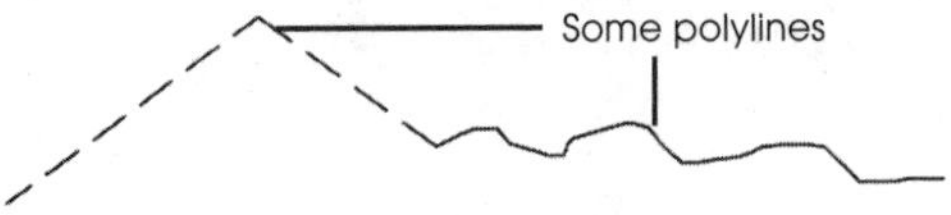

Figure 18.9

A polyline that is capable only of partially accommodating a linetype.

This problem can be further aggravated when you apply the spline or fit curve options to a polyline, which result in additional vertex points being used to draw it. The extra points result in less space between adjacent vertex points for a linetype pattern.

You can set the PLINEGEN system variable to cause AutoCAD to apply the linetype pattern continuously from one end to the other, through all the intermediate vertex points. After you turn on PLINEGEN, any new polylines are affected. To access the PLINEGEN system variable, choose Options, Linetypes, Linetype Generation or type PLINEGEN at the command prompt. PLINEGEN is on when a check mark appears next to the Linetype Generation menu item.

NOTE

To change the linetype generation setting for existing polylines, you must edit them using the Ltype gen option of the PEDIT command.

NOTE

Spline objects are similar to polylines; they have start and end points and numerous intermediate vertex points. In generating a linetype pattern for a spline object, AutoCAD considers only the distance between the ends and ignores the intermediate points. There is no equivalent of the PLINEGEN setting for splines because it is not needed.

In the following exercise, you use PLINEGEN to apply the HIDDEN linetype to the polylines representing the contour lines on the topographic map.

PLINEGEN AND LINETYPES

Continue from the previous exercise, in the CHAP18 drawing.

`Command:` *Do a ZOOM Window using the points* 220,220 *and* 1200,780	Zooms into the contour lines
`Command:` *Choose Layers (Object Properties)*	Issues DDLMODES
Select the OLD_CONTOURS *layer so that it is the only one selected. Choose* Set Ltype *then choose* Load	Opens the Load or Reload Linetypes dialog box
Select HIDDEN *from the list of available linetypes, then choose* OK	Loads the HIDDEN linetype into the drawing
Select HIDDEN *from the list of loaded linetypes*	
Choose OK *and then* OK *again*	Assigns HIDDEN to the selected layer OLD_CONTOURS

Notice that only portions of the contour lines (the polylines) appear to have the HIDDEN linetype. To apply linetypes along the entire length of an existing polyline, you have to use PEDIT.

`Command:` *Choose Pedit (Modify, Special Edit)*	Issues PEDIT

`Command: _pedit Select polyline:`
Select one of the contour lines

`Open/Join/Width/Edit vertex/ Fit/Spline/Decurve/Ltype gen /Undo/eXit <X>:` **L** ↵	Specifies the Ltype gen option
`Full PLINE linetype ON/OFF <Off>:` **ON** ↵	Turns on PLINEGEN for the selected polyline
`Open/Join/Width/Edit vertex/ Fit/Spline/Decurve/Ltype gen /Undo/eXit <X>:` ↵	Exits from PEDIT

Repeat the previous procedure, editing all the contour lines so that they have the HIDDEN linetype applied continuously. Your drawing should end up looking like figure 18.10. To affect new objects in a similar manner, turn on the system variable PLINEGEN. In the following steps, you turn PLINEGEN on and then draw a new contour line.

`Command:` *Choose* Options, Linetypes, Linetype Generation	Toggles PLINEGEN
`Command:` *Make layer* OLD_CONTOURS *the current layer*	
`Command:` *Choose Polyline (Draw, Polyline)*	Issues PLINE
`Command: _pline`	
`From point:` **455,520** ↵	Sets the start point of the polyline

Continue the polyline to point 450,550 to 450,575 to 460,600 to 475,585 to 485,555 to 475,525 and close the polyline. Notice that the HIDDEN linetype is applied continuously for the new polyline.

Save your drawing.

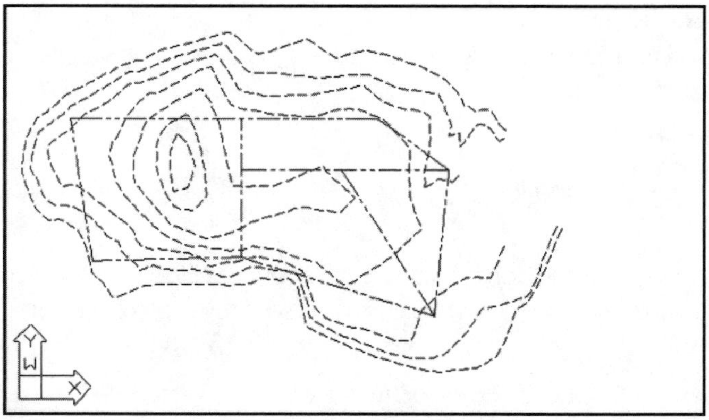

Figure 18.10

CHAP18.DWG with PLINEGEN applied to contours.

Drawing with ISO Linetypes

The linetype file ACAD.LIN includes a number of linetypes (see fig. 18.11) that meet the specifications of the International Standards Organization (ISO).

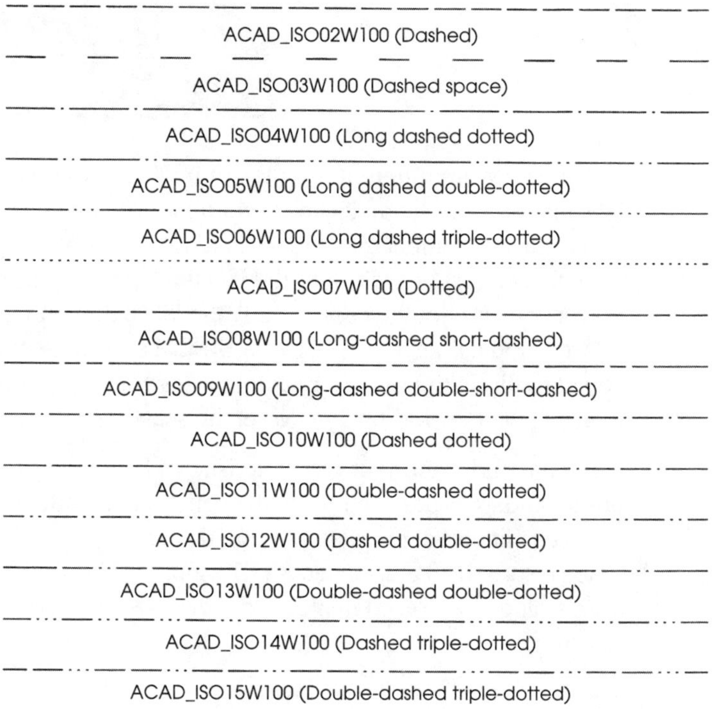

Figure 18.11

The ISO linetypes in ACAD.LIN.

An unusual characteristic of ISO linetypes is that each one has a name that begins with the prefix ACAD_ISO, but in the Select Linetype dialog box (see fig. 18.12), a different description appears in the list of loaded linetypes.

In figure 18.12, for example, the linetype ACAD_ISO02W100 is loaded in the drawing, but the description displayed in the list of loaded linetypes is Dashed. You can tell when a description in the list is of an ISO linetype because the ISO names are a mix of upper- and lowercase letters while the names and descriptions of the non-ISO linetypes are in all uppercase.

Figure 18.12

The Select Linetype dialog box with an ISO linetype.

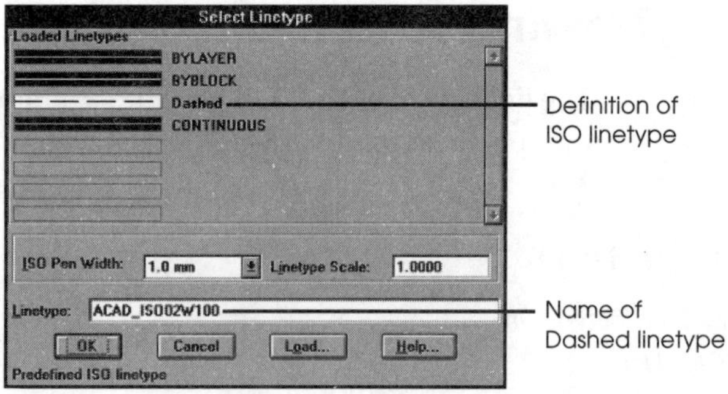

ISO linetypes are different from the other linetypes you've encountered in that the ISO linetypes can set an ISO pen width for ISO linetypes (refer to figure 18.12). The pen width assignment is a little misleading in that, at first glance, it appears that you actually can assign a width to the ISO linetypes just as you can assign a width to a polyline; this is not the case. Setting the ISO pen width to a particular value simply sets the global linetype scale factor LTSCALE to an associated value. If you choose, you can still set the LTSCALE factor just as you did for the non-ISO linetypes rather than use the pen width value to set the scale.

One final and important characteristic of ISO linetypes is that the lengths of the dashes and spaces are defined with relatively large values. For the ACAD_ISO02W100 (Dashed) linetype, for example, the dash is set to be 12 units in length while the space is set to be 3 units in length. The length values are large because the linetypes are designed to be used in metric drawing setups where each drawing unit is equal to 1 mm.

Defining Linetypes

The files in which the linetype definitions supplied with AutoCAD are stored are simple ASCII text files. To modify or create new linetypes, you use either a text editor or the LINETYPE command.

`Command:`The options of the LINETYPE command are as follows:

- **?.** This option enables you to list the linetype definitions in the linetype file you specify.
- **Create.** The Create option enables you to create a new linetype definition or replace an existing linetype definition in the linetype file you specify.

- **Load.** You use the Load option to load or reload linetype definitions from the linetype file you specify into the drawing.
- **Set.** The Set option enables you to set the current linetype. The default setting is BYLAYER.

The LINETYPE command is the predecessor of the DDLTYPE command. In general, DDLTYPE is better. LINETYPE, however, includes a Create option that enables you to modify an existing linetype definition or create a new definition without using a separate text editor.

Working with Linetype Files

Because linetype files are just text files, you can use any ASCII text editor. You can use Windows' Notepad editor, or your favorite word processor, as long as you save the file as an ASCII text file.

The two linetype files supplied with AutoCAD are ACAD.LIN and LTYPESHP.LIN, and both are located in the \ACADR13\COMMON\SUPPORT directory. You can modify the linetype definitions in these files or create or add new linetype definitions. If you choose to create your own linetype files, use the file name extension .LIN.

In the following sections, you learn how to put together the linetype definitions that go into the linetype files.

TIP

To learn how to assemble linetype definitions, print out the contents of the ACAD.LIN and LTYPESHP.LIN files and use them as examples. Before you make any changes to these files, make copies of the original files in case you need to restore them.

Defining Simple Linetypes

The simplest linetypes consist of a repeating pattern of dashes, spaces, and/or dots. The basic pattern is recorded in a linetype definition. A linetype definition always consists of two lines of text. The first line begins with an asterisk and is immediately followed by the linetype name and some optional descriptive text:

```
*linetype_name[,linetype description]
```

The linetype name can be up to 31 characters long, and can use alphanumeric characters and $, -, and _ . A linetype name cannot include spaces. You can use as many as 47 characters for the optional description text. The dash, underline, period, space, and other keyboard characters commonly are used to create a pictorial representation of the linetype that helps to document the definition within the linetype file and that appears in the Load or Reload Linetypes dialog box of the Select Linetype dialog box. As an example, the actual definition of the DASHDOT linetype stored in ACAD.LIN is as follows:

```
*DASHDOT,__ . __ . __ . __ . __ . __ . __ . __ . __ . __ . __ . __ .
A,.5,-.25,0,-.25
```

The first line consists of the linetype name and description. The second line of the definition consists of the character *A* immediately followed by a series of numbers that defines the lengths of the dashes and spaces. The *A* is the alignment type, which controls how the linetype pattern begins and ends. Currently, AutoCAD supports only one alignment type, so the second line of the definition always begins with the letter *A*.

The numbers that follow the alignment type are the lengths of the dashes and spaces in drawing units. A positive number represents a dash and a negative number represents a space. A zero represents a dot. Using a linetype scale of 1, the preceding DASHDOT linetype definition would draw a linetype consisting of a 0.50-unit-long dash followed by a 0.25-unit space, a dot, and then another 0.25-unit space.

You need only define one instance of the pattern; AutoCAD automatically repeats the pattern. A DASHDOT line is drawn by repeating the basic pattern of a dash, a space, a dot, and another space, so the definition has four numbers, one for each element. A linetype definition must always begin with a dash or a dot, never a space.

TIP

In defining a new linetype, set the lengths of the dashes and spaces in the linetype definition to be equal to what you want to see on a 1:1 scale plot.

In the following exercise, you create your own linetype definition to use for property lines.

Creating a Linetype

Continue from the previous exercise, in the CHAP18 drawing.

`Command:` **LINETYPE** ↵	Starts the LINETYPE command
`?/Create/Load/Set:` **C** ↵	Specifies the Create option
`Name of linetype to create:` **PROPERTY**↵	Specifies the name of the linetype to be created
When the Create or Append Linetype File dialog box appears, enter the file name **\IAW\IAW** *and choose* OK	Creates new file IAW.LIN in the directory \IAW

`Descriptive text:`

Type eight underscore characters, followed by one space, one underscore character, one space, one underscore character, one space, one underscore character, one space, and finally, eight underscore characters and press Enter. Your line of text should look like ________ _ _ _ ________.

`Enter pattern (on next line):`
A,1.0, -0.125, 0.125, -0.125, 0.125, -0.125, 0.125, -0.125 ↵

`New definition written to file.`

`?/Create/Load/Set:` **L** ↵	Specifies the Load option
`Linetype(s) to load:` **PROPERTY**↵	Linetype PROPERTY_LINE loaded
Specify the file \IAW\IAW *when you see the Select Linetype File dialog box*	Specifies linetype from which to load
`?/Create/Load/Set:` ↵	Ends the LINETYPE command
`Command:` *Choose Layers (Object Properties) and assign the PROPERTY linetype to the* PROPERTY_LINES *layer (see fig. 18.13)*	Because the lines on layer PROPERTY_LINES were drawn with a BYLAYER linetype setting, AutoCAD regenerates the display using the new linetype for the lines

Save your work.

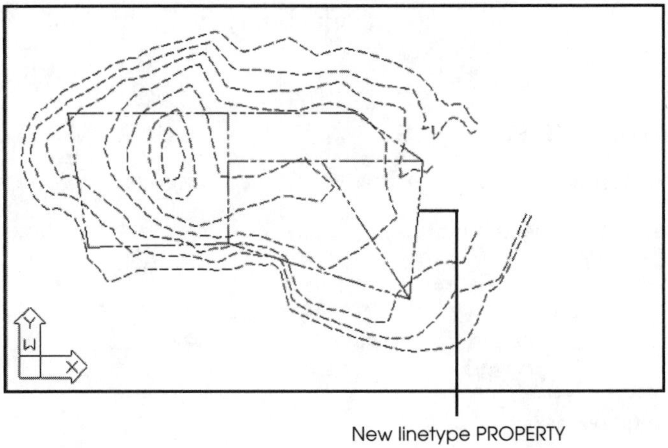

Figure 18.13

The TOPO.DWG with the new linetype PROPERTY.

In the preceding exercise, you used LINETYPE to create the new linetype pattern and store it in the file \IAW\IAW.LIN. You can examine or edit the resulting file with a text editor.

WARNING

Do not attempt to edit a linetype file that is currently open (currently accessed by the Select Linetype File dialog box or LINETYPE Load option). Most text editors will not allow you to do so; however, some editors will not protect you from doing so, which can cause errors or a loss of work.

Modifying Existing Linetype Definitions

You can modify existing linetype definitions in exactly the same manner as you create new ones. When you enter the name of an existing linetype definition at the LINETYPE command's `Name of linetype to create:` prompt, it prompts:

```
Wait, checking if linetype already defined...

DASHED already exists in this file. Current definition is:
*DASHED,__ __ __ __ __ __ __ __ __ __ __ __ __ __ __ __ __
A, 0.5, -0.25 Overwrite? <N>
```

When you respond with Y for Yes, the LINETYPE command continues with the same prompts as those for creating a new linetype, and replaces the existing definition.

You also can modify an existing linetype definition by directly editing it in the linetype definition file.

Defining Complex Linetypes

Linetype definitions which consist only of dashes, dots, and spaces are considered *simple* linetypes, and have been available in AutoCAD since the earliest versions. Beginning with Release 13, AutoCAD enables you to define and use *complex* linetypes, which can incorporate symbols and text, along with the dashes, spaces, and dots of simple linetypes (see fig.18.14).

FENCELINE2 linetype

Figure 18.14

A linetype that uses symbols.

The symbols you use in complex linetype definitions must be shape definitions. A shape definition is similar to a block definition. You insert a shape using the SHAPE command, not the INSERT command. You specify the insertion point, scale factor, and rotation angle. Defining a shape, however, is considerably more cumbersome than defining a block. The actual process of defining a shape is like that of defining a text font character, and is beyond the scope of this book.

The basic format of complex linetype definitions is similar to the format simple linetypes, except that it is has additional information.

To include a shape in the pattern, you specify the following:

```
[Shape_name,shape_file_name,S=scale_factor,R=rotation_angle,
➥X=xoffset,Y=yoffset]
```

For example, the linetype definition for the line shown in figure 18.14 is as follows:

```
*FENCELINE2,____[]_____[]____
A,.25,[BOX,ltypeshp.shx,s=.1],-.2,1
```

The required components of the shape definition portion of a linetype definition are as follows:

- **Shape_name.** The name of the shape to be inserted. In the FENCELINE2 example, the shape to be inserted is BOX.
- **Shape_file_name.** Because multiple shape definitions can be stored in a single file, you must include the shape file name. In the preceding example, the shape name is BOX, which is found in the file LTYPESHP.SHX (LTYPESHP.SHX is a shape file supplied with AutoCAD). You can include a path name in the file name if necessary.

To include a text string in the pattern, you specify the following:

```
["string",text_style,S=scale_factor, R=rotation_angle, X=x_offset,
➥Y=y_offset]
```

Figure 18.15 shows an example of a linetype with text. Its definition is similar to the preceding one:

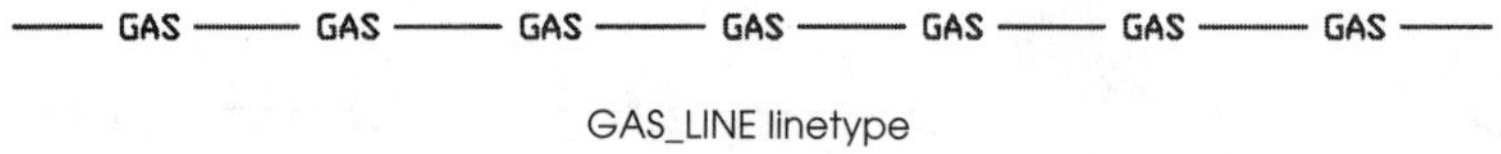

Figure 18.15

A linetype with text.

```
*GAS_LINE,——GAS——GAS
A,.5,-.2,["GAS",STANDARD,S=.1,R=0.0,X=-0.1,Y=-.05],-.25
```

The components of the text definition portion of a linetype definition are as follows:

- **String.** This is the text string that is to be drawn in the linetype. The string can be any collection of characters, including spaces, but must be enclosed in quotes. In the GAS_LINE example, the string is "GAS".
- **Text_style.** You have the option of specifying the text style name that is to be used when drawing the text. If no text style is specified, the current text style is used. In the GAS_LINE example, the text style STANDARD is specified.

Both shape and text definitions within a linetype definition have the following optional components in common:

- **Scale_factor.** The scale factor must be a real number and begin with the prefix S=. In the FENCELINE2 example, the scale factor is S=0.1. The shape BOX is a 2-by-2-unit rectangle, so the scale factor of 0.1 results in a 0.2-by-0.2-unit rectangle. If you do not explicitly set an insertion scale factor, a factor of 1 is assumed. Use a scale factor that produces the desired insertion size with a plot scale of 1=1 and a linetype scale of 1; then, you can adjust for a drawing's true plot scale by adjusting the linetype scale. In the case of text, the scale factor determines the text height. If the text style used to draw the text has a nonzero text height setting, the style's text height setting is multiplied by the scale factor. If the text style has a zero text height setting, the scale factor becomes the text height in drawing units.
- **Rotation_angle.** The rotation angle may either be an *absolute* or *relative* angle. An absolute rotation angle is measured relative to 0° of the world coordinate system. It must be a real number and begin with the prefix A=. A relative rotation angle is relative to the tangent to the line at the location of

the symbol (see 18.16). A relative rotation angle must be a real number and begin with the prefix R=. The angular value itself is assumed to be in decimal degrees unless you include a g suffix (for grads) or an r suffix (for radians) in the scale factor. If no rotation angle is specified, a relative rotation angle of 0 is assumed. Shapes are rotated about their insertion points, text strings about the left endpoint of the text string's baseline (see figure 18.17).

Figure 18.16

The effect of a rotation angle.

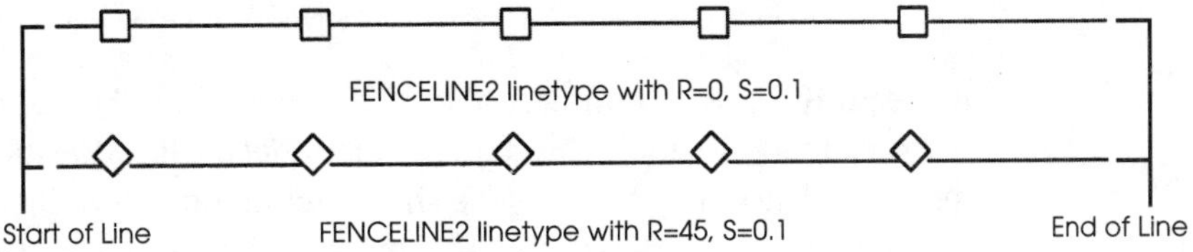

Figure 18.17

The effect of a rotation angle on GAS_LINE linetype.

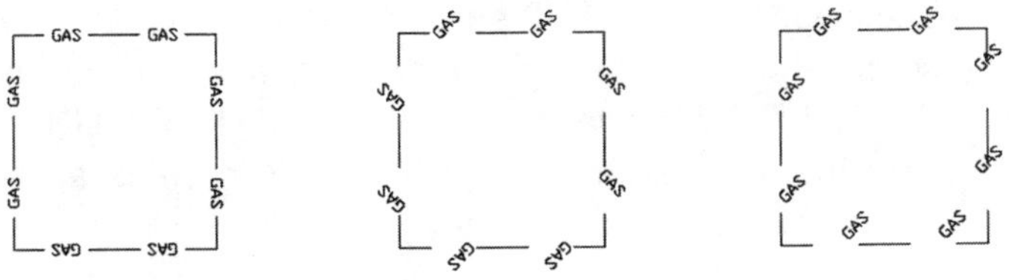

- **xoffset.** Normally, the shape or text is inserted at the end of the previous dash, dot, or space of the linetype. You can shift the insertion by specifying an x and/or a y offset. An x offset is measured along the line from the end of the last dash, dot, or space. It must be a real number and begin with X=. If the offset is a positive number, the shape is shifted in the direction of the endpoint of the line (see fig.18.18). If the offset is a negative number, the shape is shifted in the direction of the start point of the line. If no offset is specified, an offset of 0 is assumed.

- **yoffset.** A y offset is measured perpendicular to the line from the end of the last dash, dot, or space. It must be a real number and begin with Y=. The offset may be either a positive or a negative number. If no y offset is specified, an offset of 0 is assumed. The direction of a positive y offset is determined by applying the right-hand rule to the line. For example, in figure 18.18, the direction of a positive y offset is upward relative to the lines because the positive x offset direction is from the start point to the endpoint (left to right). If, however, the start and endpoints were reversed, the direction of a positive y offset would be downward relative to the line.

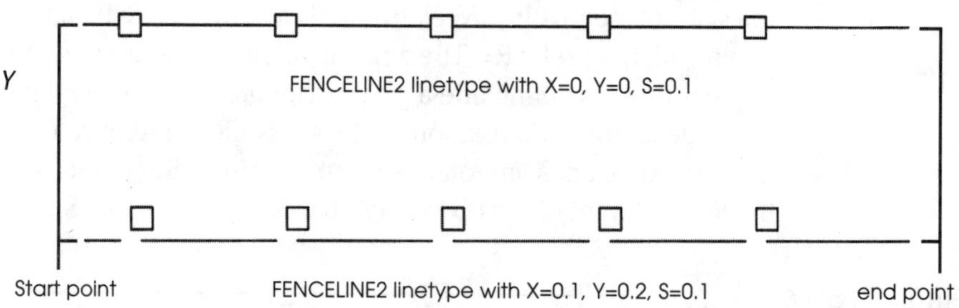

Figure 18.18

The effect of X and Y offsets.

In the FENCELINE2 example, notice that the embedded shape definition is followed with a space(–.2 value). This space ensures that the line does not go through the BOX insertion. The construction of the shape definition determines where the pen ends up after drawing the shape, but if a shape is designed to be used with linetypes, the shape definition should return the pen to the insertion point.

The shape file LTYPE.SHP is included in the AutoCAD package. LTYPE.SHP contains several shape definitions that are incorporated into the linetype definitions stored in the file LTYPESHP.LIN (see fig. 18.19). LTYPESHP.LIN also contains two linetypes that include text (see fig. 18.20). Both files are stored in the directory \R13\COM\SUPPORT.

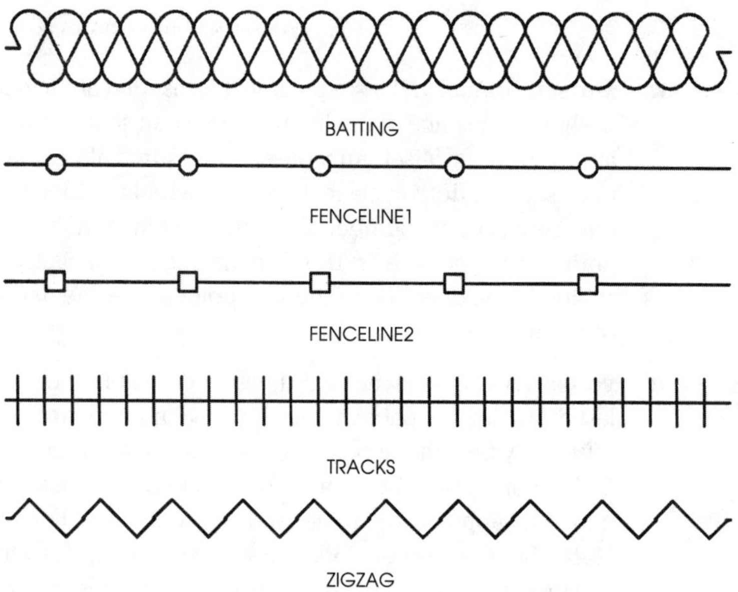

Figure 18.19

The linetypes in LTYPESHP.LIN.

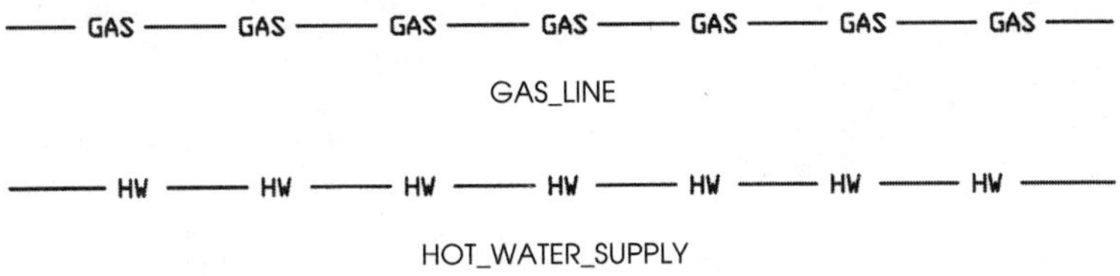

Figure 18.20

Linetypes with text in LTYPESHP.LIN.

TIP

> If you work with shape definitions that other people have defined, you can use the SHAPE command to insert each shape, to see what each looks like. By inserting each shape, you also see the position of the insertion point relative to the shape. Before you use the SHAPE command, you need to load the shape file into your drawing using the LOAD command.

You cannot use the Create option of the LINETYPE command to define any linetypes that include shapes or text. You have to use a DOS or Windows text editor to define additional complex linetypes.

In the following exercise, you apply two of the sample complex linetypes from the file LTYPESHP.LIN.

USING LINETYPES WITH SHAPES AND TEXT

Continue from the previous exercise, in the CHAP18 drawing.

`Command:` *Choose Layers (Object Properties)*	Issues DDLMODES
Make a new layer named FENCES	
Select layer FENCES *only and choose* Set Ltype	Opens the Select Linetype dialog box
Choose Load, *choose* File, *select the file* LTYPESHP.LIN *and choose* OK	Opens the linetype file LTYPESHP.LIN
Select FENCELINE2 *from the list of available linetypes and choose* OK	Loads FENCELINE2 into drawing
Select FENCELINE2 *from the list of loaded linetypes and choose* OK	Assigns FENCELINE2 to layer FENCES
Make FENCES *the current layer and choose* OK	Makes FENCES the current layer

Draw a line from 310,630 *to* 740,630 *to* 840,560 (see fig. 18.21)	Draws line with FENCELINE2 linetype

Use the DDLMODES command again to create a new layer named GAS and make it current.

Choose Set Ltype, *then choose* Load	Opens the Select Linetype dialog box and then opens the Load or Reload Linetype dialog box
Choose File, *select the file* LTYPESHP.LIN *and choose* OK	Specifies the file LTYPESHP.LIN as the file from which you want to load
Select GAS_LINE *from the list of available linetypes and choose* OK	Loads GAS_LINE into the drawing
Select GAS_LINE *from the list of loaded linetypes and choose* OK	Assigns GAS_LINE to layer GAS
Select OK	Closes the Layer Control dialog box
`Command:` *Draw a line from the point* 360,400 *to point* 790,630	Draws lines with GAS_LINE linetype (see fig. 18.22)

Save your work.

Figure 18.21

CHAP18.DWG with new fence lines drawn.

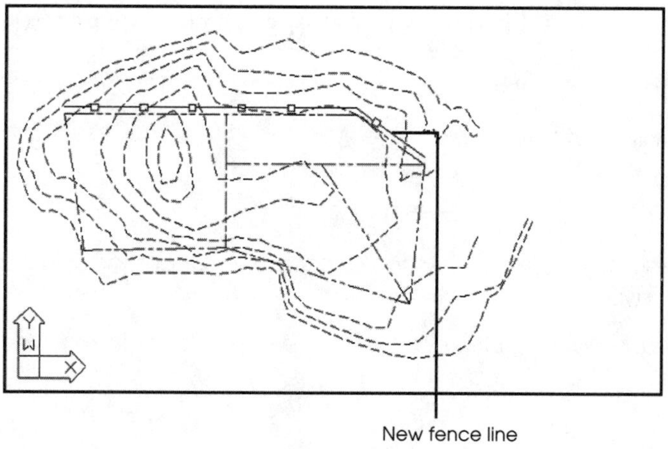

Figure 18.22

CHAP18.DWG with the gas line drawn.

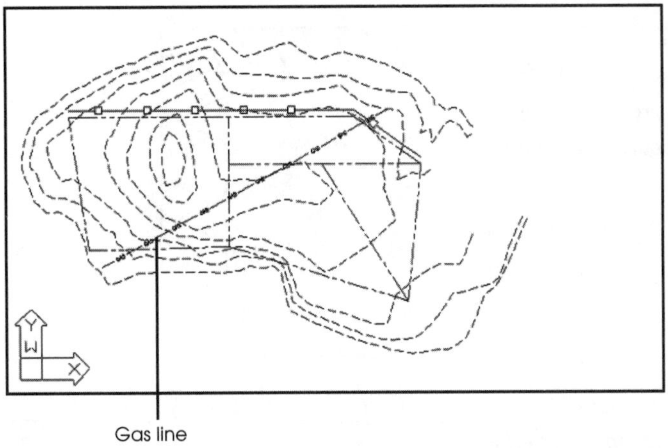

Working with Other Forms of Complex Linetypes

You can design complex linetypes that do not look like lines. A good example is the BATTING linetype (see fig. 18.23), which represents insulation in a wall section.

Figure 18.23

The BATTING linetype, meant to represent insulation in a section of wall.

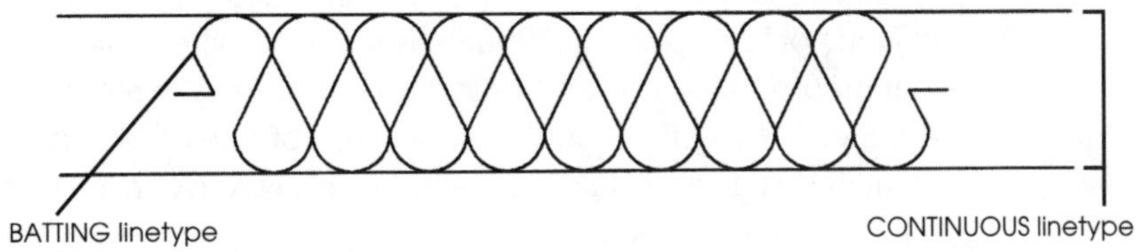

The BATTING linetype definition consists of a very short dash (0.0001 units), the shape itself, and a space. In effect, the linetype is a repetition of a single shape, end to end. Be careful about using linetypes such as BATTING when it comes to corners and intersections (see fig. 18.24). Linetypes are not automatically cleaned up correctly at corners and intersections. You must clean them up. For corners, stop one line at the corner and then continue a new line around the corner. For intersections, break one of the lines at the intersection. Refer to figure 18.25.

Figure 18.24

Drawing for BATTING for corners and intersection without any cleanup.

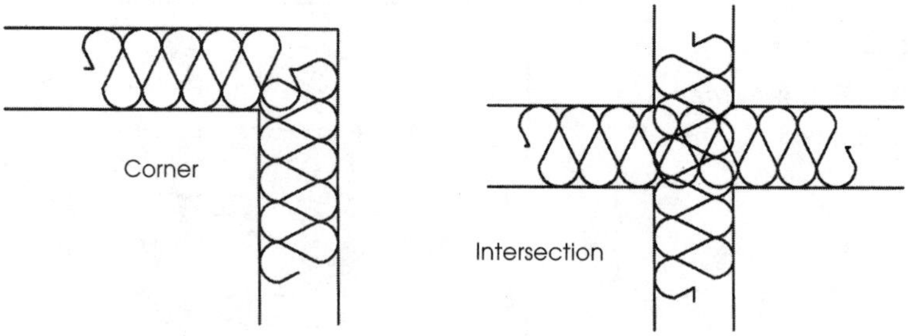

Figure 18.25

Drawing for BATTING for corners and intersections with some cleanup work.

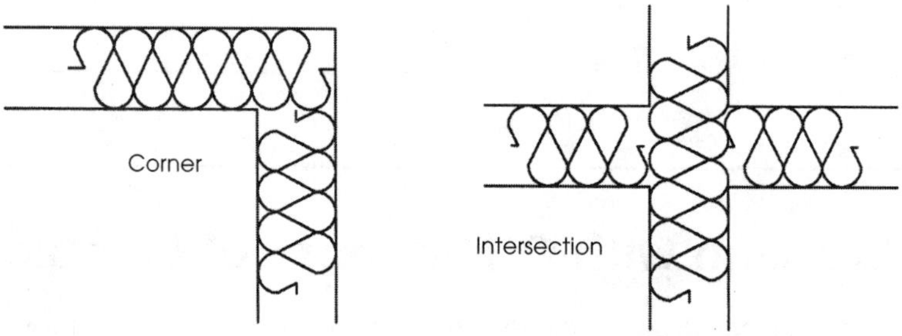

If you ever have to work with drawings created in earlier versions of AutoCAD, you might encounter objects that look like linetypes with shapes and text, but which are, in fact, not linetypes at all. Prior to Release 13, when you wanted to draw a linetype that incorporated text and/or symbols, you usually resorted to using an AutoLISP routine. The routine would draw a series of lines and text and/or symbols, which emulated a linetype. Unfortunately, the only way to convert these look-alike linetypes into true linetypes is to redraw them.

Working with Hatch Patterns

Hatching enables you to fill a selected area with a graphic pattern. AutoCAD comes with a library of over 50 hatch patterns, some of which are shown in figure 18.26.

You can find illustrations of all available hatch patterns in Appendix C of the *AutoCAD User's Guide.*

You use the BHATCH command to apply hatch patterns. BHATCH displays the Boundary Hatch dialog box (see fig. 18.27).

Figure 18.26

Some sample hatch patterns.

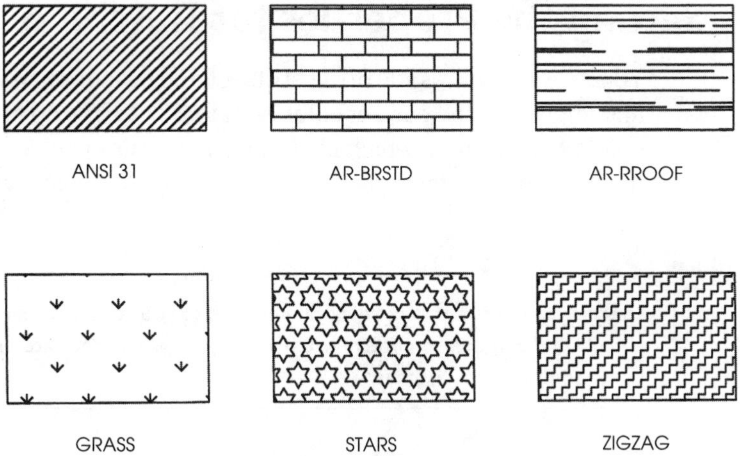

Figure 18.27

The Boundary Hatch dialog box.

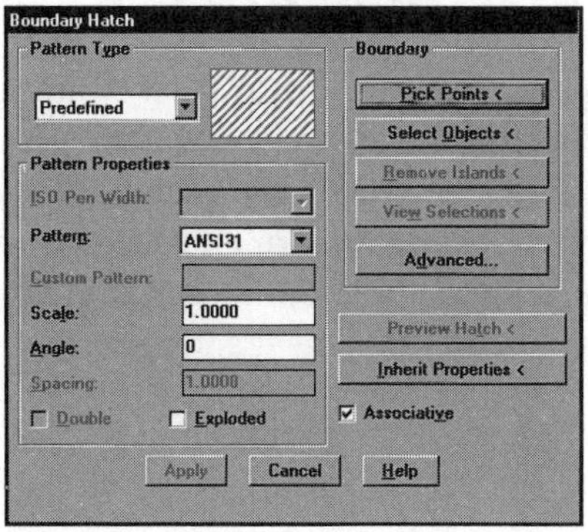

The typical procedure for drawing a hatch pattern is as follows:

1. Define the area you want to hatch.
2. Define the pattern you want to apply.
3. Apply the pattern.

NOTE

The command-line version of BHATCH is -BHATCH. -BHATCH is useful for programmers who want to incorporate hatching into their routines. There also is an obsolete and less-capable hatching command named HATCH. It is included in Release 13 for compatibility, and lacks many of the features of BHATCH. See "Using the HATCH Command," later in this chapter.

Setting the Properties for Hatching

You draw a hatch, as you do most objects, on the current layer with the current color and linetype. If the current color is set to BYLAYER, the hatch pattern takes on the color of the layer on which it is drawn. If the current color is set to a specific color, the hatch pattern takes on that color, regardless of the layer on which it is drawn.

TIP

Hatching can clutter up a drawing very quickly, so you generally want the capability to turn hatching off and on. To control hatch visibility by layer, dedicate one or more layers on which to draw your hatches.

Defining Simple Areas to Be Hatched

You apply a hatch pattern to a closed area delineated by one or more objects. In the simplest case, the area is delineated by a single closed object, such as a circle or a closed polyline. An area to be hatched can be delineated by several objects, as long as they meet end-to-end or intersect with each other to define a closed area. In figure 18.28, for example, one closed area is defined by a circle and the other by a series of lines and arcs that meet end-to-end.

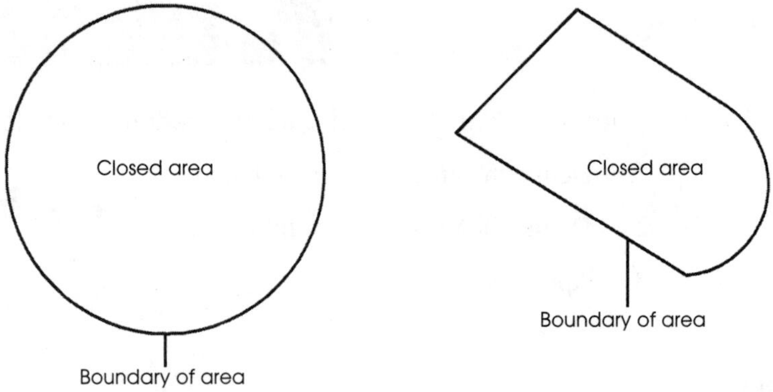

Figure 18.28

Simple areas to be hatched.

The objects that form the boundary are referred to as *boundary objects*. A simple way to select the area to be hatched is to select the boundary object(s) by choosing the Select Objects button in the Boundary Hatch dialog box (refer to figure 18.27).

Another way to define the area is to choose the Pick Points button, which requires you to select a point within the area to be hatched. BHATCH then applies the BOUNDARY command (see Chapter 8, "Drawing and Editing Polylines and Splines") to define a closed boundary surrounding the point you select.

In some situations, you find one method more appropriate than the other for defining the area to be hatched. In other situations, both methods might be equally suitable. In the exercise in the next section, you use both methods to define the areas to be hatched.

Selecting and Applying the Hatch Pattern

After you define the area to be hatched, you need to define the pattern to be applied. To define a pattern, first choose the pattern itself and then choose the parameters that control its generation.

You can choose from three types of patterns:

- **Predefined.** This category refers to the patterns defined in the file ACAD.LIN, the hatch pattern file supplied with AutoCAD. Refer to figure 18.26 for some samples.
- **User defined.** This category refers to patterns you can define using the BHATCH command. These patterns consist of one or two sets of parallel lines (see fig. 18.29). You can choose the angle and spacing of the lines in the first set, and you also can choose to have a second set of lines generated perpendicular to the first set. The second set of lines has the same spacing as the first set of lines.

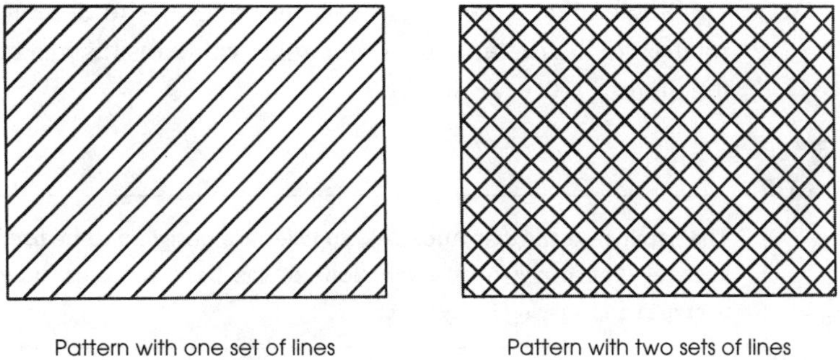

Figure 18.29

Two user-defined hatch patterns.

- **Custom.** This category refers to hatch patterns that are defined in a file other than ACAD.PAT (the default hatch pattern file). This option is discussed in greater detail in "Defining New Hatch Patterns," later in this chapter.

Setting Parameters for a Predefined Pattern

After you select the hatch pattern name from the pattern drop-down list, you need to set the parameters that control the pattern generation. For a predefined pattern, the parameters are scale and angle (see fig. 18.30).

Figure 18.30

The Boundary Hatch dialog box settings for a predefined pattern.

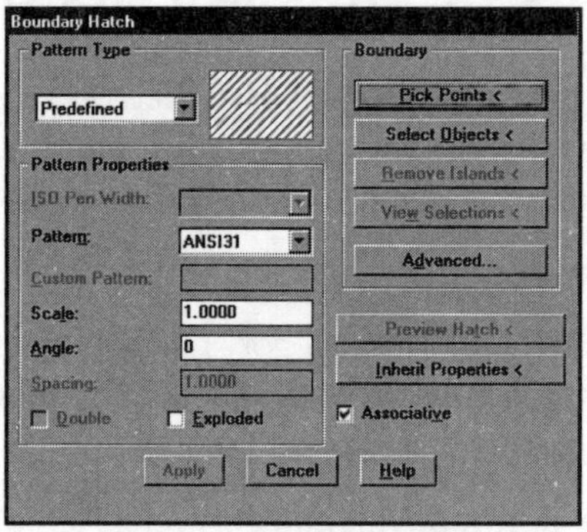

When the scale is set to 1 (default), the pattern is generated with the exact lengths specified in the hatch definition. If the scale is greater than 1, AutoCAD enlarges the pattern proportionately. If the scale factor is less than 1, AutoCAD reduces the lengths proportionately. The effect is similar to the effect that LTSCALE has on linetypes.

The angle affects the rotation of the pattern. The default value of 0 results in no rotation of the pattern; any other angle value results in a corresponding rotation of the pattern.

TIP

The hatch patterns that AutoCAD supplies are designed to be used with the continuous linetype. You can generate variations of the basic patterns, however, by using other linetypes and varying linetype scales.

Setting Parameters for a User-Defined Pattern

The parameters that define a user-defined pattern are angle, spacing, and double hatching (see fig. 18.31).

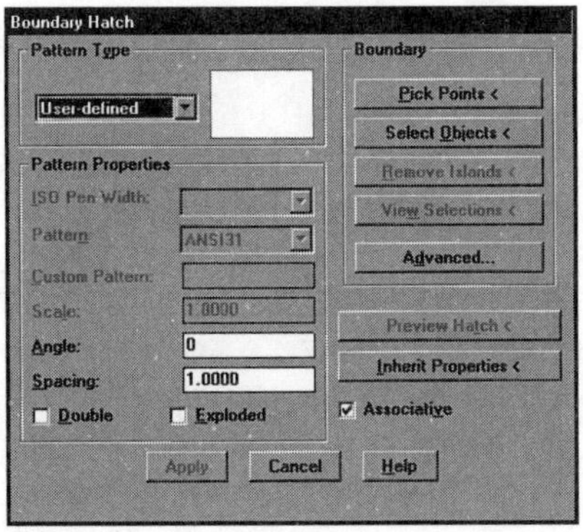

Figure 18.31

The Boundary Hatch dialog box settings for a user-defined pattern.

A user-defined pattern consists of one or two sets of parallel lines. The Angle value (default of 0) defines the angle of the lines in the first set. The Spacing value (default of 1 unit) defines the distance between the parallel lines. If you enable the Double option, AutoCAD generates a second set of parallel lines perpendicular to the first set (see fig. 18.29).

TIP

You can use a user-defined pattern with a tight line spacing to hatch an area to make it appear to be a solid filled area. Using BHATCH to fill an area is a valid use, but be careful. Tight hatch patterns usually take up a substantial amount of storage space in the drawing file. Using solids or wide polylines to fill an area is much more efficient than using a tight hatch pattern.

Previewing and Applying the Pattern

After setting the parameters for a pattern type, you can click the Preview Hatch button to view the resulting pattern without actually drawing the pattern. If you like the pattern, draw it by choosing the Apply button. If you do not like the resulting pattern, go back and change the parameters, or the pattern type itself, and preview it again. Continue to fine-tune the pattern until you like it, and then draw it by clicking on the Apply button.

To match a pattern that already exists in the drawing, click on the Inherit Properties button. Select the hatch you want to duplicate, and the pattern parameters in BHATCH are set to reproduce that hatch.

If you run into trouble or decide to abandon the hatching operation, click on the Cancel button.

In the following exercise, you use BHATCH to hatch several rectangular areas to complete the legend.

HATCHING SIMPLE AREAS

Continue from the previous exercise, or start a new drawing named CHAP18A, using the TOPO drawing from the accompanying CD as a prototype.

Turn off the layers GAS *and* OLD_CONTOURS, *then turn on the layers* BUILDINGS, LEGEND, *and* LOT_LABELS. *Create a new layer named* HATCH, *give it a unique color, and make it current.*

`Command:` *Choose Hatch (Draw, Hatch)*	Issues BHATCH
Choose ANSI32 *from the* Pattern *drop-down list*	Sets the hatch pattern to ANSI32
Set the Scale to 100 *and the Angle to* 0	Sets the scale of pattern to 100 and the angle of pattern to 0
Choose Pick Points	Specifies selection of area by picking an internal point
`Select internal point:` *Pick* ① (see fig. 18.32)	Sets start point for BOUNDARY command
`Selecting everything...`	
`Selecting everything visible...`	
`Analyzing the selected data...`	
`Analyzing internal islands...`	
`Select internal point:` ↵	Ends selection of areas
Choose Preview Hatch	Previews hatch pattern
Choose Continue	Ends preview

Set the Scale to 50	Sets scale to 50
Choose Apply	Draws hatch pattern
`Command:` ↵	Repeats BHATCH
Choose User-defined *from the* Pattern Type *drop-down list*	Sets pattern type to user-defined
Set Angle *to* 0, *set* Spacing *to* 10, *and enable* Double	Sets angle and spacing for pattern and enables the generation of two sets of parallel lines
Choose Select Objects	Specifies selection of area by selection of boundary objects
`Select objects:` *Pick* ②	Selects rectangle
`Select objects:` ↵	Ends selection
Choose Preview Hatch	Previews pattern
Choose Continue	Ends preview
Choose Apply	Draws hatch pattern; your drawing should now look like figure 18.32

Save your work.

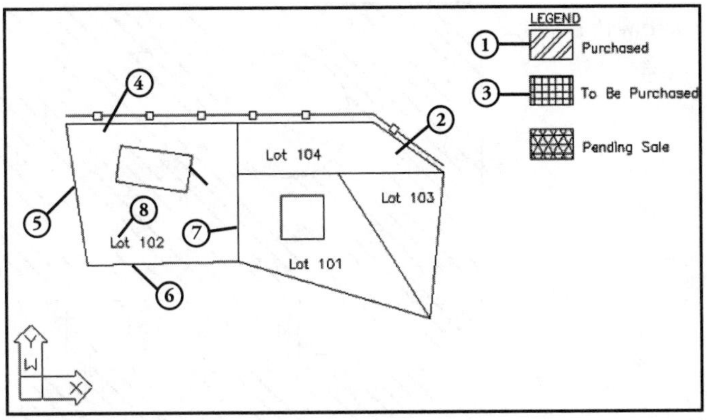

Figure 18.32

Selecting areas for hatching.

Warning

If you use a scale factor that results in a dense hatch pattern, the Preview and Apply operations might take quite some time to complete, leading you to believe that the computer has locked up. Wait several seconds, even minutes, before you decide your system has locked up and perform a warm or cold boot. If you can see any flicker of motion in the area being hatched or see that the hard drive is being accessed, BHATCH is still at work and the system is not locked up. Conversely, if you use a very large scale factor, you might think that BHATCH is failing to hatch the area because the hatched area fails to intersect any lines in the pattern. A good rule of thumb to use for setting the initial scale of the pattern is to set the scale to the inverse of the plot scale, just as you would with LTSCALE. Then, adjust the pattern scale up or down as needed. It usually is better to start with a scale setting that is too high than one that is too low because a high scale setting will not result in the computer trying to generate an extremely dense hatch pattern.

Defining Complicated Areas to Be Hatched

Quite often, you need to hatch an area but leave subareas within the overall area unhatched or hatch them with a different pattern (see fig. 18.33).

Figure 18.33

Complex area with islands.

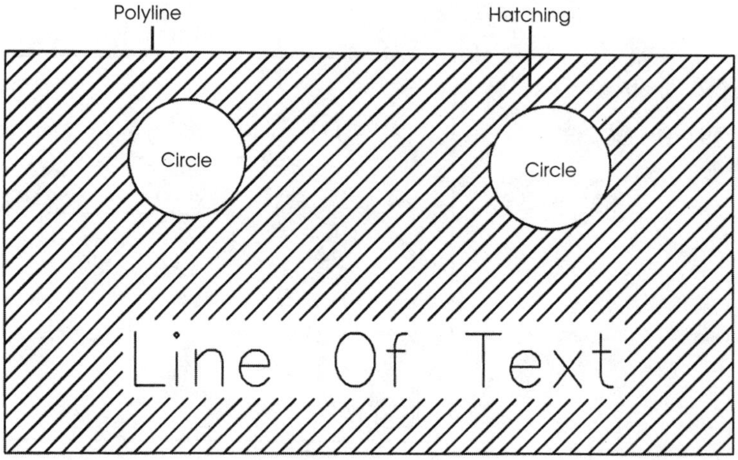

The subareas within the overall area are referred to as *islands*. As with the overall hatch area, an island must be a closed area defined by one or more objects. Text and mtext objects are also treated as islands by the BHATCH command, which ensures that they are not drawn through the text.

Defining islands is easy. If you use the Select Objects button to define the area to be hatched, all you have to do is select the objects that define the boundaries of the islands. For text or mtext objects, just selecting them is sufficient.

If you use the Pick Points button to define the areas, the islands automatically are defined as found. Sometimes this method finds islands that you don't want BHATCH to consider. In such cases, use the Remove Islands button to remove them from consideration. Be careful when you pick the point(s) used to define the boundary area and islands. The point(s) should be external to the islands you want BHATCH to consider, but internal to the overall hatch area. For example, a pick point outside of the circles but within the overall polyline would result in a hatch like that shown in figure 18.38.

In the following exercise, you hatch areas that have islands (lots 102 and 104).

Hatching Areas with Islands

Continue from the previous exercise, in the CHAP18A drawing.

`Command:` *Choose Hatch (Draw, Hatch)*	Issues BHATCH
Choose Inherit Properties	Specifies hatch settings will be set by selecting existing hatch object
`Select hatch object:` *Pick* ① *(see fig. 18.34)*	Selects hatch object to emulate
Choose Pick Points	Specifies selection of hatch are by picking points
`Select internal point:` *Pick* ②	Sets internal point for BOUNDARY

`Selecting everything...`
`Selecting everything visible...`
`Analyzing the selected data...`	

`Analyzing internal islands...`	
`Select internal point:` ↵	Ends selection of areas
Choose Preview Hatch	Previews hatch
Choose Continue	Ends preview
Choose Apply	Draws hatch
`Command:` ↵	Repeats BHATCH

Choose Inherit Properties	Specifies hatch settings will be set by selecting existing hatch object
`Select hatch object:` *Pick* ③	Selects hatch object to emulate
Choose Select Objects	Specifies hatch area is to be defined by selecting boundary objects
`Select objects:` *Pick* ④, ⑤, ⑥, ⑦, ⑧, ⑨ ↵	Selects boundary and islands
Choose Preview Hatch	Previews hatch
Choose Continue	Ends preview
Choose Apply	Draws hatch; your drawing should look like figure 18.35

Save your work.

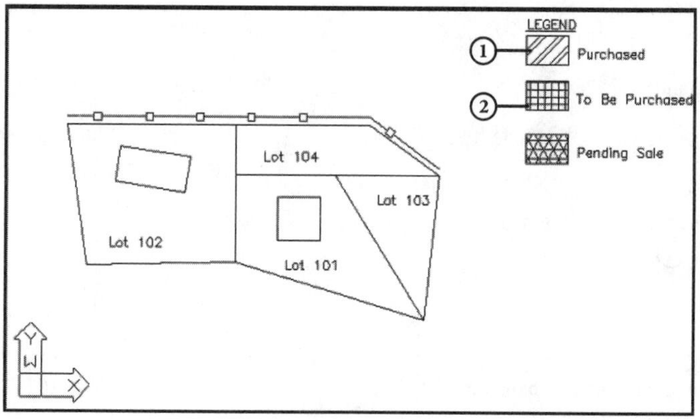

Figure 18.34

Selecting objects for hatching.

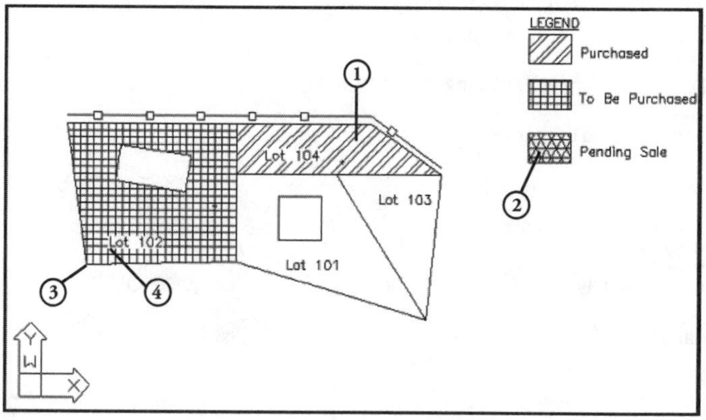

Figure 18.35

CHAP18.DWG with hatched areas.

Sometimes the BOUNDARY routine triggered by the Pick Points buttons will not define the area you had in mind. In such situations, defining the area by selecting the boundary objects, as you did in the preceding exercise, is an easy alternative.

Hatching with ISO Hatch Patterns

AutoCAD comes with several hatch patterns that conform to ISO standards. The pattern names all begin with an *ISO* prefix and can be found toward the end of the Pattern drop-down list. If you choose to use an ISO hatch pattern, you enable the ISO Pen Width option, allowing you to set the hatch scale by selecting a pen width. When you choose a particular pen width for the pattern, the Scale option automatically is set equal to the pen width. You can, if you choose, override the scale set by selecting a pen width just by entering a new value in Scale.

Like the ISO linetypes, the ISO hatch patterns are designed to be used in drawings set up for the metric system, where each drawing unit is equal to 1 mm. Keep this in mind, because the ISO hatch patterns may not be generated correctly for combinations of small areas and large scale factors.

Using the HATCH Command

A less sophisticated version of the BHATCH command is the HATCH command.

The HATCH command is the command-line predecessor of the BHATCH command. For Release 13, it has a new option that enables you to define the area to be hatched by picking points that outline the boundary. This option (not available with BHATCH) enables you to hatch an area without first having to draw objects to delineate the area, the direct hatch option.

After invoking HATCH, you are prompted for the name of the pattern to apply, its scale, and its rotation angle. After you supply these answers, the following prompt appears:

```
Select hatch boundaries or RETURN for direct hatch option,
```

Here you can select the objects that make up the hatch boundary or press Enter for the direct hatch option. If you select the direct hatch option, you see the following prompt:

```
Retain polyline? <N>
```

If you answer Yes, the polyline generated to delineate the areas to be hatched is not erased after the hatch is generated. The default answer of No results in the polyline being removed at the end of the command.

Finally, the next prompt appears:

```
From point:
```

Now you pick the beginning point of the hatch boundary, after which you see the following options:

```
Arc/Close/Length/Undo/<Next point>:
```

- **Arc.** The Arc option enables you to define an arc as part of the boundary. After you specify this option, you have several options to define the arc. The Arc options are similar to the options for the ARC command. To exit the Arc option, you need to select Close or Line.
- **Close.** This option closes the boundary and returns you to the previous prompt. You want to always end your boundary definition with the Close option to ensure a closed boundary.
- **Length.** This option draws a line of a length that is tangent to the previous line or arc segment.
- **Undo.** This option undoes the last segment.
- **Next point.** The default option is to pick the next point that defines the boundary.

After the boundary is generated, you see the following prompt:

```
From point or RETURN to apply hatch:
```

You can define another boundary (an island perhaps) or press Enter to generate the hatch and end the command. You should not define boundary lines that intersect each other; otherwise, you may not get the hatching you intend. Likewise, if you define islands, you should not select points that have previously been used to define the area.

One major drawback of the HATCH command is that it always generates nonassociative hatches, meaning that hatches generated with HATCH do not work with HATCHEDIT, nor do they update automatically when you edit the boundary objects.

Editing Hatches

After drawing a hatch, you may find that you want to change the pattern itself or change the boundaries of the area that is hatched. AutoCAD makes it easy to do both. By default, hatch objects produced by BHATCH are *associative*. This means that the parameters defining the hatch, including which objects define the hatch area, are recorded with the hatch object.

Editing Associative Hatches

To edit hatch objects, use the HATCHEDIT command. After you select the hatch object to be edited, the Hatchedit dialog box is displayed.

The Hatchedit dialog box is the same as the Boundary Hatch dialog box with many of the options disabled (see fig. 18.36).

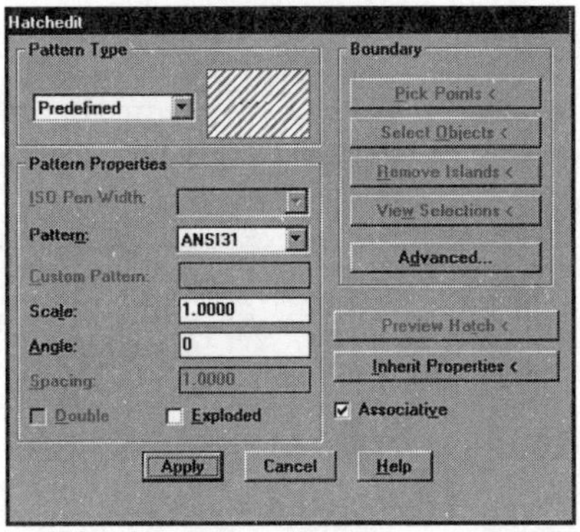

Figure 18.36

The Hatchedit dialog box.

After you select the hatch you want to edit, you can change the pattern type, the parameters controlling the pattern, the hatch style (Advanced button), and even explode the hatch (making it nonassociative). After you make a hatch nonassociative, you cannot use HATCHEDIT to edit it again.

TIP

You also can edit other properties of a hatch object, such as layer and color, with DDMODIFY, and you can access the Hatchedit dialog box from the Modify Associative Hatch dialog box that DDMODIFY displays.

If you use any edit command to change the boundary objects of an associative hatch, the hatch automatically is regenerated to fit the modified boundary. If the boundary modification results in an open boundary, the hatch will not be updated and will be changed into a nonassociative hatch. An example of such a boundary change would be to make a break in a circle that was hatched. The associativity of a hatch also is removed if you remove any boundary objects or islands that were used to generate the original hatch.

An associative hatch is updated even if it resides on a layer that has been turned off or frozen; when the layer is thawed or turned on, the hatch conforms to the modified hatch boundary. If the hatch is on a locked layer when the boundary is modified, the hatch is not updated. You must force the hatch to update by selecting the hatch with the HATCHEDIT command and then choosing the Apply button. If the hatch is nonassociative, such as those drawn with the HATCH command, the hatch is not automatically adjusted to fit the modified boundaries; you have to erase the existing hatch and hatch the modified area again.

TIP

If, for any reason, the hatch is not adjusted to conform to the modified boundaries, select the hatch with the HATCHEDIT command and choose the Apply button. As long as the hatch is associative, it will be adjusted.

When you select hatches for editing commands, the system variable PICKSTYLE plays a very important role. PICKSTYLE has four potential settings, as follows:

0 No group or associative hatch selections

1 Group selection enabled

2 Associative hatch selection enabled

3 Group and associative hatch selections enabled

The default for PICKSTYLE is 1. When PICKSTYLE is set to 2 or 3 and you select a hatch, the boundary objects associated with that hatch also are selected, sometimes leading to unwanted results. For example, if you select a hatch you want to erase with PICKSTYLE set to 3, not only do you erase the hatch, but you erase all associated boundary objects. To avoid this, leave PICKSTYLE set to 1 or 0. PICKSTYLE is not on the menu, so to set it, you need to enter it at the `Command:` prompt.

Selecting boundary objects without also selecting the hatch pattern can be tricky. Window selections work well. Grips are a very good way to edit the boundary objects of a hatch. A hatch is a special type of block; it therefore has a single grip point (unless you have grips in blocks enabled). This point is the insertion point of the hatch, which is always 0,0, no matter where the hatch actually resides on the drawing. If the view of the drawing in your window does not show the point 0,0, you never see the grip point. If you have PICKSTYLE set to 2 or 3, selecting a hatch results in the grip points of the boundary objects appearing as well. If you edit the boundary objects that have grips, the associated hatch updates to reflect the changed boundaries.

Another good way to select boundary objects without selecting the hatch is to turn off the layer the hatches are on, leaving only the boundary objects visible. Since AutoCAD automatically adjusts hatches on layers that are turned off, you do not lose anything by turning the hatch layer off.

In the next exercise, you use HATCHEDIT to adjust a pattern. You'll also change the boundaries of a hatch.

EDITING HATCHES

Continue from the previous exercise, in the CHAP18A drawing.

In the following steps, you change the hatch pattern for lot 104.

`Command:` *Choose Edit Hatch (Modify, Special Edit)*	Issues HATCHEDIT

`Command: _hatchedit`
`Select hatch object:`
Pick ① *(see fig. 18.37)*
	Selects hatch to be edited

Choose Inherit Properties	Specifies option to set hatch patterns by selecting an existing hatch
`Select hatch object:` *Pick* ②	Selects hatch to emulate
Choose Apply	Adjusts hatch to new parameters

`Analyzing associative hatch...`

In the following steps, you adjust the boundaries of lot 102.

`Command:` *Set* PROPERTY *as the current layer*	
`Command:` *Turn off layer* HATCH	Isolates the property lines from the hatching
`Command:` *Choose Stretch (Modify, Resize)*	Issues STRETCH

Select objects to stretch with the C (crossing-window) or CP (crossing-polygon) selection options.

`Select objects:` **C** ↵	Specifies crossing window
`First corner:` *Select the lower left corner of Lot 102 with a crossing window using* ③ *and* ④	Selects property lines to be stretched
`Select objects:` ↵	Ends object selection
`Base point or displacement:` **-20,-20**	Specifies displacement
`Second point of displacement:` ↵	
`Analyzing associative hatch...`	

Turn layer HATCH back on to display the adjusted hatch (see fig. 18.38).

Save your drawing.

Figure 18.37

Editing hatches.

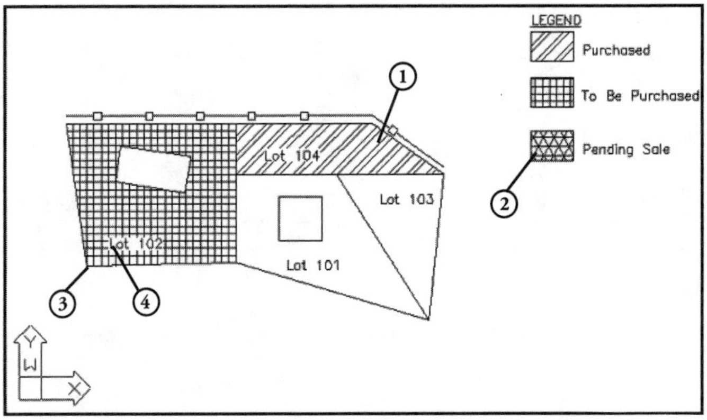

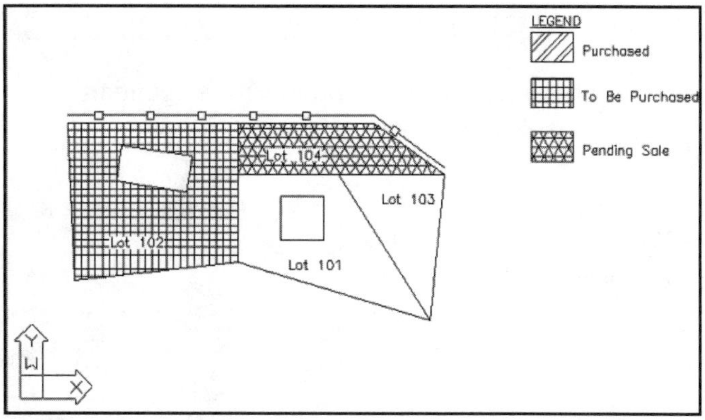

Figure 18.38

CHAP18.DWG with modified hatches.

Exploding Hatches

A hatch is a special type of block known as an *anonymous block*. Because a hatch is a block, no matter how complicated the hatching, each generated hatch is a single object. A single object is much easier to select to edit. You can, however, generate the hatch in an exploded form (as individual lines) by enabling the Exploded option in the Boundary Hatch dialog box.

In an exploded form, a hatch is not a single object but a collection of lines that form the pattern. When you edit an exploded hatch, you gain some editing flexibility within the hatched area. You can, for example, clear a portion of a hatched area by erasing the lines in the area.

However, this gain in flexibility is compromised by what you lose. An exploded hatch is not an associative hatch. Should you edit the boundary objects of the hatch, AutoCAD cannot automatically adjust the hatch to fit the new boundaries. You have to erase the old hatch and use the BHATCH command to regenerate the hatch. You cannot use HATCHEDIT on an exploded hatch.

You can use the EXPLODE command to explode an associative hatch after it has been drawn. The EXPLODE command is covered in more detail in Chapter 11, "Block Structure, Editing, Organization, and Management."

TIP

You lose more than you gain by generating an exploded hatch or by exploding an existing hatch. After you explode a hatch, you can undo the action only by using UNDO command. You are much better off working with associative hatches.

Controlling Hatch Boundaries and Style

If you choose the Advanced button in the Boundary Hatch dialog box, the Advanced Options dialog box appears (see fig. 18.39).

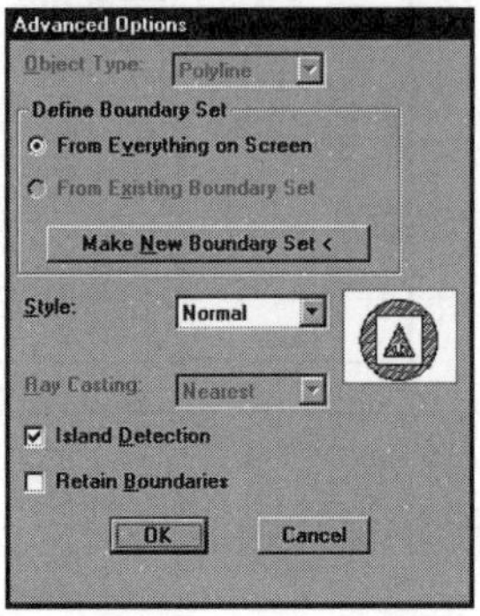

Figure 18.39

The Advanced Options dialog box.

Normally you do not need to change any of the settings in the Advanced Options dialog box to draw hatches. Understanding the options, however, gives you more control over the hatching process. The first option is Object Type, which is active only if the option Retain Boundaries (near the bottom of the dialog box) is enabled. When you create a hatch, BHATCH creates temporary polylines that delineate the area to be hatched and any islands within the area. These temporary polylines are erased by default after the hatch is drawn. You can retain them, however, by enabling the Retain Boundaries option. Furthermore, you can retain them as polylines or as regions (see Chapter 9, "Drawing with Complex Objects," for more information on regions).

You also can define the boundary set that BHATCH uses. The *boundary set* is the set of all objects that BHATCH examines when you use the Pick Points option to define the area to be hatched. Initially, the boundary set is every object in the current viewport. If you have a very crowded drawing, that boundary set might be so large that it significantly slows down the BHATCH command. If so, choose the Make New Boundary Set button to explicitly select the objects to consider as you define the area to be hatched. You can make a new boundary set anytime you want as you pick points to define hatch boundaries. If you choose to select another area to be hatched after already selecting one area to be hatched, the default boundary set is the Existing Boundary Set, the most recently used boundary set.

Another reason you might want to make a new boundary set is to hatch an area that has other objects within it that you don't want to be considered when the hatch boundaries are being formed. For example, you might have several lines going through the area to be hatched but which you don't want to be considered in the hatching process. If the stray lines are on a separate layer, you can turn it off; otherwise, you can define the boundary set to exclude the stray lines.

Tip

Normally you do not need to define your own boundary set. The default, every object visible in the current viewport, usually is satisfactory.

The Style option controls how BHATCH treats islands within islands, within the overall hatch area. The default style is Normal. The Normal style results in alternating areas being hatched, as shown in figure 18.40.

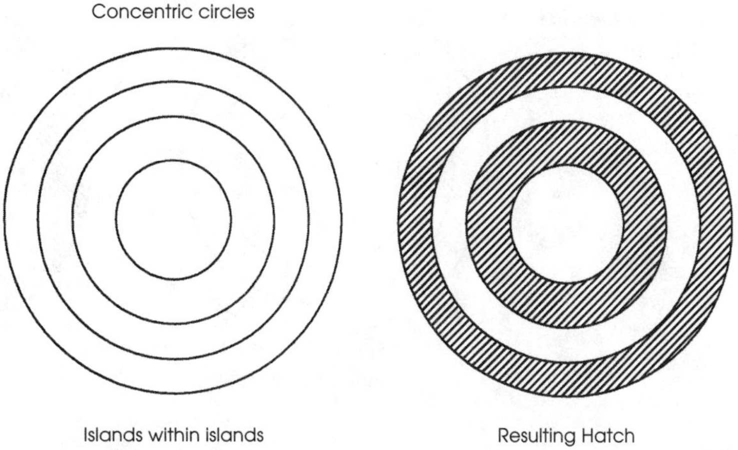

Figure 18.40

Hatching a complex area with the normal style.

You also can choose the Outermost style. The Outermost style results in the outermost area, the area between the two outermost boundaries, being hatched (see fig. 18.41).

The last style is the Ignore style, which results in the islands being ignored and the overall area being completely hatched, as shown in figure 18.42.

Figure 18.41

Hatching a complex area with the outermost style.

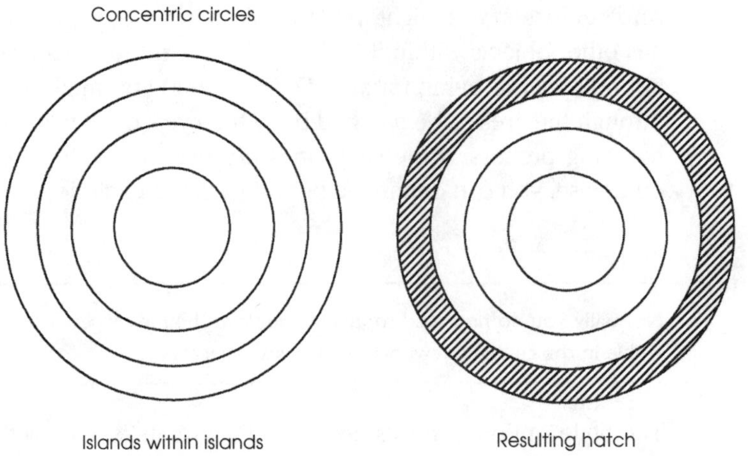

Figure 18.42

Hatching a complex area with the Ignore style.

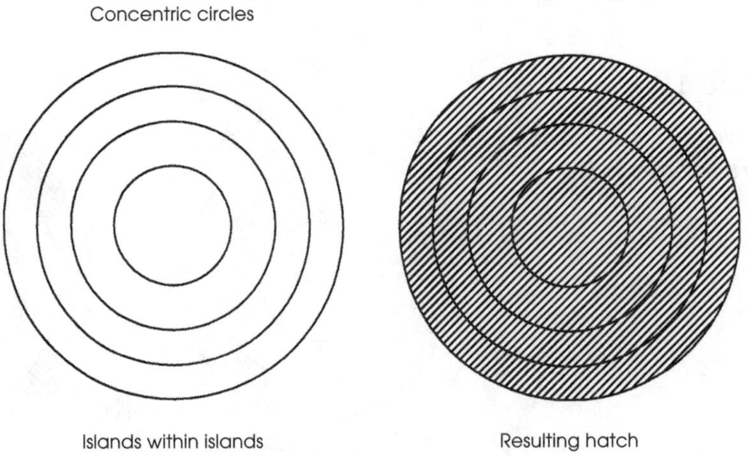

TIP

You can get the same effect, without changing the style, using the Remove Islands option to remove any islands you don't want considered. For instance, the equivalent of the Ignore style is to remove all islands within the overall boundary. The equivalent of setting the style to Outermost is to remove all islands except the outermost one.

The Ray Casting option is enabled only if the Island Detection option is disabled. *Ray casting* refers to the method used for finding a boundary when the Pick Points option is used to define the overall hatch area. A line is projected from the pick point until a boundary object is encountered, then the algorithm follows the boundary object in a counterclockwise direction until it finds another boundary object or ends up at the starting point. If the algorithm can trace a boundary to the starting point, it has successfully defined a closed area. If not, you get an error message and must try again. By default, the line is projected to the nearest object. But you can specifically direct the algorithm to project the initial line in the +x, –x, –y, or +y directions, which forces the algorithm to find a particular object first.

Defining New Hatch Patterns

Even with a library of over 50 predefined hatch patterns, you might find yourself needing additional patterns. AutoCAD does enable you to define your own hatch patterns. You can add to the ACAD.PAT file or define a new hatch pattern in its own PAT file (the Custom pattern type). In theory, hatch patterns are easy to create because each pattern is only a collection of sets of parallel lines. In practice, defining a new hatch pattern often proves complicated and time-consuming. You would be much better off purchasing one of the many hatch pattern libraries commercially available. To find out more about available products, check with your dealer, or visit the AutoCAD forum on CompuServe.

You now know how to draw objects using linetypes and how to draw hatches. AutoCAD comes with a fair sized library of predefined linetypes and hatch patterns ready for you to use. Should you need additional definitions, you can define your own or purchase them. Using linetypes and hatches is easy and can make the information on your drawing easier to comprehend.

chapter

19

INTRODUCTION TO DIMENSIONING

To communicate a design, a drawing must convey more than mere graphic entities and text. Many drawings require additional dimensions to show what lengths, angles, diameters, and sizes are required to construct the design. The necessary dimensions often are more important than the drawing itself. For example, an object not drawn to scale still might not affect the project if the dimensions are correct, but if a dimension is incorrect, you can end up with delays and additional costs to the production of the design.

You must, therefore, have accurate dimensions in your drawings. AutoCAD's dimensioning environment is dynamic. As you place dimensions on an object, AutoCAD reads the size of the object and automatically places the correct text in the dimension line. This automatic text feature forces you to construct accurate drawings before you can place your dimensions without having to edit the text to show the correct size in the dimension. When you construct your drawing accurately, you can use AutoCAD's powerful dimensioning tools to place correct dimensions on your design quickly.

This chapter covers the following topics:

- How to set up a drawing for dimensioning
- Understanding the power in associative dimensions
- Introduction to all the dimension placement commands
- How to place leaders in your drawings
- Using dimensions in the paper space environment

The dimensioning environment can be very frustrating to work with if you don't understand all the factors that control how dimensions work. After working through this chapter you will feel much more in control of the dynamic dimensioning features of AutoCAD.

The dimensioning toolbar makes entering dimension commands very quick and easy. After you open and place the dimensioning toolbar where you like it, you have access to all the dimension commands from one central location.

NOTE

When you place linear dimensions, you do not have to specify whether you want a vertical or horizontal dimension, owing to the inference dimensioning feature in Release 13. AutoCAD automatically infers the appropriate dimension command according to the direction you drag your cursor from the object you are dimensioning. This new technique makes dimensioning in AutoCAD faster and more efficient.

The DIM Mode and Equivalent Commands

When you enter DIM at the `Command:` prompt, AutoCAD enters the old (Release 12 and prior) dimensioning mode, which enables you to use the dimension subcommands from earlier releases of AutoCAD. In Release 13, the dimensioning commands are mainstreamed with all other commands and can be entered at the `Command:` prompt.

The DIM command is still available in Release 13, but only to maintain compatibility with Release 12. The following is a list of dimension commands used in the DIM mode and their Release 13 equivalents:

DIM Mode Command	*Release 13 Command*
ALIGNED	DIMALIGNED
ANGULAR	DIMANGULAR
BASELINE	DIMBASELINE
CENTER	DIMCENTER
CONTINUE	DIMCONTINUE
DIAMETER	DIMDIAMETER
HORIZONTAL	DIMLINEAR Horizontal
LEADER	LEADER
ORDINATE	DIMORDINATE
RADIUS	DIMRADIUS
ROTATED	DIMROTATE
VARIABLES	DIMSTYLE Variables
VERTICAL	DIMLINEAR Vertical

Exploring the Release 13 Dimensioning Environment

The Release 13 dimensioning commands are accessed through tools on the Dimensioning toolbar and its flyouts. Most of these tools and the commands they issue are covered in this and the next chapter

Placing dimensions in AutoCAD can be quick and easy. AutoCAD takes as much work as it can out of dimensioning by automatically calculating distances based on the size of the objects you select. Style settings control the sizing of the various parts of the dimensions, such as arrowheads, extension lines, and dimension text, by keeping all the dimensions consistent in a drawing. After you select where you want to place a dimension, AutoCAD automatically creates all the dimension parts. If you compare this process to board drafting, in which you must draw every part of every dimension, you begin to see the real power of using AutoCAD to create your drawings.

TIP

> Quick and accurate dimensioning relies more on drawing technique than on dimensioning. The accuracy of the objects in your drawing controls the accuracy of the drawing's dimensions because AutoCAD calculates dimensions based on the points you specify. When you draw an object out of scale or at an incorrect size, the drawing's dimensions reflect the incorrect size unless you override the dimension text. If you have to override the dimension text by typing the correct size every time, you defeat the speed advantage that AutoCAD provides when it calculates dimensions and places the correct text for you.
>
> Creating drawings accurately from the beginning greatly increases the speed at which you can place your dimensions. When your drawings are put together accurately you can then use object snaps or select the objects to locate the extension or lines. This will enable you to select extension line origins very quickly and accurately.

When you start a drawing from scratch, AutoCAD has a basic dimensioning environment already set up for you. This basic setup works fine for some drawings, but you might have different dimensioning needs. The problem with the basic setup is that it is so basic that it works with only one type of drawing environment and with only one scale factor. Most of the drawings you create require you to make adjustments in this basic dimensioning setup.

Preparing Your Drawing for Dimensions

Every drawing you create requires that you prepare a few settings before AutoCAD can place your dimensions. You should adhere to the following basic procedure before you place dimensions in any drawing.

Here are the five basic steps for setting up a drawing for dimensioning:

- Create a separate layer for all your dimensions. Keep your dimensions separate from all other information in your drawing.
- Create a text style to use only when you create dimensions.
- Set your dimension units to the type of measurement that you want your dimensions to reflect (decimal, architectural, engineering, and so forth), and set the precision to the smallest unit you want your dimensions to show.
- Set the Overall Scale factor (the DIMSCALE variable) in the Dimension Style dialog box to the plot scale factor of your drawing.
- Set the running object snap to ENDPoint, INTersection, and QUAdrant to speed up picking points on objects that you want to dimension.

TIP

When you create prototype drawings from which to start your new drawings, be sure to do the basic steps for setting up dimensioning in each prototype. Then whenever you start a new file, you automatically are set up for dimensioning. Otherwise, you have to go through the dimensioning setup steps every time you start a new drawing.

In the exercises in the following sections, you create a layer for dimensions, create a text style to use only for dimensions, open and place the dimensioning toolbar, set the units for dimensions, set the appropriate dimension scale factor, and turn on the running object snap for quicker placement of dimension origin points.

Creating a Dimension Layer

The first step is to create a layer for your dimensions, as shown in the following exercise.

STARTING YOUR BASIC DIMENSIONING SETUP

Create a new exercise drawing called CHAP19A. Use the DIM-EXER drawing from the Accompanying CD as a prototype.

Choose Layer (Layer Control)	Opens the Layer Control dialog box
Type **DIMS** *in the text box, then choose New*	Creates a new layer named DIMS
Select DIMS *in the* Layer Name *list box*	Selects a layer for a subsequent actions
Choose Set Color	Opens the Set Color dialog box
Choose the green color box in the Standard Colors *area*	Sets the color green for the DIMS layer
Choose OK	Exits the Set Color dialog box
Choose Current	Makes DIMS the current layer
Choose OK	Closes the Layer Control dialog box and saves the changes

The current layer is now DIMS.

Controlling Dimension Text

When you place a dimension in a drawing, the current text style dictates the dimension text. The STYLE command for text is covered in Chapter 17, "Annotation with Text." You need to create a text style called DIMS to use specifically for your dimensions so that you can control the font of the dimension text without affecting the other text in your drawing. After you create the DIMS text style, be sure to set it current before you place your dimensions.

TIP

Creating a DIMS text style enables you to set a width factor for your dimension text. If the dimension text does not fit within the extension lines of a dimension, AutoCAD places the text outside of the extension lines. Dimension text that is a little bit thinner than normal (such as .75 width) stays inside the extension lines better if, for example, the extension lines are close together.

Figure 19.1 illustrates the difference between a dimension style that has a width of 1.0 and a style that has a width of .75.

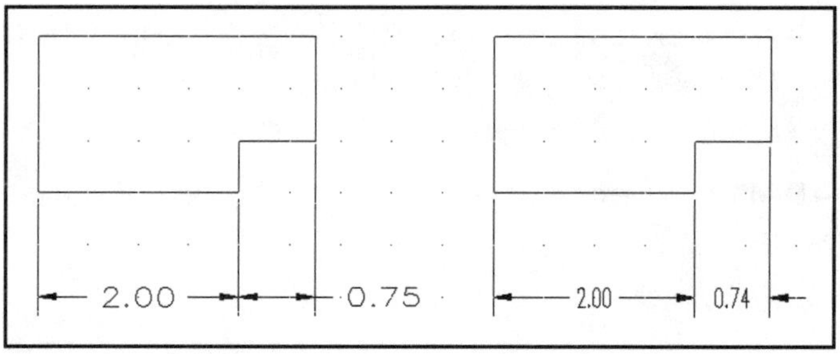

Figure 19.1

Comparing dimension text styles.

In the following exercise, you create a dimension text style called DIMS.

CREATING A TEXT STYLE FOR DIMENSION

Continuing in the CHAP19A drawing, you will now create a text style to use for dimensioning.

`Command:` *Choose* Data, Text Style	Issues the STYLE command
`_'style (or ?) <STANDARD Text style name >:` **DIMS ↵**	Creates a new text style called DIMS and opens the Select Font File dialog box

Choose Type It	Closes dialog box and prompts for file
`Font file <txt>:` **ROMANS** ↵	Searches path and loads font file
`Height <0.0000>:` ↵	Accepts the default floating text height
`Width factor <1.000>:` **.75** ↵	Specifies a thinner text width than normal
`Oblique angle <0>:` ↵	Accepts the default angle
`Backwards? <N>:` ↵	Default to forward-reading text
`Upside-down? <N>:` ↵	Default to right-side-up text
`Vertical? <N>:` ↵	Accepts the default

DIMS is now the current text style.

NOTE

You should always set the height of the text style you use for dimensions to zero so that the setting for text height in the Annotation dialog box can control the dimension's text height.

If you set the text height in the current text style to anything other than zero, the style height setting overrides the Annotation dialog box setting, which prevents the DIMTXT variable from controlling the text height. For more information, refer to Chapter 20, "Styling and Editing Dimensions."

Using Dimension Style Families

You control the appearance of your dimensions by using dimension style families. A *dimension style family* is a named set of dimension variables. There are 58 dimension variables included in each named style. Each named style can have its own settings of variables. Each named style is called the *parent style*, and within each parent style are family members, representing the different types of dimensions that you can use (LINEAR, RADIAL, ANGULAR, DIAMETER, ORDINATE, and LEADER dimensions commands).

You can apply different settings to each of the different family members. You can apply different settings to your linear commands than to your diameter commands, for example, but still use only one named dimension style, eliminating the need for a new dimension style for each type of dimension you place in the drawing.

AutoCAD's basic drawing setup includes one premade style, called STANDARD, in each new drawing you start. STANDARD gives you a foundation on which to set up the dimension variables necessary to get your dimensions to look the way you want. AutoCAD also includes drawings that you can use as prototypes to start drawings of your own. The C:\ACADWIN\COMMON\SUPPORT directory contains five drawings that can be used as prototypes: SIS_ARCH, SIS_MECH, ACADISO, US_ARCH, and US_MECH. Each of these drawings has dimension style settings to follow SIS, ISO, and US architectural and mechanical standards.

In a single drawing you might need several different types of variable settings for the different objects you dimension. Managing and editing dimension styles is covered in more detail in Chapter 20, "Styling and Editing Dimensions."

Dimension Styles Dialog Box Options

The Dimension Styles dialog box (see fig. 19.2) includes the following options:

- **Current.** Sets a dimension style current.
- **Save.** Saves the current settings to the style.
- **Name.** Creates a new dimension style name.
- **Rename.** Renames a style.
- **Parent.** Creates a style family parent.
- **Geometry.** Sets all variables for dimension components.
- **Format.** Controls text formatting and location.
- **Annotation.** Sets variables for controlling text.

See Chapter 20, "Styling and Editing Dimensions," for using the additional options and sub-dialog boxes.

NOTE

The complete list of dimension settings that make up a dimension style, along with a brief definition of each variable, are listed in Appendix F.

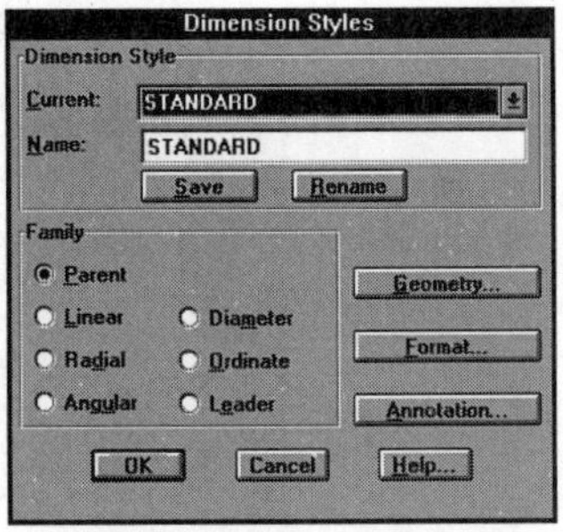

Figure 19.2

The Dimension Styles dialog box.

All dimensions use a named dimension style. The default style in the ACAD prototype is called STANDARD. You use the STANDARD dimension style (with a few minor adjustments) for your dimensions in this chapter. In Chapter 20, you design your own dimension style according to your specific needs.

In the following exercise, you will use the Dimension Styles dialog box to set the units and precision for the dimension text.

SETTING YOUR UNITS AND FEATURE SCALING

Continue in the CHAP19A drawing.

Choose Data, Dimension Style	Displays the Dimension Styles dialog box
Choose Annotation	Displays the Annotation dialog box (see fig. 19.3)
In the Primary Units *area, choose* Units	Displays the Primary Units dialog box

You want Decimal units (the default), and you will set the precision to two places.

In the Dimension *area, click in the* Precision text box	Drops down the precision list

Note the precision setting—0.00 indicates two places of precision.

Choose OK, *then* OK *again*	Closes the Primary Units and Annotation dialog boxes and accepts the changes to the precision setting

Remain in the Dimension Styles dialog box.

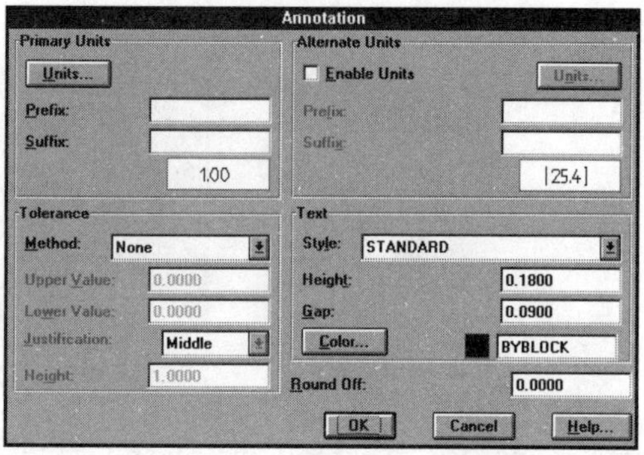

Figure 19.3

The Annotation dialog box.

Drawing Scale Factor and Dimensions

The most important dimension setting to adjust when you set up a drawing for dimensioning is the Overall Scale setting in the Geometry dialog box, which adjusts the components and distances in a dimension to the correct size for the current drawing's plotting scale factor. In a drawing plotted at 1=2 (for a drawing scale factor of 2), for example, you want to set your overall scale (DIMSCALE) to 2 (the total scale factor for the drawing). If your arrowhead size is then set to .25, AutoCAD automatically scales it up to .5. This .5-long arrowhead in the drawing is reduced to .25 long when you plot it.

To set the Overall Scale factor for your drawing, you use the Geometry dialog box in the following exercise.

Setting the Dimension Scale Factor

Continue in the CHAP19A drawing, in the Dimension Styles dialog box.

Choose Geometry	Opens the Geometry dialog box (see fig. 19.4)

In the Scale section, the default setting in the Overall Scale text box is 1.00. The scale factor for the exercise drawing is 1=1, so accept the default setting.

Choose OK	Accepts the default settings in the Annota tion dialog box
Choose Save dimension	Saves the changes to the STANDARD style
Choose OK	Exits the Dimension Styles dialog box

Save the drawing.

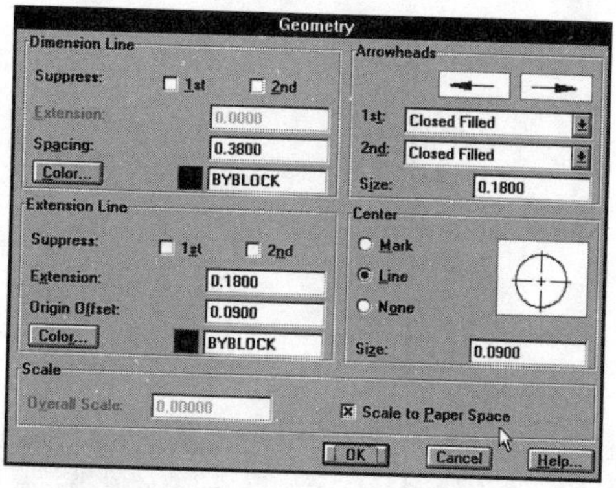

Figure 19.4

The Geometry dialog box.

TIP

You can find all the settings you need for your dimension sizes and distances in the Dimension Styles dialog box. Some people make adjusting dimension settings much more difficult than necessary by failing to use the Overall Scale setting, which forces them to calculate all the correct sizes for all the individual components of a dimension.

The best way to set up dimensioning is to set all your individual dimension component sizes and distances to the size you want them to be when you plot them and let the Overall Scale setting in the Geometry dialog box globally scale your dimensions to the correct size in the plotted AutoCAD drawing.

Placing Your Dimensioning Toolbar

You can speed up the selection of your dimension commands by having the Dimensioning toolbar open and conveniently positioned in your drawing. Figure 19.5 shows a typical placement of the Dimensioning toolbar, which you can move as a floating toolbar to any part of the drawing screen, or dock to the top, bottom, left, or right of the screen. After you place the Dimensioning toolbar, as you open other drawings it stays in its position until you close it.

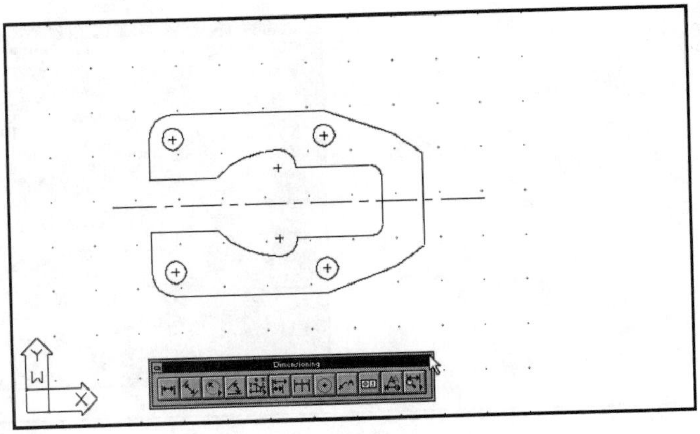

Figure 19.5

Positioning the Dimensioning toolbar.

Fast Dimensions with Automatic Object Snaps

If you create a perfectly accurate drawing, you would not want to turn around and place inaccurate dimensions by eyeballing their extension-line placement. To place dimensions accurately on objects in a drawing, you must select objects or use AutoCAD's object snap options. Object snaps are covered in Chapter 3, "Drawing Accurately."

To avoid having to enter an object snap every time you place an extension line, set your running object snap mode to ENDPoint, INTersection, QUAdrant.

TIP

One of the most important speed tips for placing dimensions is to set your running object snap mode. You use object snaps to place all your dimensions, and if you enter an object snap every time you place an extension line, you are wasting time.

Your basic dimensioning setup is now complete. Setting up for dimensions and tweaking them to work the way you want them to is covered in more detail in the next chapter. But, for now, you are ready to begin dimensioning.

Understanding the Components of a Dimension

Every dimension in AutoCAD is composed of standard components. The extension lines pull the dimension information away from the object and indicate where the dimension starts and stops. The dimension line carries the dimension text and is capped at both ends by an arrowhead or tick mark (terminator). All these component parts are grouped together like a block and edited as a single object.

Associativity

You place each dimension in a drawing with all the individual parts grouped together. *Definition points* (or *DEFPOINTS*) mark where the extension lines originate on the selected objects. If you select these points along with the objects to be edited—for example, if you select the definition points along with an object, and then stretch the object to a new length—you stretch the definition points as well, and AutoCAD automatically updates the dimension and extension lines and text to reflect the new length. This dynamic capability AutoCAD has of updating dimensions when you edit them is called *associativity*.

NOTE

In the drawing file, each dimension is a block. Dimensions are unnamed blocks. If you list all the blocks in a file and see that you have several unnamed blocks in your drawing, don't be alarmed—the dimensions in your drawing make up some of those unnamed blocks.

You can place dimensions as individual objects by turning the DIMASO variable to off. It is not recommended that you do this, however, because you lose a lot of power to make changes to your dimensions with the dimensioning edit commands.

NOTE

Any time you use associative dimensions, AutoCAD automatically creates a layer called DEFPOINTS, which holds the definition points at the origin of the extension lines and the second arrowhead. You can see the definition points on this layer, but they do not plot.

Using Dimensioning Commands

Placing dimensions in a drawing can be frustrating because dimensions don't always come in right, and controlling them seems to be a mystery. When you drew dimensions using manual board drafting techniques, you could fudge the tight areas, but when you are beginning to learn AutoCAD, this isn't as easy.

If certain features of a dimension do not fit between the extension lines, AutoCAD places the dimension as it deems appropriate. You might not like the way AutoCAD positions the dimension, and you will probably feel powerless to correct its position. Starting out by using a correct dimensioning setup, however, eliminates some of the early frustration when you begin to dimension.

As you work through the following dimension commands, you will be introduced to additional tips and techniques to give you better control of the dimensioning environment. You might recall from earlier in this chapter the technique to which you were introduced to help your dimensions come in with better control: to create a text style for dimensions that has a thinner text width. Chapter 20, "Styling and Editing Dimensions," introduces all the tools that enable you to have complete control of the way you create dimensions.

Linear Dimensions

Linear dimensions refers to a group of dimensions that measure between two points. The points can be endpoints, intersections, or any two points you can identify (usually by selecting an object or using object snap). Linear dimensions include the following types of measurements:

- **HORIZONTAL.** This linear dimension creates horizontal dimension lines. Drawn with the Linear Dimension tool (the DIMLINEAR command).
- **VERTICAL.** This linear dimension creates vertical dimension lines. Drawn with the Linear Dimension tool (the DIMLINEAR command).
- **ALIGNED.** This linear dimension creates dimension lines that are aligned (parallel) to an object or two specified points. Drawn with the Dimaligned tool (the DIMALIGNED command).
- **ROTATED.** This linear dimension creates dimension lines rotated to a specified angle, not necessarily aligned with the points. Drawn with the DIMLINEAR, using the Rotated option.
- **CONTINUE.** This linear dimension creates a series of dimensions, with each dimension using the previous dimension's second extension line as the new dimension's first extension. Drawn with the Continue Dimension tool (the DIMCONTINUE command).
- **BASELINE.** This linear dimension creates a series of dimensions, all from the same first extension line. Drawn with the Baseline Dimension tool (the DIMBASELINE command).

Automated Horizontal and Vertical Dimensions

New in Release 13 is a feature that places linear dimensions, called automated dimensioning. AutoCAD executes this feature whenever you use the DIMLINEAR dimension command. *Automated dimensioning* enables you to place a horizontal, vertical, or rotated dimension merely by selecting an object that is placed horizontally or vertically. You don't have to specify which command you want to use because AutoCAD automatically knows. This feature enables you to use one linear dimension command to place all your horizontal, vertical, and rotated dimensions simply by pressing Enter after each dimension that you place.

DIMLINEAR Command Options

The DIMLINEAR command is three dimensioning commands and two dimension text customizing commands built into one dimension command. The command options for DIMLINEAR are as follows:

- **TEXT.** Before you place a dimension, the text option enables you to specify or add to the dimension text.
- **ANGLE.** This option changes the default angle of the dimension text. Whether the default angle is aligned with the dimension line or is horizontal is controlled by the Dimension Styles dialog box—see Chapter 20, "Styling and Editing Dimensions."
- **HORIZONTAL.** This option places a horizontal dimension.
- **VERTICAL.** This option specifies a vertical dimension.
- **ROTATED.** This option rotates the dimension line to the angle you specify.

The Horizontal, Vertical, and Rotated options of DIMLINEAR function identically, except that one places the dimension line horizontally and the other places the dimension line vertically. After issuing the DIMLINEAR command, you pick one point for the first extension line and then a second point for the second extension line, or press Enter and select a single object (such as a line, arc, or circle) to place the extension origins on that object. Then, as you move the cursor to the point where you want the dimension line, AutoCAD assumes you want either a Horizontal or Vertical dimension. If you want to specify that AutoCAD place a Horizontal, Vertical, or Rotated dimension, you can enter an H, V, or R to force AutoCAD to draw that type of dimension.

Placing Horizontal Dimensions

In the following exercise you place horizontal dimensions on the CHAP19A drawing. Remember that your running object snap is set to endpoint.

Using DIMLINEAR for Horizontal Dimensions

Continue in the CHAP19A drawing, with the setup from the previous exercises.

Choose Linear Dimension	Issues the DIMLINEAR command
`Select first extension line origin or RETURN to select:` *Pick the vertical line at* ① *(see fig. 19.6)*	Sets the first extension line origin
`Second extension line origin:` *Pick the line at* ②	Sets the second extension line origin

As you move your cursor, watch it drag the dimension.

Move the cursor to the right	Drags a Vertical dimension
Move the cursor above or below the object	Drags a Horizontal dimension
`Dimension line location (Text/Angle/Horizontal/Vertical/Rotated):` *Pick* ③	Sets the dimension line location and draws the dimension

Next, place the second horizontal dimension.

`Command:` ↵	Repeats the DIMLINEAR command
DIMLINEAR `Select first extension line origin or RETURN to select:` *Pick the vertical line at* ④	Sets the first extension line origin
`Second extension line origin:` *Carefully pick the top endpoint of the center mark at* ⑤	Sets the second extension line origin
`Dimension line location (Text/Angle/Horizontal/Vertical/Rotated):` *Pick* ⑥	Sets the dimension line location and draws the dimension above the object

Save the drawing.

Figure 19.6

Placing horizontal dimensions.

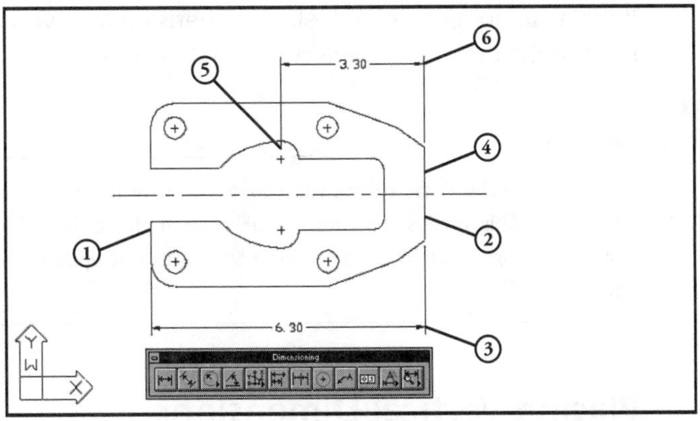

Editing Dimension Text as You Place Dimensions

Two of the options available after you specify the dimension line placement are the Text and Angle options.

The Angle option enables you to specify an angle to rotate the text in the dimension, without rotating the dimension itself.

When you enter T for the Text option, the Edit Mtext dialog box opens. The two default brackets (<>) represent the default dimension text; you can add text before or after the default brackets, which adds the text to the dimension and leaves the default text intact. Enter **Typ.** and add one space before the default brackets as shown in figure 19.7, then choose OK. The new text is added before the default dimension text. After you specify the dimension line location, you see the new text.

Figure 19.7

Editing default dimension text.

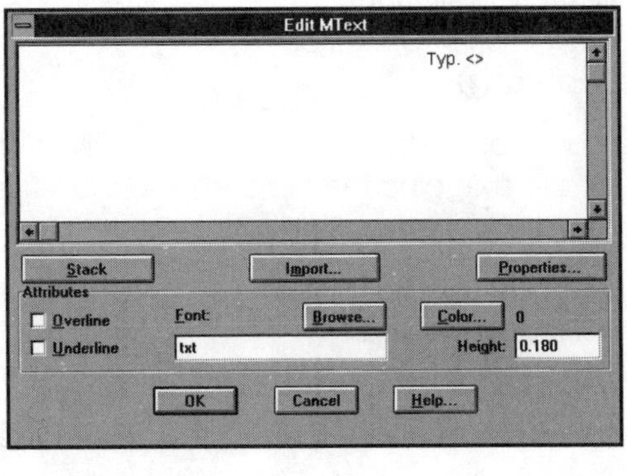

If you want to replace the default dimension text, you can press the Delete key to remove the default brackets and then type the text you need.

WARNING

If you replace the default dimension text, you lose the associativity of the text with the dimension. This means if you scale or stretch the object dimensioned, or move the dimension origin points, the dimension text does not update itself to the new dimension size.

Placing Vertical Dimensions

Now that you have placed some horizontal dimensions, you should find placing vertical dimensions similar. In the following exercise you use the DIMLINEAR command again, this time placing vertical dimensions.

ADDING VERTICAL DIMENSIONS

Continue in the CHAP19A drawing.

Choose Linear Dimension	Issues the DIMLINEAR command
`_dimlinear` `Select first extension line origin or RETURN to select:` *Carefully pick the left endpoint of the center mark at* ① *(see fig. 19.8)*	Sets the first extension line origin
`Second extension line origin:` *Carefully pick the left endpoint of the center mark at* ②	Sets the second extension line origin

Move your cursor out to the left and watch as the dimension drags an image of itself. Because you are dragging the dimension to the left of the object, the DIMLINEAR command creates a vertical dimension.

`Dimension line location (Text/Angle/Horizontal/Vertical/Rotated):` *Pick* ③	Sets the dimension line location and draws Vertical dimension

The second vertical dimension defines the hole placement off the center line.

`Command:` ↵	Repeats the DIMLINEAR command

`Select first extension line origin or RETURN to select:` *Carefully pick again at* ④	Sets the first extension line origin
`Second extension line origin:` *Pick the horizontal line at* ⑤	Sets the second extension line origin
`Dimension line location (Text/Angle/Horizontal/Vertical/Rotated):` *Pick* ⑤	Sets the dimension line location and draws Vertical dimension

Save the drawing.

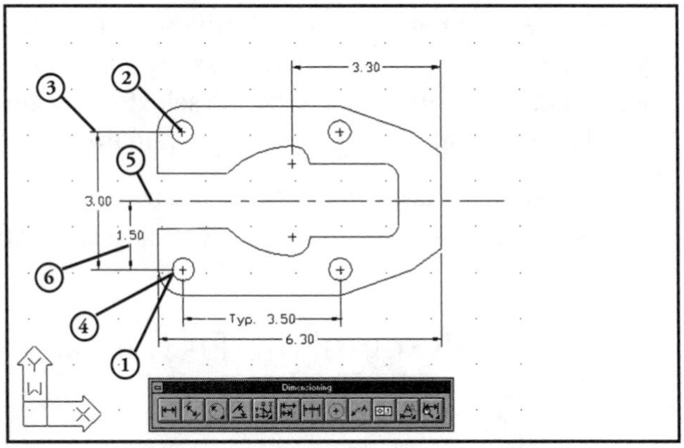

Figure 19.8

Applying vertical dimensions.

The DIMLINEAR command enables you to place horizontal, vertical, and rotated dimensions without having to enter a different command each time, thus greatly reducing the amount of time it takes to place dimensions. The Rotated, Angle, and Text options are covered in later sections.

Fast Chain Dimensions with the DIMCONTINUE Command

The DIMCONTINUE command enables you to place dimensions in single row with ease and speed. You begin a series of dimensions by using a LINEAR dimension. Next, you use the DIMCONTINUE command to string together subsequent dimensions in a series. The DIMCONTINUE command automatically begins each new dimension line at exactly the point at which the last dimension line leaves off. You do not have to specify where to place each dimension line of the series because the DIMCONTINUE command automatically uses the specified dimension's placement and lines up additional dimensions perfectly. DIMCONTINUE defaults to continue from the last linear dimension, or you can Press Enter at the prompt and then select a dimension from which to continue.

TIP

Before you begin to use the DIMCONTINUE command, make sure that the running object snap is set to ENDPoint, INTersection, or both, which enables you to pick the second extension line location very quickly. After you specify the second extension location, AutoCAD automatically asks for the next second extension line origin, and repeats until you press Enter to stop.

The following three exercises introduce the DIMCONTINUE command. In the first, you set up for DIMCONTINUE by creating a linear dimension, then continuing it as a string of dimensions. The option to select an existing dimension to start a string of continuous dimensions from is covered in the third exercise.

First, you place a horizontal dimension at the lower left corner of the gasket in the following exercise. The running object snap is already set to ENDPoint.

Placing the First Dimension

Begin a new drawing named CHAP19B, using the DIM-CONT drawing from the accompanying CD as a prototype.

Choose Linear Dimension (Dimensioning)	Issues the DIMLINEAR command
`First extension line origin or RETURN to select:` *Pick the line at* ① (see fig. 19.9)	Sets the first extension line origin
`Second extension line origin:` *Pick the line at* ②	Sets the second extension line origin
`Dimension line location (Text/Angle/Horizontal/Vertical/Rotated):` *Pick* ③	Sets the dimension line placement and and draws dimension

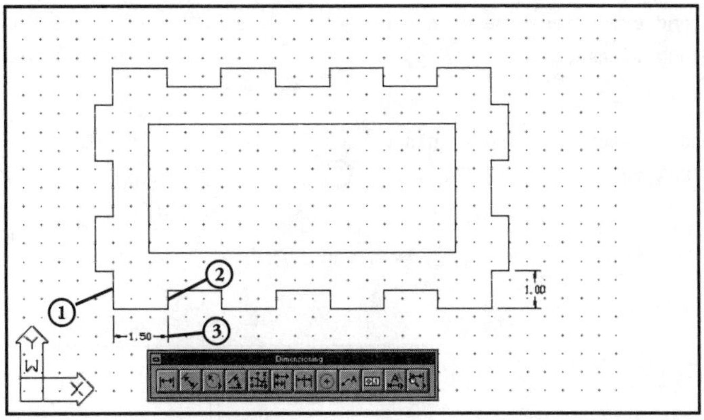

Figure 19.9

The first dimension for a chain.

NOTE

The order in which you select the extension lines is important. The DIMCONTINUE command continues from the second extension line, so make sure that the order from the first extension line to the second is in the direction you want.

After you place the first linear dimension, you can place continuous dimensions very quickly. In the following exercise, you create a continuous chain of dimensions from the first dimension, which you placed in the preceding exercise. You begin by issuing the DIMCONTINUE command.

STARTING THE CONTINUOUS CHAIN

Continue in the CHAP19 drawing.

Choose Continue Dimension (Dimensioning)	Issues the DIMCONTINUE command
`Second extension line origin or RETURN to select:` *Pick the line at* ① *(see fig. 19.10)*	Sets the second extension line origin, draws dimension, and prompts for another
`Second extension line origin or RETURN to select:` *Pick the line at* ②	Sets next second extension line origin

`Second extension line origin or RETURN to select:` *Pick* ③, ④, ⑤, and ⑥	Sets four more second extension line origins and draws dimensions
`Second extension line origin or RETURN to select:` *Pick the line at* ⑦	Sets the second extension line origin and draws dimension, placing text with a leader

Stay in the DIMCONTINUE command for the next exercise.

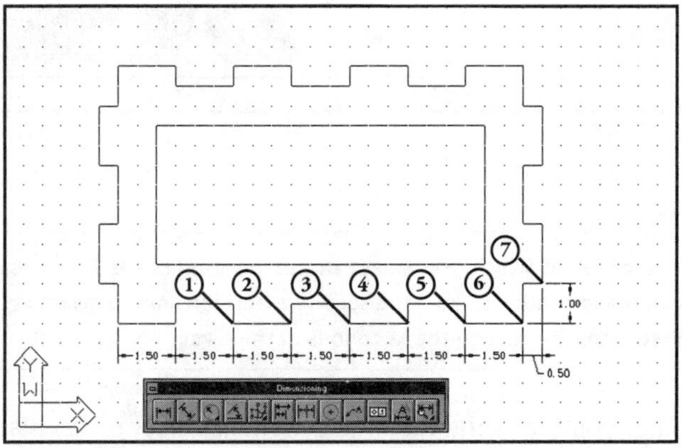

Figure 19.10

Placing continuous dimensions.

If running object snap is set to Endpoint, all you have to do is pick one feature after another and away you go. The dimension text for ⑦ wouldn't fit, so it was automatically placed with a leader.

NOTE

If you are using the DIMCONTINUE command and the text does not fit between two extension lines, AutoCAD places the text above the dimension line with a leader. When AutoCAD does this, you might need to reposition the dimension text placement. Using grips is the easiest technique to move dimension text. Using grips to reposition dimension text is covered in Chapter 20, "Styling and Editing Dimensions."

By default, the DIMCONTINUE command strings dimensions from the most recently drawn linear dimension in the current drawing session. By pressing Enter, you can then select any existing linear dimension from which to continue a string of dimensions.

Tip

When you select an existing dimension from which to create a continuous chain, the side of the dimension you select is the side from which the continuous chain is started.

In the following exercise, you begin a string of continuous dimensions from an existing dimension in the drawing. There is a vertical dimension on the lower right side of the gasket, so you will select it to start a string of dimensions from it.

Starting Continuous Dimensions from an Existing Dimension

Continue from the previous exercise, with the DIMCONTINUE command running.

`Second extension line origin or RETURN to select:` ↵	Stops sequence and prompts you to select a dimension from which to continue
`Select continued dimension:` *Pick the dimension at* ① *(see fig 19.11)*	Selects the dimension from which to continue
`Second extension line origin or RETURN to select:` *Pick* ②	Sets the second extension line origin
`Second extension line origin or RETURN to select:` *Pick* ③, ④, *and* ⑤	Sets three more second extension line origins
`Second extension line origin or RETURN to select:` ↵	Stops the sequence
`Select continued dimension:` ↵	Ends the DIMCONTINUE command

You also can use DIMCONTINUE to place continued angular dimensions. Angular dimensioning is covered later in this chapter.

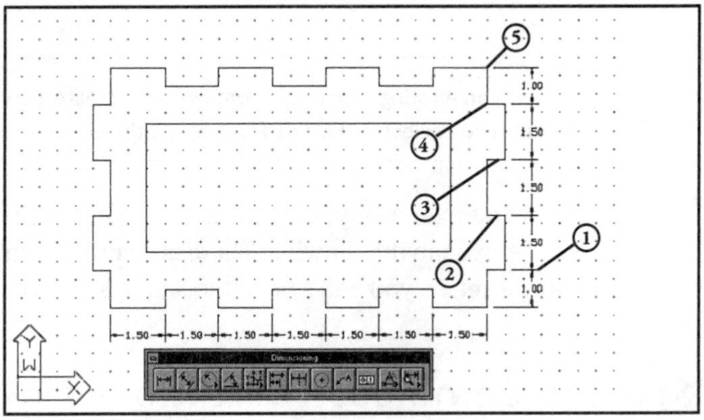

Figure 19.11

Continuing dimensions from an existing dimension.

Stacking Dimensions with BASELINE

Continuous dimensions give you the distance between each feature in a linear direction. You can use BASELINE dimensions to dimension each feature of a part, giving baseline measurements from one reference point, or *datum line*. This datum line is always the first extension line of the specified dimension, regardless of pick point or the first extension line of the default, last-created dimension.

The sequence and options for the DIMBASELINE command are the same as for the DIMCONTINUE command. In the following two exercises, you place baseline dimensions from an existing dimension, after you first place a linear dimension.

You will start by placing a horizontal dimension first. Again, remember that the running object snap is on.

APPLYING BASELINE DIMENSIONS

Start a new drawing named CHAP19C. Use the BASEDIMS drawing from the accompanying CD as a prototype.

Choose Linear Dimension (Dimensioning)	Issues the DIMLINEAR command
`First extension line origin or RETURN to select:` *Pick the line at* ① *(see fig. 19.12)*	Sets the first extension line origin
`Second extension line origin:` *Pick the top of the center mark at* ②	Sets the second extension line origin

`Dimension line location (Text/Angle/Horizontal/Vertical/Rotated):` *Pick* ③ — Places the dimension

Next, issue the DIMBASELINE command and select the second extension line origins.

Choose Baseline Dimension (Dimensioning) — Issues the DIMBASELINE command

`Second extension line origin or RETURN to select:` *Pick the top of the center mark at* ④ — Sets the second extension line origin

`Second extension line origin or RETURN to select:` *Pick the center marks at* ⑤ *and* ⑥ — Sets two more second extension line origins

`Second extension line origin or RETURN to select:`

Stay in the DIMBASELINE command for the next exercise.

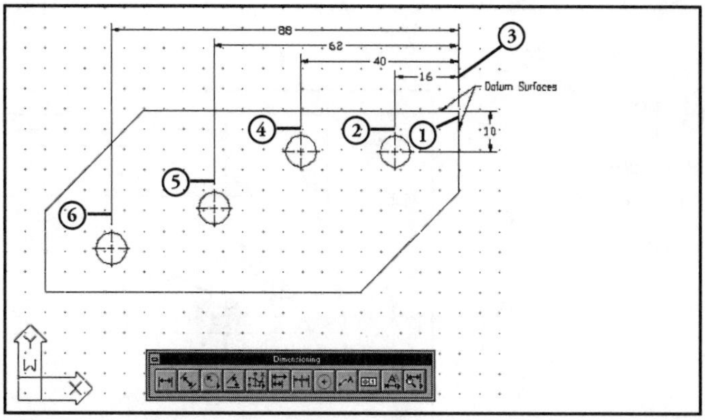

Figure 19.12

BASELINE dimensions.

In the following exercise, starting from the vertical dimension on the right of the plate drawing, you create vertical baseline dimensions using a selection to specify the initial dimension.

Baseline Dimensions from an Existing Dimension

Continue in the DIMBASELINE command from the previous exercise.

`Second extension line origin or RETURN to select:` ↵	Prompts you to select the dimension from which to start baseline dimensions
`Select base dimension:` *Pick the dimension at* ① *(see fig. 19.13)*	Selects dimension from which to start baseline dimensions
`Second extension line origin or RETURN to select:` *Pick the center mark at* ②	Specifies the second extension line origin
`Second extension line origin or RETURN to select:` *Pick the center mark at* ③	Specifies the second extension line origin
`Second extension line origin or RETURN to select:` ↵	Stops the baseline sequence
`Select base dimension:` ↵	Exits the DIMBASELINE command

Save the drawing.

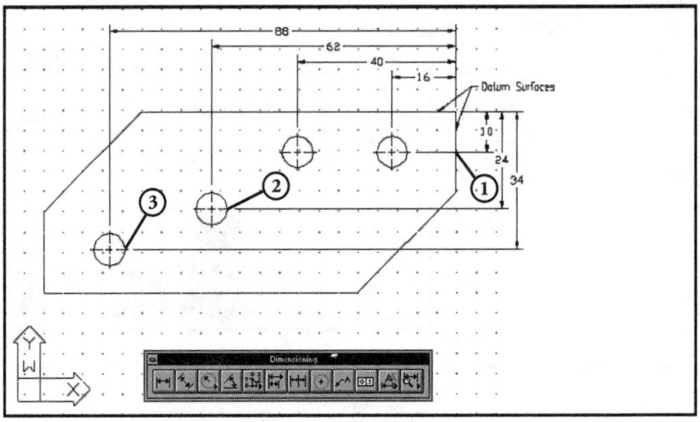

Figure 19.13

Baseline dimensions from an existing dimension.

NOTE

You can use the DIMCONTINUE and DIMBASELINE dimension commands not only on horizontal and vertical dimensions, but on any linear or angular dimension at any angle.

Using ALIGNED Dimensions

Some dimensions require the dimension line be aligned with an object, usually at an angle parallel to the extension line origins. To place a dimension with its dimension line parallel to extension line origin points, you use the DIMALIGNED command. In the following exercise, you must align the dimension for the hexagon object to follow the angle of the flat sides. Using horizontal and vertical dimensions would result in an inaccurate dimension length.

In the following exercise you place an aligned dimension to line up with the angled flat sides of a hexagon. The running object is on to speed up selection of the extension line origin points.

PLACING ALIGNED DIMENSIONS

Begin a new drawing named CHAP19D using the ALI-DIM drawing from the Accompanying CD as a prototype.

Choose Aligned Dimension (Dimensioning)	Starts the DIMALIGNED command
`First extension line origin or RETURN to select:` *Pick the line at ① (see fig. 19.14)*	Sets the first extension line origin
`Second extension line origin:` *Pick ②*	Sets the second extension line origin
`Dimension line location (Text/Angle):` *Pick ③*	Places the dimension line and draws the dimension aligned with the extension line origins

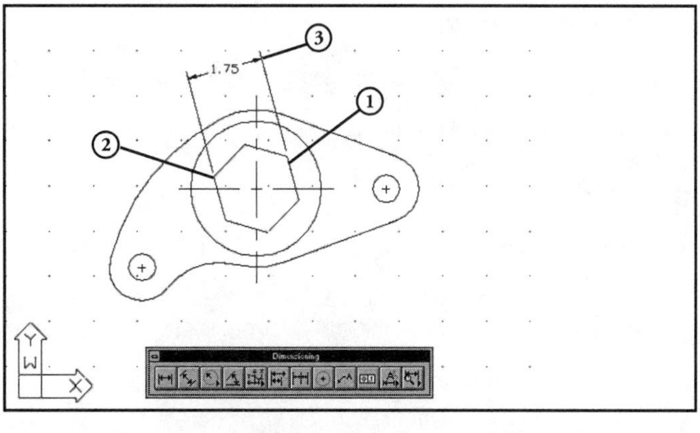

Figure 19.14

Placing an aligned dimension.

Although DIMALIGNED always aligns dimensions with the extension line origins, you sometimes need a dimension at another angle that is not parallel to an object or to the extension line origins. AutoCAD calls this a *rotated dimension*.

Applying Rotated Dimensions

You do not use the Rotated dimension as often as the other linear dimensions, but when it is needed, the Rotate option of the DIMLINEAR dimension command is the only way to get the correct measurement. In the drawing used in the following exercise (see fig. 21.19), you need to dimension the slot to show its length, and neither the aligned, horizontal, or vertical dimensions can give you the correct distance measurement.

The Rotate option in the DIMLINEAR command works perfectly here. You define the two extension line origins (which are not parallel to the line being dimensioned) and specify an angle at which to place the dimension line. The dimension line angle must be parallel to the line being dimensioned.

The DIMLINEAR Rotate option places a dimension with its dimension line set to an angle that you specify. You can access this option by choosing the Linear Dimension tool from the Dimensioning toolbar, specifying the extension line origins, then entering R for Rotated.

In the following exercise, the bracket needs a dimension placed on the slot to measure its length, so use the Rotate option in the DIMLINEAR command to place the correct dimension.

CREATING A ROTATED DIMENSION

Begin a new drawing named CHAP19E using the DIM-ROT drawing from the accompanying CD as a prototype.

Choose Linear Dimension (Dimensioning)	Issues the DIMLINEAR command
`Select first extension line origin or RETURN to select:` *Pick the angled line at ① (see fig. 19.15)*	Selects the first extension line origin
`Second extension line origin:` *Pick the line at ②*	Specifies the second extension line origin

Move the cursor around and see the dimension drag as horizontal or vertical.

`Dimension line location (Text/Angle /Horizontal/Vertical/Rotated):` **R** ↵	Enables the Rotate dimension option
`Dimension line angle <0>:` **45** ↵	Sets the angle for the dimension line
`Dimension line location (Text/Angle /Horizontal/Vertical/Rotated):` *Pick* ③	Sets the dimension line location and draws the dimension at 45°

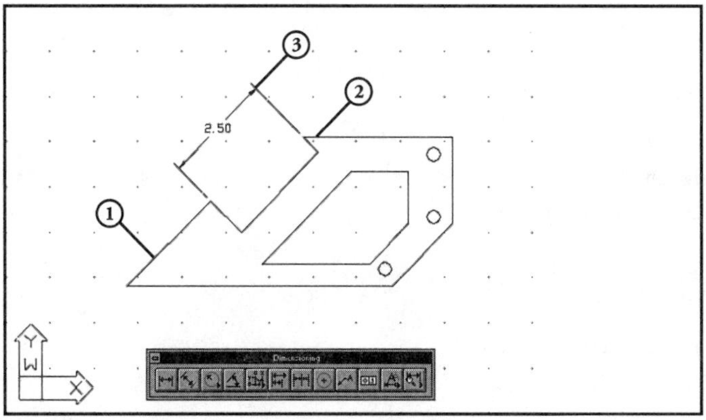

Figure 19.15

Applying a rotated dimension.

Notice that the dimension line is not parallel to the angle of the extension line origins, as in an Aligned dimension, but rather the dimension line follows the angle you specified.

Dimensioning Curved Objects

The linear dimension commands can be used to dimension circles and arcs, depending on the type of dimension information you need. The following is a list of AutoCAD dimension commands used for putting information on circles and arcs:

- **DIMRADIUS.** The DIMRADIUS command is used to specify the radius of an arc, or half the diameter of a circle.
- **DIMDIAMETER.** The DIMDIAMETER command places a dimension that shows the total distance across a circle.
- **DIMCENTER.** The DIMCENTER command places a center mark at the exact center of an arc or circle.

Placing Radius Dimensions

The DIMRADIUS command calculates an arc's radius and places the information with a leader.

The drawing in the following exercise needs several RADIUS dimensions placed.

PLACING RADIUS DIMENSIONS

Begin a new drawing named CHAP19F using the HOLE-DIM drawing from the Accompanying CD as a prototype.

Choose Radius Dimension (Dimensioning, Radial Dimension)	Starts the DIMRADIUS command
`_dimradius` `Select arc or circle:` *Pick the arc at ① (see fig. 19.16)*	Specifies the arc on which to place the radius dimension

Move the cursor and watch the leader drag.

`Dimension line location (Text/Angle):` *Pick ②*	Sets the leader and text placement, and draws dimension
`Command:` ↵	Repeats the DIMRADIUS command
`Select arc or circle:` *Pick the arc at ③*	Specifies the arc on which to place the radius dimension
`Dimension line location (Text/Angle):` *Pick ④*	Draws the dimension

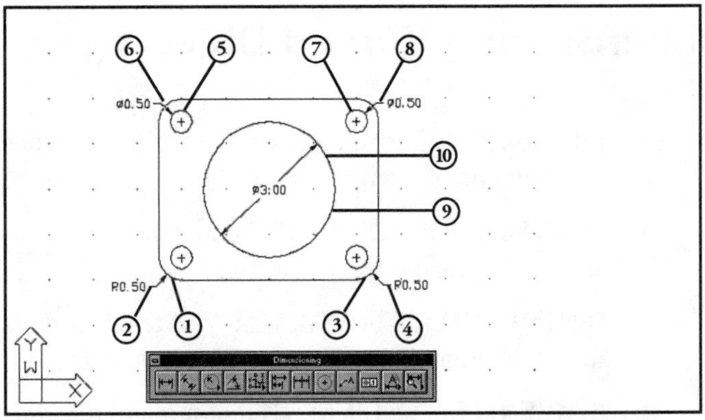

Figure 19.16

Placing radius and diameter dimensions.

The Text and Angle options work similarly to those of DIMLINEAR.

Dimensioning Circle Diameters

The DIAMETER dimension works similarly to the RADIUS command. You select the circle to dimension and then place the leader.

In the following exercise, you place some diameter dimensions in the drawing.

APPLYING DIAMETER DIMENSIONS

Continue from the previous exercise.

Choose Diameter Dimension (Dimensioning, Radial Dimension)	Issues the DIMDIAMETER command
`_dimdiameter` `Select arc or circle:` *Pick the circle at ⑤ (refer to figure 19.16)*	Selects the circle on which to place a diameter dimension
`Dimension line location (Text/Angle):` *Pick ⑥*	Sets the leader and text locations, and draws the dimension
`Command:` ↵	Repeats the DIMDIAMETER command
DIMDIAMETER	
`Select arc or circle:` *Pick the circle at ⑦*	Selects the circle on which to place a diameter dimension
`Dimension line location (Text/Angle):` *Pick ⑧*	Draws the dimension

The previous two dimensions call out the dimension with a leader and no internal dimension line because it will not fit in the circle. The next dimension adds a dimension line and puts the text in the circle because the circle is larger.

`Command:` ↵	Repeats the DIMDIAMETER command
DIMDIAMETER	
`Select arc or circle:` *Pick the circle at ⑨*	Selects the circle
`Dimension line location (Text/Angle):` *Pick ⑩*	Draws the dimension

The Text and Angle options work similarly to those for DIMLINEAR.

TIP

The size of a circle or arc determines if the text is placed inside or outside. How your text and arrowheads are positioned is controlled in the Format dialog box, which is covered in Chapter 20, "Styling and Editing Dimensions."

Adding Center Marks to Arcs and Circles

You use the DIMCENTER command to designate the center origin point of a circle or arc.

NOTE

The appropriate size of the center mark of a circle or arc is determined by the size and scale factor of the drawing. You use the DIMCEN system variable to control the size of a center mark. This variable is set by the Center area in the Geometry dialog box, within the Dimension Styles dialog box.

A positive DIMCEN setting draws only center marks. A negative setting draws center marks with extensions to just beyond the circle's quadrant points. In the Geometry dialog box, you set the size in the Size box and set the type of mark with the radio buttons. Mark (DIMCEN +) draws only center marks, Line (DIMCEN -) draws both marks and extension lines, and None (DIMCEN 0) draws neither.

In the following exercise, you use the DIMCENTER dimension command to place center marks in all the circles and at all the fillet origins.

PUTTING CENTER MARKS IN FILLETS AND HOLES

Begin a new drawing named CHAP19G using the CEN-MARK drawing from the Accompanying CD as a prototype.

Choose Center Mark (Dimensioning)	Starts the DIMCENTER command
`Select arc or circle:` *Pick the hole at ① (see fig. 19.17)*	Locates the center mark at the center of the circle

Press Enter to repeat the DIMCENTER command. Place center marks at all the remaining holes and fillets. After you finish, the HOLE drawing should look like figure 19.18.

Figure 19.17

Placing center marks.

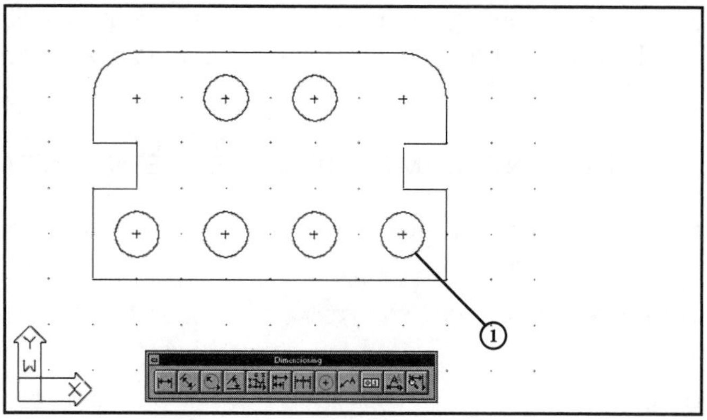

NOTE

Center marks placed by DIMCENTER are placed as individual lines, but those placed by DIMRADIUS and DIMDIAMETER are part of the associative dimension object.

Dimensioning Angles

In the design process, the relationship of two objects and the angle between them can be critical to the final product. If the angle is not correct, you can end up with a flawed design. AutoCAD has the capability to create and measure the angle between objects very accurately.

Placing ANGULAR Dimensions

You use the DIMANGULAR command to measure the angle between two objects.

If you pick an arc, DIMANGULAR dimensions it. If you pick a circle, its center sets the vertex, the pick point sets one endpoint, and DIMANGULAR prompts for the second endpoint. If you pick a line, DIMANGULAR prompts for another line and uses their intersection as the vertex and their ends as the endpoints.

NOTE

DIMANGULAR works backwards from DIMLINEAR—the default is to select an object, and you must press Enter if you want to pick points for the angle vertex and endpoints.

In the following two exercises, you place an angular dimension, then use the DIMCONTINUE command to create a string of angular dimensions.

Placing Dimensions between Angled Objects

Start a new drawing named CHAP19H using the DIMANG drawing from the accompanying CD as a prototype.

`Command:` *Choose Angular Dimension (Dimensioning)*	Issues the DIMANGULAR command
`_dimangular` `Select arc, circle, line, or RETURN:` *Pick the line at ① (see fig. 19.18)*	Selects the first line
`Second line:` *Pick the line at ②*	Selects the second line

Move the cursor around and watch the dimension drag to dimension the various inside and outside angles formed by the two lines.

`Dimension arc line location (Text/Angle):` *Pick ③*	Places the arc dimension line and text

The Text and Angle options work similarly to those of DIMLINEAR.

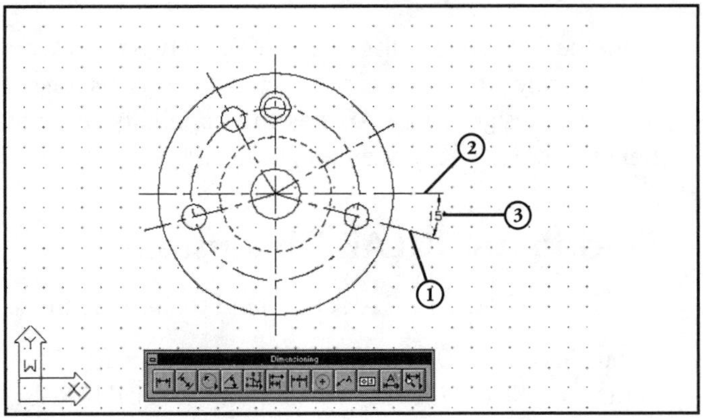

Figure 19.18

Placing an angular dimension.

TIP

You also can use DIMANGULAR to find the angle between two objects but not place the dimension. At the `Command:` prompt type DIMANGULAR and select two objects to dimension. When the dimension begins to drag and you can see the text, read the angle and then press Esc to cancel the command and not place the dimension.

Placing Drawing Notes with Leaders

You use leaders to point out a feature, then give information about that feature. Unlike dimension commands, a leader does not measure distances. A leader is composed of an arrowhead, a straight line or splined shaft, and a horizontal line called a *flat* or *hook line*. A text note of some form generally is placed at the end of the leader.

The STANDARD dimension commands put measurement information on your drawings. Sometimes you need to use text to call out information to some feature, or to point out design information. The LEADER command enables you to use a pointer to identify features and add text information.

The LEADER command has some new enhancements in Release 13. You now have many options to place information on the end of the leader. The default for annotation is single-line text. You can enter an option for multiple-line text; you can copy an existing single or multiline text, attribute definition, block, or tolerance object and attach it; or you can attach a block tolerance control frame in lieu of text. You also can specify a straight or spline-curved leader line, and whether the leader has an arrowhead. These new features greatly enhance the flexibility of the LEADER command.

NOTE

Leaders are now associative in Release 13, which means that any time you edit a leader, the arrowhead and the leader lines adjust to the new position.

Leader Command Options

The LEADER command has been enhanced to give you more capabilities with the following prompts and options:

- **Annotation.** When you press Enter to accept the default Annotation option, LEADER prompts you to enter text (Annotation) or to press Enter for other options. If you type a line of text and then press Enter, LEADER prompts `Mtext:`. If you press Enter, LEADER creates a single line of mtext. If you enter additional lines and press Enter, LEADER creates multiple lines of mtext. If you press Enter instead of entering *any* text annotation, LEADER prompts with the following:

  ```
  Tolerance/Copy/Block/None<Mtext>:
  ```

- **Tolerance.** Prompts you to create a Tolerance Control Frame to add to the end of the leader.
- **Copy.** Prompts you to select any existing text, mtext, block, attribute definition, or tolerance object to copy and attach to the leader. If you select an attribute definition, its default value is inserted as an Mtext object. If you select a text object, it is inserted as mtext.
- **Block.** Prompts you to specify a block to insert, and continues with the normal block insertion prompts.
- **None.** Draws the leader without annotation.
- **Mtext.** Pressing Enter to accept the default Mtext option opens the Edit Mtext dialog box.
- **Format.** Prompts for options for formatting the leader to be splined, straight, arrowhead, or none (no arrowhead):

  `Spline/STraight/Arrow/None/<Exit>:`

- **Spline.** Formats leader as a spline curve.
- **STraight.** Formats leader as a series of straight lines.
- **Arrow.** Places the default arrowhead style on the leader.
- **None.** Places no arrowhead on the leader.
- **Exit.** Exits format options.
- **Undo.** Undoes the last leader vertex point.

Straight leaders with arrowheads are the default each time you use leaders, so you need not use the Arrow or STraight options unless you use the None or Spline options and then change your mind.

In the drawing in the following exercise, the holes need to be called out with size information. The LEADER command is perfect for this. In the following exercise, you use the default method for text entry.

Using Leaders To Place Information

Continue in the CHAP19H drawing.	
Choose Leader (Dimensioning)	Issues the LEADER command
`_leader` `From point:` *Pick the circle at* ① *(see fig. 19.19)*	Sets the arrowhead point
`To point:` *Pick* ②	Specifies the end of the first leader
`To point (Format/Annotation /Undo)<Annotation>:` ↵	Accepts the default and prompts for annotation
`Annotation (or RETURN for options:` **HOLES THROUGH** ↵	Enters text for leader information 14 DIA-3
`MText:` ↵	Ends LEADER command and places leader and text in drawing

In the preceding exercise, LEADER automatically supplied a short hook line from the second point you picked to the text.

Figure 19.19

Placing a leader with text.

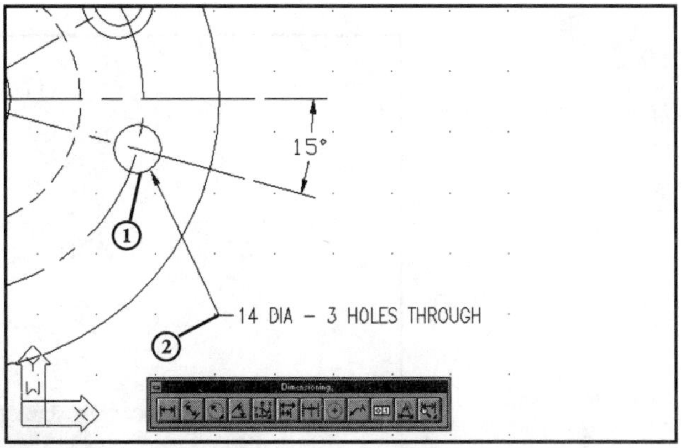

The new feature of adding multiline text to leaders enables you to add as many lines of text to your leaders as you need, which was not available in previous releases.

In the following exercise, you work through the multiline text option.

MULTILINE TEXT WITH LEADERS

Continue from the previous exercise.

Choose Leader (Dimensioning)	Issues the LEADER command
`From point:` *Pick* ① *(see fig. 19.20)*	Sets the start point for arrow
`To point:` *Pick* ②	Sets the end of leader shaft
`To point (Format/Annotation/Undo)<Annotation>:` ↵	Accepts default for Annotation
`Annotation (or RETURN for options):` ↵	Gives you further options
`Tolerance/Copy/Block/None/<Mtext>:` ↵	Displays the Edit Mtext dialog box
`Type:` **12 DIA - 18 CBORE** ↵ **12 DEEP**	Specifies text
Choose OK	Closes the Edit Mtext dialog box and draws leader and text as shown in figure 19.20

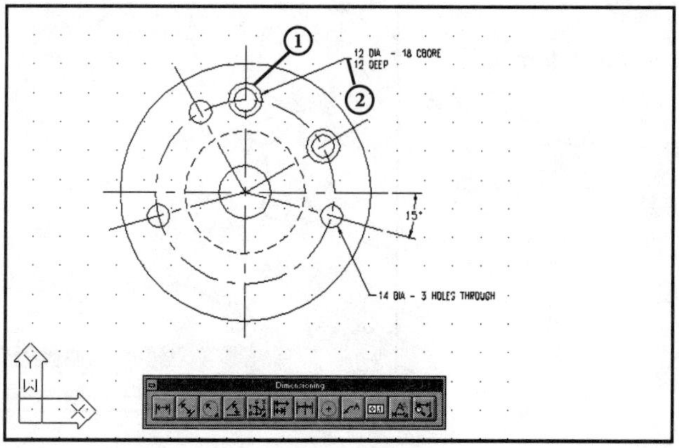

Figure 19.20

Adding multiline text to a leader.

TIP

Unless you need to specify fonts, properties, or special formatting in the Edit Mtext dialog box, it is quicker and easier to enter multiline text at the `Annotation (or RETURN for options):` prompt.

Creating Splined Leaders

One of the options in the LEADER command is to format the leader. This option gives you the ability to use splined curves for your leader shafts. You also can copy an existing text object to use for the leader you are placing.

The following exercise shows you how to use splined leaders and copy text for the leader text.

USING THE SPLINED LEADERS AND COPYING TEXT OPTIONS

Continue in the CHAP19H drawing.

Choose Leader (Dimensioning)	Issues the LEADER command
From point: *Pick ① (see fig. 19.21)*	Sets the end of the leader
To point: *Pick ②*	Sets the end of the leader shaft
To point (Format/Annotation/Undo) <Annotation>: **F** ↵	Selects the Format option
Spline/Straight/Arrow/None/<Exit>: **S** ↵	Selects the Spline option
To point (Format/Annotation/Undo) *Pick ③* ↵	Forms the spline and indicates the end of the leader spline
To point (Format/Annotation/Undo) ↵	Ends the Spline option
Annotation (or RETURN for options): ↵	Shows annotation options
Tolerance/Copy/Block/None/<Mtext>: **C** ↵	Selects the Copy option
Select an object: *Pick text at ④*	Selects the text to copied and ends the command

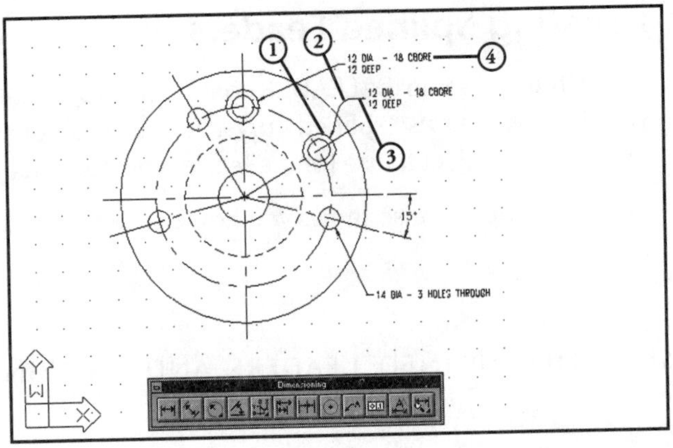

Figure 19.21

Splined leader with copied text.

NOTE

In previous versions of AutoCAD, the DIM mode LEADER command incorporated the last measured dimension in leader text if you included the string <> in the leader text. This feature is absent from the Release 13 LEADER command, but you can access the old LEADER command in DIM mode by entering DIM, then LEADER. Press Esc to exit DIM mode when finished. Leaders you create in DIM mode are not associative and only create single-line text.

Dimensioning in Paper Space

There are two methods for placing dimensions when you use paper space to plot your drawings:

- Place your dimensions in model space in a floating viewport and use automatic paper space scaling to control your dimension sizes.
- Place your dimensions in paper space.

These methods require different setups to work properly. You will begin by placing dimensions in model space in floating viewports.

Placing Dimensions in Model Space

In the following exercise, the paper space sheet is set up to plot an A-size (8.5-by-11) paper at 1=1 (full scale). The scale factor for the model space viewport is 1=25. First, set the Scale to Paper Space setting to on; you will find this setting in the Geometry dialog box in the Dimension Styles dialog box (see fig. 19.22).

Setting Dimension Scale Factor for Paper Space

Begin a new drawing named CHAP19I using the PS-DWG drawing from the accompanying CD as a prototype.

Choose Dimension Styles (Dimensioning)	Opens the Dimension Styles dialog box
Choose Geometry	Opens the Geometry dialog box
Put a check in the Scale to Paper Space box *(see fig. 19.22)*	Turns on paper space scaling
Choose OK	Exits the Geometry dialog box
Choose Save	Saves the changes to the current dimension style
Choose OK	Exits the Dimension Style dialog box

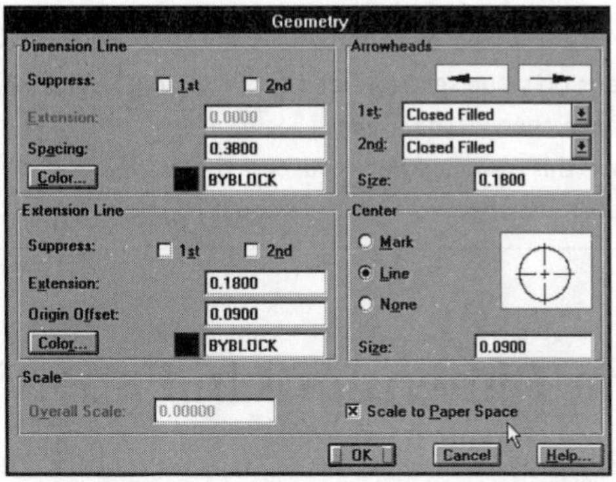

Figure 19.22

Setting paper scaling in the Geometry dialog box.

Now, make sure that model space is the current space and place linear dimensions so that your drawing looks like figure 19.23.

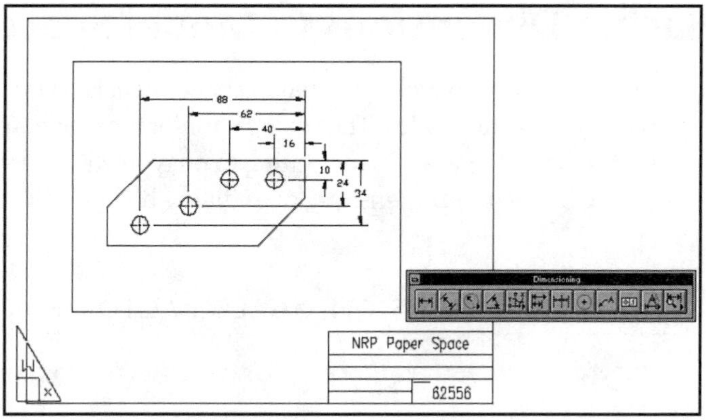

Figure 19.23

Dimensions placed in model space.

Turning on the Scale to Paper Space feature instructs AutoCAD to multiply the dimension variables settings by the zoom magnification factor for each model space viewport. This feature keeps your dimension component sizes the same size in all the viewports, regardless of the zoom scale factor in a model space viewport. For example, in the preceding exercise, you set paper space spacing on; therefore the dimensions you placed are the exact size you have set in your dimension style dialog box, no matter what zoom scale factor the viewport is set to.

TIP

The paper space environment is another reason to follow the rule mentioned in the dimension setup section. Set all your dimension variables to the size you want on the piece of paper, then let the Overall Scale setting control your dimension component sizes. If you follow this setup, when you use the Scale to Paper Space feature, the sizes of your dimensions when you plot are equal to the sizes you actually set for your variables.

Placing Dimensions in Paper Space

In the previous exercise you placed the dimensions in model space. The other option for dimensioning in the paper space environment is to place your dimensions in paper space itself, which requires a different technique to get the correct size for dimension components.

Using the DIMLFAC Variable

When you want to place your dimensions in paper space you need to set the variable DIMLFAC to match the zoom scale factor of the viewport in which you want to place dimensions.

NOTE

> The DIMLFAC dimension variable sets the linear factor for AutoCAD to scale distances when you dimension. In the following exercise, the longest dimension is 88 units long and the paper is set to 8.5-by-11, so the view of the part is only a couple units long if you try to place dimensions on it in paper space.
>
> The DIMLFAC variable scales the view of the geometry to equal its actual size, so the dimension text you place in paper space matches the geometry's actual size.

SETTING DIMLFAC FOR PAPER SPACE DIMENSIONING

Continue from the previous exercise. Erase all the dimensions and set paper space to current.

You must use the DIM mode command to set DIMLFAC for paper space.

`Command:` **DIM**	Enters DIM mode
`Dim:` **DIMLFAC** ↵	Shows DIMLFAC options
`Current value <1.0000>` `New value (Viewport):` **V**	Sets the Viewport option
`Select viewport to set scale:` Pick the viewport border at ① *(see fig. 19.24)*	Selects the viewport
`DIMLFAC set to -25.0000`	Sets DIMLFAC to the zoom scale factor of the viewport
`Dim:` **E**	Exits the DIM mode to a clear command prompt

Now use DIMLINEAR to place dimensions in paper space. As you work your way around the part, placing dimensions, notice the way AutoCAD uses the correct dimension sizes. Pick points still use object snap, snapping to objects in the floating viewport.

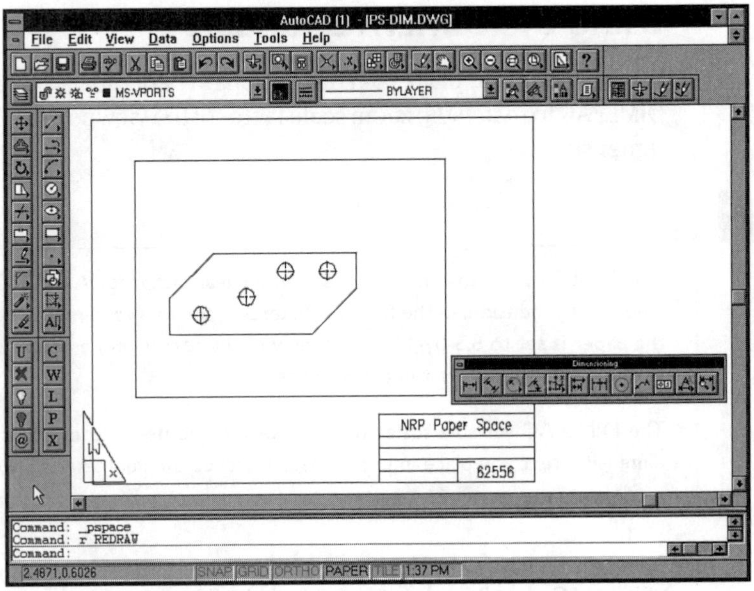

Figure 19.24

Setting to DIMLFAC to the viewport.

TIP

If both viewports are zoomed to the same scale factor, you can begin a dimension in one and end it in another.

Dimensioning is a critical skill required to create high-quality AutoCAD drawings, and one by which your professional accomplishment may often be judged. If you find that dimensioning requires an inordinate amount of time, try reviewing the techniques described in this and the next chapter.

Develop a consistent dimensioning setup from which to start all your drawings. Use object snaps, or select objects directly to be dimensioned, to quickly place accurate dimensions. Use AutoCAD's default associative dimension mode, and accept the dimension text values AutoCAD calculates, as a check on your design work. If the displayed dimension is incorrect, it probably reflects an inaccuracy in the drawing itself. Plan ahead to use CONTINUE and BASELINE dimension techniques, and recognize the importance of selecting the proper pick points. In dimensioning perhaps more than in most other aspects of using AutoCAD, improving your understanding of technique can greatly improve your efficiency.

chapter

20

Styling and Editing Dimensions

Chapter 19, "Introduction to Dimensioning," shows you how to set up the dimensioning environment and how to use the basic dimension commands. This chapter takes you through the commands and tools available to create and manipulate dimensions to make your drawings look the way you want. AutoCAD provides several options to control your drawings' dimensions.

In working through this chapter you will be introduced to the following topics:

- *Using dimension style families*
- *Editing dimension styles*
- *Controlling the individual components of a dimension*
- *Controlling the dimension text placement*
- *Managing how your dimension text looks*
- *Understanding the power of dimension associativity*
- *Managing the dimension environment in large projects*

Exploring Dimension Style Families

The individual components of a dimension are controlled by dimension variables. There is a complete list of each dimension variable and a brief definition in Appendix F of this book. You can adjust and set each dimension variable by typing the variable name at the `Command:` prompt. The easiest way, however, is to control them through the Dimension Styles dialog box, opened by the DDIM command.

The Dimension Styles dialog box also controls and creates dimension styles. A *dimension style* is a group of dimension variable settings that control how your dimensions look when placed in a drawing. All dimensions are controlled by the current dimension style at the time you place the dimension. If you do not create your own styles, you are using the default dimension style.

It is best to use your own dimension styles in a drawing. Using your own styles enables you to dimension according to your own standards or preferences, or to industry standards.

Creating a Parent Dimension Style

Because dimensions are created using whatever dimension style is current, you need to check what dimension style is current before you place your first dimension. By default, the STANDARD style is current in the ACAD prototype drawing. In addition to STANDARD, the US_ARCH prototype drawing has an ARCH dimension style, the US_MECH has an ANSI dimension style, and the ACADISO prototype has several ISO dimension styles. These are AutoCAD's generic default settings. These styles might work well for basic drawings, but you need to create your own styles for your dimensions to be created exactly the way you need them to look.

When making your own dimension style, you first set up a parent dimension style by naming and saving a style. Within this named parent style are family members that control the different types of dimensions: Linear, Radial, Angular, Diameter, Ordinate, and Leader.

For each of the family members there are three dialog boxes that control how each type of dimension will look. The three dialog boxes—Geometry, Format, and Annotation—are accessed by the buttons of the same names in the Dimension Styles dialog box (see figure 20.1). The Geometry dialog box controls the layout of the dimension's individual parts, the Format dialog box controls the placement of the dimension text, and the Annotation dialog box controls the appearance of the dimension text.

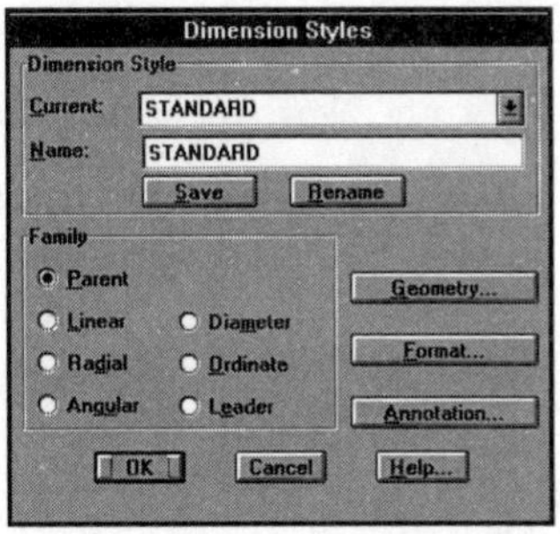

Figure 20.1

The Dimension Styles dialog box.

To start working with dimension styles, the first step is to create a new dimension style family parent. AutoCAD starts all drawings with its default STANDARD style. This style is a very basic setup, and you will want to refine the dimensioning environment to meet your specific needs.

NOTE

When you create a new dimension style, the new style's Parent inherits the settings of the currently selected family member of the current style.

In the following exercise you create a new dimension style to be used for the exercises in this chapter, and adjust the components within a dimension style.

Creating a New Dimension Style

Begin a new drawing called CHAP20A using the DIM-STYL drawing from the accompanying CD as a prototype.

Choose Dimension Styles (Dimensioning, Dimension Style)	Opens the Dimension Styles dialog box
Double-click in the Name *text box*	Highlights the text for editing
Type **PROJECT**	Names a new dimension style
Choose Save	Saves the new dimension style
Choose OK	Closes the Dimension Styles dialog box

Next, before placing some dimensions, you set the running object snap to Endpoint.

Choose Options, Running Object Snap	Opens the Running Object Snap dialog box
Choose Endpoint, then OK	Sets running object snap to Endpoint and exits the dialog box

With both the PROJECT dimension style and the running object snap set, place a couple of dimensions as shown in figure 20.2. Use the Linear Dimension (Dimensioning) tool to place the horizontal dimension shown at ① and the vertical dimension shown at ②, snapping the extension lines to the endpoints of the object.

Save your drawing.

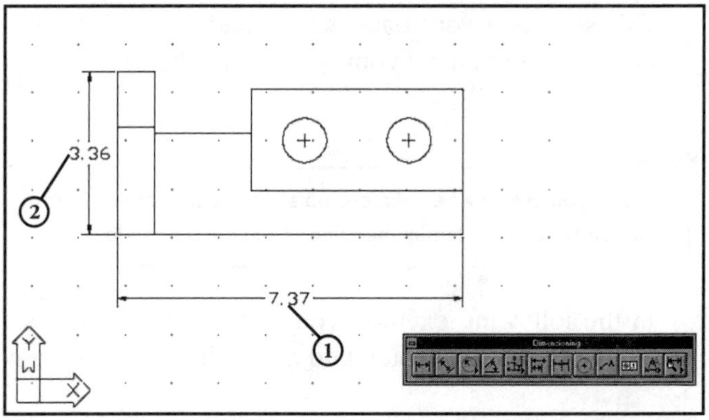

Figure 20.2

Dimensions with the new Project dimension style.

Now that you have created your own dimension style and placed some dimensions, take a look at the characteristics of dimensions that you need to control.

Understanding Associativity in Dimensioning

Dimensions by default are set to be *associative,* meaning that they have special characteristics. Each dimension is created as a single object and can be edited as a single object. The associative characteristic is controlled by the dimension variable DIMASO.

When dimensions are associative, and you change the dimensioned object or one part of the dimension, all parts of the dimension conform to the changes automatically. Associative dimensions have three definition points that are part of the dimension: a point at each extension line origin, and a point where the dimension line intersects the second extension line.

These definition points (defpoints) are placed on a layer called DEFPOINTS. This layer is automatically created when you place your first dimension in a drawing. The DEFPOINTS layer appears on-screen, but it will not plot. When you stretch an object, and you include one of the defpoints of a dimension, the dimension stretches along with the object and updates its text to reflect the object's new length.

Dimension styles also use the power of associative dimensions. When you make changes to the settings in the Dimension Styles dialog box, any dimensions defined with the affected style are automatically updated to the new settings when you exit the dialog box.

Making Adjustments to Dimension Geometry

The Geometry dialog box (see fig. 20.3) has settings for all the individual parts that make up a dimension. The individual parts consist of the dimension line, the extension lines, and the arrowheads. Center marks for circles and arcs are also controlled here, and you set the overall dimension scale factor in this dialog box.

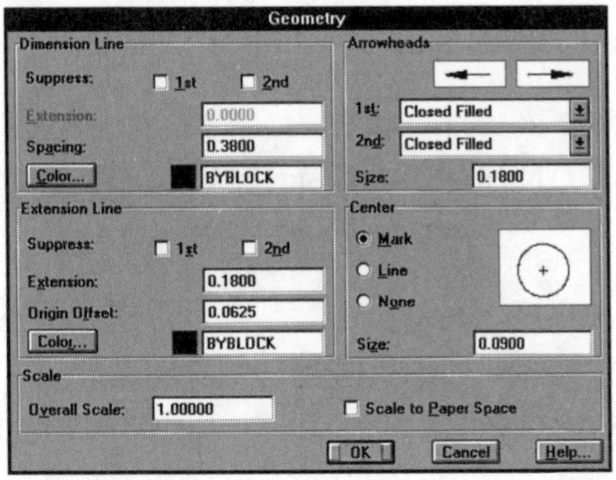

Figure 20.3

The Geometry dialog box.

Changing Dimension Lines

The Dimension Line area in the Geometry dialog box controls the variables that affect the dimension lines. The dimension line options are discussed in the following list:

- **Suppress.** The Suppress 1st and 2nd settings control the visibility of the first and second dimension line. When the text divides the dimension line in two, you can turn off the visibility of the first or second dimension line. The first dimension line is determined by the first extension line origin you select when placing the dimension.

- **Extension.** Extends the dimension line out past the extension lines. This is often used in architectural dimensioning when using oblique terminators (ticks) to give the dimension more of a hand-drawn look.
- **Spacing.** The Spacing option controls the distance between the dimension lines when they are stacked, such as when using baseline dimensions.
- **Color.** By default, your dimension's color is BYBLOCK, so dimensions adopt the current object color or layer color setting. The Color option enables you to override the color setting, using any color you want for the dimension and extension lines. The color of arrowheads matches the setting for dimension lines.

TIP

Adding color to parts of your dimensions does two things for you. First, having differently colored dimension parts helps make the dimensions easier to read on the monitor. Second, by making certain parts of the dimension a different color, you can assign different pen widths to those colors at plotting time.

In the next exercise, you make a change in the color of your dimension line.

Controlling the Color of Dimension Lines

Continue in the CHAP20A drawing.

Choose Dimension Styles (Dimensioning, Dimension Style)	Opens the Dimension Styles dialog box
Choose Geometry	Opens the Geometry dialog box
In the Dimension Line *area, choose the* Color *button*	Opens the Select Color dialog box
Choose the red *color box color*	Sets the dimension line and arrowhead to red
Choose OK	Closes the Select Color dialog box
Choose OK	Closes the Geometry dialog

Choose Save	Saves the changes to the PROJECT style
Choose OK	Closes the Dimension Styles dialog box
Save your drawing.	

Notice that the dimensions you created with the PROJECT dimension style are now updated automatically to the new extension line color setting.

Controlling Extension Lines

How you adjust your extension lines can help make your drawing easier to read. When dimensioning certain objects, set your extension lines so they don't interfere with any of the lines defining the object to be dimensioned. The following list discusses the controls in the Extension Line area of the Geometry dialog box. These controls aid in making your dimensions easier to read.

- **Suppress.** The Suppress 1st and 2nd settings control the visibility of the first and second extension line. If one or both of the extension lines is going to overlap an object line, it is best to suppress the visibility of the extension line to make the dimension easier to read. The first extension line is determined by the first dimension origin you select when placing the dimension. Defpoints are unaffected.
- **Extension.** This option controls the distance the extension lines extend past the dimension line.
- **Origin Offset.** This option controls the distance that the extension starts from the object. The defpoints are unaffected, and are still placed on the selected object or at the points you pick.
- **Color.** By default, the extension lines' color is determined by the current layer's color setting. This Color option enables you to override the layer setting, and you can pick any color you want for the extension lines.

Setting Extension Line Offset

A common adjustment that you need to make is to increase the distance the extension line is offset from the object. In the following exercise, you increase the distance for the extension line offset to make the dimensions easier to read.

Defining Extension Line Offset

Continue in the CHAP20A drawing.

Choose Dimension Styles (Dimensioning, Dimension Style)	Opens the Dimension Styles dialog box
Choose Geometry	Opens the Geometry dialog box

The origin offset is set to 0.0625 by default; set it to .125.

Double-click in the Origin Offset *text box*	Highlights the 0.0900 for editing
Type **.125**	Sets the extension line offset to 1/8"
Choose OK	Returns to the Dimension Styles dialog box
Choose Save, *then* OK	Saves the changes to the PROJECT style and exits the Dimension Styles dialog box

Save your drawing.

Notice that all the dimensions created with the PROJECT dimension style are automatically updated to the new extension line offset setting (see fig. 20.4).

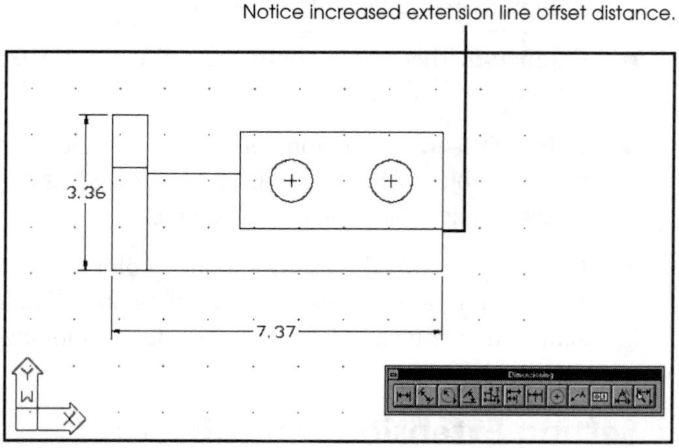

Figure 20.4

Extension line offset changes.

Suppressing Extension Lines

Good dimensioning standards require that the extension lines never overlap the object lines of the part to be dimensioned. You can suppress the first or second extension line or both extension lines so the extension lines of a dimension don't overlap object lines. In the following exercise, you apply dimensions under both of these situations.

SUPPRESSING VISIBILITY OF EXTENSION LINES

Continue in the CHAP20A drawing. You place a dimension that requires one extension line to be suppressed, and place a dimension with both extension lines to be suppressed. Start by suppressing one extension line.

Choose Dimension Styles (Dimensioning, Dimension Style)	Opens the Dimension Styles dialog box
Choose Geometry	Opens the Geometry dialog box
In the Extension Line *area, choose* Suppress 2nd	Suppresses the visibility of the second extension line
Choose OK, *then* OK *(don't save it this time)*	Closes the Geometry dialog box, then closes the Dimension Styles dialog box

Do not save the changes to the PROJECT style, or all the existing dimensions will have suppressed extension lines.

NOTE

By not choosing the Save option before exiting the Dimension Styles dialog box, you initiated a dimension override. This is indicated by a plus sign before the name (+PROJECT) in the Current Style box. This means that you did not make changes to the current dimension style, and only the following dimensions will show the changes just made to the dimension variables. Previously created dimensions are unaffected. You will learn more about overrides in the section "Overriding Style Settings" later in this chapter.

DIMENSIONING WITH SUPPRESSED EXTENSION LINES

Continue in the CHAP20A drawing.

Choose Linear Dimension (Dimensioning)	Starts the DIMLINEAR command
`First extension line origin or RETURN to select:` *Pick the line at* ① *(see fig. 20.5)*	Specifies the first extension line origin

`Second extension line origin:` *Pick the line at* ②	Specifies the second extension line origin
`Dimension line location (Text/Angle /Horizontal/Vertical/Rotated):` *Pick* ③	Sets the dimension line location

Because the second extension line would have overlapped an object line, you suppressed it (see fig. 20.5).

When both extension lines overlap object lines, you need to suppress both extension lines. In the following exercise you use an override with the PROJECT dimension style to now suppress both extension lines and place a dimension.

Choose Dimension Styles (Dimensioning, Dimension Style)	Opens the Dimension Styles dialog box
Choose Geometry	Opens the Geometry dialog box
In the Extension Line *area, choose* Suppress 1st *(2nd should already be suppressed)*	Suppresses the visibility of both extension lines
Choose OK	Closes the Geometry dialog box
Choose OK (don't save it)	Closes the Dimension Style dialog box
Choose Linear Dimension (Dimensioning)	Starts the DIMLINEAR command
`First extension line origin or RETURN to select:` *Pick the line at* ① (see fig 20.6)	Specifies the first extension line origin
`Second extension line origin:` *Pick the line at* ②	Specifies the second extension line origin
`Dimension line location (Text/Angle /Horizontal/Vertical/Rotated):` *Pick* ③	Sets the dimension line location

Save your drawing.

Notice that both extension lines are not showing on the dimension just placed (see fig. 20.6).

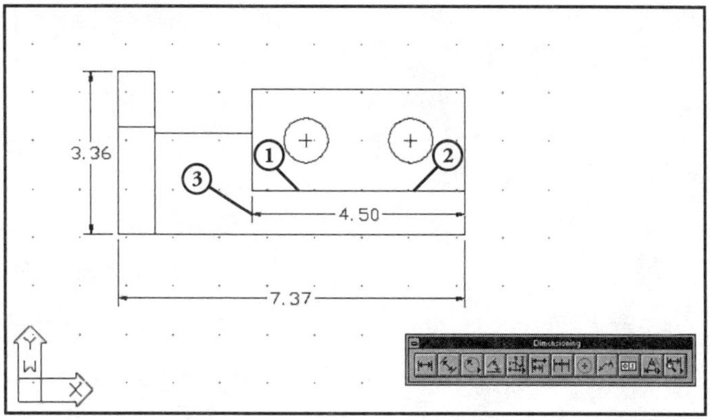

Figure 20.5

The second extension line suppressed.

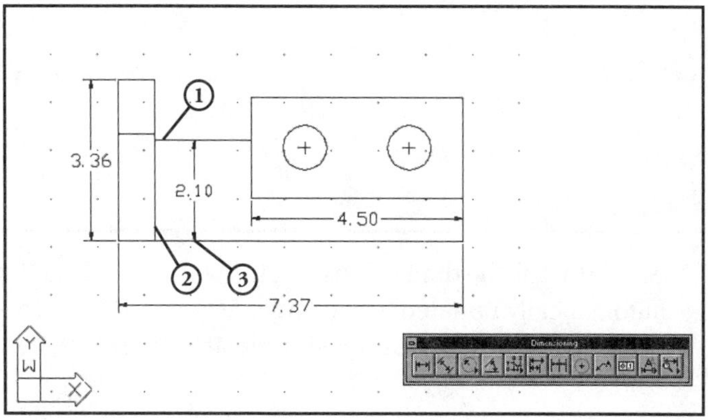

Figure 20.6

Dimension with both extension lines suppressed.

Modifying Arrowheads

At the end of dimension lines are terminators that determine the extent of the dimension. The default terminator symbol in AutoCAD is an arrowhead, which designates the point at which the dimension line is stopped by the extension line.

You can specify the type of terminator and its size in the Geometry dialog box. The default setting is Closed Filled arrowheads. The first exercise shows you how to change the size of the current arrowhead.

Changing the Arrowhead Size

Continue in the CHAP20A drawing.

In the Geometry dialog box, you have access to seven arrowhead variations. The default setting for arrowhead size is 0.1800. Change that to .25 to increase the arrowhead size for all the arrowheads in the drawing.

Choose Dimension Styles (Dimensioning, Dimension Style)	Opens the Dimension Styles dialog box

Notice that the current dimension style is +PROJECT; the plus indicates that a variable was set and not saved to the parent style. This is called an override. Next, reset the PROJECT dimension defaults.

Click in the Current *text box*	Opens the Dimension Style drop-down list
Choose PROJECT	Sets the PROJECT style current
Choose Geometry	Opens the Geometry dialog box
Press Alt+I	Highlights the arrowhead Size box
Enter **.25**	Changes the arrowhead size
Choose OK	Closes the Geometry dialog box
Choose Save	Saves the changes to the current dimension style
Choose OK	Closes the Dimension Styles dialog box

Save your drawing.

Notice that all the dimensions created with the PROJECT dimension style have been automatically updated to the larger arrowhead size. The dimensions created with overrides, however, retain their special settings (see fig. 20.7).

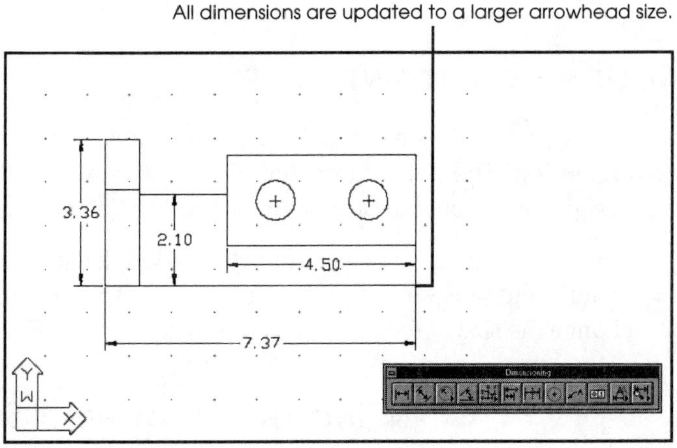

Figure 20.7

New, larger arrowhead size for all dimensions.

Arrowhead Variations

Many drafting standards require different types of terminators, and certain types of dimensioning situations—such as isometric dimensions—require custom arrowheads. AutoCAD provides eight predefined selections for dimension line terminators, plus the capability to define custom terminators. The following list explains the arrowhead controls in the Geometry dialog box for manipulating arrowhead appearance:

- **1st.** Controls the type of arrowhead placed at the first extension line.
- **2nd.** Controls the arrowhead placed at the second extension line.
- **Size.** Controls the size of the arrowheads.

The dimensions that have been placed so far with the PROJECT dimension style have used the default Closed Filled arrowhead type. In this exercise, you modify the arrowheads by changing them to the Open arrowhead type.

DEFINING ARROWHEAD TYPE

Continue in the CHAP20A drawing.

Choose Dimension Styles (Dimensioning, Dimension Style)	Opens the Dimension Styles dialog box
Choose Geometry	Opens the Geometry dialog box
Click on the 1st *arrowhead drop-down list box*	Opens a list of all the arrowhead options
Select Open	Sets the OPEN arrowhead current

Notice that the image tile for arrowheads updates automatically to show you the type of arrowhead you select.

Choose OK	Closes the Geometry dialog box
Choose Save	Saves the changes to the current dimension style
Choose OK	Closes the Dimension Styles dialog box

Watch the dynamic capability of associative dimensions as all the dimensions automatically update to the new arrowhead type (see fig. 20.8).

Save your drawing.

Figure 20.8

Detail of dimensions with different arrowheads.

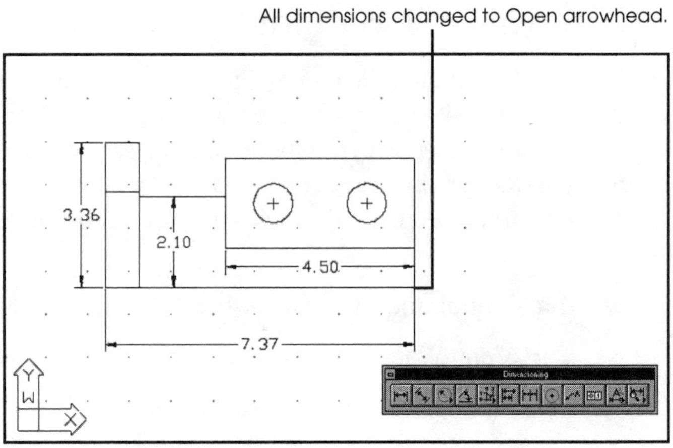

NOTE

When you set the 1st arrowhead, the 2nd arrowhead automatically changes to match. If you want different arrowheads, set the 2nd arrowhead; the 1st will not automatically change to match it.

Controlling Center Marks in Circles and Arcs

Defining the center point of circles and arcs is a standard part of placing dimension information on a drawing. AutoCAD makes this very easy with the DIMCENTER command. There are two ways to indicate your center marks. The first option is to place them without center lines going out to the perimeter; the second option is to not have the center lines placed with the center mark. Center marks are nonassociative and consist of two or more individual lines.

Center marks in circles can be placed with or without center lines extending out past the perimeter. You can set center lines on or off in the Center section of the Geometry dialog box.

PLACING CENTER LINES FOR CIRCLE DIAMETERS

Continue in the CHAP20A drawing.

In this exercise, you will place center marks with center lines. The drawing includes existing center marks without center lines. You will erase the existing center marks and place new center marks with center lines.

Choose Erase (Modify); select the four center mark lines ①, ②, ③, and ④ (see fig. 20.9); and press Enter	Issues the ERASE command and erases the four center mark lines
Choose Dimension Styles (Dimensioning, Dimension Style	Opens the Dimension Styles dialog box
Choose Geometry	Opens the Geometry dialog box
In the Center area, choose the Line *radio button*	Turns center lines on
Choose OK	Closes the Geometry dialog box
Choose OK (don't save it)	Closes the Dimension Styles dialog box

Next, use this override to place a center mark with center lines on one circle.

Choose Center Mark (Dimensioning)	Issues the DIMCENTER command
Pick the circle at ① (see fig. 20.10)	Places a center mark with center lines at the center of the circle
`Command: ↵`	Repeats the DIMCENTER command
Pick the circle at ② (see fig. 20.10)	Places a center mark with center lines at the center of the circle

Save your drawing.

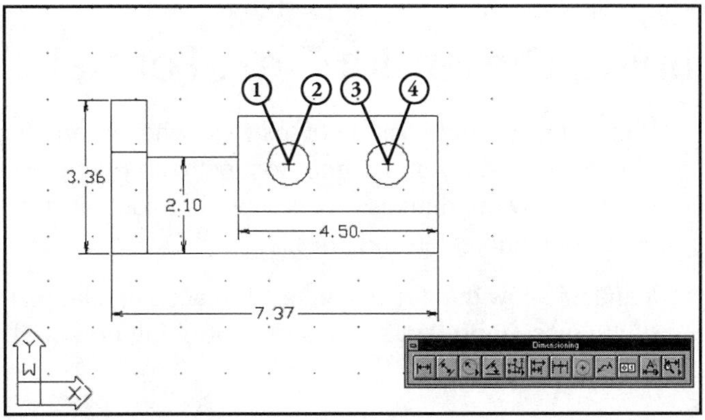

Figure 20.9

Erasing center marks.

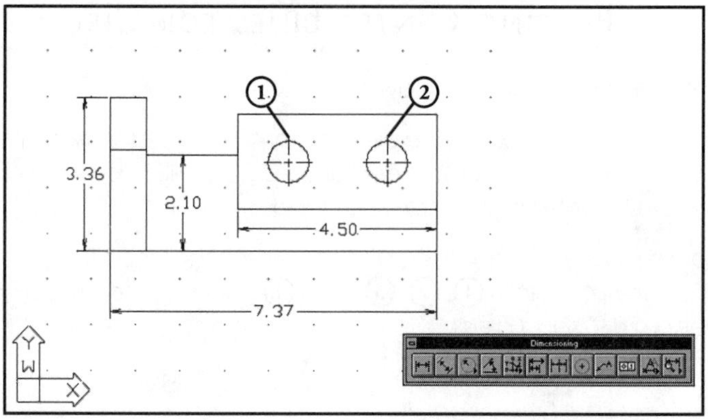

Figure 20.10

Center marks with center lines.

The DIMCENTER command has no options, but the Geometry dialog box provides the following dimension variables that control the different ways to place your center marks:

- **Mark.** This option turns on the center mark when using the DIMCENTER, DIMDIAMETER, and DIMRADIUS commands.
- **Line.** Turn this option on when you need center lines to extend from the center mark out past the perimeter of the circle.
- **None.** This option turns off the center mark. Placing radial dimensions on very small holes where the center mark would be too large is an example of when not to place a center mark.
- **Size.** This option controls the size of the center mark. The size you specify is one half the total length of the center mark. When using center lines with center marks, this setting also determines the distance the center line extends past the perimeter of the circle.

Defining Dimension Text Format

You can adjust the position of text, arrowheads, and leader lines in relation to the dimension and extension lines to meet your drafting standards. AutoCAD enables you to justify the dimension text both horizontally and vertically in relation to the dimension and extension lines.

Managing how the dimension text is placed in relation to the extension lines is one of the most important aspects of controlling how well your dimensioning works.

Chapter 19 shows how the current text style is used for dimension text. You can create a special text style for dimensions, to squeeze the text width thinner so that text fits better between the extension lines.

TIP

When placing a dimension, AutoCAD has to calculate the distance between the two extension lines and then place two arrowheads, two dimension lines, two text gaps, and the text (see fig. 20.11). If there isn't enough room for all the dimension information, AutoCAD places some of the information outside the extension lines. In addition to using a narrow text style, you can reduce the arrowhead size and the text gap size to help AutoCAD keep the information inside the extension lines.

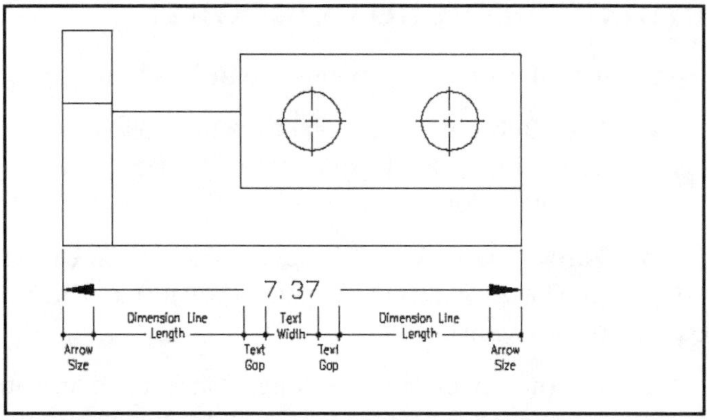

Figure 20.11

AutoCAD automatically places the dimension text and arrowheads.

The Format dialog box, accessed through the Dimension Styles dialog box, has settings to determine how the text fits within the extension lines of a dimension (see fig. 20.12). Under the Fit option, Best Fit is set as the default format. If you do not have room for both the arrowheads and the text, you can specify either the arrowheads or the text (or both) be placed outside the extension lines. A new feature under the Fit options, the Leader option, enables you to place consecutive dimensions that are very close together. The Leader option tells AutoCAD to use a leader line to place the dimension text above the dimension line when there isn't room between the extension lines.

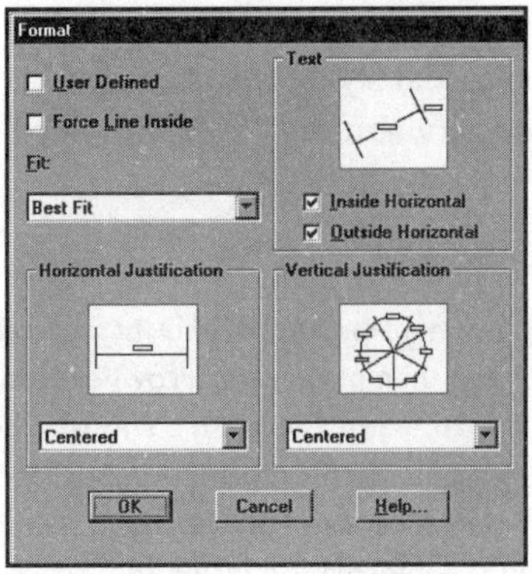

Figure 20.12

The Format dialog box.

Format Dialog Box Options

You have the following options within the Format dialog box:

- **User Defined.** When you check this option, the point you specify during dimensioning for the dimension line location also specifies where to place the dimension text.
- **Force Line Inside.** This option places a dimension line between the extension lines even when the dimension text and arrowheads are placed outside of the extension lines.
- **Fit.** This option controls dimension text and arrowhead placement in relation to the extension lines. When the extension lines of a dimension are very close together and the text and arrowheads don't fit between them, the option specified in the Fit drop-down list tells AutoCAD where to place the text and arrowhead.
- **Horizontal Justification.** Provides options for controlling the text placement along the dimension line. The available options are Centered, 1st Extension Line, 2nd Extension Line, Over 1st Extension, and Over 2nd Extension.
- **Inside Horizontal.** When checked (turned on), this option sets all the dimension text inside the extension lines to read horizontally. When off, the text aligns with the dimension line.
- **Outside Horizontal.** When checked (turned on), this option sets all the dimension text outside the extension lines to read horizontally. When off, the text aligns with the dimension line.

- **Vertical Justification.** Controls the position of the text in relation to the dimension line. The text can be placed above, centered, or below the dimension line.

Controlling Text and Extension Lines

After you select the two points for the dimension extension lines, AutoCAD calculates the distance between the two points and places the dimension lines and the dimension text accordingly. When there isn't room for the arrowheads and text, AutoCAD uses the Best Fit setting to place the information.

If you want more control over the placement of dimension text and arrowheads so that you can better follow your drafting standards, you can set a different option for the Fit setting.

In the CHAP20A drawing, there are dimensions with the text outside and the arrowheads inside. In the following exercise, you switch them so that both the arrowheads and the text are outside. You will place a new horizontal dimension and edit the text and arrowheads using the Dimension Styles dialog box.

Adjusting Arrowheads and Text Placement in a Dimension

Continue in the CHAP20A drawing.

Choose Dimension Linear (Dimensioning)	Starts the DIMLINEAR command
`First extension line origin or RETURN to select:` *Pick* ① *(see fig. 20.13)*	Selects the first extension line origin
`Second extension line origin:` *Pick* ②	Specifies the second extension line origin
`Dimension line location (Text/Angle/Horizontal/Vertical/Rotated):` *Pick* ③	Selects the dimension line location

AutoCAD places the arrowheads inside the extension lines. You now will force the arrowheads outside to go with the text.

Choose Dimension Styles (Dimensioning, Dimension Style)	Opens the Dimension Styles dialog box
Choose Format	Opens the Format dialog box

Click on the Fit *drop-down list*	Opens the options drop-down list
Select Text and Arrows	Sets Text and Arrows to be outside the extension lines
Choose OK	Closes the Format dialog box
Choose Save	Saves the setting to the PROJECT style
Choose OK	Closes the Dimension Styles dialog box

Save your drawing.

The dimension with inside arrows has been updated so that the text and the arrows are outside the extension lines (see fig. 20.14).

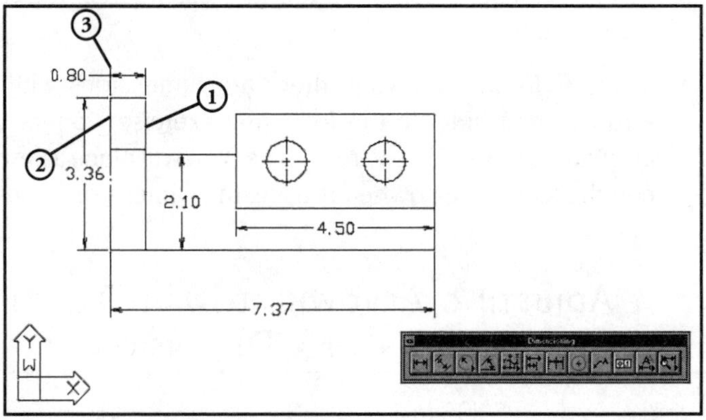

Figure 20.13

Placing a horizontal dimension.

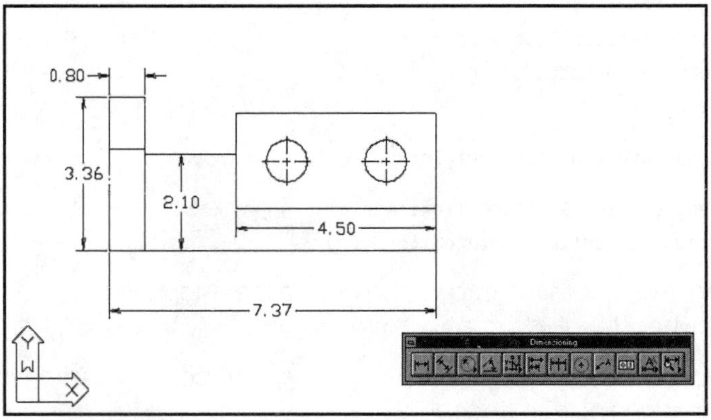

Figure 20.14

The edited text and arrowheads.

Forcing an Internal Line

When the arrowheads are placed outside the extension lines, you have an option to place a dimension line between the extension lines. This is called *forcing an internal line,* and you can set it in the Format dialog box.

The upper left dimension (0.80) has outside arrowheads and text, so you will force a dimension line inside the extension lines in the following exercise.

Forcing a Dimension Line inside Extension Lines

Continue in the CHAP20A drawing.

Choose Dimension Styles (Dimensioning, Dimension Style)	Opens the Dimension Styles dialog box
Choose Format	Opens the Format dialog box
Press Alt+L	Turns on the Force Line Inside option
Choose OK	Closes the Format dialog box
Choose Save	Saves the new setting to PROJECT style
Choose OK	Closes the Dimension Styles dialog box

Save your drawing.

Notice how the dimension is updated automatically to have an interior dimension line (see fig. 20.15).

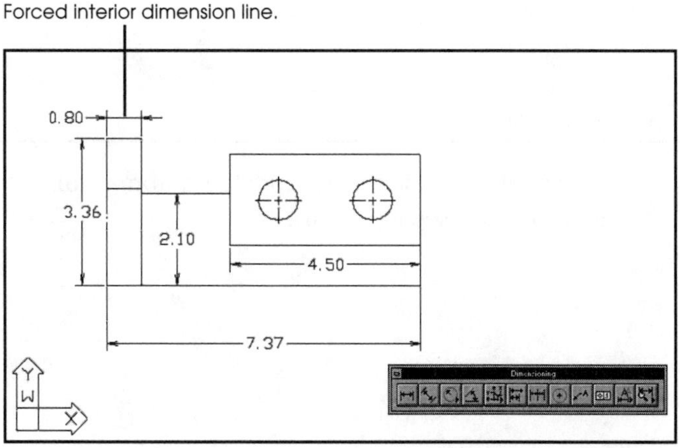

Figure 20.15

Forcing an interior dimension line.

Setting Text Orientation

Dimension text orientation in drawings uses either unilateral or bilateral placement. With the unilateral format, all the text is placed so that it reads horizontally and is read from the bottom of the drawing. In the bilateral format, the text follows the angle of the dimension line, and all vertical dimensions are read from the right side.

Text orientation is controlled in the Format dialog box. The Text section shows you an image tile of dimension text inside and outside the extension lines. The settings for inside and outside text are controlled by separate variables. The default settings for both are horizontal.

In the CHAP20A drawing, all the vertical dimensions have horizontal text. Use the Format dialog box to reset the text to follow the dimension lines. In the following exercise, you will reset all your dimensions to follow the bilateral format.

ALIGNING THE TEXT WITH THE DIMENSION LINE

Continue in the CHAP20A drawing.

Choose Dimension Styles (Dimensioning, Dimension Style)	Opens the Dimension Styles dialog box
Choose Format	Opens the Format dialog box
Clear the Inside Horizontal *and the* Outside Horizontal *check boxes*	Sets all dimension text to follow the dimension lines
Choose OK	Closes the Format dialog box
Choose Save	Saves the new setting to PROJECT style
Choose OK	Closes the dialog box and initiates the changes

Save your drawing.

The vertical dimensions are updated automatically to realign the text with the dimension line (see fig. 20.16).

Figure 20.16

Vertical dimensions with new text alignment.

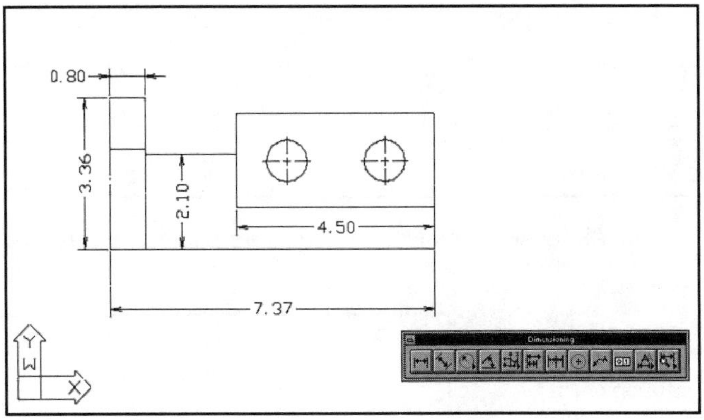

Adjusting Vertical Text Justification

How you want your text placed vertically in relation to the dimension line is controlled by the Vertical Justification section in the Format dialog box. Dimension text can be positioned above, below, or centered within the dimension line.

With ANSI standards, the text is vertically centered on the dimension line, splitting the dimension line in two. With ISO standards, the text usually is centered above the dimension line or outside the dimension line. With most architectural standards, the text is above the dimension line, and preferably centered. Depending on the drafting standards that you follow, you will want to have your dimension text either centered between or centered above the dimension lines.

In the CHAP20A drawing, all the dimension text is centered in the dimension line. You will now change it to be above the dimension line.

Positioning the Text above the Dimension Line

Continue in the CHAP20A drawing.

Choose Dimension Styles (Dimensioning, Dimension Style)	Opens the Dimension Styles dialog box
Choose Format	Opens the Format dialog box
Click in the Vertical Justification *drop-down list box*	Drops down the vertical justification options list
Select Above	Sets the text above the dimension line

Choose OK	Closes the Format dialog box
Choose Save	Saves the new setting to PROJECT style
Choose OK	Closes the dialog and initiates the changes
Save your drawing.	

The dimension text is changed to be above the dimension line (see fig. 20.17).

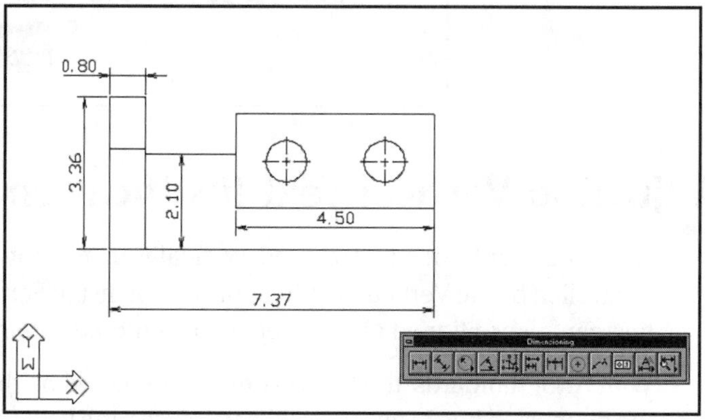

Figure 20.17

The new position of the vertical dimension text.

Managing Text Appearance in Dimensions

You have several options for controlling text appearance in dimensions. You can add prefixes and suffixes to the default text, such as RAD for radial dimensions, or a diameter symbol for diameter dimensions. Before you start to adjust the variables in a dimension style, it is a good idea to create a text style for dimensions only.

Setting Dimension Text Style

The default text style AutoCAD uses when placing a dimension is the current text style. The current text style controls the font and the width of the dimension text. Chapter 19 shows you how to create a text style called "DIMS" for dimensions, with the width of the text set to 75 percent, to help arrowheads and dimension text stay inside the extension lines more often.

So before you place any dimensions in your drawings, make sure you create—or set current—the text style that is to be used for dimensions only.

WARNING

When creating a text style, you have an option to set the height of the text. If you set the dimension text height in the style settings, it will take control of the text height, no matter what your text height is set to in the Annotation dialog box, accessed through the Dimension Styles dialog box. It is best to set the height in the text style definition to 0 and let the Annotation dialog box setting control your dimension text height. This enables you to set the text height to the size you want on the paper, and DIMSCALE can scale it to the proper size for the drawing scale.

The Annotation dialog box (see fig. 20.18) provides the settings that control how your text looks in dimensions. You have control over the following things:

- Text style to be used
- Text height
- Prefixes and suffixes for dimension text
- Adding tolerances
- The use of alternative units
- The capability to set your dimension unit's precision separate from the drawing unit's precision

Figure 20.18

The Annotation dialog box.

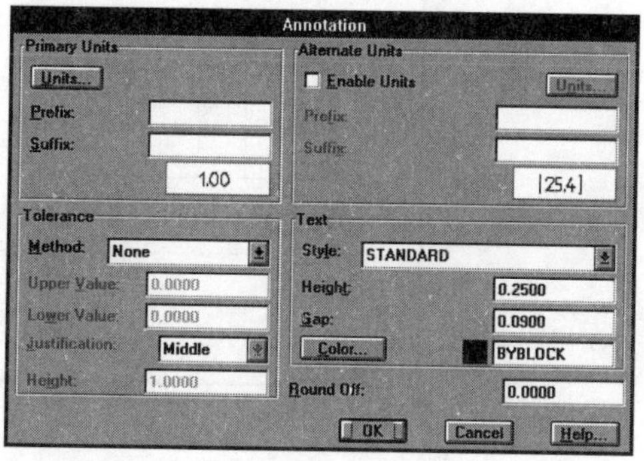

Controlling Dimension Text Height

With your current text style height set to zero, you need to control the dimension text height in the Annotation dialog box. The dimension text height in the CHAP20A drawing is set to the default height of .25. You want the dimension text to be .185, so set the text height in the Annotation dialog box in the following exercise.

Setting Dimension Text Height

Continue in the CHAP20A drawing.

Choose Dimension Styles (Dimensioning, Dimension Style)	Opens the Dimension Styles dialog box
Choose Annotation	Opens the Annotation dialog box
Press Alt+T	Highlights text Height box
Type **.185**	Sets the text height to .185
Choose OK	Closes the Annotation dialog box
Choose Save	Saves the new setting to PROJECT style
Choose OK	Closes the dialog box and initiates the changes

Save your drawing.

All the dimension text automatically updates to the new .185 text height (see fig. 20.19).

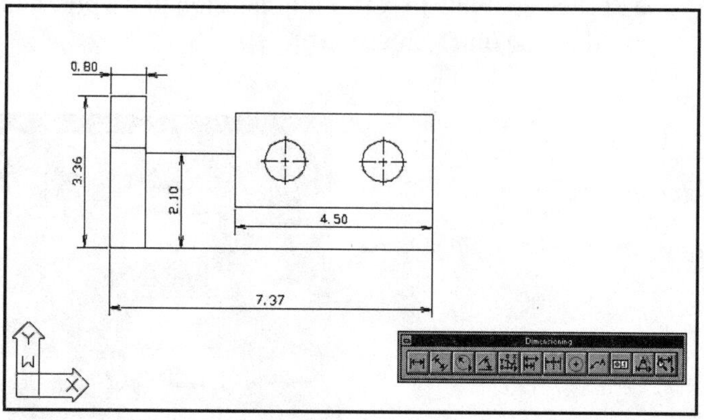

Figure 20.19

The new dimension text height.

Setting Primary Units for Dimensions

In Chapter 1 "Drawing Setup and File Management," you learned how to set the units for a drawing using the Units Control dialog box. The Units setting controls the type and precision of units you used for coordinate display and input. With Release 13, AutoCAD now has separate settings for dimension text precision within the DDIM Annotation dialog box.

You can have different units and precision for your dimensions than what is set for your drawing units. Choosing Units in the Primary Units section of the Annotation dialog box provides the option to set the type of units you want for linear and angular dimension text.

The dimension units are currently set to two decimal places. Using the Units option in the Primary Units area, set the primary units to a three-place decimal for dimension text in the following exercise.

SETTING THE UNITS FOR DIMENSIONS

Continue in the CHAP20A drawing.

Choose Dimension Styles (Dimensioning, Dimension Style)	Opens the Dimension Styles dialog box
Choose Annotation	Opens the Annotation dialog box
In the Primary Units *area, choose* Units	Opens the Primary Units dialog box
In the Dimension *area, click on the* Precision *drop-down list*	Drops down the list of dimension text precision options
Choose the three-decimal place (0.000) option	
Choose OK	Closes the Primary Units dialog box
Choose OK	Closes the Annotation dialog box
Choose Save	Saves the new setting to PROJECT style
Choose OK	Closes the dialog box and initiates the changes

Save your drawing.

All the dimension text automatically updates to the new three-decimal place precision (see fig. 20.20).

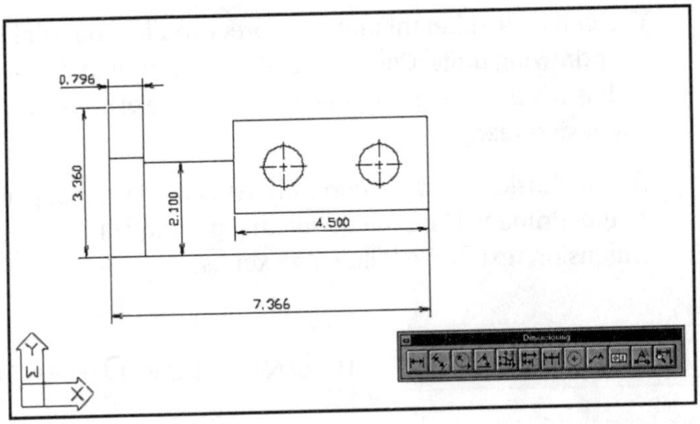

Figure 20.20

The dimensions with three-place decimal precision.

Using a Dimension Style Family

After you create a parent dimension style, such as the PROJECT dimension style you created in this chapter, you can create the family members that will make up a complete set of family settings for all the dimension commands. The family members are the different types of dimension commands such as Linear, Radial, Angular, Diameter, Ordinate, and Leader. These family members are listed in the Family section of the Dimension Styles dialog box (see fig. 20.21).

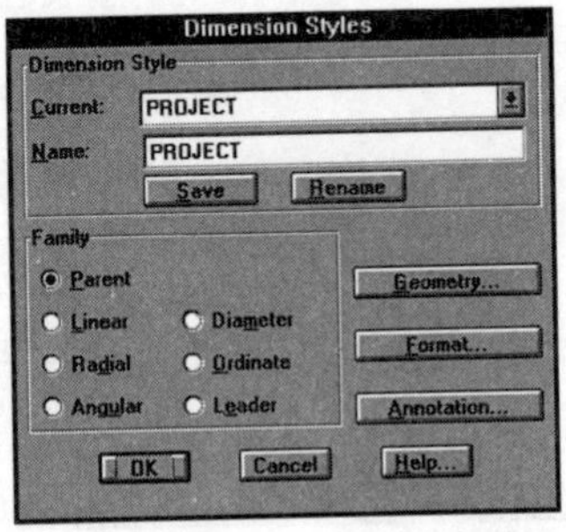

Figure 20.21

Dimension Styles dialog box family members.

Creating family members gives you the ability to set individual settings for each of the different dimension commands, even when using only one dimension style. This prevents the need for different styles when you need only a minor change in dimension settings for each type of dimension.

You should create all the individual family members because you need different settings for the different dimension commands. For example, your linear dimensions might use oblique ticks, but you want your leaders to use arrowheads. Or, you need your linear dimensions to use two-place decimal precision units, while your angular dimensions show no precision in the decimal units. Or perhaps when using radial dimensions you want your dimension text forced outside, but when using a diameter dimension you need your text forced inside.

In the following exercise you will start a dimension style family by creating the Linear and Radial family members and setting the variables. Then you will place dimensions to see the power of dimension style family members to control the different dimension commands.

Creating a Linear Family Member

Save the CHAP20A drawing as a new drawing called CHAP20B.

Choose Dimension Style (Dimensioning)	Opens the Dimension Styles dialog box
Choose Linear	Creates a Linear family member

All the following changes to the variables will apply only to the Linear family.

Choose Geometry	Opens the Geometry dialog box
In the Extension Line *area choose* Color	Opens the Select Color dialog box
Choose Magenta	Sets the extension lines to the color magenta
Choose OK	Exits the Select Color dialog box
In the Arrowheads *area click in the* 1st *image tile until* Closed Filled *appears*	Sets the terminator to Closed Filled arrowheads
Choose OK	Exits the Geometry dialog box

The Geometry settings are finished for the Linear family member. You need not set the text format variables because all the format variables that were set for the PROJECT parent style also apply to your Linear family member.

Choose Annotation	Opens the Annotation dialog box
Click in the Style *edit box in the* Text *area*	Opens the text style drop-down list
Choose DIMS	Sets DIMS as the text style for linear dimensions
In the Text area *choose* Color	Opens the Select Color dialog box
Choose Yellow	Sets dimension text to the color yellow

Choose OK	Exits the Select Color dialog box
Choose OK	Exits the Annotation dialog box
Choose Save	Saves the changes to the Linear family member
Choose OK	Exits the Dimension Styles dialog box

Notice the existing linear dimensions did not update to the new settings for linear dimensions because they were created with the Parent style.

The Linear family member under the PROJECT dimension style is now complete. The existing linear dimensions can be updated with the Apply option of the DIMSTYLE command. If they had been created with the Linear style, they would have updated automatically.

Next you will create the Radial family member. In the following exercise you will place a radial dimension using the PROJECT parent settings, because no radial family member has been created yet. Because this radial dimension will not serve your drawing needs, you will then create a Radial family member to set the variables for radius dimensions. After your Radial family member is complete you will place another radius dimension with the correct settings. This will show you the real power of dimension style family members, and why you need to create them in each parent dimension style.

CREATING A RADIAL FAMILY MEMBER

Continue in the CHAP20B drawing.

Choose Radius Dimension (Dimensioning)	Starts the DIMRADIUS command
Pick the circle at ① *(see fig. 20.22)*	Selects the circle for the radius dimension
Pick ②	Places the end of the leader

Notice in figure 20.22 that the text is above the dimension line and aligned with the leader. Those settings are not what you need for radius dimensions. You create a Radial family member in the PROJECT parent style to correct the variables so the text is horizontal and centered on the leader line.

Choose Dimension Style (Dimensioning)	Opens the Dimension Styles dialog box
Choose Radial	Creates a Radial family member

All the following changes to the variables will apply only to the Radial family.

Choose Geometry	Opens the Geometry dialog box
Choose OK	

The Geometry settings should be similar to the Linear settings.

Choose Format	Opens the Format dialog box
Press Alt+I	Changes the inside text to horizontal
Press Alt+O	Changes the outside text to horizontal
Click in the Vertical Justification *edit box*	Opens the options drop-down list
Choose Centered	Center justifies the dimension text
Choose OK	Exits the Format dialog box
Choose Save, *then* OK	Saves the style changes and closes the dialog box
Choose Radius Dimension (Dimensioning)	Issues the DIMRADIUS command
Pick ① *(see fig. 20.23)*	Selects the circle for the second radius dimension
Pick ②	Specifies the end of the leader

In figure 20.22, notice the new radius dimension was created the way you want your radius leaders to look. However, the first radius dimension was not updated to the new settings because it was created with the PROJECT parent dimension style. Later, you will learn to update existing dimensions. For now, just erase and redraw the existing radius dimension to match figure 20.22.

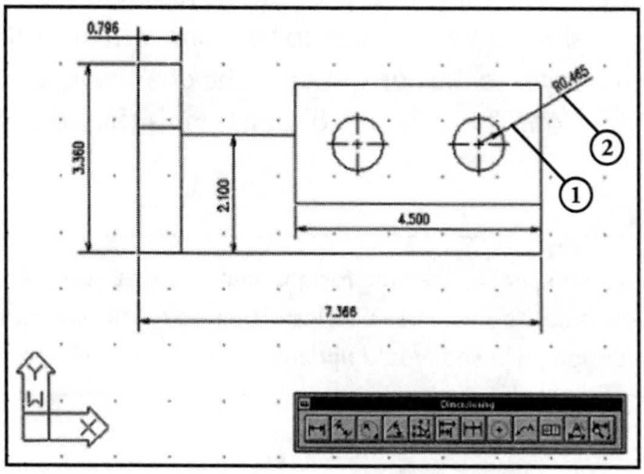

Figure 20.22

Radius dimension with incorrect variable settings.

Figure 20.23

New radius command settings under the Radical family member.

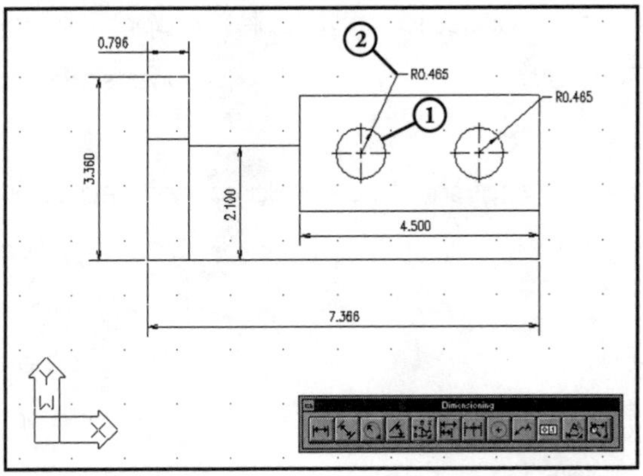

Using Dimension Style Overrides

For most of the dimensions you place in your drawings, you make an existing dimension style current and use the settings in that style to control the way your dimensions are created. At times you might want to adjust a single dimension variable to place a dimension that looks different. Rather than create a completely new style, you can override your current style's settings by changing a variable to place a single dimension. Overrides enable you to use a base dimension style, yet make small adjustments for individual dimensions that must be different. This eliminates the need to create a new dimension style for every dimension that needs a different setting.

In the CHAP20A drawing, the dimension that calls out the distance between the hole center lines and the top of the block needs to be a two place decimal. Set the dimension unit's precision to two places in the following exercise. You will not save the changes to the current style; the change in settings will be used only for the next dimension. Then place a dimension as shown in figure 20.24.

WARNING

When you set an override for a dimension that you are ready to place, do not save the changes at the Dimension Styles dialog box. This would save the change to the current dimension style and would update all the existing dimensions created with that style.

Setting Dimension Style Overrides

Continue in the CHAP20A drawing.

Choose Dimension Styles (Dimensioning, Dimension Style)	Opens the Dimension Styles dialog box
Choose Annotation	Opens the Annotation dialog box
In the Primary Units area, choose Units	Opens the Primary Units dialog box
In the Dimension *area, click in the* Precision *box*	Drops down the options list for dimension text precision
Select the two-decimal place (0.00) option	Sets the dimension units to a two place decimal
Choose OK	Closes the Primary Units dialog box
Choose OK	Closes the Annotation dialog box
Choose OK	Closes the Dimension Styles dialog box without saving the changes
Choose Linear Dimension (Dimensioning)	Issues the DIMLINEAR command
`_dimlinear` `First extension line origin or RETURN to select:` *Pick the line at* ① *(see fig. 20.24)*	Specifies the first extension line
`Second extension line origin:` *Pick the line at* ②	Specifies the second extension line origin line origin
`Dimension line location (Text/Angle/Horizontal/Vertical/Rotated):` *Pick* ③	Places the dimension line

Save your drawing.

Using this technique of changing a variable without saving it to the current style enables you to add dimensions with small variations without having to create a new dimension style (see fig. 20.24).

Figure 20.24

Placing a dimension with an override.

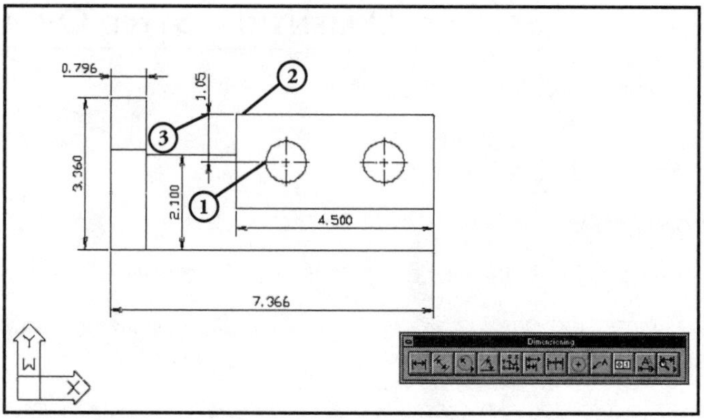

Applying Overrides to Existing Dimensions

Existing dimensions can be changed by adding an override to them. The DIMOVERRIDE command enables you to change any variable settings and then select the dimension to which you want to apply the changes. The dimension then updates to the new settings.

Using this technique requires that you type the name of the dimension variable you want to change, and you therefore need to know the name of the variable to be changed.

In the following exercise, the upper left dimension (0.796) needs its text forced inside the extension lines and the leading zero suppressed.

Applying Dimension Overrides

Continue in the CHAP20A drawing.

`Command:` **DIMOVERRIDE** ↵	Issues the DIMOVERRIDE command
`Dimension variable to override:` `(or Clear to remove overrides):` **DIMTIX** ↵ `Current value <Off> New value:` **ON** ↵	Sets the DIMTIX to ON
`Dimension variable to override:` **DIMZIN** ↵ `Current value <0> New value:` **4** ↵	Suppresses leading zeros
`Dimension variable to override:` ↵	Exits the variable prompts

`Select objects:` *Pick the upper left dimension* (0.796) `1 found`	Selects the dimension to override
`Select objects:` ↵	Exits the command and applies the overrides

The text is moved inside the extension lines, and the leading zero is suppressed (see fig. 20.25).

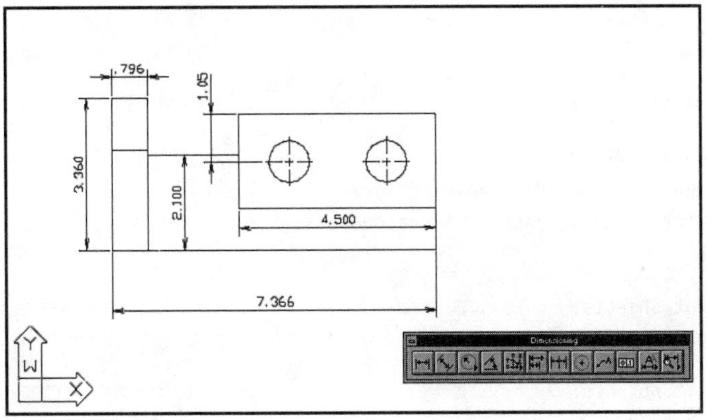

Figure 20.25

Realigning text with overrides.

TIP

There is an easier way to change existing dimensions to the overrides that you set. You can use the Dimension Styles dialog box to set dimension variables without saving them. Just choosing OK will set the variables, but will not save them to the current dimension style. Then you can use the DIMSTYLE command's Apply option to select the dimensions to which you want to apply the dimension variable changes.

Changing an Existing Dimension's Style

At times you will need to change existing dimensions to a new dimension style. Dimension styles can be applied to any existing dimension.

Using the Dimension Styles dialog box, you will set a different dimension style current and then use DIMSTYLE to select the dimensions that you want changed to that style. The existing vertical dimensions were created with the PROJECT dimension style. You will now change their dimension style to the VERT-DIMS style. The text will be switched to horizontal.

Applying a Dimension Style to an Existing Dimension

Continue in the CHAP20A drawing.

Choose Dimension Styles (Dimensioning, Dimension Style)	Opens the Dimension Styles dialog box
Click on the Current *text box*	Drops down the list of styles
Select VERT-DIMS	Selects the VERT-DIMS dimension style
Choose OK	Exits the dialog box
`Command:` **DIMSTYLE** ↵	Starts the DIMSTYLE command
`Dimension style: VERT-DIMS dimension Style Edit (Save/Restore /STatus/Variables/Apply/?)<Restore>:` **A** ↵	Specifies the Apply option
`Select objects:` *Pick all vertical dimensions*	Selects all the vertical dimensions to change to the VERT-DIMS style
`Select objects:` ↵	Ends the command and changes all selected dimensions to the VERT-DIMS style

Save your drawing.

Notice that all the vertical dimensions have text that is now horizontal and are set with two-place decimal precision (see fig. 20.26).

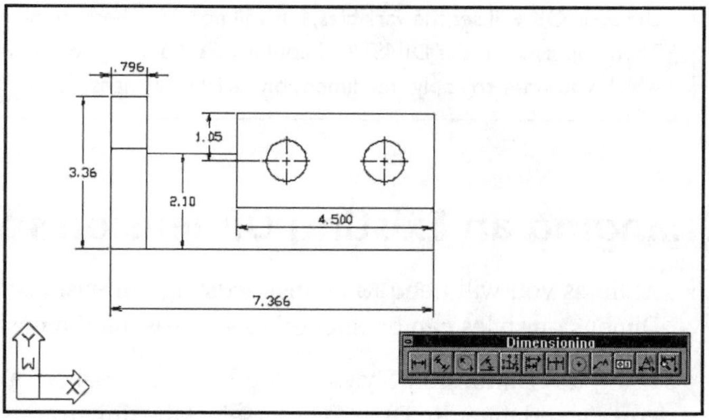

Figure 20.26

Vertical dimensions with the new style applied.

The following list describes the command options for DIMSTYLE:

- **Save.** Saves the current dimension variable settings to a new style name.
- **Restore.** Restores another dimension style's variables to make them current.
- **STatus.** Displays the current setting for all the current style's variables.
- **Variables.** Displays a list of variable settings for any dimension style without affecting the current style settings.
- **Apply.** Applies the current dimension style settings to any dimension objects you select.
- **?.** Gives you a list of the dimension styles created in the current drawing.

Getting a List of Dimension Variable Settings

To see a list of the dimension variable settings for the current dimension style, you can use the DIMSTYLE command, which you do in the following exercise.

LISTING CURRENT DIMENSION VARIABLE SETTINGS

Continue in the CHAP20A drawing.

`Command:` **DIMSTYLE** ↵	Issues the DIMSTYLE command
`dimension style: VERT-DIMS` `Dimension Style Edit (Save/Restore /STatus/Variables/Apply/?) <Restore>:` **ST** ↵	Selects the STatus option and displays the current settings in the text window

The text window lists one page of dimension variables; press Enter to see the next pages. The dimension variables are listed in Appendix F.

Save your drawing.

If you have set overrides in the Dimension Styles dialog box you can get a complete list of the current overrides by just entering the DIMSTYLE command. In the following exercise you will set one dimension variable to use as an override. Then after you set the override you will use the DIMSTYLE command to see a quick list of the current overrides that are set.

USING DIMSTYLE TO LIST OVERRIDES

Continue in the CHAP20A drawing.

Choose Dimension Styles (Dimensioning)	Opens the Dimension Styles dialog box
Choose Geometry	Opens the Geometry dialog box
Click in the first Arrowheads *image tile until* Oblique *is set*	Sets the terminator to Oblique ticks
Choose OK	Closes the Geometry dialog box

Do not save the new setting.

Choose OK	Closes the Dimension Styles dialog box
Enter **DIMSTYLE**	Starts the DIMSTYLE command
Press function key F2	Opens the AutoCAD Text Window

Above the DIMSTYLE options displays a list of the current dimension style overrides that are set (see fig. 20.27).

Press function key F2	Closes the AutoCAD Text Window
Press Esc	Cancels the DIMSTYLE command

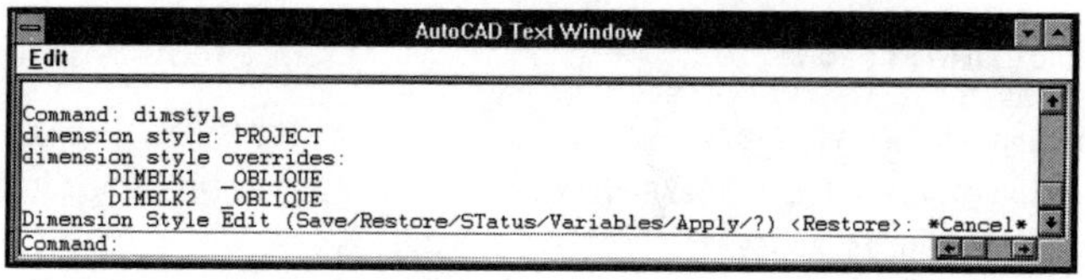

Figure 20.27

A list of current dimension style overrides.

Editing Existing Dimensions

The majority of editing dimensions can be controlled by using your style families with the Dimension Styles dialog box. At times you have to make a change to a dimension that has already been placed in a drawing, and styles will not handle what you want to do. There are dimensioning edit commands for this specific purpose.

Changing Dimension Position with Grips

When you need to move a dimension quickly, or redefine its extension line origins, you need to use grips. Grips let you edit the basic location points of a dimension, the extension line origin, the dimension line origin, and the text placement. Grips are the quickest way to change a dimension because using them doesn't even require that you enter a command. With a clear command prompt, just pick on a dimension and the unselected grip points appear. Then choose one of the unselected grip points. This unselected grip point changes to a selected grip point. You then drag that dimension part to a new position.

In the CHAP20A drawing in the following exercise, the left vertical dimension needs to be moved out farther away from the object, and the text on the right outside side vertical dimension needs to be lowered to make the two right side dimensions easier to read.

Changing Dimension Line Position

Continue in the CHAP20A drawing.

Before you start this exercise make sure you have a clear `Command:` prompt.

`Command:` *Pick the left vertical dimension*	Selects the dimension and displays its grips
Pick the unselected grip point at ① *(see fig. 20.28)*	Makes the grip point hot and starts stretch autoediting mode
`**STRETCH**` `<Stretch to point>/Base point/` `Copy/Undo/eXit:` *Drag the dimension line and pick at* ② *(see fig. 20.29)*	Moves the dimension line position

After placing the dimension line in its new position, press Esc twice to cancel the autoediting mode.

Save your drawing.

Figure 20.28

Setting a dimension grip point.

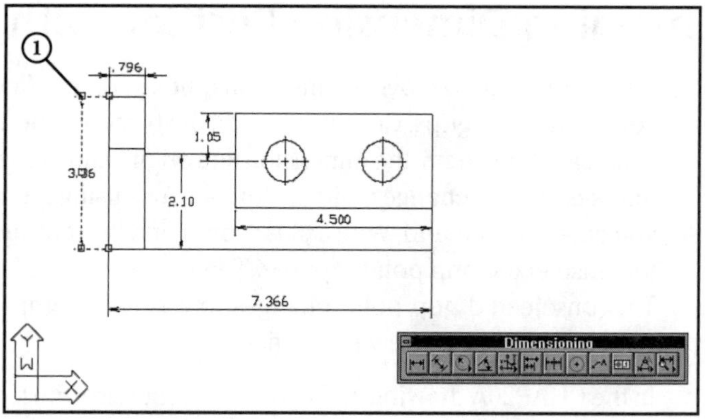

With your final autoediting completed, your drawing should look like figure 20.29.

Figure 20.29

The results of using grips to move a dimension line.

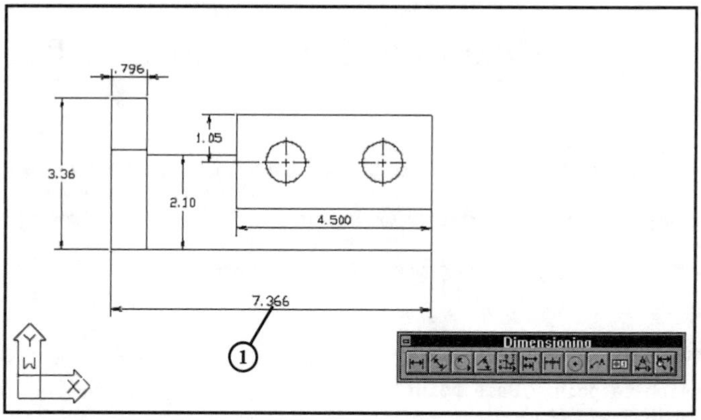

In the previous exercise you used grips to move a dimension line further from the object being dimensioned. After a dimension is placed it is very easy to change the position of the text using grips. In the following exercise you use grips to adjust the position of the text in a dimension.

Changing Dimension Text Position with Grips

Continue in the CHAP20A drawing.

`Command:` *Pick the lower horizontal dimension (see fig. 20.30)*	Selects the dimension and displays its unselected grip points

Pick the grip point at ①	Makes the grip point hot and starts the autoediting mode
Drag the text grip point and pick ② *(see fig. 20.31)*	Moves the dimension text to a new position

After placing the dimension text in its new position, press Esc twice to cancel the autoeditng mode. Your dimension text position should look like figure 20.29

Figure 20.30

Selecting the dimension text grip point.

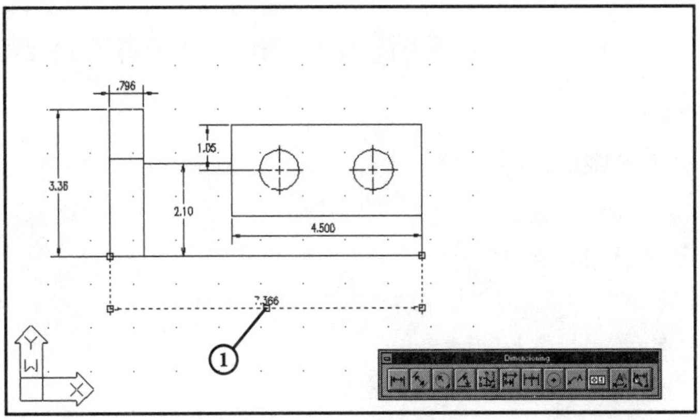

Figure 20.31

The new dimension text position.

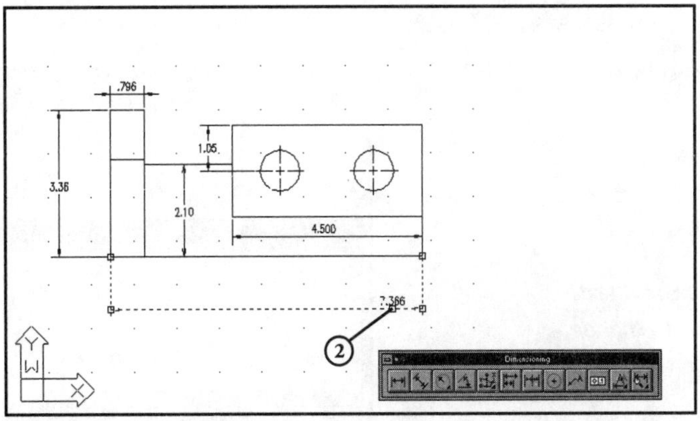

Editing Dimension Text

After you place your dimensions, you might need to adjust certain aspects of the text to have the dimension look the way you it. The DIMEDIT command provides the capability to manipulate your dimension in several ways.

In the following exercise, you use the New option in DIMEDIT to replace the overall dimension's text (7.366) with 7.500.

EDITING DIMENSION TEXT

Continue in the CHAP20A drawing.

`Command:` **DIMEDIT** ↵	Starts the DIMEDIT command
`Dimension Edit (Home/New/ Rotate/Oblique) <Home>:` **N** ↵	Selects the New option and opens the Edit MText dialog box (see fig. 20.32)

If the Select Font dialog box appears, choose Cancel (twice if necessary).

Using the Delete key, delete the default text brackets (<>)*, type* **7.500***, then choose* OK

`Select objects:` *Pick on the overall horizontal dimension* (7.366)	Selects the overall dimension for the new text
`Select objects:` ↵	Changes the dimension text to 7.500 and ends the DIMEDIT command

Save your drawing.

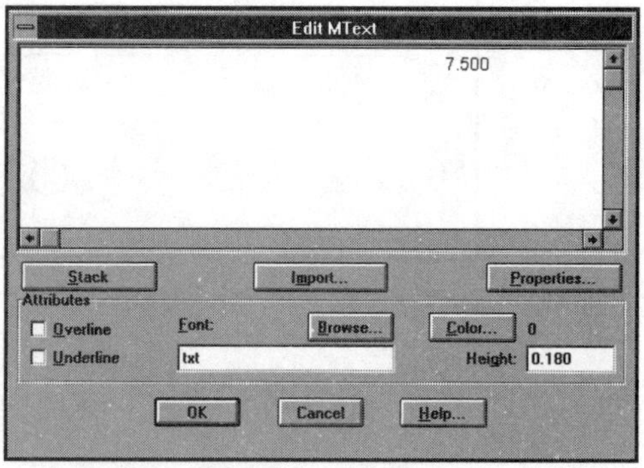

Figure 20.32

Using the Edit Mtext dialog box to change dimension text.

The dimension text changes from 7.366 to 7.500 without editing the geometry (see fig. 20.33).

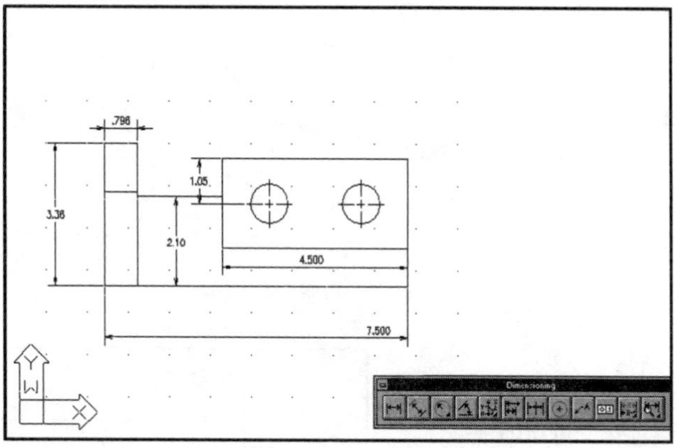

Figure 20.33

New dimension text on an overall horizontal dimension.

DIMEDIT Command Options

The DIMEDIT command provides the following options to help manage your dimension text:

- **Home.** Repositions the text back to its default position.
- **New.** Enables you to edit dimension text without having to edit the geometry to which the dimension is attached.
- **Rotate.** Rotates the dimension text without affecting the dimension geometry itself. The dimension lines will adjust to the new text width according to the DIMGAP setting.
- **Oblique.** Rotates the extension lines of a dimension to an angle you specify.

In the following exercise you will use DIMEDIT's Home option to change the overall horizontal dimension's text back to its default position.

Using DIMEDIT To Change Dimension Text to Its Home Position

Continue in the CHAP20A drawing.

Choose Home (Dimensioning)	Starts the DIMEDIT command
`Select dimension:` *Select the overall horizontal dimension*	Specifies the overall dimension
`Enter text location (Left/Right/Home/Angle): _h`	The Home option places the dimension text at the center of the dimension line (see fig. 20.34)

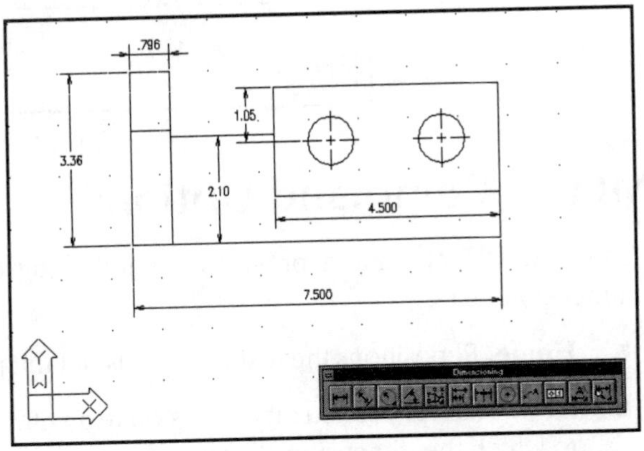

Figure 20.34

The new text position after using DIMEDIT's Home option.

The DIMEDIT command also enables you to rotate the dimension text without rotating the entire dimension. In the following exercise you use the Angle option of the DIMEDIT command to rotate the dimension text in the overall horizontal dimension.

Rotating Dimension Text

Continue in the CHAP20A drawing.

Choose Home, Rotate (Dimensioning)	Issues DIMEDIT with the Rotate option
`Select dimension:` *Pick the overall horizontal dimension*	Selects the dimension to be edited

`Enter text location (Left/Right/ Home/Angle): _a`	The tool issues the Angle option
`Enter text angle:` **45** ↵	Specifies the new text angle

The text in the overall horizontal dimension is rotated to a 45-degree angle (see fig. 20.35).

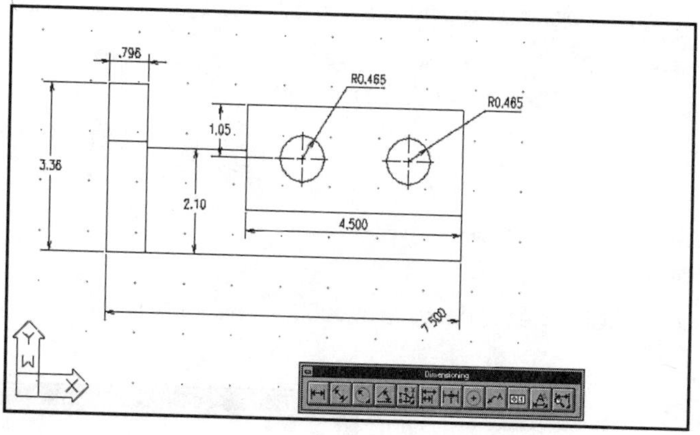

Figure 20.35

The new dimension text angle, created using the DIMEDIT command's Rotate option.

Using DDEDIT To Change Dimension Text

You can edit your dimension text in several ways. You just explored grips and the DIMEDIT command in the previous exercises. The DIMTEDIT command is covered in the next section. The quickest way to just change the text in a dimension is to use the DDEDIT command. Chapter 17, "Annotation with Text," shows you how to use the DIMEDIT command to edit your text objects in a drawing. The DDEDIT command also edits dimension text very quickly.

NOTE

The DDEDIT command uses the Edit Mtext dialog box to edit the dimension text, so you now can add multiline text in a dimension.

In the following exercise you use the DDEDIT command to change the left vertical dimension text from 3.36 to 3.25 using the DDEDIT command.

Using the DDEDIT Command with Dimension Text

Continue in the CHAP20A drawing.

Choose Edit Text (Modify, Special Edit)	Issues the DDEDIT command
`<Select a TEXT or ATTDEF object>/Undo:` *Select the left vertical dimension*	Opens the Edit Mtext dialog box

If the Select Font dialog box appears choose Cancel (twice if necessary).

In the Edit MText *dialog box, delete <> and type* **3.25** *(see fig. 20.36)*	Replaces the measured dimension with 3.25
Choose OK	Exits the Edit MText dialog box and changes the dimension text
`<Select a TEXT or ATTDEF object> /Undo:` ↵	Ends the DDEDIT command

Your vertical dimension now shows 3.25 (see fig. 20.37).

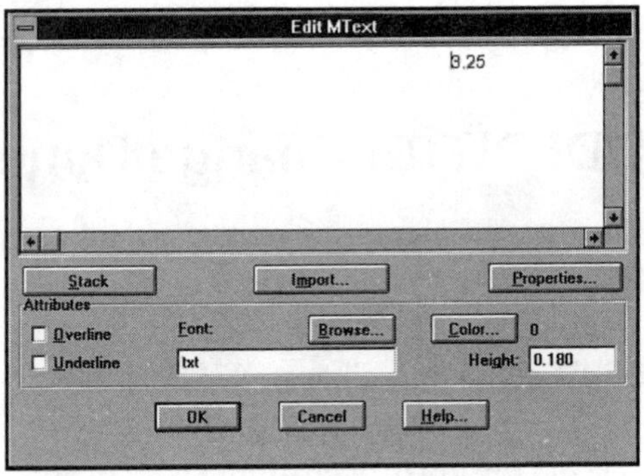

Figure 20.36

Editing the vertical dimension text in the Edit Mtext dialog box.

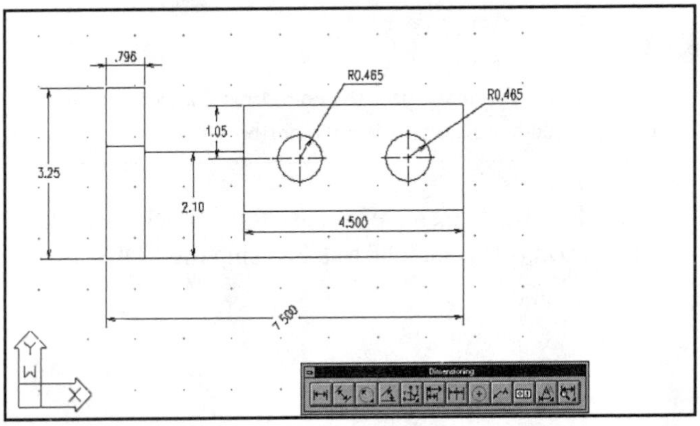

Figure 20.37

The new vertical dimension text.

Using DIMTEDIT To Edit Dimension Text

When placing dimensions, there are times when the dimensions must be placed closely together because of the limited space available. When this happens, you will need to reposition the dimensions' text to be read easily. The DIMTEDIT command gives you four options for changing the text position.

In the next exercise you use the DIMTEDIT command to move the overall horizontal dimension (7.500) to the left of the dimension line.

Using DIMTEDIT To Move Dimension Text

Continue in the CHAP20A drawing.

Choose Home, Left (Dimensioning)	Issues the DIMTEDIT command with the Left option
`Select dimension:` *Select the overall horizontal dimension* (7.500)	Specifies the dimension to be edited
`Enter text location (Left/Right/Home/Angle): _l`	The tool issues the Left option and moves the dimension text to the left of the dimension line

The overall horizontal dimension text is moved to the left of the dimension line (see fig. 20.38).

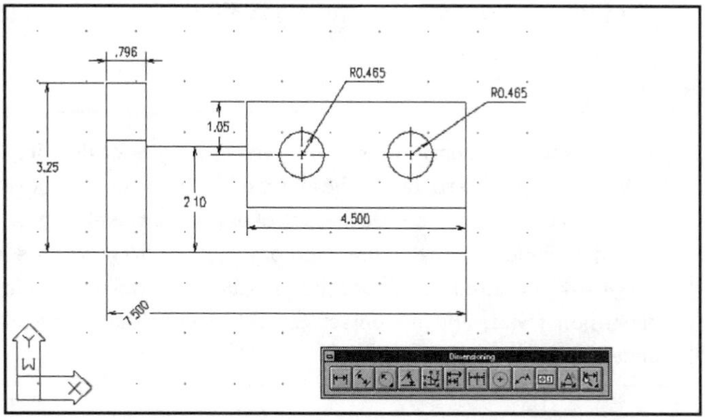

Figure 20.38

Using the DIMTEDIT Left option to move the dimension text.

DIMTEDIT Command Options

When using DIMTEDIT to change text placement, the following options are available:

- **Left.** Places the dimension text as far to the left as it can and still show a minimum dimension line length.
- **Center.** Moves the dimension text to the center of the dimension line.
- **Right.** Repositions the dimension text to the right with a minimum dimension line length.
- **Home.** Moves the text back to its original position and orientation.
- **Rotate.** Rotates the dimension text to an angle you specify.

Managing Dimensions in Projects

An important consideration in managing projects is the consistent dimensioning of all the drawings throughout all the departments. Dimension styles can be a great management tool to help accomplish this goal.

Place all your dimension styles in the prototype drawings, then, when new drawings are started from these prototypes, the dimension styles will already be available to all CAD operators, eliminating the need for each operator to define his own dimension styles. After everyone learns the dimension style to use for each dimensioning situation, all the drawings will have consistent-looking dimensions.

TIP

You can import dimension styles by inserting as a block a drawing that contains the needed styles. When you do so, cancel the insertion at the `Insertion point:` prompt and the block won't actually be inserted. Definitions of the styles as well as blocks, text styles, and other named definitions from the inserted drawing will, however, be imported. You later can purge any unwanted definitions, but it is best to insert a drawing that includes only the dimension styles, and no objects or other definitions. It need not even include any dimension objects.

A variation of the prototype drawing setup is to have a completely empty drawing file that has only the dimension styles defined. You can insert this type of drawing into any other drawing to import the defined dimension styles, which enables you to have consistent dimension styles in drawings not started from your standard prototype. You can cancel the INSERT command at the `Insertion point:` prompt—the styles will still be inserted. You also can export an existing dimension style by using the WBLOCK command to write to disk as a drawing file any dimension that uses that style. You then can open the newly created drawing file and erase the dimension—the style will remain.

Using dimension styles in your drawings gives you the ability to control how your dimensions work. With the addition of dimension style family members, you can create a complete dimension style that has specific controls for each dimension command, which greatly reduces the number of dimension styles you have to use. The power of associative dimensions and dimension edit commands gives you dynamic tools to quickly and easily edit your dimensions.

chapter

21

Techniques for Architectural and Civil Dimensioning

AutoCAD provides a great set of generic tools, but the capability to change the way AutoCAD works to meet your own standards is its greatest value. AutoCAD lends itself easily to whatever type of drawings you need to create, be it architectural, civil, mechanical, electrical, piping, or clothing design.

Both architectural and civil drawings require different dimension settings to get dimensions that look correct for that discipline. This chapter shows you how to set up the basic AutoCAD dimensioning environment for architectural and civil drawings, and then works through exercises for each. You will learn about the following:

- *Defining architectural dimension standards*
- *Creating dimension style families for architectural drawings*
- *Using hand-lettering fonts included with this book to add architectural flavor to dimensions*

- *Placing architectural dimensions*
- *Defining civil dimension standards*
- *Creating a dimension style family for civil drawings*
- *Using fonts similar to Leroy in dimensions*

When you first load AutoCAD, the dimensioning settings are set to create a very basic style of dimension. You can change certain settings so that the dimensions you place follow the standards for architectural dimensions. The architectural industry has its own type of dimension standards; most firms use oblique ticks as terminators, place the dimension text above the dimension line, and allow the dimension line to extend past the extension line. See figure 21.1 for an example of a typical floor plan dimensioned according to the dimension settings for architectural standards.

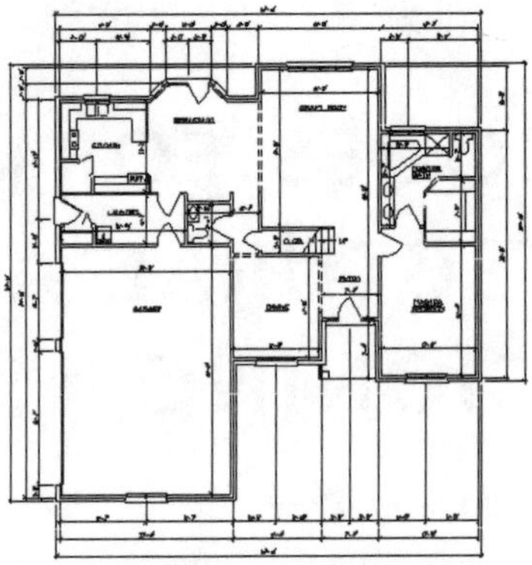

Figure 21.1

An example of architectural dimensions.

Controlling Dimension Layer Visibility in Architectural Drawings

Architectural drawings have dimensions that are specific to certain parts of the drawing. Separate dimensions might exist for the base plan, for parts of the reflected ceiling plan, and for different walls and wall types. The way you control the visibility of different types of dimensions in your drawings is very important. This is where specific layers for the different types of dimensions are used. You might need three or four layers for each type of dimension in an architectural drawing. These layers enable you to control the visibility of each set of dimensions for specific combinations of layers you need to show when plotting. For example, you might need to show a few dimensions on a reflected ceiling plan, but you do not want to show all the dimensions that might be in the architectural base plan. To control the dimensions you want to show for the reflected ceiling plan, you must have two different layers for the base plan dimensions and the reflected ceiling plan dimensions.

Creating Dimension Style Families for Architectural Drawings

Dimension style families enable you to have different settings for different types of dimensions, all within one dimension style. For example, in past releases of AutoCAD, if you used dimension styles with oblique tick marks for linear dimensioning, you had to create a new style before your leaders could have arrowheads rather than tick marks. In Release 13, you no longer need to create a new dimension style for minor changes with the different types of dimension commands. Dimension style families give you the capability to set your leaders for arrowheads and have your linear dimensions use ticks, all in one dimension style.

TIP

> Create and save your dimension styles in your prototype drawings so that all your dimension styles are immediately available when you begin a new drawing. Then all you have to do for drawings plotted at different scales is set the DIMSCALE system variable (the Overall Scale setting in the Geometry dialog box). In addition, this lends consistency to your dimensioning in all your drawings.

A prototype drawing called US_ARCH.DWG comes with your AutoCAD software, in the \ACADR13\COMMON\SUPPORT directory. The US_ARCH drawing is a good beginning of an architectural prototype, at 1/4"=1'-0" for a D size (24-by-36) sheet, but it is not complete. The dimensioning setup lacks a few features that need to be set before one could call it a complete architectural dimension style. The US_ARCH.DWG prototype is lacking the following:

- Does not have a text style that uses an architectural font
- Does not force a dimension line inside the extension lines when the text is outside the extension lines
- Does not extend the dimension lines past the extension lines
- Justifies the fractions from the bottom of the main text and does not center them on the main text

- Sets the angular dimensions to a four-place decimal (but in most architectural applications you don't need precision beyond the decimal point for angular dimensions)
- Sets the DIMRADIUS, DIMDIAMETER, and LEADER commands to use oblique ticks when they should use arrowheads
- Sets the format for text alignment to horizontal when it should align with the dimension line
- Suppressing zero inches on even foot dimensions is turned on

In the following exercises, you develop a better architectural dimension style that has complete settings. You create a dimension style called ARCH that you can use when you place dimensions on a floor plan. The dimension style has settings that are typical for architectural drawings.

CREATING AN ARCHITECTURAL DIMENSION STYLE

Begin a new drawing named CHAP21, using the FLORPLAN drawing from the IAW Disk as a prototype.

`Command:` *Choose Tools, Toolbars, Dimensioning*	Opens the Dimensioning toolbar
`Command:` *Choose Dimension Styles (Dimensioning, Dimension Style)*	Issues the DDIM command and opens the Dimension Styles dialog box (see fig. 21.2)
In the Name *edit box, enter* **ARCH**	Specifies a new dimension style name
Choose Save	Creates the ARCH style from STANDARD and sets ARCH current

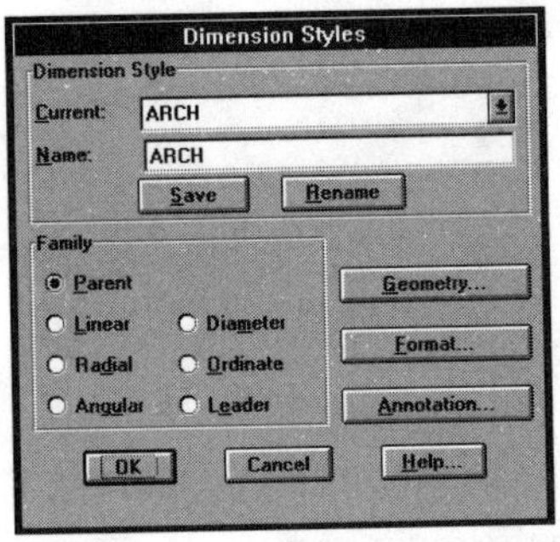

Figure 21.2

Creating a new dimension style called ARCH.

Now that you have created a new dimension style called ARCH, you need to adjust the dimension features to meet architectural standards. You created the new style from the STANDARD dimension style, which has very basic settings.

Architectural Dimension Style Family Planning

The Family area of the Dimension Styles dialog box contains radio buttons, such as the Linear button, that enable you to select the parent style of a family member. When you make changes to settings with a family member selected, the changes affect only that family member. When you make changes to the settings of the parent dimension style, they affect all family members except those that have been changed previously. After you change any setting in a specific family member, that family member ignores all further changes in the parent style. Therefore, you should plan ahead and create global settings such as overall scale and dimensioning text style before you start fine-tuning the styles of family members. There are also settings that you might want to apply to several family members. You can make these settings to the parent style first, instead of repeating them for each of several family members. Then you only need to change them in those family members to which you do not want them to apply.

In the following exercises, you make various settings that apply to all family members. Most of the settings you need to make for the Linear family member also apply to one or more of the other family members, so you'll also make the settings needed for Linear in the parent. Then, later in the chapter, you fine-tune the other family members.

Setting the Overall Dimension Scale Factor for Architectural Drawings

The most important dimension variable to set correctly is the overall plotted scale factor for your dimensions. Chapter 20, "Styling and Editing Dimensions," emphasizes the importance of setting your dimension feature sizes to the size you want on the paper. Then you set the Overall Scale factor to match your Drawing Scale factor. The Overall Scale factor multiplies the size of each dimension component and enlarges or reduces the dimension components to match the size of the drawing. The FLORPLAN is plotted at 1/4"=1'-0". You should set the Overall Dimension Scale factor to this scale, but first you must find out the correct scale factor. The easiest way to figure out the correct scale factor is to determine the number of quarter-inches in a foot, which is 48. Therefore, you should set the Overall Scale factor for this drawing to 48.

In the following exercise, you set the Overall Scale to the correct size for the FLORPLAN drawing.

SETTING THE OVERALL DIMENSION SCALE FACTOR

Continue in the Dimension Styles dialog box from the previous exercise.

Choose Geometry	Opens the Geometry dialog box (see fig. 21.3)
In the Overall Scale *edit box, type* **48**	Sets the Overall Scale factor to 48
Choose OK	Exits the Geometry dialog box
Choose Save	Saves the new settings to the ARCH parent style

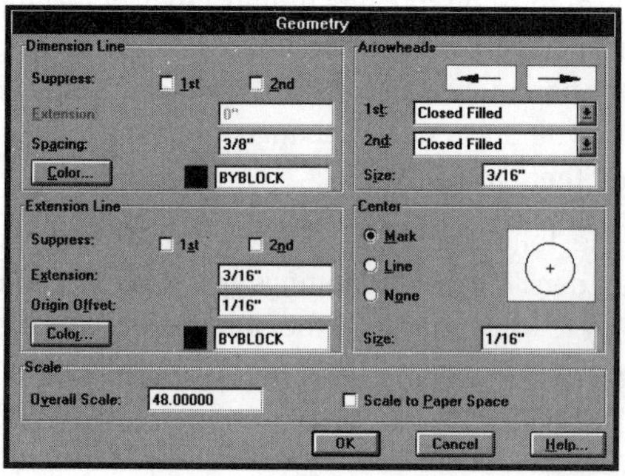

Figure 21.3

Setting the Overall Scale factor in the ARCH dimension style.

NOTE

If you use this style in other drawings at different plot scales, you can change the Overall Scale factor, which affects all dimension settings globally.

Table 23.1 lists the most common drawing scale factors in architectural drawings and the associated Dimension Scale factor settings. The Dimension Scale factor is set inside the Geometry dialog box in the Overall Scale edit box.

Table 21.1
Dimension Scale Factors in Architectural Drawings

Drawing Scale Factor	*Dimension Scale Factor*
1-1/2"=1'-0"	8
1"=1'-0"	12
3/4"=1'-0"	16
1/2"=1'-0"	24
3/8"=1'-0"	32
1/4"=1'-0"	48
1/8"=1'-0"	96
1/16"=1'-0"	192
1/32"=1'-0"	384

WARNING

After you set up family members, they ignore changes in the parent's Overall Scale. This means that if you use this ARCH style in drawings to be plotted at other scales, you must set Overall Scale individually for each family member.

Using Architectural Units for Dimensions

In AutoCAD's default drawing the default units for dimensions are set to a four-place decimal. Architectural drawings require architectural units. In the next exercise, you use the Annotation dialog box to set the units. In architectural dimensions, you want AutoCAD to display the trailing zeros for inches. The exercise also sets dimensions to use zeros for inches.

NOTE

The capability to set your dimension units separate from your drawing units is a new feature in Release 13. Within a dimension style family, each family member can now have different units settings. This means that not only can dimensions have different units from the drawing units, but each dimension command can now be set to use different units. Later in this chapter, you set angular dimensions to use different units precision from the dimension types.

SETTING ARCHITECTURAL UNITS

Continue in the Dimension Styles dialog box from the previous exercise.

Choose Annotation	Opens the Annotation dialog box
Choose Units	Opens the Primary Units dialog box
Click on the Units *edit box*	Opens a drop-down list for dimension units
Select Architectural	Sets dimension units to architectural
Choose Dimension Precision *and select* 1/64	Sets roundoff precision
Clear the 0 Inches *check box*	Turns off the suppression of trailing zeros in inches

Figure 21.4 shows the Primary Units dialog box as it should now appear.

Choose OK	Exits the Primary Units dialog box
Choose OK	Exits the Annotation dialog box
Choose Save	Saves the changes made to the ARCH style

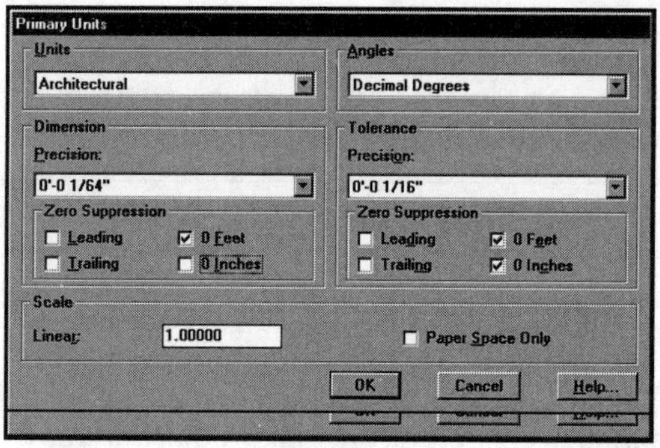

Figure 21.4

Architectural settings in the Primary Units dialog box.

Replacing Arrowheads with Tick Marks

Most architectural firms use oblique tick marks rather than arrowheads as dimension line terminators. The default setting for terminators is set to filled arrowheads.

In this exercise, you use the Geometry dialog box to set the terminators to oblique ticks.

SETTING OBLIQUE TERMINATORS

Continue in the Dimension Styles dialog box from the previous exercise.

Choose Geometry	Opens the Geometry dialog box
Click on the left arrowhead image until you get the Oblique *option in the* 1st *box (see fig. 21.5)*	*Sets the terminator to Oblique ticks*
Choose Size *and enter* **1/8**	Sets the tick size to 1/8"

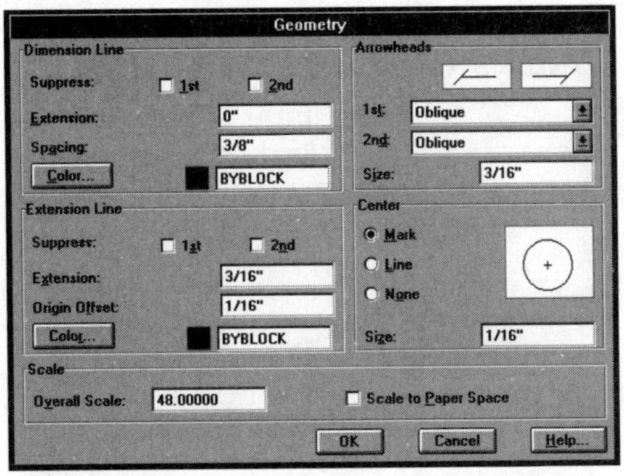

Figure 21.5

Selecting oblique terminators.

Extending Your Dimension Line

Architectural dimensions usually have the dimension line extended past the extension lines (see fig. 21.6). The setting for the dimension line extension is in the Geometry dialog box.

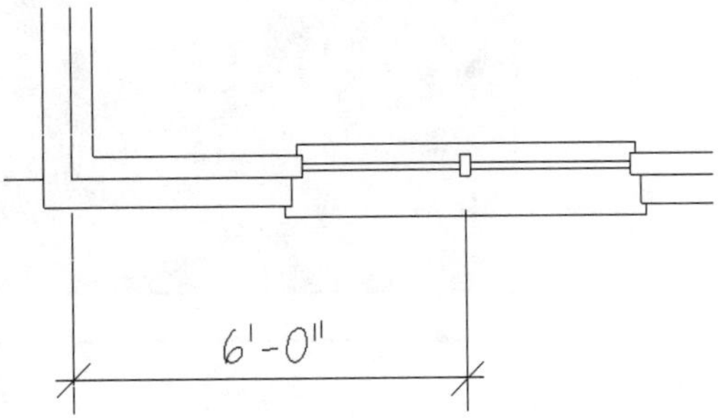

Figure 21.6

Dimension lines extended past the extension lines.

NOTE

> If you select any other arrowhead option other than Oblique, the Extension option in the Dimension Line section of the Geometry dialog box is grayed out. You cannot extend dimension lines unless you first set Arrowheads to Oblique.

Using the Geometry dialog box in the text exercise, you will set the dimension lines to extend past the extension lines 1/8". Then save the changes to the ARCH dimension style (refer to figure 21.5).

MAKING THE DIMENSION LINES EXTEND PAST THE EXTENSION LINES

Continue in the Geometry dialog box from the previous exercise.

In the Dimension Line Extension *edit box, type* **1/8** *then press* Enter *(see fig. 21.7)*	Sets the dimension line extension to 1/8" past extension lines
In the Extension Line Extension *edit box, enter* **1/8**	Sets extension line extension to 1/8" past dimension line
Choose OK	Exits the Geometry dialog box
Choose Save	Saves all the changes you made to the ARCH style, Linear dimension family member

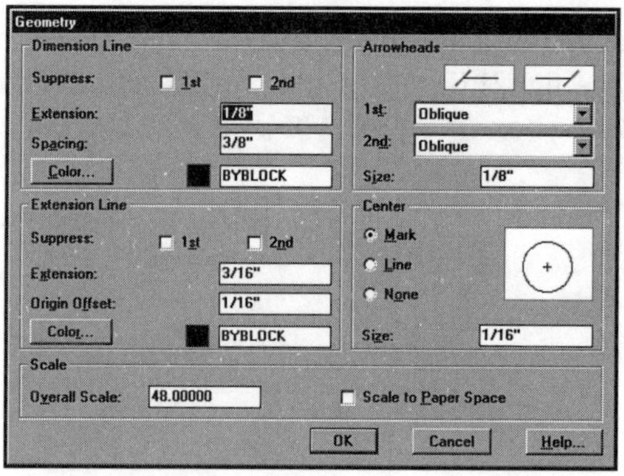

Figure 21.7

Geometry dialog box settings for Linear dimensions.

Now that you have set the dimension scale factor to 48, the units to Architectural, the arrowheads to oblique ticks, and the dimension line extension, you are ready to adjust the text format in the next exercise.

Controlling Dimension Text Location

Most architectural dimension standards require that you position the dimension line text above the dimension line. You have to set the text format so that the text aligns with the angle of the dimension line for all linear dimensions. You also set the dimension text position to be selected by the user. This enables you to slide the text to a position inside or outside the extension lines as you drag your crosshairs to place the dimension line. In the following exercise, you use the Format dialog box to set the dimension text format.

Aligning the Text with the Dimension Line

Continue from the previous exercise, with the Dimension Styles dialog box.

Choose Format	Opens the Format dialog box
Clear the Inside Horizontal *check box*	Turns off Inside Horizontal
Clear the Outside Horizontal *check box*	Turns off Outside Horizontal

The last two settings cause the dimension text to align with the dimension line at all angles.

Choose User Defined	Sets User Defined to On

User Defined causes the dimension text to be placed at the point picked to place the dimension line. This setting disables the Horizontal Justification setting.

Choose Force Line Inside	Turns on Force Line Inside

Turning on Force Line Inside forces a dimension line between the extension lines when the text is outside the extension lines, to clarify the dimension that the text is calling out.

Click in the Fit *edit box, and select* Text Only	Opens the Fit drop-down list and turns on the Text Only fit option

Text Only is the best architectural option for fitting text in extension lines. If space allows for only the text or the arrowheads (ticks) but not both, the Text Only setting places the text inside the extension lines and places the arrowheads (ticks) outside the extension lines.

Click in the Vertical Justification *image file once, then the list box shows* Above	Vertically justifies the dimension text "above" the dimension line, at any angle

Your Format dialog box should now look like figure 21.8.

Choose OK	Closes the Format dialog box
Choose Save	Saves the changes you made to the ARCH style
Choose OK	Exits the Dimension Styles dialog box and stores the settings

Save the drawing.

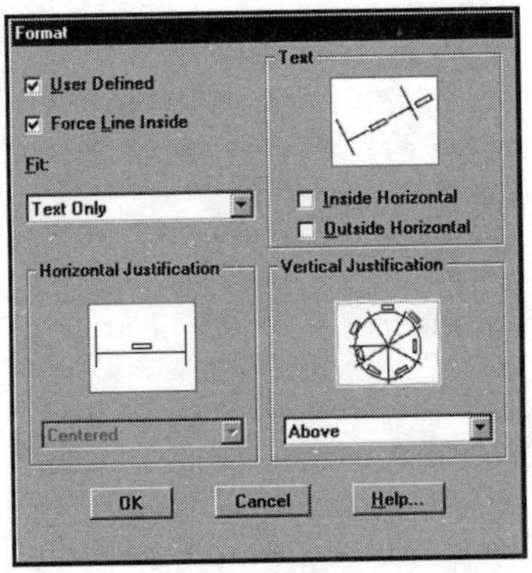

Figure 21.8

Settings for the Linear family member in the Format dialog box.

Now that you have completed a basic architectural setup, you can place the two linear dimensions shown in figure 21.9 on the floor plan. The prototype drawing had running object snap to ENDpoint and CENter, to speed up picking accurate points on features to be dimensioned.

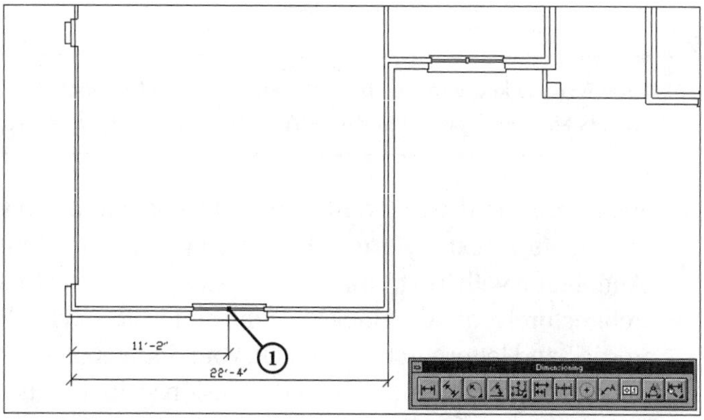

Figure 21.9

Placing dimensions on the FLORPLAN drawing.

Just place two dimensions in the following exercise, because there is more setup to be done in subsequent exercises before you place all your dimensions.

Placing Linear Architectural Dimensions

Continue in the CHAP21 drawing, with the ARCH dimension style set by the previous exercises. Zoom in to the view shown in figure 21.9.

Choose Linear Dimension (Dimensioning) and place the two dimensions shown in figure 21.9. As you pick the dimension line location, move the cursor and see it drag both the dimension line and the text. Use a MIDpoint object snap override to pick the extension line at ①.

Save the drawing.

Those dimensions look pretty good, but they'll look even better with a hand lettering-style font.

Adding Architectural Hand Lettering to Your Dimensions

One of the myths about CAD is the loss of the artistic hand-drawn techniques that make architectural drawings so unique. If you use AutoCAD in its basic form right out of the box, then this myth is partly true. But that is why you have to customize the dimension setup to follow architectural standards. Many very nice architectural hand-lettering fonts are available from third-party developers. The ARCHS architectural hand font comes on the IAW Disk that accompanies this book.

TIP

If you want to know more about the architectural font included with this book, read the ARCHS file that is placed in the IAW\DWGS directory when you install the IAW Disk.

Before you can use an Architectural style of lettering in your dimensions, you must first create a text style to which an architectural font is assigned. Chapter 17, "Annotation with Text," introduces text styles. In the following exercise, you set an architectural font, ARCHS.SHX, in the dimension style ARCH, so that you can use an artistic hand-lettering style of text in your dimensions. After you create the text style, you can apply it to your ARCH dimension style. In this exercise, you create a new DIMS text style, then use the Annotation dialog box to set the text style to DIMS.

Setting Up a Dimensioning Text Style Using a Hand-Lettering Font

Use the DDSTYLE command to create a new text style named DIMS, using the ARCHS font file. Set the width to .75, and accept defaults for the rest of the options.

`Command:` *Choose Dimension Styles (Dimensioning, Dimension Style)*	Opens the Dimension Styles dialog box
Choose Annotation	Opens the Annotation dialog box
Click in the Style *edit box, then select* DIMS	Opens the drop-down list of text styles, and selects the DIMS text style that you just created
Choose OK	Exits the Annotation dialog box
Choose Save	Saves changes to the ARCH dimension style
Choose OK	Exits the Dimension Styles dialog box and updates the linear dimensions

Save the drawing.

The dimensions that you placed now display a hand-lettering style of text (see fig. 21.10).

Figure 21.10

Dimensions with a hand-lettering font.

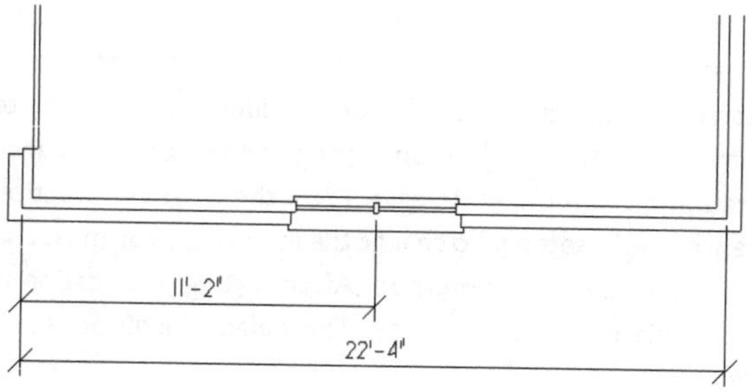

Using Stacked Fractions in Dimensions

When you use Architectural or Fractional units while dimensioning, Release 13 automatically stacks fractions. Because stacked fractions take up less space, the dimension text fits between the extension lines more often.

In the following exercise, you place a dimension to see how the new stacked fractions feature works.

Placing a Dimension with a Stacked Fraction

Zoom in to the pantry area of the kitchen and place a horizontal dimension. The resulting dimension should look like figure 21.11.

Figure 21.11

A dimension showing a stacked fraction.

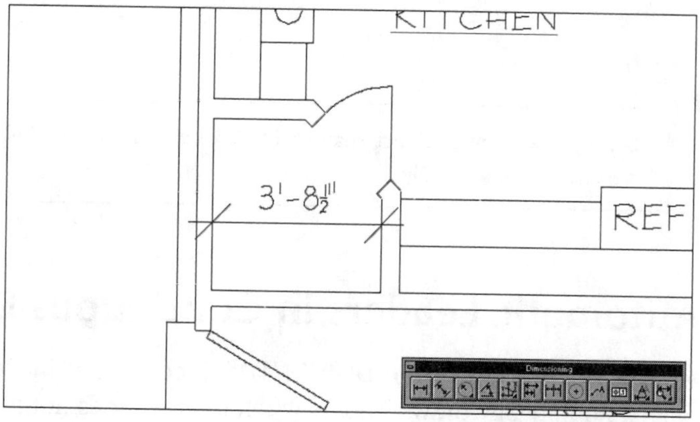

TIP

The vertical justification of the fraction in dimensions in Architectural and Fractional units is controlled by the Justification setting in the Tolerance area of the Dimension Styles, Annotation dialog box. In Release 13c4, the height of fraction text is controlled by the Tolerance Height setting. To change these settings, you must change the Tolerance Method from None to any other method. After setting Justification or Height, you can set the Tolerance Method back to None. The default justification, used by the ARCH style, is Middle.

Placing Continuous Dimensions

Continuous dimensions make up a large portion of the dimensioning you do in architectural drawings. Chapter 19, "Introduction to Dimensioning," introduces the DIMCONTINUE command. You start continuous dimensions with one of the linear or angular dimension commands, then continue a string of dimensions using the DIMCONTINUE command.

TIP

By default, DIMCONTINUE continues linear dimensions from the second extension line of the last linear dimension placed. However, you can press Enter instead and pick any extension line of any linear dimension to continue from that extension line.

TIP

Setting the running object snap to ENDPoint and CENter helps you place continuous dimensions very quickly.

Automatic Leaders in Continuous Dimensions

A new feature of the DIMCONTINUE command in Release 13 is that AutoCAD automatically draws leaders when the text does not fit inside the extension lines. This new feature greatly reduces the amount of time that you spent editing dimension text placement in earlier releases of AutoCAD. See figure 21.12 for an example of stacked fractions and the automatic leader with continuous dimensions.

In the following exercise, you place some more linear and continuous dimensions in the FLORPLAN drawing. Use figure 21.1 as a reference to place the dimensions.

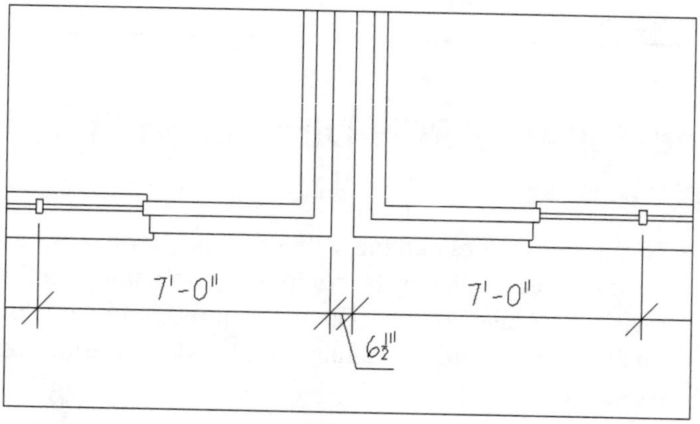

Figure 21.12

Automatic leaders and stacked fractions.

Placing Continued Dimensions

Continue in the CHAP21 drawing, with the ARCH dimension style set by the previous exercises. Zoom as needed as you work.

Choose Linear Dimension (Dimensioning) and place the 1'-8" vertical dimension at the lower left corner of the building (see fig. 21.12). Pick the lower extension line origin first, then the upper, then drag the text to place it either between the extension lines, or below the first extension line.

Choose Continue Dimension (Dimensioning)	Issues the DIMCONTINUE command
`Second extension line origin or RETURN to select:` *Pick points to continue the series from the second extension line of the 1'_8" dimension*	Continues from the last dimension
`Second extension line origin or RETURN to select:` ↵	Prompts for a dimension to continue from
`Select continued dimension:` *Pick the right extension line of the 22'_4" horizontal dimension you placed earlier*	Selects a dimension to continue from

`Second extension line origin or RETURN to select:` *Pick points to continue the series*	Continues from the selected dimension
Save the drawing.	

Fine-Tuning ARCH Dimension Style Family Members

The global settings and the settings for linear dimensions are complete. Now you need to finish the family by completing the settings for the remainder of the family members, Radial, Angular, Diameter, and Leader. You don't need to adjust settings for the Linear or Ordinate family members because the previous settings are all they need.

TIP

Even if you haven't made changes to a dimension family member, you can protect it from unintentional changes due to parental changes. Just specify the family in the Dimension Styles dialog box, open any of the Geometry, Format, or Annotation sub-dialog boxes, choose OK to close the sub-dialog box, and choose Save. Then, although the family member is still identical to the parent, subsequent changes to the parent will not affect the family member.

Ordinate dimensions are not commonly used in architectural drawings, but can be used to indicate elevations in building section or elevation drawings.

In the following exercise, you complete the settings for all the remaining family members. You also use the trick in the preceding tip to protect the Linear and Ordinate family members from global changes.

Adjusting Radial, Angular, Diameter, and Leader Family Members

Continue in the CHAP21 drawing from the previous exercise.

Choose Dimension Style (Dimensioning)	Opens the Dimension Styles dialog box
Choose Radial	Sets the following variable changes to the Radial family member

Choose Geometry	Opens the Geometry dialog box
In the Arrowheads *section, click on the left image tile until the* Right-Angle *option appears*	Sets the terminator to an open 90° arrowhead
Choose OK	Exits the Geometry dialog box
Choose Format	Opens the Format dialog box
Put a check in the Outside Horizontal *check box*	Turns the outside text position to horizontal
From the Fit *drop-down list select* Leader	Places text outside with a leader if the text and arrowhead cannot both fit
Set Vertical Justification *to* Centered	Centers the text on the leader line
Choose OK	Exits the Format dialog box
Choose Save	Saves the new changes

You have completed the Radial family member. Next, you create the Angular family member.

Choose Angular	Sets the following changes to the Angular family member
Choose Geometry	Opens the Geometry dialog box
Click on the left image tile until you get the Right-Angle *option*	Sets the terminator
Choose OK	Exits the Geometry dialog box
Choose Annotation	Opens the Annotation dialog box
Choose Units	Opens the Primary Units dialog box
In the Dimension Precision *drop-down list box, select* 0	Sets angular units to no precision past the decimal point
Choose OK	Exits the Primary Units dialog box
Choose OK	Exits the Annotation dialog box
Choose Save	Saves the new changes

The Angular family member is now complete; you are ready to start the Diameter family member.

Choose Diameter	Sets the following changes to the Diameter family member

Choose Geometry	Opens the Geometry dialog box
Under Arrowheads, *click on the left image tile until the* Right-Angle *option appears*	Sets the terminator
Choose OK	Exits the Geometry dialog box
Choose Format	Opens the Format dialog box
Put a check in the Outside Horizontal *check box*	Turns the outside text position to horizontal
In the Fit *drop-down list box, select* Leader	Sets a leader inside
Choose OK	Exits the Format dialog box
Choose Save	Saves the new settings

You now have finished the Diameter family. Next, you complete the final family member, Leaders.

Choose Leader	Creates a family member for the Leader command

When the Leader button is highlighted, changes you make to the dimension variables affect only the Leader command.

Choose Geometry	Opens the Geometry dialog box
In the 1st *drop-down list, select* Closed Filled	Sets the terminator to a closed filled arrowhead
Choose OK	Exits the Geometry dialog box
Choose Format	Opens the Format dialog box
Set the Vertical Justification *to* Centered	Sets the leader text justification to centered
Choose OK	Exits the Format dialog box
Choose Save	Saves the changes to the ARCH dimension style
Choose OK	Exits the Dimension Styles dialog box

Now place a couple leaders in the FLORPLAN drawing. Although other types of dimensions use ticks, the leaders use arrowheads, and the leader text is centered off of the leader shaft (see fig. 21.13).

Draw a couple of circles, arcs, and angled lines and try placing radial, diameter, and angular dimensions to see the effect of their family member settings.

Save the drawing.

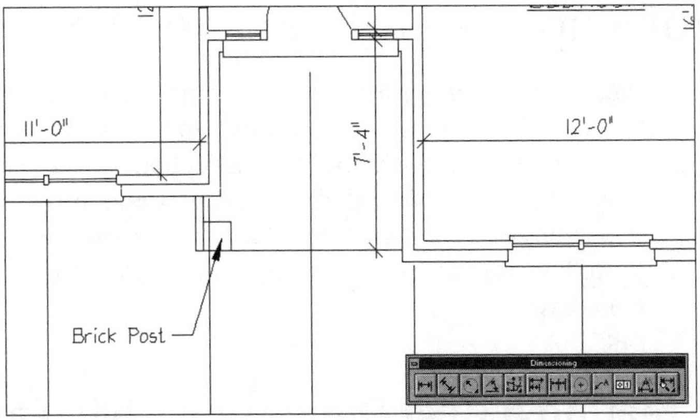

Figure 21.13

A leader note in the FLORPLAN drawing.

TIP

Although you might prefer ticks for radial diameter or angular dimensions, the dimension line extension is disabled for these family members. You can create your own tick mark that includes a dimension line extension, make a block of it, and select the User Arrow option to create a radial or angular style with extended ticks. Make the tick block one unit in size and it will be scaled correctly.

The ARCH dimension style family is now complete. All the dimension commands should now be set to follow a basic architectural standard. You can use these settings to create an architectural dimensioning setup in any drawing, or you can use WBLOCK and INSERT to export and import these settings. You might want to make some changes to fit your particular needs.

NOTE

The family members are actually stored as separate, specially named dimensions that don't show in the Dimension Styles Current drop-down list. For example, the Angular settings you made to the ARCH style have been saved as style ARCH$2. Don't mistakenly purge style family members thinking they are extraneous or not needed.

TIP

You can use the PURGE command to delete a family member's settings. $0 is Linear, $2 is Angular, $3 is Diameter, $4 is Radial, $6 is Ordinate, $7 is Leader, and $1 and $5 are unused.

Exploring the Civil Dimensioning Environment

Proper dimensioning in civil projects can require different setups, depending on the types of drawings with which you work. Site plans have different dimension information from road or bridge construction details. Plan and profile drawings also must contain specific information. Construction details use architectural units, depending on your company's standards, whereas site plans use decimal units. In the following exercises, you set up a dimension style and family members for a site plan drawing.

Creating a Civil Dimension Style Family

The architectural dimensioning setup in the first part of this chapter requires that you create a dimension style family and then create all its family members. Civil applications, from construction details to site plans, also require a complete dimension style family so that all the dimension commands work properly.

When you place information on property lines for a legal description, you use both decimal units and surveyor's units to give the length and the angle for the property line.

In the following series of exercises, you begin a new drawing using a prototype drawing from the IAW Disk, create a civil site plan dimension style, then dimension a property line and add text for the angular information.

Creating a Property Line Dimension Style

Begin a new drawing called CHAP21A, using the SITE-DIM drawing from the IAW Disk as a prototype.

Choose Dimension Styles (Dimensioning, Dimension Style)	Opens the Dimension Styles dialog box
Double-click in the Name *edit box, then enter* **PROPLINE**	Names the new dimension style family
Choose Save	Saves the new dimension style

Setting Up Units, Scale, and Text Style

Before you make settings to specific family members, you need to globally set units, scale, and the text style for the entire dimension style.

Setting Correct Dimension Units

Now that you have completed the dimension geometry and the dimension text format, you set the dimension units for the linear dimension commands.

SETTING DIMENSION UNITS AND SCALE

With the Dimension Styles dialog box still showing, you use the Annotation dialog box to set the linear dimension commands to use decimal units with two-place decimal precision.

Choose Annotation	Opens the Annotation dialog box
Choose Units	Opens the Primary Units dialog box
Click in the Precision *edit box*	Drops down the list for precision
Select 0.00	Sets the decimal precision to two places
Choose OK	Exits the Primary Units dialog box
Enter ' in the Suffix *edit box*	Sets suffix to single quote (foot mark)
Choose OK	Exits the Annotation dialog box
Choose Geometry	Opens the Geometry dialog box
In the Overall Scale *edit box, enter* **20**	Sets the dimension scale factor to 20
Choose OK	Exits the Geometry dialog box
Choose Save	Saves the changes
Choose OK	Exits the Dimension Styles dialog box

Using a Civil Lettering Style in Dimensions

The lettering that was done on the civil drawings created by hand used a lettering style called LEROY, which was named after the machine with which the lettering was created. In civil drawings done using AutoCAD, you can duplicate the LEROY lettering style very closely by using the ROMANS font that comes as a standard font with AutoCAD. You need to create a text style that uses the ROMANS font before you can apply it to your PROPLINE dimension style. In the following exercise, you create and set this new text style to be used by your dimension style.

APPLYING THE DIMS TEXT STYLE TO YOUR LINEAR FAMILY MEMBER

Continue from the preceding exercise.

Use the DDSTYLE command to create a new text style called DIMS, using the ROMANS font file. Accept the defaults for the rest of the style options.

Choose Dimension Style (Dimensioning)	Opens the Dimension Styles dialog box
Choose Annotation	Opens the Annotation dialog box
Click in the Text Style *edit box*	Drops down a list of text styles
Select DIMS	Sets the DIMS text style
Choose OK	Exits the Annotation dialog box
Choose Save	Saves the changes to the Parent style
Choose OK	Exits the Dimension Styles dialog box

Save the drawing.

Setting Up the Linear Family Member

With the parent PROPLINE dimension style created, you now will set up with the Linear family member to dimension property lines. For the Linear family member, you set the Geometry, Format, and Annotation settings.

CREATING A LINEAR DIMENSION STYLE FAMILY MEMBER

Choose Dimension Styles (Dimensioning, Dimension Style)	Opens the Dimension Styles dialog box
Choose Linear	Selects the Linear family member for the following changes
Choose Geometry	Opens the Geometry dialog box

In the Dimension Line Suppress *area, choose* 1st *and* 2nd	Suppresses both ends of dimension lines
In the Extension Line Suppress *area, choose* 1st *and* 2nd	Suppresses both extension lines
Type **20** *in the* Overall Scale *box*	Sets the overall scale to 20
Choose OK	Closes the Geometry dialog box
Choose Format	Opens the Format dialog box
Put a check in the User Defined *box*	Enables the user to specify text location
Clear the Inside Horizontal *and* Outside Horizontal *check boxes*	Sets all text to align with the dimension line
Click on the Vertical Justification *image tile until the* ABOVE *option appears*	Sets the dimension text above the dimension line

The Format dialog box should match the one shown in figure 21.14.

Choose OK	Exits the Format dialog box
Choose Save	Saves the changes to the Linear family member
Choose OK	Exits Dimension Style dialog box and saves the style changes

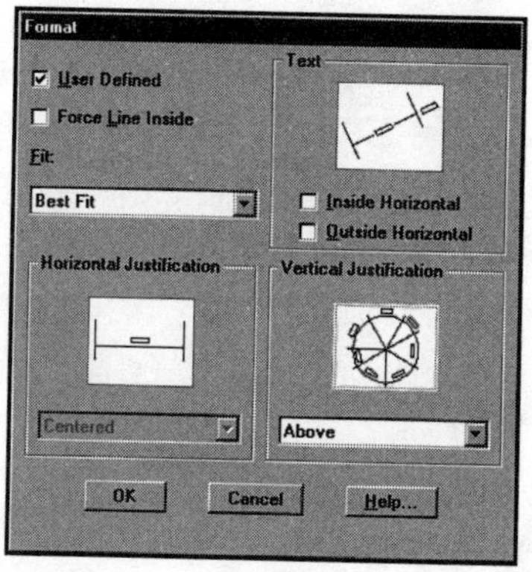

Figure 21.14

The Format dialog box settings for the Linear family member.

Creating Property Line Dimension Text

You need to place dimensional information on property lines on site plans for the angle direction and the length of each line. AutoCAD cannot place both the angle direction and the distance without editing the text. You can use the Linear dimension family member settings you made and the DIMALIGNED command to align distance text with the property lines to place dimensions that have no extension lines and no dimension lines. In Release 13, dimension text is a special form of mtext, so you can use the Edit Mtext dialog box to add the angle direction to the dimension line text.

To open the Edit Mtext dialog box for editing dimension text, you press Enter at the `Dimension line location (Text/Angle):` prompt. The Edit Mtext dialog box then displays <> to indicate the measured dimension text. You can add any other text before or after the <> , or replace the <> with whatever text you want.

In the following exercise, for the property line dimension, you add the bearing angle to the <>. To obtain the bearing angle, you use the LIST command to display it in the text window, then copy the text using the text window's Edit menu. For this to work, Surveyor angular units with N 0d00'00" E precision must be set, as they are in this drawing. Then you place the dimension using the DIMALIGNED command and the new PROPLINE dimension style, adding and editing the angle text in the Edit Mtext dialog box.

PLACING A PROPERTY LINE DIMENSION

Zoom to the area shown in figure 21.15.

`Command:` *Pick the property line at ① (see fig. 21.15), then choose List (Object Properties, Inquiry)*	Issues the LIST command and displays the selected lines on the text window
In the text window, select (press and drag on) the text `S 89d19'5" E`, *then choose* Edit, Copy	Highlights (selects) and copies the angle text to the Windows Clipboard
`Command:` *Return to the drawing window and choose Aligned Dimension (Dimensioning)*	Issues the DIMALIGNED command
`First extension line origin or RETURN to select:` ↵	Prompts you to select the line to be dimensioned

`Select object to dimension:` *Pick the property line at* ①	
`Dimension line location (Text/Angle):` **T** ↵	Opens the Edit MText dialog box (see fig. 21.16), displaying only the text <>
Press Shift+Ins, *then press the spacebar five times*	Inserts S 89d19'5" E in front of the <>
Edit the text to make it read `S89%\U+00B019'05"E   <>`	Removes spaces, changes 5" to 05", and replaces d with %\U+00B0 Unicode degree symbol string (see fig. 21.16)
Choose OK	Exits Edit Mtext dialog box (see fig. 21.16)
`Dimension line location (Text/Angle):` *Pick point* ①	Draws the dimension as S89°19'05"E 420.03'

Use the same technique to dimension the other property lines, if you want.

Save the drawing.

Figure 21.15

Placing a property line dimension.

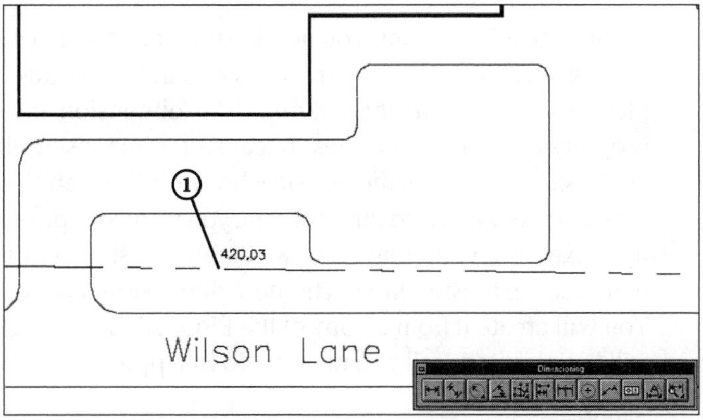

NOTE

The IAW Disk includes the PROPLINE.LSP file, which defines the NRP_DIMPL command. This command places a complete bearing and distance dimension (like the preceding exercise) automatically when you pick a line or polyline object. It requires Surveyor's units with N00d00'00"E precision and a dimension style like the one you created in the previous exercises. See Appendix G for details.

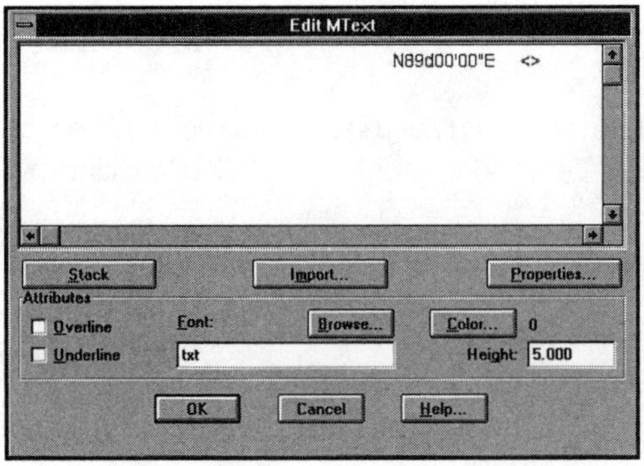

Figure 21.16

The new angle information in the Edit MText dialog box.

You now have completed the settings for your Linear family member, under the PROPLINE dimension style family. For a complete site dimensioning style, you can complete the rest of the dimension style family members, setting the options for dimension Geometry, text Format, and Annotation to follow your standards.

Placing Dimensions with No Extension Lines

When you use site plans, you need to indicate distances between two lines, such as the distance between property lines and utility easement lines. When you want to place dimensions in this manner, the dimension lines should not overlap the property and easement lines, because the extension lines can sometimes cover linetypes and confuse the person who reads the plan as to what type of line is being dimensioned. To avoid this problem, you want to suppress the extension lines. In the next exercise, you create a new dimension style and suppress the Linear family member's extension lines. The new dimension style will be called SUPPRESSED. You will create it from a copy of the PROPLINE, so the global settings of the Parent will be inherited—all you need to do is suppress the extension lines for the Linear family member.

Creating a Dimension Style with No Extension Lines

Continue from the preceding exercise, with the PROPLINE dimension style set up.

Choose Dimension Style (Dimensioning, Dimension Style)	Opens the Dimension Styles dialog box with PROPLINE current
Enter **SUPPRESSED** *in the* Name *edit box*	Names the new dimension style
Choose Save	Creates a new dimension style, identical to PPROPLINE Parent's settings

Choose Linear	Specifies Linear family member
Choose Geometry	Opens the Geometry dialog box
Enter **20** *in the* Overall Scale *edit box*	Sets the overall scale to 20
In the Extension Line Suppress *area, choose* 1st *and* 2nd	Suppresses both extension lines
Choose OK	Exits the Geometry dialog box
Choose Format	Opens the Format dialog box
Turn on User Defined, *turn off* Inside Horizontal *and* Outside Horizontal, *then choose* OK	Sets the format and closes the Format dialog box
Choose Save	Saves the changes to the new SUPPRESSED dimension style
Choose OK	Exits the Dimension Styles dialog box

Use DIMLINEAR to place some dimensions similar to the dimension in figure 21.17 in the SITEPLAN drawing.

Save the drawing.

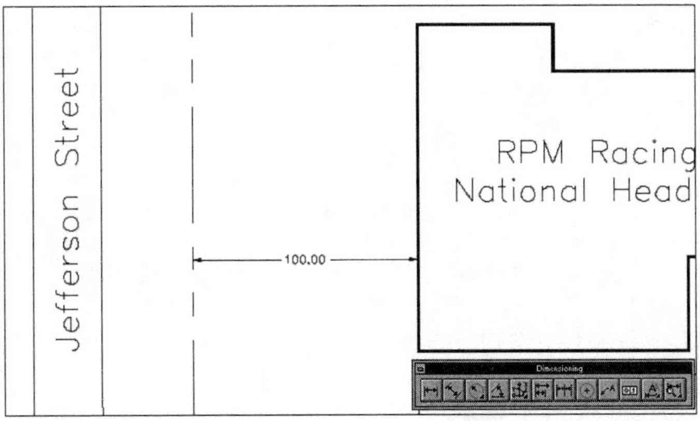

Figure 21.17

Placing dimensions with suppressed extension lines.

TIP

When you use a dimension style that has suppressed extension lines, you should use the NEArest object snap mode to place extension lines. If you need to place several dimensions, set the running object snap mode to NEArest to speed up the process.

Dimension styles give you a great amount of flexibility to create your dimensions to fit your specific application. In Release 13 with the addition of dimension style families, you can create dynamic dimension families for any application, not just architectural and civil.

chapter

22

Techniques for Mechanical Dimensioning

Completing a drawing that has dimensions both pleasing to the eye and technically correct remains a challenge. Two particular skills are required to dimension using CAD. First, you need a good understanding of the way the dimensioning commands function. Second, you must understand the technical requirements of the type of drawing with which you work.

Chapters 19 and 20 cover many of the fundamentals of dimensioning with AutoCAD. However, learning individual commands is not enough; you must develop techniques that are effective for dimensioning on the type of drawings with which you work. This chapter helps you apply AutoCAD's dimensioning commands to mechanical drawings, providing the following:

- *A brief review of general mechanical dimensioning practices and techniques*
- *A review of the specific standards as defined by the American National Standards Institute (ANSI) and International Standards Organization (ISO)*

- Techniques for styling and applying AutoCAD dimensions and dimension style families to mechanical drawings
- Coverage of AutoCAD's new ANSI-based Geometric Dimensioning and Tolerancing feature
- Emphasis on the need for using these standards in your dimension styles; several useful drawing exercises give you hands-on practice with mechanical dimensioning techniques

Understanding Dimensioning Standards

If you work in a large engineering or manufacturing company, you might be aware of existing internal design standards for mechanical drawings. Such standards usually include the following:

- Standard sheet sizes to be used for various projects
- Conventional view layout and placement
- Title blocks and notes appropriate to the drawing
- Dimension features and locations
- Tolerance specifications
- Physical size and characteristics of notes, dimension text, and arrows
- Datums and references for dimensioned objects

Even if you do not have your own standards, you probably possess a good working knowledge of mechanical drawings based on your education or experience. You might wonder about the origin of engineering specifications. Most drafting and detailing standards used in industry have their origins in one or more of the following sources:

- Senior designers who know how to implement good design practices
- Industry groups, such as automotive, aerospace, or military suppliers, who have agreed on certain standards
- Large companies, such as General Motors, who have defined their own standards

- Governmental bodies who develop their own specifications, such as Mil-Spec standards written by the Department of Defense
- National and international standards committees, such as ANSI and ISO, that have both the authority and expertise to write and administer standards that apply to all design and manufacturing activities

The current trend is away from the first three types of standards and toward universal engineering and design standards that are much more conducive to a global economy.

NOTE

Many companies develop a CAD Operations Manual. This ties in the engineering standards of the company with the way the CAD draftspersons specifically implement those standards.

Some flexibility is needed regarding how closely CAD dimensioning and tolerancing matches previous manual drafting techniques. Most CAD software, however, is written to closely emulate the current ANSI and ISO dimensioning standards, which are examined more closely later in this chapter.

Placing Dimensions Correctly

Many general rules are applied to the location and placement of dimensions in a mechanical drawing. *Placement* refers to the general part of the drawing in which the dimension is placed, and *location* refers to the distance between the view and the dimension, as well as the distance between dimensions.

NOTE

Absolute sizes and locations are based on the values that appear on the final plot. Zoom scale factors certainly affect the appearance of these features in your drawing window. The Overall Scale factor in the Geometry dialog box of the Dimension Styles settings controls all the dimension features such as text and arrowhead size.

When you create several orthogonal views of a part, you try to anticipate the amount of room that the dimensions will require. When you place dimensions in CAD, you can always reposition the views to allow for more dimensioning area. The dimensions in figure 22.1 illustrate some of the rules for dimension placement.

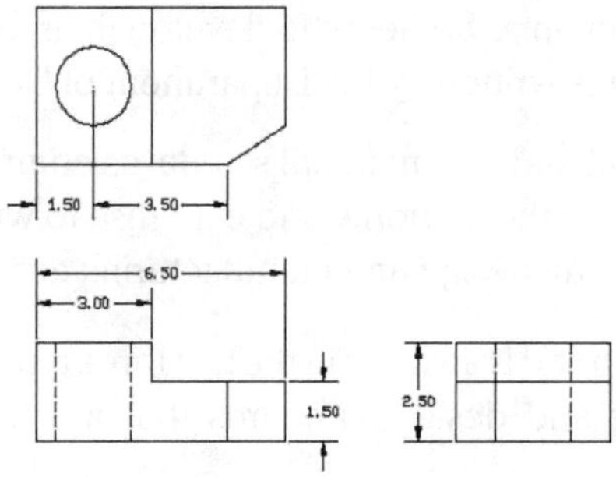

Figure 22.1

Proper location and placement of dimensions.

The specific locations of dimensions are generally related to the text size used on the drawing. For standard dimension text size of 3/16", you should place dimensions at least 7/16" from the view, and subsequent dimensions 3/8" from each other.

NOTE

When you use the baseline dimensioning feature, you can specify the distance between dimensions. The default DIMDLI setting is 3/8". This is found in the Dimension Line Spacing Text box in the Geometry portion of the Linear dimension settings.

TIP

Use proper snap and grid settings for uniform placement of dimensions.

The rules of dimension placement obviously are flexible to a certain extent in special situations. The following list emphasizes good general dimension placement guidelines.

- Place dimensions between the orthographic views
- Try to keep the dimensions off from the view itself
- Do not dimension to hidden lines or features
- Place dimensions in the view that best shows the outline of a feature
- Position the dimensions so that extension lines do not cross other extension lines or object lines

One of the most important rules of dimensioning applies to the number of dimensions used. Do not leave out dimensions required to define a part, but at the same time, do not use more dimensions than necessary.

Establishing Tolerances

Although tolerances are almost nonexistent on most architectural drawings, they are very important on mechanical drawings. Often, improper tolerancing of mating parts is one of the most costly errors that occurs in the design and manufacturing process. If you fail to sufficiently control the tolerances, mating parts might not properly fit. On the other hand, excessively close tolerances are wasteful because of the extra manufacturing costs.

Five types of tolerance specification are used in mechanical drawings, as follows:

- **Assumed Tolerance.** If you do not give a tolerance, the default tolerance is one-half of the distance between the nominal dimension value and the next logical counting number. For instance, a dimension that reads 2.83 is assumed to be between 2.825 and 2.835. The Units Control of the Annotation dimension setting enables you to specify the proper number of decimal places for a dimension.

- **General Tolerance.** You usually specify general tolerances in a tolerance block near the title block. The number of decimal places of the dimension indicates the tolerance to be used from the tolerance block.

- **Deviation Tolerance.** A deviation is shown at the dimension as the amount the dimension can vary from the nominal size. A *bilateral* tolerance, sometimes called a *symmetrical tolerance,* is an equal distance above and below the nominal value. A *unilateral* tolerance specifies a separate value for deviation above and below the nominal value. The Symmetrical and Deviation choices under the Annotation Tolerance Method specifies these tolerance types.

- **Limits Tolerance.** Limits dimensions often are easier to interpret because they consist of only two numbers: the maximum value and the minimum value of the dimension. The Limits choice under the Annotation Tolerance Method activates this type of dimension.

- **Geometric Tolerance.** Geometric dimensions and tolerances are certainly the most complicated method of tolerancing. However, they also are far superior in their capability to clearly define the intended use of a part. Geometric tolerances use many different symbols and labels that are not easy to interpret if you do not have prior knowledge of the GDT system. The new TOLERANCE tool enables you to create geometric tolerances.

NOTE

> Not specifying a tolerance is unacceptable on most mechanical drawings. Achieving an "exact" dimension in a manufacturing process is impossible.

Figure 22.2 shows a typical deviation, limits, and geometric tolerance generated in AutoCAD.

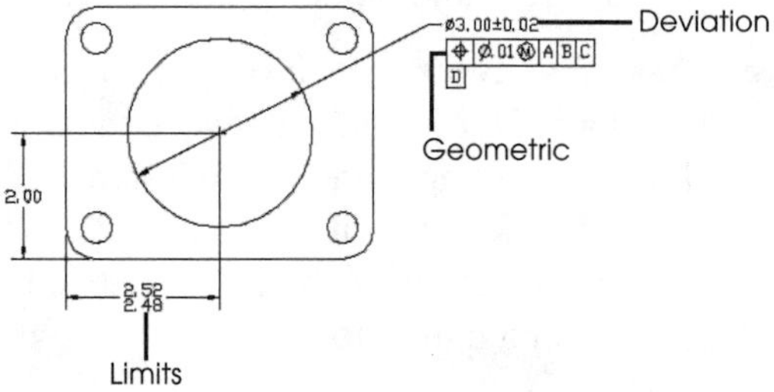

Figure 22.2

A geometric, limits, and deviation tolerance.

AutoCAD Release 13 provides the proper tools to apply all these tolerancing systems. You need to control the number of decimal places for a dimension value, and you do so best by specifying the number of decimal places for the dimension and tolerance in the Annotation group of settings found in the Dimension Style dialog box.

General tolerances are certainly the easiest to specify. Limits and deviation tolerances require additional dimension style settings, and if you use them often you should define them as separate dimension styles. Geometric tolerances are covered later in the chapter.

The following exercise reviews the dimension style settings required to generate appropriate general tolerances. Remember that in the parent/child family member relationship of dimension settings, you can have different tolerance specifications for different child categories of dimensions.

Controlling Dimension Tolerances

Begin a new drawing called CHAP22T, using the GDT-DIM drawing from the accompanying CD as a prototype.

Place the horizontal 2.50 dimension as shown in figure 22.3.

`Command:` *Choose Dimension Styles (Dimensioning, Dimension Style)*	Opens the Dimension Style dialog box

Choose the Linear *radio button, then* Annotation	Opens the Annotation dialog box for the linear family member (see fig. 22.4)
Select Limits *from the* Tolerance Method *drop-down list*	Specifies limits tolerance

Set both Upper Value and Lower Value to .02, as shown in figure 22.4.

Choose the Units *button and set the* Tolerance Precision *to 2 places* (0.00)	Opens Primary Units dialog box and sets tolerance precision
Choose OK, OK, Save, *and* OK	Saves settings and exits the dialog boxes

Place the 2.00 vertical dimension, as shown in figure 22.3.

Now set the Tolerance for the Diameter family member to Deviation in the Annotation dialog box, following a Dimension Style sequence similar to that shown in this exercise. Remember to specify tolerance value and decimal places and to save the settings.

Finish the exercise by placing the diameter dimension, as shown in figure 22.3.

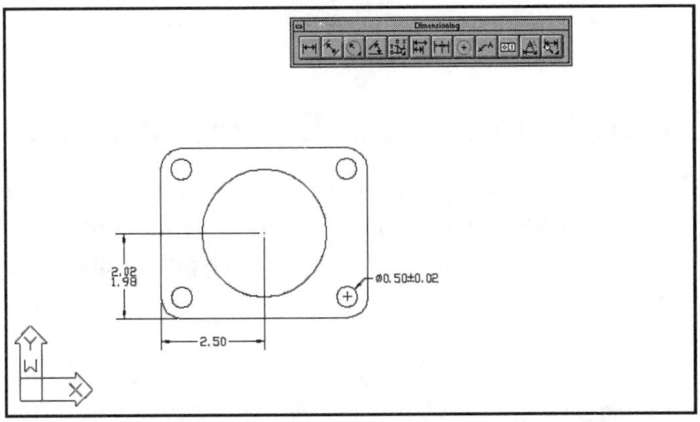

Figure 22.3

Three dimensions with different tolerance specifications.

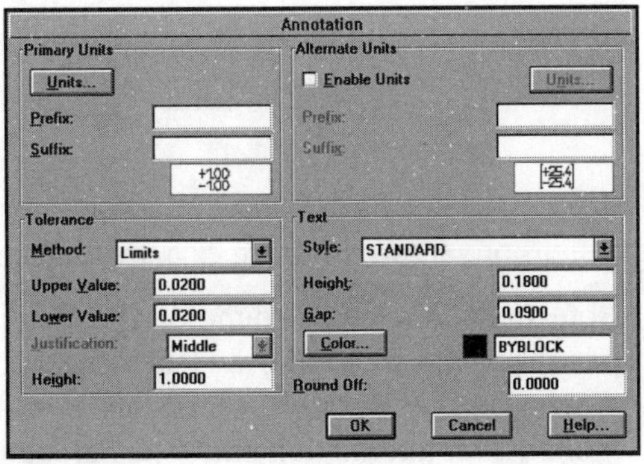

Figure 22.4

Specifying the tolerance type and value.

The use of dimension style family members enables you to set different settings for various types of dimensions, yet have the settings defined in a single dimension style.

NOTE

The Deviation and Symmetrical tolerance options are very similar. Symmetrical tolerances have the same upper and lower tolerance value, whereas the upper and lower values of deviation tolerances may vary.

Again, creating dimensions with all the proper tolerances is not always easy or convenient. However, in mechanical drawings, it is very important.

TIP

Create different dimension styles that are similar in their overall features but are set up for different types of tolerances. By doing this, you will not have to worry about which dimension settings to change each time you need a different type of tolerance.

Controlling Special Dimension Types

Several special types of dimensions are used in mechanical drawings. You must properly identify these dimensions to avoid confusing them with regular dimensions. Figure 22.5 shows three special types of dimensions.

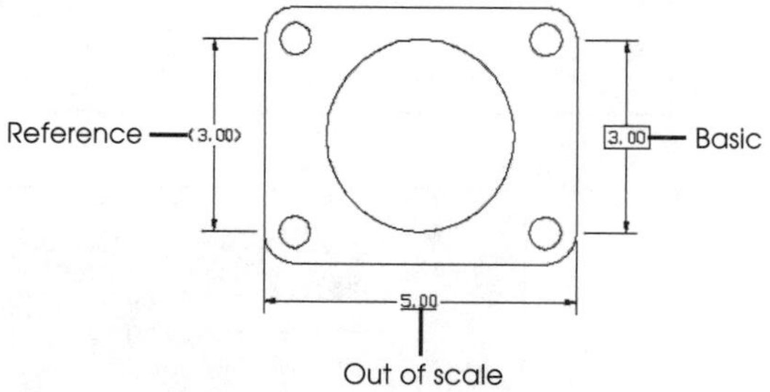

Figure 22.5

A reference, basic, and unscaled dimension.

The dimensions shown in figure 22.5 are explained in the following list:

- **Reference.** A reference dimension is identified by placing the text in parentheses or by adding the text string REF to the dimension. A reference dimension does not need a tolerance and is not required to produce the part. It often is for information only. The parentheses can be added easily to the dimension text using the DDEDIT tool.

- **Out of Scale.** Although you should always properly scale your CAD drawings, it might be necessary at times to show some objects out of the proper scale. An out-of-scale dimension is underlined to identify it as such. You simply can draw a line under the text or use the DDEDIT tool.
- **Basic.** Basic dimensions do not have tolerances because the tolerance is specified in the GDT feature control frame. The text in a basic dimension is placed in a box for easy identification. When the Basic Method of tolerancing is set in the Dimension Styles Annotation dialog box, a box is placed around the dimension text.

You might notice that Basic was one of the tolerance choices in the Dimension Styles Annotation dialog box. If you choose this feature, the dimension has the text placed in a box. Figure 22.6 shows the Edit MText dialog box, which appears if you choose the Text option in a dimensioning command.

The default brackets (<>) in the text box represent the default dimension text to be placed in the dimension. For an out-of-scale dimension, simply highlight the <> in the text window and choose the Underline button. To place parentheses around the text, add the parentheses to the <> in the text box, as shown in figure 22.6.

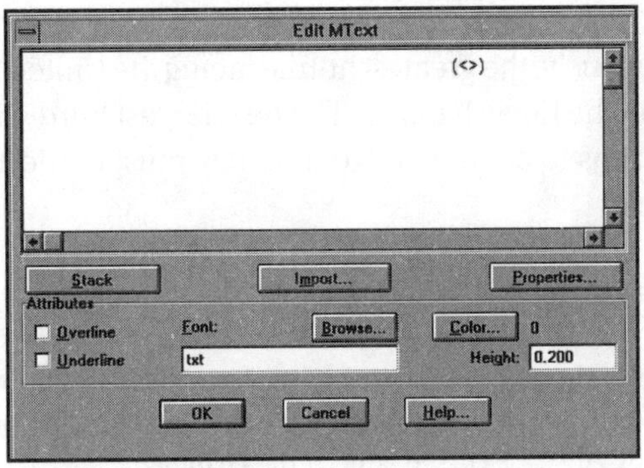

Figure 22.6

The Edit Mtext dialog box for modifying dimension text.

Applying ANSI and ISO Standards

Many companies now recognize that if they want to remain competitive, they must orient themselves to more of a global economy. Although the United States has the advantage of the universal English language, it needs to cover much ground in terms of engineering standards. Several terms need to be defined at this point.

- **ANSI.** The American National Standards Institute is a body that has the resources and the recognition to define a set of engineering standards that is recognized nationally and is compatible with international standards.

- **ASME.** The American Society of Mechanical Engineers is a national organization that publishes ANSI standards and assists in the implementation of them, among other activities.
- **ANSI Y14.4M.** This is the specific set of standards that defines proper dimensioning and tolerancing procedures. Copies of it are available directly from ASME. The Release 13 US_MECH.DWG prototype drawing contains an ANSI dimension style.
- **ISO.** The International Standards Organization is a Europe-based group that tries to coordinate and define standards that are recognized by all of the major industrial countries. The Release 13 ACADISO.DWG prototype drawing contains a set of 150 dimension styles.
- **SI Units.** The International System of Units is based on metric units. Most international standards, therefore, are defined in metric terms. The Release 13 JIS_MECH.DWG prototype drawing has a set of JIS dimension styles.
- **JIS.** The Japanese Industrial Standard is a set of engineering standards similar to ANSI.
- **DIN.** The DIN specification is an older European standard now being merged with ISO standards.

Obviously, the greatest hurdle facing the United States is its difficulty in moving away from the English units. (The next largest hurdle is probably the stubbornness of U.S. citizens to acknowledge that they must conform to any standards other than their own.)

NOTE

One of the greatest sources of conflict and confusion in many engineering departments is the process of converting between SI and English units. Creating dual dimensions in AutoCAD is discussed later in the chapter.

Interpreting the Standards

Although the latest version of a standard is written in black-and-white, many gray areas begin to appear. Textbooks often contain various translations of these standards. Trainers and consultants often are swayed by the way some large companies apply these standards. Even the programmers at Autodesk who write the code for

AutoCAD must decide how to implement these standards in the automatic dimensioning capabilities of AutoCAD.

Perhaps you have heard of the ISO 9000 series of manufacturing-related guidelines that many companies are trying to adopt. Unfortunately, it often takes a high-priced consultant to help a company determine the best way to conform to the standards.

The ANSI Y14.5M document *Dimensioning and Tolerancing* probably is the best place to start for good design standards. The document is written well and contains many useful illustrations of how to properly dimension and tolerance a mechanical drawing.

Choosing the Best Standard

Some CAD software packages come complete with several standards built-in as dimension styles or prototype drawings. You probably need to modify these settings slightly to meet your specific needs. Before Release 13, many AutoCAD users bought third-party dimensioning and tolerancing software or customized AutoCAD themselves using the capability to insert dimensioning symbols and create GDT feature control frames.

Your customer base and the type of industry with which you work probably will influence your choice of standards. AutoCAD has several different prototype drawings available for which dimensioning styles are already defined for specific standards. Figure 22.7 shows these options as they appear in a drop-down list in the International part of the Preferences dialog box. Note the English and Metric choices in that dialog box.

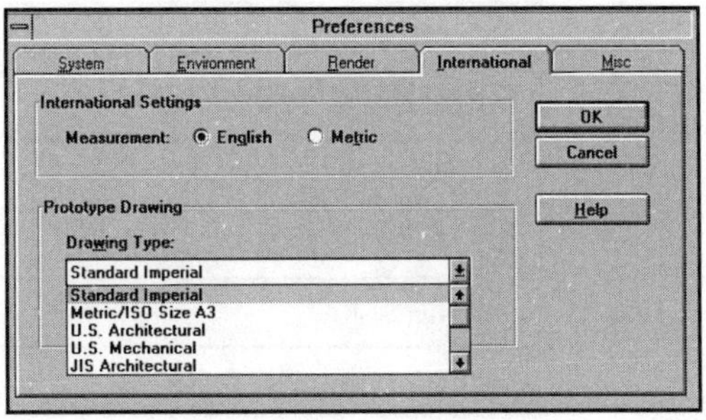

Figure 22.7

Prototype drawing options in AutoCAD.

Many standard callouts on mechanical drawings, such as the diameter or counterbore symbol, appear as icons. You can see the similarities between ANSI and ISO geometric dimensioning and tolerancing symbols in figure 22.8.

Figure 22.8

ANSI and ISO symbols.

Symbol Name	ANSI	ISO
POSITION	⌖	⌖
CONCENTRICITY/COAXIALITY	◎	◎
SYMMETRY	NONE	⌯
PARALLELISM	//	//
PERPENDICULARITY	⊥	⊥
ANGULARITY	∠	∠
CYLINDRICITY	⌭	⌭
FLATNESS	⏥	⏥
CIRCULARITY	○	○
STRAIGHTNESS	—	—
PROFILE OF A SURFACE	⌓	⌓
PROFILE OF A LINE	⌒	⌒
CIRCULAR RUNOUT	↗	↗
TOTAL RUNOUT	⌰	⌰
AT MAXIMUM MATERIAL CONDITION	Ⓜ	Ⓜ
AT LEAST MATERICAL CONDITION	Ⓛ	NONE
REGARDLESS OF FEATURE SIZE	Ⓢ	NONE
DIAMETER	Ø	Ø
DATUM	-A-	-A-
BASIC DIMENSION	50	50
REFERENCE DIMENSION	(50)	(50)
DIMENSION NOT TO SCALE	50	50
COUNTERBORE/SPOT FACE	⌴	NONE
COUNTERSINK	⌵	NONE
DEPTH	↧	NONE

Exploring GDT Dimensioning Features

Full support of Geometric dimensioning and tolerancing is a long-awaited feature in AutoCAD. As you might imagine when you look at a GDT-based mechanical drawing, it can take far longer to dimension the part than to draw it. For many AutoCAD users, the hardest part of using the new GDT features is understanding how to apply them. Of course, if you merely are trying to duplicate a drawing using AutoCAD, the thought process behind the GDT feature control frames is already complete. You need only duplicate the GDT symbols.

Warning

If you are working on a rather old drawing, or on a drawing in which proper standards were not originally used, trying to replicate the nonstandard feature control frames can become very frustrating. On some older drawings, for instance, the datum references were placed in front of the tolerance. These tolerances may have to be drawn individually.

Using the TOLERANCE Command

The new TOLERANCE command in Release 13 enables you to automatically generate most types of feature control frames.

Before you explore this command, review the parts of a typical feature control frame (see fig. 22.9).

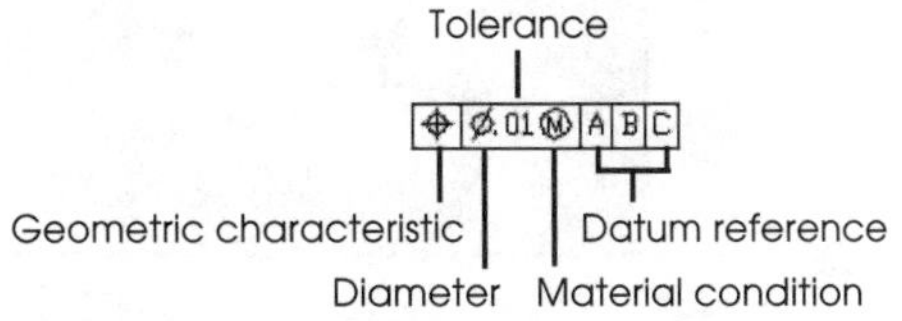

Figure 22.9

A typical feature control frame.

A brief list of explanations of the components follows.

- **Geometric characteristic.** You can choose from 1 of 14 geometric characteristics (refer to figure 22.8 for a illustration). If you do not require a symbol, simply choose OK.

- **Diameter symbol.** This diameter symbol is required on only a few of the geometric characteristics. You use it to specify a round tolerance zone, and you place it before the tolerance value.

- **Tolerance value.** You specify the total tolerance of the feature as a numeric value.
- **Material condition.** You use the material condition with some of the features to modify the tolerance value based on the true size of the feature.
- **Datum reference.** Again, you use datums with only some of the features. Depending on the application, between one and three datums are required.

The Symbol dialog box is displayed by the TOLERANCE command (see fig. 22.10). You can choose one of these tolerance symbols, or choose OK if you do not require any of them.

Figure 22.10

The Symbol dialog box.

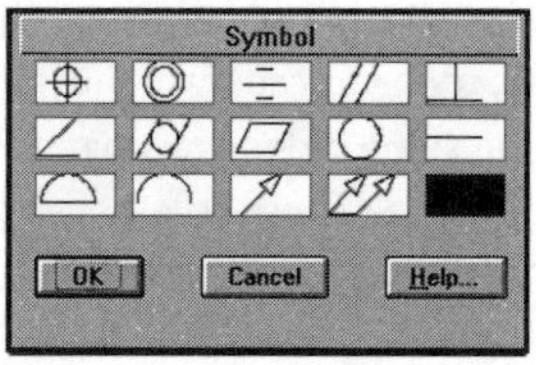

Next, after you choose OK to close the Symbol dialog box, the main Geometric Tolerance dialog box appears, as shown in figure. 22.11.

Figure 22.11

The Geometric Tolerance dialog box.

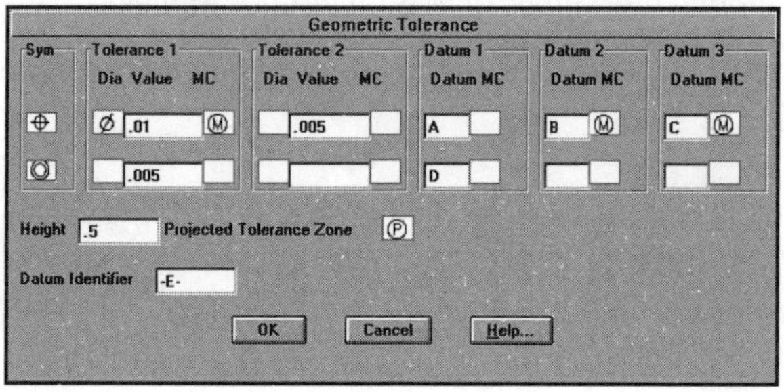

You seldom have to address all the values in the Geometric Tolerance dialog box. If you did address all the values, your complex feature control frame would appear similar to the one shown in figure 22.12.

Figure 22.12

A complex feature control frame.

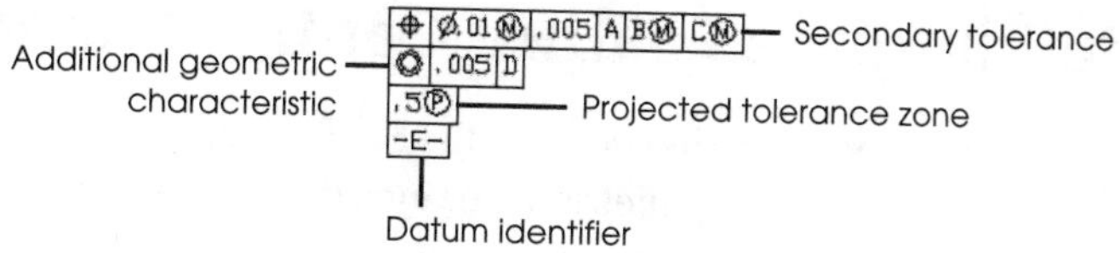

Identifying Datums

The simplest way to use the TOLERANCE command is to create a datum label. Datums are very important to GDT because they specify exactly how to set up a part in manufacturing or inspection. *Datums* typically are flat surfaces or the centerlines of cylinders. A datum should be a capital letter in a box, connected to the feature or the dimension of the feature. The datum identifier label is shown in figure 22.12.

Although you are free to name datums as you please, you really do need to call out datums in the proper order in the feature control frame. In a typical rectangular part, the *primary datum* establishes the reference plane. The *secondary datum* establishes the alignment of the part. Finally, the *tertiary datum* locates the part in the third axis of movement. Figure 22.13 shows the points that you can use to establish the respective datums.

Figure 22.13

A primary, secondary, and tertiary datum.

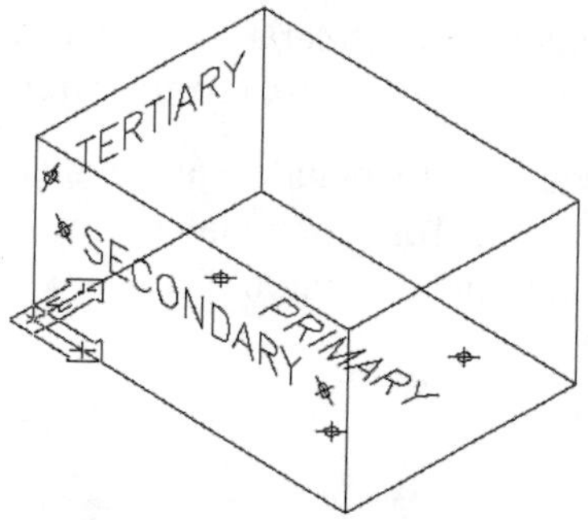

You can use the TOLERANCE command to easily create a separate datum label by choosing none of the symbols and filling in only the datum letter in the Datum 1 box of the Geometric Tolerance dialog box. If you want to add a datum identifier along with a feature control frame, fill in the datum letter in the Datum Identifier edit box.

After you identify the datums, you can reference these datums in the Datum 1, Datum 2, and Datum 3 areas of the Geometric Tolerance dialog box—the primary, secondary, and tertiary datums, respectively.

Building the Feature Control Frame

The symbol you choose from the Symbol dialog box appears in the first box in the Sym area of the Geometric Tolerance dialog box. If you click on this box, the Symbol dialog box reappears so that you can make another selection. You use any part of the second line of the Geometric Tolerance dialog box only if you want to create an additional geometric characteristic, such as that shown in figure 22.12.

TIP

You also can stack additional feature control frames by adding additional ones at a later time.

Notice that you also can activate a Projected Tolerance Zone symbol by choosing that box, as well as specify the height for that tolerance zone.

Specifying Tolerance and Material Conditions

The Tolerance 1 area of the Geometric Tolerance dialog box enables you to specify the tolerance by typing the correct value. Optionally, you can use the DIA box if you need to specify a round tolerance zone. The Tolerance 2 area enables you to specify a secondary tolerance, normally not required.

Finally, if you want to include a material condition in the tolerance or datum areas of the Geometric Tolerance dialog box, choose any of the MC boxes to open a secondary Material Condition dialog box. You have three choices (see fig. 22.14).

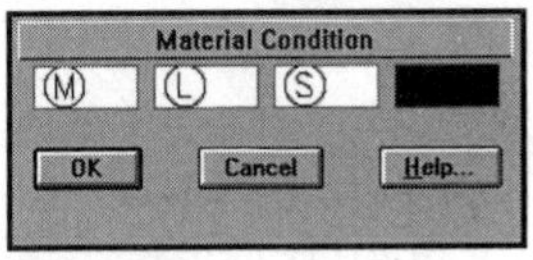

Figure 22.14

The Material Condition dialog box.

Material conditions are important to GDT. The three options are briefly explained in the following list, based on an example that deals with the locational tolerance of a hole.

- **Maximum Material Condition.** When the hole is on the small side of the tolerance, the maximum amount of material is left on the workpiece, often meaning that the location must be the most precise at this point before it can accept a mating part. When the M is present with the tolerance, as the hole is opened up towards the largest acceptable size, the locational tolerance relaxes by the difference between the maximum and minimum diameter.

- **Least Material Condition.** This defines the condition in which the hole diameter is on the large side of the tolerance, meaning that the least amount of material is present. This symbol is not used nearly as often as the M or S symbol.
- **Regardless of Feature Size.** You use the S symbol to specify that material condition does not affect the tolerance. Some argue whether the absence of this symbol altogether would not imply the same concept.

You can use a tolerance or a datum reference to specify material conditions.

NOTE

Further study of GDT applications might be necessary to determine which symbols are required and which symbols are optional for a given tolerance.

Now that you know about the TOLERANCE command and its options, you try to apply it in the following exercise. The part that you dimension has five holes that are critical to the function of the part. Instead of being located from the edge of the part, the holes are located from the theoretical center of the part. Imagine that this part needs to fit into a pocket and have all five holes align with a mating part. This is how you try to define these locations using GDT. Notice that the size tolerances are regular deviation tolerances.

You begin by drawing the side view, then you place the appropriate dimensions of size and location. Remember to identify the locational dimensions as basic. Then, you use the TOLERANCE command to label the necessary datums. Finally, you use the TOLERANCE command to create the feature control frames.

Applying GDT to a Mechanical Drawing

Begin a new drawing called CHAP22GD, using the GDT-DIM drawing from the accompanying CD as a prototype.

Use snap mode and draw the side view on layer OL, as shown in figure 22.15, then reset layer DIMS current.

Set the Dimension Style to GDT and create the 3.00 and 4.00 basic dimensions shown.

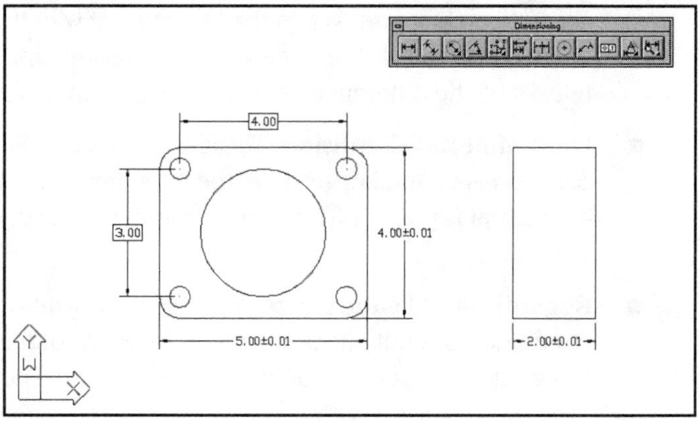

Figure 22.15

Creating the side view and linear and diameter dimensions.

Use the Annotation setting in the Dimension Styles dialog box to change the tolerance Method to Symmetrical, the tolerance value to .01, and the Primary Units tolerance precision to 2 places (0.00), then save the settings and exit the dialog box.

Create the length, width, and height dimensions as shown in figure 22.15.

Dimension both circle diameters as shown in figure 22.16.

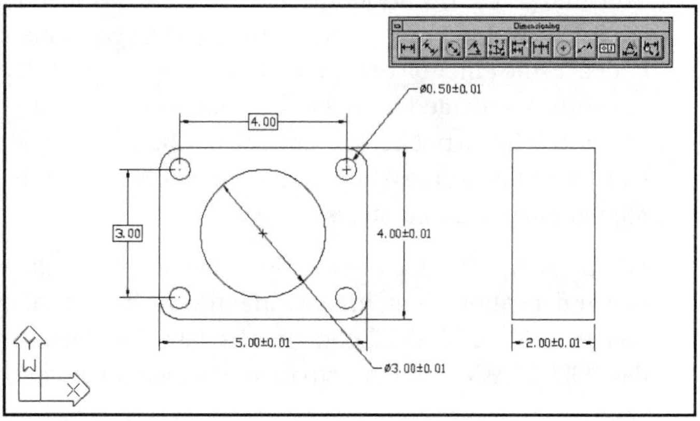

Figure 22.16

Adding the diameter dimensions.

`Command:` *Choose Tolerance (Dimensioning)*	Opens the Symbol dialog box
Choose OK	Selects no symbol and opens the Geometric Tolerance dialog box
Type **-A-** *in the* Datum 1 *box, then choose* OK	Names datum and closes dialog box
`Enter tolerance location:` *Pick at* ① *(see fig. 22.17)*	Locates datum label

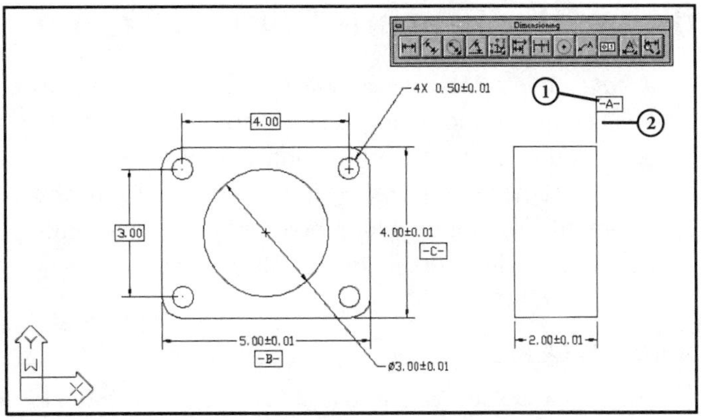

Figure 22.17

Placing the datum labels.

Draw the line at ②.

Repeat this procedure to place datum labels B and C.

`Command:` *Choose Tolerance (Dimensioning)*	Opens the Symbol dialog box
Choose the True Position *symbol, then choose* OK	Opens the Geometric Tolerance dialog box

Complete the dialog box according to the feature control frame shown in figure 22.18, then place the feature control frame near the dimension.

Repeat this process for the second feature control frame. Save your work.

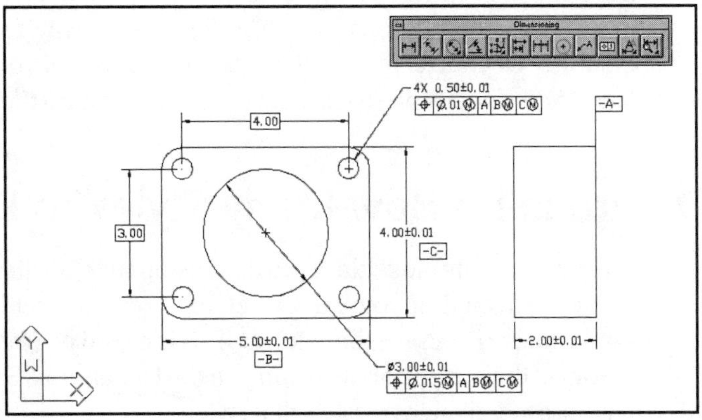

Figure 22.18

Adding the feature control frames.

Editing the Feature Control Frame

A *feature control frame* is a single object that you can move, copy, or erase. Grips also are useful for modifying feature control frames. The best way to modify the characteristics of the feature control frame is to use the DDEDIT command. When you select the feature control frame, all the current characteristics are shown in the Geometric Tolerance dialog box for you to view and edit. When you choose OK, AutoCAD updates the feature control frame.

WARNING

You cannot explode feature control frames that you create by using the TOLERANCE command. Therefore they are difficult to manually edit once they are created.

Using Dimension Style Families

As you can see from the exercises so far in this chapter, you can spend a considerable amount of time changing the Dimension Style settings for various types of dimensions, especially if tolerances are involved. Learning to utilize a number of dimension styles can help you reduce the time you spend changing the dimension style settings. Just as using several text styles is desirable, you should organize your dimensions according to dimension style.

This section focuses on how to use the Dimension Style dialog box to effectively control your dimensions, which is the easiest way to keep track of numerous variables. Of course, many shortcuts are available if you are familiar enough with AutoCAD's dimension styles and variables to control them at the `Command:` prompt.

Determining How Many Styles To Define

When you modify the settings in a dimension style, all dimensions created using that style are affected. If you want to change only the settings to create one special dimension, do not save the settings. This is called an *override,* and a + sign appears in front of the dimension style name in the Dimensions Styles dialog box to indicate that unsaved changes exist in that style.

Some common cases in which overrides are useful in a mechanical drawing include the following:

- A special tolerance not often used. An example of this would be an occasional limits Tolerance, activated by the Limits Method of the tolerance setting.
- One or both extension lines suppressed. These are controlled by check boxes in the Extension Line section of the Geometry dimension settings.
- Unique text or dimension line placement. This is controlled in the Format sections of dimensioning styles.
- Alternate units or places of precision not commonly used, which can be changed in the Annotation sections of dimensioning styles.

In other words, use overrides for special situations that occur in mechanical dimensioning.

You can anticipate certain types of dimensions when you work on mechanical drawings. Because you might need to alter several settings before you can create a certain type of dimension, always using overrides is not practical, such as in the following cases:

- Basic dimensions required on GDT-type drawings
- Common postscripts for certain dimensions
- Dual dimensioning
- Other types of tolerancing, such as limits or deviation

Often, you should save separate dimension styles so that you can quickly choose another style rather than have to check all the settings.

NOTE

In a CAD drafting department in which many different designers try to conform to a standard, a common set of dimension styles is very important. Every designer should try to use these common styles when possible.

Understanding Parent and Child Relationships

Although the concept of dimension styles is not new to AutoCAD, the parent and child relationship is new in Release 13. Using different settings for different types of dimensions is common practice; for example, the type of tolerance or the places of accuracy of a linear dimension can differ from an angular or diameter dimension.

When you define a new dimension style, you choose the Parent radio button in the Dimension Styles dialog box (see fig. 22.19). First, make all the necessary settings in the Geometry, Format, and Annotation pages of the dialog box. Try to choose settings such as units, text style, and arrows that are appropriate for most of your dimensions of that style. AutoCAD stores all these settings as parent settings.

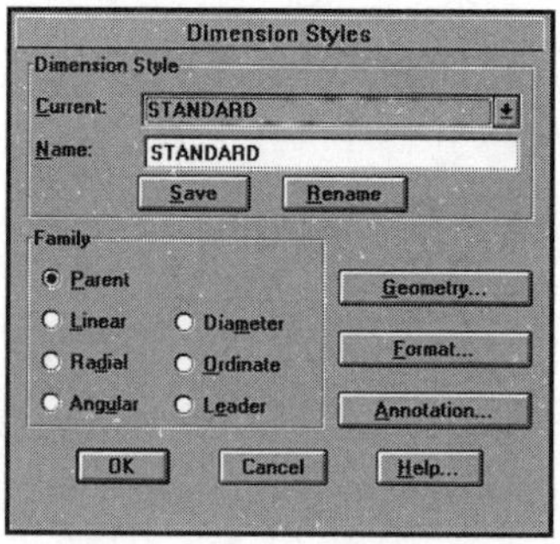

Figure 22.19

The Dimension Styles dialog box.

Next, choose one of the six child categories and alter any settings that affect only those types of dimensions. Continue to modify the various child categories until you create your best combinations of settings.

Finally, you save this dimension style and continue to define as many other different styles as you will need for your drawings. A sample of mechanical dimension styles is shown in the following list:

- **MECH-NT.** A dimension style that has no tolerance.
- **MECH-BA.** A dimension style to create basic dimensions.
- **MECH-DT.** A dimension style for creating oversize datum labels with a special font.
- **MECH-DD.** A dimension style for creating dual dimensions.

After you have included some familiar dimension styles in your prototype drawings, mechanical dimensioning should become less of a chore.

Experimenting with Other Mechanical Dimensioning Techniques

Along with Geometric dimensioning and tolerancing, you encounter many other special situations on mechanical drawings. Sometimes labeling holes or keyways according to the mating part is appropriate, assuming that the production department understands the sizes and tolerances involved. Some examples of this would be tapped holes, counterbored screw holes, or woodruff keyways. Figure 22.20 shows some examples of these notes, which are a lot less work than specifying all the exact sizes and tolerances. You can use the AutoCAD LEADER command for these notes.

Figure 22.20

Common mechanical dimensioning techniques.

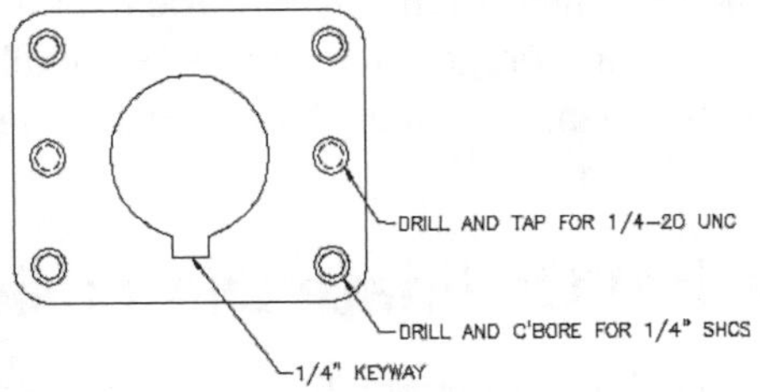

When you create a family of similar parts from a common drawing, letters or symbols can take the place of dimension values. A table is then constructed that lists several sets of values for different-sized parts, which leads to some very advanced CAD applications for which a parametric drawing is created. The actual feature size and locations are then driven by external data imported through a variety of methods that AutoCAD supports.

Controlling the Appearance of Dimensions and Tolerances

Many of the components of a dimension are controlled by the dimension style settings. In mechanical dimensioning applications, you might want to optimize the appearance of the dimensions. One item that you might want to control is the leading 0 in front of a decimal fraction. While some users feel this extra 0 is unnecessary, others want to see it because it helps the decimal point stand out if the drawing is faded and hard to read. The Units portion of the Annotation settings has a leading 0 switch for both the primary value and the tolerance. Figure 22.21 shows a dimension created with and without the leading 0.

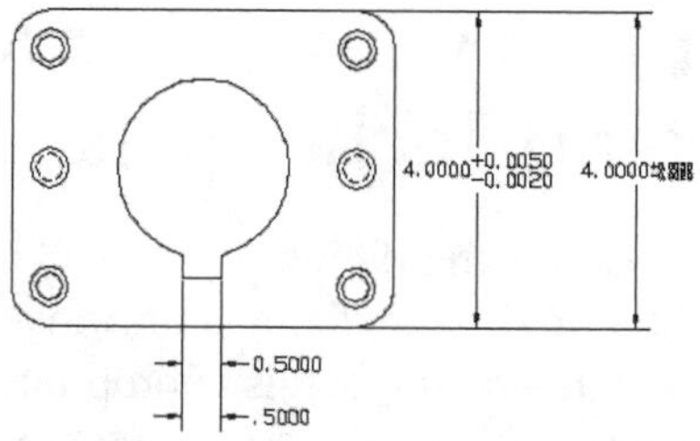

Figure 22.21

Dimensions with modified leading O and tolerance text height.

Also, in the interest of saving space, you might want to modify the text height of deviation tolerances, for which you would use the tolerance portion of the Annotation settings. Figure 22.19 also shows an example of the tolerance text at full scale and at half scale of the dimension text.

One final dimensional feature you might want to control is the color of the various dimension components. This is especially useful if you want to assign different plotting pens or plotting line widths to these components.

Creating Ordinate Dimensions

On mechanical designs that contain many features requiring locational dimensions, ordinate dimensions are very useful. Because ordinate dimensions do not use dimension lines and use only one extension line, far less clutter occurs on the drawing. You can use the DIMORDINATE command to create ordinate dimensions.

The Automatic mode of the DIMORDINATE tool determines whether the dimension will be from the X or Y datum based on the primary direction of the leader line. If you choose the X-Datum or Y-Datum options, the dimension will be taken from that datum regardless of the direction of the leader line. Figure 22.22 shows the toolbar icons for the DIMORDINATE tool.

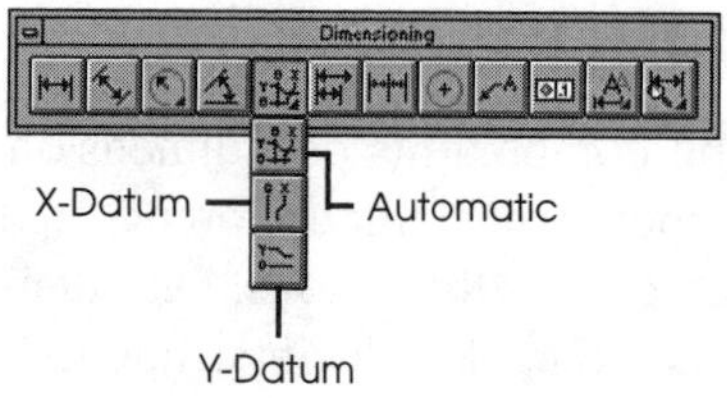

Figure 22.22

The Ordinate Dimensions toolbar.

NOTE

> Ordinate dimensioning often is referred to as datum dimensioning because all the dimensions originate from a specific datum point.

The first step of using ordinate dimensions is to set the current UCS to the dimensioning datum point. In the next exercise, you practice placing some ordinate dimensions. To help you pick points on objects and align the ordinate dimension lines, an ENDPoint running object snap is set and ortho is on in the exercise drawing.

APPLYING ORDINATE DIMENSIONS

Begin a new drawing called CHAP22O, using the BASEDIMS drawing from the accompanying CD as a prototype. Turn on ortho mode.

`Command:` *Choose View, Set UCS, Origin*	Issues the UCS command with Origin option
`Origin/ZAxis/3point/OBject/View /X/Y/Z/Prev/Restore/Save/Del/? /<World>: _o`	
`Origin point <0,0,0>:` *Pick ① (see fig. 22.23)*	Sets 0,0 to the corner of the plate
`Command:` *Choose Automatic (Dimensioning, Ordinate Dimensions)*	Issues DIMORDINATE command in automatic mode
`_dimordinate`	
`Select feature:` *Pick ②*	Selects endpoint of centerline
`Leader endpoint (Xdatum/Ydatum/Text):` *Pick point at ③*	Specifies leader length and draws dimension

Continue to add ordinate dimensions until your drawing resembles figure 22.23.

To create the 21 dimension with a staggered leader line, turn off ortho before picking ④. Otherwise, keep ortho on to ensure straight lines.

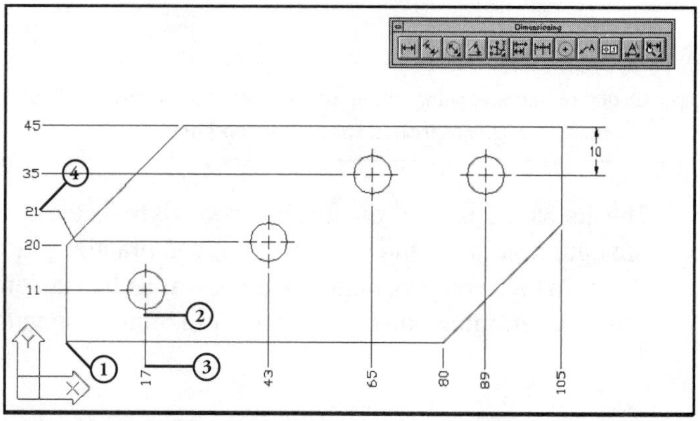

Figure 22.23

Ordinate dimensions applied to the drawing.

You can see how quickly you can dimension a detail drawing when you use ordinate dimensions. You end up with very little clutter and the extension lines do not interfere with each other.

TIP

When dimensions are very close to each other you can use a staggered leader to bring the dimension text to a better position, as shown in the 21mm dimension in figure 22.23.

Using Alternate Units

You really want to avoid creating a design that uses both SI and English units. Because of standard stock sizes, as well as standard component compatibility with items such as threads and keyways, the design must originate in either metric or English standards. Owing to customer requirements, however, or the insistence of shop workers, you sometimes must show both units in a dimension.

If you activate the Enable Units function in the Alternate Units section of the Annotation dialog box, AutoCAD automatically generates dimensions with alternate units. After you activate the alternate units, you have complete control over the units and tolerance settings of the alternate units. The most common conversion factors are 25.4 when inch units are standard, or .03937 when millimeters are standard. You should use one more place of accuracy for inch units than for decimal units. This is due to the fact that an inch is a much larger unit than a millimeter.

As you can see in figure 22.24, dual dimensioning text strings can become very long and hard to place. Local tolerances are almost out of the question.

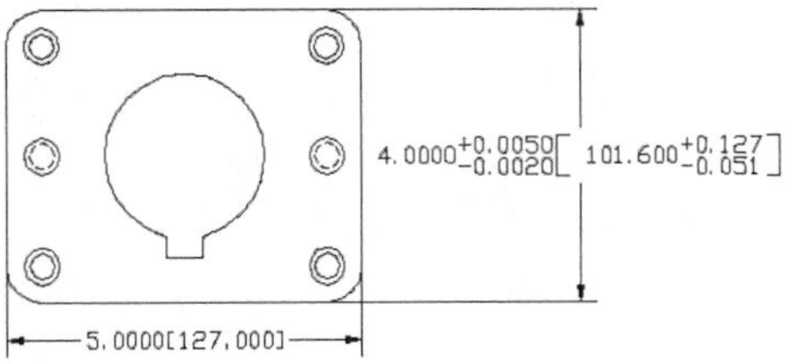

Figure 22.24

Alternate units for dual dimensioning.

Warning

You might find that in some engineering standards, dual dimensions must be placed so that the alternate units are under, rather than behind, the normal dimension text.

The first step toward developing good dimensioning skills using AutoCAD involves learning the basic dimensioning tools. Chapter 19, "Introduction to Dimensioning," introduces the dimensioning commands and demonstrates how you can apply them. Chapter 20, "Styling and Editing Dimensions," shows you how to control your dimensions by changing settings and using dimension styles. This chapter has shown you the new features in Release 13 that enable you to quickly produce the dimension details you need for mechanical drawings.

part

V

Appendices

Appendix

A

Installation and Configuration

This appendix explains the installation and configuration for AutoCAD Release 13 for Windows, Windows for Workgroups, Windows NT, and Windows 95. The information will cover the following topics:

- *System requirements for each operating system*
- *16-bit platform versus 32-bit mode*
- *Installation from diskettes or CD*
- *Basic AutoCAD configuration*

Installation Requirements

The various operating systems require different hardware components. These suggestions are based on a typical drawing size of 1 MB and are considered "minimum" requirements in most cases. In order to run multiple sessions or accommodate larger drawing size, supplemental memory is recommended.

System Requirements

Along with the follow requirements, your system needs either a 3.5" floppy drive or a CD-ROM drive to install AutoCAD. This can be an internal drive, an external drive, or a "shared" device physically attached to another PC.

Windows 3.*x* or Windows for Workgroups 3.*x*

The minimum requirements for running AutoCAD on Windows 3.*x* or Windows for Workgroups 3.*x* are as follows:

- 486-based PC or greater
- Windows 3.*x* (enhanced mode) or Windows for Workgroups 3.*x*
- MS-DOS 5.0 or later
- 16 MB RAM or more
- Minimum 35 MB hard-disk space, permanent swap file of 64 MB
- VGA (or better) display and pointing device

Windows NT 3.51

The minimum requirements for running AutoCAD on Windows NT 3.51 are as follows:

- 486-based PC or greater
- Windows NT 3.5 or later
- 32 MB RAM recommended

- Minimum 35 MB hard-disk space, permanent swap file of 64 MB
- VGA (or better) display and pointing device

Windows 95

The minimum requirements for running AutoCAD on Windows 95 are as follows:

- 486-based PC or greater
- Windows 95
- 16 MB RAM or more
- Minimum 35 MB hard-disk space and sufficient swap file space
- VGA (or better) display and pointing device

6-Bit Platform versus 32-Bit Mode

Windows and Windows for Workgroups are 16-bit operating systems. Because AutoCAD Release 13 is designed to run in 32-bit mode, there are two additional installations that you need to run for these platforms. These installations are not required when using Windows NT or Windows 95 operating systems.

Win32s

A common indicator of an existing Win32s is the game FreeCell. If you do not have FreeCell, you can search your hard drive for the WIN32S.INI file. It should be located within the following subdirectory: C:\WINDOWS\SYSTEM.

Once you have located the WIN32S.INI, you can open it and read which version you have installed on your system. This is important because only particular versions of Win32s will work with AutoCAD Release 13. To open the WIN32S.INI, locate the file through File Manager and double-click on the name, as shown in figure A.1.

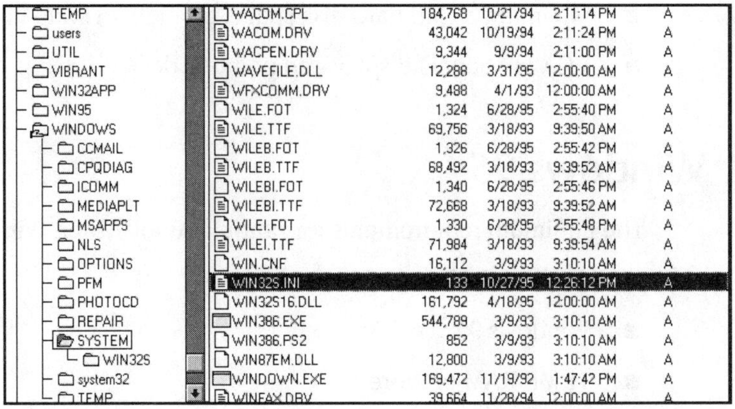

Figure A.1

Double-click on WIN32S.INI from within File Manager.

This will bring up Notepad and show you the WIN32S.INI file as seen in figure A.2.

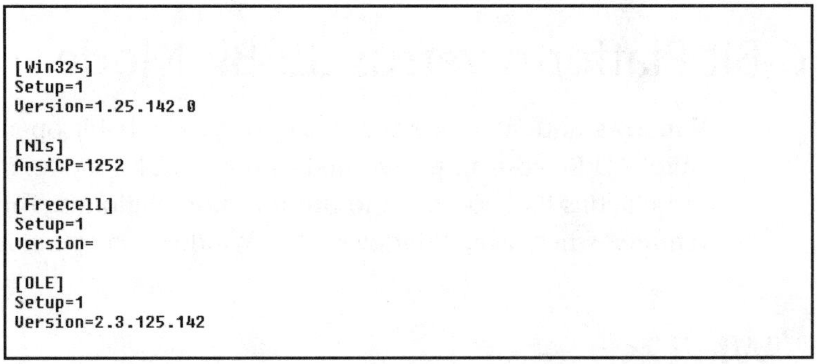

```
[Win32s]
Setup=1
Version=1.25.142.0

[Nls]
AnsiCP=1252

[Freecell]
Setup=1
Version=

[OLE]
Setup=1
Version=2.3.125.142
```

Figure A.2

The WIN32S.INI contains simple ASCII text.

The third line will tell you which version of Win32s you are running.

AutoCAD R13c0 through R13c3 runs with Win32s version 1.20 through version 1.25a, and AutoCAD R13c4 needs Win32s version 1.25 or 1.25a.

NOTE

AutoCAD will not run with a Win32s later than version 1.25a. If you have another software application that requires Win32s 1.30, AutoCAD will not run on the same PC with that program.

Installing Win32s

The following steps take you through the installation procedure for Win32s.

1. Start Windows and quit any applications that are running.
2. Insert the diskette labeled "Win32s Disk 1" into the drive. If you are installing from the CD media, insert the CD into the CD-ROM drive.
3. From the File menu within Windows, choose Run.
4. Use the Browse button and select the drive letter that matches the location of your installation disk. For the diskette installation, click on SETUP.EXE. When using CD media, you need to go to the subdirectory labeled d:\win32s\disk1 in order to find the SETUP.EXE. Choose OK. Windows will restart when the Win32s installation is completed correctly.

WinG

If you plan to install and configure the new Windows High Performance (WHIP) video display driver on a Windows 3.*x* or Windows for Workgroups 3.*x* system, you need to install Microsoft WinG. WinG is software designed to enhance performance and provide faster displays. This software is not required for the WHIP driver when using Windows NT or Windows 95.

Installing WinG

The following steps take you through the installation procedure for WinG.

1. While in Windows, insert the diskette labeled "WinG 1.0," the AutoCAD Installation CD, or the WHIP driver diskette, into the appropriate drive.
2. From the File menu within Windows, choose Run.

3. Use the Browse button and select the drive letter that matches the location of your installation disk. For the diskette installation, click on SETUP.EXE. On the CD, you will need to go to the subdirectory labeled d:\wing\disk in order to find the SETUP.EXE. Choose OK.
4. There will be prompts to follow in order to complete the installation.

NOTE

For current information regarding particular video cards and the WHIP driver, see the README.HLP that accompanies your AutoCAD installation media.

Installing AutoCAD

AutoCAD is designed to install automatically. During the installation, AutoCAD needs your personalization data and prompts for the type of installation you want: Typical, Compact, or Custom. After installing AutoCAD R13, you can explore "What's New," online help and electronic documentation. These icons install with the AutoCAD icon in your Program Group or Program Folder.

Before Installing AutoCAD

On some operating systems, there are additional software programs that install to assist in accessing the 32-bit platform of AutoCAD Release 13. The following discusses the requirements for each operating system.

Windows 3.*x* or Windows for Workgroups 3.*x*

Prior to installing AutoCAD, you need to install Win32s. If you are planning to use the WHIP video display driver, you need to install WinG. These installations are made before installing AutoCAD Release 13. Most installation guides suggest that you back up the files of your previous release of AutoCAD. See your *AutoCAD Installation Guide for Windows* for instructions about the backup procedure.

You should check two other things before installing AutoCAD:

1. VSHARE.386 must be running.
   - Double-click on the MS-DOS icon in the Main program group.
   - At the command prompt, enter **VSHARE**. If the command prompt returns, you now have VSHARE running. Otherwise, you will probably get "Bad command or filename." Check the SYSTEM.INI to see whether VSHARE.386 is loaded automatically. If VSHARE.386 is missing from your system and file, contact your dealer about acquiring the program or check in the AutoCAD forum on CompuServe (GO ACAD).
2. 32-bit file/disk access must be disabled.
   - To find the 32-bit file/disk access option, select the Control Panel icon in the Main program group.
   - Next, select the Enhanced icon.
   - Choose Virtual Memory.
   - Finally, choose Change>>.
   - At the bottom of the dialog box you will find the 32-bit file or disk access options. The adjacent boxes must be empty to disable this option. After the install program runs, you can re-enable these options by clicking on it. This places an "X" in the box.

Windows NT 3.5 or later

The Windows NT operating system does not require Win32s, WinG, or VSHARE.386. AutoCAD is written for a true 32-bit system and Windows NT provides this very thing. After ensuring that you meet the minimum system requirements, begin the installation process.

Windows 95

Like Windows NT, the Windows 95 operating system does not require Win32s, WinG, or VSHARE.386. AutoCAD is written for the 32-bit system and is Windows 95 compatible. This means that the look and feel of AutoCAD—its icons, and object linking—conform with the Windows 95 standards. After ensuring that you meet the minimum system requirements, begin the installation process.

Installing AutoCAD

The actual AutoCAD installation runs through an "Install Wizard" program that prompts you for personalization information. You can stop the installation at any time by choosing the Cancel button.

1. Insert the CD into the CD-ROM drive and your personalization diskette (also known as "Disk 1") into the appropriate drive. When installing from diskette media only, put the diskette labeled "Disk 1" in the 3.5" drive.
2. Start the installation from within Windows using the Run command. This command is in the File menu.
3. Indicate the correct drive letter in the box and type: **\setup**. For example: d:\setup. Choose OK.

WARNING

When installing from the CD, you must start from the SETUP.EXE on the CD—not on the diskette.

See the *AutoCAD Installation Guide for Windows* for in-depth information on the installation routine and its options.

Basic AutoCAD Configuration

This section will cover the basic configuration process. It discusses the minimum setup required in order to get AutoCAD running trouble-free. Once this is achieved, you can refer to your *AutoCAD Installation Guide for Windows* for information on precise device configuration.

Configuring Peripheral Devices

AutoCAD uses ADI device drivers when communicating with the peripheral components of your system. Some of these ADI drivers come with AutoCAD and their choices appear in the configuration menu for each device.

Video Display

After installing WinG, you have three video drivers from which to choose during configuration of the video device.

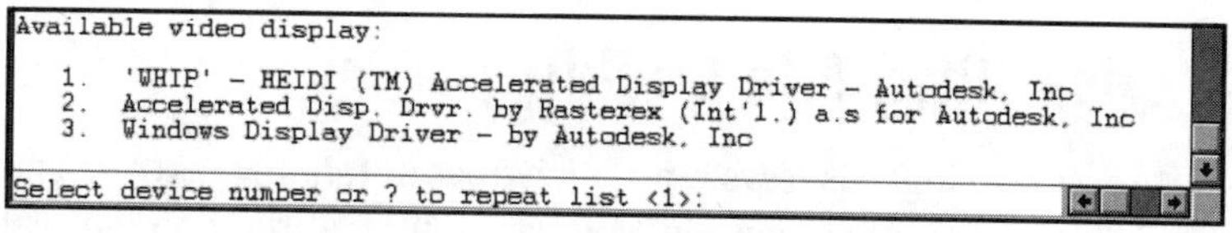

Figure A.3

Three video display drivers provided with AutoCAD in Release 13.

It is suggested that you configure for the basic "Windows Display driver" initially. Once you have verified that AutoCAD Release 13 runs correctly, you can upgrade to the "Accelerated Disp. Drvr" or the "'WHIP' - HEIDI" driver. To run the configuration routine again, simply enter **CONFIG** at the Command prompt in AutoCAD.

Digitizer

The options under Digitizer provide drivers for both a mouse and a digitizing device. You might want to choose "Current System Pointing Device" until you have tested your AutoCAD installation. Another option can be configured at a later time.

Plotter

AutoCAD comes with a variety of ADI drivers. These drivers are written specifically for the printing and plotting devices that Autodesk tests to run with AutoCAD.

Originally, you might want to choose "None" and come back later to configure for your printing or plotting device. If you do not find a driver for your plotting device, contact the manufacturer of your plotter for a compatible driver. If one is not available, ask whether your device will emulate the language of another device. The HPGL and HPGL/2 drivers are sometimes supported by devices other than Hewlett-Packard models. Your *AutoCAD Installation Guide for Windows* lists information regarding cables, port communication settings, and device options. You can consult with your guide to find a driver that uses the same settings as your unsupported device.

Entering the Login Name

Respond to the login prompt with the name you desire. This name can have spaces or special characters and must not exceed 30 characters.

Disabling File Locking

On a single-user system, which does not share files over a network, you want to enter **n**. If you are uncertain, you can enter **y** and reconfigure at a later date to change.

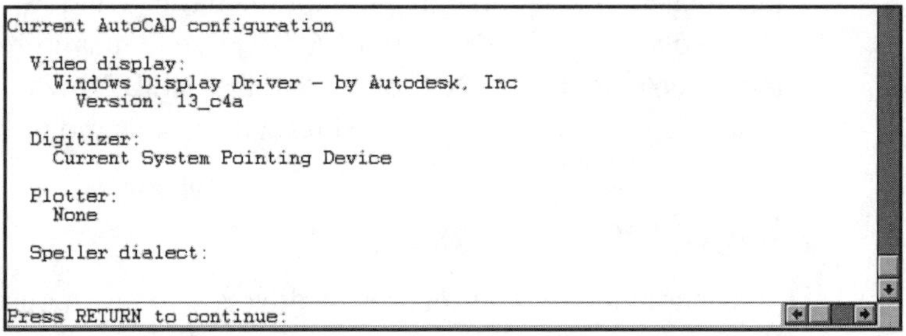

Figure A.4

Summary screen showing the current AutoCAD configuration.

After you finish configuring, you return to the configuration menu and you need to enter **y** to save your configuration settings. You will see the AutoCAD graphics area and are now able to begin a drawing session. For additional information about the configuration parameters, see "Fine-Tuning Device Configurations" in the *AutoCAD Installation Guide for Windows.*

Now that 32-bit technology is readily available, the benefits of its use are more apparent. Stability, speed, and compatibility issues become paramount when comparing 16- and 32-bit systems. Currently, add-on software, such as Win32s and WinG, is included in 32-bit programs to enable them to perform on 16-bit systems. In the future, however, expectations are that these 16-bit systems will be abandoned as new technology evolves.

Appendix B

Optimizing AutoCAD for Windows

AutoCAD Release 13 for Windows expands greatly on the use of the Windows Graphical User Interface (GUI). With toolbars and tabbed folders, such as the Object Snap toolbar and the Environment tabbed folder, the look and feel of the Windows version of AutoCAD is indistinguishable from the most advanced Windows applications.

This appendix provides an in-depth explanation of toolbars and their management and customization. This appendix also discusses setting AutoCAD preferences from the Options, Preferences dialog boxes.

NOTE

Toolbars are defined in the menu file, such as ACAD.MNU. Additions or modifications to toolbars are stored in MNS, MNR, and MNC files in the same directory of the menu. For example, changes to ACAD.MNU are stored in the ACAD.MNS, ACAD.MNR, and ACAD.MNC files, which are by default in the ACADR13\WIN\Support directory. You can restore the factory defaults by deleting these MNS, MNR, and MNC files. AutoCAD will re-create them with defaults. Toolbar settings also are stored in the ACAD.INI file; you can delete the lines referencing specific toolbars from the ACAD.INI file. To restore factory defaults, you might need to delete lines from the ACAD.INI file as well as delete MNS, MNR, and MNC files. The default ACAD.INI file is in the ACADR13\WIN directory and the ACAD.MNU file is in the ACADR13\WIN\Support directory. Changes to toolbars and preferences affect the files in these directories unless you set up different configuration (for ACAD.INI) or support (for menus) directories, as you did for the IAW setup in Chapter 1. You also must copy the menu file to the support directory. If you delete the ACAD.INI directory, AutoCAD will re-create it with its factory defaults.

Understanding Toolbars

Release 13 of AutoCAD for Windows adds numerous toolbars to the graphical user interface. Release 13 also allows for customization and creation of these toolbars. Figure B.1 shows some of the many toolbars provided with Release 13.

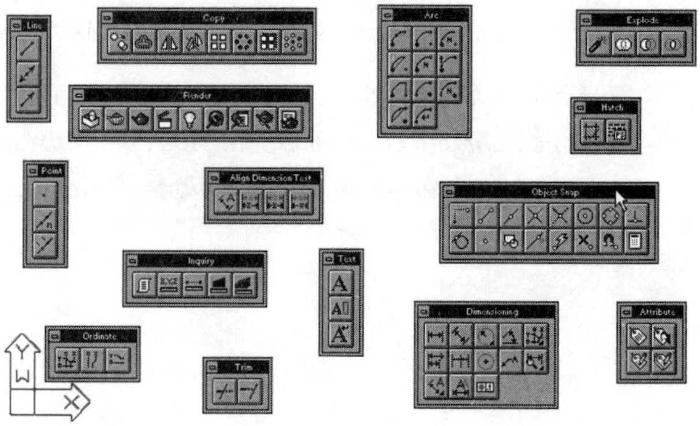

Figure B.1

Many—but far from all—of the toolbars packaged with AutoCAD Release 13.

Toolbar Examples

Figure B.2 shows the Tool Windows and Dimensioning toolbars. The Tool Windows toolbar opens other toolbars; in this case, the Dimensioning toolbar is opened by clicking on the fourth tool from the left in the Tool Windows toolbar.

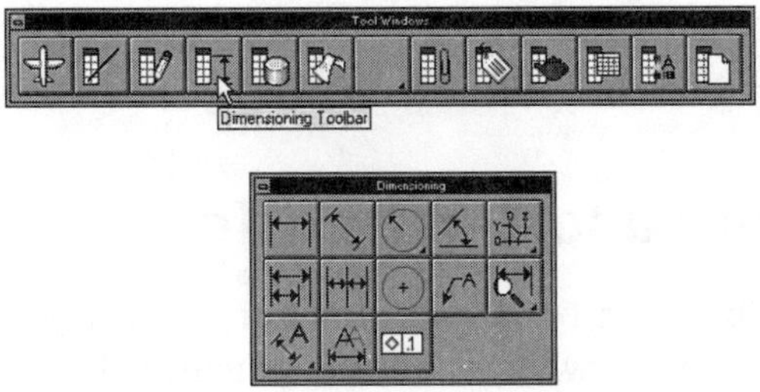

Figure B.2

The Dimensioning toolbar is launched from the Tool Windows toolbar.

Note

Toolbars can be set to two sizes, large or small. All toolbars are affected by the choice; one toolbar cannot be set for large and another for small. Toolbars set for small are shown in figure B.1 and toolbars set for large are shown in figures B.2 and B.3.

Flyouts

The triangle at the lower right of a tool icon indicates that a tool has a flyout. A *flyout* is a child toolbar that is opened by the tool on the parent toolbar; the Bind flyout is shown in figure B.3. Whichever tool on the flyout is selected last becomes the current default on the parent toolbar.

Any flyout can be opened as a separate toolbar by using the TOOLBAR command or the NRP_TBSHOW command (the Show Toolbar dialog box). To open the Show Toolbar dialog box, choose Show Toolbars from the NRO.NRP toolbar (adjacent to the Object Properties toolbar). This toolbar is installed in Chapter 1 and activated in Chapter 2.

Figure B.3

The Bind flyout on the External References toolbar.

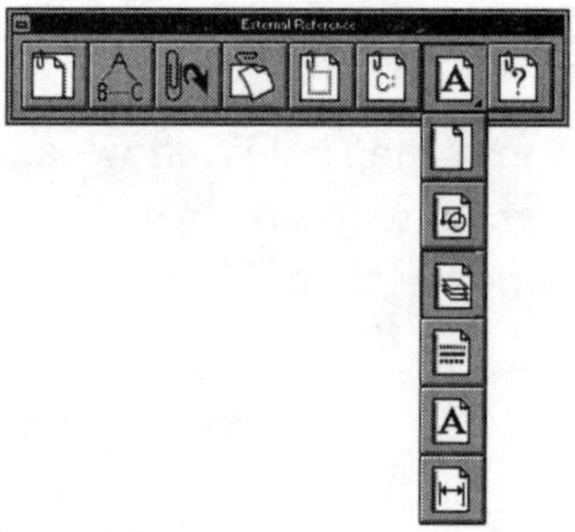

Docking and Floating Toolbars

Toolbars can be docked along the edges of the AutoCAD screen, or they can be floated anywhere on-screen. In figure B.4, the Dimension toolbar is docked on the right side of the screen, the Object Properties toolbar is docked along the top, the Modify toolbar is docked on the left side. The Tool Windows toolbar is floating in the middle of the drawing window.

Figure B.4

Four docked toolbars and one floating toolbar.

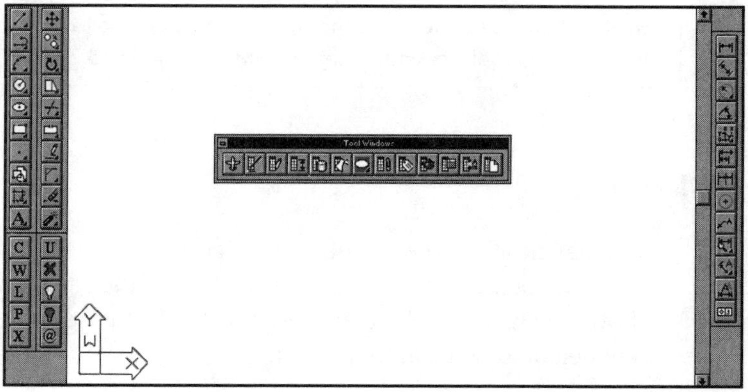

To dock a floating toolbar, position the cursor on the toolbar's title bar, press the pick button, and drag the toolbar to the desired edge of the screen. As the toolbar approaches the docking area it changes shape to illustrate how it will look in that location. After the toolbar is placed, release the pick button.

To float a docked toolbar, position the pointing device over the gray area that surrounds the tool icons in a toolbar. This gray area is referred to as the *grab region*. Press the pick button and drag the toolbar away from its docked location. When in the desired location, release the pick button.

Customizing Toolbars

A powerful feature of Release 13 is its capability to create and customize toolbars and tools. You can create new tools and toolbars, or modify and delete existing tools from existing toolbars.

Creating a Toolbar

The Toolbars dialog box is the gateway to creating and modifying toolbars. You access the Toolbars dialog box by clicking on a tool icon with the Enter button of the pointing device or by choosing Tools, Customize Toolbars. The following exercise shows how to create a toolbar.

NOTE

The easiest way to activate the Toolbars dialog box is to click on any tool in any toolbar with the Enter button of the pointing device.

Creating a New Toolbar

Command: Choose Tools, Customize Toolbars	Issues the TBCONFIG command and opens the Toolbars dialog box (see fig. B.5)
Choose New	Opens the New Toolbar dialog box (see fig. B.5)
Type **Optimize** in the Toolbar Name box	Enters a name for the toolbar
Leave ACAD as the menu group	Specifies the menu group for the toolbar configuration
Choose OK	Closes the New Toolbar dialog box and displays new toolbar entry (ACAD.Optimize) in the Toolbars list
Choose Close	Creates an empty toolbar named Optimize (see fig. B.6)

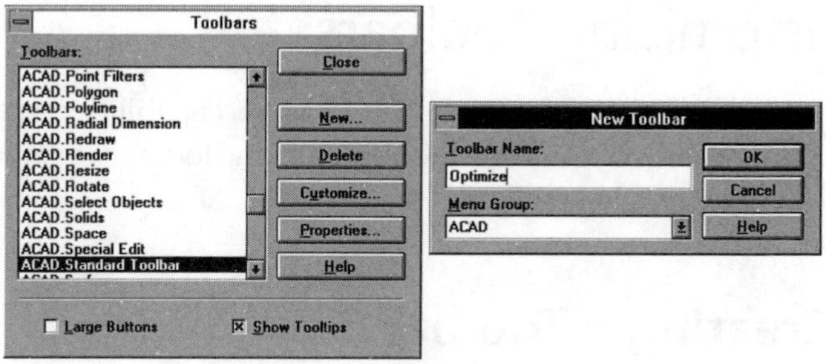

Figure B.5

The Toolbars and New Toolbar dialog boxes.

Figure B.6

The new and empty Optimize toolbar.

Adding Existing Tools to a Toolbar

You easily can add existing tools to any toolbar by performing the following steps:

1. Open the Toolbars dialog box by clicking on a tool with the Enter button or by choosing Tools, Customize Toolbars.

2. Select the toolbar from the Toolbars list. (The list defaults to the tool clicked on with the Enter button, or the first tool if opened by the pull-down menu or TBCONFIG command.)

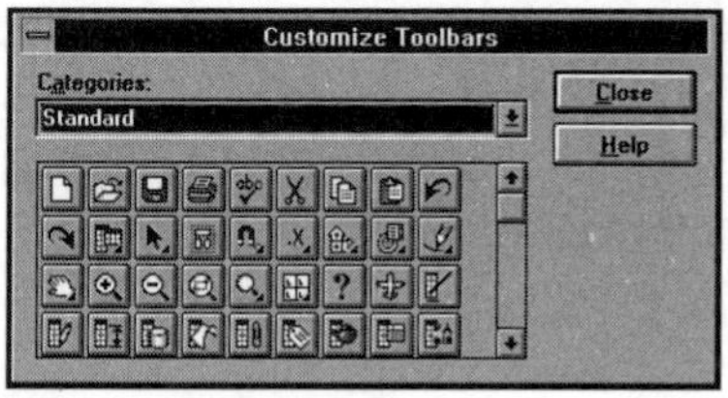

Figure B.7

The Customize Toolbars dialog box.

3. Choose Customize to open the Customize Toolbars dialog box (see fig. B.7).

4. From Categories select the appropriate category for the tool you want.

5. Using the pick button, drag the desired tool from the icon box below the Categories box and drop it on the toolbar.

Multiple tools can be dragged and dropped onto a toolbar from multiple categories. In figure B.8 tools from the Draw, Attribute, External Reference, and Miscellaneous categories have been added to the new Optimize toolbar.

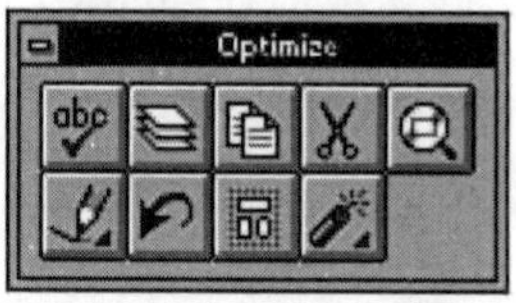

Figure B.8

Tools added to the Optimize toolbar.

Deleting, Copying, and Moving Tools

You easily can delete, move, and copy tools from toolbars or between toolbars. Perform the following steps to delete a tool from a toolbar:

1. Open the Toolbars dialog box by clicking on a tool with the Enter button or by choosing Tools, Customize Toolbars.
2. Choose Customize to open the Customize Toolbars dialog box.
3. Using the pick button, drag the tool off the toolbar. Upon releasing the pick button the tool will be deleted.

Perform the following steps to move a tool from one toolbar to another:

1. Open the Toolbars dialog box.
2. Choose Customize to open the Customize Toolbars dialog box.
3. Using the pick button, drag the tool to the new toolbar.

Perform the following steps to copy a tool:

1. Open the Toolbars dialog box.
2. Choose Customize to open the Customize Toolbars dialog box.
3. Press Ctrl on the keyboard while dragging the tool from one toolbar to the other.

Tools also can be repositioned within the toolbars. To do so, perform the following steps:

1. Open the Toolbars dialog box.
2. Choose Customize to open the Customize Toolbars dialog box.
3. Drag and drop a tool to wherever you want it positioned in that toolbar.

TIP

Space can be inserted between tools in a toolbar by using the Customize Toolbars dialog box. Choose Customize from the Toolbars dialog box and drag a tool less than halfway across the adjacent tool to create space between tools. This process can be reversed in order to remove a space between tools.

You can change the shape (aspect ratio) of a floating toolbar by dragging the bottom or side borders of that toolbar.

All toolbar dialog boxes can be opened from the `Command:` prompt. The command to open the Toolbar dialog box is TBCONFIG. The TOOLBAR command can be used to hide or show all toolbars, launch individual toolbars, and position toolbars as docked or floating.

Setting Toolbar Properties

You can use the Toolbar Properties dialog box to display or hide toolbars, change their names, assign the help string for the status bar, and verify their alias names. To open the Toolbar Properties dialog box, choose Tools, Customize Toolbars or click on a tool icon with the Enter button to open the Toolbars dialog box, then choose Properties. The Toolbar Properties dialog box appears as shown in figure B.9.

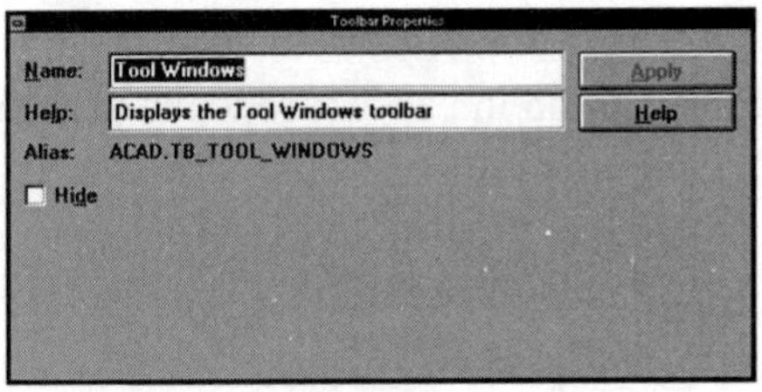

Figure B.9

The Toolbar Properties dialog box.

The following exercise illustrates how to show and hide toolbars.

SHOWING AND HIDING A TOOLBAR

Click on a tool in a toolbar with the Enter button	Opens the Toolbars dialog box
Select ACAD.Tool Windows, then choose Properties	Opens the Toolbar Properties dialog box for Tool Windows
Clear the Hide check box, then choose Apply	Displays the Tool Windows toolbar
Choose Close in the Toolbars dialog box	Closes both dialog boxes
Click on a tool in a toolbar with the Enter button	Opens the Toolbar dialog box
Select ACAD.Tool Windows, then choose Properties	Opens the Toolbar Properties dialog box for Tool Windows
You can select another toolbar name in the Toolbars dialog box without closing the Toolbar Properties dialog box.	
Put a check in the Hide check box, then choose Apply	Closes the Tool Windows toolbar
Choose Close in the Toolbar dialog box	Closes both dialog boxes

TIP

If you can remember the names of your toolbars, it is easier to show and hide toolbars by using the command line. Enter TOOLBAR, then the name of the toolbar you want to show or hide, and enter S for SHOW or H for HIDE. You also can use the NRP Show Toolbars dialog box, as described earlier in this chapter and in Chapter 2.

Alias in Toolbar Properties

AutoCAD's Alias feature serves as a link to AutoCAD's menus. A toolbars' alias includes a prefix that refers to the toolbar menu group and a name as it appears in the menu file. You must use the toolbar alias when using the TOOLBAR command to display and position a toolbar.

Help in Toolbar Properties

The text entered in the Help box is displayed in the status bar at the bottom left of the main AutoCAD window whenever the cursor is positioned in the grab area of a toolbar.

Creating and Customizing Tools

AutoCAD provides the user with the capability to create and customize tools as well as toolbars.

Creating a Tool

You can create a tool by using the Toolbars dialog box. Open the Toolbars dialog box, and then click on any non-flyout tool in the toolbar with the Enter button of the pointing device to open the Button Properties dialog box (see fig. B.10).

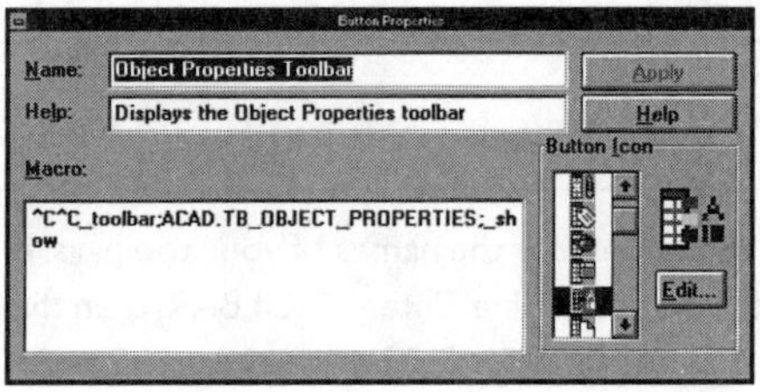

Figure B.10

The Button Properties dialog box.

To create a new tool, perform the following steps:

1. Enter a name for that tool in the Name box of the Button Properties dialog box.

2. In the Help box, type the text you want displayed in the status line.

3. In the box under Macro, enter the commands that the tool will perform. Preface transparent commands with an apostrophe and preface other commands with ^C^C to cancel pending commands.

4. Select an icon for the tool from the Button Icon list. To change a command that is performed by an existing tool, edit the commands in the Macro box.

Editing an Icon

Button icons are bitmapped images, saved as BMP files. To edit a button icon, select an icon from the Button Properties dialog box and choose Edit, which opens the Button Editor dialog box. The editing tools are limited, but similar to those found in a Paintbrush-type application.

To edit a button's icon, perform the following steps:

1. Open the Toolbar dialog box by clicking on a tool in a toolbar with the Enter button of your pointing device. Alternatively, at the command line enter **TBCONFIG**.

2. Click on the tool whose icon you want to edit with the Enter button of your pointing device. This opens the Button Properties dialog box (refer to figure B.10).

NOTE

If the icon you want to edit is on a flyout or is the child of a flyout button, you must click on the appropriate flyout tool on the parent toolbar; then click on the appropriate button on the child toolbar.

3. Choose Edit in Button Icon area of the Button Properties dialog box to edit the icon (see fig. B.11).

Figure B.11

The Button Editor dialog box for editing and creating button icons.

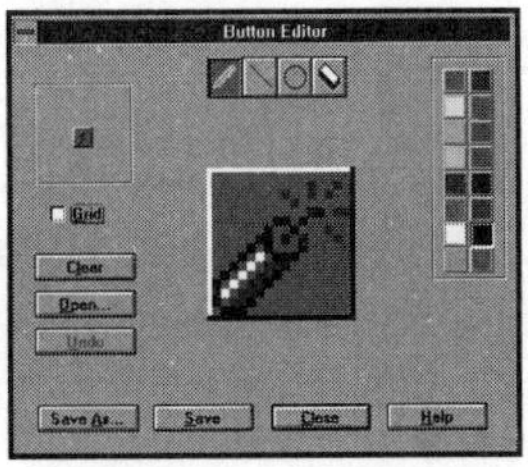

4. Select your tool of choice for editing the icon. Tools include a grid with a single box representing a single pixel. Pencil, Line, Circle, and Erase drawing tools can create or edit an icon. A color palette is available for adding color on a pixel by pixel basis.

Creating and Modifying a Flyout

To create a flyout, perform the following steps:

1. Open the Toolbars dialog box.
2. Choose Customize to open the Customize Toolbars dialog box.
3. From the bottom of the Categories list, select Custom, which displays a blank tool icon and a blank flyout tool icon (see fig. B.12).

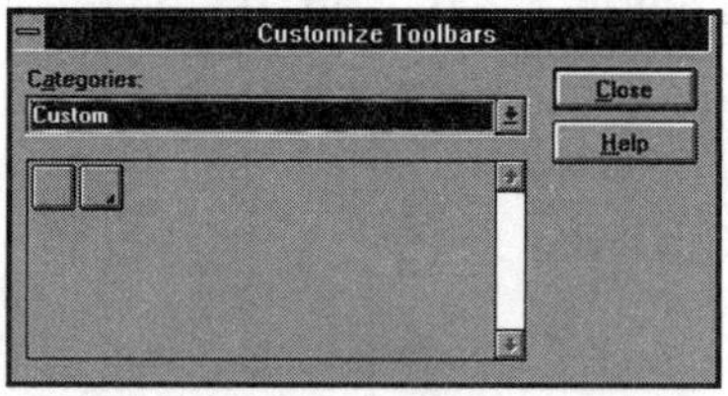

Figure B.12

A step in the creation of a flyout.

4. To add a flyout to an existing toolbar, drag the flyout icon (the button with the triangle in the lower left corner) to a toolbar and drop it. To create a flyout in a new toolbar, drag the flyout icon to any place on the screen and drop it.
5. Click on the new flyout tool with the Enter button to display the Flyout Properties dialog box.
6. In the Associated Toolbar list, select the toolbar you want associated with the flyout.
7. Select an icon from the Button Icon list to specify an icon for the flyout.

NOTE

You also can use the Flyout Properties dialog box to modify existing flyouts by clicking on the existing flyout tool with the Enter button.

Setting Preferences

User preferences can be set for the graphics window, digitizer input, fonts, colors, directories, and more in the Preferences dialog box (see fig. B.13). The Preferences dialog box is opened by the PREFERENCES command, which is issued by choosing Options, Preferences.

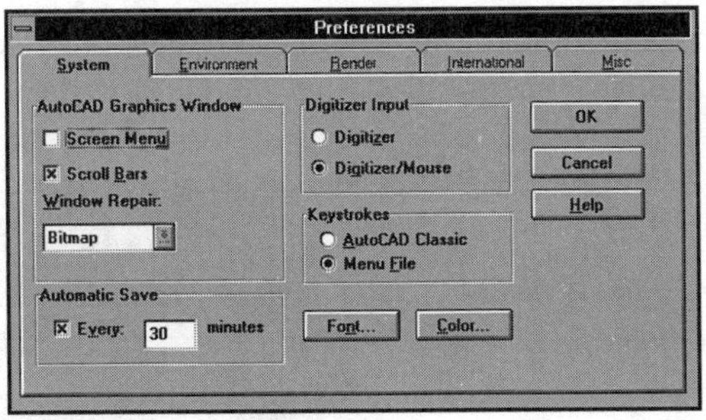

Figure B.13

The Preferences dialog box with the System tab folder open.

System

With the System tab folder open, the Screen Menu and the Scroll Bars can be turned on or off in the AutoCAD graphics window. The mode in which a graphics image is rebuilt when an overlying window is removed is selected by Window Repair. The default AutoCAD display driver is set for Bitmap. Automatic Save determines how frequently (in minutes) AutoCAD automatically saves the active drawing.

The Digitizer Input box presents a choice between Digitizer or Digitizer/Mouse. With Digitizer chosen, AutoCAD accepts input from the selected configured digitizing device. If a mouse is on the system and there is no digitizer, AutoCAD will accept the mouse input. With Digitizer/Mouse selected, AutoCAD accepts input from the last-moved pointing device.

The Keystrokes section provides the capability to choose whether you want to use accelerated keystrokes to access pull-down menu items. The choice is between AutoCAD Classic or Menu File.

The Font button enables the user to specify the font used in the graphics and text windows. Changing the font in the text window affects the fonts used on the command line and the font used in the AutoCAD Text Window. Changing the font in the graphics window affects the font used in the screen menu. To see the screen menu, it must be selected in the AutoCAD Graphics Window area.

The Color button enables you to change the appearance of the AutoCAD applications window. With this option you can change the background colors of your Graphics and Text Windows Backgrounds, the color of the text itself, and the color of the crosshairs of your AutoCAD pointing device.

Environment

The Environment tab folder (see fig. B.14) enables you to set paths for AutoCAD variables, configuration files, menus, and driver files.

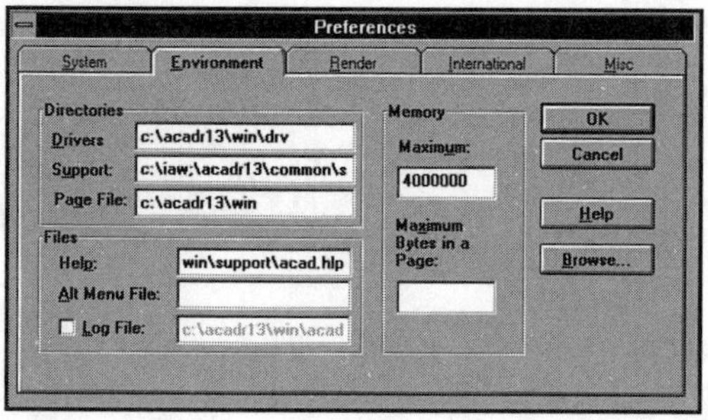

Figure B.14

The Preferences dialog box with the Environment tab folder open.

In the Directories section, Drivers sets the ACADDRV variable by specifying the search path for ADI drivers. Support sets the ACAD environment variable by telling AutoCAD which directories contain text fonts, hatch patterns, menus, and AutoLISP files. Page File sets the ACADPAGEDIR variable; it also specifies the directory for the first page file.

The Files section sets the ACADHELP environment variable. Help tells AutoCAD the name and location of the help file. The Alt Menu File text box is used to indicate the path and name of an alternate menu for the AutoCAD tablet by setting the ACADALTMENU environment variable. With Log File, the name of and path for the log file is determined. The contents of the text box will be written to the log file if the Log File check box is selected.

The AutoCAD memory pager is set up in the Memory section. The memory pager divides the current drawing between pages of memory. Data is written to disk when the memory becomes full. Maximum specifies the quantity of memory in bytes that the memory pager can receive from Windows. Autodesk recommends using this option only if it is necessary to reduce the allocation of physical memory for coexistence with another application. Maximum sets the ACADMAXMEM variable. Maximum Bytes in a Page determines the maximum amount of bytes available for the first page file. It also sets the ACADMAXPAGE variable.

Render

The Render tab folder of the Preferences dialog box (see fig. B.15) specifies directories and sets the following variables:

- **Config File Dir.** Rendering configuration file; sets the AVECFG variable.
- **Face File Dir.** Temporary storage for the faces of meshes; sets the AVEFACEDIR variable.
- **Page File Dir.** First page file; sets the AVEPAGEDIR variable.
- **Map File Path.** Map file; sets the AVERDFILE variable.

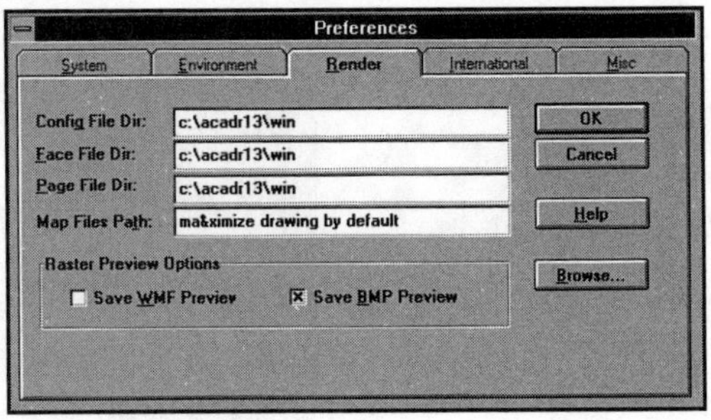

Figure B.15

The Preferences dialog box with the Render tab folder open.

International

The International tab folder (see fig. B.16) enables the user to specify either English or Metric measurements, and provides a choice between standard or metric prototype drawings.

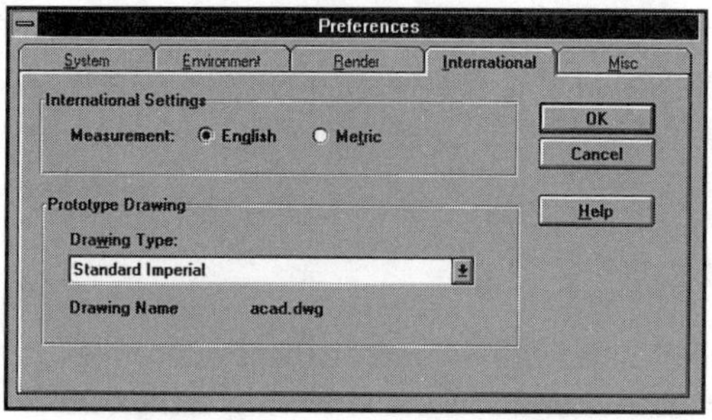

Figure B.16

The Preferences dialog box with the International tab folder open.

Miscellaneous

The final tab folder under Preferences is Misc, shown in figure B.17. In the Options section, the Text Editor box specifies the text editor used with MTEXT. Typing "Internal" in the Text Editor box specifies the AutoCAD MText Editor. Any ASCII text can be used by the MTEXT command and you specify which text editor in this dialog box.

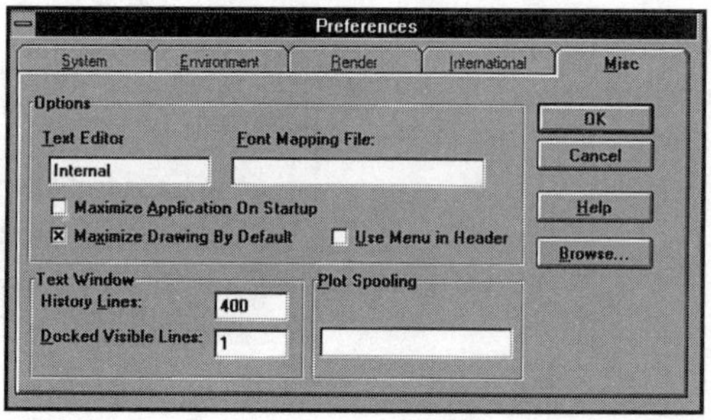

Figure B.17

The Preferences dialog box with the Misc tab folder open.

The Font Mapping File is an ASCII text file that enables you to substitute one font file for another. This option is valuable if you want a drawing to only use specific fonts. You also might want to use faster-drawing SHX fonts for drawing and higher quality, slower moving PostScript fonts for final plotting. Additionally, if your drawing contains a font that you do not have, you can use the Font Mapping File to specify which of your fonts will substitute for that font.

The font mapping file is an ASCII text file that can be created or edited with any ASCII text editor. It has an extension of .FMP.

Note

> The text editor must be in the directory specified in Support in the Directories area of the Environment tab folder (refer to fig. B.14).

Also in the Options section are settings for maximizing an application window on startup and for maximizing the AutoCAD drawing window. The checkbox for Use Menu in Header tells AutoCAD whether to use the menu file in the drawing header. If Use Menu in Header is not selected, AutoCAD uses the loaded menu file for every drawing regardless of any other menu file specified in a drawing's header.

The Text Window section enables the user to specify the number of lines visible in the command-line and text windows. History Lines specifies how many lines appear at any time above the current command line and in the text window. Docked Visible Lines specifies how many lines appear when the command-line window is docked.

The Plot Spooling option sets the ACADPLCMD environment variable and specifies conditions for using a plot spooler. A *plot spooler* buffers plot output from the computer so that the computer can become available quickly for further work while plotting is handled in the background.

The Browse button searches for files for the Text Editor, Font Mapping File, and Plot Spooling boxes.

In this appendix, you learned that AutoCAD Release 13 for Windows provides a plethora of tools for customizing its user interface. By taking advantage of the standard Windows GUI, an AutoCAD user can tailor his work environment to best suit his needs and desires. Using and working with AutoCAD's customization tools is without question the most effective way to learn how to customize your AutoCAD environment.

Appendix C

Command, Dialog Box, Menu, Tool, and Alias Equivalents

This appendix contains a table of AutoCAD commands with their dialog box names, and the pull-down menu items and tools that issue them (Table C.1). It also contains a table of command aliases (Table C.2).

In the Command Name and Option column, names and options shown in bold are new in Release 13. Many menu items and tools issue specific options along with commands. For example, the View, Zoom, All menu item and the Zoom All tool both issue the ZOOM command with the All option. These options are indicated in the Command Name and Option column for those menu items and tools, indented under the command name. In many cases, multiple options are issued; these are shown separated by commas. Often, menu items and tools issue a command, pause for input, then issue specific options; this pause for input is indicated with a backslash—for example, \,Center for the Arc Start Center End tool under the ARC command indicates that tool issues the ARC command, pauses for the user to input a start point, and then issues the Center option.

In the Dialog Box column, the names shown are those that appear in the dialog box title bar.

In the Pull Down Menu, Item column, items are shown in the form *Menuname*, *childmenuname*, *menuitemname*, and hot keys are indicated with bold and underline; for example, View, Zoom, All translates to "Choose View to open the View pull-down menu, then choose Zoom to open the Zoom child menu, then choose All to issue the ZOOM command with the All option." A few commands, such as OPEN, have keyboard shortcuts, such as Ctrl+O; these are shown in their pull-down menu item labels—such as File, Open Ctrl+O—and are therefore shown in the Menu, Item column.

Tools are listed in the form Tool Name (Toolbar name, Flyout name); for example, 3 Points (Draw, Arc) translates to "From the Arc flyout of the Draw toolbar, choose 3 Points to issue the ARC command." The tool names are those that appear in the ToolTips, and the toolbar names and flyout names are those that appear in their title bars when open as floating toolbars. Of course, if the 3 Points tool is the current default (last-used) tool from the Arc flyout, it will appear on the Draw toolbar and can be directly chosen, and if the Arc flyout is currently open as an individual toolbar, you can choose 3 Points directly from it. Tool names shown in bold are the default tools of their flyouts. These tools are the ones that initially appear (each time you start AutoCAD) on the parent toolbar and in the ToolTip of the tool that opens the flyout; however, during an AutoCAD session after you have used another tool from the flyout, it becomes the current default tool.

The — in any column indicates that an entry for the column is not applicable in that row of the table.

NOTE

The `Dim:` prompt is obsolete in Release 13. All of the R13 dimensioning commands can now be entered at the `Command:` prompt. Although the `Dim:` prompt is still present for compatibility purposes, the following commands, which were available at the `Dim:` prompt in earlier releases of AutoCAD, are obsolete and have been intentionally omitted from this table: HOMETEXT, HORIZONTAL, NEWTEXT, OBLIQUE, ROTATED, SAVE, STATUS, TROTATE, UPDATE, VARIABLES, VERTICAL.

Table C.1

Command, Dialog Box, Menu, Tool Equivalents

Command Name and Option	*Dialog Box*	*Menu, Item*	*Tool (Toolbar, Pull-Down Flyout) Name*
.X	—	—	.X (Standard, .X)
.XY	—	—	XY (Standard, .X)
.XZ	—	—	XZ (Standard, .X)
.Y	—	—	Y (Standard, .X)
.YZ	—	—	YZ (Standard, .X)
.Z	—	—	Z (Standard, .X)
3D	—	—	—
3DARRAY	—	—	—
R,\,\	—	—	3D Rectangular Array (Modify, Copy Object)
P,\,\	—	—	3D Polar Array (Modify, Copy Object)
3DFACE	—	—	3D Face (Surfaces, 3D Face)
3DMESH	—	—	3D Mesh (Surfaces, 3D Mesh)
3DPOLY	—	—	3dPolyline (Draw, Polyline)
3DSIN	3D Studio Import File	—	—
3DSOUT	3D Studio Output File	—	—
ABOUT	AUTOCAD(R)	Help, About Autocad	—
ACISIN	Select Acis File	—	—
ACISOUT	Create Acis File	—	—

continues

Table C.1, *CONTINUED*

Command, Dialog Box, Menu, Tool Equivalents

Command Name and Option	*Dialog Box*	*Menu, Item*	*Tool (Toolbar, Pull-Down Flyout) Name*
AI_BOX	—	—	Box (Surfaces, Box)
AI_DISH	—	—	Dish (Surfaces, Dish)
AI_DOME	—	—	Dome (Surfaces, Dome)
AI_MESH	—	—	Mesh (Miscella-neous, Mesh)
(AI_PROPCHK)	Modify	—	—
AI_PYRAMID	—	—	Pyramid (Surfaces, Pyramid)
AI_SPHERE	—	—	Sphere (Surfaces, Sphere)
AI_TORUS	—	—	Torus (Surfaces, Torus)
AI_WEDGE	—	—	Wedge (Surfaces, Wedge)
ALIGN	—	—	Align (Modify, Rotate)
AMECONVERT	—	—	AME Convert (Solids, AME Convert)
APPLOAD	Load AutoLISP, ADS, ARX	Tools, Applications	—
APERTURE	—	—	—
ARC	—	—	3 Points (Draw, Arc)

Command Name and Option	*Dialog Box*	*Menu, Item*	*Tool (Toolbar, Pull-Down Flyout) Name*
\,C,\	—	—	Arc Start Center End (Draw, Arc)
\,C,A	—	—	Arc Start Center Angle (Draw, Arc)
\,E,A	—	—	Arc Start End Angle (Draw, Arc)
\,E,D	—	—	Arc Start End Direction (Draw, Arc)
\,E,R	—	—	Arc Start End Radius (Draw, Arc)
\,C,\,\	—	—	Arc Center Start End (Draw, Arc)
C,\,A	—	—	Arc Center Start Angle (Draw, Arc)
C,\,L	—	—	Arc Center Start Length (Draw, Arc)
\ (Draw, Arc)	—	—	Arc Continue
AREA	—	—	Area (Object Properties, List)
ARRAY	—	—	—

continues

Table C.1, *CONTINUED*
Command, Dialog Box, Menu, Tool Equivalents

Command Name and Option	*Dialog Box*	*Menu, Item*	*Tool (Toolbar, Pull-Down Flyout) Name*
R,\,\	—	—	Rectangular Array (Modify, Copy Object)
P,\,\	—	—	Polar Array (Modify, Copy Object)
ASEADMIN	—	—	Administration (External Database, Administration)
ASEEXPORT	—	—	Export Links (External Database, Export Links)
ASELINKS	—	—	Links (External Database, Links)
ASEROWS	—	—	Rows (External Database, Rows)
ASERUNREP	—	—	—
ASESELECT	—	—	Select Objects (External Database, Select Objects)
ASESQLED	—	—	SQL Editor (External Database, SQL Editor)
ATTEDIT Globally	—	—	Edit Attribute (Attribute, Edit Attribute Globally)

Command Name and Option	Dialog Box	Menu, Item	Tool (Toolbar, Pull-Down Flyout) Name
ATTEXT	Select Template File	—	—
ATTREDEF	—	—	Redefine Attribute (Attribute, Redefine Attribute)
BHATCH	Boundary Hatch	—	Hatch (Draw, Hatch)
BLIPMODE	—	—	—
BLOCK	—	—	Block (Draw, Insert)
BMPOUT	Create BMP FIle	—	—
BOUNDARY	Boundary	—	Boundary (Draw, Rectangle)
BOX	—	—	Corner (Solids, Center)
CE,\	—	—	Center (Solids, Center)
BREAK	—	—	1 Point (Modify, 1 Point)
\,F,@	—	—	1 Point Select (Modify, 1 Point)
\,\	—	—	2 Points (Modify, 1 Point)
\,F,@	—	—	2 Points Select (Modify, 1 Point)
CAL	—	—	Calculator (Standard, Snap From)
CHAMFER	—	—	Chamfer (Modify, Chamfer)
CHANGE	—	—	—

continues

Table C.1, *CONTINUED*

Command, Dialog Box, Menu, Tool Equivalents

Command Name and Option	*Dialog Box*	*Menu, Item*	*Tool (Toolbar, Pull-Down Flyout) Name*
CHPROP	—	—	—
CIRCLE	—	—	Circle (Draw, Circle)
\,r	—	—	Circle Center Radius (Draw, Circle)
\,D	—	—	Circle Center Diameter (Draw, Circle)
2P,\	—	—	Circle 2 Point (Draw, Circle)
3P,\	—	—	Circle 3 Point (Draw, Circle)
TTR,\	—	—	Circle Tan Tan Radius (Draw, Circle)
COLOR	—	—	—
COMPILE	Select Shape, Font File	Tools, Compile	—
CONE	—	—	Center (Solids, Elliptical)
E,\	—	—	Elliptical (Solids, Elliptical)
CONFIG	—	Options, Configure	—
COPY	—	—	Copy Object (Modify, Copy Object)
COPYCLIP	—	Edit, Copy Ctrl+C	Copy (Standard)

Command Name and Option	*Dialog Box*	*Menu, Item*	*Tool (Toolbar, Pull-Down Flyout) Name*
COPYEMBED	—	—	—
COPYHIST	—	—	—
COPYLINK	—	Edit, Copy View	—
CUT	—	—	—
CUTCLIP	—	Edit, Cut Ctrl+X	Cut (Standard)
CYLINDER	—	—	Center (Solids, Elliptical)
E,\	—	—	Elliptical (Solids, Elliptical)
DBLIST	—	—	—
DDATTDEF	Attribute Definition	—	Define Attribute (Attribute, Define Attribute)
DDATTE	Attribute Edit	—	Attribute Edit (Attribute, Attribute Edit)
DDATTEXT	Attribute Extraction	—	—
DDCHPROP	Change Properties	—	—
DDCOLOR	Select Color	Data, Color	Color Control (Object Properties)
DDEDIT	Edit Text	—	Text Edit (Modify, Edit Polyline)
DDEMODES	Object Creation Modes	Data, Object Creation	Object Creation (Object Properties)
DDGRIPS	Grips	Options, Grips	—
DDIM	Dimension Styles	Data, Dimension Styles	Dimension Styles (Dimensioning, Dimension Styles)

continues

Table C.1, *CONTINUED*

Command, Dialog Box, Menu, Tool Equivalents

Command Name and Option	*Dialog Box*	*Menu, Item*	*Tool (Toolbar, Pull-Down Flyout) Name*
DDINSERT	Insert	—	Insert Block (Draw, Insert Block)
DDLMODES	Layer Control	Data, Layers	Layers (Object Properties)
DDLTYPE	Select Linetype	Data, Linetype	Linetype (Object Properties)
DDMODIFY	Modify (Varies)	Edit, Properties	Properties (Object Properties)
DDOSNAP	Running Object Snap	—	Running Object Snap (Standard, Snap From)
DDPSTYLE	Point Style	—	—
DDRENAME	Rename	Data, Rename	—
DDRMODES	Drawing Aids	Options, Drawing Aids	—
DDSELECT	Object Selection Settings	Options, Selection	—
DDSTYLE	—	—	—
DDUCS	UCS Control	View, Named UCS	Named UCS (Standard, Preset UCS)
DDUCSP	UCS Orientation	View, Preset UCS	Preset UCS (Standard, Preset UCS)
DDUNITS	Units Control	Data, Units	—
DDVIEW	View Control	View, Named Views	Named Views (Standard, Named Views)

Command Name and Option	*Dialog Box*	*Menu, Item*	*Tool (Toolbar, Pull-Down Flyout) Name*
DDVPOINT	Viewpoint Presets	—	—
DELAY	—	—	—
DIM	—	—	—
DIMALIGNED	—	—	Aligned Dimension (Dimensioning, Aligned Dimension)
DIMANGULAR	—	—	Angular Dimension (Dimensioning, Angular Dimension)
DIMBASELINE	—	—	Baseline Dimension (Dimensioning, Baseline Dimension)
DIMCENTER	—	—	Center Mark (Dimensioning, Center Mark)
DIMCONTINUE	—	—	Continue Dimension (Dimensioning, Continue Dimension)
DIMDIAMETER	—	—	Diameter Dimension (Dimensioning, Radius Dimension)
DIMEDIT	—	—	—
O,\	—	—	Oblique Dimension (Dimensioning, Dimension Styles)

continues

Table C.1, *CONTINUED*

Command, Dialog Box, Menu, Tool Equivalents

Command Name and Option	*Dialog Box*	*Menu, Item*	*Tool (Toolbar, Pull-Down Flyout) Name*
DIMLINEAR	—	—	Linear Dimension (Dimensioning, Linear Dimension)
DIMORDINATE	—	—	Automatic (Dimensioning, Automatic)
\,X	—	—	X-Datum (Dimensioning, Automatic)
\,Y	—	—	Y-Datum (Dimensioning, Automatic)
DIMRADIUS	—	—	Radius Dimension (Dimensioning, Radius Dimension)
DIMTEDIT	—	—	—
\,H	—	—	Home (Dimensioning, Home)
\,A	—	—	Rotate (Dimensioning, Home)
\,L	—	—	Left (Dimensioning, Home)
\,C	—	—	Center (Dimensioning, Home)
\,R	—	—	Right (Dimensioning, Home)

Command Name and Option	*Dialog Box*	*Menu, Item*	*Tool (Toolbar, Pull-Down Flyout) Name*
DIMSTYLE	—	—	—
DIST	—	—	Distance (Object Properties, List)
DIVIDE	—	—	Divide (Draw, Point)
DONUT	—	—	Donut (Draw, Circle)
DRAGMODE	—	—	—
DSVIEWER	—	—	Aerial View (Standard, Aerial View)
DTEXT	—	—	Dtext (Draw, Mtext)
DVIEW	—	View, 3d Dynamic View	—
DWGINFO	—	—	—
DXBIN	Select DXB File	—	—
DXFIN	Select DXF File	—	—
DXFOUT	Create DXF File	—	—
EDGE	—	—	Edge (Surfaces, Edge)
EDGESURF	—	—	Edge Surface (Surfaces, Edge Surface)
ELEV	—	—	—
ELLIPSE	—	—	Ellipse Center (Draw, Ellipse)
\,\	—	—	Ellipse Axis End (Draw, Ellipse)
A,\,\	—	—	Ellipse Arc (Draw, Ellipse)

continues

Table C.1, *CONTINUED*

Command, Dialog Box, Menu, Tool Equivalents

Command Name and Option	*Dialog Box*	*Menu, Item*	*Tool (Toolbar, Pull-Down Flyout) Name*
END	—	—	—
ERASE	—	—	Erase (Modify, Erase)
EXPLODE	—	—	Explode (Modify, Explode)
EXPORT	Export Data	File, Export	—
EXTEND	—	—	Extend (Modify, Trim)
EXTRUDE	—	—	Extrude (Solids, Extrude)
FILES	File Utilities	—	—
FILL	—	—	—
FILLET	—	—	Fillet (Modify, Chamfer)
FILTER	Object Selection Filter	—	Selection Filters (Standard, Select Window)
GIFIN	—	—	—
GRAPHSCR	—	—	—
GRID	—	—	—
GROUP	Object Grouping	—	Object Group (Standard, Object Group)
HATCH	—	—	—
HATCHEDIT	Hatchedit	—	Hatchedit (Modify, Polyline Edit)
HELP	—	Help	Help (Standard)

Command Name and Option	*Dialog Box*	*Menu, Item*	*Tool (Toolbar, Pull-Down Flyout) Name*
HIDE	—	—	Hide (Render, Hide)
ID	—	—	Locate Point (Object Properties, List)
IMPORT	Import File	File, Import	—
INSERT	—	—	—
INSERTOBJ	Insert New Object	Edit, Insert Object	—
INTERFERE	—	—	Interfere (Solids, Interfere)
INTERSECT	—	—	Intersection (Modify, Explode)
ISOPLANE	—	—	—
LAYER	—	—	—
LEADER	—	—	Leader (Dimensioning, Leader)
LENGTHEN	—	—	Lengthen (Modify, Stretch)
LIGHT	Lights	—	Lights (Render, Lights)
LIMITS	—	Data, Drawing Limits	—
LINE	—	—	Line (Draw, Line)
LINETYPE	—	—	—
LTSCALE	—	—	—
LIST	—	—	List (Object Properties, List)

continues

Table C.1, *CONTINUED*

Command, Dialog Box, Menu, Tool Equivalents

Command Name and Option	*Dialog Box*	*Menu, Item*	*Tool (Toolbar, Pull-Down Flyout) Name*
LOAD	Select Shape File	Data, Shape File	—
LOGFILEON	—	—	—
LOGFILEOFF	—	—	—
MASSPROP	—	—	Mass Properties (Object Properties, List)
MATLIB	Materials Library	—	Materials Library (Render, Materials Library)
MEASURE	—	—	Measure (Draw, Point)
MENU	Select Menu File	—	—
MENULOAD	Menu Customization	Tools, Customize Menus	—
MENUUNLOAD	Menu Customization	—	—
MINSERT	—	—	Insert Multiple Blocks (Miscellaneous, Insert Multiple Blocks)
MIRROR	—	—	Mirror (Modify, Copy Object)
MIRROR3D	—	—	3D Mirror (Modify, Copy Object)
MLEDIT	—	—	Multiline Edit (Modify, Polyline Edit)
MLINE	—	—	Multiline (Draw, Polyline)

Command Name and Option	*Dialog Box*	*Menu, Item*	*Tool (Toolbar, Pull-Down Flyout) Name*
MLSTYLE	Multiline Styles	Data, Multiline Style	Multiline Styles (Object Properties)
MOVE	—	—	(Modify, Move)
MSLIDE	Create Slide File	Tools, Slide, Save	—
MSPACE	—	View, Floating Model Space	—
MTEXT	—	—	Mtext (Draw, Mtext)
MULTIPLE	—	—	—
MVIEW	—	View, Floating Model Space	Floating Model Space (Standard, Model Space)
MVSETUP	—	—	—
NEW	Create New Drawing	File, New	New (Standard)
OFFSET	—	—	Offset (Modify, Copy Object)
OLELINKS	—	Edit, Links	—
OOPS	—	—	Oops! (Miscellaneous, Oops!)
OPEN	Open Drawing	File, Open Ctrl+O	Open (Standard)
OSNAP	—	—	—
FROM	—	—	Snap From (Standard, Snap From)
ENDP	—	—	Snap to Endpoint (Standard, Snap From)

continues

Table C.1, *CONTINUED*

Command, Dialog Box, Menu, Tool Equivalents

Command Name and Option	*Dialog Box*	*Menu, Item*	*Tool (Toolbar, Pull-Down Flyout) Name*
MIDP	—	—	Snap to Midpoint (Standard, Snap From)
INT	—	—	Snap to Intersection (Standard, Snap From)
APPINT	—	—	Snap to Apparent Intersection (Standard, Snap From)
CEN	—	—	Snap to Center (Standard, Snap From)
QUAD	—	—	Snap to Quadrant (Standard, Snap From)
PER	—	—	Snap to Perpendicular (Standard, Snap From)
TAN	—	—	Snap to Tangent (Standard, Snap From)
NODE	—	—	Snap to Node (Standard, Snap From)
INS	—	—	Snap to Insertion (Standard, Snap From)
NEA	—	—	Snap to Nearest (Standard, Snap From)

Command Name and Option	*Dialog Box*	*Menu, Item*	*Tool (Toolbar, Pull-Down Flyout) Name*
QUICK	—	—	Snap to Quick (Standard, Snap From)
NONE	—	—	Snap to None (Standard, Snap From)
PAN	—	View, Pan, Point	Pan Point (Standard, Pan Point)
\,\	—	View, Pan, Left	Pan Left (Standard, Pan Point)
\,\	—	View, Pan, Right	Pan Right (Standard, Pan Point)
\,\	—	View, Pan, Up	Pan Up (Standard, Pan Point)
\,\	—	View, Pan, Down	Pan Down (Standard, Pan Point)
\,\	—	View, Pan, Up Left	Pan Up Left (Standard, Pan Point)
\,\	—	View, Pan, Up Right	Pan Up Right (Standard, Pan Point)
\,\	—	View, Pan, Down Left	Pan Down Left (Standard, Pan Point)
\,\	—	View, Pan, Down Right	Pan Down Right (Standard, Pan Point)
PASTECLIP	—	Edit, Paste Ctrl+V	Paste (Standard)

continues

Table C.1, *CONTINUED*

Command, Dialog Box, Menu, Tool Equivalents

Command Name and Option	*Dialog Box*	*Menu, Item*	*Tool (Toolbar, Pull-Down Flyout) Name*
PASTESPEC	Paste Special	Edit, Paste Special	—
PCXIN	—	—	—
PEDIT	—	—	Polyline Edit (Modify, Polyline Edit)
PFACE	—	—	—
PLAN	—	—	—
PLINE	—	—	Polyline (Draw, Polyline)
PLOT	Plot	File, Print Ctrl+P	Print (Standard)
POINT	—	—	Point (Draw, Point)
POLYGON	—	—	Polygon (Draw, Rectangle)
PREFERENCES	Preferences	Options, Preferences	—
PSDRAG	—	—	—
PSFILL	—	—	PostScript Fill (Draw, Hatch)
PSIN	—	—	—
PSLTSCALE	—	—	—
PSOUT	—	—	—
PSPACE	—	View, Paper Space	
PURGE	—	Data, Purge	—
QSAVE	—	File, Save Ctrl+S	Save (Standard)
QTEXT	—	—	—

Command Name and Option	*Dialog Box*	*Menu, Item*	*Tool (Toolbar, Pull-Down Flyout) Name*
QUIT	—	File, Exit	—
RAY	—	—	Ray (Draw, Line)
RCONFIG	—	Options, Render Configure	—
RECOVER	—	—	—
RECTANG	—	—	Rectangle (Draw, Rectangle)
REDEFINE	—	—	—
REDO	—	Edit, Redo	Redo (Standard)
REDRAW	—	View, Redraw View	Redraw View (Standard, Redraw View)
REDRAWALL	—	View, Redraw All	Redraw All (Standard, Redraw View)
REGEN	—	—	—
REGENALL	—	—	—
REGENAUTO	—	—	—
REGION	—	—	Region (Draw, Rectangle)
REINIT	Re-Initialization	Tools, Reinitialize	—
RENAME	—	—	—
RENDER	Render	—	Render (Render, Render)
RENDSCR	—	—	—
REPLAY	Replay	Tools, Image, View	—
RESUME	—	—	—

continues

Table C.1, *CONTINUED*

Command, Dialog Box, Menu, Tool Equivalents

Command Name and Option	*Dialog Box*	*Menu, Item*	*Tool (Toolbar, Pull-Down Flyout) Name*
REVOLVE	—	—	Revolve (Solids, Revolve)
REVSURF	—	—	Revolved Surface (Surfaces, Revolved Surface)
RMAT	Materials	—	Materials (Render, Materials)
ROTATE	—	—	Rotate (Modify, Rotate)
ROTATE3D	—	—	3D Rotate (Modify, Rotate)
RPREF	Rendering Preferences	—	Rendering Preferences (Render, Rendering Preferences)
RSCRIPT	—	—	—
RULESURF	—	—	Ruled Surface (Surfaces, Ruled Surface)
SAVE	—	—	—
SAVEAS	Save Drawing As	File, Save As	—
SAVEASR12	Save Release 12 Drawing As	—	—
SAVEIMG	Save Image	Tools, Image, Save	—
SCALE	—	—	Scale (Modify, Stretch)
SCENE	Scenes	—	Scenes (Render, Scenes)

Command Name and Option	*Dialog Box*	*Menu, Item*	*Tool (Toolbar, Pull-Down Flyout) Name*
SCRIPT	Select Script File	Tools, Run Script	—
SECTION	—	—	Section (Solids, Section)
SELECT	—	—	—
W	—	—	Select Window (Standard, Select Window)
C	—	—	Select Crossing (Standard, Select Window)
G	—	—	Select Group (Standard, Select Window)
P	—	—	Select Previous (Standard, Select Window)
L	—	—	Select Last (Standard, Select Window)
ALL	—	—	Select All (Standard, Select Window)
WP	—	—	Select Window Polygon (Standard, Select Window)
CP	—	—	Select Crossing Polygon (Standard, Select Window)
F	—	—	Select Fence (Standard, Select Window)

continues

Table C.1, *CONTINUED*
Command, Dialog Box, Menu, Tool Equivalents

Command Name and Option	*Dialog Box*	*Menu, Item*	*Tool (Toolbar, Pull-Down Flyout) Name*
A	—	—	Select Add (Standard, Select Window)
R	—	—	Select Remove (Standard, Select Window)
SETVAR	—	—	—
SHADE	—	—	Shade (Render, Shade)
SHAPE	—	—	Shape (Miscellaneous, Shape)
SHELL	—	—	—
SKETCH	—	—	Sketch (Miscellaneous, Sketch)
SLICE	—	—	Slice (Solids, Slice)
SNAP	—	—	—
SOLID	—	—	2d Solid (Draw, Rectangle)
SPELL	Check Spelling	Tools, Spelling	Spelling (Standard)
SPHERE	—	—	Sphere (Solids, Sphere)
SPLINE	—	—	Spline (Draw, Polyline)
SPLINEDIT	—	—	Splinedit (Modify, Polyline Edit)

Command Name and Option	*Dialog Box*	*Menu, Item*	*Tool (Toolbar, Pull-Down Flyout) Name*
STATS	Statistics	—	Statistics (Render, Statistics)
STATUS	—	Data, Status	—
STLOUT	Create STL File	—	—
STRETCH	—	—	Stretch (Modify, Stretch)
STYLE	—	Data, Text Style	—
SUBTRACT	—	—	Subtract (Modify, Explode)
SYSWINDOWS	—	—	—
TABLET	—	Options, Tablet	—
TABSURF	—	—	Extruded Surface (Surfaces, Extruded Surface)
TBCONFIG	Toolbars	Tools, Customize Toolbars	—
TEXT	—	—	Single Line Text (Draw, Mtext)
TEXTSCR	AutoCAD Text Window	Tools, Text Window	—
TIFFIN	—	—	—
TILEMODE	—	View, Tiled Model Space	Tiled Model Space (Standard, (System variable) Model Space)
0	—	View, Paper Space	Paper Space (Standard, Model Space)
TIME	—	Data, Time	—

continues

Table C.1, *CONTINUED*
Command, Dialog Box, Menu, Tool Equivalents

Command Name and Option	*Dialog Box*	*Menu, Item*	*Tool (Toolbar, Pull-Down Flyout) Name*
TOLERANCE	Symbol	—	Tolerance (Dimensioning, Tolerance)
TOOLBAR	—	Tools, Toolbar	—
ACAD. TB_DRAW	—	Tools, Toolbar, Draw	Draw Toolbar (Standard, Aerial View)
ACAD. TB_MODIFY	—	Tools, Toolbar, Modify	Modify Toolbar (Standard, Aerial View)
ACAD.TB_ DIMENSIONING	—	Tools, Toolbar, Dimensioning	Dimensioning Toolbar (Standard, Aerial View)
ACAD. TB_SOLIDS	—	Tools, Toolbar, Solids	Solids Toolbar (Standard, Aerial View)
ACAD.TB_ SURFACES	—	Tools, Toolbar, Surfaces	Surfaces Toolbar (Standard, Aerial View)
ACAD.TB_ EXTERNAL REFRENCES	—	Tools, Toolbar, External	External References Toolbar (Standard, Aerial View)
ACAD.TB_ ATTRIBUTE	—	Tools, Toolbar, Attribute	Attribute Toolbar (Standard, Aerial View)

Command Name and Option	*Dialog Box*	*Menu, Item*	*Tool (Toolbar, Pull-Down Flyout) Name*
ACAD. TB_RENDER	—	Tools, Toolbar, Render	Render Toolbar (Standard, Aerial View)
ACAD.TB_	—	Tools, Toolbar, External	External Database Toolbar
EXTERNAL DATABASE			(Standard, Aerial View)
ACAD.TB_	—	Tools, Toolbar, Miscellaneous	Miscellaneous Toolbar
MISCELLANEOUS			
ACAD. TB_SELECT	—	Tools, Toolbar, Select	Select Objects Toolbar
_OBJECTS			Objects
ACAD. TB_OBJECT	—	Tools, Toolbar, Object Snap	Object Snap Toolbar
_SNAP			
ACAD. TB_POINT	—	Tools, Toolbar, Point Filters	Point Filters Toolbar
_FILTERS			
ACAD.TB_USC	—	Tools, Toolbar, UCS	UCS Toolbar
ACAD.TB_VIEW	—	Tools, Toolbar, View	View Toolbar
ACAD. TB_OBJECT	—	Tools, Toolbar, Objects	Object Properties
_PROPERTIES			Toolbar
ACAD. TB_TOOLBAR	—	Tools, Toolbar, Standard	Standard Toolbar Toolbar
TORUS	—	—	Torus (Solids, Torus)

continues

Table C.1, *CONTINUED*

Command, Dialog Box, Menu, Tool Equivalents

Command Name and Option	*Dialog Box*	*Menu, Item*	*Tool (Toolbar, Pull-Down Flyout) Name*
TRACE	—	—	Trace (Miscellaneous, Trace)
TREESTAT	—	—	—
TRIM	—	—	Trim (Modify, Trim)
UCS	—	—	—
W	—	View, Set UCS, World	World UCS (Standard, Preset UCS)
O	—	View, Set UCS, Origin	Origin UCS (Standard, Preset UCS)
ZA	—	View, Set UCS, ZAxis Vector	Z Axis Vector (Standard, Preset UCS)
3	—	View, Set UCS, 3 Point	3 Point (Standard, Preset UCS)
OB	—	View, Set UCS, Object	Object UCS (Standard, Preset UCS)
V	—	View, Set UCS, View	View UCS (Standard, Preset UCS)
X	—	View, Set UCS, Xaxis Rotate	X Axis Rotate (Standard, Preset UCS)
Y	—	View, Set UCS, Yaxis Rotate	Y Axis Rotate (Standard, Preset UCS)

Command Name and Option	*Dialog Box*	*Menu, Item*	*Tool (Toolbar, Pull-Down Flyout) Name*
Z	—	View, Set UCS, Zaxis Rotate	Z Axis Rotate (Standard, Preset UCS)
P	—	View, Set UCS, Previous	Previous (Standard, Preset UCS)
R	—	View, Set UCS, Restore	Restore (Standard, Preset UCS)
S	—	View, Set UCS, Save	Save (Standard, Preset UCS)
UCSICON	—	—	—
UNDEFINE	—	—	—
UNDO	—	Edit, Undo Ctrl+Z	Undo (Standard)
UNION	—	—	Union (Modify, Explode)
UNLOCK	—	—	—
VIEWRES	—	—	—
VLCONV	Visual Link Data Converter	—	—
VPLAYER	—	—	—
UNITS	—	—	—
VPOINT	—	View, 3D Viewpoint, Tripod	—
NON,0,0,1	—	View, 3D Viewpoint Presets,Top	Top View (Standard, Named Views)
NON,0,0,-1	—	View, 3D Viewpoint Presets, Bottom	Bottom View (Standard, Named Views)

continues

Table C.1, *CONTINUED*
Command, Dialog Box, Menu, Tool Equivalents

Command Name and Option	*Dialog Box*	*Menu, Item*	*Tool (Toolbar, Pull-Down Flyout) Name*
NON,-1,0,0	—	View, 3D Viewpoint Presets, Left	Left View (Standard, Named Views)
NON,1,0,0	—	View, 3D Viewpoint Presets, Right	Right View (Standard, Named Views)
NON,0,-1,0	—	View, 3D Viewpoint Presets, Front	Front View (Standard, Named Views)
NON,0,1,0	—	View, 3D Viewpoint Presets, Back	Back View (Standard, Named Views)
NON,-1,-1,1	—	View, 3D Viewpoint Presets, SW Isometric)	SW Isometric View (Standard, Named Views)
NON,1,-1,1	—	View, 3D Viewpoint Presets, SE Isometric	SE Isometric View (Standard, Named Views)
NON,1,1,1	—	View, 3D Viewpoint Presets, NE Isometric)	NE Isometric View (Standard, Named Views)
NON,-1,1,1	—	View, 3D Viewpoint Presets, NW Isometric)	NW Isometric View (Standard, Named Views)
VPORTS	—	—	—
VSLIDE	Select Slide File	Tools, Slide, View	—
WBLOCK	—	—	—

Command Name and Option	*Dialog Box*	*Menu, Item*	*Tool (Toolbar, Pull-Down Flyout) Name*
WEDGE	—	—	Corner (Solids, Center)
CE,\	—	—	Center (Solids, Center)
WMFIN	Import WMF	—	—
WMFOPTS	WMF Import Options	—	—
WMFOUT	Create WMF File	—	—
XBIND	—	—	—
B,\	—	—	Block (External Reference, All)
LA,\	—	—	Layer (External Reference, All)
LT,\	—	—	Linetype (External Reference, All)
S,\	—	—	Style (External Reference, All)
D,\	—	—	Dimension Style (External Reference, Clip)
XLINE	—	—	Construction Line (Draw, Line)
XPLODE	—	—	—
XREF	—	—	—
A,\	—	—	Attach (External Reference, Attach)
O,\	—	—	Overlay (External Reference, Overlay)
R,\	—	—	Reload (External Reference, Reload)

continues

Table C.1, *CONTINUED*
Command, Dialog Box, Menu, Tool Equivalents

Command Name and Option	*Dialog Box*	*Menu, Item*	*Tool (Toolbar, Pull-Down Flyout) Name*
D,\	—	—	Detach (External Reference, Detach)
P,\	—	—	Path (External References, Path)
?,\	—	—	List (External Reference, List)
B,\	—	—	All (External Reference, All)
XREFCLIP	—	—	Clip (External Reference, Clip)
ZOOM	—	—	—
2X	—	View, Zoom, In	Zoom In (Standard)
.5X	—	View, Zoom, Out	Zoom Out (Standard)
W	—	View, Zoom, Window	Zoom Window (Standard)
All	—	View, Zoom, All	Zoom All (Standard, Zoom)
P	—	View, Zoom, Previous	Zoom Previous (Standard, Zoom)
X	—	View, Zoom, Scale	Zoom Scale (Standard, Zoom)
D	—	View, Zoom, Dynamic	Zoom Dynamic (Standard, Zoom)
C	—	View, Zoom, Center	Zoom Center (Standard, Zoom)
Left	—	View, Zoom, Left	Zoom Left (Standard, Zoom)

Command Name and Option	Dialog Box	Menu, Item	Tool (Toolbar, Pull-Down Flyout) Name
Limits	—	View, Zoom, Limits	Zoom Limits (Standard, Zoom)
E	—	View, Zoom, Extents	Zoom Extents (Standard, Zoom)
Vmax	—	View, Zoom, Vmax	Zoom Vmax (Standard, Zoom)

Command Aliases

Aliases are abbreviations that can be entered at the `Command:` prompt to issue commands. Aliases for dimensioning commands are prefaced with D, and commands beginning with DD that open dialog boxes are prefaced with DD.

Table C.2

Command Aliases

Command Name	*Alias*	*Command Name*	*Alias*
3DARRAY	3AR	3DFACE	3DF
3DMESH	3DM	3DPOLY	3PL
AI_BOX	ABOX	AI_DISH	ADSH
AI_DOME	ADOM	AI_MESH	AMSH
AI_PYRAMID	APYR	AI_SPHERE	ASPH
AI_TORUS	ATOR	AI_WEDGE	AWED
AMECONVERT	AC	ARC	A
ARRAY	ARR	ASEADMIN	ASA
ASEEXPORT	ASX	ASELINKS	ASL
ASEROWS	ASR	ASESELECT	ASS
ASESQLED	ASQ	ATTEDIT	ATE
ATTREDEF	ATR	BHATCH	H

continues

Table C.2, *CONTINUED*
Command Aliases

Command Name	*Alias*	*Command Name*	*Alias*
BLOCK	BL	BOUNDARY	BO
BREAK	BR	CHAMFER	CH
CIRCLE	C	CONE	CO
CONFIG	CFG	COPY	CP
CYLINDER	CY	DDATTDEF	DDA
DDATTE	DAT	DDCOLOR	DDC
DDEDIT	DDT	DDEMODES	DDE
DDGRIPS	DDG	DDIM	DDI
DDINSERT	I	DDLMODES	DDL
DDLTYPE	DDLT	DDMODIFY	DDM
DDOSNAP	DDO	DDRENAME	DDRE
DDRMODES	DDR	DDSELECT	DDS
DDUCS	DDUC	DDUCSP	DDUP
DDUNITS	DDU	DDVIEW	DDV
DIMALIGNED	DALI	DIMANGULAR	DANG
DIMBASELINE	DBAS	DIMCENTER	DCEN
DIMCONTINUE	DCON	DIMDIAMETER	DDIA
DIMLINEAR	DLIN	DIMORDINATE	DORD
DIMRADIUS	DRAD	DIMTEDIT	DTE
DIVIDE	DI	DSVIEWER	AV
DTEXT	DT	DVIEW	DV
EDGE	ED	EDGESURF	ES
ELLIPSE	EL	ERASE	E
EXPLODE	EXP	EXTEND	EX
EXTRUDE	EXT	FILLET	FI

Command Name	*Alias*	*Command Name*	*Alias*
GROUP	GR	HATCHEDIT	HE
HIDE	HI	INTERFERE	INTF
INTERSECT	INTS	LAYER	LA
LEADER	LE	LIGHT	LI
LINE	L	LINETYPE	LT
LIST	LIS	MATLIB	MAL
MEASURE	ME	MINSERT	MIN
MIRROR	MI	MLEDIT	MLE
MLINE	ML	MLSTYLE	MST
MOVE	M	MSLIDE	MSL
MSPACE	MS	MTEXT	T
MVIEW	MV	OFFSET	OF
OOPS	OO	OSNAP	OS
PAN	P	PEDIT	PE
PLINE	PL	POINT	PO
POLYGON	POL	PREFERENCES	PRE
PSFILL	PSF	PSPACE	PS
PURGE	PU	RECTANG	REC
REDRAW	R	REDRAWALL	RA
REGION	REG	RENDER	REN
REVOLVE	REV	REVSURF	RS
RMAT	MA	ROTATE	RO
RPREF	RP	RULESURF	RLS
SCALE	SC	SECTION	SEC
SHADE	SH	SHAPE	SHA
SKETCH	SK	SLICE	SL
SOLID	SOL	SPELL	SP

continues

Table C.2, ***CONTINUED***

Command Aliases

Command Name	*Alias*	*Command Name*	*Alias*
SPHERE	SPH	SPLINE	SPL
SPLINEDIT	SPE	STATS	STA
STRETCH	ST	SUBTRACT	SUB
TABSURF	TS	TEXT	TE
TILEMODE	TI	TOLERANCE	TOL
TORUS	TOR	TRIM	TR
UCS	UC	UNDO	U
UNION	UN	VPOINT	VP
VSLIDE	VSL	WEDGE	WE
XBIND	XB	XLINE	XL
XREF	XR	XREFCLIP	XRC
ZOOM	Z		

Appendix

D

SYSTEM VARIABLE TABLES

This appendix contains a table of AutoCAD system variables. You can use this table to find AutoCAD's environment settings and their values. Table D.1 represents all the variables available through AutoCAD, AutoLISP, and the AutoCAD Development System. Dimension variables are in Table D.2.

The system variable name and the default AutoCAD prototype drawing (ACAD.DWG) settings are shown. A brief description is given for each variable, and the meaning is given for each code. Most variables are set by various dialog boxes or commands. These variables also can be set or checked by the SETVAR command, and most can be entered directly at the `Command:` *prompt. However, those names shown italicized can only be directly accessed by the SETVAR command because AutoCAD has a command with the same name as the variable. All values are saved with the drawing unless noted with (CFG) for ConFiGuration file or (NS) for Not Saved. The Command Name column lists the commands that set the system variables. Variables marked (RO) are read-only, which means you cannot change them.*

Table D.1
System Variables Table

Variable Name	*Default Setting*	*Command Name*	*Variable Description*
ACADPREFIX	"C:\ACADR13\COMMON\SUPPORT\;C:\ACADR13..."	—	(NS)(RO) Directory search path set by the DOS ACAD environment variable.
ACADVER	"13"	—	(NS)(RO) Release number of your copy of AutoCAD.
AFLAGS	0	DDATTDEF, ATTDEF	(NS) Current state of ATTDEF modes. The value is the sum of the following: 0 = No attribute mode selected 1 = Invisible 2 = Constant 4 = Verify 8 = Preset
ANGBASE	0.0000	DDUNITS, UNITS	The direction of angle 0 in the current UCS.
ANGDIR	0	DDUNITS, UNITS	The direction of angle measure from 0: 0 = Counterclockwise 1 = Clockwise
APERTURE	10	DDOSNAP, APERTURE	(CFG) OSNAP target size in pixels.
AREA	0.0000	AREA, LIST, DBLIST	(NS)(RO) Stores the last computed area.

Variable Name	*Default Setting*	*Command Name*	*Variable Description*
ATTDIA	0	INSERT	Controls the attribute-entry method: 0 = Attribute prompts 1 = DDATTE dialogue box
ATTMODE	1	ATTDISP	Controls attribute display: 0 = Off 1 = Normal 2 = On
ATTREQ	1	INSERT	Attribute values used by insert: 0 = Uses default 1 = Prompts for values
AUDITCTL	0	—	(CFG) Controls whether AutoCAD creates an ADT file (Audit Report): 0 = No File 1 = ADT File
AUNITS	0	DDUNITS, UNITS	Sets Angular Units mode: 0 = Decimal Degrees 1 = Degrees/minutes/ seconds 2 = Gradians 3 = Radians 4 = Surveyor's Units
AUPREC	0	DDUNITS, UNITS	Sets number of decimal places for angular units.
BACKZ	0.0000	DVIEW	(RO) The DVIEW back clipping plane offset in drawing units. (See VIEWMODE.)
BLIPMODE	1	—	Controls display of marker blips: 1 = Blips 0 = No Blips

continues

Table D.1, *CONTINUED*
System Variables Table

Variable Name	*Default Setting*	*Command Name*	*Variable Description*
CDATE	19941211.22041537	TIME	(RO)(NS) Current date and time in YYYYMMDD.HHMMSS format.
CECOLOR	"BYLAYER"	DDEMODES, COLOR	The color for new objects.
CELTSCALE	1.0000	LTSCALE, PSLTSCALE	Sets global linetype scale for new objects.
CELTYPE	"BYLAYER"	DDEMODES, LINETYPE	Sets the linetype for new objects.
CHAMFERA	0.0000	CHAMFER	The first chamfer distance.
CHAMFERB	0.0000	CHAMFER	The second chamfer distance.
CHAMFERC	0.0000	CHAMFER	The chamfer length.
CHAMFERD	0.0000	CHAMFER	The chamfer angle.
CHAMMODE	0	CHAMFER	(NS) Determines method AutoCAD uses to create chamfers: 0 = Requires two chamfer distances 1 = Requires chamfer length and angle
CIRCLERAD	0.0000	CIRCLE	(NS) Default radius value for new circles: 0 = None
CLAYER	"0"	DDLMODES, LAYER	The current layer.
CMDACTIVE	0	CMDACTIVE	(NS)(RO) (Used primarily by ADS) Indicates that an AutoCAD command is active:

Variable Name	*Default Setting*	*Command Name*	*Variable Description*
			0 = None 1 = Ordinary command 2 = Ordinary and transparent 4 = Script 8 = Dialog box
CMDDIA	1	—	(CFG) Controls whether the PLOT command uses a dialog box or command prompts: 0 = Prompts 1 = Dialog box
CMDECHO	1	—	(NS) Controls the echoing of prompts and input during AutoLISP functions: 0 = Disables echoing 1 = Enables echoing
CMDNAMES	""	—	(NS)(RO) Names of any active commands.
CMLJUST	0	DTEXT, TEXT	(CFG) Sets Multi-Line text justification: 0 = Top 1 = Middle 2 = Bottom
CMLSCALE	1.0000	DTEXT, TEXT	(CFG) Sets overall width of multi-line text: Scale factor 2 = Twice width of style def

continues

Table D.1, *CONTINUED*

System Variables Table

Variable Name	*Default Setting*	*Command Name*	*Variable Description*
			Scale Factor 0 = Collapses multiline into single line Negative Scale Factor = Flips order of offset lines
CMLSTYLE	"STANDARD"	MTEXT, DTEXT, TEXT	(CFG) Sets the style for multi-lines.
COORDS	1	[^D][F6]	Controls updating of coordinate display: 0 = Updated on pick points only 1 = Absolute continuously updated 2 = Relative only during prompts
CVPORT	2	VPORTS	The current viewport's number.
DATE	2449698.91977246	TIME	(NS)(RO) The current date and time in Julian format.
DBMOD	0	Most	(NS)(RO) Drawing modification status. Sum of the following: 0 = None 1 = Object database modified 2 = Symbol table modified 4 = Database variable modified 8 = Window modified 16 = View modified
DCTCUST	""	SPELL	(CFG) Current custom spelling dictionary and path.

Variable Name	Default Setting	Command Name	Variable Description
DCTMAIN	"enu"	SPELL	(CFG) Current main spelling dictionary file: enu = American English ena = Australian English ens = British English (ise) enz = British English (ize) ca = Catalan cs = Czech da = Danish nl = Dutch (Primary) nls = Dutch (Secondary) fi = Finnish fr = French (unaccented capitals) fra = French (accented capitals) de = German (Scharfes s) ded = German (Dopple s) it = Italian no = Norwegian (Bokmal) non = Norwegian (Nynorsk) pt = Portuguese (Iberian) ptb = Portuguese (Brazilian) ru = Russian (infrequent io) rul = Russian (frequent io) es = Spanish (unaccented capitals) esa = Spanish (accented capitals) sv = Swedish
DELOBJ	1	—	Controls whether objects used to create other objects are deleted from the database: 0 = Objects are deleted 1 = Objects are retained

continues

Table D.1, ***CONTINUED***

System Variables Table

Variable Name	*Default Setting*	*Command Name*	*Variable Description*
DIASTAT	1	DD?????	(NS)(RO) Last dialog box exit code: 0 = Cancel 1 = OK
DISPSILH	0	—	Controls display of silhouette curves of body objects in wireframe mode: 0 = Off 1 = On
DISTANCE	0.0000	DIST	(NS)(RO) Stores the distance computed by the DIST command.
DONUTID	0.5000	DONUT	(NS) Sets the default inner diameter for new donut objects.
DONUTOD	1.0000	DONUT	(NS) Sets the default outer diameter for new donut objects.
DRAGMODE	2	DRAGMODE	Controls object dragging during editing commands: 0 = No dragging 1 = On (if requested) 2 = Auto
DRAGP1	10	—	(CFG) Sets regen-drag input sampling rate.

Variable Name	Default Setting	Command Name	Variable Description
DRAGP2	25	—	(CFG) Sets fast-drag input sampling rate.
DWGCODEPAGE	"ansi_1252"	—	(RO) The code page used for the drawing.
DWGNAME	"UNNAMED"	—	(RO) The drawing name as entered by the user.
DWGPREFIX	"C:\ACADR13\WIN\"	—	(NS)(RO) The current drawing's drive and directory path.
DWGTITLED	0	NEW	(NS)(RO) Indicates whether the current drawing has been named or not: 0 = No 1 = Yes
DWGWRITE	1	OPEN	(NS) Indicates whether the current drawing is opened as read only: 0 = Read-only 1 = Read/write
EDGEMODE	0	TRIM, EXTEND	Controls determination of cutting and boundary edges: 0 = Use selected edge without extension 1 = Extends selected edge to imaginary extension of cutting or boundary object
ELEVATION	0.0000	ELEV	The current elevation in the current UCS for the current space.

continues

Table D.1, ***CONTINUED***

System Variables Table

Variable Name	*Default Setting*	*Command Name*	*Variable Description*
ERRNO	0	—	(NS) An error number generated by AutoLISP and ADS Applications. (See the AutoLISP Release 13 Programmer's Reference or the AutoCAD Development System Programmer's Reference Manual.) Not listed by SETVAR.
EXPERT	0	—	(NS) Suppresses successive level of Are you sure? warnings: 0 = None 1 = REGEN/LAYER 2 = BLOCK/WBLOCK/SAVE 3 = LINETYPE 4 = UCS/VPORT 5 = DIM
EXPLMODE	1	EXPLODE	Controls whether the EXPLODE command supports nonuniformly scaled (NUS) blocks: 0 = Does not explode NUS blocks 1 = Explodes NUS blocks
EXTMAX	-1.0000E+20,-1.0000E+20,-1.0000E+20		(RO) The X,Y coordinates of the drawing's upper right extents in the WCS.
EXTMIN	1.0000E+20,1.0000E+20,1.0000E+20		(RO) The X,Y coordinates of the drawing's lower left extents in the WCS.

Variable Name	*Default Setting*	*Command Name*	*Variable Description*
FACETRES	0.5000	HIDE, SHADE, RENDER	Adjusts smoothness of shaded and hidden-line removed objects. Valid from 0.01 to 10.0.
FFLIMIT	0	—	(CFG) Limits number of PostScript and TrueType fonts in memory. From 0 to 100. 0 is no limit.
FILEDIA	1	—	(CFG) Controls display of file dialog boxes: 0 = Only when a tilde (~) is entered 1 = On
FILLETRAD	0.0000	FILLET	Stores the current fillet radius.
FILLMODE	1	SOLID, FILL	Turns on the display of fill traces, solids, and wide polylines: 0 = Off 1 = On
FONTALT	"txt"	—	(CFG) Specifies alternative font when AutoCAD cannot locate requested font.
FONTMAP	""	—	(CFG) Specifies a mapped font file to use when AutoCAD cannot locate the font file.
FRONTZ	0.0000	DVIEW	(RO) The DVIEW front clipping plane's offset in drawing units. (See VIEWMODE.)

continues

Table D.1, *CONTINUED*
System Variables Table

Variable Name	*Default Setting*	*Command Name*	*Variable Description*
GRIDMODE	0	DDRMODES, GRID	Controls display of the grid in the current viewport: 0 = Off 1 = On
GRIDUNIT	0.0000,0.0000	DDRMODES, GRID	The X,Y grid spacing for the current viewport.
GRIPBLOCK	0	DDGRIPS	(CFG) Controls the display of grips for objects in blocks: 0 = Off 1 = On
GRIPCOLOR	5	DDGRIPS	(CFG) The current color of unselected grips. Can be any AutoCAD color from 1 to 255.
GRIPHOT	1	DDGRIPS	(CFG) The current color of selected grips. Can be any AutoCAD color from 1 to 255.
GRIPS	1	DDSELECT	(CFG) Controls the display of entity grips and grip editing: 0 = Off 1 = On
GRIPSIZE	3	DDGRIPS	(CFG) The size of grip box in pixels: 0 = PICKBOX
HANDLES	1	HANDLES	Controls the creation of entity handles for the current drawing: 1 = On

Variable Name	*Default Setting*	*Command Name*	*Variable Description*
HIGHLIGHT	1	DDRMODES	(NS) Controls object selection highlighting: 0 = Off 1 = On
HPANG	0	BHATCH, HATCH	(NS) The current hatch angle.
HPBOUND	1	BHATCH, BOUNDARY	Type of object created by the BHATCH and BOUNDARY commands: 0 = Polyline 1 = Region
HPDOUBLE	0	BHATCH, HATCH	(NS) Controls user-defined hatch pattern doubling: 0 = Off 1 = On
HPNAME	"ANSI31"	BHATCH, HATCH	(NS) The default hatch pattern for new hatches.
HPSCALE	1.0000	BHATCH, HATCH	(NS) The default hatch pattern scale. Must be nonzero.
HPSPACE	1.0000	BHATCH, HATCH	(NS) The default spacing for user-defined hatch patterns.
INSBASE	0.0000,0.0000,0.0000	BASE	Insertion base point X,Y,Z coordinate of current drawing in current space and current UCS.
INSNAME	""	DDINSERT, INSERT	(NS) Default block name for INSERT or DDINSERT.
ISOLINES	4	—	Controls number of isolines per surface on objects.

continues

Table D.1, *CONTINUED*

System Variables Table

Variable Name	*Default Setting*	*Command Name*	*Variable Description*
LASTANGLE	0.0000	ARC	(NS)(RO) The angle of the last arc entered in the current UCS for the current space.
LASTPOINT	0.0000,0.0000,0.0000	—	The last point entered in the current UCS and current space.
LENSLENGTH	50.0000	DVIEW	(RO) The lens length of the current viewport perspective.
LIMCHECK	0	LIMITS	Controls object creation outside the drawing limits: 0 = Enables object creation 1 = Disables object creation
LIMMAX	12.0000,9.0000	LIMITS	The upper right limit of the WCS in current space.
LIMMIN	0.0000,0.0000	LIMITS	The lower left limit of the WCS in current space.
LOCALE	"en"	—	(RO)(NS) The ISO language code of the AutoCAD version being used.
LOGINNAME	""	CONFIG	(CFG)(RO) User name created by the CONFIG command or input when AutoCAD is loaded.
LTSCALE	1.0000	LTSCALE	Global linetype scale factor.
LUNITS	2	DDUNITS, UNITS	The Linear units mode: 1 = Scientific 2 = Decimal 3 = Engineering 4 = Architectural 5 = Fractional

Variable Name	*Default Setting*	*Command Name*	*Variable Description*
LUPREC	4	DDUNITS, UNITS	Precision of decimal or fractional units.
MACROTRACE	0	—	(NS) Controls the Diesel, macro-debugging display. Not listed by SETVAR. 0 = On 1 = Off
MAXACTVP	16	—	(NS) Maximum number of viewports to regenerate at one time.
MAXSORT	200	—	(CFG) The maximum number of symbols and file names to be sorted in lists.
MENUCTL	1	—	(CFG) Controls page switching of the screen menu: 0 = Does not switch with keyboard command entry 1 = Does switch with keyboard command entry
MENUECHO	0	—	(NS) Controls the display of menu actions on the command line; the value is the sum of the following: 1 = Suppresses menu input 2 = Suppresses system prompts 4 = Disables ^P toggle of menu echoing 8 = Displays DIESEL input/output strings

continues

Table D.1, *CONTINUED*

System Variables Table

Variable Name	*Default Setting*	*Command Name*	*Variable Description*
MENUNAME	"C:\ACADR13\WIN\ SUPPORT\ACAD.mnc"	MENU	(NS)(RO) Name and path of currently loaded menu.
MIRRTEXT	1	MIRROR	Controls how MIRROR reflects text: 0 = Retains text direction 1 = Mirrors text
MODEMACRO	""	—	(NS) A DIESEL language expression to control status-line display.
MTEXTED	"Internal"	DDEDIT	(CFG) Name of program to use for editing mtext objects.
OFFSETDIST	-1.0000	OFFSET	(NS) Default distance for the OFFSET command. Negative value enables the THROUGH option.
ORTHOMODE	0	[^O][F8]	Sets the current Ortho mode: 0 = Off 1 = On
OSMODE	0	DDOSNAP, OSNAP	Sets the current object snap mode; value is the sum of the following: 0 = NONe 1 = ENDpoint 2 = MIDpoint 4 = CENter 8 = NODe 16 = QUAdrant 32 = INTersection

Variable Name	*Default Setting*	*Command Name*	*Variable Description*
			64 = INSertion 128 = PERpendicular 256 = TANgent 512 = NEArest 1024 = QUIck 2048 = APPint
PDMODE	0	POINT	Controls the graphic display of POINT objects.
PDSIZE	0.0000	POINT	Controls the size of POINT objects: Negative = Percentage of viewport size Positive = Absolute size 0 = 5% of graphics area height
PELLIPSE	0	ELLIPSE	The ellipse type created with ELLIPSE command: 0 = True ellipse 1 = Polyline representation of an ellipse
PERIMETER	0.0000	AREA, LIST, DBLIST	(NS)(RO) Last perimeter value calculated by AREA, LIST, DBLIST.
PFACEVMAX	4		(NS)(RO) Maximum number of vertices per face.
PICKADD	1	DDSELECT	(CFG) Controls whether selected objects are added to, or are replaced with (added with Shift + select), the current selection set: 0 = Replace (Shift to add only) 1 = Added (Shift to remove only)

continues

Table D.1, *CONTINUED*

System Variables Table

Variable Name	*Default Setting*	*Command Name*	*Variable Description*
PICKAUTO	1	DDSELECT	(CFG) Controls the implied (AUTO) windowing for object selection: 0 = Off 1 = On
PICKBOX	3	DDSELECT	(CFG) Object selection pick box size, in pixels.
PICKDRAG	0	DDSELECT	(CFG) Determines whether the pick button must be depressed during window corner picking in set selections: 0 = Off 1 = On
PICKFIRST	1	DDSELECT	(CFG) Enables entity selection before command selection (noun/verb paradigm): 0 = Off 1 = On
PICKSTYLE	1	—	(CFG) Controls group selection and associative hatch selection: 0 = No group or associative hatch selection 1 = Group selection 2 = Associative hatch selection 3 = Group and associative hatch selection

Variable Name	*Default Setting*	*Command Name*	*Variable Description*
PLATFORM	"Microsoft Windows (Intel) Version 3.10"	—	(NS)(RO) Indicates the operating system in use. String value.
PLINEGEN	0	—	Sets the linetype pattern generation around the vertices of a 2D polyline. Does not apply to polylines with tapered segments. 0 = Polylines are generated to start and end with a dash at each vertex 1 = Generates the linetype in a continuous pattern around the vertices of the polyline
PLINEWID	0.0000	PLINE	Default width for new polyline objects.
PLOTID	""	—	(CFG) Current plotter configuration description.
PLOTROTMODE	1	PLOT	Controls plot orientation: 0 = Rotation icon aligns at lower left for 0, top left for 90, top right for 180, lower right for 270 1 = Aligns lower left corner of plotting area with lower left corner of paper
PLOTTER	0	PLOT	(CFG) Current plotter configuration number.
POLYSIDES	4	POLYGON	(NS) Default number of sides for POLYGON objects (3-1024).

continues

Table D.1, *CONTINUED*
System Variables Table

Variable Name	*Default Setting*	*Command Name*	*Variable Description*
POPUPS	1	—	(NS)(RO) Status of the currently configured display driver: 0 = Does not support dialog boxes, menu bar, pull-down menus, and icon menus 1 = Supports these features
PROJMODE	1	TRIM, EXTEND	(CGF) Current projection mode for TRIM or EXTEND operations: 0 = True 3d (no projection) 1 = Project to the XY plane of the current UCS 2 = Project to the current view plane
PSLTSCALE	1	—	Paper space scaling of model space linetypes: 0 = Off 1 = On
PSPROLOG	""	—	(CFG) The name of the PostScript post-processing section of the ACAD.PSF to be appended to the PSOUT command's output.
PSQUALITY	75	PSQUALITY	(CFG) The default quality setting for rendering of images by the PSIN command.
QTEXTMODE	0	QTEXT	Sets the current state of quick text mode: 0 = Off 1 = On

Variable Name	*Default Setting*	*Command Name*	*Variable Description*
RASTER-PREVIEW	0	SAVE, SAVEAS	Controls whether a preview image is saved and in which format the image is saved: 0 = BMP only 1 = BMP and WMF 2 = WMF only 3 = No preview image created
REGENMODE	1	REGENAUTO	Indicates the current state of REGENAUTO: 0 = Off 1 = On
RIASPECT	0.0000	GIFIN, TIFFIN	(NS) Controls the aspect ratio of imported raster images.
RIBACK	0	GIFIN, TIFFIN, PCXIN	(NS) The background color of imported raster images. Based on AutoCAD colors.
RIEDGE	0	GIFIN, TIFFIN, PCXIN	(NS) Controls the edge detection feature: 0 = Disables edge detection 1-255 = Threshold for edge detection
RIGAMUT	256	GIFIN, TIFFIN, PCXIN	(NS) Number of colors used when color images are imported.
RIGREY	0	GIFIN, TIFFIN, PCXIN	(NS) Imports images as grayscale: 0 = Disables grayscale image importing >0 = Converts each pixel to grayscale

continues

Table D.1, *CONTINUED*
System Variables Table

Variable Name	*Default Setting*	*Command Name*	*Variable Description*
RITHRESH	0	GIFIN, TIFFIN, PCXIN	(NS) Controls brightness of imported images: 0 = Disables brightness control >0 = Only pixels brighter than value are imported
RE-INIT	0	REINIT	(NS) A code that specifies the type(s) of reinitializations to perform. The sum of: 1 = Digitizer port 2 = Plotter port 4 = Digitizer device 8 = Display device 16 = Reload ACAD.PGP
SAVEFILE	"AUTO.SV$"	CONFIG, PREFERENCES	(CFG)(RO) The default directory and file name for automatic file saves.
SAVENAME	""	SAVEAS	(RO)(NS) Stores the file name you save the drawing to.
SAVETIME	120	CONFIG	(CFG) The default interval between automatic file saves, in minutes: 0 = Disable automatic saves
SCREENBOXES	0	CONFIG	(CFG)(RO) The number of available screen menu boxes in the current graphics screen area.

Variable Name	*Default Setting*	*Command Name*	*Variable Description*
SCREENMODE	3	[F1]	(CFG)(RO) Indicates the active AutoCAD screen mode or window: 0 = Text 1 = Graphics 2 = Dual Screen
SCREENSIZE	1008.0000,578.0000		(RO) Size of the current viewport in pixels.
SHADEDGE	3	SHADE	Controls the display of edges and faces by the SHADE command: 0 = Faces shaded, edges not highlighted 1 = Faces shaded, edges in background color 2 = Faces not filled, edges in object color 3 = Faces in object color, edges in background color
SHADEDIF	70	SHADE	Sets the ratio of diffuse reflective light to ambient light, expressed as a percentage of diffuse reflective light.
SHPNAME	""	SHAPE	(NS) The default shape name.
SKETCHINC	0.1000	SKETCH	The recording increment for SKETCH segments.
SKPOLY	0	SKETCH	Determines whether sketch uses lines or polylines: 0 = Generate lines 1 = Generate polylines

continues

Table D.1, *CONTINUED*

System Variables Table

Variable Name	*Default Setting*	*Command Name*	*Variable Description*
SNAPANG	0	DDRMODES, SNAP	The angle of SNAP/GRID rotation in the current viewport and UCS.
SNAPBASE	0.0000,0.0000	DDRMODES, SNAP	SNAP/GRID base point in the current viewport and UCS.
SNAPISOPAIR	0	DDRMODES, SNAP, [^E], [F5]	The current isoplane for the current viewport: 0 = Left 1 = Top 2 = Right
SNAPMODE	0	DDRMODES, SNAP, [^B], [F9]	Indicates the state of SNAP for the current viewport: 0 = Off 1 = On
SNAPSTYL	0	DDRMODES, SNAP	The snap style for the current viewport: 0 = Standard 1 = Isometric
SNAPUNIT	1.0000,1.0000	DDRMODES, SNAP	The snap X,Y increment for the current viewport.
SORTENTS	96	DDSELECT	(CFG) Controls the display of object sort order: 0 = Disable SORTENTS 1 = Sorts for object selection 2 = Sorts for object snap 4 = Sorts for redraws 8 = Sorts for MSLIDE creation 16 = Sorts for REGENs 32 = Sorts for plotting 64 = Sorts for PostScript output Sum numbers to select more than one

Variable Name	Default Setting	Command Name	Variable Description
SPLFRAME	0	—	Controls display of control polygons for spline-fit polylines, defining meshes of surface-fit polygons and invisible 3D face edges: 0 = Off 1 = On
SPLINESEGS	8	—	The number of line segments in each spline curve.
SPLINETYPE	6	—	Controls the type of curve generated by PEDIT spline: 5 = Quadratic B-spline 6 = Cubic B-spline
SURFTAB1	6	—	Sets the density of a mesh in the M direction.
SURFTAB2	6	—	Sets the density of a mesh in the N direction.
SURFTYPE	6	—	Controls the type of surface generated by PEDIT Smooth: 5 = Quadratic B-spline surface 6 = Cubic B-spline surface 8 = Bezier surface
SURFU	6	—	Surface density in the M direction of 3D polygonal meshes.
SURFV	6	—	Surface density in the N direction of 3D polygonal meshes.
SYSCODEPAGE	ASCII	—	(RO) Code page used by the system.

continues

Table D.1, *CONTINUED*

System Variables Table

Variable Name	*Default Setting*	*Command Name*	*Variable Description*
TABMODE	0	TABLET	(NS) Controls the use of Tablet mode: 0 = Disables tablet mode 1 = Enables tablet mode
TARGET	0.0000,0.0000,0.0000	DVIEW	(RO) The UCS coordinates of the target point in the current viewport.
TDCREATE	2449698.91946285	TIME	(RO) Time of the creation of the current drawing in Julian format.
TDINDWG	0.00048947	TIME	(RO) Total amount of editing time elapsed on the current drawing in Julian format.
TDUPDATE	2449698.91946285	TIME	(RO) The date and time when the drawing was last saved, in Julian format.
TDUSRTIMER	0.00049144	TIME	(RO) User-controlled elapsed time in Julian format.
TEMPPREFIX	“”	CONFIG	(NS)(RO) The directory for placement of AutoCAD’s temporary files. Defaults to current drawing directory.
TEXTEVAL	0	—	(NS) Controls the checking of text input (except by DTEXT) for AutoLISP expressions: 0 = No 1 = Yes

Variable Name	*Default Setting*	*Command Name*	*Variable Description*
TEXTFILL	0	TEXT	Controls the filling of Bitstream, TrueType, and Adobe Type 1 fonts: 0 = Display as outlines 1 = Display as filled images
TEXTQLTY	50	TEXT	Controls the resolution of Bitstream, TrueType, and Adobe Type 1 fonts: 0-100 (higher is better resolution)
TEXTSIZE	0.2000	TEXT	Default height for new text objects.
TEXTSTYLE	"STANDARD"	TEXT, STYLE	Default text style for new text objects.
THICKNESS	0.0000	ELEV	Current 3D thickness.
TILEMODE	1	TILEMODE	Enables and disables paper space and viewport objects: 0 = Off 1 = On
TOOLTIPS	1	—	(CFG) Controls the display of ToolTips: 0 = Off 1 = On
TRACEWID	0.0500	TRACE	The current width of traces.
TREEDEPTH	3020	—	A code number (four digits) representing the maximum number of division for spatial database index for model space (first two digits) and paper space (last two digits).

continues

Table D.1, *CONTINUED*
System Variables Table

Variable Name	*Default Setting*	*Command Name*	*Variable Description*
TREEMAX	10000000	—	(CFG) The maximum number of nodes for spatial database organization for the current memory configuration.
TRIMMODE	1	FILLET, CHAMFER	(NS) Controls whether AutoCAD trims selected edges for fillets and chamfers: 0 = Leave edges intact 1 = Trim edges back
UCSFOLLOW	0		Controls automatic display of the plan view in the current viewport when switching to a new UCS: 0 = Off 1 = On
UCSICON	1	UCSICON	Controls the UCS icon's display. Value is the sum of the following: 0 = Off 1 = On 2 = At origin
UCSNAME	""	DDUCS, UCS	(RO) The name of the current UCS for the current space: "" = unnamed
UCSORG	0.0000,0.0000,0.0000	DDUCS, UCS	(RO) The WCS origin of the current UCS for the current space.
UCSXDIR	1.0000,0.0000,0.0000	DDUCS, UCS	(RO) The X direction of the current UCS.

Variable Name	Default Setting	Command Name	Variable Description
UCSYDIR	0.0000,1.0000,0.0000	DDUCS, UCS	(RO) The Y direction of the current UCS.
UNDOCTL	5	UNDO	(NS)(RO) The current state of UNDO. Value is the sum of the following: 1 = Enabled 2 = Single command 4 = Auto mode 8 = Group active
UNDOMARKS	0	UNDO	(NS)(RO) The current number of marks in the UNDO command's history.
UNITMODE	0	—	Controls the display of user input of fractions, feet, and inches and surveyor's angles: 0 = per LUNITS 1 = As input
USERI1-5	0	—	User integer variables. USERI1 to USERI5. Not listed by SETVAR.
USERR1-5	0.0000	—	User real-number variables USERR1 to USERR5. Not listed by SETVAR.
USERS1-5	""	—	User string variables (up to 460 characters long) USERS1 to USERS5. Not listed by SETVAR.
VIEWCTR	7.9248,4.5408,0.0000	ZOOM, PAN, VIEW	(RO) The X,Y center point coordinate of the current viewport in the current view.

continues

Table D.1, *CONTINUED*

System Variables Table

Variable Name	*Default Setting*	*Command Name*	*Variable Description*
VIEWDIR	0.0000,0.0000,1.0000	DVIEW	(RO) The camera point offset from the target in the WCS.
VIEWMODE	0	DVIEW, UCS	(RO) The current viewport's viewing mode. Value is sum of following: 0 = Disabled 1 = Perspective 2 = Front clipping on 4 = Back clipping on 8 = UCSFOLLOW On 16 = FRONTZ offset in use
VIEWSIZE	9.0816	ZOOM, VIEW	(RO) The current view's height in drawing units.
VIEWTWIST	0	DVIEW	(RO) The current viewport's view-twist angle.
VISRETAIN	0	VISRETAIN	Controls retention of Xref file zzz setting in the current drawing. 0 = Off 1 = On
VSMAX	47.5487,27.2449,0.0000	ZOOM, PAN, VIEW	(RO) The upper right X,Y coordinate of the current viewport's virtual screen for the current UCS.
VSMIN	-31.6991,-18.1632,0.00	ZOOM, PAN, VIEW	(RO) The lower left X,Y coordinate of the current viewport's virtual screen for the current UCS.

Variable Name	Default Setting	Command Name	Variable Description
WORLDUCS	1	UCS	(NS)(RO) Indicates if the current UCS = WCS: 0 = False 1 = True
WORLDVIEW	1	DVIEW,UCS	Controls the automatic changing of a UCS to the WCS during the DVIEW and VPOINT commands: 0 = Off 1 = On
XREFCTL	0	—	(CFG) Controls the creation of an XLG log file that contains XREF results: 0 = No file 1 = XLG file

Dimension Variables Table

This section of the appendix contains a table of AutoCAD dimension variables. These variables generally are set by AutoCAD's Dimension Styles dialog box (DDIM command). They also can be set or checked by entering their names at the `Command:` or `Dim:` prompts. Use this table to find AutoCAD's dimension settings and their values. Table D.2 represents all the variables available for dimensioning through AutoCAD, AutoLISP, and the AutoCAD Development System. The dimension variable name and the default AutoCAD prototype drawing (ACAD.DWG) settings are shown. A brief description is given for each variable, and the meaning is given for each code. All values are saved with the drawing unless noted with (CFG) for ConFiGuration file, or (NS) for Not Saved. Variables marked (RO) are read-only, which means you cannot change them.

Table D.2
Dimension Variables Table

Variable Name	*Default Setting*	*Variable Description*
DIMALT	Off	Enables alternate units dimensioning: 0 = Off 1 = On
DIMALTD	2	The decimal precision of the alternate units when used.
DIMALTF	25.4000	The scale factor of the alternate units when used.
DIMALTTD	2	The number of decimal places for tolerance values in alternate units.
DIMALTTZ	0	Toggles suppression of zeros for alternate unit dimension values: 0 = Off 1 = On
DIMALTU	2	Unit format for alternate units of all dimension families except angular: 1 = Scientific 2 = Decimal 3 = Engineering 4 = Architectural 5 = Fractional
DIMALTZ	0	Toggles suppression of zeroes for alternate unit dimension values: 0 = Off 1 = On
DIMAPOST	“”	The user-defined prefix and/or suffix for alternative dimension text.
DIMASO	On	Enables associative dimensioning: 0 = Off 1 = On
DIMASZ	0.1800	Controls the size of dimension arrows and affects the fit of dimension text inside dimension lines when DIMTSZ is set to 0.

Variable Name	*Default Setting*	*Variable Description*
DIMAUNIT	0	Angle format for Angular dimensions: 0 = Decimal degrees 1 = Degrees/minutes/seconds 2 = Gradians 3 = Radians 4 = Surveyor's units
DIMBLK	""	Name of block to draw rather than an arrow or a tick.
DIMBLK1	""	Name of the block for the first end of dimension lines. (See DIMSAH.)
DIMBLK2	""	Name of the block for the second end of dimension lines. (See DIMSAH.)
DIMCEN	0.0900	Controls center marks or center lines drawn by DIM commands with radii: 0 = No center marks or lines <0 = Center lines are drawn >0 = Center marks are drawn
DIMCLRD	0	The dimension line, arrow, and leader color number; any valid color number; or the following: 0 = BYBLOCK 256 = BYLAYER
DIMCLRE	0	The dimension extension line's color. (See DIMCLRD.)
DIMCLRT	0	The dimension text's color. (See DIMCLRD.)
DIMDEC	4	The number of decimal places for the tolerance values of a dimension.
DIMDLE	0.0000	The dimension line's extension distance beyond ticks when ticks are drawn (when DIMTSZ is nonzero).
DIMDLI	0.3800	The offset distance between successive baseline dimensions.

continues

Table D.2, *CONTINUED*
Dimension Variables Table

Variable Name	*Default Setting*	*Variable Description*
DIMEXE	0.1800	The length of extension lines beyond the dimension line.
DIMEXO	0.0625	The distance by which extension line origin is offset from dimensioned entity.
DIMFIT	3	Controls the placement of text relative to the dimension: 0 = Text and arrow between extension lines if enough space; otherwise, outside 1 = Text and arrows between extension lines when text fits, arrows outside; otherwise, both outside 2 = Combination of 1 and 2 3 = Places whatever will fit between extension lines 4 = Creates leader lines when there is not enough space for text between extension lines
DIMGAP	0.0900	The space between the text and the dimension line; determines when text is placed outside a dimension.
DIMJUST	0	Controls the horizontal dimension text position: 0 = Center-justifies the text 1 = Positions text next to left extension line 2 = Positions text next to second extension line 3 = Positions text above and aligned with first extension line 4 = Positions text above and aligned with second extension line
DIMLFAC	1.0000	The overall linear dimensioning scale factor; if negative, acts as the absolute value applied to paper space viewports.

Variable Name	*Default Setting*	*Variable Description*
DIMLIM	Off	Presents dimension limits as default text: 0 = Off 1 = On (See DIMTP and DIMTM.)
DIMPOST	“”	The user-defined prefix and/or suffix for dimension text, such as “mm”.
DIMRND	0.0000	The rounding interval for linear dimension text.
DIMSAH	Off	Enables the use of DIMBLK1 and DIMBLK2 instead of DIMBLK or a default terminator: 0 = Off 1 = On
DIMSCALE	1.0000	The overall scale factor applied to other dimension variables except tolerances, angles, measured lengths, or coordinates: 0 = Paper space scale
DIMSD1	Off	Suppresses drawing of first dimension line: 0 = Off 1 = On
DIMSD2	Off	Suppresses drawing of second dimension line: 0 = Off 1 = On
DIMSE1	Off	Suppresses drawing of first extension line: 0 = Off 1 = On
DIMSE2	Off	Suppresses drawing of second extension line: 0 = Off 1 = On
DIMSHO	On	Determines whether associative dimension text is updated during dragging: 0 = Off 1 = On

continues

Table D.2, *CONTINUED*

Dimension Variables Table

Variable Name	*Default Setting*	*Variable Description*
DIMSOXD	Off	Suppresses the placement of dimension lines outside the extension lines: 0 = Off 1 = On
DIMSTYLE	"STANDARD"	(RO) Holds the name of the current dimension style.
DIMTAD	0	Controls vertical position of dimension text in relation to dimension line: 0 = Centers text between extension lines 1 = Places the text above dimension line except when dimension line is not horizontal and text inside lines is forced horizontal (DIMTIH = 1); the current DIMGAP value sets the distance from dimension line to baseline of lowest line of text 2 = Places the text on opposite side of dimension line from the extension line origins 3 = Places the text for a JIS representation
DIMTDEC	4	The number of decimal places for tolerance values for a primary units dimension.
DIMTFAC	1.0000	Scale factor for dimension tolerance's text height.
DIMTIH	On	Forces dimension text inside the extension lines to be positioned horizontally rather than aligned: 0 = Off 1 = On
DIMTIX	Off	Forces dimension text inside extension lines: 0 = Off 1 = On

Variable Name	*Default Setting*	*Variable Description*
DIMTM	0.0000	The negative tolerance values used when DIMTOL or DIMLIM is on.
DIMTOFL	Off	Draws dimension lines between extension lines even if text is placed outside the extension lines: 0 = Off 1 = On
DIMTOH	On	Forces dimension text to be positioned horizontally rather than aligned when it falls outside the extension lines: 0 = Off 1 = On
DIMTOL	Off	Appends tolerance values (DIMTP and DIMTM) to the default dimension text: 0 = Off 1 = On
DIMTOLJ	1	Sets vertical justification for tolerance values relative to nominal dimension text: 0 = Bottom 1 = Middle 2 = Top
DIMTP	0.0000	When DIMTOL or DIMLIM is on, sets the maximum tolerance limit for dimension text.
DIMTSZ	0.0000	When assigned a nonzero value, forces tick marks (rather than arrows) to be drawn at the size specified by the value; affects the placement of the dimension line and text between extension lines.
DIMTVP	0.0000	Percentage of text height to offset dimension vertically.
DIMTXSTY	"STANDARD"	The text style of the dimension.

continues

Table D.2, ***CONTINUED***

Dimension Variables Table

Variable Name	*Default Setting*	*Variable Description*
DIMTXT	0.1800	Height of the dimension text, unless current text style has a fixed height.
DIMTZIN	0	Switches suppression of zeros for tolerance values: 0 = Off 1 = On
DIMUNIT	2	Sets units for all dimension-style family members except angular: 1 = Scientific 2 = Decimal 3 = Engineering 4 = Architectural 5 = Fractional
DIMUPT	Off	Controls cursor functionality for user-positioned text: 0 = Cursor controls only dimension line location 1 = Cursor controls text position as well as dimension line location
DIMZIN	0	Suppresses the display of zero inches or zero feet in dimension text, and leading and/or trailing zeros in decimal dimension text: 0 = Feet and inches 1 = Neither 2 = Inches only 3 = Feet only 4 = Leading zeros 8 = Trailing zeros 12 = Both leading and trailing zeros

Glossary

'CAL
274, 606-620

The 'CAL command invokes the calculator included with AutoCAD. Tool: Choose Calculator (Standard, Object Snap) Pull-down: Choose Tools Calculator Screen: Choose TOOLS, GeomCalc

'COLOR
84

The 'COLOR command enables you to set the current drawing color from the `Command:` prompt. Screen: Choose DATA, Color

'DDCOLOR
84

The 'DDCOLOR command enables you to set the current drawing color. Tool: Choose Color Control (Object Properties) Pull-down: Choose Data, Color Screen: Choose DATA, ColorDlg

'DDEMODES
82-83

The 'DDEMODES command enables you to set the current color, layer, linetype, text style, linetype scale, elevation, and thickness. Tool: Choose Object Creation (Object Properties) Pull-down: Choose Data, Object Creation Screen: Choose DATA, DDemode

'DDGRIPS
508-513

The 'DDGRIPS command displays the GRIPS dialog box to enable grips, control their sizes, and manage their colors. Pull-down: Choose Options, Grips Screen: Choose OPTIONS, DDgrips

'DDLTYPE
84

The 'DDLTYPE command opens the Select Linetype dialog box (refer to figure 20.4), which enables you to load linetypes from a file and set the current linetype and global linetype scale. Tool: Choose Linetype (Object Properties) Pull-down: Choose Data, Linetype Screen: Choose DATA, DDltype

'DDRMODES
21

The 'DDRMODES (Dynamic Dialog dRawing MODES) command controls drawing mode settings, such as snap, blips, ortho, axis, and isoplane. Pressing Enter after changing an X-Spacing edit box's value sets the Y-Spacing to the same value.

'DDSELECT
536

The 'DDSELECT command displays the Object Selection Settings dialog box. You use this dialog box to set object selection behavior and the pickbox size, and control the sorting of objects. Pull-down: Choose Options, Selection Screen: Choose OPTIONS, DDselec

'DIST
126, 595

The 'DIST command enables you to measure the distance and angle between any two points you pick. Tool: Choose Distance (Object Properties, Inquiry) Screen: Choose ASSIST, INQUIRY, Dist

'DSVIEWER
162-165

The 'DSVIEWER command opens the Aerial View window and enables quick screen navigation. While this window is active, you can perform zoom and pan operations without choosing additional menu or command options. Tool: Choose Aerial View (Standard, Tool Windows) NRP Toolbar: Choose Aerial View Pull-down: Choose Tools, Aerial View

'FILL
318

The 'FILL command enables you to control the visibility of the filled portion of wide polylines, multilines, traces, and solids by changing the state of the FILLMODE system variable. When the fill mode is off, AutoCAD displays or plots only the outline of filled objects. Objects regenerate and plot faster when fill mode is off. Screen: Choose OPTIONS, DISPLAY, Fill

'FILTER
571-572

The 'FILTER command opens the Object Selection Filters dialog box, which enables you to create a list of conditions that an object must satisfy to be selected. You can use FILTER at the `Command:` prompt to create filter lists to use later at a Select objects: prompt. You also can use it transparently at a Select objects: prompt to select objects to use with the current command. Tool: Choose Selection Filters (Standard, Select Objects) Screen: Choose ASSIST, Filter

'ID
99, 598

The 'ID command displays the coordinates of a selected point or displays a blip at the coordinates you type. Tool: Choose Locate Point (Object Properties, Inquiry) Screen: Choose ASSIST, INQUIRY, ID

'LAYER
69-70

The 'LAYER command provides layer control (except for paper space functions) from the `Command:` prompt. The 'LAYER command creates new layers, selects the current layer, turns layers on and off, freezes and thaws layers, locks and unlocks layers, lists defined layers, and sets the color and linetype for specified layers. The 'LAYER command is available only at the `Command:` prompt.

'LINETYPE
84

The 'LINETYPE command has options for loading linetypes, listing the contents of linetype files, setting the current linetype, and creating new linetype definitions. You must type the LINETYPE command at the `Command:` prompt because it does not appear in the menu.

'PAN
160-162

The 'PAN command shifts the drawing in the current viewport by a relative displacement. Tool: Choose Pan Point (Standard, Pan) Pull-down: Choose View, Pan Screen: Choose VIEW, Pan

'SETVAR
589-592

The 'SETVAR command enables you to view and (usually) change the current value of a system variable. Pull-down: Choose Options, System Variables Screen: Choose OPTIONS, Sys Var

'STATUS
584-585

The 'STATUS command gives you some general information about the drawing file. Pull-down: Choose Data, Status Screen: Choose DATA, Status

'TIME
585-587

The 'TIME command displays the current date and time, the date and time the drawing was created, the date and time the drawing was last updated, and the total cumulative time the drawing has been in the drawing editor. Pull-down: Choose Data, Time Screen: Choose DATA, Time

'VIEW
171, 588

The 'VIEW command enables you to save and restore named areas of the drawing. To use the command transparently, fast zooms must be on.

'ZOOM
20, 152

The 'ZOOM command alters the current magnification level of the on-screen display. It is one of the most frequently used commands in AutoCAD. Tool: Choose Zoom In, Zoom out, Zoom Window (Standard) or Zoom All (Standard, Zoom) Pull-Down: Choose View, Zoom Screen: Choose VIEW, Zoom

A

ALIGN
560-562

The ALIGN command enables you to relocate and rotate objects to align with other objects, using at most three pairs of source and destination points. You can define a move, 2D or 3D transformation, a rotation, or any combination of these operations. Tool: Choose Align (Modify, Rotate) Screen: Choose MODIFY, Align

APERTURE
122

The APERTURE command sets the size of the object snap aperture box, or target box. This command is available at the command line. The command prompts for the height of the aperture box in pixels. Acceptable values range from 1 to 50.

ARC
277-287

The ARC command enables you to create a circular arc. Three parameters enable you to choose the arc's dimensions and location. These parameters can be any combination of the start point, a point on the circumference, the endpoint, the center, the included angle, the chord length, or the tangent direction. The default method is a three-point arc that uses a starting point, a point on the circumference, and an endpoint. Tool: Choose 3 Points (Draw, Arc) Screen: Choose DRAW1, Arc

AREA
595-598

The AREA command enables you to measure the area and perimeter length of objects and defined areas. Tool: Choose Area (Object Properties, Inquiry) Screen: Choose ASSIST, INQUIRY, Area

ARRAY
393, 642-648

The ARRAY command enables you to create multiple copies of an object in a rectangular or circular (polar) pattern. Tool: Choose Rectangular Array (Modify, Copy)

ATTEDIT
453-456

The ATTEDIT command enables you to edit attribute values globally and to change properties of the attribute text. Tool: Choose Edit Attribute Globally (Attribute, Edit Attribute Globally)

ATTEXT
420-423

Extracts the attribute data specified by a template file from the drawing. You can extract data from all or selected attributes, in CDF, SDF, or DXF format.

B

BASE
380

The BASE command is used to set the INSBASE system variable. This system variable specifies the insertion base point of a file when the file is inserted into another drawing.

BHATCH
732-733

The BHATCH command enables you to draw a hatch pattern in a selected area. Tool: Choose Hatch (Draw) Screen: Choose CONSTRCT, Bhatch

BLOCK
379-380, 429-431, 587

The BLOCK command has several prompts, and one option—the ? option—to list defined blocks. AutoCAD prompts you to supply a name for the block and insertion point to use when placing the block in your drawing, and then asks you to select the objects of which the block is to consist. Tool: Choose Block (Draw, Block)

BOUNDARY
350, 738

The BOUNDARY command enables you to create a polyline or region boundary from overlapping objects. The edges of the overlapping objects must form a completely enclosed area; if the perimeter contains a gap, the command will fail. Tool: Choose Boundary (Draw, Polygon) Pull-down: Choose Construct, Bounding Polyline Screen: Choose CONSTRUCT, Boundary

BREAK
652-655

The BREAK command enables you to erase a portion of an object between two points, or to break an object into two separate objects that might share a common Endpoint. Tool: Choose one of four tools from the Break flyout toolbar (Modify, Break) Screen: Choose MODIFY, Break

C

CHAMFER
633-634, 637

The CHAMFER command enables you to chamfer two existing lines or polyline segments. Tool: Choose Chamfer (Modify, Feature) Screen: Choose CONSTRCT, Chamfer

CHANGE
439, 602-605

The CHANGE command enables you to change the object and geometric properties of selected objects. Screen: Choose MODIFY, Change

CIRCLE
119, 350

The CIRCLE command enables you to use a variety of geometric methods to draw circles. The most common (default) method requires you to specify the center point and the radius. You can drag and pick the size of the circle on-screen or specify the radius with keyboard entry. Tool: Choose Circle Center Radius (Draw, Circle) Screen: Choose DRAW1, Circle

COPY
90, 549-550

The COPY command copies objects in 2D or 3D. The original objects remain unchanged. You are prompted to specify two points or a displacement. If you specify two points, the angle and distance from the first to the second point indicates the displacement for the copy. Alternatively, if you specify a coordinate value (either X,Y or X,Y,Z, or polar or spherical) at the first prompt, Base point or displacement:, and then press Enter at the Second point of displacement: prompt, the specified coordinate value is interpreted as the displacement for the copy. In addition, you can use the Multiple option to make several copies, specifying a single base point with repeated displacement points. Tool: Choose Copy Object (Modify, Copy) Screen: Choose CONSTRCT, Copy

D

DDATTDEF
410-415, 448

The DDATTDEF command enables you to create attributes. Tool: Choose Define Attribute (Attribute) Screen: Choose CONSTRCT, DDatDef

DDATTE
450-453

The DDATTE command enables you to edit attribute values after a block reference with attributes has been inserted. Tool: Choose Edit Attribute (Attribute, Edit Attribute) Screen: Choose Modify, AttEd

DDATTEXT
420

Opens the Attribute Extraction dialog box, which extracts the attribute data specified by a template file from the drawing. You can extract data from all or selected attributes in CDF, SDF, or DXF format. Screen: Choose FILE, EXPORT, DDattEx

DDCHPROP
433, 439, 601-602

The DDCHPROP command enables you to change the object properties of selected objects. Tool: Choose Properties (Object Properties) Pull-down: Choose Edit, Properties Screen: Choose MODIFY, Ddchprop

DDEDIT
843-844

The DDEDIT command prompts for a text, mtext, or attdef (attribute definition) object and then opens a dialog box appropriate to the text type you select. The DDEDIT command enables you to edit lines and paragraphs of text, and to modify block attribute definitions. Tool: Choose Edit Text (Modify, Special Edit) Screen: Choose MODIFY, DDedit

DDIM
800

DDIM enables you to create dimension style families and to set the dimension variables. Tool: Choose Dimension Styles (Dimensioning) Pull-down: Choose Data, Dimension Style Screen: Choose DRAW DIM, DDIM

DDINSERT
380

The DDINSERT command opens the Insert dialog box, which enables you to specify a block name or a drawing filename to insert into your drawing. You also can use the Insert dialog box to specify an insertion point, scale, and rotation angle for the block. Tool: Choose Insert Block (Draw, Block) Screen: Choose DRAW2, DDINSERT

DDLMODES
33, 47, 51, 585

The DDLMODES command displays the Layer Control dialog box. You use this dialog box to set a layer current, change a layer's assigned color and linetype, add new layers to your drawing, rename layers, turn layers on and off, freeze and thaw layers, and lock and unlock layers. You can use the Filters facility to control which layers are shown in the Layer Name list box. Tool: Choose Layers (Object Properties) Pull-down: Choose Data, Layers Screen: Choose DATA, Layers

DDMODIFY
439, 592-593, 598-600

The DDMODIFY command displays the object and geometric properties of any object you select. You can view or change the properties in the DDMODIFY dialog box. Tool: Choose Properties (Object Properties) Pull-Down: Choose Edit, Properties Screen: Choose MODIFY, Modify

DDOSNAP
122, 130

The DDOSNAP command displays the Running Object Snap dialog box. The DDOSNAP command enables you to set running object snaps and to set the size of the object snap aperture box. Tool: Choose Running Object Snap (Standard, Object Snap) Pull-Down: Choose Options, Running Object Snap Screen: Choose OPTIONS, DDosnap

DDPTYPE
288

The DDPTYPE command displays the Point Style dialog box. You use this dialog box to set point object style and size. Pull-down: Choose Options, Display, Point Style Screen: Choose DRAW2, Point:, DDptype

DDRENAME
61, 495

The DDRENAME command displays the Rename dialog box, which enables you to rename blocks, layers, linetypes, text styles, dimension styles, named views, viewports, and user coordinate systems. You use this dialog box to select the object(s) by its current name and to assign the new name. You can use AutoCAD's wild cards to rename groups of objects. Pull-down: Choose Data, Rename Screen: Choose DATA, Rename

DDUNITS
17-18

The DDUNITS command displays the Units Control dialog box. It enables the current format for linear and angular units of measure to be set. The Engineering and Architectural formats appear in feet and inches and assume a unit of one inch. The other formats can represent any real-world unit. Pull-down: Choose Data, Units Screen: Choose DATA, Units

DDVIEW
174

The DDVIEW command opens the View Control dialog box, which enables you to create, restore, and delete named views. The View Control options are similar to those of the VIEW command. Tool: Choose Named Views (Standard, View) Pull-down: Choose View, Named Views Screen: Choose VIEW, DDview

DIMALIGNED
768, 781-782, 874

The DIMALIGNED command places a dimension line parallel to the origin points of the two extension lines. Tool: Choose Aligned Dimension (Dimensioning) Screen: Choose DRAW DIM, ALIGNED

DIMANGULAR
787-788

The DIMANGULAR command measures the angular distance between two objects. You can select two objects, or specify three points to calculate the angle. Tool: Choose Angular Dimension (Dimensioning) Screen: Choose DRAW DIM, ANGULAR

DIMBASELINE
768, 778-780

The DIMBASELINE command enables you to stack dimensions on top of each other, using a common first extension line. Tool: Choose Dimbaseline (Dimensioning)

DIMCENTER
783, 767-787, 812-814

The DIMCENTER command enables you to place center crosshair marks at the origins of arcs and circles. Tool: Choose Center Mark (Dimensioning)

DIMCONTINUE
768, 773-777, 864-869

The DIMCONTINUE command enables you to continue a string of dimensions in a row. Tool: Choose Continue Dimension (Dimensioning) Screen: Choose DRAW DIM, CONTINU

DIMDIAMETER
783, 785-786

The DIMDIAMETER command enables you to locate diameter information on circles. Tool: Choose Diameter Dimension (Dimensioning, Radial Dimension)

DIMEDIT
840-843

The DIMEDIT command provides the capability to assign new text to a dimension, adjust the text to its default position, rotate the text, and oblique the extension lines. The DIMEDIT command can be used to edit one or more dimensions at a time. Screen: Choose MOD DIM, DimEdit

DIMLINEAR
768-772, 807

The DIMLINEAR command is a new enhancement to AutoCAD's dimensioning features. It enables you to place horizontal, vertical, and rotated dimensions. Tool: Choose Dimlinear (Dimensioning) Screen: Choose DRAW DIM, LINEAR

DIMOVERRIDE
832-833

The DIMOVERRIDE command provides the capability to change individual dimension variables without having to create a whole new dimension style. Screen: Choose MOD DIM, Override

DIMRADIUS
783-784, 828

The DIMRADIUS command enables you to place a dimension-leader and text for the size information on circles and arcs. Tool: Choose Radius Dimension (Dimensioning) Screen: Choose DRAW DIM, RADIUS

DIMSTYLE
587, 828, 833-835

The DIMSTYLE command provides the capability to restore dimen sion styles, save the current settings to a style name, list the current variable settings, current overrides, or the settings in another dimension style, update dimensions to the current settings, and list the dimension styles that are available in a drawing. Screen Choose MOD DIM, Dim Style

DIMTEDIT
845-846

The DIMEDIT command is used to reposition text within associative dimensions. Tool: Choose Home, Rotate, Left, Center, Right (Dimensioning) Screen: Choose DRAW DIMS, DimTedt

DIVIDE
581

The DIVIDE command enables you to divide an object into a user-specified number of equal divisions. You also can use it to place a block along the divided object at each division. Tool: Choose Divide (Draw, Point) Screen: Choose DRAW2, divide

DONUT
289-291

The DONUT command enables you to create closed, filled polyline circles that can vary in width. Donuts have an inside diameter (which can be 0) and an outside diameter. Tool: Choose Donut (Draw, Circle) Screen: Choose DRAW1, Donut

DTEXT
27, 52

The DTEXT command enables you to place multiple lines of text dynamically in a drawing, which in turn enables you to preview and edit the characters as you enter them. AutoCAD prompts you for insertion point, style, justification, height, and rotation. Tool: Choose Dtext (Draw, Text) Screen: Choose DRAW2, DText

E

ELLIPSE
297-300

If the system variable PELLIPSE is set to 0, the ELLIPSE command creates true mathematical ellipses and elliptical arcs. The default method of creating an ellipse is to specify the endpoints of one axis and the distance from the center of the other axis. You can also draw an ellipse by specifying the center, one axis endpoint, and the other axis distance. The second axis can also be specified by a rotation that defines the major to minor axis ratio. Tool: Choose Ellipse (Draw, Ellipse) Screen: Choose MODIFY, Ellipse

ERASE
65, 68, 193, 535, 552

The ERASE command deletes a selected set of objects from the drawing. Any AutoCAD selection method can be used. Tool: Choose Erase (Modify) Screen: Choose MODIFY, Erase

EXPLODE
341, 581

The EXPLODE command enables you to reduce complex entities, such as 3D meshes, 3D solids, blocks, bodies, dimensions, groups, multilines, polyface meshes, polygon meshes, polylines, and regions, into their component parts. Tool: Choose Explode (Modify, Explode) Pull-down: Choose Modify, Explode Screen: Choose MODIFY, Explode

EXTEND
555

The EXTEND command enables you to project selected lines, arcs, open polylines, and rays. Valid boundary objects include polylines, arcs, circles, ellipses, floating viewports, lines, rays, regions, splines, text, and xlines. A selected object can be treated as both a boundary edge and an object to extend. The pick point in the object to extend determines which end is extended. Tool: Choose Extend (Modify, Trim) Screen: Choose MODIFY, Extend

F

FILLET
145, 534, 623-633

The FILLET command enables you to apply a fillet to two existing objects. You can apply a fillet to lines, arcs, circles, and polyline segments. Tool: Choose Fillet (Modify, Feature) Screen: Choose CONSTRCT, Fillet

G

GRID
21, 110

The GRID command controls the visibility and spacing of a visual reference grid of dots. You also can set the grid without using the GRID command by using the Drawing Aids dialog box. You can turn the grid on and off by double-clicking on the GRID box on the status bar.

GROUP
542

The GROUP command opens the Object Grouping dialog box, which enables you to create a named selection set of objects, to facilitate subsequent edits. If you enter GROUP at the `Command:` prompt, GROUP displays prompts at the command line. Tool: Choose Object Group (Standard) Screen: Choose ASSIST, Group Choose SERVICE, Group

H

HATCH
587, 743-744

The HATCH command enables you to draw a hatch pattern in a selected area. You invoke the command by typing it at the command prompt because it does not appear in the menus.

HATCHEDIT
745-748

The HATCHEDIT command enables you to edit an existing associative hatch. Tool: Choose Hatchedit (Draw, Special Edit) Screen: Choose MODIFY, HatchEd

I-K

ID
99, 598

The ID command prompts for a point and returns the X,Y,Z coordinates of the point you specify. The system variable LASTPOINT is set to the point returned. You can reference the last point by entering @ at the next prompt requesting a point. Normally, the Z coordinate is that of the current elevation. However, if you use object snap to snap to an object, the Z coordinate is the same as the selected feature of the object. Tool: Choose Locate Point (Object Properties, Inquiry)

INSERT
380, 587
The INSERT command enables you to specify a block name or a drawing filename to insert into your drawing from the `Command:` prompt. Screen: Choose DRAW2, Insert

INTERSECT
355-356
The INTERSECT command enables you to create a region from the overlapping area of two or more regions, or to create a single solid from the overlapping volumes of two or more solids. Tool: Choose Intersect (Modify, Explode) Screen: Choose DRAW 2, SOLIDS, Intrsect

L

LEADER
789-792
The LEADER command draws an arrowhead and leader and places text or other annotation objects. This enables you to point to a feature and place text information around that feature. Tool: Choose Leader (Dimensioning) Screen: Choose DRAW DIM, LEADER

LENGTHEN
562-564
The LENGTHEN command enables you to change the length of objects and the included angle of arcs, but does not let you change closed objects. You can change lengths and angles by specifying an incremental amount, percentage of its total, new absolute total, or a dynamically dragged amount. Tool: Choose Lengthen (Modify, Resize) Screen: Choose MODIFY, Lengthen

LIMITS
13, 19, 416-417
The LIMITS command defines the drawing area by the coordinates of its lower left and upper right corners. The drawing limits are 2D points in the World Coordinate System. The drawing's limits also set the extents of the grid and determine the minimum area displayed by the All option of the ZOOM command. Pull-down: Choose Data, Drawing Limits Screen: Choose DATA, Limits

LINE
47, 64, 98, 101, 350, 374
The LINE command draws a line with endpoints specified in 2D or 3D coordinates. Tool: Choose Line (Draw, Line) Screen: Choose DRAW1, Line

LIST
593-594, 691
The LIST command enables you to list the object and geometric properties of selected objects simultaneously. Tool: Choose List (Object Properties, Inquiry) Screen: Choose ASSIST, INQUIRY, List

M

MASSPROP
356-357

The MASSPROP command enables you to display various engineering data about a region or 3D solid. Tool: Choose Mass Properties (Object Properties, Inquiry) Screen: Choose ASSIST, INQUIRY, Mass Pro.

MEASURE
581

The MEASURE command enables you to place a point or a block at a specified interval along the length or circumference of an object. Tool: Choose Measure (Draw, Point) Screen: Choose DRAW2, Measure

MINSERT
380-644

The MINSERT command enables you to specify a block name or a drawing filename to insert into your drawing from the `Command:` prompt. AutoCAD then prompts you for the number of rows and columns to array the inserted block. Tool: Choose Insert Multiple Blocks (Miscellaneous, Insert Multiple Blocks) Screen: Choose DRAW2, Minsert

MIRROR
648-652

The MIRROR command enables you to create a mirror-image copy of an object. The MIRROR command includes an option that enables you to specify whether the original object is deleted after the mirrored copy is created. Tool: Choose Mirror (Modify, Copy) Screen: Choose CONSTRCT, Mirror

MLEDIT
367-374

The MLEDIT command provides a set of tools that enable you to perform various editing tasks on multiline intersections. Tool: Choose Edit Multiline (Modify, Special Edit) Screen: Choose Modify, Mledit

MLINE
587

The MLINE command enables you to create multiple parallel line objects. Tool: Choose Multiline (Draw, Polyline) Screen: Choose DRAW 1, Mline

MLSTYLE
360-367

The MLSTYLE command enables you to create, save, and load custom multiline styles. Tool: Choose Multiline Style (Object Properties) Pull-down: Choose Data, Multiline Style Screen: Choose Data, MLstyle

MOVE
207, 534, 544-549

The MOVE command relocates objects in 2D or 3D. You are prompted to specify two points or a displacement. If you specify two points, the angle and distance from the first to the second point indicates the displacement for the move. Alternatively, if you specify a coordinate value (either X,Y or X,Y,Z, or polar or spherical) at the first prompt, Base point or displacement:, and then press Enter at the Second point of displacement: prompt, the specified coordinate value is interpreted as the displacement for the move. Tool: Choose Move (Modify) Screen: Choose MODIFY, Move

MSPACE
203, 260

The MSPACE command enables you to access model space in a floating viewport while TILEMODE is off. Tool: Choose Floating Model Space (Standard, Space) Pull-down: Choose View, Floating Model Space Screen: Choose VIEW, Mspace

MTEXT
681

The MTEXT command enables you to create text paragraphs that fit within a boundary and that you treat as a single object. The boundary specifies the width and alignment of the paragraph. You also can specify the text style, height, and direction. Tool: Choose Text (Draw, Text) Screen: Choose DRAW2, MText

MTPROP
695, 699

The MTPROP command enables you to change the properties of paragraph text. You can modify both the contents (text style, height, and direction) as well as the object boundary parameters (attachment, width, and rotation). MTPROP prompts you to select an mtext object, and then opens the MText Properties dialog box.

MVIEW
199-200

The MVIEW command enables you to configure multiple floating viewports in paper space. Pull-down: Choose View, Floating Viewports Screen: Choose VIEW, Mview

MVSETUP
23

The MVSETUP command (defined by an AutoLISP program) sets up the specifications for a drawing, including units, plotting sheet size, and plotting scale. Refer to Chapter 25, "Plotting and Sheet Composition," for other MVSETUP functions. For non–paper-space use, MVSETUP must be entered at the `Command:` prompt. Pull-down: Choose View, Floating Viewports (for paper space only)

MVSETUP
23

The MVSETUP command facilitates setting up a layout in model or paperspace. Pull-down: Choose View, Floating Viewports, MVSetup

N

NEW
23, 31, 33, 47

The NEW command creates a new drawing file. Tool: Choose New (Standard) Pull-down: Choose File, New Screen: Choose FILE, New

O

OFFSET
638-642

The OFFSET command enables you to offset existing objects to create new objects. You can create the new offset object at a specific distance from the original, or create the offset object through a point. Tool: Choose Offset (Modify, Copy) Screen: Choose CONSTRCT, Offset

OOPS
383-552

The OOPS command restores the most recent set of erased objects in the current drawing session. Other commands might intervene between ERASE and OOPS. Tool: Choose Oops! (Miscellaneous) Screen: Choose MODIFY, Oops

OPEN
28

The OPEN command opens an existing drawing file. The OPEN command displays the Select File dialog box. Tool: Choose Open (Standard) Pull-down: Choose File, Open Screen: Choose FILE, Open

OSNAP
115-117, 130

The OSNAP command enables you to set running object snap modes. If you enter it at the `Command:` prompt, the following prompt appears: Object snap modes:. Specify one or more object snap modes by entering the first three letters of the mode name. Separate multiple modes with a comma. Tool: Choose Running Object Snap (Standard, Object Snap)

P

PEDIT
322-347

The PEDIT command enables you to modify 2D and 3D polyline objects and polygon meshes. You can use the PEDIT command to change the width of a polyline; add, delete, and move vertices; curve- or spline-fit the vertices; remove curve information from the vertices; adjust the tangent of a vertex; and close or open a polyline. Tool: Choose Edit Polyline (Modify, Special Edit) Pull-down: Choose Modify, Edit Polyline Screen: Choose Modify, Pedit

PLINE
350-461

The PLINE command enables you to draw polyline objects. Polylines consist of multiple straight and arc segments that you treat as a single object. Each segment also can possess width. The width of a segment can remain constant or can taper from one end to the other. Tool: Choose Polyline (Draw, Polyline) Screen: Choose Draw1, Pline

PLOT
218, 226

The PLOT command opens the Plot Configuration dialog box and enables you to generate plots on a printer or plotter. Tool: Choose Print (Standard) Pull-down: Choose File, Print Screen: Choose FILE, Print

POINT
286-288

The POINT command draws a point object with X,Y,Z coordinates anywhere in 3D space. You often use points as reference marks and as nodes to which to snap with NODe object snap mode. You can control the display style and size of points with the PDMODE and PDSIZE system Variables. Tool: Choose Point (Draw, Point) Screen: Choose DRAW2, Point

POLYGON
292-294

The POLYGON command enables you to draw regular (equilateral) polygons from 3 to 1,024 sides. Polygon objects consist of polylines of zero width. Tool: Choose Polygon (Draw, Polygon) Screen: Choose DRAW1, Polygon

PSPACE
183, 207

The PSPACE command puts you in paper space. Tool: Choose Paper Space (Standard Toolbar, Space) Pull-down: Choose View, Paper Space Screen: Choose View, Pspace

PURGE
55, 472, 869

The PURGE command deletes unreferenced (unused) blocks, dimension styles, layers, linetypes, shapes, text styles, mline styles, and registered application IDs. Pull-down: Choose Data, Purge (Option) Screen: Choose DATA, Purge

Q

QSAVE
20, 35

The QSAVE (for Quick SAVE) command saves the current, named drawing without any further user input. If QSAVE is issued and the drawing has not been named, the Save Drawing As dialog box is displayed. (Refer to SAVEAS command later in this chapter).Tool: Choose Save (Standard) Pull-down: Choose File, Save Screen: Choose FILE, Save

QTEXT
686-687

The QTEXT (Quick TEXT) command enables you to control the screen and plotted appearance of text and attributes. When QTEXT is on, AutoCAD replaces text, dimensions, and attributes by approximating rectangles. Pull-down: Choose Options, Display, Filled Text or Outline Text or Text Frame Only Screen: Choose Options, Display, Qtext

QUIT
37

The QUIT command exits AutoCAD if there have been no changes to the drawing since it was last saved. If the drawing has been changed, the Drawing Modification dialog box appears, prompting you to save or discard the changes before exiting. Pull-down Choose File, Exit Screen: Choose FILE, Exit

R

RAY
141-145

The RAY command creates a semi-infinite line. A ray has a finite starting point and extends to infinity. Tool: Choose Ray (Draw, Line) Screen: Choose DRAW1, Ray

RECTANG
137, 351, 416-417

The RECTANG command enables you to draw a rectangle by specifying the two opposite corners. Tool: Choose Rectangle (Draw, Polygon) Screen: Choose DRAW1, Rectang

REGION
350-352

The REGION command enables you to create region objects from existing closed 2D objects such as closed lines, polylines, circles, and splines. Tool: Choose Region (Draw, Polygon) Screen: Choose Construct, Region

RENAME
61

The RENAME command enables you to rename named AutoCAD items from the command line. It prompts for the old name and then the new name.

ROTATE
551-552

The ROTATE command enables you to revolve your objects selected in the X,Y plane around a specified base point, using a rotation angle relative to the current angle 0 that you point to or enter, or a relative to a reference angle that you can specify by either method. Tool: Choose Rotate (Modify, Rotate) Screen: Choose MODIFY, Rotate

S

SAVE
35-36

The SAVE command saves the current drawing either under its current name (if it is named) or under a new name. If you save the drawing under a new name, the current drawing assumes that name. AutoCAD displays the Save Drawing As dialog box that enables the graphical selection of filename, directory, and drive. The SAVE command is available only at the command line.

SAVEAS
35-36

The SAVEAS command, like SAVE, enables you to save the drawing under any name. When you issue the SAVEAS command, AutoCAD displays the Save Drawing As dialog box. Unlike the SAVE command, if the drawing is named, SAVEAS causes the current drawing name to be changed to the name under which the drawing was saved. Pull-down: Choose File, Save As Screen: Choose FILE, SaveAs

SAVEASR12
39, 676

The SAVEASR12 command provides backward compatibility with AutoCAD Release 12. When you issue the SAVEASR12 command, AutoCAD displays the Save Release 12 Drawing As dialog box, in which you enter a filename for the Release 12 drawing to be saved under. The original Release 13 drawing is saved with a BAK extension with the same name. Some of the Release 13 drawing information can be lost or altered in this process. The SAVEASR12 command is available only at the command line.

SCALE
568-570

The SCALE command enables you to change the size of existing objects relative to a specified base point, by a specified scale factor, by referencing one specified distance to another, or by using a combination of these two methods. Tool: Choose Scale (Modify, Resize) Screen: Choose MODIFY, Scale

SELECT
548

The SELECT command enables you to select objects and build a selection set that you can later recall by using the Previous object selection option. SELECT enables you to use all the selection options. Tool: Choose Select Objects (Standard) Screen: Choose ASSIST, Select

SKETCH
319-322

The SKETCH command enables you to create a contiguous series of lines or polyline segments as you move the cursor. The SKETCH command enables you to draw freehand or to trace curves from paper on a graphics tablet. The SKPOLY system variable enables you to control the type of object that you create when you use the SKETCH command. A value of 0 (the default) creates line objects; a value of 1 creates polylines. Tool: Choose Sketch (Miscella neous) Screen: Choose DRAW1, Sketch

SNAP
113-114

The SNAP command turns the snap grid on and off and sets its spacing. It also provides options for setting the snap aspect ratio (different X and Y values), rotating the snap grid around a base point, and switching to an isometric snap grid. You also use the Drawing Aids dialog box to set the snap grid.

SPELL
697-699

The SPELL command enables you to check the spelling of selected text, mtext, and attdef objects. The Check Spelling dialog box appears only if AutoCAD finds a questionable word. You can maintain custom dictionaries to minimize the unnecessary flagging of correctly spelled words. Tool: Choose Spelling (Standard) Pull-down: Choose Tools, Spelling Screen: Choose TOOLS, Spell

SPLINE
350

The SPLINE command enables you to draw 2D or 3D splines. Splines are smooth curved lines that fit to data points that you specify. You can control the tolerance of the curve to the fit-data points. SPLINE also enables you to convert spline-fit polylines into spline objects. Tool: Choose Spline (Draw, Polyline) Pull-down: Choose Draw, Spline Screen: Choose Draw1, Spline

SPLINEDIT
342-347

The SPLINEDIT command enables you to edit 2D or 3D spline objects. You can add additional control or fit-data points or move them. You can change the weight of control points and the tolerance of the spline. You also can close or open a spline and adjust the tangent information of the start and endpoints. Tool: Choose Edit Spline (Modify, Special Edit) Pull-down: Choose Modify, Edit Spline Screen: Choose MODIFY, SplinEd

STRETCH
207, 482, 565-568

The STRETCH command enables you to elongate objects selected with a crossing window. You can stretch lines, arcs, solids, traces, polylines (meshes), and 3D faces. For stretchable objects, endpoints that lie inside the crossing window are moved and endpoints that lie outside the crossing window remain fixed. All objects entirely within the window move. Text, blocks, shapes, and circles move only if their insert or center points are in the window. Tool: Choose Stretch (Modify, Resize) Screen: Choose MODIFY, Stretch

STYLE
587

The STYLE command enables you to define, name, change, and list sets of text parameters, including the font, height, width factor, obliquing angle, as well as backward, upside-down, and vertical orientation. This command also sets the current style for the drawing. Pull-down: Choose Data, Text Style Screen: Choose DATA, Style

SUBTRACT
354-356

The SUBTRACT command enables you to subtract one set of regions or solids from another region or solid. Tool: Choose Subtract (Modify, Explode) Screen: Choose DRAW 2, SOLIDS, Subtract

T

TABLET
146-147

The TABLET command enables you to calibrate the digitizing tablet to an independent coordinate system, as well as to turn tablet mode on and off and designate the tablet areas reserved for menu and screen pointing. Pull-down: Choose Options, Tablet Screen: Choose OPTIONS, Tablet

TEXT
587

The TEXT command enables you to place a single line of text in a drawing. AutoCAD prompts you for insertion point, style, justifica tion, height, and rotation. Tool: Choose Single-Line Text (Draw, Text)

TRIM
145, 304, 534, 555

The TRIM command enables you to remove portions of lines, arcs, circles, polylines, rays, and splines that cross a selected cutting edge. You can select polylines, arcs, circles, ellipses, lines, floating viewports, rays, regions, splines, text, and xlines as cutting edges. A selected object can be treated as both a cutting edge and an object to trim. The pick point on the object to trim determines which portion is trimmed. Tool: Choose Trim (Modify, Trim) Screen: Choose MODIFY, Trim

U

UCS
88-89, 587, 903

The UCS command enables you to set up and manage User Coordinate Systems. It provides a range of options, including setting the origin, specifying rotation around any axis, aligning with objects, saving, listing, and restoring. Tool: Choose UCS (Standard) Pull-down: Choose View, Set UCS Screen: Choose VIEW, UCS:

UCSICON
47, 92-95

The UCSICON command enables you to control the visibility and placement of the UCS Icon. Pull-down: Choose Options, UCS Screen: Choose OPTIONS, UCS icon

UNDO
552-554

The UNDO command enables you to reverse the effect(s) of one or more previous commands, to step back through the drawing to its state at the beginning of the drawing session. The UNDO command includes options that enable you to control the number of previous drawing steps stored, control how far back to undo previous steps, group operations as if single steps, and turn off the undo feature. Pull-down: Choose Edit, Undo Screen: Choose ASSIST, Undo

UNION
354-356

The UNION command enables you to combine multiple regions or 3D solids into a single region or 3D Solid. Tool: Choose Union (Modify, Explode) Screen: Choose DRAW 2, SOLIDS, Union

UNITS
15

The UNITS command sets linear and angular units and precision with prompts from the command line. The functionality is the same as that offered by the DDUNITS command. This command is available only by entering it at the `Command:` prompt.

V

VIEWRES
175-177

The VIEWRES command adjusts the display resolution of arcs and circles and can specify a virtual screen for quicker regenerations. A larger supplied value produces smoother curved objects; however, the value does not affect plotting. Screen: Choose OPTIONS, Viewers

VPLAYER
211-214

The VPLAYER command enables you to control the visibility of existing and new layers, per viewport. Pull-down: Choose Data, Viewport Layer Controls Screen: Choose Data, Vplayer

VPORTS
184, 588

The VPORTS command enables you to create, save, restore, delete, combine, and exit multiple tiled viewports in model space. Pull-down: Choose View, Tiled Viewports Screen: Choose VIEW, Vports

W

WBLOCK
379

The WBLOCK command enables you to create a drawing file from a block, a selection set, or an entire file, which makes the block or selections accessible from other drawing files. Pull-down: Choose File, Export Screen: Choose FILE, EXPORT, Wblock

X-Z

XBIND
494-496

The XBIND command enables you to import dependent symbols (blocks, dimension styles, text styles, layers, and linetypes) that are defined in an externally referenced drawing into the current drawing. You specify which type of symbol to bind and XBIND prompts for a specific symbol name of that type. You can enter a single name, several names separated by commas (without spaces), or

AutoCAD standard wild cards. Tool: Choose one of the XBIND tools (External Reference, Bind) Pull-down: Choose File, Bind, and one of the XBIND options Screen: Choose FILE, Xbind

XLINE
140-146

The XLINE command creates construction lines, which are infinite in length. Tool: Choose Construction Line (Draw, Line) Screen: Choose DRAW1, Xline

XPLODE
442-445, 447

The XPLODE command breaks a compound object into its component objects while enabling you to specify a new layer, color, and linetype for the component objects.

XREF
474-475, 477, 588

The XREF command enables you to attach, overlay, bind, or update external reference drawings. The xref's data resides entirely in the external drawing's database, and only a reference to the external file is placed in the current drawing's database. Tool: Choose Attach (External Reference) Pull-down: Choose File, Exter nal Reference, Attach Screen: Choose FILE, Xref

XREFCLIP
490-492

The XREFCLIP command attaches an xref, and then creates a floating viewport that displays a specified portion of the xref at a specified scale and location. Tool: Choose Clip (External Reference)

Index

Symbols

A

B

C

D

E

F

G

H

I

J-L

M

P

Q

R

S

T

U

V

X

Y-Z